한국의 토익 수험자 여러분께,

토익 시험은 세계적인 직무 영어능력 평가 시험으로, 지난 40여 년간 비즈니스 현장에서 필요한 영어능력 평가의 기준을 제시해 왔습니다. 토익 시험 및 토익스피킹, 토익라이팅 시험은 세계에서 가장 널리 통용되는 영어능력 검증 시험으로, 160여 개국 14,000여 기관이 토익 성적을 의사결정에 활용하고 있습니다.

YBM은 한국의 토익 시험을 주관하는 ETS 독점 계약사입니다.

ETS는 한국 수험자들의 효과적인 토익 학습을 돕고자 YBM을 통하여 'ETS 토익 공식 교재'를 독점 출간하고 있습니다. 또한 'ETS 토익 공식 교재' 시리즈에 기출문항을 제공해 한국의 다른 교재들에 수록된 기출을 복제하거나 변형한 문항으로 인하여 발생할 수 있는 수험자들의 혼동을 방지하고 있습니다.

복제 및 변형 문항들은 토익 시험의 출제의도를 벗어날 수 있기 때문에 기출문항을 수록한 'ETS 토익 공식 교재'만큼 시험에 잘 대비할 수 없습니다.

'ETS 토익 공식 교재'를 통하여 수험자 여러분의 영어 소통을 위한 노력에 큰 성취가 있기를 바랍니다.

감사합니다.

Dear TOEIC Test Takers in Korea,

The TOEIC program is the global leader in English-language assessment for the workplace. It has set the standard for assessing English-language skills needed in the workplace for more than 40 years. The TOEIC tests are the most widely used English language assessments around the world, with 14,000+ organizations across more than 160 countries trusting TOEIC scores to make decisions.

YBM is the ETS Country Master Distributor for the TOEIC program in Korea and so is the exclusive distributor for TOEIC Korea.

To support effective learning for TOEIC test-takers in Korea, ETS has authorized YBM to publish the only Official TOEIC prep books in Korea. These books contain actual TOEIC items to help prevent confusion among Korean test-takers that might be caused by other prep book publishers' use of reproduced or paraphrased items.

Reproduced or paraphrased items may fail to reflect the intent of actual TOEIC items and so will not prepare test-takers as well as the actual items contained in the ETS TOEIC Official prep books published by YBM.

We hope that these ETS TOEIC Official prep books enable you, as test-takers, to achieve great success in your efforts to communicate effectively in English.

Thank you.

토익® 정기시험 기출문제집 2 1000

READING

토익® 정기시험 기출문제집 2 1000 READING

발행인 허문호
발행처 YBM

편집 윤경림, 허유정
디자인 이미화, 이현숙
마케팅 정연철, 박천산, 고영노, 박찬경, 김동진, 김윤하

초판발행 2019년 12월 16일
21쇄발행 2024년 1월 2일

신고일자 1964년 3월 28일
신고번호 제 300-1964-3호
주소 서울시 종로구 종로 104
전화 (02) 2000-0515 [구입문의] / (02) 2000-0429 [내용문의]
팩스 (02) 2285-1523
홈페이지 www.ybmbooks.com

ISBN 978-89-17-23219-6

토익® 정기시험 기출문제집 2 1000 READING

Preface

Dear test taker,

English-language proficiency has become a vital tool for success. It can help you excel in business, travel the world, and communicate effectively with friends and colleagues. The TOEIC® test measures your ability to function effectively in English in these types of situations. Because TOEIC scores are recognized around the world as evidence of your English-language proficiency, you will be able to confidently demonstrate your English skills to employers and begin your journey to success.

The test developers at ETS are excited to help you achieve your personal and professional goals through the use of the ETS® TOEIC® 정기시험 기출문제집 1000 Vol. 2. This book contains test questions taken from actual, official TOEIC tests. They will help you become familiar with the TOEIC test's format and content. This book also contains detailed explanations of the question types and language points contained in the TOEIC test. These test questions and explanations have all been prepared by the same test specialists who develop the actual TOEIC test, so you can be confident that you will receive an authentic test-preparation experience.

Features of the ETS® TOEIC® 정기시험 기출문제집 1000 Vol. 2 include the following.

- Ten full-length test forms, all accompanied by answer keys and official scripts
- Specific and easy to understand explanations for learners
- The very same ETS voice actors that you will hear in an official TOEIC test administration

---

By using the ETS® TOEIC® 정기시험 기출문제집 1000 Vol. 2 to prepare for the TOEIC test, you can be assured that you have a professionally prepared resource that will provide you with accurate guidance so that you are more familiar with the tasks, content, and format of the test and that will help you maximize your TOEIC test score. With your official TOEIC score certificate, you will be ready to show the world what you know!

We are delighted to assist you on your TOEIC journey with the ETS® TOEIC® 정기시험 기출문제집 1000 Vol. 2 and wish you the best of success.

최신 기출문제 전격 공개!

'출제기관이 독점 제공한' 기출문제가 담긴 유일한 교재!

이 책에는 정기시험 기출문제 10세트가 수록되어 있다. 최신 기출문제로 실전 감각을 키워 시험에 확실하게 대비하자!

국내최고

기출 포인트를 꿰뚫는 명쾌한 해설!

최신 출제 경향을 가장 정확하게 알 수 있는 기출문제를 풀고 출제포인트가 보이는 명쾌한 해설로 토익을 정복해 보자!

독점제공

'ETS가 제공하는' 표준 점수 환산표!

출제기관 ETS가 독점 제공하는 표준 점수 환산표를 수록했다. 채점 후 환산표를 통해 자신의 실력이 어느 정도인지 가늠해 보자!

What is the TOEIC?

TOEIC은 어떤 시험인가요?

Test of English for International Communication(국제적 의사소통을 위한 영어 시험)의 약자로서, 영어가 모국어가 아닌 사람들이 일상생활 또는 비즈니스 현장에서 꼭 필요한 실용적 영어 구사 능력을 갖추었는가를 평가하는 시험이다.

시험 구성

<table>
<tr><th>구성</th><th>Part</th><th colspan="2">내용</th><th>문항수</th><th>시간</th><th>배점</th></tr>
<tr><td rowspan="4">듣기(L/C)</td><td>1</td><td colspan="2">사진 묘사</td><td>6</td><td rowspan="4">45분</td><td rowspan="4">495점</td></tr>
<tr><td>2</td><td colspan="2">질의 & 응답</td><td>25</td></tr>
<tr><td>3</td><td colspan="2">짧은 대화</td><td>39</td></tr>
<tr><td>4</td><td colspan="2">짧은 담화</td><td>30</td></tr>
<tr><td rowspan="5">읽기(R/C)</td><td>5</td><td colspan="2">단문 빈칸 채우기(문법/어휘)</td><td>30</td><td rowspan="5">75분</td><td rowspan="5">495점</td></tr>
<tr><td>6</td><td colspan="2">장문 빈칸 채우기</td><td>16</td></tr>
<tr><td rowspan="3">7</td><td rowspan="3">독해</td><td>단일 지문</td><td>29</td></tr>
<tr><td>이중 지문</td><td>10</td></tr>
<tr><td>삼중 지문</td><td>15</td></tr>
<tr><td>Total</td><td colspan="3">7 Parts</td><td>200문항</td><td>120분</td><td>990점</td></tr>
</table>

TOEIC 접수는 어떻게 하나요?

TOEIC 접수는 한국 토익 위원회 사이트(www.toeic.co.kr)에서 온라인 상으로만 접수가 가능하다. 사이트에서 매월 자세한 접수 일정과 시험 일정 등의 구체적 정보 확인이 가능하니, 미리 일정을 확인하여 접수하도록 한다.

시험장에 반드시 가져가야 할 준비물은요?

신분증 규정 신분증만 가능
(주민등록증, 운전면허증, 기간 만료 전의 여권, 공무원증 등)

필기구 연필, 지우개 (볼펜이나 사인펜은 사용 금지)

시험은 어떻게 진행되나요?

09:20	입실 (09:50 이후는 입실 불가)
09:30 - 09:45	답안지 작성에 관한 오리엔테이션
09:45 - 09:50	휴식
09:50 - 10:05	신분증 확인
10:05 - 10:10	문제지 배부 및 파본 확인
10:10 - 10:55	듣기 평가 (Listening Test)
10:55 - 12:10	독해 평가 (Reading Test)

TOEIC 성적 확인은 어떻게 하죠?

시험일로부터 약 10~11일 후, 인터넷과 ARS(060-800-0515)로 성적을 확인할 수 있다. TOEIC 성적표는 우편이나 온라인으로 발급 받을 수 있다(시험 접수시, 양자 택일). 우편으로 발급 받을 경우는 성적 발표 후 대략 일주일이 소요되며, 온라인 발급을 선택하면 유효기간 내에 홈페이지에서 본인이 직접 1회에 한해 무료 출력할 수 있다. TOEIC 성적은 시험일로부터 2년간 유효하다.

TOEIC은 몇 점 만점인가요?

TOEIC 점수는 듣기 영역(LC) 점수, 읽기 영역(RC) 점수, 그리고 이 두 영역을 합계한 전체 점수 세 부분으로 구성된다. 각 부분의 점수는 5점 단위이며, 5점에서 495점에 걸쳐 주어지고, 전체 점수는 10점에서 990점까지이며, 만점은 990점이다. TOEIC 성적은 각 문제 유형의 난이도에 따른 점수 환산표에 의해 결정된다.

토익 경향 분석

PART 1 사진 묘사 Photographs

총 6문제

1인 등장 사진
주어는 He/She, A man/woman 등이며 주로 앞부분에 나온다.

2인 이상 등장 사진
주어는 They, Some men/women/people, One of the men/women 등이며 주로 중간 부분에 나온다.

사물/배경 사진
주어는 A car, Some chairs 등이며 주로 뒷부분에 나온다.

사람 또는 사물 중심 사진
주어가 일부는 사람, 일부는 사물이며 주로 뒷부분에 나온다.

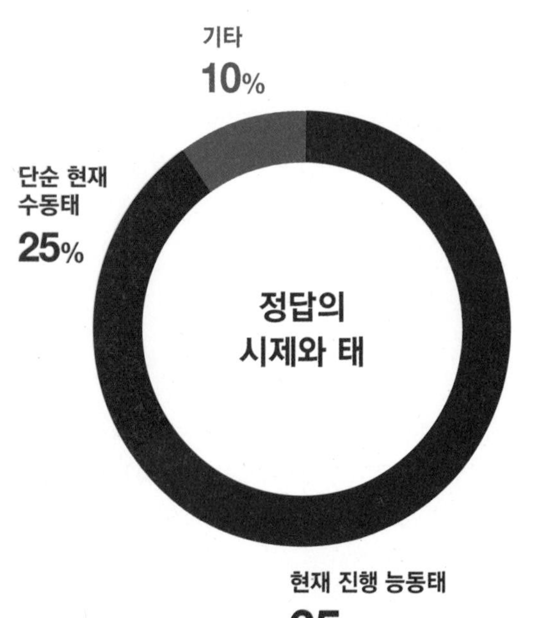

현재 진행 능동태
〈is/are + 현재분사〉 형태이며 주로 사람이 주어이다.

단순 현재 수동태
〈is/are + 과거분사〉 형태이며 주로 사물이 주어이다.

기타
〈is/are + being + 과거분사〉 형태의 현재 진행 수동태, 〈has/have + been + 과거 분사〉 형태의 현재 완료 수동태, '타동사 + 목적어' 형태의 단순 현재 능동태, There is/are와 같은 단순 현재도 나온다.

PART 2 질의 응답 Question-Response

총 25문제

평서문
질문이 아니라 객관적인 사실이나 화자의 의견 등을 나타내는 문장이다.

명령문
동사원형이나 Please 등으로 시작한다.

의문사 의문문
각 의문사마다 1~2개씩 나온다. 의문사가 단독으로 나오기도 하지만 What time ~?, How long ~?, Which room ~? 등에서처럼 다른 명사나 형용사와 같이 나오기도 한다.

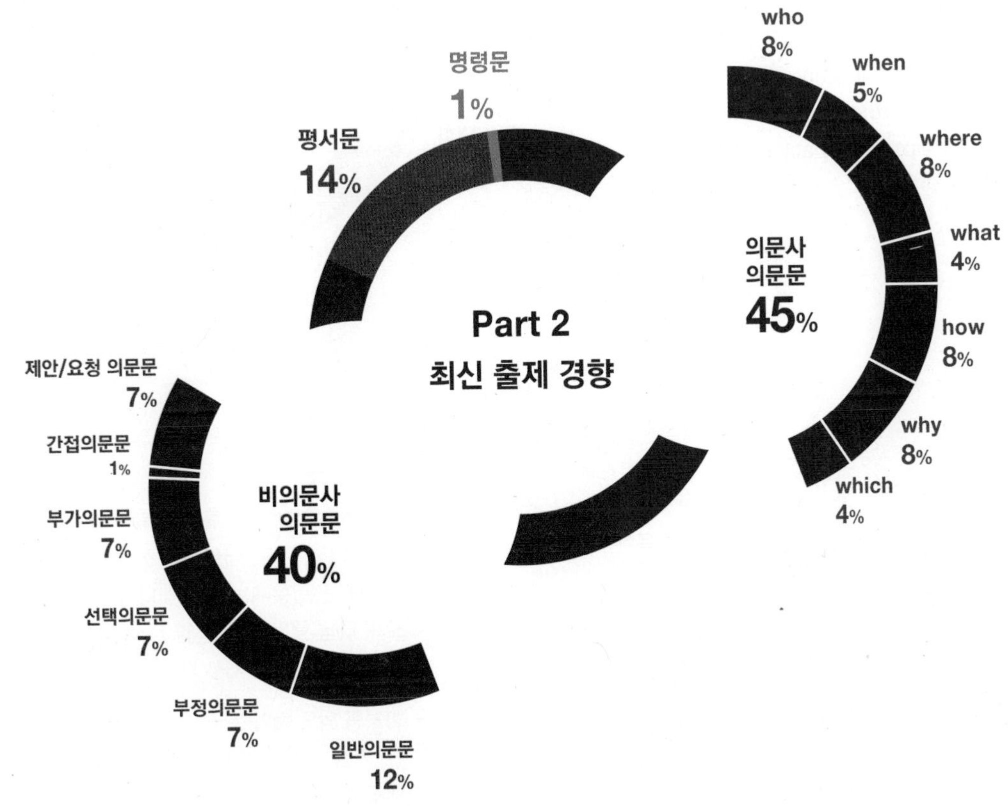

비의문사 의문문

일반(Yes/No) 의문문 적게 나올 때는 한두 개, 많이 나올 때는 서너 개씩 나오는 편이다.
부정의문문 Don't you ~?, Isn't he ~? 등으로 시작하는 문장이며 일반 긍정 의문문보다는 약간 더 적게 나온다.
선택의문문 A or B 형태로 나오며 A와 B의 형태가 단어, 구, 절일 수 있다. 구나 절일 경우 문장이 길어져서 어려워진다.
부가의문문 ~ don't you?, ~ isn't he? 등으로 끝나는 문장이며, 일반 부정 의문문과 비슷하다고 볼 수 있다.
간접의문문 의문사가 문장 처음 부분이 아니라 문장 중간에 들어 있다.
제안/요청 의문문 정보를 얻기보다는 상대방의 도움이나 동의 등을 얻기 위한 목적이 일반적이다.

PART 3 짧은 대화 Short Conversations

총 13대화문 39문제 (지문당 3문제)

- 3인 대화의 경우 남자 화자 두 명과 여자 화자 한 명 또는 남자 화자 한 명과 여자 화자 두 명이 나온다. 따라서 문제에서는 2인 대화에서와 달리 the man이나 the woman이 아니라 the men이나 the women 또는 특정한 이름이 언급될 수 있다.
- 대화 & 시각 정보는 항상 파트의 뒷부분에 나온다.
- 시각 정보의 유형으로 chart, map, floor plan, schedule, table, weather forecast, directory, list, invoice, receipt, sign, packing slip 등 다양한 자료가 골고루 나온다.

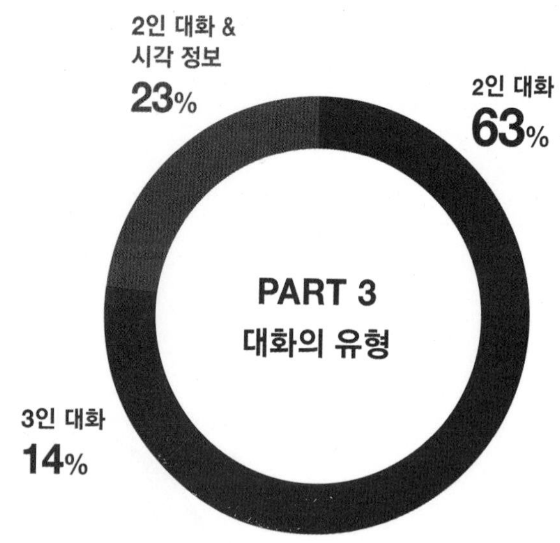

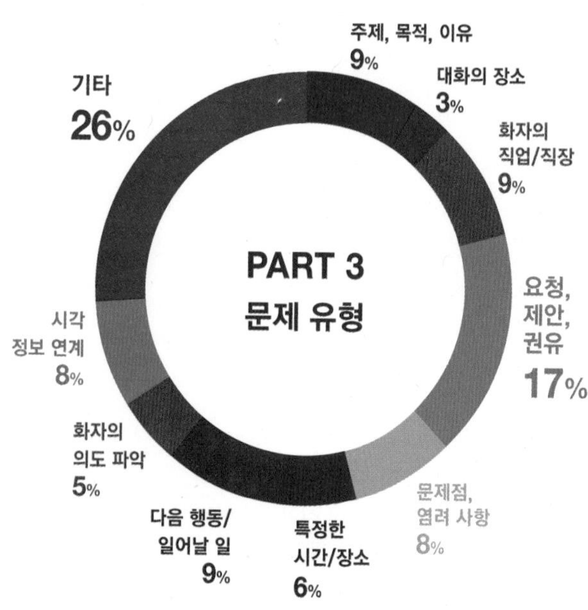

- 주제, 목적, 이유, 대화의 장소, 화자의 직업/직장 등과 관련된 문제는 주로 대화의 첫 번째 문제로 나오며 다음 행동/일어날 일 등과 관련된 문제는 주로 대화의 세 번째 문제로 나온다.
- 화자의 의도 파악 문제는 주로 2인 대화에 나오지만, 가끔 3인 대화에 나오기도 한다. 시각 정보 연계 대화에는 나오지 않고 있다.
- Part 3 안에서 화자의 의도 파악 문제는 2개가 나오고 시각 정보 연계 문제는 3개가 나온다.

PART 4 짧은 담화 Short Talks

총 10지문 30문제 (지문당 3문제)

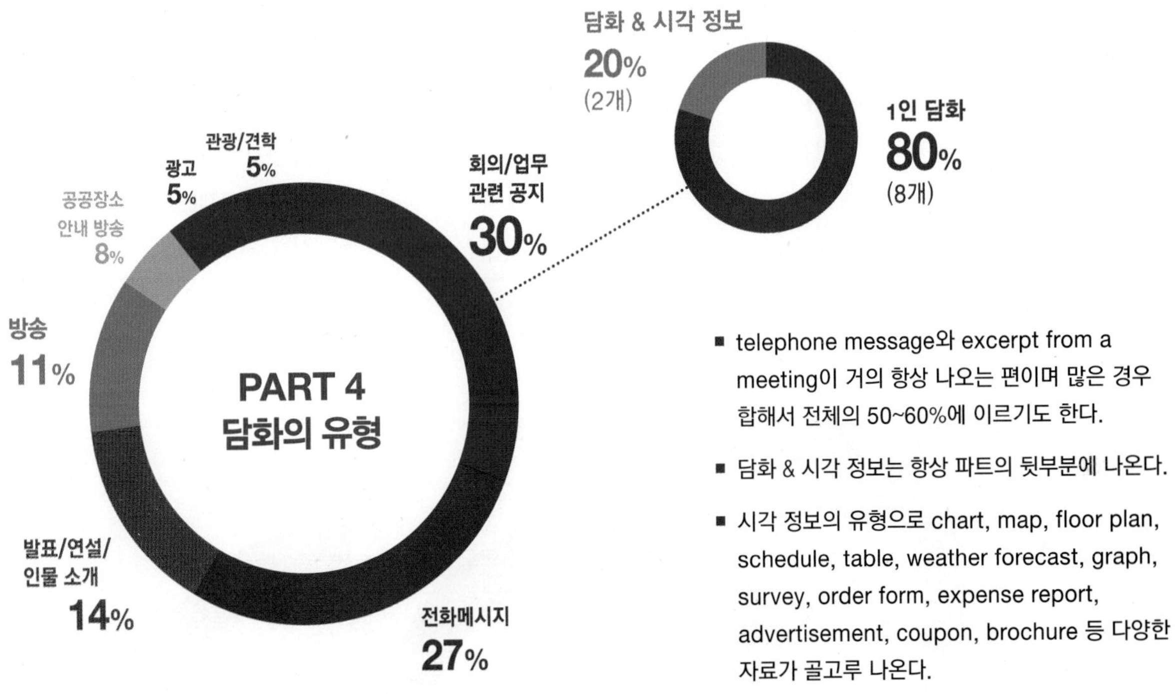

- telephone message와 excerpt from a meeting이 거의 항상 나오는 편이며 많은 경우 합해서 전체의 50~60%에 이르기도 한다.
- 담화 & 시각 정보는 항상 파트의 뒷부분에 나온다.
- 시각 정보의 유형으로 chart, map, floor plan, schedule, table, weather forecast, graph, survey, order form, expense report, advertisement, coupon, brochure 등 다양한 자료가 골고루 나온다.

- 문제 유형은 기본적으로 Part 3과 거의 비슷하다.
- 주제, 목적, 이유, 담화의 장소, 화자의 직업/직장 등과 관련된 문제는 주로 담화의 첫 번째 문제로 나오며 다음 행동/일어날 일 등과 관련된 문제는 주로 담화의 세 번째 문제로 나온다.
- Part 4 안에서 화자의 의도 파악 문제는 3개가 나오고 시각 정보 연계 문제는 2개가 나온다.

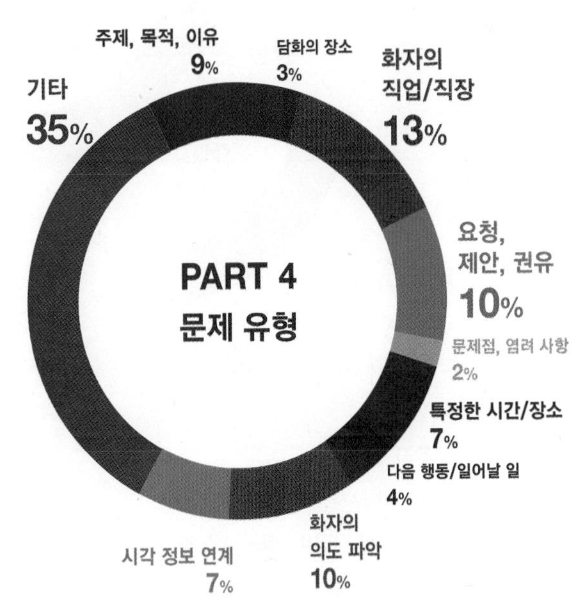

토익 경향 분석

PART 5 단문 빈칸 채우기 Incomplete Sentences 총 30문제

문법 문제

시제와 대명사와 관련된 문법 문제가 2개씩, 한정사와 분사와 관련된 문법 문제가 1개씩 나온다. 시제 문제의 경우 능동태/수동태나 수의 일치와 연계되기도 한다. 그 밖에 한정사, 능동태/수동태, 부정사, 동명사 등과 관련된 문법 문제가 나온다.

어휘 문제

동사, 명사, 형용사, 부사와 관련된 어휘 문제가 각각 2~3개씩 골고루 나온다. 전치사 어휘 문제는 3개씩 꾸준히 나오지만, 접속사나 어구와 관련된 어휘 문제는 나오지 않을 때도 있고 3개가 나올 때도 있다.

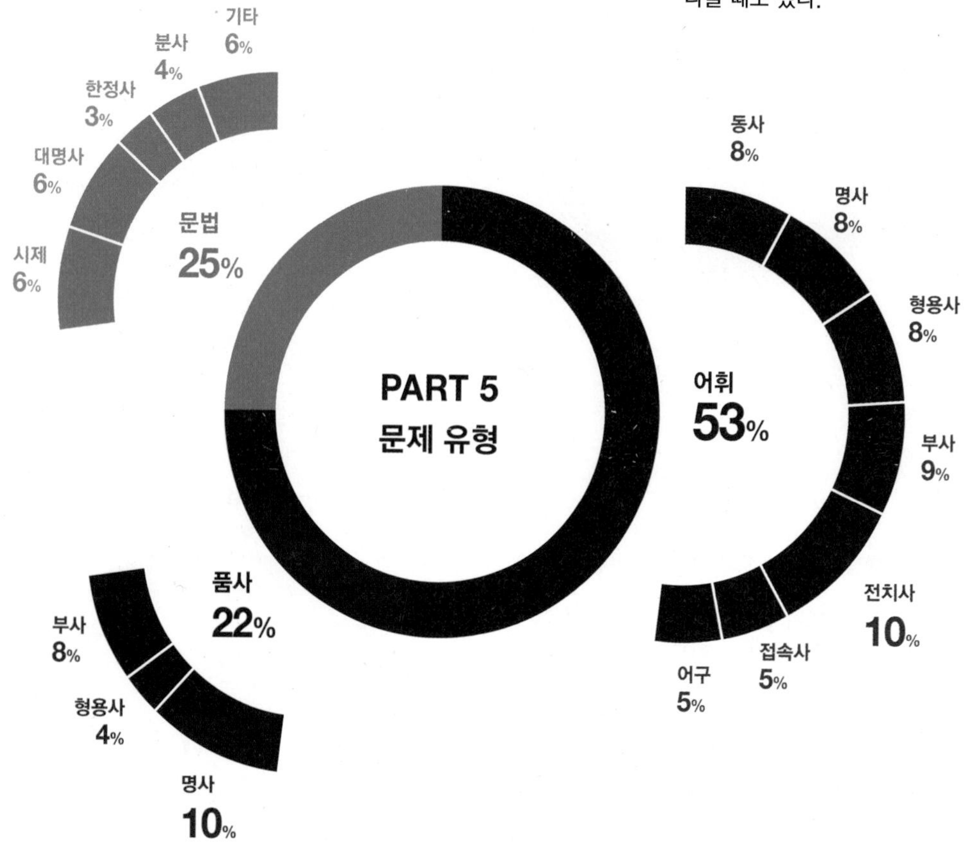

품사 문제

명사와 부사와 관련된 품사 문제가 2~3개씩 나오며, 형용사와 관련된 품사 문제가 상대적으로 적은 편이다.

PART 6 장문 빈칸 채우기 Text Completion

총 4지문 16문제 (지문당 4문제)

한 지문에 4문제가 나오며 평균적으로 어휘 문제가 2개, 품사나 문법 문제가 1개, 문맥에 맞는 문장 고르기 문제가 1개 들어간다. 문맥에 맞는 문장 고르기 문제를 제외하면 문제 유형은 기본적으로 파트 5와 거의 비슷하다.

문맥에 맞는 문장 고르기

문맥에 맞는 문장 고르기 문제는 지문당 한 문제씩 나오는데, 나오는 위치의 확률은 4문제 중 두 번째 문제, 세 번째 문제, 네 번째 문제, 첫 번째 문제 순으로 높다.

어휘 문제

동사, 명사, 부사, 어구와 관련된 어휘 문제는 매번 1~2개씩 나온다. 부사 어휘 문제의 경우 therefore(그러므로)나 however(하지만)처럼 문맥의 흐름을 자연스럽게 연결해 주는 부사가 자주 나온다.

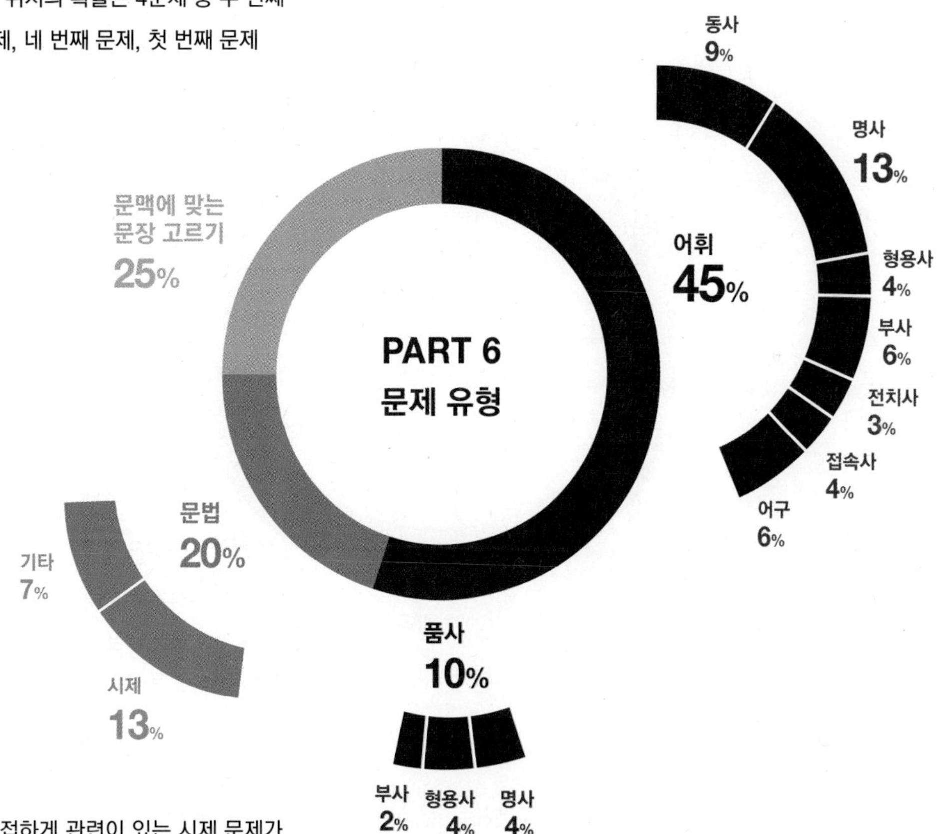

문법 문제

문맥의 흐름과 밀접하게 관련이 있는 시제 문제가 2개 정도 나오며, 능동태/수동태나 수의 일치와 연계되기도 한다. 그 밖에 대명사, 능동태/수동태, 부정사, 접속사/전치사 등과 관련된 문법 문제가 나온다.

품사 문제

명사나 형용사 문제가 부사 문제보다 좀 더 자주 나온다.

토익 경향 분석

PART 7 독해 Reading Comprehension

지문 유형	지문당 문제 수	지문 개수	비중 %
단일 지문	2문항	4개	약 15%
	3문항	3개	약 16%
	4문항	3개	약 22%
이중 지문	5문항	2개	약 19%
삼중 지문	5문항	3개	약 28%

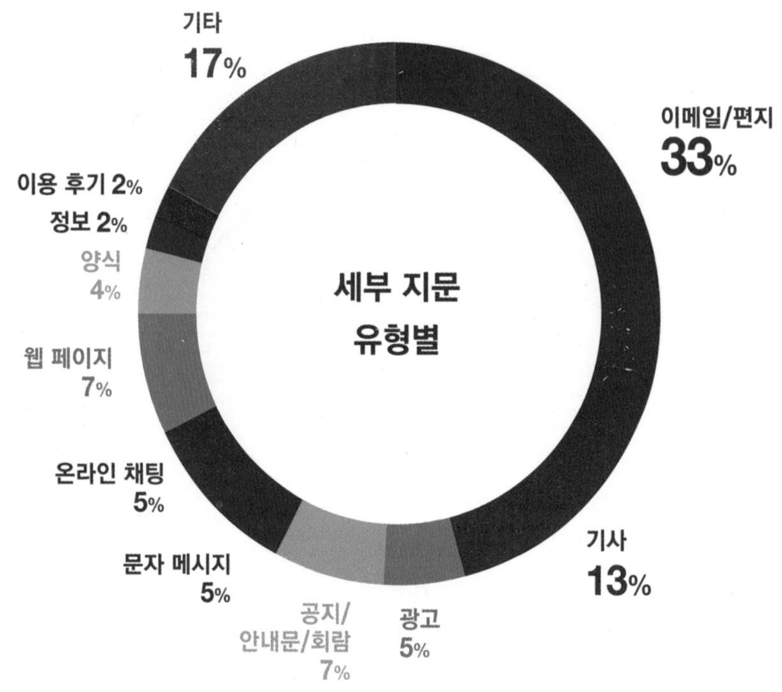

- 이메일/편지, 기사 유형 지문은 거의 항상 나오는 편이며 많은 경우 합해서 전체의 50~60%에 이르기도 한다.
- 기타 지문 유형으로 agenda, brochure, comment card, coupon, flyer, instructions, invitation, invoice, list, menu, page from a catalog, policy statement, report, schedule, survey, voucher 등 다양한 자료가 골고루 나온다.

(이중 지문과 삼중 지문 속의 지문들을 모두 낱개로 계산함 – 총 23지문)

총 15지문 54문제 (지문당 2~5문제)

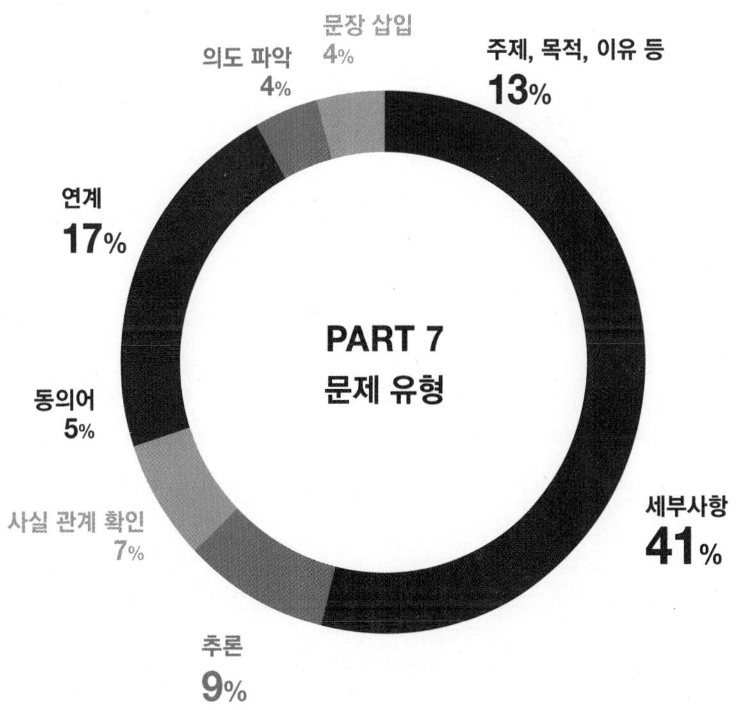

- 동의어 문제는 주로 이중 지문이나 삼중 지문에 나온다.
- 연계 문제는 일반적으로 이중 지문에서 한 문제, 삼중 지문에서 두 문제가 나온다.
- 의도 파악 문제는 문자 메시지(text-message chain)나 온라인 채팅(online chat discussion) 지문에서 출제되며 두 문제가 나온다.
- 문장 삽입 문제는 주로 기사, 이메일, 편지, 회람 지문에서 출제되며 두 문제가 나온다.

점수 환산표 및 산출법

점수 환산표 이 책에 수록된 각 Test를 풀고 난 후, 맞은 개수를 세어 점수를 환산해 보세요.

LISTENING Raw Score (맞은 개수)	LISTENING Scaled Score (환산 점수)
96-100	475-495
91-95	435-495
86-90	405-470
81-85	370-450
76-80	345-420
71-75	320-390
66-70	290-360
61-65	265-335
56-60	240-310
51-55	215-280
46-50	190-255
41-45	160-230
36-40	130-205
31-35	105-175
26-30	85-145
21-25	60-115
16-20	30-90
11-15	5-70
6-10	5-60
1-5	5-50
0	5-35

READING Raw Score (맞은 개수)	READING Scaled Score (환산 점수)
96-100	460-495
91-95	425-490
86-90	400-465
81-85	375-440
76-80	340-415
71-75	310-390
66-70	285-370
61-65	255-340
56-60	230-310
51-55	200-275
46-50	170-245
41-45	140-215
36-40	115-180
31-35	95-150
26-30	75-120
21-25	60-95
16-20	45-75
11-15	30-55
6-10	10-40
1-5	5-30
0	5-15

점수 산출 방법

아래의 방식으로 점수를 산출할 수 있다.

자신의 답안을 수록된 정답과 대조하여 채점한다. 각 Section의 맞은 개수가 본인의 Section별 '실제 점수 (통계 처리하기 전의 점수, raw score)'이다. Listening Test와 Reading Test의 정답 수를 세어, 자신의 실제 점수를 아래의 해당란에 기록한다.

	맞은 개수	환산 점수대
LISTENING		
READING		
총점		

Section별 실제 점수가 그대로 Section별 TOEIC 점수가 되는 것은 아니다. TOEIC은 시행할 때마다 별도로 특정한 통계 처리 방법을 사용하며 이러한 실제 점수를 환산 점수(converted[scaled] score)로 전환하게 된다. 이렇게 전환함으로써, 매번 시행될 때마다 문제는 달라지지만 그 점수가 갖는 의미는 같아지게 된다. 예를 들어 어느 한 시험에서 총점 550점의 성적으로 받는 실력이라면 다른 시험에서도 거의 550점대의 성적을 받게 되는 것이다.

▼

실제 점수를 위 표에 기록한 후 왼쪽 페이지의 점수 환산표를 보도록 한다. TOEIC이 시행될 때마다 대개 이와 비슷한 형태의 표가 작성되는데, 여기 제시된 환산표는 본 교재에 수록된 Test용으로 개발된 것이다. 이 표를 사용하여 자신의 실제 점수를 환산 점수로 전환하도록 한다. 즉, 예를 들어 Listening Test의 실제 정답 수가 61~65개이면 환산 점수는 265점에서 335점 사이가 된다. 여기서 실제 정답 수가 61개이면 환산 점수가 265점이고, 65개이면 환산 점수가 335점 임을 의미하는 것은 아니다. 본 책의 Test를 위해 작성된 이 점수 환산표가 자신의 영어 실력이 어느 정도인지 대략적으로 파악하는 데 도움이 되긴 하지만, 이 표가 실제 TOEIC 성적 산출에 그대로 사용된 적은 없다는 사실을 밝혀 둔다.

토익® 정기시험
기출문제집

기출 TEST

01

READING TEST

In the Reading test, you will read a variety of texts and answer several different types of reading comprehension questions. The entire Reading test will last 75 minutes. There are three parts, and directions are given for each part. You are encouraged to answer as many questions as possible within the time allowed.

You must mark your answers on the separate answer sheet. Do not write your answers in your test book.

PART 5

Directions: A word or phrase is missing in each of the sentences below. Four answer choices are given below each sentence. Select the best answer to complete the sentence. Then mark the letter (A), (B), (C), or (D) on your answer sheet.

101. Departmental restructuring will be discussed at the ------- monthly meeting.

(A) next
(B) always
(C) soon
(D) like

102. To keep ------- park beautiful, please place your nonrecyclables in the available trash cans.

(A) our
(B) we
(C) us
(D) ours

103. Mr. Hardin ------- additional images of the office building he is interested in leasing.

(A) informed
(B) asked
(C) advised
(D) requested

104. A team of agricultural experts will be brought ------- to try to improve crop harvests.

(A) because
(B) either
(C) between
(D) together

105. The board of Galaxipharm ------- Mr. Kwon's successor at yesterday's meeting.

(A) named
(B) granted
(C) founded
(D) proved

106. If your parking permit is damaged, bring it to the entrance station for a -------.

(A) replacement
(B) replacing
(C) replace
(D) replaces

107. Mr. Ahmad decided to reserve a private room for the awards dinner ------- the restaurant was noisy.

(A) rather than
(B) in case
(C) such as
(D) unless

108. Ms. Jones has provided a ------- estimate of the costs of expanding distribution statewide.

(A) conserve
(B) conserves
(C) conservative
(D) conservatively

109. Each quarter, Acaba Exports sets ------- sales goals for its staff.

(A) compact
(B) wealthy
(C) faithful
(D) realistic

110. Ms. Garcia was delighted to receive ------- that her company soon will be featured in the *In Town Times* magazine.

(A) notify
(B) notification
(C) notifying
(D) notifies

111. Children under five years of age are eligible ------- free vision tests.

(A) over
(B) down
(C) for
(D) out

112. Drivers on the Partan Expressway are reminded to drive ------- throughout July because of the ongoing construction work.

(A) caution
(B) cautiously
(C) cautious
(D) cautiousness

113. The committee will resume its weekly meetings ------- Ms. Cheon returns from Scotland on September 17.

(A) that
(B) once
(C) as well
(D) then

114. The ------- initiative aims to provide public transportation for commuters living in the outer suburbs.

(A) proposed
(B) proposing
(C) proposal
(D) propose

115. Yesterday's storm ------- interrupted the services of the Duddula, Inc., satellite communications system.

(A) annually
(B) anytime
(C) whenever
(D) temporarily

116. Even though Cabrera Pictures and Marcella Images make very different films, ------- are successful movie studios.

(A) several
(B) everybody
(C) some
(D) both

117. ------- of tasks can make a manager's job easier and help other employees learn new skills.

(A) Reputation
(B) Foundation
(C) Delegation
(D) Permission

118. Proceeds from the sale of Delcrest Corporation were equally ------- among the founder's three daughters.

(A) divisions
(B) dividing
(C) divide
(D) divided

119. ------- higher than average ticket prices, every performance of Aiden North's new play is sold out for the next six months.

(A) Throughout
(B) Except for
(C) Despite
(D) Prior to

120. Ricardo Sosa, the executive chef at Restaurant Ninal, responds to guests' suggestions -------.

(A) respect
(B) respects
(C) respectfully
(D) respected

GO ON TO THE NEXT PAGE

121. Mr. Koster is negotiating the ------- of the new contract with Arban, Inc.

(A) scope
(B) turn
(C) grip
(D) drive

122. The equipment-use guidelines ------- on our internal corporate Web site.

(A) may find
(B) can be found
(C) have found
(D) have to find

123. Professor Han created spreadsheets to calculate the farm's irrigation needs -------.

(A) dominantly
(B) precisely
(C) relatively
(D) widely

124. For hiring purposes, five years of professional experience is ------- to having achieved certification.

(A) reasonable
(B) appropriate
(C) equivalent
(D) significant

125. South Regent Aviation is adopting measures to reduce fuel expenses by ------- cargo loads.

(A) light
(B) lighten
(C) lightly
(D) lightening

126. ------- the most challenging aspect of accepting a new position is negotiating a salary that is both fair and satisfying.

(A) Perhaps
(B) Outside
(C) Every
(D) While

127. Complaints about its new line of kitchen appliances led Loxevo, Inc., to adopt higher ------- for assessing quality.

(A) standards
(B) features
(C) risks
(D) institutions

128. The chief engineer noted that constructing another bridge would be more ------- than repairing the existing structure.

(A) economy
(B) economics
(C) economically
(D) economical

129. Jansen Bus Company drivers are expected to complete regular trainings ------- maintaining their state licenses.

(A) in addition to
(B) according to
(C) inside
(D) within

130. Ms. DeSoto ------- all employees to come to last week's budget meeting even though only officers were obligated to attend.

(A) to have urged
(B) had urged
(C) will have urged
(D) was urged

PART 6

Directions: Read the texts that follow. A word, phrase, or sentence is missing in parts of each text. Four answer choices for each question are given below the text. Select the best answer to complete the text. Then mark the letter (A), (B), (C), or (D) on your answer sheet.

Questions 131-134 refer to the following notice.

Lakeview Railway Onboard Bicycle Policy

Would you like to use your bicycle to explore the Lakeview Corridor Scenic Area? Our trains have the ------- **131.** you need to safely transport your bike. When booking your ticket, just remember that reservations ------- **132.** for both you and your bicycle. Reserve your bicycle spot ------- **133.**. There are a limited number of storage racks on each train. You are responsible for stowing your bike securely. ------- **134.**. Lakeview Railway does not take responsibility for bicycles lost or damaged aboard our trains.

131. (A) stock
(B) equipment
(C) property
(D) revenue

132. (A) require
(B) requiring
(C) are required
(D) were required

133. (A) early
(B) again
(C) more
(D) instead

134. (A) Folding bicycles have become more common.
(B) Additional service fees may apply.
(C) You can obtain route maps at most stations.
(D) You must also supply your own bike lock.

GO ON TO THE NEXT PAGE →

Questions 135-138 refer to the following letter.

Corelli's Bakery
15 Middlemass Street
Youngstown, Ohio 44515

Dear Valued Customer:

For the last three years we have charged the same wholesale prices for our baked goods, including cakes, pies, cookies, and brownies. We regret that sharply rising prices for our raw ingredients, such as sugar and fruit, have forced us to raise our prices by 5 percent ------- (135.) August 1. We have made every attempt to avoid this price increase. ------- (136.), we refuse to compromise on the quality of our products. Using the best ingredients available will allow us to provide the delicious desserts your restaurant guests have come to expect. ------- (137.).
We appreciate your ------- (138.) and look forward to continuing to serve you.

Sincerely,

Tony Corelli, Owner

135. (A) actual
(B) future
(C) practical
(D) effective

136. (A) Similarly
(B) Therefore
(C) However
(D) Accordingly

137. (A) We believe you will see that our products are still a great value.
(B) Our efforts to stay profitable have not been successful.
(C) We hope our competitors will raise their prices too.
(D) Our products are healthier than traditional baked goods.

138. (A) supportive
(B) support
(C) supporter
(D) supports

Questions 139-142 refer to the following e-mail.

To: Noora Abadi
From: Alexis Palmer
Subject: Informational interview
Date: 4 February

Dear Ms. Abadi:

Thank you for taking the time to meet with me yesterday about careers in the aerospace industry. Your ------- (**139.**) were helpful and have inspired me to seek additional work experience in the field before I apply to graduate school.

I will consult the Web sites you recommended for job opportunities. As you also suggested, I will ------- (**140.**) a membership in the Eastern Aeronautics Professional Association. ------- (**141.**). I appreciate the information you shared about the organization's conference at the end of the month.

Thank you again for your ------- (**142.**) assistance.

Sincerely,

Alexis Palmer

139. (A) insights
(B) surveys
(C) improvements
(D) revisions

140. (A) resolve
(B) predict
(C) consider
(D) advertise

141. (A) I look forward to networking with other professionals in the field.
(B) My membership will expire at the end of the year.
(C) I will be giving a presentation at the conference.
(D) I would like to apply for the position soon.

142. (A) generosity
(B) generous
(C) generously
(D) generousness

GO ON TO THE NEXT PAGE

Questions 143-146 refer to the following letter.

15 October

GPO Box 985
CANBERRA ACT 6512

Dear Ms. Wilson,

On behalf of the Australia Wildlife Park Association, thank you for your donation of 40 AUD to our national park. -------. Individual contributions have helped it stay open to visitors for more than 50 years. Our goal is to keep the park system running effectively for future ------- to enjoy.
143. / **144.**

Enclosed please find a copy of our brochure, which lists various programmes ------- to benefit both park visitors and our wildlife habitats. Please consider ------- one of these programmes in the future. The money would be used wisely and would be deeply appreciated.
145. / **146.**

Sincerely,

Akosua Masika, Membership Chair

143. (A) The association grants scholarships for those studying zoology.
(B) Supporters like you help preserve the park for public use.
(C) We hope you enjoyed your visit to the park today.
(D) Interested parties can volunteer to clean wildlife habitats.

144. (A) generations
(B) lifestyles
(C) committees
(D) planners

145. (A) designer
(B) designs
(C) designing
(D) designed

146. (A) researching
(B) organizing
(C) leading
(D) funding

PART 7

Directions: In this part you will read a selection of texts, such as magazine and newspaper articles, e-mails, and instant messages. Each text or set of texts is followed by several questions. Select the best answer for each question and mark the letter (A), (B), (C), or (D) on your answer sheet.

Questions 147-148 refer to the following Web page.

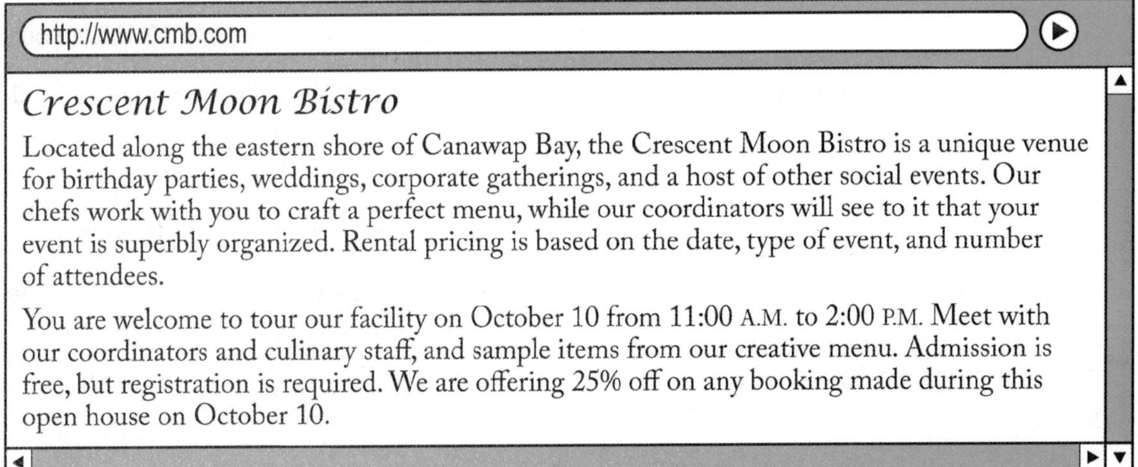

http://www.cmb.com

Crescent Moon Bistro

Located along the eastern shore of Canawap Bay, the Crescent Moon Bistro is a unique venue for birthday parties, weddings, corporate gatherings, and a host of other social events. Our chefs work with you to craft a perfect menu, while our coordinators will see to it that your event is superbly organized. Rental pricing is based on the date, type of event, and number of attendees.

You are welcome to tour our facility on October 10 from 11:00 A.M. to 2:00 P.M. Meet with our coordinators and culinary staff, and sample items from our creative menu. Admission is free, but registration is required. We are offering 25% off on any booking made during this open house on October 10.

147. What is being advertised?

(A) A vacation rental
(B) A new hotel
(C) An event space
(D) A summer camp

148. What will be offered on October 10 ?

(A) A discounted reservation rate
(B) A special concert
(C) A famous recipe book
(D) A class by a famous chef

GO ON TO THE NEXT PAGE

Questions 149-150 refer to the following memo.

To: Processing Plant Managers
From: Sunlight Sugar Executive Board
Date: June 15
Subject: News

We are pleased to announce that, following our strongest quarter in over three years, we were ranked as the number-two sugar distributor in the region in the June 1 edition of *Sugar Industry Times*. We are extremely grateful to all our employees, who helped make this possible through their hard work and dedication.

To celebrate this achievement, we would like to recognize employees with a bonus to be added to their July 15 paycheck. Plant managers at each location should inform staff at the next plant meeting on July 1. Thank you for helping us achieve our goals.

149. What is indicated about Sunlight Sugar?

(A) It is changing the payday schedule.
(B) It publishes the *Sugar Industry Times*.
(C) It was established more than three years ago.
(D) It was previously the number-one distributor of sugar.

150. When will plant managers announce an employee bonus?

(A) On June 1
(B) On June 15
(C) On July 1
(D) On July 15

Questions 151-152 refer to the following online chat discussion.

Ella Santos [10:02 A.M.]
Good morning. I purchased two tickets to Friday night's performance. However, my business trip was rescheduled, and I won't be in London on Friday. Can I get a refund for this purchase?

Mai Tong, Customer Service [10:04 A.M.]
Thank you for contacting us. Unfortunately, the Mosella Palladium's policies do not allow refunds. We offer exchanges for tickets of equal or lesser value. You can view our entire season, which has a variety of music, dance, and theatre, at www.mosellapalladium.co.uk.

Ella Santos [10:07 A.M.]
I reviewed the season schedule before contacting you. Can you switch the tickets now, or must I call your phone number? I've already made a selection.

Mai Tong, Customer Service [10:08 A.M.]
I can help with that. What would you like to see instead?

Ella Santos [10:10 A.M.]
I'd like two tickets to the Gaperstein Orchestra on 22 October.

151. What most likely is the Mosella Palladium?

(A) A sports stadium
(B) A performance venue
(C) A dance company
(D) A theatrical group

152. At 10:08 A.M., what does Ms. Tong mean when she writes, "I can help with that"?

(A) She will send a brochure.
(B) She will arrange a phone call.
(C) She can process a refund.
(D) She can exchange some tickets.

GO ON TO THE NEXT PAGE →

Questions 153-154 refer to the following e-mail.

E-mail

To: Ted Lee <ted.lee@comconnecting.com>

From: Agnaldo Paes <apaes@manosinc.com>

Date: May 3

Subject: Interview

Dear Mr. Lee,

Thank you for your interest in the master electrician position here at Manos Contracting, Inc. Your résumé is very impressive, and I would like to schedule an in-person interview sometime next week. Does next Tuesday afternoon work for you? I am usually in the office until 6 p.m. If Tuesday is not convenient, perhaps Wednesday morning would be acceptable? Any time after 9 a.m. works for me. My office is on the second floor of our main building, which is located at the end of Elkton Street. Since this is only our first meeting in the interview process, I do not expect it to last longer than one hour. I look forward to hearing from you soon.

Sincerely,

Agnaldo Paes
Assistant Director of Human Resources
Manos Contracting, Inc.

153. What is probably true about Mr. Lee?

(A) He is moving to a new town.
(B) He is an experienced electrician.
(C) He has recently received professional certification.
(D) He will be offered a job at the interview.

154. When is Mr. Paes most likely NOT available for an interview?

(A) Tuesday at 3:15 P.M.
(B) Tuesday at 6:30 P.M.
(C) Wednesday at 9:30 A.M.
(D) Wednesday at 11:30 A.M.

Questions 155-157 refer to the following Web page.

http://www.mazullospizza.com

Home | **About** | Our Ingredients | Order Online

Mazullo's Deep-Dish Pizza

Get a taste of the best pizza in Chicago!

We have been serving authentic deep-dish Chicago-style pizza since Tonia Mazullo opened the original restaurant in a humble shop in Bridgeport. Thirty-five years later, her children and grandchildren continue to craft delectable pizzas using traditional Mazullo-family dough and tomato sauce recipes.

We offer dine-in, carryout, and delivery service within three miles of our locations.

- All pizzas are made fresh to order and include your choice of three toppings. Every pizza is served with a large beverage and our famous garlic rolls.
- A variety of salads and pastas make optional side dishes.
- All vegetable toppings are local, organic, and farm-to-table.

Click on a location to get directions, phone numbers, and restaurant hours.

Bridgeport | Lincoln Park | Edgewater | Avondale

155. What is true about Mazullo's Bridgeport shop?

(A) It has recently expanded.
(B) It is under new management.
(C) It does not offer delivery.
(D) It was the first location to open.

156. What is indicated about Mazullo's pizzas?

(A) They are reasonably priced.
(B) They are imported from Chicago.
(C) Their sauce is made from a family recipe.
(D) Their vegetable toppings come from Mazullo-owned farms.

157. What is NOT included with a deep-dish pizza order?

(A) Garlic rolls
(B) Pasta
(C) Toppings
(D) A beverage

GO ON TO THE NEXT PAGE

Questions 158-160 refer to the following letter.

Kendinburgh Transit
64 Ponteland Rd
Kendinburgh, TD9 5UW

Callum Stevenson
42 Leicester Road
Girvaton, P24 9QS

3 January

Dear Mr. Stevenson,

— [1] —. We are happy to have you as part of the Kendinburgh Transit team. Prior to your receiving training on the vehicle you will be assigned to, we must first ensure that your medical documentation is up-to-date. — [2] —.

The main priority of public transport is the safety of passengers and other motorists. Your ability to safely operate a bus in city traffic and changing weather conditions depends in part on your good health. For this purpose, you will need to undergo a pre-employment physical checkup. To make an appointment, please call (0500) 555 0140. — [3] —. Your examination will be performed by a physician selected by Kendinburgh Transit, and you will not be charged for it. — [4] —. Please present the physician's report to your supervisor on your first day.

We look forward to working with you.

Kristine Yerkes
Kendinburgh Transit

158. Who most likely is Mr. Stevenson?

(A) A driver
(B) A mechanic
(C) A medical assistant
(D) A city official

159. What is Mr. Stevenson asked to do by phone?

(A) Extend his medical leave
(B) Schedule an examination
(C) Contact his supervisor
(D) Inquire about weather conditions

160. In which of the positions marked [1], [2], [3], and [4] does the following sentence best belong?

"To that end, we need you to complete one more task before beginning employment with us next month."

(A) [1]
(B) [2]
(C) [3]
(D) [4]

Questions 161-163 refer to the following article.

A Changing of the Guard at Rolidge Motors

by Nathan Kekana

DURBAN—Rolidge Motors has announced that Cara Walters will be the next CEO of the Durban-based company. Ms. Walters succeeds Thomas Hsing, who has served in the role for fifteen years and is retiring. Most recently, Ms. Walters was executive vice president for Cermak & Holden Ltd., which she helped to grow into one of the largest electronics firms in South Africa.

This marks Ms. Walters' return to Rolidge Motors, where she began her career after graduating from university. She completed the Rolidge Leadership Programme and stayed for seven years before moving on to Cermak & Holden.

"Ms. Walters has both the leadership experience and inside knowledge of Rolidge Motors to make her tenure here successful," remarked Mr. Hsing. "We are excited to have Ms. Walters join us," added Matilde Bekwa, Rolidge Motors' chairman of the board. "Her work at Cermak & Holden has been remarkable, and we look forward to benefiting from her visionary leadership."

161. What does the article mainly discuss?

(A) The benefits of a leadership training program
(B) A successful electronics company
(C) The appointment of a new CEO
(D) A company opening in Durban

162. What is indicated about Ms. Walters?

(A) She worked in several departments at Cermak & Holden.
(B) She was hired by Rolidge Motors after finishing university.
(C) She was a professor before starting her own company.
(D) She specializes in saving struggling companies.

163. Which of Ms. Walters' qualifications is mentioned by both Mr. Hsing and Ms. Bekwa?

(A) Her popularity among colleagues
(B) Her innovations at Cermak & Holden
(C) Her academic credentials
(D) Her reputation as a business leader

GO ON TO THE NEXT PAGE →

Questions 164-167 refer to the following e-mail.

E-mail

To: skim@jigyeapartments.com
From: larue@waterservices.org
Subject: Water Shut-off
Date: 7 January

Dear Mr. Kim,

Because of a maintenance project, the water to Jigye Apartments will be turned off for several hours next Wednesday, 12 January. The interruption will begin at 11:00 A.M. Water service will be restored by 5:00 P.M. Please inform all of your building's tenants in advance about the interruption, as well as these general guidelines:

1. After the water is turned back on, air in the pipes may cause sudden bursts of water. You can fix this problem by running water slowly at first.

2. For any other issues that occur after water service is returned, call our Customer Service desk at the number listed on our Web site for your specific area.

3. Maintenance workers do their best to work quickly and finish as scheduled.

This service interruption is necessary to improve the quality of your water service in the future. We apologize for any inconvenience and thank you for your patience.

Best regards,

Pierrick de la Rue

164. According to the e-mail, when can residents expect to use water again?

(A) At 7:00 A.M.
(B) At 11:00 A.M.
(C) At 3:00 P.M.
(D) At 5:00 P.M.

165. Who most likely is Mr. Kim?

(A) A plumber
(B) A building manager
(C) A construction worker
(D) A customer-service agent

166. What potential issue does Mr. de la Rue mention?

(A) There could be an additional maintenance charge.
(B) There could be a leak in the main water line.
(C) There might be problems with the water flow.
(D) There might be a follow-up check in a week.

167. What is indicated about the residents of Jigye Apartments?

(A) They should call a specific number with any concerns.
(B) They should try to decrease their water usage.
(C) They have complained to the Customer Service desk.
(D) They have scheduled a tenant meeting on January 12.

Questions 168-171 refer to the following memo.

To: South Street Bank staff
From: William Rees-Yates, Chief Executive Officer
Date: May 12

I am pleased to announce that our bank is expanding. Thanks to our creative marketing and award-winning customer service, the demand for our services has been growing. — [1] —. We will therefore be opening a branch in Leesburg this year.

Although the new branch will not be in operation until July 1, it is already virtually ready to open. — [2] —. There remain, however, a couple of job openings to be filled that can be viewed at www.southstreetbank.com/jobs. If any of our current staff are interested in transferring to the Leesburg branch, we encourage you to review the vacancies soon and apply at the Web site listed above. Please contact Human Resources with any questions. — [3] —.

Meanwhile, our business continues to thrive and grow in other ways. — [4] —. We have recently been nominated for the Business of the Year award by the Chamber of Commerce. This is a significant achievement, due in no small part to the dedicated work of our outstanding team. On behalf of our management team, thank you very much and congratulations.

168. What is the memo mainly about?

(A) A merger with another company
(B) The hiring of several new staff
(C) A temporary closing for renovations
(D) The opening of a new branch

169. What are staff invited to do?

(A) Join a local business group
(B) Attend a celebratory gathering
(C) Review information on a Web site
(D) Submit ideas for better customer service

170. What is one achievement Mr. Rees-Yates mentions?

(A) An award nomination
(B) A positive review in a local publication
(C) An invitation to a popular event
(D) An unexpected increase in investment

171. In which of the positions marked [1], [2], [3], and [4] does the following sentence best belong?

"Most Leesburg staff have already been recruited."

(A) [1]
(B) [2]
(C) [3]
(D) [4]

GO ON TO THE NEXT PAGE

Questions 172-175 refer to the following online chat discussion.

Monday, 8 May

Gabriel Li (9:10 A.M.)	Good morning, everyone. I want to remind you that Larkin Landscaping will be here at Derryco tomorrow morning to remove the trees from the front parking area. My workers will block off the area before the contractor arrives, so you and your staff should plan to find parking elsewhere or use public transit.
Ava Abberton (9:11 A.M.)	I have a client, Jan McGonagle, who will be driving in from Belfast to meet with me at 10:00 A.M. What should I tell her? Can she contact the facilities department?
Martin Beattie (9:12 A.M.)	There's heavy rain in the forecast. Are you sure the tree work will go forward?
Gabriel Li (9:13 A.M.)	Yes, give Ms. McGonagle my mobile phone number and have her call me when she arrives. I will direct her around the back. The spots there will be reserved for visitors only.
Gabriel Li (9:14 A.M.)	And yes, Larkin assured me the crew comes out rain or shine.
Daniel Deegan (9:15 A.M.)	Remember, too, that we can approve team members to work from home tomorrow. Just make sure that all conference calls are listed on the master schedule on the intranet.
Gabriel Li (9:16 A.M.)	Right. Thank you, all.

172. Who most likely is Mr. Li?

(A) A landscaping crew member
(B) A delivery coordinator
(C) A warehouse worker
(D) A facilities supervisor

173. Why will Ms. McGonagle contact Mr. Li?

(A) To schedule a visit with him
(B) To obtain parking assistance
(C) To get a list of directions to the office
(D) To advise him of transit delays

174. What is likely to happen on May 9 ?

(A) Some Derryco employees will work at home.
(B) Derryco will be closed for business.
(C) Ms. McGonagle will stay in a local hotel.
(D) Mr. Deegan will cancel a conference call.

175. At 9:14 A.M., what does Mr. Li mean when he writes, "the crew comes out rain or shine"?

(A) The weather forecast is probably wrong.
(B) The outdoor work will proceed as scheduled.
(C) Larkin Landscaping employs an outstanding group of workers.
(D) Derryco employees should prepare for bad weather.

GO ON TO THE NEXT PAGE

Questions 176-180 refer to the following Web page and e-mail.

http://www.sunriseaerospace.co.au/companynews

Sunrise Aerospace

HOME	**COMPANY NEWS**	CONTACT	REVIEWS

We are pleased to announce that our latest design, the Suppliss Seat, will be introduced on Honshu Express's Tokyo–Osaka service route, which is scheduled to debut soon. Since last February, our design team has worked closely with Honshu Express to produce a comfortable seat that meets the most stringent safety standards. Like all our products, it is made of lightweight yet durable materials, resulting in significant fuel-cost savings over time. The prototype for the Suppliss Seat has received high marks from designers and was nominated for a Henry Design Award in January.

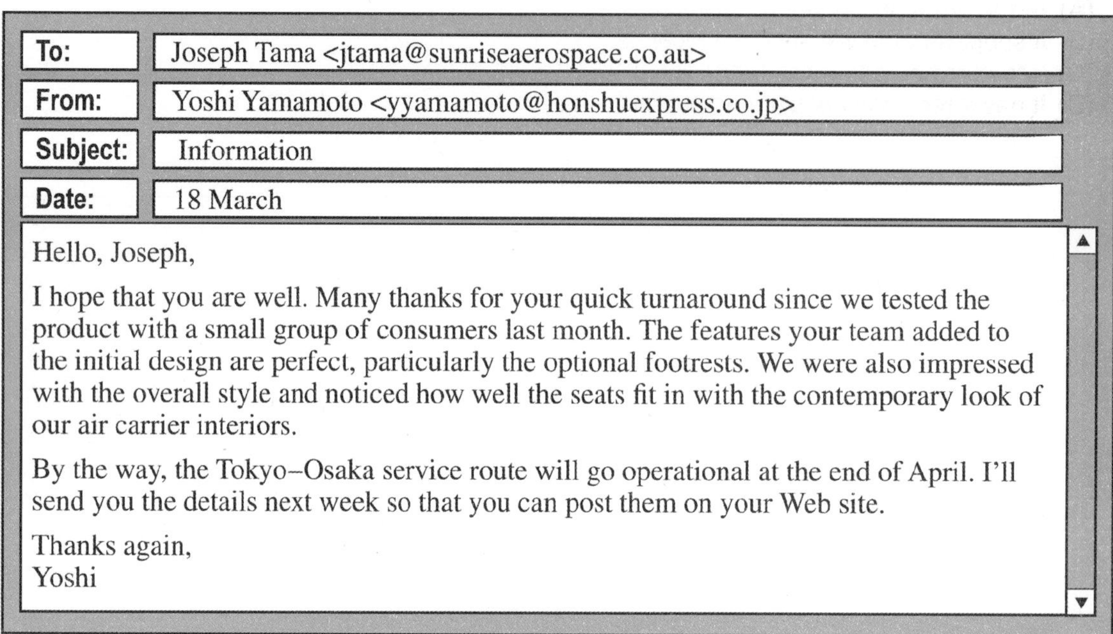

To: Joseph Tama <jtama@sunriseaerospace.co.au>

From: Yoshi Yamamoto <yyamamoto@honshuexpress.co.jp>

Subject: Information

Date: 18 March

Hello, Joseph,

I hope that you are well. Many thanks for your quick turnaround since we tested the product with a small group of consumers last month. The features your team added to the initial design are perfect, particularly the optional footrests. We were also impressed with the overall style and noticed how well the seats fit in with the contemporary look of our air carrier interiors.

By the way, the Tokyo–Osaka service route will go operational at the end of April. I'll send you the details next week so that you can post them on your Web site.

Thanks again,
Yoshi

176. What is the purpose of the Web page?
(A) To invite feedback about a service
(B) To announce a business merger
(C) To publicize a successful product
(D) To nominate a product for an award

177. What type of industry does the design team support?
(A) Airline
(B) Technology
(C) Education
(D) City transit systems

178. What characteristic of the Suppliss Seat is NOT mentioned?
(A) It is lightweight.
(B) It supports the feet.
(C) It features a contemporary style.
(D) It has a reclining position.

179. What does the e-mail indicate about the consumer tests?
(A) They have not yet been completed.
(B) They resulted in design changes.
(C) They took place on a specific route.
(D) They did not meet all safety standards.

180. When will the Suppliss Seat come into regular use?
(A) In January
(B) In February
(C) In March
(D) In April

GO ON TO THE NEXT PAGE

Questions 181-185 refer to the following advertisement and e-mail.

Leasing Opportunities

La Gardina Mall offers a unique shopping experience in a beautiful setting of landscaped gardens, courtyards, and fountains. The mall features retail shops that range from well-known chain stores to one-of-a-kind boutiques, as well as a large variety of restaurants and cafés.

With 300,000 square meters of pedestrian-only retail space, La Gardina Mall attracts more than four million visitors per year. It is a shopping and dining destination for local Bay Shore residents and tourists alike.

If you would like more information about leasing retail or restaurant space at La Gardina, please contact Cecilia Goncalves, our Leasing Administrator, at cgoncalves@lagardina.com. While most of our space is occupied by long-term lessees, a limited number of seasonal contracts (four months minimum) are available.

E-mail

To:	Cecilia Goncalves <cgoncalves@lagardina.com>
From:	Marco Sabatini <msabatini@sabatinileather.com>
Date:	25 March
Subject:	Retail space
Attachment:	List of products

Dear Ms. Goncalves:

As owner of Sabatini Leather Goods, I would like to express interest in a short-term leasing opportunity at La Gardina Mall.

Sabatini Leather Goods is a small company that manufactures and sells souvenir handbags and wallets. Our high-quality leather products are imprinted with the name of the tourist destination where they are sold. I have attached some images of our best-selling items from our most recent temporary shop in Glastonbury, where we had our best sales performance in the company's history. We have sold our products in 24 different locations so far, all with great success.

We have been looking for a place in Bay Shore for a while, and La Gardina Mall seems to be a good fit. We would like a space of about 150 square meters for a three-month period over the summer tourism season. Could you please call me at 555-0125 so that we can discuss this matter further?

Respectfully,

Marco Sabatini

181. What is suggested about La Gardina Mall?

(A) It is located in Bay Shore.
(B) It is open only in the summer.
(C) It recently added many new shops.
(D) It features mainly fashion boutiques.

182. In the advertisement, the word "occupied" in paragraph 3, line 3, is closest in meaning to

(A) filled
(B) captured
(C) kept busy
(D) made steady

183. What is the main purpose of the e-mail?

(A) To promote a new botanical garden
(B) To profile a popular company
(C) To inquire about a potential business deal
(D) To ask about job opportunities at a mall

184. What is indicated about Sabatini Leather Goods products?

(A) They are sold online.
(B) They are often discounted.
(C) They are marketed to tourists.
(D) They are manufactured in Glastonbury.

185. What will Mr. Sabatini and Ms. Goncalves most likely have to negotiate?

(A) The location of a store
(B) The length of a contract
(C) The size of a retail space
(D) The cost of a monthly lease Questions

GO ON TO THE NEXT PAGE

Questions 186-190 refer to the following chart, e-mail, and article.

TYCHE FINE CARPETS—Pleiades Collection Product Availability (updated daily)					
Name	**Size** (cm)	**Shipping Weight**	**Quantity Available** (today)	**Quantity Available** (in 30 days)	**Quantity Available** (in 60 days)
Artemis	190 x 280	13 kg	30	60	0
Hera	190 x 280	14 kg	16	20	0
Janus	160 x 230	11 kg	0	0	20
Iris	120 x 170	9 kg	10	15	15

To: Frieda Zuckerman

From: Miles Sorrell

Date: February 5

Subject: Logistical arrangements

Attachment: Photos

Dear Ms. Zuckerman:

I regret to inform you that Tyche Fine Carpets, the supplier we selected for the carpets in The Pavel Hotel's lobby and lounge areas, will not have our chosen pattern available until after the hotel's anticipated opening date of March 1. Attached are photographs of several alternative selections that I believe will work well with the décor. They are all made of the same material as the previous selection, and the prices are comparable. With the grand opening less than a month away, I need a decision from you as soon as possible. Even with this last-minute change, I am certain that The Pavel Hotel will provide the ambience we have set out to create.

Thank you,

Miles Sorrell

Pavel Hotel Open
by Lavonne Coe

(Centerville—March 2) Former city court judge Mildred Simpson joined owner Patrice Snell yesterday to celebrate the opening of The Pavel Hotel in downtown Centerville, between the library and the visitors center. Once the city's courthouse and Ms. Simpson's workplace, the existing structure had been vacant for the past nine years. Now the space boasts 34 elegant rooms, an inviting lounge with a fireplace, and a gorgeous lobby. An on-site café is expected to open next month. The interior, designed by Miles Sorrell, retains the old features of the building, such as expansive windows and high ceilings, while creating a warm and inviting space.

186. What does the chart indicate about all the carpets in the Pleiades Collection?

(A) They will be available in 60 days.
(B) They are currently in stock.
(C) They have different weights.
(D) They are the same size.

187. What carpet did Mr. Sorrell originally order?

(A) Artemis
(B) Hera
(C) Janus
(D) Iris

188. What does Mr. Sorrell ask Ms. Zuckerman to do?

(A) Delay the hotel's opening
(B) Select a substitute item
(C) Order some different furniture
(D) Send photographs of the lobby

189. According to the article, what occupied the building prior to The Pavel Hotel?

(A) A library
(B) A visitors center
(C) A courthouse
(D) A café

190. What is indicated about The Pavel Hotel?

(A) It opened on schedule.
(B) It was under construction for nine years.
(C) It is becoming a tourist destination.
(D) It is managed by Ms. Simpson.

GO ON TO THE NEXT PAGE

Questions 191-195 refer to the following memo, schedule, and e-mail.

From: Optieris Office of Parking and Transportation
To: All Optieris staff
Date: December 20
Subject: Upcoming enhancements to our shuttle bus system

In direct response to your helpful feedback, we would like to announce a number of improvements to the shuttle system that connects the Optieris campus with the Morbrook and Nesse train stations. The following changes will go into effect on January 2:

(1) A third bus will be added to our fleet to increase service frequency as well as capacity in case one bus is ever down for maintenance. Buses will now run every 15 minutes instead of 30 minutes.

(2) A second campus stop will be added. Besides the current stop at the main administration building on the east side of the Optieris campus, there will be a second stop to better accommodate all our staff.

(3) A service will be added in the evening. It will depart the Optieris campus 30 minutes later than the current last service of the day.

Thanks again for your input. For the sake of our environment, we are proud to facilitate your use of public transportation by making our shuttle bus service more convenient than ever.

Shuttle Bus Schedule—Weekday Mornings
(Updated January 2)

Morbrook Station →	Nesse Station →	East Campus →	West Campus
7:15	7:21	7:39	7:42
7:30	7:36	7:54	7:57
7:45	7:51	8:09	8:12
8:00	8:06	8:24	8:27
8:15	8:21	8:39	8:42
8:30	8:36	8:54	8:57

E-mail

From:	Sofia Edgren <sofiaedgren@lekmail.com>
To:	Sharani Khamis <s.khamis@optieris.com>
Subject:	Applicant interview at Optieris
Date:	January 25

Dear Ms. Khamis,

Thanks for inviting me to an interview with Mr. Rochon next week on the Optieris campus. I am certainly excited to be a finalist for this position in quality control. I also appreciate your sending me the company shuttle bus schedule. I will take a train arriving at Nesse Station at 7:55 A.M. and then your shuttle bus upon arrival, which should get me to your West Campus at a reasonable time.

Sincerely,

Sofia Edgren

191. What reason is given for updating the shuttle bus system?

(A) Optieris employees provided feedback.
(B) The current bus fleet is getting old.
(C) More staff are coming to work by train.
(D) Optieris has built new facilities on its campus.

192. What will be one change to the bus system from January 2 ?

(A) Buses will create less air pollution.
(B) Buses will be more frequent.
(C) Each bus will follow a different route.
(D) The first morning bus will run earlier.

193. What bus stop will be added to the route?

(A) Morbrook Station
(B) Nesse Station
(C) East Campus
(D) West Campus

194. Why will Ms. Edgren visit the Optieris campus?

(A) To finalize a contract between her company and Optieris
(B) To run a quality-control check
(C) To attend a training session
(D) To pursue an employment opportunity

195. What time does Ms. Edgren expect to get off her bus at Optieris?

(A) At 7:57 A.M.
(B) At 8:12 A.M.
(C) At 8:27 A.M.
(D) At 8:42 A.M.

GO ON TO THE NEXT PAGE →

Questions 196-200 refer to the following invoice, review, and e-mail.

Bright Now Home

Order Number: 92584
Customer Name: Jesse Beeby
Preferred Store: Northwest store

Item Number	Item Name	Quantity	Price
BN-101	Coastland Gray	2 gallons	$50.00
BN-102	Linwall Gray	1 gallon	$25.00
BN-116	Darby Olive	1 gallon	$25.00
BN-118	Brightwyn Green	2 gallons	$50.00
BN-126	Foxdell Green	1 gallon	$25.00
			Total $175.00

Pick Up in Store: Bright Now Home–Northwest store
348 Main Street
(720) 555-0112
customerservice@brightnowhome.com

Additional locations:
Northeast store: 986 14th Street
Southwest store: 1455 Smith Road
Southeast flagship store: 152 32nd Avenue

http://www.uopine.com/business/bright-now-home 

September 18

I used Bright Now Home's new in-store customer pickup for the first time this week. The service was a big time-saver because my order was ready for me when I got to the store. Since I had already paid online, I didn't have to wait in the regular line in the store.

Unfortunately, I didn't double-check my order before I left the store. When I arrived at the house I was working on, I realized I had received only one of the two gallons of BN-101 paint I had ordered. I called the store immediately, and the manager arranged for me to pick up the missing gallon of paint at the location closest to where I was working. Also, he gave me my money back for both gallons. I will definitely use this service again!

Jesse Beeby

To:	Jesse Beeby <jbeeby@jbeebyinc.com>
From:	Hattie Jones <hattie.jones@brightnowhome.com>
Date:	September 19
Subject:	Online Order

Mr. Beeby,

We are glad to have served your business recently. We saw the comments you posted about us on uopine.com, and we are grateful to you. It was nice to hear that our flagship location was so convenient to your work site and that you were able to pick up your missing paint there.

We stand behind our products and services and look forward to seeing you again soon. After all, the rainy season is almost here, so now is a great time to come in and get the tools you need for those upcoming roof jobs!

Hattie Jones
Customer Service Manager
Bright Now Home

196. What most likely is Mr. Beeby's job?

(A) Salesclerk
(B) Housepainter
(C) Delivery driver
(D) Real estate agent

197. What item did Mr. Beeby need more of?

(A) Coastland Gray
(B) Linwall Gray
(C) Brightwyn Green
(D) Foxdell Green

198. Where did Mr. Beeby pick up the item missing from his order?

(A) At the northwest store
(B) At the northeast store
(C) At the southwest store
(D) At the southeast store

199. What is indicated about Bright Now Home?

(A) It has design experts in stores.
(B) It provides same-day delivery service.
(C) It sells supplies for building maintenance.
(D) It offers coupons on its Web site.

200. What is one purpose of Ms. Jones's e-mail?

(A) To introduce a new service
(B) To thank a customer
(C) To announce a seasonal sale
(D) To explain a policy change

Stop! This is the end of the test. If you finish before time is called, you may go back to Parts 5, 6, and 7 and check your work.

토익® 정기시험
기출문제집

RC

기출 TEST

02

READING TEST

In the Reading test, you will read a variety of texts and answer several different types of reading comprehension questions. The entire Reading test will last 75 minutes. There are three parts, and directions are given for each part. You are encouraged to answer as many questions as possible within the time allowed.

You must mark your answers on the separate answer sheet. Do not write your answers in your test book.

PART 5

Directions: A word or phrase is missing in each of the sentences below. Four answer choices are given below each sentence. Select the best answer to complete the sentence. Then mark the letter (A), (B), (C), or (D) on your answer sheet.

101. The new interns have been very mindful of ------- parking regulations.

(A) theirs
(B) ours
(C) our
(D) they

102. To help the arts center improve its programming, please indicate which aspect of the workshop was most -------.

(A) informative
(B) primary
(C) enthusiastic
(D) financial

103. Mr. Gupta explained the ------- of the upgraded customer database to the sales team.

(A) beneficial
(B) benefits
(C) benefited
(D) benefiting

104. Buses leaving the city terminal were delayed due to icy conditions ------- the roads.

(A) on
(B) out
(C) from
(D) until

105. If you have recently ------- a digital camera and want to learn how to use it, this course is for you.

(A) purchased
(B) purchase
(C) purchasing
(D) to purchase

106. The upcoming ------- of Tantino Airport will ease congestion and modernize guest accommodations.

(A) performance
(B) supplement
(C) deadline
(D) renovation

107. The study showed that customers aged 35 to 44 paid with a Sonoka credit card ------- than customers in any other age-group.

(A) frequently
(B) frequent
(C) more frequently
(D) frequency

108. You need to ------- a business plan before your loan application can be processed.

(A) donate
(B) request
(C) confess
(D) submit

109. The hotel's ------- shuttle bus will take guests to Hong Kong's major landmarks.

(A) compliments
(B) complimentary
(C) compliment
(D) complimenting

110. ------- months of work to sell the Apton Building, the realtor finally succeeded last week.

(A) Besides
(B) After
(C) Still
(D) For

111. We will review all four custodial-service bids and choose ------- that suits our needs.

(A) some
(B) one
(C) others
(D) either

112. The client asked for ------- to the images in the advertising text.

(A) standards
(B) drawings
(C) revisions
(D) duplications

113. Please be advised ------- we have had to cancel your order because of a difficulty with our shipping agent.

(A) that
(B) of
(C) whether
(D) between

114. Tin Creek Corporation ------- that its paper towels are the most absorbent on the market.

(A) obtains
(B) competes
(C) inquires
(D) claims

115. KCLN Associates will enter into a business ------- with the contractor as soon as some of the terms are renegotiated.

(A) agreed
(B) agreement
(C) agreeable
(D) agreeing

116. ------- registering for online banking is not required, we strongly recommend it to all of our customers.

(A) Although
(B) Instead
(C) Regardless
(D) Despite

117. Viewers can easily ------- to the main character in the popular television series *Autumn Mystery*.

(A) related
(B) relatable
(C) relating
(D) relate

118. Fairlawn Medical Clinic offers a full ------- of services as part of its community wellness programs.

(A) center
(B) surplus
(C) range
(D) type

119. The rear entrance to RC Bank will be closed for repairs and not ------- next Monday.

(A) accessible
(B) accessing
(C) access
(D) accesses

120. Mr. Carson wants to see Carson audio products -------, even in remote regions of the world.

(A) decidedly
(B) furthermore
(C) rather
(D) everywhere

GO ON TO THE NEXT PAGE

121. We can buy office ------- such as desks and printers from any of our company's approved vendors.

(A) equip
(B) equipping
(C) equipment
(D) equipped

122. When taking a book order, agents must record the customer's name and the ------- price of each item.

(A) assembled
(B) listed
(C) addressed
(D) earned

123. The building will be furnished ------- the supervisors do their inspection.

(A) with
(B) these
(C) once
(D) just

124. In a strong display of confidence, the firm's board of directors ------- approved the merger.

(A) superficially
(B) regularly
(C) magnificently
(D) unanimously

125. When recently -------, residents of Mill Creek Park said that street disrepair is the issue that concerns them most.

(A) poll
(B) polls
(C) pollster
(D) polled

126. Ms. Rivera agreed to work on the holiday ------- Mr. Grant could attend the conference.

(A) considering
(B) so that
(C) as if
(D) wherever

127. The clerk collects packages from each department twice a day and takes them to the mail room -------.

(A) throughout
(B) all along
(C) too much
(D) downstairs

128. Please inform Ms. Erwin of any complaints ------- those already discussed in today's meeting.

(A) beyond
(B) between
(C) during
(D) against

129. The Tonsin Writers League is a reputable organization with highly ------- members.

(A) accomplishes
(B) accomplishment
(C) accomplished
(D) accomplish

130. As Mr. Nakata's assistant, Ms. Bain is in charge of ------- him on the latest financial news.

(A) discussing
(B) briefing
(C) resuming
(D) narrating

PART 6

Directions: Read the texts that follow. A word, phrase, or sentence is missing in parts of each text. Four answer choices for each question are given below the text. Select the best answer to complete the text. Then mark the letter (A), (B), (C), or (D) on your answer sheet.

Questions 131-134 refer to the following e-mail.

To: Bai Chang <bchang@lexrg.com>
From: customerservice@sprtech.com
Date: September 28
Subject: Order 255646

Dear Ms. Chang:

Thank you for your purchase on September 27. Your package has shipped and is due to arrive on October 1. ------- **131.** . Simply visit www.sprtech.com/shipping/status, enter your order number, and press "Search."

When you receive your package, we ------- **132.** you to take a short survey at www.sprtech.com/survey. It is through customer feedback that we are ------- **133.** to monitor our level of service. Upon ------- **134.** of the survey, you will receive a 10% discount toward your next order.

Sprtech.com Customer Service

131. (A) You will receive a full refund.
(B) A replacement is on back order.
(C) Tracking your order is easy.
(D) We will answer your question soon.

132. (A) invited
(B) invite
(C) were inviting
(D) have invited

133. (A) able
(B) skillful
(C) suitable
(D) equal

134. (A) publication
(B) production
(C) introduction
(D) completion

GO ON TO THE NEXT PAGE

Questions 135-138 refer to the following information.

Conference Room 120 can be booked for meetings and conference calls. First, make a reservation request online at www.gzpoffice.com/confroom. When your request ------- (**135.**), the system automatically checks for availability. Your request will be accepted if no other event is scheduled at that time. The system will then immediately send you an e-mail message to ------- (**136.**) your reservation. However, if another meeting is scheduled that conflicts with yours, you will be notified that the request has been declined. ------- (**137.**). It is therefore ------- (**138.**) that you schedule your event well ahead of time. This way, if a given time slot is already reserved, you will be able to reschedule your meeting.

135. (A) is received
(B) receiving
(C) to receive
(D) received

136. (A) move
(B) cancel
(C) change
(D) confirm

137. (A) Thank you for accepting our invitation to the event.
(B) Please prepare discussion points before the meeting.
(C) Note that reservations are on a first-come, first-served basis.
(D) The time of the next meeting will be announced in due course.

138. (A) fortunate
(B) advisable
(C) previous
(D) flexible

Questions 139-142 refer to the following e-mail.

From: Karel Authier <k.authier@codetouchmag.com>
To: Honorato Quinones <quinones@voyacon.com.es>
Date: Tuesday, July 18 11:04 A.M.
Subject: Voyacon Feature

Dear Mr. Quinones:

I am delighted to inform you that Voyacon has been selected as one of this year's *Code Touch Magazine*'s Top 25 Emerging Technology Firms. We will be ------- **139.** your company in our September issue. This is considered a great honor by our readers, as our list includes only ------- **140.** that advance the industry in significant ways.

As Voyacon's founder, could you e-mail us a digital photograph of yourself to use in the article? ------- **141.**. We would need to receive it ------- **142.** August 5. Otherwise, we will use a public-domain photo.

Thanks for your help, and congratulations.

Sincerely,

Karel Authier
Editor-in-Chief

139. (A) profile
(B) profiling
(C) profiles
(D) profiled

140. (A) publications
(B) machines
(C) techniques
(D) enterprises

141. (A) Hundreds of companies were initially considered.
(B) We will forward several copies as soon as possible.
(C) This is the fifth year we will be publishing this list.
(D) It should be a high-resolution, full-color image.

142. (A) by
(B) at
(C) within
(D) among

GO ON TO THE NEXT PAGE

Questions 143-146 refer to the following memo.

To: All Employees
From: Carmen Phelps, Central City Museum Director
Re: Special Exhibitions Curator
Date: November 15

To All Staff,

Please note that an advertisement will be placed in this Wednesday's newspaper regarding a new position at the Central City Museum. After the ------- **143.** of *Bloom Outside the Box*, our recent exhibition showcasing the artwork of local sculptor Leanne Bloom, the museum board has decided to allocate a new position dedicated to creating new quarterly exhibitions. The position title is Special Exhibitions Curator. The successful applicant ------- **144.** work on January 2.

------- **145.** . Proven knowledge of local and regional artists is preferred. ------- **146.** museum staff are encouraged to apply. Please contact Liliana Wells at extension 449 with questions.

Thank you.

Carmen

143. (A) popularity
(B) winner
(C) goal
(D) awareness

144. (A) started
(B) will start
(C) has started
(D) was starting

145. (A) Board nominations close at the end of the day on Friday.
(B) Critic Tony Watanabe gave the exhibition a five-star review.
(C) The position requires extensive experience.
(D) We look forward to hosting this event.

146. (A) Expressed
(B) Observed
(C) Depended
(D) Qualified

PART 7

Directions: In this part you will read a selection of texts, such as magazine and newspaper articles, e-mails, and instant messages. Each text or set of texts is followed by several questions. Select the best answer for each question and mark the letter (A), (B), (C), or (D) on your answer sheet.

Questions 147-148 refer to the following e-mail.

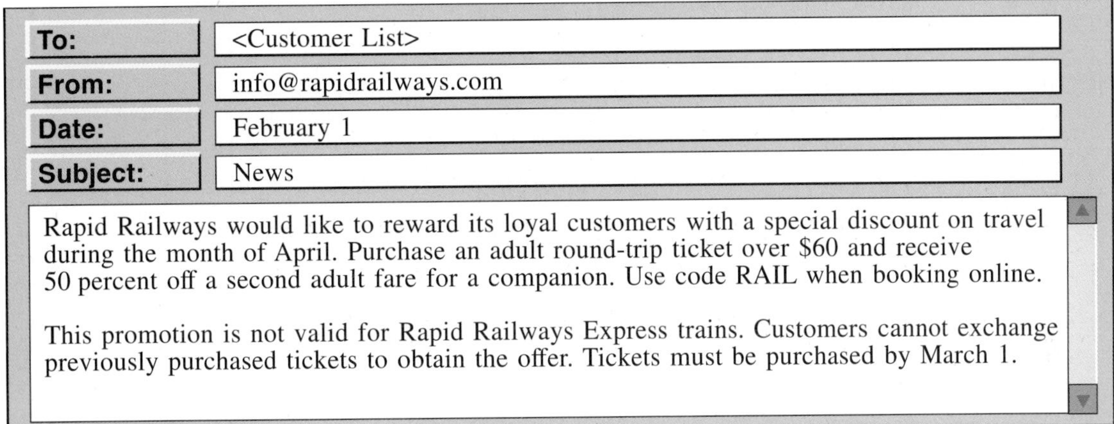

To:	<Customer List>
From:	info@rapidrailways.com
Date:	February 1
Subject:	News

Rapid Railways would like to reward its loyal customers with a special discount on travel during the month of April. Purchase an adult round-trip ticket over $60 and receive 50 percent off a second adult fare for a companion. Use code RAIL when booking online.

This promotion is not valid for Rapid Railways Express trains. Customers cannot exchange previously purchased tickets to obtain the offer. Tickets must be purchased by March 1.

147. What is the purpose of the e-mail?

(A) To publicize an updated service
(B) To attract first-time customers
(C) To increase the sale of April tickets
(D) To promote Rapid Railways Express

148. What is true about the special discount?

(A) It includes children.
(B) It requires that tickets be purchased over the phone.
(C) It applies only to tickets already purchased.
(D) It is offered to two people traveling together.

GO ON TO THE NEXT PAGE

Questions 149-150 refer to the following invitation.

Clearhaven Chamber of Commerce

Breakfast Club

Guest Speaker Philippa Dixton of Dixton Advertising
"Social Media Trends for Business Success"

Wednesday, September 26
7:30–9:00 A.M.

Kelly's Café
17 Richards Street
Clearhaven, Virginia 20101

$8.00 per person
Includes full breakfast buffet

Registration required, limited seating available
RSVP by September 20
Clearhaven Chamber of Commerce, 540-555-0112

149. What topic will be discussed at the event?

(A) Social media
(B) Successful investments
(C) Setting up a small business
(D) Coping with staff turnover

150. What is indicated about the event?

(A) It is held once a month.
(B) It takes place on a weekend.
(C) Registration is not necessary.
(D) Space is limited.

Questions 151-152 refer to the following notice.

Harrod Automotive Manufacturing

Andrew Dunn, Director
Laura Bradley, Site Manager

Welcome to Harrod Automotive Manufacturing! We are serious about maintaining a safe workplace environment. We ask that the following rules be strictly observed while you are touring the assembly floor. Anyone found in violation of these rules will be asked to leave the premises. For concerns about compliance, please contact the site manager.

ALWAYS:
- Stay with your tour guide.
- Wear safety glasses and helmet.
- Respond to alarm signals and obey evacuation instructions.
- Request permission from your guide before taking photographs.

NEVER:
- Leave your group.
- Enter areas marked "Danger" or "Staff Only."
- Touch equipment.

151. For whom is the notice most likely intended?

(A) Maintenance workers
(B) Security guards
(C) Safety inspectors
(D) Factory visitors

152. According to the notice, why should someone contact Ms. Bradley?

(A) To praise an employee
(B) To inquire about a policy
(C) To submit photographs
(D) To obtain a schedule

TEST 2

GO ON TO THE NEXT PAGE

Questions 153-154 refer to the following text-message chain.

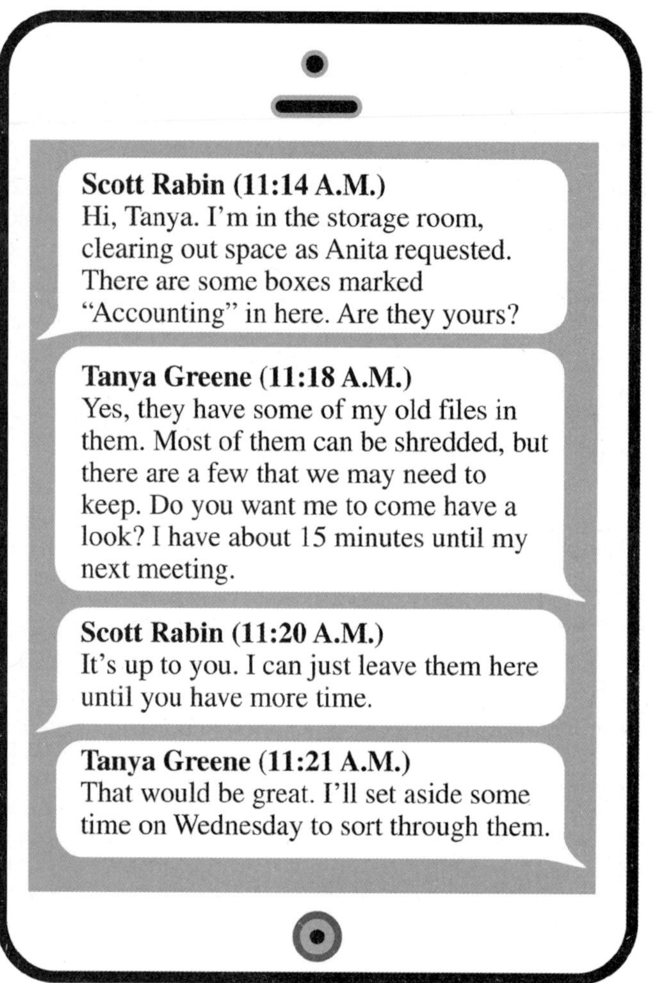

Scott Rabin (11:14 A.M.)
Hi, Tanya. I'm in the storage room, clearing out space as Anita requested. There are some boxes marked "Accounting" in here. Are they yours?
Tanya Greene (11:18 A.M.)
Yes, they have some of my old files in them. Most of them can be shredded, but there are a few that we may need to keep. Do you want me to come have a look? I have about 15 minutes until my next meeting.
Scott Rabin (11:20 A.M.)
It's up to you. I can just leave them here until you have more time.
Tanya Greene (11:21 A.M.)
That would be great. I'll set aside some time on Wednesday to sort through them.

153. Why did Mr. Rabin send a message to Ms. Greene?

(A) To ask if she needs more storage space
(B) To find out if some files belong to her
(C) To get her help moving some boxes
(D) To ask where some files should be put

154. At 11:20 A.M., what does Mr. Rabin mean when he writes, "It's up to you"?

(A) He will sort some documents when Ms. Greene wants him to.
(B) He can arrange for a time to unlock the storage room.
(C) Ms. Greene can decide when she prefers to look at some files.
(D) Ms. Greene can choose the type of boxes she wants to use.

Questions 155-157 refer to the following article.

NAIROBI (2 November)—Agosti, the popular Italian shoe retailer, will launch its first outlet store in East Africa this week when Agosti Nairobi opens. Customers will find all the bright colours and unique designs for which Agosti is known. — [1] —.

Agosti Nairobi will feature a unique hands-on approach to fashion, with touch-screen display stations positioned throughout the store. — [2] —. These stations will allow shoppers to browse through product information, read customer reviews, and identify best-selling styles.

— [3] —. The store will also feature a foot plantar pressure sensor. By standing on the sensor, customers will be able to determine their precise foot measurements and choose the best shoe size for their feet. Shoes will be available in a variety of lengths and widths not usually found in competitor stores.

"We at Agosti see East Africa as an important place for new fashion," said Raffael Zito, Agosti's marketing director. According to Mr. Zito, the opening of the Nairobi store is only the first step of an ambitious expansion plan. — [4] —.

155. What aspect of the Agosti Nairobi store does the article highlight?

(A) Its spacious interior
(B) Its knowledgeable sales team
(C) Its wide selection of brands
(D) Its interactive displays

156. What is true about Agosti shoes?

(A) They are available in new designs.
(B) They are very expensive.
(C) They are made in hard-to-find sizes.
(D) They are mostly handmade.

157. In which of the positions marked [1], [2], [3], and [4] does the following sentence best belong?

"In fact, the company is currently scouting locations for a new design facility in the region."

(A) [1]
(B) [2]
(C) [3]
(D) [4]

TEST 2

GO ON TO THE NEXT PAGE

Questions 158-160 refer to the following form.

http://www.pinecrestofficepark.com/requestform

Pinecrest Office Park
Request Form
Judy Blanch, Office Manager
215.555.0118, extension 2

Date of Request: April 2
Tenant: Lerner and Randall, LLC
Office: Suite B, Third floor
Tenant Contact Name: Amy Randall

Type of Problem:
Structural ☑
Electrical ☐
Plumbing ☐

Brief Description of Work Needed:
The ceiling over the window has developed a water leak, and the wall is beginning to discolor.

Additional Instructions:
Before coming over, please call my office at 215.555.0127. My partner, Zach Lerner, and I would like to be present when the building staff is there. There is very expensive office equipment directly under that part of the ceiling. We will need to move it before any repairs are made.

To Be Filled Out by Pinecrest Management:
Date Received: April 3
Assigned to: In-Su Kim
Approved: Yes ☑ No ☐
Approved by: Judy Blanch

Notes:
Please investigate this problem early tomorrow morning after you call Ms. Randall. If roofing repairs are needed, e-mail John Roper (Roper Roofers – john@roperroofers.com), and set up an appointment for an estimate.

158. What is the purpose of the form?
(A) To apply for a job
(B) To request a lease
(C) To report a problem
(D) To change an address

159. Who will first contact Ms. Randall about her April 2 request?
(A) Mr. Kim
(B) Mr. Lerner
(C) Mr. Roper
(D) Ms. Blanch

160. Why does Ms. Randall mention some office equipment?
(A) It is for sale.
(B) It needs to be moved.
(C) It has been damaged.
(D) It needs to be replaced.

Questions 161-163 refer to the following press release.

FOR IMMEDIATE RELEASE
Media contact: Andrea Óladóttir / +613 555 0124

Babson Vehicles Ltd. Enthusiastically Implements Deluxident's Newest Product

OTTAWA (10 June)—Babson Vehicles Ltd., a leading Canadian manufacturer, has just adopted a new fingerprint entry system aimed at improving company security. Created by Icelandic firm Deluxident, the system enables employees to enter campus buildings simply by scanning their fingerprints.

According to Babson's CEO Daniel Deems, Deluxident's fingerprint-scanning system is a significant improvement over other security products the company has tried in the past.

"Deluxident's fingerprint scanner has been a tremendous asset. In the past, we always accessed our buildings by using photographic and electronic identification badges," said Deems. "Producing and replacing lost badges, however, was expensive. In addition, they posed a significant security threat. Employees sometimes forgot their badges, adding to traffic through our security office. All in all, the badges were costly and risky."

For the past decade, Deluxident has been offering high-tech workplace solutions with its innovative digital products. Headquartered in Reykjavík, Deluxident delivers items worldwide and offers 24-hour technical assistance by telephone. For further details about the new fingerprint-scanning entry system, visit www.deluxident.is.

161. What is implied about Mr. Deems?

(A) He oversees multiple buildings.
(B) He makes frequent trips abroad.
(C) He is a successful inventor.
(D) He often misplaces his identification badge.

162. Why does Mr. Deems prefer Deluxident's new product over previous products?

(A) It facilitates campus entry for visitors.
(B) It lowers expenses in the long term.
(C) It requires photo identification.
(D) It allows employees to quickly locate each other.

163. What is true about Deluxident?

(A) It ships its products internationally.
(B) It is based in Canada.
(C) It provides on-site consulting services.
(D) It plans to merge with Babson Vehicles Ltd.

GO ON TO THE NEXT PAGE

Questions 164-167 refer to the following letter.

> Maria Cleary
> 2289 Coolidge Street
> Great Falls, MT 59401
>
> Paul Donnell
> 5267 Cotton Vale
> Helena, MT 59624
>
> Dear Mr. Donnell,
>
> After searching through Lewis and Clark County's public property tax records online, I discovered that you are the owner of the building that was once a general store on the corner of Waller Avenue and Main Street. As far as I can tell, the building has been boarded up and unoccupied for quite a few years. — [1] —. I would like to know if you would be interested in selling it.
>
> I have been planning to open a café in the area, and I believe that with some modest improvements, your building could be the perfect location. I would want to keep as much of the original structure intact as possible. — [2] —. Any modifications would be minor.
>
> I realize there are other buildings for sale in the business district, but they do not have the same connection to the community. — [3] —. I have spoken with many Helena residents who have fond memories of your building, and they would like to see it transformed into a usable structure again. — [4] —. I am confident that my plan would be welcomed by the community.
>
> Thank you for considering my offer. If you would like to discuss details, I can be reached at 406-555-0181.
>
> Sincerely,
>
> *Maria Cleary*
>
> Maria Cleary

164. What is indicated about Lewis and Clark County?

(A) It is well-known for its restaurants.
(B) It enforces strict building regulations.
(C) It provides property information over the Internet.
(D) It is seeking feedback on a development project.

165. What is suggested about the general store building?

(A) It is currently open to the public.
(B) It has changed ownership many times.
(C) It is undergoing extensive renovations.
(D) It has been vacant for several years.

166. Why most likely is Ms. Cleary interested in Mr. Donnell's property?

(A) It is popular with local residents.
(B) It is located in the city center.
(C) It is being sold for a low price.
(D) It features a spacious floor plan.

167. In which of the positions marked [1], [2], [3], and [4] does the following sentence best belong?

"I think the exposed brick siding, for example, is essential to the building's charm."

(A) [1]
(B) [2]
(C) [3]
(D) [4]

Questions 168-171 refer to the following information.

Bulletin boards at Quenten Advertising

The physical bulletin boards in our facilities are overseen by the administrative assistant in the Human Resources Department. The bulletin boards are in locked glass cabinets, and the administrative assistant is responsible for the cabinet keys and for ensuring that all postings are kept current.

- **The bulletin board by the elevator** is used to convey general information to all employees, such as important company news or reminders.
- **The bulletin board outside the conference rooms** is used solely for information relating to upcoming meetings and events scheduled for those rooms.
- **The staff lounge bulletin board** may be used for announcements not sponsored by Quenten Advertising that may be of general interest to coworkers, such as personal items for sale, local festivals, and other community events. To post these notices, staff must first submit a request to Human Resources and include contact information as well as a photocopy of the posting. These announcements cannot be posted more than two weeks before the event date.

All bulletin boards will be checked regularly to ensure compliance with their intended purposes.

168. What is the purpose of the information?

(A) To describe a job opening
(B) To explain a company policy
(C) To provide building information to visitors
(D) To help clients navigate a Web site

169. Where is important company news most likely posted?

(A) Near the elevator
(B) In the staff lounge
(C) Inside the conference rooms
(D) In the Human Resources Department

170. According to the information, why should employees contact Human Resources?

(A) To pick up their office keys
(B) To have their notices approved
(C) To register for company events
(D) To submit photocopy requests

171. Why are bulletin boards checked regularly?

(A) To confirm that the cabinets are kept locked
(B) To confirm that personal items have been sold
(C) To ensure that postings are appropriate at each location
(D) To ensure that postings are interesting to all employees

GO ON TO THE NEXT PAGE

Questions 172-175 refer to the following online chat discussion.

Live Chat

Satoru Hashimoto (10:42 A.M.)	I just logged in to my guest loyalty program account and noticed that the nights I stayed at the Grand Jurong Hotel last month haven't been credited. Are my loyalty points being processed?
Franca Russo (10:44 A.M.)	Thank you for contacting the Customer Care Centre. I'm looking at your account and see that the loyalty points are not there at the moment. Points are good for one year after the check-out date. I am adding Mr. Han Sai Wong from the Grand Jurong to this chat to confirm your stay at the hotel. What were the dates of your stay so that he can look up the reservation?
Han Sai Wong (10:46 A.M.)	Already got it. I can confirm Mr. Hashimoto stayed four nights with a check-in date of March 7.
Satoru Hashimoto (10:47 A.M.)	March 7 through March 11.
Franca Russo (10:50 A.M.)	Mr. Hashimoto, I have added the points to your account. With your new points, you are eligible to either upgrade your room for the stay you reserved next month, or you may apply the points toward one free night on a future booking. May I assist you in upgrading your current reservation or in completing a booking for a future stay?
Satoru Hashimoto (10:51 A.M.)	Not at this time. Thank you for your help!

172. Why did Mr. Hashimoto contact Customer Care?

(A) To provide feedback on a recent stay
(B) To book a room using his loyalty points
(C) To change an existing reservation
(D) To inquire about missing loyalty points

173. At 10:46 A.M., what does Mr. Wong mean when he writes, "Already got it"?

(A) He has found some information.
(B) He is pointing out a mistake made by Ms. Russo.
(C) He is going to call Mr. Hashimoto.
(D) He will complete Mr. Hashimoto's reservation.

174. What does Ms. Russo offer to do for Mr. Hashimoto?

(A) Award him extra points
(B) Issue a refund
(C) Provide an upgrade on a future stay
(D) Transfer his account to a different points program

175. What is NOT indicated about the loyalty points program?

(A) Points earned on a stay remain valid for a year.
(B) Points can be used to upgrade a reservation.
(C) Points are credited after a guest leaves the hotel.
(D) Points can be doubled under certain conditions.

GO ON TO THE NEXT PAGE →

Questions 176-180 refer to the following e-mail and employee handbook.

To:	Munahid Awad
From:	Abby Fordyce
Subject:	Information
Date:	2 February
Attachment:	Handbook

Dear Mr. Awad,

Good morning. I hope your first day at Epmedin Medical Supplies is going well.

Please find details about our employment policies and practices attached. By the way, you have already been assigned your own personal parking space, but you will need to contact the transportation operations department to obtain a parking permit for display purposes.

As we discussed last week, we need to make travel arrangements for you to visit our other facilities. Your first trip will be to our headquarters next week, followed by visits to the rest of our facilities at the end of the month. Wendy Leighton will assist with your reservations and can be reached at wleighton@epmedin.co.uk.

Please let me know if there is anything else you need.

Sincerely,

Abby

Epmedin Medical Supplies

Employee Handbook

Dress Code

Workplace dress codes vary by location. Headquarters in London and the Glasgow office require staff to wear formal business attire, while business casual attire is approved for staff at our Dublin and Belfast manufacturing plants. Formal business attire is defined as a business suit, including a jacket, dress pants or a dress skirt, and a tie (for men). Business casual attire is trousers or khakis, a dress shirt or blouse, or a dress or skirt.

Transportation

Parking at the London office is reserved for delivery and security vehicles. Monthly bus and train passes can be purchased through Human Resources at half the regular fare.

Because of limited on-site parking at our Glasgow and Dublin production facilities, staff can park for free at designated parking garages. Employees need a permit, which can be obtained through the transportation operations department. Permits must be renewed annually online.

Employees at the Belfast facility must obtain a permit for a designated parking space from the transportation operations department.

176. What is a purpose of the e-mail?

(A) To issue an invitation to a celebration
(B) To give notice of a policy change
(C) To forward a company document
(D) To approve a vacation request

177. In the e-mail, the word "going" in paragraph 1, line 1, is closest in meaning to

(A) departing
(B) proceeding
(C) selling
(D) visiting

178. What is indicated about Mr. Awad?

(A) He revised the employee handbook.
(B) He has met Ms. Leighton.
(C) He takes public transportation to work.
(D) He will be traveling in February.

179. Where does Mr. Awad most likely work?

(A) In London
(B) In Glasgow
(C) In Dublin
(D) In Belfast

180. According to the handbook, what do all Epmedin office locations have in common?

(A) Parking garages are not available.
(B) Parking permits are not required.
(C) Employees need to comply with specific dress codes.
(D) Factory workers follow very strict safety regulations.

GO ON TO THE NEXT PAGE

Questions 181-185 refer to the following e-mail and agenda.

E-mail

To: Management Team
From: Fiona Watson
Date: March 19
Subject: Spring meeting
Attachment: Final Agenda

Dear Colleagues,

This is a reminder that Contiera Corporation's spring management meeting is scheduled for 9 A.M. tomorrow. The final agenda is attached. Please note that I have added an item to the original meeting agenda. Mai Tran, our publications supervisor, wants to update everyone on this season's product line. She should not take more than twenty minutes.

To prepare for the meeting, please review our most recent marketing plan so that we all have a clear idea of our goals for the quarter. It would also help if each of you brought copies of your latest budget report and projected cost estimates for next quarter.

I look forward to seeing you tomorrow.

Fiona Watson

Spring Management Meeting—Final Agenda

Date and Time: March 20, 9 A.M.
Location: Conference Room 2

Topic	Description	Leader
Community events	– Learn about local outreach opportunities	Paul Ranier, president of the Arborville Business Association
Budget review	– Discuss department budgets	Fiona Watson
Online advertising	– Review cost of Web ads – Analyze areas for growth	Marcia Dover
Web site updates	– Present recent changes to ski-apparel page – Demonstrate new content management software	Barry Callahan
Print publications	– Review final changes to spring sportswear catalog	Mai Tran

181. In the e-mail, what does Ms. Watson imply about the meeting?

(A) Some clients will be attending it.
(B) A recently hired supervisor will be leading it.
(C) It will take more time than originally planned.
(D) Its location has been changed.

182. What item on the agenda is new?

(A) Community events
(B) Online advertising
(C) Web site updates
(D) Print publications

183. What does Ms. Watson ask people to bring to the meeting?

(A) Updated financial documents
(B) A list of new hires
(C) A copy of the agenda
(D) Revised vendor contracts

184. What does the agenda indicate about Mr. Ranier?

(A) He teaches a course in online advertising.
(B) He will be joining the meeting by telephone.
(C) He used to work with Ms. Watson.
(D) He represents a local organization.

185. What does Contiera Corporation most likely sell?

(A) Books and magazines
(B) Gardening supplies
(C) Athletic clothing
(D) Computer software

GO ON TO THE NEXT PAGE

Questions 186-190 refer to the following article, e-mail, and program.

Film Festival Returns to Wales

SWANSEA (24 May)—The Penglais Film Festival returns to town with a full slate of exciting new films. The festival has gained international recognition for the talent it has attracted over the years. It also boasts of having launched the careers of a growing number of celebrity filmmakers.

The week-long festival will run from 9 to 15 August and will feature animated, documentary, and feature films. The festival is open to the public, with the exception of the closing event on 15 August, which is by invitation only. Tickets for all public events must be purchased in advance and are expected to sell out quickly.

Ticket sales will begin at 10 a.m. on 3 June. Please note that tickets for individual film showings must be purchased separately.

A full schedule of screenings is now available on the festival's Web site at www.penglaisfest.co.uk.

E-mail

To:	Desmond Griffith <d_griffith@docsnow.co.uk>
From:	Ioan Driscoll <ioan.driscoll@penglaisfest.co.uk>
Subject:	Re: Penglais Award Ceremony
Date:	28 May

Dear Mr. Griffith,

I am excited and honoured to hear that you will be able to accept your prize in person at this year's Penglais Award Ceremony. The ceremony will take place at the Wynford Blue Hotel at 5 P.M. on Friday, 15 August. You will be introduced by the festival's president, Ms. Sarah Wu, and you will have the opportunity to give a speech. We kindly request that you limit this speech to no more than 10 minutes.

Please provide me with the e-mail addresses of up to five guests you would like to invite to the ceremony. I will be sure to send them each a link to download their ticket electronically within ten days of the event.

Congratulations,

Ioan Driscoll

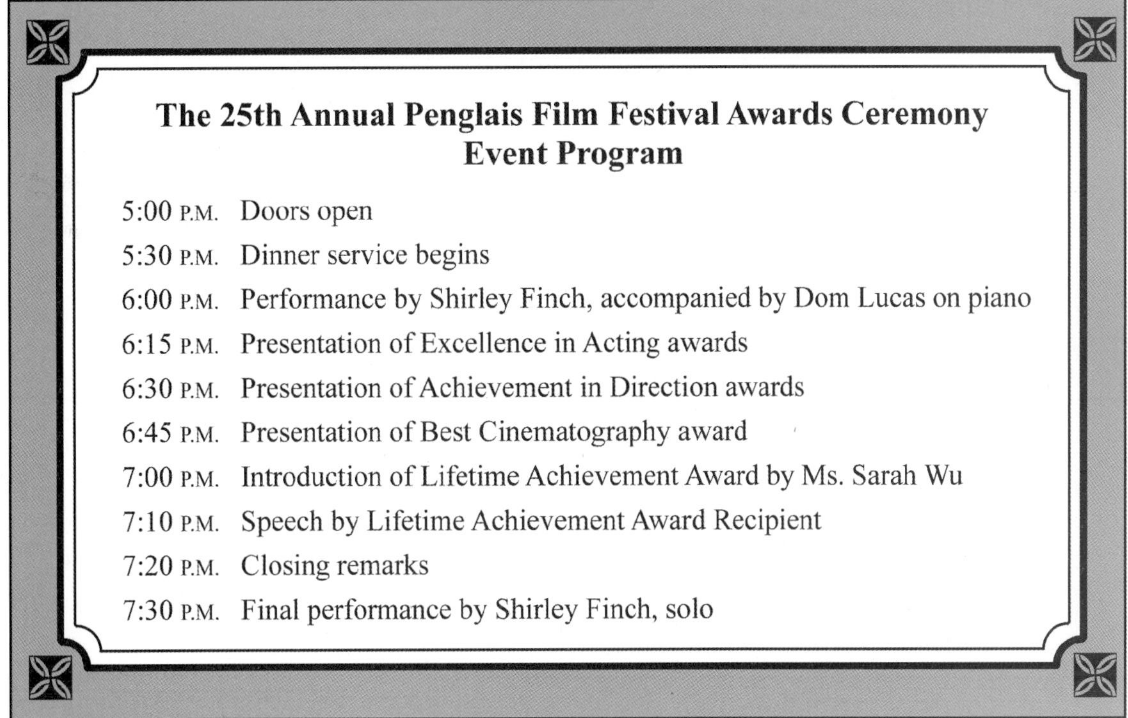

The 25th Annual Penglais Film Festival Awards Ceremony
Event Program

5:00 P.M. Doors open
5:30 P.M. Dinner service begins
6:00 P.M. Performance by Shirley Finch, accompanied by Dom Lucas on piano
6:15 P.M. Presentation of Excellence in Acting awards
6:30 P.M. Presentation of Achievement in Direction awards
6:45 P.M. Presentation of Best Cinematography award
7:00 P.M. Introduction of Lifetime Achievement Award by Ms. Sarah Wu
7:10 P.M. Speech by Lifetime Achievement Award Recipient
7:20 P.M. Closing remarks
7:30 P.M. Final performance by Shirley Finch, solo

186. What is indicated about the Penglais Film Festival?

(A) It is new to Wales.
(B) Many past participants have become famous.
(C) It focuses on classic films from the past.
(D) Tickets to feature films have sold out.

187. Why is Mr. Driscoll pleased?

(A) He will receive an award.
(B) His film will be shown at the festival.
(C) Mr. Griffith will attend an event.
(D) Mr. Griffith has invited him to speak.

188. What is suggested about tickets for the awards ceremony?

(A) They cannot be purchased.
(B) They cannot be accessed online.
(C) They will become available on May 3.
(D) They are included with the purchase of individual film tickets.

189. Who most likely is Shirley Finch?

(A) An event host
(B) An entertainer
(C) An award presenter
(D) A festival director

190. What award will Mr. Griffith most likely receive?

(A) Excellence in Acting
(B) Best Cinematography
(C) Lifetime Achievement
(D) Achievement in Direction

GO ON TO THE NEXT PAGE

Questions 191-195 refer to the following e-mails and letter.

To:	a.raman@bgi.co.in
From:	s.kapoor@imail.co.in
Date:	15 April
Subject:	Thank-you note

Dear Mr. Raman,

Thanks for encouraging me to apply for the position at Neela Advertising and for writing such a glowing referral on my behalf.

Mr. Nirmal, Neela's chief recruiting officer, expressed his admiration for the television commercials I produced for Delhi Works, but he explained that his company in fact needs someone who can also create Web content and applications. I was therefore not offered the position.

Kindly let me know if you happen to hear of any other positions that might be a good fit for me. Thank you in advance.

Best regards,

Shreya

---

17 May

Shreya Kapoor
21 Hammam Street
Mumbai

Dear Ms. Kapoor,

I am pleased that you will be joining Mumbai Canning Ltd. on 1 June. I was impressed with the knowledge you displayed at the time you interviewed at our offices. Your specific experience at Delhi Works, Inc., will be of tremendous value here.

I am enclosing some documents that you should complete, sign, and bring with you when you report to Human Resources at 9:30 A.M. on your first day. You will receive a brief administrative orientation at that time. Your assigned mentor, Ms. Meera Sethi, will meet you there at 10:30 to escort you to your department, where she will review your training plan and the projects the team is currently working on. At noon she will be taking you to our cafeteria for lunch in the company of some of your colleagues. I hope to join you there as well.

Welcome to Mumbai Canning Ltd.!

Sincerely,

Zara Mehta

Zara Mehta
Mumbai Canning Ltd.

To:	a.raman@bgi.co.in
From:	s.kapoor@imail.co.in
Date:	20 May
Subject:	Good news

Dear Mr. Raman,

Thank you for your last referral. The director offered me the position during our interview, and I will be starting on 1 June. I will be happy to provide you with details about my duties once I get settled.

Best,

Shreya

191. Why was Ms. Kapoor turned down for a position at Neela Advertising?

(A) She failed to provide adequate referrals.
(B) She did not meet the criteria for the job.
(C) She missed the application deadline.
(D) She was not available for a follow-up interview.

192. What is suggested about Ms. Kapoor?

(A) She left her job at Delhi Works, Inc., several years ago.
(B) She used to work with Mr. Nirmal at Delhi Works, Inc.
(C) She will produce television commercials for Mumbai Canning Ltd.
(D) She has recently switched careers.

193. Who most likely is Ms. Sethi?

(A) A cafeteria manager
(B) A payroll accountant
(C) A marketing team member
(D) A budget director

194. According to the letter, where will Ms. Mehta be at noon on June 1 ?

(A) In a design meeting
(B) On a business trip
(C) At a job interview
(D) At a dining facility

195. How was Ms. Kapoor offered her new job?

(A) In person
(B) In a letter
(C) By e-mail
(D) Over the telephone

GO ON TO THE NEXT PAGE →

Questions 196-200 refer to the following e-mails and memo.

To:	Kyung-Jin Sohn
From:	Darius Jackson
Date:	November 8
Subject:	Solutions to a problem

Dear Ms. Sohn,

As you know, competition for use of the printers has been causing a great deal of delay for members of the legal department. Everyone has had to wait to print documents at some point. Some of us have had to start coming to work earlier, and others are staying late. This is having a negative impact on our productivity and morale.

We could improve the situation for the remainder of the year by posting a sign-up sheet next to the printers. To be fair, each employee should sign up for only two fifteen-minute blocks per day. We could also reserve the lunch hour for unscheduled printing. And we should consider discontinuing the use of color printers until the situation is under control—color printing is up to five times as expensive as black-and-white printing. Let me know what you think.

Regards,

Darius Jackson
Legal Administrator, Reeder and Kelter, Inc.

MEMO

To: All Reeder and Kelter, Inc., Staff
From: Kyung-Jin Sohn, Support Manager
Date: November 24
Subject: Printer use

We have purchased two new printers, a multicolor UX212 and a black-and-white UY120 Truzynx. Unfortunately, they will not be arriving until December 18. In the meantime, please continue to schedule your printer-use times using the online link I e-mailed you on November 10. Using this document, you may reserve up to two fifteen-minute printing periods per day. Please do not schedule consecutive sessions, and remember that we have set aside time both in the morning and in the afternoon for emergency printing. Also, please use the color printers only when absolutely necessary. We have been purchasing more color ink than usual because staff members are using the color printers for scanning and printing when the black-and-white printers are in use.

To:	kjsohn@reederandkelter.com
From:	lsullivan@truzynx.com
Date:	December 22
Subject:	Truzynx purchase

Dear Ms. Sohn,

Thank you for your recent purchase of two Truzynx printers for your company. Your purchase includes two years of free maintenance for each machine. Your first regularly scheduled servicing date will be one month from delivery. We also offer discounted prices on our extended maintenance plans within 60 days of equipment purchase. Please let me know if you are interested in these plans for your new printers.

Are you looking to improve your efficiency? We also have Truzplan. With this affordable remote-printing service, we can securely print your scanned documents and bring them to your office when you need them. Please let me know if you would like more information.

Sincerely,

Leilani Sullivan
Sales Representative

196. According to the first e-mail, how have some employees coped with a problem?

(A) By reducing operational costs
(B) By working outside their regular hours
(C) By hiring temporary staff
(D) By outsourcing a maintenance service

197. Which of Mr. Jackson's suggestions did Ms. Sohn implement?

(A) Allowing employees two fifteen-minute printing periods per day
(B) Allotting a one-hour period at midday for emergency printing
(C) Posting a sign-up sheet next to the printers
(D) Discontinuing the use of color printers

198. According to the memo, what is the problem with the color printers?

(A) They have not been ordered.
(B) They regularly break down.
(C) They fail to scan documents.
(D) They are being overused.

199. What is true about the new printers purchased by Reeder and Kelter, Inc.?

(A) They were delivered on November 24.
(B) They include a three-year maintenance plan.
(C) They will be serviced on January 18.
(D) They came with free remote printing during the first month.

200. What does Truzplan offer?

(A) Delivery of printed documents
(B) Equipment insurance
(C) Suggestions for accessories
(D) Training in the use of equipment

Stop! This is the end of the test. If you finish before time is called, you may go back to Parts 5, 6, and 7 and check your work.

토익® 정기시험
기출문제집

기출 TEST

03

READING TEST

In the Reading test, you will read a variety of texts and answer several different types of reading comprehension questions. The entire Reading test will last 75 minutes. There are three parts, and directions are given for each part. You are encouraged to answer as many questions as possible within the time allowed.

You must mark your answers on the separate answer sheet. Do not write your answers in your test book.

PART 5

Directions: A word or phrase is missing in each of the sentences below. Four answer choices are given below each sentence. Select the best answer to complete the sentence. Then mark the letter (A), (B), (C), or (D) on your answer sheet.

101. The event planner determined that Tuesday's forum will require ------- chairs.

(A) addition
(B) additions
(C) additional
(D) additionally

102. Ms. Hu will check the storage closet before she ------- more office supplies.

(A) contains
(B) orders
(C) writes
(D) copies

103. All sales staff are asked to acknowledge their ------- in Monday's workshop.

(A) participate
(B) participates
(C) participated
(D) participation

104. The commercial for Zhou's Café was ------- Sunn Agency's best advertisement of the year.

(A) easy
(B) ease
(C) easiest
(D) easily

105. Use coupon code SAVE20 to purchase ------- perfume or cologne for 20 percent off.

(A) any
(B) few
(C) single
(D) many

106. Talk-Talk Cell Phone Company will soon be merging with its main -------.

(A) competitor
(B) competing
(C) competitive
(D) competitively

107. Ms. Ellis designed one of the most ------- marketing campaigns the department had seen.

(A) create
(B) creation
(C) creative
(D) creatively

108. Last month we received numerous ------- comments from customers on our blog.

(A) eventual
(B) probable
(C) close
(D) positive

109. Beginning on August 1, patients will be asked to complete a short survey ------- each visit.

(A) inside
(B) after
(C) where
(D) whenever

110. Viewing the beautiful landscape outside her door ------- inspires Elia Colao to paint.

(A) continually
(B) continue
(C) continual
(D) continued

111. Although the parts are made in China, the ------- of Jamy bicycles is done in Canada.

(A) vision
(B) meeting
(C) approach
(D) assembly

112. Many businesses promote carpooling ------- traffic congestion.

(A) is prevented
(B) prevent
(C) to prevent
(D) prevented

113. ------- the repairs are complete, only essential personnel are allowed in the building.

(A) Despite
(B) Finally
(C) Until
(D) During

114. We apologize for having used the wrong colors on the Slarott Architecture brochures and will deliver ------- on Friday.

(A) replacing
(B) replaces
(C) replaced
(D) replacements

115. Employees must store all tools ------- at the end of the shift.

(A) properly
(B) restfully
(C) truly
(D) finely

116. An ------- to renovate the old factory was submitted to the city council.

(A) application
(B) establishment
(C) experience
(D) accomplishment

117. Customers ------- wish to return a defective item may do so within twenty days of the date of purchase.

(A) whose
(B) who
(C) which
(D) whichever

118. The Golubovich House will be open ------- a special living-history program on Sunday.

(A) from
(B) around
(C) for
(D) by

119. Mr. Wijaya is reviewing the résumés to select the candidate best ------- for the position.

(A) qualify
(B) qualifications
(C) qualifying
(D) qualified

120. Tourists praise Navala City's world-class beaches ------- its historical attractions.

(A) as well as
(B) yet
(C) so that
(D) when

GO ON TO THE NEXT PAGE

121. Mr. Chandling will cover any time-sensitive work ------- Mr. Tan is on vacation.

(A) along
(B) besides
(C) while
(D) then

122. Laura Gless promotes faculty-led study programs in ------- such as France and Italy.

(A) destinations
(B) ambitions
(C) purposes
(D) intentions

123. Mr. Stafford e-mailed the clients to ask ------- there is a train station near their office.

(A) so
(B) about
(C) whether
(D) of

124. Last year, the city ------- nearly 500 building permits to small-business owners.

(A) regarded
(B) issued
(C) performed
(D) constructed

125. Local merchants are hopeful that if this new business succeeds, ------- will also benefit.

(A) theirs
(B) them
(C) their
(D) themselves

126. Following the retirement of Mr. Whalen, the company ------- a search for a new CEO.

(A) connected
(B) launched
(C) persuaded
(D) treated

127. Ms. Travaglini filed the paperwork with the facilities department ------- a week ago.

(A) beyond
(B) over
(C) past
(D) through

128. After the lease -------, customers have the option of purchasing the car or returning it to their local dealer.

(A) expired
(B) is expiring
(C) will be expiring
(D) expires

129. The *Jones News Hour* is broadcast ------- on radio and television.

(A) instinctively
(B) simultaneously
(C) collectively
(D) mutually

130. Ms. Choi would have been at the keynote address if her train ------- on time.

(A) arrives
(B) will arrive
(C) had arrived
(D) arriving

PART 6

Directions: Read the texts that follow. A word, phrase, or sentence is missing in parts of each text. Four answer choices for each question are given below the text. Select the best answer to complete the text. Then mark the letter (A), (B), (C), or (D) on your answer sheet.

Questions 131-134 refer to the following advertisement.

Philadelphia's PH11-TV invites you to download our new traffic app for your mobile device. The app ------- **131.** the station's traffic coverage. Use it to get traffic news if you are away from your television and are unable to watch our traffic reports. ------- **132.**. Plus, you can program your daily commute into the app to receive personalized alerts ------- **133.** on your mobile device when any traffic-related event occurs along your route. Avoid traffic delays by downloading the PH11-TV traffic app today, ------- **134.** tune in to our live broadcast beginning at 5:00 A.M. and 4:00 P.M. daily.

131. (A) displaces
(B) observes
(C) commands
(D) supplements

132. (A) Our city is substantial in size.
(B) Text messages are subject to service fees.
(C) We send our newscasters to all areas of the city.
(D) The app features frequent updates.

133. (A) direction
(B) directly
(C) directing
(D) directs

134. (A) or
(B) well
(C) quick
(D) only

GO ON TO THE NEXT PAGE

Questions 135-138 refer to the following Web page.

http://www.midwestartisanalcheeseguild.org

The Midwest Artisanal Cheese Guild (MACG) organizes trade shows and conducts educational seminars ------- **135.** the cheese-crafting trade within the midwestern United States. Cheeses from this region are recognized internationally. Many of ------- **136.** cheeses are used by chefs at restaurants around the world.

The MACG puts on the region's largest cheese-maker exposition, held each year in April. The prestigious Wizard of Cheese contest is held at this event. ------- **137.**. Dan Travella was last year's ------- **138.**. His aged cheddar cheese received a winning score of 98.7 out of 100.

135. (A) is advancing
(B) to advance
(C) has advanced
(D) will advance

136. (A) these
(B) each
(C) when
(D) instead

137. (A) Local firm Bromatel demonstrates the latest in cheese-making technology.
(B) Next year some new conference activities are planned.
(C) Cheese makers from around the country compete.
(D) Hotel reservations can be made on our Web site.

138. (A) speaker
(B) expert
(C) judge
(D) champion

Questions 139-142 refer to the following information.

Most of the -------(139.) to *Zien Travel Quarterly* are professional writers with whom we have an ongoing relationship. -------(140.) , we always like to encourage and support new talent. We try to include at least one article per issue from a new writer, but with just four issues a year, the opportunities for publication are quite limited.

Before submitting an idea for publication, please read the guidelines at www.zientravel.com/writers, as they outline our specific areas of interest in detail. -------(141.) .

Note that we aim to respond to all correspondence in a timely manner, but there may be times when we are slow to respond. For this reason, we ask that you please be -------(142.) .

139. (A) contributes
(B) contribution
(C) contributing
(D) contributors

140. (A) With that said
(B) For instance
(C) In other words
(D) In that case

141. (A) There are dozens of ways to improve one's writing skills.
(B) That is why an editorial calendar is so important to our publication.
(C) This will increase the likelihood of your proposal being accepted.
(D) While this story is excellent, it does not meet our needs at this time.

142. (A) patient
(B) secondary
(C) cautious
(D) precise

GO ON TO THE NEXT PAGE

Questions 143-146 refer to the following e-mail.

To: bgosnell@bvb.org
From: sluu@luumarketing.com
Subject: Online marketing research
Date: April 3

Dear Mr. Gosnell,

Below are some preliminary conclusions and recommendations based on our analysis of the design of the Brookside Visitors Bureau Web site.

First, the site is not as ------- (**143.**) as it should be. We recommend updating its appearance and adding information that meets the demands of today's tourists. Note also that your organization's logo is not used consistently ------- (**144.**) your Web site.

You should also consider supplementing the imagery used to promote the city. ------- (**145.**). We therefore recommend uploading some professionally made videos featuring the various attractions Brookside has to offer. ------- (**146.**), we suggest adding a page to the Web site that allows residents and visitors to upload their own photos and videos of city attractions.

Please contact me at your earliest convenience to discuss the next steps.

Best regards,

Shelly Luu
Luu Marketing

143. (A) effectiveness
(B) effectively
(C) effective
(D) effecting

144. (A) upon
(B) toward
(C) among
(D) throughout

145. (A) No photos can be used without my written authorization.
(B) A display of photos is not enough to attract prospective visitors.
(C) A systematic way of filing photos is essential for easy retrieval.
(D) Photos that were not in the proper format have been rejected.

146. (A) So that
(B) In addition
(C) To clarify
(D) After all

PART 7

Directions: In this part you will read a selection of texts, such as magazine and newspaper articles, e-mails, and instant messages. Each text or set of texts is followed by several questions. Select the best answer for each question and mark the letter (A), (B), (C), or (D) on your answer sheet.

TEST 3

Questions 147-148 refer to the following ticket.

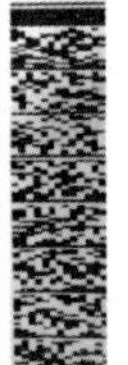

Bellevue Transport

Adult off-peak value ticket*

The bearer of this ticket is entitled to unlimited round-trip passage between destinations on the date of issue.

Please retain this ticket until completing your travel, as it may be inspected by crew members on the ferry.

*Off-peak value tickets are valid for travel Monday to Thursday, 9:00 A.M. to 4:00 P.M. only. Passengers who wish to travel at other times may upgrade to a regular fare ticket for $5.00.

Between Bellevue Beach and Kipsky Island

Between Bellevue Beach and Port Canary

147. What is true about the ticket?

(A) It was purchased for $5.00.
(B) It can be returned for a cash refund.
(C) It is valid for more than one journey.
(D) It is good for 24 hours.

148. For what mode of transportation is the ticket?

(A) A bus
(B) A boat
(C) A train
(D) A taxi

GO ON TO THE NEXT PAGE

Questions 149-150 refer to the following advertisement.

Graphic Design Associate Needed

The Zachary Township Floral Garden (ZTFG) is seeking a creative and career-oriented person to join our dynamic team. Duties include helping to design, publicize, and market ZTFG activities to schools and media outlets in the surrounding community. Qualifications include proficiency in office and design software and previous experience in a graphic design firm. Flexible work schedule. To apply, e-mail a cover letter, résumé, and two professional references to jobs@ztfg.org by May 5. To learn more, stop by any morning Monday through Friday for a tour of the garden.

149. What is a requirement of the job?

(A) Prior employment with a nonprofit organization
(B) Knowledge of organic gardening principles
(C) The ability to identify some garden flowers
(D) Competency with graphic design software

150. How can job applicants get more information?

(A) By viewing a video
(B) By taking a class
(C) By visiting the garden
(D) By contacting some references

Questions 151-152 refer to the following memo.

MEMO

To: All Employees
From: Don Wunder, Director of Facilities
Subject: Chanti Workspaces
Date: February 11

In a special partnership with Chanti Workspaces, five standing desks will be available to employees on a trial basis from February 20 to March 15. Standing desks allow you to stand comfortably while working. We will use the new Chanti B45 model, which is adjustable, so you can alternate between sitting and standing at the perfect height for you. Research suggests that standing desks can negate some of the harmful physical effects of sitting too much. They may also improve mood and overall health. Those wishing to take advantage of this opportunity should contact me. If we have more interest than desks, the recipients will be those who contact me first. Those using the desks will be asked to take a survey about their experience to help us determine whether we should make standing desks available to all employees.

151. What is the purpose of the memo?

(A) To ask for help in assembling some furniture
(B) To offer staff a chance to try a new type of furniture
(C) To encourage employees to take exercise classes
(D) To survey worker preferences about office equipment

152. What is indicated about the Chanti B45 model?

(A) It can be difficult to get used to.
(B) It will increase worker productivity.
(C) It can be adjusted to different heights.
(D) It is the most expensive standing desk.

GO ON TO THE NEXT PAGE

Questions 153-154 refer to the following text-message chain.

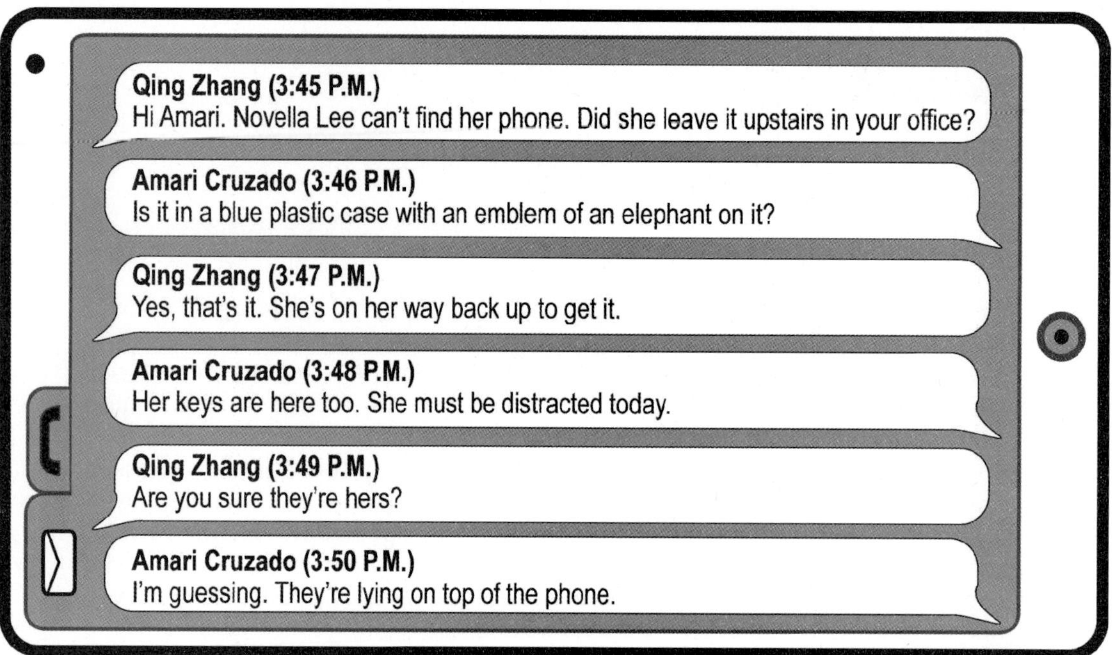

Qing Zhang (3:45 P.M.)
Hi Amari. Novella Lee can't find her phone. Did she leave it upstairs in your office?
Amari Cruzado (3:46 P.M.)
Is it in a blue plastic case with an emblem of an elephant on it?
Qing Zhang (3:47 P.M.)
Yes, that's it. She's on her way back up to get it.
Amari Cruzado (3:48 P.M.)
Her keys are here too. She must be distracted today.
Qing Zhang (3:49 P.M.)
Are you sure they're hers?
Amari Cruzado (3:50 P.M.)
I'm guessing. They're lying on top of the phone.

153. What will Ms. Lee most likely do next?

(A) Retrieve some things from upstairs
(B) Order some accessories for her phone
(C) E-mail Mr. Cruzado's assistant
(D) Borrow Ms. Zhang's phone

154. At 3:50 P.M., what does Mr. Cruzado mean when he writes, "I'm guessing"?

(A) He believes that Ms. Lee is often forgetful.
(B) He thinks that Ms. Zhang spoke incorrectly.
(C) He assumes that the keys belong to Ms. Lee.
(D) He wonders if the keys belong to Ms. Zhang.

Questions 155-157 refer to the following property listing.

> Ideal for a new business! This recently constructed property contains nearly 2,000 square metres of office space, with an additional 1,000 square metres of storage space and a 3,000-square-metre car garage. — [1] —. Easily accessible from downtown Cloverdale, the property is within 500 metres of several restaurants and a brand-new shopping centre. — [2] —. The sleek, modern design features floor-to-ceiling windows that provide an abundance of natural light. — [3] —. The standard lease is for twelve months with monthly payments and a security deposit. — [4] —. For a lease application or to view the property in person, call Danna Pulley at (519) 555-0139.

155. How large is the parking area?

(A) 500 square meters
(B) 1,000 square meters
(C) 2,000 square meters
(D) 3,000 square meters

156. What is NOT mentioned as an advantage of the property?

(A) It is close to restaurants and stores.
(B) It is a short drive from the airport.
(C) It allows for plenty of sunlight.
(D) It is a relatively new building.

157. In which of the positions marked [1], [2], [3], and [4] does the following sentence best belong?

"Longer terms can be negotiated, depending on the needs of the applicant."

(A) [1]
(B) [2]
(C) [3]
(D) [4]

GO ON TO THE NEXT PAGE

Questions 158-160 refer to the following e-mail.

To:	Rafael Vargas
From:	Bon-Hwa Oh
Subject:	Information
Date:	1 October

Dear Rafael:

The opening at the new airport office here is now set for Monday, 3 November, because of a delay caused by some unexpected construction in Terminal A. I will e-mail you more details later this week, along with a request that you join us here. It would be great to have someone attend from the corporate office.

As I have planned, we will celebrate our relocation with a month of special deals on all car rentals. I have also arranged for us to partner with Moonray Airways for special flight and car travel packages. Although we expect many of our customers will continue to be business travelers, we hope to attract tourists, too.

I hope to see you next month.

Bon-Hwa Oh

158. The word "set" in paragraph 1, line 1, is closest in meaning to

(A) scheduled
(B) attached
(C) trained
(D) raised

159. What does Mr. Oh suggest in his e-mail?

(A) He has corrected a mistake.
(B) He has visited the corporate office.
(C) He is a newly hired employee.
(D) He is responsible for an office relocation.

160. What is expected to open on November 3 ?

(A) An airport terminal
(B) A car rental business
(C) A tourist agency
(D) A construction company

Questions 161-163 refer to the following letter.

Saunderson Medical Group • 46 Manuka Road • Karori, Wellington 6012

12 September

Dear Saunderson Medical Group Patient:

Saunderson Medical Group (SMG) thanks you for choosing us as your health care provider. Throughout our 35-year history, we have successfully treated thousands of patients in Karori. Given the rapid changes in the health care market, we have looked for the best way to continue to provide the best experience for our patients. Toward that end, we are pleased to announce that SMG will join with Keefe Health effective 1 October.

What does this mean for you? Only our name will change; beginning next month we will become Keefe Health Karori. Your physician will remain the same, and you may continue to see your doctor at our Karori location. However, we will now have available all of the talented doctors and specialists from the Keefe Health network to offer you a broader range of diagnostic services and treatments. Keefe Health is consistently ranked at the top of all medical providers in the larger metropolitan area for expertise and patient outcomes.

To learn more about Keefe Health, visit its Web site at www.keefehealth.co.nz. If you wish to schedule an appointment, please use our existing phone number.

We look forward to continuing to care for you.

Sincerely,

Saunderson Medical Group

161. What is the purpose of the letter?

(A) To thank patients for their patronage
(B) To advise patients about a business merger
(C) To introduce a new doctor on staff
(D) To announce the opening of a branch office

162. What is suggested about Keefe Health?

(A) It offers medical options that SMG does not offer.
(B) Its location is inconvenient for Karori residents.
(C) Its patients will soon receive the letter.
(D) It has been in business for 35 years.

163. According to the letter, what should recipients do to schedule an appointment?

(A) Visit Keefe Health's Web page
(B) Go to Keefe Health's main office
(C) Send an e-mail request to the SMG receptionist
(D) Call the same phone number as in the past

TEST 3

GO ON TO THE NEXT PAGE

Questions 164-167 refer to the following online chat discussion.

Will Frankel (4:32 P.M.):	Are the instructors that are being sent over to our company ready to begin the safety training sessions on Monday?
Donna Davis (4:33 P.M.):	Yes. They'll arrive there at ZRC Tech at 2:30 on Monday afternoon. Someone will meet them at the security desk and show them where they'll be teaching, right?
Will Frankel (4:34 P.M.):	My assistant can help with that.
Donna Davis (4:35 P.M.):	Will the rooms be set up with computers and whiteboards?
Violet Menja (4:35 P.M.):	As Will stated, I'll meet the instructors at the security desk and get them visitor passes.
Will Frankel (4:37 P.M.):	We'll be using two large conference rooms that will have everything the instructors need.
Violet Menja (4:38 P.M.):	The lab technicians will finish up their shifts just before 3:00, so they can go straight to their sessions. I'll be around to help get everyone settled.
Donna Davis (4:41 P.M.):	Excellent. The sessions end at 5:00. Will either of you be there? Do the instructors need to lock up?
Will Frankel (4:42 P.M.):	I'll be there to lock up the rooms when they finish.
Donna Davis (4:43 P.M.):	Good. That's it, then.
Will Frankel (4:44 P.M.):	I'm here until 5:30 if you need anything else this afternoon.

164. Why did Mr. Frankel contact Ms. Davis?

(A) To propose a change to a schedule
(B) To request a security form
(C) To order laboratory supplies
(D) To confirm special arrangements

165. When will Ms. Menja be at the security desk?

(A) At 2:30 P.M.
(B) At 3:00 P.M.
(C) At 5:00 P.M.
(D) At 5:30 P.M.

166. What is indicated about the lab technicians?

(A) They have recently been hired.
(B) They will attend training sessions after work.
(C) They will have a break in the afternoon.
(D) They have previously met Ms. Davis.

167. At 4:43 P.M., what does Ms. Davis mean when she writes, "That's it, then"?

(A) She does not have any more questions.
(B) She does not think the doors should be locked.
(C) She believes that Mr. Frankel has a good idea.
(D) She has finished closing up the rooms.

Questions 168-171 refer to the following e-mail.

E-mail

From:	Kira Takamatsu
To:	Eric Sutherland
Subject:	Meeting follow-up
Date:	March 8

Dear Eric,

Thank you for sharing your concerns about your workload. — [1] —. We do our best to distribute projects so that employees can complete them during the regular workweek. — [2] —. Since we recently added book-cover design to your already full list of responsibilities, we have decided to assign an assistant to you, a new team member named Hugo Rynkowski. — [3] —. You will oversee his work, including all poster, logo, and catalog layout projects.

When Mr. Rynkowski arrives next Monday, you will need to share with him all of your clients' information, including general descriptions and specific requirements. You will be responsible for instructing him on our design software as well as all other systems that you are using.

If you have any other concerns, please do not hesitate to share them with me. — [4] —.

Kind regards,

Kira Takamatsu

168. Who most likely is Mr. Sutherland?

(A) A computer programmer
(B) A graphic designer
(C) A company manager
(D) A writer

169. What problem did Mr. Sutherland report?

(A) Inconvenient scheduling
(B) Outdated software
(C) Long commutes
(D) Too much work

170. What is Mr. Sutherland asked to do next week?

(A) Prepare a report
(B) Meet a potential client
(C) Train a new employee
(D) Create a job description

171. In which of the positions marked [1], [2], [3], and [4] does the following sentence best belong?

"This new hire will support you in most of your tasks."

(A) [1]
(B) [2]
(C) [3]
(D) [4]

GO ON TO THE NEXT PAGE

Questions 172-175 refer to the following article.

Perth Daily Tribune

Beneath the Bright Blue Sea

(2 November)—If you are looking for Sara Nannup, start by checking under the sea. That's where she has captured all the images in her latest book of photography, *Beneath the Bright Blue Sea.*

Ms. Nannup began taking pictures when her father gave her an easy-to-use instant camera for her fifth birthday. When she went to university, however, she put the camera down to pursue a career in print journalism.

After she graduated, Ms. Nannup was hired as a staff writer by the *Perth Daily Tribune* and had little time for taking pictures. That changed when she attended an underwater photography workshop while on vacation in Bali, Indonesia. There her interest in photography was renewed, and she eventually left her job at the newspaper to devote herself to photography full-time.

Although she started with a child's instant camera, Ms. Nannup now works with advanced underwater cameras. To deal with wear and tear, she updates her equipment every few years. "Salt water and sand pose challenges for underwater photography equipment beyond those that an everyday camera would face," she said.

After years now of diving and taking pictures, she has yet to tire of her profession. "I still love being able to show people images of creatures and places that they have never seen," says Ms. Nannup.

Most of Ms. Nannup's work, including her latest release, focuses on the ocean around Australia. In May, however, she will travel to Greece to photograph underwater ruins in the Mediterranean for her next book.

Visit www.saranannup.com.au for more information on Ms. Nannup and her work.

172. What is the purpose of the article?

(A) To profile a former newspaper employee
(B) To offer photography advice
(C) To promote an online newspaper column
(D) To advertise a photography exhibition

173. What inspired Ms. Nannup to take underwater photographs?

(A) Advice from her father
(B) A job in Indonesia
(C) A special workshop
(D) A journalism class

174. The word "pose" in paragraph 4, line 6, is closest in meaning to

(A) model
(B) check
(C) ask
(D) present

175. What is indicated about Ms. Nannup?

(A) She is an experienced diver.
(B) She will soon publish her first book.
(C) She has taken photographs in Greece.
(D) She has used the same camera for many years.

GO ON TO THE NEXT PAGE

Questions 176-180 refer to the following brochure and article.

WESTWOOD PROPERTIES, INC.

Residential Communities

Westwood Properties, Inc. (WPI), has two residential apartment communities in the city of Kentville.

HILLSIDE MANOR **222 Jackson Rd.**	**LAKEVIEW OAKS** **119 E. Corfu St.**
Features: • 2- and 3-bedroom units with washer and dryer • Swimming pool plus basketball and tennis courts • Children's park nearby • Top-rated schools in the area • Five minutes from the business district • Pet-friendly environment	Features: • 1-bedroom units with large kitchens and baths • Hardwood floors • Community laundry room on each floor • Fitness center and outdoor swimming pool • Ten minutes from business district • Access to multiple bus lines right outside your door • Pet-friendly environment

Visit our Web site at www.westwoodproperties.com to view floor plans or to schedule a personal tour. Sales agents are available at our offices to answer your questions Monday through Friday from 9:00 A.M. to 5:00 P.M., and on Saturday and Sunday from 12:00 noon to 5:00 P.M.

WPI Announces Expansion

KENTVILLE (March 16)—Westwood Properties, Inc. (WPI), in partnership with the Kentville city government, will be constructing its third residential development in Kentville. The new development, Green Valley Court, will consist of 150 freestanding homes.

Work will begin in April and is expected to be completed in eighteen months. WPI will bear 60 percent of the costs, while the remainder will be borne by the city government.

WPI has built a reputation for providing comfortable living at affordable prices. Its current residential developments, Hillside Manor and Lakeview Oaks, were built five years ago and are much in demand, with long waiting lists.

According to Helen Hart, a marketing executive for WPI, Green Valley Court will be located twenty minutes from the business district. Ms. Hart went on to say that "Green Valley Court will be ideal for retirees and those longing for some rest and relaxation after a hard day's work."

176. What is stated about Westwood Properties, Inc.?

(A) Its offices are open daily.
(B) It lists available units online.
(C) It offers hourly personal tours.
(D) Its headquarters are located in Kentville.

177. What is NOT listed as a feature of the units at Lakeview Oaks?

(A) Recreational facilities
(B) Laundry facilities
(C) Covered parking
(D) Hardwood flooring

178. What does the article suggest about the units at Hillside Manor and Lakeview Oaks?

(A) They were built in eighteen months.
(B) They were completed in April.
(C) Many people find them expensive.
(D) Many people want to live in them.

179. What does the article mention about Green Valley Court?

(A) It will contain two apartment buildings.
(B) It will be managed by Ms. Hart.
(C) Its construction costs will be partly paid for by the government.
(D) It is restricted to people who have retired.

180. How will Green Valley Court differ from the other two developments?

(A) It will allow residents to have pets.
(B) It will be farther from the business district.
(C) It will include special features for elderly residents.
(D) It will allow people to buy homes as well as rent them.

GO ON TO THE NEXT PAGE

Questions 181-185 refer to the following e-mails.

To:	Dennis Maki
From:	Nigella Smith
Date:	Thursday, November 8, 2:15 P.M.
Subject:	Update

Dennis:

The heads of accounting and sales have chosen the finalists for the job openings in their departments here at Plumsted Aynes. Susan Tsai would like to invite Marco Garcia and Danielle Jenkins to return for second interviews for the accounting position, and Rajesh Kapoor wants to invite Melanie Yu for a second interview for the medical sales position.

I would like you to call the finalists, schedule interviews with them, and then make lunch arrangements accordingly. Keep in mind that Susan will be out of the office next week for a conference.

Thank you for your assistance with this search so far. I'm especially grateful that you were able to work on a short deadline when I asked you to set up the initial interviews.

Regards,

Nigella Smith
Human Resources Director

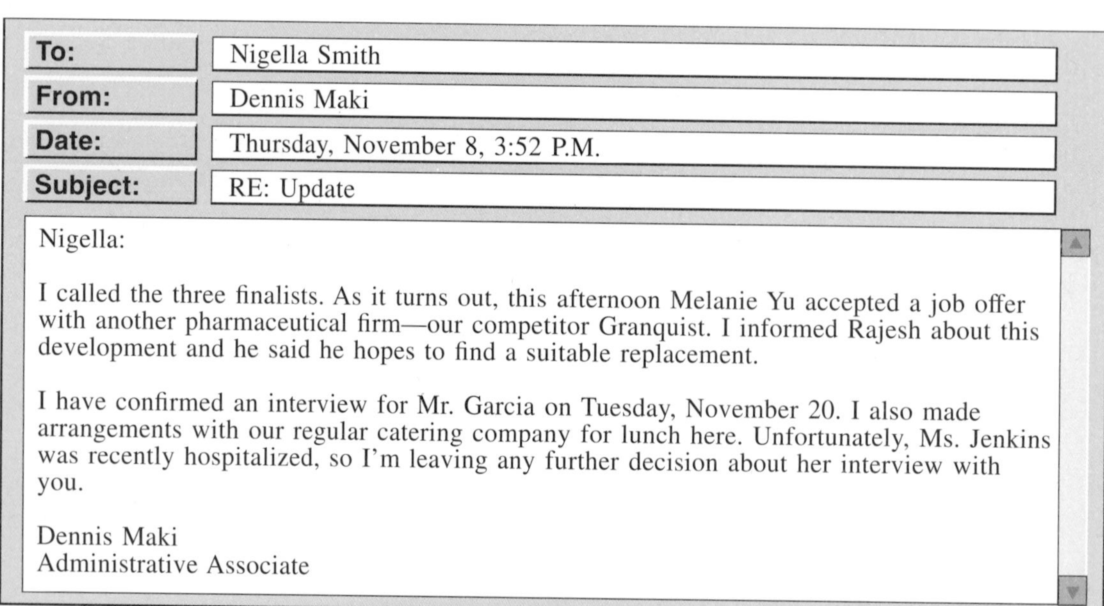

To:	Nigella Smith
From:	Dennis Maki
Date:	Thursday, November 8, 3:52 P.M.
Subject:	RE: Update

Nigella:

I called the three finalists. As it turns out, this afternoon Melanie Yu accepted a job offer with another pharmaceutical firm—our competitor Granquist. I informed Rajesh about this development and he said he hopes to find a suitable replacement.

I have confirmed an interview for Mr. Garcia on Tuesday, November 20. I also made arrangements with our regular catering company for lunch here. Unfortunately, Ms. Jenkins was recently hospitalized, so I'm leaving any further decision about her interview with you.

Dennis Maki
Administrative Associate

181. What is one purpose of the first e-mail?

(A) To announce a job opening
(B) To make an offer to a job applicant
(C) To request that applicants be contacted
(D) To check a job candidate's references

182. What type of company most likely is Plumsted Aynes?

(A) An accounting firm
(B) A medical clinic
(C) A caterer
(D) A pharmaceutical company

183. What is suggested about Ms. Jenkins?

(A) She has visited Plumsted Aynes before.
(B) She will be interviewed by Ms. Smith.
(C) She previously worked for Granquist.
(D) She is interested in a sales position.

184. What will Mr. Kapoor most likely do?

(A) Meet with Mr. Garcia
(B) Attend a conference
(C) Make reservations at a restaurant
(D) Select a new candidate to interview

185. What was Mr. Maki NOT able to do?

(A) Order food to be delivered
(B) Schedule all the appointments within a given time frame
(C) Have a conversation with Ms. Yu
(D) Assist Ms. Smith with setting up the initial interviews

GO ON TO THE NEXT PAGE

Questions 186-190 refer to the following article, Web page, and online order form.

KELOWNA (2 June)—A new enterprise is revolutionizing mealtime in Kelowna. Fine Fresh Foods is a meal-delivery service that was founded one year ago by Kathryn Mishra. The service allows users to go online and browse hundreds of recipes. They select the recipes they like and have the ingredients, with cooking instructions, shipped to them on a weekly basis.

Ms. Mishra first thought of the idea when she observed her friends' hectic lives. "My friends were too busy to plan, shop, and cook for themselves," she explained. "Most nights they would go to a restaurant and get takeout food. Some wanted to cook at home in their kitchens but didn't feel confident in their abilities."

Ms. Mishra has found a way to streamline the whole process. Fine Fresh Foods works with local suppliers—often small farms—that are required to be organic. The focus on working with local partners, as well as the convenience and reasonable price of the service, has made the business extremely popular. At the moment, Fine Fresh Foods delivers only within Kelowna, but expansion to other areas is planned in the coming year.

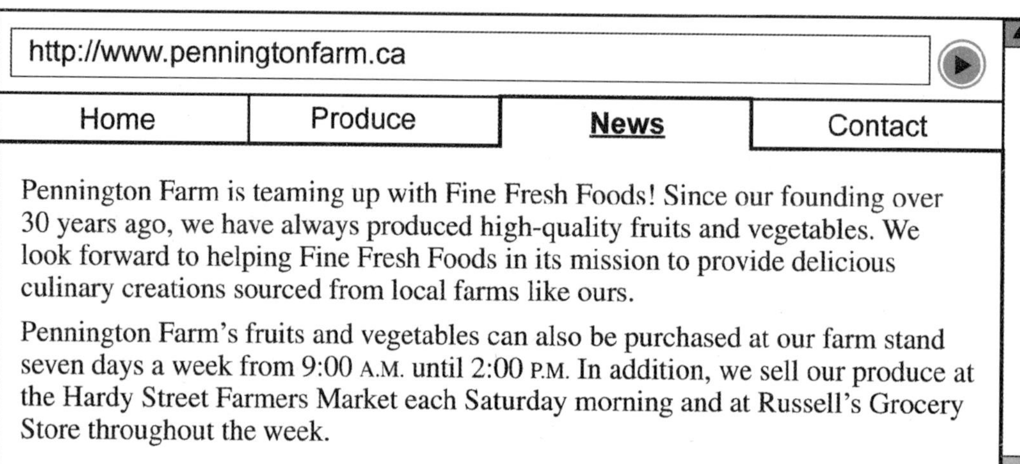
http://www.penningtonfarm.ca

Home | Produce | **News** | Contact

Pennington Farm is teaming up with Fine Fresh Foods! Since our founding over 30 years ago, we have always produced high-quality fruits and vegetables. We look forward to helping Fine Fresh Foods in its mission to provide delicious culinary creations sourced from local farms like ours.

Pennington Farm's fruits and vegetables can also be purchased at our farm stand seven days a week from 9:00 A.M. until 2:00 P.M. In addition, we sell our produce at the Hardy Street Farmers Market each Saturday morning and at Russell's Grocery Store throughout the week.

http://www.finefreshfoods.ca/orderform

Fine Fresh Foods

Order Form

Name: Darren Soun
E-mail: dsoun@email.ca
Phone: 250-555-0193
Selected Recipes: #11—Stir-fried chicken and vegetables (serves four)
#32—Pork tenderloin with asparagus (serves four)
#56—Vegetable barley soup (serves two)
Total: $50.00 (Charged to credit card ending in 4873)
Delivery Day and Time: Tuesday, 13 June, at 6:00 P.M.

186. What is the article mainly about?

(A) How a food-service company got started
(B) What recipes a cooking class will cover
(C) Why a local restaurant is popular
(D) Where to buy inexpensive kitchen equipment

187. According to the article, what is one reason customers like Fine Fresh Foods?

(A) Its hours are convenient.
(B) Its prices are affordable.
(C) It has several locations.
(D) It offers free delivery.

188. What is announced on the Pennington Farm Web page?

(A) A job opportunity
(B) An upcoming sale
(C) A business partnership
(D) An anniversary celebration

189. What most likely is true about Pennington Farm?

(A) It is a family-run business.
(B) It recently opened a second farm stand.
(C) It sells exclusively to Russell's Grocery Store.
(D) It is an organic farm.

190. What is suggested about Mr. Soun?

(A) He does not eat meat.
(B) He lives in Kelowna.
(C) He is having a dinner party on June 12.
(D) He is one of Ms. Mishra's friends.

GO ON TO THE NEXT PAGE

Questions 191-195 refer to the following e-mails and chart.

E-mail

To: Kate Millerson
From: Daniel Friedman
Date: January 25
Subject: Upcoming focus group

Hi, Kate,

The next focus group to test the new fruit-flavored beverage ideas will be held on February 1 in the Greenville office. Mari Kobayashi will be leading it.

Please design a questionnaire to collect the group's feedback using the one you created last month as a template and send it over to Mari. After the focus group takes place, please tally the results in the form of a chart. I need to incorporate this information into my monthly report to the chief marketing officer.

Thanks,

Daniel

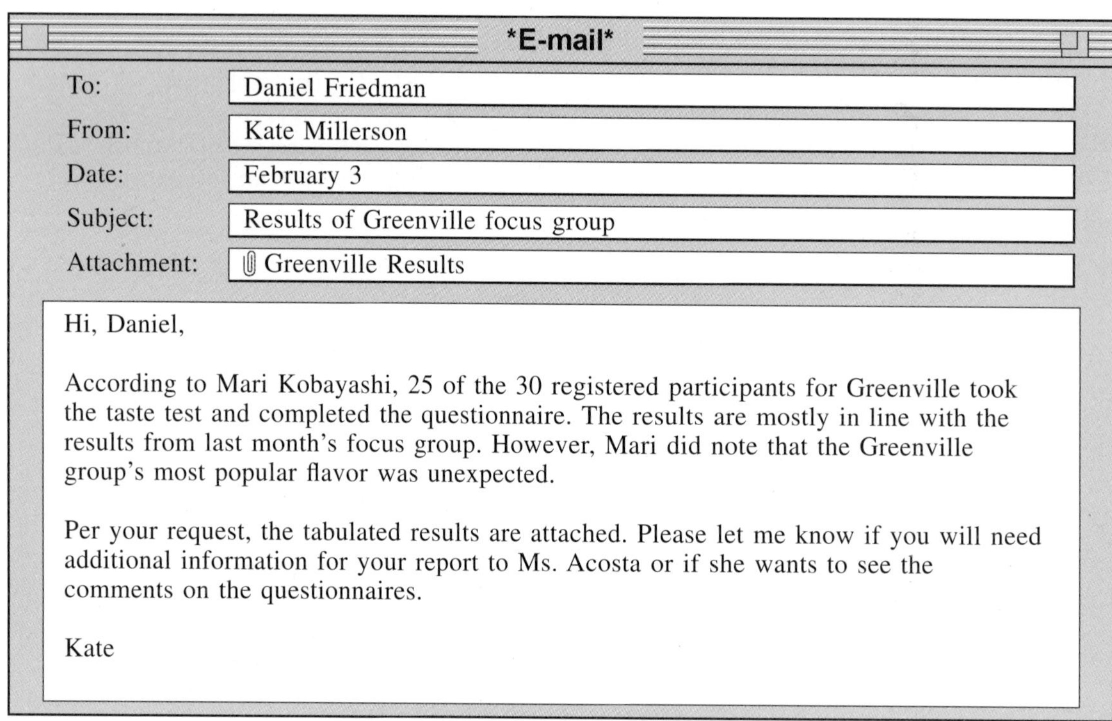

E-mail

To: Daniel Friedman
From: Kate Millerson
Date: February 3
Subject: Results of Greenville focus group
Attachment: Greenville Results

Hi, Daniel,

According to Mari Kobayashi, 25 of the 30 registered participants for Greenville took the taste test and completed the questionnaire. The results are mostly in line with the results from last month's focus group. However, Mari did note that the Greenville group's most popular flavor was unexpected.

Per your request, the tabulated results are attached. Please let me know if you will need additional information for your report to Ms. Acosta or if she wants to see the comments on the questionnaires.

Kate

Greenville Focus Group

February 1

(Numbers indicate how many participants preferred each option.)

Type of drink:	Carbonated (8)		Noncarbonated (17)	
Highest price willing to pay:	$1.25 (5)	$1.50 (12)	$2.00 (5)	$2.50 (3)
Flavor:	Cherry (2)	Lemon (7)	Lime (13)	Orange (3)

TEST 3

191. In the first e-mail, what is indicated about Ms. Millerson?

(A) She has designed questionnaires before.
(B) She will lead a focus group on February 1.
(C) She will interview Ms. Kobayashi.
(D) She has been transferred to the Greenville office.

192. What does Mr. Friedman say he will do with Ms. Millerson's data?

(A) Distribute it to his staff
(B) Show it to a new client
(C) Include it in a report
(D) Write an article based on it

193. Who most likely is Ms. Acosta?

(A) The director of Human Resources
(B) The chief marketing officer
(C) A focus group leader
(D) An information technology expert

194. What does Ms. Millerson suggest about the Greenville focus group?

(A) Some people arrived late.
(B) The group will meet again soon.
(C) Each attendee received a payment.
(D) There were fewer participants than expected.

195. Which flavor preference surprised Ms. Kobayashi?

(A) Cherry
(B) Lemon
(C) Lime
(D) Orange

GO ON TO THE NEXT PAGE

Questions 196-200 refer to the following Web site, online review, and booking confirmation.

http://www.zabokahaiti.ht

French | **English**

Zaboka Guesthouse
99 rue Hibbert, Pétion-Ville, Haiti

The Zaboka Guesthouse, situated in the hills above Haiti's capital city of Port-au-Prince, occupies the top four floors of a gorgeous building in a historic district. Our guesthouse is centrally located and just a short walk to markets, restaurants, art galleries, and nightclubs.

Details:

- Amenities include wireless Internet, kitchen facilities, and luggage storage.
- All guests are also entitled to a free Haitian-style breakfast including locally grown coffee.
- The room rate is $45 per night per guest ($15 is charged up front to secure each reservation; the remainder must be paid upon arrival).
- Check-in starts at 1:00 P.M.; checkout is no later than 11:30 A.M.
- A minimum stay of two nights is required.
- Parties arriving after 7:00 P.M. will be charged a late-night check-in fee of $5.00 per reservation.

http://www.travelfair.com

Pétion-Ville, Haiti: Zaboka Guesthouse
Posted by Wilford Gaines on October 7

I stayed at the Zaboka Guesthouse for three nights in April. There are several other hotels in the area, but in my view, this is certainly the nicest option within the price range. The lively courtyard and huge communal kitchen both present a great environment for meeting other guests. That was without a doubt my favorite aspect. If you plan to arrive in the evening, make sure you get the code to enter into the electronic keypad at the door, as the street level entrance is locked after 7 P.M. This isn't something I was made aware of, so I had to wait a short while to be let in. Other than that, I really enjoyed my stay!

http://www.zabokahaiti.ht/receipt167642

Thank you for your reservation! Please print a copy of these details for your records.

Guest Name: Melinda Le
Number of Guests: 1
Booking Reference Number: 167642
Date and Time of Check-in: 2 June at 8:00 P.M.
Date and Time of Checkout: 3 June at 11:00 A.M.
Amount Paid: $15.00 deposit
+ $5.00 late-night check-in fee
= $20.00 total paid via card ending in -8990
Amount Due on Arrival: $30.00
Total: $50.00

Send a message to reception@zabokahaiti.ht or call + 509 2555 0161 if you have any questions prior to your arrival. We look forward to hosting you!

196. Where is the Zaboka Guesthouse located?

(A) Next to a history museum
(B) Near an urban transit center
(C) In an old area of the town
(D) In a new residential area

197. What does the Web site mention about the Zaboka Guesthouse?

(A) It provides a complimentary breakfast.
(B) It can be reserved for special evening events.
(C) It offers tours to local attractions.
(D) It requires full payment in advance.

198. What did Mr. Gaines like most about the Zaboka Guesthouse?

(A) Its friendly staff
(B) Its spacious rooms
(C) Its social atmosphere
(D) Its attractive architecture

199. How did the Zaboka Guesthouse make an exception for Ms. Le?

(A) By extending her checkout time
(B) By waiving a nighttime check-in fee
(C) By charging a lower price for her room
(D) By allowing her to stay only one night

200. What is suggested about Ms. Le?

(A) She made her reservation over the phone.
(B) She will need a code to enter the guesthouse.
(C) She will be traveling with extra luggage.
(D) She requested a room that overlooks the courtyard.

Stop! This is the end of the test. If you finish before time is called, you may go back to Parts 5, 6, and 7 and check your work.

토익® 정기시험
기출문제집

기출 TEST

04

READING TEST

In the Reading test, you will read a variety of texts and answer several different types of reading comprehension questions. The entire Reading test will last 75 minutes. There are three parts, and directions are given for each part. You are encouraged to answer as many questions as possible within the time allowed.

You must mark your answers on the separate answer sheet. Do not write your answers in your test book.

PART 5

Directions: A word or phrase is missing in each of the sentences below. Four answer choices are given below each sentence. Select the best answer to complete the sentence. Then mark the letter (A), (B), (C), or (D) on your answer sheet.

101. ------- account will be credited after we receive the returned merchandise.

(A) You
(B) Yours
(C) Your
(D) Yourself

102. Late entries for the cake decoration contest will not be -------.

(A) solved
(B) accepted
(C) decided
(D) earned

103. The newspaper has seen an ------- in the number of subscribers who read the online version.

(A) increase
(B) increases
(C) increasingly
(D) increased

104. Every attorney at the firm of Duncan and Hulce has practiced law ------- more than ten years.

(A) at
(B) for
(C) on
(D) by

105. Prethart Tool Company has created a more ------- drill than its previous models.

(A) powerful
(B) powers
(C) powerfully
(D) power

106. To find out if an item on this Web site is in stock, ------- highlight the item and click the "Check on it" button.

(A) mostly
(B) simply
(C) enough
(D) quite

107. Mr. Jones ------- Ms. Cheng's clients while she is on a business trip to Hong Kong.

(A) will assist
(B) assisted
(C) to assist
(D) is assisted

108. The Jossty Company offers insurance policies to renters at the lowest rates -------.

(A) ready
(B) strong
(C) available
(D) agreeable

109. ------- the Editorial Department receives the author's final approval, the manuscript should be sent to the printer.

(A) As soon as
(B) Still
(C) In the meantime
(D) For example

110. Sidewalks in the town of Newburgh are ------- one meter wide.

(A) general
(B) generally
(C) generalize
(D) generalization

111. The housing authority has formed a ------- to look for new construction locations.

(A) member
(B) building
(C) frontier
(D) committee

112. A recent study has found that those ------- regularly read food labels tend to be healthier.

(A) what
(B) where
(C) who
(D) when

113. If you are not ------- with your Electoshine toothbrush, you may return it for a full refund.

(A) satisfaction
(B) satisfying
(C) satisfied
(D) satisfy

114. DG Feed Supply has shown strong growth heading ------- the end of the fiscal year.

(A) among
(B) into
(C) around
(D) between

115. Book fair volunteers may be asked to work longer shifts if the need -------.

(A) arise
(B) arises
(C) had arisen
(D) arising

116. On Tuesday, Mr. Molina will visit the Seoul office for the first time ------- becoming vice-president of operations.

(A) under
(B) past
(C) until
(D) since

117. Attendees said the fireworks were the most ------- part of the festival.

(A) impression
(B) impressive
(C) impresses
(D) impressed

118. The interview panel felt that Dinah Ong's education fit the job description of junior accountant -------.

(A) perfectly
(B) recently
(C) routinely
(D) occasionally

119. The new software makes it possible to track purchases ------- at multiple points-of-sale.

(A) rely
(B) reliable
(C) reliant
(D) reliably

120. ------- the next few months, Camion Vehicles will add more features to its sedans.

(A) Provided
(B) Applying
(C) Toward
(D) Over

GO ON TO THE NEXT PAGE

121. Altona Printing is expecting a ------- upturn in holiday card orders in the next few weeks.

(A) considerable
(B) wide
(C) central
(D) dominant

122. By creating innovative packaging -------, EK2 Beverages hopes consumers will reuse their water bottles.

(A) designed
(B) designs
(C) designing
(D) designers

123. Throughout her tenure at LPID Systems, Ms. Patterson has ------- at defining complex concepts in simple terms.

(A) excelled
(B) organized
(C) instructed
(D) simplified

124. Winslet Food Service has ------- to expand the cafeteria's menu offerings.

(A) promptly
(B) before
(C) although
(D) promised

125. ------- the results of the customer survey, we may consider extending the store's evening hours until 9 P.M.

(A) Because
(B) Depending on
(C) Whereas
(D) In order for

126. Yerrow Cameras' lenses have a long telephoto reach yet an ------- lightweight casing.

(A) exceptions
(B) exception
(C) excepting
(D) exceptionally

127. After postponing her studies for many years, Ms. Ruiz ------- earned a degree in law.

(A) thoroughly
(B) distinctly
(C) eventually
(D) already

128. A favorable report on the ------- of Seesom Eyewear convinced the partners to invest in the company.

(A) profitability
(B) profitable
(C) profited
(D) profitably

129. In Monday's meeting, Mr. Ito ------- the need to hire enough workers for the peak season.

(A) hesitated
(B) emphasized
(C) dominated
(D) launched

130. Pugh Tower won the Best New Building Award for its creative ------- of sustainable materials.

(A) routine
(B) accessory
(C) incorporation
(D) submission

PART 6

Directions: Read the texts that follow. A word, phrase, or sentence is missing in parts of each text. Four answer choices for each question are given below the text. Select the best answer to complete the text. Then mark the letter (A), (B), (C), or (D) on your answer sheet.

Questions 131-134 refer to the following memo.

From: Janine Farber
To: Barker Marketing Group employees
Date: September 25
Subject: Entryway improvements

As many of you have noticed, the main entrance of our building is in ------- **131.** condition. It is in desperate need of attention. Therefore, beginning at 6 P.M. on Friday, the main entrance ------- **132.** for approximately one month as it is renovated. The changes will give the entryway a more streamlined and contemporary appearance.

------- **133.** the main entrance is closed, employees and visitors may use the side entrances to gain access to the building. ------- **134.**.

131. (A) poor
(B) stable
(C) physical
(D) excellent

132. (A) close
(B) was closing
(C) will be closed
(D) had been closed

133. (A) While
(B) During
(C) Sometimes
(D) In the meantime

134. (A) All ground floor offices will remain accessible.
(B) The construction firm has won several awards.
(C) The building is more than 50 years old.
(D) The board of directors is discussing the project.

GO ON TO THE NEXT PAGE

Questions 135-138 refer to the following article.

(May 2)—Automotive-manufacturing company Lybera, Inc., today announced that Harvey Ramirez has been appointed as the new chairperson of its board of directors. He ------- (135.) Helen McGavick, who has resigned in order to pursue a new business venture.

"We thank Ms. McGavick for her service and wish her success in her ------- (136.) endeavors," said Fen Wang, Lybera's president and CEO.

Mr. Ramirez has spent ten years as CEO of aerospace-engineering firm Elia Aviation. ------- (137.), he held a variety of senior management roles across public and private sectors.

"Mr. Ramirez's familiarity with sophisticated technology, combined with his leadership experience, makes him well suited to lead our company," said Mr. Wang. "------- (138.)."

135. (A) replaces
(B) was replacing
(C) has been replaced
(D) would have replaced

136. (A) advancing
(B) future
(C) certain
(D) instant

137. (A) Again
(B) Consequently
(C) Previously
(D) However

138. (A) These meetings take place on a regular basis.
(B) The product is currently being developed.
(C) We hope to learn more about the position.
(D) We look forward to his guidance.

Questions 139-142 refer to the following letter.

25 February

Dear Ms. Nguyen,

We appreciate your feedback regarding Medusa Airways' flight 859, which was scheduled to depart at 9:35 A.M. on 19 February. We are sorry that this flight -------. We have decided to
139.
compensate you for the -------. We have refunded the unused portion of your ticket, valued at
140.
$410. Also, we will reimburse the $200 you paid in hotel charges resulting ------- the disruption.
141.
-------. Please allow up to five business days for the transactions to process.
142.

Sincerely,

Yeeking Lai
Customer Relations Manager

139. (A) was canceled
(B) will be canceled
(C) had to cancel
(D) is canceling

140. (A) work
(B) time
(C) drawback
(D) inconvenience

141. (A) above
(B) near
(C) from
(D) beyond

142. (A) We hope you have an enjoyable trip.
(B) Both amounts have been credited to your account.
(C) Your complaint will soon be reviewed.
(D) Thank you for your understanding.

GO ON TO THE NEXT PAGE

Questions 143-146 refer to the following e-mail.

To: Film crew
From: Sandeep Goswami
Date: Monday, October 2
Subject: Barn scene retake

Dear Crew,

This is a reminder that on Saturday we will be doing a retake of the advertisement featuring the horses at Willow Stables. Filming with animals can be unpredictable, and last week we were not able to get the footage we needed. ------- **143.** , I would like to begin promptly at 8:00 A.M. so that we can film from a number of angles before lunch. As long as everyone is punctual and everything goes well, we should get the footage we need by then. ------- **144.** .

I also want to ------- **145.** the fact that the set is closed to all who are not absolutely essential to the filming of the scene. Anyone else will be too much of a ------- **146.** .

Sandeep Goswami
Monarda Productions

143. (A) Otherwise
(B) In either case
(C) If possible
(D) Alternatively

144. (A) I was impressed by the rehearsal.
(B) Luckily, it is not noticeable to viewers.
(C) We will need different equipment.
(D) However, it may take the full day.

145. (A) research
(B) challenge
(C) avoid
(D) stress

146. (A) distraction
(B) distracting
(C) distracted
(D) distract

PART 7

Directions: In this part you will read a selection of texts, such as magazine and newspaper articles, e-mails, and instant messages. Each text or set of texts is followed by several questions. Select the best answer for each question and mark the letter (A), (B), (C), or (D) on your answer sheet.

Questions 147-148 refer to the following notice.

STAR DESIGNS

Dear Customers:

For many years, we at Star Designs have strived to offer quality apparel at competitive prices. Unfortunately, as a quick glance at our online store shows, we have been forced to increase our prices recently. Every effort has been made to avoid this, but because of the growing costs of cotton and most fabrics that we use to sew our colorful shirts and formal wear, we could no longer afford to maintain our prices. However, we will continue to provide the excellent quality and customer-oriented approach that you have come to appreciate with Star Designs.

Thank you for your understanding and your continued loyalty!

147. What does Star Designs produce?

(A) Software
(B) Clothing
(C) Cosmetics
(D) Furniture

148. What is being announced?

(A) A grand opening
(B) An expanded product line
(C) A change in prices
(D) An upgraded online store

GO ON TO THE NEXT PAGE

Questions 149-150 refer to the following brochure.

Acadetech

Over ten years serving individuals as well as small- and mid-sized businesses

What we do:

- Responsive Web site design with secure e-commerce functionality
- Multilingual content development and management
- Branding and marketing

Prices begin at $200 for a basic five-page Web site in English. Expedited design available. Call or e-mail us today for a consultation!

Customer reviews:

"My business has had a boost since the launch of the great new Web site designed by Mr. Alexander. The super-secure e-commerce tools make shopping easy and safe for my customers."
—*Julia Melo*, Flowers To Go

"Acadetech is the best! I needed to accommodate a large variety of customers, and they listened. Thanks to their responsive design, my site is just as functional on mobile phones and tablets as on big desktop screens."
—*Erik Schroeder*, Jamestown Catering

149. What is suggested about Acadetech?

(A) It works mainly with large companies.
(B) It investigates Web site security breaches.
(C) It offers a variety of Web site designs.
(D) It provides delivery service for online-shopping businesses.

150. With what feature is Mr. Schroeder particularly pleased?

(A) The security
(B) The speed
(C) The simplicity
(D) The adaptability

Questions 151-153 refer to the following e-mail.

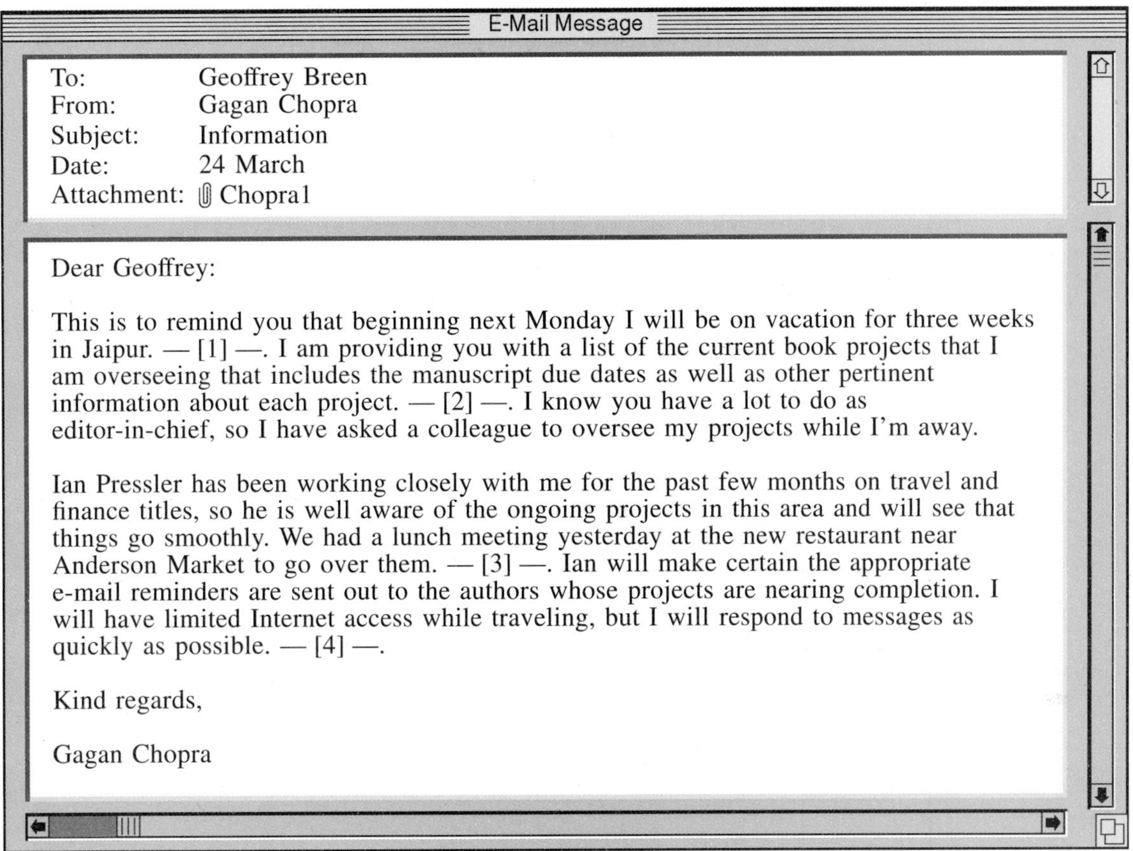

E-Mail Message

To: Geoffrey Breen
From: Gagan Chopra
Subject: Information
Date: 24 March
Attachment: Chopra1

Dear Geoffrey:

This is to remind you that beginning next Monday I will be on vacation for three weeks in Jaipur. — [1] —. I am providing you with a list of the current book projects that I am overseeing that includes the manuscript due dates as well as other pertinent information about each project. — [2] —. I know you have a lot to do as editor-in-chief, so I have asked a colleague to oversee my projects while I'm away.

Ian Pressler has been working closely with me for the past few months on travel and finance titles, so he is well aware of the ongoing projects in this area and will see that things go smoothly. We had a lunch meeting yesterday at the new restaurant near Anderson Market to go over them. — [3] —. Ian will make certain the appropriate e-mail reminders are sent out to the authors whose projects are nearing completion. I will have limited Internet access while traveling, but I will respond to messages as quickly as possible. — [4] —.

Kind regards,

Gagan Chopra

151. Where most likely does Mr. Chopra work?

(A) At a travel agency
(B) At a publishing company
(C) At a restaurant
(D) At a financial consulting company

152. What does Mr. Chopra write that Mr. Pressler will do?

(A) Go to the market
(B) Plan a lunch meeting
(C) Begin a new project
(D) Send some e-mails

153. In which of the positions marked [1], [2], [3], and [4] does the following sentence best belong?

"While there, we put together a project list, which includes all of the associated tasks."

(A) [1]
(B) [2]
(C) [3]
(D) [4]

GO ON TO THE NEXT PAGE

Questions 154-155 refer to the following text-message chain.

Soraya Channa 8:45 A.M.
Hi, Ru. I'm supposed to greet the new marketing interns at 9:00 and begin the first training session, but my train just left the station.

Ru Liao 8:46 A.M.
What happened?

Soraya Channa 8:47 A.M.
I think it was a weather-related delay. Maybe there was ice on the tracks? In any event, I'm not going to be able to make it to the office in time.

Ru Liao 8:48 A.M
OK. In that case, I'll greet the interns and lead the first session, and you can join us when you arrive. Then you could lead the session on our demographic research in the afternoon.

Soraya Channa 8:49 A.M.
Yes, that definitely works. Thanks!

154. What is Ms. Channa's problem?

(A) She missed her train.
(B) She has been delayed.
(C) She is not prepared to give a presentation.
(D) She forgot to contact the interns.

155. At 8:49 A.M., what does Ms. Channa mean when she writes, "Yes, that definitely works"?

(A) A train has started to move.
(B) A machine is operating correctly.
(C) The suggested plan is a good one.
(D) She was able to change her travel schedule.

Questions 156-158 refer to the following article.

Small Business News

By Anna Fortin

PRESTON (29 August)—The town's small business boom continues, creating new jobs and strengthening local markets. In fact, Preston's small businesses employed 4,300 people last year, equaling 25 percent of the local labor force.

"Small businesses are definitely a key economic driver," explains Dr. Henry Belanger, who teaches finance at Lackland University. "Start-up businesses are a significant engine for job creation."

According to Belanger, Preston is part of a province-wide trend.

"Last year, the province saw job expansion above the national average, adding more than 19,000 jobs overall," Dr. Belanger said. "About 17 percent were in small businesses. Moreover, thanks to the personal income generated by small companies, larger, established businesses benefited too."

Parties interested in starting a business can access the government's Provincial Small Business Center for help in creating a business plan, finding capital, and learning marketing strategies.

TEST 4

156. The word "boom" in paragraph 1, line 2, is closest in meaning to

(A) sound
(B) discovery
(C) growth
(D) surprise

157. Who most likely is Dr. Belanger?

(A) The president of the Provincial Small Business Center
(B) A small-business owner
(C) The mayor of Preston
(D) A university professor

158. What does Dr. Belanger state about small businesses?

(A) The government has opened a new office to help them.
(B) Their impact extends to larger organizations.
(C) They provide inexperienced employees with training.
(D) They are closing throughout the province.

GO ON TO THE NEXT PAGE

Questions 159-160 refer to the following e-mail.

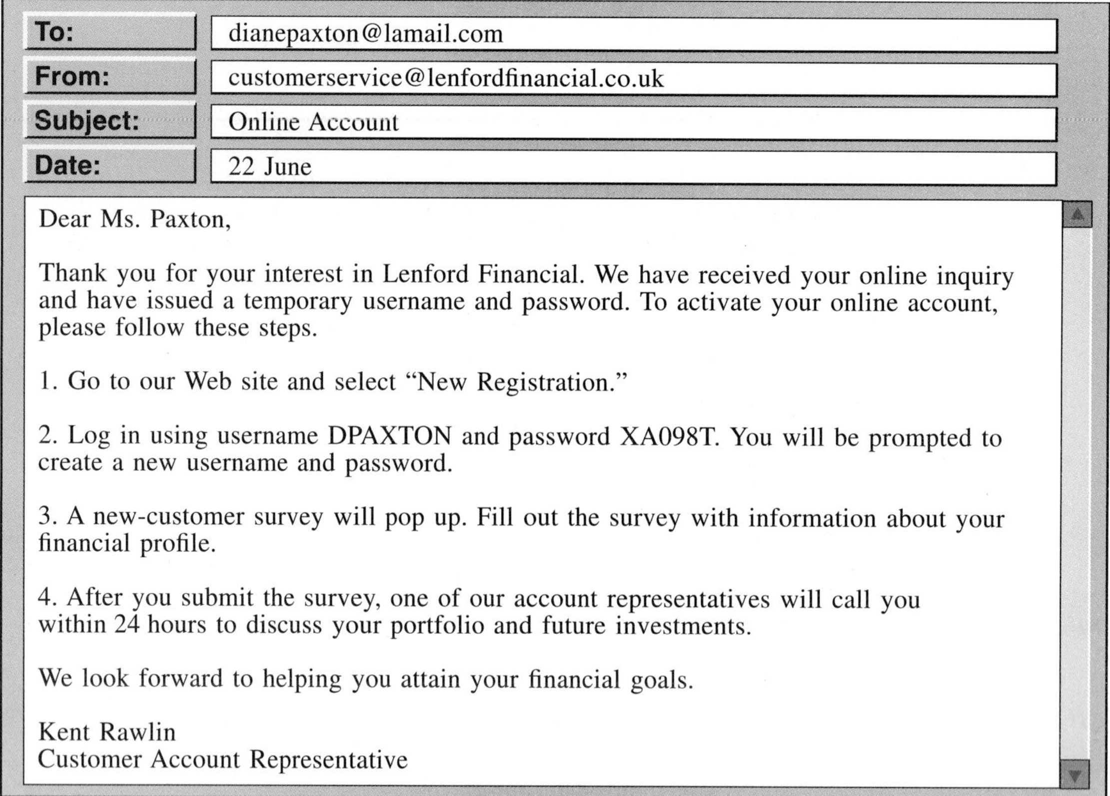

To:	dianepaxton@lamail.com
From:	customerservice@lenfordfinancial.co.uk
Subject:	Online Account
Date:	22 June

Dear Ms. Paxton,

Thank you for your interest in Lenford Financial. We have received your online inquiry and have issued a temporary username and password. To activate your online account, please follow these steps.

1. Go to our Web site and select "New Registration."

2. Log in using username DPAXTON and password XA098T. You will be prompted to create a new username and password.

3. A new-customer survey will pop up. Fill out the survey with information about your financial profile.

4. After you submit the survey, one of our account representatives will call you within 24 hours to discuss your portfolio and future investments.

We look forward to helping you attain your financial goals.

Kent Rawlin
Customer Account Representative

159. What does the e-mail suggest about Ms. Paxton?

(A) She has requested information from Lenford Financial.
(B) She is a finance professional.
(C) She has been a Lenford Financial customer for many years.
(D) She was not able to log in to her account.

160. What is Ms. Paxton instructed to do?

(A) Call an account representative
(B) Request a temporary password
(C) Take a survey over the phone
(D) Submit a form online

Questions 161-163 refer to the following job advertisement.

Green Rock University Seeks Assistant for Technology Lab

Because of student demand, Green Rock University's Technology Lab will now be open during the evening. As a result of these extended hours, we are seeking an evening lab assistant. The successful candidate should possess a range of relevant knowledge and skills in 3-D printing, basic coding, graphic design programs, and movie-making software.

We are looking for a person who is patient, creative, and enjoys helping others. The ideal candidate will also enjoy learning new things and sharing that knowledge with other people. Applicants chosen for interviews will be asked to bring examples of technology-related projects they have worked on and should be prepared to discuss those projects. Interested applicants should send a letter of interest and résumé to tech@greenrockuniversity.edu.

161. Why is the lab-assistant position being offered?

(A) Building renovations have been completed.
(B) Equipment has been modernized.
(C) Some employees have left.
(D) Hours of operation have changed.

162. What is NOT a requirement of the job?

(A) A degree in graphic design
(B) A desire to help others
(C) Coding knowledge
(D) Creativity

163. How should applicants apply for the position?

(A) By telephone
(B) By e-mail
(C) By express mail
(D) In person

GO ON TO THE NEXT PAGE

Questions 164-167 refer to the following e-mail.

To:	Alan Rogerson <arogerson@rogersoncorp.ca>
From:	Yoshi Takeda <ytakeda@dskt.co.jp>
Subject:	Greenhouse system
Date:	18 November
Attachment:	DSKTgs

Dear Mr. Rogerson,

I am glad we got a chance to talk at the agricultural technology trade show in Dublin last week. Per your request, I have attached an electronic version of our booklet on the DSKT greenhouse system. — [1] —.

I am aware that your greenhouses are located some distance from one another. — [2] —. Using our environmental monitoring system, you could check the temperature, humidity, and air quality of each greenhouse remotely. You would no longer need to be on-site to make observations every night. DSKT sends the readings to your smartphone or computer. — [3] —.

You might also be interested in our crop irrigation systems. — [4] —. Let me know if you would like more information; I will be happy to answer questions about any of our products.

Sincerely,

Yoshi Takeda

164. Why did Mr. Takeda send the e-mail?

(A) To inquire about attending a trade show
(B) To discuss an upcoming meeting
(C) To follow up on a recent conversation
(D) To schedule a product demonstration

165. What is suggested about Mr. Rogerson?

(A) He rarely travels for work.
(B) He is involved in farming.
(C) He specializes in environmental science.
(D) He designed a smartphone application.

166. According to the e-mail, what can the DSKT greenhouse system do?

(A) Water plants
(B) Disable machinery
(C) Control lighting
(D) Transmit information

167. In which of the positions marked [1], [2], [3],and [4] does the following sentence best belong?

"I am confident it will illustrate how our system can meet your needs."

(A) [1]
(B) [2]
(C) [3]
(D) [4]

Questions 168-171 refer to the following notice.

"Expressions in Form and Color"
March 30
5:30 P.M.–9:00 P.M.

Event Description: The Summerlake University Art Department is pleased to present its annual showcase, opening today at 5:30 P.M. in the campus art gallery located in Building 4. Come see new artwork—including paintings, photographs, drawings, and sculptures—while enjoying beverages and appetizers.

Student artists will be on hand to speak about their work to visitors at the gallery from 5:30 P.M. to 7:30 P.M. this evening. At 7:30 P.M., Fin Olson, sculptor of *Delivered*, will give a presentation about how his study abroad in Milan influenced his work. Mr. Olson, who will finish his degree in April, has already sold many pieces to private collectors and teaches workshops to children.

This event is open to students, faculty, and the public. Parking is available in the designated areas next to Buildings 4 and 8. Please note that the area by Building 4 requires a permit, but the area by Building 8 is free to the public.

For more information, including a list of featured artwork, please visit the Art Department's Web site at www.summerlake.edu/artdepartment/events.

168. What is the purpose of the notice?

(A) To advertise an art class
(B) To promote a yearly exhibition
(C) To publicize the sale of a sculpture
(D) To announce the opening of a museum

169. What is indicated about the works of art?

(A) They were produced by students.
(B) They represent a common theme.
(C) They include some pieces from private collections.
(D) They are mostly paintings.

170. What is mentioned about Mr. Olson?

(A) He is a recent university graduate.
(B) He manages a Web site.
(C) He has a parking permit.
(D) He traveled to another country.

171. What is NOT suggested about the event?

(A) Refreshments will be served.
(B) Artists will speak with attendees.
(C) Free parking is available.
(D) Demonstrations will be given.

GO ON TO THE NEXT PAGE

Questions 172-175 refer to the following online chat discussion.

Ichiro Watanabe (9:30 A.M.)	Does anyone have ideas before the Friday department meeting for improving the inspection process for dental offices?
Suzanne Parrin (9:31 A.M.)	There is too much paperwork. Perhaps inspectors could complete forms electronically.
Zachary Qian (9:32 A.M.)	Great idea. That would eliminate paper completely.
Ichiro Watanabe (9:33 A.M.)	That's an effective way for us to save time and money, but how do we transition from using the current forms to electronic ones? How would inspectors be trained?
Suzanne Parrin (9:35 A.M.)	What if inspectors continue to use paper forms while they're learning how to use the new electronic version?
Zachary Qian (9:36 A.M.)	That way, they would gain some experience with the electronic forms. And maybe we could hire instructors to train our inspectors so they're ready for the transition.
Suzanne Parrin (9:38 A.M.)	Exactly. We could hold the training sessions here at the Labor Department.
Ichiro Watanabe (9:40 A.M.)	Great. I'll propose these ideas at the meeting.

172. What are the writers discussing?

(A) Changing a work procedure
(B) Hiring experienced inspectors
(C) Staffing a new department
(D) Creating additional paper forms

173. What is suggested about the writers?

(A) They train dental assistants.
(B) They manage other employees.
(C) They are determining a budget.
(D) They are purchasing computers.

174. At 9:38 A.M., what does Ms. Parrin most likely mean when she writes, "Exactly"?

(A) She knows how many years of experience are required.
(B) She wants to make sure all the paperwork is accurate.
(C) She thinks Mr. Qian's idea will resolve a problem.
(D) She believes Mr. Watanabe's estimate is correct.

175. What will Mr. Watanabe most likely do on Friday?

(A) Present a lesson to the inspectors
(B) Distribute a survey to the trainers
(C) Learn to use an electronic form
(D) Suggest a solution to a problem

TEST 4

GO ON TO THE NEXT PAGE

Questions 176-180 refer to the following memo and form.

MEMO

To: All Staff
From: Shondra Brown, Director of Benefits
Date: August 4
Re: Wellness Classes

In the interest of promoting a healthy and productive workforce, Lellar Manufacturing will begin offering monthly wellness classes. While participation is not required, we do hope that everyone will take advantage of this opportunity. Part- and full-time regular employees are eligible for these classes at no cost. All other workers and trainees will be required to pay a small enrollment fee.

Local nurses from Union City Hospital will run the classes on-site, so you do not have to travel anywhere. Classes will be held the first Friday morning of each month, and the class topics will change each month. The class topics in order, starting in September and going through December, will be as follows: Easy Stretching, Good Food Choices, Tips for Better Sleep, and Starting an Exercise Group.

Supervisor approval is necessary. The first step is to complete a class request form and send it to the Benefits Department. If you have any questions, contact our benefits counselors Don Herrell at ext. 249 or Leah Katzen at ext. 199.

Lellar Manufacturing

WELLNESS CLASS REQUEST FORM

Name:	*Alfredo De Santos*
Title:	*Production Trainee*
Name/Title of Immediate Supervisor:	*Galen Sanders, Production Manager*
Requested Class Date:	*September 2*
Enrollment Fee Paid:	☑
Received by Benefits Counselor:	*Leah Katzen*

176. What is the purpose of the memo?

(A) To explain a new requirement
(B) To inform staff about a benefit
(C) To suggest a process improvement
(D) To introduce cost-saving measures

177. Where will a company activity take place?

(A) At Lellar Manufacturing
(B) At Union City Hospital
(C) At a local doctor's office
(D) At a nearby production facility

178. What topic will be covered in September?

(A) Easy Stretching
(B) Good Food Choices
(C) Tips for Better Sleep
(D) Starting an Exercise Group

179. Why has Mr. De Santos paid a fee?

(A) He returned his training materials late.
(B) He needs to replace some training items.
(C) He is not a regular employee.
(D) He requested an extra class.

180. Who must provide an approval?

(A) Ms. Brown
(B) Mr. Herrell
(C) Ms. Katzen
(D) Mr. Sanders

GO ON TO THE NEXT PAGE

Questions 181-185 refer to the following Web page and e-mail.

 http://www.barrowstreetpost.co.uk/tori-fadulu/ 

Tori Fadulu has been a writer with *Barrow Street Post* for the past two years. Previously, she worked as a freelance writer for the *Caldwell Times* and the *Andover Daily News*. She is the author of *Stones in Moonlight*, for which she received the prestigious Klockner Prize for new novelists. Ms. Fadulu holds a degree in journalism from MacDougal University. She has lived in London her entire life but loves to travel.

Recent *Barrow Street Post* Articles by Tori Fadulu

"Culture Up Close," 4 December
People from a village in Mongolia warmly welcome the writer into their homes to share their culture and traditions.

"A Night Out in London," 19 October
With so many things to see and do in London, how do real Londoners choose to spend their nights out? Ms. Fadulu speaks to some to find out.

"Exploring on a Budget," 28 September
Alberta natives Besha Phelan and Hayley Luongo have been travelling across Canada for the past three years and have spent far less money than they did when they were renting an apartment in Calgary.

"Hiking South America," 5 August
Patagonia is a hiker's paradise, and its natural beauty is not to be missed. Ms. Fadulu joins several hikers on the trails to learn what keeps them going back.

To:	Tori Fadulu
From:	Jamie Tsang
Subject:	Column idea
Date:	15 December

Hi, Tori,

We have been getting a lot of positive e-mails and letters from readers about your December piece. You did some very nice work. Because the article was so popular, I would like to see the concept become a recurring column focusing on your experiences living with and learning from people in different regions of the world.

Let's set up a time to discuss the details. Are you free tomorrow at noon? We could talk over lunch.

My best,

Jamie Tsang, Senior Editor

181. To whom is the Klockner Prize awarded?

(A) Journalism professors
(B) Publishers
(C) Newspaper editors
(D) Book authors

182. What is suggested about Ms. Fadulu?

(A) She is based in Andover.
(B) She often goes to Canada to see her relatives.
(C) She has interviewed people who live in her hometown.
(D) She studied several languages at university.

183. In the e-mail, the word "nice" in paragraph 1, line 2, is closest in meaning to

(A) polite
(B) good
(C) happy
(D) delicate

184. What article does Mr. Tsang want to develop into a column?

(A) "Culture Up Close"
(B) "A Night Out in London"
(C) "Exploring on a Budget"
(D) "Hiking South America"

185. What does Mr. Tsang want to do on December 16 ?

(A) Try a new restaurant
(B) Watch a show
(C) Have a meeting
(D) Teach a class

TEST 4

GO ON TO THE NEXT PAGE

Questions 186-190 refer to the following proposal forms and e-mail.

PROPOSAL

Project For:
Sethi Technologies
34 Carnaby Street
San Francisco, CA 94129

Contractor Information:
Geo Carpet Care
541 Grantham Avenue
San Francisco, CA 94128

Scope of Work
Cleaning of all carpets and upholstered furniture in common areas and personal work spaces. Includes furniture moving as needed. Temporary floor protector pads provided. Spot removal included.
*Note: We use all-natural, odorless cleaning products.

Company Proposal
We, Geo Carpet Care, propose the above scope of work for the amount of $2,650 plus tax.
Price includes a 10% discount for first-time customers.
50% due at acceptance; balance due upon completion.
Price remains valid for 30 days after proposal submission.

Submitted by: Martin Acosta
Date: June 1

Customer Approval: ________
Date: ________

FRESHEN CARPETS: PROPOSAL
8423 Golden Way
San Francisco, CA 94124

Customer: Sethi Technologies
Address: 34 Carnaby Street, San Francisco, CA 94129
Date: June 5

Freshen Carpets proposes to clean the entire carpeted area of customer's premises and clean all upholstered furniture. Clearing of floor space to be completed by customer. Spot removal extra.

Cost: $1,900 + tax (reflects the standard reduced price for new customers)
Payment due to representative upon completion of service. This proposal is good for 30 days.

Prepared by: Richard Wang
Purchaser Acceptance: ________
Date: ________

To:	All Sethi Technologies Employees
From:	Joe Tierney, Facilities Department
Subject:	Carpet Cleaning
Date:	June 25

On Saturday morning, all of the carpets and upholstered furniture will be cleaned. In preparation for the work, some of our facilities staff members will be moving furniture as necessary on Friday evening so that the cleaning crew can access the areas to be cleaned. In addition, we ask that before you leave on Friday, you remove any fragile or valuable personal items from your work space. Please do not leave any confidential work material in plain view. The carpets and furniture will be dry by Monday. Do not come in over the weekend; work at home if necessary.

TEST 4

186. Who most likely is Mr. Acosta?

(A) The owner of Sethi Technologies
(B) A colleague of Mr. Tierney
(C) A facilities manager
(D) A representative of Geo Carpet Care

187. When should customers pay Freshen Carpets for their services?

(A) Upon signing the proposal
(B) Within thirty days of the proposal's submission
(C) The day the cleaning is completed
(D) Upon receiving an invoice in the mail

188. What do both companies offer to customers?

(A) A monthly payment plan
(B) A choice of cleaning products
(C) A service warranty
(D) A discount for new customers

189. What does Mr. Tierney ask all employees to do?

(A) Move desks and chairs
(B) Remove breakable items
(C) Work at home on Friday
(D) Review two proposals

190. What is suggested about Sethi Technologies?

(A) It hired Freshen Carpets.
(B) It will close later than usual on Friday, June 26.
(C) It is a long-time customer of Geo Carpet Care.
(D) Its facilities staff will open the office early on Monday.

GO ON TO THE NEXT PAGE

Questions 191-195 refer to the following text message, article, and review.

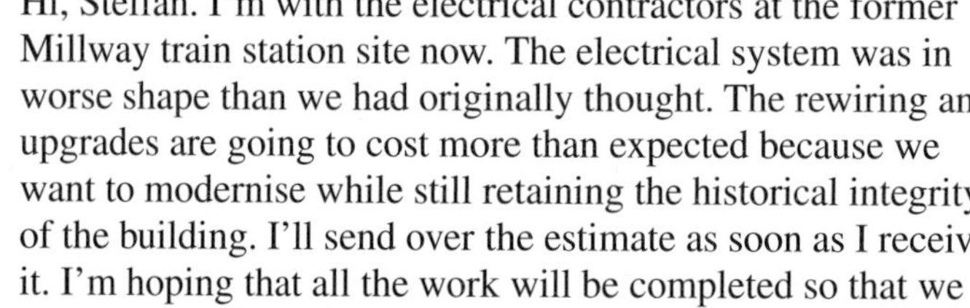

From: Fausto Forletti [11:02 A.M.]
To: Steffan Griffiths <029 2018 0743>

Hi, Steffan. I'm with the electrical contractors at the former Millway train station site now. The electrical system was in worse shape than we had originally thought. The rewiring and upgrades are going to cost more than expected because we want to modernise while still retaining the historical integrity of the building. I'll send over the estimate as soon as I receive it. I'm hoping that all the work will be completed so that we can open as planned in May.

New Hotel to Open in South Wales

CARDIFF (18 April)—The Millway Road Hotel is scheduled to open on 14 May. The building was once a busy train station that was designed by Arthur Lewison over 150 years ago.

For almost three decades the building had been left unoccupied. It was purchased two years ago by Steffan Griffiths, president of Griffiths Hoteliers.

According to project coordinator Fausto Forletti, the old building required extensive renovation not only to turn it into a hotel but also to update the electrical, heating, and plumbing systems.

The hotel has 25 guest rooms, a meeting room, and a restaurant with banquet facilities. All of Mr. Griffiths' facilities are noted for their world-class dining experiences. The hotel's Bayside Café has award-winning Welsh chef Mal Davies to create a menu and oversee the restaurant.

In the near future, Mr. Griffiths plans to expand the property's garden.

For information and reservations, visit www.millwayroadhotel.co.uk.

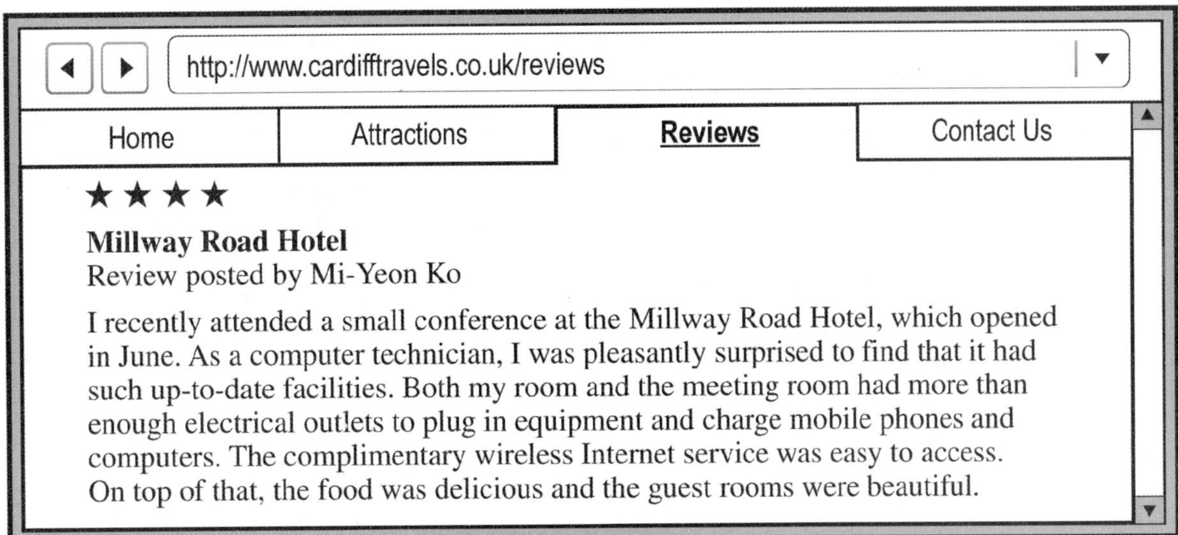
http://www.cardifftravels.co.uk/reviews

Home | Attractions | **Reviews** | Contact Us

★★★★

Millway Road Hotel
Review posted by Mi-Yeon Ko

I recently attended a small conference at the Millway Road Hotel, which opened in June. As a computer technician, I was pleasantly surprised to find that it had such up-to-date facilities. Both my room and the meeting room had more than enough electrical outlets to plug in equipment and charge mobile phones and computers. The complimentary wireless Internet service was easy to access. On top of that, the food was delicious and the guest rooms were beautiful.

191. Why did Mr. Forletti send the text message?

(A) To explain why a project's cost will increase
(B) To ask for help in solving an electrical problem
(C) To warn that a delivery will be delayed
(D) To discuss a problem with a contractor

192. Where was Mr. Forletti when he sent the text message?

(A) On a train
(B) At a restaurant
(C) At a proposed hotel site
(D) In an electrical contractor's office

193. What does the article suggest about Mr. Lewison?

(A) He is purchasing a hotel.
(B) He created a dining menu.
(C) He was the architect of a building.
(D) He is the coordinator of a renovation.

194. What does the article indicate about the Millway Road Train Station?

(A) It included a world-class restaurant.
(B) It was owned by Mr. Griffiths' father.
(C) It was located near a famous garden.
(D) It had been abandoned for many years.

195. What is suggested in Ms. Ko's review?

(A) The hotel's guest rooms are quite large.
(B) The hotel did not open as scheduled.
(C) A café is located on the hotel's top floor.
(D) Internet access was too expensive.

GO ON TO THE NEXT PAGE

Questions 196-200 refer to the following e-mails and schedule.

E-mail

To: All Staff

From: Leila Hedlund

Subject: November software training

Date: October 30

Attachment: Software Training Schedule

Dear Staff,

Throughout November, we will be holding mandatory training sessions for two of our major software products.

Training in the Abacus Deepthink software will be required for all staff members and can be completed in a single online session. Several possible session times are available. The software has gone through several changes recently, so even longtime users must attend.

The Optisafe software training will be offered in person and is a requirement only for Drug Safety department members. This past year, major upgrades have been made to the software, and all department staff will need to learn how to use its new capabilities.

Please look over the attached schedule and go to the company training Web site to sign up.

Thank you,

Leila Hedlund
Kodarex Pharmaceuticals

Software Training Schedule			
Date	**Title**	**Time**	**Location**
November 6	Abacus Deepthink	9 A.M.–11 A.M.	Online
November 9	Optisafe	9 A.M.–1 P.M.	Building C, Room 822
November 14	Abacus Deepthink	1 P.M.–3 P.M.	Online
November 17	Abacus Deepthink	10 A.M.–12 P.M.	Online
November 22	Optisafe	1 P.M.–5 P.M.	Building C, Room 822
November 27	Abacus Deepthink	3 P.M.–5 P.M.	Online
The online lessons can be accessed at https://www.abacusdeepthink.com			

E-mail

To:	Leila Hedlund
From:	Diego Ramos-Toro
Re:	November software training
Date:	October 31

Dear Leila,

I need to attend both software trainings, but I had planned to take off work from November 6 through November 18. Also, I must attend an all-day client meeting on November 22 that we cannot reschedule. Will there be any alternative sessions for the Optisafe training that I could attend?

Thank you,

Diego Ramos-Toro

196. According to the first e-mail, what is true about the Optisafe software?

(A) It is replacing another software program.
(B) It is used for data analysis.
(C) It has undergone significant updates.
(D) It is the focus of monthly trainings.

197. According to the schedule, what do the Abacus Deepthink trainings have in common?

(A) They are given on the same day of the month.
(B) They are taught by the same instructor.
(C) They are delivered through a Web site.
(D) They all start at the same time.

198. Why did Mr. Ramos-Toro write to Ms. Hedlund?

(A) To register for a training session
(B) To ask for help resolving a conflict
(C) To report a software malfunction
(D) To request additional time off

199. What is suggested about Mr. Ramos-Toro?

(A) He works in the Drug Safety department.
(B) He completed a required training.
(C) He is Ms. Hedlund's supervisor.
(D) He wants an alternative position in the company.

200. When will Mr. Ramos-Toro most likely complete a training?

(A) On November 14
(B) On November 17
(C) On November 22
(D) On November 27

Stop! This is the end of the test. If you finish before time is called, you may go back to Parts 5, 6, and 7 and check your work.

토익® 정기시험
기출문제집

기출 TEST

05

READING TEST

In the Reading test, you will read a variety of texts and answer several different types of reading comprehension questions. The entire Reading test will last 75 minutes. There are three parts, and directions are given for each part. You are encouraged to answer as many questions as possible within the time allowed.

You must mark your answers on the separate answer sheet. Do not write your answers in your test book.

PART 5

Directions: A word or phrase is missing in each of the sentences below. Four answer choices are given below each sentence. Select the best answer to complete the sentence. Then mark the letter (A), (B), (C), or (D) on your answer sheet.

101. The custodial staff ------- that we clean our dishes before leaving the kitchen.

(A) requests
(B) behaves
(C) uses
(D) visits

102. If customers lose their original warranty -------, they can download a new one from the Web site.

(A) certify
(B) certificate
(C) certifiable
(D) certifiably

103. Our Portview branch is located ------- the central business district, between Burnside Avenue and Everett Street.

(A) on
(B) to
(C) for
(D) in

104. None of the employees ------- that Mr. Annan planned to retire at the end of the year.

(A) knowingly
(B) known
(C) knew
(D) to know

105. Apply to Joneston Stores today so as not to miss ------- chance to join a great sales team.

(A) you
(B) your
(C) yours
(D) yourself

106. Employees are eligible to receive a ------- salary if they complete a special marketing course.

(A) possible
(B) frequent
(C) closed
(D) higher

107. *Keeping the Deal*, Jan Butler's latest volume on management style, is her most commercially ------- book to date.

(A) successfully
(B) successful
(C) succeed
(D) success

108. Present this postcard to a sales ------- at any of our stores and receive a £5.00 gift card.

(A) accessory
(B) associate
(C) faculty
(D) formula

109. Lakeside Shopping Center has undergone ------- renovations in the last decade.

(A) multiple
(B) multiply
(C) multiples
(D) multiplied

110. There is a mandatory meeting today for everyone involved in managing or recruiting -------.

(A) staplers
(B) volunteers
(C) devices
(D) headquarters

111. The Smeeville bus system will accept only Rove Fare cards ------- May 1 onward.

(A) now
(B) from
(C) while
(D) when

112. Relocating for work is ------- a difficult decision, but it can be rewarding.

(A) understandably
(B) understanding
(C) understood
(D) understand

113. Last week Parmax Corporation ------- a disagreement with its main competitor concerning patent infringement.

(A) settling
(B) settler
(C) settle
(D) settled

114. Khoury Dairy's upgraded milk-bottling system has ------- increased productivity in the Tallahassee plant.

(A) consistency
(B) consistencies
(C) consistent
(D) consistently

115. The Rinka 2000 blender has not received a single ------- in the New Products Web forum.

(A) complained
(B) complaint
(C) complaining
(D) complain

116. After raising $45 million last year, Yamamoto Technologies is now ------- Seattle's best-funded companies.

(A) into
(B) over
(C) among
(D) across

117. Deangelo's Delights was so popular that the owner opened two ------- bakeries.

(A) allowable
(B) additional
(C) uninterested
(D) inclusive

118. Chef Octavia Farina took over Fratelli's Restaurant ------- the previous chef left to open a new restaurant.

(A) unless
(B) rather than
(C) as if
(D) after

119. The director of Wingstom Foods commended Ms. Weiss for increasing ------- in the bakery division.

(A) produced
(B) producing
(C) production
(D) productive

120. Greg Owens, founder of multi-national Hermes Taxi Service, used to drive a taxi -------.

(A) he
(B) his
(C) himself
(D) his own

GO ON TO THE NEXT PAGE

121. Starlight Theaters is proud to announce record earnings for the third quarter, far exceeding -------.

(A) adjustments
(B) endorsements
(C) computations
(D) expectations

122. Employees can attend one of the many workshops offered, ------- seems most interesting.

(A) whichever
(B) however
(C) everyone
(D) much

123. ------- her strong negotiation skills, Marie Russel was made Sanwa, Inc.'s lead sales contact.

(A) Given
(B) Deciding
(C) Finding
(D) Because

124. A locked suggestion box will allow employees to submit feedback to management -------.

(A) anonymously
(B) approximately
(C) expressly
(D) patiently

125. A new strategy is under development to ------- our products more aggressively overseas.

(A) invest
(B) compete
(C) participate
(D) market

126. ------- on the city's ongoing revitalization project, Mayor Owen promised that residents would be pleased with the results.

(A) Comment
(B) Comments
(C) Commented
(D) Commenting

127. -------, repairs to the plumbing pipes in the Moffett Building will be costly.

(A) Tremendously
(B) Unfortunately
(C) Casually
(D) Enormously

128. The CEO's speech will be recorded in its ------- and made available to employees who could not attend the meeting.

(A) entirety
(B) system
(C) perception
(D) estimation

129. Trails on the southeast side of the mountain are often closed ------- because storms tend to occur without warning.

(A) accidentally
(B) coincidentally
(C) steeply
(D) unexpectedly

130. Please submit your hours ------- any work-related expense reports by Friday.

(A) as well as
(B) above all
(C) in addition
(D) in case that

PART 6

Directions: Read the texts that follow. A word, phrase, or sentence is missing in parts of each text. Four answer choices for each question are given below the text. Select the best answer to complete the text. Then mark the letter (A), (B), (C), or (D) on your answer sheet.

Questions 131-134 refer to the following notice.

Power Outage Scheduled at City Hall

On Friday, April 14, the city hall's electricity is scheduled to be shut down at 7 A.M. and restored at 6 P.M. The building ------- (**131.**) for the day. During the power outage, the emergency lighting system will be upgraded. ------- (**132.**), all circuit panels will be replaced to bring them into compliance with current safety codes.

------- (**133.**) exiting city hall offices on Thursday, please disconnect all desktop computers, wireless servers, and other computer-related equipment. Furthermore, employees are asked to remove any personal contents from the kitchenette. ------- (**134.**). Please direct questions or concerns to the director of building maintenance.

131. (A) has closed
(B) closing
(C) will close
(D) was closing

132. (A) In that case
(B) Regularly
(C) Rather than
(D) Specifically

133. (A) Inside
(B) Beyond
(C) Without
(D) Before

134. (A) Any items left behind will be discarded.
(B) The contents of each refrigerator must be labeled.
(C) Employees should report to work as usual.
(D) Emergency lighting will allow each department to remain operational.

GO ON TO THE NEXT PAGE

Questions 135-138 refer to the following e-mail.

To: Annette Schreiber <aschreiber@www.aschreiber.net>
From: Herbert Peraino, General Manager <hperaino@partyon.com>
Date: May 5
Subject: Private Party

Hello Ms. Schreiber,

Thank you for considering Partyon for your upcoming event. We welcome the opportunity to inform you about the areas we have available.

------- **135.** Our patio, for instance, can hold up to 15 people. This space is ------- **136.** for small get-togethers. Our lounge area can fit up to 40 people. It is best suited for informal ------- **137.**. Then there's our grand dining room, intended for more formal parties. It offers accommodations for up to 60 guests. Moreover, we can ------- **138.** design either a lunch or dinner menu for you according to your specifications.

If you have any further questions, please do not hesitate to contact us.

Sincerely,

Herbert Peraino

135. (A) We offer different settings depending on the size of your party.
(B) We are happy to answer any query you have about available dates.
(C) We are interested in hearing your opinion about our services.
(D) We offer lunch and dinner catering options for various types of events.

136. (A) worried
(B) exact
(C) ideal
(D) ultimate

137. (A) gatherings
(B) locales
(C) collections
(D) methods

138. (A) easy
(B) easily
(C) ease
(D) easier

Questions 139-142 refer to the following article.

TAYLORSVILLE (October 4)—Mayor Bo Crandell of the town of Taylorsville announced plans for a bicycle-share program this week. Past efforts to encourage the use of bicycles for transportation failed because there were no convenient areas to park bicycles downtown. Additionally, cyclists ------- (**139.**) to share narrow streets with cars and trucks, raising safety concerns.

With the new bicycle-share initiative, bicycle stations will be placed ------- (**140.**) at eight locations around Taylorsville. One important purpose of the initiative is to ease the limited vehicle parking in the downtown area. "------- (**141.**), I want to encourage local residents to spend more time outdoors and enjoy our beautiful town," added the mayor at the end of his remarks. ------- (**142.**).

139. (A) were forced
(B) force
(C) will be forcing
(D) have forced

140. (A) strategizing
(B) strategy
(C) strategic
(D) strategically

141. (A) Otherwise
(B) Rather
(C) Moreover
(D) Similarly

142. (A) People who use the program have created Web-site accounts.
(B) In a recent survey, many respondents mentioned a concern for safety.
(C) Nearby Grandmont's bicycle-share program is in its fifth successful year.
(D) He aims to have the bicycle stations ready for use as early as next April.

GO ON TO THE NEXT PAGE

Questions 143-146 refer to the following e-mail.

To: All employees
From: Alex Muresianu
Date: 28 June
Subject: New employee handbook training

Klok Financial has recently updated its employee handbook. -------. (**143.**) Although the information concerning benefits and terms of employment remains the same, other important modifications have been made. This version of the handbook includes new policies concerning e-mail privacy, Internet use, and use of mobile devices. Our travel guidelines have also been -------. (**144.**) The process for reimbursement after a trip is now much more efficient.

All employees must attend an informational session about the policies. One-hour sessions will be held at 10 A.M. on 9 July and 16 July. -------, (**145.**) employees will be required to sign a form acknowledging that they have received, read, and understood the information contained in the handbook and that they accept the terms. Please arrange with your manager ------- (**146.**) one of these sessions.

Alex Muresianu

143. (A) Thank you for adhering to the policies.
(B) Our new logo is displayed on the cover.
(C) This is the first change in over ten years.
(D) Corporate lawyers were hired to write it.

144. (A) revised
(B) deleted
(C) discussed
(D) notified

145. (A) In summary
(B) On the other hand
(C) As a matter of fact
(D) Immediately afterward

146. (A) to attend
(B) who attended
(C) while attending
(D) in attendance at

PART 7

Directions: In this part you will read a selection of texts, such as magazine and newspaper articles, e-mails, and instant messages. Each text or set of texts is followed by several questions. Select the best answer for each question and mark the letter (A), (B), (C), or (D) on your answer sheet.

Questions 147-148 refer to the following notice.

Sales Lunch Workshop

Attention sales associates! Are you new to CMG Direct Retail? Is your sales sheet looking a little short? Do you want to increase your commissions but can't seem to find new clients? Come to this month's lunch workshop, where Senior Sales Manager Chad Avakian will share his secrets for locating, securing, and expanding new accounts! Lunch is not provided, so be sure to pack something for yourself. After the meeting, a digital recording of the full presentation will be made available on the company's training Web site, so there's no need to bring a laptop for notes. Please RSVP to the training department at events@cmgdr.com to reserve your space.

147. What are attendees advised to bring to the meeting?

(A) Some food
(B) Sales sheets
(C) Registration forms
(D) A laptop computer

148. Who will most likely benefit from the event?

(A) Senior sales managers
(B) Staff in the training department
(C) New clients of CMG Direct Retail
(D) Recently hired sales professionals

TEST 5

GO ON TO THE NEXT PAGE

Questions 149-150 refer to the following online form.

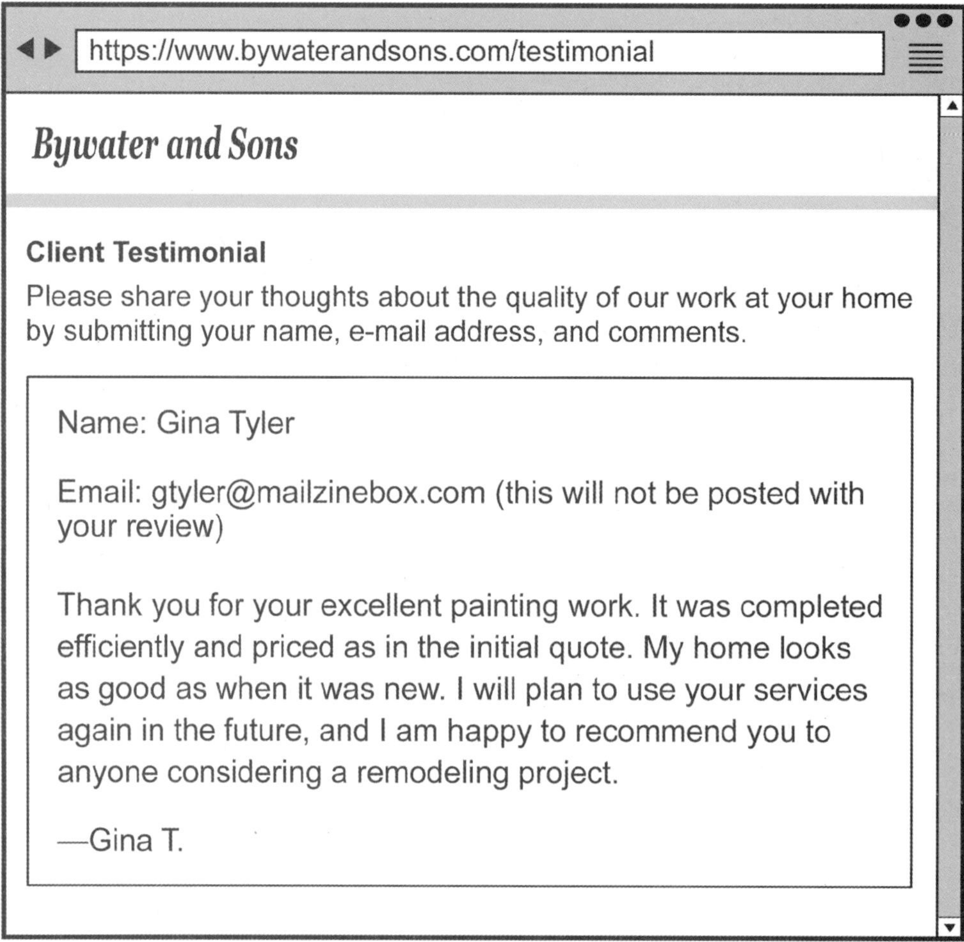

https://www.bywaterandsons.com/testimonial

Bywater and Sons

Client Testimonial

Please share your thoughts about the quality of our work at your home by submitting your name, e-mail address, and comments.

Name: Gina Tyler

Email: gtyler@mailzinebox.com (this will not be posted with your review)

Thank you for your excellent painting work. It was completed efficiently and priced as in the initial quote. My home looks as good as when it was new. I will plan to use your services again in the future, and I am happy to recommend you to anyone considering a remodeling project.

—Gina T.

149. What kind of business is Bywater and Sons?

(A) A renovation contractor
(B) A property management office
(C) A moving company
(D) A delivery service

150. What is indicated about e-mail addresses?

(A) They will be used to send invoices.
(B) They will be kept private.
(C) They will be stored in a company database.
(D) They are necessary to receive a free price quote.

Questions 151-152 refer to the following online customer service chat.

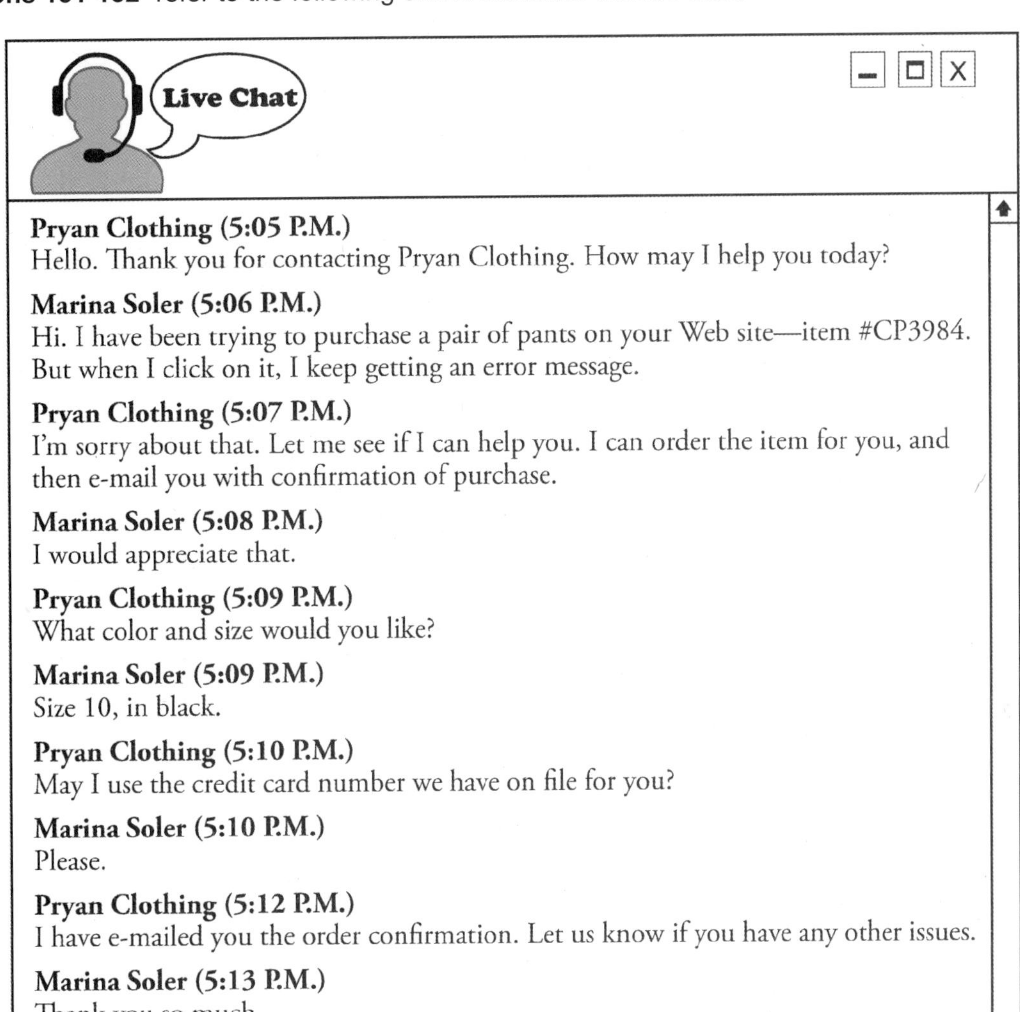

151. Why does Ms. Soler contact Pryan Clothing?

(A) She wants to return an item.
(B) She is having trouble ordering.
(C) She never received an order she purchased.
(D) She has a complaint about customer service.

152. At 5:08 P.M., what does Ms. Soler most likely mean when she writes, "I would appreciate that"?

(A) She will accept the help being offered.
(B) She has received her confirmation e-mail.
(C) She would like to choose a different color.
(D) She is thankful that the item is still on sale.

TEST 5

GO ON TO THE NEXT PAGE

Questions 153-154 refer to the following article.

Bower Technical Institute to Host Guest Students

(April 27)—According to a recent government report, the demand for diesel mechanics is expected to increase by 15 percent in the next ten years. There is a growing need for diesel mechanics in the construction, oil, and power industries. Most of the positions pay very well and only require a high school diploma and technical training. Bower Technical Institute in Centerville provides that training.

On May 1, Bower Technical Institute invites you to be a guest student from 9 A.M. to 2 P.M. After a question-and-answer session about the profession, guest students will observe actual diesel mechanic classes that focus on power trains and engine management systems. Later, guest students can participate in hands-on sessions to experience some of the day-to-day tasks involved in the field.

The event is free, but space is limited. Participants must have a high school diploma or equivalent credential. E-mail Taneisha Hill at thill@bowertech.com to reserve a spot.

153. What is indicated about industries that rely on diesel mechanics?

(A) They have increased their profits by 15 percent.
(B) They will need more trained technicians.
(C) Their workers are underpaid.
(D) They are growing quickly in Centerville.

154. What will guest students NOT be able to do at the event?

(A) Ask questions about the field
(B) Attend free classes
(C) Take part in practice tasks
(D) Earn credit toward a diploma

Questions 155-157 refer to the following e-mail.

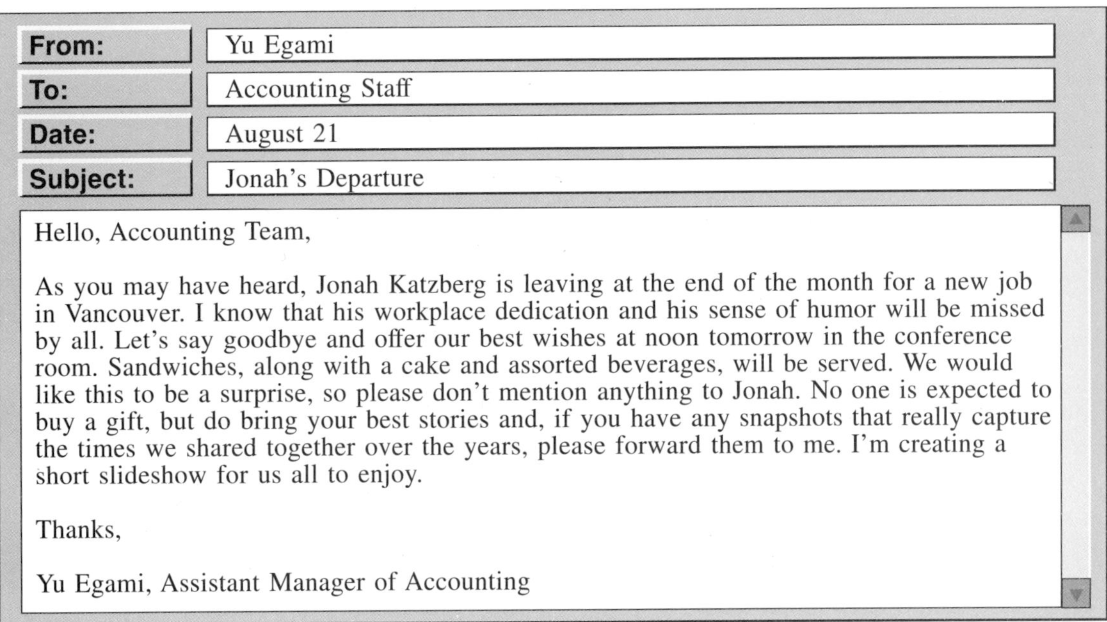

From:	Yu Egami
To:	Accounting Staff
Date:	August 21
Subject:	Jonah's Departure

Hello, Accounting Team,

As you may have heard, Jonah Katzberg is leaving at the end of the month for a new job in Vancouver. I know that his workplace dedication and his sense of humor will be missed by all. Let's say goodbye and offer our best wishes at noon tomorrow in the conference room. Sandwiches, along with a cake and assorted beverages, will be served. We would like this to be a surprise, so please don't mention anything to Jonah. No one is expected to buy a gift, but do bring your best stories and, if you have any snapshots that really capture the times we shared together over the years, please forward them to me. I'm creating a short slideshow for us all to enjoy.

Thanks,

Yu Egami, Assistant Manager of Accounting

155. What is suggested about Mr. Katzberg?

(A) He is a well-liked colleague.
(B) He is transferring to another department.
(C) He is preparing a presentation.
(D) He is not able to attend an event.

156. What does Mr. Egami ask team members to do?

(A) Contribute to a gift purchase
(B) Keep a secret
(C) Prepare some food
(D) Pose for a group photo

157. The word "capture" in paragraph 1, line 6, is closest in meaning to

(A) gain
(B) represent
(C) conclude
(D) get control of

TEST 5

GO ON TO THE NEXT PAGE

Questions 158-160 refer to the following information.

Factory Staff: Break Times

Full-time factory staff are entitled to three breaks daily and are encouraged to use them. Please attend to any personal business during these break times. — [1] —. Those who work a full eight-hour shift may take a fifteen-minute break in the morning and another fifteen-minute break in the afternoon. Lunch breaks are 30 minutes long.

There is a break area on the ground level that includes a kitchen and a staff lounge. — [2] —. Please note that the refrigerator is cleaned out every Friday evening, so be sure to take home any leftover food that you want to save.

There are lockers in the staff lounge for storing personal items. — [3] —. Employees are welcome to use the restrooms adjacent to the staff lounge. — [4] —.

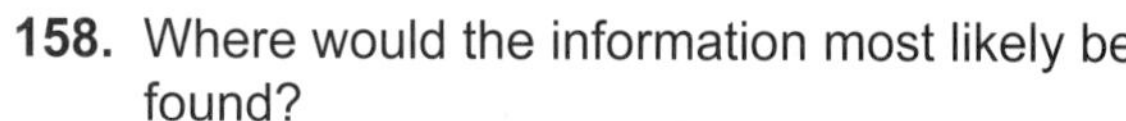

158. Where would the information most likely be found?

(A) In a product manual
(B) In a sales department invoice
(C) In an employee handbook
(D) In a company press release

159. What is indicated about the staff break area?

(A) It has just been renovated.
(B) It has several vending machines.
(C) It is on the second floor.
(D) It has a refrigerator.

160. In which of the positions marked [1], [2], [3], and [4] does the following sentence best belong?

"This includes making phone calls, texting, and using social media."

(A) [1]
(B) [2]
(C) [3]
(D) [4]

Questions 161-163 refer to the following article.

Saxal Paper Goods, Inc., Acquires Bear Industrial

TORONTO (May 9)—Last month, Saxal Paper Goods, Inc. (SPG), located in Missassauga, announced that it had acquired Bear Industrial. The distributor of food packaging and paper products said the deal for Bear Industrial will help it establish a base in a new area as part of an initiative to expand as well as to break into sales of disposable food-service supplies. Bear Industrial serves many institutional settings in Quebec and the surrounding areas.

"Bear Industrial is one of the oldest and most reputable distributors in Quebec, and we are thrilled to acquire such a fine company and expand into the region," President Arne Wellington told local reporters at a press conference. "We welcome Bear Industrial employees to SPG and look forward to working together for the benefit of all." He added that no workers are expected to lose their jobs as a result of the acquisition.

"The Bear Industrial acquisition is a key step in SPG's strategy to establish our company as one of Canada's leading providers of food packaging, paper products, and food-service disposables," Wellington said. "Our goal is to expand our geographic reach through partnerships with industry-leading companies and operators."

161. Why did SPG purchase Bear Industrial?

(A) SPG needed to be closer to its suppliers.
(B) SPG wished to expand its business in a different region.
(C) Bear Industrial had more advanced manufacturing equipment.
(D) Bear Industrial was going out of business.

162. What is true about the products produced by Bear Industrial?

(A) They are intended to be thrown away after use.
(B) They are used in fine restaurants.
(C) They are imported to Quebec.
(D) They are undergoing redesign.

163. According to the article, what will SPG likely do in the future?

(A) Reduce staff
(B) Relocate its headquarters to Quebec
(C) Work with other companies similar to Bear Industrial
(D) Appoint a new president

TEST 5

GO ON TO THE NEXT PAGE

Questions 164-167 refer to the following text message chain.

Shari Shu [9:35 A.M.]
Did you see the e-mail I sent you earlier? Our company has organized a company-wide donation drive next month. We will be collecting used computers and electronics for a nonprofit group.

Jennifer Bech [9:37 A.M.]
Yes, I saw it. Thanks for sharing. I can help circulate the information on social media if you'd like.

Shari Shu [9:38 A.M.]
That would be good. You're online a lot. Also, haven't you been in touch with the editor for the Yakima Daily News before? I'd like to contact the editor, but I can't find an address online.

Jennifer Bech [9:39 A.M.]
Yes, but it has been years. I think there's a new editor now. Let me check.

Shari Shu [9:40 A.M.]
We wrote a press release that we want to e-mail to various news outlets tomorrow.

Jennifer Bech [9:44 A.M.]
Yes, there's a new editor: Dale Korman. I don't have his e-mail address, but from the old contacts I have, it looks like they all use the same naming convention. I'd try d.korman@yakimanews.com. That's my best guess.

164. What is Ms. Shu's company doing next month?

(A) Making a charitable donation
(B) Offering a product discount
(C) Recruiting new employees
(D) Working with a business consultant

165. What does Ms. Bech offer to do?

(A) Find a venue
(B) Promote an event
(C) Locate a news article
(D) Contact a potential client

166. At 9:38 A.M., what does Ms. Shu most likely mean when she writes, "You're online a lot"?

(A) An article will need more research.
(B) A Web site could benefit from some revisions.
(C) Ms. Bech is well suited for a task.
(D) Ms. Bech may already be familiar with a company.

167. What does Ms. Bech indicate about *Yakima Daily News* staff members?

(A) Their e-mail addresses can be found on the editorial page.
(B) Their e-mail addresses are likely structured the same way.
(C) They often receive news tips from the public by e-mail.
(D) They might not respond to e-mails in a timely manner.

TEST 5

GO ON TO THE NEXT PAGE

Questions 168-171 refer to the following article.

Ready, Set—Jamboree!

NASSAU (20 June)—Every other year, Nassau is overrun by lovers of Afrobeat, a music style that fuses rhythms of the African dance tradition with jazz and funk music. The Fourth Biennial Afrobeat Jamboree, better known as "Afrojam," will run between 18 July and 22 July. — [1] —.

Afrojam will feature musicians from around the globe, including Nigeria, the United Kingdom, and, of course, the Bahamas. Recent ticket sales indicate that this year's Afrojam will draw an even bigger crowd than it did two years ago, which explains the move to the Ashanti Amphitheatre. — [2] —. Additional details about the event are available at www.afrojam.org.bs.

Visitors to afrojam.org.bs can also enjoy video clips featuring some of the greatest moments of the past, such as the surprise appearance of the world-famous Strawberry Jam, a favourite with many city residents. — [3] —.

This year's event offers a new feature: discounts on meals. Festival attendees need only to present their ticket stubs at participating restaurants to receive 10 percent off their bill. The discount is only good on concert evenings. — [4] —.

The organizers encourage local restaurateurs from across Nassau to consider getting involved. Those interested can call 555-0171 or complete an application at www.afrojam.org.bs/sponsors.

168. What is NOT indicated about Afrojam?

(A) It takes place once every two years.
(B) It has become more popular over time.
(C) It has been organized three times before.
(D) It is usually held in the Ashanti Amphitheatre.

169. What most likely is Strawberry Jam?

(A) A ticket sales company
(B) A video streaming site
(C) A food establishment
(D) A musical group

170. What must festivalgoers do to receive a discount?

(A) Fill out a survey
(B) Show a concert ticket
(C) Contact the event organizers
(D) Visit the festival Web site

171. In which of the positions marked [1], [2], [3], and [4] does the following sentence best belong?

"A complete list of food vendors will be posted on the event Web site by 15 July."

(A) [1]
(B) [2]
(C) [3]
(D) [4]

Questions 172-175 refer to the following e-mail.

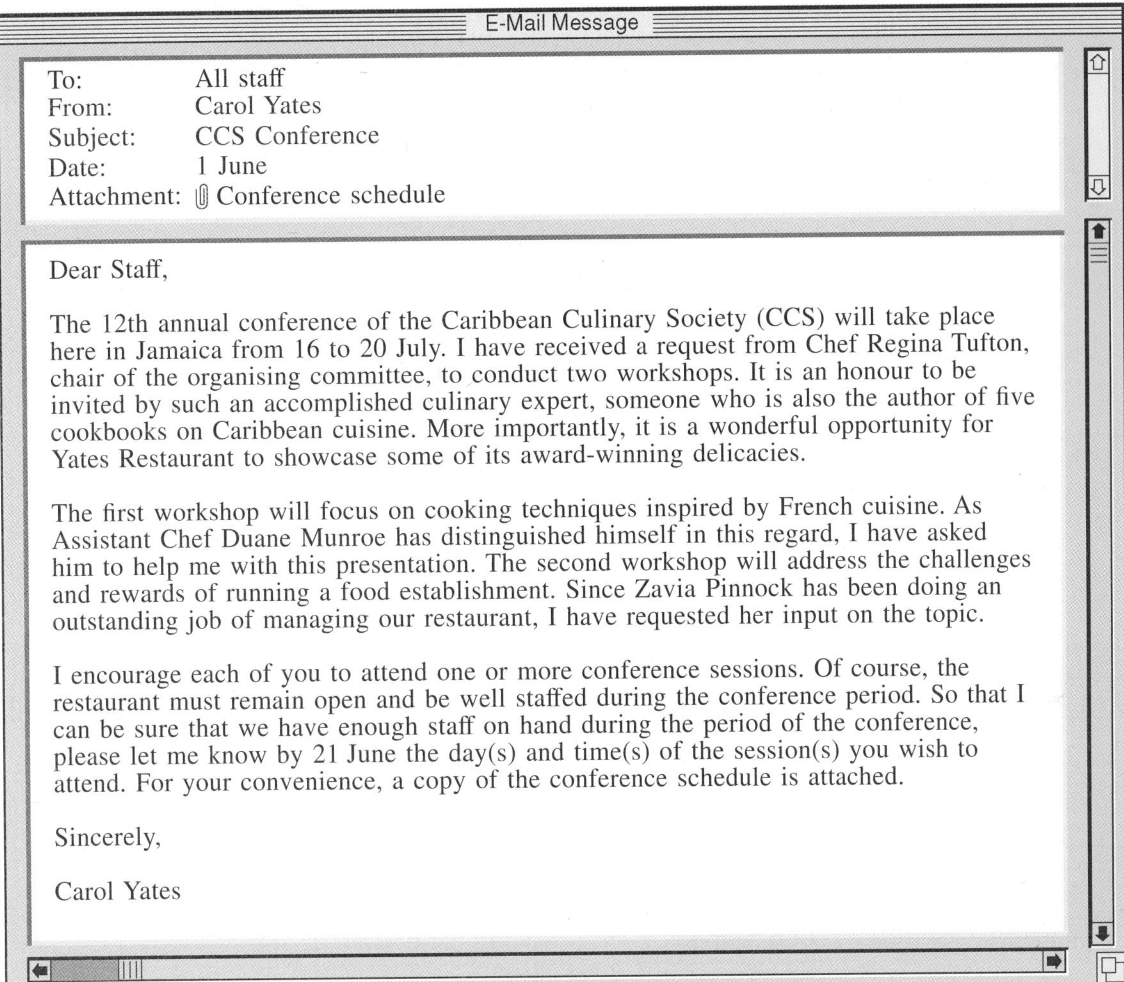

E-Mail Message

To: All staff
From: Carol Yates
Subject: CCS Conference
Date: 1 June
Attachment: Conference schedule

Dear Staff,

The 12th annual conference of the Caribbean Culinary Society (CCS) will take place here in Jamaica from 16 to 20 July. I have received a request from Chef Regina Tufton, chair of the organising committee, to conduct two workshops. It is an honour to be invited by such an accomplished culinary expert, someone who is also the author of five cookbooks on Caribbean cuisine. More importantly, it is a wonderful opportunity for Yates Restaurant to showcase some of its award-winning delicacies.

The first workshop will focus on cooking techniques inspired by French cuisine. As Assistant Chef Duane Munroe has distinguished himself in this regard, I have asked him to help me with this presentation. The second workshop will address the challenges and rewards of running a food establishment. Since Zavia Pinnock has been doing an outstanding job of managing our restaurant, I have requested her input on the topic.

I encourage each of you to attend one or more conference sessions. Of course, the restaurant must remain open and be well staffed during the conference period. So that I can be sure that we have enough staff on hand during the period of the conference, please let me know by 21 June the day(s) and time(s) of the session(s) you wish to attend. For your convenience, a copy of the conference schedule is attached.

Sincerely,

Carol Yates

172. What is the purpose of the e-mail?

(A) To establish an organization
(B) To report on staff promotions
(C) To announce participation in an event
(D) To honor the recipients of an award

173. What is stated about Ms. Tufton?

(A) She will be visiting Yates Restaurant in July.
(B) She has written several recipe books.
(C) She began her career in Jamaica.
(D) She is presenting at a conference.

174. What is indicated about Mr. Munroe and Ms. Pinnock?

(A) They improved some cooking techniques.
(B) They once managed a restaurant together.
(C) They have led workshops before.
(D) They are skilled in their roles.

175. What are staff asked to do?

(A) Submit some information
(B) Photocopy some material
(C) Help keep the restaurant clean
(D) Schedule a meeting with Ms. Yates

TEST 5

GO ON TO THE NEXT PAGE

Questions 176-180 refer to the following e-mail and Web page.

From:	Hiroaki Yoneya <hyoneya@westernstatesmilling.net>
To:	Clay Crosby <ccrosby@westernstatesmilling.net>
Date:	June 1
Subject:	Baseball night

Clay,

You may remember that we recently discussed ideas for an outing for the employees and their families. I think the best idea is to go to a baseball game. I have always enjoyed taking my family to see the Billington Buffaloes, our local team. You might have noticed that several of the photos in my office were taken at the stadium! And since I usually see other staff members at the games, I think this will appeal to most of our group.

Could you please set this up for June 28? I believe it can all be done online if you prefer. By my calculations, we will need 45 tickets in total, but please double-check this number. Also, I would like food to be provided. Let's limit our cost to under $20 per person and make sure the seating is covered just in case the weather is poor. Please send me the details as soon as the tickets are purchased.

Thanks,

Hiroaki Yoneya, Associate Manager
Western States Milling, Inc.

http://www.billingtonbuffaloes.com/grouptickets

Group Areas	Maximum Capacity	Price	Covered Seating
Home Run Pavilion	60 people	$17 per person	Yes
First Base Dugout Den	50 people	$19 per person	No
North Side Party Deck	60 people	$25 per person	No
Deluxe Suites	50 people	$30 per person	Yes

Group Ticket Policies

- Each group member in the Home Run Pavilion, First Base Dugout Den, and North Side Party Deck areas will receive a hot dog, chips, and a soda. The Deluxe Suites include an all-you-can-eat buffet for each guest.
- Each group will receive a special visit from the mascot, Bobby Buffalo.
- Groups will be welcomed to the stadium over the announcement system.
- Everyone in the group will receive 10% off team merchandise (on game day only).
- A 25% deposit is required when booking. The remaining balance is due no later than two weeks in advance of the date booked. Tickets will be mailed when the balance is paid.
- Please call the box office at (406) 555-0192 with any questions.

176. What is the purpose of the e-mail?

(A) To ask an employee to arrange an event
(B) To discuss a baseball team's request
(C) To inform employees about ticket prices
(D) To solicit suggestions for a company outing

177. What is indicated about Mr. Yoneya?

(A) He found an error on the team's Web site.
(B) He regularly attends baseball games.
(C) He wants to change the date of an event.
(D) He recently moved to Billington.

178. What section of the stadium is best for the Western States Milling staff?

(A) Home Run Pavilion
(B) First Base Dugout Den
(C) North Side Party Deck
(D) Deluxe Suites

179. What is NOT an additional benefit available to group ticket holders?

(A) A visit from Bobby Buffalo
(B) A welcome announcement
(C) A discount on merchandise
(D) A group photograph

180. According to the Web page, what must Mr. Crosby do in order to make a reservation?

(A) Make a deposit
(B) Have his supervisor sign a form
(C) Call the box office
(D) Complete an online ticket request

GO ON TO THE NEXT PAGE

Questions 181-185 refer to the following article and Web page.

GRI Ready for Action

By Antoine Williams

Although considered by many to be the running capital of Ontario, the city of Barrie is also home to several public swimming establishments, including the Galewood Recreation Institute (GRI). The institute boasts two indoor pools, one used for recreational swimming and the other reserved for special programmes, such as swimming lessons and lifeguard certification.

This summer, the institute will add intensive swimming and safety certification classes. "It is our high season," said Herbert Gagnon, institute director. "Our pools are indoors, which allows for swimming all year, but in the summer people naturally have more time for recreation and new activities in general." Summer classes will be offered mornings, afternoons, and evenings. "We hope that we can accommodate everybody's schedule," continued Gagnon. "Our classes aim to serve not just children, but all age ranges and levels of experience." For additional information, please call 905-555-0142 or visit www.galewoodrec.org.

http://www.galewoodrec.org/employment

Employment Opportunities
Job Title: Swimming Instructors
Date posted: March 20

The Galewood Recreation Institute has an ongoing need for certified swimming instructors to work at one or both of our swimming pools. Instructors perform lifeguard duties, teach weekly swimming lessons, lead safety certification courses, and carry out other standard duties. The need for staff is especially acute during the busy summer months. Institute staff are expected to provide top-quality service to patrons at all times, so applicants should be energetic and have strong interpersonal skills.

In addition to regular positions, we are looking to select two instructors interested in being part of a unique summer education programme for teenagers. Along with having the same skills required by the regular position, these special instructors will be required to implement a curriculum designed and supervised by the Ontario Foundation for Teaching and Learning. The selected candidates will first complete a paid monthlong training course during May. They must be available to work Tuesday evenings and Wednesday evenings from June 1 through the end of the summer.

Candidates must have a minimum of six months of teaching experience and hold current certification from an accredited training programme. When applying, please upload your certifications along with your résumé.

181. What does the article suggest about residents of Barrie?

(A) They believe that the city is growing too rapidly.
(B) They wish that the city had another public sports facility.
(C) They find that local running events disrupt traffic.
(D) They place an emphasis on exercise activities.

182. In the article, the word "allows" in paragraph 2, line 6, is closest in meaning to

(A) gives permission
(B) makes possible
(C) replaces
(D) includes

183. What is stated in both the article and the Web page?

(A) A new program begins on March 20.
(B) GRI has two outdoor swimming pools.
(C) The summer is a busy time for GRI.
(D) GRI is collaborating with the Ontario Foundation for Teaching and Learning.

184. What qualification is desired for the jobs listed on the Web page?

(A) The ability to relate well with others
(B) Three to four years of experience
(C) A willingness to do administrative work
(D) A valid driver's license

185. What is suggested about the education program for teenagers?

(A) It was designed by experts.
(B) It trains professional athletes.
(C) It was created by institute staff.
(D) It is scheduled to be one month long.

TEST 5

GO ON TO THE NEXT PAGE

Questions 186-190 refer to the following online form, search results, and e mail.

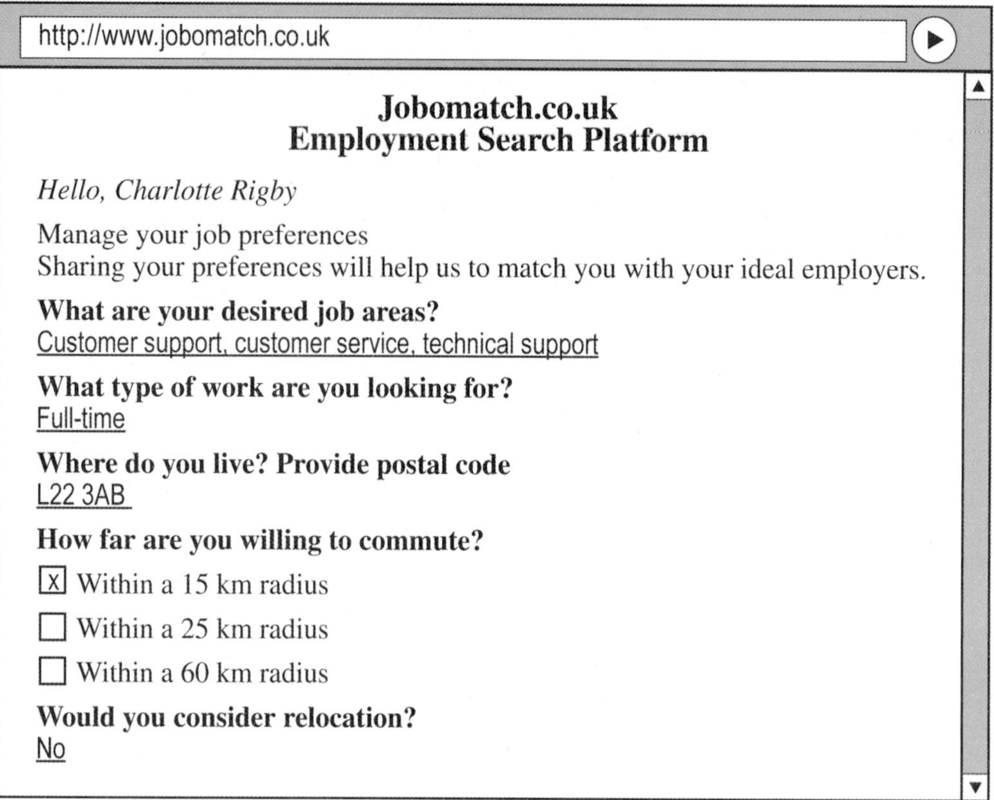

http://www.jobomatch.co.uk

Jobomatch.co.uk
Employment Search Platform

Hello, Charlotte Rigby

Manage your job preferences
Sharing your preferences will help us to match you with your ideal employers.

What are your desired job areas?
Customer support, customer service, technical support

What type of work are you looking for?
Full-time

Where do you live? Provide postal code
L22 3AB

How far are you willing to commute?

[X] Within a 15 km radius

[ ] Within a 25 km radius

[ ] Within a 60 km radius

Would you consider relocation?
No

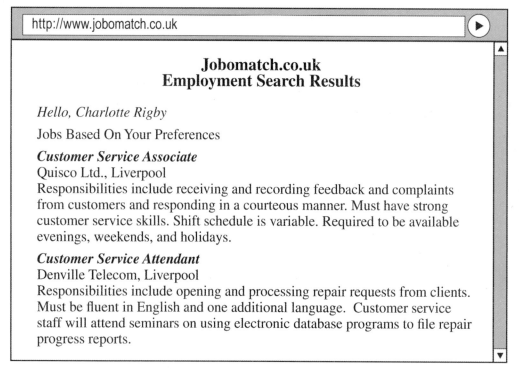

http://www.jobomatch.co.uk

Jobomatch.co.uk
Employment Search Results

Hello, Charlotte Rigby

Jobs Based On Your Preferences

Customer Service Associate
Quisco Ltd., Liverpool
Responsibilities include receiving and recording feedback and complaints from customers and responding in a courteous manner. Must have strong customer service skills. Shift schedule is variable. Required to be available evenings, weekends, and holidays.

Customer Service Attendant
Denville Telecom, Liverpool
Responsibilities include opening and processing repair requests from clients. Must be fluent in English and one additional language. Customer service staff will attend seminars on using electronic database programs to file repair progress reports.

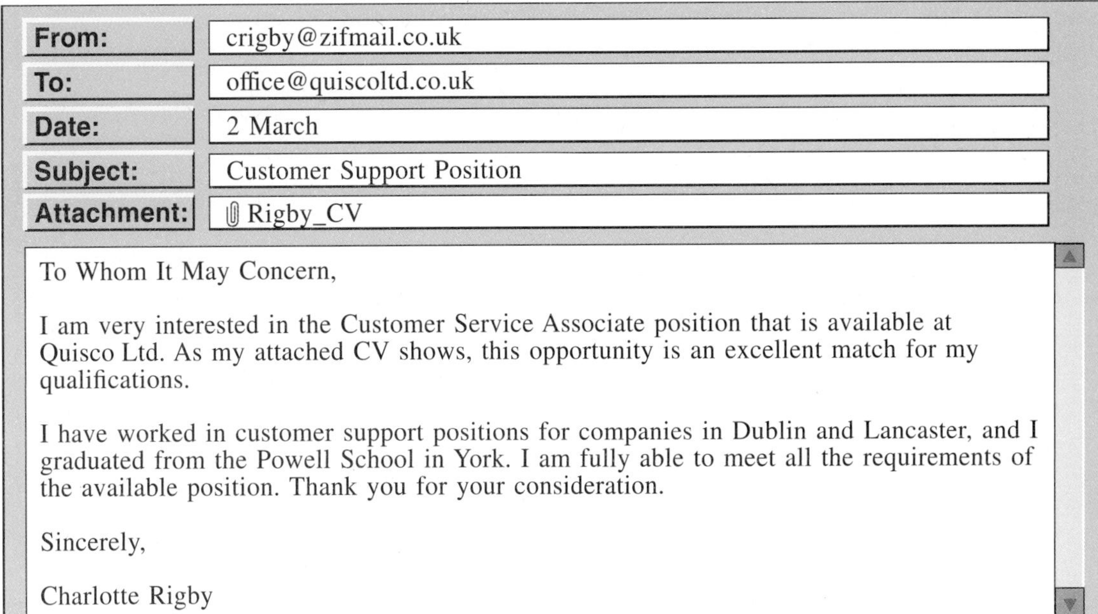

From: crigby@zifmail.co.uk
To: office@quiscoltd.co.uk
Date: 2 March
Subject: Customer Support Position
Attachment: Rigby_CV

To Whom It May Concern,

I am very interested in the Customer Service Associate position that is available at Quisco Ltd. As my attached CV shows, this opportunity is an excellent match for my qualifications.

I have worked in customer support positions for companies in Dublin and Lancaster, and I graduated from the Powell School in York. I am fully able to meet all the requirements of the available position. Thank you for your consideration.

Sincerely,

Charlotte Rigby

186. According to the form, what type of employment is Ms. Rigby seeking?

(A) A part time position
(B) A job working from home
(C) A position working directly with clients
(D) A job requiring relocation for a new career

187. Where does Ms. Rigby most likely live?

(A) Liverpool
(B) Dublin
(C) Lancaster
(D) York

188. What is required for the position at Quisco Ltd.?

(A) Knowledge of multiple languages
(B) Resolving customer problems
(C) Scheduling repair requests
(D) Attending training seminars

189. What does training at Denville Telecom involve?

(A) Learning safety procedures
(B) Traveling internationally
(C) Communicating with customers
(D) Using specialized software

190. What is likely true about Ms. Rigby?

(A) She is willing to work irregular hours.
(B) She is willing to organize seminars.
(C) She will change work departments.
(D) She will teach at the Powell School.

GO ON TO THE NEXT PAGE

Questions 191-195 refer to the following letter, meeting minutes, and advertisement.

Regal Properties
34 Weston Road, Halifax NS B3J 3P4

January 3

Dear District Council Members,

My firm is interested in purchasing the building at 1210 Prince Street. Since this property has been on the market for almost five years, it has fallen into disrepair. Regal Properties is willing to invest what is necessary to update the building.

In addition, we would like to convert three of the apartment units on the ground floor facing the street into space for businesses. However, the property is zoned only for residential use. Would you consider rezoning the property to allow for mixed residential and business use?

Sincerely,

John Stone

John Stone, Owner

District Council of Halifax
Meeting Minutes of January 21

In attendance: Mayor Stuart Kaplan and all council members

Old business

- Council member Amanda Mueller reported satisfactory progress on the Wells Park cleanup project.
- Council member Harold Glass submitted a final version of next year's budget. The proposed budget was unanimously approved.

New business

Community resident and building manager Carla Phillips spoke to express opposition to the rezoning of 1210 Prince Street under consideration by the council. Ms. Phillips is concerned that the increased pedestrian and vehicular traffic will make the street too crowded. She thinks it will also be difficult for residents of her building, Lighthouse Apartments, located at 1208 Prince Street, to park in the neighborhood.

The council agreed to consider the zoning issue at their February monthly meeting to give additional residents on Prince Street an opportunity to voice their opinions.

You can have it all!

Enjoy a wonderful lifestyle at 1210 Prince Street!

- Newly renovated apartments with one or two bedrooms
- Contemporary upscale kitchens
- Triple-pane insulated windows
- Coffee shop, dry cleaners, and convenience store on street level
- Expanded parking area exclusively for residents of 1208 and 1210 Prince Street starting in December

Visit www.lifeonprincestreet.com or call 866-555-0122 for more information.

191. What does Mr. Stone's letter suggest about a property?

(A) It has not been maintained for several years.
(B) It is priced too high for his budget.
(C) It is located close to an area for shopping.
(D) It is no longer for sale.

192. According to the meeting minutes, who presented a financial plan to the district council?

(A) Harold Glass
(B) Stuart Kaplan
(C) Amanda Mueller
(D) Carla Phillips

193. How did the district council most likely respond to Mr. Stone's letter?

(A) It supported the renovation of a community hall.
(B) It scheduled a presentation by Regal Properties.
(C) It canceled a February meeting.
(D) It approved a zoning change for a building.

194. What is indicated about the residents of Lighthouse Apartments?

(A) Many of them are small-business owners.
(B) They will vote at the next district council meeting.
(C) They will have more parking options in December.
(D) Many of them walk to their jobs.

195. What is a feature of the apartments in the advertisement?

(A) Large bedrooms
(B) Updated kitchen designs
(C) Free Wi-Fi
(D) Floor-to-ceiling windows

TEST 5

GO ON TO THE NEXT PAGE

Questions 196-200 refer to the following e-mails and proposed agenda.

To:	Linton Business Alliance members
From:	Robin Fowler
Date:	June 12
Subject:	Organizational meeting
Attachment:	Proposed agenda

Hello everyone,

I am reaching out to you to determine when we can meet. Since news about the creation of our Business Alliance is generating interest within the community, it is time to create some written materials to promote ourselves.

I would like to spend time at our meeting formulating an action plan for soliciting members. I have attached a draft agenda. It should not take long to coordinate our assignments for speaking to local business owners, but we could probably save meeting time by doing this online before the meeting.

Please send me an e-mail with your availability for the next few weeks. I understand that Sasha Zimmer is out of town until early July, but I still hope we can find a meeting date and time that will work for everyone.

Robin Fowler

Organizational meeting—Proposed agenda

10:00 A.M.	Introductions
10:15 A.M.	**Item 1**—Discussion to define mission statement and identify three initiatives for the year
11:00 A.M.	**Item 2**—Media training workshop with Brandon Clark *
12:00 noon	**Item 3**—Assign tasks for creation of Alliance communications: press release, letter to local business owners, brochure, and a Web page highlighting membership
12:30 P.M.	**Item 4**—Assign Alliance members to speak with business owners
12:45 P.M.	Adjourn

* Brandon Clark, a news anchor at the Ulani News Network, has offered to lead a workshop about interacting with the media. He will emphasize the importance of preparing talking points and staying on message.

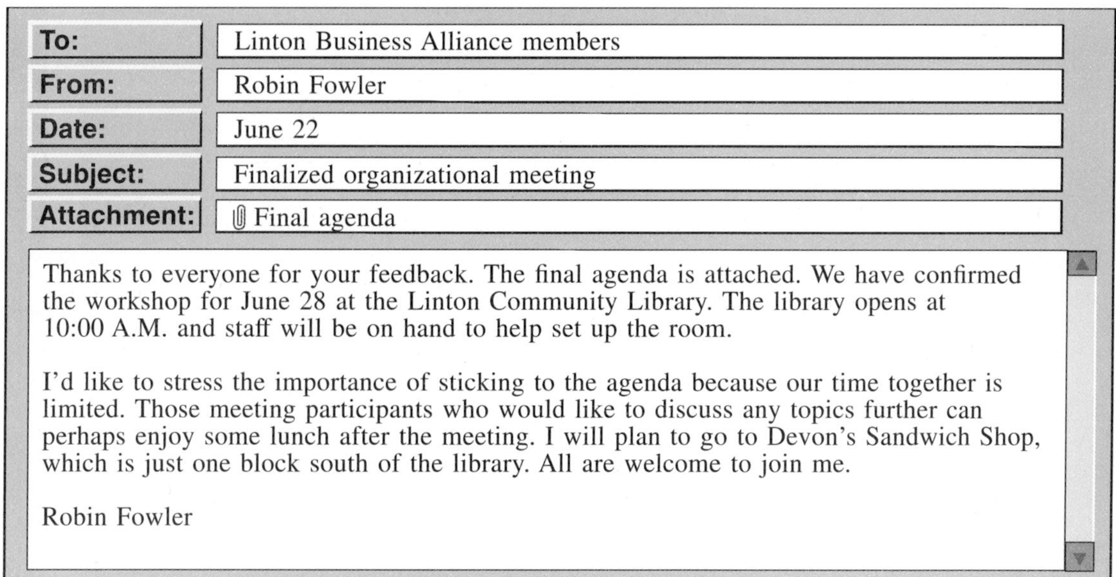

To:	Linton Business Alliance members
From:	Robin Fowler
Date:	June 22
Subject:	Finalized organizational meeting
Attachment:	Final agenda

Thanks to everyone for your feedback. The final agenda is attached. We have confirmed the workshop for June 28 at the Linton Community Library. The library opens at 10:00 A.M. and staff will be on hand to help set up the room.

I'd like to stress the importance of sticking to the agenda because our time together is limited. Those meeting participants who would like to discuss any topics further can perhaps enjoy some lunch after the meeting. I will plan to go to Devon's Sandwich Shop, which is just one block south of the library. All are welcome to join me.

Robin Fowler

196. Based on the first e-mail, what is most likely true about the Linton Business Alliance?

(A) It opposes a city policy.
(B) It is a new organization.
(C) It charges membership fees.
(D) It is led by city officials.

197. What item does Ms. Fowler suggest could be removed from the proposed agenda?

(A) Item 1
(B) Item 2
(C) Item 3
(D) Item 4

198. What does the proposed agenda indicate about Mr. Clark?

(A) He is applying for membership.
(B) He will be a guest speaker.
(C) He is a retired journalist.
(D) He will take notes during a discussion.

199. What can be concluded about the upcoming meeting?

(A) It will be open to the general public.
(B) It will receive significant media attention.
(C) It will be missing at least one group member.
(D) It will require attendees to bring some equipment.

200. In the second e-mail, what information about lunch does Ms. Fowler provide?

(A) The time of a reservation
(B) The number of attendees
(C) The cost
(D) The location

Stop! This is the end of the test. If you finish before time is called, you may go back to Parts 5, 6, and 7 and check your work.

토익® 정기시험
기출문제집

기출 TEST

06

READING TEST

In the Reading test, you will read a variety of texts and answer several different types of reading comprehension questions. The entire Reading test will last 75 minutes. There are three parts, and directions are given for each part. You are encouraged to answer as many questions as possible within the time allowed.

You must mark your answers on the separate answer sheet. Do not write your answers in your test book.

PART 5

Directions: A word or phrase is missing in each of the sentences below. Four answer choices are given below each sentence. Select the best answer to complete the sentence. Then mark the letter (A), (B), (C), or (D) on your answer sheet.

101. While the director of communications is away, all e-mails and calls will be forwarded to ------- assistant.

(A) she
(B) her
(C) hers
(D) herself

102. Mr. Srour's flight arrived ------- late for him to attend the reception.

(A) so
(B) ever
(C) too
(D) already

103. Mr. Wagner will arrange the schedule of events for the ------- of the flagship store.

(A) opening
(B) openness
(C) openly
(D) opens

104. ------- the final award had been presented, Ms. Ryu acknowledged the support of the event's sponsors.

(A) During
(B) Then
(C) After
(D) Next

105. Chunto Consultancy Service recommended a ------- way of balancing the annual budget.

(A) succeed
(B) success
(C) successful
(D) successfully

106. Press lightly ------- the pedal with your left foot to release the vehicle's parking brake.

(A) up
(B) on
(C) of
(D) in

107. Hikers are invited ------- the information center for trail maps of Far Valley Park.

(A) visiting
(B) to visit
(C) visits
(D) having visited

108. Danton Estate Brokerage offers an online educational program to help ------- home buyers choose a property.

(A) unmistakable
(B) incomplete
(C) unused
(D) inexperienced

109. Iolana Dance Troupe stands out because the group knows ------- to integrate a variety of dance styles.

(A) how
(B) that
(C) since
(D) about

110. The Lafayette Hill Public Library requires that the ------- of mobile phones be restricted to the conversation rooms.

(A) use
(B) model
(C) time
(D) call

111. Major airlines have ------- been using self-serve ticketing systems to reduce wait times.

(A) increases
(B) increasing
(C) increased
(D) increasingly

112. A book of songs written by Pakistani singer Ayesha Saad was sold at auction yesterday ------- an undisclosed amount.

(A) from
(B) to
(C) off
(D) for

113. There is ------- more important to maintaining dental health than brushing your teeth twice a day.

(A) other
(B) neither
(C) nothing
(D) whatever

114. Taste tests suggest that most people ------- Dairysmooth's red-bean-flavored ice cream very appetizing.

(A) find
(B) feel
(C) take
(D) like

115. Regardless of ------- a candidate is offered a job, all applications are kept on file for six months.

(A) even
(B) whether
(C) although
(D) including

116. ------- the Nye Research Center, performing assigned duties for 30 minutes while standing increases productivity.

(A) Not only
(B) In case of
(C) As though
(D) According to

117. This booklet is intended to inform drivers of ------- on bridge travel for oversized vehicles.

(A) restricts
(B) restricting
(C) restrictive
(D) restrictions

118. Customers can now enjoy ------- food seven days a week at the recently renovated Novani Grill.

(A) exceptional
(B) surpassing
(C) effective
(D) dominant

119. No one at the Anshelt Corporation campaigned ------- for expansion of the internship program than Melody Ahn.

(A) energetic
(B) most energetic
(C) energetically
(D) more energetically

120. Monday's workshop will help restaurant owners ------- their ability to effectively recruit, train, and retain staff.

(A) cover
(B) prepare
(C) progress
(D) evaluate

GO ON TO THE NEXT PAGE

121. The digital advertising campaign has generated ------- interest in the clothing line.

(A) substance
(B) substances
(C) substantial
(D) substantially

122. The seminar leader stated that addressing customer concerns ------- was one crucial element for financial success.

(A) consistently
(B) largely
(C) hugely
(D) identically

123. Although the desk was slightly damaged during assembly, it is still ------- .

(A) function
(B) functional
(C) functionally
(D) functioned

124. ------- its discounts for new customers, Teratran Phone's service plans are considered inferior by many.

(A) Far from
(B) Despite
(C) Among
(D) Instead of

125. Now that Ms. Nakamura ------- to the London headquarters, a new manager is running our Tokyo office.

(A) has transferred
(B) transferring
(C) transfer
(D) to transfer

126. ------- the kitchen cabinets arrived late, the contractor installed them without putting the job behind schedule.

(A) Even though
(B) Instead of
(C) In addition to
(D) On top of

127. The proposal for the Seascape project will be ready tomorrow ------- we receive the budget analysis today.

(A) expecting
(B) if not
(C) unlike
(D) as long as

128. The Ortimate 3 home theater system is Hyong Electronics' most ------- priced configuration.

(A) closely
(B) sparsely
(C) reasonably
(D) absolutely

129. The Oakwood Restaurant ------- a special dinner menu on Saturdays for the past decade.

(A) is offering
(B) has been offering
(C) will be offering
(D) would have been offering

130. Mr. de Tonnancour has a speaking ------- on Tuesday, November 15.

(A) engagement
(B) term
(C) subject
(D) employment

PART 6

Directions: Read the texts that follow. A word, phrase, or sentence is missing in parts of each text. Four answer choices for each question are given below the text. Select the best answer to complete the text. Then mark the letter (A), (B), (C), or (D) on your answer sheet.

Questions 131-134 refer to the following article.

DODOMA (21 May)—Dodoma Gas and Electric (DGE) and Arusha Power (Arupo) have announced today that they ------- **131.** into one company. The effective date of the merger is 1 July. The soon-to-be ------- **132.** company will operate under the new name Tanzania Energy Solutions. DGE serves about 250,000 households and businesses, while Arupo serves about 90,000. ------- **133.** . In a joint statement, CEOs Johnathan Gashaza of DGE and Coretha Komba of Arupo assured customers they will not see any service changes. ------- **134.** also said there will be no employee layoffs.

131. (A) have been merging
(B) will be merging
(C) have merged
(D) are merged

132. (A) renovated
(B) informed
(C) created
(D) acquired

133. (A) The financial terms of the agreement have yet to be disclosed.
(B) The energy sector is vital to Tanzania's development.
(C) Both companies have an exceptional grasp of the international financial market.
(D) Both companies have an excellent reputation in their respective industries.

134. (A) We
(B) It
(C) They
(D) She

GO ON TO THE NEXT PAGE

Questions 135-138 refer to the following letter.

29 August

Alvin Mangubat
Director of Human Resources
Farsten Products, Ltd.
549 Castor Boulevard
Winnipeg MB R3E 2S2

Dear Mr. Mangubat,

I am writing to apply for the mechanical engineer position advertised on your Web site. I think I have much to offer Farsten Products' design ------- (**135.**) as an employee.

------- (**136.**). I am currently an engineer at Yount Systems, where I have worked on machine and engine designs for the last six years. ------- (**137.**) that, I was employed by Zelenka Industries, where I helped develop efficient methods for recycling scrap steel.

I have enclosed my résumé, which ------- (**138.**) more details about my work history and my educational background. I look forward to meeting with you to discuss how my skills and experience can benefit Farsten Products.

Sincerely,

Gail Paek
Encl.

135. (A) phase
(B) department
(C) consultant
(D) expertise

136. (A) Your Web site also listed an internship that would be a great opportunity.
(B) The job description said that applicants should have an advanced degree.
(C) My manager replied to your request last week.
(D) My extensive experience makes me an ideal fit for your company.

137. (A) Regarding
(B) Following
(C) Contrary to
(D) Prior to

138. (A) give
(B) gave
(C) gives
(D) is giving

Questions 139-142 refer to the following e-mail.

To: Lathifah Suryani <lsuryani@cmail.com>
From: Jabari Evers <eversj@pems.com>
Date: May 18
Subject: Text Messages

Dear Ms. Suryani,

In order to ------- (139.) our patients as effectively and reliably as possible, we are now offering them the option of receiving appointment reminders and other relevant information via our text-messaging system. You are currently registered to receive our materials via e-mail. ------- (140). If you would like to add text messaging to your mode of communication with us or would like to change your ------- (141.) from e-mail to text messaging, please let us know at your earliest convenience. ------- (142.) goal is to give you relevant and useful information about your health and about the products and services we offer in a timely fashion.

Jabari Evers
Customer Care Representative
Professional Eye Care Management Services

139. (A) serve
(B) care
(C) work
(D) provide

140. (A) You have not been in our office recently.
(B) No action is required if you like your current service.
(C) We have great products you can buy.
(D) E-mail messages are not available to all patients.

141. (A) prefer
(B) preferential
(C) preferred
(D) preference

142. (A) Their
(B) My
(C) Your
(D) Our

TEST 6

GO ON TO THE NEXT PAGE

Questions 143-146 refer to the following article.

TOFTLUND (10 June)—Row after row of electric cars in local parking areas seem to indicate that the city of Toftlund has begun to give up on gasoline-fueled cars. In fact, 20 percent of the cars on Toftlund city streets are electric, but this number is changing at a ------- **143.** pace.

To some extent, this is due to the city's generous tax ------- **144.** offered to electric car drivers. According to Anne Rasmussen, president of Toftlund Green Business, more attractive designs and longer-lasting batteries have ------- **145.** made a difference. Ms. Rasmussen predicts the number of electric cars in Toftlund will more than double in the coming years. ------- **146.**.

143. (A) rapid
(B) brief
(C) narrow
(D) valuable

144. (A) beneficial
(B) benefitting
(C) benefits
(D) to benefit

145. (A) just
(B) over
(C) very
(D) also

146. (A) Moreover, she likes the convenience of having recharging stations on highways.
(B) In fact, she believes that in twenty years only electric cars will be sold here.
(C) Therefore, she feels that the price of electric cars is too high.
(D) She notes that the population of Toftlund has been decreasing steadily.

PART 7

Directions: In this part you will read a selection of texts, such as magazine and newspaper articles, e-mails, and instant messages. Each text or set of texts is followed by several questions. Select the best answer for each question and mark the letter (A), (B), (C), or (D) on your answer sheet.

Questions 147-148 refer to the following invitation.

You are cordially invited to the
Dr. Jatin Sachdeva Memorial Lecture

delivered by

Dr. Seema Razdan
Director, National Centre for Research and author of
Improving Your Bedside Manner: Essential Skills in Health Care

Topic: Patient Care
Date: 15 May, 9:30–10:30 A.M.
Venue: Nadkarni Auditorium

This lecture is open only to Jalandhar Hospital medical personnel who interact daily with patients. Seating is limited. E-mail Mr. Arnav Gopal to hold your spot.

147. For whom is the invitation most likely intended?

(A) Health insurance providers
(B) Hospital gift-shop workers
(C) Doctors and nurses
(D) Administrators and managers

148. What are interested individuals asked to do?

(A) Review notes from a lecture
(B) Read Dr. Razdan's book
(C) Arrive early at the auditorium
(D) Contact Mr. Gopal

GO ON TO THE NEXT PAGE

Questions 149-150 refer to the following instructions.

Welcome to Rosen Valley Bank! To activate your debit card online, follow these steps:

1. Go to www.rosenvalleybank.com and click on the "Debit Card" tab.
2. Enter your full, 16-digit debit card number.
3. Type in your temporary PIN number. For security purposes, a 4-digit number should have been mailed to you in a separate letter to serve as a temporary password for card activation purposes. If you have not received this letter, please contact your local branch.
4. You will be prompted to create your own unique 4-digit debit card PIN. You will be required to provide this number each time you use your card for purchases or to access cash.
5. Click the "Activate" icon at the bottom of the screen. You may now begin using your Rosen Valley debit card.

ROSEN VALLEY BANK

149. For whom are the instructions most likely intended?

(A) New customers
(B) Bank loan applicants
(C) Employees in training
(D) Customer service representatives

150. What is the reader asked to do?

(A) Sign and return a letter
(B) Create an online username
(C) Verify contact information
(D) Update a secure code

Questions 151-152 refer to the following text-message chain.

(5:34 P.M.) Daniel Haney
Abdul, are you still in the office?

(5:35 P.M.) Abdul Ahmed
Yes. Getting ready to leave soon. Why?

(5:36 P.M.) Daniel Haney
I can't remember my new password to the remote computer system. Why does the company make us change it so often!

(5:37 P.M.) Abdul Ahmed
Do you have it written down somewhere?

(5:38 P.M.) Daniel Haney
Yes. On a piece of paper on my desk.

(5:40 P.M.) Abdul Ahmed
There's a lot of paper on your desk.

(5:41 P.M.) Daniel Haney
Sorry! It's a little yellow piece. Look all the way at the bottom-left corner.

(5:43 P.M.) Abdul Ahmed
OK. I think I've got it: RV5cc. Is that what you're looking for?

(5:44 P.M.) Daniel Haney
Yes. Thanks so much, Abdul. You're a lifesaver!

151. What is Mr. Haney's problem?
(A) He is locked out of his office.
(B) He needs help finding a report.
(C) He has forgotten important information.
(D) He did not turn off his work computer.

152. At 5:40 P.M., what does Mr. Ahmed imply when he writes, "There's a lot of paper on your desk"?
(A) He is unable to work at Mr. Haney's desk.
(B) He needs more specific instructions.
(C) Mr. Haney should be more organized.
(D) Mr. Haney is not finished with his work.

GO ON TO THE NEXT PAGE →

Questions 153-154 refer to the following e-mail.

E-mail

From: Tracy Felsenthal
To: Jon Davies
Date: December 8
Subject: Information
Attachment: Letter

Dear Mr. Davies:

Attached please find the details for your trip to Bratislava, Slovakia. It includes your itinerary, hotel confirmation, and confirmation of your participation in the conference of the World Federation of Flight Attendants (WFFA). There are also instructions for requesting reimbursement for any expenses you incur. Please print and sign a copy of the attached letter and return it to me at your earliest convenience; it serves as acknowledgment that you have received the information. You may wish to print a copy for your records as well.

If you have any questions, please let me know.

Regards,

Tracy Felsenthal
Staff Development Coordinator
Aileron Airways

153. What is a purpose of the e-mail?

(A) To acknowledge completion of travel arrangements
(B) To announce the implementation of a travel policy
(C) To provide information about the WFFA
(D) To request approval for a conference presentation

154. What is Mr. Davies instructed to do?

(A) Confirm that his records are current
(B) Submit details about a conference
(C) Book a hotel room
(D) Sign a document

Questions 155-157 refer to the following form.

WORK AGREEMENT

MORITZ-CONNELLY LANDSCAPERS 

E-mail: info@moritzconnelly.com
Web site: www.moritzconnelly.com
Phone: 215-555-0128

Customer name:	Ana Arellano
Customer phone number:	215-555-0193
Work site:	4 Market Street, Philadelphia, PA
Type of project:	Home garden
Project date:	May 9
Arrival time:	9:00 A.M.
Anticipated time of completion:	12:00 Noon

Service	**Price**
Monthly lawn maintenance (May)	$39.95
Fertilization of garden soil	$150.00
Delivery and planting of flowers	$395.00

Project total:	$584.95
Deposit (Paid, May 1):	$200.00
Balance due upon completion:	**$384.95**

155. What is indicated about the project?

(A) It will begin in the afternoon.
(B) It has been paid in full.
(C) It requires the removal of plants.
(D) It includes a service offered regularly.

156. Where will the work take place?

(A) At a park
(B) At a floral shop
(C) At Ms. Arellano's residence
(D) At the offices of Moritz-Connelly Landscapers

157. What amount will Moritz-Connelly Landscapers receive on May 9 ?

(A) $39.95
(B) $200.00
(C) $384.95
(D) $584.95

TEST 6

GO ON TO THE NEXT PAGE

Questions 158-160 refer to the following press release.

FOR IMMEDIATE RELEASE
Contact: Eloise Bassett, bassett@edmond.com.jm

Montego Bay (23 July)—Edmond Limited is pleased to announce the completion of its latest project, South Montego Bay Court. — [1] —. The complex has only 200 townhouses still available; most of the units were presold when construction first began.

Each townhouse features a well-equipped kitchen, a spacious family room, two to three comfortable bedrooms, and two full bathrooms. The family room opens to a patio, so residents can enjoy the peaceful setting. — [2] —. Every unit also includes modern amenities, such as central air conditioning and an energy-efficient oven, dishwasher, and clothes washer/dryer.

The South Montego Bay Court complex is ideally situated close to shops and restaurants as well as several popular beaches. — [3] —. Additionally, residents have access to an outdoor pool and a playground on the property.

You are welcome to drop in at South Montego Court and visit any of the available units. — [4] —. If you wish to schedule a private tour, you may do so by calling 876-555-0176.

158. What most likely is Edmond Limited?

(A) An interior design firm
(B) A housing developer
(C) A housing loan provider
(D) A home inspection group

159. What is indicated about the townhouses?

(A) They have all been sold.
(B) They have private gardens.
(C) They include some appliances.
(D) They each have two parking spaces.

160. In which of the positions marked [1], [2], [3], and [4] does the following sentence best belong?

"They are open for viewing Tuesday through Saturday from 10:00 A.M. to 7:00 P.M."

(A) [1]
(B) [2]
(C) [3]
(D) [4]

Questions 161-163 refer to the following job announcement.

Field Trip Coordinator Needed

Somerset Falls Parks Department is looking for an outdoor enthusiast to lead our Environmental Education School Field Trip Program. The job description includes researching and preparing field trip lessons, evaluating each program after facilitation, and assisting in the coordination and scheduling of all field trip groups.

Qualifications include a degree in biology, environmental science, or a related subject. Qualified applicants must also have previous experience in managing teams and should be familiar with the parks, nature organizations, and environmental resources in the city. The ability to assist in marketing and outreach is a plus, though not required.

To apply, e-mail a cover letter, résumé, and professional references to jobs@somersetfallsparks.com by March 25.

Visit www.somersetfallsparks.com/jobs/FAQs for a list of frequently asked questions about available positions and our hiring process.

TEST 6

161. What is a required qualification for the job?

(A) Knowledge of the area's parks
(B) A background in teaching
(C) Experience in advertising
(D) A driver's license

162. The word "plus" in paragraph 2, line 5, is closest in meaning to

(A) reward
(B) addition
(C) benefit
(D) tip

163. How can more information about the job be obtained?

(A) By checking a schedule
(B) By contacting a field trip facilitator
(C) By sending an e-mail
(D) By visiting a Web site

GO ON TO THE NEXT PAGE →

Questions 164-167 refer to the following online chat discussion.

Hannah Ward [2:01 P.M.]	Before we begin our discussion about the upcoming meeting with Coral City government officials, I have some exciting news to report: one of our most recent designs, Chatillion House, will be featured in next month's issue of Residential Life.
Mahdi Naser [2:02 P.M.]	Wow, that's excellent news! I really enjoyed working on that assignment.
Elaine Lau [2:02 P.M.]	Fantastic! This will mean increased exposure for the firm.
Mahdi Naser [2:03 P.M.]	My thoughts exactly. The magazine has a readership that spans many countries.
Hannah Ward [2:04 P.M.]	Let's not forget the magnificent job that the people from Vistarama did.
Elaine Lau [2:05 P.M.]	That company has become vital to our work.
Hannah Ward [2:07 P.M.]	Particularly since we wanted the house to blend in with the greenery that adorns the neighborhood. Using a variety of plants, trees, and flowers, the crew from Vistarama created a scenery that is absolutely stunning.
Mahdi Naser [2:08 P.M.]	Yes, the area that surrounds the house looks absolutely fabulous.
Hannah Ward [2:08 P.M.]	OK, let's move on. Elaine, any new information about the requirements for Coral City's new courthouse?
Elaine Lau [2:09 P.M.]	Yes, there is. This morning I discussed them with Jerica Ogilvie, a city official. I'll go over them with you right away.

164. What information did Ms. Ward share with her coworkers?

(A) Details of the results of a report
(B) Findings of a recently concluded study
(C) A valuable opportunity for the company
(D) An update about a forthcoming project

165. At 2:03 P.M., what does Mr. Naser mean when he writes, "My thoughts exactly"?

(A) The firm will gain greater visibility.
(B) The firm's creations can be found in many parts of the world.
(C) It was gratifying to work on the firm's latest project.
(D) It is important to talk about developments within the firm.

166. What business is Vistarama in?

(A) Building design
(B) Legal services
(C) Landscaping
(D) Publishing

167. What will Ms. Lau most likely do next?

(A) Ask Ms. Ogilvie to provide information about the courthouse
(B) Provide details about the scenery near Chatillion House
(C) Discuss the requests from Coral City officials
(D) Contact other Coral City officials

TEST 6

GO ON TO THE NEXT PAGE

Questions 168-171 refer to the following e-mail.

To:	team@comlor.com
From:	theo_shanner@comlor.com
Date:	Saturday, July 9
Subject:	Flooring Update
Attachment:	Document_1

Dear Staff,

Please note that the office will be closed again on Monday because the contractor needs more time than initially anticipated to complete the floor installation. I will update you on the progress of the project as details become available. While at home, though, continue to follow up on project leads and to support your customer accounts.

Obviously, we will have to postpone the meeting scheduled for Monday until later in the week. On that occasion we will go over our earnings and revenue of the previous quarter. I have attached the relevant information so that you can review it ahead of time. Additionally, we will be looking at some recent trends in sustainable building design and construction.

Finally, I apologize for the disruption this renovation project has caused. Then again, I hope you have been seizing this opportunity to find new ways to work effectively and to enjoy work-life balance.

Best regards,

Theo Shanner
Comlor Ltd.

168. What is mentioned about the flooring installation project?

(A) It is part of a larger renovation project.
(B) It is taking longer than anticipated.
(C) It will be inspected upon completion.
(D) It has been temporarily stopped.

169. What are employees expected to do on Monday?

(A) Start at a different time
(B) Request details from clients
(C) Work from a remote location
(D) Submit agenda items

170. What did Mr. Shanner include with the e-mail?

(A) Financial summaries
(B) Training documents
(C) A list of sales contacts
(D) A detailed project schedule

171. What type of business most likely is Comlor Ltd.?

(A) An office furniture company
(B) An industrial parts manufacturer
(C) A financial consulting firm
(D) An architecture firm

Questions 172-175 refer to the following article.

Considering Flextime?

by Romy Johnson

Many employees wish to work a nonstandard schedule, available through a system known as "flextime." Flextime may involve working nontraditional hours or working more hours on some days and fewer on others. — [1] —. Although commonly viewed as a benefit to workers, flextime can also benefit employers by increasing employee satisfaction, helping in recruitment of new talent, and permitting longer hours of coverage at the business without increasing the number of employees or incurring overtime costs.

Employers who are interested in such arrangements should first consider several factors. — [2] —. They include the number of workers who want to take advantage of the program, how employees' hours will be tracked, and whether flextime will interfere with daily business.

Then a policy must be created that includes details specific to the company's needs and preferences. — [3] —. Employers should revisit this information from time to time and make changes as necessary. And of course, prior to implementation, employers will want to consult with their legal team to make sure the proposed policy complies with laws concerning wages and hours. — [4] —.

172. For whom is the article mainly intended?

(A) Teams of lawyers
(B) Leaders of companies
(C) Payroll processors
(D) Newspaper reporters

173. What is NOT mentioned as a benefit of flextime?

(A) It is easy to begin implementing.
(B) It makes a company appealing to job applicants.
(C) It can enable a company to extend its operating hours.
(D) It increases workers' happiness.

174. According to the article, what should take place periodically?

(A) A simplification of payments
(B) An adjustment of job descriptions
(C) A review of policies
(D) A reduction of hours

175. In which of the positions marked [1], [2], [3], and [4] does the following sentence best belong?

"For example, employers may choose to allow only employees with certain job titles to participate."

(A) [1]
(B) [2]
(C) [3]
(D) [4]

TEST 6

GO ON TO THE NEXT PAGE

Questions 176-180 refer to the following Web page and e-mail.

Morlen Museum Visitor Information

Welcome! Located just minutes from High Street Station in Richford's shopping district, the Morlen Museum offers visitors a chance to explore scientific topics in engaging, hands-on exhibits. Tours can be arranged for those seeking even more detailed information. Parking is available in a nearby city garage. And don't forget to visit the museum shop with its wide range of unique and interesting items.

Admission:

Ticket Type	Price	Provides
Basic	£15.00	• Access to the museum's permanent exhibits
Basic Plus	£20.00	• Basic access AND access to the Van Zandt Planetarium Show
Super Saver	£25.00	• Basic Plus access AND access to the Geology Lab
Full Access	£30.00	• Super Saver access AND access to special exhibits

Special Exhibits:

- Sports: The Way We Move (1 January–31 March)
- Butterflies: Color in Motion (1 April–30 June)
- Mathematical Beauty: How Numbers Shape Our World (1 July–30 September)
- Earth, Fire, Water, Wind: Future Power Sources (1 October–31 December)

To: tlin@morlenmusuem.org
From: acordell@talvix.com
Date: 2 October
Subject: Upcoming excursion

Dear Ms. Lin,

I'm writing on behalf of the Talvix Energy Professionals Partnership (TEPP). The TEPP pairs young adults considering careers in the energy sector with engineers and executives from Talvix. Each quarter we arrange an educational trip for the program participants.

On 12 October we are planning for a group of six mentors and twelve mentees to visit the Morlen Museum. We plan to visit the Geology Lab to examine the origins of fossil fuels. We believe an in-depth tour would be quite beneficial to the mentees. Would you be able to provide us with a tour of the lab? If so, what would be the cost in addition to the ticket price? We also want to spend time at the special exhibit.

Thank you in advance for your assistance.

Alton Cordell

Director, TEPP

176. What is suggested about the Morlen Museum?

(A) It offers on-site parking.
(B) It is conveniently located.
(C) Its admission prices were recently raised.
(D) Its museum shop is currently closed.

177. Why did Mr. Cordell write the e-mail?

(A) To inquire about an advertised job
(B) To offer a volunteer opportunity
(C) To request information about a museum tour
(D) To propose a topic for a special exhibit

178. According to the e-mail, what is the TEPP?

(A) A mentoring program
(B) A staffing company
(C) A travel agency
(D) A geology club

179. What type of ticket will members of the TEPP group most likely require?

(A) Basic
(B) Basic Plus
(C) Super Saver
(D) Full Access

180. What exhibit will the TEPP group most likely visit?

(A) Sports
(B) Butterflies
(C) Mathematical Beauty
(D) Earth, Fire, Water, Wind

GO ON TO THE NEXT PAGE

Questions 181-185 refer to the following notice and e-mail.

HJP Transport Solutions, Ltd.

Powell Internship Programme

HJP Transport Solutions, Ltd., headquartered in London, seeks university students to fill ten intern positions in its Powell Internship Programme (PIP). Interns will be placed in one of HJP's three regional offices: Birmingham, Manchester, or Bristol. Applicants should email a statement of interest and résumé to pip@hjp.co.uk by 31 March. Successful candidates will have the honour of being the first recipients of the Powell Internship.

Background:

PIP is the initiative of Tristan Powell, who wanted to honour the ingenuity of Henry J. Powell, the founder of HJP Transport Solutions, Ltd. The programme seeks to inspire young engineering students to follow in Henry J. Powell's footsteps and propose and develop innovative solutions to shipping and transport problems. Having earned his doctorate degree in engineering, Henry J. Powell went on to found HJP Transport Solutions, Ltd. Over time, he built the company into a successful, internationally renowned business. Having served four decades as company president, he retired last year and was succeeded by his son, Tristan.

To:	Joseph Chen <jchen@sunnydale.ac.uk>
From:	Padma Vithana <pvithana@hjp.co.uk>
Date:	25 April
Subject:	Information

Dear Mr. Chen,

Thank you for promptly returning the paperwork relevant to your internship. You will receive your intern packet within a week.

As for your inquiry about housing, I appreciate your concern that the two-hour train ride from London to your assigned location makes for an arduous daily commute. Regrettably, HJP does not provide accommodations for interns. I suggest that you contact Mr. Daniel Anders who is in charge of the mentorship program in our Bristol office. He has lived in the city for many years and presumably will have some advice about housing options there. Good luck, and I hope you will enjoy working at HJP.

Sincerely,

Padma Vithana
Director of Recruiting, HJP Transport Solutions, Ltd.

181. What is the purpose of the notice?

(A) To list volunteer opportunities at a company
(B) To describe the history of a company
(C) To advertise a company's new program
(D) To announce the retirement of a company's president

182. Who is Tristan Powell?

(A) The founder of a business
(B) The head of a company
(C) A university instructor
(D) An internship candidate

183. What is one reason for Ms. Vithana's e-mail?

(A) To congratulate Mr. Chen
(B) To inquire about a problem
(C) To send Mr. Chen paperwork
(D) To answer a question

184. What is true about Mr. Chen?

(A) He has worked with Mr. Anders in the past.
(B) He requested help with a project.
(C) He is an engineering student.
(D) He is transferring to a different office.

185. Where will Mr. Chen be working?

(A) In Birmingham
(B) In Bristol
(C) In London
(D) In Manchester

TEST 6

GO ON TO THE NEXT PAGE

Questions 186-190 refer to the following Web page, e-mail, and information sheet.

http://www.euroful.it/glasscontainers

Euroful Glass

Euroful is celebrating 125 years of providing quality glass containers to Italy and beyond!

Glass bottles and jars have long been the standard for beautiful, functional containers. Consider all the desirable attributes of this useful material.

1. Neutrality	Glass containers do not interact with the products they hold. Glass has no flavor or odor and is thus ideal for storing food or personal care products.
2. Impermeability	Glass is impermeable to air and water. Products stored in glass containers are well protected and remain fresh longer.
3. Environmentally Responsible	Glass is made of sand, limestone, and soda ash—natural ingredients that do not harm the Earth. Glass can be reused and recycled.
4. Convenience	Glass is easy to clean and dishwasher safe.
5. Style	Glass has endless design possibilities. Choose from our catalog or work with our Euroful designers who can assist you in customizing a vessel for your product.

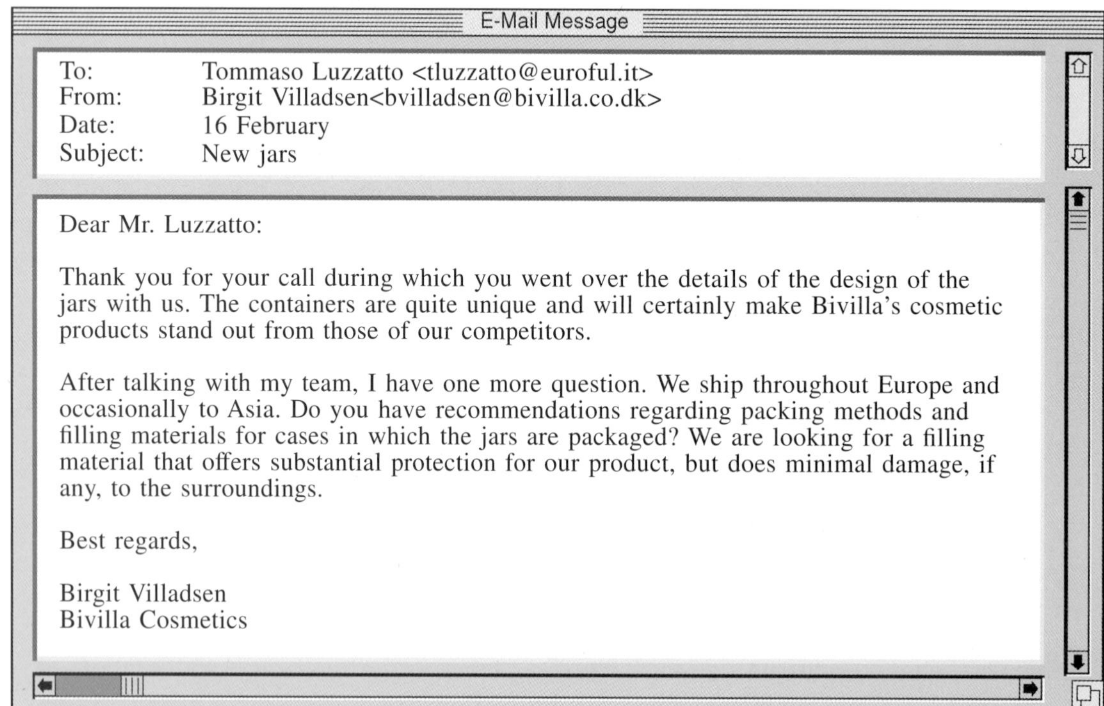

E-Mail Message

To: Tommaso Luzzatto <tluzzatto@euroful.it>
From: Birgit Villadsen<bvilladsen@bivilla.co.dk>
Date: 16 February
Subject: New jars

Dear Mr. Luzzatto:

Thank you for your call during which you went over the details of the design of the jars with us. The containers are quite unique and will certainly make Bivilla's cosmetic products stand out from those of our competitors.

After talking with my team, I have one more question. We ship throughout Europe and occasionally to Asia. Do you have recommendations regarding packing methods and filling materials for cases in which the jars are packaged? We are looking for a filling material that offers substantial protection for our product, but does minimal damage, if any, to the surroundings.

Best regards,

Birgit Villadsen
Bivilla Cosmetics

Tips for shipping products in glass containers

Overpacking is the safest method of transporting delicate items. Overpacking simply means packing the box containing the product inside another larger box. An absorbent filling material is inserted between the two boxes, cushioning the smaller box from vibrations and movement during transit. Depending on your specific needs, any of the following materials could be used as filler.

Filler	Protection	Earth friendly
Recycled paper strips	light	++
Plastic air pillows	high	–
Styrofoam packing peanuts	medium	– –
Expanding bio foam	high	++

186. What is indicated about Euroful?

(A) It is a new company.
(B) It sells cardboard boxes.
(C) It can make customized products.
(D) Its products are sold primarily in Asia.

187. Why did Ms. Villadsen send Mr. Luzzatto the e-mail?

(A) To ask for advice
(B) To propose a change
(C) To explain a procedure
(D) To recommend a supplier

188. What attribute of Euroful's glass containers did Ms. Villadsen and Mr. Luzzatto discuss?

(A) Attribute 2
(B) Attribute 3
(C) Attribute 4
(D) Attribute 5

189. According to the information sheet, what does overpacking require?

(A) Extra product samples
(B) Boxes of different sizes
(C) Individually wrapped jars
(D) Special instructions for delivery

190. What packaging filler would best meet the needs of Bivilla Cosmetics?

(A) Recycled paper strips
(B) Plastic air pillows
(C) Styrofoam packing peanuts
(D) Expanding bio foam

GO ON TO THE NEXT PAGE

Questions 191-195 refer to the following article, schedule, and e-mail.

City to Upgrade Aging Gas Pipes

(September 1)—During the month of October, Nairobi Energy Services, Inc., (NESI) plans to replace two kilometers of cast-iron underground gas pipes with plastic-coated steel pipes as part of its commitment to maintaining the city's energy infrastructure.

"The increase in pressure provided by the new pipes will better support today's high-efficiency furnaces, water heaters, clothes dryers, and other gas appliances," said Ms. Esther Cheptumo, the gas company's vice president. "The new system will ensure safe and reliable gas delivery for years to come."

Some streets in Nairobi will be closed to traffic between 9:00 A.M. and 4:00 P.M. while pipes are replaced. The gas company is working with city officials to develop a schedule that will minimize the inconvenience. The schedule will be updated daily on the company's Web site as well as in all local newspapers. Customers who experience a significant problem due to the work schedule should contact the gas company with their concerns.

GAS SYSTEM UPGRADE SCHEDULE

Monday, October 16:	Wollaston St.
Tuesday, October 17:	Moringa Rd.
Wednesday, October 18:	Blackwood St.
Thursday, October 19:	Satinwood Ave.
Friday, October 20:	No work scheduled (national holiday)

When work on your street has been completed, a NESI technician will come to your house to connect your service line.

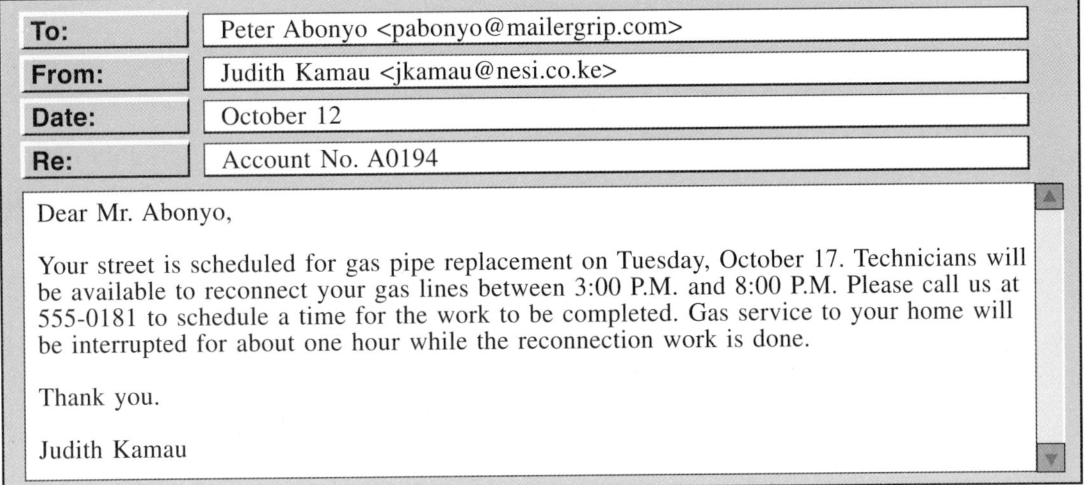

To:	Peter Abonyo <pabonyo@mailergrip.com>
From:	Judith Kamau <jkamau@nesi.co.ke>
Date:	October 12
Re:	Account No. A0194

Dear Mr. Abonyo,

Your street is scheduled for gas pipe replacement on Tuesday, October 17. Technicians will be available to reconnect your gas lines between 3:00 P.M. and 8:00 P.M. Please call us at 555-0181 to schedule a time for the work to be completed. Gas service to your home will be interrupted for about one hour while the reconnection work is done.

Thank you.

Judith Kamau

191. According to the article, what is true about the new pipes?

(A) They will help modern appliances run better.
(B) They will be installed more quickly than cast-iron pipes.
(C) They will be replaced in several years.
(D) They will be installed at night.

192. What does the article indicate about the work schedule?

(A) It will not be approved by city officials.
(B) It has been posted by Ms. Cheptumo.
(C) It contains several errors.
(D) It has not been finalized.

193. What will happen on October 16 ?

(A) A meeting of NESI technicians will be held.
(B) A national holiday will be celebrated.
(C) A city street will be closed to traffic.
(D) A NESI customer's complaint will be resolved.

194. What is suggested about Mr. Abonyo?

(A) He requested some information.
(B) He lives on Moringa Road.
(C) He recently spoke to Ms. Kamau.
(D) He is not at home in the evening.

195. Who most likely is Ms. Kamau?

(A) A city official
(B) A NESI employee
(C) An appliance technician
(D) An executive at a factory.

GO ON TO THE NEXT PAGE

Questions 196-200 refer to the following brochure and e-mails.

Elvinna's

Located just outside of Nassau, the capital city of The Bahamas, Elvinna's is the ideal venue for your reception, banquet, or business meeting. Away from the hustle and bustle of the city, it is surrounded by lush gardens featuring a variety of beautiful sculptures.

The Alameda Room seats between 100 and 250 people comfortably, and our largest space, the Bougainvillea Room, is perfect for up to 300 guests. For business meetings, the Tamarind Room can accommodate up to 50 guests, while the Waterfall Room, slightly larger, seats up to 80 people. Our two business meeting spaces are outfitted with the latest technology to support productive and efficient meetings.

Our elegant restaurant, the Candlewood Tree, offers an ample menu that takes into account many dietary restrictions and preferences. Plan ahead to join us on July 10 when we offer a special Independence Day dinner menu!

To book an event, visit elvinnas.bs. First-time reservations for select days receive a 15 percent discount. For further information call 242-555-0135.

To:	Tanika Nichols
From:	Brian Darville
Date:	18 February
Subject:	Anniversary planning

Hello, Tanika,

I visited Elvinna's and looked at the space that you suggested might be right for our company's anniversary celebration. Their catering menu would suit the various preferences of our expected guests, now numbering over 250. Currently the room is available on two Saturdays, 15 July and 5 August; it is also available on Wednesday, 23 August. Note that this last date would qualify for a nice discount.

Let me know if I have your approval to book this room. We need to make a decision quickly before other parties reserve those dates. I'll be in touch soon about rescheduling the awards ceremony in May.

Brian

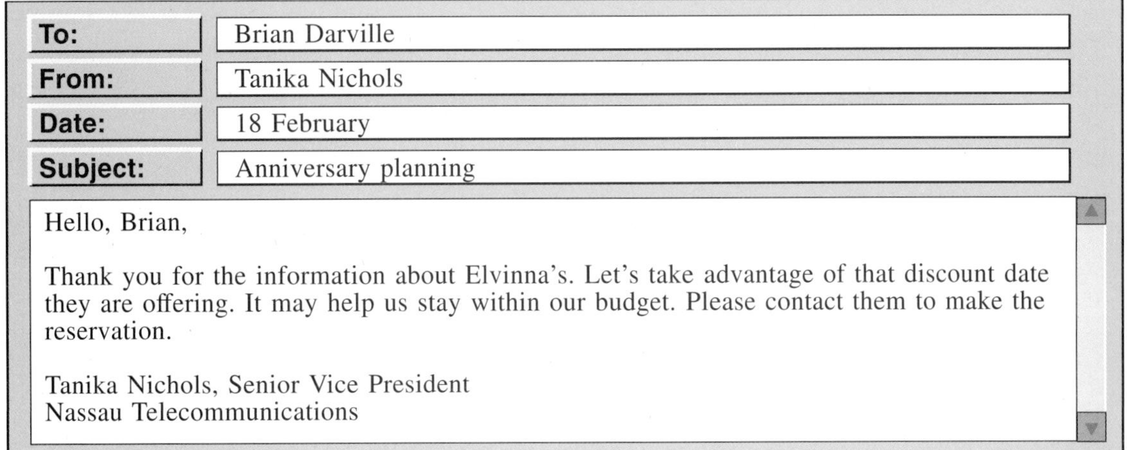

To:	Brian Darville
From:	Tanika Nichols
Date:	18 February
Subject:	Anniversary planning

Hello, Brian,

Thank you for the information about Elvinna's. Let's take advantage of that discount date they are offering. It may help us stay within our budget. Please contact them to make the reservation.

Tanika Nichols, Senior Vice President
Nassau Telecommunications

196. What does the brochure mention about Elvinna's?

(A) It is able to host groups of various types.
(B) It is conveniently located in downtown Nassau.
(C) It has hired a new chef for its restaurant.
(D) It plans to renovate a business center.

197. What does Mr. Darville indicate about the plan for his company's celebration?

(A) It should feature a simple menu.
(B) It will need to be rescheduled.
(C) It will include an awards ceremony.
(D) It is a decision he cannot make alone.

198. Where will the company's anniversary celebration most likely be held?

(A) In the Alameda Room
(B) In the Bougainvillea Room
(C) In the Tamarind Room
(D) In the Waterfall Room

199. Why is Mr. Darville concerned?

(A) Not enough people have responded to an invitation.
(B) He thinks that a different venue might cost less.
(C) A venue that he likes might be reserved by another group.
(D) He has not been able to secure entertainment.

200. When will Nassau Telecommunications' celebration most likely take place?

(A) On July 10
(B) On July 15
(C) On August 5
(D) On August 23

Stop! This is the end of the test. If you finish before time is called, you may go back to Parts 5, 6, and 7 and check your work.

토익® 정기시험
기출문제집

RC

기출 TEST

07

READING TEST

In the Reading test, you will read a variety of texts and answer several different types of reading comprehension questions. The entire Reading test will last 75 minutes. There are three parts, and directions are given for each part. You are encouraged to answer as many questions as possible within the time allowed.

You must mark your answers on the separate answer sheet. Do not write your answers in your test book.

PART 5

Directions: A word or phrase is missing in each of the sentences below. Four answer choices are given below each sentence. Select the best answer to complete the sentence. Then mark the letter (A), (B), (C), or (D) on your answer sheet.

101. Mr. Guo ------- with an electrician yesterday about the rewiring project.

(A) consults
(B) is consulting
(C) to consult
(D) consulted

102. Ms. Lan Le will complete ------- internship at the George Cake Shop next week.

(A) she
(B) her
(C) hers
(D) herself

103. Every Thursday the Lifelong Reading Club meets to ------- novels written by local authors.

(A) create
(B) discuss
(C) perform
(D) dictate

104. Skymills Insurance ------- grew from a small business to a midsize company with 350 employees.

(A) quick
(B) quickly
(C) quicker
(D) quickest

105. Local shop owners are invited to the ------- of Clyde Bank's downtown branch.

(A) open
(B) opened
(C) opening
(D) openly

106. All e-mail messages regarding legal issues should be ------- in a separate folder.

(A) stored
(B) escaped
(C) served
(D) determined

107. Hiring an ------- for Ms. Tsai must be our top priority, as her workload has increased.

(A) assist
(B) assistant
(C) assisted
(D) assistance

108. The ------- Ladoff Building was constructed in 1923 and stood two stories tall.

(A) origin
(B) originated
(C) originally
(D) original

109. If you have questions about your most ------- credit card statement, call Mr. Hassan.

(A) central
(B) consecutive
(C) actual
(D) recent

110. The Rinzlite dishwasher was ranked higher ------- all other dishwashers in its class.

(A) to
(B) past
(C) than
(D) by

111. So far, the Grantley store ------- 20 percent more mobile phones than it did last year.

(A) will sell
(B) was sold
(C) has sold
(D) are selling

112. In the event of a power failure, unplug computers until power is ------- restored.

(A) fully
(B) fullness
(C) fullest
(D) full

113. Although Mr. Akiyama retired last year, he ------- visits the office each week.

(A) next
(B) yet
(C) still
(D) finally

114. At the panel discussion, Ms. Yang made a ------- argument for environmentally responsible business practices.

(A) convince
(B) convincing
(C) convinced
(D) convincingly

115. The Hokodo Orchestra will hold ------- for new string musicians next Tuesday.

(A) attention
(B) investigations
(C) motivation
(D) auditions

116. Although the team members ------- were not available after the game, the coach was happy to be interviewed.

(A) themselves
(B) they
(C) theirs
(D) them

117. Ms. Schwimmer's application was not ------- reviewed until November 5.

(A) relatively
(B) occasionally
(C) completely
(D) enormously

118. Managers are encouraged to give their staff ------- feedback during the annual performance-review meetings.

(A) construction
(B) constructively
(C) constructive
(D) constructing

119. Deckermark Enterprises offers employees flexible scheduling and telecommuting ------.

(A) statements
(B) exchanges
(C) precautions
(D) options

120. Ms. Summer can estimate the cost for the land-clearing project in Fosterville, ------- before the details are finalized.

(A) even
(B) some
(C) such
(D) else

GO ON TO THE NEXT PAGE

121. The company's transition from paper paychecks to electronic paychecks was ------- smooth.

(A) impressive
(B) impression
(C) impressively
(D) impress

122. All temporary workers should contact Ms. Fierro to ------- an identification badge.

(A) combine
(B) obtain
(C) gather
(D) approach

123. We will pay your insurance claim ------- we receive the official damage report.

(A) once
(B) since
(C) like
(D) except

124. Neither of the ------- in the debate was willing to take a stand on the riverfront development controversy.

(A) politicians
(B) politicize
(C) political
(D) politically

125. ------- the additional funding, Central City Medical School expects to double the size of its research team.

(A) Over
(B) On
(C) At
(D) With

126. The clients have indicated that a reception area of 60 square meters will be ------- in the new building.

(A) sufficient
(B) flexible
(C) capable
(D) calculating

127. Ms. Lau would like to know ------- Mr. Cole called the main office yesterday.

(A) whatever
(B) while
(C) why
(D) who

128. Koffler Law hired more paralegals ------- meet its commitment to clients.

(A) consequently
(B) in order to
(C) in any case
(D) additionally

129. The newest edition of the *Biltmire Road Atlas* has plastic-coated pages for extra -------.

(A) familiarity
(B) persistence
(C) durability
(D) replacement

130. Job seekers should prepare a list of professional references ------- applying for positions.

(A) prior to
(B) outside of
(C) in front of
(D) according to

PART 6

Directions: Read the texts that follow. A word, phrase, or sentence is missing in parts of each text. Four answer choices for each question are given below the text. Select the best answer to complete the text. Then mark the letter (A), (B), (C), or (D) on your answer sheet.

Questions 131-134 refer to the following article.

TOKYO (2 June)—Toda Entertainment announced this morning that it will be revealing its latest video game later this week. A preview of the game ------- **131.** a presentation from the developers will be broadcast on the company's Web site on Friday at 4:00 P.M. Japan Standard Time. Until now, no details have been revealed about the game. Many consumers are already ------- **132.** that it will be a sequel to the company's popular *Todashi Adventure* series. The first game in that series, released two years ago, was a ------- **133.** success for the company, selling over 400,000 copies in Japan. ------- **134.**.

131. (A) but
(B) even though
(C) how
(D) as well as

132. (A) confirming
(B) speculating
(C) requesting
(D) analyzing

133. (A) remarkable
(B) remarkably
(C) remarking
(D) remark

134. (A) The company was not able to meet this goal.
(B) Toda Entertainment will announce its new CEO next week.
(C) Its worldwide sales were double that number.
(D) Consumers can now purchase it for the first time.

Questions 135-138 refer to the following letter.

July 11

Dear Mr. Wong:

It was good to speak with you today about the opening in the accounts receivable department at Riedeberg Realty. ------- **135.** . My prior experience has prepared me particularly well for this ------- **136.** . Strong writing skills, assertiveness, and accuracy ------- **137.** in my last two jobs. I am also able to work effectively with coworkers, especially in a fast-paced environment.

I appreciate the time you took to ------- **138.** me. I look forward to hearing from you when you make your final hiring decision.

Sincerely,

Jon Troughman

135. (A) The job seems like an ideal match for my skills and interests.
(B) The company had an outstanding reputation nationally.
(C) Note that I have applied for a number of other jobs as well.
(D) Please contact me to discuss additional scheduling options.

136. (A) event
(B) incident
(C) position
(D) exception

137. (A) all requiring
(B) had all required
(C) all requirements
(D) were all required

138. (A) train
(B) recommend
(C) entertain
(D) interview

Questions 139-142 refer to the following Web page.

Protection & Conservation

The Garner Museum of Art (GMA) ensures the preservation of its collection by carefully ------- (139.) the lighting of its galleries. Certain artifacts—many of which are thousands of years old—are particularly sensitive to light. ------- (140.), the museum does not showcase any of its pieces in areas with windows. Nor does it keep artwork in areas with certain kinds of ------- (141.), potentially harmful bulbs. ------- (142.). By taking such measures, the GMA hopes that its collection will be enjoyed for generations to come.

139. (A) monitoring
(B) acquiring
(C) performing
(D) guarding

140. (A) After all
(B) For instance
(C) On the contrary
(D) For this reason

141. (A) bright
(B) brightly
(C) brighten
(D) brightness

142. (A) Therefore, the museum will place some of its older pieces on loan.
(B) Also, flash photography is not permitted.
(C) Only a few staff members possess these specialized skills.
(D) Unfortunately, it can be difficult to determine an object's age.

TEST 7

GO ON TO THE NEXT PAGE

Questions 143-146 refer to the following e-mail.

To: All Managers
From: Bert Pizarro
Date: October 10
Subject: Staff banquet

Dear Managers,

December is quickly approaching, and the Human Resources team is working out the details for this year's staff banquet. As you know, this ------- (143.) event is an opportunity for us to thank our entire staff for their service and to reflect on the past twelve months. In addition, it will provide everyone with the opportunity ------- (144.) time with their colleagues in a relaxed social setting.

We know that the distance to last year's banquet in Riverdale made it difficult for several employees to attend the event. To make it easier for everyone to participate in this celebration, we are looking for a ------- (145.) that is closer to our office building. ------- (146.).

We plan to send out further details soon.

Kind regards,

Bert Pizarro
Human Resources Manager

143. (A) initial
(B) annual
(C) favoring
(D) hiring

144. (A) to spend
(B) having spent
(C) spending
(D) will spend

145. (A) result
(B) transport
(C) capacity
(D) venue

146. (A) Driving directions are attached.
(B) We apologize for the confusion.
(C) Please reply with any suggestions.
(D) Remember to confirm your attendance.

PART 7

Directions: In this part you will read a selection of texts, such as magazine and newspaper articles, e-mails, and instant messages. Each text or set of texts is followed by several questions. Select the best answer for each question and mark the letter (A), (B), (C), or (D) on your answer sheet.

Questions 147-148 refer to the following notice.

Our Return Pledge

If the products you purchased from Things Galore do not perform to your expectations, please return to our store for an exchange or a refund. Refunds may be issued on full-price purchases only. See Thingsgalore.com/help for details.

147. Where would the notice likely appear?

(A) On a coupon
(B) On a Web site
(C) On a product label
(D) On a sales receipt

148. What is suggested about Things Galore?

(A) It will not issue a refund for all items.
(B) It does not sell discounted products.
(C) It has recalled defective items.
(D) It is having an annual sale.

TEST 7

GO ON TO THE NEXT PAGE

Questions 149-150 refer to the following text-message chain.

Ed Singh (9:46 A.M.) Hi Marisa, has David Yuen stopped by your office?

Marisa Viteli (9:48 A.M.) Not that I know of. I just got here.

Ed Singh (9:49 A.M.) OK. He's having a hard time debugging a program and I told him to ask you to look at it. I hope you don't mind.

Marisa Viteli (9:50 A.M.) Not at all. He's on the Zandos project, right?

Ed Singh (9:51 A.M.) Yes, they're building an order-tracking system and it has to be delivered in a few weeks.

Marisa Viteli (9:52 A.M.) Ah, that's a huge program. I can see why he's having coding problems.

149. For whom do the writers most likely work?

(A) A home repair business
(B) A food delivery business
(C) A building construction company
(D) A software development company

150. At 9:50 A.M., what does Ms. Viteli most likely mean when she writes, "Not at all"?

(A) She does not know David Yuen.
(B) She has not been to her office yet.
(C) She is willing to help a coworker.
(D) She is part of the Zandos project team.

Questions 151-152 refer to the following e-mail.

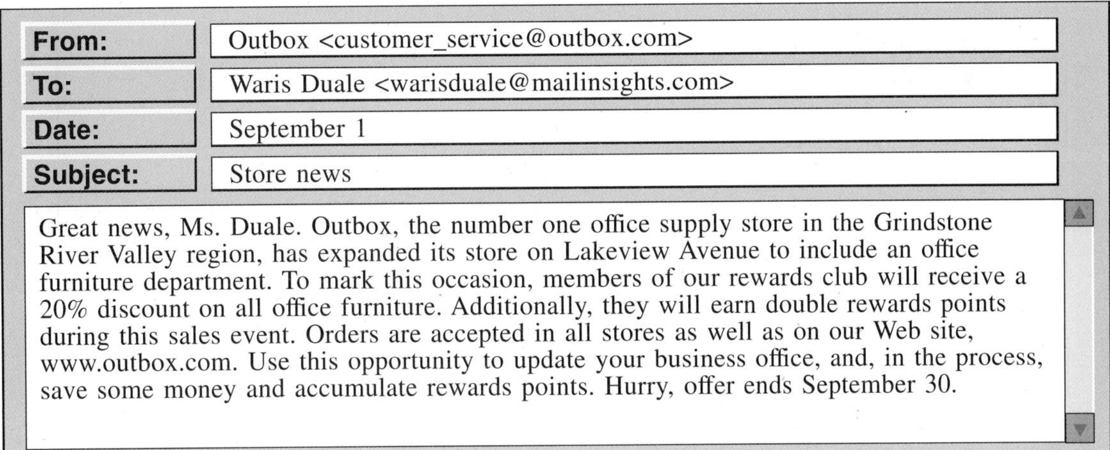

From:	Outbox <customer_service@outbox.com>
To:	Waris Duale <warisduale@mailinsights.com>
Date:	September 1
Subject:	Store news

Great news, Ms. Duale. Outbox, the number one office supply store in the Grindstone River Valley region, has expanded its store on Lakeview Avenue to include an office furniture department. To mark this occasion, members of our rewards club will receive a 20% discount on all office furniture. Additionally, they will earn double rewards points during this sales event. Orders are accepted in all stores as well as on our Web site, www.outbox.com. Use this opportunity to update your business office, and, in the process, save some money and accumulate rewards points. Hurry, offer ends September 30.

151. Why was the e-mail sent?

(A) To introduce an online ordering process
(B) To announce a new store location
(C) To mention a special offer
(D) To explain a new program

152. What is indicated about the store on Lakeview Avenue?

(A) It was recently enlarged.
(B) It has updated its Web site.
(C) It often hosts sales events for rewards club members.
(D) It was the first Outbox store in the region.

TEST 7

GO ON TO THE NEXT PAGE →

Questions 153-155 refer to the following memo.

MEMO

To: All Staff
From: Donaldo Mata, Facilities Supervisor
Date: July 22
Subject: Drilling process

As I reported at last week's staff meeting, we are now in the final planning stages for the new addition to our headquarters building. — [1] —. As part of the process, contractors will be drilling holes tomorrow in the north, east, and west sides of the building to do structural analysis. — [2] —. The drilling is expected to take several hours, and the work will be very noisy. I realize that this type of noise can be very distracting to employees who are trying to speak with customers or conduct meetings. — [3] —. I have requested that the contractors begin drilling on the east side, closest to the Customer Service Office, so that drilling can be finished before peak service hours. Please keep windows on all sides of the building shut to minimize the noise and prevent any exhaust fumes from the drilling rig from entering the building.

— [4] —. I will be here all day supervising the process and will be available to answer any questions. I sincerely apologize for the inconvenience.

153. Why are the holes being drilled?

(A) To identify the best location for a well
(B) To install an improved drainage system
(C) To facilitate planning of a building project
(D) To analyze the soil quality for landscaping

154. What does Mr. Mata ask staff to do tomorrow?

(A) Work from home
(B) Close all windows
(C) Tour the new office space
(D) Reschedule client meetings

155. In which of the positions marked [1], [2], [3], and [4] does the following sentence best belong?

"However, there is little that can be done regarding noise levels."

(A) [1]
(B) [2]
(C) [3]
(D) [4]

Questions 156-158 refer to the following press release.

> **FOR IMMEDIATE RELEASE**
> **Contact:** Pilar Rios, Media Communications, prios@belledevelopment.org
>
> LOS ANGELES (April 18)—California-based Belle Development has entered into an agreement to collaborate with the firm Holden Assets, which is based in London. The companies will join forces to remodel and transform open spaces in airports, train stations, hotels, and office buildings for retailers. According to Belle spokesperson Irina Carson, "The projects will improve both the experience of customers and the revenue streams of the property owners." During the press conference on Monday, Carson said the two companies had been so successful when they worked together previously remodeling an airport in Naples, Italy, that they "decided to make it a long-term relationship." The venture begins next month with the redesign of shops and restaurants at a train station in Barcelona.

156. What does the press release announce?

(A) The launch of a new product line
(B) The relocation of a company's headquarters
(C) The increased earnings of a real estate firm
(D) The start of a lengthy business partnership

157. The word "spaces" in paragraph 1, line 4, is closest in meaning to

(A) holes
(B) areas
(C) seats
(D) parks

158. Where does the press release indicate a project was completed?

(A) In Los Angeles
(B) In London
(C) In Naples
(D) In Barcelona

TEST 7

GO ON TO THE NEXT PAGE

Questions 159-161 refer to the following notice.

Dear Visitors:

Heylin Park is a rugged wilderness site. Our trails are grassy and unpaved, and many contain protruding tree roots, rocks, and stumps. Licensed park rangers will remove fallen debris if a trail becomes impassable, but in order to maintain a healthy habitat for wildlife, the land is otherwise kept in its natural state. To support our efforts, we ask that you please take nothing home with you aside from photographs and memories. Please allow the flowers to grow wild and leave sticks and stones where they are.

If you would like to learn about the different trees, shrubs, and flowers growing in our park, you can join a free ranger-guided hike. These are held every Saturday from 2:00 p.m. to 3:30 p.m. Just add your name to the sign-up sheet at the check-in kiosk, located near the park entrance.

Thank you and enjoy your hike!

Sincerely,

Heylin Park Management

159. What is suggested about Heylin Park?

(A) It is an undeveloped area.
(B) It was affected by a recent storm.
(C) Its entrance fees are being raised.
(D) It is the location of many research projects.

160. What is prohibited at Heylin Park?

(A) Camping overnight
(B) Hiking without a guide
(C) Visiting without a permit
(D) Collecting natural objects

161. What can visitors do at the check-in kiosk?

(A) Register for a tour
(B) Subscribe to a newsletter
(C) View photographs of plants
(D) Volunteer to help build trails

Questions 162-163 refer to the following article.

Bryson Business Development Network Expands Its Learning Program

(March 14)—Last summer, after offering on-site courses for over ten years, Calgary-based Bryson Business Development Network began offering a different set of workshops for people who have recently started a business. Hundreds of new business owners signed up for the online sessions, which focused on topics such as Web site development, marketing, and advertising. This summer, the company will introduce some new learning opportunities.

"We are excited to announce the launch of a wide variety of in-depth courses led by experts in the field," director Rosa Gonzales said. "To enable everyone to learn more about the courses, we have created a brief video highlighting the main points that will be covered in each course. Customers are invited to view this introductory presentation free of charge on our Web site to help them decide which of our offerings best meet their needs."

Registration and more information are available at www.brysonbdn.ca.

162. What is the purpose of the article?

(A) To announce a company merger
(B) To provide marketing tips
(C) To introduce a new director
(D) To publicize online courses

163. What does Ms. Gonzales encourage people to do?

(A) Make a payment
(B) Complete a form
(C) Watch a video
(D) Contact an expert

Questions 164-167 refer to the following online chat discussion.

Live Chat

Ariana Jones (1:18 P.M.):
Hi, Renalto and Janice. How are things coming along with those blogs I asked you to start?

Janice Canto (1:20 P.M.):
I am thinking of profiling the members of our team of investment advisors.

Ariana Jones (1:22 P.M.):
Could you give me more details on that?

Janice Canto (1:24 P.M.):
Well, I want to feature an interview with a different team member every month. I could get a little personal and professional background information, and inquire about the member's views on investment strategies, that sort of thing.

Ariana Jones (1:25 P.M.):
Nice. Our customers would really like that. What about you, Renalto?

Renalto Pereira (1:27 P.M.):
I'm thinking of reporting on emerging stock market trends. I've already collected a lot of material about this topic.

Janice Canto (1:27 P.M.):
Sorry, I have to leave for a meeting in about five minutes.

Ariana Jones (1:28 P.M.):
Sounds interesting. Do you need assistance with the research?

Renalto Pereira (1:29 P.M.):
Thanks, but I think I've got it covered.

Ariana Jones (1:30 P.M.):
OK, I'd like both of you to get back to me by Monday with your progress on these ideas.

164. In what industry do the participants most likely work?

(A) Finance
(B) Health care
(C) Technology
(D) Real estate

165. What is suggested about Ms. Jones?

(A) She will help Mr. Pereira with his research.
(B) She supervises Ms. Canto's work.
(C) She will be out of the office on Monday.
(D) She needs information about a job applicant.

166. What is indicated about Ms. Canto's blogs?

(A) They will be ready by the end of the day.
(B) They will be written by several team members.
(C) They will be published once a month.
(D) They will be designed for internal company use.

167. At 1:28 P.M., what does Ms. Jones mean when she writes, "Sounds interesting"?

(A) She wants to know more about Ms. Canto's meeting.
(B) She likes the subject matter of Mr. Pereira's blog.
(C) She is pleased with recent stock market trends.
(D) She likes to receive positive customer feedback.

GO ON TO THE NEXT PAGE

Questions 168-171 refer to the following meeting minutes.

Corbissin Corporation

Minutes of Quarterly Finance Team Meeting
Thursday, 18 October

Present: Lorenzo Abeyta (Chair), Dolores Tengco, Perla Buenaflor, Omar Mayuga, and Cora Odevilas

Absent: Juan Carlos Serapio (attending International Technology Conference)

The meeting was called to order at 10:30 A.M. by Lorenzo Abeyta.

The minutes from the 20 June meeting were approved unanimously.

Financial Summary (presented by Omar Mayuga)
- Revenue from the last quarter was up by 10 percent.
- The budget has been approved for the hiring of additional sales personnel and customer service associates.
- Discussion of the proposed internship program was postponed until more research has been done. Perla Buenaflor will look into this proposal and present a report at the next meeting.
- The "We All Tell a Story" marketing campaign is under way. The project features testimonials from small-business owners whose office operations improved after installation of our products.

Announcements
Dolores Tengco confirmed that the launch of our new line of printers and copiers is set for 10 November. There will be commercials on TV and radio, online, and in print media. Stores in Mandaluyong and Taguig are planning full-day events. More information on other sales events in stores will be released soon.

The meeting was adjourned at 11:30 A.M. by Lorenzo Abeyta.

168. What is indicated about the Corbissin Corporation?
(A) Its finance team meets monthly.
(B) Its sales personnel received a pay raise.
(C) It manufactures and sells office technology.
(D) It has recently opened a store in Taguig.

169. What is suggested about Mr. Serapio?
(A) He wrote the meeting minutes.
(B) He scheduled the previous team meeting.
(C) He recently gave a presentation at a conference.
(D) He was away on business on October 18.

170. Who will gather more information on a topic?
(A) Mr. Abeyta
(B) Ms. Tengco
(C) Ms. Buenaflor
(D) Mr. Mayuga

171. What will happen in November?
(A) The finance team will travel.
(B) New products will be released.
(C) Some equipment will be repaired.
(D) A user guide will be updated.

Questions 172-175 refer to the following letter.

Harding Environmental Group

September 6

Jelani Campbell
Norden Water Commission
329 Route 15
Norden City, AZ 86310

Dear Mr. Campbell,

I appreciate the Norden Water Commission's interest in my serving as a member of your board of directors. As we discussed, I am currently unable to assume any additional responsibilities. — [1] —. However, I would like to take this opportunity to voice my support for Ms. Lauren Birrell to serve as a board member.

Ms. Birrell, the Director of Development at Harding Environmental Group, began her career here as a water analyst. She was quickly promoted to multiple supervisory roles as her expert knowledge and skills became apparent. — [2] —. For example, a recent research study led by Ms. Birrell found deficiencies with Norden City's water pumping system. — [3] —. She provided guidance on necessary upgrades in a timely and cost-effective manner. The upgraded system, which requires much less maintenance, has saved Norden City thousands of dollars over the past five years.

Additionally, Ms. Birrell has built strong relationships with the Great Valley Watershed, the Norden Department of Environmental Protection, and other government agencies. — [4] —. Ms. Birrell would be an invaluable contributor to your organization.

Should you have any questions, please contact me directly at 928-555-0176.

Sincerely,

Saniya Mathur

Saniya Mathur
President, Harding Environmental Group

172. Why did Ms. Mathur send the letter?

(A) To describe her job responsibilities
(B) To recommend a colleague for a position
(C) To welcome a new member to the board of directors
(D) To congratulate a coworker on a promotion

173. What is mentioned about Harding Environmental Group?

(A) It conducts research studies.
(B) It provides legal services.
(C) It manufactures water pumps.
(D) It is a government agency.

174. What is suggested about Norden City's water system?

(A) It must be updated in the next five years.
(B) It is inspected regularly by Ms. Birrell.
(C) Its maintenance costs have decreased.
(D) Its pumps are in need of repair.

175. In which of the positions marked [1], [2], [3], and [4] does the following sentence best belong?

"Your organization would benefit from these connections."

(A) [1]
(B) [2]
(C) [3]
(D) [4]

TEST 7

GO ON TO THE NEXT PAGE

Questions 176-180 refer to the following e-mail and Web page.

To:	Hyo-Jung Cho
From:	Julian Katz
Date:	14 June
Subject:	Information

Dear Ms. Cho:

Since you were away last week, you might not yet know all the details of the situation with the Web site. Shannon Gehring, our Web designer, was in the middle of revising the site when a severe thunderstorm hit our area. Our servers were struck by lightning and sustained some damage. While they were being repaired, the museum's Web site was down for two days.

I know you are planning to send an e-mail to members today, asking them to help us meet a fund-raising goal by 30 June, the end of our fiscal year. Our site is back online now, and includes a new comment page that can be used for this fund-raising event. Please let me know if you need additional information.

Sincerely,

Julian Katz
IT Coordinator
Knight Museum of Art

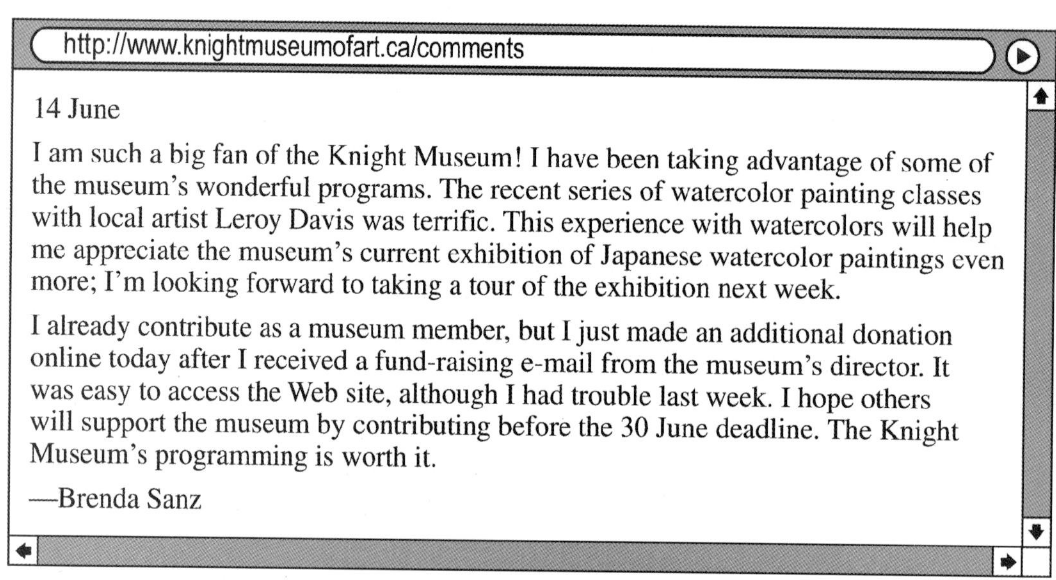

http://www.knightmuseumofart.ca/comments

14 June

I am such a big fan of the Knight Museum! I have been taking advantage of some of the museum's wonderful programs. The recent series of watercolor painting classes with local artist Leroy Davis was terrific. This experience with watercolors will help me appreciate the museum's current exhibition of Japanese watercolor paintings even more; I'm looking forward to taking a tour of the exhibition next week.

I already contribute as a museum member, but I just made an additional donation online today after I received a fund-raising e-mail from the museum's director. It was easy to access the Web site, although I had trouble last week. I hope others will support the museum by contributing before the 30 June deadline. The Knight Museum's programming is worth it.

—Brenda Sanz

176. Why did Mr. Katz contact Ms. Cho?

(A) To introduce a new employee
(B) To provide an update
(C) To request details about an event
(D) To ask for assistance

177. In the e-mail, the word "meet" in paragraph 2, line 1, is closest in meaning to

(A) connect
(B) fulfill
(C) encounter
(D) assemble

178. Who is Ms. Cho?

(A) The museum director
(B) The IT coordinator
(C) A Web designer
(D) A local artist

179. What is Ms. Sanz eager to do?

(A) Help with the Web site
(B) Lead tours for members
(C) Enroll in an art class
(D) Attend an exhibition

180. What does Ms. Sanz suggest in her comment?

(A) She made a donation before the end of the fiscal year.
(B) She has visited Japan.
(C) She recently accessed the museum's online art collection.
(D) She purchased a painting by Leroy Davis.

GO ON TO THE NEXT PAGE

Questions 181-185 refer to the following e-mail and invoice.

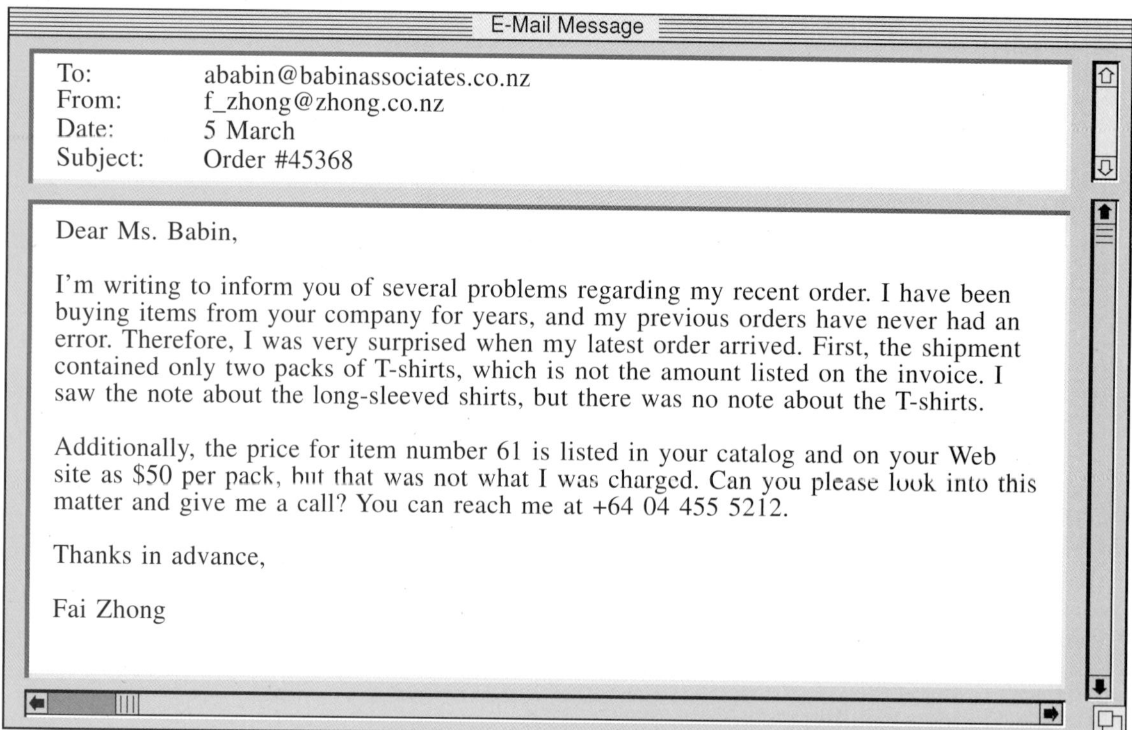

E-Mail Message

To: ababin@babinassociates.co.nz
From: f_zhong@zhong.co.nz
Date: 5 March
Subject: Order #45368

Dear Ms. Babin,

I'm writing to inform you of several problems regarding my recent order. I have been buying items from your company for years, and my previous orders have never had an error. Therefore, I was very surprised when my latest order arrived. First, the shipment contained only two packs of T-shirts, which is not the amount listed on the invoice. I saw the note about the long-sleeved shirts, but there was no note about the T-shirts.

Additionally, the price for item number 61 is listed in your catalog and on your Web site as $50 per pack, but that was not what I was charged. Can you please look into this matter and give me a call? You can reach me at +64 04 455 5212.

Thanks in advance,

Fai Zhong

From:
Babin and Associates
25 Caledonia Street, Strathmore
Wellington 6022

To:
Fai Zhong
Zhong Restaurant and Catering
76 Romeo Street, Thorndon
Wellington 6011

PAYMENT IS DUE UPON RECEIPT OF INVOICE

Order #45368

Item Number	**Item Description**	**Amount Ordered**	**Price per Pack**	**Total Price**
32A	T-shirts, white with logo, assorted sizes	3 packs	$125.00	$375.00
32B* *See note below*	Long-sleeved shirts, white with logo, assorted sizes	3 packs	$175.00	$525.00
61	Black aprons, limited edition, knee-length	5 packs	$60.00	$300.00
118	Black trousers, assorted sizes	2 packs	$200.00	$400.00
		TOTAL	**GST Inclusive**	**$1,600.00**

* We had only one pack of long-sleeved shirts in stock. We included it with this shipment and will send the others in 7–10 business days. There will be no additional shipping charge for these items.

181. Babin and Associates is most likely what type of business?

(A) A laundry service
(B) A clothing company
(C) A catering firm
(D) A shipping service

182. What is indicated about Mr. Zhong?

(A) He uses several addresses.
(B) He prefers overnight shipping.
(C) He has ordered from Babin and Associates before.
(D) He is expanding his business.

183. What does Mr. Zhong request?

(A) An updated catalog
(B) A new logo design
(C) A return phone call
(D) Shipment to a different location

184. According to the invoice, what is true about the long-sleeved shirts?

(A) They are being billed at a discount.
(B) They are available in many colors.
(C) Some of them were damaged in the warehouse.
(D) Some of them will be shipped at a later date.

185. What is one problem that Mr. Zhong identifies?

(A) Too many trousers were delivered.
(B) The wrong amount was charged for aprons.
(C) The T-shirts do not fit well.
(D) The logo on the shirts is incorrect.

TEST 7

GO ON TO THE NEXT PAGE

Questions 186-190 refer to the following e-mail, ticket, and schedule.

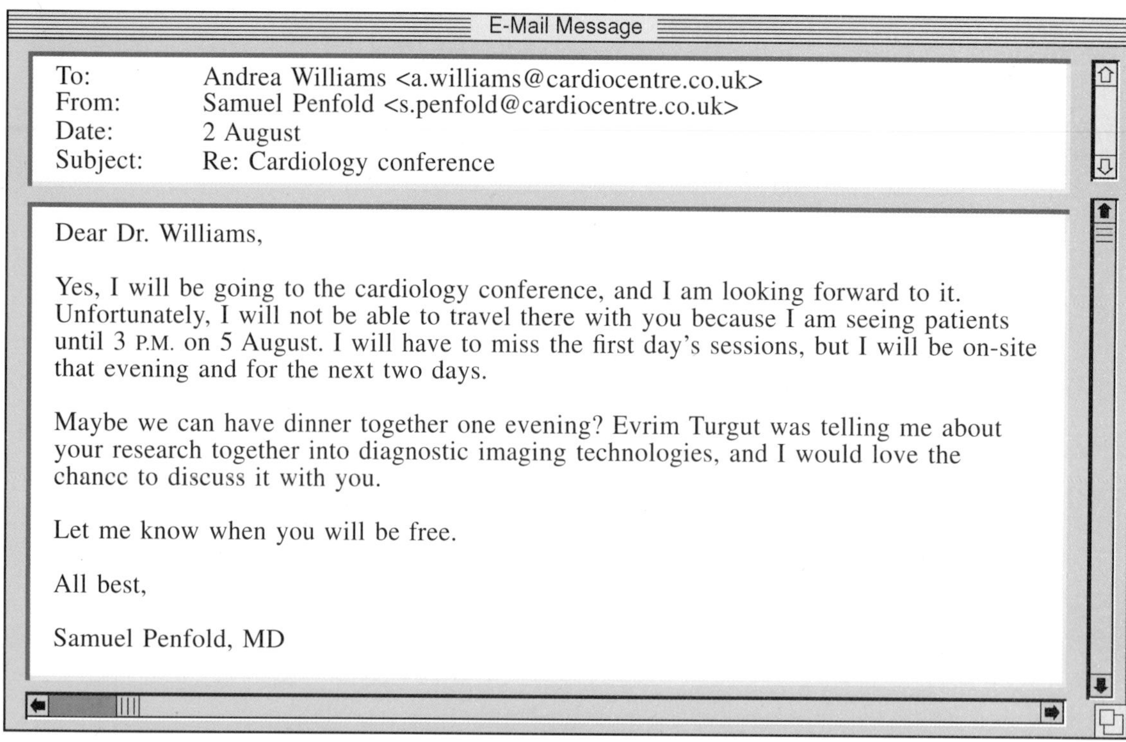

E-Mail Message

To: Andrea Williams <a.williams@cardiocentre.co.uk>
From: Samuel Penfold <s.penfold@cardiocentre.co.uk>
Date: 2 August
Subject: Re: Cardiology conference

Dear Dr. Williams,

Yes, I will be going to the cardiology conference, and I am looking forward to it. Unfortunately, I will not be able to travel there with you because I am seeing patients until 3 P.M. on 5 August. I will have to miss the first day's sessions, but I will be on-site that evening and for the next two days.

Maybe we can have dinner together one evening? Evrim Turgut was telling me about your research together into diagnostic imaging technologies, and I would love the chancc to discuss it with you.

Let me know when you will be free.

All best,

Samuel Penfold, MD

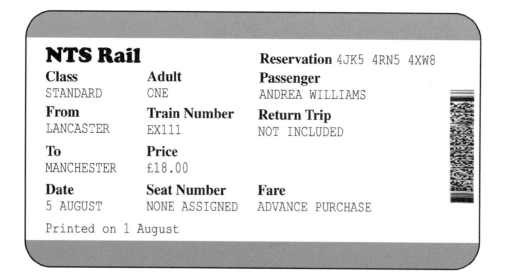

NTS Rail

		Reservation 4JK5 4RN5 4XW8
Class STANDARD	**Adult** ONE	**Passenger** ANDREA WILLIAMS
From LANCASTER	**Train Number** EX111	**Return Trip** NOT INCLUDED
To MANCHESTER	**Price** £18.00	
Date 5 AUGUST	**Seat Number** NONE ASSIGNED	**Fare** ADVANCE PURCHASE

Printed on 1 August

Train Schedule—NTS Rail Lancaster to Manchester				
Train Number	**Departure Time**	**Duration**	**Arrival Time**	**Price**
EX111	7:00 A.M.	55 min	7:55 A.M.	£20.00
RN902	8:30 A.M.	1 h 01 min	9:31 A.M.	£20.00
EX224	10:15 A.M.	1 h 15 min	11:30 A.M.	£18.00
RN516	12:30 P.M.	1 h 25 min	1:55 P.M.	£18.00
EX670	2:00 P.M.	1 h 35 min	3:35 P.M.	£18.00
RN823	4:45 P.M.	1 h 05 min	5:50 P.M.	£20.00

Purchasing tickets online at https://www.ntsrail.co.uk more than 24 hours before your trip entitles you to a 10 percent discount off the above-listed fares. Full-price tickets are available at all NTS Rail kiosks.

186. Who most likely is Evrim Turgut?

(A) A medical doctor
(B) An office manager
(C) A conference organizer
(D) A customer service representative

187. What does the ticket indicate about Dr. Williams' trip?

(A) She will be traveling in first class.
(B) She will be changing trains during her trip.
(C) She will be using the same ticket for her return trip.
(D) She will be able to choose where to sit.

188. Based on his availability, what train will Dr. Penfold most likely take?

(A) EX111
(B) EX224
(C) RN516
(D) RN823

189. What is suggested about Dr. Williams?

(A) She works in Manchester.
(B) She travels by train on a regular basis.
(C) She bought her ticket at a reduced price.
(D) She made her reservation at the Lancaster train station.

190. According to the schedule, what is true about the train trips?

(A) They last the same length of time.
(B) They are cheaper in the morning.
(C) They will end at the same destination.
(D) They must be purchased in person.

GO ON TO THE NEXT PAGE

Questions 191-195 refer to the following article, e-mail, and form.

Community Project to Showcase Pottersville Artists

By Laurence du Bois

POTTERSVILLE (May 21)—At the opening of this year's Small Business Fair in Pottersville Central Park yesterday, the Pottersville Chamber of Commerce announced Images of Success, a community initiative that seeks to promote Pottersville businesses by way of public art. Through the project, local artists will work with area business owners to create original murals on storefronts throughout the city.

To apply, business owners must submit a description of their business's role in the community and document that their business has been in its current location for at least two years. Artists interested in participating must complete an application in which they describe their connection to Pottersville and submit samples of their own original artwork.

Both business owners and artists should submit applications to Timothy Freel at tfreel@pottersvillecoc.gov by June 15. The city will reimburse artists for approved supplies up to a limit of $150.

To:	Timothy Freel
From:	Haruka Goto
Date:	June 24
Subject:	Images of Success inquiry
Attachment:	Draft #2

Dear Mr. Freel,

It was a pleasure meeting with you earlier this week at Jam Café to talk about the design for the Images of Success mural project. I hadn't been to Jam Café since it reopened, and it was great to see the finished renovations. In fact, the owner of the café recently bought one of my paintings to display in the café.

As you suggested, I have adjusted the color scheme to include only the colors from Jam Café's interior. Please let me know as soon as possible whether you would like me to make additional changes.

Best,

Haruka Goto

Pottersville Chamber of Commerce Reimbursement Form

Complete the entire form and attach a record of the purchase. Allow two weeks for processing.

Name: Haruka Goto

Date: June 25

Event: Images of Success

Description:

Supplies purchased at Pottersville Art Supply for Images of Success mural project.

Copy of receipt dated June 24 attached.

Product	Unit Price	Quantity	Total Price
Soft green spray paint, 18 oz. can	$11.99	2	$23.98
Emerald green paint, ½ gallon	$18.99	1	$18.99
Forest green paint, 1 gallon	$34.99	1	$34.99
Set of paintbrushes	$24.99	1	$24.99
	Total (including tax)		$111.14

Approved by: T. Freel **Approval Date:** July 3

191. According to the article, where will artists display their work?

(A) In Pottersville Central Park
(B) At area businesses
(C) At the Chamber of Commerce
(D) On government Web sites

192. What is the purpose of the e-mail?

(A) To request approval of a design
(B) To extend an offer of employment
(C) To place an order for art materials
(D) To arrange an appointment

193. What is indicated about the supplies Ms. Goto purchased?

(A) They were ordered online.
(B) They are not sold in Pottersville.
(C) Their cost will be reimbursed in full.
(D) Their approval has been denied.

194. What needs to be included with the form?

(A) A tax statement
(B) A copy of the design
(C) The project application
(D) The sales receipt

195. What is most likely true about Jam Café?

(A) It sells local artwork.
(B) Its logo was designed by Ms. Goto.
(C) It is closed for remodeling.
(D) It has a green interior.

TEST 7

GO ON TO THE NEXT PAGE

Questions 196-200 refer to the following Web page, e-mail, and article.

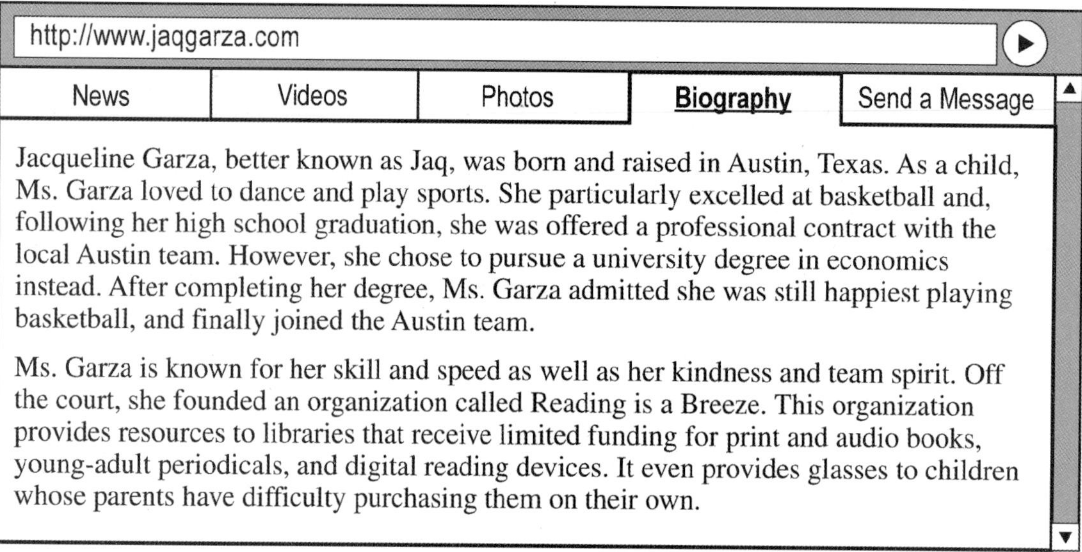
http://www.jaqgarza.com

News | Videos | Photos | **Biography** | Send a Message

Jacqueline Garza, better known as Jaq, was born and raised in Austin, Texas. As a child, Ms. Garza loved to dance and play sports. She particularly excelled at basketball and, following her high school graduation, she was offered a professional contract with the local Austin team. However, she chose to pursue a university degree in economics instead. After completing her degree, Ms. Garza admitted she was still happiest playing basketball, and finally joined the Austin team.

Ms. Garza is known for her skill and speed as well as her kindness and team spirit. Off the court, she founded an organization called Reading is a Breeze. This organization provides resources to libraries that receive limited funding for print and audio books, young-adult periodicals, and digital reading devices. It even provides glasses to children whose parents have difficulty purchasing them on their own.

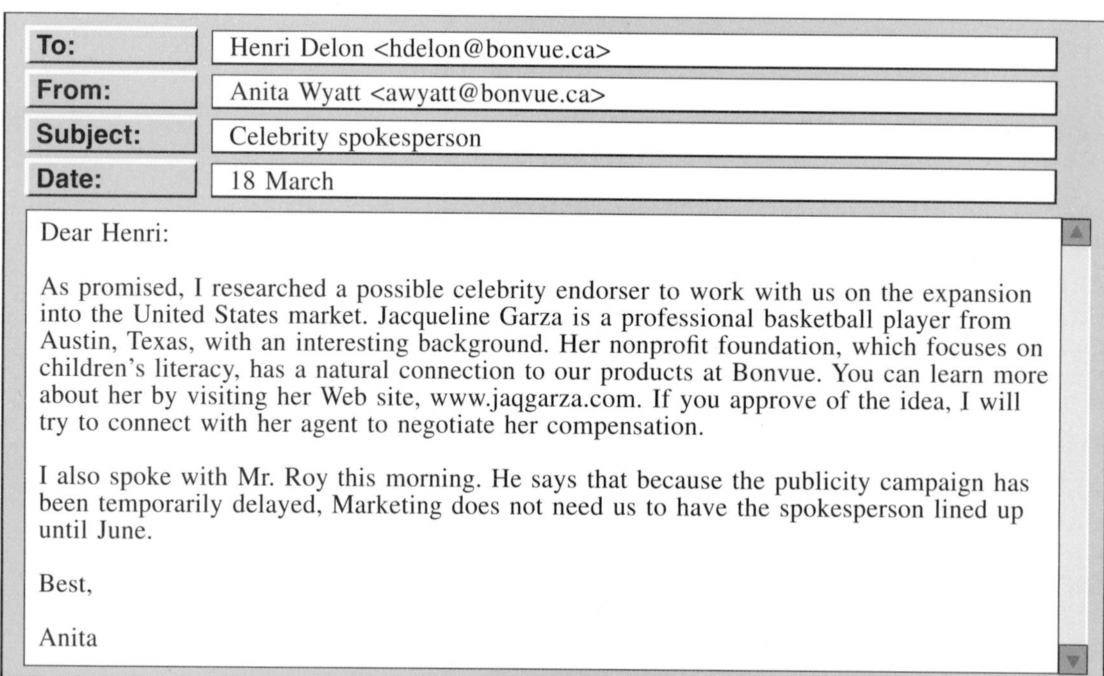
To: Henri Delon <hdelon@bonvue.ca>

From: Anita Wyatt <awyatt@bonvue.ca>

Subject: Celebrity spokesperson

Date: 18 March

Dear Henri:

As promised, I researched a possible celebrity endorser to work with us on the expansion into the United States market. Jacqueline Garza is a professional basketball player from Austin, Texas, with an interesting background. Her nonprofit foundation, which focuses on children's literacy, has a natural connection to our products at Bonvue. You can learn more about her by visiting her Web site, www.jaqgarza.com. If you approve of the idea, I will try to connect with her agent to negotiate her compensation.

I also spoke with Mr. Roy this morning. He says that because the publicity campaign has been temporarily delayed, Marketing does not need us to have the spokesperson lined up until June.

Best,

Anita

Bonvue Expands into the U.S.

Austin (May 11)—Bonvue, the French designer eyewear company, has announced its entry into the United States market. Austin-based basketball star Jacqueline "Jaq" Garza has signed up as the company's celebrity endorser. A video clip featuring Ms. Garza announcing the collaboration was released on Monday, and a full line of advertisements will be rolled out next week.

Founded and headquartered in Paris, the eyewear company is currently under the direction of CEO Martin Oliveira. Bonvue expanded into Canadian retail stores eight years ago in Ottawa. The company's popular eyeglasses and sunglasses will now be sold at stores across the U.S.

196. According to the Web page, what did Ms. Garza receive before joining a professional team?

(A) A university degree
(B) A donation of books
(C) Dance lessons
(D) Funding for a project

197. Why does Ms. Wyatt consider Ms. Garza a suitable celebrity endorser?

(A) Her charity distributes eyeglasses.
(B) Her teamwork skills are strong.
(C) Bonvue is based in Austin.
(D) Bonvue makes basketball apparel.

198. What does the e-mail suggest about Mr. Roy?

(A) He is Ms. Garza's talent agent.
(B) He has visited Ms. Garza's Web page.
(C) He is a former representative for Bonvue.
(D) He works with Ms. Wyatt and Mr. Delon.

199. What is indicated about Ms. Garza?

(A) She is a longtime Bonvue customer.
(B) She does not receive money from Bonvue.
(C) She recently appeared in a movie.
(D) She joined the Bonvue publicity campaign ahead of schedule.

200. What information about Bonvue is included in the article?

(A) The number of years it has been in business
(B) The location of its head office
(C) The slogan for its advertising campaign
(D) The price of its most popular product

Stop! This is the end of the test. If you finish before time is called, you may go back to Parts 5, 6, and 7 and check your work.

토익® 정기시험
기출문제집

기출 TEST

08

READING TEST

In the Reading test, you will read a variety of texts and answer several different types of reading comprehension questions. The entire Reading test will last 75 minutes. There are three parts, and directions are given for each part. You are encouraged to answer as many questions as possible within the time allowed.

You must mark your answers on the separate answer sheet. Do not write your answers in your test book.

PART 5

Directions: A word or phrase is missing in each of the sentences below. Four answer choices are given below each sentence. Select the best answer to complete the sentence. Then mark the letter (A), (B), (C), or (D) on your answer sheet.

101. Kanelek Limited and Evensohn LLC have entered a strategic partnership to ------- their market share.

(A) increased
(B) increasing
(C) increases
(D) increase

102. Glenwick Organic Farm stands out from other farms for its environmentally ------- practices.

(A) exposed
(B) communal
(C) friendly
(D) considerable

103. Our ------- is responsible for performing quality-control reviews during production.

(A) divided
(B) division
(C) divisive
(D) dividing

104. Because of a mechanical failure in the production facility, Fizzy Bottlers will be closed ------- further notice.

(A) around
(B) through
(C) except
(D) until

105. Interviewees are asked not to talk among ------- while waiting in the reception area.

(A) themselves
(B) theirs
(C) them
(D) their

106. The accounting department reminds all staff to submit expense reports ------- after returning from a trip.

(A) very
(B) enough
(C) rather
(D) soon

107. Olayinka Boutique ------- hosts special shopping events for members of its loyalty club.

(A) occasion
(B) occasions
(C) occasional
(D) occasionally

108. For homeowners seeking to reduce their electricity bills, the energy-saving ideas in this brochure should be -------.

(A) lengthy
(B) immediate
(C) helpful
(D) perceptive

109. The Delmar Highway Department ------- an online list of current road closures.

(A) maintenance
(B) maintains
(C) maintaining
(D) is maintained

110. ------- reducing staff, management made the decision to decrease administrative bonuses.

(A) Rather than
(B) Whether
(C) Just as
(D) Namely

111. The doorways, which arch so -------, were left intact during the renovation of the historic Dersten Building.

(A) graceful
(B) grace
(C) gracefully
(D) graces

112. Ms. Maeda was ------- that her art submission was used on the cover of the firm's annual report.

(A) performed
(B) flattered
(C) welcomed
(D) challenged

113. The primary ------- is whether the cost of the car repair is reasonable considering the amount of labor involved.

(A) method
(B) relation
(C) concern
(D) source

114. Norvo Financial has built an ------- client base in a short period of time.

(A) impressive
(B) impress
(C) impressively
(D) impresses

115. We ------- all employees to wear formal business attire when meeting with clients in the office.

(A) monitor
(B) require
(C) confirm
(D) include

116. ------- Ms. Chang nor Mr. Kao received the e-mail outlining the project proposal.

(A) Both
(B) None
(C) Neither
(D) Whoever

117. In case of inclement weather, employees are encouraged to work ------- rather than travel to the office.

(A) carefully
(B) remotely
(C) eventually
(D) closely

118. Long-term maintenance fees ------- according to the type of industrial printing machine purchased.

(A) copy
(B) repair
(C) support
(D) vary

119. Ms. Kwon made it absolutely ------- that hiring decisions require her approval.

(A) clearing
(B) clear
(C) clearly
(D) cleared

120. Sookie Choi's latest children's book is being ------- by Chung-He Park.

(A) illustrating
(B) illustrated
(C) illustration
(D) illustrates

GO ON TO THE NEXT PAGE

121. The Stoneport Gallery is hosting a ------- next week to showcase the works of sculptor Fabrice Pepin.

(A) scene
(B) society
(C) formality
(D) reception

122. Mr. Soto will run 5 kilometers every other day in order to ------- for the Leesburg Corporate Challenge half marathon.

(A) translate
(B) listen
(C) wait
(D) train

123. All employees are expected to behave ------- when they are traveling on company business.

(A) responsible
(B) responsibly
(C) responsibility
(D) responsibleness

124. ------- he is now retired, Mr. Matilla is able to pursue his hobby of woodworking.

(A) During
(B) Therefore
(C) When
(D) Because

125. ------- for press coverage of the music festival will receive official responses by June 30.

(A) Applies
(B) Application
(C) Applicants
(D) Applying

126. All employees should back up crucial data ------- switching over to the new software system on August 5.

(A) before
(B) of
(C) what
(D) so

127. A label on each box should indicate the production date as well as the place of ------- of the contents.

(A) importance
(B) safety
(C) foundation
(D) origin

128. Ms. Jha assured the client that ------- would deliver the contract that afternoon.

(A) her
(B) she
(C) hers
(D) herself

129. During negotiations, management appeared ------- to the idea of increasing the staff's wages.

(A) agree
(B) agreement
(C) agreeable
(D) agrees

130. Employees ------- several departments have been encouraged to minimize costs.

(A) across
(B) into
(C) between
(D) despite

PART 6

Directions: Read the texts that follow. A word, phrase, or sentence is missing in parts of each text. Four answer choices for each question are given below the text. Select the best answer to complete the text. Then mark the letter (A), (B), (C), or (D) on your answer sheet.

Questions 131-134 refer to the following advertisement.

Italy has so much to offer—museums, gardens, beautiful scenery, and great food. For one low price, the All-Italy Pass provides access to more than a hundred popular attractions across the country. The more you ------- **131.** it, the better value you will get.

------- **132.** . Passes must be purchased online before you leave your home country and are activated when you visit your first attraction. They will remain ------- **133.** for 21 days.

Purchase of the pass ------- **134.** includes a decorative travel pin and full-color souvenir guidebook.

131. (A) user
(B) using
(C) use
(D) used

132. (A) The offer is only available to international visitors.
(B) Tourists cannot see all the sites in a week.
(C) The attractions are very crowded in the summer.
(D) Several companies offer tour guides.

133. (A) open
(B) valid
(C) constant
(D) ordinary

134. (A) besides
(B) also
(C) after
(D) beyond

TEST 8

GO ON TO THE NEXT PAGE

Questions 135-138 refer to the following e-mail.

To: Weiyi Shan <wshan@strategiccomm.org>
From: Arvin Flores <aflores@floresmanufacturing.com>
Date: April 5
Subject: March 28 workshops

Dear Mr. Shan,

I am writing to share our -------(135.) for the workshops Alana Hughes delivered at our corporate headquarters on March 28. Some employees -------(136.) a concern regarding the usefulness of improvisation training in a business setting. These same employees participated fully throughout the day and even inquired about the possibility of follow-up sessions. We asked participants to complete our company's evaluation form -------(137.) to better gauge the effectiveness of the workshops. Results were mainly positive, with 90 percent of participants stating that their communication skills are now stronger. -------(138.). Please let me know if you would like to discuss the workshops in more detail.

Best regards,

Arvin Flores

135. (A) appreciate
(B) appreciative
(C) appreciated
(D) appreciation

136. (A) express
(B) are expressing
(C) were to be expressed
(D) had expressed

137. (A) afterward
(B) often
(C) since
(D) instead

138. (A) The workshop will be rescheduled for later in the week.
(B) A few participants said they would have liked more practice.
(C) An additional workshop in team building is occasionally offered.
(D) We will provide you with an invoice requesting payment.

Questions 139-142 refer to the following e-mail.

To: Li Cheung <lcheung@broadwayos.com>
From: Travis Juno <tjuno@hiraokaarchitecture.com>
Date: November 18
Subject: Monthly order

Dear Mr. Cheung:

We need to make an adjustment to Hiraoka Architecture's ------- **139.** order. Fewer of our presenters are using dry-erase whiteboards in their presentations, and as a result, we are using fewer BR1608 dry-erase markers. ------- **140.**, I would like to reduce the number in our order to only twelve of those beginning next month. Please raise the number of GN2280 all-purpose markers to fourteen.

We will eventually phase out the BR1608 markers entirely. However, I ------- **141.** you plenty of notice before then, probably by late next year.

Can you send a statement with the revised monthly bill? ------- **142.**.

Best,

Travis Juno
Hiraoka Architecture

139. (A) still
(B) overdue
(C) standing
(D) redundant

140. (A) Therefore
(B) Typically
(C) Similarly
(D) Nevertheless

141. (A) give
(B) have been given
(C) gave
(D) will give

142. (A) We have not yet used up our inventory.
(B) You can find it in your e-mail inbox.
(C) Our finance department will need it.
(D) Employees are happy with the product.

TEST 8

GO ON TO THE NEXT PAGE

Questions 143-146 refer to the following letter.

13 March

Dennis Carrera
Lejos Plumbing and Heating
San Antonio, Texas

Dear Mr. Carrera:

Congratulations! Mallorca Construction ------- **143.** the bid of Lejos Plumbing and Heating to provide enhancements to the County Courthouse. Your workers will have access to the ------- **144.** on May 5. As specified by the district building code, Lejos Plumbing and Heating will be responsible for securing the required permits. The enclosed plan outlines the scope of the project. ------- **145.**, the document lists the other contractors we are partnering with, and it reveals how your firm's work fits into the overall project.

We are requesting no significant adjustments to the blueprints and specifications you submitted with your proposal. Please contact my office if you need additional information. ------- **146.**.

Sincerely,

Petra Rojas, Manager
Mallorca Construction Ltd.

Enclosure

143. (A) may accept
(B) would accept
(C) has accepted
(D) was accepting

144. (A) site
(B) data
(C) results
(D) product

145. (A) However
(B) In addition
(C) As a result
(D) On the other hand

146. (A) Unfortunately, your bid arrived after the deadline.
(B) We will inform you of our final decision soon.
(C) Best wishes again on your recent expansion.
(D) We will provide it to you promptly.

PART 7

Directions: In this part you will read a selection of texts, such as magazine and newspaper articles, e-mails, and instant messages. Each text or set of texts is followed by several questions. Select the best answer for each question and mark the letter (A), (B), (C), or (D) on your answer sheet.

Questions 147-148 refer to the following notice.

Thank you for choosing the River Street Hotel!

In an effort to bring our guests the very best experience, we've extended our complimentary shuttle bus service to include the city's downtown area. The shuttle loops around the downtown's most popular tourist attractions with several stops, including all historic sites, the outdoor market, and the theater district. While these destinations are all within walking distance from the hotel, the shuttle will allow you to reach them more quickly. The route is ideal for first-time and regular visitors. The shuttle will also make additional stops during special events and festivals.

Shuttle schedules are posted in the hotel lobby. As with our airport service, rewards club members can book a shuttle ahead of time.

River Street Hotel

147. What is being offered?

(A) A free transportation service
(B) Discounted passes to a festival
(C) Membership in a rewards program
(D) A guided tour of the theater district

148. What is suggested about the River Street Hotel?

(A) It is a historic building.
(B) It is a highly rated hotel.
(C) It is near the city's downtown area.
(D) It is popular with business travelers.

TEST 8

GO ON TO THE NEXT PAGE

Questions 149-150 refer to the following text-message chain.

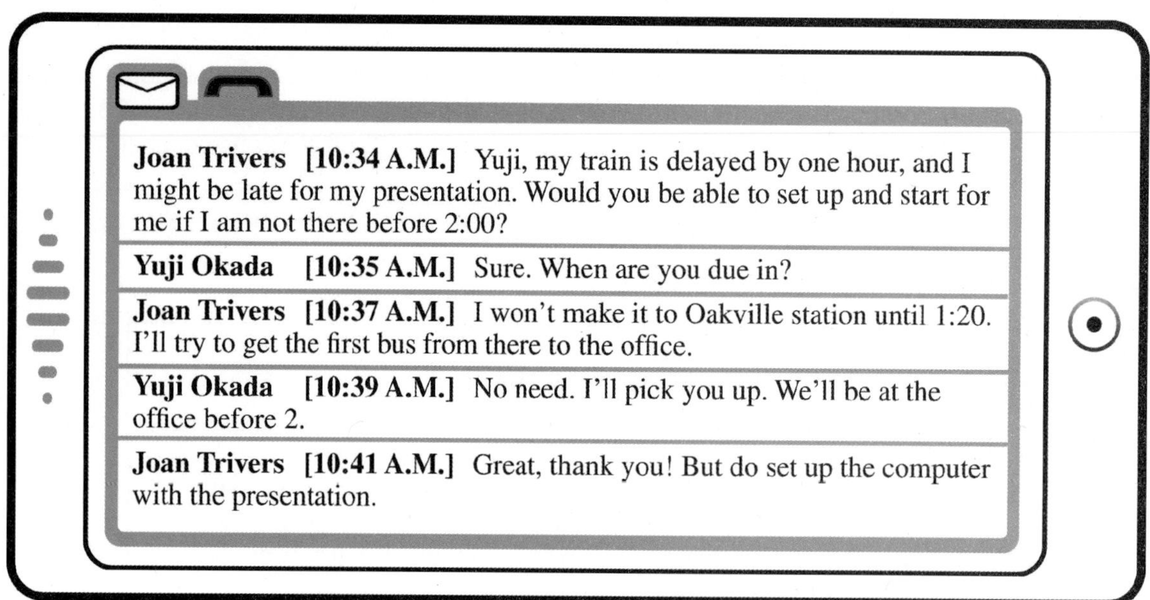

Joan Trivers [10:34 A.M.] Yuji, my train is delayed by one hour, and I might be late for my presentation. Would you be able to set up and start for me if I am not there before 2:00?

Yuji Okada [10:35 A.M.] Sure. When are you due in?

Joan Trivers [10:37 A.M.] I won't make it to Oakville station until 1:20. I'll try to get the first bus from there to the office.

Yuji Okada [10:39 A.M.] No need. I'll pick you up. We'll be at the office before 2.

Joan Trivers [10:41 A.M.] Great, thank you! But do set up the computer with the presentation.

149. What is Ms. Trivers concerned about?

(A) Arriving at the office by a certain time
(B) Missing a colleague's presentation
(C) Catching a connecting train
(D) Finding a bus station

150. At 10:39 A.M., what does Mr. Okada most likely mean when he writes, "No need"?

(A) They will not have to go to Oakville.
(B) They will not need a computer.
(C) Ms. Trivers does not need to take a bus.
(D) Ms. Trivers does not have to come to the office.

Questions 151-153 refer to the following article.

Sheldon Business News

SHELDON (August 4)—Downing Way announced on Tuesday that it will be creating many new jobs in the city of Sheldon. The restaurant's spokesperson, Daniel Vacher, said the restaurant is slated to open on September 26 at 1091 Downing Boulevard. Management is looking to fill 50 positions before the doors open. Positions range from servers to pastry chefs to managers. Because of the number of positions, Downing Way will host a one-day career fair on August 16. Open interviews will be conducted at the event.

Downing Way's newest location will be the only restaurant in Sheldon that harvests its own vegetables and herbs in a garden on the premises. It also specializes in regional cuisine. "We are pleased to be able to contribute to growing the local job base," said Marie Fontaine, founder and CEO of Downing Way. "We are looking to hire team members with a passion for food and first-class hospitality skills. We offer our staff a competitive pay rate and excellent benefits." Interested candidates who are unable to attend the career fair may instead apply online at downingway-sheldon.com.

151. What is the article about?

(A) The relocation of a restaurant
(B) Job opportunities at a new restaurant
(C) Local gardening trends
(D) Training to develop new job skills

152. What is indicated about the event on August 16 ?

(A) It is intended for local restaurant owners.
(B) Job seekers must attend the event to be interviewed.
(C) Attendees will sample representative restaurant dishes.
(D) There will be 50 available positions.

153. How is Downing Way unique?

(A) It grows its own produce.
(B) It offers the best wages.
(C) It has been in the same family for generations.
(D) Its Web site has won a number of industry awards.

TEST 8

GO ON TO THE NEXT PAGE

Questions 154-157 refer to the following memo.

MEMO

To: Customer Service Personnel
Subject: Meeting next Friday
Date: November 19

Last week we conducted a study to gather opinions about our customer service. The data are in and they look good. Most people expressed satisfaction with their communication with our representatives. Their questions about packaging services, shipping charges, and the status of their parcels were answered professionally and promptly.

One area that we need to address is the low number of referrals. Few customers we approached reported telling others about our services. Based on the answers, most people are repeat customers who always rely on us for their shipping needs, or they choose us based on our advertising. Clearly, we fail to request referrals properly.

Therefore, our meeting next Friday will center around this topic. I will design materials and practice activities to correct this shortcoming. But I would also appreciate it if you could come up with some creative ways to improve our referral rate. Send me your suggestions and I will be sure to include them in our discussion. I look forward to hearing from you all.

Janice Wells, Senior Customer Service Coordinator

154. Where does Ms. Wells probably work?

(A) At a market research firm
(B) At a delivery company
(C) At an insurance agency
(D) At an advertising company

155. What information did Ms. Wells review?

(A) Prices for materials
(B) Shipping dates
(C) Survey results
(D) Sales figures

156. What problem does Ms. Wells mention?

(A) Few customers recommend the company to others.
(B) Some orders were not processed promptly.
(C) Advertising expenses have increased.
(D) The customer service department is understaffed.

157. What are staff asked to do?

(A) Complete an online form
(B) Recruit additional customer service staff
(C) Propose an alternate day for a meeting
(D) Submit ideas for a discussion

Questions 158-159 refer to the following e-mail.

E-mail

To:	Barbara Treloar <btreloar@questor.ca>
From:	Amy Dunstan <adunstan@bluetern.co.nz>
Subject:	Cover
Date:	20 April

Dear Barbara:

You will be receiving an e-mail from the Blue Tern marketing team before the end of the week. The e-mail describes the marketing process, and it gives you a link to an online questionnaire for authors. Although the design team will have the final say on your book's cover, you do have some input. Do you feel strongly about anything that you do or do not want to see on the cover? Please let me know.

Sincerely,

Amy Dunstan
Senior Developmental Editor

158. Who most likely is Ms. Treloar?

(A) An author
(B) A publicist
(C) An advertising executive
(D) A marketing team member

159. According to the e-mail, what should soon arrive?

(A) A book
(B) A cover photo
(C) Some editorial suggestions
(D) Some marketing information

TEST 8

GO ON TO THE NEXT PAGE

Questions 160-162 refer to the following letter.

Ms. Julia Gandarillas
1896 Bartlett Avenue
Southfield, MI 48075

November 10

Dear Ms. Gandarillas,

Thank you for renewing your contract with Liu Web Works. We have enclosed your quarterly invoice for our Web site hosting services. — [1] —. You'll notice that the amount of $20.00 was added to the regular maintenance cost. — [2] —. As a reminder, Liu Web Works performed a major upgrade in June to ensure that your Web site is compatible with the latest devices. Your customers will now see and interact with the same content, regardless of whether they are using a computer, tablet, or smartphone. — [3] —.

Please let us know how these enhancements have affected your Web site and business. — [4] —. Complete our online survey by logging in to your account with us and clicking the link that appears at the top of the page. As a token of our appreciation for your suggestions, you will receive a 10 percent discount on a future bill.

Thanks for your continued business!
Shaun Liu
Liu Web Works

160. Why did the fee change?

(A) Liu Web Works removed a discount.
(B) Liu Web Works improved its services.
(C) Ms. Gandarillas added an online store to her Web site.
(D) Ms. Gandarillas requested additional equipment.

161. What does Mr. Liu ask Ms. Gandarillas to do?

(A) Send a reminder to her customers
(B) Renew her yearly contract
(C) Update her account information
(D) Complete a feedback form

162. In which of the positions marked [1], [2], [3], and [4] does the following sentence best belong?

"We e-mailed you in May about this increase."

(A) [1]
(B) [2]
(C) [3]
(D) [4]

Questions 163-166 refer to the following online chat discussion.

Jorge Avila 10:18 A.M.
You may have noticed that the air-conditioning is not functioning in parts of the building.

Simon Miano 10:19 A.M.
I noticed. The temperature and humidity are rising fast in here.

Jorge Avila 10:20 A.M.
A condenser is down, and the fix is not quick or cheap. The last time one broke it took a week to get a replacement. I'm glad that it's not too hot this week. The technician is on the way, but for now, feel free to plug in a fan.

Simon Miano 10:24 A.M.
I'm afraid the computer servers may overheat. Do we have any portable units we could set up in the Information Technology office?

April Denner 10:25 A.M.
We really can't afford to lose them.

Jorge Avila 10:26 A.M.
Not in this building. With Ms. Denner's OK, we could use the van to pick up the ones in the warehouse in Mindones. I think we have 3 or 4 there. But the earliest I could get back is tonight.

April Denner 10:28 A.M.
Jorge, I'm authorizing you to make an emergency purchase of portable AC units for the IT office right away. Please decide on the number of units needed, determine the cost, and report back to me as soon as you have set up the purchase.

Jorge Avila 10:28 A.M.
I'll get started on that now.

April Denner 10:29 A.M.
If you can't get a local appliance outlet to deliver by the afternoon, send someone in the delivery van to pick them up.

163. What is the problem?

(A) The delivery van needs repairs.
(B) The cooling system is not working.
(C) Condensers are too expensive to replace.
(D) Authorization for a purchase has been denied.

164. At 10:26 A.M., what does Mr. Avila mean when he writes, "Not in this building"?

(A) The technician is not available.
(B) He does not have an office in IT.
(C) The computer servers are fine where he is.
(D) There are no portable air conditioners nearby.

165. Why most likely does Ms. Denner decide against using the units in Mindones?

(A) There are not enough of them.
(B) They will take too long to arrive.
(C) They do not work effectively.
(D) There is not enough space for them.

166. What will most likely happen next?

(A) Mr. Avila will arrange a purchase.
(B) The fans will be delivered to the IT office.
(C) Mr. Miano will drive to the warehouse.
(D) The technician will replace the servers.

GO ON TO THE NEXT PAGE

Questions 167-168 refer to the following e-mail.

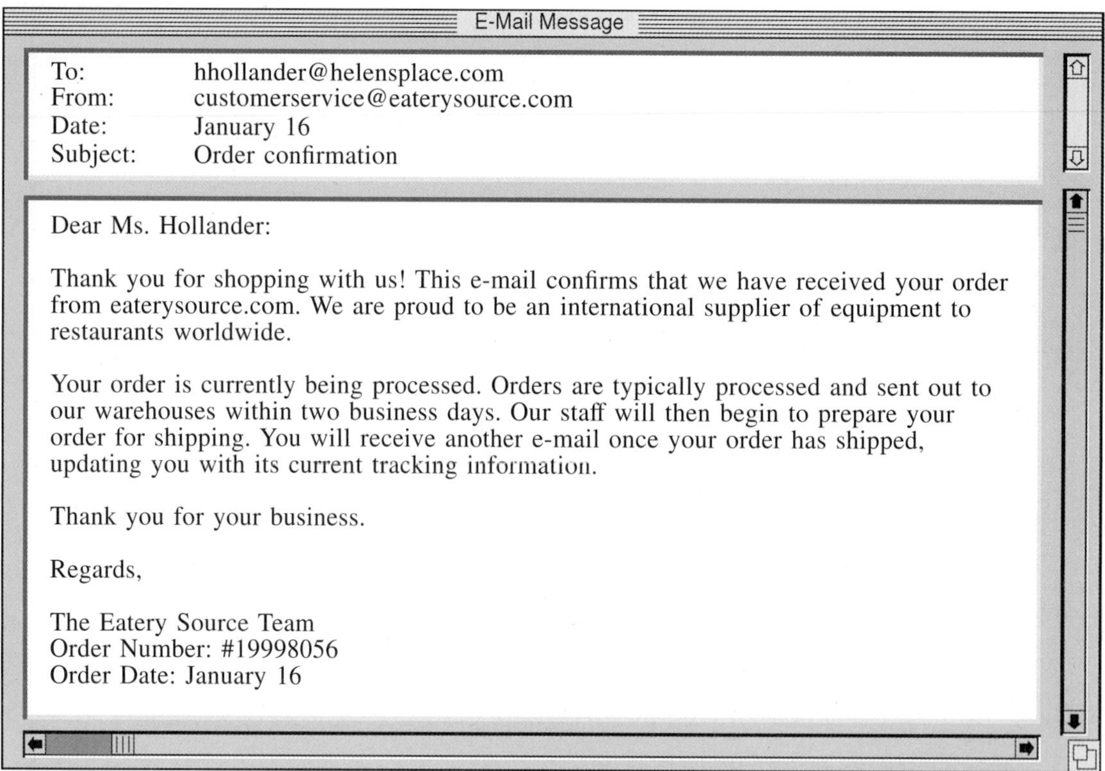

E-Mail Message

To: hhollander@helensplace.com
From: customerservice@eaterysource.com
Date: January 16
Subject: Order confirmation

Dear Ms. Hollander:

Thank you for shopping with us! This e-mail confirms that we have received your order from eaterysource.com. We are proud to be an international supplier of equipment to restaurants worldwide.

Your order is currently being processed. Orders are typically processed and sent out to our warehouses within two business days. Our staff will then begin to prepare your order for shipping. You will receive another e-mail once your order has shipped, updating you with its current tracking information.

Thank you for your business.

Regards,

The Eatery Source Team
Order Number: #19998056
Order Date: January 16

167. For what type of business does Ms. Hollander most likely work?

(A) A restaurant
(B) A supermarket
(C) A food supplier
(D) A shipping company

168. According to the e-mail, when will Ms. Hollander receive another e-mail from Eatery Source?

(A) When she makes a payment
(B) When she places another order
(C) When new products become available
(D) When her order has left the warehouse

Questions 169-171 refer to the following e-mail.

From:	Tronica LLC Customer Service
To:	Nossis Software Subscribers
Date:	14 September
Subject:	Version 3.1

Dear Nossis Software Subscribers,

Later this month, Tronica LLC will release version 3.1 of Nossis, our online software for creating commercial artwork. Beginning at 11 p.m. GMT on 29 September, Nossis will be unavailable while our technicians roll out the new version. You need take no action. We will back up all portfolios containing customer files stored in our online database; thus, they will be fully protected during the process. All users will be notified on the morning of 30 September upon completion of the process. After receiving the notification, customers can resume using Nossis.

New features include a redesigned interface for streamlined workflow, innovative design themes, new backgrounds and fonts, and interactive tracking tools for markups and revisions. We are confident that you will enjoy these new features.

Sincerely,

Tronica LLC Customer Service

169. What is the purpose of the e-mail?

(A) To advertise a sale
(B) To attract new subscribers
(C) To explain how to use a program
(D) To inform customers about changes

170. What does the e-mail indicate will happen on September 29 ?

(A) A computer application will become inaccessible.
(B) Tronica LLC will hire new technicians.
(C) An e-mail will be sent to Nossis users.
(D) New software will be made available for purchase.

171. The phrase "roll out" in paragraph 1, line 3, is closest in meaning to

(A) flatten
(B) remove
(C) introduce
(D) spread across

GO ON TO THE NEXT PAGE

Questions 172-175 refer to the following article.

Saying Yes to Financial Success

EDINBURGH (3 April)—Yolanda Abascal had intended to study fashion design when she first entered university in Manchester 30 years ago. But while working one summer at a small clothing boutique, she discovered a love for retail. — [1] —. To pursue her new dream, she earned a business degree instead and opened a small store in her hometown of Edinburgh called Say Yes To Yolanda.

Fast-forward to today, and Ms. Abascal's small store has expanded to a successful enterprise that earns millions of pounds each year. — [2] —. This success is in part due to the magic of Vihaan Kulkarni, whom Ms. Abascal hired four years ago to develop a parallel virtual store, YesYolanda.com. It was Mr. Kulkarni's idea to rename the flagship store Yes Yolanda to match its digital identity.

Ms. Abascal is a strong proponent of personal interaction, and she loves engaging with her customers. — [3] —. However, she realizes that an online presence is important. Yes Yolanda expects earnings from online sales alone to rise to more than £140 million this year. Nearly two-thirds of these sales will come from outside Scotland, mainly the United States, Singapore, and Australia.

Yes Yolanda's workforce has expanded accordingly. Besides hiring people with technical skills to update and run the Web site, the company has just added an in-house photography studio.

"The studio ensures that items are photographed in a timely fashion for online display," said Ms. Abascal. "This is a necessity, since new products are added every week." — [4] —.

Although Ms. Abascal says she does not know what the future holds, it would seem that the only direction for Yes Yolanda is up.

172. What is the purpose of the article?

(A) To profile several local companies
(B) To discuss fashion trends in Scotland
(C) To illustrate how a business has grown
(D) To advertise a new photography service

173. What is indicated about Yes Yolanda?

(A) Its sales have held steady for years.
(B) It opened its first store in Manchester.
(C) Its Web designer recently won an award.
(D) It used to be known by a different name.

174. The word "fashion" in paragraph 5, line 2, is closest in meaning to

(A) form
(B) style
(C) event
(D) manner

175. In which of the positions marked [1], [2], [3], and [4] does the following sentence best belong?

"She still believes she can best meet their needs when they shop at her physical store."

(A) [1]
(B) [2]
(C) [3]
(D) [4]

TEST 8

GO ON TO THE NEXT PAGE

Questions 176-180 refer to the following online form and e-mail.

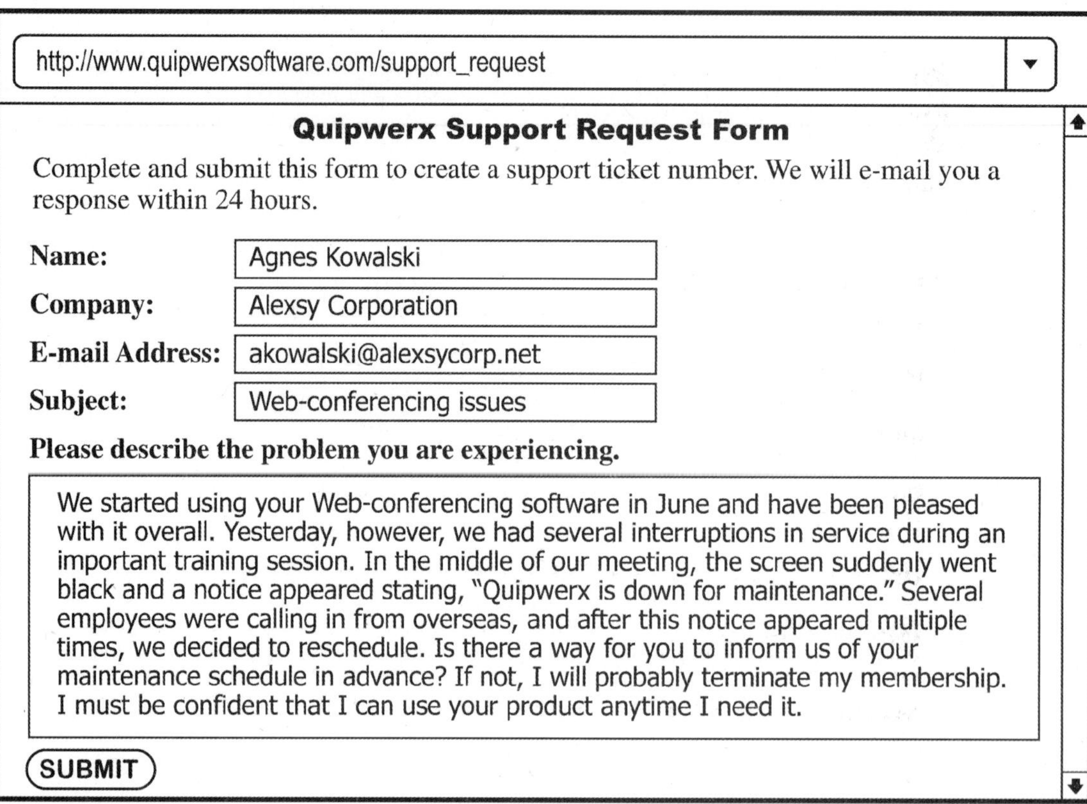

http://www.quipwerxsoftware.com/support_request

Quipwerx Support Request Form

Complete and submit this form to create a support ticket number. We will e-mail you a response within 24 hours.

Name: Agnes Kowalski

Company: Alexsy Corporation

E-mail Address: akowalski@alexsycorp.net

Subject: Web-conferencing issues

Please describe the problem you are experiencing.

We started using your Web-conferencing software in June and have been pleased with it overall. Yesterday, however, we had several interruptions in service during an important training session. In the middle of our meeting, the screen suddenly went black and a notice appeared stating, "Quipwerx is down for maintenance." Several employees were calling in from overseas, and after this notice appeared multiple times, we decided to reschedule. Is there a way for you to inform us of your maintenance schedule in advance? If not, I will probably terminate my membership. I must be confident that I can use your product anytime I need it.

SUBMIT

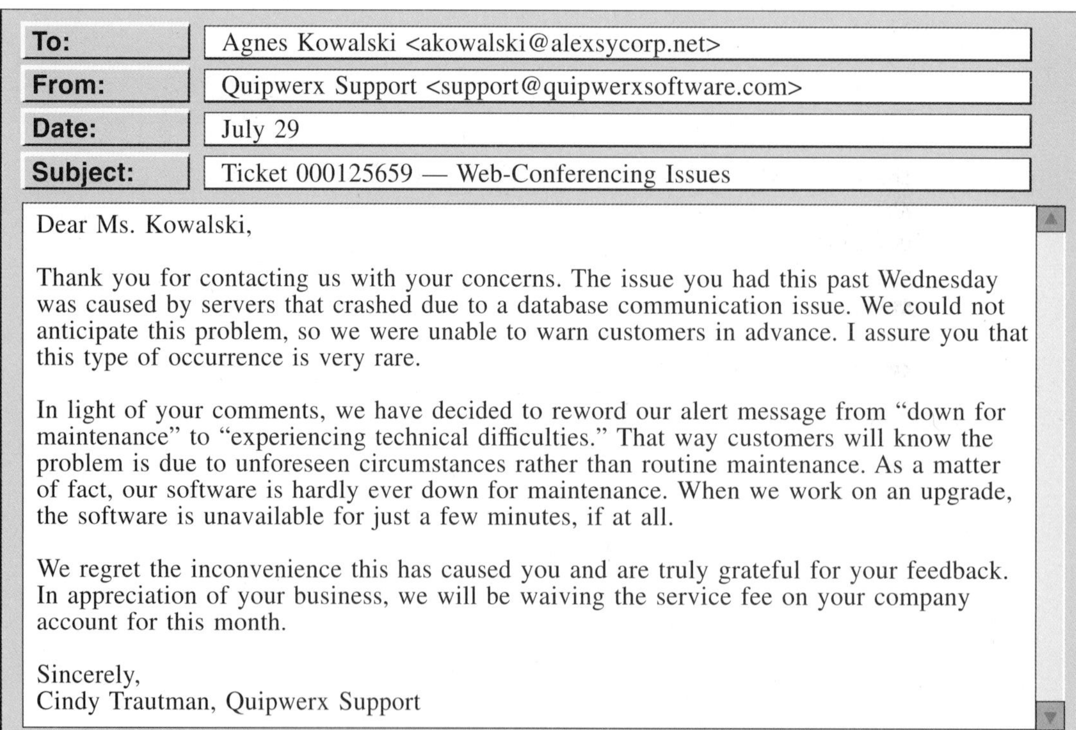

To: Agnes Kowalski <akowalski@alexsycorp.net>

From: Quipwerx Support <support@quipwerxsoftware.com>

Date: July 29

Subject: Ticket 000125659 — Web-Conferencing Issues

Dear Ms. Kowalski,

Thank you for contacting us with your concerns. The issue you had this past Wednesday was caused by servers that crashed due to a database communication issue. We could not anticipate this problem, so we were unable to warn customers in advance. I assure you that this type of occurrence is very rare.

In light of your comments, we have decided to reword our alert message from "down for maintenance" to "experiencing technical difficulties." That way customers will know the problem is due to unforeseen circumstances rather than routine maintenance. As a matter of fact, our software is hardly ever down for maintenance. When we work on an upgrade, the software is unavailable for just a few minutes, if at all.

We regret the inconvenience this has caused you and are truly grateful for your feedback. In appreciation of your business, we will be waiving the service fee on your company account for this month.

Sincerely,
Cindy Trautman, Quipwerx Support

176. What does Ms. Kowalski request on the online form?

(A) A membership cancellation
(B) A maintenance calendar
(C) A call from customer support
(D) A new time for a training session

177. What is suggested about Ms. Kowalski?

(A) She used to work for Quipwerx.
(B) She joined Alexsy Corporation in June.
(C) She uses Web-conferencing software regularly.
(D) She conducts training sessions every Wednesday.

178. What is Ms. Kowalski's complaint regarding Quipwerx conferencing software?

(A) It does not serve her current purposes.
(B) It is incompatible with her computer.
(C) It is unreliable.
(D) It cannot be used by her overseas clients.

179. What does Ms. Trautman say Quipwerx will change?

(A) Its malfunction message
(B) Its customer agreement
(C) Its Web-conferencing software
(D) Its maintenance schedule

180. What is indicated about Alexsy Corporation?

(A) It services its system regularly.
(B) It hires new staff every week.
(C) It recently upgraded its software.
(D) It pays a monthly fee to Quipwerx.

GO ON TO THE NEXT PAGE

Questions 181-185 refer to the following e-mail and instructions.

From:	He-Ran Kim, Wheeling Travel Associates
To:	Mihir Sukbara
Subject:	Travel Plans for Sports Trade Show
Sent:	3 July
Attachment:	Sydney-Perth Itinerary

Dear Mr. Sukbara,

Per your request, I have reserved your round-trip ticket to Perth. Departure from Sydney is 20 July, and return from Perth is 24 July, which should perfectly accommodate your 21–23 July Trade Show. The itinerary is attached.

In reply to your question whether your samples can be brought along, the skis and snowboards can be checked as luggage. My contact at Canberra Airways tells me there is a $75 AUD fee for each piece of oversized luggage. If this fee is paid in advance, oversized items can be dropped at the express drop-off kiosk when you check in. Make sure that your items do not exceed the airline's maximum allowable weight and size requirements. Please let me know how many items you wish to check so that I can make the prepayment for you.

Best,

He-Ran Kim
Wheeling Travel Associates

Canberra Airways

Express Luggage Drop-Off Service—Instructions

Upon arrival at the airport, please follow these simple steps:

1. Print out your boarding pass at any of our check-in kiosks as you enter the terminal.
2. Follow directions to the express drop-off kiosk and place your items on the scales. Show your photo ID and boarding pass to one of our agents, who will ask how many bags you are checking.
3. Our agent will tag your bags and return your papers so you can proceed to Security without delay.

NOTE: Express drop-off service is currently available only in Sydney, Melbourne, and Brisbane.

181. According to the e-mail, why is Mr. Sukbara most likely going to Perth?

(A) To compete in a sports event
(B) To negotiate a corporate merger
(C) To promote his company's products
(D) To visit clients near the city

182. What is true about Mr. Sukbara's oversized luggage?

(A) It consists of sports equipment.
(B) It exceeds the weight limit.
(C) It will be packed by Ms. Kim.
(D) It was purchased at a trade show.

183. What does Ms. Kim offer to do for Mr. Sukbara?

(A) Make hotel reservations
(B) Handle a fee
(C) Schedule a delivery
(D) Arrange shuttle transportation

184. What is indicated about a boarding pass?

(A) It is attached to Ms. Kim's e-mail.
(B) It must be printed at home.
(C) It can be obtained only from an airline agent.
(D) It must be presented at a drop-off kiosk.

185. What is suggested about Mr. Sukbara regarding his return flight?

(A) Mr. Sukbara will be flying back to Sydney overnight.
(B) Mr. Sukbara will be purchasing his own return ticket.
(C) Mr. Sukbara will be unable to use the express drop-off service.
(D) Mr. Sukbara will be unable to modify his itinerary.

GO ON TO THE NEXT PAGE

Questions 186-190 refer to the following Web page, e-mail, and article

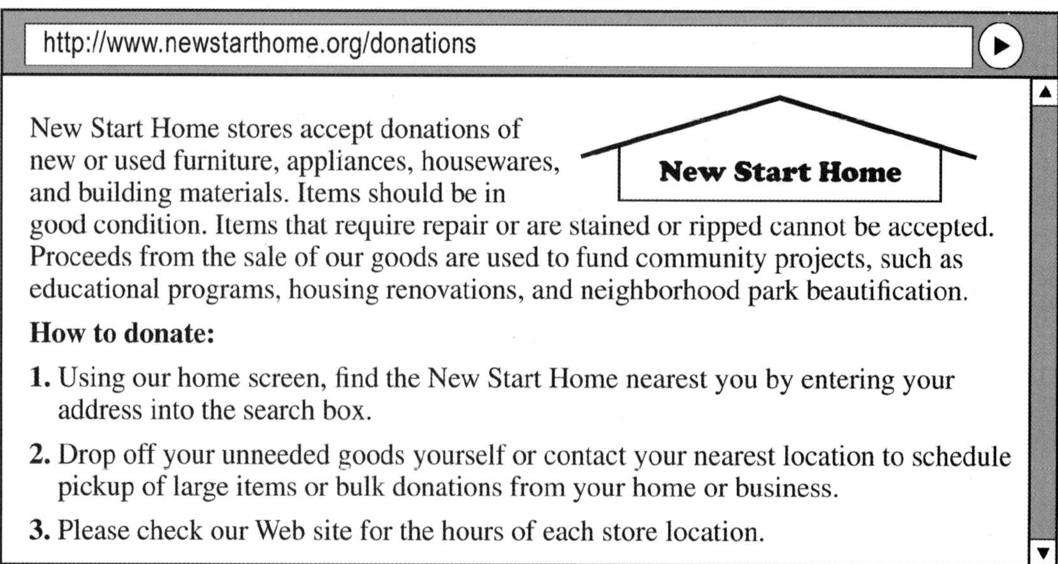

http://www.newstarthome.org/donations

New Start Home

New Start Home stores accept donations of new or used furniture, appliances, housewares, and building materials. Items should be in good condition. Items that require repair or are stained or ripped cannot be accepted. Proceeds from the sale of our goods are used to fund community projects, such as educational programs, housing renovations, and neighborhood park beautification.

How to donate:

1. Using our home screen, find the New Start Home nearest you by entering your address into the search box.

2. Drop off your unneeded goods yourself or contact your nearest location to schedule pickup of large items or bulk donations from your home or business.

3. Please check our Web site for the hours of each store location.

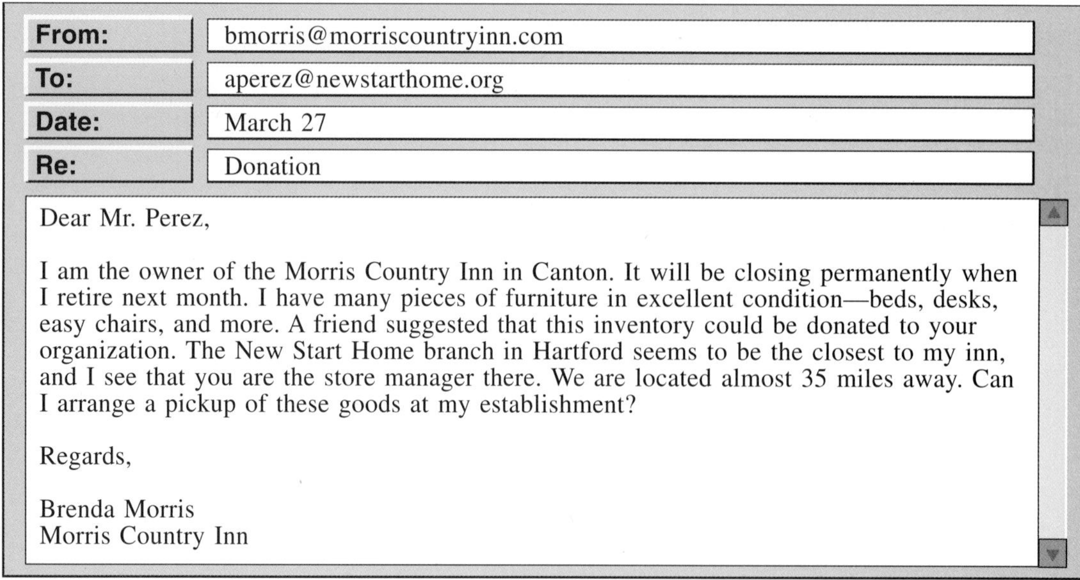

From: bmorris@morriscountryinn.com

To: aperez@newstarthome.org

Date: March 27

Re: Donation

Dear Mr. Perez,

I am the owner of the Morris Country Inn in Canton. It will be closing permanently when I retire next month. I have many pieces of furniture in excellent condition—beds, desks, easy chairs, and more. A friend suggested that this inventory could be donated to your organization. The New Start Home branch in Hartford seems to be the closest to my inn, and I see that you are the store manager there. We are located almost 35 miles away. Can I arrange a pickup of these goods at my establishment?

Regards,

Brenda Morris
Morris Country Inn

Morris Country Inn Shutting Its Doors

CANTON (April 27)—Brenda Morris watched the New Start Home truck drive away, full of furnishings from the Morris Country Inn. She has been the owner-operator of the inn, a local landmark, for 40 years. "I am happy to be heading to Seaview Point, with its beaches and warm weather," remarked Ms. Morris. "And I now plan to spend time volunteering and just relaxing. But the inn has been a big part of my life, and it will be hard leaving this community."

The property that the Morris Country Inn currently stands on has been sold to the Brent Valley Development Group, which plans to convert the building into apartment units over the coming year.

186. According to the Web page, what does New Start Home do with items it receives?

(A) It sells them.
(B) It donates them to schools.
(C) It sends them to be recycled.
(D) It repairs them.

187. How did Ms. Morris most likely learn the name of a manager at New Start Home?

(A) By searching online
(B) By e-mailing other organizations
(C) By reading an article in the local newspaper
(D) By participating in a community project

188. What is indicated about Ms. Morris in the e-mail?

(A) She visited New Start Home with a friend.
(B) She is seeking a new job.
(C) She has decided to close a business.
(D) She needs directions to a business.

189. What is suggested about the New Start Home branch in Hartford?

(A) It furnishes hotels.
(B) It is staffed by students.
(C) It has sold out of its current inventory.
(D) It picks up donations in nearby towns.

190. According to the article, where is Ms. Morris planning to live next?

(A) In Hartford
(B) In Seaview Point
(C) In Canton
(D) In Brent Valley

TEST 8

GO ON TO THE NEXT PAGE

Questions 191-195 refer to the following e-mails and order form.

To:	Imogen Chambers <ichambers@championos.com>
From:	Reginald Lee <rlee@cooperandcolsonlaw.org>
Re:	Office supplies order
Date:	March 20

Dear Ms. Chambers,

We have a standing order filled by Champion Office Supply, with automatic delivery to us on the first day of each month. I am writing because we would like to modify our usual order for the upcoming month as outlined on the attached form. Please note that we would like the ink toner that we have ordered in the past to be replaced by a different brand as indicated. Furthermore, we would like to add item WB918 to the order only this month, as we have recently hired new attorneys and we are preparing additional office spaces for them. Please use our credit card account that you have on file.

We continue to be pleased with the quality of your merchandise, especially the recycled stationery products with our firm's logo.

Thank you.

Reginald Lee, Office Manager
Cooper and Colson Law

Order for: Cooper and Colson Law **Delivery date:** April 1
Contact: Reginald Lee

Item Description	Item Number	Quantity	Price Per Unit	Itemized Total
Printed letterhead	LH228	10 Reams	54.00	540.00
Whiteboard pens	WP263	10 Packages of 4	4.99	49.90
Cytronics ink toner cartridge	CP576	8	42.00	336.00
Witeglow Magnetic Whiteboard (50" x 35")	WB918	4	79.99	319.96
Champion Office Supply			**TAX:**	74.75
			TOTAL:	$1320.61

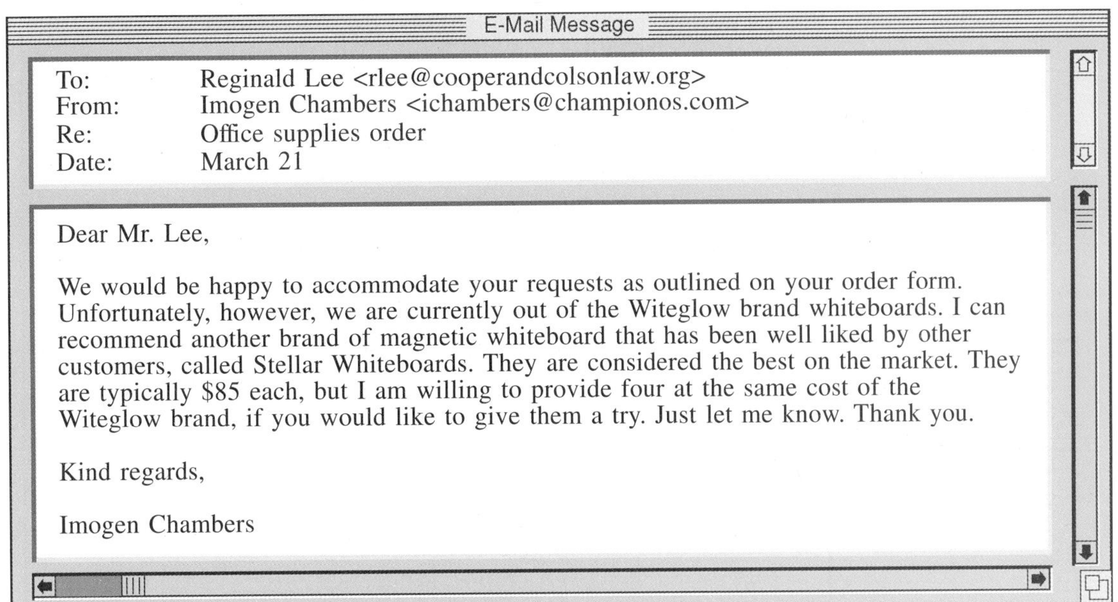
E-Mail Message

To: Reginald Lee <rlee@cooperandcolsonlaw.org>
From: Imogen Chambers <ichambers@championos.com>
Re: Office supplies order
Date: March 21

Dear Mr. Lee,

We would be happy to accommodate your requests as outlined on your order form. Unfortunately, however, we are currently out of the Witeglow brand whiteboards. I can recommend another brand of magnetic whiteboard that has been well liked by other customers, called Stellar Whiteboards. They are considered the best on the market. They are typically $85 each, but I am willing to provide four at the same cost of the Witeglow brand, if you would like to give them a try. Just let me know. Thank you.

Kind regards,

Imogen Chambers

191. What is the purpose of the first e-mail?

(A) To amend a regular order
(B) To report a delivery error
(C) To make a complaint about a product
(D) To confirm a delivery date

192. In the first e-mail, what is indicated about Cooper and Colson Law?

(A) It has just installed a new photocopier.
(B) It is currently expanding.
(C) It is in the process of relocating.
(D) It has just hired a new office manager.

193. What product is Mr. Lee particularly pleased with?

(A) Paper with company letterhead
(B) Whiteboard pens
(C) The Witeglow magnetic whiteboard
(D) The Cytronics ink toner cartridge

194. What item number identifies a replacement for a regularly ordered product?

(A) LH228
(B) WP263
(C) CP576
(D) WB918

195. How much will the law firm pay for each Stellar brand whiteboard?

(A) $49.90
(B) $54.00
(C) $79.99
(D) $85.00

TEST 8

GO ON TO THE NEXT PAGE

Questions 196-200 refer to the following schedule and e-mails.

Brenton Solutions
Building 3 Conference Room Calendar
Mondays in March

This schedule shows the meetings regularly scheduled in conference rooms on Mondays in the month of March. Keep in mind that management may request a room with minimal advance notice. If this occurs, you may contact Janet Marten at jmarten@brentonsolutions.com to inquire about rooms in other buildings on campus.

Time Slot	Room 3A (Capacity: 35)	Room 3B (Capacity: 50)
Morning 1 9:00–10:00 A.M.	Available	Sales Team (Use Room 3A for dividing into project groups, if necessary.)
Morning 2 10:30–11:45 A.M.	Human Resources	Summer Events Planning
Afternoon 1 2:00–2:45 P.M.	Customer Service	Technology and Engineering
Afternoon 2 3:00–4:00 P.M.	Available	Marketing Group

To: Team Leaders
From: Janet Marten
Subject: Conference Room Calendars
Date: February 27

To All Team Leads:

Please be informed that both Building 3 conference rooms will be unavailable throughout the day on Monday, March 12, as our division of Brenton Solutions will be hosting the Corporate Management team. These meetings are expected to begin promptly at 9:30 A.M. and to extend one full hour past the time that afternoon meetings usually end. Any team leads in need of conference space on this date should send me their request no later than Friday by replying directly to this e-mail. Space will be reserved on a first-come, first-served basis. Thanks!

Janet Marten, Corporate Secretary

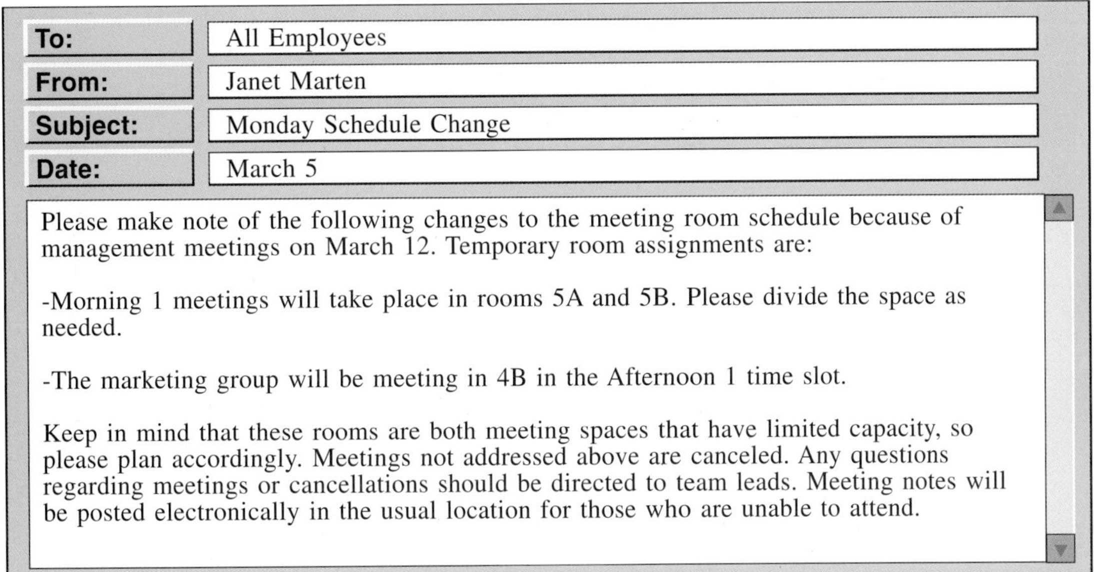

To:	All Employees
From:	Janet Marten
Subject:	Monday Schedule Change
Date:	March 5

Please make note of the following changes to the meeting room schedule because of management meetings on March 12. Temporary room assignments are:

-Morning 1 meetings will take place in rooms 5A and 5B. Please divide the space as needed.

-The marketing group will be meeting in 4B in the Afternoon 1 time slot.

Keep in mind that these rooms are both meeting spaces that have limited capacity, so please plan accordingly. Meetings not addressed above are canceled. Any questions regarding meetings or cancellations should be directed to team leads. Meeting notes will be posted electronically in the usual location for those who are unable to attend.

196. According to the schedule, what is true about Brenton Solutions?

(A) Its maximum room capacity is 35.
(B) It has multiple buildings.
(C) It releases room schedules yearly.
(D) Its employees meet once a month.

197. Why should team leads reply to the first e-mail?

(A) To reserve a room
(B) To meet with corporate managers
(C) To get meeting minutes
(D) To request more staff

198. When will the Corporate Management visit most likely end?

(A) At 11:45 A.M.
(B) At 2:45 P.M.
(C) At 4:00 P.M.
(D) At 5:00 P.M.

199. Who will NOT have a meeting on March 12?

(A) The sales team
(B) The marketing group
(C) Management
(D) Human Resources

200. What is indicated about employees who miss a meeting?

(A) They should contact Janet Marten.
(B) They must meet with their team lead.
(C) They can access meeting information online.
(D) They can attend a second session in 3B.

Stop! This is the end of the test. If you finish before time is called, you may go back to Parts 5, 6, and 7 and check your work.

토익® 정기시험 기출문제집

기출 TEST

09

READING TEST

In the Reading test, you will read a variety of texts and answer several different types of reading comprehension questions. The entire Reading test will last 75 minutes. There are three parts, and directions are given for each part. You are encouraged to answer as many questions as possible within the time allowed.

You must mark your answers on the separate answer sheet. Do not write your answers in your test book.

PART 5

Directions: A word or phrase is missing in each of the sentences below. Four answer choices are given below each sentence. Select the best answer to complete the sentence. Then mark the letter (A), (B), (C), or (D) on your answer sheet.

101. The review board published a list of companies ------- considers to be the most charitable.

(A) it
(B) its
(C) itself
(D) its own

102. Anyone who was unable to ------- yesterday's budget meeting may contact Mr. Kwon for his notes.

(A) recognize
(B) achieve
(C) attend
(D) inform

103. The evening's dance ------- was made possible with support from Taglet's Emporium.

(A) presented
(B) presents
(C) presenting
(D) presentation

104. All ------- candidates for the marketing position should submit a cover letter and résumé.

(A) increasing
(B) qualified
(C) beneficial
(D) modified

105. Because experts ------- a strong allergy season, Chowlan Pharmacy has increased its stock of preventative medicine.

(A) predict
(B) prediction
(C) are predicted
(D) predictably

106. The mayor applauded the Wilton Clinic ------- its leadership in promoting the city's public health programs.

(A) at
(B) for
(C) of
(D) to

107. Liao Uniform Services has been a leading ------- of medical apparel for more than 30 years.

(A) supplies
(B) supplying
(C) supplier
(D) supplied

108. Please adjust the budget to include the ------- of a fountain in the garden.

(A) schedule
(B) determination
(C) result
(D) installation

109. The speed limit on all ------- streets in Benton has been changed to 40 kilometers per hour.

(A) residential
(B) residing
(C) residences
(D) residentially

110. ------- visitors generally prefer to set their own pace, the aquarium now offers user-friendly audio tours.

(A) Except
(B) Since
(C) How
(D) That

111. The salmon dish at Salia's Café ------- with a brown sugar, mustard, and pepper glaze.

(A) to serve
(B) will serve
(C) is served
(D) was serving

112. Due to the uneven terrain of the Chilman Trail, proper hiking footwear is ------- recommended.

(A) closely
(B) highly
(C) nearly
(D) roughly

113. Visitors may tour the new printing plant facilities ------- the hours of 4 P.M. and 6 P.M.

(A) always
(B) between
(C) in
(D) only

114. Given the current economic climate, Playablanca Financial is ------- to make new acquisitions.

(A) hesitant
(B) delinquent
(C) worthy
(D) empty

115. Mr. Fitzpatrick memorized his lines ------- weeks before the filming of the movie began.

(A) perfectly
(B) perfected
(C) perfect
(D) perfecting

116. Ms. Amari has scanned the grant applications, and they will be submitted ------- the deadline.

(A) along
(B) over
(C) during
(D) before

117. Good design and quality material are ------- important to Krasner Laboratory's product development team.

(A) gradually
(B) enough
(C) equally
(D) well

118. We make our ------- of pet treats with only the best ingredients.

(A) usage
(B) line
(C) result
(D) addition

119. Dr. Wu provides patients with exceptional dental care at an ------- price.

(A) affords
(B) affordable
(C) affordably
(D) affordability

120. ------- two additional designers are hired, current staffers will not need to work overtime to complete projects on time.

(A) Whether
(B) Already
(C) Instead
(D) If

GO ON TO THE NEXT PAGE

121. All safety policies will be ------- reviewed by the Human Resources Department before publication.

(A) extensively
(B) extensive
(C) extension
(D) extending

122. Some roadside farmers markets in Dublin run year-round, while others ------- only in the summer and fall.

(A) grow
(B) operate
(C) raise
(D) promise

123. We do not have enough fabric samples, so please promptly return ------- ones you borrowed.

(A) what
(B) whomever
(C) whichever
(D) whose

124. ------- it does not rain tomorrow, tents will be set up for any scheduled outdoor events.

(A) Though
(B) Even if
(C) Almost
(D) Besides that

125. The network is expected to be unavailable for ------- two hours.

(A) no more than
(B) hardly any
(C) as far as
(D) that many

126. Consumer advocates advise against blindly accepting ------- opinions about a product.

(A) total
(B) biased
(C) profitable
(D) competitive

127. ------- of tasks makes a supervisor's job easier and helps team members learn new skills.

(A) Promotion
(B) Commission
(C) Provision
(D) Delegation

128. Scientists at Lipkin Pharmaceuticals described findings similar to those reported -------.

(A) elsewhere
(B) beyond
(C) furthermore
(D) wherever

129. All four walls of the greenhouse ------- of fully tempered glass.

(A) construct
(B) constructing
(C) have constructed
(D) will be constructed

130. The increase in tourism in Mariondale can be ------- to the various attractions the city has added in recent years.

(A) deducted
(B) confirmed
(C) attributed
(D) amplified

PART 6

Directions: Read the texts that follow. A word, phrase, or sentence is missing in parts of each text. Four answer choices for each question are given below the text. Select the best answer to complete the text. Then mark the letter (A), (B), (C), or (D) on your answer sheet.

Questions 131-134 refer to the following e-mail.

To: Eriford Hotel Staff
From: Seth Park
Subject: Conserving resources
Date: 15 March

To all housekeeping staff:

Hotel management has decided to implement a new policy ------- **131.** the daily laundering of towels. Going forward, all towels left on the floor by guests will be collected and washed each day, but any used towels hung up on hooks or racks will be left in the room for guests to reuse. This policy will ------- **132.** our daily laundry load. ------- **133.**, our electricity and power use will be reduced.
Notices will be posted in each room informing our guests of this policy. ------- **134.**. The management is deeply committed to conservation.

Thank you,

Seth Park
Hospitality Manager, Eriford Hotel

131. (A) regards
(B) regardless
(C) regarding
(D) regarded

132. (A) minimize
(B) double
(C) require
(D) eliminate

133. (A) Despite this
(B) However
(C) As a result
(D) Evidently

134. (A) We would greatly appreciate your cooperation with this effort.
(B) Please inform us if you identify any maintenance needs.
(C) During this time, please try to limit showers to ten minutes.
(D) You will be asked to share all of your ideas at the staff meeting.

GO ON TO THE NEXT PAGE

Questions 135-138 refer to the following notice.

Attention Travelers:

Was your luggage damaged while in transit? If so, ------- (135.) it to the Cloud Express Airlines baggage office as soon as possible after arrival. Domestic travelers are asked to report damage within 24 hours of reaching their destination, and international travelers must submit a report within five days of an incident. ------- (136.). Office personnel will review and evaluate all ------- (137.). Be advised that Cloud Express Airlines is not responsible for preexisting conditions or broken zippers or buckles related to overpacking or ------- (138.) wear.

135. (A) brings
(B) brought
(C) bring
(D) bringing

136. (A) Cloud Express has recently expanded its international routes.
(B) Cloud Express hires only the most qualified employees.
(C) The baggage office will be temporarily closed this week.
(D) Please complete the baggage damage form as instructed.

137. (A) claims
(B) agendas
(C) passports
(D) rates

138. (A) normality
(B) normal
(C) normally
(D) normalize

Questions 139-142 refer to the following memo.

To: Broome Library Staff
From: Ainsley Mason
Re: Community Rooms
Date: March 20

I am pleased to report that construction of our new community rooms will be complete by the end of this month. The four rooms will be ------- (139.) from the main lobby.

The new rooms range in occupancy from 10 to 25 people and are intended for meetings and study groups. ------- (140.). Ms. Sundquist will be temporarily responsible for reserving the spaces until the end of March. ------- (141.), she will return to her role as Library Information Specialist. An advertisement will be posted soon for a permanent Community Liaison. This individual will be in charge of ------- (142.) bookings for the new rooms.

139. (A) accessible
(B) assorted
(C) appropriate
(D) acceptable

140. (A) Interviews will be conducted in early May.
(B) Lynn Sundquist has led many meetings.
(C) All rooms must be reserved in advance.
(D) Staff parking spaces will be marked clearly.

141. (A) Nonetheless
(B) At that time
(C) Likewise
(D) In a word

142. (A) oversee
(B) oversees
(C) overseen
(D) overseeing

TEST 9

GO ON TO THE NEXT PAGE

Questions 143-146 refer to the following e-mail.

To: tkhan@smolermanufacturing.co.uk
From: lpreston@emmetestate.co.uk
Date: 9 March
Subject: 1161 Coral Lane

Dear Ms. Khan,

Thank you for asking about the 200-square-metre warehouse space at 1161 Coral Lane. I checked my real estate database, and -------(143.) this property has been taken off the market.

If you would like to give me an idea of what specifically you are looking for, I -------(144.) you in finding something else. Just respond to this e-mail with your price range, size needs, preferred area of town, and any other important requirements. -------(145.) .

If you wish, you may also sign up for -------(146.) . This way you will receive instant e-mail or text-message notifications whenever new property listings become available.

Best regards,

Lloyd Preston
Emmet Estate Agents

143. (A) briefly
(B) considerably
(C) apparently
(D) primarily

144. (A) am assisting
(B) can assist
(C) have been assisting
(D) assist

145. (A) For example, you need approval before anything is upgraded.
(B) I will be showing this property to potential buyers on Thursday.
(C) It is an interesting trend in the real estate industry.
(D) Then I will search for commercial buildings that meet these criteria.

146. (A) alerts
(B) payments
(C) activities
(D) inspections

PART 7

Directions: In this part you will read a selection of texts, such as magazine and newspaper articles, e-mails, and instant messages. Each text or set of texts is followed by several questions. Select the best answer for each question and mark the letter (A), (B), (C), or (D) on your answer sheet.

Questions 147-148 refer to the following e-mail.

To:	j.parnthong@trottermail.co.uk
From:	l.florinsmith@gaseau.co.uk
Date:	22 January
Subject:	Your purchase
Attachment:	recipes

Dear Ms. Parnthong,

Thank you for your recent purchase of four Gaseau bamboo cooking utensils. As you know, all Gaseau products are made of 100 percent natural bamboo and are meant to last a lifetime. They are light, durable, and safe for use with nonstick cookware as well as metal pots and pans. Please remember to hand-wash your new utensils with mild soap and water.

To thank you for your business, I have attached a few simple recipes that you can create using your new products.

If you have not already done so, please leave a review on our Web site concerning your experience with us. You can use this link: www.gaseau.co.uk/reviews.

Regards,

Liane Florin-Smith
Customer Service Representative

147. What is indicated about the utensils?

(A) They are made of natural materials.
(B) They cannot be used on metal surfaces.
(C) They must be washed with a special cleaning product.
(D) They are best-selling products.

148. What is Ms. Parnthong asked to do?

(A) Confirm receipt of her purchase
(B) Give some feedback online
(C) Review a recipe
(D) Enter a contest

TEST 9

GO ON TO THE NEXT PAGE

Questions 149-150 refer to the following product description.

Zevk Black Tea

Turkey boasts some of the best premium black tea blends in the world. Zevk (the Turkish word for "delight") is no exception—and has fifty years of commercial success to prove it. To be truly hospitable to your guests Turkish style, serve it in tall clear glasses so that they can admire the changing colors of Zevk tea as it brews. Accompany with biscuits or sweets.

Directions: Fill a pouch with Zevk tea and put it in a glass.
Pour in boiling water and let steep. Sweeten to taste.

Product of Turkey
Net Weight 250 g.
Packaged exclusively for ABD Exports.
Use within six months of package date for best taste.

149. What advice is given to Zevk tea consumers?

(A) How to keep it fresh over time
(B) The food items to serve with it
(C) The amount of sugar to add
(D) How long to let a pouch steep in a glass

150. According to the product description, what is true about Zevk tea?

(A) It is a relatively new product.
(B) It has a fruity flavor to it.
(C) It is sold outside of Turkey.
(D) It comes in boxes containing 250 tea pouches each.

Questions 151-152 refer to the following text-message chain.

Bishwa Poudel [9:27 A.M.]
I missed my train to Jaipur. Apparently it leaves from another station. No other trains can get me to the business forum in time for my keynote address. Any ideas?

Shraddha Kher [9:32 A.M.]
No problem. I'll send a car for you.

Bishwa Poudel [9:33 A.M.]
What a relief! Thank you. The dinner begins at 7 P.M., so if I leave New Delhi within two hours, I should arrive on time.

Shraddha Kher [9:34 A.M.]
Where shall the driver collect you?

Bishwa Poudel [9:35 A.M.]
At the Safdarjung station, Entrance 1. Please confirm when the car is on the way.

151. At 9:32 A.M., what does Ms. Kher most likely mean when she writes, "No problem"?

(A) She appreciates that Mr. Poudel is thankful.
(B) She will help Mr. Poudel get to the correct station.
(C) She will change the time of Mr. Poudel's keynote address.
(D) She knows how she can help Mr. Poudel.

152. What is suggested about Mr. Poudel?

(A) He is going to miss his dinner engagement.
(B) He is within driving distance of the business forum.
(C) He will be going to a different restaurant.
(D) He needs to pick up a colleague at 7 P.M.

TEST 9

GO ON TO THE NEXT PAGE

Questions 153-154 refer to the following instructions.

How to Connect Your New Apereta Modem

Use this insert as a form to keep track of your installation information and progress.

1. First, plug the **black** AC adaptor into a wall outlet and then connect it to the first port on your modem, labeled "Power."
2. Next, plug one end of the **blue** cable into a wall-mounted phone jack near your modem. Plug the other end into the second port on your modem, labeled "Service."
3. Finally, plug the **red** cable into a USB port in your computer. Then plug the other end into the third port on your modem, labeled "Computer."
4. Open an Internet browser. The Apereta home page should load automatically. Click the "Agree" button to be guided through the sign-up process. When you are finished, you will be e-mailed a Web link with your service password.
   Note your password here: Rt17ya-52p
5. To reset your service password, click the "Reset" button at the bottom of the sign-in page, then enter a password of your choice.
   Note your new password here: ____________________

153. What is the red cable intended to connect?

(A) The modem and the power outlet
(B) The modem and the phone jack
(C) The computer and the modem
(D) The computer and the power outlet

154. What has the user of the instructions most likely NOT done yet?

(A) Clicked the "Agree" button
(B) Received an e-mail message
(C) Connected all of the cables
(D) Reset the service password

Questions 155-157 refer to the following invitation.

A Night of Creativity and Inspiration at The Centre Creative

Thursday, 22 September
6:30 P.M. to 9:00 P.M.

The Centre Creative
42 Danvers Road, Cardiff, Wales

The Centre Creative is now ten years old! To celebrate a decade of supporting the arts throughout the United Kingdom, we are hosting A Night of Creativity and Inspiration. We invite all who have supported our fund-raising campaigns over the years to join us for art, food, and networking. Mingle with local artists and fellow art enthusiasts as you enjoy sculptures by Ming Young that are currently being featured in our gallery. Also enjoy appetizers and a variety of gourmet pastries prepared by Chef Diego Espina from the Sundial Café, which just opened on the lower level. Curator Olivia Richards will present a talk on the history of the centre. Proceeds from refreshments purchased during the evening will be used to fund the Painting Kids initiative at local schools.

Please contact Ian Griffin (igriffin@centrecreative.co.uk) to register to attend. Note that once capacity is reached, registration will close.

155. For whom is the invitation most likely intended?

(A) Art instructors
(B) Previous donors
(C) Restaurant patrons
(D) School administrators

156. The word "just" in paragraph 1, line 8, is closest in meaning to

(A) fairly
(B) exactly
(C) recently
(D) currently

157. What is indicated about the event?

(A) It will feature paintings for sale.
(B) It requires a fee to attend.
(C) It is limited to a specific number of attendees.
(D) It will include a cooking demonstration.

GO ON TO THE NEXT PAGE

Questions 158-161 refer to the following article.

A New Rail Line for Salvador

By Leonel Menendez

(14 November)—The government of the state of Bahia has finally arrived at a decision about who will take charge of the railway project between Salvador and Paripe. — [1] —. After an unexpectedly long selection process, the Secretariat for Urban Development announced last week that a proposal had finally been selected.

A joint venture between SOA International and ROOV Project Management was chosen to receive the contract. — [2] —. The Secretariat had insisted that a Brazilian firm be included in the contract. SOA International has long been involved in rail projects throughout Brazil, Spain, and the Middle East. The Swiss company, ROOV Project Management, was recently selected as Project Management Company of the Year by the International Project Management Institute. — [3] —.

The line will be constructed in two phases. The first phase will make use of an existing rail line that runs from Salvador to Plataforma, but the track will be replaced to accommodate the light-rail cars that SOA will build. The second phase will continue with the construction of a new track from Plataforma to Paripe. The long delay in settling on a vendor has caused the Secretariat to offer incentives for the project to be completed in 30 months. — [4] —. However, Spokesperson David Rios of ROOV has said that 36 months would be the minimum reasonable time to complete the project because of unpredictable weather, labor, and supplies.

158. Why was the article written?

(A) To solicit bids for a construction project
(B) To announce the awarding of a contract
(C) To explain a possible merger
(D) To criticize a policy decision

159. What is implied about SOA International?

(A) It collaborated with ROOV before.
(B) It built the existing rail line.
(C) It has won many industry awards.
(D) It is a Brazilian-based company.

160. What does the article indicate about the project?

(A) It is the first of its kind in Brazil.
(B) Its delay is caused by insufficient funds.
(C) Its second phase involves building a new rail line.
(D) It will most likely be completed in 30 months.

161. In which of the positions marked [1], [2], [3], and [4] does the following sentence best belong?

"Last year the government solicited proposals to build, operate, and maintain a light-rail system."

(A) [1]
(B) [2]
(C) [3]
(D) [4]

Questions 162-164 refer to the following post.

http://www.dealdirect.co.ke/buyerforum

Thread>Order not received

Posted on 15 May 11:49 AM by Frederick Wambu

Two weeks ago I ordered a shipment of books through dealdirect.co.ke. I did not receive the shipment, which was scheduled for 20 April. I called the shipping company, and the representative said that she has a record of someone accepting the package, but the signature is not legible. I called Deal Direct to make sure that the address they have on file for me is correct, and it was. I'm trying to figure out what my next step should be. I'm open to your ideas. So far, I've put up notices in my apartment building, but no one has responded. I wonder if I should just forget about it and reorder books from a different company or spend more time trying to resolve the matter.

162. What is something that Mr. Wambu has NOT done?

(A) Called Deal Direct
(B) Checked with the shipping company
(C) Reordered the products
(D) Posted notices

163. What is the purpose of the post?

(A) To ask for advice
(B) To request a refund
(C) To offer a solution
(D) To answer a question

164. In paragraph 1, line 15, the word "resolve" is closest in meaning to

(A) discover
(B) settle
(C) decide
(D) consider

TEST 9

GO ON TO THE NEXT PAGE

Questions 165-167 refer to the following article.

Ashby Logo Gets a New Look

(30 July)—A new logo for the city of Ashby was unveiled by Mayor Charles Cavanaugh on Tuesday. The logo and its accompanying slogan, "Ashby Connects," will be put to official use immediately. — [1] —.

The new design uses elements from Ashby's original logo, including the red banner and the year of the city's founding. — [2] —. But an image of the city's skyline in silhouette gives the new design a more contemporary feel. The slogan communicates Ashby's focus on creating community connections. — [3] —.

While Mayor Cavanaugh insists that the new logo is popular, not everyone is happy. "Why all the fuss?" asked lifelong resident Noelle Davidson. "The old logo was very recognizable. I don't know why they went to the trouble of replacing it." — [4] —.

Local maps and the letterhead for official correspondence have already been printed with the new logo. Residents will also soon see it in promotional campaigns for events in the area, such as the annual used-clothing drive and the summer music festival. The logo and slogan are registered trademarks and may not be used without permission. For more information, go to www.ashbyconnects.co.uk.

165. What is a feature of the new design?

(A) The mayor's name
(B) The current date
(C) An additional color
(D) An updated picture

166. What is NOT mentioned as a place the new logo will appear?

(A) On maps of the area
(B) On city stationery
(C) On clothing
(D) On event posters

167. In which of the positions marked [1], [2], [3], and [4] does the following sentence best belong?

"Nevertheless, most residents expressed approval, saying it was time for a change."

(A) [1]
(B) [2]
(C) [3]
(D) [4]

Questions 168-171 refer to the following e-mail.

To:	s.gillis@stephengillis.net
From:	pete@bartharchitecture.com
Date:	Thursday, October 2
Subject:	Re: Contract

Dear Mr. Gillis:

Thank you for sending me your signed contract. It was good to meet with you last week and to hear about your vision for the woodworking business you hope to create.

Based on the features you want your woodshop to have, I have some solid ideas with which to move forward. From our conversation, I also understand that you have some cost concerns. I will certainly be conscious of this when working on the design plans and will be sure to use materials that are both structurally sound and economical. You can expect some preliminary sketches within the next two weeks. Once you have looked them over, let's set a time to meet again, at which point any adjustments can be made and finalized.

I have already noted where your large pieces of machinery will be located. However, please let me know if you change your mind about anything, as I will need to figure out where the high-powered electrical outlets should be installed. For the purpose of safety, I am required to ensure that all large pieces of equipment such as table saws have their own dedicated circuits.

I am looking forward to collaborating with you to turn your ideas into reality.

Best regards,

Pete Barth

168. What is the purpose of the e-mail?

(A) To clarify a billing procedure
(B) To explain the roles of various contractors
(C) To discuss the next phases of a project
(D) To request some new design ideas

169. What is indicated about Mr. Gillis?

(A) He plans to relocate his shop.
(B) He has a well-established business.
(C) He needs to renew his permits.
(D) He has a limited budget.

170. According to the e-mail, how should Mr. Gillis prepare for the next meeting?

(A) By reviewing some drawings
(B) By making a written agenda
(C) By signing an updated contract
(D) By visiting some potential building sites

171. Why does Mr. Barth want to know about the large machinery?

(A) To determine a room's correct measurements
(B) To make sure all safety policies are being followed
(C) To determine the size of the work crew he will need to assemble
(D) To make sure a plan will not interfere with another project

GO ON TO THE NEXT PAGE

Questions 172-175 refer to the following online chat discussion.

Luke Orlan [8:30 A.M.]
Good morning, everyone. I would like an update on the grand opening at the Carter Street Mall.

Pamela Cooke [8:31 A.M.]
The opening went well. The shops and restaurants got a lot of pedestrian traffic and the customers seemed happy. We are still compiling the customer-satisfaction surveys. The Red Moon Restaurant was popular.

Luke Orlan [8:32 A.M.]
Please send me that data once you have it. Anything else I need to know?

Alena Santiago [8:33 A.M.]
Well, there were some issues with the parking area during the grand opening. The lighting did not work right. It didn't function as it should have when it got dark.

Luke Orlan [8:34 A.M.]
Oh?

Alena Santiago [8:34 A.M.]
We discovered that a timer was not set correctly.

Luke Orlan [8:35 A.M.]
I'm glad that was easily resolved. What about maintenance in general?

Marcus Afolayan [8:35 A.M.]
We want to make sure that management works closely with the Maintenance Department. We have staff on-site for routine housekeeping, and we have outside contractors taking care of the landscaping and maintenance of the escalators.

Luke Orlan [8:36 A.M.]
Everything seems to be running smoothly. Let's continue these online meetings weekly. I hope to travel there in February to see everything firsthand. Thanks.

172. Who most likely is Mr. Orlan?

(A) A corporate representative
(B) A restaurant chef
(C) An architect
(D) A maintenance worker

173. At 8:32 A.M., what does Mr. Orlan mean when he writes, "Please send me that data once you have it"?

(A) He wants to know the amount of revenue collected over the last week.
(B) He is interested in knowing visitors' reactions to the mall.
(C) He is concerned about increases in the operating budget.
(D) He needs an updated list of recently hired staff.

174. What problem is mentioned in the discussion?

(A) Surveys were sent out late.
(B) A restaurant was too crowded.
(C) Management has not yet hired enough landscapers.
(D) A parking area was not well lit.

175. What is suggested about the Carter Street Mall?

(A) Ms. Santiago oversees its personnel office.
(B) It is being renovated.
(C) It has several empty retail spaces.
(D) Mr. Orlan has not visited it yet.

GO ON TO THE NEXT PAGE

Questions 176-180 refer to the following job advertisement and e-mail.

Vos Communications, Inc.—Current Openings

Vos Communications, Inc. (VCI), is headquartered in Johannesburg, with a print division in Cape Town and a digital media division in Pretoria. We produce scientific publications with a focus on health and wellness in Africa and have been expanding rapidly in the three years following our launch. To meet our current needs, we are seeking applicants with a solid understanding of the medical communications industry for the following positions:

Senior Medical Writer
Develops original print materials. Requirements include a master's degree in clinical medicine, at least five years of experience as a medical writer, excellent communication skills, and the ability to work both independently and collaboratively. The successful candidate will be based in our print division.

Assistant Editor
Works as a member of the Editorial Panel in our print division. Requirements include a bachelor's degree in journalism or related field, excellent copyediting skills, and experience using editing software.

Medical Writer/Quality Control Reviewer
Works closely with other members of the print division team to ensure the accuracy of all print division publications. Based in our print division.

Applicants should submit a cover letter, a résumé, and a writing sample to Mr. Leon Madisha at lmadisha@vci.co.za. Interviews will be conducted from 7 through 12 May at our headquarters, at which time three letters of recommendation must be presented. Only candidates selected for an interview will be contacted.

To:	Leon Madisha < lmadisha@vci.co.za >
From:	Amina Buys <buysam@mailworks.net.za>
Date:	1 May
Subject:	Assistant editor position
Attachment:	buys_application_materials

Dear Mr. Madisha,

I am writing to express my interest in the assistant editor position.

I hold a bachelor's degree in communications from the University of Richards Bay. I have been working as an editorial assistant at Luxor Publishing House in Durban for six years. My position has enabled me to develop long-term collaborative relationships with clients.

I believe my experience in the publishing industry and attentiveness to detail make me a perfect fit. Attached please find the relevant application materials. Incidentally, I will be attending a conference near your headquarters at the time of the scheduled interview period, so if I do get selected, getting to the interview will not be a problem.

Sincerely,

Amina Buys

176. What is indicated about VCI?

(A) It has been in operation for three years.
(B) It currently has jobs available in various cities.
(C) Its publications center around issues of finance.
(D) Its staff is dedicated to improving its publications.

177. In the advertisement, the word "solid" in paragraph 1, line 4, is closest in meaning to

(A) hard
(B) constant
(C) thorough
(D) dense

178. Which qualification is required by all the job openings?

(A) An ability to work as part of a team
(B) A master's degree in a science field
(C) Strong software skills
(D) A medical background

179. What most likely was NOT an application document submitted by Ms. Buys?

(A) An illustration of her writing capabilities
(B) An expression of her interest for the job
(C) A description of her qualifications and experience
(D) An employer's evaluation of her abilities and knowledge

180. Where will Ms. Buys attend a conference?

(A) In Cape Town
(B) In Durban
(C) In Johannesburg
(D) In Pretoria

TEST 9

GO ON TO THE NEXT PAGE

Questions 181-185 refer to the following online article and reader comment.

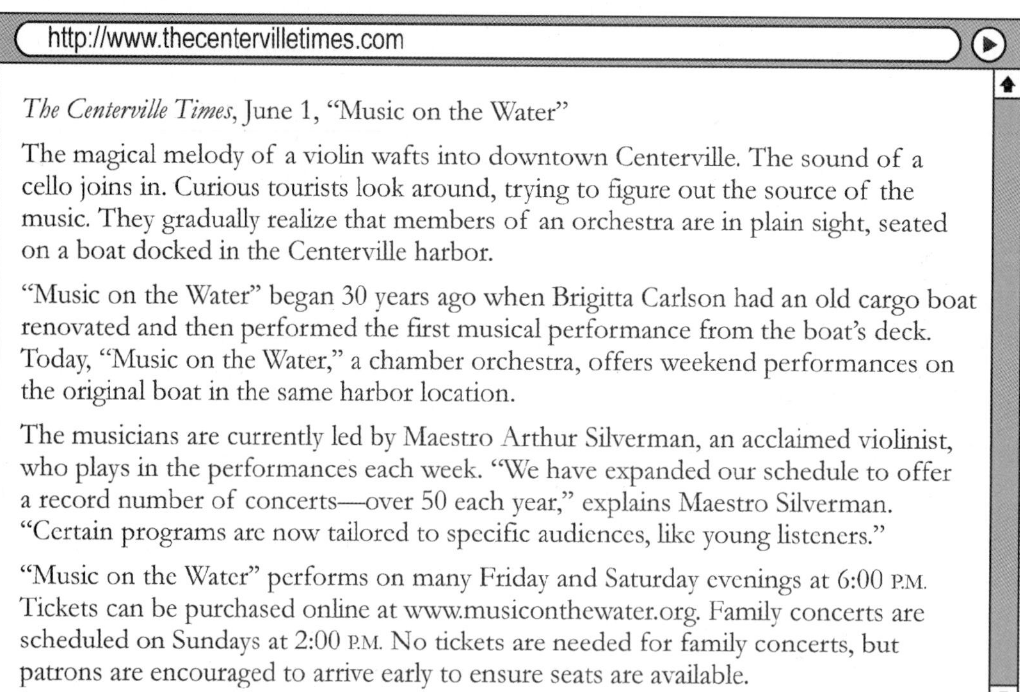

http://www.thecentervilletimes.com

The Centerville Times, June 1, "Music on the Water"

The magical melody of a violin wafts into downtown Centerville. The sound of a cello joins in. Curious tourists look around, trying to figure out the source of the music. They gradually realize that members of an orchestra are in plain sight, seated on a boat docked in the Centerville harbor.

"Music on the Water" began 30 years ago when Brigitta Carlson had an old cargo boat renovated and then performed the first musical performance from the boat's deck. Today, "Music on the Water," a chamber orchestra, offers weekend performances on the original boat in the same harbor location.

The musicians are currently led by Maestro Arthur Silverman, an acclaimed violinist, who plays in the performances each week. "We have expanded our schedule to offer a record number of concerts—over 50 each year," explains Maestro Silverman. "Certain programs are now tailored to specific audiences, like young listeners."

"Music on the Water" performs on many Friday and Saturday evenings at 6:00 P.M. Tickets can be purchased online at www.musiconthewater.org. Family concerts are scheduled on Sundays at 2:00 P.M. No tickets are needed for family concerts, but patrons are encouraged to arrive early to ensure seats are available.

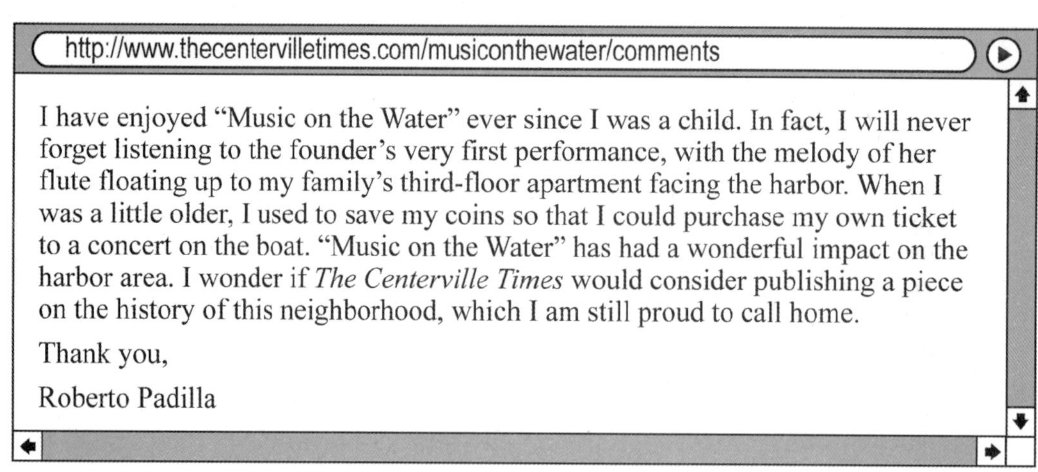

http://www.thecentervilletimes.com/musiconthewater/comments

I have enjoyed "Music on the Water" ever since I was a child. In fact, I will never forget listening to the founder's very first performance, with the melody of her flute floating up to my family's third-floor apartment facing the harbor. When I was a little older, I used to save my coins so that I could purchase my own ticket to a concert on the boat. "Music on the Water" has had a wonderful impact on the harbor area. I wonder if *The Centerville Times* would consider publishing a piece on the history of this neighborhood, which I am still proud to call home.

Thank you,

Roberto Padilla

181. What is suggested about "Music on the Water" performances?

(A) They have recently increased seating capacity.
(B) They are held in an unexpected location.
(C) They take place only during the summer.
(D) They sell out quickly.

182. What does the article suggest about the family concerts?

(A) Seating is not guaranteed.
(B) Recordings are available for purchase.
(C) Audience members may request favorite pieces.
(D) Interviews with the concert musicians are posted online.

183. What is suggested about Ms. Carlson?

(A) She studied music with Maestro Silverman.
(B) She organized tours of the harbor.
(C) She played the flute.
(D) She owned a boat-repair shop.

184. What does Mr. Padilla request?

(A) Additional weekly performances
(B) Improving the sound quality of concerts
(C) An article on a particular topic
(D) Reduced ticket prices for neighborhood residents

185. What does the reader comment imply about Mr. Padilla?

(A) He has recently bought concert tickets.
(B) He is a journalist for *The Centerville Times*.
(C) He was inspired to become a musician himself.
(D) He has lived in Centerville since his childhood.

TEST 9

GO ON TO THE NEXT PAGE

Questions 186-190 refer to the following advertisement, form, and e-mail.

Carson Office Supplies

SALE!

This weekend only, May 25–26, we're having our biggest sale of the year!

50% off select printers	$15.99 for a 10-ream case of paper	25% off all Sonama televisions	$150 off all Rigkuere office desks	$10 off all Herbrot ink cartridges

Shop in store or online. Only while supplies last!

Carson Office Supplies

Return Authorization Request

Order Number: 300034122
Account Number: Business5271
Name: Jane Mori
E-mail: j.mori@welsomf.com
Subject: Recent purchase
Reason for Return:

I am the purchasing manager at Welso Manufacturing, and we have a business account with Carson Office Supplies. Last week I purchased the following items: 3 Rigkuere office desks, 15 Herbrot ink cartridges, 30 notepads, and 5 boxes of envelopes. Today I noticed in an advertisement for your upcoming weekend sale that some of the items I purchased are going to be heavily discounted. Would it be possible for me to get a refund for the applicable items and then rebuy them at the lower weekend sale price?

To:	Jane Mori <j.mori@welsomf.com>
From:	Sheridan Homel <homel@cos.com>
Date:	May 22
Subject:	Re: Exchange
Attachment:	Coupon, returns & exchanges

Dear Ms. Mori:

Thank you for your message and your continued business with Carson Office Supplies. Unfortunately, only items purchased on the official sale dates are eligible for the sale prices.

Because you have a business account with us, however, you automatically receive a 20 percent discount on bulk items (purchases of fifteen or more of the same item), which is deducted when you make a purchase through our online business portal. I can see from your order that this was the case for some of your items.

I can also offer you a 10 percent off coupon on your next purchase. The coupon is attached—it specifies the access code that you can use online. I will also attach our return and exchange procedures for your future reference.

Do not hesitate to contact me with any questions or concerns.

Sheridan Homel
Branch Manager
Carson Office Supplies

186. What is probably true about Ms. Mori?

(A) She owns a business.
(B) She is a first-time customer.
(C) She received a discount on a printer.
(D) She purchased her items before May 25.

187. Why does Ms. Mori ask about returning some of her items?

(A) She received the wrong order.
(B) The items were broken when they arrived.
(C) The desks she ordered are too small.
(D) She wants to purchase items during the weekend sale.

188. According to the e-mail, why did Ms. Mori receive a discount on her bulk purchases?

(A) She redeemed a coupon.
(B) She used a business account.
(C) She entered a special code online.
(D) She shopped during an exclusive sale for members.

189. What items from Ms. Mori's purchase qualified for the bulk discount?

(A) The office desks and notepads
(B) The ink cartridges and boxes of envelopes
(C) The ink cartridges and notepads
(D) The boxes of envelopes and the office desks

190. What was included with the e-mail?

(A) An updated return form
(B) A document about store policy
(C) An application for a new account
(D) A receipt for Ms. Mori's purchase

TEST 9

GO ON TO THE NEXT PAGE

Questions 191-195 refer to the following online message board, e-mail, and Web page.

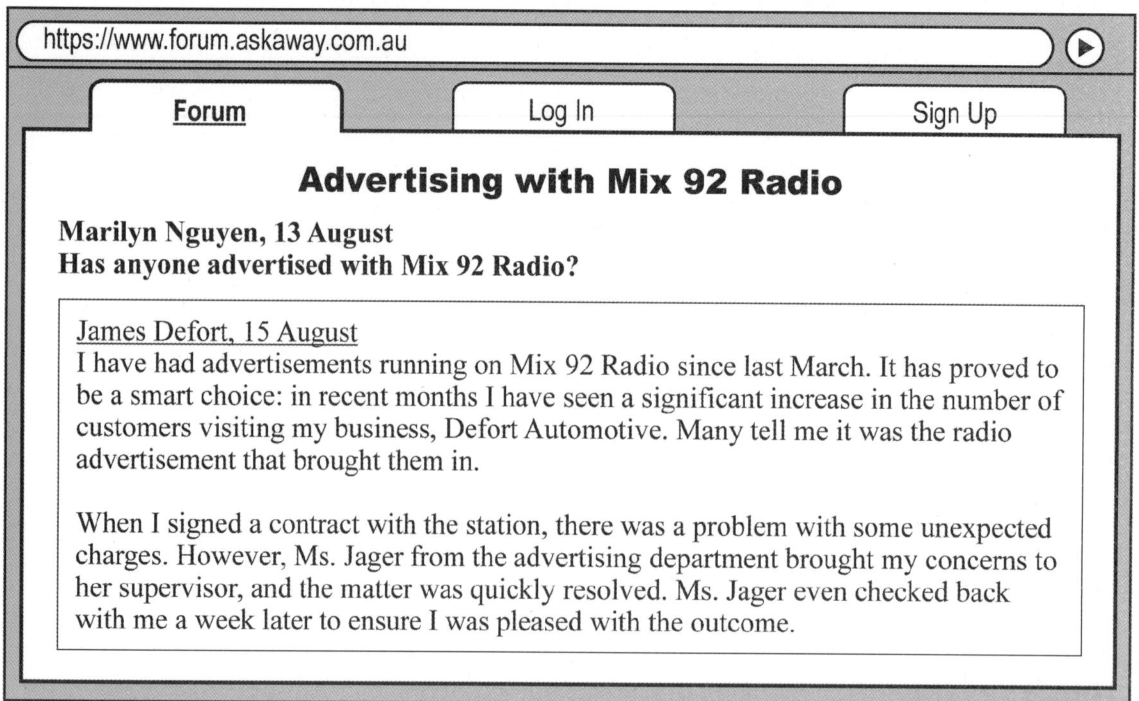
https://www.forum.askaway.com.au

Forum | Log In | Sign Up

Advertising with Mix 92 Radio

Marilyn Nguyen, 13 August
Has anyone advertised with Mix 92 Radio?

James Defort, 15 August
I have had advertisements running on Mix 92 Radio since last March. It has proved to be a smart choice: in recent months I have seen a significant increase in the number of customers visiting my business, Defort Automotive. Many tell me it was the radio advertisement that brought them in.

When I signed a contract with the station, there was a problem with some unexpected charges. However, Ms. Jager from the advertising department brought my concerns to her supervisor, and the matter was quickly resolved. Ms. Jager even checked back with me a week later to ensure I was pleased with the outcome.

E-mail

To: All staff
From: Kathrin Jager
Date: 29 September
Subject: Final broadcast

Dear All,

As my internship at Mix 92 Radio draws to a close, please know that working here has been a wonderful experience for me. I am grateful for the training and advice I have received over the past twelve months. I especially want to thank my boss and mentor, Alison Alvey, from whom I have not only learned the fundamentals of radio advertising, but also how to meet customers' needs. Her nomination for this year's Australis Trophy speaks volumes about her dedication to her clients and staff.

I also appreciate the video recording you presented to me, showing me at work and at play here. I will miss joining many of you for lunches at the Hot Spot Café.

Best wishes,

Kathrin Jager

https://www.cba.com.au/aawinners/advertising_and_social_media

Australis Small Business Trophy Winners
Advertising and Social Media Category

Platinum: Ravi Vedantam, Social Media Technology, Mix 92 Radio

Gold: Zixuan Li, Marketing, Streiler's Clothing Stores

Silver: Jorge Beltran, Beltran Publicity Company

Bronze: Alison Alvey, Advertising, Mix 92 Radio

Winners were selected from over 50 nominations. The recipient of the Platinum Australis Trophy will be profiled in the December issue of *Canberra Business Today*. Awards will be presented by the Canberra Business Association at a gala event in the banquet hall of the Fourth Street Hotel on 12 October.

191. What does Mr. Defort indicate about Mix 92 Radio?
(A) It resolved his problem adequately.
(B) It is a rapidly growing company.
(C) It advertises local businesses only.
(D) It charges an extra fee to new clients.

192. What is suggested about Mr. Defort?
(A) He has been a client of Mix 92 Radio for many years.
(B) He was assisted by an intern at Mix 92 Radio.
(C) He recently experienced a decline in his car sales.
(D) He runs the biggest automotive business in the area.

193. Why did Ms. Jager send the e-mail?
(A) To ask for help from coworkers
(B) To organize a luncheon
(C) To arrange a video recording session
(D) To thank staff members

194. What award will be presented to Ms. Jager's supervisor?
(A) Platinum
(B) Gold
(C) Silver
(D) Bronze

195. What does the Web page suggest?
(A) The gala event is open to the public.
(B) Fewer awards nominations were received this year.
(C) Mr. Vedantam and Ms. Alvey are colleagues.
(D) Winners will receive a free subscription to *Canberra Business Today*.

TEST 9

GO ON TO THE NEXT PAGE

Questions 196-200 refer to the following article, invitation, and e-mail.

Olinawe is a Fusion of Flavours

DONCASTER (21 March)—After many years of hard work, chef Amina Ikegami is opening her own restaurant in downtown Doncaster.

Ms. Ikegami trained at Chesterfield Culinary Academy and worked as a junior sous chef at the Sisra Bistro for three years. She spent the last twelve years on staff at Delmourel's, where she held the title of executive chef for the past four years.

Ms. Ikegami has won several awards, including the UK Innovative Chef Award. Although she is sad to leave Delmourel's, she is thrilled to fulfill her longtime dream of owning her own restaurant.

Ms. Ikegami's new restaurant, Olinawe, features a menu influenced by the many varied flavours of her childhood. She was raised in England in a family with French, Senegalese, and Japanese heritage. Being exposed to so many different food traditions is what inspired her to become a chef.

"My mother and father are great cooks themselves," says Ms. Ikegami. "I loved having all these cuisines in one house, and I always strive to bring that fusion of cultures into my cooking."

Olinawe opens officially on 25 April and will serve lunch and dinner Tuesdays through Sundays.

Join Us!
Enjoy delicious fusion cuisine
at
Olinawe
a new restaurant from
Chef Amina Ikegami

Saturday, 2 April
7:00 P.M.–11:00 P.M.

All food and drinks are included.
This is an invitation-only event.
Please bring this invitation with you.

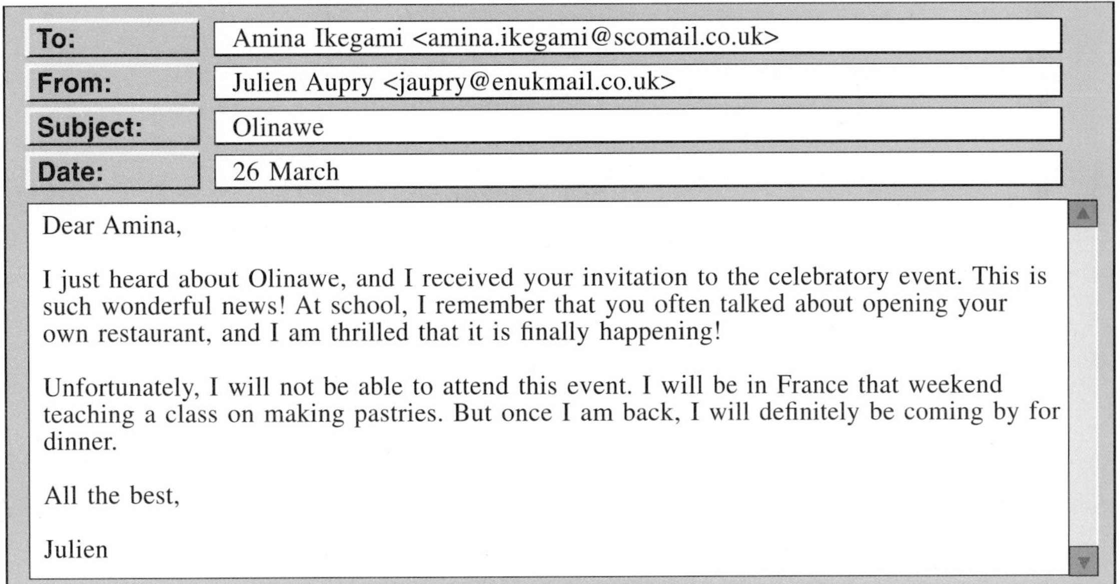

To:	Amina Ikegami <amina.ikegami@scomail.co.uk>
From:	Julien Aupry <jaupry@enukmail.co.uk>
Subject:	Olinawe
Date:	26 March

Dear Amina,

I just heard about Olinawe, and I received your invitation to the celebratory event. This is such wonderful news! At school, I remember that you often talked about opening your own restaurant, and I am thrilled that it is finally happening!

Unfortunately, I will not be able to attend this event. I will be in France that weekend teaching a class on making pastries. But once I am back, I will definitely be coming by for dinner.

All the best,

Julien

196. What is the purpose of the article?

(A) To describe a new style of cooking
(B) To announce the opening of a new restaurant
(C) To advertise classes at a cooking school
(D) To profile different dining establishments in Doncaster

197. What inspired Ms. Ikegami to enter the cooking profession?

(A) A childhood trip to Japan
(B) A fellow chef at Delmourel's
(C) Her former professor at school
(D) Her diverse family background

198. What is true about the event on April 2 ?

(A) It requires reservations.
(B) It is open to the general public.
(C) It takes place before Olinawe officially opens.
(D) It is being sponsored by the Sisra Bistro.

199. Why does Mr. Aupry send the e-mail?

(A) To decline an invitation
(B) To make a reservation for dinner
(C) To welcome Ms. Ikegami to France
(D) To ask Ms. Ikegami to teach a class

200. What is indicated about Mr. Aupry?

(A) He has eaten at Olinawe.
(B) He used to work for Ms. Ikegami.
(C) He attended Chesterfield Culinary Academy.
(D) He is the executive chef at Delmourel's.

TEST 9

Stop! This is the end of the test. If you finish before time is called, you may go back to Parts 5, 6, and 7 and check your work.

토익® 정기시험
기출문제집

RC

기출 TEST

10

READING TEST

In the Reading test, you will read a variety of texts and answer several different types of reading comprehension questions. The entire Reading test will last 75 minutes. There are three parts, and directions are given for each part. You are encouraged to answer as many questions as possible within the time allowed.

You must mark your answers on the separate answer sheet. Do not write your answers in your test book.

PART 5

Directions: A word or phrase is missing in each of the sentences below. Four answer choices are given below each sentence. Select the best answer to complete the sentence. Then mark the letter (A), (B), (C), or (D) on your answer sheet.

101. Sunwirth Sneakers has several ------- in the greater metropolitan area.

(A) locations
(B) locate
(C) located
(D) location

102. Cimber CPAs offers clients the convenience of ------- their invoices online and by mail.

(A) buying
(B) paying
(C) going
(D) eating

103. The new software at Patel Industries has been working ------- since it was installed last year.

(A) reliable
(B) to rely
(C) more reliable
(D) reliably

104. Best practices in customer service are outlined ------- the training handbook.

(A) along
(B) toward
(C) over
(D) throughout

105. The Scratch software will help us migrate our client records -------.

(A) simple
(B) simpler
(C) simply
(D) simplicity

106. The comedian said that ------- sense of humor was inherited from a grandparent.

(A) herself
(B) her
(C) she
(D) hers

107. Starting this August, Gavelton Bike Tours will be leading group cycling trips ------- Paris to Berlin.

(A) from
(B) beside
(C) along
(D) after

108. We hope to ------- an agreement with Mason Cooper, Inc., within the next week.

(A) reach
(B) talk
(C) reason
(D) put

109. Factory-floor managers must submit an inspection report at the end ------- their shift.

(A) if
(B) to
(C) of
(D) as

110. ------- a retail store, Seedum International will now sell merchandise only through its Web site.

(A) Sometimes
(B) Later
(C) Formerly
(D) Frequently

111. Remarkably, neither Ms. Chen ------- Mr. Gillespie had been notified that the board meeting was canceled.

(A) or
(B) and
(C) with
(D) nor

112. The new microwave soup containers are ------- than the previous ones.

(A) rigid
(B) most rigidly
(C) rigidly
(D) more rigid

113. The Banly Tourism Society is ------- to present the first issue of its publication, *The Banly Quarterly*.

(A) regular
(B) general
(C) proud
(D) favorite

114. Konixer Printers is conducting a thorough ------- of current requests for equipment upgrades.

(A) evaluate
(B) evaluation
(C) evaluator
(D) evaluative

115. ------- the addition of 300 spaces, the ferry terminal's parking area is still full by 9:00 A.M. every day.

(A) Despite
(B) Across
(C) Besides
(D) Inside

116. Justlox, Inc., is planning to ------- redesign Model 543Q with its partners in Britain to ensure a better product.

(A) collaboration
(B) collaborative
(C) collaboratively
(D) collaborate

117. Each box of Lane Permanent Markers contains an ------- of surprising colors.

(A) assortment
(B) excitement
(C) account
(D) industry

118. We were pleased by the ------- and courteous reply we received from Astella Airlines concerning the change in itinerary.

(A) safe
(B) close
(C) clean
(D) prompt

119. The rising employment rate is one factor contributing to ------- in the housing construction trade.

(A) grow
(B) growth
(C) grew
(D) grown

120. The color of the new chairs was not ------- on the invoice.

(A) specify
(B) specified
(C) specifying
(D) specification

GO ON TO THE NEXT PAGE

121. Two hours is the ------- amount of time needed to complete the assignment.

(A) minimum
(B) temporary
(C) bottom
(D) durable

122. A successful digital marketing campaign has helped Fossler Electronics ------- its profit margins.

(A) stabilized
(B) stability
(C) stabilizing
(D) stabilize

123. Applicants for the position of data manager are expected to have a minimum of three years' ------- experience.

(A) supervisors
(B) supervisory
(C) supervise
(D) supervises

124. The mayor's speech at Monday's business breakfast ------- and will be broadcast later this week.

(A) record
(B) recording
(C) being recorded
(D) was recorded

125. The researchers ------- tested different formulas until the desired results were achieved.

(A) soon
(B) suddenly
(C) well
(D) repeatedly

126. Loan specialists at Newton Bank can help your company ------- equipment purchases.

(A) commit
(B) associate
(C) reserve
(D) finance

127. ------- our partnership with Shox Gym, we are able to provide employees with a free membership to the fitness center.

(A) After all
(B) Because of
(C) For this reason
(D) As long as

128. Mr. Tran asked the department whether ------- could work overtime on Friday.

(A) anyone
(B) anywhere
(C) anyway
(D) anyhow

129. Canyonland Corporation will research the potential ------- of expanding its overseas market to East Africa.

(A) deadline
(B) availability
(C) profitability
(D) emphasis

130. Chef Lind's cookbook, ------- will be available next week, contains only dessert recipes.

(A) who
(B) what
(C) which
(D) whose

PART 6

Directions: Read the texts that follow. A word, phrase, or sentence is missing in parts of each text. Four answer choices for each question are given below the text. Select the best answer to complete the text. Then mark the letter (A), (B), (C), or (D) on your answer sheet.

Questions 131-134 refer to the following notice.

Pro Unis is now hiring for positions in our production, human resources, and accounting departments. As one of the region's largest employers, Pro Unis ------- **131.** workforces with uniforms for over 70 years. Since our founding, Pro Unis has been committed to employee retention and ------- **132.**. We offer competitive wages, job training, and regular opportunities for promotion. To learn more about ------- **133.**, visit prounis.com/careers. Interested job-seekers will be directed to fill out an online application and upload a résumé. ------- **134.**.

131. (A) outfitted
(B) will outfit
(C) is outfitting
(D) has been outfitting

132. (A) advanced
(B) an advance
(C) they advance
(D) advancement

133. (A) issues
(B) events
(C) openings
(D) investments

134. (A) They must also pass a background check to be eligible for employment.
(B) Let Pro Unis design work uniforms for your company.
(C) You can now follow us on social media.
(D) We recently hired a new director of human resources.

GO ON TO THE NEXT PAGE

Questions 135-138 refer to the following information.

WS Dental is pleased to announce that our practice is ------- (135.). Our second office is now open at 242 Union Street in Lambton, offering greater ------- (136.) for patients living on the north side of the city. Our original clinic will continue to operate at 12 Finn Place. Dr. Walbeck and Dr. Steiner are committed to providing ------- (137.) care at both locations.

WS Dental provides a full range of dental services at both offices. They are both open from 8 A.M. to 5 P.M., Monday through Friday. ------- (138.). Extended evening hours will be considered in the coming season.

135. (A) training
(B) expanding
(C) calling
(D) moving

136. (A) collection
(B) production
(C) performance
(D) convenience

137. (A) exception
(B) exceptions
(C) exceptional
(D) exceptionally

138. (A) Our Finn Place office is also open on Saturday mornings.
(B) This area has a rich history and a vibrant downtown.
(C) The facility is comfortable, clean, and bright.
(D) Once there, take a right onto Mountain View Road.

Questions 139-142 refer to the following e-mail.

To: jroux@xmail.com
From: josephbelle@perilleuxrealestate.com
Date: March 2
Subject: Your job inquiry

Dear Ms. Roux:

Your résumé ------- (139.) to me by a colleague. ------- (140.). We appreciate your interest in Perilleux Real Estate and will keep your ------- (141.) on file in case a full-time position opens up in the future.

------- (142.), would you consider working for us part-time on a special project? Our CEO needs administrative support on an ambitious advertising campaign. The project should last until the end of July.

Kindly let me know if this opportunity interests you.

Sincerely,

Joseph Belle, Vice President
Human Resources

139. (A) to pass on
(B) will pass on
(C) is passing on
(D) was passed on

140. (A) It was nice to meet you at the networking event.
(B) Our firm is now six years old.
(C) We are happy to have you as part of our team.
(D) Unfortunately, we do not have an open receptionist position.

141. (A) documents
(B) analysis
(C) descriptions
(D) reports

142. (A) First of all
(B) As mentioned
(C) In the meantime
(D) In order that

GO ON TO THE NEXT PAGE

Questions 143-146 refer to the following article.

Hurst Airlines Improves its Customer Service Offerings

LOS ANGELES (September 22)—Hurst Airlines has started installing self-check-in kiosks where passengers can scan their identification, print their own boarding passes, and tag their own luggage to be loaded onto the aircraft. These new ------- **143.** are already in place at two airports in California. ------- **144.** will soon be available at all airports where Hurst Airlines flies. According to Hurst Airlines CEO Roxana Ghazi, the company aims for all its service areas ------- **145.** equipped with kiosks by the end of the summer.

The intent of these kiosks is to make the check-in process run more quickly. Said Ms. Ghazi, "We have limited staff, and lines can often be quite long. ------- **146.**. These new kiosks are expected to significantly reduce the amount of time spent in line."

143. (A) devices
(B) positions
(C) materials
(D) regulations

144. (A) It
(B) She
(C) They
(D) Either

145. (A) to be
(B) that are
(C) they were
(D) having been

146. (A) Unfortunately, we are changing our routes.
(B) Passengers should arrive two hours before a flight.
(C) We expect to hire more staff soon.
(D) This is especially true during peak operating times.

PART 7

Directions: In this part you will read a selection of texts, such as magazine and newspaper articles, e-mails, and instant messages. Each text or set of texts is followed by several questions. Select the best answer for each question and mark the letter (A), (B), (C), or (D) on your answer sheet.

Questions 147-148 refer to the following job posting.

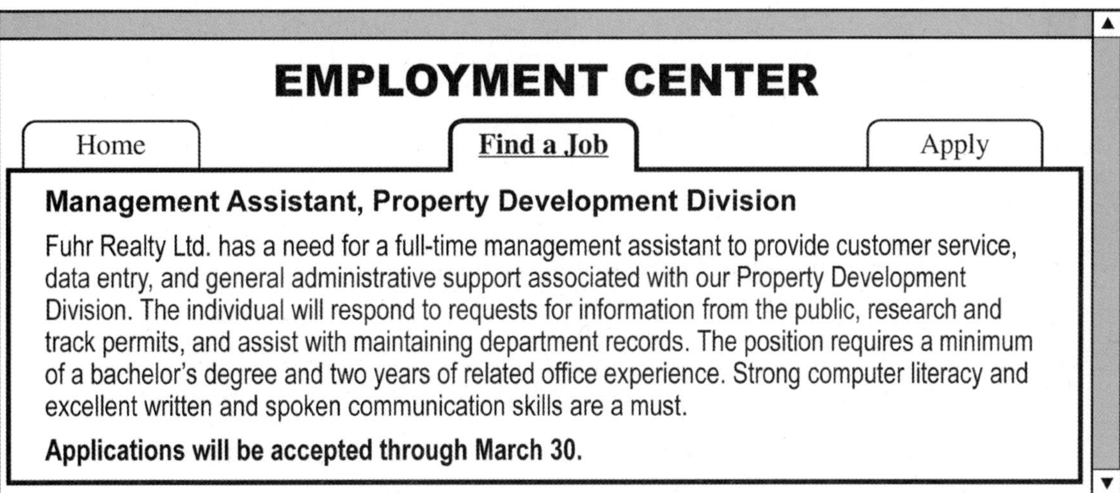

EMPLOYMENT CENTER

Home | Find a Job | Apply

Management Assistant, Property Development Division

Fuhr Realty Ltd. has a need for a full-time management assistant to provide customer service, data entry, and general administrative support associated with our Property Development Division. The individual will respond to requests for information from the public, research and track permits, and assist with maintaining department records. The position requires a minimum of a bachelor's degree and two years of related office experience. Strong computer literacy and excellent written and spoken communication skills are a must.

Applications will be accepted through March 30.

147. What is included in the job posting?

(A) The location of Fuhr Realty Ltd.
(B) A starting date for the position
(C) A description of job responsibilities
(D) Information about employment benefits

148. What qualification is necessary for the position?

(A) A degree in accounting
(B) A professional certification
(C) Experience as a manager
(D) Good computer skills

GO ON TO THE NEXT PAGE →

Questions 149-150 refer to the following text-message chain.

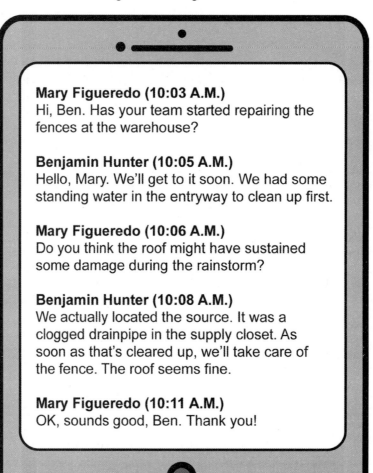

Mary Figueredo (10:03 A.M.)
Hi, Ben. Has your team started repairing the fences at the warehouse?

Benjamin Hunter (10:05 A.M.)
Hello, Mary. We'll get to it soon. We had some standing water in the entryway to clean up first.

Mary Figueredo (10:06 A.M.)
Do you think the roof might have sustained some damage during the rainstorm?

Benjamin Hunter (10:08 A.M.)
We actually located the source. It was a clogged drainpipe in the supply closet. As soon as that's cleared up, we'll take care of the fence. The roof seems fine.

Mary Figueredo (10:11 A.M.)
OK, sounds good, Ben. Thank you!

149. What most likely is Mr. Hunter's profession?

(A) Receptionist
(B) Interior decorator
(C) Maintenance worker
(D) Security guard

150. At 10:05 A.M., why does Mr. Hunter write, "We'll get to it soon"?

(A) His team will begin a task shortly.
(B) His team will continue a project.
(C) His team will arrive at a location quickly.
(D) His team will clean up some water.

Questions 151-152 refer to the following notice.

Attention Line 75 Riders

All Metrowestern passengers should be aware of the following temporary changes for bus line 75. Due to construction, service on Eighth Avenue between Taylor Street and Forbes Boulevard will be suspended during the following periods. We apologize for any inconvenience.

Monday, April 5, 10:00 A.M.–4:00 P.M.
Wednesday, April 7, 11:00 A.M.–4:30 P.M.
Friday, April 9, 6:30 P.M.–10:00 P.M.
Saturday, April 10, 9:00 A.M.–5:00 P.M.

As usual, all Metrowestern bus service ends at 11:30 P.M. All buses begin running again at 5:45 A.M. daily.

151. What is the purpose of the notice?

(A) To introduce a new express bus route
(B) To announce temporary changes in bus service
(C) To report on the completion of a construction project
(D) To request that riders avoid travel during peak hours

152. According to the notice, when will the bus route be available?

(A) On April 5 at 11:30 A.M.
(B) On April 7 at 5:30 A.M.
(C) On April 9 at 3:00 P.M.
(D) On April 10 at 4:00 P.M.

TEST 10

GO ON TO THE NEXT PAGE

Questions 153-154 refer to the following e-mail.

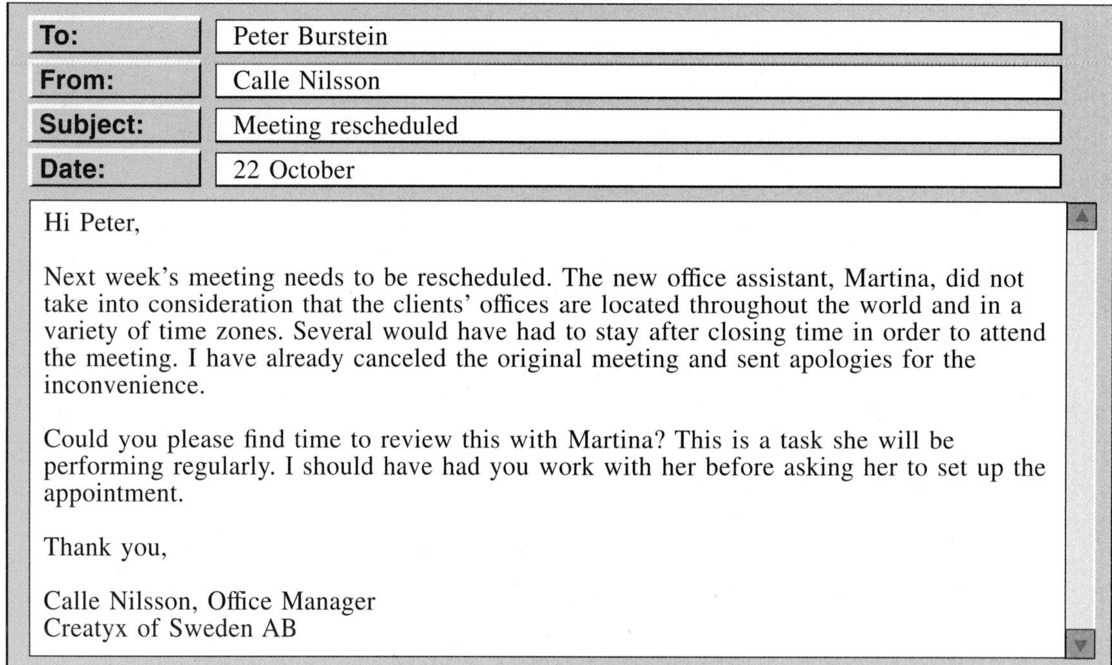

To:	Peter Burstein
From:	Calle Nilsson
Subject:	Meeting rescheduled
Date:	22 October

Hi Peter,

Next week's meeting needs to be rescheduled. The new office assistant, Martina, did not take into consideration that the clients' offices are located throughout the world and in a variety of time zones. Several would have had to stay after closing time in order to attend the meeting. I have already canceled the original meeting and sent apologies for the inconvenience.

Could you please find time to review this with Martina? This is a task she will be performing regularly. I should have had you work with her before asking her to set up the appointment.

Thank you,

Calle Nilsson, Office Manager
Creatyx of Sweden AB

153. Why did Ms. Nilsson send the e-mail?

(A) To set up an interview
(B) To suggest a new client
(C) To announce a new calendar system
(D) To request that an employee be trained

154. What was wrong with the original time of the meeting?

(A) It was scheduled during an office holiday.
(B) It was not convenient for international clients.
(C) Ms. Nilsson was not available on that date.
(D) The room was being used by Mr. Burstein.

Questions 155-157 refer to the following e-mail.

E-mail

To: Bradley Watkins
From: Aiko Yamashita
Subject: New software
Date: April 4

Bradley, I've come across a new software program that I think will be very useful for creating checklists to organize our projects. — [1] —. It's called Close Project, and it seems fairly easy to work with. — [2] —. Users log in to view a list of items that need to be completed for each project they are working on. — [3] —. This helps to keep better track of the progress of each project. There's even a mobile application that allows users to take photographs to show an actual problem, such as a broken pipe. — [4] —. I've downloaded a sample program. Would you be interested in coming to my office this afternoon to go through it with me? Let me know.

Aiko

155. Why did Ms. Yamashita send the e-mail to Mr. Watkins?

(A) To reschedule an appointment
(B) To confirm that he has received a sample
(C) To inform him about a new product
(D) To find out whether he has completed a project

156. What does Ms. Yamashita ask Mr. Watkins to do?

(A) Contact her
(B) Call a subcontractor
(C) Send some photographs
(D) Write some project notes

157. In which of the positions marked [1], [2], [3], and [4] does the following sentence best belong?

"Then they check 'Completed' when each task is finished."

(A) [1]
(B) [2]
(C) [3]
(D) [4]

GO ON TO THE NEXT PAGE

Questions 158-160 refer to the following announcement.

Win Free Juice for the Summer!

Here at Fresh Burst we want to celebrate the approaching summer! We'll reward the customer who comes up with a juice flavour that is brand-new. The lucky winner will receive a case of twenty-four 250 ml. bottles of the new juice every month from 1 July through 30 September! We'll also take photographs of you with your new juice to use in our advertising campaigns.

All you have to do is leave a comment describing your idea for a new flavour on our Fresh Burst social media page, then share your post with your friends. In your post, don't forget to include the creative name you've invented for your new juice!

The contest runs from 6 January until 14 February. The winner will be notified by 25 April. Please note that the competition is only open to people aged 18 and over. Please also note that we cannot accept entries that include logos, product names, or other materials that are copyrighted by other companies.

158. What type of organization most likely is Fresh Burst?

(A) A local newspaper
(B) A photography studio
(C) A social media platform
(D) A beverage manufacturer

159. When is the deadline to enter the competition?

(A) January 6
(B) February 14
(C) April 25
(D) September 30

160. What is NOT a requirement for entering the competition?

(A) Being at least 18 years old
(B) Including a logo with the entry
(C) Sharing a post on social media
(D) Creating a name for the new product

Questions 161-163 refer to the following chart.

Mergystic Industries (MI) Plant Operations Workflow

1. Trucks deliver materials to MI plant. Nonrecyclable items are removed; recyclables are put on a conveyor belt. Discarded items are transferred to trucks for landfill disposal.
2. Rotating discs lift out cardboard. Smaller items pass through the screen. Boxes are cleaned and flattened.
3. Paper passes under a low barrier to a holding area, while other objects continue on. Paper items are shredded.
4. A magnet removes metal objects from the conveyor belt. Metal objects are automatically sorted by type and crushed.
5. Glass items are manually removed from the belt. Glass objects are shattered.
6. An optical scanner separates plastics by type using a printed-on code. All processed items are sent to manufacturers as raw materials.

161. What type of business most likely is Mergystic Industries?

(A) A manufacturing firm
(B) A package-printing company
(C) A recycling plant
(D) A shipping company

162. According to the chart, what happens to cardboard boxes in the process?

(A) They are put behind a screen.
(B) They are cleaned.
(C) They are filled with products.
(D) They are crushed.

163. What items are most likely removed from the conveyor belt at stage 4 ?

(A) Milk cartons
(B) Glass jars
(C) Steel cans
(D) Plastic bottles

GO ON TO THE NEXT PAGE

Questions 164-167 refer to the following article.

New and Notable in Tarryville

Many in our small city thought we would never have a restaurant-delivery service. — [1] —. But thanks to two enterprising young people, we now have TVL Delivers! Alicia Kazarian and Theresa Cho were in their final year at the local university when they came up with their plan last May. "We were studying for exams one night and wanted to avoid going out for dinner. We were frustrated by the limited options available in Tarryville for food delivery. We wanted an easy way to find, order, and pay for our meals. — [2] —. But no such service existed here," said Ms. Cho.

In an effort to fill the food-delivery gap in Tarryville, TVL Delivers connects diners and restaurants on an online platform that serves each of their needs. — [3] —. Restaurants can reach a broader clientele, and customers can choose from an impressively diverse list of vendors, select and order their food, and pay through one of a number of online payment methods, all from the convenience of their home or office. The restaurants partnering with TVL Delivers are spread across most of Tarryville's neighborhoods and offer food options to suit any budget. — [4] —. "We think we're off to a good start, but we already have improvements in mind," said Ms. Kazarian. "Some food-delivery services promise that orders will be delivered in as little as 30 minutes. We hope eventually to deliver within a specified time, but we need to ensure that all aspects of our service are working properly before officially making that promise."

The head of the Tarryville Business Council, Barry Porter, expressed enthusiasm for the new business. "Of course, I am always excited for a new business to open here in Tarryville. But this is a business that local residents have long wished for. And, with the recent opening of Crisley Office Park on the south side of the city, I am sure TVL Delivers will be a success."

164. What is the purpose of the article?

(A) To review a restaurant that just opened
(B) To interview a famous Tarryville resident
(C) To report on the construction of a new city building
(D) To describe a recently launched business

165. According to the article, what is NOT offered by TVL Delivers?

(A) Guaranteed delivery times
(B) Online menus
(C) Convenient payment options
(D) A variety of participating vendors

166. What does Mr. Porter suggest about the businesses at Crisley Office Park?

(A) They will soon move to another location.
(B) They will order from TVL Delivers.
(C) Some of them will be restaurants.
(D) Some of them will hire local university students.

167. In which of the positions marked [1], [2], [3], and [4] does the following sentence best belong?

"We also wanted to be able to choose from a range of cuisines and price points."

(A) [1]
(B) [2]
(C) [3]
(D) [4]

GO ON TO THE NEXT PAGE

Questions 168-171 refer to the following letter.

3 November

Rhys Tomasen
Hiring Manager
Slepoy Marketing Ltd.
Level 7, 500 Exeton Street
Sydney, NSW 2000

Dear Mr. Tomasen,

I would like to thank you again for the opportunity to interview for the position of staff photographer with Slepoy Marketing. Although I am disappointed that I was not chosen, I enjoyed meeting you and your staff. Your decision to go with another candidate does not diminish my belief that your company is a first-rate marketing firm, which rightfully deserves the many awards it has won.

Incidentally, during our meeting you happened to mention your upcoming mountain-themed campaign as well as the fact that your company often hires freelance photographers. I will be traveling in Asia for the next three months, and plan to shoot landscape photographs that might be appropriate for this campaign. Should you be interested, I would be happy to send you some of those pictures.

Thanks again for meeting with me. I hope to have another opportunity to speak with you at this year's Graphic Arts Conference in Brisbane.

Sincerely,

Ye-Eun Whang

Ye-Eun Whang

168. Why did Ms. Whang send the letter?

(A) To decline a job offer
(B) To offer her services
(C) To inquire about a job opening
(D) To suggest a candidate for a position

169. What is Ms. Whang's opinion of Slepoy Marketing?

(A) It is worthy of its many awards.
(B) It offers services that are in high demand.
(C) It has good hiring practices.
(D) It values staff collaboration.

170. What does Ms. Whang want to send Mr. Tomasen?

(A) A list of references
(B) Some marketing ideas
(C) A conference program
(D) Some photographs

171. When does Ms. Whang hope to see Mr. Tomasen again?

(A) At a second interview
(B) At a marketing meeting
(C) At a photography session
(D) At a professional conference

GO ON TO THE NEXT PAGE

Questions 172-175 refer to the following online chat discussion.

CHAT

Nora O'Byrne (9:36 A.M.) Ms. Klimek, I just purchased plane tickets to our presentation meeting with the Madrid retailer next week.

Anna Klimek (9:37 A.M.) Great. Did you manage to book a flight for Thursday?

Nora O'Byrne (9:37 A.M.) Yes, at 4:00 P.M. We'll arrive there in the evening, with enough time to rest before the Friday meeting. Back to Dublin on Saturday, as planned.

Anna Klimek (9:38 A.M.) Perfect. Could you also take care of travel insurance?

Nora O'Byrne (9:38 A.M.) To cover both health and merchandise examples?

Anna Klimek (9:39 A.M.) Yes, we're taking fabrics, designs, and a few selections from our line. Can you use the same insurance agent as last time?

Nora O'Byrne (9:40 A.M.) Mr. Daly, could you prepare an insurance package for Ms. Klimek and me? International travel, covering health and sample goods we will be bringing.

Fergal Daly (9:40 A.M.) With pleasure. Can I have your flight and baggage details?

Nora O'Byrne (9:41 A.M.) Next Thursday to Saturday. Dublin to Madrid and return, on Air Conaway. Lightweight baggage, mainly apparel and fashion accessories.

Fergal Daly (9:59 A.M.) OK, I've just forwarded you an electronic policy.

Nora O'Byrne (10:01 A.M.) Thank you! I've just provided my electronic signature. I'll wire the money now.

Fergal Daly (10:02 A.M.) Take your time. The insurance company allows two days, so you have until Wednesday.

Send

172. In what industry do Ms. O'Byrne and Ms. Klimek most likely work?

(A) Insurance
(B) Advertising
(C) Clothing
(D) Health care

173. When will a presentation probably be given?

(A) On Wednesday
(B) On Thursday
(C) On Friday
(D) On Saturday

174. What are Ms. O'Byrne and Ms. Klimek planning to take on board the airplane?

(A) Customers' orders
(B) Training materials
(C) Heavy luggage
(D) Product samples

175. At 10:02 A.M., what does Mr. Daly mean when he writes, "Take your time"?

(A) A payment does not need to be made immediately.
(B) A signature is not needed until next week.
(C) A document will be sent tomorrow.
(D) A flight has been delayed.

TEST 10

GO ON TO THE NEXT PAGE

Questions 176-180 refer to the following articles.

New Theatre Almost Ready

By Nigel Smith

LIVERPOOL (15 August)—Work is nearing completion on a new theatre, which will become the first new theatre in the city for the past 20 years. The Cricket Theatre, which is being built on the site of the former Fletcher shoe factory, will have an auditorium that can seat 400 patrons. The theatre will be operated by the Watts-Spicer Group, which owns three other theatres, two in London and one in York.

The venue is expected to open in October, said Watts-Spicer's chairperson, Colin Watts. "We have just completed the longest stage of the project, which was slower than expected due to back-ordered seats from Australia. We are expecting to open with the musical *Backup* on 30 October." The Cricket Theatre will host a variety of productions, from traditional plays to special engagements with artists of all kinds.

Cricket Theatre's *Backup* Is Wonderful

By Clara Kennedy

LIVERPOOL (2 December)—The Cricket Theatre's first production, *Backup*, opened last night to a full house. Theatregoers were clearly delighted by this new musical, which is based on a true story. *Backup* follows Babette Jones, a young backup singer for famous musical acts, through her 23-year struggle to become a successful solo act. Liverpool native Tami McClure, as Ms. Jones, thrilled the audience with her wide-ranging vocals. Paul Robinson, who played her fearless manager, also put in a strong performance. Costume designer Sophie Wright's fashions were exquisite.

Backup's strong production values and the Cricket Theatre's reasonable ticket prices point to a long and successful future for this new theatre. *Backup* runs until 5 February at the Cricket Theatre.

176. What is indicated about the Watts-Spicer Group?

(A) It runs multiple theaters.
(B) It owned the Fletcher shoe factory.
(C) It is an Australian company.
(D) It operates the oldest theater in the city.

177. In the first article, the word "stage" in paragraph 2, line 4, is closest in meaning to

(A) phase
(B) platform
(C) scene
(D) presentation

178. What is implied about the Cricket Theatre?

(A) Its prices are very high.
(B) Its shows will mainly be musical comedies.
(C) Its expected opening was delayed.
(D) Its next production begins in January.

179. According to the second article, what is indicated about *Backup*?

(A) It had low ticket sales.
(B) It disappointed the audience.
(C) Its story is fictional.
(D) Its story takes place over several decades.

180. Who is Ms. McClure?

(A) A performer
(B) A manager
(C) A costume designer
(D) A set designer

TEST 10

GO ON TO THE NEXT PAGE

Questions 181-185 refer to the following article and online review.

KENT (26 February)—Stellar Chocolates is a local business offering a wide selection of handcrafted delicacies. With two shops in Kent, the business is well-known in the area. Recently, however, Stellar Chocolates gained national recognition by earning top awards from the Chocolate Council last month.

Stephanie Davidson, who co-owns the shops with Brian Markus, emphasises the sources and quality of Stellar Chocolates. "Before launching the business, Brian and I spent several months travelling to areas of the world known for quality cacao-bean production. We inspected the plants and learned about traditional harvesting and roasting processes," she said. In fact, production started only after the co-owners had secured the finest ingredients for their products. They now incorporate a variety of other ingredients such as chili, basil, and even wasabi, to create a unique line of chocolates.

Demand for Stellar's line has continued to grow, and the firm expects to open a third shop in Bath later this year. Ms. Davidson noted that they have found additional space in an old mill to be converted for retail use. "The new shop will be our largest, and we plan to establish a mail-order business so that we can ship not just domestically but also internationally," she said.

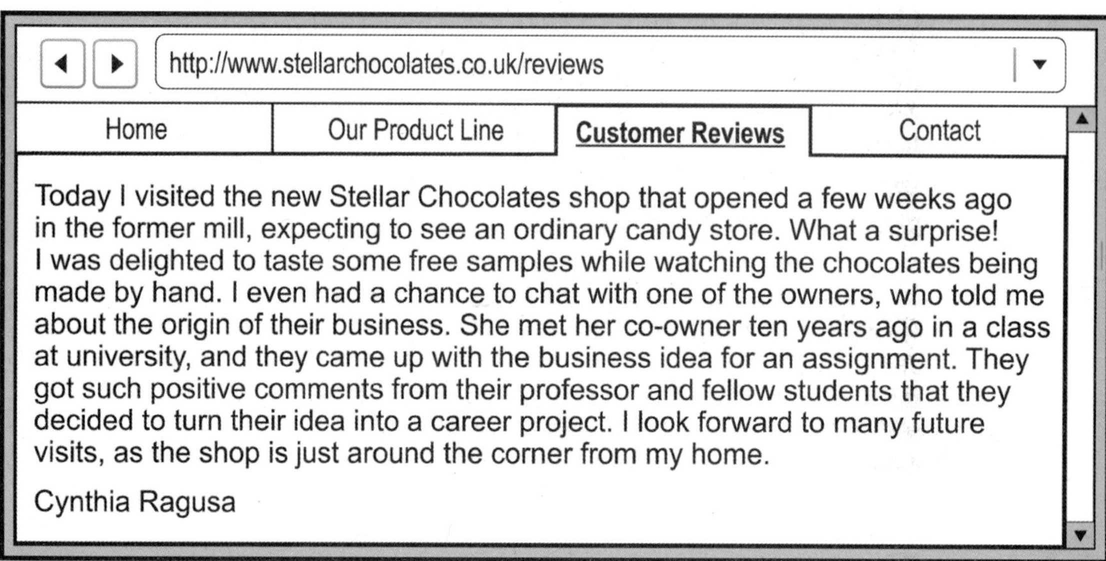

http://www.stellarchocolates.co.uk/reviews

Home | Our Product Line | **Customer Reviews** | Contact

Today I visited the new Stellar Chocolates shop that opened a few weeks ago in the former mill, expecting to see an ordinary candy store. What a surprise! I was delighted to taste some free samples while watching the chocolates being made by hand. I even had a chance to chat with one of the owners, who told me about the origin of their business. She met her co-owner ten years ago in a class at university, and they came up with the business idea for an assignment. They got such positive comments from their professor and fellow students that they decided to turn their idea into a career project. I look forward to many future visits, as the shop is just around the corner from my home.

Cynthia Ragusa

181. What is stated about Stellar Chocolates in the article?

(A) It sells a variety of items in addition to chocolates.
(B) It does most of its business through mail orders.
(C) It has been recognized for excellence in chocolate making.
(D) It has recently automated its manufacturing process.

182. What is indicated about Mr. Markus?

(A) He was interviewed for the article.
(B) He is a frequent customer.
(C) He met Ms. Davidson at university.
(D) He oversaw the conversion of the mill.

183. In the article, the word "finest" in paragraph 2, line 11, is closest in meaning to

(A) healthiest
(B) best
(C) thinnest
(D) most common

184. What is suggested about Ms. Ragusa?

(A) She seldom eats chocolate.
(B) She used to work in a mill in Kent.
(C) She is a colleague of Ms. Davidson's.
(D) She lives in Bath.

185. What is indicated about the newest Stellar Chocolates shop?

(A) Its opening was delayed.
(B) Its hours have been extended.
(C) It is located in a former post office.
(D) It offers complimentary samples.

TEST 10

GO ON TO THE NEXT PAGE

Questions 186-190 refer to the following e-mail, Web page, and form.

To:	Alex Gulin <alex.gulin@senmail.ca>
From:	Kohek Apparel <orders@kohekapparel.com>
Date:	August 27
Subject:	Kohek Apparel order confirmation

Dear Alex:

Thank you for your online order from Kohek Apparel! Your order should arrive within 5–10 business days. See below for details:

Order Number: 96781

Deliver To: 22 Exeter Street, Toronto, M4B 1B3 CANADA

Order Summary:

Description	Item Number	Color	Size	Price
Jogging suit	P394	Charcoal gray	Large	$78.00
Cotton shirt	S963	Bright white	Large	$36.00
Wool sweater	SW852	Sky blue	Large	$45.00
Fleece jacket	J109	Moss green	Large	$65.00
			Total $224.00	

We appreciate your repeated business! To receive a coupon for 10 percent off your next order, visit our website and enter the promotional code RC008.

http://www.kohekapparel.com/returns 

KOHEK APPAREL—Return Policy

Kohek Apparel strives to create high-quality, great-fitting items at a reasonable price. We want you to be completely satisfied with your order and would like to make the return process as easy as possible.

To return an item, request a shipping label by emailing customersupport@kohekapparel.com. A printable shipping label will be emailed to you. Once you receive it, place the item in the same box it arrived in, along with a completed return request form (found on the back of your invoice), and tape the shipping label to the box. If you no longer have the original box, place the item in a different box. Your purchase will be fully refunded once we receive the package.

Returns within the United States are completely free. For returns from Canada, a $6 shipping charge will be deducted from your refund. From all other countries, the shipping charge is $12.

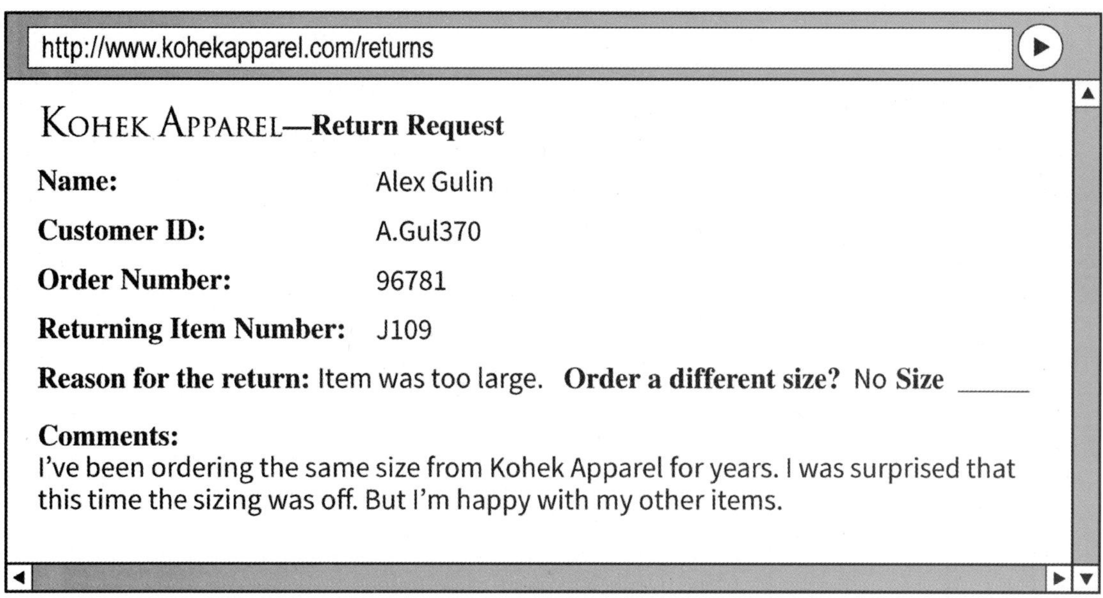

http://www.kohekapparel.com/returns

KOHEK APPAREL—**Return Request**

Name: Alex Gulin

Customer ID: A.Gul370

Order Number: 96781

Returning Item Number: J109

Reason for the return: Item was too large. **Order a different size?** No **Size** _____

Comments:
I've been ordering the same size from Kohek Apparel for years. I was surprised that this time the sizing was off. But I'm happy with my other items.

186. What is suggested about Kohek Apparel?
(A) It has added several new items to its inventory.
(B) It offers discounts to returning customers.
(C) It specializes in summer apparel.
(D) It does not ship items internationally.

187. What do all of the items in Mr. Gulin's order have in common?
(A) They are made from the same material.
(B) They are the same price.
(C) They are manufactured in Canada.
(D) They are the same size.

188. What do customers need to do when returning an item?
(A) Use a box of a specific size
(B) Submit a form online
(C) Print out a shipping label
(D) Use a specific delivery company

189. What item is Mr. Gulin returning?
(A) A jogging suit
(B) A shirt
(C) A sweater
(D) A jacket

190. What is indicated about Mr. Gulin?
(A) He will be charged a return shipping fee.
(B) He is dissatisfied with the refund policy.
(C) He is going to order a replacement item.
(D) He will not buy clothes again from Kohek Apparel.

GO ON TO THE NEXT PAGE

Questions 191-195 refer to the following schedule, newsletter article, and form.

Kuraki Motors Canadian Dealer Annual Meeting
Schedule for Friday, June 8

7:30 A.M.	Breakfast	East Ballroom
9:00 A.M.	Keynote Address CEO Katsuhiko Nakamuro	South Ballroom
10:30 A.M.	Kuraki Business Outlook Vice President Jiro Higa	South Ballroom
Noon	Lunch	East Ballroom
1:30 P.M.	New Product Debuts Chief Designer Yuna Yamashita	South Ballroom
4:00 P.M.	Dealer-Led Seminars: The Modern Dealership Digital Campaigns	 Mara Room Flora Room
6:00 P.M.	Dinner	East Ballroom

Canadian Dealer Meeting

By Josie Hopkins, *Kuraki Now* Staff Writer

Executives from Kuraki Motors returned to Toronto for an annual meeting of the nearly 1,000 Canadian representatives of the brand. The two-day event kicked off on Friday morning with CEO Katsuhiko Nakamuro, who gave a keynote address highlighting progress on the company's new manufacturing plant in Toronto. He was followed by Vice President Jiro Higa detailing increased production levels and expected growth. Attendees then had the opportunity to attend two days of seminars. But the highlight of the event was the unveiling of two new models, the sleek Daino sedan and Kuraki's new hybrid, the Pura. The models will be rolling into dealerships in August.

Kuraki Motors Canadian Dealer Annual Meeting—Survey Form

Thank you for attending this year's dealer meeting. We would appreciate your feedback. Please use the following rating scale to rate each of the seminars you attended.

Rating Scale: 4 = excellent; 3 = very good; 2 = satisfactory; 1 = poor

Seminars	Rating
The Modern Dealership	4
Digital Campaigns	n/a
Proven Methods to Attract Salespeople	4
Internet Sales Success	n/a
The Business Model of the Future	n/a
Standing Out from the Competition	4

Comments:

The seminars on both days were informative as always. I wish that some were not scheduled at the same time and that more were offered before lunch on Saturday. Some of my colleagues were unable to stay for the afternoon sessions.

Name: Howard Gellman

191. In which location did Kuraki's senior executives make presentations?

(A) East Ballroom
(B) South Ballroom
(C) Mara Room
(D) Flora Room

192. What is one purpose of the article?

(A) To summarize the events that took place at an annual meeting
(B) To review the features of a new car model
(C) To provide details about seminars being offered
(D) To announce the promotion of Mr. Nakamuro

193. When were the Daino and the Pura most likely introduced to meeting attendees?

(A) At 7:30 A.M.
(B) At 9:00 A.M.
(C) At 1:30 P.M.
(D) At 6:00 P.M.

194. What is indicated about Mr. Gellman?

(A) He attended a seminar on Friday.
(B) He left before lunch on Saturday.
(C) He works in digital advertising for Kuraki.
(D) He plans to lead a seminar at next year's meeting.

195. What is Mr. Gellman's complaint about the seminars?

(A) They were too long.
(B) The topics were boring.
(C) It was not possible to attend them all.
(D) He did not like the presenters.

GO ON TO THE NEXT PAGE

Questions 196-200 refer to the following invitation, brochure, and e-mail.

Creative Tech Conference

Join us for the Tenth Annual Creative Tech Conference. Explore the latest technologies with the top innovators in their fields. Enjoy a full day of presentations, workshops, discussions, and exhibitions, culminating with a keynote address by Ayana Gonzalez, the founder of Grutenhur Tech.

May 12, 9 A.M.–6 P.M.
Bondal University
22 Markus Street
Ione, California

Purchase tickets online at www.creativetechcon.com/tickets.

Interested in being a sponsor? See the attached sponsor benefits brochure.

Creative Tech Conference
Sponsor Benefits

We couldn't run the Creative Tech Conference without the help of sponsors. In addition to supporting entrepreneurs and innovators, sponsorship is a great way to get the name of your business out to our 500+ attendees in various tech fields. See below for sponsorship levels.

Innovator—$5,000
- Your company's logo on a large banner displayed during the keynote address
- Free four-hour exhibitor booth
- Your company's logo featured on our Web site and conference program
- Half-price tickets for all employees that attend the conference

Creator—$3,000
- Your company's logo on a large banner displayed during the final reception
- Free four-hour exhibitor booth
- Your company's logo featured on our Web site and conference program

Entrepreneur—$2,000
- Your company's logo featured on our Web site and conference program
- Free four-hour exhibitor booth

Patron—$1,000
- Your company's logo featured on our Web site and conference program

Please contact sponsors@creativetechconference.com for more information.

E-mail

To:	All Orlavel Analytics Staff
From:	Edsel Skyers
Subject:	Creative Tech Conference
Date:	May 2

Dear Staff,

I hope you will attend the Creative Tech Conference on May 12. It is taking place nearby at Bondal University. I have gone the past two years, and it is a great way to network and stay informed about the newest trends in our field. And because we are a sponsor of the event, our employees receive a discount on tickets. Plus, as some of you may know, the keynote speaker is a former employee! Let me know if you have any questions.

Edsel Skyers
Product Development Director
Orlavel Analytics

196. What does the invitation state about the Creative Tech Conference?

(A) It is organized by university professors.
(B) University students can request free tickets.
(C) It is a one-day conference.
(D) This is the first year the conference will take place.

197. According to the brochure, what is a benefit of sponsoring the conference?

(A) Sponsors can give a presentation at the conference.
(B) Sponsors are invited to a special reception.
(C) Sponsors can advertise their business to potential customers.
(D) Sponsors get free product samples.

198. Why did Mr. Skyers write the e-mail?

(A) To introduce his staff to a new employee
(B) To encourage his staff to attend an event
(C) To tell his staff about new technology
(D) To announce a research partnership with a university

199. What is indicated about Ms. Gonzalez?

(A) She is a sponsor of the Creative Tech Conference.
(B) She lives in Ione, California.
(C) She opened a business 10 years ago.
(D) She previously worked for Orlavel Analytics.

200. What type of sponsor is Orlavel Analytics?

(A) Innovator
(B) Creator
(C) Entrepreneur
(D) Patron

Stop! This is the end of the test. If you finish before time is called, you may go back to Parts 5, 6, and 7 and check your work.

ANSWER SHEET

ETS® TOEIC® 토익® 정기시험 기출문제집

수험번호 | | | | | | |

응시일자 : 20 년 월 일

성명		
	한 글	
	한 자	
	영 자	

Test 01 (Part 5~7)

No.		No.		No.		No.		No.	
101	ⓐ ⓑ ⓒ ⓓ	121	ⓐ ⓑ ⓒ ⓓ	141	ⓐ ⓑ ⓒ ⓓ	161	ⓐ ⓑ ⓒ ⓓ	181	ⓐ ⓑ ⓒ ⓓ
102	ⓐ ⓑ ⓒ ⓓ	122	ⓐ ⓑ ⓒ ⓓ	142	ⓐ ⓑ ⓒ ⓓ	162	ⓐ ⓑ ⓒ ⓓ	182	ⓐ ⓑ ⓒ ⓓ
103	ⓐ ⓑ ⓒ ⓓ	123	ⓐ ⓑ ⓒ ⓓ	143	ⓐ ⓑ ⓒ ⓓ	163	ⓐ ⓑ ⓒ ⓓ	183	ⓐ ⓑ ⓒ ⓓ
104	ⓐ ⓑ ⓒ ⓓ	124	ⓐ ⓑ ⓒ ⓓ	144	ⓐ ⓑ ⓒ ⓓ	164	ⓐ ⓑ ⓒ ⓓ	184	ⓐ ⓑ ⓒ ⓓ
105	ⓐ ⓑ ⓒ ⓓ	125	ⓐ ⓑ ⓒ ⓓ	145	ⓐ ⓑ ⓒ ⓓ	165	ⓐ ⓑ ⓒ ⓓ	185	ⓐ ⓑ ⓒ ⓓ
106	ⓐ ⓑ ⓒ ⓓ	126	ⓐ ⓑ ⓒ ⓓ	146	ⓐ ⓑ ⓒ ⓓ	166	ⓐ ⓑ ⓒ ⓓ	186	ⓐ ⓑ ⓒ ⓓ
107	ⓐ ⓑ ⓒ ⓓ	127	ⓐ ⓑ ⓒ ⓓ	147	ⓐ ⓑ ⓒ ⓓ	167	ⓐ ⓑ ⓒ ⓓ	187	ⓐ ⓑ ⓒ ⓓ
108	ⓐ ⓑ ⓒ ⓓ	128	ⓐ ⓑ ⓒ ⓓ	148	ⓐ ⓑ ⓒ ⓓ	168	ⓐ ⓑ ⓒ ⓓ	188	ⓐ ⓑ ⓒ ⓓ
109	ⓐ ⓑ ⓒ ⓓ	129	ⓐ ⓑ ⓒ ⓓ	149	ⓐ ⓑ ⓒ ⓓ	169	ⓐ ⓑ ⓒ ⓓ	189	ⓐ ⓑ ⓒ ⓓ
110	ⓐ ⓑ ⓒ ⓓ	130	ⓐ ⓑ ⓒ ⓓ	150	ⓐ ⓑ ⓒ ⓓ	170	ⓐ ⓑ ⓒ ⓓ	190	ⓐ ⓑ ⓒ ⓓ
111	ⓐ ⓑ ⓒ ⓓ	131	ⓐ ⓑ ⓒ ⓓ	151	ⓐ ⓑ ⓒ ⓓ	171	ⓐ ⓑ ⓒ ⓓ	191	ⓐ ⓑ ⓒ ⓓ
112	ⓐ ⓑ ⓒ ⓓ	132	ⓐ ⓑ ⓒ ⓓ	152	ⓐ ⓑ ⓒ ⓓ	172	ⓐ ⓑ ⓒ ⓓ	192	ⓐ ⓑ ⓒ ⓓ
113	ⓐ ⓑ ⓒ ⓓ	133	ⓐ ⓑ ⓒ ⓓ	153	ⓐ ⓑ ⓒ ⓓ	173	ⓐ ⓑ ⓒ ⓓ	193	ⓐ ⓑ ⓒ ⓓ
114	ⓐ ⓑ ⓒ ⓓ	134	ⓐ ⓑ ⓒ ⓓ	154	ⓐ ⓑ ⓒ ⓓ	174	ⓐ ⓑ ⓒ ⓓ	194	ⓐ ⓑ ⓒ ⓓ
115	ⓐ ⓑ ⓒ ⓓ	135	ⓐ ⓑ ⓒ ⓓ	155	ⓐ ⓑ ⓒ ⓓ	175	ⓐ ⓑ ⓒ ⓓ	195	ⓐ ⓑ ⓒ ⓓ
116	ⓐ ⓑ ⓒ ⓓ	136	ⓐ ⓑ ⓒ ⓓ	156	ⓐ ⓑ ⓒ ⓓ	176	ⓐ ⓑ ⓒ ⓓ	196	ⓐ ⓑ ⓒ ⓓ
117	ⓐ ⓑ ⓒ ⓓ	137	ⓐ ⓑ ⓒ ⓓ	157	ⓐ ⓑ ⓒ ⓓ	177	ⓐ ⓑ ⓒ ⓓ	197	ⓐ ⓑ ⓒ ⓓ
118	ⓐ ⓑ ⓒ ⓓ	138	ⓐ ⓑ ⓒ ⓓ	158	ⓐ ⓑ ⓒ ⓓ	178	ⓐ ⓑ ⓒ ⓓ	198	ⓐ ⓑ ⓒ ⓓ
119	ⓐ ⓑ ⓒ ⓓ	139	ⓐ ⓑ ⓒ ⓓ	159	ⓐ ⓑ ⓒ ⓓ	179	ⓐ ⓑ ⓒ ⓓ	199	ⓐ ⓑ ⓒ ⓓ
120	ⓐ ⓑ ⓒ ⓓ	140	ⓐ ⓑ ⓒ ⓓ	160	ⓐ ⓑ ⓒ ⓓ	180	ⓐ ⓑ ⓒ ⓓ	200	ⓐ ⓑ ⓒ ⓓ

Test 02 (Part 5~7)

No.		No.		No.		No.		No.	
101	ⓐ ⓑ ⓒ ⓓ	121	ⓐ ⓑ ⓒ ⓓ	141	ⓐ ⓑ ⓒ ⓓ	161	ⓐ ⓑ ⓒ ⓓ	181	ⓐ ⓑ ⓒ ⓓ
102	ⓐ ⓑ ⓒ ⓓ	122	ⓐ ⓑ ⓒ ⓓ	142	ⓐ ⓑ ⓒ ⓓ	162	ⓐ ⓑ ⓒ ⓓ	182	ⓐ ⓑ ⓒ ⓓ
103	ⓐ ⓑ ⓒ ⓓ	123	ⓐ ⓑ ⓒ ⓓ	143	ⓐ ⓑ ⓒ ⓓ	163	ⓐ ⓑ ⓒ ⓓ	183	ⓐ ⓑ ⓒ ⓓ
104	ⓐ ⓑ ⓒ ⓓ	124	ⓐ ⓑ ⓒ ⓓ	144	ⓐ ⓑ ⓒ ⓓ	164	ⓐ ⓑ ⓒ ⓓ	184	ⓐ ⓑ ⓒ ⓓ
105	ⓐ ⓑ ⓒ ⓓ	125	ⓐ ⓑ ⓒ ⓓ	145	ⓐ ⓑ ⓒ ⓓ	165	ⓐ ⓑ ⓒ ⓓ	185	ⓐ ⓑ ⓒ ⓓ
106	ⓐ ⓑ ⓒ ⓓ	126	ⓐ ⓑ ⓒ ⓓ	146	ⓐ ⓑ ⓒ ⓓ	166	ⓐ ⓑ ⓒ ⓓ	186	ⓐ ⓑ ⓒ ⓓ
107	ⓐ ⓑ ⓒ ⓓ	127	ⓐ ⓑ ⓒ ⓓ	147	ⓐ ⓑ ⓒ ⓓ	167	ⓐ ⓑ ⓒ ⓓ	187	ⓐ ⓑ ⓒ ⓓ
108	ⓐ ⓑ ⓒ ⓓ	128	ⓐ ⓑ ⓒ ⓓ	148	ⓐ ⓑ ⓒ ⓓ	168	ⓐ ⓑ ⓒ ⓓ	188	ⓐ ⓑ ⓒ ⓓ
109	ⓐ ⓑ ⓒ ⓓ	129	ⓐ ⓑ ⓒ ⓓ	149	ⓐ ⓑ ⓒ ⓓ	169	ⓐ ⓑ ⓒ ⓓ	189	ⓐ ⓑ ⓒ ⓓ
110	ⓐ ⓑ ⓒ ⓓ	130	ⓐ ⓑ ⓒ ⓓ	150	ⓐ ⓑ ⓒ ⓓ	170	ⓐ ⓑ ⓒ ⓓ	190	ⓐ ⓑ ⓒ ⓓ
111	ⓐ ⓑ ⓒ ⓓ	131	ⓐ ⓑ ⓒ ⓓ	151	ⓐ ⓑ ⓒ ⓓ	171	ⓐ ⓑ ⓒ ⓓ	191	ⓐ ⓑ ⓒ ⓓ
112	ⓐ ⓑ ⓒ ⓓ	132	ⓐ ⓑ ⓒ ⓓ	152	ⓐ ⓑ ⓒ ⓓ	172	ⓐ ⓑ ⓒ ⓓ	192	ⓐ ⓑ ⓒ ⓓ
113	ⓐ ⓑ ⓒ ⓓ	133	ⓐ ⓑ ⓒ ⓓ	153	ⓐ ⓑ ⓒ ⓓ	173	ⓐ ⓑ ⓒ ⓓ	193	ⓐ ⓑ ⓒ ⓓ
114	ⓐ ⓑ ⓒ ⓓ	134	ⓐ ⓑ ⓒ ⓓ	154	ⓐ ⓑ ⓒ ⓓ	174	ⓐ ⓑ ⓒ ⓓ	194	ⓐ ⓑ ⓒ ⓓ
115	ⓐ ⓑ ⓒ ⓓ	135	ⓐ ⓑ ⓒ ⓓ	155	ⓐ ⓑ ⓒ ⓓ	175	ⓐ ⓑ ⓒ ⓓ	195	ⓐ ⓑ ⓒ ⓓ
116	ⓐ ⓑ ⓒ ⓓ	136	ⓐ ⓑ ⓒ ⓓ	156	ⓐ ⓑ ⓒ ⓓ	176	ⓐ ⓑ ⓒ ⓓ	196	ⓐ ⓑ ⓒ ⓓ
117	ⓐ ⓑ ⓒ ⓓ	137	ⓐ ⓑ ⓒ ⓓ	157	ⓐ ⓑ ⓒ ⓓ	177	ⓐ ⓑ ⓒ ⓓ	197	ⓐ ⓑ ⓒ ⓓ
118	ⓐ ⓑ ⓒ ⓓ	138	ⓐ ⓑ ⓒ ⓓ	158	ⓐ ⓑ ⓒ ⓓ	178	ⓐ ⓑ ⓒ ⓓ	198	ⓐ ⓑ ⓒ ⓓ
119	ⓐ ⓑ ⓒ ⓓ	139	ⓐ ⓑ ⓒ ⓓ	159	ⓐ ⓑ ⓒ ⓓ	179	ⓐ ⓑ ⓒ ⓓ	199	ⓐ ⓑ ⓒ ⓓ
120	ⓐ ⓑ ⓒ ⓓ	140	ⓐ ⓑ ⓒ ⓓ	160	ⓐ ⓑ ⓒ ⓓ	180	ⓐ ⓑ ⓒ ⓓ	200	ⓐ ⓑ ⓒ ⓓ

ANSWER SHEET

ETS® TOEIC® 토익® 정기시험 기출문제집

수험번호						

응시일자 : 20 년 월 일

성명	한 글	
	한 자	
	영 자	

Test 03 (Part 5~7)

No.		No.		No.		No.		No.	
101	ⓐ ⓑ ⓒ ⓓ	121	ⓐ ⓑ ⓒ ⓓ	141	ⓐ ⓑ ⓒ ⓓ	161	ⓐ ⓑ ⓒ ⓓ	181	ⓐ ⓑ ⓒ ⓓ
102	ⓐ ⓑ ⓒ ⓓ	122	ⓐ ⓑ ⓒ ⓓ	142	ⓐ ⓑ ⓒ ⓓ	162	ⓐ ⓑ ⓒ ⓓ	182	ⓐ ⓑ ⓒ ⓓ
103	ⓐ ⓑ ⓒ ⓓ	123	ⓐ ⓑ ⓒ ⓓ	143	ⓐ ⓑ ⓒ ⓓ	163	ⓐ ⓑ ⓒ ⓓ	183	ⓐ ⓑ ⓒ ⓓ
104	ⓐ ⓑ ⓒ ⓓ	124	ⓐ ⓑ ⓒ ⓓ	144	ⓐ ⓑ ⓒ ⓓ	164	ⓐ ⓑ ⓒ ⓓ	184	ⓐ ⓑ ⓒ ⓓ
105	ⓐ ⓑ ⓒ ⓓ	125	ⓐ ⓑ ⓒ ⓓ	145	ⓐ ⓑ ⓒ ⓓ	165	ⓐ ⓑ ⓒ ⓓ	185	ⓐ ⓑ ⓒ ⓓ
106	ⓐ ⓑ ⓒ ⓓ	126	ⓐ ⓑ ⓒ ⓓ	146	ⓐ ⓑ ⓒ ⓓ	166	ⓐ ⓑ ⓒ ⓓ	186	ⓐ ⓑ ⓒ ⓓ
107	ⓐ ⓑ ⓒ ⓓ	127	ⓐ ⓑ ⓒ ⓓ	147	ⓐ ⓑ ⓒ ⓓ	167	ⓐ ⓑ ⓒ ⓓ	187	ⓐ ⓑ ⓒ ⓓ
108	ⓐ ⓑ ⓒ ⓓ	128	ⓐ ⓑ ⓒ ⓓ	148	ⓐ ⓑ ⓒ ⓓ	168	ⓐ ⓑ ⓒ ⓓ	188	ⓐ ⓑ ⓒ ⓓ
109	ⓐ ⓑ ⓒ ⓓ	129	ⓐ ⓑ ⓒ ⓓ	149	ⓐ ⓑ ⓒ ⓓ	169	ⓐ ⓑ ⓒ ⓓ	189	ⓐ ⓑ ⓒ ⓓ
110	ⓐ ⓑ ⓒ ⓓ	130	ⓐ ⓑ ⓒ ⓓ	150	ⓐ ⓑ ⓒ ⓓ	170	ⓐ ⓑ ⓒ ⓓ	190	ⓐ ⓑ ⓒ ⓓ
111	ⓐ ⓑ ⓒ ⓓ	131	ⓐ ⓑ ⓒ ⓓ	151	ⓐ ⓑ ⓒ ⓓ	171	ⓐ ⓑ ⓒ ⓓ	191	ⓐ ⓑ ⓒ ⓓ
112	ⓐ ⓑ ⓒ ⓓ	132	ⓐ ⓑ ⓒ ⓓ	152	ⓐ ⓑ ⓒ ⓓ	172	ⓐ ⓑ ⓒ ⓓ	192	ⓐ ⓑ ⓒ ⓓ
113	ⓐ ⓑ ⓒ ⓓ	133	ⓐ ⓑ ⓒ ⓓ	153	ⓐ ⓑ ⓒ ⓓ	173	ⓐ ⓑ ⓒ ⓓ	193	ⓐ ⓑ ⓒ ⓓ
114	ⓐ ⓑ ⓒ ⓓ	134	ⓐ ⓑ ⓒ ⓓ	154	ⓐ ⓑ ⓒ ⓓ	174	ⓐ ⓑ ⓒ ⓓ	194	ⓐ ⓑ ⓒ ⓓ
115	ⓐ ⓑ ⓒ ⓓ	135	ⓐ ⓑ ⓒ ⓓ	155	ⓐ ⓑ ⓒ ⓓ	175	ⓐ ⓑ ⓒ ⓓ	195	ⓐ ⓑ ⓒ ⓓ
116	ⓐ ⓑ ⓒ ⓓ	136	ⓐ ⓑ ⓒ ⓓ	156	ⓐ ⓑ ⓒ ⓓ	176	ⓐ ⓑ ⓒ ⓓ	196	ⓐ ⓑ ⓒ ⓓ
117	ⓐ ⓑ ⓒ ⓓ	137	ⓐ ⓑ ⓒ ⓓ	157	ⓐ ⓑ ⓒ ⓓ	177	ⓐ ⓑ ⓒ ⓓ	197	ⓐ ⓑ ⓒ ⓓ
118	ⓐ ⓑ ⓒ ⓓ	138	ⓐ ⓑ ⓒ ⓓ	158	ⓐ ⓑ ⓒ ⓓ	178	ⓐ ⓑ ⓒ ⓓ	198	ⓐ ⓑ ⓒ ⓓ
119	ⓐ ⓑ ⓒ ⓓ	139	ⓐ ⓑ ⓒ ⓓ	159	ⓐ ⓑ ⓒ ⓓ	179	ⓐ ⓑ ⓒ ⓓ	199	ⓐ ⓑ ⓒ ⓓ
120	ⓐ ⓑ ⓒ ⓓ	140	ⓐ ⓑ ⓒ ⓓ	160	ⓐ ⓑ ⓒ ⓓ	180	ⓐ ⓑ ⓒ ⓓ	200	ⓐ ⓑ ⓒ ⓓ

Test 04 (Part 5~7)

No.		No.		No.		No.		No.	
101	ⓐ ⓑ ⓒ ⓓ	121	ⓐ ⓑ ⓒ ⓓ	141	ⓐ ⓑ ⓒ ⓓ	161	ⓐ ⓑ ⓒ ⓓ	181	ⓐ ⓑ ⓒ ⓓ
102	ⓐ ⓑ ⓒ ⓓ	122	ⓐ ⓑ ⓒ ⓓ	142	ⓐ ⓑ ⓒ ⓓ	162	ⓐ ⓑ ⓒ ⓓ	182	ⓐ ⓑ ⓒ ⓓ
103	ⓐ ⓑ ⓒ ⓓ	123	ⓐ ⓑ ⓒ ⓓ	143	ⓐ ⓑ ⓒ ⓓ	163	ⓐ ⓑ ⓒ ⓓ	183	ⓐ ⓑ ⓒ ⓓ
104	ⓐ ⓑ ⓒ ⓓ	124	ⓐ ⓑ ⓒ ⓓ	144	ⓐ ⓑ ⓒ ⓓ	164	ⓐ ⓑ ⓒ ⓓ	184	ⓐ ⓑ ⓒ ⓓ
105	ⓐ ⓑ ⓒ ⓓ	125	ⓐ ⓑ ⓒ ⓓ	145	ⓐ ⓑ ⓒ ⓓ	165	ⓐ ⓑ ⓒ ⓓ	185	ⓐ ⓑ ⓒ ⓓ
106	ⓐ ⓑ ⓒ ⓓ	126	ⓐ ⓑ ⓒ ⓓ	146	ⓐ ⓑ ⓒ ⓓ	166	ⓐ ⓑ ⓒ ⓓ	186	ⓐ ⓑ ⓒ ⓓ
107	ⓐ ⓑ ⓒ ⓓ	127	ⓐ ⓑ ⓒ ⓓ	147	ⓐ ⓑ ⓒ ⓓ	167	ⓐ ⓑ ⓒ ⓓ	187	ⓐ ⓑ ⓒ ⓓ
108	ⓐ ⓑ ⓒ ⓓ	128	ⓐ ⓑ ⓒ ⓓ	148	ⓐ ⓑ ⓒ ⓓ	168	ⓐ ⓑ ⓒ ⓓ	188	ⓐ ⓑ ⓒ ⓓ
109	ⓐ ⓑ ⓒ ⓓ	129	ⓐ ⓑ ⓒ ⓓ	149	ⓐ ⓑ ⓒ ⓓ	169	ⓐ ⓑ ⓒ ⓓ	189	ⓐ ⓑ ⓒ ⓓ
110	ⓐ ⓑ ⓒ ⓓ	130	ⓐ ⓑ ⓒ ⓓ	150	ⓐ ⓑ ⓒ ⓓ	170	ⓐ ⓑ ⓒ ⓓ	190	ⓐ ⓑ ⓒ ⓓ
111	ⓐ ⓑ ⓒ ⓓ	131	ⓐ ⓑ ⓒ ⓓ	151	ⓐ ⓑ ⓒ ⓓ	171	ⓐ ⓑ ⓒ ⓓ	191	ⓐ ⓑ ⓒ ⓓ
112	ⓐ ⓑ ⓒ ⓓ	132	ⓐ ⓑ ⓒ ⓓ	152	ⓐ ⓑ ⓒ ⓓ	172	ⓐ ⓑ ⓒ ⓓ	192	ⓐ ⓑ ⓒ ⓓ
113	ⓐ ⓑ ⓒ ⓓ	133	ⓐ ⓑ ⓒ ⓓ	153	ⓐ ⓑ ⓒ ⓓ	173	ⓐ ⓑ ⓒ ⓓ	193	ⓐ ⓑ ⓒ ⓓ
114	ⓐ ⓑ ⓒ ⓓ	134	ⓐ ⓑ ⓒ ⓓ	154	ⓐ ⓑ ⓒ ⓓ	174	ⓐ ⓑ ⓒ ⓓ	194	ⓐ ⓑ ⓒ ⓓ
115	ⓐ ⓑ ⓒ ⓓ	135	ⓐ ⓑ ⓒ ⓓ	155	ⓐ ⓑ ⓒ ⓓ	175	ⓐ ⓑ ⓒ ⓓ	195	ⓐ ⓑ ⓒ ⓓ
116	ⓐ ⓑ ⓒ ⓓ	136	ⓐ ⓑ ⓒ ⓓ	156	ⓐ ⓑ ⓒ ⓓ	176	ⓐ ⓑ ⓒ ⓓ	196	ⓐ ⓑ ⓒ ⓓ
117	ⓐ ⓑ ⓒ ⓓ	137	ⓐ ⓑ ⓒ ⓓ	157	ⓐ ⓑ ⓒ ⓓ	177	ⓐ ⓑ ⓒ ⓓ	197	ⓐ ⓑ ⓒ ⓓ
118	ⓐ ⓑ ⓒ ⓓ	138	ⓐ ⓑ ⓒ ⓓ	158	ⓐ ⓑ ⓒ ⓓ	178	ⓐ ⓑ ⓒ ⓓ	198	ⓐ ⓑ ⓒ ⓓ
119	ⓐ ⓑ ⓒ ⓓ	139	ⓐ ⓑ ⓒ ⓓ	159	ⓐ ⓑ ⓒ ⓓ	179	ⓐ ⓑ ⓒ ⓓ	199	ⓐ ⓑ ⓒ ⓓ
120	ⓐ ⓑ ⓒ ⓓ	140	ⓐ ⓑ ⓒ ⓓ	160	ⓐ ⓑ ⓒ ⓓ	180	ⓐ ⓑ ⓒ ⓓ	200	ⓐ ⓑ ⓒ ⓓ

ANSWER SHEET

ETS® TOEIC® 토익® 정기시험 기출문제집

수험번호						

응시일자 : 20 년 월 일

성명		
	한 글	
	한 자	
	영 자	

Test 05 (Part 5~7)

101	ⓐ ⓑ ⓒ ⓓ	121	ⓐ ⓑ ⓒ ⓓ	141	ⓐ ⓑ ⓒ ⓓ	161	ⓐ ⓑ ⓒ ⓓ	181	ⓐ ⓑ ⓒ ⓓ
102	ⓐ ⓑ ⓒ ⓓ	122	ⓐ ⓑ ⓒ ⓓ	142	ⓐ ⓑ ⓒ ⓓ	162	ⓐ ⓑ ⓒ ⓓ	182	ⓐ ⓑ ⓒ ⓓ
103	ⓐ ⓑ ⓒ ⓓ	123	ⓐ ⓑ ⓒ ⓓ	143	ⓐ ⓑ ⓒ ⓓ	163	ⓐ ⓑ ⓒ ⓓ	183	ⓐ ⓑ ⓒ ⓓ
104	ⓐ ⓑ ⓒ ⓓ	124	ⓐ ⓑ ⓒ ⓓ	144	ⓐ ⓑ ⓒ ⓓ	164	ⓐ ⓑ ⓒ ⓓ	184	ⓐ ⓑ ⓒ ⓓ
105	ⓐ ⓑ ⓒ ⓓ	125	ⓐ ⓑ ⓒ ⓓ	145	ⓐ ⓑ ⓒ ⓓ	165	ⓐ ⓑ ⓒ ⓓ	185	ⓐ ⓑ ⓒ ⓓ
106	ⓐ ⓑ ⓒ ⓓ	126	ⓐ ⓑ ⓒ ⓓ	146	ⓐ ⓑ ⓒ ⓓ	166	ⓐ ⓑ ⓒ ⓓ	186	ⓐ ⓑ ⓒ ⓓ
107	ⓐ ⓑ ⓒ ⓓ	127	ⓐ ⓑ ⓒ ⓓ	147	ⓐ ⓑ ⓒ ⓓ	167	ⓐ ⓑ ⓒ ⓓ	187	ⓐ ⓑ ⓒ ⓓ
108	ⓐ ⓑ ⓒ ⓓ	128	ⓐ ⓑ ⓒ ⓓ	148	ⓐ ⓑ ⓒ ⓓ	168	ⓐ ⓑ ⓒ ⓓ	188	ⓐ ⓑ ⓒ ⓓ
109	ⓐ ⓑ ⓒ ⓓ	129	ⓐ ⓑ ⓒ ⓓ	149	ⓐ ⓑ ⓒ ⓓ	169	ⓐ ⓑ ⓒ ⓓ	189	ⓐ ⓑ ⓒ ⓓ
110	ⓐ ⓑ ⓒ ⓓ	130	ⓐ ⓑ ⓒ ⓓ	150	ⓐ ⓑ ⓒ ⓓ	170	ⓐ ⓑ ⓒ ⓓ	190	ⓐ ⓑ ⓒ ⓓ
111	ⓐ ⓑ ⓒ ⓓ	131	ⓐ ⓑ ⓒ ⓓ	151	ⓐ ⓑ ⓒ ⓓ	171	ⓐ ⓑ ⓒ ⓓ	191	ⓐ ⓑ ⓒ ⓓ
112	ⓐ ⓑ ⓒ ⓓ	132	ⓐ ⓑ ⓒ ⓓ	152	ⓐ ⓑ ⓒ ⓓ	172	ⓐ ⓑ ⓒ ⓓ	192	ⓐ ⓑ ⓒ ⓓ
113	ⓐ ⓑ ⓒ ⓓ	133	ⓐ ⓑ ⓒ ⓓ	153	ⓐ ⓑ ⓒ ⓓ	173	ⓐ ⓑ ⓒ ⓓ	193	ⓐ ⓑ ⓒ ⓓ
114	ⓐ ⓑ ⓒ ⓓ	134	ⓐ ⓑ ⓒ ⓓ	154	ⓐ ⓑ ⓒ ⓓ	174	ⓐ ⓑ ⓒ ⓓ	194	ⓐ ⓑ ⓒ ⓓ
115	ⓐ ⓑ ⓒ ⓓ	135	ⓐ ⓑ ⓒ ⓓ	155	ⓐ ⓑ ⓒ ⓓ	175	ⓐ ⓑ ⓒ ⓓ	195	ⓐ ⓑ ⓒ ⓓ
116	ⓐ ⓑ ⓒ ⓓ	136	ⓐ ⓑ ⓒ ⓓ	156	ⓐ ⓑ ⓒ ⓓ	176	ⓐ ⓑ ⓒ ⓓ	196	ⓐ ⓑ ⓒ ⓓ
117	ⓐ ⓑ ⓒ ⓓ	137	ⓐ ⓑ ⓒ ⓓ	157	ⓐ ⓑ ⓒ ⓓ	177	ⓐ ⓑ ⓒ ⓓ	197	ⓐ ⓑ ⓒ ⓓ
118	ⓐ ⓑ ⓒ ⓓ	138	ⓐ ⓑ ⓒ ⓓ	158	ⓐ ⓑ ⓒ ⓓ	178	ⓐ ⓑ ⓒ ⓓ	198	ⓐ ⓑ ⓒ ⓓ
119	ⓐ ⓑ ⓒ ⓓ	139	ⓐ ⓑ ⓒ ⓓ	159	ⓐ ⓑ ⓒ ⓓ	179	ⓐ ⓑ ⓒ ⓓ	199	ⓐ ⓑ ⓒ ⓓ
120	ⓐ ⓑ ⓒ ⓓ	140	ⓐ ⓑ ⓒ ⓓ	160	ⓐ ⓑ ⓒ ⓓ	180	ⓐ ⓑ ⓒ ⓓ	200	ⓐ ⓑ ⓒ ⓓ

Test 06 (Part 5~7)

101	ⓐ ⓑ ⓒ ⓓ	121	ⓐ ⓑ ⓒ ⓓ	141	ⓐ ⓑ ⓒ ⓓ	161	ⓐ ⓑ ⓒ ⓓ	181	ⓐ ⓑ ⓒ ⓓ
102	ⓐ ⓑ ⓒ ⓓ	122	ⓐ ⓑ ⓒ ⓓ	142	ⓐ ⓑ ⓒ ⓓ	162	ⓐ ⓑ ⓒ ⓓ	182	ⓐ ⓑ ⓒ ⓓ
103	ⓐ ⓑ ⓒ ⓓ	123	ⓐ ⓑ ⓒ ⓓ	143	ⓐ ⓑ ⓒ ⓓ	163	ⓐ ⓑ ⓒ ⓓ	183	ⓐ ⓑ ⓒ ⓓ
104	ⓐ ⓑ ⓒ ⓓ	124	ⓐ ⓑ ⓒ ⓓ	144	ⓐ ⓑ ⓒ ⓓ	164	ⓐ ⓑ ⓒ ⓓ	184	ⓐ ⓑ ⓒ ⓓ
105	ⓐ ⓑ ⓒ ⓓ	125	ⓐ ⓑ ⓒ ⓓ	145	ⓐ ⓑ ⓒ ⓓ	165	ⓐ ⓑ ⓒ ⓓ	185	ⓐ ⓑ ⓒ ⓓ
106	ⓐ ⓑ ⓒ ⓓ	126	ⓐ ⓑ ⓒ ⓓ	146	ⓐ ⓑ ⓒ ⓓ	166	ⓐ ⓑ ⓒ ⓓ	186	ⓐ ⓑ ⓒ ⓓ
107	ⓐ ⓑ ⓒ ⓓ	127	ⓐ ⓑ ⓒ ⓓ	147	ⓐ ⓑ ⓒ ⓓ	167	ⓐ ⓑ ⓒ ⓓ	187	ⓐ ⓑ ⓒ ⓓ
108	ⓐ ⓑ ⓒ ⓓ	128	ⓐ ⓑ ⓒ ⓓ	148	ⓐ ⓑ ⓒ ⓓ	168	ⓐ ⓑ ⓒ ⓓ	188	ⓐ ⓑ ⓒ ⓓ
109	ⓐ ⓑ ⓒ ⓓ	129	ⓐ ⓑ ⓒ ⓓ	149	ⓐ ⓑ ⓒ ⓓ	169	ⓐ ⓑ ⓒ ⓓ	189	ⓐ ⓑ ⓒ ⓓ
110	ⓐ ⓑ ⓒ ⓓ	130	ⓐ ⓑ ⓒ ⓓ	150	ⓐ ⓑ ⓒ ⓓ	170	ⓐ ⓑ ⓒ ⓓ	190	ⓐ ⓑ ⓒ ⓓ
111	ⓐ ⓑ ⓒ ⓓ	131	ⓐ ⓑ ⓒ ⓓ	151	ⓐ ⓑ ⓒ ⓓ	171	ⓐ ⓑ ⓒ ⓓ	191	ⓐ ⓑ ⓒ ⓓ
112	ⓐ ⓑ ⓒ ⓓ	132	ⓐ ⓑ ⓒ ⓓ	152	ⓐ ⓑ ⓒ ⓓ	172	ⓐ ⓑ ⓒ ⓓ	192	ⓐ ⓑ ⓒ ⓓ
113	ⓐ ⓑ ⓒ ⓓ	133	ⓐ ⓑ ⓒ ⓓ	153	ⓐ ⓑ ⓒ ⓓ	173	ⓐ ⓑ ⓒ ⓓ	193	ⓐ ⓑ ⓒ ⓓ
114	ⓐ ⓑ ⓒ ⓓ	134	ⓐ ⓑ ⓒ ⓓ	154	ⓐ ⓑ ⓒ ⓓ	174	ⓐ ⓑ ⓒ ⓓ	194	ⓐ ⓑ ⓒ ⓓ
115	ⓐ ⓑ ⓒ ⓓ	135	ⓐ ⓑ ⓒ ⓓ	155	ⓐ ⓑ ⓒ ⓓ	175	ⓐ ⓑ ⓒ ⓓ	195	ⓐ ⓑ ⓒ ⓓ
116	ⓐ ⓑ ⓒ ⓓ	136	ⓐ ⓑ ⓒ ⓓ	156	ⓐ ⓑ ⓒ ⓓ	176	ⓐ ⓑ ⓒ ⓓ	196	ⓐ ⓑ ⓒ ⓓ
117	ⓐ ⓑ ⓒ ⓓ	137	ⓐ ⓑ ⓒ ⓓ	157	ⓐ ⓑ ⓒ ⓓ	177	ⓐ ⓑ ⓒ ⓓ	197	ⓐ ⓑ ⓒ ⓓ
118	ⓐ ⓑ ⓒ ⓓ	138	ⓐ ⓑ ⓒ ⓓ	158	ⓐ ⓑ ⓒ ⓓ	178	ⓐ ⓑ ⓒ ⓓ	198	ⓐ ⓑ ⓒ ⓓ
119	ⓐ ⓑ ⓒ ⓓ	139	ⓐ ⓑ ⓒ ⓓ	159	ⓐ ⓑ ⓒ ⓓ	179	ⓐ ⓑ ⓒ ⓓ	199	ⓐ ⓑ ⓒ ⓓ
120	ⓐ ⓑ ⓒ ⓓ	140	ⓐ ⓑ ⓒ ⓓ	160	ⓐ ⓑ ⓒ ⓓ	180	ⓐ ⓑ ⓒ ⓓ	200	ⓐ ⓑ ⓒ ⓓ

ANSWER SHEET

ETS® TOEIC® 토익® 정기시험 기출문제집

수험번호						

응시일자 : 20 년 월 일

성명	한 글	
	한 자	
	영 자	

Test 07 (Part 5~7)

101	ⓐ ⓑ ⓒ ⓓ	121	ⓐ ⓑ ⓒ ⓓ	141	ⓐ ⓑ ⓒ ⓓ	161	ⓐ ⓑ ⓒ ⓓ	181	ⓐ ⓑ ⓒ ⓓ
102	ⓐ ⓑ ⓒ ⓓ	122	ⓐ ⓑ ⓒ ⓓ	142	ⓐ ⓑ ⓒ ⓓ	162	ⓐ ⓑ ⓒ ⓓ	182	ⓐ ⓑ ⓒ ⓓ
103	ⓐ ⓑ ⓒ ⓓ	123	ⓐ ⓑ ⓒ ⓓ	143	ⓐ ⓑ ⓒ ⓓ	163	ⓐ ⓑ ⓒ ⓓ	183	ⓐ ⓑ ⓒ ⓓ
104	ⓐ ⓑ ⓒ ⓓ	124	ⓐ ⓑ ⓒ ⓓ	144	ⓐ ⓑ ⓒ ⓓ	164	ⓐ ⓑ ⓒ ⓓ	184	ⓐ ⓑ ⓒ ⓓ
105	ⓐ ⓑ ⓒ ⓓ	125	ⓐ ⓑ ⓒ ⓓ	145	ⓐ ⓑ ⓒ ⓓ	165	ⓐ ⓑ ⓒ ⓓ	185	ⓐ ⓑ ⓒ ⓓ
106	ⓐ ⓑ ⓒ ⓓ	126	ⓐ ⓑ ⓒ ⓓ	146	ⓐ ⓑ ⓒ ⓓ	166	ⓐ ⓑ ⓒ ⓓ	186	ⓐ ⓑ ⓒ ⓓ
107	ⓐ ⓑ ⓒ ⓓ	127	ⓐ ⓑ ⓒ ⓓ	147	ⓐ ⓑ ⓒ ⓓ	167	ⓐ ⓑ ⓒ ⓓ	187	ⓐ ⓑ ⓒ ⓓ
108	ⓐ ⓑ ⓒ ⓓ	128	ⓐ ⓑ ⓒ ⓓ	148	ⓐ ⓑ ⓒ ⓓ	168	ⓐ ⓑ ⓒ ⓓ	188	ⓐ ⓑ ⓒ ⓓ
109	ⓐ ⓑ ⓒ ⓓ	129	ⓐ ⓑ ⓒ ⓓ	149	ⓐ ⓑ ⓒ ⓓ	169	ⓐ ⓑ ⓒ ⓓ	189	ⓐ ⓑ ⓒ ⓓ
110	ⓐ ⓑ ⓒ ⓓ	130	ⓐ ⓑ ⓒ ⓓ	150	ⓐ ⓑ ⓒ ⓓ	170	ⓐ ⓑ ⓒ ⓓ	190	ⓐ ⓑ ⓒ ⓓ
111	ⓐ ⓑ ⓒ ⓓ	131	ⓐ ⓑ ⓒ ⓓ	151	ⓐ ⓑ ⓒ ⓓ	171	ⓐ ⓑ ⓒ ⓓ	191	ⓐ ⓑ ⓒ ⓓ
112	ⓐ ⓑ ⓒ ⓓ	132	ⓐ ⓑ ⓒ ⓓ	152	ⓐ ⓑ ⓒ ⓓ	172	ⓐ ⓑ ⓒ ⓓ	192	ⓐ ⓑ ⓒ ⓓ
113	ⓐ ⓑ ⓒ ⓓ	133	ⓐ ⓑ ⓒ ⓓ	153	ⓐ ⓑ ⓒ ⓓ	173	ⓐ ⓑ ⓒ ⓓ	193	ⓐ ⓑ ⓒ ⓓ
114	ⓐ ⓑ ⓒ ⓓ	134	ⓐ ⓑ ⓒ ⓓ	154	ⓐ ⓑ ⓒ ⓓ	174	ⓐ ⓑ ⓒ ⓓ	194	ⓐ ⓑ ⓒ ⓓ
115	ⓐ ⓑ ⓒ ⓓ	135	ⓐ ⓑ ⓒ ⓓ	155	ⓐ ⓑ ⓒ ⓓ	175	ⓐ ⓑ ⓒ ⓓ	195	ⓐ ⓑ ⓒ ⓓ
116	ⓐ ⓑ ⓒ ⓓ	136	ⓐ ⓑ ⓒ ⓓ	156	ⓐ ⓑ ⓒ ⓓ	176	ⓐ ⓑ ⓒ ⓓ	196	ⓐ ⓑ ⓒ ⓓ
117	ⓐ ⓑ ⓒ ⓓ	137	ⓐ ⓑ ⓒ ⓓ	157	ⓐ ⓑ ⓒ ⓓ	177	ⓐ ⓑ ⓒ ⓓ	197	ⓐ ⓑ ⓒ ⓓ
118	ⓐ ⓑ ⓒ ⓓ	138	ⓐ ⓑ ⓒ ⓓ	158	ⓐ ⓑ ⓒ ⓓ	178	ⓐ ⓑ ⓒ ⓓ	198	ⓐ ⓑ ⓒ ⓓ
119	ⓐ ⓑ ⓒ ⓓ	139	ⓐ ⓑ ⓒ ⓓ	159	ⓐ ⓑ ⓒ ⓓ	179	ⓐ ⓑ ⓒ ⓓ	199	ⓐ ⓑ ⓒ ⓓ
120	ⓐ ⓑ ⓒ ⓓ	140	ⓐ ⓑ ⓒ ⓓ	160	ⓐ ⓑ ⓒ ⓓ	180	ⓐ ⓑ ⓒ ⓓ	200	ⓐ ⓑ ⓒ ⓓ

Test 08 (Part 5~7)

101	ⓐ ⓑ ⓒ ⓓ	121	ⓐ ⓑ ⓒ ⓓ	141	ⓐ ⓑ ⓒ ⓓ	161	ⓐ ⓑ ⓒ ⓓ	181	ⓐ ⓑ ⓒ ⓓ
102	ⓐ ⓑ ⓒ ⓓ	122	ⓐ ⓑ ⓒ ⓓ	142	ⓐ ⓑ ⓒ ⓓ	162	ⓐ ⓑ ⓒ ⓓ	182	ⓐ ⓑ ⓒ ⓓ
103	ⓐ ⓑ ⓒ ⓓ	123	ⓐ ⓑ ⓒ ⓓ	143	ⓐ ⓑ ⓒ ⓓ	163	ⓐ ⓑ ⓒ ⓓ	183	ⓐ ⓑ ⓒ ⓓ
104	ⓐ ⓑ ⓒ ⓓ	124	ⓐ ⓑ ⓒ ⓓ	144	ⓐ ⓑ ⓒ ⓓ	164	ⓐ ⓑ ⓒ ⓓ	184	ⓐ ⓑ ⓒ ⓓ
105	ⓐ ⓑ ⓒ ⓓ	125	ⓐ ⓑ ⓒ ⓓ	145	ⓐ ⓑ ⓒ ⓓ	165	ⓐ ⓑ ⓒ ⓓ	185	ⓐ ⓑ ⓒ ⓓ
106	ⓐ ⓑ ⓒ ⓓ	126	ⓐ ⓑ ⓒ ⓓ	146	ⓐ ⓑ ⓒ ⓓ	166	ⓐ ⓑ ⓒ ⓓ	186	ⓐ ⓑ ⓒ ⓓ
107	ⓐ ⓑ ⓒ ⓓ	127	ⓐ ⓑ ⓒ ⓓ	147	ⓐ ⓑ ⓒ ⓓ	167	ⓐ ⓑ ⓒ ⓓ	187	ⓐ ⓑ ⓒ ⓓ
108	ⓐ ⓑ ⓒ ⓓ	128	ⓐ ⓑ ⓒ ⓓ	148	ⓐ ⓑ ⓒ ⓓ	168	ⓐ ⓑ ⓒ ⓓ	188	ⓐ ⓑ ⓒ ⓓ
109	ⓐ ⓑ ⓒ ⓓ	129	ⓐ ⓑ ⓒ ⓓ	149	ⓐ ⓑ ⓒ ⓓ	169	ⓐ ⓑ ⓒ ⓓ	189	ⓐ ⓑ ⓒ ⓓ
110	ⓐ ⓑ ⓒ ⓓ	130	ⓐ ⓑ ⓒ ⓓ	150	ⓐ ⓑ ⓒ ⓓ	170	ⓐ ⓑ ⓒ ⓓ	190	ⓐ ⓑ ⓒ ⓓ
111	ⓐ ⓑ ⓒ ⓓ	131	ⓐ ⓑ ⓒ ⓓ	151	ⓐ ⓑ ⓒ ⓓ	171	ⓐ ⓑ ⓒ ⓓ	191	ⓐ ⓑ ⓒ ⓓ
112	ⓐ ⓑ ⓒ ⓓ	132	ⓐ ⓑ ⓒ ⓓ	152	ⓐ ⓑ ⓒ ⓓ	172	ⓐ ⓑ ⓒ ⓓ	192	ⓐ ⓑ ⓒ ⓓ
113	ⓐ ⓑ ⓒ ⓓ	133	ⓐ ⓑ ⓒ ⓓ	153	ⓐ ⓑ ⓒ ⓓ	173	ⓐ ⓑ ⓒ ⓓ	193	ⓐ ⓑ ⓒ ⓓ
114	ⓐ ⓑ ⓒ ⓓ	134	ⓐ ⓑ ⓒ ⓓ	154	ⓐ ⓑ ⓒ ⓓ	174	ⓐ ⓑ ⓒ ⓓ	194	ⓐ ⓑ ⓒ ⓓ
115	ⓐ ⓑ ⓒ ⓓ	135	ⓐ ⓑ ⓒ ⓓ	155	ⓐ ⓑ ⓒ ⓓ	175	ⓐ ⓑ ⓒ ⓓ	195	ⓐ ⓑ ⓒ ⓓ
116	ⓐ ⓑ ⓒ ⓓ	136	ⓐ ⓑ ⓒ ⓓ	156	ⓐ ⓑ ⓒ ⓓ	176	ⓐ ⓑ ⓒ ⓓ	196	ⓐ ⓑ ⓒ ⓓ
117	ⓐ ⓑ ⓒ ⓓ	137	ⓐ ⓑ ⓒ ⓓ	157	ⓐ ⓑ ⓒ ⓓ	177	ⓐ ⓑ ⓒ ⓓ	197	ⓐ ⓑ ⓒ ⓓ
118	ⓐ ⓑ ⓒ ⓓ	138	ⓐ ⓑ ⓒ ⓓ	158	ⓐ ⓑ ⓒ ⓓ	178	ⓐ ⓑ ⓒ ⓓ	198	ⓐ ⓑ ⓒ ⓓ
119	ⓐ ⓑ ⓒ ⓓ	139	ⓐ ⓑ ⓒ ⓓ	159	ⓐ ⓑ ⓒ ⓓ	179	ⓐ ⓑ ⓒ ⓓ	199	ⓐ ⓑ ⓒ ⓓ
120	ⓐ ⓑ ⓒ ⓓ	140	ⓐ ⓑ ⓒ ⓓ	160	ⓐ ⓑ ⓒ ⓓ	180	ⓐ ⓑ ⓒ ⓓ	200	ⓐ ⓑ ⓒ ⓓ

ANSWER SHEET

ETS® TOEIC® 토익® 정기시험 기출문제집

수험번호						

응시일자 : 20 년 월 일

성명		
	한 글	
	한 자	
	영 자	

Test 09 (Part 5~7)

101	ⓐ ⓑ ⓒ ⓓ	121	ⓐ ⓑ ⓒ ⓓ	141	ⓐ ⓑ ⓒ ⓓ	161	ⓐ ⓑ ⓒ ⓓ	181	ⓐ ⓑ ⓒ ⓓ
102	ⓐ ⓑ ⓒ ⓓ	122	ⓐ ⓑ ⓒ ⓓ	142	ⓐ ⓑ ⓒ ⓓ	162	ⓐ ⓑ ⓒ ⓓ	182	ⓐ ⓑ ⓒ ⓓ
103	ⓐ ⓑ ⓒ ⓓ	123	ⓐ ⓑ ⓒ ⓓ	143	ⓐ ⓑ ⓒ ⓓ	163	ⓐ ⓑ ⓒ ⓓ	183	ⓐ ⓑ ⓒ ⓓ
104	ⓐ ⓑ ⓒ ⓓ	124	ⓐ ⓑ ⓒ ⓓ	144	ⓐ ⓑ ⓒ ⓓ	164	ⓐ ⓑ ⓒ ⓓ	184	ⓐ ⓑ ⓒ ⓓ
105	ⓐ ⓑ ⓒ ⓓ	125	ⓐ ⓑ ⓒ ⓓ	145	ⓐ ⓑ ⓒ ⓓ	165	ⓐ ⓑ ⓒ ⓓ	185	ⓐ ⓑ ⓒ ⓓ
106	ⓐ ⓑ ⓒ ⓓ	126	ⓐ ⓑ ⓒ ⓓ	146	ⓐ ⓑ ⓒ ⓓ	166	ⓐ ⓑ ⓒ ⓓ	186	ⓐ ⓑ ⓒ ⓓ
107	ⓐ ⓑ ⓒ ⓓ	127	ⓐ ⓑ ⓒ ⓓ	147	ⓐ ⓑ ⓒ ⓓ	167	ⓐ ⓑ ⓒ ⓓ	187	ⓐ ⓑ ⓒ ⓓ
108	ⓐ ⓑ ⓒ ⓓ	128	ⓐ ⓑ ⓒ ⓓ	148	ⓐ ⓑ ⓒ ⓓ	168	ⓐ ⓑ ⓒ ⓓ	188	ⓐ ⓑ ⓒ ⓓ
109	ⓐ ⓑ ⓒ ⓓ	129	ⓐ ⓑ ⓒ ⓓ	149	ⓐ ⓑ ⓒ ⓓ	169	ⓐ ⓑ ⓒ ⓓ	189	ⓐ ⓑ ⓒ ⓓ
110	ⓐ ⓑ ⓒ ⓓ	130	ⓐ ⓑ ⓒ ⓓ	150	ⓐ ⓑ ⓒ ⓓ	170	ⓐ ⓑ ⓒ ⓓ	190	ⓐ ⓑ ⓒ ⓓ
111	ⓐ ⓑ ⓒ ⓓ	131	ⓐ ⓑ ⓒ ⓓ	151	ⓐ ⓑ ⓒ ⓓ	171	ⓐ ⓑ ⓒ ⓓ	191	ⓐ ⓑ ⓒ ⓓ
112	ⓐ ⓑ ⓒ ⓓ	132	ⓐ ⓑ ⓒ ⓓ	152	ⓐ ⓑ ⓒ ⓓ	172	ⓐ ⓑ ⓒ ⓓ	192	ⓐ ⓑ ⓒ ⓓ
113	ⓐ ⓑ ⓒ ⓓ	133	ⓐ ⓑ ⓒ ⓓ	153	ⓐ ⓑ ⓒ ⓓ	173	ⓐ ⓑ ⓒ ⓓ	193	ⓐ ⓑ ⓒ ⓓ
114	ⓐ ⓑ ⓒ ⓓ	134	ⓐ ⓑ ⓒ ⓓ	154	ⓐ ⓑ ⓒ ⓓ	174	ⓐ ⓑ ⓒ ⓓ	194	ⓐ ⓑ ⓒ ⓓ
115	ⓐ ⓑ ⓒ ⓓ	135	ⓐ ⓑ ⓒ ⓓ	155	ⓐ ⓑ ⓒ ⓓ	175	ⓐ ⓑ ⓒ ⓓ	195	ⓐ ⓑ ⓒ ⓓ
116	ⓐ ⓑ ⓒ ⓓ	136	ⓐ ⓑ ⓒ ⓓ	156	ⓐ ⓑ ⓒ ⓓ	176	ⓐ ⓑ ⓒ ⓓ	196	ⓐ ⓑ ⓒ ⓓ
117	ⓐ ⓑ ⓒ ⓓ	137	ⓐ ⓑ ⓒ ⓓ	157	ⓐ ⓑ ⓒ ⓓ	177	ⓐ ⓑ ⓒ ⓓ	197	ⓐ ⓑ ⓒ ⓓ
118	ⓐ ⓑ ⓒ ⓓ	138	ⓐ ⓑ ⓒ ⓓ	158	ⓐ ⓑ ⓒ ⓓ	178	ⓐ ⓑ ⓒ ⓓ	198	ⓐ ⓑ ⓒ ⓓ
119	ⓐ ⓑ ⓒ ⓓ	139	ⓐ ⓑ ⓒ ⓓ	159	ⓐ ⓑ ⓒ ⓓ	179	ⓐ ⓑ ⓒ ⓓ	199	ⓐ ⓑ ⓒ ⓓ
120	ⓐ ⓑ ⓒ ⓓ	140	ⓐ ⓑ ⓒ ⓓ	160	ⓐ ⓑ ⓒ ⓓ	180	ⓐ ⓑ ⓒ ⓓ	200	ⓐ ⓑ ⓒ ⓓ

Test 10 (Part 5~7)

101	ⓐ ⓑ ⓒ ⓓ	121	ⓐ ⓑ ⓒ ⓓ	141	ⓐ ⓑ ⓒ ⓓ	161	ⓐ ⓑ ⓒ ⓓ	181	ⓐ ⓑ ⓒ ⓓ
102	ⓐ ⓑ ⓒ ⓓ	122	ⓐ ⓑ ⓒ ⓓ	142	ⓐ ⓑ ⓒ ⓓ	162	ⓐ ⓑ ⓒ ⓓ	182	ⓐ ⓑ ⓒ ⓓ
103	ⓐ ⓑ ⓒ ⓓ	123	ⓐ ⓑ ⓒ ⓓ	143	ⓐ ⓑ ⓒ ⓓ	163	ⓐ ⓑ ⓒ ⓓ	183	ⓐ ⓑ ⓒ ⓓ
104	ⓐ ⓑ ⓒ ⓓ	124	ⓐ ⓑ ⓒ ⓓ	144	ⓐ ⓑ ⓒ ⓓ	164	ⓐ ⓑ ⓒ ⓓ	184	ⓐ ⓑ ⓒ ⓓ
105	ⓐ ⓑ ⓒ ⓓ	125	ⓐ ⓑ ⓒ ⓓ	145	ⓐ ⓑ ⓒ ⓓ	165	ⓐ ⓑ ⓒ ⓓ	185	ⓐ ⓑ ⓒ ⓓ
106	ⓐ ⓑ ⓒ ⓓ	126	ⓐ ⓑ ⓒ ⓓ	146	ⓐ ⓑ ⓒ ⓓ	166	ⓐ ⓑ ⓒ ⓓ	186	ⓐ ⓑ ⓒ ⓓ
107	ⓐ ⓑ ⓒ ⓓ	127	ⓐ ⓑ ⓒ ⓓ	147	ⓐ ⓑ ⓒ ⓓ	167	ⓐ ⓑ ⓒ ⓓ	187	ⓐ ⓑ ⓒ ⓓ
108	ⓐ ⓑ ⓒ ⓓ	128	ⓐ ⓑ ⓒ ⓓ	148	ⓐ ⓑ ⓒ ⓓ	168	ⓐ ⓑ ⓒ ⓓ	188	ⓐ ⓑ ⓒ ⓓ
109	ⓐ ⓑ ⓒ ⓓ	129	ⓐ ⓑ ⓒ ⓓ	149	ⓐ ⓑ ⓒ ⓓ	169	ⓐ ⓑ ⓒ ⓓ	189	ⓐ ⓑ ⓒ ⓓ
110	ⓐ ⓑ ⓒ ⓓ	130	ⓐ ⓑ ⓒ ⓓ	150	ⓐ ⓑ ⓒ ⓓ	170	ⓐ ⓑ ⓒ ⓓ	190	ⓐ ⓑ ⓒ ⓓ
111	ⓐ ⓑ ⓒ ⓓ	131	ⓐ ⓑ ⓒ ⓓ	151	ⓐ ⓑ ⓒ ⓓ	171	ⓐ ⓑ ⓒ ⓓ	191	ⓐ ⓑ ⓒ ⓓ
112	ⓐ ⓑ ⓒ ⓓ	132	ⓐ ⓑ ⓒ ⓓ	152	ⓐ ⓑ ⓒ ⓓ	172	ⓐ ⓑ ⓒ ⓓ	192	ⓐ ⓑ ⓒ ⓓ
113	ⓐ ⓑ ⓒ ⓓ	133	ⓐ ⓑ ⓒ ⓓ	153	ⓐ ⓑ ⓒ ⓓ	173	ⓐ ⓑ ⓒ ⓓ	193	ⓐ ⓑ ⓒ ⓓ
114	ⓐ ⓑ ⓒ ⓓ	134	ⓐ ⓑ ⓒ ⓓ	154	ⓐ ⓑ ⓒ ⓓ	174	ⓐ ⓑ ⓒ ⓓ	194	ⓐ ⓑ ⓒ ⓓ
115	ⓐ ⓑ ⓒ ⓓ	135	ⓐ ⓑ ⓒ ⓓ	155	ⓐ ⓑ ⓒ ⓓ	175	ⓐ ⓑ ⓒ ⓓ	195	ⓐ ⓑ ⓒ ⓓ
116	ⓐ ⓑ ⓒ ⓓ	136	ⓐ ⓑ ⓒ ⓓ	156	ⓐ ⓑ ⓒ ⓓ	176	ⓐ ⓑ ⓒ ⓓ	196	ⓐ ⓑ ⓒ ⓓ
117	ⓐ ⓑ ⓒ ⓓ	137	ⓐ ⓑ ⓒ ⓓ	157	ⓐ ⓑ ⓒ ⓓ	177	ⓐ ⓑ ⓒ ⓓ	197	ⓐ ⓑ ⓒ ⓓ
118	ⓐ ⓑ ⓒ ⓓ	138	ⓐ ⓑ ⓒ ⓓ	158	ⓐ ⓑ ⓒ ⓓ	178	ⓐ ⓑ ⓒ ⓓ	198	ⓐ ⓑ ⓒ ⓓ
119	ⓐ ⓑ ⓒ ⓓ	139	ⓐ ⓑ ⓒ ⓓ	159	ⓐ ⓑ ⓒ ⓓ	179	ⓐ ⓑ ⓒ ⓓ	199	ⓐ ⓑ ⓒ ⓓ
120	ⓐ ⓑ ⓒ ⓓ	140	ⓐ ⓑ ⓒ ⓓ	160	ⓐ ⓑ ⓒ ⓓ	180	ⓐ ⓑ ⓒ ⓓ	200	ⓐ ⓑ ⓒ ⓓ

ANSWER SHEET

ETS® TOEIC® 토익® 정기시험 기출문제집

수험번호						

응시일자 : 20 년 월 일

성명	한 글	
	한 자	
	영 자	

Test (Part 5~7)

101	ⓐ	ⓑ	ⓒ	ⓓ	121	ⓐ	ⓑ	ⓒ	ⓓ	141	ⓐ	ⓑ	ⓒ	ⓓ	161	ⓐ	ⓑ	ⓒ	ⓓ	181	ⓐ	ⓑ	ⓒ	ⓓ
102	ⓐ	ⓑ	ⓒ	ⓓ	122	ⓐ	ⓑ	ⓒ	ⓓ	142	ⓐ	ⓑ	ⓒ	ⓓ	162	ⓐ	ⓑ	ⓒ	ⓓ	182	ⓐ	ⓑ	ⓒ	ⓓ
103	ⓐ	ⓑ	ⓒ	ⓓ	123	ⓐ	ⓑ	ⓒ	ⓓ	143	ⓐ	ⓑ	ⓒ	ⓓ	163	ⓐ	ⓑ	ⓒ	ⓓ	183	ⓐ	ⓑ	ⓒ	ⓓ
104	ⓐ	ⓑ	ⓒ	ⓓ	124	ⓐ	ⓑ	ⓒ	ⓓ	144	ⓐ	ⓑ	ⓒ	ⓓ	164	ⓐ	ⓑ	ⓒ	ⓓ	184	ⓐ	ⓑ	ⓒ	ⓓ
105	ⓐ	ⓑ	ⓒ	ⓓ	125	ⓐ	ⓑ	ⓒ	ⓓ	145	ⓐ	ⓑ	ⓒ	ⓓ	165	ⓐ	ⓑ	ⓒ	ⓓ	185	ⓐ	ⓑ	ⓒ	ⓓ
106	ⓐ	ⓑ	ⓒ	ⓓ	126	ⓐ	ⓑ	ⓒ	ⓓ	146	ⓐ	ⓑ	ⓒ	ⓓ	166	ⓐ	ⓑ	ⓒ	ⓓ	186	ⓐ	ⓑ	ⓒ	ⓓ
107	ⓐ	ⓑ	ⓒ	ⓓ	127	ⓐ	ⓑ	ⓒ	ⓓ	147	ⓐ	ⓑ	ⓒ	ⓓ	167	ⓐ	ⓑ	ⓒ	ⓓ	187	ⓐ	ⓑ	ⓒ	ⓓ
108	ⓐ	ⓑ	ⓒ	ⓓ	128	ⓐ	ⓑ	ⓒ	ⓓ	148	ⓐ	ⓑ	ⓒ	ⓓ	168	ⓐ	ⓑ	ⓒ	ⓓ	188	ⓐ	ⓑ	ⓒ	ⓓ
109	ⓐ	ⓑ	ⓒ	ⓓ	129	ⓐ	ⓑ	ⓒ	ⓓ	149	ⓐ	ⓑ	ⓒ	ⓓ	169	ⓐ	ⓑ	ⓒ	ⓓ	189	ⓐ	ⓑ	ⓒ	ⓓ
110	ⓐ	ⓑ	ⓒ	ⓓ	130	ⓐ	ⓑ	ⓒ	ⓓ	150	ⓐ	ⓑ	ⓒ	ⓓ	170	ⓐ	ⓑ	ⓒ	ⓓ	190	ⓐ	ⓑ	ⓒ	ⓓ
111	ⓐ	ⓑ	ⓒ	ⓓ	131	ⓐ	ⓑ	ⓒ	ⓓ	151	ⓐ	ⓑ	ⓒ	ⓓ	171	ⓐ	ⓑ	ⓒ	ⓓ	191	ⓐ	ⓑ	ⓒ	ⓓ
112	ⓐ	ⓑ	ⓒ	ⓓ	132	ⓐ	ⓑ	ⓒ	ⓓ	152	ⓐ	ⓑ	ⓒ	ⓓ	172	ⓐ	ⓑ	ⓒ	ⓓ	192	ⓐ	ⓑ	ⓒ	ⓓ
113	ⓐ	ⓑ	ⓒ	ⓓ	133	ⓐ	ⓑ	ⓒ	ⓓ	153	ⓐ	ⓑ	ⓒ	ⓓ	173	ⓐ	ⓑ	ⓒ	ⓓ	193	ⓐ	ⓑ	ⓒ	ⓓ
114	ⓐ	ⓑ	ⓒ	ⓓ	134	ⓐ	ⓑ	ⓒ	ⓓ	154	ⓐ	ⓑ	ⓒ	ⓓ	174	ⓐ	ⓑ	ⓒ	ⓓ	194	ⓐ	ⓑ	ⓒ	ⓓ
115	ⓐ	ⓑ	ⓒ	ⓓ	135	ⓐ	ⓑ	ⓒ	ⓓ	155	ⓐ	ⓑ	ⓒ	ⓓ	175	ⓐ	ⓑ	ⓒ	ⓓ	195	ⓐ	ⓑ	ⓒ	ⓓ
116	ⓐ	ⓑ	ⓒ	ⓓ	136	ⓐ	ⓑ	ⓒ	ⓓ	156	ⓐ	ⓑ	ⓒ	ⓓ	176	ⓐ	ⓑ	ⓒ	ⓓ	196	ⓐ	ⓑ	ⓒ	ⓓ
117	ⓐ	ⓑ	ⓒ	ⓓ	137	ⓐ	ⓑ	ⓒ	ⓓ	157	ⓐ	ⓑ	ⓒ	ⓓ	177	ⓐ	ⓑ	ⓒ	ⓓ	197	ⓐ	ⓑ	ⓒ	ⓓ
118	ⓐ	ⓑ	ⓒ	ⓓ	138	ⓐ	ⓑ	ⓒ	ⓓ	158	ⓐ	ⓑ	ⓒ	ⓓ	178	ⓐ	ⓑ	ⓒ	ⓓ	198	ⓐ	ⓑ	ⓒ	ⓓ
119	ⓐ	ⓑ	ⓒ	ⓓ	139	ⓐ	ⓑ	ⓒ	ⓓ	159	ⓐ	ⓑ	ⓒ	ⓓ	179	ⓐ	ⓑ	ⓒ	ⓓ	199	ⓐ	ⓑ	ⓒ	ⓓ
120	ⓐ	ⓑ	ⓒ	ⓓ	140	ⓐ	ⓑ	ⓒ	ⓓ	160	ⓐ	ⓑ	ⓒ	ⓓ	180	ⓐ	ⓑ	ⓒ	ⓓ	200	ⓐ	ⓑ	ⓒ	ⓓ

Test (Part 5~7)

101	ⓐ	ⓑ	ⓒ	ⓓ	121	ⓐ	ⓑ	ⓒ	ⓓ	141	ⓐ	ⓑ	ⓒ	ⓓ	161	ⓐ	ⓑ	ⓒ	ⓓ	181	ⓐ	ⓑ	ⓒ	ⓓ
102	ⓐ	ⓑ	ⓒ	ⓓ	122	ⓐ	ⓑ	ⓒ	ⓓ	142	ⓐ	ⓑ	ⓒ	ⓓ	162	ⓐ	ⓑ	ⓒ	ⓓ	182	ⓐ	ⓑ	ⓒ	ⓓ
103	ⓐ	ⓑ	ⓒ	ⓓ	123	ⓐ	ⓑ	ⓒ	ⓓ	143	ⓐ	ⓑ	ⓒ	ⓓ	163	ⓐ	ⓑ	ⓒ	ⓓ	183	ⓐ	ⓑ	ⓒ	ⓓ
104	ⓐ	ⓑ	ⓒ	ⓓ	124	ⓐ	ⓑ	ⓒ	ⓓ	144	ⓐ	ⓑ	ⓒ	ⓓ	164	ⓐ	ⓑ	ⓒ	ⓓ	184	ⓐ	ⓑ	ⓒ	ⓓ
105	ⓐ	ⓑ	ⓒ	ⓓ	125	ⓐ	ⓑ	ⓒ	ⓓ	145	ⓐ	ⓑ	ⓒ	ⓓ	165	ⓐ	ⓑ	ⓒ	ⓓ	185	ⓐ	ⓑ	ⓒ	ⓓ
106	ⓐ	ⓑ	ⓒ	ⓓ	126	ⓐ	ⓑ	ⓒ	ⓓ	146	ⓐ	ⓑ	ⓒ	ⓓ	166	ⓐ	ⓑ	ⓒ	ⓓ	186	ⓐ	ⓑ	ⓒ	ⓓ
107	ⓐ	ⓑ	ⓒ	ⓓ	127	ⓐ	ⓑ	ⓒ	ⓓ	147	ⓐ	ⓑ	ⓒ	ⓓ	167	ⓐ	ⓑ	ⓒ	ⓓ	187	ⓐ	ⓑ	ⓒ	ⓓ
108	ⓐ	ⓑ	ⓒ	ⓓ	128	ⓐ	ⓑ	ⓒ	ⓓ	148	ⓐ	ⓑ	ⓒ	ⓓ	168	ⓐ	ⓑ	ⓒ	ⓓ	188	ⓐ	ⓑ	ⓒ	ⓓ
109	ⓐ	ⓑ	ⓒ	ⓓ	129	ⓐ	ⓑ	ⓒ	ⓓ	149	ⓐ	ⓑ	ⓒ	ⓓ	169	ⓐ	ⓑ	ⓒ	ⓓ	189	ⓐ	ⓑ	ⓒ	ⓓ
110	ⓐ	ⓑ	ⓒ	ⓓ	130	ⓐ	ⓑ	ⓒ	ⓓ	150	ⓐ	ⓑ	ⓒ	ⓓ	170	ⓐ	ⓑ	ⓒ	ⓓ	190	ⓐ	ⓑ	ⓒ	ⓓ
111	ⓐ	ⓑ	ⓒ	ⓓ	131	ⓐ	ⓑ	ⓒ	ⓓ	151	ⓐ	ⓑ	ⓒ	ⓓ	171	ⓐ	ⓑ	ⓒ	ⓓ	191	ⓐ	ⓑ	ⓒ	ⓓ
112	ⓐ	ⓑ	ⓒ	ⓓ	132	ⓐ	ⓑ	ⓒ	ⓓ	152	ⓐ	ⓑ	ⓒ	ⓓ	172	ⓐ	ⓑ	ⓒ	ⓓ	192	ⓐ	ⓑ	ⓒ	ⓓ
113	ⓐ	ⓑ	ⓒ	ⓓ	133	ⓐ	ⓑ	ⓒ	ⓓ	153	ⓐ	ⓑ	ⓒ	ⓓ	173	ⓐ	ⓑ	ⓒ	ⓓ	193	ⓐ	ⓑ	ⓒ	ⓓ
114	ⓐ	ⓑ	ⓒ	ⓓ	134	ⓐ	ⓑ	ⓒ	ⓓ	154	ⓐ	ⓑ	ⓒ	ⓓ	174	ⓐ	ⓑ	ⓒ	ⓓ	194	ⓐ	ⓑ	ⓒ	ⓓ
115	ⓐ	ⓑ	ⓒ	ⓓ	135	ⓐ	ⓑ	ⓒ	ⓓ	155	ⓐ	ⓑ	ⓒ	ⓓ	175	ⓐ	ⓑ	ⓒ	ⓓ	195	ⓐ	ⓑ	ⓒ	ⓓ
116	ⓐ	ⓑ	ⓒ	ⓓ	136	ⓐ	ⓑ	ⓒ	ⓓ	156	ⓐ	ⓑ	ⓒ	ⓓ	176	ⓐ	ⓑ	ⓒ	ⓓ	196	ⓐ	ⓑ	ⓒ	ⓓ
117	ⓐ	ⓑ	ⓒ	ⓓ	137	ⓐ	ⓑ	ⓒ	ⓓ	157	ⓐ	ⓑ	ⓒ	ⓓ	177	ⓐ	ⓑ	ⓒ	ⓓ	197	ⓐ	ⓑ	ⓒ	ⓓ
118	ⓐ	ⓑ	ⓒ	ⓓ	138	ⓐ	ⓑ	ⓒ	ⓓ	158	ⓐ	ⓑ	ⓒ	ⓓ	178	ⓐ	ⓑ	ⓒ	ⓓ	198	ⓐ	ⓑ	ⓒ	ⓓ
119	ⓐ	ⓑ	ⓒ	ⓓ	139	ⓐ	ⓑ	ⓒ	ⓓ	159	ⓐ	ⓑ	ⓒ	ⓓ	179	ⓐ	ⓑ	ⓒ	ⓓ	199	ⓐ	ⓑ	ⓒ	ⓓ
120	ⓐ	ⓑ	ⓒ	ⓓ	140	ⓐ	ⓑ	ⓒ	ⓓ	160	ⓐ	ⓑ	ⓒ	ⓓ	180	ⓐ	ⓑ	ⓒ	ⓓ	200	ⓐ	ⓑ	ⓒ	ⓓ

ANSWER SHEET

ETS® TOEIC® 토익® 정기시험 기출문제집

수험번호						

응시일자 : 20 년 월 일

성명		
	한 글	
	한 자	
	영 자	

Test (Part 5~7)

101	ⓐ ⓑ ⓒ ⓓ	121	ⓐ ⓑ ⓒ ⓓ	141	ⓐ ⓑ ⓒ ⓓ	161	ⓐ ⓑ ⓒ ⓓ	181	ⓐ ⓑ ⓒ ⓓ
102	ⓐ ⓑ ⓒ ⓓ	122	ⓐ ⓑ ⓒ ⓓ	142	ⓐ ⓑ ⓒ ⓓ	162	ⓐ ⓑ ⓒ ⓓ	182	ⓐ ⓑ ⓒ ⓓ
103	ⓐ ⓑ ⓒ ⓓ	123	ⓐ ⓑ ⓒ ⓓ	143	ⓐ ⓑ ⓒ ⓓ	163	ⓐ ⓑ ⓒ ⓓ	183	ⓐ ⓑ ⓒ ⓓ
104	ⓐ ⓑ ⓒ ⓓ	124	ⓐ ⓑ ⓒ ⓓ	144	ⓐ ⓑ ⓒ ⓓ	164	ⓐ ⓑ ⓒ ⓓ	184	ⓐ ⓑ ⓒ ⓓ
105	ⓐ ⓑ ⓒ ⓓ	125	ⓐ ⓑ ⓒ ⓓ	145	ⓐ ⓑ ⓒ ⓓ	165	ⓐ ⓑ ⓒ ⓓ	185	ⓐ ⓑ ⓒ ⓓ
106	ⓐ ⓑ ⓒ ⓓ	126	ⓐ ⓑ ⓒ ⓓ	146	ⓐ ⓑ ⓒ ⓓ	166	ⓐ ⓑ ⓒ ⓓ	186	ⓐ ⓑ ⓒ ⓓ
107	ⓐ ⓑ ⓒ ⓓ	127	ⓐ ⓑ ⓒ ⓓ	147	ⓐ ⓑ ⓒ ⓓ	167	ⓐ ⓑ ⓒ ⓓ	187	ⓐ ⓑ ⓒ ⓓ
108	ⓐ ⓑ ⓒ ⓓ	128	ⓐ ⓑ ⓒ ⓓ	148	ⓐ ⓑ ⓒ ⓓ	168	ⓐ ⓑ ⓒ ⓓ	188	ⓐ ⓑ ⓒ ⓓ
109	ⓐ ⓑ ⓒ ⓓ	129	ⓐ ⓑ ⓒ ⓓ	149	ⓐ ⓑ ⓒ ⓓ	169	ⓐ ⓑ ⓒ ⓓ	189	ⓐ ⓑ ⓒ ⓓ
110	ⓐ ⓑ ⓒ ⓓ	130	ⓐ ⓑ ⓒ ⓓ	150	ⓐ ⓑ ⓒ ⓓ	170	ⓐ ⓑ ⓒ ⓓ	190	ⓐ ⓑ ⓒ ⓓ
111	ⓐ ⓑ ⓒ ⓓ	131	ⓐ ⓑ ⓒ ⓓ	151	ⓐ ⓑ ⓒ ⓓ	171	ⓐ ⓑ ⓒ ⓓ	191	ⓐ ⓑ ⓒ ⓓ
112	ⓐ ⓑ ⓒ ⓓ	132	ⓐ ⓑ ⓒ ⓓ	152	ⓐ ⓑ ⓒ ⓓ	172	ⓐ ⓑ ⓒ ⓓ	192	ⓐ ⓑ ⓒ ⓓ
113	ⓐ ⓑ ⓒ ⓓ	133	ⓐ ⓑ ⓒ ⓓ	153	ⓐ ⓑ ⓒ ⓓ	173	ⓐ ⓑ ⓒ ⓓ	193	ⓐ ⓑ ⓒ ⓓ
114	ⓐ ⓑ ⓒ ⓓ	134	ⓐ ⓑ ⓒ ⓓ	154	ⓐ ⓑ ⓒ ⓓ	174	ⓐ ⓑ ⓒ ⓓ	194	ⓐ ⓑ ⓒ ⓓ
115	ⓐ ⓑ ⓒ ⓓ	135	ⓐ ⓑ ⓒ ⓓ	155	ⓐ ⓑ ⓒ ⓓ	175	ⓐ ⓑ ⓒ ⓓ	195	ⓐ ⓑ ⓒ ⓓ
116	ⓐ ⓑ ⓒ ⓓ	136	ⓐ ⓑ ⓒ ⓓ	156	ⓐ ⓑ ⓒ ⓓ	176	ⓐ ⓑ ⓒ ⓓ	196	ⓐ ⓑ ⓒ ⓓ
117	ⓐ ⓑ ⓒ ⓓ	137	ⓐ ⓑ ⓒ ⓓ	157	ⓐ ⓑ ⓒ ⓓ	177	ⓐ ⓑ ⓒ ⓓ	197	ⓐ ⓑ ⓒ ⓓ
118	ⓐ ⓑ ⓒ ⓓ	138	ⓐ ⓑ ⓒ ⓓ	158	ⓐ ⓑ ⓒ ⓓ	178	ⓐ ⓑ ⓒ ⓓ	198	ⓐ ⓑ ⓒ ⓓ
119	ⓐ ⓑ ⓒ ⓓ	139	ⓐ ⓑ ⓒ ⓓ	159	ⓐ ⓑ ⓒ ⓓ	179	ⓐ ⓑ ⓒ ⓓ	199	ⓐ ⓑ ⓒ ⓓ
120	ⓐ ⓑ ⓒ ⓓ	140	ⓐ ⓑ ⓒ ⓓ	160	ⓐ ⓑ ⓒ ⓓ	180	ⓐ ⓑ ⓒ ⓓ	200	ⓐ ⓑ ⓒ ⓓ

Test (Part 5~7)

101	ⓐ ⓑ ⓒ ⓓ	121	ⓐ ⓑ ⓒ ⓓ	141	ⓐ ⓑ ⓒ ⓓ	161	ⓐ ⓑ ⓒ ⓓ	181	ⓐ ⓑ ⓒ ⓓ
102	ⓐ ⓑ ⓒ ⓓ	122	ⓐ ⓑ ⓒ ⓓ	142	ⓐ ⓑ ⓒ ⓓ	162	ⓐ ⓑ ⓒ ⓓ	182	ⓐ ⓑ ⓒ ⓓ
103	ⓐ ⓑ ⓒ ⓓ	123	ⓐ ⓑ ⓒ ⓓ	143	ⓐ ⓑ ⓒ ⓓ	163	ⓐ ⓑ ⓒ ⓓ	183	ⓐ ⓑ ⓒ ⓓ
104	ⓐ ⓑ ⓒ ⓓ	124	ⓐ ⓑ ⓒ ⓓ	144	ⓐ ⓑ ⓒ ⓓ	164	ⓐ ⓑ ⓒ ⓓ	184	ⓐ ⓑ ⓒ ⓓ
105	ⓐ ⓑ ⓒ ⓓ	125	ⓐ ⓑ ⓒ ⓓ	145	ⓐ ⓑ ⓒ ⓓ	165	ⓐ ⓑ ⓒ ⓓ	185	ⓐ ⓑ ⓒ ⓓ
106	ⓐ ⓑ ⓒ ⓓ	126	ⓐ ⓑ ⓒ ⓓ	146	ⓐ ⓑ ⓒ ⓓ	166	ⓐ ⓑ ⓒ ⓓ	186	ⓐ ⓑ ⓒ ⓓ
107	ⓐ ⓑ ⓒ ⓓ	127	ⓐ ⓑ ⓒ ⓓ	147	ⓐ ⓑ ⓒ ⓓ	167	ⓐ ⓑ ⓒ ⓓ	187	ⓐ ⓑ ⓒ ⓓ
108	ⓐ ⓑ ⓒ ⓓ	128	ⓐ ⓑ ⓒ ⓓ	148	ⓐ ⓑ ⓒ ⓓ	168	ⓐ ⓑ ⓒ ⓓ	188	ⓐ ⓑ ⓒ ⓓ
109	ⓐ ⓑ ⓒ ⓓ	129	ⓐ ⓑ ⓒ ⓓ	149	ⓐ ⓑ ⓒ ⓓ	169	ⓐ ⓑ ⓒ ⓓ	189	ⓐ ⓑ ⓒ ⓓ
110	ⓐ ⓑ ⓒ ⓓ	130	ⓐ ⓑ ⓒ ⓓ	150	ⓐ ⓑ ⓒ ⓓ	170	ⓐ ⓑ ⓒ ⓓ	190	ⓐ ⓑ ⓒ ⓓ
111	ⓐ ⓑ ⓒ ⓓ	131	ⓐ ⓑ ⓒ ⓓ	151	ⓐ ⓑ ⓒ ⓓ	171	ⓐ ⓑ ⓒ ⓓ	191	ⓐ ⓑ ⓒ ⓓ
112	ⓐ ⓑ ⓒ ⓓ	132	ⓐ ⓑ ⓒ ⓓ	152	ⓐ ⓑ ⓒ ⓓ	172	ⓐ ⓑ ⓒ ⓓ	192	ⓐ ⓑ ⓒ ⓓ
113	ⓐ ⓑ ⓒ ⓓ	133	ⓐ ⓑ ⓒ ⓓ	153	ⓐ ⓑ ⓒ ⓓ	173	ⓐ ⓑ ⓒ ⓓ	193	ⓐ ⓑ ⓒ ⓓ
114	ⓐ ⓑ ⓒ ⓓ	134	ⓐ ⓑ ⓒ ⓓ	154	ⓐ ⓑ ⓒ ⓓ	174	ⓐ ⓑ ⓒ ⓓ	194	ⓐ ⓑ ⓒ ⓓ
115	ⓐ ⓑ ⓒ ⓓ	135	ⓐ ⓑ ⓒ ⓓ	155	ⓐ ⓑ ⓒ ⓓ	175	ⓐ ⓑ ⓒ ⓓ	195	ⓐ ⓑ ⓒ ⓓ
116	ⓐ ⓑ ⓒ ⓓ	136	ⓐ ⓑ ⓒ ⓓ	156	ⓐ ⓑ ⓒ ⓓ	176	ⓐ ⓑ ⓒ ⓓ	196	ⓐ ⓑ ⓒ ⓓ
117	ⓐ ⓑ ⓒ ⓓ	137	ⓐ ⓑ ⓒ ⓓ	157	ⓐ ⓑ ⓒ ⓓ	177	ⓐ ⓑ ⓒ ⓓ	197	ⓐ ⓑ ⓒ ⓓ
118	ⓐ ⓑ ⓒ ⓓ	138	ⓐ ⓑ ⓒ ⓓ	158	ⓐ ⓑ ⓒ ⓓ	178	ⓐ ⓑ ⓒ ⓓ	198	ⓐ ⓑ ⓒ ⓓ
119	ⓐ ⓑ ⓒ ⓓ	139	ⓐ ⓑ ⓒ ⓓ	159	ⓐ ⓑ ⓒ ⓓ	179	ⓐ ⓑ ⓒ ⓓ	199	ⓐ ⓑ ⓒ ⓓ
120	ⓐ ⓑ ⓒ ⓓ	140	ⓐ ⓑ ⓒ ⓓ	160	ⓐ ⓑ ⓒ ⓓ	180	ⓐ ⓑ ⓒ ⓓ	200	ⓐ ⓑ ⓒ ⓓ

토익® 정기시험 기출문제집 2

1000

READING

정답 및 해설

기출 TEST 1

101 (A)	102 (A)	103 (D)	104 (D)	105 (A)
106 (A)	107 (B)	108 (C)	109 (D)	110 (B)
111 (C)	112 (B)	113 (B)	114 (A)	115 (D)
116 (D)	117 (C)	118 (D)	119 (C)	120 (C)
121 (A)	122 (B)	123 (B)	124 (C)	125 (D)
126 (A)	127 (A)	128 (D)	129 (A)	130 (B)
131 (B)	132 (C)	133 (A)	134 (D)	135 (D)
136 (C)	137 (A)	138 (B)	139 (A)	140 (C)
141 (A)	142 (B)	143 (B)	144 (A)	145 (D)
146 (D)	147 (C)	148 (A)	149 (C)	150 (C)
151 (B)	152 (D)	153 (B)	154 (B)	155 (D)
156 (C)	157 (B)	158 (A)	159 (B)	160 (B)
161 (C)	162 (B)	163 (D)	164 (D)	165 (B)
166 (C)	167 (A)	168 (D)	169 (C)	170 (A)
171 (B)	172 (D)	173 (B)	174 (A)	175 (B)
176 (C)	177 (A)	178 (D)	179 (B)	180 (D)
181 (A)	182 (A)	183 (C)	184 (C)	185 (B)
186 (C)	187 (C)	188 (B)	189 (C)	190 (A)
191 (A)	192 (B)	193 (D)	194 (D)	195 (C)
196 (B)	197 (A)	198 (D)	199 (C)	200 (B)

PART 5

101 형용사 자리 _ 명사구 수식

해설 빈칸이 정관사 the와 명사구 monthly meeting 사이에 있으며, 문맥상 '월례 회의'를 수식하는 형용사가 빈칸에 들어가야 자연스럽다. 따라서 '다음의'라는 뜻의 형용사로 쓰일 수 있는 (A) next가 정답이다. (D) like는 형용사로 쓰일 경우 '비슷한'이라는 의미가 되어 빈칸에 적절하지 않다.

번역 부서별 구조 조정이 다음 달 월례 회의에서 논의될 예정이다.

어휘 departmental 부서의 restructuring 구조 조정

102 인칭대명사의 격 _ 소유격

해설 빈칸은 to부정사구 「To keep+목적어(park)+목적격 보어(beautiful)」에서 목적어 park를 한정 수식하는 자리이므로, 소유격 인칭대명사 (A) our가 정답이다.

번역 우리 공원을 아름답게 유지하려면, 재활용되지 않는 것들은 이용 가능한 쓰레기통에 넣어 주십시오.

어휘 nonrecyclables 재활용되지 않는 것들 available 이용 가능한

103 동사 어휘

해설 해당 절에서 직접목적어 역할을 하는 additional images of the office building과 가장 잘 어울리는 타동사를 선택해야 한다. 따라서 images와 같은 사물을 목적어로 취할 수 있는 (D) requested (요청했다)가 정답이다. (B) asked 또한 '요청했다'라는 의미로 쓰일 수 있지만, 사물 명사를 목적어로 취하려면 전치사 for와 함께 쓰여야 한다. (A) informed는 '알렸다, 통지했다', (C) advised는 '조언했다, 알렸다'라는 뜻으로, 알림 또는 조언을 받는 대상을 목적어로 취하므로 빈칸에는 적절하지 않다.

번역 하딘 씨는 자신이 임대하고 싶은 사무용 건물의 이미지를 추가로 요청했다.

어휘 additional 추가의 lease 임대[임차]하다

104 부사 자리 _ 구동사(phrasal verb) _ 어휘

해설 빈칸 없이도 완전한 문장이며 빈칸이 수동태 동사 be brought와 to 부정사 사이에 있으므로, 보기 중 부사를 선택해야 한다. 문맥상 '작물 수확량을 늘리기 위해 농업 전문가들로 구성된 팀이 모이게 될 것이다'라는 내용이 되어야 자연스러우므로, bring과 함께 구동사를 이루어 '모이게 하다, 합치다'라는 의미를 완성하는 (D) together가 정답이다. (B) either는 부사로 쓰일 경우 부정문에서 '또한, 역시'라는 의미를 나타내며, 전치사/부사인 (C) between은 '~ 사이에'라는 의미이므로 빈칸에 적절하지 않다. (A) because는 접속사로 품사상 빈칸에 들어갈 수 없다.

번역 작물 수확량을 늘리기 위해 농업 전문가들로 구성된 팀이 모이게 될 것이다.

어휘 agricultural 농업의 expert 전문가 improve 늘리다, 개선하다 crop 작물 harvest 수확(량)

105 동사 어휘

해설 빈칸은 주어 The board of Galaxipharm의 동사 자리로, 명사구 Mr. Kwon's successor를 목적어로 취하고 있다. 따라서 빈칸에는 주어 및 목적어와 어울리는 동사가 들어가야 한다. '갤럭시팜 이사회'와 '권 씨의 후임자'의 관계를 보았을 때, 전자는 지명하는 주체, 후자는 지명되는 대상으로 보는 것이 가장 자연스러우므로, '지명했다, 임명했다'라는 의미의 (A) named가 정답이다. (B) granted가 '수여했다, 승인했다'라는 의미로 쓰일 경우 간접목적어(대상자)와 직접목적어(대상물)가 모두 있어야 하므로 정답이 될 수 없고, (C) founded는 '설립했다, 기초를 세웠다', (D) proved는 '입증했다, ~임이 판명되었다'라는 뜻으로 빈칸에 적절하지 않다.

번역 갤럭시팜 이사회는 어제 회의에서 권 씨의 후임자를 지명했다.

어휘 board 이사회 successor 후임자

106 명사 자리 _ 전치사의 목적어

해설 빈칸은 부정관사 a 뒤에 오는 명사 자리로, 전치사 for의 목적어 역할을 한다. 따라서 '교체[대체]물'이라는 의미의 명사인 (A) replacement가 정답이다. (B) replacing을 '교체'라는 뜻의 동명사라고 가정하더라도, 부정관사 a와 쓰일 수는 없으므로 빈칸에 알맞지 않다. 동사 (C) replace와 (D) replaces는 품사상 빈칸에 들어갈 수 없다.

번역 주차 허가증이 훼손된 경우, 입구 건물로 가져와 다른 것으로 받아 가십시오.

어휘 parking permit 주차 허가증 damaged 훼손된 entrance 입구 replace 교체[대체]하다

107 부사절 접속사

해설 빈칸은 두 개의 완전한 절을 이어 주는 접속사 자리이다. 따라서 (B) in case와 (D) unless 중 하나를 선택해야 한다. 별실을 예약하기로 결정한 것(decided to reserve a private room)은 식당이 시끄러운(the restaurant was noisy) 경우를 대비했다고 보는 것이 자연스러우므로, '~할 것을 대비하여'라는 뜻의 (B) in case가 정답이다. (D) unless는 '~하지 않으면, ~이 아닌 경우에는'이라는 의미로 문맥상 어색하다. (A) rather than은 '~라기보다는'이라는 의미의 상관접속사로 쓰일 수 있으나, 해당 문장의 빈칸에 들어가 두 개의 완전한 절을 이어 줄 수는 없다. (C) such as 역시 완전한 절을 이끌 수 없으므로 오답이다.

번역 아마드 씨는 식당이 시끄러울 경우를 대비하여 시상식 만찬을 위해 별실을 예약하기로 결정했다.

어휘 decide 결정하다 reserve 예약하다 private room 프라이빗 룸, 별실 awards dinner 시상식 만찬

108 형용사 자리 _ 명사 수식

해설 빈칸은 부정관사 a 뒤에서 명사 estimate를 수식하는 형용사 자리이므로, '(수나 양을) 적게 잡은, 보수적인'이라는 의미의 형용사 (C) conservative가 정답이다. (A) conserve와 (B) conserves는 명사/동사, (D) conservatively는 부사로 품사상 빈칸에 들어갈 수 없다.

번역 존스 씨는 주 전체로 유통을 확대하는 데 드는 비용을 적게 잡은 추정치를 제공했다.

어휘 provide 제공하다, 산출하다 estimate 추정치 expand 확대하다 distribution 유통, 배급 statewide 주 전체로 conserve 보존하다; 과일 잼

109 형용사 어휘

해설 빈칸은 동사 sets의 목적어 역할을 하는 sales goals를 수식하고 있다. 따라서 직원들을 위해 설정된 판매 목표의 특성을 적절히 묘사하는 형용사가 들어가야 하므로, '현실적인, 실현 가능한'이라는 의미의 (D) realistic이 정답이다. (A) compact는 '소형의, 작은', (B) wealthy는 '부유한', (C) faithful은 '충실한, 충직한'이라는 뜻으로 모두 문맥상 빈칸에 적절하지 않다.

번역 아카바 수출은 분기마다 직원들을 위한 현실적인 판매 목표를 설정한다.

어휘 quarter 분기

110 명사 자리 _ 동사의 목적어

해설 빈칸은 to부정사의 동사원형 receive의 목적어 역할을 하는 명사 자리로, 빈칸 뒤 that이 이끄는 명사절(that her company ~ magazine)과 동격 관계를 이룬다. 따라서 '통지, 알림'이라는 의미의 명사 (B) notification이 정답이다. (C) notifying을 '통지하기'라는 뜻의 동명사로 본다고 하더라도, 뒤에 통지를 받는 대상이 나오지 않으며, 의미상 receive(받다)의 목적어가 될 수 없으므로 오답이다. (A) notify와 (D) notifies는 동사로 품사상 빈칸에 적절하지 않다.

번역 가르시아 씨는 자신의 회사가 곧 〈인 타운 타임즈〉 잡지에 실린다는 통지를 받고 기뻐했다.

어휘 delighted 기뻐하는 receive 받다 feature 특별히 포함하다, 대서특필하다

111 전치사 어휘

해설 '자격이 있는'이라는 의미의 형용사 eligible과 어울려 쓰이는 전치사를 선택해야 한다. 따라서 '~에 적합한, ~에 맞는'이라는 뜻을 지닌 (C) for가 정답이다. 참고로, eligible은 to부정사와도 함께 쓰인다.

번역 5세 미만 어린이는 무료 시력 검사를 받을 수 있다.

어휘 vision test 시력 검사

112 부사 자리 _ 동사 수식

해설 빈칸은 to부정사의 동사원형 drive를 수식하는 부사 자리이므로, '조심해서'라는 의미의 부사 (B) cautiously가 정답이다. (A) caution은 명사/동사, (C) cautious는 형용사, (D) cautiousness는 명사로 품사상 빈칸에 들어갈 수 없다.

번역 파르탄 고속도로 운전자들은 진행 중인 공사 때문에 7월 내내 조심해서 운전해야 한다는 점을 주지해야 한다.

어휘 remind 상기시키다 ongoing 진행 중인 construction 공사, 건설 caution 조심, 경고; 경고하다 cautious 조심스러운 cautiousness 조심성

113 부사절 접속사

해설 빈칸은 두 개의 완전한 절을 이어 주는 접속사 자리이므로, 접속사로 쓰일 수 있는 (A) that과 (B) once 중 하나를 선택해야 한다. 빈칸 앞 주절에서는 미래 시제를 사용하여 주간 회의를 재개할 것(will resume)이라고 하고, 뒤에 오는 종속절에서는 현재 시제를 사용하여 천 씨가 돌아올(returns) 미래 상황을 나타내고 있다. 따라서 '일단 ~하면, ~하자마자'라는 의미의 시간 부사절 접속사 (B) once가 정답이다.

번역 위원회는 천 씨가 9월 17일에 스코틀랜드에서 돌아오는 대로 주간 회의를 재개할 것이다.

어휘 committee 위원회 resume 재개하다

114 형용사 자리 _ 분사

해설 빈칸이 정관사 The와 명사 initiative 사이에 있으므로, initiative를 수식하는 형용사나 initiative와 복합명사를 이루는 명사가 들어갈 수 있다. 따라서 형용사 역할을 하는 과거분사 (A) proposed와 현재분사 (B) proposing, 명사 (C) proposal 중 하나를 선택해야 한다. 대중교통을 제공하고자 하는(aims to provide public transportation) 계획안은 제안되는 것이므로, 수동의 의미를 내포한 과거분사 (A) proposed가 정답이다. (C) proposal은 '제안(서), 계획안'이라는 의미로 initiative와 복합명사를 이룰 수 없으며, (D) propose는 동사로 품사상 빈칸에 들어갈 수 없다.

번역 제안된 계획안은 외곽의 교외에 사는 통근자들에게 대중교통을 제공하는 것을 목표로 한다.

어휘 initiative 계획(안), 방안 aim 목표로 하다 public transportation 대중교통 commuter 통근자 outer 외곽의 suburb 교외

115 부사 어휘

해설 빈칸은 동사 interrupted를 수식하는 부사 자리로, 어제의 폭풍(Yesterday's storm)이 서비스를 중단시킨(interrupted the services) 방식이나 빈도를 묘사하는 부사가 들어가야 자연스럽다. 따라서 '일시적으로'라는 의미의 (D) temporarily가 정답이다. (A) annually는 '매년', (B) anytime은 '언제나'라는 의미로 문맥상 빈칸에 적절하지 않고, (C) whenever는 '언제라도'라는 뜻의 부사로 쓰일 수 있지만 문맥상 어색하며 위치상으로도 빈칸에 들어갈 수 없다.

번역 어제 폭풍으로 위성 통신 시스템인 더둘라사의 서비스가 일시 중단되었다.

어휘 temporarily 일시적으로, 임시로 interrupt 중단시키다, 방해하다 satellite communication 위성 통신

116 대명사 어휘

해설 빈칸은 be동사 are의 주어 자리로, 보어인 영화사들(movie studios)과 같은 대상을 가리키는 대명사가 들어가야 한다. 따라서 부사절의 주어인 두 회사 Cabrera Pictures and Marcella Images를 대신할 수 있는 (D) both(둘 다)가 정답이다.

번역 카브레라 픽처스와 마르셀라 이미지스는 매우 다른 영화를 만들지만, 둘 다 성공한 영화사이다.

어휘 even though 비록 ~이지만 different 다른 several 몇몇(의)

117 명사 어휘

해설 빈칸은 문장의 주어 역할을 하는 명사 자리로, 전치사구 of tasks의 수식을 받는다. 관리자의 일을 수월하게 하고(make a manager's job easier) 다른 직원들이 새로운 기술을 배울 수 있도록 도와줄 수 있는(help other employees learn new skills) 것과 상응하는 단어가 들어가야 하므로, '(권한·업무 등의) 위임'이라는 뜻의 (C) Delegation이 정답이다. (A) Reputation은 '평판, 명성', (B) Foundation은 '토대, 설립, 재단', (D) Permission은 '허락, 허가'라는 뜻으로 모두 문맥상 빈칸에 적절하지 않다.

번역 업무를 위임하면 관리자의 일을 수월하게 하고 다른 직원들이 새로운 기술을 배우게끔 해 줄 수 있다.

어휘 delegation 위임, 대표단

118 동사 어형 _ 태

해설 빈칸이 be동사 were와 부사 equally 뒤에 있으므로, 현재분사 (B) dividing과 과거분사 (D) divided 중 하나를 선택해야 한다. '수익(금)'이라는 의미의 주어 Proceeds는 분배되는 대상이므로, 수동의 의미를 내포한 (D) divided가 정답이다. (A) divisions는 명사로 부사 equally의 수식을 받을 수 없고, (C) divide는 동사원형으로 be동사와 함께 쓰일 수 없으므로 빈칸에 들어갈 수 없다.

번역 델크레스트사의 매각 수익은 창업자의 세 딸에게 균등하게 분배되었다.

어휘 proceeds 수익(금) equally 균등하게, 동등하게 divide 분배하다 founder 창업자, 설립자

119 전치사 어휘

해설 빈칸은 명사구 higher than average ticket prices를 목적어로 취하는 전치사 자리로, 빈칸을 포함한 전치사구가 콤마 뒤 절을 수식하고 있다. 따라서 명사구와 해당 절을 가장 자연스럽게 연결하는 전치사가 들어가야 한다. 평균보다 높은 티켓 가격의 영향을 받지 않고 모든 공연이 매진되었다(every performance ~ is sold out)는 내용의 문장이므로, '~에도 불구하고'라는 의미의 (C) Despite가 정답이다. (A) Throughout은 '~의 도처에, ~ 내내', (B) Except for는 '~을 제외하고', (D) Prior to는 '~ 전에, ~에 앞서'라는 뜻으로 모두 문맥상 빈칸에 적절하지 않다.

번역 평균보다 높은 티켓 가격에도 불구하고, 에이든 노스의 신작 연극은 향후 6개월치 공연이 전부 매진되었다.

어휘 average 평균의; 평균 performance 공연

120 부사 자리 _ 동사 수식

해설 빈칸은 동사 responds를 수식하는 부사 자리이므로, '정중하게'라는 의미의 부사인 (C) respectfully가 정답이다. (A) respect, (B) respects는 동사/명사로 품사상 빈칸에 들어갈 수 없으며, (D) respected를 과거분사로 본다고 하더라도 명사 suggestions가 이미 guests'의 한정 수식을 받고 있으므로, 빈칸에는 적합하지 않다.

번역 니날 레스토랑의 총주방장 리카도 소사는 손님들의 제안에 정중하게 응대한다.

어휘 executive chef 총주방장 respond 응대하다 suggestion 제안 respect 존경, 존중; 존경[존중]하다 respects (공손한) 안부 respected 존경[존중]받는

121 명사 어휘

해설 빈칸은 동사구 is negotiating의 목적어 역할을 하는 명사 자리로, 전치사구 of the new contract with Arban, Inc.의 수식을 받는다. 따라서 계약 시 협상(negotiate)해야 할 대상을 나타내는 명사가 빈칸에 들어가야 하므로, '범위'라는 의미의 (A) scope가 정답이다. (B) turn은 '전환, 차례', (C) grip은 '움켜쥠, 이해, 통제', (D) drive는 '운동, 추진력'이라는 뜻으로 문맥상 빈칸에 적절하지 않다.

번역 코스터 씨는 아반사와 새 계약의 범위를 협상중이다.

어휘 negotiate 협상하다 contract 계약

122 동사 어형 _ 태

해설 알맞은 동사 형태를 선택하는 문제이다. 주어 The equipment-use guidelines(장비 사용 지침)는 웹사이트에서 찾을 수 있는 대상이므로, 수동태 동사 (B) can be found가 정답이다. (A) may find, (C) have found, (D) have to find는 모두 목적어를 취하는 능동태 동사이므로 빈칸에 들어갈 수 없다.

번역 장비 사용 지침은 우리 회사 내부 웹사이트에서 찾을 수 있다.

어휘 equipment 장비 internal 내부의 corporate 기업의

123 부사 어휘

해설 빈칸은 to부정사의 동사원형 calculate를 수식하는 부사 자리이다. 따라서 빈칸에는 '계산하다'와 가장 잘 어울리는 부사가 들어가야 하므로, '정확하게'라는 의미의 (B) precisely가 정답이다. (A) dominantly는 '지배적으로, 우세하게', (C) relatively는 '비교적, 상대적으로', (D) widely는 '널리, 다방면에 걸쳐'라는 뜻으로 문맥상 빈칸에 적절하지 않다.

번역 한 교수는 농장의 관개 필요량을 정확하게 계산하기 위해 스프레드시트를 만들었다.

어휘 calculate 계산하다 irrigation 관개

124 형용사 어휘

해설 빈칸에는 주어 five years of professional experience에 대해 설명하며 to having achieved certification과 자연스럽게 연결되는 형용사가 들어가야 한다. 채용에 있어 직무 경력과 자격증은 서로 비교되는 대상이므로, '동등한, ~에 상당하는'이라는 의미의 (C) equivalent가 정답이다. 참고로, equivalent는 전치사 to와 자주 쓰인다. (A) reasonable은 '합당한, 적당한', (B) appropriate는 '적절한, 알맞은', (D) significant는 '중요한, 상당한'이라는 뜻으로 문맥상 빈칸에 적절하지 않다.

번역 채용 시 5년의 직무 경력은 자격증을 취득한 것과 동등하게 간주된다.

어휘 professional 직무의 achieve 획득하다, 달성하다 certification 자격(증)

125 동명사 _ 전치사의 목적어

해설 빈칸이 전치사 by와 복합명사 cargo loads 사이에 있으므로, 빈칸에는 cargo loads를 수식하는 형용사나 이를 목적어로 취하는 동명사가 들어갈 수 있다. 문맥상 해당 부분이 연료비를 절감하는 방안(measures to reduce fuel expenses)을 설명하는 내용이 되어야 자연스러우므로, by와 함께 '가볍게 함으로써'라는 의미를 완성하는 동명사 (D) lightening이 정답이다. (B) lighten은 동사, (C) lightly는 부사로 품사상 빈칸에 들어갈 수 없다.

번역 사우스 리젠트 항공은 화물 하중을 가볍게 해 연료비를 줄이는 방안을 채택 중이다.

어휘 aviation 항공 adopt 채택하다 measure 방안 reduce 줄이다 fuel 연료 expense 비용 lighten 가볍게 하다 cargo 화물 load 짐의 양, 적재량

126 부사 자리 _ 어휘

해설 빈칸이 '가장 어려운 측면은 임금을 협상하는 것이다'라는 완전한 문장 앞에 있으므로, 문장 전체를 수식하는 부사가 들어가야 한다. 따라서 '아마도'라는 뜻의 부사인 (A) Perhaps가 정답이다. (B) Outside는 부사로 쓰일 경우 문장 전체를 수식할 수 없고, 전치사로 쓰여 도치될 수 있다고 가정하더라도 문맥상 어색하므로 정답이 될 수 없다. (C) Every는 한정사, (D) While은 부사절 접속사로 품사상 빈칸에 들어갈 수 없다.

번역 아마도 새로운 직책을 수락할 때 가장 어려운 측면은 타당하면서도 만족스러운 임금 협상일 것이다.

어휘 challenging 어려운 accept 수락하다 negotiate 협상하다 fair 타당한, 공정한 satisfying 만족스러운

127 명사 어휘

해설 빈칸은 to부정사의 동사원형 adopt의 목적어 역할을 하는 명사 자리로, 비교급 형용사 higher의 수식을 받고 있다. 따라서 품질 평가에 있어서(for assessing quality) 더 엄격히 채택해야 하는 대상을 나타내는 명사가 들어가야 하므로, '기준, 수준'이라는 의미의 (A) standards가 정답이다. (B) features는 '특징, 특집', (C) risks는 '위험, 위험 요인', (D) institutions는 '기관, 사회 제도'라는 뜻으로 문맥상 빈칸에 적절하지 않다.

번역 새로운 주방 가전 제품 라인에 대한 불만 때문에 로제보사는 품질 평가에 있어서 더 높은 기준을 채택했다.

어휘 appliance 가전 제품 adopt 채택하다 assess 평가하다

128 형용사 자리 _ 주격 보어

해설 빈칸은 that절의 주어 constructing another bridge를 보충 설명하는 보어 자리로, 명사나 형용사가 들어갈 수 있다. 교량을 하나 더 건설하는 것(constructing another bridge)과 기존 구조물을 수리하는 것(repairing the existing structure)을 비교하고 있으므로, 빈칸에는 특성이나 상태를 묘사하는 형용사가 들어가야 자연스럽다. 따라서 more ~ than과 함께 '~보다 더 경제적인'이라는 표현을 완성하는 형용사 (D) economical이 정답이다.

번역 수석 엔지니어는 기존 구조물을 수리하는 것보다 교량을 하나 더 건설하는 편이 더 경제적일 거라고 말했다.

어휘 construct 건설하다 economical 경제적인 repair 수리하다 existing 기존의 structure 구조(물) economy 경제, 경기 economics 경제학, 경제 상태 economically 경제적으로

129 전치사 어휘

해설 빈칸은 동명사구 maintaining their state licenses를 목적어로 취하는 전치사 자리로, 빈칸을 포함한 전치사구가 앞에 있는 동사구를 수식하고 있다. 따라서 빈칸에는 이들을 가장 잘 연결해 주는 전치사가 들어가야 한다. 정기 교육을 수료하는 것과 주 면허를 유지하는 것은 버스 운전자가 동시에 충족해야 할 요건이므로, '~에 더하여, ~외에도'라는 의미의 (A) in addition to가 정답이다. (B) according to는 '~에 따라', (C) inside는 '~ 안에', (D) within은 '~ 이내에'라는 뜻으로 문맥상 빈칸에 적절하지 않다.

번역 젠슨 버스 회사 운전자들은 자신들의 주 면허를 유지하는 것 외에도 정기 교육을 수료해야 한다.

어휘 be expected to ~해야 한다 regular 정기적인 maintain 유지하다

130 동사 어형 _ 태 _ 시제

해설 빈칸은 주어 Ms. DeSoto의 동사 자리로, 빈칸 뒤 all employees를 목적어로 취한다. 따라서 본동사 역할을 할 수 있는 (B) had urged, (C) will have urged, (D) was urged 중 하나를 선택

해야 한다. 주어인 Mr. DeSoto는 직원들에게 회의 참석을 촉구하는 주체이고, even though가 이끄는 부사절의 동사가 과거(were obligated)이므로, 빈칸에는 능동태 과거(완료) 시제가 들어가야 한다. 따라서 (B) had urged가 정답이다. (A) to have urged는 to부정사이므로 동사 자리에 들어갈 수 없다.

번역 임원들만 참석할 의무가 있음에도 불구하고 데소토 씨는 모든 직원에게 지난주 예산 회의에 참석하라고 촉구했다.

어휘 urge 촉구하다 budget 예산 officer 임원, 간부
be obligated to ~할 의무가 있다

PART 6

131-134 공지

레이크뷰 철도 자전거 휴대 승차 정책

자전거를 이용해 레이크뷰 코리더 경관 지구를 둘러보고 싶으신가요? 저희 열차에는 자전거를 안전하게 운반할 수 있는 [131]**장비**가 있습니다. 표를 예매할 때, 고객님과 자전거 모두 예약이 [132]**이루어져야** 한다는 점만 기억하십시오. 자전거 자리를 [133]**일찌감치** 예약하십시오. 각 열차의 자전거 보관대 수가 제한되어 있습니다. 자전거를 안전하게 실어야 할 책임은 고객님께 있습니다. [134]**자전거 자물쇠도 스스로 구비해야 합니다.** 레이크뷰 철도는 열차에서 분실 또는 파손된 자전거에 대해 책임지지 않습니다.

어휘 explore 탐험하다 scenic area 경관 지구 transport 운반[운송]하다 reservation 예약 limited 제한된 storage 보관 rack 대, 선반 be responsible for ~에 책임이 있다 stow 싣다 securely 안전하게 take responsibility for ~에 대해 책임지다 aboard (기차·배 등)에서, 탑승[승차]한

131 명사 어휘

해설 빈칸은 동사 have의 목적어 역할을 하는 명사 자리로, which 또는 that이 생략된 관계사절(you need to safely transport your bike)의 수식을 받는다. 따라서 빈칸에는 자전거를 안전하게 운반하기 위해 필요한 것을 나타내는 명사가 들어가야 하므로, '장비, 장치'라는 의미의 (B) equipment가 정답이다. (A) stock은 '재고, 주식', (C) property는 '재산, 부동산, 건물', (D) revenue는 '수익, 세입'이라는 뜻으로 모두 문맥상 빈칸에 적절하지 않다.

132 동사 어형_태_시제

해설 빈칸은 that절의 주어 reservations의 동사 자리이므로, 본동사 역할을 할 수 있는 (A) require, (C) are required, (D) were required 중 하나를 선택해야 한다. 해당 부분은 티켓 예약 규정과 관련된 내용이므로 현재 시제를 사용하는 것이 적절하며, 주어인 reservations는 요구되는 대상이므로, 수동태 현재 동사인 (C) are required가 정답이 된다. (B) requiring은 동명사/현재분사이므로 동사 자리에 들어갈 수 없다.

133 부사 어휘

해설 명령문의 동사원형 Reserve를 적절히 수식하는 부사를 선택하는 문제이다. 바로 뒤 문장에서 각 열차의 자전거 보관대 수가 제한되어 있다(There are a limited number of storage racks on each train)고 했으므로, 해당 부분은 이와 연관된 권고 사항을 나타내는 것이 자연스럽다. 따라서 '일찌감치 예약하십시오'라는 내용을 완성하는 (A) early가 정답이다.

134 문맥에 맞는 문장 고르기

번역 (A) 접이식 자전거가 더 흔해졌습니다.
(B) 추가 서비스 요금이 적용될 수 있습니다.
(C) 대다수 역에서 노선도를 얻을 수 있습니다.
(D) 자전거 자물쇠도 스스로 구비해야 합니다.

해설 빈칸 앞 문장에서 자전거를 안전하게 실어야 할 책임은 고객에게 있다(You are responsible for stowing your bike securely)고 했고, 뒤 문장에서 레이크뷰 철도는 열차에서 분실 또는 파손된 자전거에 대해 책임지지 않는다(Lakeview Railway does not take responsibility ~ our trains)고 했다. 따라서 빈칸에도 고객의 책임과 관련된 내용이 들어가야 문맥상 자연스러우므로, (D)가 정답이다.

어휘 common 흔한 additional 추가의 obtain 얻다 route map 노선도

135-138 편지

코렐리스 베이커리
미들매스 가 15번지
영스타운, 오하이오 주 44515

소중한 고객님께:

지난 3년 동안 저희는 케이크, 파이, 쿠키, 브라우니를 포함한 제과 제품의 도매 가격을 동일하게 유지했습니다. 유감스럽게도, 설탕, 과일 등 원재료 가격이 급등하면서 8월 1일을 [135]**기하여** 어쩔 수 없이 가격을 5퍼센트 인상하게 되었습니다. 저희는 이번 가격 인상을 피하기 위해 모든 노력을 다했습니다. [136]**그러나** 제품의 품질에 대한 타협은 거부하기로 했습니다. 저희가 이용 가능한 최상의 재료를 사용해야 고객님 레스토랑의 손님들이 기대하는 맛있는 디저트를 제공할 수 있습니다. [137]**여전히 저희 제품의 가치가 크다는 점을 아시게 되리라 믿습니다.** 고객님의 [138]**성원**에 감사드리며 앞으로도 계속 고객님께 제품을 납품해 드릴 수 있기를 바랍니다.

토니 코렐리, 사장

어휘 charge (요금을) 부과하다 wholesale price 도매가 raw ingredient 원 재료 attempt 노력, 시도 avoid 피하다 refuse 거부하다 compromise 타협하다 appreciate 감사하다 serve (상품이나 서비스를) 제공하다

135 형용사 어휘

해설 빈칸은 문장 구조상으로 보면 to부정사구와 날짜를 이어 주는 전치사가 들어가야 하는 자리이다. 따라서 보기의 형용사 중 전치사처

럼 쓰일 수 있는 (D) effective가 정답이 된다. effective는 시간이나 날짜 표현 앞에 쓰여 '~를 기하여, ~부터'라는 의미를 나타낸다. (A) actual은 '실제의, 사실상의', (B) future는 '미래의, 향후의', (C) practical은 '실질적인, 실용적인'이라는 뜻의 형용사로 빈칸에 적절하지 않다.

136 접속부사

해설 빈칸 앞뒤 문장을 의미상 자연스럽게 연결하는 접속부사를 선택하는 문제이다. 빈칸 앞 문장에서 이번 가격 인상을 피하기 위해 모든 노력을 다했다(We have made every attempt to avoid this price increase)고 했지만, 뒤 문장에서는 제품의 품질에 대한 타협은 거부하기로 했다(we refuse to compromise on the quality of our products), 즉 품질을 유지하기 위해서는 가격 인상이 불가피하다는 점을 피력하고 있다. 따라서 빈칸에는 대조적인 내용을 이어 주는 접속부사가 들어가야 자연스러우므로, '그러나, 하지만'이라는 의미의 (C) However가 정답이다. (A) Similarly는 '마찬가지로, 유사하게', (B) Therefore는 '그러므로, 그 결과', (D) Accordingly는 '따라서, 그에 맞춰'라는 뜻으로 문맥상 빈칸에 적절하지 않다.

137 문맥에 맞는 문장 고르기

번역 (A) 여전히 저희 제품의 가치가 크다는 점을 아시게 되리라 믿습니다.
(B) 수익성을 유지하기 위한 저희 노력은 성공하지 못했습니다.
(C) 경쟁 업체들도 가격을 올리리라 생각합니다.
(D) 저희 제품은 전통적인 제과 제품보다 더 건강에 좋습니다.

해설 빈칸 앞 문장에서 최상의 재료를 사용해야 레스토랑의 손님들이 기대하는 맛있는 디저트를 제공할 수 있다(Using the best ingredients available ~ to provide the delicious desserts your restaurant guests have come to expect)고 했고, 뒤 문장에서 계속 제품을 납품할 수 있기를 바란다(look forward to continuing to serve you)고 했으므로, 빈칸에는 제품의 품질이 여전히 좋다는 것을 어필하는 내용이 들어가야 자연스럽다. 따라서 (A)가 정답이다.

어휘 profitable 수익성 있는 competitor 경쟁 업체

138 명사 자리 _ 동사의 목적어 _ 어휘

해설 빈칸은 동사 appreciate의 목적어 역할을 하는 명사 자리이므로, (B) support, (C) supporter, (D) supports 중 하나를 선택해야 한다. '감사하다'라는 의미의 appreciate는 감사함을 느끼는 이유를 목적어로 취하므로, '성원, 지지'라는 의미의 불가산 명사인 (B) support가 정답이다. (C) supporter는 '지지자', (D) supports는 '버팀대, 지주'라는 의미로 문맥상 어색하며, (A) supportive는 형용사로 품사상 빈칸에 들어갈 수 없다.

139-142 이메일

수신: 누라 아바디
발신: 알렉시스 파머
제목: 정보 제공 면담
날짜: 2월 4일

아바디 씨께,

어제 제게 시간을 내 주시고 항공 우주 업계에서의 진로에 대해 이야기해 주셔서 감사합니다. 귀하의 139**식견**은 도움이 되었고, 그로 인해 대학원 지원 전에 그 분야에서 추가로 업무 경험을 쌓을까 하는 마음이 생겼습니다.

추천해 주신 웹사이트를 참고해 취업 기회를 살펴보겠습니다. 제안하신 대로, 동부 항공 전문 협회에 가입하는 것을 140**고려해** 보겠습니다. 141**저는 그 분야의 다른 전문가들과 인맥을 쌓게 되기를 기대합니다.** 이번 달 말에 있을 협회 회의에 대한 정보를 공유해 주셔서 감사합니다.

142**큰** 도움을 주신 데 대해 다시 한번 감사드립니다.

알렉시스 파머

어휘 aerospace 항공 우주 (산업) industry 산업, 업계 inspire 고무하다, ~할 마음이 들게 하다 graduate school 대학원 consult 참고하다 opportunity 기회 association 협회 organization 단체 assistance 도움

139 명사 어휘

해설 빈칸은 Your의 수식을 받으며, 동사구 were helpful and have inspired의 주어 역할을 하는 명사 자리이다. 앞 문장에서 항공 우주 업계에서의 진로에 대해(about careers in the aerospace industry) 이야기해 주어 감사하다고 했으므로, 빈칸에는 아바디 씨가 제공한 것 중 도움이 될 만한 것을 나타내는 명사가 들어가야 자연스럽다. 따라서 '식견'이라는 의미의 (A) insights가 정답이다. (B) surveys는 '설문 조사', (C) improvements는 '향상, 개선', (D) revisions는 '수정 (사항)'이라는 뜻으로 문맥상 빈칸에 적절하지 않다.

140 동사 어휘

해설 빈칸은 a membership을 목적어로 취하는 동사 자리이며, 빈칸이 포함된 절은 As가 이끄는 부사절(As you also suggested)의 수식을 받고 있다. 따라서 빈칸에는 협회 가입과 관련하여 아바디 씨의 제안에 따라 파머 씨가 하고자 하는 행위를 나타내는 동사가 들어가야 하므로, '고려하다, 생각해 보다'라는 의미의 (C) consider가 정답이다. (A) resolve는 '해결하다, 결심하다', (B) predict는 '예측하다, 예견하다', (D) advertise는 '광고하다'라는 뜻으로 문맥상 빈칸에 적절하지 않다.

141 문맥에 맞는 문장 고르기

번역 (A) 저는 그 분야의 다른 전문가들과 인맥을 쌓게 되기를 기대합니다.
(B) 연말에 제 회원 자격이 만료됩니다.
(C) 저는 그 회의에서 발표할 예정입니다.
(D) 곧 그 직책에 지원하고 싶습니다.

해설 빈칸 앞 문장에서 협회 가입을 고려하겠다(I will consider a membership ~ Association)고 했고, 뒤 문장에서는 이번 달 말에 있을 협회 회의(the organization's conference)에 대한 정보를 공유해 주어 고맙다고 했으므로, 빈칸에는 협회 가입에 대한 기대감을 표현하는 내용이 들어가야 문맥상 자연스럽다. 따라서 (A)가 정답이다.

어휘 expire 만료되다

142 형용사 자리 _ 명사 수식

해설 빈칸이 소유격 인칭대명사 your와 명사 assistance 사이에 있으므로, 빈칸에는 assistance를 수식하는 형용사나 assistance와 복합명사를 이루는 명사가 들어갈 수 있다. 문맥상 도움(assistance)의 특성을 묘사하는 말이 빈칸에 들어가는 것이 자연스러우므로, '큰, 관대한'이라는 의미의 형용사 (B) generous가 정답이다. (A) generosity는 '관대한 태도/행위', (D) generousness는 '관대함'을 뜻하므로 assistance와 복합명사를 이룰 수 없고, (C) generously는 부사로 품사상 빈칸에 들어갈 수 없다.

143-146 편지

> 10월 15일
>
> 중앙우체국 사서함 985
> 캔버라 ACT 6512
>
> 윌슨 씨께,
>
> 호주 야생동물 공원 협회를 대표하여, 저희 국립공원에 40호주 달러를 기부해 주신 것에 대해 감사드립니다. [143]**귀하와 같은 후원자들께서 공원을 공공 용도로 보존할 수 있도록 도와주십니다.** 개인 기부금 덕분에 국립공원이 50년 이상 방문객에게 개방될 수 있었습니다. 저희 목표는 미래 [144]**세대**가 즐길 수 있게 공원 시스템을 효율적으로 운영하는 것입니다.
>
> 공원 방문객과 야생동물 서식지 모두에 도움이 되도록 [145]**고안된** 다양한 프로그램들을 정리한 소책자 1부를 동봉합니다. 향후 이러한 프로그램 중 하나에 [146]**자금 지원**을 고려해 주세요. 그 자금은 현명하게 사용될 것이며 매우 감사히 여겨질 것입니다.
>
> 아코수아 마시카, 회원 관리 위원장
>
> 어휘 on behalf of ~을 대표하여 wildlife 야생동물 donation 기부 contribution 기부금 effectively 효율적으로 generation 세대 benefit 도움이 되다 habitat 서식지

143 문맥에 맞는 문장 고르기

번역 (A) 협회는 동물학을 공부하는 사람들에게 장학금을 줍니다.
(B) 귀하와 같은 후원자들께서 공원을 공공 용도로 보존할 수 있도록 도와주십니다.
(C) 오늘 공원 방문이 즐거우셨기를 바랍니다.
(D) 관심 있는 사람들은 자원해서 야생동물 서식지를 청소할 수 있습니다.

해설 빈칸 앞 문장에서 국립공원에 기부한 것에 대한 감사(thank you for your donation ~ to our national park)를 전했고, 뒤 문장에서 개인 기부금 덕분에 국립공원이 50년 이상 방문객에게 개방될 수 있었다(Individual contributions have helped it stay open to visitors for more than 50 years)고 했으므로, 빈칸에도 개인 기부의 선한 영향력과 관련된 내용이 들어가야 문맥상 자연스럽다. 따라서 (B)가 정답이다.

어휘 grant 주다 preserve 보존하다 volunteer 자원하다 interested party 관심 있는 사람, 이해 당사자

144 명사 어휘

해설 빈칸은 전치사 for의 목적어 역할을 하는 명사 자리로, 형용사 future의 수식을 받는다. 또한 to 부정사 to enjoy의 의미상 주어 역할을 한다. 따라서 빈칸에는 미래에 공원을 즐겁게 이용할 주체를 나타내는 명사가 들어가야 하므로, '세대'라는 의미의 (A) generations가 정답이다. (B) lifestyles는 '생활 방식', (C) committees는 '위원회', (D) planners는 '설계자'라는 뜻으로 문맥상 빈칸에 적절하지 않다.

145 형용사 자리 _ 분사

해설 빈칸은 동사 lists의 목적어 역할을 하는 명사 programmes를 뒤에서 수식하는 형용사 자리이다. 따라서 형용사와 같은 역할을 할 수 있는 현재분사 (C) designing과 과거분사 (D) designed 중 하나를 선택해야 한다. 여기서 말하는 프로그램은 고안되는 대상이므로, 수동의 의미를 내포한 (D) designed가 정답이다. (A) designer는 명사, (B) designs는 동사/명사로 품사상 빈칸에 들어갈 수 없다.

146 동사 어휘

해설 빈칸 뒤 명사구 one of these programmes를 목적어로 취하면서, 명령문의 동사 consider의 목적어 역할을 하는 동명사 자리이다. 뒤 문장에서 그 자금이 현명하게 사용될 것이며 감사히 여겨질 것(The money would be used wisely and would be deeply appreciated)이라고 했으므로, 빈칸에는 프로그램을 위해 모금하는 것과 관련된 동사가 들어가야 글의 흐름이 자연스러워진다. 따라서 '자금 지원'이라는 의미의 (D) funding이 정답이다. (A) researching은 '연구하기, 조사하기', (B) organizing은 '준비하기, 조직하기', (C) leading '이끌기, 안내하기'라는 의미로 앞뒤 문맥상 빈칸에 적절하지 않다.

PART 7

147-148 웹페이지

> http://www.cmb.com
>
> **초승달 식당**
>
> [147]**캐너웹 만 동쪽 연안을 따라 자리잡은 초승달 식당은 생일 파티, 결혼식, 기업 모임, 그리고 기타 사교 행사에 적합한 독특한 장소입니다.** 저희 요리사들은 여러분을 위한 완벽한 메뉴를 공들여 만들고 있으며 코디네이터들은 여러분의 행사가 멋들어지게 준비되도록 심혈을 기울일 것입니다. 대여료는 날짜, 행사 종류, 참석자 수를 토대로 결정됩니다.
>
> 10월 10일 오전 11시부터 오후 2시까지 저희 시설을 둘러보십시오. 코디네이터와 조리사를 만나 보시고 창의적인 저희 메뉴를 시식하십시오. 입장료는 무료지만 등록이 필요합니다. [148]**10월 10일 공개일에 예약하시면 25퍼센트 할인을 제공합니다.**

어휘 venue 장소 corporate 회사[기업]의 gathering 모임 superbly 멋들어지게, 최상으로 organize 준비하다 facility 시설 culinary 요리의 admission 입장(료) registration 등록

147 주제 / 목적

번역 광고되고 있는 것은?

(A) 민박
(B) 새로운 호텔
(C) 행사 공간
(D) 여름 캠프

해설 첫 번째 단락에서 초승달 식당은 생일 파티, 결혼식, 기업 모임, 기타 사교 행사에 적합한 독특한 장소(the Crescent Moon Bistro is a unique venue for birthday parties ~ other social events)라고 했으므로, (C)가 정답이다.

▸▸ Paraphrasing 지문의 a unique venue for birthday parties ~ other social events
→ 정답의 An event space

148 세부 사항

번역 10월 10일에 제공되는 것은?

(A) 예약 요금 할인
(B) 특별 콘서트
(C) 유명한 요리책
(D) 유명 요리사의 강좌

해설 마지막 단락에서 10월 10일 공개일에 예약하면 25퍼센트 할인이 제공된다(We are offering 25% off on any booking ~ on October 10)고 했으므로, (A)가 정답이다.

어휘 rate 요금

▸▸ Paraphrasing 지문의 25% off on any booking
→ 정답의 A discounted reservation rate

149-150 회람

수신: 가공 공장 관리자들
발신: 선라이트 슈가 이사회
날짜: 6월 15일
제목: 소식

[149]**우리가 3년여 만에 분기 실적이 최강세를 보인 데 이어 6월 1일자 〈슈가 인더스트리 타임즈〉에서 지역 설탕 유통 업체 2위에 올랐음을 알리게 되어 기쁩니다.** 노고와 헌신으로 이를 가능하게 만든 모든 직원에게 진심으로 감사합니다.

[150]**이 성과를 기념하기 위해 7월 15일 급여에 보너스를 추가로 지급하여 직원들의 공로를 치하하고자 합니다. 각 입지에 있는 공장 관리자는 7월 1일에 있을 다음 공장 회의에서 직원들에게 알리십시오.** 목표를 달성할 수 있게 도와주어 고맙습니다.

어휘 processing 가공, 처리 executive board 이사회 distributor 유통 업체 extremely 지극히 grateful 감사하는 dedication 헌신 celebrate 기념[축하]하다 achievement 성과 recognize 공로를 인정하다 location 입지 achieve 달성하다

149 사실 관계 확인

번역 선라이트 슈가에 관해 명시된 것은?

(A) 급여일 일정을 변경하고 있다.
(B) 〈슈가 인더스트리 타임즈〉를 발간한다.
(C) 설립된 지 3년이 넘었다.
(D) 과거 1위 설탕 유통 업체였다.

해설 첫 번째 단락에서 3년여 만에 분기 실적이 최강세를 보였다(following our strongest quarter in over three years)고 했으므로, 설립된 지 3년이 넘었다는 것을 알 수 있다. 따라서 (C)가 정답이다.

어휘 payday 급여일 publish 발간하다 establish 설립하다 previously 과거에

▸▸ Paraphrasing 지문의 in over three years
→ 정답의 more than three years ago

150 세부 사항

번역 공장 관리자들은 언제 직원 보너스를 알릴 것인가?

(A) 6월 1일
(B) 6월 15일
(C) 7월 1일
(D) 7월 15일

해설 두 번째 단락에서 보너스를 추가로 지급하여 직원들의 공로를 치하(recognize employees with a bonus ~ paycheck)하겠다고 한 후, 관리자들에게 7월 1일에 있을 회의 때 직원들에게 알리라(inform staff ~ on July 1)고 지시했으므로, (C)가 정답이다.

▸▸ Paraphrasing 지문의 inform staff
→ 질문의 announce an employee bonus

151-152 온라인 채팅

엘라 산토스 [오전 10시 2분]
안녕하세요. 금요일 밤 공연 티켓을 두 장 구입했습니다. 그런데 출장 일정이 조정되어서 제가 금요일에 런던에 없을 거예요. 이번 구매에 대해 환불받을 수 있을까요?

마이 통, 고객 서비스 [오전 10시 4분]
연락 주셔서 감사합니다. [151]**아쉽지만 모젤라 팔라디움 방침상 환불은 불가능합니다.** 동일한 금액 또는 더 저렴한 가격의 티켓으로 교환해 드립니다. [151]**www.mosellapalladium.co.uk에서 다양한 음악, 무용, 연극 등 모든 공연을 확인할 수 있습니다.**

엘라 산토스 [오전 10시 7분]
연락드리기 전에 시즌 일정을 살펴봤어요. [152]**지금 티켓 교환이 가능한가요, 아니면 전화로 해야 하나요?** 벌써 골랐거든요.

마이 통, 고객 서비스 [오전 10시 8분]
제가 도와 드릴게요. [152]대신 어떨 걸 보시겠어요?

엘라 산토스 [오전 10시 10분]
10월 22일 게이퍼스타인 오케스드라 표 두 장이요.

어휘 purchase 구매하다 performance 공연 reschedule 일정을 조정하다 refund 환불 unfortunately 아쉽게도 policy 방침 selection 선택

151 추론 / 암시

번역 모젤라 팔라디움은 무엇이겠는가?

(A) 스포츠 경기장
(B) 공연장
(C) 무용단
(D) 극단

해설 통 씨가 오전 10시 4분 메시지에서 모젤라 팔라디움 웹사이트에서 다양한 음악, 무용, 연극 등 모든 공연을 확인할 수 있다(You can view our entire season, which has a variety of music, dance, and theatre)고 했으므로, 모젤라 팔라디움이 공연장임을 추론할 수 있다. 따라서 (B)가 정답이다.

▸▸ Paraphrasing 지문의 **a variety of music, dance, and theatre** → 정답의 **performance**

152 의도 파악

번역 오전 10시 8분에 통 씨가 "제가 도와 드릴게요"라고 적은 의도는 무엇인가?

(A) 소책자를 보낼 것이다.
(B) 통화를 주선할 것이다.
(C) 환불을 처리할 수 있다.
(D) 표를 교환할 수 있다.

해설 산토스 씨가 오전 10시 7분 메시지에서 온라인 채팅으로 티켓 교환이 가능한지 아니면 전화로 해야 할지(Can you switch the tickets now, or must I call your phone number?) 문의했고, 이에 대해 통 씨가 '제가 도와 드릴게요(I can help with that)'라고 한 후 어떤 공연을 원하는지(What would you like to see instead) 물었다. 따라서 (D)가 정답이다.

▸▸ Paraphrasing 지문의 **switch the tickets** → 정답의 **exchange some tickets**

153-154 이메일

이메일

수신: 테드 리 〈ted.lee@comconnecting.com〉
발신: 아그날도 파에스 〈apaes@manosinc.com〉
날짜: 5월 3일
제목: 면접

리 씨께,

[153]**이곳 마노스 컨트랙팅의 수석 전기 기사직에 관심을 가져 주셔서 감사합니다. 귀하의 이력서가 무척 인상 깊어서 다음 주 중에 대면 면접 일정을 잡고 싶습니다.** [154]**다음 주 화요일 오후 괜찮으신가요? 저는 보통 오후 6시까지 사무실에 있습니다. 만약 화요일이 어려우시면, 혹시 수요일 오전은 괜찮으신가요? 저는 오전 9시 이후 아무때나 괜찮습니다.** 제 사무실은 엘크턴 가 끝에 있는 본관 2층에 있습니다. 이번이 면접 절차에서 첫 만남이므로 한 시간을 넘기지는 않을 겁니다. 곧 답장 주시길 기다리겠습니다.

아그날도 파에스
인사부 과장
마노스 컨트랙팅사

어휘 electrician 전기 기술자 impressive 인상 깊은 in-person interview 대면 면접 convenient 편리한 acceptable 괜찮은, 받아들일 수 있는 process 절차

153 추론 / 암시

번역 리 씨에 관해 무엇이 사실이겠는가?

(A) 새로운 도시로 이사할 것이다.
(B) 숙련된 전기 기사이다.
(C) 최근 전문 자격증을 받았다.
(D) 면접에서 일자리를 제안받을 것이다.

해설 초반부에서 마노스 컨트랙팅의 수석 전기 기사직(the master electrician position)에 관심을 가져 준 것에 대해 리 씨에게 감사를 표한 후 이력서가 무척 인상 깊다(Your résumé is very impressive)고 덧붙였다. 따라서 리 씨가 숙련된 전기 기술자임을 추론할 수 있으므로, (B)가 정답이다.

어휘 experienced 숙련된 recently 최근 certification 자격증

154 추론 / 암시

번역 파에스 씨는 언제 면접이 불가능하겠는가?

(A) 화요일 오후 3시 15분
(B) 화요일 오후 6시 30분
(C) 수요일 오전 9시 30분
(D) 수요일 오전 11시 30분

해설 중반부를 보면, 파에스 씨는 리 씨에게 다음 주 화요일 오후가 괜찮은지(Does next Tuesday afternoon work for you?) 물어본 후 자신이 보통 오후 6시까지 사무실에 있다(I am usually in the office until 6 p.m.)고 했다. 이어 화요일이 어렵다면 수요일 오전은 괜찮은지(Wednesday morning would be acceptable?) 문의한 후 오전 9시 이후 아무때나 괜찮다(Any time after 9 a.m. works for me)고 했으므로, (A), (C), (D)는 가능한 시간으로 보인다. 따라서 (B)가 정답이다.

155-157 웹페이지

http://www.mazullospizza.com

홈	소개	재료	온라인 주문

마줄로스 딥-디시 피자

시카고 최상의 피자를 맛보세요!

[155]**저희는 토니아 마줄로가 브리지포트의 단출한 상가에 처음 식당을 연 이래 정통 딥-디시 시카고 스타일 피자를 제공해 왔습니다.** [156]**35년 후 마줄로 씨의 자녀와 손주들이 정통 마줄로 가 도우와 토마토 소스 조리법을 이용해 맛있는 피자를 계속 만들고 있습니다.**

식당 내 식사, 테이크아웃, 지점에서 3마일 이내 배달 서비스를 제공합니다.

- [157(C)]**모든 피자는 주문 즉시 바로 만들며 고르신 3가지 토핑이 포함됩니다.** [157(A)/(D)]**모든 피자는 대형 사이즈 음료와 유명한 마늘 롤이 함께 제공됩니다.**
- 사이드 메뉴로 다양한 샐러드와 파스타가 있습니다.
- 모든 채소 토핑은 현지 유기농 채소로 농장에서 직접 가져옵니다.

길 안내, 전화번호, 식당 운영 시간은 지점을 클릭하세요.

브리지포트	링컨 공원	에지워터	애본데일

어휘 authentic 정통적인 humble 단출한, 소박한 craft 공들여 만들다 delectable 아주 맛있는 carryout 포장해서 들고 가는 음식 delivery 배달

155 사실 관계 확인

번역 마줄로의 브리지포트 가게에 관해 사실인 것은?

(A) 최근 확장했다.
(B) 새로운 경영진이 운영하고 있다.
(C) 배달 서비스를 제공하지 않는다.
(D) 처음 문을 연 매장이다.

해설 두 번째 단락에서 토니 마줄로가 브리지포트의 단출한 상가에 처음 식당(the original restaurant in a humble shop in Bridgeport)을 연 이래 정통 딥-디시 시카고 스타일 피자를 제공해 왔다고 했으므로, (D)가 정답이다.

▸▸ **Paraphrasing** 지문의 **the original restaurant**
→ 정답의 **the first location**

156 사실 관계 확인

번역 마줄로스 피자에 관해 명시된 것은?

(A) 가격이 적당하다.
(B) 시카고에서 수입한다.
(C) 소스는 가정 조리법으로 만든다.
(D) 채소 토핑은 마줄로가 소유한 농장에서 가져온다.

해설 두 번째 단락에서 정통 마줄로 가 도우와 토마토 소스 조리법(using traditional Mazullo-family dough and tomato sauce recipes)을 이용해 맛있는 피자를 계속 만들고 있다고 했으므로, (C)가 정답이다.

어휘 reasonably priced 가격이 적당한 import 수입하다

▸▸ **Paraphrasing** 지문의 **traditional Mazullo-family ~ tomato sauce recipes** → 정답의 **a family recipe**

157 사실 관계 확인

번역 딥-디시 피자 주문에 포함되지 않는 것은?

(A) 마늘 롤
(B) 파스타
(C) 토핑
(D) 음료

해설 주문 관련 첫 번째 항목에서 모든 피자에는 3가지 토핑(three toppings)이 포함되며 대형 사이즈 음료와 마늘 롤(a large beverage and ~ garlic rolls)이 함께 제공된다고 했으므로, (A), (C), (D)가 주문에 포함되는 것을 확인할 수 있다. 하지만 두 번째 항목에서 파스타는 사이드 메뉴(optional side dishes)라고 했으므로, (B)가 정답이다.

158-160 편지

켄딘버러 트랜지트
폰티랜드 로 64번지
켄딘버러, TD9 5UW

캘럼 스티븐슨
레스터 로 42번지
거베이튼, P24 9QS

1월 3일

스티븐슨 씨께,

켄딘버러 트랜지트 팀의 일원으로 모시게 되어 기쁩니다. [158/160]**배정 받으실 차량에서 교육을 받으시기 전에 우선 귀하의 의료 기록이 최신인지 저희 측에서 확인해야 합니다.** 그렇게 할 수 있도록, 다음 달에 업무를 시작하시기 전에 한 가지 일을 더 마무리해 주셨으면 합니다.

대중교통에서 최우선 순위는 승객과 다른 운전자의 안전입니다. 도시의 교통 체증과 변하는 날씨 상황 속에서 버스를 안전하게 운행하는 능력은 건강에도 일부 좌우됩니다. [159]**그렇기 때문에 근무 시작 전 신체 검사를 거쳐야 합니다. 예약하시려면 (0500) 555 0140으로 전화하십시오.** 검진은 켄딘버러 트랜지트가 선정한 의사가 수행하며, 비용이 귀하에게 부과되지 않습니다. 첫날 귀하의 상사에게 의사의 진단서를 제출하십시오.

함께 일하기를 고대합니다.

크리스틴 예커스
켄딘버러 트랜지트

어휘 transit 수송, 통행 prior to ~ 전에 assign 배정하다 ensure 확실히 하다 documentation 서류 up-to-date 최신 정보를 포함하는 priority 우선 순위 passenger 승객 motorist 자동차 운전자 ability 능력 undergo 거치다 employment 근무, 고용 appointment 예약 physician 의사 supervisor 상사

158 추론 / 암시

번역 스티븐슨 씨는 누구이겠는가?

(A) 운전사
(B) 정비공
(C) 의사 보조직
(D) 시 공무원

해설 첫 번째 단락에서 배정받을 차량에서 교육을 받기 전에(Prior to your receiving training on the vehicle you will be assigned to) 먼저 의료 기록이 최신인지 확인해야 한다고 했으므로, 스티븐슨 씨가 운전사임을 추론할 수 있다. 따라서 (A)가 정답이다.

어휘 mechanic 정비공

159 세부 사항

번역 스티븐슨 씨가 전화해서 하도록 요청받은 일은?

(A) 병가를 연장한다.
(B) 검진 일정을 잡는다.
(C) 상사에게 연락한다.
(D) 날씨 상황에 대해 묻는다.

해설 두 번째 단락에서 근무 시작 전 신체 검사를 받아야 한다(you will need to undergo a pre-employment physical checkup)고 한 후, 예약하려면 전화를 하라(To make an appointment, please call ~)고 요청했다. 따라서 (B)가 정답이다.

▸▸ **Paraphrasing** 지문의 **call** → 질문의 **by phone**
지문의 **a pre-employment physical checkup** → 정답의 **an examination**
지문의 **make an appointment** → 정답의 **Schedule**

160 문장 삽입

번역 [1], [2], [3], [4]로 표시된 곳 중에서 다음 문장이 들어가기에 가장 적합한 곳은?

"그렇게 할 수 있도록, 다음 달에 업무를 시작하시기 전에 한 가지 일을 더 마무리해 주셨으면 합니다."

(A) [1]
(B) [2]
(C) [3]
(D) [4]

해설 주어진 문장이 '그렇게 할 수 있도록, 그 목적을 달성하기 위해'라는 뜻의 접속부사로 시작했으므로, 이 앞에 스티븐슨 씨에게 요청하는 일(one more task)의 목적이 언급되어야 한다. 스티븐슨 씨가 추가적으로 해야 할 일은 신체 검사(physical checkup)이며, 이는 그의 의료 기록이 최신인지 확인(ensure ~ medical documentation is up-to-date)하기 위함이므로, (B) [2]가 정답이다.

161-163 기사

롤리지 모터스 파수꾼 바뀌다

네이선 케카나

더반 – [161]**더반을 근거지로 하는 롤리지 모터스는 카라 월터스가 회사의 차기 CEO가 될 것이라고 발표했다.** 월터스 씨는 15년간 CEO로 재임하고 은퇴하는 토마스 싱 씨의 후임이다. 얼마 전까지 월터스 씨는 서맥 앤 홀든사 부사장으로 일했는데, 그녀는 이 회사를 남아프리카 최대의 전자 회사 중 하나로 성장하도록 도왔다.

[162]**이로써 월터스 씨는 롤리지 모터스로 복귀하는 것이 되는데, 롤리지 모터스는 그녀가 대학 졸업 후 직장 생활을 시작한 곳이다.** 월터스 씨는 롤리지 리더십 프로그램을 수료하고 7년간 근무하다가 서맥 앤 홀든사로 옮겼다.

"[163]**월터스 씨는 리더십 경험을 갖고 있고 롤리지 모터스의 내부 사정에도 훤해 재임 동안 성공할 겁니다." 싱 씨가 말했다.** "월터스 씨가 합류하게 되어 설렙니다." [163]**롤리지 모터스 이사회 의장 마틸드 베콰가 덧붙였다. "월터스 씨가 서맥 앤 홀든에서 훌륭한 일을 해냈기에, 우리도 그녀의 통찰력 있는 리더십을 통해 도움을 받을 수 있길 기대합니다."**

어휘 retire 은퇴하다 electronics firm 전자 회사 tenure 재임 기간 chairman of the board 이사회 의장 benefit 도움을 받다 visionary 선견지명이 있는, 통찰력 있는

161 주제 / 목적

번역 주로 무엇에 관한 기사인가?

(A) 리더십 교육 프로그램의 장점
(B) 성공한 전자 회사
(C) 새로운 CEO 임명
(D) 더반에서 문을 여는 회사

해설 첫 번째 단락을 보면, 카라 월터스가 회사의 차기 CEO가 될 거라고 롤리지 모터스에서 발표했다(Rolidge Motors has announced that Cara Walters will be the next CEO)고 했으므로, 새로운 CEO 임명에 관한 기사임을 알 수 있다. 따라서 (C)가 정답이다.

162 사실 관계 확인

번역 월터스 씨에 관해 명시된 것은?

(A) 서맥 앤 홀든의 여러 부서에서 일했다.
(B) 대학을 마친 후 롤리지 모터스에 채용되었다.
(C) 교수로 있다가 자신의 회사를 창업했다.
(D) 곤경에 빠진 회사를 구하는 데 특별한 재능이 있다.

해설 두 번째 단락에서 월터스 씨가 대학 졸업 후 롤리지 모터스에서 직장 생활을 시작했다(Rolidge Motors, where she began her career after graduating from university)고 했으므로, (B)가 정답이다.

어휘 struggling 곤경에 빠진, 고투하는

▸▸ **Paraphrasing** 지문의 **she began her career after graduating from university**
→ 정답의 **She was hired ~ after finishing university**

163 세부 사항

번역 월터스 씨의 자질 중 싱 씨와 베콰 씨 모두 언급한 것은?

(A) 동료들 사이의 인기
(B) 서맥 앤 홀든에서 보여 준 혁신
(C) 학위
(D) 업계 지도자로서 명성

해설 마지막 단락을 보면, 싱 씨는 월터스 씨가 리더십 경험을 갖고 있고(Ms. Walters has both the leadership experience and inside knowledge) 롤리지 모터스의 내부 사정에도 훤해 재임 동안 성공할 것이라고 했다. 베콰 씨는 월터스 씨가 서맥 앤 홀든에서 훌륭한 일을 해냈기에 그녀의 통찰력 있는 리더십을 통해 도움을 받을 수 있길 바란다(we look forward to benefiting from her visionary leadership)고 했다. 싱 씨와 베콰 씨 모두 월터스 씨의 리더십을 언급했으므로, (D)가 정답이다.

어휘 popularity 인기 credential 자격증 reputation 명성

164-167 이메일

이메일

수신: skim@jigyeapartments.com
발신: larue@waterservices.org
제목: 단수
날짜: 1월 7일

김 씨께,

정비 작업 때문에 다음 주 수요일, 1월 12일 몇 시간 동안 지계 아파트가 단수됩니다. 단수는 오전 11시에 시작됩니다. [164]**수도 서비스는 오후 5시에 복구될 예정입니다.** [165]**다음과 같은 일반 지침과 함께 단수에 관해 미리 건물 입주자 모두에게 알려 주세요.**

1. [166]**수도가 복구되면 수도관 속에 있던 공기 때문에 물이 갑자기 쏟아질 수 있습니다.** 처음에는 천천히 물을 흐르게 하면 이 문제가 해결됩니다.

2. [167]**수도 서비스가 재개된 후 발생하는 다른 문제는 웹사이트에 나와 있는 해당 지역 번호의 고객 서비스 데스크로 문의하십시오.**

3. 정비 담당자들은 신속히 작업해서 예정대로 끝내기 위해 최선을 다합니다.

이번 서비스 중단은 향후 수도 서비스의 질을 개선하기 위해 필요합니다. 불편을 끼쳐 드려 죄송하며 양해해 주시면 감사하겠습니다.

피에릭 드 라 루

어휘 maintenance 정비 interruption 중단 tenant 입주자, 세입자 burst 파열, 폭발 inconvenience 불편함 patience 인내심

164 세부 사항

번역 이메일에 의하면 주민들이 다시 수도를 쓸 수 있는 시간은?

(A) 오전 7시
(B) 오전 11시
(C) 오후 3시
(D) 오후 5시

해설 첫 번째 단락에서 수도 서비스는 오후 5시에 복구될 예정(Water service will be restored by 5:00 P.M.)이라고 했으므로, (D)가 정답이다.

▸▸ Paraphrasing 지문의 **Water service will be restored**
→ 질문의 **use water again**

165 추론 / 암시

번역 김 씨는 누구이겠는가?

(A) 배관공
(B) 건물 관리인
(C) 공사 현장 작업자
(D) 고객 서비스 직원

해설 첫 번째 단락에서 단수에 관해 미리 건물 입주자들에게 알릴 것(Please inform all of your building's tenants)을 김 씨에게 요청했으므로, 김 씨가 건물 관리인임을 추론할 수 있다. 따라서 (B)가 정답이다.

166 세부 사항

번역 드 라 루 씨가 언급하는 잠재적 문제는?

(A) 추가 유지 비용이 있을 수 있다.
(B) 주 수도관에 누수가 있을 수 있다.
(C) 수돗물 흐름에 문제가 있을 수 있다.
(D) 일주일 후에 후속 점검이 있을 수 있다.

해설 지침의 첫 번째 항목을 보면, 수도가 복구된 후 수도관 속에 있던 공기 때문에 물이 갑자기 쏟아질 수 있다(air in the pipes may cause sudden bursts of water)고 했으므로, (C)가 정답이다.

▸▸ Paraphrasing 지문의 **may cause** → 질문의 **potential issue**
지문의 **sudden bursts of water**
→ 정답의 **problems with the water flow**

167 사실 관계 확인

번역 지계 아파트 주민들에 관해 명시된 것은?

(A) 우려 사항이 있으면 특정 번호로 전화해야 한다.
(B) 물 사용을 줄이려고 노력해야 한다.
(C) 고객 서비스 데스크에 불만을 제기했다.
(D) 1월 12일에 입주자 회의가 잡혀 있다.

해설 지침의 두 번째 항목을 보면, 다른 문제가 있을 시 웹사이트에 나와 있는 해당 지역 번호의 고객 서비스 데스크로 전화하라(For any other issues ~ call our Customer Service desk at the number listed on our Web site)고 요청했다. 따라서 (A)가 정답이다.

▸▸ **Paraphrasing** 지문의 For any other issues that occur
→ 정답의 with any concerns
지문의 our Customer Service desk at the number ~ for your specific area
→ 정답의 a specific number

168-171 회람

수신: 사우스 스트리트 은행 직원
발신: 윌리엄 리스-예이츠, 최고 경영자
날짜: 5월 12일

우리 은행의 사세가 확장되고 있다는 것을 알리게 되어 기쁩니다. 창의적인 마케팅과 수상 경력에 빛나는 고객 서비스 덕분에 서비스에 대한 수요가 증가하고 있습니다. [168]**따라서 우리는 올해 리즈버그에 지점을 개설할 예정입니다.**

새 지점은 7월 1일이 되어야 운영되지만 이미 사실상 개점 준비를 마쳤습니다. 리즈버그 직원 대다수는 이미 채용되었습니다. [171]**그러나 충원되어야 할 자리가 몇 개 남아 있으며, 이는 www.southstreetbank.com/jobs에서 확인할 수 있습니다.** [169]**현재 우리 직원 중 누구라도 리즈버그 지점으로 전출 갈 의향이 있다면, 위에 적힌 웹사이트에서 얼른 공석을 확인하고 지원하십시오.** 궁금한 점은 인사부에 문의하십시오.

한편, 우리 회사는 다른 방식으로도 계속 번창하고 성장하고 있습니다. [170]**우리는 최근 상공회의소로부터 올해의 업체상 후보에 올랐습니다.** 이는 의미 있는 성과로, 뛰어난 우리 팀 여러분의 헌신적인 노력 덕분입니다. 경영진을 대표해, 매우 감사하고 축하한다는 말을 전합니다.

어휘 expand 확장하다[되다] award-winning 수상 경력이 있는 demand 수요 operation 운영, 가동 virtually 사실상 current 현재의 transfer 전출 가다 vacancy 공석 thrive 번창하다 nominate 후보에 오르다 Chamber of Commerce 상공회의소 significant 의미 있는 achievement 업적 in no small part 크게, 주로 dedicated 헌신적인 outstanding 뛰어난 on behalf of ~을 대표해 management 경영진

168 주제 / 목적

번역 주로 무엇에 관한 회람인가?
(A) 다른 회사와 합병
(B) 몇몇 신입 사원 채용
(C) 수리로 인한 임시 휴업
(D) 새 지점 개점

해설 첫 번째 단락에서 회사가 올해 리즈버그에 지점을 개설할 예정(We will therefore be opening a branch in Leesburg this year)이라고 한 후, 이에 대해 이어서 설명하고 있다. 따라서 (D)가 정답이다.

어휘 merger 합병 temporary 임시의

▸▸ **Paraphrasing** 지문의 be opening a branch
→ 정답의 The opening of a new branch

169 세부 사항

번역 직원들이 권유 받은 일은?
(A) 지역 업체 단체에 합류하기
(B) 축하 모임 참석하기
(C) 웹사이트 정보 확인하기
(D) 더 나은 고객 서비스를 위한 아이디어 제출하기

해설 두 번째 단락에서 리즈버그 지점으로 전출 갈 의향이 있다면 웹사이트에서 공석을 확인하고 지원하라(we encourage you to review the vacancies soon and apply at the Web site)고 권유했으므로, (C)가 정답이다.

어휘 celebratory 축하하는 submit 제출하다

▸▸ **Paraphrasing** 지문의 review the vacancies
→ 정답의 Review information

170 세부 사항

번역 리스-예이츠 씨가 언급한 한 가지 업적은?
(A) 수상 후보 지명
(B) 지역 출판물의 긍정적 후기
(C) 인기 행사에 초대받음
(D) 예상치 못한 투자 증가

해설 마지막 단락에서 회사가 최근 올해의 업체상 후보에 올랐다(nominated for the Business of the Year award)고 했으므로, (A)가 정답이다.

어휘 unexpected 예상치 못한

▸▸ **Paraphrasing** 지문의 been nominated for the Business of the Year award
→ 정답의 An award nomination

171 문장 삽입

번역 [1], [2], [3], [4]로 표시된 곳 중에서 다음 문장이 들어가기에 가장 적합한 곳은?
"리즈버그 직원 대다수는 이미 채용되었습니다."
(A) [1]
(B) [2]
(C) [3]
(D) [4]

해설 주어진 문장에서 리즈버그 직원 대다수가 이미 채용되었다(Most Leesburg staff have already been recruited)고 했으므로, 앞 또는 뒤 문장에서도 직원 채용과 관련된 내용이 언급되어야 한다. [2] 뒤에서 충원되어야 할 자리가 몇 개 남아 있으며(There remain a couple of job openings to be filled), 이는 웹사이트에서 확인할 수 있다고 했으므로, (B)가 정답이다.

어휘 recruit 채용하다

172-175 온라인 채팅

[174]5월 8일 월요일

가브리엘 리 (오전 9시 10분)
여러분, 안녕하세요. 다시 말씀드리지만 내일 아침 라킨 조경이 이곳 데리코로 와서 앞쪽 주차장에서 나무를 제거할 겁니다. 도급 업체가 도착하기 전에 [172]**제 직원들이 주차장을 폐쇄할 예정이니** 여러분과 직원들은 다른 주차장을 찾든지 대중교통을 이용하든지 계획을 세워야 합니다.

애바 애버턴 (오전 9시 11분)
제 고객인 잰 맥고너글 씨가 오전 10시에 저를 만나러 벨파스트에서 차를 몰고 옵니다. 그녀에게 뭐라고 말해야 할까요? [172]**그녀가 시설부로 연락하면 될까요?**

마틴 비티 (오전 9시 12분)
[175]**예보에는 비가 많이 온다고 하네요. 나무 작업이 정말 진행될까요?**

가브리엘 리 (오전 9시 13분)
[172/173]**예, 맥고너글 씨에게 제 휴대폰 번호를 주시고 도착하면 전화하라고 하세요.** [173]**제가 그녀를 뒤쪽으로 안내할게요. 거기에는 방문객 전용으로 따로 둔 곳이 있어요.**

가브리엘 리 (오전 9시 14분)
[175]**예,** 라킨이 비가 오든 화창하든 작업반이 온다고 확인해 주었어요.

다니엘 디건 (오전 9시 15분)
이것도 기억하세요, [174]**내일 팀원이 재택 근무할 수 있도록 허락할 수 있어요.** 내부 전산망 기본 일정에 반드시 전화 회의를 전부 올려 놓기만 하세요.

가브리엘 리 (오전 9시 16분)
알겠습니다. 모두 고마워요.

어휘 landscaping 조경 remove 제거하다 contractor 도급 업체 facility 시설 forecast 예보 reserve 따로 잡아 두다 approve 승인하다 intranet 내부 전산망

172 추론 / 암시

번역 리 씨는 누구이겠는가?
(A) 조경 작업반원
(B) 배송 담당자
(C) 창고 직원
(D) 시설 관리자

해설 리 씨가 오전 9시 10분에 도급 업체가 오기 전에 자신의 직원들이 주차장을 폐쇄할 예정(My workers will block off the area)이라고 하자, 9시 11분에 애버턴 씨가 자신의 고객인 맥고너글 씨가 도착하면 시설부로 연락하라고 해도 되는지(Can she contact the facilities department?) 물었다. 이에 리 씨가 9시 13분 메시지에서 '예(Yes)'라고 응답한 후 맥고너글 씨에게 자신의 휴대폰 번호를 주라(give Ms. McGonagle my mobile phone number)고 했으므로, 리 씨가 시설 관리자임을 추론할 수 있다. 따라서 (D)가 정답이다.

173 세부 사항

번역 맥고너글 씨가 리 씨에게 연락하는 이유는?
(A) 방문 일정을 정하기 위해
(B) 주차에 도움을 받기 위해
(C) 사무실 길 안내 목록을 얻기 위해
(D) 수송 지연을 알리기 위해

해설 리 씨는 오전 9시 13분 메시지에서 맥고너글 씨에게 자신의 휴대폰 번호를 주고 도착하면 전화하게 하라(have her call me when she arrives)고 말한 후, 자신이 맥고너글 씨를 방문객 전용 공간으로 안내할 것(I will direct her ~ reserved for visitors only)이라고 했다. 따라서 맥고너글 씨가 리 씨에게 연락하면 주차에 도움을 받을 수 있을 것이므로, (B)가 정답이다.

어휘 obtain 얻다 transit 수송, 교통

174 추론 / 암시

번역 5월 9일에 무슨 일이 있겠는가?
(A) 일부 데리코 직원들이 집에서 일할 것이다.
(B) 데리코사가 폐업할 것이다.
(C) 맥고너글 씨가 지역 호텔에 머물 것이다.
(D) 디건 씨가 전화 회의를 취소할 것이다.

해설 질문에 주어진 5월 9일은 온라인 채팅 회의가 있는 5월 8일 다음날이다. 오전 9시 15분 메시지에서 디건 씨가 내일 팀원들의 재택 근무를 허락할 수 있다(we can approve team members to work from home tomorrow)고 했으므로, 5월 9일에 일부 직원이 집에서 일할 것이라고 추론할 수 있다. 따라서 (A)가 정답이다.

▸▸ **Paraphrasing** 지문의 **to work from home**
→ 정답의 **work at home**

175 의도 파악

번역 오전 9시 14분에 리 씨가 "비가 오든 화창하든 작업반이 온다"고 적은 의도는 무엇인가?
(A) 일기 예보가 아마 틀릴 수도 있다.
(B) 실외 작업이 예정대로 진행될 것이다.
(C) 라킨 조경은 뛰어난 작업자들을 고용한다.
(D) 데리코 직원들은 악천후에 대비해야 한다.

해설 비티 씨가 오전 9시 12분 메시지에서 비가 많이 온다는 일기 예보(There's heavy rain in the forecast)를 언급한 후, 작업이 진행될 수 있을지(Are you sure the tree work will go forward?) 문의했다. 이에 대해 리 씨가 그렇다고 하며 '비가 오든 화창하든 작업반이 온다(the crew comes out rain or shine)'라고 응답한 것이므로, 날씨에 관계없이 실외 작업이 예정대로 진행될 것임을 알 수 있다. 따라서 (B)가 정답이다.

▸▸ **Paraphrasing** 지문의 **the tree work will go forward**
→ 정답의 **The outdoor work will proceed**

176-180 웹페이지 + 이메일

http://www.sunriseaerospace.co.au/companynews

선라이즈 [177]항공 산업

홈	회사 소식	연락처	후기

[176/180]곧 시작될 혼슈 익스프레스의 도쿄-오사카 노선에 당사 최신 디자인인 서플리스 시트가 도입된다는 것을 발표하게 되어 기쁩니다. [177]지난 2월부터, 저희 디자인팀은 혼슈 익스프레스와 긴밀히 협조해 가장 엄격한 안전 기준을 충족하는 안락한 의자를 생산했습니다. [178(A)]당사 제품이 모두 그렇듯, 이 의자는 가볍지만 튼튼한 자재로 제작되어 시간이 흐를수록 연료비가 상당히 절감될 것입니다. [176]서플리스 시트 시제품은 디자이너들에게 호평을 받았으며 1월에 헨리 디자인상 후보에 올랐습니다.

어휘 comfortable 안락한 stringent 엄격한 lightweight 가벼운 durable 튼튼한 significant 상당한 prototype 시제품

수신: 조셉 타마 〈jtama@sunriseaerospace.co.au〉
발신: 요시 야마모토 〈yyamamoto@honshuexpress.co.jp〉
제목: 정보
날짜: 3월 18일

안녕하세요, 조셉,

잘 지내시죠. **[179]지난달 소규모 소비자 집단으로 제품을 테스트한 후 신속히 생각을 전환해 주셔서 진심으로 감사드립니다. [178(B)/179]처음 디자인에 귀사의 팀이 추가한 사양, 특히 발판 옵션은 완벽합니다. [178(C)]전체적인 스타일 역시 인상 깊었고 의자가 현대적인 항공기 내부 모습에 잘 어울렸습니다.**

[180]그런데 도쿄-오사카 노선이 4월 말부터 운항됩니다. 웹사이트에 게시할 수 있도록 다음 주에 세부 내용을 드리겠습니다.

다시 한번 감사합니다.
요시

어휘 turnaround 방향 전환 feature 기능, 사양 optional 선택의, 옵션의 footrest 발판 overall 전체적인 contemporary 현대적인 air carrier 수송기 operational 사용[운행] 가능한

176 주제 / 목적

번역 웹페이지의 목적은?

(A) 서비스에 대한 의견 요청
(B) 업체 합병 발표
(C) 성공적인 제품 홍보
(D) 제품 수상 후보로 추천하기

해설 첫 번째 줄에서 서플리스 시트가 혼슈 익스프레스의 도쿄-오사카 노선에 도입된다는 것(our latest design, the Suppliss Seat, will be introduced ~ service route)을 알렸고, 마지막 줄에서 시제품이 디자이너들의 호평을 받았으며(received high marks from designers) 디자인상 후보에도 지명되었다(was nominated for a Henry Design Award)고 했다. 따라서 (C)가 정답이다.

어휘 publicize 홍보하다, 알리다

177 세부 사항

번역 디자인팀은 어떤 업계를 지원하는가?

(A) 항공
(B) 기술
(C) 교육
(D) 시 교통 시스템

해설 웹페이지 상단의 회사명을 보면 선라이즈 항공 산업(Sunrise Aerospace)이라고 되어 있고, 세 번째 줄에서 회사의 디자인팀이 혼슈 익스프레스와 긴밀히 협조해(our design team has worked closely with Honshu Express) 안락한 의자를 생산했다고 했으므로, 디자인팀이 항공 업계를 지원하고 있음을 알 수 있다. 따라서 (A)가 정답이다.

▸▸ Paraphrasing 지문의 **has worked closely with**
→ 질문의 **support**

178 연계

번역 서플리스 시트의 특징으로 언급되지 않은 것은?

(A) 가볍다.
(B) 발을 받쳐 준다.
(C) 현대적인 스타일이다.
(D) 등받이를 젖힐 수 있다.

해설 웹페이지의 다섯 번째 줄 '의자가 가볍지만 튼튼한 자재로 제작된다(it is made of lightweight yet durable materials)'에서 (A)를 확인할 수 있다. 그리고 이메일의 첫 번째 단락에서 발판(footrests)이 완벽하고 의자가 현대적인(contemporary) 항공기와 잘 어울린다고 칭찬한 부분에서 (B)와 (C)를 확인할 수 있다. 따라서 언급되지 않은 (D)가 정답이다.

어휘 recline (의자) 등받이를 젖히다

▸▸ Paraphrasing 지문의 **the optional footrests**
→ 보기 **(B)의 supports the feet**

179 사실 관계 확인

번역 소비자 테스트에 관해 이메일에 명시된 것은?

(A) 아직 마무리되지 않았다.
(B) 디자인 변경으로 이어졌다.
(C) 특정 노선에서 일어났다.
(D) 안전 기준을 전부 충족하지는 못했다.

해설 이메일의 첫 번째 단락에서 소비자 테스트 이후 신속히 생각을 전환해 준 것(your quick turnaround)에 대해 감사하다고 한 후, 처음 디자인에 추가한 사양은 완벽했다(The features your team added to the initial design are perfect)고 했다. 따라서 소비자 테스트의 결과가 디자인 변경으로 이어졌음을 확인할 수 있으므로, (B)가 정답이다.

>> **Paraphrasing** 지문의 we tested the product with a small group of consumers
→ 질문의 the consumer tests
지문의 features ~ added to the initial design
→ 정답의 design changes

180 연계

번역 서플리스 시트는 언제 정식으로 사용될 것인가?

(A) 1월
(B) 2월
(C) 3월
(D) 4월

해설 웹페이지의 첫 번째 줄에서 서플리스 시트가 혼슈 익스프레스의 도쿄-오사카 노선에 도입된다(our latest design, the Suppliss Seat, will be introduced ~ service route)고 발표했다. 이메일의 마지막 단락을 보면 서플리스 시트가 도입된 도쿄-오사카 노선이 4월 말부터 운항된다(the Tokyo-Osaka service route will go operational at the end of April)고 했으므로, (D)가 정답이다.

181-185 광고 + 이메일

임차 기회

라 가디나 몰은 조경 정원, 안뜰, 분수가 멋지게 꾸며진 곳에서의 독특한 쇼핑 경험을 선사합니다. 몰에는 유명한 체인점부터 단 하나뿐인 부티크까지 망라한 소매점들뿐만 아니라 아주 다양한 식당과 카페도 있습니다.

30만 제곱미터에 이르는 보행자 전용 소매 공간을 갖춘 라 가디나 몰은 해마다 4백만 명이 넘는 방문객을 끌어들이고 있습니다. [181]**이곳은 베이 쇼어 현지 주민과 관광객 모두를 위한 쇼핑 및 식사 장소입니다.**

라 가디나에서 소매 또는 식당 공간을 임대하는 것에 관한 정보가 더 필요하시면 cgoncalves@lagardina.com으로 임대 담당자인 세실리아 곤캐브즈에게 연락하세요. 공간 대부분은 장기 임차인들이 [182]**점유**하고 있지만 [185]**제한된 수의 계절 한정 계약(최소 4개월)도 가능합니다.**

어휘 retail 소매의 one-of-a-kind 하나뿐인 pedestrian 보행자 attract 끌어들이다, 유치하다 destination 장소, 행선지 lessee 임차인

이메일

수신: 세실리아 곤캐브즈 〈cgoncalves@lagardina.com〉
발신: 마르코 사바티니 〈msabatini@sabatinileather.com〉
날짜: 3월 25일
제목: 소매 공간
첨부: 제품 목록

곤캐브즈 씨께:

[183/185]**사바티니 가죽 제품 소유주로서 라 가디나 몰 단기 임차 기회에 관심을 표합니다.**

사바티니 가죽 제품은 기념품 핸드백과 지갑을 제조, 판매하는 작은 회사입니다. [184]**저희 고급 가죽 제품에는 제품이 판매되는 관광지의 이름이 각인되어 있습니다.** 글래스턴베리에 있는 저희의 가장 최근 임시 매장에서 가장 많이 판매된 제품들의 이미지를 첨부합니다. 그 매장에서 회사 역사상 최고의 판매 실적을 올렸습니다. 지금까지 스물네 군데의 각기 다른 장소에서 제품을 팔았는데 모두 큰 성공을 거두었습니다.

[181]**저희는 한동안 베이 쇼어에 있는 장소를 물색하고 있었는데, 라 가디나 몰이 딱 적당해 보입니다.** [185]**저희는 여름 관광철에 3개월 동안 150 제곱미터 정도의 공간을 원합니다.** 이 문제를 더 논의할 수 있게 555-0125로 제게 전화해 주시겠습니까?

마르코 사바티니

어휘 short-term 단기의 manufacture 제조하다 souvenir 기념품 imprint 각인하다 temporary 임시의 sales performance 판매 실적

181 연계

번역 라 가디나 몰에 관해 암시된 것은?

(A) 베이 쇼어에 있다.
(B) 여름에만 문을 연다.
(C) 최근 새 매장을 많이 추가했다.
(D) 주로 패션 부티크가 있다.

해설 광고의 두 번째 단락에서 라 가디나 몰이 베이 쇼어 현지 주민과 관광객 모두를 위한(for local Bay Shore residents and tourists alike) 쇼핑 및 식사 장소라고 소개했다. 또한 이메일의 마지막 단락에서 사바티니 씨의 회사가 베이 쇼어에 있는 장소를 물색하고 있었는데, 라 가디나 몰이 딱 적당해 보인다(We have been looking for a place in Bay Shore ~ La Gardina Mall seems to be a good fit)고 했으므로, 라 가디나 몰이 베이 쇼어에 위치해 있음을 추론할 수 있다. 따라서 (A)가 정답이다.

182 동의어 찾기

번역 광고에서 세 번째 단락 3행의 "occupied"와 의미가 가장 가까운 단어는?

(A) 채워진
(B) 포착된
(C) 혼잡해진
(D) 안정된

해설 "occupied"가 포함된 부분은 '공간 대부분은 장기 임차인들이 점유하고 있지만(While most of our space is occupied by long-term lessees)'이라는 의미로, 여기서 occupied는 '점유된, 차지된'이라는 뜻으로 쓰였다. 따라서 '채워진, 메워진'이라는 뜻의 (A) filled가 정답이다.

183 주제 / 목적

번역 이메일의 주 목적은?

(A) 새 식물원 홍보
(B) 유명한 회사 개요 소개
(C) 잠재적인 사업 거래 문의
(D) 몰의 일자리 문의

해설 첫 번째 단락에서 사바티니 가죽 제품 소유주로서(As owner of Sabatini Leather Goods) 라 가디나 몰 단기 임차 기회에 관심을 표한다(express interest in a short-term leasing opportunity at La Gardina Mall)고 했으므로, 앞으로 할 가능성이 있는 거래에 대해 문의하기 위한 이메일임을 알 수 있다. 따라서 (C)가 정답이다.

184 사실 관계 확인

번역 사바티니 가죽 제품의 상품에 관해 명시된 것은?

(A) 온라인에서 판매된다.
(B) 종종 할인된다.
(C) 관광객에게 판매한다.
(D) 글래스턴베리에서 제조된다.

해설 이메일의 두 번째 단락에서 사바티니사의 고급 가죽 제품에는 제품이 판매되는 관광지의 이름이 각인되어 있다(imprinted with the name of the tourist destination where they are sold)고 했으므로, 관광객을 대상으로 판매된다는 사실을 확인할 수 있다. 따라서 (C)가 정답이다.

185 연계

번역 사바티니 씨와 곤캐브즈 씨는 무엇을 두고 협상해야 하겠는가?

(A) 매장 위치
(B) 계약 기간
(C) 소매 공간 규모
(D) 월세 비용

해설 사바티니 씨는 이메일의 첫 번째 단락에서 단기 임차(short-term leasing opportunity at La Gardina Mall)에 대한 관심을 표한 후, 마지막 단락에서 여름 관광철에 3개월 동안 150제곱미터 정도의 공간(a space ~ for a three-month period over the summer tourism season)을 원한다고 했다. 하지만 광고의 마지막 단락을 보면 계약 기간이 최소 4개월(four months minimum)은 되어야 한다고 했으므로, 임대 담당자(Leasing Administrator)인 곤캐브즈 씨와 계약 기간을 협상해야 한다는 것을 추론할 수 있다. 따라서 (B)가 정답이다.

186-190 차트 + 이메일 + 기사

티케 파인 카펫 – 플레이아데스 콜렉션
출고 가능 제품 (매일 업데이트)

이름	크기	[186]**배송 무게**	[187]**출고 가능 물량 (오늘)**	출고 가능 물량 (30일 후)	출고 가능 물량 (60일 후)
아르테미스	190x280	**13kg**	30	60	0
헤라	190x280	**14kg**	16	20	0
야누스	160x230	**11kg**	[187]**0**	0	20
아이리스	120x170	**9kg**	10	15	15

어휘 availability 이용 가능성, 이용 가능한 것

수신: 프리다 주커만
발신: 마일즈 소렐
날짜: 2월 5일
제목: 물류 준비
첨부: 사진

주커만 씨께:

[187/190]**유감스럽게도 우리가 파벨 호텔 로비 및 라운지 공간에 깔 카펫 공급 업체로 선정한 티케 파인 카펫에서 3월 1일 호텔 개업 예정일이 지나서야 우리가 선택한 패턴을 입수할 수 있다고 합니다.** [188]**실내 장식과 잘 어울릴 것 같은 대안 제품 몇 가지의 사진을 첨부합니다.** 모두 이전에 선택한 것과 동일한 재료로 제조되었고, 가격은 비슷합니다. [188]**개업이 한 달도 남지 않은 상황이니 가능한 한 빨리 결정해야 합니다.** 이렇게 막판에 변경 사항이 있긴 하지만, 파벨 호텔이 우리가 만들려고 했던 분위기를 제공할 것으로 확신합니다.

감사합니다.

마일즈 소렐

어휘 supplier 공급 업체 anticipated 예상했던 alternative 대안의 décor (실내) 장식 previous 이전의 comparable 비슷한 ambience 분위기

파벨 호텔 개업
라본느 코

(센터빌 – [190]**3월 2일) 전 시 법원 판사 밀드러드 심슨은 소유주 패트리스 스넬과 함께 어제 파벨 호텔 개업을 축하했다.** 파벨 호텔은 센터빌 시내의 도서관과 관광 안내소 사이에 있다. [189]**한때 시 법원 청사이자 심슨 씨의 일터였던 기존의 구조물은 지난 9년 동안 비어 있었다.** 이제 이 공간은 34개의 우아한 객실과 벽난로가 있는 매력적인 라운지, 그리고 멋진 로비를 자랑한다. 다음 달에는 건물 내 카페가 문을 열 예정이다. 마일즈 소렐이 디자인한 인테리어는 널찍한 창문과 높은 천장 등 건물의 오랜 특징을 고스란히 간직하면서 따뜻하고 매력적인 공간을 만들어 낸다.

어휘 celebrate 축하하다 visitors center 관광 안내소 courthouse 법원 청사 existing 기존의 structure 구조물 vacant 비어 있는 boast 자랑하다 inviting 매력적인, 마음을 끄는 on-site 건물 내의, 현장의 be expected to ~할 예정이다 retain 유지하다 feature 특징 expansive 넓은 ceiling 천장

186 사실 관계 확인

번역 차트에서 플레이아데스 콜렉션의 모든 카펫에 관해 명시된 것은?

(A) 60일 후 출고할 수 있다.
(B) 현재 재고가 있다.
(C) 무게가 다르다.
(D) 크기가 같다.

해설 차트의 배송 무게(Shipping Weight) 항목에서 모든 카펫의 무게가 다르다는 것을 확인할 수 있으므로, (C)가 정답이다.

187 연계

번역 소렐 씨가 원래 주문한 카펫은?

(A) 아르테미스
(B) 헤라
(C) 야누스
(D) 아이리스

해설 이메일의 첫 번째 문장을 보면, 카펫 공급 업체인 티케 파인 카펫에서 소렐 씨 회사가 선택한 패턴을 3월 1일 이후에나 입수할 수 있다(Tyche Fine Carpets, ~ will not have our chosen pattern available until after ~ March 1)고 했으므로, 원래 주문했던 카펫이 현재 재고가 없다는 것을 알 수 있다. 차트에서 현재 재고가 없는 카펫이 '야누스(Janus)'임을 확인할 수 있으므로, (C)가 정답이다.

188 세부 사항

번역 소렐 씨가 주커만 씨에게 부탁한 일은?

(A) 호텔 개업 연기
(B) 대체 품목 선택
(C) 다른 가구 주문
(D) 로비 사진 보내기

해설 소렐 씨가 주커만 씨에게 보낸 이메일을 보면, 주문한 카펫의 재고가 없어 몇 가지 대안으로 선택할 만한 제품의 사진을 첨부했다(Attached are photographs of several alternative selections)고 한 후, 개업이 한 달도 남지 않은 상황이니 가능한 한 빨리 결정을 해 줄 것(With the grand opening less than a month away, I need a decision from you as soon as possible)을 요청했다. 따라서 (B)가 정답이다.

어휘 substitute 대체의, 대용의

▸▸ Paraphrasing 지문의 alternative → 정답의 substitute

189 세부 사항

번역 기사에 따르면 파벨 호텔 이전에 들어섰던 건물은?

(A) 도서관
(B) 관광 안내소
(C) 법원 청사
(D) 카페

해설 기사의 중반부에서 파벨 호텔 부지가 한때 시 법원 청사였다(Once the city's courthouse)고 했으므로, (C)가 정답이다.

190 연계

번역 파벨 호텔에 관해 명시된 것은?

(A) 예정대로 개업했다.
(B) 9년 동안 건설했다.
(C) 관광지가 되었다.
(D) 심슨 씨가 운영한다.

해설 기사가 작성된 날짜가 3월 2일(March 2)이고, 기사의 첫 번째 문장에서 전 시 법원 판사 밀드러드 심슨은 어제(yesterday) 호텔 소유주 패트리스 스넬과 함께 파벨 호텔 개업을 축하했다(to celebrate the opening of The Pavel Hotel)고 했으므로, 파벨 호텔의 개업 행사가 3월 1일이었음을 알 수 있다. 이메일의 첫 번째 문장을 보면, 3월 1일이 파벨 호텔 개업 예정일(the hotel's anticipated opening date of March 1)이라고 했으므로, (A)가 정답이다.

191-195 회람 + 일정표 + 이메일

발신: 옵티어리스 주차 및 교통 사무소
수신: [191]**옵티어리스 전 직원**
날짜: 12월 20일
제목: 곧 시행될 셔틀버스 시스템 개선 사항

[191]**여러분의 유용한 의견에 바로 부응하여 옵티어리스 구내와 모브룩, 네스 기차역을 연결하는 셔틀 시스템의 몇 가지 개선 사항을 발표하고자 합니다.** [192]**다음 변경 사항은 1월 2일부터 시행됩니다:**

(1) [192]**전체 버스에 세 번째 버스를 추가해 버스 한 대가 정비로 운행 정지될 경우에 대비해 운행 빈도와 수용인원을 늘리겠습니다. 버스는 이제 30분이 아니라 15분 간격으로 운행됩니다.**

(2) 두 번째 구내 정류장이 추가됩니다. [193]**현재 옵티어리스 구내 동쪽에 있는 본관 건물에서 정차하는 것 외에, 직원 모두의 편의를 더욱 잘 도모하기 위해 두 번째 정류장이 생깁니다.**

(3) 저녁 운행편이 추가됩니다. 현재의 마지막 운행 시간보다 30분 늦게 옵티어리스 구내에서 출발합니다.

다시 한번 의견에 감사합니다. 환경을 위해, 그 어느 때보다도 편리한 셔틀버스 서비스를 제공하여 여러분의 대중교통 이용을 촉진한다는 점에 자부심을 느낍니다.

어휘 enhancement 향상, 개선(사항) in response to ~에 부응하여 improvement 개선(사항) connect 연결하다 campus 구내, (기업에 속한) 부지와 건물 go into effect 시행되다 fleet (한 기관이 소유한 배·버스 등) 무리 frequency 빈도 capacity 수용 인원 maintenance 정비 accommodate 편의를 도모하다 depart 출발하다 input 의견 environment 환경 facilitate 촉진하다 public transportation 대중교통 convenient 편리한

셔틀 버스 일정 – 평일 오전
(1월 2일 업데이트)

모브룩 역	→ 네스 역	→ [193]**동쪽 부지**	→ [193]**서쪽 부지**
7:15	7:21	7:39	7:42
7:30	7:36	7:54	7:57
7:45	7:51	8:09	8:12
8:00	[195]**8:06**	8:24	[195]**8:27**
8:15	8:21	8:39	8:42
8:30	8:36	8:54	8:57

이메일

발신: 소피아 에즈런 <sofiaedgren@lekmail.com>
수신: 샤라니 카미스 <s.khamis@optieris.com>
제목: 옵티어리스 지원자 면접
날짜: 1월 25일

카미스 씨께,

[194]다음 주 옵티어리스 구내에서 있을 로숀 씨와의 면접에 불러 주셔서 감사합니다. 품질 관리 분야에서 이 직책에 지원한 최종 후보자가 되어 정말 설렙니다. 또한 회사 셔틀버스 시간표를 보내 주셔서 감사합니다. **[195]저는 오전 7시 55분에 네스 역에 도착하는 기차를 타고, 도착하면 귀사의 셔틀버스를 타려고 합니다. 그러면 적당한 시간에 서쪽 부지로 갈 수 있을 겁니다.**

소피아 에즈런

어휘 quality control 품질 관리 appreciate 감사하다 reasonable 적당한

191 세부 사항

번역 셔틀 버스 시스템을 개선한 이유로 제시된 것은?

(A) 옵티어리스 직원들이 의견을 냈다.
(B) 현재 버스가 노후화되고 있다.
(C) 더 많은 직원들이 기차로 출근하고 있다.
(D) 옵티어리스가 구내에 새로운 시설을 건설했다.

해설 회람의 수신인이 옵티어리스 전 직원(All Optieris staff)이고, 첫 번째 단락에서 직원들의 유용한 의견에 부응하여(In direct response to your helpful feedback) 옵티어리스 구내와 모브룩, 네스 기차역을 연결하는 셔틀 시스템의 몇 가지 개선 사항을 발표한다(announce a number of improvements to the shuttle system)고 했다. 따라서 (A)가 정답이다.

▸▸ Paraphrasing 지문의 **a number of improvements to the shuttle system**
→ 질문의 **updating the shuttle bus system**

192 세부 사항

번역 1월 2일부터 버스 시스템에 있을 변화 한 가지는?

(A) 버스가 대기 오염을 덜 일으킬 것이다.
(B) 버스가 더 자주 운행될 것이다.
(C) 각 버스의 노선이 달라질 것이다.
(D) 첫 번째 오전 버스가 더 일찍 운행될 것이다.

해설 질문에서 언급된 1월 2일은 변경 사항이 시행되는 날(The following changes will go into effect on January 2)임을 회람에서 확인할 수 있다. 첫 번째 변경 사항에서 세 번째 버스를 추가해 운행 빈도와 수용 인원을 늘리겠다(A third bus will be added ~ to increase service frequency as well as capacity)고 했으므로, (B)가 정답이다.

어휘 pollution 오염

▸▸ Paraphrasing 지문의 **increase service frequency**
→ 정답의 **be more frequent**

193 연계

번역 어떤 버스 정류장이 노선에 추가될 예정인가?

(A) 모브룩 역
(B) 네스 역
(C) 동쪽 부지
(D) 서쪽 부지

해설 회람의 두 번째 변경 사항에서 옵티어리스 구내 동쪽에 있는 본관 건물 정류장에 이어 두 번째 정류장이 생긴다(Besides the current stop ~ the east side of the Optieris campus, there will be a second stop)고 했다. 일정표를 보면, 기존의 동쪽 부지(East Campus) 다음에 새로 생기는 정류장이 서쪽 부지(West Campus)임을 확인할 수 있으므로, (D)가 정답이다.

▸▸ Paraphrasing 지문의 **Besides the current stop**
→ 질문의 **added to the route**

194 세부 사항

번역 에즈런 씨가 옵티어리스 구내를 방문하는 이유는?

(A) 자신의 회사와 옵티어리스 간 계약을 마무리하기 위해
(B) 품질 관리를 점검하기 위해
(C) 교육에 참석하기 위해
(D) 취업 기회를 잡기 위해

해설 에즈런 씨가 보낸 이메일의 첫 번째 문장을 보면, 옵티어리스 구내에서 있을 로숀 씨와의 면접에 불러 줘서 감사하다(Thanks for inviting me to an interview ~ on the Optieris campus)고 한 후, 품질 관리 분야의 직책에 지원한 최종 후보자가 되어 기쁘다(I am ~ to be a finalist for this position in quality control)고 했다. 따라서 취업 기회를 잡고자 옵티어리스 구내를 방문하는 것임을 알 수 있으므로, (D)가 정답이다.

▸▸ Paraphrasing 지문의 **to be a finalist for this position**
→ 정답의 **an employment opportunity**

195 연계

번역 에즈런 씨는 버스를 타고 몇 시에 옵티어리스에 내릴 것으로 예상되는가?

(A) 오전 7시 57분
(B) 오전 8시 12분
(C) 오전 8시 27분
(D) 오전 8시 42분

해설 이메일의 후반부에서 오전 7시 55분에 네스 역에 도착해서 바로 셔틀버스를 타면(take a train arriving at Nesse Station at 7:55 A.M. and then your shuttle bus upon arrival) 적당한 시간에 서쪽 부지에 도착할 것(which should get me to your West Campus at a reasonable time)이라고 했다. 일정표를 보면, 에즈

런 씨가 오전 7시 55분에 네스 역에 도착할 경우 바로 탈 수 있는 버스가 8시 6분에 있으며, 이 버스가 8시 27분에 서부 부지에 도착할 예정임을 알 수 있다. 따라서 (C)가 정답이다.

196-200 송장 + 후기 + 이메일

브라이트 나우 홈

주문 번호: 92584
고객 이름: 제시 비비
선호 매장: 노스웨스트 매장

품번	품명	수량	가격
[197]**BN-101**	[197]**코스트랜드 그레이**	2갤런	50달러
BN-102	린월 그레이	1갤런	25달러
BN-116	다비 올리브	1갤런	25달러
BN-118	브라이트윈 그린	2갤런	50달러
BN-126	폭스델 그린	1갤런	25달러
			총 175.00달러

매장 픽업: 브라이트 나우 홈 - 노스웨스트 매장
메인 가 348번지
(720) 555-0112
customerservice@brightnowhome.com

추가 매장:
노스이스트 매장: 14번 가 986번지
사우스웨스트 매장: 스미스 로 1455번지
[198]**사우스이스트 플래그십 매장: 32번 가 152번지**

어휘 additional 추가의

http://www.uopine.com/business/bright-now-home

9월 18일

이번 주에 브라이트 나우 홈의 새로운 매장 고객 픽업을 이용했습니다. 이 서비스 덕분에 시간이 많이 절약되었어요. 매장에 도착했을 때 주문품이 준비되어 있었거든요. 온라인으로 이미 결제했기 때문에 매장에서 줄을 서서 기다릴 필요가 없었죠.

아쉽게도 저는 매장을 떠나기 전에 주문품을 재차 확인하지 않았습니다. [196/197]**제가 작업하고 있는 집에 도착해서야 2갤런 주문했던 BN-101 페인트를 1갤런밖에 받지 못했다는 것을 알았어요.** 즉시 매장에 전화했고 매니저는 제가 작업하고 있는 곳과 가장 가까운 매장에서 받지 못한 페인트를 가져가도록 처리해 주었습니다. 또 매니저는 2갤런 값을 돌려주었어요. 이 서비스를 꼭 다시 이용할 겁니다!

제시 비비

어휘 realize 깨닫다 receive 받다 immediately 즉시 arrange 처리하다 definitely 반드시

수신: 제시 비비 〈jbeeby@jbeebyinc.com〉
발신: 해티 존스 〈hattie.jones@brightnowhome.com〉
날짜: 9월 19일
제목: 온라인 주문

비비 씨께,

최근 저희와 거래해 주셔서 감사합니다. [200]**고객님께서 uopine.com에 올린 글을 보고 감사한 마음이 들었습니다.** [198]**플래그십 매장이 고객님의 작업 현장에서 아주 가까웠고 그곳에서 누락되었던 페인트를 픽업하실 수 있었다는 소식을 들어 다행이었습니다.**

저희는 당사 제품과 서비스의 품질을 보장하며, 곧 고객님을 다시 만나기를 고대하고 있습니다. [199]**무엇보다도 장마철이 다가오니, 지금이 저희 가게에 방문하셔서 곧 있을 지붕 작업에 필요한 도구들을 구하기 딱 좋은 시기입니다!**

해티 존스
고객 서비스 부장
브라이트 나우 홈

어휘 recently 최근 convenient 가까운 upcoming 다가오는

196 추론 / 암시

번역 비비 씨의 직업은 무엇이겠는가?

(A) 영업 사원
(B) 주택 도장공
(C) 배송 기사
(D) 부동산 중개인

해설 비비 씨가 작성한 후기의 두 번째 단락을 보면, 작업하고 있는 집에 도착해서(When I arrived at the house I was working on) 보니 2갤런 주문했던 BN-101 페인트를 1갤런밖에 받지 못했다(I had received only one of the two gallons of BN-101 paint I had ordered)고 했다. 따라서 비비 씨가 주택 도장공임을 추론할 수 있으므로, (B)가 정답이다.

197 연계

번역 비비 씨가 더 필요했던 품목은?

(A) 코스트랜드 그레이
(B) 린월 그레이
(C) 브라이트윈 그린
(D) 폭스델 그린

해설 비비 씨가 쓴 후기의 두 번째 단락에서 BN-101 페인트를 2갤런 주문했는데 1갤런밖에 받지 못했다(I had received only one of the two gallons of BN-101 paint I had ordered)고 했으므로, BN-101 품목이 더 필요했다는 것을 알 수 있다. 송장의 품번(Item Number) 항목에서 BN-101이 코스트랜드 그레이(Coastland Gray)임을 확인할 수 있으므로, (A)가 정답이다.

198 연계

번역 비비 씨는 주문품에서 빠진 품목을 어디에서 픽업했는가?

(A) 노스웨스트 매장
(B) 노스이스트 매장
(C) 사우스웨스트 매장
(D) 사우스이스트 매장

해설 존스 씨가 비비 씨에게 보낸 이메일의 첫 단락을 보면, 플래그십 매장이 비비 씨의 작업 현장에서 아주 가까웠고 누락되었던 페인트를 그곳에서 픽업할 수 있었다는 소식을 들었다(our flagship location was so convenient ~ you were able to pick up your missing paint there)고 했다. 송장을 보면 플래그십 매장이 사우스이스트(Southeast flagship store)에 있음을 확인할 수 있으므로, (D)가 정답이다.

199 사실 관계 확인

번역 브라이트 나우 홈에 관해 명시된 것은?

(A) 매장에 디자인 전문가를 보유하고 있다.
(B) 당일 배송 서비스를 제공한다.
(C) 건물 관리 비품을 판매한다.
(D) 웹사이트에서 쿠폰을 제공한다.

해설 이메일의 마지막 단락에서 장마철이 다가오니 지금이 지붕 작업에 필요한 도구들을 구하기 딱 좋은 시기(now is a great time to ~ get the tools you need for those upcoming roof jobs)라며 브라이트 나우 홈을 홍보하고 있다. 따라서 브라이트 나우 홈이 건물 관리 비품을 판매한다는 것을 알 수 있으므로, (C)가 정답이다.

어휘 expert 전문가 supplies 비품

200 주제 / 목적

번역 존스 씨 이메일의 목적 중 하나는?

(A) 새로운 서비스 소개하기
(B) 고객에게 감사하기
(C) 계절 할인 알리기
(D) 방침 변경 설명하기

해설 이메일의 첫 번째 단락에서 비비 씨가 uopine.com에 올린 글을 보고 감사한 마음이 들었다(We saw the comments you posted ~ and we are grateful to you)고 했으므로, 이메일을 보낸 목적 중 하나가 후기를 남긴 고객에게 감사를 전하기 위함임을 알 수 있다. 따라서 (B)가 정답이다.

▸▸ **Paraphrasing** 지문의 **are grateful to you**
→ 정답의 **thank a customer**

기출 TEST 2

101 (C)	102 (A)	103 (B)	104 (A)	105 (A)
106 (D)	107 (C)	108 (D)	109 (B)	110 (B)
111 (B)	112 (C)	113 (A)	114 (D)	115 (B)
116 (A)	117 (D)	118 (C)	119 (A)	120 (D)
121 (C)	122 (B)	123 (C)	124 (D)	125 (D)
126 (B)	127 (D)	128 (A)	129 (C)	130 (B)
131 (C)	132 (B)	133 (A)	134 (D)	135 (A)
136 (D)	137 (C)	138 (B)	139 (B)	140 (D)
141 (D)	142 (A)	143 (A)	144 (B)	145 (C)
146 (D)	147 (C)	148 (D)	149 (A)	150 (D)
151 (D)	152 (B)	153 (B)	154 (C)	155 (D)
156 (C)	157 (D)	158 (C)	159 (A)	160 (B)
161 (A)	162 (B)	163 (A)	164 (C)	165 (D)
166 (A)	167 (B)	168 (B)	169 (A)	170 (B)
171 (C)	172 (D)	173 (A)	174 (C)	175 (D)
176 (C)	177 (B)	178 (D)	179 (D)	180 (C)
181 (C)	182 (D)	183 (A)	184 (D)	185 (C)
186 (B)	187 (C)	188 (A)	189 (B)	190 (C)
191 (B)	192 (C)	193 (C)	194 (D)	195 (A)
196 (B)	197 (A)	198 (D)	199 (C)	200 (A)

PART 5

101 인칭대명사의 격 _ 소유격

해설 빈칸은 전치사 of의 목적어 역할을 하는 복합명사 parking regulations를 한정 수식하는 자리이다. 따라서 소유격 인칭대명사 (C) our가 정답이다.

번역 새로 온 인턴사원들은 우리 주차 규정을 각별히 유념하고 있다.

어휘 mindful 유념하는 regulation 규정

102 형용사 어휘

해설 빈칸에는 아트 센터의 프로그램 편성 개선에 도움을 주기 위해(To help the arts center improve its programming) 알려 주어야 할 워크숍의 측면을 묘사하는 형용사가 들어가야 자연스럽다. 따라서 '유익한'이라는 의미의 (A) informative가 정답이다. (B) primary는 '주요한', (C) enthusiastic은 '열렬한, 열광적인', (D) financial은 '재정의'라는 뜻으로 문맥상 빈칸에 적절하지 않다.

번역 아트 센터의 프로그램 편성 개선을 도와주시려면, 워크숍의 어떤 측면이 가장 유익했는지 알려 주세요.

어휘 improve 개선하다 indicate 표현[표시]하다

103 명사 자리 _ 동사의 목적어

해설 빈칸은 동사 explained의 목적어 역할을 하는 명사 자리로, 전치사구 of the upgraded customer database의 수식을 받고 있다. 따라서 '이점, 혜택'이라는 뜻의 명사로 쓰일 수 있는 (B) benefits가 정답이다. (D) benefiting을 동명사라고 가정하더라도, 정관사 the와 of로 시작하는 전치사구 사이에는 들어갈 수 없으므로 정답이 될 수 없다. (A) beneficial은 형용사, (C) benefited는 과거동사/과거분사로 품사상 빈칸에 들어갈 수 없다.

번역 굽타 씨는 업그레이드된 고객 데이터베이스의 이점을 영업팀에 설명했다.

어휘 explain 설명하다

104 전치사 어휘

해설 빈칸은 명사구 the roads를 목적어로 취하는 전치사 자리로, 빈칸을 포함한 전치사구가 명사구 icy conditions를 수식하고 있다. 따라서 빈칸에는 '빙판 상태'와 '도로'를 자연스럽게 연결하는 전치사가 들어가야 한다. 빙판 상태는 도로 표면에 나타나므로, '~ 위에'라는 의미의 (A) on이 정답이다.

번역 도로 위 빙판으로 인해 시 터미널에서 출발하는 버스가 지연되었다.

어휘 delay 지연시키다

105 동사 어형

해설 빈칸에는 have와 결합하여 현재완료 시제를 이루며 부사 recently의 수식을 받는 과거분사가 들어가야 한다. 따라서 (A) purchased가 정답이다. (B) purchase는 동사원형/명사, (C) purchasing은 동명사/현재분사, (D) to purchase는 to부정사로 빈칸에 들어갈 수 없다.

번역 최근에 디지털 카메라를 구입했고 사용법을 배우고 싶다면, 이 강좌가 여러분에게 딱입니다.

어휘 recently 최근 purchase 구입하다

106 명사 어휘

해설 빈칸은 형용사 upcoming의 수식을 받으며 동사 ease 및 modernize의 주어 역할을 하는 명사 자리이다. 따라서 혼잡을 완화하고(ease congestion) 고객 숙박 시설을 현대화할(modernize guest accommodations) 수 있는 방안을 나타내는 명사가 들어가야 하므로, '수리, 개·보수'라는 의미의 (D) renovation이 정답이다. (A) performance는 '수행, 성과, 공연', (B) supplement는 '보완, 추가', (C) deadline은 '기한'이라는 뜻으로 문맥상 빈칸에 적절하지 않다.

번역 곧 있을 탄티노 공항의 개·보수 공사로 혼잡이 완화되고 고객 숙박 시설이 현대화될 것이다.

어휘 upcoming 곧 있을, 다가오는 congestion 혼잡, 밀집

107 부사 자리 _ 동사 수식 _ 비교급

해설 빈칸은 that이 이끄는 명사절의 동사 paid를 수식하는 부사 자리이므로, 부사의 원급인 (A) frequently와 비교급인 (C) more frequently 중 하나를 선택해야 한다. 서로 다른 대상을 비교한 문장이며 빈칸 뒤에 than이 있으므로, (C) more frequently가 정답이 된다. (B) frequent는 형용사의 원급, (D) frequency는 명사로 품사상 빈칸에 들어갈 수 없다.

번역 이 연구는 35세에서 44세 사이의 고객이 여타 연령층의 고객보다 더 자주 소노카 신용카드로 지불했다는 것을 보여 주었다.

어휘 frequently 자주 frequent 빈번한 frequency 빈도, 잦음

108 동사 어휘

해설 빈칸은 명사구 a business plan을 목적어로 취하는 to부정사의 동사원형 자리로, 대출 신청서가 처리될 수 있기 전에(before your loan application can be processed) 사업 계획서로 해야 할 행위를 나타내는 동사가 들어가야 한다. 따라서 '제출하다'라는 의미의 (D) submit가 정답이다. (A) donate는 '기부하다, 기증하다', (B) request는 '요청하다, 요구하다', (C) confess는 '자백하다, 인정하다'라는 뜻으로 문맥상 빈칸에 적절하지 않다.

번역 대출 신청서가 처리될 수 있으려면 그 전에 먼저 사업 계획서를 제출해야 합니다.

어휘 loan 대출(금) application 신청(서) process 처리하다

109 형용사 자리 _ 명사 수식 _ 어휘

해설 빈칸은 소유격 The hotel's와 복합명사 shuttle bus 사이에서 shuttle bus를 수식하는 형용사 자리로, 문맥상 호텔에서 제공하는 셔틀버스의 특성을 나타내는 단어가 들어가야 자연스럽다. 따라서 '무료의'라는 뜻의 형용사 (B) complimentary가 정답이다. 참고로, complimentary는 '칭찬의, 경의를 표하는'이라는 의미로도 쓰인다. (A) compliments와 (C) compliment는 명사/동사로 품사상 빈칸에 들어갈 수 없다.

번역 호텔의 무료 셔틀버스는 홍콩의 주요 명소로 투숙객들을 실어나를 것이다.

어휘 landmark 명소 compliment 칭찬; 칭찬하다

110 전치사 자리 _ 어휘

해설 빈칸은 명사구 months of work를 목적어로 취하는 전치사 자리이다. 건물을 매각하기 위한 수개월의 노력(months of work to sell the Apton Building)과 마침내 성공했다(finally succeeded)는 내용을 적절히 연결하는 전치사가 들어가야 하므로, '~ 후에'라는 의미의 (B) After가 정답이다. (A) Besides는 '~ 외에', (D) For는 '~를 위해, ~ 동안' 등의 의미로 문맥상 어색하며, (C) Still은 부사/형용사로 품사상 빈칸에 적절하지 않다.

번역 부동산 중개인은 몇 달 동안 앱턴 빌딩을 매각하기 위해 노력한 끝에 지난주에 마침내 성공했다.

어휘 realtor 부동산 중개인

111 부정대명사

해설 빈칸은 동사 choose의 목적어 역할을 하는 명사 자리로, 주격 관계대명사절(that suits our needs)의 수식을 받고 있다. 따라서 관계대명사절의 단수동사(suits)와 수가 일치하며 가산명사 all four custodial-service bids를 대신할 수 있는 대명사가 들어가야 하므로, '(그중) 하나'라는 의미인 (B) one이 정답이다. (A) some은 가산명사를 대신할 경우 복수동사와 쓰여야 하고, (D) either는 둘 중 하나를 선택할 때 쓰이므로 정답이 될 수 없다.

번역 우리는 네 건의 관리 서비스 입찰을 검토하고 우리 필요에 맞는 것을 선택할 것이다.

어휘 custodial 관리의 bid 입찰 suit ~에 맞다

112 명사 어휘

해설 '~을 요청했다'라는 의미의 asked for 및 전치사구 to the images와 어울려 쓰이는 명사를 선택하는 문제이다. 광고 텍스트의 이미지(the images in the advertising text)와 관련하여 요청할 수 있는 사항을 나타내는 단어가 빈칸에 들어가야 한다. 따라서 전치사 to와 함께 '~에 대한 수정 (사항)'이라는 의미를 완성하는 (C) revisions가 정답이다. (A) standards는 '기준, 수준', (B) drawings는 '그림', (D) duplications는 '복사[복제]품'이라는 뜻으로 문맥상 빈칸에 적절하지 않다.

번역 그 고객은 광고 텍스트에 있는 이미지들을 수정해 달라고 요청했다.

어휘 advertising 광고

113 명사절 접속사

해설 빈칸이 이끄는 절을 포함한 명령문은 「advise(알리다, 안내하다)+간접목적어(you)+that절」의 구조가 수동태로 변형된 것이므로, (A) that이 정답이다. (C) whether도 명사절을 이끌 수 있지만 '~인지 아닌지'라는 의미로 문맥상 어색하고, (B) of와 (D) between은 전치사로 절을 이끌 수 없으므로 오답이다.

번역 해운 대리점과 문제가 있어 고객님의 주문을 취소해야 했다는 것을 알려 드립니다.

어휘 cancel 취소하다 difficulty 어려움 shipping agent 해운 대리점

114 동사 어휘

해설 빈칸은 that이 이끄는 명사절(that its paper towels are ~ on the market)을 목적어로 취하는 타동사 자리이다. 따라서 '(~라고) 주장하다'라는 뜻의 (D) claims가 정답이다. (A) obtains는 '얻다, 획득하다', (C) inquires는 '묻다, 알아보다'라는 뜻으로 that절과 어울리지 않고, (B) competes는 '경쟁하다, 겨루다'라는 뜻의 자동사로 전치사 없이 바로 목적어를 취할 수 없다.

번역 틴 크릭사는 자사의 종이 타월이 시중에서 가장 흡수력이 좋은 제품이라고 주장한다.

어휘 absorbent 흡수력이 좋은

115 명사 자리 _ 복합명사

해설 빈칸에는 business와 복합명사를 이루는 명사 또는 business를 뒤에서 수식하는 형용사/분사가 들어갈 수 있다. 동사 enter into가 '(논의·협약 등을) 체결하다, 시작하다'라는 뜻이며, 이를 도급 업체와 함께(with the contractor) 한다고 했으므로, 빈칸에는 도급 업체와 체결해야 하는 것을 나타내는 명사가 들어가야 한다. 따라서 '협약, 계약'이라는 뜻의 명사인 (B) agreement가 정답이다. 참고로, (C) agreeable은 '동의하는, 받아들일 수 있는'이라는 의미의 형용사로, 전치사 to와 주로 쓰인다.

번역 KCLN 어소시에이츠는 일부 계약 조건이 재협상되는 대로 도급 업체와 업무 협약을 체결할 예정이다.

어휘 contractor 도급 업체 terms (계약 등의) 조건 renegotiate 재협상하다 agree 동의[합의]하다

116 부사절 접속사

해설 빈칸은 완전한 절(registering for ~ is not required)을 이끄는 접속사 자리이므로, '비록 ~일지라도, ~이긴 하지만'이라는 뜻의 부사절 접속사 (A) Although가 정답이다. (B) Instead와 (C) Regardless는 부사, (D) Despite는 전치사로, 완전한 절을 이끌 수 없다.

번역 온라인 뱅킹 등록이 필수는 아니지만, 저희는 모든 고객에게 적극 추천합니다.

어휘 register for ~에 등록하다 required 필수의 recommend 추천하다 instead 대신에 regardless 개의치 않고 despite ~임에도 불구하고

117 동사 자리 _ 조동사 + 동사원형

해설 빈칸 앞에 조동사 can과 부사 easily가 있으므로, 빈칸에는 동사원형이 들어가야 한다. 따라서 (D) relate가 정답이다. relate to는 '~와 관련되다' 이외에 '~에 공감하다'라는 뜻으로 자주 쓰인다. (A) related는 형용사/과거동사/과거분사, (B) relatable는 형용사, (C) relating은 동명사/현재분사로 빈칸에 들어갈 수 없다.

번역 시청자들은 인기 텔레비전 시리즈 〈가을 미스터리〉의 주인공에게 쉽게 공감할 수 있다.

어휘 viewer 시청자 main character 주인공 related 연관된 relatable 공감할 수 있는

118 명사 어휘

해설 빈칸은 형용사 full의 수식을 받으며 「a+full+명사+of」 구조를 이루어 services를 수식하고 있다. 지역 사회 건강 프로그램(community wellness programs)의 일환으로 다양한 서비스를 제공한다는 내용이 되어야 자연스러우므로, '범위, (특정 범위 내의) 다양함'이라는 의미의 (C) range가 정답이다. 참고로, a range of 역시 '폭넓은, 다양한'이라는 뜻을 지닌다. (A) center는 '중심, 중앙', (B) surplus는 '나머지, 잉여', (D) type은 '종류, 유형'이라는 뜻으로 「a+full+명사+of」 구조로 쓰여 명사를 수식할 수 없다.

번역 페어론 병원은 지역 사회 건강 프로그램의 일환으로 폭넓은 서비스를 제공한다.

어휘 community 지역 사회 wellness 건강

119 형용사 자리 _ 주격 보어

해설 해당 문장은 등위접속사 and가 두 개의 구를 연결하고 있는 구조로, not 앞뒤로 will과 be가 생략되어 있다. 주어 The rear entrance(후문)는 이용 가능한 대상이므로, '이용할 수 있는, 접근 가능한'이라는 의미의 형용사 (A) accessible이 정답이 된다. 참고로, access가 동사로 쓰일 경우 뒤에 바로 목적어가 와야 한다.

번역 RC 은행 후문은 수리를 위해 폐쇄되며 다음 주 월요일에는 이용할 수 없다.

어휘 rear 뒤쪽의 entrance 입구 repair 수리 access 이용, 접근; 이용[접근]하다

120 부사 어휘

해설 to부정사의 동사원형 see를 적절히 수식하는 부사를 선택하는 문제이다. 카슨 씨가 세계의 외딴 지역에서도(even in remote regions of the world) 자신의 회사 제품을 보고 싶어 한다는 내용의 문장이므로, 빈칸에도 장소와 관련된 부사가 들어가야 자연스럽다. 따라서 '어디나, 모든 곳에'라는 의미의 (D) everywhere가 정답이다. (A) decidedly는 '확실히, 분명히'라는 뜻으로 문맥상 어색하며, (B) furthermore는 '더욱이', (C) rather는 '다소, 차라리'라는 뜻의 부사로 문맥상 어색하고 위치상으로도 빈칸에 들어갈 수 없다.

번역 카슨 씨는 세계의 외딴 지역에서도 카슨 오디오 제품을 보고 싶어 한다.

어휘 remote 외딴, 먼

121 명사 자리 _ 복합명사

해설 가산명사인 office 앞에 한정사(관사, 소유격 등)가 없으므로, 빈칸에는 office와 복합명사를 이루는 명사가 들어가야 한다. 따라서 '장비, 용품'이라는 뜻의 명사 (C) equipment가 정답이다. 참고로, equipment는 불가산명사로 단수 취급되며, 앞에 한정사가 오지 않아도 된다. (A) equip은 동사, (B) equipping은 동명사/현재분사, (D) equipped는 과거분사로 품사상 빈칸에 들어갈 수 없다.

번역 우리는 회사가 승인한 판매 업체로부터 책상과 프린터 같은 사무용품을 살 수 있다.

어휘 approved 공인된, 승인된 vendor 판매 업자[업체] equip 장비를 갖추다

122 형용사 어휘 _ 과거분사

해설 명사 price를 적절히 수식하는 과거분사를 선택하는 문제이다. 고객명과 함께 기록해야(must record) 하는 가격과 가장 잘 어울리는 보기는 '표시된, 나열된'이라는 의미의 (B) listed이다. (A) assembled는 '모인, 조립된,' (C) addressed는 '호명된, 주소가 적힌', (D) earned는 '얻은, 획득한'이라는 뜻으로 문맥상 빈칸에 적절하지 않다.

번역 대리점은 도서 주문을 받을 때 고객의 이름과 각 품목의 표시 가격을 기록해야 한다.

어휘 agent 대리점[인]

123 부사절 접속사

해설 빈칸은 완전한 두 절을 이어 주는 접속사 자리이므로, '일단 ~하면, ~하자마자'라는 의미의 부사절 접속사 (C) once가 정답이다. 참고로, once는 '한 번, 한때'라는 의미의 부사로도 쓰일 수 있다. (A) with는 전치사, (B) these는 지시대명사/지시형용사, (D) just는 부사/형용사로 완전한 절을 이끌 수 없으므로 빈칸에 들어갈 수 없다.

번역 감독관들이 건물 준공 검사를 하면 가구가 비치될 것이다.

어휘 furnish 가구를 비치하다 supervisor 감독관 inspection 점검, (건물) 준공 검사

124 부사 어휘

해설 빈칸은 동사 approved를 수식하는 부사 자리이므로, 합병 찬성(approved the merger)이 이루어진 방식을 적절히 묘사하는 부사가 들어가야 한다. 따라서 '만장일치로'라는 의미의 (D) unanimously가 정답이다. (A) superficially는 '표면적으로', (B) regularly는 '정기적으로, 규칙적으로', (C) magnificently는 '장대하게, 당당하게'라는 뜻으로 문맥상 빈칸에 적절하지 않다.

번역 회사 이사회는 강한 자신감을 보이며 만장일치로 합병에 찬성했다.

어휘 confidence 자신감 board of directors 이사회 approve 찬성하다, 승인하다 merger 합병

125 분사 구문

해설 빈칸 앞에 부사절 접속사 When과 부사 recently가 있으므로, 빈칸에는 과거분사 또는 현재분사가 들어갈 수 있다. 따라서 과거분사인 (D) polled가 정답이다. 참고로, 주어 residents of Mill Creek Park는 여론 조사를 받는 대상이므로, 수동의 의미를 내포한 과거분사가 쓰여야 한다. (A) poll, (B) polls는 명사/동사, (C) pollster는 명사로 품사상 빈칸에 들어갈 수 없다.

번역 최근 여론 조사에서 밀 크리크 공원의 주민들은 도로 파손이 가장 걱정스러운 문제라고 말했다.

어휘 disrepair 파손 concern 걱정을 끼치다 poll 여론 조사를 하다 pollster 여론 조사 요원

126 부사절 접속사_어휘

해설 빈칸 앞뒤 절을 가장 자연스럽게 연결하는 부사절 접속사를 선택하는 문제이다. 리베라 씨가 휴일에 일하기로 동의한 것(Ms. Rivera agreed to work on the holiday)은 그랜트 씨가 회의에 참석할 수 있게(Mr. Grant could attend the conference) 하기 위함이므로, 목적을 나타낼 때 쓰이는 (B) so that이 정답이다. (A) considering (that)은 '~을 고려하면, ~을 감안하면', (C) as if는 '마치 ~인 것처럼', (D) wherever는 '어디든지, 어디에나'라는 뜻으로 문맥상 빈칸에 적절하지 않다.

번역 리베라 씨는 그랜트 씨가 회의에 참석할 수 있도록 휴일에 일하기로 동의했다.

어휘 attend 참석하다

127 부사 어휘

해설 동사 takes 및 전치사구 to the mail room과 가장 잘 어울리는 부사를 선택하는 문제이다. 소포(them=packages)를 가져가는 우편실의 위치를 나타내는 부사가 빈칸에 들어가야 자연스러우므로, '아래층으로, 아래층에서'라는 의미의 (D) downstairs가 정답이다. (A) throughout은 '도처에, 내내', (B) all along은 '내내', (C) too much는 '너무, 몹시'라는 뜻으로 문맥상 빈칸에 적절하지 않다.

번역 그 사원은 하루에 두 번 각 부서에서 소포를 수거해 아래층 우편실로 가져간다.

128 전치사 어휘

해설 빈칸은 those already discussed in today's meeting을 목적어로 취하는 전치사 자리이며, 여기서 those는 complaints를 뜻한다. 회의에서 이미 논의된 불만 사항은 다시 알릴(inform) 필요가 없으므로, '~ 이외에'라는 의미의 (A) beyond가 정답이다. (B) between은 '~ 사이에, ~ 중간에', (C) during은 '~ 동안, ~하는 중에', (D) against는 '~에 반대하여'라는 뜻으로 문맥상 빈칸에 적절하지 않다.

번역 오늘 회의에서 이미 논의된 것들 외에 다른 불만 사항이 있으면 어윈 씨에게 알려 주세요.

어휘 complaint 불만 사항 discuss 논의하다

129 형용사 자리

해설 빈칸은 부사 highly의 수식을 받으며 명사 members를 꾸며 주는 형용사 자리이므로, '기량이 뛰어난'이라는 의미의 형용사 (C) accomplished가 정답이다. (A) accomplishes와 (D) accomplish는 동사, (B) accomplishment는 명사로 품사상 빈칸에 들어갈 수 없다.

번역 톤신 작가 연합은 매우 기량이 뛰어난 회원들이 있는 평판 좋은 단체이다.

어휘 reputable 평판이 좋은 organization 조직, 단체

130 동사 어휘

해설 빈칸은 Mr. Nakata를 가리키는 him을 목적어로 취하는 동명사 자리이다. 최신 금융 소식과 관련하여(on the latest financial news) 베인 씨가 나카타 씨를 위해 해야 할 일을 나타내는 동사가 빈칸에 들어가야 하므로, '(~에게) 보고하기'라는 의미의 (B) briefing이 정답이다. 참고로, 동사 brief는 「brief+사람 명사+on+보고 주제」의 구조로 자주 쓰인다. (A) discussing은 '논의하기'라는 뜻으로 뒤에 사람 명사가 올 경우 전치사 with와 쓰여야 하고, (C) resuming은 '(~를) 다시 시작하기', (D) narrating은 '(~에 대해) 이야기하기'라는 뜻으로 빈칸에 적절하지 않다.

번역 베인 씨는 나카타 씨의 비서로서 최신 금융 뉴스를 그에게 보고하는 일을 담당하고 있다.

어휘 assistant 비서, 조수 in charge of ~을 담당하는

PART 6

131-134 이메일

수신: 바이 창 〈bchang@lexrg.com〉
발신: customerservice@sprtech.com
날짜: 9월 28일
제목: 주문 255646

창 씨께:

9월 27일 구매 건에 대해 감사드립니다. 고객님의 소포는 이미 배송되었고 10월 1일에 도착할 예정입니다. [131]**주문품을 추적하는 것은 쉽습**

니다. www.sprtech.com/shipping/status를 방문해 고객님의 주문 번호를 입력하고 "검색"을 누르십시오.

소포를 받으시면 www.sprtech.com/survey에서 간단한 설문 조사에 응해 [132]**주시기 바랍니다.** 저희는 고객의 의견을 통해서 저희의 서비스 수준을 확인[133]**할 수 있습니다.** 설문을 [134]**완료하시면** 다음 주문 시 10퍼센트를 할인받을 수 있습니다.

Sprtech.com 고객 서비스

어휘 purchase 구매(품) be due to ~할 예정이다 survey 설문 조사 monitor 감시하다, 확인하다

131 문맥에 맞는 문장 고르기

번역 (A) 전액 환불받으실 겁니다.
(B) 교체품이 이월 주문됩니다.
(C) 주문품을 추적하는 것은 쉽습니다.
(D) 곧 문의에 답변 드리겠습니다.

해설 빈칸 앞 문장에서 창 씨의 소포가 10월 1일 도착할 예정(Your package ~ is due to arrive on October 1)이라고 했고, 뒤 문장에서 배송 상태를 확인하는 방법(Simply visit ~ and press "Search")을 구체적으로 설명했다. 따라서 빈칸에도 소포의 배송과 관련된 내용이 들어가야 문맥상 자연스러우므로, (C)가 정답이다.

어휘 refund 환불 replacement 교체(품) back order 이월 주문, 미뤄진 주문

132 동사 어형 _ 시제

해설 빈칸은 주어 we의 동사 자리이다. When이 이끄는 부사절의 동사가 현재 시제(receive)이며, 주절에서 말을 하는 동시에 요청하는(invite) 행위를 하고 있으므로, 빈칸에는 단순 현재 시제 동사가 들어가야 자연스럽다. 따라서 (B) invite가 정답이다.

133 형용사 어휘

해설 주어 we의 보어 역할을 하며 to부정사와 어울려 쓰이는 형용사를 선택하는 문제이다. 고객 의견(customer feedback)은 서비스 수준을 확인(monitor our level of service)할 수 있게 하는 수단이므로, '~할 수 있는'이라는 의미의 (A) able이 정답이다. (C) suitable은 '적합한, 적절한'이라는 뜻으로, to부정사와 쓰일 수 있지만 문맥상 빈칸에 적절하지 않다. (B) skillful은 '숙련된'이라는 뜻으로 주로 전치사 at, in과 쓰이고, (D) equal은 '동일한, 동등한'이라는 뜻으로 전치사 to와 함께 쓰인다.

134 명사 어휘

해설 빈칸은 전치사 Upon의 목적어 역할을 하는 명사 자리로, of the survey의 수식을 받고 있다. 다음 주문 시 10퍼센트 할인을 받는 것(receive a 10% discount toward your next order)은 설문 조사(survey)를 완료한 후 받을 수 있는 혜택이므로, '완료, 완성'이라는 의미의 (D) completion이 정답이다. (A) publication은 '출판, 발표', (B) production은 '생산, 제작', (C) introduction은 '소개, 도입'이라는 뜻으로 문맥상 빈칸에 적절하지 않다.

135-138 정보문

120호 회의실은 회의 및 전화 회의 용도로 예약할 수 있습니다. 먼저, www.gzpoffice.com/confroom에서 온라인으로 예약 요청을 하십시오. 요청이 [135]**접수되면** 시스템에서 자동으로 이용 가능 여부를 확인합니다. 만약 그 시간에 다른 행사가 예정되어 있지 않다면 요청이 승인될 것입니다. 그러고 나서 시스템에서 예약을 [136]**확정하기** 위해 즉시 이메일 메시지를 발송할 겁니다. 하지만 당신의 회의와 겹치는 다른 회의가 예정되어 있는 경우, 요청이 거부되었다는 통지를 받게 됩니다. [137]**예약은 선착순이라는 점 유념하십시오.** 따라서 미리 행사 일정을 잡는 것이 [138]**바람직합니다.** 이렇게 하면, 해당 시간대가 이미 예약되어 있을 경우 회의 일정을 다시 잡을 수 있습니다.

어휘 book 예약하다 conference call 전화 회의 reservation 예약 availability 이용 가능함 accept 수락하다 immediately 즉시 confirm 확정하다 conflict (일정이) 겹치다 notify 통지하다 decline 거부하다 well ahead of time 미리 reschedule 일정을 다시 잡다

135 동사 어형 _ 태

해설 빈칸은 When이 이끄는 부사절의 동사 자리이므로, (A) is received와 (D) received 중 하나를 선택해야 한다. 주어인 your request가 접수되는 대상이며 주절에 현재 시제(checks)가 쓰였으므로, 수동태 현재 동사인 (A) is received가 정답이 된다. (B) receiving은 동명사/현재분사, (C) to receive는 to부정사로 동사 자리에 들어갈 수 없다.

136 동사 어휘

해설 빈칸 앞 문장에서 그 시간에 다른 행사가 예정되어 있지 않으면 요청은 승인될 것(Your request will be accepted ~ at that time)이라고 했으므로, 해당 부분은 그 후 예약을 확정하는 이메일이 발송될 거라는 내용이 되어야 자연스럽다. 따라서 '확정하다, 확인하다'라는 의미의 (D) confirm이 정답이다. (A) move는 '움직이다, 옮기다', (B) cancel은 '취소하다, 무효화하다', (C) change는 '변하다, 바꾸다'라는 뜻으로 문맥상 빈칸에 적절하지 않다.

137 문맥에 맞는 문장 고르기

번역 (A) 행사 초대를 수락해 주셔서 감사합니다.
(B) 회의 전에 논점을 준비하세요.
(C) 예약은 선착순이라는 점 유념하십시오.
(D) 다음 회의 시간은 적절한 때에 발표하겠습니다.

해설 빈칸 앞 문장에서 일정이 겹치는 다른 회의가 예정되어 있으면 예약 신청이 거부될 것(if another meeting is scheduled ~ declined)이라고 했고, 뒤 문장에서는 행사 일정을 미리 잡으라(schedule your event well ahead of time)고 조언하고 있다. 따라서 빈칸에는 그 이유를 설명하는 내용이 들어가야 문맥상 자연스러우므로, (C)가 정답이다.

어휘 first-come, first-served basis 선착순 in due course 적절한 때에

TEST 2

138 형용사 어휘

해설 일정이 겹치는 다른 회의가 예정되어 있으면 예약 신청이 거부될 것(if another meeting is scheduled ~ declined)이니 행사 일정을 미리 잡으라(schedule your event well ahead of time)고 조언하는 내용이므로, '바람직한, 권할 만한'이라는 의미의 (B) advisable이 정답이다. (A) fortunate는 '운이 좋은', (C) previous는 '이전의', (D) flexible은 '융통성 있는, 유연한'이라는 뜻으로 문맥상 빈칸에 적합하지 않다.

139-142 이메일

발신: 카렐 오티에 〈k.authier@codetouchmag.com〉
수신: 오노라토 퀴노네스 〈quinones@voyacon.com.es〉
날짜: 7월 18일 화요일 오전 11시 4분
제목: 보야콘 특집 기사

퀴노네스 씨께:

보야콘이 〈코드 터치 매거진〉 올해의 25대 신생 기술 기업 중 하나로 선정되었음을 알려 드리게 되어 기쁩니다. 저희는 9월 호에 귀사의 [139]**연혁을 소개할** 예정입니다. 명단에는 주목할 만한 방식으로 산업을 발전시키는 [140]**기업들**만 포함되므로, 저희 독자들은 이를 큰 영예로 여깁니다.

보야콘의 창립자로서, 해당 기사에 사용할 귀하의 디지털 사진을 이메일로 보내 주시겠습니까? [141]**고해상도 컬러 이미지여야 합니다.** 8월 5일[142]**까지** 받았으면 합니다. 그렇지 않으면 공개된 사진을 사용하겠습니다.

협조에 감사드리며, 축하를 보냅니다.

카렐 오티에

편집장

어휘 select 선정하다 emerging 신생[신흥]의 enterprise 기업 advance 발전시키다; 진보 significant 중요한, 주목할 만한 founder 창립자 article 기사 public-domain 공개된, 공공의

139 동사 어형 _ 태

해설 빈칸 앞에 will be, 뒤에 목적어 역할을 하는 명사구 your company가 있으므로, 빈칸에는 타동사의 현재분사가 들어가야 한다. 따라서 (B) profiling이 정답이다. (D) profiled가 과거분사로 쓰일 경우, will be 뒤에 올 수는 있지만 목적어를 취할 수 없으므로 빈칸에 들어갈 수 없다.

어휘 profile (약력·연혁을) 소개하다; 프로필

140 명사 어휘

해설 빈칸은 동사 includes의 목적어 역할을 하는 명사 자리로, 주격 관계대명사절(that advance the industry in significant ways)의 수식을 받고 있다. 따라서 산업을 발전시키는 주체인 동시에, 신생 기술 기업 명단(our list)에 포함되는 대상이 빈칸에 들어가야 하므로, '기업'이라는 의미의 (D) enterprises가 정답이다. (A) publications는 '출판물', (B) machines는 '기계', (C) techniques는 '기술, 기법'이라는 뜻으로 문맥상 빈칸에 적절하지 않다.

141 문맥에 맞는 문장 고르기

번역 (A) 처음에는 수많은 기업들이 고려되었습니다.
(B) 최대한 빨리 몇 부를 전달하겠습니다.
(C) 이번이 이 명단을 발표하는 다섯 번째 해입니다.
(D) 고해상도 컬러 이미지여야 합니다.

해설 빈칸 앞 문장에서 기사에 사용할 디지털 사진을 이메일로 보내 달라(e-mail us a digital photograph ~ in the article)고 요청했고, 뒤 문장에서 제출 시한(August 5)을 안내했다. 따라서 빈칸에도 기사용 사진과 관련된 내용이 들어가야 문맥상 자연스러우므로, (D)가 정답이다.

어휘 initially 처음에 publish 출간하다, 발표하다 high-resolution 고해상도

142 전치사 어휘

해설 빈칸 뒤에 사진을 받아야 하는 기한(August 5)이 나왔으므로, '~까지, ~가 끝나기 전에'라는 의미의 (A) by가 정답이다. (C) within은 '~ 이내에'라는 뜻으로 뒤에 특정한 기간을 나타내는 명사가 와야 한다.

143-146 회람

수신: 전 직원
발신: 카르멘 펠프스, 센트럴 시티 박물관장
관련: 특별전 큐레이터
날짜: 11월 15일

전 직원에게,

이번 주 수요일 신문에 센트럴 시티 박물관의 새 직책에 관한 광고가 게재될 것임을 알려 드립니다. 최근 현지 조각가 린 블룸의 작품을 전시한 〈블룸 아웃사이드 더 박스〉가 [143]**인기**를 얻은 이후, 박물관 이사회는 새로운 분기별 전시회를 여는 데 전념할 새로운 직책을 배치하기로 결정했습니다. 직함은 특별전 큐레이터입니다. 합격자는 1월 2일에 업무를 [144]**시작할 겁니다.**

[145]**이 직책은 경험이 풍부해야 합니다.** 현지 및 지역 예술가에 대한 지식이 검증될 경우 우대합니다. [146]**자격을 갖춘** 박물관 직원은 지원하기 바랍니다. 문의 사항은 내선 449번으로 릴리아나 웰스에게 연락하십시오.

감사합니다.

카르멘

어휘 place an advertisement 광고를 게재하다 regarding ~에 관한 exhibition 전시(회) showcase 전시하다 sculptor 조각가 allocate 배치[배정]하다 dedicated to ~에 전념하는 quarterly 분기의 applicant 지원자 proven 검증[입증]된 regional 지방[지역]의 encourage 장려[권장]하다 extension 내선 (번호)

143 명사 어휘

해설 빈칸은 After의 목적어 자리로, 빈칸을 포함한 전치사가 콤마 뒤 주절(the museum board ~ quarterly exhibitions)을 수식하고 있다. 따라서 빈칸에는 〈블룸 아웃사이드 더 박스〉 전시회 이후 분기별 전시회에 전념할 새로운 직책을 배치하기로 한 이유를 나타내는 단어가 들어가야 하므로, '인기'라는 의미의 (A) popularity가 정답이다. (B) winner는 '우승자', (C) goal은 '목표, 득점', (D) awareness는 '인식'이라는 뜻으로 문맥상 빈칸에 적절하지 않다.

144 동사 어형 _ 시제

해설 앞서 특별전 큐레이터가 새로 채용될 예정이라고 했고, 회람이 작성된 날짜(Date: November 15)를 기준으로 합격자가 업무를 시작하는 시점(January 2)은 미래이므로, (B) will start가 정답이다.

145 문맥에 맞는 문장 고르기

번역 (A) 위원회 추천은 금요일 퇴근 시 마감됩니다.
(B) 비평가 토니 와타나베는 이 전시회를 평가하며 별점 5개를 줬습니다.
(C) 이 직책은 경험이 풍부해야 합니다.
(D) 우리는 이 행사를 주최하기를 고대합니다.

해설 앞 문단에서 새롭게 채용할 직책에 대해 설명했고, 빈칸 뒤 문장에서 우대 조건(Proven knowledge ~ is preferred)을 언급했으므로, 빈칸에도 새 직책과 관련된 내용이 들어가야 문맥상 자연스럽다. 따라서 (C)가 정답이다.

어휘 nomination 추천, 지명 extensive 풍부한

146 형용사 어휘 _ 과거분사

해설 주어 museum staff를 적절히 수식하는 형용사(과거분사)를 선택하는 문제이다. 새로 채용할 직책의 지원 요건과 우대 조건을 설명한 후 지원을 독려하고 있으므로, 지원 권유를 받는 직원의 특성을 나타내는 단어가 빈칸에 들어가야 자연스럽다. 따라서 '자격을 갖춘'이라는 의미의 (D) Qualified가 정답이다. (A) Expressed는 '표현된, 나타난', (B) Observed는 '관찰된, 준수된'이라는 의미로 문맥상 빈칸에 부적절하다. (C) Depended는 자동사의 과거분사로 명사를 앞에서 수식할 수 없다.

PART 7

147-148 이메일

수신: 〈고객 목록〉
발신: info@rapidrailways.com
날짜: 2월 1일
제목: 소식

[147]래피드 철도는 4월 한 달 동안 여행을 특별 할인해 단골 고객님들께 보답하고자 합니다. [148]60달러 이상의 성인 왕복 티켓을 구입하고 동반자 1인의 성인 요금을 50퍼센트 할인받으세요. 온라인 예약 시 코드 RAIL을 사용하십시오.

이번 판촉 행사는 래피드 철도 고속 열차에는 해당되지 않습니다. 이전에 구입한 티켓을 교환해 할인을 받을 수 없습니다. 티켓은 3월 1일까지 구입해야 합니다.

어휘 reward 보답하다 loyal customer 단골 고객 purchase 구입하다 adult 성인 round-trip 왕복의 fare 요금 companion 동반자 promotion 판촉 (행사) valid 유효한 exchange 교환하다 previously 이전에 obtain 받다

147 주제 / 목적

번역 이메일의 목적은?
(A) 개선된 서비스 홍보하기
(B) 첫 이용 고객 유치하기
(C) 4월 티켓 판매량 늘리기
(D) 래피드 철도 고속 열차 광고하기

해설 첫 번째 단락에서 4월 한 달 동안 여행을 특별 할인해(a special discount on travel during the month of April) 단골 고객에게 보답하고자 한다고 했으므로, 4월의 티켓 판매량을 늘리고자 보낸 메일임을 알 수 있다. 따라서 (C)가 정답이다.

어휘 publicize 홍보하다

148 사실 관계 확인

번역 특별 할인에 관해 사실인 것은?
(A) 어린이를 포함한다.
(B) 전화로 티켓을 구매해야 한다.
(C) 이미 구입한 티켓에만 적용된다.
(D) 함께 여행하는 2인에게 제공된다.

해설 첫 번째 단락에서 60달러 이상의 성인 왕복 티켓을 구입하면 동반자 1인의 성인 요금을 50퍼센트 할인받을 수 있다(receive 50 percent off a second adult fare for a companion)고 했으므로, (D)가 정답이다.

▸▸ Paraphrasing 지문의 50 percent off a second adult fare for a companion
→ 질문의 the special discount

149-150 초대장

클리어헤이븐 상공회의소
조식 클럽

초청 연사: 딕스턴 광고의 필리파 딕스턴
"[149]**사업 성공을 위한 소셜 미디어 동향**"

9월 26일 수요일
오전 7:30–9:00

켈리스 카페
리처즈 가 17번지
클리어헤이븐, 버지니아 20101

1인당 8달러
조식 뷔페 포함

[150]**등록 필요, 이용 가능 좌석 한정**
9월 20일까지 회답 주시기 바랍니다
클리어헤이븐 상공회의소, 540-555-0112

어휘 Chamber of Commerce 상공회의소 registration 등록 limited 한정된 RSVP 회신 바람

149 세부 사항

번역 행사에서 논의될 주제는?

(A) 소셜 미디어
(B) 성공 투자
(C) 중소 업체 설립하기
(D) 직원 이직 대처하기

해설 초대장 상단에서 초청 연사(Guest Speaker)인 딕스턴 씨가 '사업 성공을 위한 소셜 미디어 동향(Social Media Trends for Business Success)'이라는 주제로 발표한다는 것을 확인할 수 있다. 따라서 (A)가 정답이다.

어휘 cope with ~에 대처하다 turnover 이직(률)

150 사실 관계 확인

번역 행사에 관해 명시된 것은?

(A) 한 달에 한 번 열린다.
(B) 주말에 열린다.
(C) 등록하지 않아도 된다.
(D) 공간에 제약이 있다.

해설 초대장 하단에서 이용 가능한 좌석이 한정(limited seating available)되어 있어 등록이 필요하다고 했으므로, (D)가 정답이다.

▸▸ Paraphrasing 지문의 **limited seating available**
→ 정답의 **Space is limited**

151-152 공지

해로드 자동차 제조사

앤드류 던, 이사
[152]**로라 브래들리, 현장 소장**

[151]**해로드 자동차 제조사에 오신 것을 환영합니다!** 저희는 안전한 작업 환경을 유지하는 것을 중요시합니다. [151]**조립 작업장을 둘러보실 때 다음 규칙을 엄수해 주시기 바랍니다.** 이 규칙을 위반한 것으로 드러난 사람은 구내를 떠나라는 요청을 받을 것입니다. [152]**규정 준수에 관한 문제는 현장 소장에게 문의하십시오.**

항상:
▶ 견학 안내인 곁을 떠나지 마십시오.
▶ 보안경과 헬멧을 착용하십시오.
▶ 경고 신호에 부응하고 대피 지시에 따르십시오.
▶ 사진을 찍기 전에 안내인에게 허락을 구하십시오.

금지:
▶ 무리에서 이탈하기.
▶ "위험" 또는 "관계자 외 출입 금지" 표시된 곳에 들어가기.
▶ 장비 만지기.

어휘 environment 환경 strictly 엄격히 observe 지키다 assembly 조립 floor 작업장 violation 위반 premise 구내 obey 따르다 evacuation 대피 permission 허락

151 추론 / 암시

번역 공지의 대상은 누구이겠는가?

(A) 보수 작업자
(B) 경비원
(C) 안전 조사원
(D) 공장 방문자

해설 첫 번째 단락에서 해로드 자동차 제조사에 온 것을 환영한다(Welcome to Harrod Automotive Manufacturing!)고 한 후 조립 작업장을 둘러볼 때 다음 규칙을 엄수하기를 바란다(We ask ~ while you are touring the assembly floor)고 했다. 따라서 공장 방문자를 위한 공지임을 추론할 수 있으므로, (D)가 정답이다.

152 세부 사항

번역 공지에 따르면 누군가 브래들리 씨에게 연락해야 하는 이유는?

(A) 직원 칭찬
(B) 정책 문의
(C) 사진 제출
(D) 일정 받기

해설 공지의 상단에서 브래들리 씨가 현장 소장(Laura Bradley, Site Manager)임을 확인할 수 있고, 첫 번째 단락을 보면 규정 준수에 관한 문제는 현장 소장인 브래들리 씨에게 문의하라(For concerns about compliance, please contact the site manager)고 되어 있다. 따라서 (B)가 정답이다.

어휘 praise 칭찬하다 obtain 받다

▸▸ Paraphrasing 지문의 **For concerns about compliance**
→ 정답의 **To inquire about a policy**

153-154 문자 메시지

스콧 라빈 (오전 11시 14분)
안녕하세요, 타냐. 아니타가 요청한 대로 창고에서 공간을 비우고 있어요. [153]**여기 "회계"라고 표시된 상자들이 몇 개 있네요. 당신 건가요?**

타냐 그린 (오전 11시 18분)

예, 153**안에 제 예전 파일 일부가 들어 있어요.** 대부분은 파쇄해도 되지만 보관해야 되는 것들도 몇 개 있어요. 154**제가 가서 볼까요? 다음 회의까지 15분 정도 시간이 있어요.**

스콧 라빈 (오전 11시 20분)

당신이 정하세요. 154**당신한테 시간이 좀 더 생길 때까지 그냥 여기 두어도 돼요.**

타냐 그린 (오전 11시 21분)

그래 주시면 좋겠네요. 수요일에 시간을 내서 분류할게요.

어휘 storage 저장 shred 파쇄하다 sort through 분류하다

153 세부 사항

번역 라빈 씨가 그린 씨에게 메시지를 보낸 이유는?

(A) 저장 공간이 더 필요한지 물으려고
(B) 일부 파일이 그녀 것인지 알아보려고
(C) 상자를 옮기는 데 도움을 얻으려고
(D) 일부 파일을 어디에 두어야 하는지 물으려고

해설 라빈 씨가 오전 11시 14분 메시지에서 창고에 "회계"라고 표시된 상자들(There are some boxes marked "Accounting" in here)이 그린 씨의 것인지(Are they yours?) 문의했고, 이에 대해 그린 씨가 자신의 예전 파일 일부가 그 상자 안에 있다고 했다. 따라서 (B)가 정답이다.

154 의도 파악

번역 오전 11시 20분에 라빈 씨가 "당신이 정하세요"라고 적은 의도는 무엇인가?

(A) 그린 씨가 원할 때 자신이 서류를 분류할 것이다.
(B) 자신이 시간을 내서 창고 문을 열 수 있다.
(C) 그린 씨는 파일을 보고 싶을 때를 결정할 수 있다.
(D) 그린 씨는 자신이 사용하기를 원하는 상자를 고를 수 있다.

해설 그린 씨는 오전 11시 18분 메시지에서 자신이 창고에 가서 봐야 할지(Do you want me to come have a look?) 라빈 씨에게 물은 후, 다음 회의까지 15분 정도 시간이 있다(I have about 15 minutes until my next meeting)고 했다. 이에 대해 라빈 씨가 '당신이 정하세요(It's up to you)'라고 답한 후 그린 씨에게 시간이 좀 더 생길 때까지 그냥 창고에 두어도 된다(I can just leave them here until you have more time)고 했으므로, 그린 씨가 원할 때 파일을 확인하라는 의도임을 파악할 수 있다. 따라서 (C)가 정답이다.

155-157 기사

나이로비(11월 2일) - 이탈리아의 인기 신발 소매점 아고스티는 아고스티 나이로비가 개업하는 이번 주에 동아프리카에서의 첫 할인 매장을 여는 게 된다. 고객들은 아고스티가 유명한 이유인 밝은 색상과 독특한 디자인을 모두 보게 될 것이다.

155**아고스티 나이로비는 매장 곳곳에 터치스크린 디스플레이를 비치해서 직접 손으로 조작하여 패션에 접근하는 독특한 방식을 선보일 예정이다.** 이 디스플레이를 통해 쇼핑객은 제품 정보를 검색하고, 고객 후기를 읽고, 가장 잘 팔리는 스타일을 식별할 수 있게 된다.

155**매장에는 발바닥 압력 센서도 설치된다.** 고객은 센서 위에 서서 자신의 정확한 발 치수를 판단할 수 있고 발에 가장 잘 맞는 신발 사이즈를 선택할 수 있게 된다. 156**보통 다른 경쟁 업체 매장에서는 찾아 볼 수 없는 다양한 길이와 폭의 신발들을 구매할 수 있을 것이다.**

"저희 아고스티는 동아프리카를 새로운 패션에 적합한 중요 장소로 보고 있습니다." 아고스티 마케팅 이사 라파엘 지토는 말했다. 157**지토 씨에 따르면 나이로비 매장 개점은 야심 찬 확장 계획의 첫 단계일 뿐이다.** 실제로, 회사는 현재 이 지역에서 새로운 디자인 시설을 위한 장소를 물색하고 있다.

어휘 retailer 소매점 feature 특별히 포함하다, 특색으로 삼다 hands-on 직접 손으로 만지는, 직접 해 보는 approach 접근 방식 identify 식별하다 plantar 발바닥의 determine 결정하다 precise 정확한 measurement 치수 available 입수할 수 있는, 이용 가능한 competitor 경쟁 업체 expansion 확장

155 세부 사항

번역 기사는 아고스티 나이로비 매장의 어떤 면을 강조하는가?

(A) 넓은 실내
(B) 박식한 영업팀
(C) 다양한 브랜드 구색
(D) 쌍방향 디스플레이

해설 두 번째 단락에서 아고스티 나이로비가 매장 곳곳에 터치스크린 디스플레이(touchscreen display stations)를 비치해서 고객이 직접 손으로 조작하여 패션에 접근하는 독특한 방식을 선보일 예정이라고 한 후, 디스플레이의 구체적인 용도를 설명했다. 또 세 번째 단락에서는 발바닥 압력 센서(foot plantar pressure sensor)에 대해 자세히 언급했다. 따라서 (D)가 정답이다.

어휘 spacious 넓은 knowledgeable 박식한 interactive 쌍방향의

156 사실 관계 확인

번역 아고스티 신발에 관해 사실인 것은?

(A) 새 디자인으로 구입할 수 있다.
(B) 매우 비싸다.
(C) 구하기 힘든 사이즈로도 제조된다.
(D) 대체로 수제품이다.

해설 세 번째 단락에서 아고스티 나이로비 매장에서는 다른 경쟁 업체 매장에서는 찾아 볼 수 없는 다양한 길이와 폭의 신발들을 구매할 수 있을 것(Shoes will be available in a variety of lengths and widths not usually found in competitor stores)이라고 했다. 따라서 (C)가 정답이다.

▸▸ **Paraphrasing** 지문의 **in a variety of lengths and widths not usually found in competitor stores**
→ 정답의 **in hard-to-find sizes**

157 문장 삽입

번역 [1], [2], [3], [4]로 표시된 곳 중에서 다음 문장이 들어가기에 가장 적합한 곳은?

"실제로, 회사는 현재 이 지역에서 새로운 디자인 시설을 위한 장소를 물색하고 있다."

(A) [1]
(B) [2]
(C) [3]
(D) [4]

해설 주어진 문장에서 실제로 회사가 현재 나이로비 지역에서 새로운 디자인 시설을 위한 장소를 물색 중(the company is currently scouting locations for a new design facility)이라고 했으므로, 앞에서 먼저 확장 관련 내용이 언급되어야 한다. [4] 앞에서 나이로비 매장 개점은 야심 찬 확장 계획의 첫 단계일 뿐(the opening of the Nairobi store is only the first step of an ambitious expansion plan)이라는 내용이 왔고, 이 다음에 주어진 문장이 들어가야 문맥상 자연스럽다. 따라서 (D)가 정답이다.

158-160 양식

http://www.pinecrestofficepark.com/requestform

파인크레스트 오피스 파크
요청서
주디 블랜치, 사무장
215.555.0118, 내선 2

요청일: 4월 2일
입주자: 러너 앤 랜들, LLC
사무소: 스위트룸 B, 3층
입주자 연락명: 에이미 랜들

158**문제 유형:**
구조물 ☑
전기 ☐
배관 ☐

158**필요한 작업 간단 설명:**
창문 위 천장에 누수가 진행되었고 벽은 변색하기 시작했습니다.

추가 지시 사항:
오시기 전에 215.555.0127 제 사무실로 전화 주세요. 건물 담당 직원이 사무실에 올 때 제 파트너인 잭 러너와 제가 있었으면 합니다. 160**천장 그 부분 바로 밑에 아주 비싼 사무 장비가 있어요. 수리를 시작하기 전에 우리가 그걸 옮겨야 합니다.**

파인크레스트 관리소 작성:
수령일: 4월 3일 **승인:** 예 ☑ 아니오 ☐
159**배정: 인수 김** **승인자:** 주디 블랜치

유의 사항:
159**랜들 씨에게 전화한 후 내일 아침 일찍 이 문제를 조사해 주세요.** 지붕 수리가 필요하면 존 로퍼(로퍼 루퍼스-john@roperroofers.com)에게 이메일을 보내 견적 받을 날을 정하세요.

어휘 tenant 입주자 description 설명 ceiling 천장 leak 새는 곳, 누출 discolor 변색되다 repair 수리 investigate 조사하다 estimate 견적(서)

158 주제 / 목적

번역 양식의 목적은?

(A) 일자리 지원
(B) 임대 요청
(C) 문제 보고
(D) 주소 변경

해설 양식의 문제 유형(Type of Problem) 항목에 '구조물(Structural)'이 체크되어 있고, 필요한 작업을 설명하는 부분(Brief Description of Work Needed)에 창문 위 천장에 누수가 진행되었으며(The ceiling over the window has developed a water leak) 벽은 변색하기 시작한다(the wall is beginning to discolor)고 적혀 있다. 따라서 문제점을 보고하고 수리를 요청하기 위해 작성된 양식임을 알 수 있으므로, (C)가 정답이다.

159 세부 사항

번역 4월 2일 요청과 관련하여 가장 먼저 랜들 씨에게 연락할 사람은?

(A) 김 씨
(B) 러너 씨
(C) 로퍼 씨
(D) 블랜치 씨

해설 양식 하단에 파인크레스트 관리소가 작성한 유의 사항(Notes) 부분을 보면, 랜들 씨에게 전화한 후 문제를 조사하라(Please investigate this problem ~ after you call Ms. Randall)고 적혀 있다. 따라서 일을 배정받은(Assigned to) 김 씨가 가장 먼저 랜들 씨에게 연락할 것임을 알 수 있으므로, (A)가 정답이다.

160 세부 사항

번역 랜들 씨가 사무 장비에 관해 언급한 이유는?

(A) 판매용이다.
(B) 옮겨야 한다.
(C) 파손되었다.
(D) 교체되어야 한다.

해설 양식 중반의 추가 지시 사항(Additional Instructions)란을 보면, 누수가 진행 중인 천장 바로 밑에 비싼 사무 장비가 있고(There is very expensive office equipment) 이를 수리 시작 전에 옮겨야 한다(We will need to move it before any repairs are made)고 쓰여 있다. 따라서 (B)가 정답이다.

어휘 replace 교체하다

161-163 보도 자료

즉시 보도용
언론 연락: 안드레아 올라도티르/+613 555 0124

밥슨 자동차사, 디럭시던트의 최신 상품 의욕적으로 도입

오타와(6월 10일) – 캐나다의 선두적 제조 업체인 밥슨 자동차사는 회사의 보안 개선을 목표로 새로운 지문 인식 출입 시스템을 막 도입했다. 161**아이슬란드 회사인 디럭시던트가 만든 이 시스템으로 직원들은 지문을 스캔하기만 하면 구내 건물들에 들어갈 수 있다.**

[161]**뱁슨의 CEO 다니엘 딤스에 따르면, 디럭시던트의 지문 인식 시스템은 회사가 과거에 시도했던 다른 보안 제품들에 비해 상당히 개선된 것이라고 한다.**

"[162]**디럭시던트의 지문 인식기가 큰 자산이 되고 있습니다. 과거에는 항상 사진과 전자 신분증을 사용해 건물에 출입했었죠.**" 딤스가 말했다. "하지만 신분증을 제작하고 분실 신분증을 교체하려면 [162]**비용이 많이 들었어요.** 게다가 보안에도 상당한 위협이 되었죠. 직원들이 가끔 신분증을 깜박하고 와서 경비실을 오가는 사람이 많아지기도 했었죠. 전반적으로 [162]**신분증은 비용이 많이 들고** 위험했어요."

지난 10년 동안 디럭시던트는 혁신적인 디지털 제품으로 첨단 기술 업무 현장에 솔루션을 제공해 왔다. [163]**레이캬비크에 본사를 둔 디럭시던트는 전 세계에 물품을 배송하며 전화로 24시간 기술 지원을 제공한다.** 새로운 지문 인식 출입 시스템에 관한 자세한 내용을 보려면 www.deluxident.is를 방문하면 된다.

어휘 enthusiastically 의욕적으로 implement 시행하다, 도입해서 사용하다 adopt 도입하다 aim 목표로 하다 enable 가능하게 하다 significant 상당한 tremendous 엄청난 asset 이점, 자산 identification 신분 증명 replace 교체하다 threat 위협 traffic 왕래 costly 비싼 risky 위험한 decade 10년

161 추론 / 암시

번역 딤스 씨에 관해 암시된 것은?

(A) 여러 동의 건물을 관리한다.
(B) 자주 해외로 나간다.
(C) 성공한 발명가다.
(D) 자주 신분증 둔 곳을 잊는다.

해설 두 번째 단락에서 딤스 씨가 뱁슨 자동차사의 CEO(Babson's CEO Daniel Deems)임을 알 수 있고, 첫 번째 단락에서 디럭시던트가 만든 새 지문 인식 출입 시스템으로 뱁슨사 직원들이 지문을 스캔하기만 하면 구내 건물들에 들어갈 수 있다(enter campus buildings simply by scanning their fingerprints)고 했다. 따라서 뱁슨 자동차의 CEO인 딤스 씨가 여러 동의 구내 건물을 관리한다고 추론할 수 있으므로, (A)가 정답이다.

어휘 oversee 관리하다 frequent 빈번한 inventor 발명가 misplace 잘못 두다, 둔 곳을 잊다

162 세부 사항

번역 딤스 씨가 과거 제품보다 디럭시던트의 신제품을 선호하는 이유는?

(A) 방문객의 구내 진입을 수월하게 한다.
(B) 장기적으로 비용을 낮춘다.
(C) 사진이 있는 신분증이 필요하다.
(D) 직원들이 서로의 위치를 빨리 찾게 해 준다.

해설 세 번째 단락에서 딤스 씨는 디럭시던트의 신제품인 지문 인식기가 큰 자산(a tremendous asset)이 되고 있다며 과거에 신분증을 사용했을 때는 비용이 많이 들었다(expensive, costly)고 했다. 따라서 그가 디럭시던트의 신제품을 선호하는 이유가 비용적인 측면과 연관되어 있음을 알 수 있으므로, (B)가 정답이다.

어휘 facilitate 수월하게 하다 locate (위치를) 찾다

▸▸ Paraphrasing 지문의 other security products the company has tried in the past
→ 질문의 previous products

163 사실 관계 확인

번역 디럭시던트에 관해 사실인 것은?

(A) 제품을 해외로 배송한다.
(B) 캐나다에 본사가 있다.
(C) 현장 컨설팅 서비스를 제공한다.
(D) 뱁슨 자동차사와 합병할 계획이다.

해설 마지막 단락에서 디럭시던트가 전 세계에 물품을 배송한다(Deluxident delivers items worldwide)고 했으므로, (A)가 정답이다.

▸▸ Paraphrasing 지문의 delivers items worldwide
→ 정답의 ships its products internationally

164-167 편지

마리아 클리어리
쿨리지 가 2289번지
그레이트 폴스, 몬태나 주 59401

폴 도넬
코튼 베일 5267번지
헬레나, MT 59624

도넬 씨께,

[164]**온라인으로 루이스 앤 클라크 카운티의 공공 재산세 기록을 열람해 보고, 귀하가 월러 애비뉴와 메인 스트리트 모퉁이에 있는, 한때 잡화점이었던 건물의 소유자라는 것을 알게 되었습니다.** [165]**제가 알기로 그 건물은 몇 년 동안 판자로 막혀 비어 있었습니다.** 그것을 매각하실 의향이 있는지 알고 싶습니다.

저는 그 지역에 카페를 열 계획이고, 조금만 고치면 귀하의 건물이 완벽한 입지가 될 수 있으리라 믿습니다. [167]**저는 가능한 한 원래의 구조물을 온전하게 유지하고 싶습니다.** 예를 들어 노출된 벽돌 외장은 건물의 멋에 필수라고 생각합니다. 개조하더라도 소규모로 할 것입니다.

상업 지구에 매물로 나온 다른 건물들이 있다는 건 알지만, 그것들은 귀하의 건물처럼 지역사회와 연결되어 있지는 않습니다. [166]**저는 많은 헬레나 주민과 이야기를 나누었는데, 그들은 귀하의 건물에 좋은 추억을 가지고 있고, 건물이 다시 사용할 수 있는 구조물로 바뀌는 것을 보고 싶어 합니다.** 제 계획이 공동체의 환영을 받을 것이라고 확신합니다.

제 제안을 고려해 주시면 감사하겠습니다. 자세하게 논의하고 싶으시면 406-555-0181번으로 연락 주십시오.

마리아 클리어리

어휘 property tax 재산세 general store 잡화점 board up (문·창문 등을) 판자로 막다 unoccupied 비어 있는 modest 약간의, 소규모의 intact 온전한 transform 바뀌다

TEST 2

164 사실 관계 확인

번역 루이스 앤 클라크 카운티에 관해 명시된 것은?

(A) 식당들로 유명하다.
(B) 엄격한 건축 규정을 시행한다.
(C) 인터넷으로 부동산 정보를 제공한다.
(D) 개발 프로젝트에 관한 의견을 구하고 있다.

해설 첫 번째 단락을 보면, 클리어리 씨는 온라인으로 루이스 앤 클라크 카운티의 공공 재산세 기록을 열람해 본 후(After searching through Lewis and Clark County's public property tax records online) 도넬 씨가 건물의 소유주임을 알게 되었다고 했다. 따라서 (C)가 정답이다.

▸▸ **Paraphrasing** 지문의 **public property tax records**
→ 정답의 **property information**
지문의 **online** → 정답의 **over the Internet**

165 추론 / 암시

번역 잡화점 건물에 관해 암시된 것은?

(A) 현재 일반에게 공개되어 있다.
(B) 주인이 여러 번 바뀌었다.
(C) 대대적으로 개보수 중이다.
(D) 수년 동안 비어 있다.

해설 첫 번째 단락에서 잡화점 건물이 몇 년 동안 판자로 막혀 비어 있다(As far as I can tell, the building has been ~ unoccupied for quite a few years)고 했으므로, (D)가 정답이다.

어휘 undergo 겪다 extensive 대대적인 vacant 비어 있는

▸▸ **Paraphrasing** 지문의 **unoccupied for quite a few years**
→ 정답의 **vacant for several years**

166 추론 / 암시

번역 클리어리 씨가 도넬 씨의 부동산에 관심을 갖는 이유는 무엇이겠는가?

(A) 지역 주민에게 인기가 있다.
(B) 도심에 위치한다.
(C) 저렴한 가격에 팔리고 있다.
(D) 넓은 평면도가 특징이다.

해설 세 번째 단락에서 많은 헬레나 주민이 도넬 씨의 건물에 좋은 추억을 가지고 있고(many Helena residents ~ have fond memories of your building), 건물이 다시 사용할 수 있는 구조물로 바뀌는 것을 보고 싶어 한다(they would like to see it transformed into a usable structure again)고 했다. 따라서 도넬 씨의 건물이 지역 주민들에게 인기가 있어 클리어리 씨가 관심을 갖는 것으로 볼 수 있으므로, (A)가 정답이다.

▸▸ **Paraphrasing** 지문의 **many Helena residents**
→ 정답의 **local residents**

167 문장 삽입

번역 [1], [2], [3], [4]로 표시된 곳 중에서 다음 문장이 들어가기에 가장 적합한 곳은?

"예를 들어 노출된 벽돌 외장은 건물의 멋에 필수라고 생각합니다."

(A) [1]
(B) [2]
(C) [3]
(D) [4]

해설 주어진 문장에서 노출된 벽돌 외장은 건물의 멋에 필수(the exposed brick siding ~ is essential to building's charm)라며 건물에서 그대로 두어야 하는 부분을 예를 들어(for example) 설명했으므로, 앞에서 먼저 이와 관련된 내용이 언급되어야 한다. [2] 앞에서 가능한 한 원래의 구조물을 온전하게 유지하고 싶다(keep as much of the original structure intact as possible)는 의견을 밝혔으므로, (B)가 정답이다.

어휘 exposed 노출된 siding 외장 essential 필수적인 charm 멋, 매력

168-171 정보문

퀜텐 광고 게시판

우리 시설의 실물 게시판은 인사부 사무 보조원이 관리하고 있습니다. 게시판은 자물쇠로 잠긴 유리 캐비닛 안에 있고 사무 보조원이 캐비닛 열쇠를 관리하며 모든 게시물을 최신 상태로 유지할 책임이 있습니다.

• [169]**엘리베이터 옆 게시판은 중요한 회사 소식이나 알림 같은, 전 직원을 대상으로 하는 일반적인 정보를 전달하는 데 사용됩니다.**

• **회의실 밖 게시판**은 회의실에 예정된 임박한 회의와 행사 관련 정보에만 사용됩니다.

• **직원 휴게실 게시판**에는 퀜텐 광고가 올리는 공지가 아닌, 개인 물품 판매, 지역 축제, 그리고 기타 지역 행사와 같이 동료들이 관심을 가질 만한 공지를 올리는 데 사용할 수 있습니다. [170]**이런 공고를 게시하려면 먼저 인사부에 신청해야 하며 게시물 사본뿐 아니라 연락처 정보를 포함해야 합니다.** 이 공지들은 행사일 전 2주 내로만 게시할 수 있습니다.

[171]**모든 게시판이 의도된 용도에 맞게 사용될 수 있도록 주기적으로 점검할 예정입니다.**

어휘 physical 실물의, 눈에 보이는 oversee 관리하다 responsible for ~을 책임지는 reminder 알림 solely 오로지 compliance 준수

168 주제 / 목적

번역 정보문의 목적은?

(A) 공석에 대해 설명하기 위해
(B) 회사 정책을 설명하기 위해
(C) 방문객에게 건물 정보를 제공하기 위해
(D) 고객의 웹사이트 탐색을 돕기 위해

해설 지문 전반에서 회사 내 게시판의 용도 및 관리와 관련된 정보를 제공하고 있다. 따라서 게시판과 관련된 회사 정책을 설명하기 위한 정보문임을 알 수 있으므로, (B)가 정답이다.

169 추론 / 암시

번역 중요한 회사 소식은 어디에 게시되겠는가?

(A) 엘리베이터 근처
(B) 직원 휴게실 내부
(C) 회의실 내부
(D) 인사부 내부

해설 게시판별 설명의 첫 번째 항목에서 엘리베이터 옆 게시판은 중요한 회사 소식이나 알림 같이 전 직원을 대상으로 하는 일반적인 정보를 전달하는 데 사용된다(The bulletin board by the elevator is used to convey ~ such as important company news or reminders)고 했으므로, (A)가 정답이다.

▸▸ **Paraphrasing** 지문의 **by the elevator**
→ 정답의 **Near the elevator**

170 세부 사항

번역 정보문에 의하면, 직원들이 인사부에 연락해야 하는 이유는?

(A) 사무실 열쇠를 받기 위해
(B) 공지를 승인받기 위해
(C) 회사 행사에 등록하기 위해
(D) 복사 신청서를 제출하기 위해

해설 게시판별 설명의 세 번째 항목에서 퀜텐 광고가 올리는 공지 외에 동료들이 관심을 가질 만한 기타 공지를 올리려면 먼저 인사부에 신청해야 한다(To post these notices, staff must first submit a request to Human Resources)고 했으므로, (B)가 정답이다.

▸▸ **Paraphrasing** 지문의 **staff must first submit a request to**
→ 질문의 **should employees contact**
지문의 **To post these notices**
→ 정답의 **To have their notices approved**

171 세부 사항

번역 게시판을 주기적으로 점검하는 이유는?

(A) 캐비닛이 잠겨 있는지 확인하려고
(B) 개인 물품이 판매되었는지 확인하려고
(C) 게시물이 각 위치에 적합한지 확인하려고
(D) 전 직원에게 흥미로운 게시물인지 확인하려고

해설 마지막 단락에서 모든 게시판이 의도된 용도에 맞게 사용될 수 있도록(to ensure compliance with their intended purposes) 주기적으로 점검할 예정이라고 했으므로, (C)가 정답이다.

▸▸ **Paraphrasing** 지문의 **to ensure compliance with their intended purposes** → 정답의 **To ensure that postings are appropriate at each location**

172-175 온라인 채팅

실시간 채팅

사토루 하시모토 (오전 10시 42분):
[172]**우수 고객 보상 프로그램 계정에 막 접속했는데 지난달 그랜드 주롱 호텔에 묵었던 숙박 일수가 적립되지 않았다는 것을 알게 되었어요. 제 우수 고객 포인트가 처리되는 중인가요?**

프랑카 루소 (오전 10시 44분):
고객 관리 센터에 연락 주셔서 감사합니다. 고객님 계정을 보니 현재 우수고객 포인트가 없네요. [175(A)/(C)]**포인트는 체크아웃한 후로부터 1년간 유효합니다.** [173]**그랜드 주롱의 한 사이 웡 씨를 이 대화에 초대해서 고객님의 호텔 숙박에 대해 확인할게요. 그가 예약을 검색할 수 있도록 숙박하신 날짜를 말씀해 주시겠어요?**

한 사이 웡 (오전 10시 46분):
이미 가지고 있어요. [173]**하시모토 씨가 3월 7일 체크인해서 4박 숙박하셨음을 확인해 드립니다.**

사토루 하시모토 (오전 10시 47분):
3월 7일부터 3월 11일까지에요.

프랑카 루소 (오전 10시 50분):
하시모토 씨, 고객님의 계정에 포인트를 추가했습니다. [175(B)]**새 포인트로 다음 달에 묵기로 예약하신 객실을 업그레이드하거나** 포인트를 적용해 향후 예약 시 1박을 무료로 숙박하실 수 있습니다. [174]**현재의 예약 업그레이드를 도와 드릴까요, 아니면 향후 숙박 예약을 도와 드릴까요?**

사토루 하시모토 (오전 10시 51분):
이번엔 안 쓸게요. 도와주셔서 고마워요!

어휘 guest loyalty program 우수 고객 보상 프로그램(단골 고객에게 포인트 적립, 할인 등의 혜택을 주는 제도) credit (금액을 계정에) 기입하다, 입금하다 process 처리하다 eligible ~할 수 있는, ~할 자격이 있는

172 세부 사항

번역 하시모토 씨가 고객 관리 부서에 연락한 이유는?

(A) 최근 숙박에 대한 의견을 제공하려고
(B) 우수 고객 포인트를 사용해 객실을 예약하려고
(C) 기존 예약을 바꾸려고
(D) 누락된 우수 고객 포인트에 관해 문의하려고

해설 하시모토 씨가 오전 10시 42분 메시지에서 우수 고객 보상 프로그램 계정에 자신이 지난달 그랜드 주롱 호텔에 묵었던 숙박 일수가 적립되지 않았다(the nights I stayed at the Grand Jurong Hotel ~ haven't been credited)는 문제점을 언급한 후, 우수 고객 포인트가 처리되고 있는지(Are my loyalty point being processed?) 문의했다. 따라서 (D)가 정답이다.

어휘 recent 최근의 existing 기존의

TEST 2

173 의도 파악

번역 오전 10시 46분에 웡 씨가 "이미 가지고 있어요"라고 적은 의도는 무엇인가?

(A) 정보를 찾았다.
(B) 루소 씨가 한 실수를 지적하고 있다.
(C) 하시모토 씨에게 전화를 하려고 한다.
(D) 하시모토 씨의 예약을 마무리하려고 한다.

해설 루소 씨가 오전 10시 44분 메시지에서 그랜드 주롱의 웡 씨를 대화에 초대해서 호텔 숙박에 대해 확인하겠다(I am adding Mr. Han Sai Wong ~ to confirm your stay at the hotel)고 한 후, 웡 씨가 예약을 검색할 수 있도록 하시모토 씨에게 언제 숙박했는지(What were the dates of your stay so that he can look up the reservation?) 물었다. 이에 대해 초대를 받은 웡 씨가 '이미 가지고 있어요(Already got it)'라고 한 후 루소 씨가 원했던 정보(Mr. Hashimoto stayed four nights with a check-in date of March 7)를 제공했다. 따라서 (A)가 정답이다.

174 세부 사항

번역 루소 씨가 하시모토 씨를 위해 하겠다고 제안한 일은?

(A) 추가 포인트 증정
(B) 환불
(C) 향후 숙박 시 업그레이드 제공
(D) 그의 계정을 다른 포인트 프로그램으로 이전

해설 루소 씨는 오전 10시 50분 메시지에서 하시모토 씨에게 새로 적립된 포인트로 다음 달에 숙박하기로 예약한 방을 업그레이드할 수 있다(you are eligible to ~ upgrade your room for the stay you reserved next month)고 말한 후, 해당 예약을 업그레이드해 주길 원하는지(May I assist you in upgrading your current reservation) 물었다. 따라서 (C)가 정답이다.

▸▸ Paraphrasing 지문의 **the stay you reserved next month**
→ 정답의 **a future stay**

175 사실 관계 확인

번역 우수 고객 포인트 프로그램에 관해 명시되지 않은 것은?

(A) 숙박으로 획득한 포인트는 1년간 계속 유효하다.
(B) 포인트를 예약 업그레이드에 사용할 수 있다.
(C) 투숙객이 호텔을 떠난 뒤 포인트가 적립된다.
(D) 일정한 조건에서는 포인트가 2배가 될 수 있다.

해설 루소 씨가 쓴 오전 10시 44분 메시지의 '포인트는 체크아웃한 후로부터 1년간 유효하다(Points are good for one year after the check-out date)'에서 (A)와 (C)를, 오전 10시 50분 메시지의 '새 포인트로 다음 달에 숙박하기로 예약한 객실을 업그레이드할 수 있다(With your new points, you are eligible to ~ upgrade your room for the stay you reserved next month)'에서 (B)를 확인할 수 있다. 따라서 언급되지 않은 (D)가 정답이다.

▸▸ Paraphrasing 지문의 **Points are good for one year**
→ 보기 (A)의 **Points ~ remain valid for a year**
지문의 **after the check-out date**
→ 보기 (C)의 **after a guest leaves the hotel**

176-180 이메일 + 직원 편람

수신: 무나히드 아와드
발신: 애비 포다이스
제목: 정보
날짜: [178]**2월 2일**
첨부: 편람

아와드 씨께,

안녕하세요. 에프메딘 메디컬 서플라이즈에서의 첫날을 잘 [177]**보내고 계시길** 바랍니다.

[176]**당사의 고용 정책 및 관행에 대한 자세한 내용을 첨부하니 참고하십시오.** [179]**그건 그렇고, 이미 전용 주차 공간을 배정받으셨겠지만, 교통 운영부에 연락해 제시용 주차 허가증을 받으셔야 할 겁니다.**

지난주에 논의한 대로, 귀하가 다른 시설들을 방문하실 수 있도록 저희가 교통편을 준비해 드려야 합니다. [178]**다음 주에 본사로 첫 번째 출장을 가실 거고, 이후 월말에 나머지 시설들을 방문하시게 될 예정입니다.** 웬디 레이턴이 예약에 도움을 드릴 것이며, wleighton@epmedin.co.uk로 연락하시면 됩니다.

더 필요한 것이 있으면 제게 알려 주세요.

애비

어휘 employment 고용 practice 관행 assign 배정하다 permit 허가증 arrangement 준비 reach 연락하다

에프메딘 메디컬 서플라이즈
직원 편람

복장 규정

[180]**직장 복장 규정은 장소에 따라 다르다. 런던 본사와 글래스고 사무소 직원은 정장을 입어야 하며, 더블린과 벨파스트 제조 공장 직원은 간편복도 허용된다.** 정장은 재킷, 드레스 팬츠 또는 드레스 스커트, 넥타이(남성)가 포함된 비즈니스 슈트로 정의한다. 간편복은 바지 또는 카키 팬츠, 드레스 셔츠나 블라우스, 또는 드레스나 스커트다.

교통편

런던 사무소 주차 공간은 배송과 보안 차량용으로 지정되어 있다. 버스와 기차 월 정기권은 인사부를 통해 정가의 절반 가격에 구매할 수 있다.

글래스고와 더블린 생산 시설에는 현장 주차 공간이 제한되어 있으므로 직원은 지정된 주차장에 무료로 주차할 수 있다. 직원은 허가증이 필요하며, 이는 교통 운영부를 통해 얻을 수 있다. 허가증은 온라인에서 해마다 갱신해야 한다.

[179]**벨파스트 시설 직원은 지정 주차 공간을 쓰려면 교통 운영부에서 허가증을 받아야 한다.**

어휘 vary 다르다 headquarters 본사 attire 복장 approve 허용하다 define 정의하다 reserve 따로 두다 vehicle 차량 fare 요금 garage 주차장 obtain 얻다 renew 갱신하다 designated 지정된

176 주제 / 목적

번역 이메일의 목적 중 하나는?

(A) 축하 행사 초대장 발급
(B) 정책 변경 공지
(C) 회사 문서 전달
(D) 휴가 요청 승인

해설 이메일 두 번째 단락에서 회사의 고용 정책 및 관행에 대한 자세한 내용을 첨부하며 참고하라(Please find ~ our employment policies and practices attached)고 했으므로, 이메일을 보낸 목적 중 하나가 회사 문서를 전달하기 위함임을 알 수 있다. 따라서 (C)가 정답이다.

▸▸ Paraphrasing 지문의 our employment policies and practices → 정답의 a company document

177 동의어 찾기

번역 이메일에서 첫 번째 단락 1행의 "going"과 의미가 가장 가까운 단어는?

(A) 출발하는
(B) 진행되고 있는
(C) 판매하는
(D) 방문하는

해설 "going"이 포함된 문장은 '첫날을 잘 보내고 있길 바란다'라는 내용으로, 여기서 going은 '되는, 되어 가는'이라는 뜻으로 쓰였다. 따라서 '진행되고 있는'이라는 의미의 (B) proceeding이 정답이다.

178 사실 관계 확인

번역 아와드 씨에 관해 명시된 것은?

(A) 직원 편람을 수정했다.
(B) 레이턴 씨를 만났다.
(C) 대중교통을 타고 출근한다.
(D) 2월에 출장을 갈 예정이다.

해설 이메일의 세 번째 단락에서 아와드 씨가 다음 주에 본사로 첫 번째 출장을 가고, 이후 월말에 나머지 시설들을 방문할 예정(Your first trip will be to our headquarters next week, followed by visits ~ at the end of the month)이라고 했다. 이메일이 작성된 날짜(Date: 2 February)를 보면, 아와드 씨의 출장이 2월에 있을 예정임을 확인할 수 있으므로, (D)가 정답이다.

179 연계

번역 아와드 씨는 어디에서 일하겠는가?

(A) 런던
(B) 글래스고
(C) 더블린
(D) 벨파스트

해설 이메일의 두 번째 단락에서 전용 주차 공간을 받았더라도 교통 운영부에 연락해 제시용 주차 허가증을 받아야 한다(you will need to contact the transportation operations department to obtain a parking permit for display purposes)고 했다. 직원 편람의 '교통편(Transportation)' 부분 마지막 단락을 보면, 벨파스트 시설 직원은 지정된 주차 공간을 쓰려면 교통 운영부에서 허가증을 받아야 한다(Employees at the Belfast facility must obtain a permit ~ from the transportation operations department)고 되어 있다. 따라서 아와드 씨가 벨파스트 시설에서 근무한다고 추론할 수 있으므로, (D)가 정답이다.

180 세부 사항

번역 편람에 의하면, 모든 에프메딘 사무소의 공통점은?

(A) 주차장을 쓸 수 없다.
(B) 주차 허가증이 필요 없다.
(C) 직원은 특정 복장 규정을 지켜야 한다.
(D) 공장 직원들은 매우 엄격한 안전 규정을 따른다.

해설 직원 편람의 '복장 규정(Dress Code)' 부분에서 직장 복장 규정은 장소에 따라 다르다(Workplace dress codes vary by location)고 한 후, 각 지역별 복장 규정(Headquarters in London and the Glasgow office ~ formal business attire, while business casual attire ~ our Dublin and Belfast manufacturing plants)을 명시했다. 따라서 (C)가 정답이다.

어휘 comply with ~을 지키다 strict 엄격한 regulation 규정

▸▸ Paraphrasing 지문의 dress codes vary by location → 정답의 specific dress codes

181-185 이메일 + 안건

수신: 경영진
발신: 피오나 왓슨
날짜: 3월 19일
제목: 춘계 회의
첨부: 최종 안건

동료들께,

콘티에라사의 춘계 관리자 회의가 내일 오전 9시로 예정되어 있음을 알려 드립니다. 최종 안건을 첨부합니다. 181/182**제가 원래 회의 안건에 한 가지 항목을 추가했다는 점 유념하십시오.** 182/185**출판물 관리자인 마이 트란이 모두에게 이번 시즌 제품군에 대해 알려 주고 싶어 합니다.** 181**20분 이상 걸리지는 않을 겁니다.**

회의를 준비하기 위해, 가장 최근의 마케팅 계획을 검토해 모두 이번 분기의 목표를 명확히 숙지하도록 하십시오. 183**또한 각자 최신 예산 보고서 사본과 다음 분기 예상 비용 견적을 가져오시면 도움이 되겠습니다.**

내일 뵙겠습니다.

피오나 왓슨

어휘 agenda 안건 publication 출판(물) quarter 분기 budget 예산(안) projected 예상되는 estimate 견적(서)

춘계 관리자 회의 – 최종 안건		
날짜와 시간: 3월 20일 오전 9시 장소: 2회의실		
주제	**설명**	**진행자**
지역 행사	– 지역 봉사활동 기회 알아보기	[184]**폴 래니어, 아버빌 비즈니스 협회 회장**
예산안 검토	– 부서 예산안 토의	피오나 왓슨
온라인 광고	– 웹 광고 비용 검토 – 성장 분야 분석	마르샤 도버
웹사이트 업데이트	– 스키복 페이지 최근 변경 사항 발표 – 새 콘텐트 관리 소프트웨어 시연	베리 캘러핸
[182]**출판물 출간**	– [185]**춘계 스포츠웨어 카탈로그 최종 변경 사항 검토**	[182]**마이 트란**

어휘 community 지역 (사회) outreach 봉사[지원]활동 opportunity 기회 analyze 분석하다 present 발표하다 apparel 의류 demonstrate 시연하다

181 추론 / 암시

번역 이메일에서 왓슨 씨가 회의에 관해 암시하는 것은?

(A) 일부 고객이 참석할 것이다.
(B) 최근 고용된 관리자가 진행할 것이다.
(C) 당초 계획보다 시간이 더 걸릴 것이다.
(D) 장소가 변경되었다.

해설 이메일의 첫 번째 단락에서 원래 회의 안건에 한 가지 항목을 추가했다(Please note that I have added an item to the original meeting agenda)고 한 후 20분 이상 걸리지는 않을 것(She should not take more than twenty minutes)이라고 했다. 따라서 회의가 당초 계획보다 더 길어질 것임을 추론할 수 있으므로, (C)가 정답이다.

182 연계

번역 안건에서 새로운 항목은?

(A) 지역 행사
(B) 온라인 광고
(C) 웹사이트 업데이트
(D) 출판물 출간

해설 이메일의 첫 번째 단락에서 원래 회의 안건에 한 가지 항목을 추가했다(Please note that I have added an item to the original meeting agenda)고 한 후, 출판물 관리자인 마이 트란이 모두에게 이번 시즌 제품군에 대해 알려 주고 싶어 한다(Mai Tran ~ wants to update everyone on this season's product line)고 덧붙였다. 안건 목록의 마지막 항목을 보면 트란 씨가 출판물 출간(Print publications) 관련 회의를 진행한다는 것을 확인할 수 있으므로, (D)가 정답이다.

183 세부 사항

번역 왓슨 씨가 사람들에게 회의에 가져오라고 요청하는 것은?

(A) 업데이트된 재무 관련 서류
(B) 신입 사원 목록
(C) 안건 사본
(D) 수정된 판매 업자 계약서

해설 이메일의 두 번째 단락에서 각자 최신 예산 보고서 사본과 다음 분기 예상 비용 견적(copies of your latest budget report and projected cost estimates for next quarter)을 가져오길 바란다고 했으므로, (A)가 정답이다.

▸▸ **Paraphrasing** 지문의 **copies of your latest budget report and projected cost estimates**
→ 정답의 **Updated financial documents**

184 사실 관계 확인

번역 안건에서 래니어 씨에 관해 명시된 것은?

(A) 온라인 광고 강좌를 가르친다.
(B) 전화로 회의에 합류할 것이다.
(C) 과거 왓슨 씨와 함께 일한 적이 있다.
(D) 지역 단체를 대표한다.

해설 안건의 진행자(Leader) 목록을 보면, 첫 번째 진행자인 폴 래니어 씨가 아버빌 비즈니스 협회 회장(president of the Arborville Business Association)이라고 나와 있다. 따라서 (D)가 정답이다.

어휘 represent 대표하다

▸▸ **Paraphrasing** 지문의 **president of the Arborville Business Association**
→ 정답의 **represents a local organization**

185 연계

번역 콘티에라사는 무엇을 판매하겠는가?

(A) 책과 잡지
(B) 원예용품
(C) 운동복
(D) 컴퓨터 소프트웨어

해설 이메일의 첫 번째 단락에서 출판물 관리자인 마이 트란이 모두에게 이번 시즌 제품군에 대해 알려 주고 싶어 한다(Mai Tran ~ wants to update everyone on this season's product line)고 했다. 안건에서 해당 회의 주제에 대해 설명한 부분(Despcription)을 보면, 콘티에라사의 상품군이 스포츠웨어(sportswear)임을 알 수 있다. 따라서 (C)가 정답이다.

▸▸ **Paraphrasing** 지문의 **sportswear** → 정답의 **Athletic clothing**

186-190 기사 + 이메일 + 프로그램

영화제 웨일스로 돌아오다

스완지(5월 24일) – 펜글레스 영화제가 흥미진진한 새 영화 후보작들과 함께 도시로 돌아온다. 이 영화제는 수년간 인재들을 유치해 국제적으로 인정받고 있다. [186]**또한 점점 더 많은 유명 영화 제작자들이 경력을 쌓는 발판이 되어 오고 있다고 자랑한다.**

1주일간 열리는 영화제는 8월 9일부터 15일까지 진행될 예정이며 애니메이션, 다큐멘터리, 장편 영화 등을 선보인다. [188]**영화제는 초청자만 참석하는 8월 15일 폐막 행사를 제외하고 일반에 공개된다.** 모든 일반 행사 티켓은 미리 구입해야 하며 빨리 매진될 것으로 예상된다.

티켓 판매는 6월 3일 오전 10시에 시작된다. 개별 영화 상영 티켓은 별도로 구입해야 한다는 점 유의해야 한다.

전체 상영 일정은 현재 영화제 웹사이트 www.penglaisfest.co.uk에서 볼 수 있다.

어휘 slate 후보자[작] 명단 gain 얻다 recognition 인정 attract 유치하다 boast of ~을 자랑하다 celebrity 유명 인사 feature film 장편 (특작) 영화 with the exception of ~을 제외하고 individual 개별의 separately 별도로

이메일

수신: 데스몬드 그리피스 〈d_griffith@docsnow.co.uk〉
발신: 요안 드리스콜 〈ioan.driscoll@penglaisfest.co.uk〉
제목: Re: 펜글레스 시상식
날짜: 5월 28일

그리피스 씨께,

[187]**귀하가 올해 펜글레스 시상식에서 직접 수상하실 수 있다는 소식을 듣게 되어 설레고 영광스럽습니다.** [188]**시상식은 8월 15일 금요일 오후 5시에 윈포드 블루 호텔에서 열립니다.** [190]**영화제 위원장인 사라 우 씨의 소개를 받고 연설할 수 있는 기회를 가지실 겁니다.** 연설을 10분 이내로 제한해 주실 것을 정중히 부탁드립니다.

시상식에 초대하고 싶은 내빈의 이메일 주소를 5명까지 알려 주세요. 행사 10일 이내에 전자 기기로 티켓을 다운로드할 수 있는 링크를 모두에게 꼭 보내도록 하겠습니다.

축하합니다.

요안 드리스콜

어휘 in person 직접, 몸소 take place 일어나다 ceremony 기념식 electronically 전자기기로, 인터넷으로

제25회 연례 펜글레스 영화제 시상식
행사 프로그램

오후 5:00 개막
오후 5:30 만찬 서비스 시작
오후 6:00 [189]**셜리 핀치 공연, 돔 루카스 피아노 반주**
오후 6:15 최우수 연기상 시상
오후 6:30 감독상 시상
오후 6:45 최고 촬영상 시상
오후 7:00 [190]**공로상 소개, 사라 우 씨**
오후 7:10 [190]**공로상 수상자 연설**
오후 7:20 폐회사
오후 7:30 [189]**셜리 핀치 마지막 공연, 솔로**

어휘 performance 공연 direction 감독 cinematography 촬영술 lifetime achievement award 공로상

186 사실 관계 확인

번역 펜글레스 영화제에 관해 명시된 것은?
(A) 웨일스에서 처음 열린다.
(B) 다수의 과거 참가자들이 유명해졌다.
(C) 과거의 고전 영화에 집중한다.
(D) 장편 영화 티켓은 매진되었다.

해설 기사의 첫 번째 단락에서 펜글레스 영화제가 점점 더 많은 유명 영화 제작자들이 경력을 쌓는 발판이 되어 오고 있다(It also boasts of having launched the careers of a growing number of celebrity filmmakers)고 했다. 따라서 (B)가 정답이다.

어휘 participant 참가자

187 세부 사항

번역 드리스콜 씨가 기뻐하는 이유는?
(A) 상을 받을 것이다.
(B) 자신의 영화가 영화제에 상영 예정이다.
(C) 그리피스 씨가 행사에 참석할 것이다.
(D) 그리피스 씨가 그를 연설에 초청했다.

해설 이메일의 첫 번째 단락에서 그리피스 씨가 펜글레스 시상식에서 직접 수상할 수 있다(you will be able to accept your prize in person at ~ Penglais Award Ceremony)는 소식을 듣게 되어 설레고 영광스럽다고 했다. 따라서 (C)가 정답이다.

▸▸ **Paraphrasing** 지문의 **excited and honoured**
→ 질문의 **pleased**
지문의 **accept your prize in person at ~ Penglais Award Ceremony**
→ 정답의 **attend an event**

188 연계

번역 시상식 티켓에 관해 암시된 것은?
(A) 구매할 수 없다.
(B) 온라인으로 이용할 수 없다.
(C) 5월 3일에 구입이 가능해진다.
(D) 개별 영화 티켓 구매 시 포함된다.

해설 이메일의 첫 번째 단락에서 시상식은 8월 15일 금요일 오후 5시에 윈포드 블루 호텔에서 열린다(The ceremony will take place ~ on Friday, 15 August)고 했는데, 기사의 두 번째 단락을 보면 8월 15일 폐막 행사는 초청받은 사람만 참석할 수 있다(the closing event on 15 August, which is by invitation only)고 나와 있다. 따라서 (A)가 정답이다.

189 추론 / 암시

번역 셜리 핀치는 누구이겠는가?

(A) 행사 진행자
(B) 연예인
(C) 시상자
(D) 영화제 감독

해설 프로그램을 보면, 셜리 핀치가 오후 6시(Performance by Shirley Finch, accompanied by Dom Lucas on piano)와 오후 7시 30분(Final Performance by Shirley Finch, solo)에 공연을 한다고 적혀 있다. 따라서 (B)가 정답이다.

190 연계

번역 그리피스 씨는 무슨 상을 받겠는가?

(A) 연기상
(B) 최고 촬영상
(C) 공로상
(D) 감독상

해설 이메일의 첫 번째 단락에서 그리피스 씨가 영화제 위원장인 사라 우 씨의 소개를 받고 연설할 수 있는 기회를 가질 것(You will be introduced by ~ Ms. Sarah Wu, and you will have the opportunity to give a speech)이라고 했다. 프로그램에 따르면 우 씨의 소개를 받고(Introduction of Lifetime Achievement Award by Ms. Sarah Wu) 연설을 하는 수상자는(Speech by Lifetime Achievement Award Recipient) 공로상을 받는 사람이므로, (C)가 정답이다.

191-195 이메일 + 편지 + 이메일

수신: a.raman@bgi.co.in
발신: s.kapoor@imail.co.in
날짜: 4월 15일
제목: 감사 편지

라만 씨께,

제가 닐라 광고 직책에 지원하도록 격려해 주시고 저를 그토록 극찬하는 추천서를 써 주셔서 감사합니다.

191/192/193**닐라의 수석 채용 담당관인 니르말 씨는 제가 델리 웍스를 위해 제작한 텔레비전 광고를 칭찬했지만, 그의 회사는 사실상 웹 콘텐트와 애플리케이션도 만들 수 있는 사람이 필요하다고 설명했습니다.** 191**따라서 저는 그 자리를 제안받지 못했습니다.**

저에게 적합해 보이는 다른 자리를 혹시 보시면 알려 주셨으면 합니다. 미리 감사드립니다.

슈레야

어휘 encourage 격려하다 glowing 극찬하는 referral 추천서 behalf 자기편, 지지 admiration 칭찬 commercial 광고 fit 딱 맞는 것, 적합한 사람

5월 17일

슈레야 카푸르
함맘 가 21번지
뭄바이

카푸르 씨께,

194**귀하가 6월 1일 뭄바이 캐닝사에 입사하시게 되어 기쁩니다.** 저희 사무실에서 면접 시 보여 주신 식견에 감탄했습니다. 192/193**델리 웍스 사에서 쌓으신 특별한 경험이 이곳에서 굉장한 가치를 지니게 될 것입니다.**

첫날 오전 9시 30분에 인사부에 보고할 때 작성하고 서명해서 갖고 오셔야 할 서류를 동봉합니다. 그때 간단한 행정 관련 오리엔테이션을 받으시게 됩니다. 193**담당 멘토인 미라 세티 씨가 10시 30분에 그곳에서 귀하를 맞이해 부서로 안내할 예정이며, 그곳에서 교육 계획과 팀이 현재 진행하고 있는 프로젝트를 다시 한번 알려 드릴 것입니다.** 194**정오에는 동료 몇 사람과 함께 점심식사를 하기 위해 회사 구내식당으로 귀하를 모셔갈 것입니다. 저도 거기서 합류했으면 합니다.**

뭄바이 캐닝사에 오신 것을 환영합니다!

자라 메타
뭄바이 캐닝사

어휘 tremendous 엄청난 complete 작성하다 administrative 행정의 assigned 배정된 currently 현재

수신: a.raman@bgi.co.in
발신: s.kapoor@imail.co.in
날짜: 5월 20일
제목: 희소식

라만 씨께,

지난번 추천서 감사합니다. 195**면접 도중 이사님이 그 자리를 제안하셨고, 저는 6월 1일에 근무를 시작합니다.** 자리가 잡히면 제 업무에 대한 자세한 내용을 기꺼이 알려 드리겠습니다.

슈레야

어휘 duty 업무 settle 자리 잡다, 정착하다

191 세부 사항

번역 카푸르 씨가 닐라 광고 직책에 불합격한 이유는?

(A) 적합한 추천서를 제공하지 못했다.
(B) 자리에 맞는 자격을 충족하지 못했다.
(C) 지원 마감일을 놓쳤다.
(D) 후속 면접에 갈 수 없었다.

해설 카푸르 씨가 쓴 첫 번째 이메일의 두 번째 단락을 보면, 닐라 광고가 웹 콘텐트와 애플리케이션도 만들 수 있는 사람(someone who can also create Web content and applications)을 필요로 해서 자신이 일자리를 제안받지 못했다(I was therefore not offered the position)고 했다. 따라서 (B)가 정답이다.

어휘 adequate 적합한 criteria 자격, 조건, 기준

▸▸ Paraphrasing 지문의 was not offered the position
→ 질문의 was turned down for a position
지문의 who can also create Web content and applications
→ 정답의 the criteria for the job

192 연계

번역 카푸르 씨에 관해 암시된 것은?

(A) 몇 해 전 자신의 직장인 델리 웍스사를 떠났다.
(B) 과거에 델리 웍스사에서 니르말 씨와 함께 일한 적이 있다.
(C) 뭄바이 캐닝사에서 텔레비전 광고를 만들 것이다.
(D) 최근 직업을 바꾸었다.

해설 편지의 첫 번째 단락에서 카푸르 씨가 델리 웍스사에서 쌓은 경험이 뭄바이 캐닝사에서 굉장한 가치를 지니게 될 것(Your specific experience ~ will be of tremendous value)이라고 했다. 카푸르 씨가 쓴 첫 번째 이메일의 두 번째 단락을 보면, 그녀가 델리 웍스 텔레비전 광고를 제작했음(the television commercials I produced for Delhi Works)을 알 수 있다. 따라서 카푸르 씨가 뭄바이 캐닝사에서도 텔레비전 광고를 만들 것임을 추론할 수 있으므로, (C)가 정답이다.

193 연계

번역 세티 씨는 누구이겠는가?

(A) 구내식당 매니저
(B) 급여 담당 경리
(C) 마케팅 팀원
(D) 예산 담당 이사

해설 편지의 두 번째 단락에서 담당 멘토인 세티 씨가 카푸르 씨를 부서로 안내할 예정이며, 그곳에서 교육 계획과 팀이 현재 진행하고 있는 프로젝트를 다시 한번 알려 줄 예정(Your assigned mentor, Ms. Meera Sethi ~ will review your training plan and the projects the team is currently working on)이라고 했다. 카푸르 씨는 광고를 제작하는 업무를 하게 될 것이므로, 카푸르 씨의 멘토인 세티 씨 역시 광고 관련 부서에서 근무한다고 추론할 수 있다. 따라서 (C)가 정답이다.

194 세부 사항

번역 편지에 의하면, 6월 1일 정오에 메타 씨는 어디에 있겠는가?

(A) 디자인 회의
(B) 출장
(C) 취업 면접
(D) 식당

해설 메타 씨가 쓴 편지의 첫 번째 단락을 보면, 6월 1일이 카푸르 씨가 뭄바이 캐닝사에 입사하는 날(you will be joining Mumbai Canning Ltd. on 1 June)임을 확인할 수 있다. 두 번째 단락에서 그날 정오에 세티 씨가 카푸르 씨를 회사 구내식당으로 데려갈 예정(At noon she will be taking you to our cafeteria for lunch)이며 자신도 거기서 합류하고 싶다(I hope to join you there as well)고 했으므로, (D)가 정답이다.

▸▸ Paraphrasing 지문의 cafeteria → 정답의 dining facility

195 세부 사항

번역 카푸르 씨는 어떻게 새 일자리를 제안받았는가?

(A) 직접
(B) 편지로
(C) 이메일로
(D) 전화로

해설 두 번째 이메일의 두 번째 문장에서 면접 도중 이사가 그 자리를 제안했다(The director offered me the position during our interview)고 했으므로, (A)가 정답이다.

▸▸ Paraphrasing 지문의 The director offered me the position during our interview → 정답의 In person

196-200 이메일 + 회람 + 이메일

수신: 경진 손
발신: 다리우스 잭슨
날짜: 11월 8일
제목: 문제에 대한 해법

손 씨께,

[196]**아시다시피, 프린터를 사용하기 위한 경쟁으로 인해 법무팀 팀원들에게 상당한 지연이 초래되고 있습니다.** 어느 시점에서부터인가 모두가 문서를 출력하기 위해 기다려야 하게 되었습니다. [196]**우리 중 몇몇은 더 일찍 출근해야 하기 시작했고, 다른 사람들은 늦게까지 남아 있습니다.** 이는 생산성과 의욕에 부정적인 영향을 미치고 있죠.

프린터 옆에 신청표를 붙여 올해 남은 기간 동안 이러한 상황을 개선할 수 있습니다. [197]**공정하게 하려면, 직원마다 하루에 15분씩 두 구간만 신청해야 합니다.** 또한 점심시간은 예정에 없던 출력을 위해 따로 비워 둘 수 있습니다. 그리고 상황이 통제될 때까지 컬러 프린터의 사용을 중단하는 것도 고려해야 합니다. 컬러 출력은 흑백 출력보다 최대 5배 비싸거든요. 여러분의 의견을 알려 주세요.

다리우스 잭슨

법무팀 서무, 리더 앤 켈터사

어휘 competition 경쟁 impact 영향 productivity 생산성 morale 사기, 의욕 remainder 남은 것 fair 공정한 reserve 따로 비워 두다 discontinue 중단하다 expensive 비싼

TEST 2

회람

수신: 리더 앤 켈터사 전 직원
발신: 경진 손, 총무 담당자
날짜: 11월 24일
제목: 프린터 사용

[199]**멀티컬러 UX212와 흑백 UY120 트루징스 두 대의 새 프린터를 구입했습니다.** 프린터들은 아쉽게도 12월 18일이 되어야 도착합니다. 그동안 11월 10일에 제가 보낸 온라인 링크를 사용해 계속해서 프린터 사용 시간 일정을 잡아 주시기 바랍니다. [197]**이 문서를 사용해서 하루에 최대 15분의 출력 기간을 두 번까지 예약할 수 있습니다.** 시간을 연달아 예약하지 마시고, 비상 출력을 위해 오전과 오후 모두에 시간을 따로 확보해 두었다는 점 기억하십시오. 또한 컬러 프린터는 반드시 필요한 경우에만 사용하십시오. [198]**흑백 프린터가 사용 중일 때 직원들이 컬러 프린터를 사용해 스캔하고 출력하기 때문에 컬러 잉크를 평소보다 더 많이 구입해오고 있습니다.**

어휘 purchase 구입하다 unfortunately 아쉽게도 consecutive 연이은 set aside 따로 떼어 두다 emergency 비상, 긴급 absolutely 정말로, 반드시 necessary 필요한

수신: kjsohn@reederandkelter.com
발신: lsullivan@truzynx.com
날짜: 12월 22일
제목: 트루징스 구입

손 씨께,

[199]**최근 트루징스 프린터 두 대를 구입해 주셔서 감사합니다.** 구매에는 각 기계에 대해 2년간의 무상 유지 보수 서비스가 포함됩니다. [199]**첫 정기 서비스 날짜는 배송일로부터 한 달 후입니다.** 저희는 또한 장비 구입 후 60일 동안은 연장된 유지 보수 서비스 플랜을 할인된 가격에 제공합니다. 새 프린터를 위한 이 플랜에 관심 있으시면 알려 주시기 바랍니다.

효율성을 개선하고 싶으신가요? [200]**저희에게는 트루즈플랜도 있습니다. 이 저렴한 원격 출력 서비스를 통해 스캔한 문서를 안전하게 출력해 필요할 때 사무실로 가져다 드립니다.** 더 자세한 정보를 원하시면 말씀해 주십시오.

릴라니 설리반
영업 사원

어휘 maintenance 유지 보수 delivery 배송 extended 연장된 efficiency 효율성 affordable (가격이) 알맞은, 저렴한

196 세부 사항

번역 첫 번째 이메일에 의하면, 일부 직원들이 문제에 대처하는 방법은?

(A) 운영비를 절감해서
(B) 정규 시간 이외에 근무해서
(C) 임시직을 고용해서
(D) 유지 보수 서비스를 외부에 위탁해서

해설 첫 번째 이메일의 첫 번째 단락에서 프린터 사용 경쟁으로 초래된 업무 지연(competition for use of the printers has been causing a great deal of delay)으로 인해 직원들 중 몇몇은 더 일찍 출근해야 하기 시작했고, 다른 사람들은 늦게까지 남아 있다(Some of us have had to start coming to work earlier, and others are staying late)고 했다. 따라서 (B)가 정답이다.

어휘 temporary 임시의 outsource 외주로 돌리다, 외부에 위탁하다

▸▸ Paraphrasing 지문의 **coming to work earlier, staying late**
→ 정답의 **working outside their regular hours**

197 연계

번역 잭슨 씨의 제안 중 손 씨가 실행한 것은?

(A) 직원에게 하루 두 차례 15분간 출력 허용하기
(B) 비상 출력으로 정오에 1시간 할당하기
(C) 프린터 옆에 신청표 붙이기
(D) 컬러 프린터 사용 중단하기

해설 첫 번째 이메일의 두 번째 단락에서 잭슨 씨는 직원마다 하루에 15분씩 두 구간만 신청해야 한다(each employee should sign up for only two fifteen-minute blocks per day)고 제안했다. 손 씨가 쓴 회람의 중반부를 보면, 15분의 출력 기간을 하루에 최대 두 번까지 예약할 수 있다(you may reserve up to two fifteen-minute printing periods per day)고 했으므로, (A)가 정답이다. 아침과 오후에 비상 출력이 가능하고(set aside time both in the morning and in the afternoon for emergency printing), 사용 신청은 온라인 링크로 할 수 있으며(schedule your printer-use times using the online link), 필요시 컬러 프린터를 사용할 수 있으므로(use the color printers only when ~ necessary), 나머지 보기는 오답이다.

198 세부 사항

번역 회람에 의하면, 컬러 프린터의 문제는?

(A) 주문이 되지 않았다.
(B) 자주 고장 난다.
(C) 문서 스캔이 안 된다.
(D) 지나치게 사용되고 있다.

해설 회람의 후반부에서 흑백 프린터가 사용 중일 때 직원들이 컬러 프린터를 사용해 스캔하고 출력하기(staff members are using the color printers ~ when the black-and-white printers are in use) 때문에 컬러 잉크를 평소보다 더 많이 구입해오고 있다(We have been purchasing more color ink than usual)고 했다. 따라서 (D)가 정답이다.

199 연계

번역 리더 앤 켈터사가 구입한 새 프린터들에 관해 사실인 것은?

(A) 11월 24일에 배송되었다.
(B) 3년 유지 보수 계획이 포함된다.
(C) 1월 18일에 서비스를 받을 것이다.
(D) 처음 한 달은 무료 원격 출력이 제공된다.

해설 회람의 초반부에서 리더 앤 켈터사가 구매한 두 대의 프린터(We have purchased two new printers)가 12월 18일이 되어야 도착한다(they will not be arriving until December 18)고 했다. 두 번째 이메일의 첫 번째 단락을 보면, 최근 리더 앤 켈터사가 구입한 프린터(Thank you for your recent purchase of two Truzynx printers for your company)의 첫 정기 서비스 날짜는 배송일로부터 한 달이 지난 시점(Your first regularly scheduled servicing date will be one month from delivery)이라고 쓰여 있다. 따라서 1월 18일에 첫 정기 서비스를 받을 것임을 알 수 있으므로, (C)가 정답이다.

200 세부 사항

번역 트루즈플랜이 제공하는 것은?

(A) 출력 문서 배송
(B) 장비 보험
(C) 부속품 제안
(D) 장비 사용 교육

해설 두 번째 이메일의 두 번째 단락에서 '트루즈플랜(Truzplan)'이라는 저렴한 원격 출력 서비스를 통해 스캔한 문서를 안전하게 출력하여 사무실로 가져다 줄 수 있다(we can securely print your scanned documents and bring them to your office)고 했다. 따라서 (A)가 정답이다.

▸▸ **Paraphrasing** 지문의 **print your scanned documents and bring them to your office**
→ 정답의 **Delivery of printed documents**

기출 TEST 3

101 (C)	102 (B)	103 (D)	104 (D)	105 (A)
106 (A)	107 (C)	108 (D)	109 (B)	110 (A)
111 (D)	112 (C)	113 (C)	114 (D)	115 (A)
116 (A)	117 (B)	118 (C)	119 (D)	120 (A)
121 (C)	122 (A)	123 (C)	124 (B)	125 (A)
126 (B)	127 (B)	128 (D)	129 (B)	130 (C)
131 (D)	132 (D)	133 (B)	134 (A)	135 (B)
136 (A)	137 (C)	138 (D)	139 (D)	140 (A)
141 (C)	142 (A)	143 (C)	144 (D)	145 (B)
146 (B)	147 (C)	148 (B)	149 (D)	150 (C)
151 (B)	152 (C)	153 (A)	154 (C)	155 (D)
156 (B)	157 (D)	158 (A)	159 (D)	160 (B)
161 (B)	162 (A)	163 (D)	164 (D)	165 (A)
166 (B)	167 (A)	168 (B)	169 (D)	170 (C)
171 (C)	172 (A)	173 (C)	174 (D)	175 (A)
176 (A)	177 (C)	178 (D)	179 (C)	180 (B)
181 (C)	182 (D)	183 (A)	184 (D)	185 (B)
186 (A)	187 (B)	188 (C)	189 (D)	190 (B)
191 (A)	192 (C)	193 (B)	194 (D)	195 (C)
196 (C)	197 (A)	198 (C)	199 (D)	200 (B)

PART 5

101 형용사 자리 _ 명사 수식

해설 빈칸이 동사 require와 명사 chairs 사이에 있으므로, 빈칸에는 chairs를 수식하는 형용사 또는 chairs와 복합명사를 이루는 명사가 들어갈 수 있다. 문맥상 의자가 더 필요할 것이라는 내용이 되어야 자연스러우므로, '추가적인'이라는 의미의 형용사 (C) additional이 정답이다. 명사 addition(s)은 '추가(물)'이라는 뜻으로 chairs와 복합명사를 이루지 않으며, (D) additionally는 부사로 품사상 빈칸에 들어갈 수 없다.

번역 행사 기획자는 화요일 포럼에 의자가 추가로 필요할 것이라고 판단했다.

어휘 determine 판단하다 require 필요(로) 하다

102 동사 어휘

해설 빈칸은 주어 she의 동사 자리로, more office supplies를 목적어로 취한다. 따라서 사람이 사무용품을 대상으로 하는 행위를 나타내는 동사가 들어가야 하므로, '주문하다'라는 의미의 (B) orders가 정답이다. (A) contains는 '포함하다, 억누르다', (C) writes는 '쓰다, 작성하다', (D) copies는 '복사하다, 모방하다'라는 뜻으로 모두 문맥상 빈칸에 적절하지 않다.

번역 후 씨는 사무용품을 더 주문하기 전에 수납장을 확인할 것이다.

어휘 storage closet 수납장 supplies 용품, 비품

103 명사 자리 _ 동사의 목적어

해설 빈칸은 소유격 their의 한정 수식을 받는 명사 자리로, acknowledge의 목적어 역할을 한다. 따라서 '참석, 참여'라는 의미의 명사 (D) participation이 정답이다. (A) participate와 (B) participates는 동사, (C) participated는 동사/과거분사로 모두 품사상 빈칸에 들어갈 수 없다.

번역 영업 사원 전원은 월요일 워크숍 참석 여부를 알려 주시기 바랍니다.

어휘 acknowledge 알리다, 인정하다

104 부사 자리 _ 최상급 강조

해설 빈칸 없이도 완전한 문장이며, 빈칸이 be동사와 주격 보어인 Sunn Agency's best advertisement 사이에 있으므로, 빈칸에는 부사가 들어가야 한다. 따라서 '단연, 확실히'라는 의미로 최상급 표현을 강조할 때 쓰이는 부사 (D) easily가 정답이다. (A) easy는 형용사의 원급, (C) easiest는 형용사의 최상급, (B) ease는 명사/동사로 품사상 빈칸에 들어갈 수 없다.

번역 저우즈 카페의 광고는 선 에이전시의 올해 광고 중 단연 최고였다.

어휘 commercial 광고 (방송) advertisement 광고

105 형용사 어휘

해설 빈칸은 불가산명사 perfume or cologne을 한정 수식하는 자리이므로, 불가산명사와 수가 일치하는 (A) any가 정답이다. 참고로, any는 불가산명사뿐만 아니라 단수 가산명사와 복수 가산명사 모두를 수식할 수 있다. (B) few와 (D) many는 복수 가산명사를 수식하며, '단일의'라는 의미의 (C) single은 「a + single + 단수명사」 구조로 쓰인다.

번역 쿠폰 코드 SAVE20을 사용해 향수나 콜론을 20퍼센트 할인된 가격에 구입하세요.

어휘 purchase 구입하다

106 명사 자리 _ 전치사의 목적어

해설 빈칸은 소유격 its와 형용사 main의 수식을 받는 명사 자리로, 전치사 with의 목적어 역할을 한다. 따라서 '경쟁 업체, 경쟁자'라는 의미의 명사 (A) competitor가 정답이다. (B) competing은 동명사/현재분사, (C) competitive는 형용사, (D) competitively는 부사로 빈칸에 들어갈 수 없다.

번역 톡-톡 휴대폰 회사는 곧 주요 경쟁 업체와 합병할 것이다.

어휘 merge 합병하다 competitive 경쟁하는, 경쟁력 있는 competitively 경쟁적으로

107 형용사 자리 _ 명사 수식

해설 빈칸은 the most와 함께 최상급을 이루어 marketing campaigns를 수식하는 형용사 자리이므로, '창의적인'이라는 의미의 형용사 (C) creative가 정답이다. (A) create는 동사, (B) creation은 명사, (D) creatively는 부사로 모두 품사상 빈칸에 들어갈 수 없다.

번역 엘리스 씨는 그 부서에서 가장 창의적인 마케팅 캠페인 중 하나를 기획했다.

어휘 department 부서

108 형용사 어휘

해설 빈칸은 received의 목적어 comments를 수식하는 형용사 자리로, 고객들로부터 받은 의견(comments from customers)을 가장 잘 묘사하는 형용사가 들어가야 한다. 따라서 '긍정적인, 호의적인'이라는 의미의 (D) positive가 정답이다. (A) eventual은 '궁극적인, 최종적인', (B) probable은 '있음직한, 그럴듯한', (C) close는 '가까운, 긴밀한'이라는 뜻으로 문맥상 빈칸에 적절하지 않다.

번역 지난달에 우리는 블로그에서 고객들로부터 긍정적인 의견을 많이 받았다.

어휘 receive 받다 numerous 많은

109 전치사 자리 _ 어휘

해설 빈칸은 명사구 each visit을 목적어로 취하는 전치사 자리로, 빈칸을 포함한 전치사구가 complete a short survey를 수식하고 있다. 문맥상 설문 조사를 작성하는 시점을 나타내는 전치사가 빈칸에 들어가야 자연스러우므로, '~ 후에'라는 뜻의 (B) after가 정답이다. (A) inside는 주로 장소를 나타내며, 시간 관련 표현 앞에 올 경우 '~ 이내에'라는 뜻으로 쓰인다. (C) where는 부사/대명사/접속사, (D) whenever는 부사/접속사로 품사상 빈칸에 들어갈 수 없다.

번역 8월 1일부터 환자들은 매번 방문 후 간단한 설문 조사를 작성하도록 요청받을 것이다.

어휘 patient 환자 complete 작성하다, 완료하다 survey 설문 조사

110 부사 자리 _ 동사 수식

해설 빈칸이 주어 역할을 하는 동명사구(Viewing ~ her door)와 동사 inspires 사이에 있으므로, 빈칸에는 동명사 Viewing 또는 동사 inspires를 수식하는 부사가 들어갈 수 있다. 따라서 '계속, 끊임없이'라는 의미의 부사 (A) continually가 정답이다. 참고로, continually는 문맥상 inspires를 수식한다. (B) continue는 동사, (C) continual은 형용사, (D) continued는 동사/과거분사로 품사상 빈칸에 들어갈 수 없다.

번역 자신의 문밖의 아름다운 풍경을 감상하는 일은 엘리아 콜라오가 계속 그림을 그리도록 영감을 불어넣는다.

어휘 landscape 풍경 inspire 영감을 불어넣다

111 명사 어휘

해설 빈칸은 동사 is done의 주어 역할을 하는 명사 자리로, 전치사구 of Jamy bicycles의 수식을 받는다. 자전거 부품은 중국에서 제조되지만(Although the parts are made in China) 다른 작업은 캐나다에서 이루어진다는 내용의 문장이므로, 빈칸에는 자전거 제작 과정과 관련된 명사가 들어가야 한다. 따라서 '조립'이라는 의미의 (D) assembly가 정답이다. (A) vision은 '시각, 통찰력', (B) meeting은 '회의, 만남', (C) approach는 '접근법, 처리 방법'이라는 뜻으로 모두 문맥상 빈칸에 적절하지 않다.

번역 제이미 자전거의 부품은 중국에서 제조되지만 조립은 캐나다에서 이루어진다.

어휘 part 부품

112 to부정사 _ 부사적 용법

해설 빈칸은 traffic congestion을 목적어로 취하면서 앞에 있는 완전한 절(Many business promote carpooling)을 수식하는 역할을 한다. 따라서 to부정사인 (C) to prevent가 정답이다. 해당 문장에 이미 동사(promote)가 있기 때문에 (A) is prevented, (B) prevent, (D) prevented는 빈칸에 들어갈 수 없다. (D) prevented를 과거분사로 본다고 하더라도 traffic congestion을 목적어로 취할 수 없으므로, (D)는 정답이 될 수 없다.

번역 많은 사업체들이 교통 체증을 막기 위해 카풀을 장려한다.

어휘 promote 장려하다 prevent 막다 traffic congestion 교통 체증

113 부사절 접속사

해설 빈칸 뒤 완전한 절(the repairs are complete)을 이끄는 접속사 자리이므로, '~할 때까지'라는 의미의 부사절 접속사 (C) Until이 정답이다. 참고로, until은 전치사로도 쓰일 수 있다. (A) Despite(~에도 불구하고)와 (D) During(~ 동안)은 전치사, (B) Finally(마침내, 마지막으로)는 부사로 완전한 절을 이끌 수 없다.

번역 수리가 완료될 때까지 건물에는 필수 인원만 들어갈 수 있다.

어휘 repair 수리 essential 필수적인 personnel 인원

114 명사 자리 _ 동사의 목적어

해설 빈칸은 동사 will deliver의 목적어 역할을 하는 명사 자리로, 배송의 대상이 되는 사물 명사가 들어가야 한다. 따라서 '교체품'이라는 의미의 명사 (D) replacements가 정답이다. (A) replacing은 동명사/현재분사, (B) replaces는 동사, (C) replaced는 동사/과거분사로 품사상 빈칸에 들어갈 수 없다.

번역 슬래롯 건축 소책자에 엉뚱한 색을 사용한 것에 대해 사과드리며 금요일에 교체품을 배송하겠습니다.

어휘 apologize for ~에 대해 사과하다 architecture 건축 brochure 소책자 deliver 배송하다

115 부사 어휘

해설 동사 store를 적절히 수식하는 부사를 선택하는 문제이다. 공구 보관(store all tools)과 관련하여 당부하는 내용의 문장이므로, '적절히, 제대로'라는 의미의 (A) properly가 정답이다. (B) restfully는 '편안하게', (C) truly는 '진심으로, 엄밀하게', (D) finely는 '멋지게, 섬세하게'라는 뜻으로 문맥상 빈칸에 적절하지 않다.

번역 직원들은 교대 근무 후 모든 공구를 적절히 보관해야 한다.

어휘 employee 직원 store 보관하다 tool 공구 shift 교대 근무

116 명사 어휘

해설 빈칸은 동사 was submitted의 주어 역할을 하는 명사 자리로, to부정사구(to renovate the old factory)의 수식을 받는다. 따라서 빈칸에는 공장 보수를 위해 시 의회에 제출된 것을 나타내는 명사가 들어가야 하므로, '신청서, 지원서'라는 의미의 (A) application이 정답이다. (B) establishment는 '기관, 설립', (C) experience는 '경험, 경력', (D) accomplishment는 '성취, 업적'이라는 뜻으로 문맥상 빈칸에 적절하지 않다.

번역 오래된 그 공장을 보수하겠다는 신청서가 시 의회에 제출되었다.

어휘 application 신청(서) renovate 보수하다 submit 제출하다 council 의회

117 관계대명사 _ 주격

해설 빈칸은 주어가 없는 불완전한 절(wish to return a defective item)을 이끄는 접속사 자리로, 빈칸이 이끄는 절이 Customers를 수식하고 있다. 따라서 사람 명사(Customers)를 대신하여 불완전한 절의 주어 역할을 할 수 있는 관계대명사가 빈칸에 들어가야 하므로, (B) who가 정답이다. (A) whose는 소유격 관계대명사로 뒤에 명사가 와야 하며, (C) which는 사물 명사를 대신할 때 쓰이므로 빈칸에 들어갈 수 없다. (D) whichever는 명사절/부사절을 이끄는 접속사로 앞에 오는 명사를 수식할 수 없다.

번역 불량품을 반품하고자 하는 고객은 구매일로부터 20일 이내에 할 수 있다.

어휘 customer 고객 defective 결함이 있는 purchase 구매(품)

118 전치사 어휘

해설 빈칸은 명사구 a special living-history program을 목적어로 취하는 전치사 자리로, 빈칸 이하의 전치사구가 will be open을 수식하고 있다. 따라서 빈칸에는 will be open과 a special living-history program을 가장 잘 연결하는 전치사가 들어가야 한다. 특별 생활사 프로그램은 골루보비치 하우스가 일요일에 문을 여는 목적이라고 할 수 있으므로, '~를 위해'라는 의미의 (C) for가 정답이다.

번역 골루보비치 하우스는 특별 생활사 프로그램을 위해 일요일에 문을 열 것이다.

어휘 living-history 생활사

119 형용사 자리 _ 명사 수식

해설 빈칸은 명사구 the candidate을 뒤에서 수식하는 형용사 자리로, 부사 best와 전치사구 for the position의 수식을 받는다. 따라서 형용사와 같은 역할을 하는 현재분사 (C) qualifying(자격을 주는, 한정하는)과, 과거분사 (D) qualified(자격을 갖춘, 자격이 있는) 중 하나를 선택해야 한다. 지원자(candidate)는 자격을 갖춘 사람이며, 문맥상 '가장 적합한 지원자'라는 내용이 되어야 자연스러우므로, (D) qualified가 정답이다. 참고로, qualified는 전치사 for 또는 to 부정사와 함께 자주 쓰인다. (A) qualify는 동사, (B) qualifications는 명사로 품사상 빈칸에 들어갈 수 없다.

번역 위자야 씨는 그 직책에 가장 적합한 지원자를 선정하기 위해 이력서를 검토하고 있다.

어휘 review 검토하다 résumé 이력서 candidate 지원자, 후보자

120 상관접속사

해설 빈칸은 동사 praise의 목적어 역할을 하는 명사구 Navala City's world-class beaches와 its historical attractions를 연결하는 접속사 자리이다. '세계적인 수준의 해변'과 '역사적 명소' 모두를 칭찬하는 내용의 문장이므로, '~뿐만 아니라 …도'라는 의미의 상관접속사 (A) as well as가 정답이다. 등위접속사 (B) yet은 문맥상/위치상 빈칸에 적합하지 않고, (C) so that과 (D) when은 두 개의 명사구를 연결할 수 없으므로 빈칸에 들어갈 수 없다.

번역 관광객들은 나발라 시티의 역사적 명소뿐만 아니라 세계적인 수준의 해변에 찬사를 보낸다.

어휘 praise 찬사를 보내다 historical 역사적인 attraction 명소

121 부사절 접속사

해설 빈칸은 두 개의 완전한 절을 이어 주는 접속사 자리이므로, '~하는 동안'이라는 의미의 부사절 접속사 (C) while이 정답이다. (A) along과 (B) besides는 전치사/부사, (D) then은 부사/형용사로 빈칸에 들어가 두 개의 절을 이어 줄 수 없다.

번역 챈들링 씨는 탠 씨가 휴가 중일 때 시각을 다투는 일을 처리할 것이다.

어휘 time-sensitive 시각을 다투는 on vacation 휴가 중인

122 명사 어휘

해설 빈칸은 전치사 in의 목적어 역할을 하는 명사 자리로, 예시를 보여주는 전치사구 such as France and Italy의 수식을 받는다. 따라서 빈칸에는 프랑스와 이탈리아 같은 장소를 포괄하는 명사가 들어가야 하므로, '행선지, 목적지'라는 의미의 (A) destinations가 정답이다. (B) ambitions는 '야망, 포부', (C) purposes는 '목적, 용도', (D) intentions는 '의도, 의사'라는 뜻으로 문맥상 빈칸에 적합하지 않다.

번역 로라 글레스는 프랑스와 이탈리아 같은 장소에서 열리는 교수진 주도의 학습 프로그램을 홍보한다.

어휘 faculty 교수진

123 명사절 접속사

해설 빈칸은 완전한 절(there is a train station near their office)을 이끄는 접속사 자리이며, 빈칸 이하의 절이 타동사 ask의 목적어 역할을 하고 있다. 따라서 '~인지 (아닌지)'라는 의미로 명사절을 이끌 수 있는 (C) whether가 정답이다. (A) so는 등위접속사로 명사절을 이끌 수 없고, (B) about과 (D) of는 전치사이므로 품사상 빈칸에 들어갈 수 없다.

번역 스태포드 씨는 고객들에게 이메일을 보내 그들의 사무실 근처에 기차역이 있는지 물었다.

어휘 client 고객

124 동사 어휘

해설 빈칸은 주어 the city의 동사 자리로, 명사구 (nearly 500) building permits를 목적어로 취한다. 따라서 시(the city)에서 허가증으로 할 수 있는 행위를 나타내는 동사가 들어가야 하므로, '발급했다, 발행했다'라는 의미의 (B) issued가 정답이다. (A) regarded는 주로 전치사 as와 쓰여 '~라고 간주했다'라는 뜻으로 쓰이고, (C) performed는 '수행했다, 공연했다', (D) constructed는 '건설했다, 구성했다'라는 뜻이므로 문맥상 빈칸에 적절하지 않다.

번역 지난해 시는 소상공인에게 거의 500건의 건축 허가증을 발급했다.

어휘 nearly 거의, 약 permit 허가(증)

125 소유대명사

해설 빈칸은 that절의 동사 will benefit의 주어 역할을 하는 명사 자리이므로, 소유대명사인 (A) theirs가 정답이다. 참고로, theirs는 their(local merchants') businesses를 대신한다. (B) them은 목적격 인칭대명사, (C) their는 소유격 인칭대명사, (D) themselves는 재귀대명사로 모두 주어 자리에 들어갈 수 없다.

번역 지역 상인들은 이 신규 사업이 성공하면 자신들의 사업도 혜택을 볼 것으로 기대하고 있다.

어휘 local 지역의 merchant 상인 benefit 혜택을 보다

126 동사 어휘

해설 주어 the company 및 목적어 a search (for a new CEO)와 어울려 쓰이는 동사를 선택하는 문제이다. 웨일런 씨의 은퇴 이후 (Following the retirement of Mr. Whalen)에 회사에서 새로운 CEO를 찾기 시작했다는 내용이 되어야 자연스러우므로, '시작했다, 착수했다'라는 의미의 (B) launched가 정답이다. (A) connected는 '연결했다', (C) persuaded는 '설득했다', (D) treated는 '다루었다, 치료했다'라는 뜻으로 문맥상 빈칸에 적절하지 않다.

번역 웨일런 씨의 은퇴에 이어 회사는 새로운 CEO를 찾기 시작했다.

어휘 following ~후에, ~에 이어 retirement 은퇴

127 전치사 어휘

해설 빈칸은 a week ago와 함께 동사구를 수식하고 있다. 따라서 a week ago 앞에 쓰여 '일주일도 전에'라는 표현을 완성하는 (B) over(~ 이상)가 정답이다. (A) beyond는 '~를 넘어서, ~를 지나서', (C) past는 '지나서', (D) through는 '~를 통해, ~까지'라는 뜻으로 문맥상 빈칸에 적절하지 않다.

번역 트라바글리니 씨는 일주일도 전에 시설부에 서류를 제출했다.

어휘 file (서류를) 제출하다, 철하다 paperwork 서류 facility 시설

128 동사 어형 _ 시제

해설 빈칸은 After가 이끄는 부사절의 주어 the lease의 동사 자리이다. 주절의 동사가 현재 시제(have)이며, 자동차 리스와 관련된 정책을 나타내는 문장이므로, 빈칸에도 단순 현재 시제 동사가 들어가야 자연스럽다. 따라서 (D) expires가 정답이다.

번역 임대 기간이 만료된 후, 고객들은 그 차를 구입하거나 지역 영업소에 반환할 수 있다.

어휘 lease 임대 (기간) expire 만료되다 purchase 구입하다

129 부사 어휘

해설 전치사구 on radio and television과 함께 동사 is broadcast를 적절히 수식하는 부사를 선택하는 문제이다. 프로그램이 라디오 및 텔레비전 모두에서 방송된다는 내용의 문장이므로, '동시에'라는 의미의 (B) simultaneously가 정답이다. (A) instinctively는 '본능적으로, 직관적으로', (C) collectively는 '집합적으로, 총괄하여', (D) mutually는 '서로, 상호간에'라는 뜻으로 문맥상 빈칸에 적절하지 않다.

번역 〈존스 뉴스 아워〉는 라디오와 텔레비전을 통해 동시에 방송된다.

어휘 broadcast 방송하다

130 동사 어형 _ 시제 _ 가정법 과거완료

해설 빈칸은 주어 her train의 동사 자리로, 빈칸을 포함한 if절이 앞에 있는 주절(Ms. Choi would have been at the keynote address)을 수식하고 있다. 주절의 동사가 would have been이며 과거(참석하지 못했다)와 반대되는 상황(참석했을 것이다)을 가정하고 있으므로, 해당 문장이 가정법 과거완료 구문이라는 것을 알 수 있다. 가정법 과거완료 구문은 「If+주어+had+p.p. ~, 주어+조동사 과거형+have+p.p. ~.」 구조로 쓰인다. 따라서 (C) had arrived가 정답이다.

번역 기차가 제시간에 도착했다면 최 씨는 기조 연설에 참석했을 것이다.

어휘 keynote address 기조 연설 on time 제시간에

PART 6

131-134 광고

필라델피아의 PH11-TV는 여러분의 모바일 기기에 저희가 새로 출시한 교통 앱을 다운로드하실 것을 권합니다. 이 앱은 방송국의 교통 안내 방송을 131**보완합니다.** TV와 떨어져 있어서 교통 방송을 볼 수 없다면 이 앱을 이용해 교통 소식을 받으세요. 132**이 앱에는 소식이 자주 업데이트됩니다.** 또한, 여러분이 매일 이용하는 통근 경로를 앱에 설정해 두면, 해당 경로를 따라 교통 관련 사건이 발생할 경우 모바일 기기에서 개인 맞춤형 알림을 133**바로** 받을 수 있습니다. 오늘 PH11-TV 교통 앱을 다운로드해 교통 정체를 피하시거나, 134**혹은** 매일 오전 5시와 오후 4시에 시작하는 저희의 생방송을 시청하세요.

어휘 device 기기 coverage 방송, 보도 be unable to ~할 수 없다 commute 통근 거리[경로] personalized 개인 맞춤형의 alert 알림, 경고 occur 발생하다 avoid 피하다 tune in (라디오, 텔레비전을) 틀다, 주파수를 맞추다

TEST 3

131 동사 어휘

해설 빈칸에 적절한 동사를 선택하는 문제이다. 앞 문장에서 PH11-TV가 새로운 교통 앱을 출시했다고 했고, 뒤 문장에서는 TV로 교통 방송을 볼 수 없을 경우 이 앱을 이용해 교통 소식을 받으라(get traffic news if you ~ are unable to watch our traffic reports)고 권했다. 따라서 이 앱이 방송국의 교통 방송(the station's traffic coverage)을 보완하는 역할을 한다고 설명하는 것이 가장 자연스러우므로, '보완하다, 보충하다'라는 의미의 (D) supplements가 정답이다. (A) displaces는 '대체하다'라는 뜻으로 쓰일 수 있지만, 앱과 TV 교통 방송 둘 다 이용 가능하기 때문에 정답이 될 수 없다. (B) observes는 '관찰하다, 준수하다', (C) commands는 '명령하다, 지시하다'라는 뜻으로 문맥상 빈칸에 적합하지 않다.

132 문맥에 맞는 문장 고르기

번역 (A) 우리 도시는 규모가 상당합니다.
(B) 문자 메시지는 서비스 요금이 부과됩니다.
(C) 우리는 도시 전 지역으로 뉴스 프로 진행자들을 보냅니다.
(D) 이 앱에는 소식이 자주 업데이트됩니다.

해설 빈칸 앞 문장에서 방송국이 새로 출시한 교통 앱의 역할(The app supplements the station's traffic coverage)을 언급했고, 뒤 문장에서 앱의 기능(to receive personalized alerts ~ along your route)에 대해 설명했다. 따라서 빈칸에도 교통 앱과 관련된 내용이 들어가야 문맥상 자연스러우므로, (D)가 정답이다.

어휘 substantial 상당한 be subject to ~의 대상이다 fee 요금 feature 특징으로 하다, (특별히) 포함하다 frequent 빈번한

133 부사 자리 _ 동사 수식

해설 빈칸은 전치사구 on your mobile device와 함께 to receive를 수식하는 부사 자리이므로, '바로, 직접'이라는 의미의 부사인 (B) directly가 정답이다. (A) direction은 명사, (C) directing은 동명사/현재분사, (D) directs는 동사로 모두 품사상 빈칸에 들어갈 수 없다.

어휘 direction 방향, 지시 direct 지시하다, 겨냥하다; 직접적인

134 등위접속사

해설 빈칸에는 두 개의 명령문을 연결할 수 있는 접속사가 들어가야 하므로, '또는, 혹은'이라는 의미의 등위접속사 (A) or가 정답이다. (B) well과 (D) only는 부사, (C) quick은 형용사/부사로 품사상 빈칸에 들어갈 수 없다.

135-138 웹페이지

http://www.midwestartisanalcheeseguild.org

중서부 치즈 장인 조합(MACG)은 미국 중서부의 치즈 제조업을 [135]**발전시키기 위해** 무역 박람회를 조직하고 교육 세미나를 실시합니다. 이 지역의 치즈는 세계적으로 인정받고 있습니다. [136]**이들** 치즈 중 다수가 전 세계 식당 주방장들에 의해 사용됩니다.

MACG는 매년 4월에 열리는 이 지역 최대 규모의 치즈 제조 업체 박람회를 개최합니다. 이 행사에서 권위 있는 '치즈 마법사' 대회가 열립니다. [137]**전국에서 온 치즈 제조 업자들이 경쟁합니다.** 댄 트래블라가 지난해 [138]**우승자**였습니다. 그의 숙성된 체다 치즈는 100점 만점에 98.7점을 받아 우승했습니다.

어휘 artisanal 장인의 organize 조직하다 conduct 실시하다, 수행하다 trade 사업, 무역 region 지역 recognize 인정하다 put on (행사 등을) 개최하다 exposition 박람회 prestigious 권위 있는 wizard 마법사 aged (치즈 등이) 숙성된

135 to부정사

해설 빈칸 앞에 완전한 절이 왔고, 뒤에 명사구 the cheese-crafting trade가 있으므로, 빈칸에는 준동사(to부정사, 동명사, 분사)가 들어가야 한다. 따라서 '치즈 제조업을 발전시키기 위해'라는 의미의 to부정사 (B) to advance가 정답이다. 이미 문장에 동사(organizes, conducts)가 있으므로, (A) is advancing, (C) has advanced, (D) will advance는 빈칸에 들어갈 수 없다.

어휘 advance 발전시키다

136 지시형용사 _ 수 일치

해설 빈칸은 복수명사 cheeses를 한정 수식하는 자리이므로, 복수명사와 수가 일치하는 지시형용사 (A) these가 정답이다. (B) each는 단수명사를 수식하므로 정답이 될 수 없으며, (C) when은 부사/접속사/대명사, (D) instead는 부사로 품사상 빈칸에 들어갈 수 없다.

137 문맥에 맞는 문장 고르기

번역 (A) 지역 기업 브로마텔이 최신 치즈 제조 기술을 시연합니다.
(B) 내년에 몇 가지 새로운 회의 활동들이 계획되어 있습니다.
(C) 전국에서 온 치즈 제조 업자들이 경쟁합니다.
(D) 호텔 예약은 저희 웹사이트에서 할 수 있습니다.

해설 앞 문장에서 치즈 제조 업체 박람회 행사에서 권위 있는 '치즈 마법사' 대회가 열린다(The prestigious Wizard of Cheese contest is held at this event)고 했고, 뒤에서 참가자(Dan Travella)의 우승 점수(a winning score)가 나왔으므로, 빈칸에도 이 대회와 관련된 내용이 들어가야 문맥상 자연스럽다. 따라서 대회 참가자(Cheese makers from around the country)를 언급한 (C)가 정답이다.

어휘 firm 기업 demonstrate 시연하다 latest 최신의 compete 경쟁하다 reservation 예약

138 명사 어휘

해설 빈칸에는 소유격 last year's의 수식을 받으며 주어 Dan Travella와 동격 관계를 이루는 명사가 들어가야 한다. 앞 문장에서 '치즈 마법사' 대회(Wizard of Cheese contest)가 열린다고 했고, 뒤에서 트래블라 씨의 숙성된 체다 치즈가 100점 만점에 98.7점을 받아 우승했다(received a winning score ~ 100)고 했으므로, '우승자'라는 의미의 (D) champion이 정답이다. (A) speaker는 '연사, 발표자', (B) expert는 '전문가', (C) judge는 '심사위원, 판사'라는 뜻으로 문맥상 빈칸에 적절하지 않다.

139-142 정보문

〈계간 지엔 트래블〉의 대다수 [139]**기고가들**은 전문 작가들로, 지금도 저희와 지속적인 관계를 유지하고 있습니다. [140]**그렇기는 하지만**, 저희는 항상 새로운 인재들을 격려하고 지원하고자 합니다. 새로운 작가의 기사를 1호당 적어도 한 편은 포함시키려고 노력하지만, 일년에 단 4호만 발행하므로 출판 기회가 상당히 제한되어 있습니다.

출판을 위한 아이디어를 제출하기 전에 www.zientravel.com/writers에서 지침을 읽어 보십시오. 이 지침에는 당사의 특정 관심 분야에 대해 자세히 설명되어 있습니다. [141]**이렇게 하면 귀하의 제안이 수용될 가능성이 높아집니다.**

빠른 시일 내에 모든 서신에 응답하는 것을 목표로 삼고 있지만, 회신이 늦어지는 경우도 있을 수 있다는 점 유의하십시오. 그러므로 [142]**인내심을 가지고** 기다려 주시기 바랍니다.

어휘 quarterly 계간지 ongoing 지속적인, 계속 진행 중인 encourage 격려하다 talent 인재 article 기사 issue 호 opportunity 기회 publication 출판, 발행 limited 제한된 submit 제출하다 specific 특정한 respond 응답하다 correspondence 서신 in a timely manner 적시에, 빠른 시일 내에

139 명사 자리

해설 빈칸은 정관사 the의 한정 수식을 받는 명사 자리로, 보기에서 명사인 (B) contribution과 (D) contributors 중 하나를 선택해야 한다. 문장의 주어인 Most of ------- to *Zien Travel Quarterly*가 보어인 professional writers와 동격 관계를 이루어야 하므로, 빈칸에는 사람 명사가 들어가야 한다. 따라서 '기고가들'이라는 의미의 (D) contributors가 정답이다. (A) contributes는 동사, (C) contributing은 동명사/현재분사로 품사상 빈칸에 들어갈 수 없다.

어휘 contribute 기여하다, 기고하다 contribution 기여, 기고문

140 접속부사

해설 빈칸 앞뒤 문장을 의미상 자연스럽게 연결하는 접속부사를 선택하는 문제이다. 빈칸 앞 문장에서 〈계간 지엔 트래블〉의 대다수 기고가들은 전문 작가들(Most of the contributors to *Zien Travel Quarterly* are professional writers)이라고 했으나, 빈칸 뒤에서는 항상 새로운 인재들을 격려하고 지원하고자 한다(we always like to encourage and support new talent)고 했다. 따라서 빈칸에는 대조적인 내용을 연결하는 접속부사가 들어가야 하므로, '그렇기는 하지만, 그런데도'라는 의미의 (A) With that said가 정답이다. 참고로, (With) That being said, Having said that으로도 쓰일 수 있다. (B) For instance는 '예를 들어', (C) In other words는 '다시 말해서, 즉', (D) In that case는 '그렇다면'이라는 뜻으로 문맥상 빈칸에 적절하지 않다.

141 문맥에 맞는 문장 고르기

번역 (A) 글솜씨를 향상시키는 방법은 수십 가지가 있습니다.
(B) 이래서 편집 일정이 당사의 출판물에 그토록 중요합니다.
(C) 이렇게 하면 귀하의 제안이 수용될 가능성이 높아집니다.
(D) 이 기사는 훌륭하지만, 지금은 저희 요구를 충족하지 못합니다.

해설 빈칸 앞 문장에서 출판을 위한 아이디어를 제출하기 전에 자사의 특정 관심 분야에 대해 자세히 설명하는 지침을 읽어 볼 것(please read the guidelines ~ as they outline our specific areas of interest in detail)을 권고했다. 따라서 이러한 조언을 한 이유가 이어지는 것이 문맥상 자연스러우므로, (C)가 정답이다.

어휘 improve 향상시키다 editorial 편집의 calendar 일정 increase 높이다 likelihood 가능성 accept 수용하다 meet the needs 요구를 충족하다

142 형용사 어휘

해설 앞 문장에서 빠른 시일 내에 모든 서신에 응답하려고 노력하지만 회신이 늦어질 수 있다(there may be times when we are slow to respond)고 했고, 해당 문장에서는 이와 관련된 당부를 하고 있다. 따라서 빈칸에는 회신이 늦어지는 상황에서 주어 you에게 요구되는 태도를 묘사하는 형용사가 들어가야 하므로, '인내심 있는'이라는 의미의 (A) patient가 정답이다. (B) secondary는 '부차적인, 부수적인', (C) cautious는 '조심스러운, 신중한', (D) precise는 '정확한, 꼼꼼한'이라는 뜻으로 문맥상 빈칸에 적절하지 않다.

143-146 이메일

수신: bgosnell@bvb.org
발신: sluu@luumarketing.com
제목: 온라인 마케팅 조사
날짜: 4월 3일

고스넬 씨께,

아래는 브룩사이드 관광청 웹사이트의 디자인을 분석해 이를 바탕으로 내린 몇 가지 예비 결론 및 권고 사항입니다.

첫째, 이 사이트는 기대만큼 [143]**효과적이지** 않습니다. 외관을 수정하고 오늘날 관광객들의 요구에 맞는 정보를 추가할 것을 권고합니다. 또한 귀사의 기관 로고가 웹사이트 [144]**전반에 걸쳐** 일관성 없이 사용되고 있다는 점도 유의하십시오.

또한 도시를 홍보하는 데 사용되는 시각 자료를 보완하는 것도 고려해야 합니다. [145]**사진을 전시하는 것만으로는 잠재 방문객을 유치하기에 충분하지 않습니다.** 따라서 브룩사이드가 제공하는 다양한 볼거리를 보여주는 전문적으로 만든 비디오를 업로드할 것을 추천합니다. [146]**덧붙여** 주민과 방문객이 직접 도시 명소의 사진과 동영상을 올릴 수 있는 페이지를 웹사이트에 추가할 것을 제안합니다.

다음 단계를 논의할 수 있도록 최대한 빨리 연락 주십시오.

셸리 루
루 마케팅

어휘 preliminary 예비의 conclusion 결론 recommendation 권고 (사항) analysis 분석 Visitors Bureau 관광청 appearance 외관 demand 요구, 수요 organization 기관, 조직 consistently 일관되게 supplement 보완하다 attraction 볼거리, 명소

143 형용사 자리 _ 주격 보어

해설 빈칸은 원급 비교 구문에 쓰이는 'as ... as' 사이에서 주어 the site를 보충 설명하는 주격 보어 자리이다. 따라서 '효과적인'이라는 뜻의 형용사 (C) effective가 정답이다. (D) effecting은 '(어떤 결과를) 가져오는'이라는 뜻으로 주격 보어 역할을 할 수 없고, (A) effectiveness는 명사, (B) effectively는 부사로 품사상 빈칸에 들어갈 수 없다.

144 전치사 어휘

해설 동사구 is not used consistently와 명사구 your Web site를 가장 잘 연결하는 전치사를 선택하는 문제이다. 기관 로고가 일관성 없게 사용되는 것은 웹사이트 전반에 걸쳐 나타나는 현상이므로, '도처에, 내내'라는 의미의 (D) throughout이 정답이다.

145 문맥에 맞는 문장 고르기

번역 (A) 저의 서면 동의 없이는 어떤 사진도 사용할 수 없습니다.
(B) 사진을 전시하는 것만으로는 잠재 방문객을 유치하기에 충분하지 않습니다.
(C) 쉽게 검색하려면 체계적으로 사진을 정리하는 방법이 필수입니다.
(D) 올바른 형식이 아닌 사진은 받지 않습니다.

해설 빈칸 앞 문장에서 도시를 홍보하는 데 사용되는 시각 자료를 보완하라(consider supplementing the imagery)고 조언했고, 뒤 문장에서 빈칸을 근거로 들며(therefore) 전문적으로 만든 비디오를 업로드할 것(uploading some professionally made videos ~ offer)을 추천했다. 따라서 시각 자료를 보완하는 방법으로 비디오를 추천하는 이유가 빈칸에 들어가야 자연스러우므로, (B)가 정답이다.

어휘 authorization 승인 essential 필수적인 attract 유치하다 prospective 장래의, 예비의 retrieval 검색, 회수 proper 올바른 reject 거부하다

146 접속부사

해설 앞 문장에서 추천 사항(We therefore recommend ~ offer)을, 빈칸 뒤에서 제안 사항(we suggest adding a page to the Web site ~ attractions)을 언급했으므로, 빈칸에는 유사한 내용을 연결하는 접속부사가 들어가야 글의 흐름이 자연스러워진다. 따라서 '게다가, 또한'이라는 뜻의 (B) In addition이 정답이다. (A) So that은 접속사로 뒤에 바로 완전한 절이 이어져야 하고, (C) To clarify는 '명확하게 말하자면', (D) After all은 '결국에는'이라는 뜻으로 문맥상 적절하지 않다.

PART 7

147-148 표

벨뷰 교통 성인 비수기 정액권* [147]**이 표 소지자는 발행일에 목적지 간 왕복 구간을 무제한으로 이용할 수 있습니다.**	벨뷰 해안과 킵스키 섬 구간
[148]**여객선 승무원이 검사할 수 있으므로 여행이 끝날 때까지 이 표를 보관하십시오.** *비수기 정액권은 월요일에서 목요일 오전 9시부터 오후 4시까지 여행에만 유효합니다. 다른 시간에 여행하고자 하는 승객은 5달러를 내고 정규 운임표로 업그레이드하시면 됩니다.	벨뷰 해안과 카나리아 항구 구간

어휘 off-peak 비수기의, 사용자가 적은 be entitled to ~할 권리가 있다 unlimited 무제한의 passage 구간 destination 목적지 retain 보유하다 inspect 검사하다 valid 유효한 passenger 승객

147 사실 관계 확인

번역 표에 관해 사실인 것은?
(A) 5달러에 구입했다.
(B) 현금으로 환불할 수 있다.
(C) 한 번 이상 사용할 수 있다.
(D) 24시간 유효하다.

해설 첫 번째 문단에서 표 소지자는 발행일에 목적지 간 왕복 구간을 무제한으로 이용할 수 있다(unlimited round-trip passage between destinations)고 했으므로, (C)가 정답이다.

어휘 purchase 구입하다 good 유효한

▸▸ **Paraphrasing** 지문의 **unlimited round-trip passage**
→ 정답의 **more than one journey**

148 세부 사항

번역 어떤 교통편에 해당하는 표인가?
(A) 버스
(B) 배
(C) 기차
(D) 택시

해설 두 번째 문장에서 여객선 승무원이 표를 검사할 수 있다(it may be inspected by crew member on the ferry)고 했으므로, (B)가 정답이다.

▸▸ **Paraphrasing** 지문의 **ferry** → 정답의 **boat**

149-150 구인 공고

그래픽 디자인 직원 구함

재커리 타운십 플로럴 가든(ZTFG)에서 역동적인 저희 팀에 합류할 창의적이고 커리어를 중시하는 사람을 찾고 있습니다. 업무에는 ZTFG 활동을 고안하고 홍보하며 주변 지역 사회의 학교 및 각종 매체에 광고하는 일이 포함됩니다. [149]**사무용 소프트웨어 및 디자인 소프트웨어에 능숙해야 하며 이전에 그래픽 디자인 회사에서 근무한 경력이 있어야 합니다.** 탄력 근무제입니다. 지원하려면 5월 5일까지 이메일 jobs@ztfg.org로 자기소개서와 이력서, 직장 추천서 2부를 보내십시오. [150]**더 자세한 사항을 알고 싶다면 월요일부터 금요일까지 언제든 오전에 들러 화원을 둘러보십시오.**

어휘 associate 직원, 동료 career-oriented 커리어를 중시하는, 출세 지향적인 publicize 홍보하다 qualification 자격(증) proficiency 능숙함 previous 이전의 flexible work schedule 탄력 근무제

149 세부 사항

번역 일자리의 자격 요건은?

(A) 과거 비영리 단체 근무 경력
(B) 유기농 원예 방법에 대한 지식
(C) 몇몇 정원 화초 식별 능력
(D) 그래픽 디자인 소프트웨어 역량

해설 중반부에서 사무용 소프트웨어와 디자인 소프트웨어에 능숙해야 한다(Qualifications include proficiency in office and design software)고 했으므로, (D)가 정답이다.

어휘 nonprofit 비영리의 principle 원리, 방법 identify 식별하다 competency 능숙함, 역량

▸▸ Paraphrasing 지문의 Qualifications
→ 질문의 requirement of the job
지문의 proficiency in ~ design software
→ 정답의 Competency with graphic design software

150 세부 사항

번역 구직자들이 더 자세한 정보를 얻을 수 있는 방법은?

(A) 동영상 시청하기
(B) 강좌 듣기
(C) 화원 방문하기
(D) 추천인에게 연락하기

해설 마지막 문장에서 더 알아보고 싶다면 월요일부터 금요일까지 언제든 오전에 들러 화원을 둘러보라(To learn more, stop by ~ for a tour of the garden)고 조언했으므로, (C)가 정답이다.

▸▸ Paraphrasing 지문의 learn more
→ 질문의 get more information
지문의 stop by ~ for a tour of the garden
→ 정답의 visiting the garden

151-152 회람

회람

수신: 전 직원
발신: 돈 분더, 시설부장
제목: 샨티 워크스페이시즈
날짜: 2월 11일

[151]**샨티 워크스페이시즈와의 특별 제휴로, 직원들은 2월 20일부터 3월 15일까지 5개의 스탠딩 데스크를 시범 사용할 수 있습니다.** 스탠딩 데스크를 쓰면 일할 때 편안하게 서 있을 수 있습니다. [152]**높낮이 조절이 가능한 샨티 B45 신형 모델을 사용하게 될 것이므로, 본인에게 완벽한 높이로 앉았다 일어났다를 번갈아 가며 할 수 있습니다.** 연구 결과에 따르면, 스탠딩 데스크는 너무 오래 앉아 있는 것이 신체에 미치는 해로운 영향을 없앨 수 있다고 합니다. 또한 기분과 전반적인 건강을 증진시킬 수 있습니다. 이 기회를 이용하고 싶은 분은 저에게 연락하세요. 관심 있는 사람이 책상 수보다 많으면 저에게 먼저 연락한 사람이 책상을 받을 것입니다. 전 직원이 스탠딩 데스크를 사용할 수 있게 해야 할지 저희가 판단할 수 있게끔, 책상을 사용하는 사람은 자신의 경험에 대한 설문 조사에 응하라는 요청받을 것입니다.

어휘 available 이용할 수 있는 trial 시범의 comfortably 편안하게 adjustable 조절할 수 있는 alternate 번갈아 가며 하다 height 높이 negate 상쇄하다 harmful 해로운 physical 신체의 effect 영향 improve 개선하다 overall 전반적인 take advantage of ~을 이용하다 opportunity 기회 recipient 수령자 determine 판단하다

151 주제 / 목적

번역 회람의 목적은?

(A) 몇몇 가구를 조립하는 데 도움을 요청하기 위해
(B) 직원들에게 새로운 유형의 가구를 사용해 볼 기회를 제공하기 위해
(C) 직원들에게 운동 수업을 받으라고 장려하기 위해
(D) 사무 장비에 대한 직원들의 선호도를 조사하기 위해

해설 첫 번째 줄에서 샨티 워크스페이시즈와의 특별 제휴로 직원들이 5개의 스탠딩 데스크를 시범 사용할 수 있다(five standing desks will be available to employees on a trial basis)고 한 후 관련 내용을 설명했으므로, 직원들에게 새로운 유형의 가구를 사용해 볼 기회를 제공하기 위한 회람임을 알 수 있다. 따라서 (B)가 정답이다.

152 사실 관계 확인

번역 샨티 B45 모델에 관해 명시된 것은?

(A) 적응하기 어려울 수 있다.
(B) 직원 생산성을 높일 것이다.
(C) 다양한 높이로 조절할 수 있다.
(D) 가장 비싼 스탠딩 데스크이다.

해설 네 번째 줄에서 높낮이 조절이 가능한 샨티 B45 신형 모델을 사용하게 되어 본인에게 완벽한 높이로 앉았다 일어났다를 번갈아 가며 할 수 있다(We will use the new Chanti B45 model, which is adjustable, so you can alternate ~ at the perfect height for you)고 했으므로, (C)가 정답이다.

어휘 increase 높이다 productivity 생산성 adjust 조절하다 expensive 비싼

▸▸ Paraphrasing 지문의 can alternate ~ at the perfect height for you
→ 정답의 can be adjusted to different heights

153-154 문자 메시지

칭 장 (오후 3시 45분)
안녕하세요, 아마리. [153]**노벨라 리가 휴대폰을 못 찾고 있어요. 위층 당신 사무실에 놓고 왔나요?**

아마리 크루자도 (오후 3시 46분)
코끼리 무늬가 있는 파란색 플라스틱 케이스 안에 있나요?

칭 장 (오후 3시 47분)
예, 그거예요. [153]**지금 가지러 올라가고 있어요.**

아마리 크루자도 (오후 3시 48분)
[153]**그녀의 열쇠도 여기 있네요.** 오늘 정신이 없었나 봐요.

칭 장 (오후 3시 49분)
[153/154]**열쇠도 그녀의 것이 확실해요?**

아마리 크루자도 (오후 3시 50분)
[153]그런 것 같아요. [154]**그 휴대폰 위에 놓여 있어요.**

어휘 upstairs 위층으로[에] distracted 정신이 산란한

153 추론 / 암시

번역 리 씨는 다음으로 무엇을 하겠는가?

(A) 위층에서 물건들을 되찾아온다.
(B) 폰 액세서리를 주문한다.
(C) 크루자도 씨의 비서에게 이메일을 보낸다.
(D) 장 씨의 폰을 빌린다.

해설 장 씨가 오후 3시 45분 메시지에서 리 씨가 휴대폰을 못 찾고 있다(Novella Lee can't find her phone)며 위층에 있는 크루자도 씨의 사무실에 놓고 왔는지(Did she leave it upstairs in your office?) 물었다. 크루자도 씨가 자신의 사무실에 있는 휴대폰을 묘사하며 이것이 맞냐고 되묻자, 장 씨가 맞다고 확인해 주며 리 씨가 지금 가지러 올라가고 있다(She's on her way back up to get it)고 했다. 또한 크루자도 씨의 사무실에 리 씨 것으로 보이는 열쇠도 있다고 했으므로, 리 씨가 위층에서 자신의 물건들을 되찾아올 것임을 추론할 수 있다. 따라서 (A)가 정답이다.

어휘 retrieve 되찾아오다

154 의도 파악

번역 오후 3시 50분에 크루자도 씨가 "그런 것 같아요"라고 적은 의도는 무엇인가?

(A) 리 씨가 자주 깜박한다고 생각한다.
(B) 장 씨가 잘못 말했다고 생각한다.
(C) 열쇠가 리 씨 것이라고 추측한다.
(D) 열쇠가 장 씨 것인지 궁금하다.

해설 장 씨가 오후 3시 49분 메시지에서 열쇠도 리 씨의 것이 확실한지(Are you sure they're hers?) 물었고, 이에 대해 크루자도 씨가 '그런 것 같아요(I'm guessing)'라고 한 후, 리 씨의 휴대폰 위에 놓여 있다(They're lying on top of the phone)고 덧붙였다. 따라서 열쇠가 리 씨 것이라고 추측했음을 알 수 있으므로, (C)가 정답이다.

어휘 assume 추측하다, 가정하다

155-157 부동산 광고

신규 사업체에 안성맞춤! [155/156(D)]**최근 건설된 이 건물에는 약 2,000제곱미터의 사무 공간 외에도 1,000제곱미터의 창고 공간 및 3,000제곱미터의 주차장이 있습니다.** [156(A)]**이 건물은 클로버데일 도심에서 쉽게 갈 수 있으며, 500미터 이내에 식당 여러 곳과 새로운 쇼핑센터가 있습니다.** [156(C)]**매끈하고 현대적인 디자인으로 바닥부터 천장까지 전면 유리로 되어 있어 자연광이 풍부하게 들어옵니다.** [157]**표준 임대 기간은 12개월이며 월세와 임대 보증금을 냅니다.** 신청자의 필요에 따라 기간을 더 길게 협상할 수 있습니다. 임대 신청이나 직접 건물을 보시려면 (519) 555-0139번으로 대나 풀리에게 전화하세요.

어휘 recently 최근 property 건물, 부동산 contain 포함하다 additional 추가의 garage 주차장 accessible 접근할 수 있는 sleek 매끈한 an abundance of 풍부한 security deposit 임대 보증금 in person 직접

155 세부 사항

번역 주차장의 규모는?

(A) 500제곱미터
(B) 1,000제곱미터
(C) 2,000제곱미터
(D) 3,000제곱미터

해설 두 번째 문장에서 약 2,000제곱미터의 사무 공간 외에도 1,000제곱미터의 창고 공간 및 3,000제곱미터짜리 주차장이 있다(This recently constructed property contains ~ a 3,000-square-metre car garage)고 했으므로, (D)가 정답이다.

156 사실 관계 확인

번역 건물의 장점으로 언급되지 않은 것은?

(A) 식당, 가게와 가깝다.
(B) 공항에서 자동차로 잠깐이다.
(C) 햇빛이 많이 든다.
(D) 비교적 새 건물이다.

해설 네 번째 줄 '500미터 이내에 식당 여러 곳과 새로운 쇼핑센터가 있다(the property is within 500 metres of several restaurants and ~ shopping centre)'에서 (A)를, 여섯 번째 줄 '바닥부터 천장까지 전면 유리로 되어 있어 자연광이 풍부하게 들어온다(floor-to-ceiling windows that provide an abundance of natural light)'에서 (C)를 확인할 수 있다. 또한 첫 번째 줄에서 건물이 최근에 지어졌다(This recently constructed property)고 했으므로, (D)도 확인할 수 있다. 따라서 언급되지 않은 (B)가 정답이다.

어휘 relatively 비교적

▸▸ Paraphrasing 지문의 **within 500 metres of several restaurants and a brand-new shopping centre** → 보기 (A)의 **close to restaurants and stores**
지문의 **provide an abundance of natural light** → 보기 (C)의 **allows for plenty of sunlight**
지문의 **This recently constructed property** → 보기 (D)의 **a relatively new building**

157 문장 삽입

번역 [1], [2], [3], [4]로 표시된 곳 중에서 다음 문장이 들어가기에 가장 적합한 곳은?

"신청자의 필요에 따라 기간을 더 길게 협상할 수 있습니다."

(A) [1]
(B) [2]
(C) [3]
(D) [4]

해설 주어진 문장에서 신청자의 필요에 따라 기간을 더 길게 협상할 수 있다(Longer terms can be negotiated, depending on the needs of the applicant)고 했으므로, 앞에서 먼저 일반적인 임대 기간에 관련된 내용이 언급되어야 한다. [4] 앞에서 표준 임대 기간은 12개월이며 월세와 임대 보증금을 낸다(The standard lease is for twelve months with ~ a security deposit)는 내용이 왔으므로, 이 다음에 주어진 문장이 이어져야 글의 흐름이 자연스러워진다. 따라서 (D)가 정답이다.

158-160 이메일

수신: 라파엘 바르가스
발신: 본화 오
제목: 정보
날짜: 10월 1일

라파엘에게:

[160]이곳 신공항 사무소 오픈이 11월 3일 월요일로 [158]정해졌는데, 이는 예상치 못한 터미널 A 공사에 따른 지연 때문입니다. [159]이번 주 후반에 이곳에 합류해 달라는 요청과 함께 더 자세한 내용을 이메일로 보내 드리겠습니다. 본사 사무실에서 누군가 참석하면 좋겠습니다.

[159/160]제가 계획한 대로, 모든 차량 임대에 한 달 동안 특가를 제공해 이전을 기념하려고 합니다. 또한 문레이 항공과 제휴해 특별편 및 자동차 여행 패키지를 준비했습니다. 고객 중 다수는 여전히 출장 여행자일 것으로 예상하지만, 저희는 관광객도 유치하기를 바랍니다.

다음 달에 보게 되기를 바랍니다.

본화 오

어휘 unexpected 예상치 못한 celebrate 축하[기념]하다 relocation 이전 arrange 준비하다 attract 유치하다

158 동의어 찾기

번역 첫 번째 단락 1행의 "set"과 의미가 가장 가까운 단어는?

(A) 예정된
(B) 첨부된
(C) 훈련된
(D) 인상된

해설 "set"이 포함된 부분은 '이곳 신공항 사무소 오픈이 11월 3일 월요일로 정해졌다(The opening at the new airport office here is now set for Monday, 3 November)'라는 내용으로, 여기서 set은 '예정된, 정해진'이라는 뜻으로 쓰였다. 따라서 '일정이 잡힌, 예정된'이라는 의미의 (A) scheduled가 정답이다.

159 추론 / 암시

번역 오 씨가 이메일에서 암시한 것은?

(A) 실수를 바로잡았다.
(B) 회사 사무실을 방문했다.
(C) 새로 채용된 직원이다.
(D) 사무소 이전을 책임지고 있다.

해설 첫 번째 단락에서 오 씨는 바르가스 씨에게 사무소 오픈에 대한 소식을 전한 후, 합류해 달라는 요청과 함께 더 자세한 사항을 이메일로 전달하겠다(I will e-mail you more details ~ you join us here)고 했다. 또한 자신이 계획한 대로(As I have planned) 모든 차량 임대에 한 달 동안 특가를 제공해 이전을 기념하려 한다(celebrate our relocation)고 했으므로, 오 씨가 사무실 이전을 계획한 책임자임을 추론할 수 있다. 따라서 (D)가 정답이다.

어휘 correct 바로잡다 be responsible for ~을 책임지다

160 세부 사항

번역 11월 3일에 문을 열 예정인 것은?

(A) 공항 터미널
(B) 렌터카 업체
(C) 여행사
(D) 건설사

해설 첫 번째 단락에서 11월 3일에 신공항 사무소 오픈이 예정되어 있다(The opening at the new airport office ~ Monday, 3 November)고 했고, 두 번째 단락에서 모든 차량 임대에 한 달 동안 특가를 제공해 이전을 기념할 계획(As I have planned, we will celebrate our relocation with ~ special deals on all car rentals)이라고 했다. 따라서 (B)가 정답이다.

161-163 편지

사운더슨 메디컬 그룹 • 마누카 로 46번지 • 카로리, 웰링턴 6012

9월 12일

[161]사운더슨 메디컬 그룹 환우 여러분:

사운더슨 메디컬 그룹(SMG)을 의료 서비스 제공자로 선택해 주셔서

TEST 3

감사합니다. 35년의 역사에 걸쳐 저희는 카로리에서 수많은 환자들을 성공적으로 치료해 왔습니다. 의료 서비스 시장의 급격한 변화를 감안하여, 저희는 환자에게 최상의 경험을 지속적으로 제공할 수 있는 최선의 방법을 모색해 왔습니다. **[161]이를 위해, SMG가 10월 1일부로 키프 헬스와 함께하게 된다는 것을 발표하게 되어 기쁩니다.**

이것이 여러분에게 무엇을 의미할까요? 단지 이름만 바뀔 뿐입니다. 다음 달부터 저희는 키프 헬스 카로리가 됩니다. 여러분의 주치의는 그대로 유지되며, 카로리에서 계속 주치의에게 진찰을 받으실 수 있습니다. **[162]하지만, 이제 키프 헬스 네트워크의 재능 있는 의사와 전문가 모두가 여러분에게 더 광범위한 진단 서비스와 치료법을 제공할 수 있게 됩니다.** 키프 헬스는 전문 지식과 환자 치료 결과로 규모가 더 큰 대도시권의 모든 의료 서비스 공급자 중 상위권에 지속적으로 올라 있습니다.

키프 헬스에 대한 자세한 내용은 웹사이트 www.keefehealth.co.nz를 방문하십시오. **[163]예약하시려면 기존 전화 번호를 사용하십시오.**

여러분을 계속 치료하게 되기를 바랍니다.

사운더슨 메디컬 그룹

어휘 patient 환자 treat 치료하다 physician 의사 diagnostic 진단의 consistently 계속 expertise 전문 지식 appointment 예약 existing 기존의

161 주제 / 목적

번역 편지의 목적은?

(A) 이용해 준 환자들에게 감사하기
(B) 업체 합병에 대해 환자들에게 알리기
(C) 새로 온 의사 소개하기
(D) 지점 개소 발표하기

해설 첫 번째 단락에서 SMG가 10월 1일부로 키프 헬스와 함께하게 된다는 것을 발표하게 되어 기쁘다(we are pleased to announce that SMG will join with Keefe Health)고 했으므로, 편지의 수신인인 사운더스 메디컬 그룹 환자들(Dear Saunderson Medical Group Patent)에게 업체 합병을 알리기 위한 편지임을 알 수 있다. 따라서 (B)가 정답이다.

어휘 patronage 단골 거래, 이용 advise (~에 대해) 알리다

▸▸ **Paraphrasing** 지문의 to announce that SMG will join with Keefe Health → 정답의 To advise ~ about a business merger

162 추론 / 암시

번역 키프 헬스에 관해 암시된 것은?

(A) SMG가 제공하지 않는 의료 옵션을 제공한다.
(B) 위치가 카로리 주민에게 불편하다.
(C) 환자들이 곧 편지를 받을 것이다.
(D) 35년째 운영되고 있다.

해설 두 번째 단락에서 합병하게 되면 키프 헬스 네트워크의 재능 있는 의사와 전문가 모두가 환자들에게 더 광범위한 진단 서비스와 치료법을 제공할 수 있게 된다(offer you a broader range of diagnostic services and treatments)고 했으므로, SMG에서는 제공하지 않는 의료 서비스를 키프 헬스에서 제공한다고 추론할 수 있다. 따라서 (A)가 정답이다.

어휘 inconvenient 불편한

163 세부 사항

번역 편지에 의하면, 수취인이 예약하기 위해 해야 하는 것은?

(A) 키프 헬스 웹페이지 방문
(B) 키프 헬스 본사 가기
(C) SMG 접수원에게 이메일로 요청하기
(D) 과거와 같은 전화번호로 전화하기

해설 세 번째 단락에서 예약을 하려면 기존 전화 번호를 사용하라(If you wish to schedule an appointment, please use our existing phone number)고 안내했으므로, (D)가 정답이다.

▸▸ **Paraphrasing** 지문의 use our existing phone number → 정답의 Call the same phone number as in the past

164-167 온라인 채팅

윌 프랭클 (오후 4시 32분): **[164]우리 회사로 파견되는 강사들이 월요일에 안전교육을 시작할 준비가 되었나요?**

도나 데이비스 (오후 4시 33분): 예. **[165]월요일 오후 2시 30분에 ZRC 테크에 도착할 예정입니다. 누군가 경비실로 마중 나가서 교육할 곳으로 안내하는 거 맞죠?**

윌 프랭클 (오후 4시 34분): 제 비서가 도울 겁니다.

도나 데이비스 (오후 4시 35분): 방에는 컴퓨터와 화이트보드가 설치될 건가요?

바이올렛 멘자 (오후 4시 35분): **[165]윌이 말한 것처럼 제가 경비실에서 강사들을 맞이해 방문객 출입증을 주겠습니다.**

윌 프랭클 (오후 4시 37분): 강사들에게 필요한 것을 전부 갖추고 있는 대회의실 2개를 사용할 겁니다.

바이올렛 멘자 (오후 4시 38분): **[166]실험실 기사들이 3시 직전에 교대 근무를 마치니까 바로 교육에 갈 수 있어요.** 모두들 자리 잡을 수 있게 제가 곁에서 도울게요.

도나 데이비스 (오후 4시 41분): 좋아요. **[167]교육은 5시에 끝납니다. 두 사람 중 누가 거기 가나요? 강사들이 문을 잠가야 할까요?**

윌 프랭클 (오후 4시 42분): **[167]제가 거기 가서 끝나면 문을 잠글게요.**

도나 데이비스 (오후 4시 43분): 좋아요. 그러면 됐습니다.

윌 프랭클 (오후 4시 44분): 제가 여기 5시 30분까지 있을 테니 오늘 오후에 혹시 더 필요한 게 있다면 말해주세요.

어휘 instructor 강사 assistant 비서, 조수 state 말하다 lab technician 실험실 기사 shift 교대 근무

164 세부 사항

번역 프랭클 씨가 데이비스 씨에게 연락한 이유는?

(A) 일정 변경을 제안하려고
(B) 보안 서식을 요청하려고
(C) 실험실 비품을 주문하려고
(D) 특별한 준비 사항을 확인하려고

해설 프랭클 씨는 오후 4시 32분 메시지에서 회사로 파견되는 강사들이 월요일에 안전 교육을 시작할 준비가 되었는지(Are the instructors ~ ready to begin the safety training sessions on Monday?) 데이비스 씨에게 물었고, 이후 4시 35분 메시지에서 강의에 필요한 장비들(computers and whiteboards)도 설치되었는지 확인했다. 따라서 (D)가 정답이다.

어휘 arrangement 준비, 계획

165 세부 사항

번역 멘자 씨는 언제 경비실에 있겠는가?

(A) 오후 2시 30분
(B) 오후 3시
(C) 오후 5시
(D) 오후 5시 30분

해설 데이비스 씨는 오후 4시 33분 메시지에서 강사들이 월요일 오후 2시 30분에 ZRC 테크에 도착할 예정(They'll arrive there at ZRC Tech at 2:30 on Monday)이라고 한 후, 이때 경비실로 마중 나가서 교육할 곳으로 강사들을 안내할 사람이 있는지(Someone will meet them at the security desk ~ right?) 확인했다. 이에 대해 프랭클 씨의 비서인 멘자 씨가 4시 35분 메시지에서 자신이 경비실에서 강사들을 맞이해 방문객 출입증을 주겠다(I'll meet the instructors at the security desk ~ visitor passes)고 했으므로, (A)가 정답이다.

166 사실 관계 확인

번역 실험실 기사들에 관해 명시된 것은?

(A) 최근 고용되었다.
(B) 근무 후 교육에 참석할 것이다.
(C) 오후에 휴식을 취할 것이다.
(D) 이전에 데이비스 씨를 만난 적이 있다.

해설 멘자 씨가 오후 4시 38분 메시지에서 실험실 기사들이 3시 직전에 교대 근무를 마친 후 바로 교육에 갈 수 있다(The lab technicians will finish up their shifts ~ can go straight to their sessions)고 했으므로, (B)가 정답이다.

▸▸ **Paraphrasing** 지문의 **go ~ to their sessions**
→ 정답의 **attend training sessions**

167 의도 파악

번역 오후 4시 43분에 데이비스 씨가 "그러면 됐습니다"라고 적은 의도는 무엇인가?

(A) 더 이상 질문거리가 없다.
(B) 문을 잠글 필요가 없다고 생각한다.
(C) 프랭클 씨의 아이디어가 좋다고 생각한다.
(D) 자신이 방 문을 닫았다.

해설 데이비스 씨는 오후 4시 41분 메시지에서 프랭클 씨와 멘자 씨 중 누가 교육에 가는지(Will either of you be there?), 강사들이 문을 잠가야 하는지(Do the instructors need to lock up?) 등에 대해 문의했고, 이에 대해 프랭클 씨가 오후 4시 42분 메시지에서 자신이 교육에 갈 예정이며 끝나면 문을 잠글 것(I'll be there ~ they finish)이라고 응답했다. 프랭클 씨의 답변을 받은 데이비스 씨가 '그러면 됐습니다(That's it, then)'라고 한 것이므로, 더 이상 문의사항이 없다는 의도로 쓴 메시지임을 알 수 있다. 따라서 (A)가 정답이다.

168-171 이메일

발신: 키라 타카마츠
수신: 에릭 서덜랜드
제목: 후속 회의
날짜: 3월 8일

에릭에게,

[169]**업무량에 대한 걱정을 공유해 줘서 고마워요.** 우리는 직원들이 정규 주당 근무 시간에 마칠 수 있게끔 프로젝트를 배분하려고 최선을 다하고 있습니다. [168/171]**이미 꽉 찬 당신의 업무 목록에 최근 책 표지 디자인을 추가했기 때문에, 휴고 린코우스키라는 새로운 팀원을 당신의 보조로 배정하기로 결정했어요.** 이 신입 사원이 대부분의 업무에서 당신을 지원할 겁니다. 당신은 모든 포스터, 로고, 카탈로그 레이아웃 프로젝트를 포함해 그의 작업을 감독하게 됩니다.

[170]**다음 주 월요일 린코우스키 씨가 도착하면, 전반적인 설명과 구체적인 요구 사항을 포함해 고객들의 모든 정보를 공유해 주세요. 당신이 사용하고 있는 우리의 디자인 소프트웨어뿐만 아니라 기타 모든 시스템에 대해서도 그에게 알려 줄 책임이 있습니다.**

다른 고민이 있으면 주저하지 마시고 저에게 알려 주세요.

키라 타카마츠

어휘 concerns 걱정 workload 업무량 distribute 배분하다 complete 완료하다 responsibility 책임, 임무 assign 배정하다 oversee 감독하다 description 설명 specific 구체적인 requirement 요건 be responsible for ~에 책임이 있다 instruct 알려 주다, 가르치다 hesitate 주저하다

168 추론 / 암시

번역 서덜랜드 씨는 누구이겠는가?

(A) 컴퓨터 프로그래머
(B) 그래픽 디자이너
(C) 회사 매니저
(D) 작가

해설 첫 번째 단락에서 이미 꽉 찬 서덜랜드 씨의 업무 목록에 최근 책 표지 디자인을 추가했기 때문에(Since we recently added book-cover design to your already full list of responsibilities) 새로운 팀원을 보조로 배정하기로 결정했다고 했으므로, 서덜랜드 씨가 그래픽 디자이너임을 추론할 수 있다. 따라서 (B)가 정답이다.

169 세부 사항

번역 서덜랜드 씨가 보고한 문제는?

(A) 불편한 일정
(B) 구식 소프트웨어
(C) 긴 통근 거리
(D) 과중한 업무

해설 첫 번째 단락에서 서덜랜드 씨에게 업무량에 대한 걱정을 공유해 줘서 고맙다(Thank you for sharing your concerns about your workload)고 했으므로, (D)가 정답이다.

어휘 outdated 구식의 commute 통근 (거리)

170 세부 사항

번역 서덜랜드 씨가 다음 주에 요청받은 일은?

(A) 보고서 준비
(B) 잠재 고객 면담
(C) 신입 사원 교육
(D) 업무 분장표 작성

해설 두 번째 단락에서 다음 주 월요일 린코우스키 씨가 도착하면(When Mr. Rynkowski arrives next Monday), 고객 관련 정보를 모두 공유하고(share with him all of your clients' information) 디자인 소프트웨어와 기타 시스템에 대해 알려 줄 것(You will be responsible for instructing him on our design software as well as all other systems that you are using)을 서덜랜드 씨에게 요청했다. 따라서 (C)가 정답이다.

어휘 potential 잠재적인 job description 사무분장표

▸▸ Paraphrasing 지문의 **next Monday** → 질문의 **next week**
지문의 **instructing him(Mr. Rynkowski)** → 정답의 **Train a new employee**

171 문장 삽입

번역 [1], [2], [3], [4]로 표시된 곳 중에서 다음 문장이 들어가기에 가장 적합한 곳은?

"이 신입 사원이 대부분의 업무에서 당신을 지원할 겁니다."

(A) [1]
(B) [2]
(C) [3]
(D) [4]

해설 주어진 문장에서 '이 신입 사원이 대부분의 업무에서 당신을 지원할 겁니다'(This new hire will support you in most of your tasks)라고 했으므로, 앞에서 This new hire가 누구인지 먼저 언급되어야 한다. [3] 앞에서 휴고 린코우스키라는 새로운 팀원(a new team member named Hugo Rynkowski)을 서덜랜드 씨의 보조로 배정하기로 결정했다는 내용이 왔으므로, 이 다음에 주어진 문장이 이어져야 글의 흐름이 자연스러워진다. 따라서 (C)가 정답이다.

172-175 기사

퍼스 데일리 트리뷴

맑고 푸른 바닷속

(11월 2일)－사라 나눕을 찾고 있다면, 바닷속부터 확인해야 한다. 그곳이 바로 그녀가 자신의 최근 사진집 〈맑고 푸른 바닷속〉에 실린 모든 이미지를 포착한 곳이다.

나눕 씨는 아버지가 자신의 다섯 번째 생일에 사용하기 쉬운 즉석 카메라를 주었을 때부터 사진을 찍기 시작했다. 하지만 대학에 입학하고 출판 저널리즘 분야로 진로를 잡으면서 그녀는 카메라를 내려놓았다.

172졸업 후 나눕 씨는 〈퍼스 데일리 트리뷴〉 전속 기자로 채용되어 사진 찍을 시간이 거의 없었다. 173사정이 바뀐 건 그녀가 인도네시아 발리에서 휴가를 보내다 수중 사진 워크숍에 참석했을 때였다. 172/173그곳에서 사진에 대한 관심이 되살아났고 결국 그녀는 사진에만 전념하기 위해 직장인 신문사를 떠났다.

비록 어린 시절 즉석카메라로 시작했지만, 나눕 씨는 현재 고급 수중 카메라로 작업하고 있다. 그녀는 마모에 대처하기 위해 몇 년마다 장비를 업데이트한다. "소금물과 모래는 일반 카메라가 직면하는 것 이상으로 수중 사진 장비에 문제를 **174초래합니다**"라고 그녀는 말했다.

175몇 년 동안 다이빙을 하고 사진을 찍었지만, 그녀는 아직 자신의 직업에 싫증내지 않는다. "사람들에게 한 번도 보지 못한 생물과 장소의 이미지를 보여 줄 수 있다는 것이 여전히 좋아요"라고 나눕 씨는 말한다.

최근 공개된 사진을 포함, 나눕 씨의 작품 대부분은 호주 주변의 바다에 초점을 맞추고 있다. 하지만 5월에 그녀는 그리스로 가서 다음 책을 위해 지중해 해저 유적을 촬영할 예정이다.

나눕 씨와 그녀의 작품에 대한 자세한 정보는 www.sarananmnup.com.au를 방문하면 된다.

어휘 capture 포착하다 pursue 추구하다 renew 되살아나다 eventually 결국 wear and tear 마모 equipment 장비 pose 제기하다, 가하다 profession 직업 ruins 유적

172 주제 / 목적

번역 기사의 목적은?

(A) 전 신문사 직원 소개하기
(B) 사진에 관해 조언하기
(C) 온라인 신문 칼럼 홍보하기
(D) 사진 전시회 광고하기

해설 해당 기사는 〈퍼스 데일리 트리뷴〉에서 작성한 것으로, 전반에 걸쳐 사진 작가인 사라 나눕 씨에 대해 소개하고 있다. 세 번째 단락을 보면, 그녀가 졸업 후 〈퍼스 데일리 트리뷴〉에서 전속 기자로 근무하다가 사진에 전념하기 위해 떠났다(After she graduated, Ms. Nannup was hired as a staff writer by the *Perth Daily Tribune* ~ left her job at the newspaper)고 되어 있으므로, (A)가 정답이다.

> ▸▸ Paraphrasing 지문의 she ~ left her job at the newspaper
> → 정답의 a former newspaper employee

173 세부 사항

번역 나눕 씨가 수중 사진을 찍도록 영감을 준 것은?

(A) 아버지의 조언
(B) 인도네시아 직장
(C) 특정 워크숍
(D) 저널리즘 수업

해설 세 번째 단락에서 나눕 씨가 인도네시아 발리에서 휴가를 보내던 중 참석했던 수중 사진 워크숍(an underwater photography workshop)에서 사진에 대한 관심이 되살아났다(There her interest in photography was renewed)고 했다. 따라서 (C)가 정답이다.

> ▸▸ Paraphrasing 지문의 an underwater photography workshop → 정답의 A special workshop

174 동의어 찾기

번역 네 번째 단락 6행의 "pose"와 의미가 가장 가까운 단어는?

(A) 모형을 만들다
(B) 점검하다
(C) 묻다
(D) 야기하다

해설 "pose"가 포함된 부분은 '소금물과 모래가 수중 사진 장비에 문제를 초래한다(Salt water and sand pose challenges for underwater photography equipment)'라는 내용으로, 여기서 pose는 '(문제 등을) 초래하다, 제기하다'라는 뜻으로 쓰였다. 따라서 '(문제 등을) 야기하다, 제시하다'라는 의미의 (D) present가 정답이다.

175 사실 관계 확인

번역 나눕 씨에 관해 명시된 것은?

(A) 숙련된 다이버다.
(B) 곧 첫 번째 책을 출간할 예정이다.
(C) 그리스에서 사진을 찍었다.
(D) 여러 해째 같은 카메라를 쓰고 있다.

해설 다섯 번째 단락에서 몇 년 동안 다이빙을 하고 사진을 찍었지만, 나눕 씨는 아직 자신의 직업에 싫증내지 않는다(After years now of diving and taking pictures, she has yet to tire of her profession)고 했다. 따라서 나눕 씨가 숙련된 다이버임을 알 수 있으므로, (A)가 정답이다.

> ▸▸ Paraphrasing 지문의 After years now of diving
> → 정답의 an experienced diver

176-180 소책자 + 기사

웨스트우드 부동산 회사
주거 단지

웨스트우드 부동산 회사(WPI)는 캔트빌 시에 주거용 아파트 단지 두 곳을 소유하고 있습니다.

힐사이드 매너 잭슨 로 222번지	레이크뷰 오크스 E. 코르푸 가 119번지
사양: • 세탁기와 건조기가 있는 침실 2개, 3개짜리 아파트 • 수영장, 농구장, 테니스 코트 • 근처에 어린이 공원 • 지역에 일류 학교들 • [180]**상업 지구에서 5분 거리** • 반려동물 친화적인 환경	사양: • 넓은 주방과 욕실이 있는 침실 1개짜리 아파트 • [177(D)]**원목마루** • [177(B)]**각 층에 공용 세탁실** • [177(A)]**헬스장과 야외 수영장** • [180]**상업 지구에서 10분 거리** • 바로 집 앞에 다수 버스 노선 이용 가능 • 반려동물 친화적인 환경

웹사이트 www.westwoodproperties.com에서 평면도를 보시거나 개별 투어 일정을 잡으세요. [176]**월요일부터 금요일까지는 오전 9시에서 오후 5시까지, 토요일과 일요일은 정오 12시부터 오후 5시까지 당사 영업 사원들이 사무실에서 문의에 답변해 드립니다.**

어휘 residential 주거의 laundry 세탁

WPI 확장 발표

캔트빌(3월 16일) – 웨스트우드 부동산 회사(WPI)가 캔트빌 시 정부와 협력하여 캔트빌에 세 번째 주거 단지를 건설할 예정이다. 새로운 주택 단지인 그린 밸리 코트는 150채의 단독 주택으로 구성된다.

공사는 4월에 시작해 18개월 후에 완공될 것으로 예상된다. [179]**WPI가 비용의 60퍼센트를 부담하고 나머지는 시 정부가 부담한다.**

WPI는 부담 없는 가격에 편안한 주거를 제공하여 명성을 쌓았다. [178]**현재 회사가 소유하고 있는 주택 단지인 힐사이드 매너와 레이크뷰 오크스는 5년 전에 건설되었고 수요가 많아 대기자 명단이 길다.**

[180]**WPI 마케팅 담당 임원인 헬렌 하트에 따르면, 그린 밸리 코트는 상업 지구에서 20분 거리에 위치할 것이라고 한다.** 이어서 하트 씨는 이렇게 말했다. "그린 밸리 코트는 은퇴자와 고된 하루 일과를 마친 후 평안과 휴식을 원하는 사람에게 안성맞춤일 겁니다."

어휘 development 주택 단지, 개발지 freestanding 독립된 remainder 나머지 bear 부담하다 reputation 명성 affordable (가격이) 적당한, 부담 없는 demand 수요 retiree 은퇴자

176 사실 관계 확인

번역 웨스트우드 부동산 회사에 관해 언급된 것은?

(A) 매일 사무실을 연다.
(B) 이용할 수 있는 가구를 온라인에 게시한다.
(C) 매시간 개별 투어를 제공한다.
(D) 본사가 켄트빌에 있다.

해설 소책자의 마지막 문장에서 월요일부터 금요일까지는 오전 9시에서 오후 5시까지, 토요일과 일요일은 정오 12시부터 오후 5시까지 자사의 영업 사원들이 사무실에서 문의에 답변한다(Sales agents are available ~ Monday through Friday ~ and on Saturday and Sunday from 12:00 noon to 5:00 P.M.)고 했으므로, 웨스트우드 부동산 회사가 매일 영업한다는 것을 알 수 있다. 따라서 (A)가 정답이다.

▸▸ **Paraphrasing** 지문의 **Monday through Friday ~ and on Saturday and Sunday** → 정답의 **daily**

177 사실 관계 확인

번역 레이크뷰 오크 아파트의 사양이 아닌 것은?

(A) 여가 시설
(B) 세탁 시설
(C) 덮개가 있는 주차장
(D) 원목마루

해설 소책자에 나온 레이크뷰 오크 아파트의 사양(features) 중 '헬스장과 야외 수영장(Fitness center and outdoor swimming pool)'에서 (A)를, '각 층에 공용 세탁실(Community laundry room on each floor)'에서 (B)를, '원목마루(Hardwood floors)'에서 (D)를 확인할 수 있다. 하지만 주차장에 대해서는 언급되지 않았으므로, (C)가 정답이다.

▸▸ **Paraphrasing** 지문의 **Fitness center and outdoor swimming pool**
→ 보기 (A)의 **Recreational facilities**
지문의 **Community laundry room**
→ 보기 (B)의 **Laundry facilities**
지문의 **Hardwood floors**
→ 보기 (D)의 **Hardwood flooring**

178 추론 / 암시

번역 기사가 힐사이드 매너와 레이크뷰 오크 가구에 관해 암시하는 것은?

(A) 18개월 만에 건설되었다.
(B) 4월에 완공되었다.
(C) 많은 사람들이 비싸다고 생각한다.
(D) 많은 사람들이 살고 싶어 한다.

해설 기사의 세 번째 단락에서 힐사이드 매너와 레이크뷰 오크는 5년 전에 건설되었고 수요가 많아 대기자 명단이 길다(Hillside Manor and Lakeview Oaks, ~ are much in demand, with long waiting lists)고 했다. 따라서 많은 사람들이 그곳에서 살고 싶어한다는 것을 추론할 수 있으므로, (D)가 정답이다.

▸▸ **Paraphrasing** 지문의 **much in demand, with long waiting lists**
→ 정답의 **Many people want to live in them**

179 사실 관계 확인

번역 그린 밸리 코트에 관해 기사에서 언급한 것은?

(A) 아파트 2개 동이 포함될 것이다.
(B) 하트 씨가 관리할 것이다.
(C) 건설 비용 일부를 정부에서 지불할 것이다.
(D) 은퇴한 사람들만 이용이 가능할 것이다.

해설 기사의 두 번째 단락을 보면, 그린 밸리 코트 건설 시 WPI가 비용의 60퍼센트를 부담하고 나머지는 시 정부가 부담한다(WPI will bear 60 percent of the costs, while the remainder will be borne by the city government)고 했으므로, (C)가 정답이다.

어휘 restrict 제한하다

▸▸ **Paraphrasing** 지문의 **the remainder will be borne by the city government** → 정답의 **will be partly paid for by the government**

180 연계

번역 그린 밸리 코트가 다른 두 주택 단지와 다른 점은?

(A) 주민들이 반려동물을 키울 수 있을 것이다.
(B) 상업 지구에서 더 멀 것이다.
(C) 노령 거주자를 위한 특별 사양이 포함될 것이다.
(D) 주택 임대뿐 아니라 구입도 가능할 것이다.

해설 소책자에서 힐사이드 매너는 상업 지구에서 5분 거리(Five minutes from the business district)이고, 레이크뷰 오크는 10분 거리(Ten minutes from business district)라고 했지만, 기사의 마지막 단락을 보면 그린 밸리 코트는 상업 지구에서 20분 거리에 위치할 것(Green Valley Court will be located twenty minutes from the business district)이라고 했다. 따라서 (B)가 정답이다.

181-185 이메일 + 이메일

수신: 데니스 마키
발신: 나이젤라 스미스
날짜: 11월 8일 목요일 오후 2시 15분
제목: 업데이트

데니스:

회계와 영업 책임자들이 이곳 플럼스테드 에인즈에서 자신들의 부서에 채용할 최종 후보자를 선정했습니다. 182/183/184**수잔 차이는 회계직 2차 면접에 마르코 가르시아와 다니엘 젠킨스를 부르고 싶어 하며, 라제시 카푸어는 멜라니 유를 의료 영업직 2차 면접에 또 부르고 싶어 합니다.**

181**최종 후보자들에게 전화를 걸어 면접 일정을 잡은 다음 그에 따라 점심을 준비해 주셨으면 합니다.** 수잔은 회의 때문에 다음 주에 사무실에 없다는 점 유의하세요.

지금까지 이번 구인에 협조해 주셔서 고마워요. 특히 1차 면접을 준비하라고 했을 때 마감이 빠듯했을텐데 일을 해내서 감사하게 생각해요.

나이젤라 스미스
인사부장

어휘 accounting 회계, 경리 arrangement 준비 accordingly 그에 따라 assistance 도움, 지원 initial 1차의

수신: 나이젤라 스미스
발신: 데니스 마키
날짜: 11월 8일 목요일 오후 3시 52분
제목: RE: 업데이트

나이젤라:

최종 후보자 세 사람에게 전화했습니다. 182/184**알고 보니 오늘 오후 멜라니 유가 다른 제약 회사이자 우리의 경쟁사인 그랜퀴스트의 취업 제의를 받아들였더군요.** 184**저는 라제시에게 이 진행 상황에 대해 알렸고 그는 다른 적임자를 찾았으면 한다고 말했습니다.**

11월 20일 화요일에 가르시아 씨의 면접을 확정했습니다. 그리고 단골 출장요리 업체가 이곳에서 점심 식사를 준비하도록 했습니다. 185**아쉽게도 젠킨스 씨는 최근 입원을 했고, 따라서 그녀의 면접에 관한 추후 결정은 당신께 맡기도록 하겠습니다.**

데니스 마키
사무 보조

어휘 pharmaceutical 제약의 competitor 경쟁사 suitable 적절한 replacement 대신하는 사람, 대체물 hospitalize 입원시키다

181 주제 / 목적

번역 첫 번째 이메일의 한 가지 목적은?

(A) 공석 발표
(B) 구직자에게 제안하기
(C) 지원자 연락 요청
(D) 구직자 추천서 확인

해설 첫 번째 이메일의 두 번째 단락을 보면, 최종 후보자들에게 전화를 걸어 면접 일정을 잡은 다음 그에 따라 점심을 준비해 줄 것(I would like you to call the finalists, schedule interviews ~ lunch arrangements accordingly)을 요청했다. 따라서 (C)가 정답이다.

어휘 job applicant[candidate] 구직자

▸▸ Paraphrasing 지문의 call the finalists
→ 정답의 applicants (should) be contacted

182 연계

번역 플럼스테드 에인즈는 어떤 회사이겠는가?

(A) 회계 법인
(B) 병원
(C) 출장요리 업체
(D) 제약 회사

해설 플럼스테드 에인즈의 인사부장인 스미스 씨가 쓴 첫 번째 이메일의 첫 단락을 보면, 라제시 카푸어가 멜라니 유를 의료 영업직 2차 면접에 부르고 싶어 한다(Rajesh Kapoor wants to invite Melanie Yu for a second interview for the medical sales position)고 했다. 하지만 두 번째 이메일의 첫 단락에서 멜라니 유가 다른 제약 회사이자 경쟁사인 그랜퀴스트의 취업 제의를 받아들였다(Melanie Yu accepted a job offer with another pharmaceutical firm—our competitor Granquist)고 했다. 따라서 플럼스테드 에인즈도 제약 회사임을 추론할 수 있으므로, (D)가 정답이다.

183 추론 / 암시

번역 젠킨스 씨에 관해 암시된 것은?

(A) 전에 플럼스테드 에인즈를 방문한 적이 있다.
(B) 스미스 씨가 면접을 볼 것이다.
(C) 이전에 그랜퀴스트에서 일했다.
(D) 영업직에 관심이 있다.

해설 첫 번째 이메일의 첫 번째 단락에서 수잔 차이가 회계직 2차 면접에 마르코 가르시아와 다니엘 젠킨스를 또 부르고 싶어 한다(Susan Tsai would like to invite ~ Danielle Jenkins to return for second interviews for the accounting position)고 했다. 따라서 젠킨스 씨가 1차 면접 때 플럼스테드 에인즈를 방문했다고 추론할 수 있으므로, (A)가 정답이다.

184 연계

번역 카푸어 씨는 무엇을 하겠는가?

(A) 가르시아 씨 만나기
(B) 회의 참석하기
(C) 식당 예약하기
(D) 면접할 새 후보자 선정하기

해설 첫 번째 이메일의 첫 단락에서 라제시 카푸어가 멜라니 유를 의료 영업직 2차 면접에 부르고 싶어 한다(Rajesh Kapoor wants to invite Melanie Yu for a second interview)고 했지만, 두 번째 이메일의 첫 단락을 보면 멜라니 유가 다른 제약 회사의 취업 제의를 받아들여(Melanie Yu accepted a job offer with another pharmaceutical firm) 카푸어 씨가 다른 적임자를 찾고 싶어 한다(he hopes to find a suitable replacement)고 했다. 따라서 카푸어 씨가 멜라니 유를 대신할 새 면접자를 선정할 것임을 추론할 수 있으므로, (D)가 정답이다.

▸▸ Paraphrasing 지문의 a suitable replacement
→ 정답의 a new candidate

TEST 3

185 세부 사항

번역 마키 씨가 할 수 없었던 일은?

(A) 배달 음식 주문하기
(B) 주어진 시간 안에 약속 일정 전부 잡기
(C) 유 씨와 대화하기
(D) 스미스 씨를 도와 1차 면접 준비하기

해설 마키 씨가 쓴 두 번째 이메일의 마지막 단락을 보면, 젠킨스 씨가 최근 입원했으니 그녀의 면접에 관한 추후 결정은 스미스 씨에게 맡기도록 하겠다(Ms. Jenkins was recently hospitalized, so I'm leaving any further decision about her interview with you)고 했다. 따라서 마키 씨가 면접 일정 잡는 일을 마무리하지 못했다는 것을 알 수 있으므로, (B)가 정답이다.

186-190 기사 + 웹페이지 + 온라인 주문서

킬로나(6월 2일) – 킬로나에서 신생 기업이 식사 시간에 혁명을 일으키고 있다. [186]**파인 프레시 푸즈는 1년 전 캐서린 미쉬라가 설립한 식사 배달 서비스다.** 이 서비스로 사용자들은 온라인에 접속해 수백 가지 조리법을 찾아볼 수 있다. 이들은 자신들이 좋아하는 조리법을 선택하고 조리 설명서와 함께 재료를 매주 배송받는다.

[186]**미쉬라 씨는 친구들의 바쁜 생활을 관찰하면서 처음 아이디어를 떠올렸다.** "친구들이 너무 바빠서 스스로 계획하고, 장을 보고, 요리를 할 수 없었죠." 그녀가 설명했다. "저녁이면 대개 식당에 가서 음식을 포장해 왔어요. 일부는 자신의 집 주방에서 요리하고 싶어 했지만 솜씨에 자신이 없었죠."

미쉬라 씨는 모든 과정을 간소화할 방법을 찾았다. [189]**파인 프레시 푸즈는 지역 공급 업자들(주로 소규모 농장)과 협력하는데, 이들은 유기농으로 재배하도록 요구된다.** [187]**지역 업체와의 협력에 중점을 두었다는 점과 더불어 서비스의 편리함 및 합리적인 가격으로 인해 이 업체는 큰 인기를 얻게 되었다.** [190]**현재 파인 프레시 푸즈는 킬로나에만 배달되지만, 이듬해에 다른 지역으로 확장이 계획되어 있다.**

어휘 enterprise 기업 revolutionize 혁명을 일으키다 ingredient 재료 instruction 지침, 설명서 observe 관찰하다 confident 자신 있는 streamline 간소화하다 supplier 공급업자 convenience 편리함 reasonable 합리적인 expansion 확장

http://www.penningtonfarm.ca

홈	농산물	소식	연락처

[188/189]**페닝턴 농장이 파인 프레시 푸즈와 협력할 예정입니다!** 30년 전 설립된 이래 저희는 항상 고품질의 과일과 채소를 생산해 왔습니다. 저희 같은 지역 농장을 공급자로 해서 맛있는 요리를 제공하고자 하는 파인 프레시 푸즈의 사명에 도움이 되기를 바랍니다.

페닝턴 농장의 과일과 채소는 한 주 내내 오전 9시부터 오후 2시까지 농장 판매대에서도 구입하실 수 있습니다. 덧붙여 저희는 매주 토요일 오전 하디 가 농산물 직판장, 한 주 내내 러셀 식료품점에서도 농산물을 판매합니다.

어휘 produce 농산물; 생산하다 founding 설립 culinary 요리의 purchase 구매하다

http://www.finefreshfoods.ca/orderform

파인 프레시 푸즈
주문서

이름: [190]**대런 사운**
이메일: dsoun@email.ca
전화: 250-555-0193
선택 조리법: #11 – 닭고기와 채소 볶음 (4인분)
#32 – 아스파라거스를 곁들인 돼지고기 안심 (4인분)
#56 – 채소 보리 수프 (2인분)
총: $50.00 (4873으로 끝나는 신용카드로 청구)
배송 날짜 및 시간: [190]**6월 13일 화요일, 오후 6시**

어휘 stir-fried 볶음 요리 tenderloin 안심 barley 보리

186 주제 / 목적

번역 주로 무엇에 관한 기사인가?

(A) 음식 서비스 회사의 창업 경위
(B) 요리 교실에서 다룰 조리법
(C) 지역 식당이 인기 있는 이유
(D) 저렴한 주방 기구를 살 수 있는 곳

해설 기사의 첫 번째 단락에서 파인 프레시 푸즈는 1년 전 캐서린 미쉬라가 설립한 식사 배달 서비스(Fine Fresh Foods is a meal-delivery service that was founded ~ by Kathryn Mishra)라고 소개했고, 두 번째 단락에서 미쉬라 씨가 친구들의 바쁜 생활을 관찰하면서 사업체에 대해 처음 아이디어를 떠올렸다(Ms. Mishra first thought of the idea when she observed her friends' hectic lives)고 했다. 따라서 파인 프레시 푸즈의 창업 경위와 관련된 기사라고 볼 수 있으므로, (A)가 정답이다.

187 세부 사항

번역 기사에 의하면, 고객들이 파인 프레시 푸즈를 좋아하는 한 가지 이유는?

(A) 시간이 편리하다.
(B) 가격이 적당하다.
(C) 지점이 여러 군데 있다.
(D) 무료 배송을 제공한다.

해설 기사의 마지막 단락에서 지역 업체와의 협력에 중점을 두었다는 점과 더불어 서비스의 편리함 및 합리적인 가격으로 인해 이 업체는 큰 인기를 얻게 되었다(The focus on working with local partners, ~ reasonable price of the service, has made the business extremely popular)고 했다. 따라서 (B)가 정답이다.

▸▸ Paraphrasing 지문의 extremely popular
→ 질문의 customers like
지문의 reasonable price of the service
→ 정답의 Its prices are affordable

188 세부 사항

번역 페닝턴 농장 웹페이지에서 발표된 것은?

(A) 취업 기회
(B) 곧 있을 할인
(C) 업무 제휴
(D) 기념일 축하 행사

해설 웹페이지의 첫 번째 단락에서 페닝턴 농장이 파인 프레시 푸즈와 협력 예정이라(Pennington Farm is teaming up with Fine Fresh Foods!)고 발표했으므로, (C)가 정답이다.

▸▸ **Paraphrasing** 지문의 is teaming up with Fine Fresh Foods → 정답의 A business partnership

189 연계

번역 페닝턴 농장에 관해 무엇이 사실이겠는가?

(A) 가족이 운영하는 업체다.
(B) 최근 두 번째 농장 판매대를 열었다.
(C) 러셀 식료품점에 독점 판매한다.
(D) 유기농 농장이다.

해설 웹페이지의 첫 번째 단락에서 페닝턴 농장이 파인 프레시 푸즈와 협력할 예정이라(Pennington Farm is teaming up with Fine Fresh Foods!)고 발표했고, 기사의 마지막 단락에서 파인 프레시 푸즈와 협력하는 지역 공급 업자들(주로 소규모 농장)은 유기농으로 재배하도록 요청받는다(Fine Fresh Foods works with local suppliers—often small farms—that are required to be organic)고 했다. 따라서 파인 프레시 푸즈와 협력하는 페닝턴 농장이 유기농 농장임을 추론할 수 있으므로, (D)가 정답이다.

190 연계

번역 사운 씨에 관해 암시된 것은?

(A) 고기를 먹지 않는다.
(B) 킬로나에 산다.
(C) 6월 12일에 디너 파티를 연다.
(D) 미쉬라 씨의 친구다.

해설 주문서(Order Form)를 보면 사운 씨가 6월 13일에 파인 프레시 푸즈에 배달을 요청한 주문자(Name: Darren Soun)임을 확인할 수 있고, 6월에 작성된 기사의 마지막 단락에서 현재 파인 프레시 푸즈가 킬로나에만 배달되지만, 이듬해에 다른 지역으로 확장할 계획(At the moment, Fine Fresh Foods delivers only within Kelowna ~ in the coming year)이라고 했다. 따라서 주문자인 사운 씨가 현재 킬로나에 거주한다고 추론할 수 있으므로, (B)가 정답이다.

191-195 이메일 + 이메일 + 차트

이메일

수신: 케이트 밀러슨
발신: 다니엘 프리드먼
날짜: 1월 25일
제목: 곧 있을 포커스 그룹 토론

안녕하세요, 케이트,

새로운 과일 맛 음료 아이디어를 테스트하기 위한 다음 포커스 그룹 토론이 2월 1일 그린빌 사무실에서 열립니다. 마리 고바야시 씨가 주도할 겁니다.

191**지난달에 견본으로 당신이 작성했던 설문지를 사용해 해당 그룹의 피드백을 수집할 설문지를 만든 후 마리에게 보내세요.** 포커스 그룹 토론이 실시된 후 결과를 차트 형태로 집계하세요. 192/193**제가 이 정보를 최고 마케팅 경영자에게 보내는 월간 보고서에 포함해야 합니다.**

감사합니다.

다니엘

어휘 focus group 포커스 그룹 (시장 조사를 위해 선발한 소규모 집단 혹은 그 토론) questionnaire 설문지 template 견본, 원형 tally 집계하다 incorporate 포함하다

이메일

수신: 다니엘 프리드먼
발신: 케이트 밀러슨
날짜: 2월 3일
제목: 그린빌 포커스 그룹 토론 결과
첨부: 그린빌 결과

안녕하세요, 다니엘,

194**마리 고바야시에 따르면 그린빌 그룹 등록 참가자 30명 중 25명이 맛 테스트를 보고 설문지를 작성했다고 합니다.** 결과는 지난달 포커스 그룹 토론의 결과와 대부분 일치합니다. 195**그러나 마리는 그린빌 그룹에서 가장 인기 있는 맛은 예상 밖이었다고 언급했습니다.**

요청하신 대로, 표로 작성한 결과를 첨부합니다. 193**아코스타 씨에게 올릴 보고서용으로 추가 정보가 필요하게 되거나, 아코스타 씨가 설문지 의견을 보고 싶어 하면 알려 주세요.**

케이트

어휘 registered 등록된 participant 참가자 in line with ~와 일치하는 unexpected 예상 밖의 tabulated 표로 만든 additional 추가의

그린빌 포커스 그룹
2월 1일
(숫자는 각 옵션을 선호하는 참가자의 수)

음료 유형:	탄산 (8)		비탄산 (17)	
기꺼이 지불할 수 있는 최고 가격:	1.25달러 (5)	1.5달러 (12)	2달러 (5)	2.5달러 (3)
맛:	체리 (2)	레몬 (7)	195**라임** 195**(13)**	오렌지 (3)

어휘 prefer 선호하다 carbonated 탄산이 든

191 사실 관계 확인

번역 첫 번째 이메일에서 밀러슨 씨에 관해 명시된 것은?

(A) 전에 설문지를 만든 적이 있다.
(B) 2월 1일 포커스 그룹 토론을 진행할 것이다.
(C) 고바야시 씨를 인터뷰할 것이다.
(D) 그린빌 사무소로 전출되었다.

해설 첫 번째 이메일의 두 번째 단락을 보면, 다니엘 프리드먼 씨는 케이트 밀러슨 씨에게 지난달에 그녀가 견본으로 작성했던 설문지를 사용해 포커스 그룹의 피드백을 수집할 설문지를 만들 것(Please design a questionnaire ~ using the one you created last month as a template)을 요청했다. 따라서 밀러슨 씨가 전에도 설문지를 만들었음을 알 수 있으므로, (A)가 정답이다.

192 세부 사항

번역 프리드먼 씨는 밀러슨 씨의 자료로 무엇을 할 것이라고 말하는가?

(A) 직원에게 배포한다.
(B) 신규 고객에게 보여 준다.
(C) 보고서에 포함한다.
(D) 자료를 토대로 기사를 쓴다.

해설 첫 번째 이메일의 두 번째 단락을 보면, 프리드먼 씨는 밀러슨 씨가 집계한 정보를 최고 마케팅 경영자에게 보내는 월간 보고서에 포함할 것(I need to incorporate this information into my monthly report)이라고 했다. 따라서 (C)가 정답이다.

어휘 distribute 배포하다

▸▸ **Paraphrasing** 지문의 **incorporate this information into my monthly report**
→ 정답의 **Include it in a report**

193 연계

번역 아코스타 씨는 누구이겠는가?

(A) 인사부장
(B) 최고 마케팅 경영자
(C) 포커스 그룹 리더
(D) 정보 기술 전문가

해설 프리드먼 씨에게 보낸 이메일의 두 번째 단락에서 밀러슨 씨는 아코스타 씨에게 올릴 보고서용으로 추가 정보가 필요하게 되면 자신에게 알려 달라(Please let me know if you will need additional information for your report to Ms. Acosta)고 했다. 첫 번째 이메일의 두 번째 단락을 보면, 프리드먼 씨가 보고서를 제출할 대상은 최고 마케팅 경영자(my monthly report to the chief marketing officer)임을 알 수 있다. 따라서 (B)가 정답이다.

어휘 expert 전문가

194 추론 / 암시

번역 밀러슨 씨가 그린빌 포커스 그룹에 관해 암시한 것은?

(A) 일부가 늦게 도착했다.
(B) 곧 다시 모일 것이다.
(C) 모든 참석자가 대금을 받았다.
(D) 예상보다 참석자가 적었다.

해설 밀러슨 씨가 쓴 두 번째 이메일의 첫 번째 단락에서 그린빌 그룹에 등록한 참가자 30명 중 25명이 맛 테스트를 보고 설문지를 작성했다(25 of the 30 registered participants for Greenville ~ completed the questionnaire)고 했다. 따라서 등록한 참가자보다 실제 참가자가 적었음을 추론할 수 있으므로, (D)가 정답이다.

▸▸ **Paraphrasing** 지문의 **25 of the 30 registered participants**
→ 정답의 **fewer participants than expected**

195 연계

번역 고바야시 씨를 놀라게 한 맛 선호도는?

(A) 체리
(B) 레몬
(C) 라임
(D) 오렌지

해설 두 번째 이메일의 첫 번째 단락에서 고바야시 씨가 그린빌 그룹에서 가장 인기 있는 맛이 예상 밖이라고 언급했다(Mari did note that the Greenville group's most popular flavor was unexpected)고 했다. 차트 하단을 보면, 라임(Lime) 맛이 13표로 가장 높은 선호도를 보인 것을 확인할 수 있으므로, (C)가 정답이다.

196-200 웹사이트 + 온라인 후기 + 예약 확인

http://www.zabokahaiti.ht

불어 | **영어**

자보카 게스트하우스
히버트 가 99번지, 페티옹-빌, 아이티

[196]**아이티 수도 포르토프랭스가 내려다보이는 언덕에 위치한 자보카 게스트하우스는 유서 깊은 지역에 있는 멋진 건물의 꼭대기 4개층을 차지하고 있습니다.** 저희 게스트하우스는 도심에 위치해 조금만 걸어가면 되는 거리에 시장, 식당, 미술관, 나이트클럽이 있습니다.

세부 사항:

- 무선 인터넷, 주방 시설, 짐 보관소를 포함한 편의 시설.
- [197]**또한 모든 투숙객에게 현지에서 재배된 커피를 포함한 아이티 스타일 무료 조식이 제공됩니다.**
- 객실 요금은 1박에 1인당 45달러(예약을 확보하기 위해 선불로 15달러가 부과됨; 잔금은 도착 시 지불해야 함)입니다.
- 체크인은 오후 1시부터 시작되며 체크아웃은 늦어도 오전 11시 30분까지입니다.
- [199]**숙박은 최소 2박 이상이어야 합니다.**
- 오후 7시 이후에 도착하는 일행은 예약당 5달러의 심야 체크인 요금이 부과됩니다.

어휘 situated 위치한 occupy 차지하다 amenity 편의 시설 storage 보관(소) be entitled to ~을 받을 자격이 있다 up front 선불의 secure 확보하다 remainder 나머지

http://www.travelfair.com

페티옹-빌, 아이티: 자보카 게스트하우스

윌포드 게인즈, 10월 7일 게시

저는 4월에 자보카 게스트하우스에 3박 묵었습니다. 이 지역에는 다른 호텔도 몇 군데 있지만 제가 보기엔 이곳이 분명 해당 가격대에서 가장 훌륭한 선택입니다. [198]**활력이 넘치는 안뜰과 넓은 공용 주방은 다른 투숙객들을 만나기에 아주 좋은 환경을 제공합니다. 확실히 저는 이 점이 가장 마음에 들었습니다.** [200]**거리로 통하는 입구가 오후 7시면 잠기므로 저녁에 도착할 계획이라면 출입문의 전자 키패드 비밀번호를 반드시 받도록 하세요.** 저는 이걸 몰라서 잠시 기다렸다가 들어가야 했습니다. 이것 말고는 묵는 동안 정말 즐거웠어요!

어휘 communal 공용의 environment 환경

http://www.zabokahaiti.ht/receipt167642

예약해 주셔서 감사합니다! 보관용으로 이 세부 내용을 1부 출력해 두세요.

투숙객 이름: [199/200]**멜린다 르**
투숙객 수: 1명
예약 조회 번호: 167642
[199/200]**체크인 날짜 및 시간: 6월 2일 오후 8시**
[199]**체크아웃 날짜 및 시간: 6월 3일 오전 11시**
지불액: 15달러 보증금
+ 5달러 심야 체크인 요금
= 20달러 -8990으로 끝나는 카드로 지불한 총액
도착 시 지불액: 30달러
총: 50달러

도착 전 문의 사항이 있으면 reception@zabokahaiti.ht로 메시지를 보내거나 +509 2555 0161로 전화하세요. 모시게 되기를 기대합니다!

어휘 deposit 보증금 prior to ~ 전에

196 세부 사항

번역 자보카 게스트하우스는 어디에 있는가?

(A) 역사 박물관 옆
(B) 시 환승역 인근
(C) 시에서 오래된 지역
(D) 새로 조성된 주거 지역

해설 웹사이트의 첫 번째 문장에서 자보카 게스트하우스가 유서 깊은 지역에 있는 멋진 건물의 꼭대기 4개층을 차지하고 있다(The Zaboka Guesthouse ~ occupies the top four floors of a gorgeous building in a historic district)고 했으므로, (C)가 정답이다.

어휘 transit center 환승역

▸▸ **Paraphrasing** 지문의 **in a historic district**
→ 정답의 **In an old area of the town**

197 사실 관계 확인

번역 웹사이트에서 자보카 게스트하우스에 관해 언급한 것은?

(A) 무료 조식을 제공한다.
(B) 특별한 저녁 행사를 예약할 수 있다.
(C) 지역 명소 투어를 제공한다.
(D) 미리 전액을 지불해야 한다.

해설 웹사이트의 세부 사항(Details) 중 두 번째 항목을 보면, 모든 투숙객에게 현지에서 재배된 커피를 포함한 아이티 스타일 무료 조식이 제공된다(All guests are also entitled to a free Haitian-style breakfast including locally grown coffee)고 적혀 있다. 따라서 (A)가 정답이다.

어휘 complimentary 무료의 attraction 명소 in advance 미리

▸▸ **Paraphrasing** 지문의 **a free ~ breakfast**
→ 정답의 **a complimentary breakfast**

198 세부 사항

번역 게인즈 씨가 자보카 게스트하우스에서 가장 마음에 들었던 것은?

(A) 친절한 직원
(B) 넓은 객실
(C) 사교적인 분위기
(D) 마음을 끄는 건축

해설 게인즈 씨가 작성한 온라인 후기의 세 번째 줄을 보면, 활력이 넘치는 안뜰과 넓은 공용 주방은 다른 투숙객들을 만나기에 아주 좋은 환경을 제공한다(The lively courtyard and huge communal kitchen both present a great environment for meeting other guests)고 했다. 이후 그 점이 가장 마음에 들었던 부분(That was without a doubt my favorite aspect)이라고 덧붙였으므로, (C)가 정답이다.

▸▸ **Paraphrasing** 지문의 **my favorite aspect**
→ 질문의 **Mr. Gaines like(d) most**
지문의 **a great environment for meeting other guests**
→ 정답의 **Its social atmosphere**

199 연계

번역 자보카 게스트하우스는 르 씨에게 어떤 예외를 적용했는가?

(A) 체크아웃 시간 연장
(B) 심야 체크인 요금 면제
(C) 객실 요금 인하
(D) 하룻밤 숙박 허용

해설 웹페이지의 세부 사항(Details) 중 다섯 번째 항목에서 숙박은 최소 2박 이상이어야 한다(A minimum stay of two nights is required)고 명시했다. 하지만 예약 확인서의 체크인/아웃 날짜와 시간을 보면, 6월 2일 오후 8시(2 June at 8:00 P.M.)와 6월 3일 오전 11시(3 June at 11:00 A.M.)라고 적혀 있으므로, 투숙객인 르 씨가 하룻밤만 숙박했다는 것을 확인할 수 있다. 따라서 (D)가 정답이다.

어휘 extend 연장하다 waive 면제하다

200 연계

번역 르 씨에 관해 암시된 것은?

(A) 전화로 예약했다.
(B) 게스트하우스로 들어가려면 비밀번호가 필요할 것이다.
(C) 허용 한도가 초과된 짐을 가지고 여행할 것이다.
(D) 안뜰이 내려다보이는 객실을 요청했다.

해설 예약 확인서의 체크인 날짜와 시간: 6월 2일 오후 8시(Date and Time of Check-in: 2 June at 8:00 P.M.)에서 르 씨가 저녁에 도착할 예정임을 알 수 있고, 온라인 후기의 중반부를 보면 거리로 통하는 입구가 오후 7시면 잠기므로 저녁에 도착할 계획이라면 출입문의 전자 키패드 비밀번호를 받아야 한다(make sure you get the code to enter into the electronic keypad at the door ~ after 7 P.M.)고 나와 있다. 따라서 7시 이후에 도착 예정인 르 씨가 게스트하우스에 들어가려면 비밀번호가 필요할 것임을 추론할 수 있으므로, (B)가 정답이다.

기출 TEST 4

101 (C)	102 (B)	103 (A)	104 (B)	105 (A)
106 (B)	107 (A)	108 (C)	109 (A)	110 (B)
111 (D)	112 (C)	113 (C)	114 (B)	115 (B)
116 (D)	117 (B)	118 (A)	119 (D)	120 (D)
121 (A)	122 (B)	123 (A)	124 (D)	125 (B)
126 (D)	127 (C)	128 (A)	129 (B)	130 (C)
131 (A)	132 (C)	133 (A)	134 (A)	135 (A)
136 (B)	137 (C)	138 (D)	139 (A)	140 (D)
141 (C)	142 (B)	143 (C)	144 (D)	145 (D)
146 (A)	147 (B)	148 (C)	149 (C)	150 (D)
151 (B)	152 (D)	153 (C)	154 (B)	155 (C)
156 (C)	157 (D)	158 (B)	159 (A)	160 (D)
161 (D)	162 (A)	163 (B)	164 (C)	165 (B)
166 (D)	167 (A)	168 (B)	169 (A)	170 (D)
171 (D)	172 (A)	173 (B)	174 (C)	175 (D)
176 (B)	177 (A)	178 (A)	179 (C)	180 (D)
181 (D)	182 (C)	183 (B)	184 (A)	185 (C)
186 (D)	187 (C)	188 (D)	189 (B)	190 (A)
191 (A)	192 (C)	193 (C)	194 (D)	195 (B)
196 (C)	197 (C)	198 (B)	199 (A)	200 (D)

PART 5

101 인칭대명사의 격 _ 소유격

해설 빈칸은 주어 역할을 하는 명사 account를 한정 수식하는 자리이므로, 소유격 인칭대명사 (C) Your가 정답이다.

번역 저희가 반품된 상품을 받은 후에 고객님 계좌로 입금됩니다.

어휘 credit 입금하다 receive 받다 merchandise 상품

102 동사 어휘

해설 빈칸은 will not be와 함께 수동태 미래 동사를 이루어 주어 Late entries ~ contest에 대해 설명하는 과거분사 자리이다. 따라서 늦게 제출한 출품작은 어떻게 되는지를 나타내는 단어가 들어가야 하므로, will not be와 함께 '접수되지 않을 것이다'라는 의미를 완성하는 (B) accepted가 정답이다. (A) solved는 '해결된', (C) decided는 '결정된', (D) earned는 '얻은, 받은'이라는 뜻으로 문맥상 빈칸에 적절하지 않다.

번역 케이크 데커레이션 경연 대회에 늦게 제출한 출품작은 접수되지 않습니다.

어휘 entry 출품작 decoration 장식

103 명사 자리 _ 동사의 목적어

해설 빈칸은 부정관사 an 뒤에 이어지는 명사 자리로, 동사 has seen의 목적어 역할을 한다. 따라서 an과 수가 일치하는 단수명사 (A) increase가 정답이다. (B) increases는 복수명사/동사, (C) increasingly는 부사, (D) increased는 동사/과거분사로 빈칸에 들어갈 수 없다.

번역 신문의 온라인 판을 읽는 구독자 수가 증가했다.

어휘 subscriber 구독자 increase 증가; 증가하다 increasingly 점점 더

104 전치사 어휘

해설 현재완료 동사 has practiced와 기간을 나타내는 명사구 more than ten years를 적절히 연결하는 전치사를 선택해야 한다. 따라서 '~ 동안'이라는 의미로 특정 기간을 나타내는 표현과 함께 쓰이는 (B) for가 정답이다. (A) at, (C) on, (D) by는 특정 시점과 어울려 쓰이므로, 빈칸에 적절하지 않다.

번역 던컨 앤 헐스 사무소의 모든 변호사는 10년 이상 변호사 업무를 했다.

어휘 attorney 변호사 practice (전문직을) 업으로 하다

105 형용사 자리 _ 명사 수식

해설 빈칸은 more와 함께 비교급을 이루어 명사 drill을 수식하는 형용사 자리이므로, 보기 중 형용사인 (A) powerful이 정답이다. (B) powers와 (D) power는 명사/동사, (C) powerfully는 부사로 품사상 빈칸에 들어갈 수 없다.

번역 프렛하트 공구사는 자사의 이전 모델보다 더 강력한 드릴을 만들었다.

어휘 previous 이전의 power 힘, 권한; 작동시키다 powerfully 강력하게

106 부사 어휘

해설 빈칸 뒤에 오는 명령문을 적절히 수식하는 부사를 선택하는 문제이다. 재고 확인을 하려면(To find out ~ in stock) 해당 물품에 강조 표시를 하고 확인 버튼을 클릭하면 된다는 내용의 문장이므로, 빈칸에는 이 과정이 얼마나 간단한지를 강조하는 부사가 들어가야 자연스럽다. 따라서 '그냥, 간단히'라는 의미의 (B) simply가 정답이다. (A) mostly는 '주로, 일반적으로', (C) enough는 '충분히', (D) quite는 '꽤, 정말'이라는 뜻으로, 문맥상 빈칸에 적절하지 않다. 참고로, (C) enough가 부사로 쓰일 경우 수식하는 대상의 뒤에 와야 한다.

번역 이 웹사이트에 있는 물품이 재고가 있는지 알아보려면 해당 물품에 강조 표시를 하고 "확인" 버튼만 클릭하세요.

어휘 in stock 재고가 있는

107 동사 어형 _ 시제 _ 태

해설 빈칸은 주어 Mr. Jones의 동사 자리이므로, 보기에서 (A) will assist, (B) assisted, (D) is assisted 중 하나를 선택해야 한다. 주어 Mr. Jones가 고객을 도와주는 주체이고, while이 이끄는 부사절의 동사가 현재(is)이므로, 빈칸에는 능동태 현재/미래 시제의 동사가 들어가야 한다. 따라서 능동태 미래 시제인 (A) will assist가 정답이 된다. (C) to assist는 to부정사로 동사 자리에 들어갈 수 없다.

번역 청 씨가 홍콩으로 출장 간 사이 존스 씨가 청 씨의 고객을 도울 것이다.

어휘 client 고객 business trip 출장

TEST 4

108 형용사 어휘

해설 앞에 오는 명사 rates를 적절히 수식하는 형용사를 선택하는 문제이다. '가능한 최저 요금에 보험을 제공한다'라는 내용이 되어야 자연스러우므로, '이용 가능한'이라는 뜻으로 명사를 뒤에서 수식해 줄 수 있는 (C) available이 정답이다. (A) ready는 '준비된', (B) strong은 '강력한', (D) agreeable은 '유쾌한, 받아들일 수 있는'이라는 의미로, 문맥상/위치상 빈칸에 적절하지 않다.

번역 조스티사는 가능한 최저 요금에 임차인에게 보험을 제공한다.

어휘 insurance policy 보험 (증권) renter 임차인 rate 요금

109 부사절 접속사

해설 빈칸 뒤 완전한 절(the Editorial Department receives the ~ approval)을 이끄는 접속사 자리이므로, '~하자마자'라는 의미의 부사절 접속사 (A) As soon as가 정답이다. (B) Still(여전히, 그럼에도), (C) In the meantime(그 동안에), (D) For example(예를 들어)은 모두 부사로 완전한 절을 이끄는 자리에 들어갈 수 없다.

번역 편집부에서 저자의 최종 승인을 받는 대로 원고는 인쇄 업체에 발송되어야 한다.

어휘 author 저자 approval 승인 manuscript 원고

110 부사 자리 _ 형용사 수식

해설 빈칸은 are one meter wide를 수식하는 부사 자리이므로, '대체로, 일반적으로'라는 의미의 부사인 (B) generally가 정답이다. (A) general은 형용사/명사, (C) generalize는 동사, (D) generalization은 명사로 모두 품사상 빈칸에 들어갈 수 없다.

번역 뉴버그 시의 보도는 대체로 너비가 1미터이다.

어휘 sidewalk 보도 general 일반적인; 사령관 generalize 일반화하다 generalization 일반화

111 명사 어휘

해설 빈칸은 동사 has formed의 목적어 역할을 하는 명사 자리로, 빈칸 뒤 to부정사구(to look for ~ locations)의 수식을 받는다. 따라서 빈칸에는 신규 건설 장소 물색을 위해 결성한 것을 나타내는 명사가 들어가야 하므로, '위원회'라는 의미의 (D) committee가 정답이다. (A) member는 '구성원, 일원', (B) building은 '건물, 건축', (C) frontier는 '국경, 한계'라는 뜻으로 문맥상 빈칸에 적절하지 않다.

번역 주택 공사 당국은 신규 건설 장소를 물색하기 위해 위원회를 결성했다.

어휘 authority 당국 construction 건설 location 장소

112 관계대명사 _ 주격

해설 빈칸은 주어가 없는 불완전 절(regularly read food labels)을 이끄는 접속사 자리로, 빈칸이 이끄는 절이 지시대명사 those를 수식하고 있다. 따라서 불완전한 절의 주어 역할을 할 수 있는 관계대명사가 빈칸에 들어가야 하므로, those와 함께 '~하는 사람들'이라는 의미를 완성하는 (C) who가 정답이다. (A) what은 불완전한 절을 이끌 수 있지만 앞에 있는 명사를 수식할 수 없고, (B) where와 (D) when은 관계부사로 빈칸에 들어갈 수 없다.

번역 최근 연구에 따르면 식품 라벨을 자주 읽는 사람이 더 건강한 편이라고 한다.

어휘 recent 최근의 regularly 자주, 주기적으로 tend to ~하는 경향이 있다

113 형용사 자리 _ 주격 보어

해설 빈칸은 주어 you를 보충 설명하는 주격 보어 자리이므로, 보기에서 명사 (A) satisfaction, 현재분사 (B) satisfying, 과거분사 (C) satisfied 중 하나를 선택해야 한다. 주어 you는 상품(toothbrush)으로 인해 만족감이나 불만족감을 느끼게 되는 것이므로, 전치사 with와 쓰여 수동의 의미를 나타내는 과거분사 (C) satisfied(만족스러워하는)가 정답이 된다. (D) satisfy는 동사로 품사상 빈칸에 들어갈 수 없다.

번역 일렉토샤인 칫솔에 만족하지 못하신다면 반품하여 전액 환불받을 수 있습니다.

어휘 full refund 전액 환불 satisfaction 만족 satisfying 만족감을 주는 satisfy 만족시키다

114 전치사 어휘

해설 '~를 향해 가는'이라는 의미의 현재분사 heading과 명사구 the end of the fiscal year를 적절히 연결하는 전치사를 선택하는 문제이다. 문맥상 시간의 흐름을 나타내는 전치사가 들어가야 자연스러우므로, '~로, ~를 향해'라는 의미의 (B) into가 정답이다.

번역 DG 피드 서플라이는 회계 연도 말로 향해 가면서 강력한 성장세를 보였다.

어휘 fiscal year 회계 연도

115 동사 어형 _ 시제 _ 수 일치

해설 빈칸은 if가 이끄는 부사절의 주어 the need의 동사 자리이므로, 보기에서 현재 동사 (A) arise와 (B) arises, 과거완료 동사 (C) had arisen 중 하나를 선택해야 한다. 주절의 동사가 현재 시제(may be asked)로 가능성을 나타내고 있으며, 주어 the need가 3인칭 단수이므로, (B) arises가 정답이 된다. (D) arising은 동명사/현재분사로 동사 자리에 들어갈 수 없다.

번역 도서 박람회 자원봉사자들은 필요시 연장 근무를 요청받을 수도 있다.

어휘 fair 박람회 shift 교대 근무 (시간)

116 전치사 어휘

해설 for the first time과 becoming vice-president of operations를 적절히 연결하는 전치사를 선택하는 문제이다. 문맥상 영업 부서장이 된 이후 처음으로 서울 사무소를 방문할 예정이라는 내용이 되어야 자연스러우므로, '~ 이래로'라는 의미의 (D) since가 정답이다. (A) under는 '~ 하에, ~ 중에', (B) past는 '~을 지나', (C) until은 '~까지'라는 뜻으로 문맥상 빈칸에 적절하지 않다.

번역 화요일에 몰리나 씨는 영업 부서장이 된 이후 처음으로 서울 사무소를 방문할 예정이다.

어휘 operations 영업 활동[전략]

117 형용사 자리 _ 명사 수식

해설 빈칸은 the most와 함께 최상급을 이루어 명사 part를 수식하는 형용사 자리이므로, 보기에서 형용사 (B) impressive와 형용사 역할을 할 수 있는 과거분사 (D) impressed 중 하나를 선택해야 한다. 축제의 일부(part of the festival)인 불꽃놀이(fireworks)는 강한 인상을 주는 주체이므로, '인상 깊은'이라는 뜻의 형용사 (B) impressive가 정답이 된다. (D) impressed는 '깊은 인상을 받은'이라는 뜻으로 감정을 느끼는 주체를 묘사할 때 쓰인다. (A) impression은 명사, (C) impresses는 동사로 품사상 빈칸에 들어갈 수 없다.

번역 참가자들은 불꽃놀이가 축제에서 가장 인상 깊은 부분이었다고 말했다.

어휘 attendee 참석자 impression 인상, 감명 impress 깊은 인상을 주다

118 부사 어휘

해설 '들어맞다, 어울리다'라는 의미의 동사 fit을 적절히 수식하는 부사를 선택하는 문제이다. 따라서 어울리는 정도를 묘사하는 부사가 빈칸에 들어가야 자연스러우므로, '완벽하게, 완전히'라는 의미의 (A) perfectly가 정답이다. (B) recently는 '최근에', (C) routinely는 '관례대로, 정기적으로', (D) occasionally는 '가끔, 때때로'라는 뜻으로 문맥상 빈칸에 적절하지 않다.

번역 면접단은 디나 옹의 학력이 초급 회계사의 직무 요건에 완벽하게 들어맞는다고 생각했다.

어휘 job description 직무 요건, 직무 기술서 accountant 회계사

119 부사 자리 _ 동사 수식

해설 빈칸은 to부정사의 동사원형 track을 수식하는 부사 자리이므로, '확실하게, 신뢰할 수 있게'라는 뜻의 부사인 (D) reliably가 정답이다. (A) rely는 동사, (B) reliable과 (C) reliant는 형용사로 품사상 빈칸에 들어갈 수 없다. 참고로, 해당 문장은 「make + 가목적어(it) + 목적격 보어(possible) + 진목적어(to track ~ points-of-sale」의 구조로 쓰였다.

번역 새로운 소프트웨어로 여러 매장에서 이루어진 구매 건을 정확하게 추적할 수 있다.

어휘 track 추적하다 purchase 구매 multiple 많은 points-of-sale 매장 rely 의지하다 reliable 신뢰할 수 있는 reliant 의지하는

120 전치사 자리 _ 어휘

해설 빈칸 뒤에 기간을 나타내는 명사구 the next few months가 있으므로, 이를 목적어로 취할 수 있는 현재분사 (B) Applying(~을 적용하여), 전치사 (C) Toward(~을 향해, ~ 무렵)와 (D) Over(~ 동안, ~을 넘어) 중 하나를 선택해야 한다. 문맥상 다음 몇 달 동안 차량에 기능을 추가할 거라는 내용이 되어야 자연스러우므로, '~ 동안'이라는 의미의 (D) Over가 정답이다. (A) Provided (that)는 '~라면'이라는 의미의 접속사로 뒤에 완전한 절이 와야 한다.

번역 앞으로 몇 달 동안 캐미언 자동차 회사는 자사의 세단에 더 많은 기능을 추가할 예정이다.

어휘 add 추가하다 feature 기능, 특징, 사양

121 형용사 어휘

해설 빈칸 뒤 명사 upturn을 적절히 수식하는 형용사를 선택하는 문제이다. 따라서 상승의 정도를 묘사하는 형용사가 빈칸에 들어가야 자연스러우므로, '상당한, 많은'이라는 의미의 (A) considerable이 정답이다. (B) wide는 '폭넓은, 광범위한', (C) central은 '가장 중요한, 중앙의', (D) dominant는 '우세한, 지배적인'이라는 뜻으로 문맥상 빈칸에 적절하지 않다.

번역 알토나 인쇄소는 앞으로 몇 주 동안 명절용 카드 주문량이 상당히 증가할 것으로 예상하고 있다.

어휘 expect 예상하다 upturn 상승, 호전

122 명사 자리 _ 복합명사

해설 빈칸은 packaging과 복합명사를 이루어 동명사 creating(만들기)의 목적어 역할을 하는 명사 자리이다. 따라서 만들어지는 대상을 나타내는 명사가 빈칸에 들어가야 하므로, '디자인(된 형태)'을 의미하는 (B) designs가 정답이다. (A) designed를 과거분사로 보더라도 packaging을 수식하기에는 어색하며, (C) designing은 명사로 쓰일 경우 '설계, 디자인(술)'을 뜻하므로 문맥상 빈칸에 적절하지 않다.

번역 EK2 음료는 혁신적인 포장 디자인을 만들어 소비자들이 자사의 물병을 재사용하기를 바란다.

어휘 innovative 혁신적인 beverage 음료 consumer 소비자 reuse 재사용하다

123 동사 어휘

해설 빈칸은 has와 현재완료 동사를 이루어 주어 Ms. Patterson에 대해 설명하는 과거분사 자리로, 전치사구 at defining complex concepts in simple terms(복잡한 개념을 단순한 용어로 정의하는 데 있어)와 어울려 쓰이는 자동사가 들어가야 한다. 따라서 '뛰어났다, 탁월했다'라는 의미의 (A) excelled가 정답이다. (B) organized는 '조직했다, 정리했다', (C) instructed는 '지시했다, 가르쳤다', (D) simplified는 '간소화했다'라는 의미의 타동사로 빈칸에 들어갈 수 없다.

번역 패터슨 씨는 LPID 시스템즈 재임 기간 내내 복잡한 개념을 단순한 용어로 정의하는 데 탁월했다.

어휘 tenure 재임 (기간) define 정의하다 term 용어, 말

124 동사 어형 _ have + 과거분사

해설 빈칸이 has와 to expand 사이에 있으므로, 빈칸에는 has와 함께 현재완료 동사를 이루는 과거분사가 들어가야 한다. 따라서 '약속했다'라는 의미로 to expand ~ menu offerings를 목적어로 취할 수 있는 (D) promised가 정답이다. (A) promptly는 부사, (B) before는 부사/전치사/접속사, (C) although는 접속사로 품사상 빈칸에 들어갈 수 없다.

번역 윈슬렛 푸드 서비스는 구내식당에서 제공되는 메뉴를 확대하겠다고 약속했다.

어휘 expand 확대하다 promptly 즉시

125 전치사 자리

해설 빈칸은 명사구 the results of the customer survey를 목적어로 취하는 전치사 자리로, 빈칸을 포함한 전치사구가 콤마 뒤 절을 수식하고 있다. 따라서 전치사가 들어간 (B) Depending on과 (D) In order for 중 하나를 선택해야 한다. 고객 설문 조사의 결과는 영업 시간 연장을 고려하는 데 영향을 미치므로, '~에 따라'라는 의미의 (B) Depending on이 정답이다. 참고로, (D) In order for는 「In order for+목적격+to부정사」의 구조로 쓰여 '~가 …하기 위해'라는 뜻을 나타낸다. (A) Because와 (C) Whereas는 접속사로 뒤에 완전한 절이 이어져야 한다.

번역 고객 설문 조사 결과에 따라 우리는 매장의 저녁 시간을 오후 9시까지 연장하는 방안을 검토할 수도 있다.

어휘 survey (설문) 조사 extend 연장하다 whereas ~인 반면에

126 부사 자리 _ 형용사 수식

해설 빈칸 뒤 형용사 lightweight를 수식하는 부사 자리이므로, '유난히, 특별히'라는 뜻의 부사인 (D) exceptionally가 정답이다. (A) exceptions와 (B) exception은 명사, (C) excepting은 전치사로 모두 품사상 빈칸에 들어갈 수 없다.

번역 예로우 카메라즈의 렌즈는 망원 초점 길이가 길지만 덮개가 유난히 가볍다.

어휘 telephoto 망원 사진 reach (닿을 수 있는) 거리[범위] lightweight 가벼운 exception 예외 excepting ~를 제외하고

127 부사 어휘

해설 '취득했다'라는 의미의 동사 earned를 적절히 수식하는 부사를 선택하는 문제이다. 수년간 학업을 연기한 후에(After postponing her studies for many years) 학위를 취득한(earned a degree) 것이므로, '결국, 마침내'라는 의미의 (C) eventually가 정답이다. (A) thoroughly는 '철저히, 완전히', (B) distinctly는 '뚜렷이, 명백히', (D) already는 '이미, 벌써'라는 뜻으로 문맥상 빈칸에 적절하지 않다.

번역 루이스 씨는 수년간 학업을 연기한 끝에 결국 법학 학위를 취득했다.

어휘 postpone 연기하다 earn 얻다, 취득하다 degree 학위

128 명사 자리 _ 전치사의 목적어

해설 빈칸은 정관사 the와 전치사 of 사이의 명사 자리이므로, '수익성'이라는 의미의 명사인 (A) profitability가 정답이다. (B) profitable은 형용사, (C) profited는 동사/과거분사, (D) profitably는 부사로 모두 품사상 빈칸에 들어갈 수 없다.

번역 시솜 아이웨어의 수익성에 관해 긍정적인 입장을 보인 보고서는 제휴 업체들로 하여금 그 회사에 투자하도록 했다.

어휘 favorable (전망이) 밝은, 유망한 convince 설득시키다 invest 투자하다 profitable 수익성이 있는, 유익한 profit 이익을 얻다[주다]; 이익 profitably 이익이 되게, 유익하게

129 동사 어휘

해설 to부정사구(to hire ~ for the peak season)의 수식을 받는 명사구 the need를 목적어로 취하는 동사를 선택하는 문제이다. 따라서 '인력 고용의 필요성'과 어울리는 동사가 빈칸에 들어가야 하므로, '강조했다'라는 의미의 (B) emphasized가 정답이다. (A) hesitated는 '주저했다, 망설였다', (C) dominated는 '지배했다, 우세했다', (D) launched는 '출시했다, 개시했다'라는 뜻으로 문맥상 빈칸에 적절하지 않다.

번역 월요일 회의에서 이토 씨는 성수기를 맞아 충분한 인력을 채용해야 한다고 강조했다.

어휘 peak season 성수기

130 명사 어휘

해설 빈칸을 포함한 전치사구 for its ~ materials가 상을 받게 된 이유를 나타내고 있으므로, 빈칸에는 지속 가능 자재(sustainable materials)로 한 행위를 나타내는 명사가 들어가야 한다. 따라서 creative와 함께 '창의적 결합'이라는 의미를 완성하는 (C) incorporation이 정답이다. (A) routine은 '일상, 관례', (B) accessory는 '장신구, 부대용품', (D) submission은 '제출'이라는 뜻으로 문맥상 빈칸에 적절하지 않다.

번역 퓨 타워는 지속 가능 자재를 창의적으로 결합해 최우수 신축 건물상을 수상했다.

어휘 creative 창의적인 sustainable (환경을 파괴하지 않고) 지속 가능한

PART 6

131-134 회람

발신: 재닌 파버
수신: 바커 마케팅 그룹 직원
날짜: 9월 25일
제목: 입구 개량 공사

많은 분들이 알고 계시다시피, 우리 건물 정문이 [131]**엉망인** 상태입니다. 수리가 절실히 필요합니다. 따라서 금요일 오후 6시부터, 수리가 진행되는 약 한 달간 정문이 [132]**폐쇄될 예정입니다.** 이 변화로 입구는 좀 더 깔끔하고 현대적인 외관을 갖추게 될 것입니다.

정문이 폐쇄되는 [133]**동안**, 직원과 방문객은 측면 출입구를 이용해 건물에 들어올 수 있습니다. [134]**모든 1층 사무실은 계속 접근이 가능합니다.**

어휘 improvement 개량 (공사) desperate 절실한 attention 주의, 수리 approximately 대략 renovate 수리하다 streamlined 간결한, 깔끔한 contemporary 현대적인 appearance 외관 gain access to ~에 접근하다

131 형용사 어휘

해설 명사 condition을 적절히 수식하는 형용사를 선택하는 문제이다. 뒤에 나오는 문장에서 건물 정문이 수리가 절실히 필요하다(It is in desperate need of attention)고 했으므로, 빈칸에는 그러한 상태(condition)를 적절히 묘사하는 형용사가 들어가야 한다. 따라서 '볼품 없는, 엉망인'이라는 의미의 (A) poor가 정답이다. (B) stable은 '안정적인', (C) physical은 '신체의, 물질적인', (D) excellent는 '탁월한, 훌륭한'이라는 뜻으로 문맥상 빈칸에 적절하지 않다.

132 동사 어형 _ 태 _ 시제

해설 빈칸에 적절한 동사 형태를 선택하는 문제이다. 빈칸을 수식하는 beginning at 6 P.M. on Friday와 부사절 as it is renovated를 통해 정문(main entrance)이 앞으로 폐쇄될 예정임을 알 수 있으므로, 수동태 미래 시제인 (C) will be closed가 정답이다. 참고로, close는 자동사로 쓰일 수도 있지만, (A) close의 경우 주어와 수가 일치하지 않으므로 빈칸에 들어갈 수 없다.

133 부사절 접속사

해설 빈칸은 완전한 절(the main entrance is closed)을 이끄는 접속사 자리이므로, '~하는 동안'이라는 의미의 접속사 (A) While이 정답이다. (B) During(~하는 동안)은 전치사, (C) Sometimes(때때로, 가끔)와 (D) In the meantime(그 동안에, 그 사이에)은 부사로 완전한 절을 이끌 수 없다.

134 문맥에 맞는 문장 고르기

번역 (A) 모든 1층 사무실은 계속 접근이 가능합니다.
(B) 건설사는 여러 상을 수상했습니다.
(C) 건물은 지어진 지 50년이 넘었습니다.
(D) 이사회가 프로젝트를 논의 중입니다.

해설 빈칸 앞 문장에서 정문이 폐쇄되는 동안 직원과 방문객은 측면 출입구를 이용해 건물에 들어올 수 있다(employees and visitors may use the side entrances to gain access to the building)고 했으므로, 빈칸에도 건물 출입과 관련된 내용이 들어가야 문맥상 자연스럽다. 따라서 (A)가 정답이다.

어휘 accessible 접근[이용]할 수 있는 board of directors 이사회

135-138 기사

(5월 2일) – 자동차 제조 업체인 리베라사는 하비 라미레즈가 이사회 신임 의장으로 임명되었다고 오늘 발표했다. 그는 새로운 벤처 사업을 추진하기 위해 사임한 헬렌 맥가빅의 135**후임자가 된다**.

"우리는 맥가빅 씨의 노고에 감사하며 그녀가 136**앞으로 하려는** 시도에 성공이 있기를 기원합니다." 리베라사의 회장 겸 CEO인 펜 왕 씨가 말했다.

라미레즈 씨는 우주 공학 회사인 엘리아 항공의 CEO로 10년간 근무해왔다. 137**그에 앞서**, 그는 공공 부문과 민간 부문에 걸쳐 다양한 고위 간부직을 역임했다.

"라미레즈 씨는 리더십 경험과 더불어 정교한 기술에 대한 지식이 깊어 우리 회사를 이끌기에 아주 적합합니다." 왕 씨가 말했다. "138**우리는 그의 지도를 기대합니다.**"

어휘 manufacturing 제조 appoint 임명하다 chairperson 의장 board of directors 이사회 resign 사퇴하다 pursue 추구하다 endeavor 노력, 시도 previously 이전에 private sector 민간 부문 familiarity 잘 알고 있음 sophisticated 정교한 suited 적합한

135 동사 어형 _ 태 _ 시제

해설 빈칸은 주어 He(Harvey Ramirez)의 동사 자리로, Helen McGavick을 목적어로 취한다. 따라서 보기에서 능동태인 (A) replaces와 (B) was replacing 중 하나를 선택해야 한다. 빈칸 뒤에서 현재완료 시제(has resigned)를 사용하여 맥가빅 씨가 사임했다고 했고, 후임자가 되는 것은 그 후의 일이므로, 현재 시제인 (A) replaces(대신하다, 후임자가 되다)가 정답이 된다.

136 형용사 어휘

해설 명사 endeavors를 적절히 수식하는 형용사를 선택하는 문제이다. 앞 문장에서 맥가빅 씨가 새로운 벤처 사업을 추진하기 위해(to pursue a new business venture) 사임했다고 했으므로, 빈칸이 포함된 부분은 앞으로 그녀가 할 시도에 성공을 기원한다는 내용이 되어야 자연스럽다. 따라서 '미래의, 향후의'라는 의미의 (B) future가 정답이다. (A) advancing은 '나이가 들어가는, 전진하는', (C) certain은 '어떤, 확신하는', (D) instant는 '즉각적인'이라는 뜻으로 모두 문맥상 빈칸에 적절하지 않다.

137 접속부사

해설 빈칸 앞뒤 문장을 의미상 자연스럽게 연결하는 접속부사를 선택하는 문제이다. 앞 문장에서 현재완료시제(has spent)를 사용하여 라미레즈 씨가 엘리아 항공의 CEO로 10년간 근무해 왔다고 했는데, 빈칸 뒤에서는 과거 시제(held)를 사용하여 다양한 고위 간부직을 역임했다고 했다. 따라서 빈칸에 '이전에, 그에 앞서'라는 의미의 (C) Previously가 들어가야 글의 흐름이 자연스러워진다. (A) Again은 '한 번 더, 다시', (B) Consequently는 '그 결과, 따라서', (D) However는 '하지만'이라는 뜻으로 문맥상 빈칸에 적절하지 않다.

138 문맥에 맞는 문장 고르기

번역 (A) 이 모임들은 정기적으로 열립니다.
(B) 그 제품은 현재 개발 중입니다.
(C) 우리는 그 직책에 대해 더 알고 싶습니다.
(D) 우리는 그의 지도를 기대합니다.

해설 빈칸 앞 문장에서 라미레즈 씨가 리더십 경험과 더불어 정교한 기술에 대한 지식이 깊어 회사를 이끌기에 아주 적합하다(Mr. Ramirez's familiarity with sophisticated technology ~ makes him well suited to lead our company)며 임명된 이유를 설명했으므로, 빈칸에도 그의 지도력과 관련된 내용이 들어가는 것이 자연스럽다. 따라서 (D)가 정답이다.

어휘 on a regular basis 정기적으로 currently 현재 guidance 지도

139-142 편지

> 2월 25일
>
> 응우옌 씨께,
>
> 2월 19일 오전 9시 35분 출발 예정이었던 메두사 항공 859편에 대한 의견 감사드립니다. 이 항공편이 139**취소되어** 유감입니다. 저희는 고객님께서 겪으신 140**불편**에 대해 보상하기로 결정했습니다. 티켓의 미사용 부분인 410달러를 환불해 드렸습니다. 또한, 운항에 생긴 지장 141**으로 인해** 고객님께서 지불하신 호텔비 200달러를 환급해 드립니다. 142**두 금액 모두 고객님 계좌에 입금 조치하였습니다.** 입금 처리가 완료되기까지 영업일을 기준으로 최대 5일이 소요될 수 있습니다.
>
> 이킹 라이
> 고객 관리 부장
>
> 어휘 appreciate 감사하다 regarding ~에 대한 be scheduled to ~할 예정이다 depart 출발하다 cancel 취소하다 compensate 보상하다 inconvenience 불편 refund 환불하다 unused 사용하지 않은 reimburse 환급하다 disruption 중단, 지장 transaction 거래, 처리 process 처리하다[되다]

139 동사 어형_태_시제

해설 빈칸은 주어 the flight의 동사 자리이며 항공편은 취소되는 대상이므로, 수동태인 (A) was canceled와 (B) will be canceled 중 하나를 선택해야 한다. 앞 문장에서 2월 19일 출발 예정이었던 메두사 항공 859편(Medusa Airways' flight 859, which was scheduled to depart ~ on 19 February)에 대한 의견에 감사하다고 했고, 편지를 쓴 날짜가 2월 25일(25 February)이므로, 항공편이 과거에 취소된 것임을 알 수 있다. 따라서 (A) was canceled가 정답이 된다.

140 명사 어휘

해설 빈칸에는 전치사 for의 목적어 역할을 하며 보상을 해 주는(to compensate you) 이유를 나타내는 명사가 들어가야 한다. 앞 문장에서 항공편이 취소되어 유감이라(We are sorry that this flight was canceled)고 했으므로, 보기 중 이와 관련된 단어를 선택해야 한다. 따라서 '불편(함)'이라는 의미의 (D) inconvenience가 정답이다. (A) work는 '일, 작품', (B) time은 '시간, 시기', (C) drawback은 '결점, 문제점'이라는 뜻으로 문맥상 빈칸에 적절하지 않다.

141 전치사 어휘

해설 현재분사 resulting과 어울려 쓰이는 전치사를 선택하는 문제이다. 호텔비 200달러를 지불한 것(the $200 you paid in hotel charges)은 항공편 운항에 지장(the disruption)이 생겨 발생한 결과이므로, '~로 (인해)'라는 뜻으로 쓰일 수 있는 (C) from이 정답이다.

142 문맥에 맞는 문장 고르기

번역 (A) 즐거운 여행 되시길 바랍니다.
(B) 두 금액 모두 고객님 계좌에 입금 조치하였습니다.
(C) 불만 사항은 곧 검토하겠습니다.
(D) 이해해 주셔서 감사합니다.

해설 빈칸 앞 부분에서 비행기 티켓의 미사용 부분에 해당하는 410달러(the unused portion of your ticket, valued at $410)와 호텔비 200달러(the $200 you paid in hotel charges)를 환급해 준다고 했고, 뒤 문장에서 입금 처리가 완료되기까지 영업일을 기준으로 최대 5일이 소요될 수 있다(Please allow up to five business days for the transactions to process)고 했다. 따라서 빈칸에도 환급 절차와 관련된 내용이 들어가야 자연스러우므로, (B)가 정답이다.

어휘 credit 돈을 넣어 주다, 입금하다 complaint 불만

143-146 이메일

> 수신: 촬영팀
> 발신: 샌딥 고스와미
> 날짜: 10월 2일 월요일
> 제목: 헛간 장면 재촬영
>
> 촬영팀에게,
>
> 월로우 마구간 말들이 나오는 광고를 토요일에 재촬영하게 된다는 점 다시 한번 알려 드립니다. 동물과 함께 하는 촬영은 예측이 불가능해서 지난주에 필요한 장면을 얻지 못했죠. 점심 전에 다양한 앵글로 촬영할 수 있도록 143**가능하면** 오전 8시 정각에 시작했으면 합니다. 모두 시간을 지키고 다 순조롭게 진행된다면 그때까지 필요한 장면을 얻을 수 있을 겁니다. 144**하지만 하루 종일 걸릴지도 모릅니다.**
>
> 해당 장면 촬영에 반드시 필요한 사람이 아니면 세트장 출입이 금지된다는 점 또한 145**강조하고** 싶네요. 그렇지 않은 사람은 큰 146**방해**가 될 테니까요.
>
> 샌딥 고스와미
> 모나다 프로덕션즈
>
> 어휘 barn 헛간 retake 재촬영 advertisement 광고 featuring ~가 출연하는 stable 마구간 unpredictable 예측할 수 없는 footage 장면 promptly 정각에 punctual 시간을 지키는 absolutely 절대적으로, 반드시 essential 필수적인

143 접속부사

해설 빈칸 앞뒤 문장을 의미상 자연스럽게 연결하는 접속부사를 선택하는 문제이다. 앞 문장에서 지난주에 필요한 장면을 얻지 못했다(last week we were not able to get the footage we needed)고 했고, 빈칸 뒤에서는 이를 해결하기 위해 오전 8시 정각에 시작하고 싶다(I would like to begin ~ from a number of angles before lunch)고 했다. 따라서 '가능하면, 되도록이면'이라는 의미로 바람을 표현할 때 쓰이는 (C) If possible이 정답이다. (A) Otherwise는 '그렇지 않으면', (B) In either case는 '어느 경우에나', (D) Alternatively는 '대신에'라는 뜻으로 문맥상 빈칸에 적절하지 않다.

144 문맥에 맞는 문장 고르기

번역 (A) 리허설에 감명을 받았습니다.
(B) 다행히 관객들은 눈치 채지 못했습니다.
(C) 다른 장비가 필요할 것입니다.
(D) 하지만 하루 종일 걸릴지도 모릅니다.

해설 앞 문장에서 모두 시간을 지키고 다 순조롭게 진행된다면 점심 전까지 필요한 장면을 얻을 수 있을 것 같다(As long as everyone is punctual ~ we should get the footage we need by then)고 가정했으므로, 빈칸에도 촬영 시간 및 진행에 관한 내용이 들어가야 자연스럽다. 따라서 (D)가 정답이다.

어휘 noticeable 눈에 띄는, 뚜렷한

145 동사 어휘

해설 빈칸은 the fact that 이하를 목적어로 취하는 동사 자리이다. 해당 장면 촬영에 절대적으로 필요한 사람이 아니면 세트장 출입이 금지된다는 점(the set is closed to all ~ filming of the scene)을 당부하는 내용의 문장이므로, '강조하다'라는 의미의 (D) stress가 정답이다. (A) research는 '연구하다, 조사하다', (B) challenge는 '도전하다, 이의를 제기하다', (C) avoid는 '피하다, 모면하다'라는 뜻으로 문맥상 빈칸에 적절하지 않다.

146 명사 자리_전치사의 목적어

해설 빈칸은 부정관사 a 뒤에 이어지는 명사 자리로, 전치사 of의 목적어 역할을 한다. 따라서 '산만, 방해(하는 것)'이라는 의미의 명사 (A) distraction이 정답이다. (B) distracting은 현재분사/동명사, (C) distracted는 과거동사/과거분사, (D) distract는 동사로 품사상 빈칸에 들어갈 수 없다.

어휘 distracting 산만하게 하는 distracted 산만해진 distract 산만하게 하다

PART 7

147-148 공지

스타 디자인즈

고객님들께:

[147]**저희 스타 디자인즈는 양질의 의류를 경쟁력 있는 가격에 제공하고자 오랫동안 노력해 왔습니다.** [148]**온라인 매장을 잠깐 살펴보면 아시겠지만, 아쉽게도 저희는 최근에 어쩔 수 없이 가격을 인상했습니다.** 가격 인상을 피하기 위해 모든 노력을 다했지만 컬러 셔츠와 정장 제작에 쓰이는 면과 대다수 직물 비용이 상승해 가격을 그대로 유지할 수 없었습니다. 그러나, 여러분께서 저희 스타 디자인즈에 대해 높이 평가하시는 탁월한 품질과 고객 중심의 접근법은 앞으로 계속 제공하도록 하겠습니다.

양해해 주시고 변함 없이 이용해 주셔서 감사합니다!

어휘 strive 애쓰다 apparel 의류 competitive 경쟁력 있는 unfortunately 아쉽게도 be forced to 어쩔 수 없이 ~하다 increase 인상하다 recently 최근 avoid 피하다 afford to ~할 형편이 되다 customer-oriented 고객 중심의 approach 접근법 appreciate 인정하다, 높이 사다 loyalty 충성(심)

147 세부 사항

번역 스타 디자인즈가 생산하는 것은?
(A) 소프트웨어
(B) 의류
(C) 화장품
(D) 가구

해설 첫 번째 문장에서 스타 디자인즈가 양질의 의류를 경쟁력 있는 가격에 제공하고자 오랫동안 노력해 왔다(we at Star Designs have strived to offer quality apparel at competitive prices)고 했으므로, (B)가 정답이다.

▸▸ Paraphrasing 지문의 apparel → 정답의 Clothing

148 주제 / 목적

번역 무엇을 알리고 있는가?
(A) 개업
(B) 생산 라인 확장
(C) 가격 변동
(D) 온라인 매장 개선

해설 두 번째 문장에서 아쉽게도 최근에 어쩔 수 없이 가격을 인상했다(Unfortunately, ~ we have been forced to increase our prices recently)고 한 후 그 이유를 설명하고 있으므로, 가격 변동을 알리는 공지임을 알 수 있다. 따라서 (C)가 정답이다.

어휘 expand 확장하다

▸▸ Paraphrasing 지문의 to increase our prices
→ 정답의 A change in prices

149-150 안내책자

아케이드테크
10년 이상 개인 및 중소기업에 서비스 제공 중

하는 일:
- [149]**안전 전자 상거래 기능을 갖춘 반응형 웹사이트 디자인**
- 다국어 콘텐트 개발 및 관리
- 브랜딩과 마케팅

[149]**기본 5페이지 영문 웹사이트 비용 200달러부터 시작.** 긴급 디자인 가능. 오늘 전화 또는 이메일로 상담 받으세요!

고객 후기:
"알렉산더 씨가 디자인한 근사한 새 웹사이트를 개설한 후 제 사업이 날개를 달았습니다. 아주 안전한 전자 상거래 툴 덕분에 고객들의 쇼핑이

쉽고 안전해졌어요."
–*줄리아 멜로*, 플라워즈 투 고

"아케이드테크가 최고예요! [150]**아주 다양한 고객을 수용해야 했는데 이 회사가 귀를 기울여 줬어요. 반응형 디자인 덕분에 커다란 데스크톱 화면뿐 아니라 휴대전화와 태블릿에서도 웹사이트가 잘 작동해요.**"
–[150]***에릭 슈뢰더***, 제임스타운 케이터링

어휘 responsive 반응형의 secure 안전한 e-commerce 전자 상거래 functionality 기능(성) multilingual 다국어의 expedited 긴급한 boost 부양, 증가 accommodate 수용하다

149 추론 / 암시

번역 아케이드테크에 관해 암시된 것은?

(A) 주로 대기업과 일한다.
(B) 웹사이트 해킹을 조사한다.
(C) 다양한 웹사이트 디자인을 제공한다.
(D) 온라인 쇼핑 업체에 배송 서비스를 제공한다.

해설 하는 일(What we do) 항목의 '안전 전자 상거래 기능을 갖춘 반응형 웹사이트 디자인(Responsive Web site design with secure e-commerce functionality)'과 '기본 5페이지 영문 웹사이트 가격 200달러부터 시작(Prices begin at $200 for a basic five-page Web site in English)'이라는 문구로 보아 아케이드테크가 다양한 웹사이트 디자인을 제공한다는 것을 추론할 수 있다. 따라서 (C)가 정답이다.

어휘 investigate 조사하다 security breach 해킹 delivery 배송

150 세부 사항

번역 슈뢰더 씨가 특히 좋아하는 기능은?

(A) 보안
(B) 속도
(C) 간결함
(D) 적용성

해설 고객 후기(Customer reviews)에서 슈뢰더 씨는 아주 다양한 고객을 수용해야 했는데(I needed to accommodate a large variety of customers), 아케이드 테크의 반응형 디자인 덕분에 커다란 데스크톱 화면뿐 아니라 휴대전화와 태블릿에서도 자신의 웹사이트가 잘 작동한다(Thanks to their responsive design, ~ as functional on mobile phones and tablets as on big desktop screens)며 기뻐했다. 따라서 (D)가 정답이다.

151-153 이메일

이메일 메시지

수신: 제프리 브린
발신: 가간 초프라
제목: 정보
날짜: 3월 24일
첨부: ⓪ 초프라 1

제프리 씨께:

제가 다음 주 월요일부터 자이푸르에서 3주 동안 휴가를 보내게 된다는 점 다시 한번 알려 드립니다. [151]**제가 현재 관리하고 있는 원고의 마감일, 그리고 각 프로젝트에 관한 정보들이 담긴 도서 프로젝트 목록을 보내드립니다.** 편집장으로서 할 일이 많으시다는 걸 알기에 제가 없는 동안 제 프로젝트를 관리해 달라고 동료에게 부탁했습니다.

지난 몇 달 동안 이안 프레슬러는 저와 긴밀히 협조해 여행, 금융 관련 책들을 만들었습니다. 따라서 그는 이 분야에 진행 중인 프로젝트들을 잘 알고 있으며, 업무가 순조롭게 진행되도록 살필 것입니다. [153]**어제 점심 때 앤더슨 마켓 근처에 새로 생긴 식당에서 만나 이 프로젝트들을 검토했습니다.** 거기서 관련 업무를 전부 포함한 프로젝트 목록을 만들었습니다. [152]**이안은 프로젝트가 거의 마무리되어 가는 단계에 있는 작가들에게 적절한 이메일 알림 메시지가 발송되도록 조치할 것입니다.** 여행 중에는 인터넷 접속에 제약이 있겠지만, 가능한 한 빨리 메시지에 응답하겠습니다.

가간 초프라

어휘 oversee 관리[감독]하다 manuscript 원고 due date 마감일 pertinent 관련 있는 colleague 동료 appropriate 적절한 respond 응답하다

151 추론 / 암시

번역 초프라 씨는 어디에서 근무하겠는가?

(A) 여행사
(B) 출판사
(C) 식당
(D) 재무 컨설팅 회사

해설 첫 번째 단락에서 초프라 씨가 자신이 현재 관리하고 있는 원고의 마감일, 그리고 각 프로젝트에 관한 정보들이 담긴 도서 프로젝트 목록을 보낸다(I am providing you with a list of the current book projects that I am overseeing ~ about each project)고 했으므로, 그가 출판사에서 근무한다는 것을 추론할 수 있다. 따라서 (B)가 정답이다.

152 세부 사항

번역 초프라 씨는 프레슬러 씨가 무엇을 할 것이라고 쓰는가?

(A) 시장에 간다.
(B) 점심 회의를 계획한다.
(C) 신규 프로젝트를 시작한다.
(D) 이메일을 보낸다.

해설 두 번째 단락에서 프레슬러 씨가 프로젝트 마무리 단계에 있는 작가들에게 적절한 이메일 알림 메시지가 발송되도록 조치할 것(the appropriate e-mail reminders are sent out to the authors ~ completion)이라고 했으므로, (D)가 정답이다.

▸▸ **Paraphrasing** 지문의 **make certain the appropriate e-mail reminders are sent out**
→ 정답의 **Send some e-mails**

153 문장 삽입

번역 [1], [2], [3], [4]로 표시된 곳 중에서 다음 문장이 들어가기에 가장 적합한 곳은?

"거기서 관련 업무를 전부 포함한 프로젝트 목록을 만들었습니다."

(A) [1]
(B) [2]
(C) [3]
(D) [4]

해설 주어진 문장에서 '거기서(While there) 관련 업무를 전부 포함한 프로젝트 목록을 만들었다'고 했으므로, 앞에서 먼저 there가 대신하는 장소가 언급되어야 한다. [3] 앞에서 어제 점심 때 앤더슨 마켓 근처 새로 생긴 식당에서 만나 프로젝트들을 검토했다(We had a lunch meeting yesterday at the new restaurant near Anderson Market)며 there가 대신하는 구체적인 장소를 밝혔다. 따라서 (C)가 정답이다.

어휘 associated 관계된

154-155 문자 메시지

소라야 찬나 오전 8시 45분
안녕하세요, 루. 9시에 새로 온 마케팅 인턴 사원들과 만나서 첫 번째 교육을 시작하기로 되어 있는데 제가 탄 기차가 막 역을 출발했어요.

루 리아오 오전 8시 46분
무슨 일이에요?

소라야 찬나 오전 8시 47분
날씨 때문에 지연된 것 같아요. 철로에 얼음이 있어서 그런 것 같아요? [154/155]**아무튼 제시간에 사무실에 도착할 수 없을 거예요.**

루 리아오 오전 8시 48분
알겠어요. [155]**그렇다면 제가 인턴 사원들을 맞이하고 첫 번째 시간을 진행할게요. 도착하면 합류하세요. 그 후 오후에 인구 통계 조사에 관한 시간을 진행하시면 되죠.**

소라야 찬나 오전 8시 49분
예, 정말 그러면 되겠어요. 고마워요!

어휘 be supposed to ~하기로 되어 있다 delay 지연 make it 시간에 맞춰서 가다 demographic 인구 통계의 definitely 정말, 반드시

154 세부 사항

번역 찬나 씨의 문제는?

(A) 기차를 놓쳤다.
(B) 지연되었다.
(C) 발표할 준비가 되지 않았다.
(D) 깜박하고 인턴 사원과 연락하지 않았다.

해설 찬나 씨가 오전 8시 47분 메시지에서 기차가 지연되어 제시간에 사무실에 도착할 수 없을 것이라(In any event, I'm not going to be able to make it to the office in time)고 했으므로, (B)가 정답이다.

155 의도 파악

번역 오전 8시 49분에 찬나 씨가 "예, 정말 그러면 되겠어요"라고 적은 의도는 무엇인가?

(A) 기차가 움직이기 시작했다.
(B) 기계가 제대로 작동하고 있다.
(C) 제안된 계획이 괜찮다.
(D) 자신의 여행 일정을 바꿀 수 있었다.

해설 리아오 씨가 오전 8시 48분 메시지에서 찬나 씨의 지각 문제에 대한 해결 방안(In that case, I'll greet the interns ~ you could lead the session on our demographic research in the afternoon)을 제안했다. 이에 대해 찬나 씨가 '예, 정말 그러면 되겠어요(Yes, that definitely works)'라고 응답 한 후, 감사(Thanks!)를 표했으므로, 리아오 씨의 제안을 긍정적으로 받아들였음을 알 수 있다. 따라서 (C)가 정답이다.

156-158 기사

중소기업 소식
글 안나 포틴

프레스턴 (8월 29일) – 시에서 중소기업 [156]**호황**이 계속되고 있어 일자리가 새로 생기고 지역 시장이 탄탄해지고 있다. 사실 프레스턴의 중소기업들은 지난해 지역 인력의 25퍼센트에 해당하는 4,300명을 고용했다.

"중소기업은 확실히 경제의 핵심 동력입니다." [157]**랙랜드대학에서 재무학을 가르치는 헨리 비랭거 박사가 설명한다.** "신생기업들은 일자리 창출의 중요한 동력입니다."

비랭거에 따르면 프레스턴은 주 전반에 걸쳐 나타난 동향의 일부라고 한다.

"지난해 주에는 총 19,000개 이상의 일자리가 추가되어 일자리 확충에 있어서 국내 평균치를 웃돌았습니다." 비랭거 박사가 말했다. "약 17퍼센트가 중소기업이었습니다. [158]**더욱이 중소기업에서 창출되는 개인 소득 덕분에 규모가 더 크고 이미 입지가 탄탄한 기업들도 이득을 보았습니다.**"

창업에 관심이 있는 당사자들은 정부의 주립 중소기업 센터를 찾아 사업계획서 작성, 자본 물색, 마케팅 전략 학습에 도움을 청할 수 있다.

어휘 strengthen 강화하다 labor force 인력 significant 현저한 province 주, 도 expansion 확장 personal income 개인 소득 generate 창출하다 established 입지가 탄탄한 benefit 이득[혜택]을 보다 access 접근하다 capital 자본 strategy 전략

156 동의어 찾기

번역 첫 번째 단락 2행의 "boom"과 의미가 가장 가까운 단어는?

(A) 소리
(B) 발견
(C) 성장
(D) 놀라움

해설 "boom"이 포함된 부분은 '시의 중소기업 호황이 계속되고 있다(The town's small business boom continues)'라는 내용으로, 여기서 boom은 '호황, 붐'이라는 뜻으로 쓰였다. 따라서 '성장, 증가'라는 의미의 (C) growth가 정답이다.

157 추론 / 암시

번역 비랭거 박사는 누구이겠는가?

(A) 주 중소기업 센터 소장
(B) 중소기업 소유주
(C) 프레스턴 시장
(D) 대학 교수

해설 두 번째 단락에서 '랙랜드대학에서 재무학을 가르치는 헨리 비랭거 박사(Dr. Henry Belanger, who teaches finance at Lackland University)'라고 했으므로, 비랭거 박사가 대학 교수임을 추론할 수 있다. 따라서 (D)가 정답이다.

▸▸ Paraphrasing 지문의 who teaches finance at Lackland University → 정답의 A university professor

158 사실 관계 확인

번역 비랭거 박사가 중소기업에 관해 언급하는 것은?

(A) 정부가 중소기업을 돕기 위해 새 사무소를 개설했다.
(B) 더 큰 조직까지 영향력이 확대된다.
(C) 경험이 부족한 직원들에게 훈련을 제공한다.
(D) 주 전역에 걸쳐 폐업을 하고 있다.

해설 네 번째 단락에서 중소기업에서 창출되는 개인 소득 덕분에 규모가 더 크고 이미 입지가 탄탄한 기업들도 이득을 보았다(thanks to the personal income generated by small companies, larger, established businesses benefited too)고 했으므로, (B)가 정답이다.

어휘 impact 영향 extend 확대되다 inexperienced 경험이 부족한

▸▸ Paraphrasing 지문의 larger, established businesses → 정답의 larger organizations

159-160 이메일

수신: dianepaxton@lamail.com
발신: customerservice@lenfordfinancial.co.uk
제목: 온라인 계정
날짜: 6월 22일

팩스턴 씨께,

렌포드 파이낸셜에 관심 가져 주셔서 감사합니다. [159]**고객님의 온라인 문의를 접수하여 임시 사용자명과 비밀번호를 발급했습니다.** 온라인 계정을 활성화하려면 다음 단계를 따르세요.

1. 웹사이트로 가서 "신규 등록"을 선택합니다.
2. 사용자명 DPAXTON, 비밀번호 XA098T를 이용해 로그인합니다. 새 사용자명과 비밀번호를 생성하라는 요청을 받으실 겁니다.
3. [160]**신규 고객 조사서가 나타납니다. 고객님의 재무 개요에 관한 정보를 조사서에 기입합니다.**
4. [160]**조사서를 제출한 후,** 계정 담당자 중 한 명이 24시간 이내에 전화를 걸어 포트폴리오와 향후 투자에 대해 논의하게 됩니다.

고객님의 재무 목표를 이룰 수 있게 저희가 도와드리기를 기대합니다.

켄트 롤린
고객 계정 담당자

어휘 inquiry 문의 issue 발급하다 temporary 임시의 activate 활성화하다 registration 등록 prompt (컴퓨터 상에서) ~하라고 요청하다 submit 제출하다 representative 담당자, 직원 investment 투자 attain 이루다

159 추론 / 암시

번역 이메일이 팩스턴 씨에 관해 암시하는 것은?

(A) 렌포드 파이낸셜에 정보를 요청했다.
(B) 재무 전문가다.
(C) 오랫동안 렌포드 파이낸셜 고객이었다.
(D) 자신의 계정에 로그인할 수 없었다.

해설 첫 번째 단락에서 온라인 문의를 접수하여 임시 사용자명과 비밀번호를 발급했다(We have received your online inquiry and have issued a temporary username and password)고 했으므로, 수신자인 팩스턴 씨가 먼저 해당 정보를 요청했음을 추론할 수 있다. 따라서 (A)가 정답이다.

160 세부 사항

번역 팩스턴 씨가 하라고 지시 받은 일은?

(A) 계정 담당자에게 연락한다.
(B) 임시 비밀번호를 요청한다.
(C) 전화로 설문 조사를 받는다.
(D) 양식을 온라인으로 제출한다.

해설 온라인 계정을 활성화하기 위해 따라야 할 단계를 보면, 웹사이트에 방문해(Go to our Web site) 신규 고객 조사서에 재무 개요에 관한 정보를 작성한 후(Fill out the survey with information about your financial profile) 제출하라(After you submit the survey)고 나와 있다. 따라서 (D)가 정답이다.

▸▸ Paraphrasing 지문의 Web site → 정답의 online
지문의 A new-customer survey → 정답의 a form

161-163 구인 공고

그린록대학에서 기술연구소 조교 구함

학생들의 요구 때문에 그린록대학 기술연구소는 이제 저녁에도 문을 엽니다. [161]**이처럼 연장된 시간으로 인해 저녁에 일할 연구소 조교를 구하고 있습니다.** [162(C)]**합격자는 3-D 프린팅, 기초 코딩, 그래픽 디자인 프로그램 및 영상 제작 소프트웨어 관련 다양한 지식과 기술을 보유해야 합니다.**

[162(B)/(D)]**저희는 끈기 있고 창의적이며 남을 잘 돕는 사람을 찾고 있습니다.** 새로운 것을 배우기 좋아하고 이 지식을 타인과 공유하기 좋아하는 지원자라면 더할 나위 없이 좋습니다. 면접 대상으로 선정된 지원자는 직접 작업한 기술 관련 프로젝트 샘플을 가져오라는 요청을 받을 것이며, 해당 프로젝트에 관해 설명할 준비가 되어 있어야 합니다. [163]**관심 있는 지원자는 tech@greenrockuniversity.edu로 자기소개서와 이력서를 보내십시오.**

어휘 lab 연구소, 실험실 demand 요구 extended 연장된 candidate 지원자 possess 소유하다 a range of 다양한 relevant 관련된 patient 끈기 있는 applicant 지원자

161 세부 사항

번역 연구소 조교 직을 제안하는 이유는?

(A) 건물 수리가 마무리되었다.
(B) 장비가 현대화되었다.
(C) 일부 직원이 떠났다.
(D) 운영 시간이 변경되었다.

해설 첫 번째 단락에서 운영 시간이 연장되어 저녁에 일할 연구소 조교를 구하고 있다(As a result of these extended hours, we are seeking an evening lab assistant)고 했으므로, (D)가 정답이다.

▸▸ Paraphrasing 지문의 **these extended hours**
→ 정답의 **Hours of operation have changed**

162 사실 관계 확인

번역 일자리의 요건이 아닌 것은?

(A) 그래픽 디자인 학위
(B) 남을 돕고자 하는 마음
(C) 코딩 지식
(D) 창의성

해설 두 번째 단락의 '끈기 있고 창의적이며 남을 잘 돕는 사람을 찾고 있다(We are looking for a person who is patient, creative and enjoys helping others)'에서 (B)와 (D)를, 첫 번째 단락의 '합격자는 3-D 프린팅, 기초 코딩, 그래픽 디자인 프로그램 및 영상 제작 소프트웨어 관련 다양한 지식과 기술을 보유해야 한다(The successful candidate should possess a range of relevant knowledge and skills in 3-D printing ~ movie-making software)'에서 (C)를 확인할 수 있다. 따라서 언급되지 않은 (A)가 정답이다.

▸▸ Paraphrasing 지문의 **enjoys helping others**
→ 보기 (B)의 **A desire to help others**
지문의 **relevant knowledge and skills in ~ basic coding**
→ 보기 (C)의 **Coding knowledge**

163 세부 사항

번역 지원자는 어떻게 그 자리에 지원해야 하는가?

(A) 전화로
(B) 이메일로
(C) 속달우편으로
(D) 직접

해설 두 번째 단락의 마지막 문장에서 이메일 주소를 알려 주며 관심 있는 지원자는 자기소개서와 이력서를 보내라(Interested applicants should send a letter of interest and résumé to tech@greenrockuniversity.edu)고 했으므로, (B)가 정답이다.

어휘 in person 직접, 몸소

▸▸ Paraphrasing 지문의 **send ~ to tech@greenrockuniversity.edu** → 정답의 **By e-mail**

164-167 이메일

수신: 앨런 로저슨 〈arogerson@rogersoncorp.ca〉
발신: 요시 타케다 〈ytakeda@dskt.co.jp〉
제목: 온실 시스템
날짜: 11월 18일
첨부: DSKTgs

로저슨 씨께,

[164]**지난주 더블린에서 열린 농업 기술 무역 박람회에서 이야기를 나눌 기회를 가져서 기쁩니다.** [164/167]**귀하의 요청에 따라, DSKT 온실 시스템에 관한 전자 버전 소책자를 첨부합니다.** 어떻게 저희 시스템이 귀하의 요구를 충족할 수 있는지 이것이 보여 줄 것으로 확신합니다.

[165]**귀하의 온실들이 서로 약간 떨어진 곳에 있다고 알고 있습니다.** 저희 환경 감시 시스템을 사용하면 각 온실의 온도, 습도, 그리고 공기 질을 원격으로 확인하실 수 있습니다. 더 이상 매일 밤 관측하느라 현장에 갈 필요가 없습니다. [166]**DSKT가 측정값을 스마트폰이나 컴퓨터로 전송합니다.**

[165]**저희 농작물 관개 시스템에도 관심이 있으실 겁니다.** 더 많은 정보를 원하시면 알려 주세요. 저희 제품에 대해서라면 어떤 질문이든 기꺼이 답변해 드리겠습니다.

요시 타케다

어휘 agricultural 농업의 distance 거리 environmental 환경의 temperature 온도 humidity 습도 remotely 원격으로 on-site 현장의 observation 관측 reading 측정값 crop 농작물 irrigation 관개

164 주제 / 목적

번역 타케다 씨가 이메일을 보낸 이유는?

(A) 무역 박람회 참가에 관해 문의하기 위하여
(B) 곧 있을 회의에 관해 의논하기 위하여
(C) 최근 대화에 이어 후속 조치를 취하기 위하여
(D) 제품 시연 일정을 잡기 위하여

해설 첫 번째 단락에서 지난주 더블린에서 열린 농업 기술·무역 박람회에서 이야기 나눴던 것(I am glad we got a chance to talk ~ last week)을 언급한 후, 로저슨 씨의 요청에 따라 DSKT 온실 시스템에 관한 전자 버전 소책자를 첨부한다(Per your request, I have attached an electronic version of ~ the DSKT greenhourse system)고 했다. 따라서 최근 대화에 이어 후속 조치를 취하기 위한 이메일임을 알 수 있으므로, (C)가 정답이다.

어휘 follow up 후속 조치를 취하다 recent 최근의 product demonstration 제품 시연

▸▸ Paraphrasing 지문의 we got a chance to talk ~ last week
→ 정답의 a recent conversation

165 추론 / 암시

번역 로저슨 씨에 관해 암시된 것은?

(A) 출장을 거의 다니지 않는다.
(B) 농업에 종사하고 있다.
(C) 환경 과학 전문가다.
(D) 스마트폰 애플리케이션을 설계했다.

해설 두 번째 단락에서 로저슨 씨의 온실(your greenhouses)을 언급했고, 세 번째 단락에서 로저슨 씨가 농작물 관개 시스템에도 관심이 있을 것(You might also be interested in our crop irrigation systems)으로 추측했으므로, 로저슨 씨가 농업에 종사한다고 추론할 수 있다. 따라서 (B)가 정답이다.

어휘 involved 종사하는, 관여하는

166 세부 사항

번역 이메일에 따르면, DSKT 온실 시스템이 할 수 있는 것은?

(A) 식물에 물 주기
(B) 기계 작동 멈추기
(C) 조명 통제하기
(D) 정보 전송하기

해설 두 번째 단락에서 DSKT가 온도, 습도 등의 측정값을 스마트폰이나 컴퓨터로 전송한다(DSKT sends the readings to your smartphone or computer)고 했으므로, (D)가 정답이다.

어휘 disable (기계 등을) 작동 못하게 하다 transmit 전송하다

▸▸ Paraphrasing 지문의 sends the readings
→ 정답의 Transmit information

167 문장 삽입

번역 [1], [2], [3], [4]로 표시된 곳 중에서 다음 문장이 들어가기에 가장 적합한 곳은?

"어떻게 저희 시스템이 귀하의 요구를 충족할 수 있는지 이것이 보여 줄 것으로 확신합니다."

(A) [1]
(B) [2]
(C) [3]
(D) [4]

해설 주어진 문장에서 어떻게 자사의 시스템이 로저슨 씨의 요구를 충족할 수 있는지 이것이 보여 줄 것이라(it will illustrate how our system can meet your needs)고 했으므로, 앞에서 먼저 it이 대신하는 대상이 나와야 한다. [1] 앞에서 로저슨 씨의 요청에 따라 DSKT 온실 시스템에 관한 전자 버전 소책자를 첨부한다(an electronic version of our booklet on the DSKT greenhouse system)며 it이 가리키는 자료를 언급했으므로, (A)가 정답이다.

168-171 공지

"형태와 색채의 표현"
3월 30일
오후 5시 30분 - 오후 9시

행사 설명: [168]**서머레이크대학 미술학과는 오늘 오후 5시 30분 4동에 위치한 교내 미술관에서 연례 전시회를 열게 되어 기쁩니다.** [171(A)]**오셔서 음료와 전채 요리를 즐기면서 회화, 사진, 소묘, 조각 등 새로운 미술 작품을 관람하세요.**

[169/171(B)]**학생 예술가들이 오늘 저녁 오후 5시 30분부터 7시 30분까지 미술관에서 방문객에게 자신들의 작품에 대해 직접 이야기합니다.** [170]**오후 7시 30분, 〈구출되다〉의 조각가 핀 올슨이 밀라노 유학이 자신의 작품에 미친 영향에 대해 발표하겠습니다.** 올슨 씨는 4월에 학위를 마치는데 이미 개인 소장가에게 많은 작품을 판매했고 아동을 대상으로 워크숍을 지도하고 있습니다.

이번 행사는 학생, 교수, 그리고 일반에게 공개됩니다. [171(C)]**4동과 8동 옆에 있는 지정 구역에 주차 가능합니다. 4동 옆 구역은 허가증이 필요하지만 8동 옆 구역은 일반에게 무료입니다.**

전시 작품 목록을 포함한 자세한 정보를 보려면 미술학과 웹사이트 www.summerlake.edu/artdepartment/events를 방문하세요.

어휘 sculpture 조각(품) beverage 음료 appetizer 전채 요리 be on hand 참석하다 sculptor 조각가 influence 영향을 미치다 piece 작품 faculty 교수진 designated 지정된 permit 허가증

168 주제 / 목적

번역 공지의 목적은?

(A) 미술 강좌 광고
(B) 연례 전시회 홍보
(C) 조각품 판매 홍보
(D) 미술관 개관 발표

해설 첫 번째 단락에서 연례 전시회를 열게 되어 기쁘다(The Summerlake University Art Department is pleased to present its annual showcase)고 한 후 관련 정보를 안내하고 있으므로, 연례 전시회 홍보를 위한 공지임을 알 수 있다. 따라서 (B)가 정답이다.

어휘 advertise 광고하다 promote 홍보하다 exhibition 전시회 publicize 홍보하다

▸▸ Paraphrasing 지문의 annual showcase
→ 정답의 a yearly exhibition

169 사실 관계 확인

번역 미술 작품에 관해 명시된 것은?

(A) 학생들이 제작했다.
(B) 공통 주제를 표현한다.
(C) 일부 개인 소장 작품들이 포함된다.
(D) 주로 회화로 구성된다.

해설 두 번째 단락에서 학생 예술가들이 저녁에 미술관에서 방문객에게 자신들의 작품에 대해 직접 이야기한다(Student artists will be on hand to speak about their work ~ this evening)고 했으므로, 학생들이 제작한 작품임을 알 수 있다. 따라서 (A)가 정답이다.

어휘 represent 표현하다

170 사실 관계 확인

번역 올슨 씨에 관해 언급된 것은?

(A) 최근 대학을 졸업했다.
(B) 웹사이트를 운영한다.
(C) 주차 허가증이 있다.
(D) 외국으로 여행했다.

해설 두 번째 단락에서 핀 올슨이 밀라노 유학이 자신의 작품에 미친 영향에 대해 발표할 예정(Fin Olson ~ will give a presentation about how his study abroad in Milan influenced his work)이라고 했으므로, 올슨 씨가 외국에 갔던 경험이 있음을 알 수 있다. 따라서 (D)가 정답이다.

▸▸ Paraphrasing 지문의 **his study abroad**
→ 정답의 **He traveled to another country**

171 추론 / 암시

번역 행사에 관해 암시된 것이 아닌 것은?

(A) 다과가 제공될 것이다.
(B) 예술가들이 참석자들과 이야기를 나눌 것이다.
(C) 무료 주차가 가능하다.
(D) 시연회가 열릴 것이다.

해설 첫 번째 단락의 '음료와 전채 요리를 즐기면서 새로운 미술 작품을 관람하세요(Come see new artwork ~ while enjoying beverages and appetizers)'에서 (A)를, 두 번째 단락의 '학생 예술가들이 방문객에게 자신들의 작품에 대해 직접 이야기합니다(Student artists will be on hand to speak about their work to visitors)'에서 (B)를, 세 번째 단락의 '8동 옆 구역은 일반에게 무료입니다(the area by Building 8 is free to the public)'에서 (C)를 추론할 수 있다. 따라서 언급되지 않은 (D)가 정답이다.

어휘 refreshment 다과 available 이용 가능한

▸▸ Paraphrasing 지문의 **beverages and appetizers**
→ 보기 (A)의 **Refreshments**
지문의 **speak ~ to visitors**
→ 보기 (B)의 **speak with attendees**
지문의 **the area by Building 8 is free to the public** → 보기 (C)의 **Free parking**

172-175 온라인 채팅

이치로 와타나베 (오전 9시 30분)
[172/175]**금요일 부서 회의 전에 치과 점검 과정을 개선할 아이디어 있으신가요?**

수잔 패린 (오전 9시 31분)
서류 작업이 너무 많아요. 조사관이 양식을 컴퓨터로 완성해도 될 텐데요.

재커리 챈 (오전 9시 32분)
좋은 생각이에요. 그러면 종이를 완전히 없앨 수 있겠어요.

이치로 와타나베 (오전 9시 33분)
시간과 돈을 절약하는 효과적인 방안이 되겠네요. 하지만 어떻게 해야 현재 양식 대신 전자 양식을 사용하게 될 수 있을까요? [173]**조사관들이 어떻게 교육을 받으면 좋을까요?**

수잔 패린 (오전 9시 35분)
조사관들이 새로운 전자 버전 사용법을 익히는 동안은 종이 양식을 계속 쓰면 어때요?

재커리 챈 (오전 9시 36분)
그렇게 하면 전자 양식을 어느 정도 경험할 수 있을 거예요. [173/174]**조사관들이 이행에 대비할 수 있게 이들을 교육할 강사를 채용해도 될 것 같아요.**

수잔 패린 (오전 9시 38분)
맞아요. [173/174]**이곳 노동부에서 교육 세션을 열면 돼요.**

이치로 와타나베 (오전 9시 40분)
좋아요. [175]**회의에서 이런 아이디어를 제안해 볼게요.**

어휘 improve 개선하다 inspection 점검 electronically 컴퓨터로 eliminate 제거하다 completely 완전히 effective 효과적인 transition 이행, 전환; 이행하다 current 현재의

172 주제 / 목적

번역 글쓴이들이 논의하고 있는 것은?

(A) 업무 절차 변경
(B) 숙련된 조사관 채용
(C) 신설 부서 직원 배치
(D) 추가 종이 양식 만들기

해설 와타나베 씨가 오전 9시 30분 메시지에서 치과 점검 과정을 개선할 아이디어가 있는지(Does anyone have ideas ~ for improving the inspection process for dental offices?) 물었고, 이후 현재 사용하는 양식 대신 전자 양식을 사용하여 서류 작업을 줄일 방안에 대해 논의했다. 따라서 (A)가 정답이다.

▸▸ Paraphrasing 지문의 **improving the inspection process**
→ 정답의 **Changing a work procedure**

173 추론 / 암시

번역 글쓴이들에 관해 암시된 것은?

(A) 치과 보조원을 교육한다.
(B) 다른 직원들을 관리한다.
(C) 예산을 결정하고 있다.
(D) 컴퓨터를 구매하고 있다.

TEST 4

해설 와타나베 씨가 오전 9시 33분 메시지에서 조사관들이 어떻게 교육받는 것이 좋을지(How would inspectors be trained?) 물어본 것과, 이후 챈 씨와 패린 씨가 방안을 제시한 것(hire instructors, hold the training session here at the Labor Department)으로 보아 이들이 다른 직원들을 관리하는 일을 한다고 추론할 수 있다. 따라서 (B)가 정답이다.

어휘 budget 예산 purchase 구매하다

174 의도 파악

번역 오전 9시 38분에 패린 씨가 "맞아요"라고 적은 의도는 무엇이겠는가?

(A) 몇 년의 경험이 필요한지 알고 있다.
(B) 모든 서류 작업이 정확한지 확인하고 싶다.
(C) 챈 씨의 아이디어가 문제를 해결할 것으로 생각한다.
(D) 와타나베 씨의 판단이 정확하다고 믿는다.

해설 챈 씨가 오전 9시 36분 메시지에서 조사관을 교육할 강사를 채용해도 될 것 같다(And maybe we could hire instructors to train our inspectors)고 제안했다. 이에 대해 패린 씨가 '맞아요(Exactly)'라고 응답한 후 노동부에서 교육 세션을 열면 된다(We could hold the training sessions here at the Labor Department)며 챈 씨의 의견에 동조했다. 따라서 (C)가 정답이다.

어휘 accurate 정확한 resolve 해결하다 estimate 판단

175 추론 / 암시

번역 와타나베 씨는 금요일에 무엇을 하겠는가?

(A) 조사관 상대로 강의하기
(B) 교육 담당자들에게 설문 조사지 배포하기
(C) 전자 양식 사용법을 배우기
(D) 문제 해결책을 제안하기

해설 와타나베 씨가 오전 9시 30분 메시지에서 금요일 부서 회의 참석 전에 치과 점검 과정을 개선할 아이디어가 있는지(Does anyone have ideas ~ for improving the inspection process for dental offices?) 물었고, 오전 9시 40분 메시지에서 함께 논의한 아이디어를 회의할 때 제안해 보겠다(I'll propose these ideas at the meeting)고 했다. 따라서 와타나베 씨가 금요일 부서 회의에서 과도한 서류 작업 문제에 대한 해결책을 제안할 것으로 추론할 수 있으므로, (D)가 정답이다.

어휘 distribute 배포하다 solution 해결책

176-180 회람 + 양식

회람

수신: 전 직원
발신: 숀드라 브라운, 복지 담당 이사
날짜: 8월 4일
제목: 건강 강좌

[176/177]**직원 건강과 생산성을 촉진하기 위해, 렐라 제조는 매달 건강 강좌를 제공할 예정입니다.** 참가가 필수는 아니지만, 모두가 이 기회를 이용했으면 합니다. [179]**시간제 및 상근 정규 직원은 무료로 이 강좌를 들을 수 있습니다. 나머지 직원 모두와 수습 직원은 소정의 등록비를 지불해야 합니다.** [177]**유니언 시티 병원의 지역 간호사들이 현장에서 강좌를 진행하므로 다른 곳으로 갈 필요가 없습니다.** 강좌는 매월 첫 번째 금요일 아침에 열리며 강좌 주제는 매달 바뀝니다. [178]**9월에 시작해 12월까지 이어지는 순서별 강좌 주제는 '하기 쉬운 스트레칭', '음식 선택 잘하기', '더 나은 수면을 위한 조언', '단체 운동 시작하기'입니다.**

[180]**상사의 승인이 필요합니다.** 첫 번째 단계는 강좌 요청서를 작성해 복지과로 보내는 것입니다. 질문이 있으시면 복지 상담사 돈 헤럴에게 내선 249번 또는 레아 캐젠에게 내선 199번으로 연락하십시오.

어휘 benefits (회사의) 복지, 수당 wellness 건강 productive 생산적인 take advantage of ~을 이용하다 opportunity 기회 eligible for ~에 자격이 되는 at no cost 무료로 enrollment 등록 on-site 현장의 supervisor 관리자, 상사

렐라 제조
건강 강좌 신청서

이름:	알프레도 데 산토스
[179]**직위:**	**생산부 수습 직원**
[180]**직속 상사 이름/직위:**	게일런 샌더스, 생산부장
신청 강좌 날짜:	9월 2일
등록비 납부:	☑
수령 복지 상담사:	레아 캐젠

어휘 immediate supervisor 직속 상사

176 주제 / 목적

번역 회람의 목적은?

(A) 새로운 요건 설명
(B) 복지 혜택에 관해 직원에게 알림
(C) 절차 개선 방안 제안
(D) 비용 절감 조치 소개

해설 회람의 첫 번째 단락에서 직원 건강과 생산성을 촉진하기 위해 매달 건강 강좌를 제공할 예정(In the interest of promoting a healthy and productive workforce, Lellar Manufacturing will begin offering monthly wellness classes)이라고 했으므로, 회사의 복지 혜택에 관해 알리기 위한 회람임을 알 수 있다. 따라서 (B)가 정답이다.

어휘 measure 조치

▸▸ **Paraphrasing** 지문의 **offering monthly wellness classes**
→ 정답의 **a benefit**

177 세부 사항

번역 회사 활동은 어디에서 일어나는가?

(A) 렐라 제조
(B) 유니언 시티 병원
(C) 지역 의원
(D) 인근 생산 시설

해설 회람의 두 번째 단락에서 유니언 시티 병원의 지역 간호사들이 현장에서 강좌를 진행하기 때문에 다른 곳으로 갈 필요가 없다(Local nurses ~ will run the classes on-site, so you do not have to travel anywhere)고 했다. 따라서 렐라 제조에서 교육이 진행될 예정임을 알 수 있으므로, (A)가 정답이다.

어휘 facility 시설

▸▸ Paraphrasing 지문의 on-site
→ 정답의 At Lellar Manufacturing

178 세부 사항

번역 9월에 다룰 주제는?

(A) 하기 쉬운 스트레칭
(B) 음식 선택 잘하기
(C) 더 나은 수면을 위한 조언
(D) 단체 운동 시작하기

해설 회람의 두 번째 단락에서 9월에 시작해 12월까지 이어지는 강좌 주제를 순서대로 나열(The class topics in order, starting in September and going through December, will be as follows) 했으므로, 첫 번째로 나온 '하기 쉬운 스트레칭(Easy Stretching)'이 9월 강좌 주제라는 것을 확인할 수 있다. 따라서 (A)가 정답이다.

179 연계

번역 데 산토스 씨가 비용을 지불한 이유는?

(A) 교육 자료를 늦게 반납했다.
(B) 교육 물품을 대체해야 한다.
(C) 정규직이 아니다.
(D) 추가 강좌를 신청했다.

해설 회람의 첫 번째 단락에서 시간제 및 상근 정규 직원은 무료로 강좌를 들을 수 있지만(Part- and full-time regular employees are eligible for these classes at no cost), 나머지 직원들과 수습 직원은 소정의 등록비를 지불해야 한다(All other workers and trainees will be required to pay a small enrollment fee)고 했다. 데 산토스 씨가 제출한 양식을 보면 생산부 수습 직원(Production Trainee)이라고 되어 있으므로, 그가 정규 직원이 아니어서 등록비를 납부했음을 알 수 있다. 따라서 (C)가 정답이다.

어휘 replace 대체하다

180 연계

번역 승인해야 하는 사람은?

(A) 브라운 씨
(B) 헤럴 씨
(C) 캐젠 씨
(D) 샌더스 씨

해설 회람의 마지막 단락에서 상사의 승인이 필요하다(Supervisor approval is necessary)고 했는데, 데 산토스 씨가 제출한 양식을 보면 그의 직속 상사가 게일런 샌더스 씨(Name/Title of Immediate Supervisor: Galen Sanders, Production Manager)임을 알 수 있다. 따라서 (D)가 정답이다.

181-185 웹페이지 + 이메일

http://www.barrowstreetpost.co.uk/tori-fadulu/

토리 파둘루는 지난 2년 동안 〈배로우 스트리트 포스트〉 기자였습니다. 이전에 그녀는 〈콜드웰 타임스〉, 〈앤도버 데일리 뉴스〉 프리랜서 기자로 일했습니다. [181]**그녀는 〈달빛 아래 바위들〉 저자로, 이 책으로 권위 있는 클로크너상의 신인 소설가 부문에서 수상했습니다.** 파둘루 씨는 맥두걸대학에서 언론학 학위를 받았습니다. [182]**그녀는 평생 런던에서 살았지만 여행을 좋아합니다.**

최근 토리 파둘루가 작성한 〈배로우 스트리트 포스트〉 기사

[184]**"문화 밀착 취재", 12월 4일**
몽골의 한 마을 사람들이 자신들의 집에서 기자를 따뜻하게 환대해서 문화와 전통을 공유한다.

"런던의 밤 외출", 10월 19일
[182]**볼거리도 할 일도 아주 많은 런던에서 진짜 런던 사람들은 밤 외출 시 무엇을 할까? 파둘루 씨가 몇몇 시민들과 이야기를 나누면서 알아본다.**

"저예산 탐험", 9월 28일
앨버타주 원주민인 베샤 펠런과 헤일리 루온고가 지난 3년 동안 캐나다 전역을 여행했는데 캘거리에서 아파트를 임대해 살 때보다 훨씬 적은 돈을 썼다.

"남아메리카 하이킹", 8월 5일
파타고니아는 등반가의 낙원으로 자연의 아름다움을 놓칠 수 없는 곳이다. 파둘루 씨가 등산로에서 등반가 몇 사람을 만나 그들을 계속 돌아오게 하는 것이 무엇인지 알아본다.

어휘 previously 이전에 prestigious 권위 있는 trail 등산로

수신: 토리 파둘루
발신: 제이미 창
제목: 칼럼 아이디어
날짜: [185]**12월 15일**

안녕하세요, 토리,

[184]**당신의 12월 기사에 대해 독자들에게 긍정적인 이메일과 편지를 많이 받고 있어요.** 정말 [183]잘하셨어요. [184]**그 기사가 아주 인기가 많았기 때문에, 동일한 콘셉트로 세계 여러 지역의 사람들과 함께 살면서 배우는 당신의 경험에 초점을 맞추어 계속 칼럼을 실었으면 해요.**

[185]**시간을 정해 자세한 이야기를 나눕시다. 내일 정오에 시간 되시나요? 점심 먹으면서 이야기하면 좋겠어요.**

제이미 창, 수석 편집자

어휘 article 기사 recurring 계속 되풀이되는

181 세부 사항

번역 클로크너상은 누구에게 수여되었는가?

(A) 언론학 교수
(B) 출판업자
(C) 신문 편집자
(D) 책 저자

해설 웹페이지의 첫 번째 단락에서 파둘루 씨가 〈달빛 아래 바위들〉이라는 책을 집필해 권위 있는 클로크너상의 신인 소설가 부문에서 수상했다(She is the author of *Stone in Moonlight*, for which she received the prestigious Klockner Prize for new novelists)고 했으므로, (D)가 정답이다.

어휘 publisher 출판업자

182 추론 / 암시

번역 파둘루 씨에 관해 암시된 것은?

(A) 앤도버가 근거지다.
(B) 친척을 보러 자주 캐나다로 간다.
(C) 고향에 사는 사람들을 인터뷰했다.
(D) 대학에서 몇 가지 언어를 공부했다.

해설 웹페이지의 첫 번째 단락에서 파둘루 씨가 평생 런던에서 살았다(She has lived in London her entire life)고 했는데, 10월 19일자 기사("A Night Out in London") 개요를 보면 진짜 런던 사람들이 밤 외출 시 무엇을 하는지 알아보기 위해 그녀가 몇몇 시민들과 이야기를 나누었음(how do real Londoners choose to spend ~ Ms. Fadulu speaks to some to find out)을 알 수 있다. 따라서 (C)가 정답이다.

▸▸ Paraphrasing 지문의 **speaks** → 정답의 **has interviewed**
지문의 **Londoners**
→ 정답의 **people who live in her hometown**

183 동의어 찾기

번역 이메일에서 첫 번째 단락 2행의 "nice"와 의미가 가장 가까운 단어는?

(A) 공손한
(B) 훌륭한
(C) 행복한
(D) 섬세한

해설 "nice"를 포함한 문장은 '정말 잘하셨어요(You did some very nice work)'라는 의미로, 여기서 nice는 '훌륭한'이라는 뜻으로 쓰였다. 따라서 (B) good이 정답이다.

184 연계

번역 창 씨가 칼럼으로 전개하고 싶은 기사는?

(A) 문화 밀착 취재
(B) 런던의 밤 외출
(C) 저예산 탐험
(D) 남아메리카 하이킹

해설 창 씨는 이메일의 첫 번째 단락에서 파둘루 씨의 12월 기사에 대해 독자들에게 긍정적인 이메일과 편지를 많이 받고 있다(We have been getting ~ from readers about your December piece)고 한 후, 동일한 콘셉트로 계속 칼럼을 이어 갔으면 좋겠다(Because the article was so popular, I would like to see the concept become a recurring column ~ the world)고 제안했다. 웹페이지에 따르면 12월에 파둘루 씨가 쓴 기사는 '문화 밀착 취재(Culture Up Close)'이므로, (A)가 정답이다.

▸▸ Paraphrasing 지문의 **would like to see ~ become a recurring column**
→ 질문의 **want to develop into a column**

185 세부 사항

번역 창 씨가 12월 16일에 하려는 일은?

(A) 새로 생긴 식당에 가 보기
(B) 쇼 관람하기
(C) 회의하기
(D) 수업하기

해설 12월 16일은 창 씨가 파둘루 씨에게 이메일을 쓴(Date: 15 December) 다음 날이다. 이메일의 마지막 단락에서 내일 시간이 되면 점심 먹으면서 이야기하면 좋겠다(Are you free tomorrow ~ We could talk over lunch)고 했으므로, 그가 12월 16일에 자세한 사항을 논의하기 위해(to discuss the details) 파둘루 씨와 회의를 하고자 함을 알 수 있다. 따라서 (C)가 정답이다.

186-190 제안서 + 제안서 + 이메일

제안서

사업 대상:	186**도급 업체 정보:**
세티 테크놀로지스	186**지오 카펫 케어**
캐너비 가 34번지	그랜덤 가 541번지
샌프란시스코, CA 94129	샌프란시스코, CA 94128

작업 범위

공동 구역 및 개인 작업 공간의 카펫과 천을 댄 가구 전부. 190**필요시 가구 옮기는 일 포함.** 임시 바닥 보호 패드 제공. 얼룩 제거 포함.
*비고: 당사는 100퍼센트 천연 무취 세척 제품을 사용합니다.

회사 제안

지오 카펫 케어는 상기 작업 범위를 2,650달러(세금 별도)에 제안합니다.
188**첫 거래 고객에게 제공하는 10퍼센트 할인이 포함된 가격입니다.**
수락 시 50퍼센트 지불; 잔액은 완료 시 지불.
제안서 제출 후 30일 동안 가격 유효.

186**제출자:** 마틴 아코스타 **고객 승인:** ____________
날짜: 6월 1일 **날짜:** ____________

어휘 contractor 도급 업체 scope 범위 upholstered 천을 댄 temporary 임시의 protector 보호 장치 spot 얼룩 removal 제거 odorless 무취의 due 지불해야 하는, 지불 기일이 된 acceptance 수락 balance 잔액 completion 완성 valid 유효한 submission 제출

프레션 카펫: 제안서
골든 웨이 8423번지
샌프란시스코, CA 94124

고객: 세티 테크놀로지스
주소: 캐너비 가 34번지, 샌프란시스코, CA 94129
날짜: 6월 5일

프레션 카펫은 부지 내 카펫이 깔린 전 구역과 천을 댄 가구 전부에 대한 청소 용역을 제안합니다. [190]**바닥 공간 치우기는 고객이 완료.** 얼룩 제거 별도.

비용: 1,900달러 + 세금 [188](신규 고객 표준 할인가 적용)
[187]**용역 완료 시 대표자에게 비용 지급.** 본 제안은 30일 동안 유효함.

작성: 리처드 왕
구매자 수락:
날짜:

어휘 premises 부지, 구내 representative 대표

수신: 세티 테크놀로지스 전 직원
발신: 조 티어니, 시설부
제목: 카펫 청소
날짜: 6월 25일

토요일 아침, 카펫과 천을 댄 가구 전부를 청소할 예정입니다. [190]**작업에 대비해, 청소 작업반이 청소할 구역에 접근할 수 있도록 시설 담당 직원 몇 명이 금요일 저녁에 가구를 필요한 만큼 옮길 것입니다.** [189]**덧붙여, 금요일 퇴근하기 전 업무 공간에서 깨지기 쉽거나 값비싼 개인 물품들을 치워 주세요.** 기밀 업무 자료는 잘 보이는 곳에 두지 마세요. 카펫과 가구는 월요일이면 건조됩니다. 주말에 오지 마시고 필요하면 집에서 일하십시오.

어휘 access 접근하다 fragile 깨지기 쉬운 valuable 값비싼 confidential 기밀의 in plain view 잘 보이는 곳에 if necessary 필요시

186 추론 / 암시

번역 아코스타 씨는 누구이겠는가?
(A) 세티 테크놀로지스 소유주
(B) 티어니 씨의 동료
(C) 시설부장
(D) 지오 카펫 케어 대표

해설 첫 번째 제안서 상단의 '도급 업체 정보: 지오 카펫 케어(Contractor Information: Geo Carpet Care)'와 하단의 '제출자: 마틴 아코스타(Submitted by: Martin Acosta)'에서 아코스타 씨가 지오 카펫 케어 소속임을 추론할 수 있다. 따라서 (D)가 정답이다.

187 세부 사항

번역 고객은 언제 프레션 카펫에 용역비를 지불해야 하는가?
(A) 제안서 서명 시
(B) 제안서 제출 30일 이내
(C) 청소가 완료되는 날
(D) 우편으로 송장 수령 시

해설 프레션 카펫이 제출한 두 번째 제안서를 보면, 가격(Cost) 아래 부분에 '용역 완료 시 대표자에게 비용 지급(Payment due to representative upon completion of service)'이라고 명시되어 있다. 따라서 (C)가 정답이다.

▸▸ **Paraphrasing** 지문의 **upon completion of service**
→ 정답의 **The day of the cleaning is completed**

188 연계

번역 두 회사가 고객에게 제공하는 것은?
(A) 월납 결제 방식
(B) 청소 제품 선택
(C) 서비스 보증
(D) 신규 고객 할인

해설 첫 번째 제안서의 회사 제안(Company Proposal) 부분을 보면, 지오 카펫 케어가 첫 거래 고객에게 10퍼센트 할인(a 10% discount for first-time customers)을 제공한다는 것을 알 수 있다. 두 번째 제안서의 가격(Cost) 부분에서 프레션 카펫 역시 신규 고객 표준 할인가(the standard reduced price for new customers)를 적용한다는 것을 알 수 있으므로, (D)가 정답이다.

189 세부 사항

번역 티어니 씨가 전 직원에게 요청하는 일은?
(A) 책상과 의자 옮기기
(B) 깨지기 쉬운 물건 치우기
(C) 금요일에 재택 근무하기
(D) 두 가지 제안서 검토하기

해설 이메일 중반부에서 금요일 퇴근하기 전 업무 공간에서 깨지기 쉽거나 값비싼 개인 물품들을 치워 달라(remove any fragile or valuable personal items from your work space)고 했으므로, (B)가 정답이다.

어휘 breakable 깨지기 쉬운

▸▸ **Paraphrasing** 지문의 **fragile** → 정답의 **breakable**

190 연계

번역 세티 테크놀로지스에 관해 암시된 것은?
(A) 프레션 카펫을 고용했다.
(B) 6월 26일 금요일에는 평소보다 늦게 마칠 예정이다.
(C) 지오 카펫 케어의 오랜 고객이다.
(D) 시설 담당 직원이 월요일 일찍 사무실 문을 열 것이다.

해설 이메일을 보면, 작업에 대비해 청소 작업반이 청소할 구역에 접근할 수 있도록 시설 담당 직원 몇 명이 금요일 저녁에 가구를 필요한 만큼 옮길 예정(In preparation for the work, some of our facilities staff members will be moving furniture)이라고 되어 있다. 첫 번째 제안서에서 지오 카펫 케어는 필요시 가구 옮기는 일도 작업에 포함된다(Includes furniture moving as needed)고 했지만, 두 번째 제안서에서 프레션 카펫은 바닥 공간을 치우는 일은 고객이 해야 한다(Clearing of floor space to be completed by customer)고 했다. 따라서 시설 담당 직원이 직접 가구를 옮길 예정인 세티 테크놀로지스는 프레션 카펫을 고용했음을 추론할 수 있으므로, (A)가 정답이다.

191-195 문자 메시지 + 기사 + 후기

발신: 파우스토 폴레티 [오전 11시 02분]
수신: 스테판 그리피스 〈029 2018 0743〉

안녕하세요, 스테판. [192]**저는 지금 예전 밀웨이 기차역 부지에 전기 공사 도급 업자와 있어요.** 전기 시스템이 우리가 당초 생각했던 것보다 훨씬 엉망이었어요. [191]**우리가 건물의 역사적인 모습을 온전하게 보존하면서 현대화를 원하기 때문에 전선 교체와 개량 공사에 예상보다 비용이 많이 들겠어요. 견적서를 받는 대로 보내 드릴게요.** 계획대로 5월에 문을 열 수 있도록 모든 작업이 완료되었으면 하는 바람이에요.

어휘 electrical contractor 전기 공사 도급 업자 originally 당초 rewire 전선을 갈다 retain 보존하다 integrity 온전한 상태 estimate 견적(서)

사우스 웨일스에 새 호텔 개관 예정

카디프(4월 18일) – [192/195]**밀웨이 로드 호텔이 5월 14일 문을 열 예정이다.** [192/193]**건물은 한때 붐비는 기차역이었는데, 이 역은 아서 루이슨이 150년도 더 전에 설계했던 것이었다.**

[194]**이 건물은 30년 가까이 비어 있었다.** 2년 전 그리피스 호텔리어 회장인 스테판 그리피스가 매입했다.

프로젝트 진행자 파우스토 폴레티에 따르면 예전 건물을 호텔로 바꾸는 일뿐 아니라 전기, 난방, 배관 시스템도 개선하려면 대대적인 개보수가 필요하다고 한다.

호텔에는 객실 25개, 회의실 1개, 연회 시설을 갖춘 식당 1개가 있다. 그리피스 씨의 시설들은 세계적인 수준의 식사 서비스로 유명하다. 호텔의 베이사이드 카페에는 웨일스 출신 주방장으로 수상 경력이 있는 맬 데이비스가 메뉴를 꾸리고 식당을 총괄한다.

머지 않아 그리피스 씨는 이 부동산의 정원을 확장할 계획이다.

정보와 예약을 원하면 www.millwayroadhotel.co.uk를 방문하면 된다.

어휘 decade 10년 unoccupied 비어 있는 purchase 구매하다 extensive 대규모의 plumbing 배관 oversee 총괄하다 expand 확장하다 property 부동산 reservation 예약

http://www.cardifftravels.co.uk/reviews

홈	명소	후기	문의

★★★★
밀웨이 로드 호텔
후기 게시자 미연 고

[195]**최근 6월에 문을 연 밀웨이 로드 호텔에서 소규모 회의에 참석했습니다.** 컴퓨터 기술자로서 호텔이 뜻밖의 첨단 시설을 갖추고 있어서 기분이 좋았어요. 숙박했던 객실과 회의실에 장비를 꽂고 휴대전화와 컴퓨터를 충전할 콘센트가 아주 많았답니다. 무료 무선 인터넷 서비스도 이용하기 쉬웠습니다. 무엇보다 음식이 맛있고 객실이 근사했어요.

어휘 recently 최근 up-to-date 첨단의 electrical outlet 콘센트 complimentary 무료의

191 주제 / 목적

번역 폴레티 씨가 문자를 보낸 이유는?

(A) 프로젝트 비용이 상승한 이유를 설명하기 위해
(B) 전기 문제를 해결하는 데 도움을 요청하려고
(C) 배송이 지연된다고 주의를 주려고
(D) 도급업자와 문제를 상의하려고

해설 문자의 중반부에서 건물의 역사적인 모습을 온전하게 보존하면서 현대화하기를 원하기 때문에 전선 교체와 개량 공사에 예상보다 비용이 많이 들 것(The rewiring and upgrades are going to cost more than expected ~ remaining the historical integrity of the building)이라며 견적서를 받는대로 보내겠다고 했으므로, (A)가 정답이다.

▸▸ Paraphrasing 지문의 cost more than expected
→ 정답의 cost will increase

192 연계

번역 문자를 보낼 때 폴레티 씨는 어디에 있었는가?

(A) 기차
(B) 식당
(C) 예정된 호텔 부지
(D) 전기 도급 업자의 사무실

해설 문자의 초반부를 보면, 폴레티 씨가 예전 밀웨이 기차역 부지(I'm ~ at the former Millway train station site now)에서 문자를 보냈다는 것을 알 수 있다. 기사의 첫 번째 단락에서 5월 14일 문을 열 예정인 밀웨이 로드 호텔 건물이 한때 붐비는 기차역이었다(The Millway Road Hotel is scheduled to open ~ once a busy train station)고 했으므로, (C)가 정답이다.

193 추론 / 암시

번역 기사가 루이슨 씨에 관해 암시하는 것은?

(A) 호텔을 매입 중이다.
(B) 식사 메뉴를 꾸렸다.
(C) 건물 건축가였다.
(D) 개보수 공사 진행자다.

해설 기사의 첫 번째 단락에서 호텔 건물이 한때 붐비는 기차역이었으며, 이 역은 아서 루이슨이 150년도 더 전에 설계한 것(a busy train station that was designed by Arthur Lewison over 150 years ago)이라고 했으므로, 루이슨 씨가 건축가였음을 추론할 수 있다. 따라서 (C)가 정답이다.

▸▸ Paraphrasing 지문의 a busy train station that was designed by Arthur Lewison
→ 정답의 He was the architect of a building

194 사실 관계 확인

번역 기사가 밀웨이 로드 기차역에 관해 명시한 것은?

(A) 세계적인 수준의 식당이 포함되었다.
(B) 그리피스 씨의 아버지 소유였다.
(C) 유명한 정원 근처에 있었다.
(D) 오랫동안 방치되었다.

해설 기사의 두 번째 단락에서 밀웨이 로드 기차역 건물이 30년 가까이 비어 있었다(For almost three decades the building had been left unoccupied)고 했으므로, (D)가 정답이다.

어휘 abandoned 방치된

▸▸ Paraphrasing 지문의 For almost three decades
→ 정답의 for many years
지문의 left unoccupied → 정답의 abandoned

195 연계

번역 고 씨의 후기에 암시된 것은?

(A) 호텔 객실이 꽤 크다.
(B) 호텔이 예정대로 문을 열지 않았다.
(C) 카페는 호텔 꼭대기 층에 있다.
(D) 인터넷 사용료가 너무 비쌌다.

해설 후기의 첫 번째 문장을 보면, 고 씨는 최근 6월에 문을 연 밀웨이 로드 호텔에서 소규모 회의에 참석했다(I recently attended a small conference at the Millway Road Hotel, which opened in June)고 했다. 하지만 기사의 첫 번째 단락에서 밀웨이 로드 호텔이 5월 14일 문을 열 예정(The Millway Road Hotel is scheduled to open on 14 May)이라고 했으므로, 호텔 개업이 늦어졌음을 추론할 수 있다. 따라서 (B)가 정답이다.

196-200 이메일 + 일정표 + 이메일

이메일

수신: 전 직원
발신: 릴러 헤들런드
제목: 11월 소프트웨어 교육
날짜: 10월 30일
첨부: 소프트웨어 교육 일정

직원들께,

11월 내내, 우리 회사의 주요 소프트웨어 제품 두 개에 대한 의무 교육을 실시할 예정입니다.

아바쿠스 딥싱크 소프트웨어 교육은 전 직원이 받아야 하며 온라인 세션 한 번으로 완료 가능합니다. 이용 가능한 세션 시간대가 여러 개 있습니다. 이 소프트웨어는 최근 몇 가지 변경을 거쳤기 때문에 오래 사용한 사람도 반드시 참석해야 합니다.

[196/199]옵티세이프 소프트웨어 교육은 면대면으로 제공되며, 약품안 전부 직원들만 필수입니다. [196]지난해 소프트웨어가 대폭 업그레이드되었으므로 부서 전 직원이 새로운 기능의 사용법을 배워야 합니다.

첨부된 일정표를 보시고 회사 교육 웹사이트로 가서 등록하세요.

감사합니다.

릴러 헤들런드
코다렉스 제약 회사

어휘 mandatory 의무의 recently 최근에 in person 직접, 면대면으로 requirement 필수요건 capability 기능, 역량

소프트웨어 교육 일정

날짜	제목	시간	위치
11/6	[197]**아바쿠스 딥싱크**	오전 9시-오전 11시	[197]**온라인**
11/9	옵티세이프	오전 9시-오후 1시	C동 822호
11/14	[197]**아바쿠스 딥싱크**	오후 1시-오후 3시	[197]**온라인**
11/17	[197]**아바쿠스 딥싱크**	오전 10시-오후 12시	[197]**온라인**
11/22	옵티세이프	오후 1시-오후 5시	C동 822호
[200]**11/27**	[197]**아바쿠스 딥싱크**	오후 3시-오후 5시	[197]**온라인**

온라인 수업은 https://www.abacusdeepthink.com에서 접속할 수 있습니다.

어휘 access (컴퓨터에) 접속하다, 이용하다

이메일

수신: 릴러 헤들런드
발신: 디에고 라모스-토로
제목: 11월 소프트웨어 교육
날짜: 10월 31일

릴러에게,

[198/199/200]저는 모든 소프트웨어 교육에 참석해야 하는데, 11월 6일부터 11월 18일까지 휴가를 갈 계획이었어요. [198/200]게다가 11월 22일 하루 종일 고객 회의에 참석해야 하는데 이 일정은 바꿀 수가 없어요. [198]제가 참석할 수 있는 다른 옵티세이프 교육 세션이 있을까요?

감사합니다.

디에고 라모스-토로

어휘 reschedule 일정을 조정하다 alternative 대체의, 다른

TEST 4

196 사실 관계 확인

번역 첫 번째 이메일에 의하면 옵티세이프 소프트웨어에 관해 사실인 것은?

(A) 다른 소프트웨어 프로그램을 대체하고 있다.
(B) 데이터 분석에 활용된다.
(C) 상당히 개선되었다.
(D) 월간 교육의 핵심이다.

해설 첫 번째 이메일의 세 번째 단락에서 지난해 옵티세이프 소프트웨어가 대폭 업그레이드되어(This past year, major upgrades have been made to the software) 부서 전 직원이 새로운 기능의 사용법을 배워야 한다고 했으므로, (C)가 정답이다.

어휘 significant 상당한, 현저한 focus 주안점, 핵심

▸▸ Paraphrasing 지문의 **major upgrades have been made**
→ 정답의 **has undergone significant updates**

197 세부 사항

번역 일정에 의하면, 아바쿠스 딥싱크 교육의 공통점은?

(A) 해당 월의 같은 날에 이루어진다.
(B) 같은 강사가 가르친다.
(C) 웹사이트로 진행된다.
(D) 모두 같은 시간에 시작한다.

해설 소프트웨어 교육 일정(Software Training Schedule)을 보면, 모든 아바쿠스 딥싱크(Abacus Deepthink) 교육이 온라인(Online)으로 진행될 예정임을 확인할 수 있다. 따라서 (C)가 정답이다.

▸▸ Paraphrasing 지문의 **Online** → 정답의 **through a Web site**

198 주제 / 목적

번역 라모스-토로 씨가 헤들런드 씨에게 메일을 쓴 이유는?

(A) 교육 세션에 등록하려고
(B) 겹치는 일정을 해결하는 데 도움을 요청하려고
(C) 소프트웨어 오작동을 보고하려고
(D) 추가 휴가를 요청하려고

해설 두 번째 이메일에서 라모스-토로 씨는 예정된 휴가(I had planned to take off work from November 6 through November 18)와 고객 회의(I must attend an all-day client meeting on November 22) 일정 때문에 소프트웨어 교육을 참석할 수 없다고 한 후, 자신이 참석할 수 있는 다른 옵티세이프 소프트웨어 교육 세션이 있을지(Will there be any alternative sessions for the Optisafe training that I could attend?) 문의했다. 따라서 (B)가 정답이다.

어휘 conflict (일정) 겹침 malfunction 오작동, 고장

199 추론 / 암시

번역 라모스-토로 씨에 관해 암시된 것은?

(A) 약품 안전부에서 일한다.
(B) 필요한 교육을 마쳤다.
(C) 헤들런드 씨의 상사다.
(D) 회사에서 다른 직책을 원한다.

해설 두 번째 이메일에서 라모스-토로 씨는 자신이 모든 소프트웨어 교육에 참석해야 한다고 했는데, 첫 번째 이메일의 세 번째 단락을 보면 옵티세이프 소프트웨어 교육이 약품 안전부 직원들에게만 필수라는 것(The Optisafe software training ~ is a requirement only for Drug Safety department members)을 알 수 있다. 따라서 두 교육 모두 참석해야 하는 라모스-토로 씨가 약품 안전부 소속임을 추론할 수 있으므로, (A)가 정답이다.

어휘 supervisor 상사

200 연계

번역 라모스-토로 씨는 교육 하나를 언제 마치겠는가?

(A) 11월 14일
(B) 11월 17일
(C) 11월 22일
(D) 11월 27일

해설 두 번째 이메일에서 라모스-토로 씨는 자신이 11월 6일부터 11월 18일까지 휴가를 갈 계획(I had planned to take off work from November 6 through November 18)이고, 11월 22일에는 하루 종일 고객 회의에 참석해야 한다(I must attend an all-day client meeting on November 22)고 했다. 소프트웨어 교육 일정(Software Training Schedule)을 보면, 라모스-토로 씨가 11월 27일에 아바쿠스 딥싱크 소프트웨어 교육을 받을 수 있음을 추론할 수 있다. 따라서 (D)가 정답이다.

기출 TEST 5

101 (A)	102 (B)	103 (D)	104 (C)	105 (B)
106 (D)	107 (B)	108 (B)	109 (A)	110 (B)
111 (B)	112 (A)	113 (D)	114 (D)	115 (B)
116 (C)	117 (B)	118 (D)	119 (C)	120 (C)
121 (D)	122 (A)	123 (A)	124 (A)	125 (D)
126 (D)	127 (B)	128 (A)	129 (D)	130 (A)
131 (C)	132 (D)	133 (D)	134 (A)	135 (A)
136 (C)	137 (A)	138 (B)	139 (A)	140 (D)
141 (C)	142 (D)	143 (C)	144 (A)	145 (D)
146 (A)	147 (A)	148 (D)	149 (A)	150 (B)
151 (B)	152 (A)	153 (B)	154 (D)	155 (A)
156 (B)	157 (B)	158 (C)	159 (D)	160 (A)
161 (B)	162 (A)	163 (C)	164 (A)	165 (B)
166 (C)	167 (B)	168 (D)	169 (D)	170 (B)
171 (D)	172 (C)	173 (B)	174 (D)	175 (A)
176 (A)	177 (B)	178 (A)	179 (D)	180 (A)
181 (D)	182 (B)	183 (C)	184 (A)	185 (A)
186 (C)	187 (A)	188 (B)	189 (D)	190 (A)
191 (A)	192 (A)	193 (D)	194 (C)	195 (B)
196 (B)	197 (D)	198 (B)	199 (C)	200 (D)

PART 5

101 동사 어휘

해설 빈칸은 주어 The custodial staff의 동사 자리로, that이 이끄는 명사절(that we clean our dishes before leaving the kitchen)을 목적어로 취한다. 따라서 빈칸에는 that절을 목적어로 취할 수 있는 타동사가 들어가야 한다. 주방에서 나가기 전 설거지를 하라는 것은 관리 직원들이 당부할 만한 사항이므로, '요청하다, 요구하다'라는 의미의 (A) requests가 정답이다. 참고로, request와 같이 제안, 요청, 명령 등의 동사 뒤에 오는 that절에는 (should +)동사원형이 쓰인다. (B) behaves는 '행동하다, 처신하다', (C) uses는 '사용하다, 쓰다', (D) visits는 '방문하다, 찾아가다'라는 뜻으로 빈칸에 적절하지 않다.

번역 관리 직원들은 우리에게 주방에서 나가기 전에 설거지를 하라고 요청한다.

어휘 custodial (건물 등을) 관리하는

102 명사 자리 _ 복합명사

해설 빈칸에는 동사 lose를 수식하는 부사 또는 warranty와 복합명사를 이루어 lose의 목적어 역할을 하는 명사가 들어갈 수 있다. 보기에서 명사 (B) certificate와 부사 (D) certifiably 중 하나를 선택해야 하는데, 잃어버릴 수 있는 대상이 빈칸에 들어가야 문맥상 자연스럽다. 따라서 warranty와 함께 '보증서'라는 의미를 완성하는 명사 (B) certificate가 정답이다. (D) certifiably는 '보증할 수 있게'라는 의미로 빈칸에 적절하지 않다. (A) certify는 동사, (C) certifiable은 형용사로 품사상 빈칸에 들어갈 수 없다.

번역 고객들은 품질 보증서 원본을 잃어버릴 경우 웹사이트에서 새 보증서를 다운로드할 수 있다.

어휘 warranty 품질 보증(서) certify 증명하다, 자격증을 교부하다 certificate 증서 certifiable 보증할 수 있는

103 전치사 어휘

해설 동사 is located와 장소를 나타내는 명사구 the central business district를 적절히 연결하는 전치사를 선택하는 문제이다. 중심 상업 지구는 주어 Our Portview branch가 속한 장소이므로, '~ 안에'라는 의미의 (D) in이 정답이다. 참고로, (A) on은 '~ (위)에'라는 의미로, avenue, street과 같은 장소 앞에 쓰인다.

번역 저희 포트뷰 지점은 중심 상업 지구의 번사이드 가와 에버렛 가 사이에 있습니다.

어휘 district 지구, 지역

104 동사 자리

해설 빈칸은 주어 None of the employees의 동사 자리이므로, 과거 동사인 (C) knew가 정답이다. (A) knowingly는 부사, (B) known은 과거분사, (D) to know는 to부정사이므로, 동사 자리에 들어갈 수 없다.

번역 직원 중 누구도 애넌 씨가 연말에 퇴직하기로 계획한 것을 알지 못했다.

어휘 retire 퇴직하다, 은퇴하다

105 인칭대명사의 격 _ 소유격

해설 빈칸은 to부정사(to miss)의 목적어 역할을 하는 명사 chance를 한정 수식하는 자리이므로, 소유격 인칭대명사 (B) your가 정답이다.

번역 훌륭한 영업팀에 합류할 기회를 놓치지 않으려면 오늘 존스턴 스토어즈에 지원하세요.

어휘 so as to ~하기 위해서

106 형용사 어휘

해설 receive의 목적어 역할을 하는 salary를 적절히 수식하는 형용사를 선택하는 문제이다. 특별 마케팅 과정을 수료할 경우(if they complete a special marketing course) 혜택의 일환으로 급여를 더 많이 받게 될 수 있다는 내용이 되어야 자연스럽다. 따라서 '더 높은'이라는 의미의 (D) higher가 정답이다. (A) possible은 '가능한, 있을 수 있는', (B) frequent는 '빈번한', (C) closed는 '닫힌, 폐쇄적인'이라는 뜻으로 문맥상 빈칸에 적절하지 않다.

번역 직원들은 특별 마케팅 과정을 수료하면 더 높은 급여를 받을 자격을 갖추게 된다.

어휘 be eligible to ~할 자격이 있다 complete 완료[수료]하다

107 형용사 자리

해설 빈칸이 부사 commercially와 명사 book 사이에 있으므로, 빈칸에는 commercially의 수식을 받는 동시에 book을 수식하는 형용사가 들어가야 한다. 따라서 '성공한, 성공적인'이라는 의미의 형용사인 (B) successful이 정답이다. (A) successfully는 부사, (C) succeed는 동사, (D) success는 명사로 품사상 빈칸에 들어갈 수 없다.

번역 경영 방식에 관한 잔 버틀러의 최근 저서 〈거래 유지하기〉는 지금까지 나온 그녀의 책 중 상업적으로 가장 성공한 책이다.

어휘 commercially 상업적으로

108 명사 어휘

해설 빈칸은 sales와 복합명사를 이루어 전치사 to의 목적어 역할을 하는 명사 자리로, 엽서를 제시할(Present this postcard to) 대상을 나타내는 사람 명사가 들어가야 한다. 따라서 sales와 함께 '영업[판매] 사원'이라는 의미를 완성하는 (B) associate가 정답이다. (A) accessory는 '장신구, 부대용품', (C) faculty는 '교수단, 능력', (D) formula는 '공식, 방식'이라는 뜻으로 문맥상 빈칸에 적절하지 않다.

번역 저희 매장 중 아무 곳에서나 판매 사원에게 이 엽서를 제시하고 5파운드짜리 상품권을 받으세요.

109 형용사 자리 _ 명사 수식

해설 빈칸은 동사 has undergone의 목적어 역할을 하는 명사 renovations를 수식하는 형용사 자리이므로, 형용사 (A) multiple(다수의)과 형용사 역할을 할 수 있는 과거분사 (D) multiplied(곱해진, 증가된) 중 하나를 선택해야 한다. 문맥상 보수 작업이 이루어진 횟수를 나타내는 형용사가 더 어울리므로, (A) multiple이 정답이 된다. 참고로, multiple은 '배수'라는 뜻의 명사로도 쓰일 수 있다.

번역 레이크사이드 쇼핑 센터는 지난 10년간 여러 번 보수를 거쳐 오고 있다.

어휘 renovation 개조, 보수 multiply 곱하다

110 명사 어휘

해설 빈칸은 or가 연결하는 동명사 managing과 recruiting의 목적어 역할을 하는 명사 자리이므로, 관리 또는 채용의 대상이 되는 사람 명사가 들어가야 한다. 따라서 '자원봉사자'라는 의미의 (B) volunteers가 정답이다. (A) staplers는 '스테이플러', (C) devices는 '장치, 방책', (D) headquarters는 '본사, 본부'라는 뜻으로 문맥상 빈칸에 적절하지 않다.

번역 오늘 자원봉사자 관리 및 채용에 관련된 모든 사람이 의무적으로 참석해야 하는 회의가 있다.

어휘 mandatory 의무적인 involved in ~에 관련된

111 전치사 자리

해설 빈칸은 May 1를 목적어로 취하는 전치사 자리이므로, '~로부터'라는 의미의 전치사 (B) from이 정답이다. (A) now는 부사/명사/접속사, (C) while은 접속사, (D) when은 부사/접속사/대명사로 품사상 빈칸에 들어갈 수 없다. 참고로, from은 부사 onward와 짝을 이루어 '~부터 (계속)'라는 뜻을 나타낸다.

번역 스미빌 버스 시스템은 5월 1일부터 로브 페어 카드만 받을 예정이다.

112 부사 자리

해설 빈칸 없이도 「주어(Relocating for work)+be동사(is)+주격 보어(a difficult decision)」의 완전한 구조를 이루고 있다. 따라서 빈칸에는 부사만 들어갈 수 있으므로, '당연히'라는 의미의 부사 (A) understandably가 정답이다. 동명사인 (B) understanding이 빈칸에 들어갈 경우 '어려운 결정을 이해하는 것이다'라는 뜻이 되어 어색해진다. (C) understood는 동사/과거분사, (D) understand는 동사로 품사상 빈칸에 들어갈 수 없다.

번역 일 때문에 이사하는 것은 당연히 어려운 결정이지만 득이 될 수도 있다.

어휘 relocate 이전하다 rewarding 보람 있는, 득이 되는

113 동사 어형 _ 시제

해설 빈칸은 주어 Parmax Corporation의 동사 자리이므로, 보기에서 (C) settle과 (D) settled 중 하나를 선택해야 한다. 분쟁을 해결한 것은 지난 주(Last week)이므로, 과거 시제인 (D) settled가 정답이 된다. (A) settling은 현재분사/동명사, (B) settler는 명사로 품사상 빈칸에 들어갈 수 없다.

번역 파맥스사는 지난주에 주요 경쟁 업체와의 특허권 침해 관련 분쟁을 해결했다.

어휘 settle a disagreement 분쟁을 해결하다 concerning 관련된 patent infringement 특허권 침해 settler 정착민

114 부사 자리

해설 빈칸이 현재완료 동사를 이루는 has와 increased 사이에 있으므로, 빈칸에는 과거분사 increased를 수식하는 부사가 들어가야 한다. 따라서 '한결같이, 지속적으로'라는 의미의 부사 (D) consistently가 정답이다. (A) consistency와 (B) consistencies는 명사, (C) consistent는 형용사로 품사상 빈칸에 들어갈 수 없다.

번역 코우리 데어리의 향상된 우유 주입 시스템은 탤러해시 공장의 생산성을 지속적으로 높여 왔다.

어휘 productivity 생산성 consistency 일관성 consistent 지속적인

115 명사 자리 _ 동사의 목적어

해설 빈칸은 부정관사 a와 형용사 single 뒤에 이어지는 명사 자리로, 동사 has not received의 목적어 역할을 한다. 따라서 '불만 사항, 불평'이라는 의미의 명사 (B) complaint가 정답이다. (A) complained는 동사/과거분사, (C) complaining은 동명사/현재분사, (D) complain은 동사로 품사상 빈칸에 들어갈 수 없다.

번역 링카 2000 블렌더는 뉴 프로덕츠 웹 포럼에서 불만 사항이 한 건도 접수되지 않았다.

116 전치사 어휘

해설 빈칸에 적절한 전치사를 선택하는 문제이다. Yamamoto Technologies가 시애틀에서 투자를 가장 많이 받은 회사들(Seattle's best-funded companies) 중 하나라는 내용이 되어야 자연스러우므로, '~ 중에, ~ 사이에'라는 의미의 (C) among이 정답이다. (A) into는 '~ 안으로', (B) over은 '~ 위에, ~ 이상', (D) across는 '~을 가로질러, ~ 전역에'라는 뜻으로 문맥상 빈칸에 적절하지 않다.

번역 작년에 4,500만 달러를 모은 이후, 야마모토 테크놀로지스는 현재 시애틀에서 투자를 가장 많이 받은 회사 중 하나가 되었다.

어휘 well-funded 투자를 많이 받은, 충분한 재원이 마련된

117 형용사 어휘

해설 two와 명사 bakeries 사이에 들어갈 형용사를 선택하는 문제이다. 딘젤로스 딜라이츠가 아주 인기가 높아서(Deangelo's Delights was so popular) 주인이 두 곳의 제과점을 더 열었다는 내용이 되어야 자연스러우므로, '추가적인'이라는 의미의 (B) additional이 정답이다. (A) allowable은 '허용되는, 정당한', (C) uninterested는 '무관심한, 흥미 없는', (D) inclusive는 '포함하여, 포괄적인'이라는 뜻으로 문맥상 빈칸에 적절하지 않다.

번역 딘젤로스 딜라이츠는 아주 인기가 높아서 주인이 두 곳의 제과점을 추가로 열었다.

118 접속사 어휘

해설 앞뒤 완전한 절을 자연스럽게 이어 주는 부사절 접속사를 선택하는 문제이다. 레스토랑을 인수한 것(took over Fratelli's Restaurant)은 이전 요리사가 새 음식점을 개업하기 위해 떠난 뒤 발생한 일이므로, '~ 후에'라는 뜻의 (D) after가 정답이다.

번역 요리사 옥타비아 파리나 씨는 이전 요리사가 새 음식점을 개업하기 위해 떠난 뒤 프라텔리즈 레스토랑을 인수했다.

어휘 take over (기업 등을) 인수하다, 인계받다

119 명사 자리 _ 동명사의 목적어

해설 빈칸은 동명사 increasing의 목적어 역할을 하는 명사 자리이므로, '생산(량)'이라는 의미의 명사인 (C) production이 정답이다. (A) produced는 동사/과거분사, (B) producing은 동명사/현재분사, (D) productive는 형용사로 품사상 빈칸에 들어갈 수 없다.

번역 윙스톰 푸즈의 이사는 제과 부문에서 생산량을 늘린 것에 대해 바이스 씨를 칭찬했다.

어휘 commend A for B B에 대해 A를 칭찬하다 produce 생산하다 productive 생산적인

120 재귀대명사 _ 강조 용법

해설 빈칸이 완전한 문장(Greg Owens ~ used to drive a taxi) 뒤에 있으므로, 빈칸에는 문장 구성에 영향을 주지 않는 대명사가 들어가야 한다. 따라서 '직접, 그 자신도'라는 의미로 주어 Greg Owens를 강조하는 재귀대명사 (C) himself가 정답이다. 참고로, (D) his own의 경우 '직접, 스스로'라는 의미가 되려면 앞에 전치사 on이 있어야 한다.

번역 다국적 기업인 에르메스 택시 서비스의 창립자 그레그 오웬즈 씨는 그 자신도 택시 운전을 하곤 했다.

121 명사 어휘

해설 빈칸은 현재분사 exceeding의 목적어 역할을 하는 명사 자리로, 빈칸을 포함한 분사구가 앞에 나온 record earnings를 수식하고 있다. 따라서 빈칸에는 기록적인 수익(record earnings)이 뛰어넘은(exceeding) 대상을 나타내는 명사가 들어가야 하므로, '예상(치)'라는 의미의 (D) expectations가 정답이다. (A) adjustments는 '조절, 조정', (B) endorsements는 '보증, 이서', (C) computations는 '계산'이라는 뜻으로 문맥상 빈칸에 적절하지 않다.

번역 스타라이트 극장은 3분기에 예상치를 훨씬 뛰어넘는 기록적인 수익을 발표하게 되어 자랑스럽습니다.

어휘 earnings 수익, 이익

122 복합관계대명사

해설 빈칸은 주어가 없는 불완전한 절(seems most interesting)을 이끄는 접속사 자리이다. 따라서 문장의 주어 역할을 하며 불완전한 절을 이끌 수 있는 복합관계대명사 (A) whichever(어느 것이든지)가 정답이다. 참고로, (B) however가 복합관계부사로 부사절을 이끌 경우에는 뒤에 완전한 절이 와야 한다. (C) everyone은 대명사, (D) much는 대명사/한정사/부사로 앞뒤 절을 연결할 수 없으므로 빈칸에 들어갈 수 없다.

번역 직원들은 제공되는 그 많은 워크숍 중 어느 것이든 가장 흥미로워 보이는 것 하나에 참석할 수 있다.

123 전치사 / 분사 자리

해설 빈칸에는 명사구 her strong negotiation skills를 목적어로 취하는 전치사나 현재분사가 들어갈 수 있다. 뛰어난 협상 기술(strong negotiation skills)은 Marie Russel이 판매부장직에 임명될 때 반영되었을 사항이므로, '~을 고려해 볼 때'라는 의미의 (A) Given이 정답이다. (B) Deciding은 '결정하며', (C) Finding은 '발견하며'라는 뜻으로 문맥상 빈칸에 어색하고, (D) Because는 접속사로 뒤에 완전한 절이 이어져야 하므로 빈칸에 들어갈 수 없다.

번역 뛰어난 협상 기술로 마리 러셀 씨는 산와 주식회사의 판매부장이 됐다.

어휘 negotiation 협상

124 부사 어휘

해설 to부정사구 to submit feedback to management를 적절히 수식하는 부사를 선택하는 문제이다. 자물쇠가 달린 건의함(A locked suggestion box)이 의견 제출(submit feedback) 방식에 미칠 영향을 나타내는 부사가 빈칸에 들어가야 자연스러우므로, '익명으로'라는 의미의 (A) anonymously가 정답이다. (B) approximately는 '대략, 거의', (C) expressly는 '분명히, 특별히', (D) patiently는 '끈기 있게, 참을성 있게'라는 뜻으로 문맥상 빈칸에 적절하지 않다.

번역 자물쇠가 달린 건의함으로 직원들은 경영진에게 익명으로 의견을 제출할 수 있게 될 것이다.

어휘 management 경영(진)

125 동사 어휘

해설 목적어 역할을 하는 명사구 our products 및 부사구 more aggressively와 가장 잘 어울리는 타동사를 선택하는 문제이다. 제품은 해외에서 적극적으로 판매하거나 홍보해야 할 대상이므로, '시장에 내놓다, 홍보하다'라는 의미의 타동사인 (D) market이 정답이다. (A) invest는 '(시간·노력 등을) 투자하다'라는 뜻으로 문맥상 빈칸에 적합하지 않고, (B) compete는 '경쟁하다, 겨루다', (C) participate는 '참가하다, 참석하다'라는 뜻의 자동사로 빈칸에 들어갈 수 없다.

번역 우리 제품을 해외에서 더욱 더 적극적으로 선보이기 위해 새 전략을 개발 중이다.

어휘 aggressively 적극[공격]적으로

126 분사 구문

해설 빈칸은 전치사구 on the city's ongoing revitalization project와 함께 콤마 뒤 완전한 절(Mayor Owen promised that ~ the results)을 수식하는 분사 자리이다. 따라서 과거분사 (C) Commented와 현재분사 (D) Commenting 중 하나를 선택해야 하는데, 주어인 Mayor Owen은 발언을 하는(comment) 주체이므로, 능동의 의미를 내포하는 현재분사 (D) Commenting이 정답이 된다. (A) Comment와 (B) Comments는 명사/동사로 품사상 빈칸에 들어갈 수 없다.

번역 오웬 시장은 현재 진행되는 시의 경기 부양 프로젝트에 대해 이야기하며 주민들이 결과에 만족할 것이라고 약속했다.

어휘 revitalization 경기 부양화, 경제 활성화

127 부사 어휘

해설 빈칸은 콤마 뒤에 이어지는 문장 전체를 수식하는 부사 자리로, 많은 수리 비용이 드는 상황(repairs ~ will be costly)을 가장 잘 묘사하는 부사가 들어가야 한다. 따라서 '유감스럽게도, 불행히도'라는 의미의 (B) Unfortunately가 정답이다. (A) Tremendously는 '엄청나게', (C) Casually는 '무심코, 약식으로', (D) Enormously는 '엄청나게, 대단히'라는 뜻으로 문맥상 빈칸에 적절하지 않다.

번역 유감스럽게도, 모펫 빌딩의 배관 파이프 수리는 많은 비용이 들 것이다.

어휘 costly 많은 비용이 드는

128 명사 어휘

해설 빈칸 앞 its는 주어인 The CEO's speech를 대신하는 소유격이며, 빈칸을 포함한 전치사구(in its -------)가 동사구 will be recorded를 수식하고 있다. 따라서 빈칸에는 CEO의 연설이 녹음되는 방식이나 형태와 관련된 명사가 들어가야 하므로, in its와 함께 '전부, 완전한 형태로'라는 뜻을 완성하는 (A) entirety(전부, 전체)가 정답이다. (B) system은 '체계, 체제', (C) perception은 '지각, 인지', (D) estimation은 '판단, 평가'라는 뜻으로 문맥상 빈칸에 적절하지 않다.

번역 최고 경영책임자의 연설은 전부 녹음되어 회의에 참석하지 못한 직원들이 들을 수 있게 될 것이다.

어휘 attend 참석하다

129 부사 어휘

해설 동사 are closed를 적절히 수식하는 부사를 선택하는 문제이다. 폭풍우가 기상 경보 없이 발생하는 경향이 있기 때문에(because storms tend to occur without warning) 트레일 코스도 종종 예고 없이 폐쇄된다는 내용이 되어야 자연스럽다. 따라서 '예상외로, 갑자기'라는 의미의 (D) unexpectedly가 정답이다. (A) accidently는 '우연히, 우발적으로', (B) coincidentally는 '동시 발생적으로, 우연히', (C) steeply는 '가파르게'라는 뜻으로 문맥상 빈칸에 적절하지 않다.

번역 폭풍우가 경보 없이 발생하는 경향이 있어서 산의 남동부 트레일 코스는 종종 갑작스럽게 폐쇄된다.

130 상관접속사

해설 빈칸은 동사 submit의 목적어 역할을 하는 두 명사구 your hours와 any work-related expense reports를 연결하는 역할을 하므로, 등위 또는 상관접속사가 들어가야 한다. 따라서 '~뿐만 아니라, ~에 더하여'라는 의미의 상관접속사 (A) as well as가 정답이다. (B) above all(무엇보다도, 특히)과 (C) in addition(게다가, 더하여)은 부사, (D) in case that(~할 경우를 대비해)은 부사절 접속사로 빈칸에 들어갈 수 없다.

번역 근무 시간 및 업무와 관련된 일체의 경비 보고서를 금요일까지 제출하세요.

PART 6

131-134 공지

시청 단전 예정

4월 14일 금요일, 시청의 전력 공급이 오전 7시에 중단되었다가 오후 6시에 다시 복구될 예정입니다. 해당 일자에 시청 건물은 [131]**폐쇄됩니다.** 정전 중에 비상용 점등 시스템이 업그레이드될 것입니다. [132]**구체적으로 말하면**, 현행 안전 규정을 준수할 수 있도록 모든 회로 패널이 교체될 예정입니다.

목요일에 시청 사무실에서 나가기 [133]**전에**, 모든 데스크톱 컴퓨터와 무선 서버, 기타 컴퓨터 관련 장비의 전원을 분리해 주십시오. 아울러 직원들은 주방에서 모든 개인 물품을 치워야 합니다. [134]**남겨진 모든 물품은 폐기될 예정입니다.** 질문이나 우려 사항은 건물 유지보수 담당자에게 문의해 주십시오.

어휘 power outage 전력 공급 중단, 정전 restore 복구하다, 회복시키다 circuit 회로 replace 교체하다 compliance 준수 safety code 안전 규정[규율] equipment 장비 furthermore 게다가 maintenance 유지 보수

131 동사 어형 _ 시제

해설 빈칸은 주어 The building의 동사 자리이므로, 보기에서 (A) has closed, (C) will close, (D) was closing 중 하나를 선택해야 한다. 전력 공급이 중단될 예정(the city hall's electricity is scheduled to be shut down)인 4월 14일 금요일(On Friday, April 14 = for the day)에 건물이 폐쇄되는 것이므로, 빈칸에도 미래를 나타내는 시제가 들어가야 한다. 따라서 (C) will close가 정답이다. 참고로, close는 타동사로도 쓰이기 때문에 수동태 미래 시제(will be closed)도 가능하다. (B) closing은 동명사/현재분사로 동사 자리에 들어갈 수 없다.

132 부사 자리 _ 접속부사 _ 어휘

해설 앞뒤 문장을 의미상 자연스럽게 연결해 주는 접속부사를 선택하는 문제이다. 앞 문장에서 비상용 점등 시스템이 업그레이드된다(the emergency lighting system will be upgraded)고 했고, 빈칸 뒤에서 현행 안전 규정을 준수할 수 있도록 모든 회로 패널이 교체될 예정(all circuit panels will be replaced)이라며 업그레이드되는 사항을 구체적으로 명시했다. 따라서 '구체적으로 말해, 특별히'라는 의미의 (D) Specifically가 정답이다. (A) In that case는 '그런 경우에, 그렇다면', (B) Regularly는 '정기적으로, 규칙적으로'라는 뜻으로 문맥상 어색하며, (C) Rather than은 접속사/전치사로 쓰이므로 빈칸에 들어갈 수 없다.

133 전치사 어휘

해설 빈칸에 적절한 전치사를 선택하는 문제이다. 컴퓨터나 기타 장비의 전원을 분리하는 것(disconnect all desktop computers ~ equipment)은 사무실을 나가기 전에 해야 할 일이므로, '~ 전에'라는 뜻의 시간 전치사 (D) Before가 정답이다. (A) Inside는 '~ 안에, 내부에', (B) Beyond는 '~ 너머, ~을 능가하는', (C) Without은 '~ 없이'라는 의미로 문맥상 빈칸에 적절하지 않다.

134 문맥에 맞는 문장 고르기

번역 (A) 남겨진 모든 물품은 폐기될 예정입니다.
(B) 각 냉장고 안의 물품은 라벨을 붙여야 합니다.
(C) 직원들은 평소대로 출근해야 합니다.
(D) 비상용 조명은 각 부서가 계속 운영되도록 할 것입니다.

해설 빈칸 앞 문장에서 직원들에게 주방에서 모든 개인 물품을 치울 것(employees are asked to remove any personal contents from the kitchenette)을 요청했으므로, 빈칸에도 이와 관련된 내용이 들어가야 문맥상 자연스럽다. 따라서 (A)가 정답이다.

어휘 discard 버리다, 폐기하다 report to work 출근하다

135-138 이메일

수신: 아네트 슈라이버 〈aschreiber@www.aschreiber.net〉
발신: 허버트 페라이노, 총지배인 〈hperaino@partyon.com〉
날짜: 5월 5일
제목: 비공개 파티

안녕하세요, 슈라이버 씨.

곧 있을 행사에 저희 파티온을 고려해 주셔서 감사합니다. 저희가 제공할 수 있는 공간을 안내해 드릴 기회가 주어져 기쁩니다.

135**저희는 파티 규모에 따라 다양한 장소를 제공합니다.** 예를 들어, 저희 테라스는 15명까지 수용할 수 있습니다. 이 공간은 소규모 모임에 136**이상적**입니다. 라운지 구역은 40명까지 들어갈 수 있습니다. 편안한 137**모임**을 갖기에 가장 적합합니다. 그리고 좀 더 격식 있는 파티에 맞는 대규모 식당이 있습니다. 최대 60명의 손님을 위한 공간을 제공합니다. 게다가 지정하신 대로 점심 또는 저녁 식사 메뉴를 138**쉽게** 구성해 드릴 수 있습니다.

궁금하신 점이 더 있으시면, 언제든 저희에게 연락 주십시오.

허버트 페라이노 드림

어휘 upcoming 다가오는, 앞으로 있을 get-together 모임, 파티 informal 격식을 차리지 않은, 편안한 intended for ~를 위해 의도된[만들어진] accommodation 시설, 자리 according to the specifications 지정한 대로

135 문맥에 맞는 문장 고르기

번역 (A) 저희는 파티 규모에 따라 다양한 장소를 제공합니다.
(B) 이용 가능한 날짜에 대해 질문이 있으시면 기꺼이 답해 드리겠습니다.
(C) 저희 서비스에 대한 귀하의 의견을 듣고 싶습니다.
(D) 다양한 종류의 행사를 위한 점심 및 저녁 식사 선택 사항을 제공합니다.

해설 빈칸 뒤에서 수용 인원 및 용도에 따른 공간(patio, lounge area, grand dining room)을 예를 들어(for instance) 나열하고 있으므로, 빈칸에서 먼저 이들을 포괄하는 내용이 언급되어야 문맥상 자연스럽다. 따라서 (A)가 정답이다.

136 형용사 어휘

해설 빈칸은 주어 This space의 보어 역할을 하는 형용사 자리로, 빈칸 뒤 용도를 나타내는 전치사구 for small get-togethers의 수식을 받는다. 따라서 빈칸에는 for와 어울려 쓰이며 공간의 특성을 나타내는 형용사가 들어가야 하므로, '이상적인, 가장 알맞은'이라는 의미의 (C) ideal이 정답이다. (A) worried는 '걱정하는', (B) exact는 '정확한, 꼼꼼한', (D) ultimate는 '궁극의, 최후의'라는 뜻으로 문맥상 빈칸에 적절하지 않다.

137 명사 어휘

해설 빈칸은 전치사 for의 목적어 역할을 하는 명사 자리로, 형용사 informal의 수식을 받는다. 해당 문장의 주어 It이 앞에 언급된 Our lounge area를 가리키므로, 빈칸에는 라운지 구역이 무엇에 적합한지(best suited for) 나타내는 명사가 들어가야 한다. 따라서 '모임'이라는 의미의 (A) gatherings가 정답이다. (B) locales는 '현장, (소설·영화 등의) 배경', (C) collections는 '수집(품), 모금', (D) methods는 '방법, 체계'라는 뜻으로 문맥상 빈칸에 적절하지 않다.

138 부사 자리 _ 동사원형 수식

해설 빈칸이 조동사 can과 동사원형 design 사이에 있으므로, 빈칸에는 design을 수식하는 부사가 들어가야 한다. 따라서 '쉽게'라는 의미의 부사 (B) easily가 정답이다. (A) easy는 형용사, (C) ease는 명사/동사, (D) easier는 비교급 형용사로 품사상 빈칸에 들어갈 수 없다.

139-142 기사

테일러스빌 (10월 4일) – 테일러스빌의 보 크랜델 시장은 자전거 공유 프로그램에 관한 계획을 이번 주에 발표했다. 교통 수단으로써 자전거 이용을 독려하고자 했던 과거의 노력은 시내에 자전거를 주차할 만한 편리한 공간이 없어서 실패했다. 더구나 자전거를 타는 사람들이 좁은 길을 차, 트럭 등과 함께 달려야 [139]**했어서** 안전에 관한 우려를 불러 일으켰다.

새로운 자전거 공유 계획으로, 테일러스빌 여덟 곳에 자전거 보관소가 [140]**전략적으로** 세워질 예정이다. 이 계획의 중요한 의도 중 하나는 시내 지역의 한정된 주차 공간 문제를 완화하는 것이다. "[141]**더욱이,** 지역 주민들이 야외에서 더 많은 시간을 보내고 우리의 아름다운 도시를 누릴 수 있게 하고 싶습니다"라고 크랜델 시장은 발표 말미에 덧붙였다. [142]**그는 빠르면 내년 4월에 자전거 보관소를 이용할 수 있도록 할 계획이다.**

어휘 additionally 게다가 raise concerns 우려를 불러 일으키다 initiative 계획, 방침 encourage 장려하다, 고무하다 remark 발언, 말

139 동사 어형 _ 태

해설 빈칸에 적절한 동사 형태를 선택하는 문제이다. 주어인 cyclists는 어쩔 수 없는 상황에서 차, 트럭 등과 함께 좁은 길을 달리게 되었던 것이므로, '(어쩔 수 없이) ~하게 되었다'라는 의미의 수동태 동사 (A) were forced가 정답이다. force는 '~하게 하다, 강요하다'라는 뜻의 타동사로 강요 당하는 대상을 목적어로 취한다. 따라서 능동태인 (B) force, (C) will be forcing, (D) have forced는 빈칸에 들어갈 수 없다.

140 부사 자리 _ 동사 수식

해설 빈칸은 완전한 절(bicycle stations will be placed) 뒤에서 동사 will be placed를 수식하는 부사 자리이므로, '전략적으로, 전략상'이라는 의미의 부사 (D) strategically가 정답이다. (A) strategizing은 동명사/현재분사, (B) strategy는 명사, (C) strategic은 형용사로 품사상 빈칸에 들어갈 수 없다.

어휘 strategize 전략을 짜다 strategy 전략 strategic 전략적인

141 접속부사

해설 앞뒤 문장을 의미상 자연스럽게 연결해 주는 접속부사를 선택하는 문제이다. 앞 문장에서 자전거 공유 프로그램의 의도(One important purpose ~ to ease the limited vehicle parking in the downtown area)가 소개되었고, 빈칸 뒤에서 해당 계획과 관련하여 테일러스빌 시장이 추가적으로 바라는 바(I want to encourage local residents to ~ enjoy our beautiful town)가 언급되었다. 따라서 '더욱이, 또한'이라는 의미의 (C) Moreover가 정답이다. (A) Otherwise는 '그렇지 않으면, 달리', (B) Rather는 '오히려, 차라리', (D) Similarly는 '마찬가지로, 유사하게'라는 뜻으로 문맥상 빈칸에 적절하지 않다.

142 문맥에 맞는 문장 고르기

번역 (A) 프로그램을 이용하는 사람들은 웹사이트 계정을 만들었다.
(B) 최근 설문 조사에서 많은 응답자들이 안전 관련 우려 사항을 언급했다.
(C) 인근 그랜몬트의 자전거 공유 프로그램은 5년째 성공을 거두고 있다.
(D) 그는 빠르면 내년 4월에 자전거 보관소를 이용할 수 있도록 할 계획이다.

해설 빈칸 앞에서 자전거 공유 프로그램을 위해 보관소가 전략적으로 설치될 예정(bicycle stations will be placed ~ Taylorsville)이라고 했고, 해당 프로그램의 의도와 테일러스빌 시장의 바람이 언급되었다. 따라서 프로그램 계획 관련 내용이 이어지는 것이 자연스러우므로, (D)가 정답이다.

어휘 respondent 응답자

143-146 이메일

수신: 전 직원
발신: 알렉스 뮤레시아누
날짜: 6월 28일
제목: 새로운 직원 안내서 교육

클록 파이낸셜은 최근 직원 안내서를 업데이트했습니다. [143]**10년 넘는 기간 동안 처음으로 변경된 것입니다.** 복리 후생 및 고용 조건에 관한 정보는 그대로지만, 다른 중요 사항에 대한 수정이 이뤄졌습니다. 이번 안내서에는 이메일 개인 정보, 인터넷 사용, 모바일 기기 사용에 관한 새로운 정책이 포함되어 있습니다. 출장 지침 또한 [144]**개정되었습니다.** 출장 후 환급 절차가 이제 훨씬 더 효율적이게 되었습니다.

전 직원은 정책 관련 설명회에 필히 참석해야 합니다. 7월 9일과 7월 16일 오전 10시에 한 시간짜리 세션이 열릴 예정입니다. [145]**이후 바로,** 직원들은 안내서에 포함된 정보를 받아서 읽었고 이해했으며, 조건을 받아들인다는 사실을 인정하는 양식에 서명해야 합니다. 관리자와 상의하여 두 세션 중 하나에 [146]**참석하도록** 하십시오.

알렉스 뮤레시아누

어휘 concerning ~에 관련된 terms 조건 modification 수정, 변경 reimbursement 환급, 상환 efficient 효율적인 informational 정보를 제공하는 acknowledge 인정하다 arrange 계획을 세우다, 준비하다

143 문맥에 맞는 문장 고르기

번역 (A) 정책을 잘 지켜 주셔서 감사합니다.
(B) 저희 새 로고가 표지에 그려져 있습니다.
(C) 10년 넘는 기간 동안 처음으로 변경된 것입니다.
(D) 이를 작성하기 위해 사내 변호사들이 채용됐습니다.

해설 빈칸 앞 문장에서 클록 파이낸셜이 최근 직원 안내서를 업데이트했다(Klok Financial has recently updated its employee handbook)고 했고, 뒤 문장에서 변경된 사항(Although the information concerning ~ remains the same, other important modifications have been made)을 대략적으로 설명했으므로, 빈칸에도 직원 안내서 업데이트와 관련된 내용이 들어가야 자연스럽다. 따라서 (C)가 정답이다.

어휘 adhere to ~를 고수하다, ~를 충실히 지키다 corporate 회사의

144 동사 어휘

해설 빈칸 앞에서 직원 안내서의 몇 가지 중요한 사항이 수정되었다며 새 정책들을 나열했다. 이에 덧붙여 출장 지침(travel guidelines)을 언급한 것이므로, 이 역시(also) 수정되었다는 내용이 되어야 자연스럽다. 따라서 '개정된, 수정된'이라는 의미의 (A) revised가 정답이다. 빈칸 뒤에 관련 절차가 더 효율적으로 바뀌었다(now much more efficient)고 했기 때문에 '삭제된'이라는 뜻의 (B) deleted는 빈칸에 들어갈 수 없다. (C) discussed는 '논의된', (D) notified는 '통지를 받은'이라는 뜻으로 문맥상 빈칸에 적절하지 않다.

145 접속부사

해설 앞뒤 문장을 의미상 자연스럽게 연결해 주는 접속부사를 선택하는 문제이다. 빈칸 앞 문장에서 예정된 설명회 일정(One-hour sessions ~ on 9 July and 16 July)을, 뒤에서 직원들이 요청받게 될 사항(employees will be required to sign a form acknowledging ~ the terms)을 언급했으므로, 빈칸에는 전후 상황을 연결하는 접속부사가 들어가야 자연스럽다. 따라서 '이후 바로'라는 의미의 (D) Immediately afterward가 정답이다. (A) In summary는 '요약하면', (B) On the other hand는 '다른 한편으로, 반면에', (C) As a matter of fact는 '사실은'이라는 뜻으로 문맥상 빈칸에 적절하지 않다.

146 to부정사

해설 관리자와 상의하여 미래에 열릴 예정인 설명회에 참석하라는 내용의 문장이므로, 목적을 나타내는 to부정사 (A) to attend가 정답이다. (B) who attended(참석했던), (C) while attending(참석하는 동안에), (D) in attendance at(참석하는)은 문맥상 빈칸에 적절하지 않다.

PART 7

147-148 공지

영업부 점심 워크숍

[148]**영업 사원 여러분들은 주목하세요! CMG 다이렉트 리테일에 새로 입사하셨나요?** 여러분의 판매 집계표가 다소 모자라 보이십니까? 수수료를 더 많이 받고 싶은데 새로운 고객을 찾을 수가 없습니까? 이번 달 점심 워크숍에 참석하세요. 수석 영업 관리자인 채드 아바키안 씨가 신규 고객을 찾고 확보하고 늘리는 비결을 공유해 드립니다! [147]**점심 식사는 제공되지 않으니 먹을 것을 각자 가져오세요.** 워크숍이 끝나면 발표 전체를 디지털 녹화한 내용을 회사 교육 웹사이트에서 볼 수 있습니다. 따라서 메모를 위해 노트북을 가져오실 필요가 없습니다. 좌석 예약을 위해 인력 개발부 이메일 events@cmgdr.com으로 참석 여부를 알려 주시기 바랍니다.

어휘 sales associate 영업 사원 sales sheet 판매 집계표 commission 수수료 secure 확보하다 expand 확대하다, 늘리다 account 고객 reserve 예약하다

147 세부 사항

번역 참석자들은 워크숍에 무엇을 가져오라는 조언을 받았는가?
(A) 음식
(B) 판매 집계표
(C) 신청서
(D) 노트북 컴퓨터

해설 공지의 중반부에서 점심 식사가 제공되지 않으니 먹을 것을 각자 가져오라(Lunch is not provided, so be sure to pack something for yourself)고 안내했으므로, (A)가 정답이다.

▸▸ **Paraphrasing** 지문의 **to pack** → 질문의 **to bring**

148 추론 / 암시

번역 행사를 통해 누가 가장 혜택을 받을 것인가?
(A) 수석 영업 관리자들
(B) 인력 개발부 직원들
(C) CMG 다이렉트 리테일 신규 고객들
(D) 최근 채용된 영업 사원들

해설 공지의 초반부에서 영업 사원들은 주목하라(Attention sales associates!)고 한 후, 회사에 새로 입사해서(Are you new to CMG Direct Retail?) 영업에 어려움을 겪고 있다면 채드 아바키안 씨가 진행하는 워크숍에 오라고 초청했다. 따라서 (D)가 정답이다.

▸▸ **Paraphrasing** 지문의 **sales associates** → 정답의 **sales professionals**
지문의 **new to CMG Direct Retail** → 정답의 **Recently hired**

TEST 5

149-150 온라인 양식

https://www.bywaterandsons.com/testimonial

바이워터 앤 선즈

고객 추천

[149]**고객님 댁에서 저희가 한 작업의 품질에 대해 의견을 말씀해 주세요.** 성함과 이메일 주소, 의견을 제출하시면 됩니다.

이름: 지나 타일러

[150]**이메일: gtyler@mailzinebox.com (고객님의 후기에 이메일 주소는 게시되지 않음)**

페인트 작업을 훌륭히 해 주셔서 감사합니다. 효율적으로 완료됐고 비용이 원래 견적대로 나왔어요. 저희 집은 새 집이었을 때만큼 멋집니다. 나중에 서비스를 다시 이용할 계획입니다. [149]**리모델링을 고려하는 사람들에게 기꺼이 귀사를 추천할 거예요.**

- 지나 타일러

어휘 initial 처음의 quote 견적

149 세부 사항

번역 바이워터 앤 선즈는 어떤 종류의 업체인가?

(A) 보수 도급 업체
(B) 부동산 관리 사무실
(C) 이사 업체
(D) 배송 서비스 업체

해설 양식 상단에 바이워터 앤 선즈가 한 작업의 품질에 대한 의견을 달라(Please share your thoughts about the quality of our work at your home)고 쓰여 있고, 타일러 씨가 작성한 내용을 보면, 마지막 부분에 리모델링을 고려하는 사람들에게 바이워터 앤 선즈를 추천하고 싶다(I am happy to recommend you to anyone considering a remodeling project)고 되어 있다. 따라서, 바이워터 앤 선즈가 보수 도급 업체임을 알 수 있으므로, (A)가 정답이다.

어휘 contractor 도급 업자, 하청 업체 property 부동산, 재산

▸▸ Paraphrasing 지문의 remodeling project → 정답의 renovation

150 사실 관계 확인

번역 이메일 주소에 대해 명시된 것은?

(A) 청구서 발송에 쓰일 것이다.
(B) 공개되지 않을 것이다.
(C) 회사 데이터베이스에 저장될 것이다.
(D) 무료 가격 견적서를 받는 데 필요하다.

해설 고객 의견에 이메일(Email) 주소가 적힌 부분을 보면, 타일러 씨의 후기에 이메일 주소는 게시되지 않는다(this will not be posted with your review)고 쓰여 있다. 따라서 (B)가 정답이다.

어휘 invoice 송장, 청구서

▸▸ Paraphrasing 지문의 will not be posted → 정답의 will be kept private

151-152 온라인 고객 서비스 채팅

실시간 채팅

프리안 의류 (오후 5시 5분)
안녕하세요. 프리안 의류에 연락 주셔서 감사합니다. 어떻게 도와 드릴까요?

마리나 솔러 (오후 5시 6분)
안녕하세요. [151]**웹사이트에서 바지를 구입하려고 하는데요.** #CP3984 제품이요. [151]**그런데 클릭하면 계속 오류 메시지가 뜹니다.**

프리안 의류 (오후 5시 7분)
죄송합니다. 도와 드릴 수 있는지 한번 보겠습니다. [152]**제가 그 제품을 주문해 드리고 이메일로 구매 확인서를 보내 드릴 수 있습니다.**

마리나 솔러 (오후 5시 8분)
그렇게 해 주시면 감사하겠습니다.

프리안 의류 (오후 5시 9분)
어떤 색상과 사이즈를 원하세요?

마리나 솔러 (오후 5시 9분)
사이즈 10에 검은색이요.

프리안 의류 (오후 5시 10분)
저희가 파일에 가지고 있는 고객님의 신용카드 번호를 사용해도 될까요?

마리나 솔러 (오후 5시 10분)
그렇게 해 주세요.

프리안 의류 (오후 5시 12분)
주문 확인서를 이메일로 보내 드렸습니다. 다른 문제가 있으면 알려 주십시오.

마리나 솔러 (오후 5시 13분)
정말 감사합니다.

어휘 confirmation 확인(서) issue 문제, 말썽거리

151 세부사항

번역 솔러 씨가 프리안 의류에 연락하는 이유는?

(A) 제품을 환불받고 싶어 한다.
(B) 주문하는 데 문제가 있다.
(C) 구입한 주문품을 받지 못했다.
(D) 고객 서비스에 대해 불만이 있다.

해설 솔러 씨가 오후 5시 6분 메시지에서 웹사이트에서 바지를 구입하려고 하는데(I have been trying to purchase ~ on your Web site), 클릭하면 계속 오류 메시지가 뜬다(when I click on it, I keep getting an error message)고 했다. 따라서 주문하는 데 문제가 생겨 연락을 한 것이므로, (B)가 정답이다.

▸▸ **Paraphrasing** 지문의 **keep getting an error message**
→ 정답의 **having trouble**

152 의도 파악

번역 오후 5시 8분에 솔러 씨가 "그렇게 해 주시면 감사하겠습니다"라고 쓸 때, 그 의도는 무엇인가?

(A) 제안된 도움을 받을 것이다.
(B) 확인 이메일을 받았다.
(C) 다른 색상을 선택하고 싶다.
(D) 해당 제품을 여전히 판매해서 감사하게 생각한다.

해설 솔러 씨가 주문에 문제가 있다고 하자, 프리안 의류는 오후 5시 7분 메시지에서 제품을 대신 주문한 후 이메일로 구매 확인서를 보내 주겠다(I can order the item for you ~ e-mail you with confirmation of purchase)고 제안했다. 이에 대해 솔러 씨가 '그렇게 해 주시면 감사하겠습니다(I would appreciate that)'라고 응답한 것이므로, (A)가 정답이다.

153-154 기사

바우어 기술 학교, 초빙 학생 맞아

(4월 27일) - 최근 정부 보고서에 따르면 향후 10년간 디젤 정비공에 대한 수요가 15퍼센트 증가할 전망입니다. [153]**건설, 정유, 전력 업계에서 디젤 정비공 수요가 늘고 있습니다.** 해당 직책은 대부분 급여가 매우 높으며, 고등학교를 졸업하고 [153]**기술 교육**만 받으면 됩니다. 센터빌에 있는 바우어 기술 학교에서 해당 교육을 제공합니다.

바우어 기술 학교는 5월 1일 오전 9시부터 오후 2시까지 여러분을 초빙 학생으로 모십니다. [154(A)]**이 직업에 대한 질의응답 시간이 끝나면** 초빙 학생들은 전동 장치와 엔진 관리 시스템에 초점을 둔 실제 디젤 정비공 수업을 참관합니다. [154(C)]**이후 해당 분야에 관련된 일상 업무를 체험하는 실전 시간에 참여할 수 있습니다.**

[154(B)]**본 행사는 무료이나,** 좌석이 한정되어 있습니다. 참여자는 고등학교 졸업장 또는 이에 상응하는 자격증을 보유해야 합니다. 좌석을 예약하려면 타니샤 힐에게 thill@bowertech.com으로 이메일을 보내주세요.

어휘 mechanic 정비공 diploma 졸업장 profession 직업 observe 관찰하다 power train 전동 장치 hands-on 직접 해 보는 involved in ~에 관련된 equivalent 동등한 credential 자격(증)

153 사실 관계 확인

번역 디젤 정비공을 필요로 하는 업계들에 대해 명시된 것은?

(A) 수익을 15퍼센트 증가시켰다.
(B) 훈련을 받은 기술자가 더 필요할 것이다.
(C) 업계 종사자들은 적은 급여를 받는다.
(D) 센터빌에서 빠르게 성장하고 있다.

해설 첫 번째 단락에서 건설, 정유, 전력 업계에서 디젤 정비공 수요가 늘고 있다(There is a growing need for diesel mechanics in the construction, oil, and power industries)고 한 후, 해당 직책을 맡으려면 기술 교육(technical training)을 받는 것이 요구된다(require)고 했다. 따라서 (B)가 정답이다.

어휘 underpaid 제대로 급여를 못 받는, 급여가 적은

154 사실 관계 확인

번역 초빙 학생들이 행사에서 할 수 없는 것은?

(A) 해당 분야에 대해 질문하기
(B) 무료 강좌 참석하기
(C) 실습에 참여하기
(D) 졸업장을 위한 학점 따기

해설 기사의 두 번째 단락의 '질의응답 시간이 끝나면(After a question-and-answer session about the profession)'에서 (A)를, 세 번째 단락의 '본 행사는 무료이다(The event is free)'에서 (B)를, 두 번째 단락의 '해당 분야에 관련된 일상 업무를 체험하는 실전 시간에 참여할 수 있다(guest students can ~ experience some of the day-to-day tasks involved in the field)'에서 (C)를 확인할 수 있다. 따라서 언급되지 않은 (D)가 정답이다.

어휘 earn credits 학점을 따다

▸▸ **Paraphrasing** 지문의 **a question-and-answer session about the profession**
→ 보기 (A)의 **Ask questions about the field**
지문의 **The event is free**
→ 보기 (B)의 **free classes**
지문의 **participate in hands-on sessions to experience some of the day-to-day tasks**
→ 보기 (C)의 **Take part in practice tasks**

155-157 이메일

발신: 유 에가미
수신: 회계팀 직원
날짜: 8월 21일
제목: 요나 씨의 사직

안녕하세요, 회계팀 여러분.

이미 들으셨겠지만 요나 카츠버그 씨가 이번 달 말에 밴쿠버에 새 직장을 구해 떠납니다. [155]**카츠버그 씨의 직장에 대한 헌신과 유머 감각은 우리 모두가 그리워할 것 같습니다.** 내일 정오에 회의실에서 작별의 인사를 전하고 행운을 빌어 줍시다. 케이크, 각종 음료와 함께 샌드위치가 제공될 예정입니다. [156]**깜짝 파티로 하고 싶으니 요나 씨에게는 아무 말도 하지 말아 주세요.** 선물은 가져오지 마시고 멋진 이야기를 준비해 오세요. 그리고 지난 몇 년간 함께 했던 순간을 잘 [157]**담아낸** 사진이 있으면 저에게 전달해 주세요. 제가 내일 모두 함께 볼 간단한 슬라이드쇼를 준비하고 있습니다.

감사합니다.
유 에가미, 회계팀 부팀장

어휘 accounting 회계 dedication 헌신

TEST 5

155 추론 / 암시

번역 카츠버그 씨에 대해 암시된 것은?

(A) 인기 있는 동료이다.
(B) 다른 부서로 이동한다.
(C) 발표를 준비하고 있다.
(D) 행사에 참석할 수 없다.

해설 이메일의 두 번째 문장에서 카츠버그 씨의 직장에 대한 헌신과 유머 감각은 모두가 그리워할 것 같다(his workplace dedication and his sense of humor will be missed by all)고 했으므로, 그가 인기 있는 동료임을 추론할 수 있다. 따라서 (A)가 정답이다.

어휘 colleague 동료 transfer 이동하다, 이전하다

156 세부 사항

번역 에가미 씨는 팀원들에게 무엇을 부탁하는가?

(A) 선물 구입비 보태기
(B) 비밀 지키기
(C) 음식 준비하기
(D) 단체 사진을 위한 포즈 취하기

해설 이메일의 중반부에서 깜짝 파티로 하고 싶으니 카츠버그 씨에게는 말하지 말라(We would like this to be a surprise, so please don't mention anything to Jonah)고 요청했으므로, (B)가 정답이다.

어휘 contribute to ~에 기부하다

▸▸ Paraphrasing 지문의 **don't mention anything**
→ 정답의 **Keep a secret**

157 동의어 찾기

번역 첫 번째 단락 6행의 "capture"와 의미가 가장 가까운 단어는?

(A) 얻다
(B) 나타내다
(C) 결론을 내다
(D) 통제하다

해설 "capture"가 포함된 부분은 '함께했던 순간을 잘 담아낸 사진'이라는 뜻으로, 여기서 capture는 '담아내다, 포착하다'라는 의미로 쓰였다. 따라서 '나타내다, 표현하다'라는 뜻인 (B) represent가 정답이다.

158-160 정보

[158]공장 직원: 휴식 시간

[158]공장 정규직 직원들에게는 하루 3회의 휴식 시간이 부여되며 직원들은 이를 사용하는 것이 좋습니다. [160]이 휴식 시간 동안 개인적인 일을 처리하십시오. 여기에는 전화하기, 메시지 보내기, 소셜미디어 이용하기 등이 포함됩니다. 8시간 교대 근무를 하는 사람은 오전에 15분의 휴식 시간이, 오후에 다시 15분의 휴식 시간이 주어집니다. 점심 시간은 30분입니다.

[158]1층에 주방과 직원 라운지가 있는 휴식 공간이 있습니다. [159]매주 금요일 저녁에 냉장고를 청소하니 보관을 원하는 남은 음식은 집으로 가져가시기 바랍니다.

직원 라운지에는 개인 물품을 보관할 수 있는 사물함이 있습니다. 직원들은 직원 라운지 근처 화장실을 사용해도 좋습니다.

어휘 be entitled to ~할 자격이 주어지다 attend to ~를 처리하다 leftover 나머지의; 남은 음식 adjacent to ~에 인접한

158 추론 / 암시

번역 해당 정보는 어디에서 볼 수 있겠는가?

(A) 제품 사용 설명서
(B) 영업부 송장
(C) 직원 안내서
(D) 회사 보도 자료

해설 공장 직원의 휴식 시간(Factory Staff: Break Times)과 관련하여 공장 직원에게 주어지는 3회의 휴식 시간(three breaks daily), 휴식 공간(break area) 및 이용 가능한 시설(kitchen, staff lounge, refrigerator, lockers) 등에 대해 설명한 정보문이다. 이러한 정보는 직원 안내서에서 볼 수 있으므로, (C)가 정답이다.

159 사실 관계 확인

번역 직원 휴식 공간에 대해 명시된 것은?

(A) 막 개조 공사를 했다.
(B) 여러 대의 자동판매기가 있다.
(C) 2층에 있다.
(D) 냉장고가 있다.

해설 두 번째 단락에서 매주 금요일 저녁에 냉장고를 청소하니(Please note that the refrigerator is cleaned out every Friday evening) 남은 음식은 집에 가져가라고 당부했다. 이에 따라 휴식 공간에 냉장고가 있음을 알 수 있으므로, (D)가 정답이다.

어휘 renovate 개조하다, 보수하다

160 문장 삽입

번역 [1], [2], [3], [4]로 표시된 곳 중에서 다음 문장이 들어가기에 가장 적합한 곳은?

"여기에는 전화하기, 메시지 보내기, 소셜미디어 이용하기 등이 포함됩니다."

(A) [1]
(B) [2]
(C) [3]
(D) [4]

해설 주어진 문장에서 '여기에는 전화하기, 메시지 보내기, 소셜미디어 이용하기 등이 포함된다(This includes making phone calls, texting, and using social media)'고 했으므로, 앞에서 먼저 This가 가리키는 대상이 나와야 한다. [1] 앞에서 휴식 시간 동안 개인적인 일(any personal business)을 처리하라며 주어진 예시를 모두 포괄하는 대상을 언급했으므로, (A)가 정답이다.

161-163 기사

삭설 제지용품 주식회사, 베어 인더스트리얼 인수해

토론토 (5월 9일) – 지난달, 미사소거에 있는 삭설 제지용품 주식회사(SPG)는 베어 인더스트리얼을 인수했다고 발표했다. [161/162]**이 식품 포장재 및 제지용품 유통 업체는 자사의 사세 확장 및 요식업 일회용품 판매 시작 계획의 일환으로 새로운 지역에 기반을 마련하는 데 있어서 베어 인더스트리얼 인수 거래가 도움이 될 것이라고 말했다.** 베어 인더스트리얼은 퀘벡 및 인근 지역에서 많은 기관에 제품을 공급한 업체다.

"베어 인더스트리얼은 퀘벡에서 역사가 가장 오래되고 평판이 좋은 유통 업체입니다. [161]**저희는 이렇게 훌륭한 회사를 인수하고 해당 지역으로 진출하게 되어 매우 기쁩니다.**" 아르네 웰링턴 회장은 기자회견에서 지역 기자들에게 이와 같이 밝혔다. "베어 인더스트리얼 직원 여러분을 SPG로 모셔서 모두를 위해 협력할 것을 기대합니다." 그는 어떤 근로자도 인수의 결과로 일자리를 잃게 되지 않을 것이라고 덧붙였다.

"베어 인더스트리얼 인수는 캐나다 제일의 식품 포장재, 제지용품, 요식업 일회용품 공급 업체 중 하나로 자리매김하려는 SPG의 전략에 있어 중요한 단계입니다." 웰링턴 회장은 말했다. "[163]**저희의 목표는 업계를 선도하는 회사 및 업체들과의 제휴를 통해 지리적으로 영역을 확장하는 것입니다.**"

어휘 acquire 얻다, 인수하다 distributor 유통 업자[업체] establish a base 기반을 마련하다 initiative 계획 disposable 일회용의; 일회용품 institutional 기관의 serve (상품·서비스를) 제공하다 surrounding area 주변 지역 reputable 평판이 좋은 press conference 기자회견 for the benefit of ~를 위해 acquisition 인수 geographic 지리적인 reach (닿을 수 있는) 범위, 권한

161 세부 사항

번역 SPG가 베어 인더스트리얼을 인수한 이유는?

(A) SPG는 공급 업체와 더 가까워져야 했다.
(B) SPG는 다른 지역으로의 사업 확장을 원했다.
(C) 베어 인더스트리얼에게는 더 앞선 제조 장비가 있었다.
(D) 베어 인더스트리얼은 도산을 앞두고 있었다.

해설 첫 번째 단락에서 사세 확장 및 요식업 일회용품 판매 시작 계획의 일환으로 새로운 지역에 기반을 마련하는 데 있어서 베어 인더스트리얼 인수 거래가 도움이 될 것(the deal for Bear Industrial will help it establish a base in a new area ~ to break into sales of disposable food-service supplies)이라고 했다. 또한 두 번째 단락에서 베어 인더스트리얼이 퀘벡에서 평판이 좋다고 하며, 해당 지역으로 진출하게 되어 기쁘다(we are thrilled to ~ expand into the region)고 했다. 따라서 SPG가 다른 지역으로 사업을 확장하고 싶어 베어 인더스트리얼을 인수했다는 것을 알 수 있으므로, (B)가 정답이다.

어휘 advanced 선진의 manufacturing 제조

▸▸ Paraphrasing 지문의 **establish a base in a new area, expand into the region** → 정답의 **expand its business in a different region**

162 사실 관계 확인

번역 베어 인더스트리얼이 생산한 제품에 대해 맞는 것은?

(A) 사용 후 버리도록 만들어진다.
(B) 고급 음식점에서 사용된다.
(C) 퀘벡으로 수입된다.
(D) 다시 디자인하고 있다.

해설 첫 번째 단락을 보면 식품 포장재 및 제지용품 유통 업체인 SPG가 베어 인더스트리얼 인수를 통해 요식업 일회용품 판매(sales of disposable food-service supplies)를 시작할 수 있게 되었다는 것을 알 수 있다. 따라서 (A)가 정답이다.

어휘 undergo ~을 받다, 겪다

▸▸ Paraphrasing 지문의 **disposable**
→ 정답의 **be thrown away after use**

163 추론 / 암시

번역 기사에 따르면, SPG는 향후 무엇을 하겠는가?

(A) 직원 감축
(B) 퀘벡으로 본사 이전
(C) 베어 인더스트리얼과 유사한 다른 업체들과 협력
(D) 새로운 회장 임명

해설 마지막 단락에서 SPG의 목표는 업계를 선도하는 회사 및 업체들과의 제휴를 통해 지리적으로 영역을 확장하는 것(Our goal is to expand ~ through partnerships with industry-leading companies and operators)이라고 했다. 따라서 베어 인더스트리얼 같은 업체들과의 제휴를 추진할 것임을 추론할 수 있으므로, (C)가 정답이다.

어휘 relocate 이전하다 appoint 임명하다

▸▸ Paraphrasing 지문의 **through partnerships with industry-leading companies and operators**
→ 정답의 **Work with other companies**

164-167 문자 메시지

샤리 슈 (오전 9시 35분)
제가 아까 보낸 이메일 보셨나요? [164]**우리 회사가 다음 달에 열릴 전사 규모의 기부 운동을 준비했어요.** 비영리 단체를 위해 중고 컴퓨터와 전자 제품을 모을 겁니다.

제니퍼 베크 (오전 9시 37분)
네, 봤어요. 공유해 주셔서 감사합니다. [165/166]**원하시면 소셜미디어에서 정보를 퍼뜨리는 데 도움을 드릴 수 있어요.**

샤리 슈 (오전 9시 38분)
[166]**그거 좋겠네요.** 온라인상에 자주 게시니까요. 그리고 전에 〈야키마 데일리 뉴스〉 편집자와 연락하시지 않았나요? 편집자에게 연락을 하고 싶은데 온라인에서 주소를 못 찾겠어요.

제니퍼 베크 (오전 9시 39분)
네, 그런데 몇 년이나 지났어요. 지금은 새로운 편집자가 있을 겁니다. 확인해 볼게요.

TEST 5

샤리 슈 (오전 9시 40분)
내일 다양한 언론 매체에 이메일로 보내고자 하는 보도 자료를 작성했어요.

제니퍼 베크 (오전 9시 44분)
네, 새로운 편집자 데일 콜만 씨가 있네요. [167]**이메일 주소는 없지만 제가 가지고 있는 예전 연락처들을 보면 모두 같은 방식으로 주소명을 만드는 것 같아요.** 제가 d.korman@yakimanews.com으로 보내 볼게요. 이렇게만 추측이 되네요.

어휘 company-wide 회사 전체의 donation drive 기부 운동 nonprofit group 비영리 단체 news outlet 언론 매체 convention 관례, 규정

164 세부 사항

번역 슈 씨의 회사는 다음 달에 무엇을 할 것인가?

(A) 자선 기부
(B) 제품 할인
(C) 신입 사원 채용
(D) 경영 고문과 협력

해설 슈 씨가 오전 9시 35분 메시지에서 자신의 회사가 다음 달에 열릴 전사 규모의 기부 운동을 준비했다(Our company has organized a company-wide donation drive next month)고 했으므로, (A)가 정답이다.

어휘 charitable 자선의, 자선을 베푸는

165 세부 사항

번역 베크 씨는 무엇을 하겠다고 제안하는가?

(A) 장소 찾기
(B) 행사 홍보하기
(C) 뉴스 기사 찾기
(D) 잠재 고객에게 연락하기

해설 베크 씨가 오전 9시 37분 메시지에서 소셜미디어에서 행사 관련 정보를 퍼뜨리는 데 도움을 줄 수 있다(I can help circulate the information on social media)는 제안을 했으므로, (B)가 정답이다.

▸▸ Paraphrasing 지문의 **circulate the information on social media** → 정답의 **Promote an event**

166 의도 파악

번역 오전 9시 38분에 슈 씨가 "온라인상에 자주 있으시니까요"라고 말할 때, 그 의도는 무엇인가?

(A) 기사는 조사를 더 해야 한다.
(B) 웹사이트는 몇 군데 수정하면 이익이 될 수 있다.
(C) 베크 씨는 그 일에 매우 적합하다.
(D) 베크 씨는 회사를 이미 잘 알고 있을 수도 있다.

해설 베크 씨가 오전 9시 37분에 메시지에서 소셜미디어에서 행사 관련 정보를 퍼뜨리는 데 도움을 줄 수 있다(I can help circulate the information on social media)는 제안을 했는데, 슈 씨가 이를 수락(That would be good)한 후 '온라인상에 자주 있으시니까요(You're online a lot)'라며 베크 씨의 제안을 받아들인 이유를 덧붙였다. 이는 베크 씨가 소셜미디어에서 홍보하는 일에 적합하다고 생각해서 한 말이므로, (C)가 정답이다.

어휘 revision 정정, 수정

167 사실 관계 확인

번역 베크 씨가 〈야키마 데일리 뉴스〉 직원들에 대해 명시한 것은?

(A) 그들의 이메일 주소를 사설란에서 확인할 수 있다.
(B) 그들의 이메일 주소는 같은 방식으로 구성된 것 같다.
(C) 그들은 종종 대중으로부터 이메일로 뉴스 정보를 받는다.
(D) 그들은 적절한 때에 이메일 회신을 하지 않을 수도 있다.

해설 베크 씨가 오전 9시 44분 메시지에서 〈야키마 데일리 뉴스〉 편집자의 이메일 주소는 없지만 예전 연락처들을 보면 모두 같은 방식으로 주소명을 만드는 것 같다(they all use the same naming convention)고 했으므로, (B)가 정답이다.

어휘 editorial page 사설란 in a timely manner 시기 적절하게

▸▸ Paraphrasing 지문의 **the same naming convention** → 정답의 **structured the same way**

168-171 기사

준비, 시작, 잼버리!

나소 (6월 20일)–나소는 2년마다 아프로비트 애호가로 넘쳐난다. 아프로비트는 아프리카 전통 춤의 리듬에 재즈와 펑키 뮤직을 융합한 음악이다. [168(A)/(C)]**아프로잼으로 더 잘 알려진 제4회 비엔날레 아프로비트 잼버리가 7월 18일부터 22일까지 개최될 예정이다.**

[169]**아프로잼에는 나이지리아, 영국, 그리고 바하마 등 전 세계 출신 음악가들이 출연한다.** [168(B)]**최근 입장권 판매량은 올해의 아프로잼이 2년 전보다 더 많은 관중을 유치할 것임을 보여 주며,** 이로 인해 행사는 아샨티 원형 극장으로 옮겨졌다. 행사에 관한 추가 세부 사항은 www.afrojam.org.bs에서 확인 가능하다.

[169]**afrojam.org.bs 방문자는 많은 시민이 가장 좋아하는 세계적인 스트로베리 잼의 깜짝 출연 등 과거의 멋진 순간들이 담긴 동영상도 시청할 수 있다.**

올해 행사에서는 새롭게 식사 할인이 제공된다. [170/171]**축제 참가자들은 행사 참여 식당에서 자신이 소지한 반쪽 티켓을 제시하고 10퍼센트 할인을 받으면 된다.** 할인은 콘서트 당일 저녁에만 유효하다. 식당 전체 목록은 7월 15일 행사 웹사이트에 게시될 예정이다.

주최측은 나소 전역의 식당 경영주들에게 참여를 독려하고 있다. 관심이 있는 사람은 555-0171로 전화하거나 www.afrojam.org.bs/sponsors에서 신청서를 작성하면 된다.

어휘 overrun 가득 차다 fuse 융합하다 biennial 2년에 한 번씩의 feature 출연시키다, 특별히 포함하다; 특징 indicate 보여 주다, 시사하다 amphitheatre 원형 극장, 돔 경기장 appearance 출연 ticket stub (필요한 부분을 절취한 후 남은) 반쪽 티켓 restaurateur 식당 경영자 complete an application 신청서를 작성하다

168 사실 관계 확인

번역 아프로잼에 대해 명시되지 않은 것은?

(A) 2년마다 개최된다.
(B) 시간이 지날수록 인기를 더하고 있다.
(C) 이전에 세 차례 조직됐다.
(D) 보통 아샨티 원형 극장에서 개최된다.

해설 첫 번째 단락의 '아프로비트 잼으로 더 잘 알려진 제4회 비엔날레 아프로비트 잼버리가 7월 18일부터 22일까지 개최될 예정이다(The Fourth Biennial Afrobeat Jamboree ~ between 18 July and 22 July)'에서 (A)와 (C)를, 두 번째 단락의 '최근 입장권 판매량은 올해의 아프로잼이 2년 전보다 더 많은 관중을 유치할 것(this year's Afrojam will draw an even bigger crowd than ~ two years ago)임을 보여 준다'에서 (B)를 확인할 수 있다. 하지만 두 번째 단락 후반부에서 관중이 늘어나 제4회 행사가 아샨티 원형 극장으로 옮겨졌다(the move to the Ashanti Amphitheatre)고 했으므로, 행사가 주로 아샨티 원형극장에서 개최된다고 볼 수는 없다. 따라서 (D)가 정답이다.

▸▸ Paraphrasing 지문의 **Biennial** → 보기 (A)의 **every two years**
지문의 **draw an even bigger crowd** → 보기 (B)의 **become more popular**
지문의 **The Fourth Biennial Afrobeat Jamboree** → 보기 (C)의 **been organized three times before**

169 추론 / 암시

번역 스트로베리 잼은 무엇이겠는가?

(A) 입장권 판매 업체
(B) 비디오 스트리밍 사이트
(C) 식품 관련 시설
(D) 음악 그룹

해설 세 번째 단락에서 웹사이트 방문자는 세계적인 스트로베리 잼의 깜짝 출연 등 과거의 멋진 순간들이 담긴 동영상도 시청할 수 있다(Visitors to afrojam.org.bs can also enjoy video clips ~ such as the surprise appearance of the world-famous Strawberry Jam)고 했다. 따라서 스트로베리 잼이 아프로잼에 참가했음을 추론할 수 있다. 두 번째 단락에서 아프로잼에는 전 세계 출신 음악가들이 출연한다(Afrojam will feature musicians from around the globe)고 했으므로, (D)가 정답이다.

어휘 establishment 시설, 기관

170 세부 사항

번역 축제 참가자들은 할인을 받기 위해 무엇을 해야 하는가?

(A) 설문 조사 작성하기
(B) 콘서트 티켓 제시하기
(C) 행사 주최측에게 연락하기
(D) 축제 웹사이트 방문하기

해설 네 번째 단락에서 축제 참가자들은 행사 참여 식당에서 자신이 소지한 반쪽 티켓을 제시하고 10퍼센트 할인을 받으면 된다(Festival attendees need only to present their ticket stubs ~ to receive 10 percent off their bill)고 했으므로, (B)가 정답이다.

▸▸ Paraphrasing 지문의 **Festival attendees** → 질문의 **festivalgoers**
지문의 **10 percent off their bill** → 질문의 **a discount**
지문의 **present their ticket stubs** → 정답의 **Show a concert ticket**

171 문장 삽입

번역 [1], [2], [3], [4]로 표시된 곳 중에서 다음 문장이 들어가기에 가장 적합한 곳은?

"식당 전체 목록은 7월 15일 행사 웹사이트에 게시될 예정이다."

(A) [1]
(B) [2]
(C) [3]
(D) [4]

해설 주어진 문장에서 식당 전체 목록이 행사 웹사이트에 게시될 예정(A complete list of food vendors will be posted on the event Web site)이라고 했으므로, 앞이나 뒤에 식당과 관련된 내용이 언급되어야 한다. [4] 앞에서 축제 참가자들이 식당에서 할인 혜택을 받을 수 있는 방법을 알려 주었으므로, 이 뒤에 주어진 문장이 이어져야 자연스럽다. 따라서 (D)가 정답이다.

어휘 vendor 판매 업체

TEST 5

172-175 이메일

수신: 전 직원
발신: 캐롤 예이츠
제목: CCS 회의
날짜: 6월 1일
첨부: 회의 일정

직원 여러분께,

[172]**카리브해 요리 소사이어티(CCS)의 제12차 연례 회의가 7월 16일부터 20일까지 이곳 자메이카에서 개최됩니다.** [172/173]**저는 조직 위원회 위원장인 요리사 레지나 터프톤 씨께 두 개의 워크숍을 개최해 달라는 요청을 받았습니다.** [173]**출중한 요리 대가이자 카리브해 음식에 관한 요리책을 5권이나 낸 저자에게 초청을 받게 된 것은 큰 영광입니다.** 더 중요한 사실은, 우리 예이츠 레스토랑이 수상에 빛나는 요리를 선보일 멋진 기회가 된다는 점입니다.

첫 번째 워크숍은 프랑스 요리에서 영감을 얻은 조리법에 초점을 맞출 것입니다. [174]**보조 요리사인 듀안 먼로 씨가 이 분야에 뛰어나시기 때문에 발표를 도와 달라고 요청을 드렸습니다.** 두 번째 워크숍은 음식점 운영의 어려움과 보상에 대해 다룰 예정입니다. [174]**자비아 피노크 씨가 우리 식당 경영을 아주 잘 해 왔기 때문에 그녀에게 이 주제에 대한 조언을 요청했습니다.**

[175]**여러분 모두 한 개 이상의 회의에 참석하실 것을 권장합니다.** 물론 회의 기간에도 식당은 계속 문을 열어야 하고 직원도 충분히 있어야 할 것입니다. [175]**회의 기간 중 충분한 직원을 확보할 수 있도록, 6월 21일까지 참석을 원하는 세션의 요일과 시간을 저에게 알려 주십시오.** 여러분의 편의를 위해 회의 일정을 첨부합니다.

캐롤 예이츠

어휘 culinary 요리의 take place 개최되다, 열리다 organizing committee 조직 위원회 accomplished 기량이 뛰어난 delicacy 진미, 별미 distinguish oneself 뛰어나다, 두각을 드러내다 address 다루다 establishment 시설, 기관 well-staffed 직원이 잘 갖춰진 attach 첨부하다

172 주제 / 목적

번역 이메일을 쓴 목적은?

(A) 기관 설립
(B) 직원 승진 보고
(C) 행사 참여 발표
(D) 수상자 기념

해설 첫 번째 단락에서 카리브해 요리 소사이어티(CCS)의 제12차 연례 회의가 개최된다(The 12th annual conference of the Caribbean Culinary Society (CCS) will take place)고 한 후 조직위원회 위원장인 요리사 터프톤 씨로부터 두 개의 워크숍을 개최해 달라는 요청을 받았다(I have received a request from Chef Regina Tufton ~ to conduct two workshops)고 했다. 이후 워크숍에 대해 설명하며 일정을 첨부했으므로, 행사 참여를 알리기 위한 이메일이라고 볼 수 있다. 따라서 (C)가 정답이다.

어휘 promotion 승진 recipient 수령인

173 사실 관계 확인

번역 터프톤 씨에 대해 명시된 것은?

(A) 7월에 예이츠 레스토랑을 방문할 것이다.
(B) 여러 권의 요리책을 썼다.
(C) 자메이카에서 일을 시작했다.
(D) 회의에 참석할 것이다.

해설 첫 번째 단락에서 조직 위원회 위원장인 요리사 터프톤 씨가 출중한 요리 대가이자 카리브해 음식에 관한 요리책을 5권이나 낸 저자(Chef Regina Tufton, ~ who is also the author of five cookbooks on Caribbean cuisine)라고 했으므로, (B)가 정답이다.

▸▸ Paraphrasing 지문의 **the author of five cookbooks**
→ 정답의 **has written several recipe books**

174 사실 관계 확인

번역 먼로 씨와 피노크 씨에 대해 명시된 것은?

(A) 몇 가지 조리법을 향상시켰다.
(B) 함께 음식점을 경영한 적이 있다.
(C) 전에 워크숍을 진행한 적이 있다.
(D) 자신들의 직무에서 숙련된 사람들이다.

해설 두 번째 단락에서 보조 요리사인 먼로 씨에게 도움을 요청한 이유가 첫 번째 워크숍과 관련된 분야에 뛰어나기(Assistant Chef Duane Munroe has distinguished himself in this regard) 때문이라고 했고, 피노크 씨에게 두 번째 워크숍의 주제와 관련한 조언을 구했던 이유가 식당 경영을 아주 잘 해 왔기(Zavia Pinnock has been doing an outstanding job of managing our restaurant) 때문이라고 했다. 따라서 (D)가 정답이다.

175 세부 사항

번역 직원들은 무엇을 하라고 요청받았는가?

(A) 정보 제출하기
(B) 자료 복사하기
(C) 식당 청결을 유지하도록 돕기
(D) 예이츠 씨와의 회의 일정 잡기

해설 마지막 단락에서 직원들 모두 한 개 이상의 회의에 참석할 것을 권장한다(I encourage each of you to attend one or more conference sessions)고 한 후, 참석을 원하는 세션의 요일과 시간을 알려 달라(please let me know ~ the day(s) and time(s) of the session(s) you wish to attend)고 요청했다. 따라서 (A)가 정답이다.

어휘 photocopy 복사하다

▸▸ Paraphrasing 지문의 **let me know ~ the day(s) and time(s) of the session(s) you wish to attend**
→ 정답의 **Submit some information**

176-180 이메일 + 웹페이지

발신: 히로아키 요네야 <hyoneya@westernstatesmilling.net>
수신: 클레이 크로스비 <ccrosby@westernstatesmilling.net>
날짜: 6월 1일
제목: 야구의 밤

클레이,

[176]**우리가 최근 직원과 그 가족을 위한 야유회에 대해 논의한 것을 기억하실 겁니다. 가장 좋은 아이디어는 야구 경기를 보러 가는 것이라고 생각해요.** [177]**저는 우리 지역 팀인 빌링턴 버팔로즈의 경기에 항상 가족들을 데려 가고 있어요.** 제 사무실에 있는 사진 중 몇 장이 경기장에서 찍은 거라는 사실을 알아차리셨을 겁니다! 보통 경기를 볼 때 다른 직원들도 마주치기 때문에 야구를 보러 가는 게 우리 회사 대다수의 흥미를 끌 거라고 생각해요.

[176]**6월 28일로 준비해 주실 수 있나요?** 원하시면 온라인으로 모두 해결할 수 있습니다. 제 계산에 따르면 총 45장의 표가 필요하겠지만 숫자를 다시 한번 확인해 주세요. 음식도 제공되었으면 합니다. [178]**비용을 1인당 20달러 아래로 제한하고 날씨가 좋지 않을 경우를 대비해 지붕이 있는 좌석으로 합시다.** 표를 구입하는 대로 세부 사항을 저에게 보내 주세요.

감사합니다.

히로아키 요네야, 부실장
웨스턴 스테이츠 밀링 주식회사

어휘 outing 야유회 notice 알아차리다 appeal 관심[흥미]을 끌다 calculation 계산 purchase 사다, 구입하다

http://www.billingtonbuffaloes.com/grouptickets

단체 구역	최대 수용 인원	가격	좌석 지붕
178**홈런 파빌리온**	60인	178**1인당 17달러**	178**있음**
퍼스트 베이스 더그아웃 덴	50인	1인당 19달러	없음
노스 슬라이드 파티 데크	60인	1인당 25달러	없음
디럭스 스위트	50인	1인당 30달러	있음

단체 표 관련 정책

- 홈런 파빌리온, 퍼스트 베이스 더그아웃 덴, 노스 슬라이드 파티 테크 구역에 앉는 단체 일원은 각각 핫도그, 칩스, 탄산음료를 제공받습니다. 디럭스 스위트는 모든 관람객을 위한 뷔페 식사를 포함합니다.
- 179(A)**각 단체로 마스코트 바비 버팔로가 특별 방문합니다.**
- 179(B)**단체는 경기장 안내 방송으로 환영의 인사를 받습니다.**
- 179(C)**단체의 모든 일원은 팀 관련 상품 구입 시 10퍼센트 할인을 받습니다.** (경기 당일 한정)
- 180**예약 시 25퍼센트의 보증금을 지불해야 합니다.** 나머지 금액은 늦어도 예약 일자 2주 전까지 납부해야 합니다. 지불이 이루어지면 표를 우편으로 발송해 드립니다.
- 질문이 있으시면 매표소 (406) 555-0192로 전화하세요.

어휘 merchandise 물품, 상품 deposit 보증금 remaining balance 잔여 금액 no later than 늦어도 ~까지는

176 주제 / 목적

번역 이메일을 쓴 목적은?

(A) 직원에게 행사 준비를 부탁하려고
(B) 야구 팀의 요청에 대해 의논하려고
(C) 직원들에게 표 가격을 알려 주려고
(D) 회사 야유회에 대한 제안을 들으려고

해설 이메일의 첫 번째 단락에서 직원과 그 가족을 위한 야유회(an outing for the employees and their families)로 가장 좋은 아이디어는 야구 경기를 보러 가는 것(I think the best idea is to go to a baseball game)이라고 제안한 후, 두 번째 단락에서 크로스비 씨에게 6월 28일로 준비해 달라(Could you please set this up for June 28?)고 요청했다. 따라서 행사 준비를 부탁하기 위한 이메일이라고 볼 수 있으므로, (A)가 정답이다.

어휘 arrange 준비하다, 마련하다 solicit 간청하다, 구하다

▸▸ Paraphrasing 지문의 set this up
→ 정답의 arrange an event

177 사실 관계 확인

번역 요네야 씨에 대해 명시된 것은?

(A) 팀 웹사이트에서 오류를 발견했다.
(B) 정기적으로 야구 경기를 보러 간다.
(C) 행사 일자를 변경하고 싶어 한다.
(D) 최근 빌링턴으로 이사했다.

해설 이메일의 첫 번째 단락에서 요네야 씨는 자신의 지역 팀인 빌링턴 버팔로즈의 경기에 항상 가족들을 데려 가고 있다(I have always enjoyed taking my family to see ~ our local team)고 했으므로, (B)가 정답이다.

▸▸ Paraphrasing 지문의 see the Billington Buffaloes, our local team
→ 정답의 attends baseball games

178 연계

번역 경기장의 어떤 구역이 웨스턴 스테이트 밀링 직원들에게 가장 적합한가?

(A) 홈런 파빌리온
(B) 퍼스트 베이스 더그아웃 덴
(C) 노스 사이드 파티 데크
(D) 디럭스 스위트

해설 이메일의 두 번째 단락에서 요네야 씨가 비용은 1인당 20달러 아래로 제한하고 날씨가 좋지 않을 경우를 대비해 지붕이 있는 좌석으로 하자(Let's limit our cost to under $20 per person ~ the seating is covered just in case the weather is poor)고 제안했다. 웹페이지의 표를 보면 요네야 씨의 제안에 가장 부합하는 구역은 홈런 파빌리온(Home Run Pavilion)이므로, (A)가 정답이다.

179 사실 관계 확인

번역 단체 표 소지자들에게 추가 혜택으로 제공되지 않는 것은?

(A) 바비 버팔로의 방문
(B) 환영 안내 방송
(C) 상품 할인
(D) 단체 사진

해설 웹페이지에 명시된 단체 표 관련 정책(Group Ticket Policies)의 두 번째 항목(Each group will receive a special visit from the mascot, Bobby Buffalo)에서 (A)를, 세 번째 항목(Groups will be welcomed to the stadium over the announcement system)에서 (B)를, 네 번째 항목(Everyone in the group will receive 10% off team merchandise)에서 (C)를 확인할 수 있다. 따라서 언급되지 않은 (D)가 정답이다.

▸▸ Paraphrasing 지문의 a special visit → 보기 (A)의 A visit
지문의 be welcomed to the stadium over the announcement system
→ 보기 (B)의 A welcome announcement
지문의 10% off → 보기 (C)의 A discount

180 세부 사항

번역 웹페이지에 따르면, 크로스비 씨는 예약을 하기 위해 무엇을 해야 하는가?

(A) 보증금 내기
(B) 관리자에게 서류에 서명 받기
(C) 매표소에 전화하기
(D) 온라인 표 요청서 작성하기

TEST 5

해설 단체 표 관련 정책(Group Ticket Policies)의 다섯 번째 항목에서 예약 시 25퍼센트의 보증금을 지불해야 한다(A 25% deposit is required when booking)고 했으므로, (A)가 정답이다.

▸▸ Paraphrasing 지문의 **when booking**
→ 질문의 **in order to make a reservation**
지문의 **A 25% deposit is required**
→ 정답의 **(must) Make a deposit**

181-185 기사 + 웹페이지

GRI, 본격적인 개시 준비 마쳐

글 안토인 윌리엄스

[181]**많은 사람이 배리 시를 온타리오 주의 육상 중심지로 여기고 있지만, 배리 시는 게일우드 레크리에이션 인스티튜트(GRI)를 포함한 여러 공공 수영 시설의 본고장이기도 하다.** GRI는 두 개의 실내 수영장을 보유하고 있는데 하나는 여가 수영에 사용되고 다른 하나는 수영 강습이나 안전 요원 자격증 같은 특별 프로그램만을 위한 곳이다.

[183]**올 여름 GRI에서는 수영 집중 강습 및 안전 자격증 강습을 추가할 예정이다.** 센터장인 허버트 가뇽 씨는 "[183]**지금은 저희 성수기입니다.** 저희 수영장은 실내에 있어서 연중 내내 수영을 [182]**할 수 있긴 합니다**만, 사람들은 보통 여름에 휴양과 새로운 활동을 할 시간이 더 많거든요." 여름 강습은 오전, 오후, 저녁에 제공될 예정이다. "모든 분의 일정에 맞춰 드릴 수 있었으면 합니다." 가뇽 씨가 말을 이었다. "저희 강습은 아동뿐 아니라 모든 연령대와 경험 수준을 목표로 합니다." 추가 정보를 원하면 905-555-0142로 전화하거나 www.galewoodrec.org를 방문하면 된다.

어휘 capital 수도, 중심지 establishment 시설, 기관 boast ~를 갖고 있다, 자랑하다 reserved for ~를 위해 따로 둔 certification 자격, 인증 high season 성수기 in general 보통, 대개 accommodate ~에 맞추다

http://www.galewoodrec.org/employment

채용 기회

직책: 수영 강사

게시일자: 3월 20일

게일우드 레크리에이션 인스티튜트는 저희 수영장 한 곳이나 두 곳 모두에서 일할 자격증이 있는 수영 강사를 계속 모집합니다. 강사는 안전 요원의 직무를 실행하고 매주 있는 수영 강습을 지도하며 안전 자격증 과정을 진행하고 기타 기본 직무를 수행합니다. [183]**직원 수요는 분주한 여름철에 특히 높아집니다.** [184]**센터 직원은 항상 고객에게 최고의 서비스를 제공해야 하므로 지원자는 활기 넘치고 대인 관계 능력이 좋아야 합니다.**

정규 직책과 더불어, 십 대를 위한 특별 여름 교육 프로그램의 일원이 되고 싶은 두 분의 강사를 선발하려고 합니다. [185]**특별 강사는 정규직에서 요하는 것과 동일한 역량을 갖추는 동시에 온타리오 교육 및 학습 재단에서 고안하고 감독하는 교육 과정을 실시해야 합니다.** 선발된 지원자는 5월에 한 달간 진행되는 유급 교육 과정을 이수합니다. 6월 1일부터 여름이 끝날 때까지 화요일 저녁과 수요일 저녁에 근무할 수 있어야 합니다.

지원자는 최소 6개월의 강습 경험이 있어야 하며 공인 교육 프로그램의 통용 자격증을 소지하고 있어야 합니다. 지원 시 이력서와 함께 자격증을 업로드하십시오.

어휘 ongoing 계속 진행중인 certified 자격[증]을 갖춘 carry out 수행하다 acute 극심한 patron 후원자, 고객 applicant 지원자 interpersonal 대인 관계에 관련된 implement 수행하다 candidate 후보자, 지원자 monthlong 한 달 간의 current 통용되는 accredited 공인된, 인가를 받은

181 추론 / 암시

번역 기사에서 배리 시민들에 대해 암시된 것은?

(A) 시가 너무 빠르게 성장하고 있다고 믿는다.
(B) 시에 다른 공공 스포츠 시설이 있었으면 하고 바란다.
(C) 지역에서 진행하는 육상 행사가 교통에 지장을 준다는 것을 안다.
(D) 체육 활동에 중점을 둔다.

해설 기사의 첫 번째 단락에서 많은 사람이 배리 시를 온타리오 주의 육상 중심지로 여기고 있지만, 배리 시는 게일우드 레크리에이션 인스티튜트(GRI)를 포함한 여러 공공 수영 시설의 본고장이기도 하다(Although considered ~ the running capital of Ontario, the city of Barrie is also home to several public swimming establishments)고 소개했다. 따라서 달리기와 수영 같은 체육 활동에 중점을 두는 도시라고 추론할 수 있으므로, (D)가 정답이다.

어휘 disrupt 방해하다, 지장을 주다 place an emphasis on ~에 중점을 두다

182 동의어 찾기

번역 기사의 두 번째 단락 6행의 "allows"와 의미가 가장 가까운 단어는?

(A) 허가해 주다
(B) 가능하게 하다
(C) 대신하다
(D) 포함하다

해설 "allows"를 포함한 부분은 '수영장이 실내에 있어서 연중 내내 수영을 할 수 있다(Our pools are indoors, which allows for swimming all year)'라는 내용으로, 여기서 allows는 '할 수 있게 하다, 가능하게 하다'라는 뜻으로 쓰였다. 따라서 '가능하게 하다'라는 의미의 (B) makes possible이 정답이다.

183 연계

번역 기사와 웹페이지에 모두 명시된 것은?

(A) 3월 20일에 새로운 프로그램이 시작된다.
(B) GRI는 실외 수영장 두 개가 있다.
(C) 여름은 GRI에게 가장 바쁜 시기이다.
(D) GRI는 온타리오 교육 및 학습 재단과 협력하고 있다.

해설 기사의 두 번째 단락에서 수영 집중 강습 및 안전 자격증 강습을 추가할 예정(This summer, the institute will add intensive swimming and safety certification classes)인 여름이 GRI의

성수기(It is our high season)라고 했는데, 웹페이지의 첫 번째 단락에서도 직원 수요는 분주한 여름철에 특히 높아진다(The need for staff is especially acute during the busy summer months)고 했다. 따라서 (C)가 정답이다.

어휘 collaborate with ~와 협력하다

▸▸ Paraphrasing 지문의 high season → 정답의 a busy time

184 세부 사항

번역 웹페이지에 게시된 직책은 어떤 자질이 요구되는가?

(A) 다른 사람들과 좋은 관계를 맺는 능력
(B) 3-4년의 경력
(C) 행정 업무를 할 의향
(D) 유효한 운전면허증

해설 웹페이지의 첫 번째 단락에서 센터 직원은 항상 고객에게 최고의 서비스를 제공해야 하므로 지원자는 활기 넘치고 대인 관계 능력이 좋아야 한다(applicants should be energetic and have strong interpersonal skills)고 했으므로, (A)가 정답이다.

어휘 relate well with ~와 좋은 관계를 맺다, 잘 지내다
administrative 행정상의, 관리상의

▸▸ Paraphrasing 지문의 strong interpersonal skills
→ 정답의 The ability to relate well with others

185 추론 / 암시

번역 십 대를 위한 교육 프로그램에 대해 암시된 것은?

(A) 전문가가 고안했다.
(B) 전문 운동 선수들을 훈련시킨다.
(C) 기관 직원이 만들었다.
(D) 한 달 일정이다.

해설 웹페이지의 두 번째 단락에서 십 대를 위한 여름 교육 프로그램(a unique summer education programme for teenagers)의 특별 강사는 정규직에서 요하는 것과 동일한 역량을 갖추는 동시에 온타리오 교육 및 학습 재단에서 고안하고 감독하는 교육 과정을 실시해야 한다(these special instructors will be required to implement a curriculum designed and supervised by the Ontario Foundation for Teaching and Learning)고 했다. 따라서 십 대를 위한 교육 프로그램이 전문가에 의해 고안되었음을 추론할 수 있으므로, (A)가 정답이다.

▸▸ Paraphrasing 지문의 the Ontario Foundation for Teaching and Learning → 정답의 experts

186-190 온라인 양식 + 조사 결과 + 이메일

http://www.jobomatch.co.uk

Jobomatch.co.uk
채용 검색 플랫폼

안녕하세요, 샬롯 릭비 씨

당신의 취업 선호도를 관리하세요
선호도를 공유해 주시면 귀하에게 이상적인 고용 업체와 연결해 드리는 데 도움이 됩니다.

186원하시는 직무 영역은 무엇입니까?
186고객 지원, 고객 서비스, 기술 지원

어떤 유형의 일자리를 찾고 계십니까?
정규직

어디에 살고 계십니까? 우편 번호를 기재하십시오.
L22 3AB

얼마나 먼 거리까지 통근할 의향이 있으십니까?
☒ 반경 15킬로미터 이내
☐ 반경 25킬로미터 이내
☐ 반경 60킬로미터 이내

187이동을 고려하고 계십니까?
187아니요

어휘 employment 채용, 취업 job preference 취업 선호도 postal code 우편 번호 commute 통근하다 radius 반경 relocation 재배치

http://www.jobomatch.co.kr

Jobomatch.co.uk
채용 검색 결과

안녕하세요, 샬롯 릭비 씨

187귀하의 취업 선호도에 따른 일자리

고객 서비스 상담원
187리버풀, 퀴스코 유한회사
188직무에는 고객으로부터 의견과 불만 사항을 받아서 기록하고 정중하게 응대하는 일이 포함됩니다. 뛰어난 고객 서비스 능력이 있어야 합니다. 190근무 교대 스케줄이 일정하지 않습니다. 저녁, 주말, 휴일에 근무 가능해야 합니다.

고객 서비스 직원
187리버풀, 덴빌 텔레콤
직무에는 고객의 수리 요청에 착수해 처리하는 일이 포함됩니다. 영어와 다른 언어 한 가지를 유창하게 구사해야 합니다. **189고객 서비스 직원은 수리 경과 보고서 정리를 위한 전자 데이터베이스 프로그램 사용 관련 세미나에 참석할 겁니다.**

어휘 courteous 공손한, 정중한 variable 변동이 많은, 가변적인 progress report 경과 보고서

발신: crigby@zifmail.co.uk
수신: office@quiscoltd.co.uk
날짜: 3월 2일
제목: 고객 지원 직책

첨부: Rigby_CV

관계자께,

[190]**저는 퀴스코 유한회사의 고객 서비스 상담원 직책에 매우 관심이 있습니다.** 첨부한 이력서에 나와 있듯 저의 자질에 아주 잘 맞는 기회라고 생각합니다.

저는 더블린과 랭커스터에 있는 회사들의 고객 지원 업무를 담당했으며, 요크에 있는 포웰 스쿨을 졸업했습니다. [190]**공석의 모든 자격 요건을 충족합니다.** 감사합니다.

샬롯 릭비

어휘 qualification 자질, 자격[증] meet the requirements 요건을 충족시키다

186 세부 사항

번역 양식에 따르면, 릭비 씨는 어떤 고용 형태를 찾고 있는가?

(A) 시간제 일자리
(B) 재택 근무 일자리
(C) 고객을 직접 응대하는 직책
(D) 새로 이동이 필요한 일자리

해설 '원하시는 직무 영역은 무엇입니까?(What are your desired job areas?)'라는 질문에 '고객 지원, 고객 서비스, 기술 지원(Customer support, customer service, technical support)'이라고 응답했으므로, (C)가 정답이다.

▸▸ Paraphrasing 지문의 **customer** → 정답의 **clients**

187 연계

번역 릭비 씨는 어디에 거주하겠는가?

(A) 리버풀
(B) 더블린
(C) 랭커스터
(D) 요크

해설 온라인 서식의 '이동을 고려하고 계십니까?(Would you consider relocation?)'라는 질문에 릭비 씨가 '아니요(No)'라는 응답을 했는데, 채용 검색 결과(Employment Search Results)를 보면 릭비 씨의 선호도에 따라(Jobs Based On Your Preferences) 리버풀 소재의 회사 두 곳(Quisco Ltd., Liverpool/Denville Telecomm, Liverpool)을 추천했다. 따라서 릭비 씨가 리버풀에 살고 있다고 볼 수 있으므로, (A)가 정답이다.

188 세부 사항

번역 퀴스코 유한회사의 직책은 무엇을 요구하는가?

(A) 여러 개의 언어에 관한 지식
(B) 고객의 문제 해결
(C) 수리 요청 일정 잡기
(D) 교육 세미나 참가

해설 채용 검색 결과(Employment Search Results)에서 퀴스코 유한회사의 직무에는 고객으로부터 의견과 불만 사항을 받아서 기록하고 정중하게 응대하는 일(receiving and recording feedback and complaints from customers and responding in a courteous manner)이 포함되어 있으며, 뛰어난 고객 서비스 능력이 있어야 한다(Must have strong customer service skills)고 했다. 따라서 (B)가 정답이다.

어휘 resolve 해결하다

▸▸ Paraphrasing 지문의 **Must have** → 질문의 **is required**
지문의 **complaints from customers**
→ 정답의 **customer problems**

189 세부 사항

번역 덴빌 텔레콤의 교육 과정에는 무엇이 포함되는가?

(A) 안전 수칙 배우기
(B) 해외 출장
(C) 고객과의 소통
(D) 전문 소프트웨어 사용하기

해설 채용 검색 결과(Employment Search Results)에서 덴빌 텔레콤의 고객 서비스 직원은 전자 데이터베이스 프로그램 사용 관련 세미나에 참석할 거라(Customer service staff will attend seminars on using electronic database programs)고 했으므로, (D)가 정답이다.

어휘 safety procedure 안전 수칙

▸▸ Paraphrasing 지문의 **electronic database programs**
→ 정답의 **specialized software**

190 연계

번역 릭비 씨에 대해 맞는 것은?

(A) 불규칙적인 시간에 근무할 의향이 있다.
(B) 세미나를 준비하고 싶어 한다.
(C) 업무 부서 변경을 원한다.
(D) 포웰 스쿨에서 가르친다.

해설 릭비 씨가 이메일 첫 번째 단락에서 퀴스코 유한회사의 고객 서비스 상담원 직책에 매우 관심이 있다(I am very interested in ~ position that is available at Quisco Ltd.)고 한 후, 두 번째 단락에서 공석의 모든 자격 요건을 충족한다(I am fully able to meet all the requirements of the available position)고 했다. 채용 검색 결과(Employment Search Results)를 보면, 퀴스코 유한회사의 근무 교대 스케줄이 일정하지 않아(Shift schedule is variable) 저녁, 주말, 휴일에 근무할 수 있어야 한다(Required to be available evenings, weekends, and holidays)고 되어 있다. 따라서 릭비 씨가 불규칙한 업무 시간을 수용할 의향이 있음을 추론할 수 있으므로, (A)가 정답이다.

어휘 irregular 불규칙적인

▸▸ Paraphrasing 지문의 **Shift schedule is variable**
→ 정답의 **work irregular hours**

191-195 편지 + 회의록 + 광고

리걸 부동산
34 웨스턴 로, 핼리팩스 NS B3J 3P4

1월 3일

지방 자치구 의회 의원 여러분께,

저희 업체는 프린스 가 1210번지에 있는 건물 구입에 관심이 있습니다. [191]**거의 5년 동안 매물로 나와 있었기 때문에 이 건물은 황폐해졌습니다.** 리걸 부동산은 건물 보수에 필요한 것을 투자할 용의가 있습니다.

아울러 거리 쪽을 바라보는 1층 아파트 세 채를 사무용 공간으로 전환하고 싶습니다. 그러나 이 건물은 주거용으로만 분류되어 있습니다. [193]**이 건물을 주거용 및 업무용으로 모두 이용할 수 있도록 분류를 변경해 주실 수 있을까요?**

존 스톤, 사업주

어휘 property 재산, 부동산, 건물 fall into disrepair 황폐해지다 convert A into B A를 B로 전환시키다 residential 주거의 rezone 재구분하다, 분류를 변경하다

핼리팩스 지방 자치구 의회
1월 21일 회의록

참석자: 스튜어트 캐플란 시장 및 의회 의원 전원

기존 안건
- 아만다 월러 의원은 웰스 공원 정화 프로젝트에 대해 만족스러운 경과를 보고했다.
- [192]**해럴드 글래스 의원은 내년 최종 예산안을 제출했다.** 제안된 예산안은 만장일치로 승인이 이루어졌다.

새로운 안건
지역 주민이자 건물 관리인인 칼라 필립스는 의회에서 검토 중인 프린스 가 1210번지 재분류 건에 대해 반대 의사를 표명했다. 필립스 씨는 보행자 및 차량 통행 증가로 거리가 너무 혼잡해질 것을 우려한다. [194] **또한 자신이 관리하는 건물인 프린스 가 1208번지의 라이트하우스 아파트 거주자들이 인근에 주차하는 것 역시 어려워질 것이라고 생각한다.**

의회는 프린스 가의 다른 거주민들에게 의견을 말할 기회를 주기 위해 2월 월례 회의에서 해당 분류 건을 검토하기로 했다.

어휘 in attendance 참석한 unanimously 만장일치로 express opposition to ~에 반대를 표명하다 pedestrian 보행자의 vehicular 차량의 neighborhood 인근 consider (결정을 내리기 위해) 논의하다, 검토하다 voice one's opinion 의견을 말하다

모든 것을 누릴 수 있습니다!

프린스 가 1210번지에서 멋진 삶을 즐기세요!
- [193]**1개 또는 2개의 침실이 있는 새로 개조한 아파트**
- [195]**현대적이고 고급스러운 주방**
- 3중 단열 창문
- [193]**1층에 커피숍, 드라이클리닝, 편의점**
- [194]**12월부터 프린스 가 1208 및 1210번지의 거주자만을 위한 주차 공간 확장**

더 자세한 정보를 원하시면 www.lifeonpricestreet.com을 방문하시거나 866-555-0122로 전화하세요.

어휘 renovate 개조하다, 보수하다 contemporary 현대의, 동시대의 insulated 단열 처리가 된 exclusively 독점적으로

191 추론 / 암시

번역 스톤 씨의 편지는 건물에 대해 무엇을 암시하고 있는가?
(A) 건물이 몇 년 동안 관리되지 않았다.
(B) 예산보다 가격이 너무 높게 책정됐다.
(C) 쇼핑 지역과 가까운 위치에 있다.
(D) 더 이상 판매하지 않는다.

해설 편지의 첫 번째 단락에서 거의 5년 동안 매물로 나와 있었기 때문에 건물이 황폐해졌다(Since this property has been on the market for almost five years, it has fallen into disrepair)고 했으므로, 그 동안 건물이 관리되지 않았음을 추론할 수 있다. 따라서 (A)가 정답이다.

▸▸ Paraphrasing 지문의 for almost five years
→ 정답의 for several years
지문의 has fallen into disrepair
→ 정답의 has not been maintained

192 세부 사항

번역 회의록에 따르면, 지방 자치구 의회에 재무 계획서를 제출한 사람은?
(A) 해럴드 글래스
(B) 스튜어트 캐플란
(C) 아만다 월러
(D) 칼라 필립스

해설 회의록의 기존 안건(Old business) 부분에서 해럴드 글래스 의원이 내년 최종 예산안을 제출했다(Council member Harold Glass submitted a final version of next year's budget)고 했으므로, (A)가 정답이다.

▸▸ Paraphrasing 지문의 submitted ~ next year's budget
→ 질문의 presented a financial plan

193 연계

번역 지방 자치구 의회에서는 스톤 씨의 편지에 어떻게 반응했겠는가?
(A) 지역 회관 개조를 지원했다.
(B) 리걸 부동산의 발표 일정을 잡았다.
(C) 2월 회의를 취소했다.
(D) 건물 분류 변경을 승인했다.

해설 스톤 씨는 편지의 마지막 부분에서 프린스 가 1210번지에 있는 건물을 주거용 및 업무용으로 모두 이용할 수 있도록 분류를 변경해 줄

TEST 5

것(Would you consider rezoning the property to allow for mixed residential and business use?)을 요청했다. 회의록에서는 결과를 알 수 없지만 해당 건물의 광고를 보면, '1개 또는 2개의 침실이 있는 새로 개조한 아파트(Newly renovated apartments with one or two bedrooms)'와 '커피숍, 드라이클리닝, 편의점(Coffee shop, dry cleaners, and convenience store on street level)'이 있다고 쓰여 있으므로, 스톤 씨의 요청이 승인되었음을 추론할 수 있다. 따라서 (D)가 정답이다.

194 연계

번역 라이트하우스 아파트 거주자들에 대해 명시된 것은?

(A) 그들 중 다수가 소규모 자영업자들이다.
(B) 다음 번 지방 자치구 의회에서 투표를 할 것이다.
(C) 그들은 12월에 주차 공간을 더 많이 갖게 될 것이다.
(D) 그들 중 다수가 걸어서 출근한다.

해설 회의록의 새로운 안건(New business) 부분을 보면, 건물 분류를 변경할 경우 프린스 가 1208번지의 라이트하우스 아파트 거주자들이 인근에 주차하기 어려워질 것(it will also be difficult for residents of her building, Lighthouse Apartments ~ to park in the neighborhood)이라는 우려가 있다고 되어 있다. 하지만 광고에서 프린스 가 1208 및 1210번지의 거주자만을 위한 주차 공간이 12월부터 늘어난다(Expanded parking area exclusively for residents of 1208 and 1210 Prince Street starting in December)고 했으므로, (C)가 정답이다.

▸▸ Paraphrasing 지문의 Expanded parking area
→ 정답의 have more parking options

195 세부 사항

번역 광고에 나온 아파트의 특징은?

(A) 넓은 침실
(B) 새로워진 주방 디자인
(C) 무료 와이파이
(D) 전면 창문

해설 아파트 특징 중 하나로 현대적이고 고급스러운 주방(Contemporary upscale kitchens)이 언급되었으므로, (B)가 정답이다.

▸▸ Paraphrasing 지문의 Contemporary upscale kitchens
→ 정답의 Updated kitchen designs

196-200 이메일 + 제안서 + 이메일

수신: 린톤 기업 연합 직원
발신: 로빈 파울러
날짜: 6월 12일
제목: 조직 회의
첨부: 안건 제안서

여러분, 안녕하십니까?

우리가 만날 시기를 결정하고자 연락 드렸습니다. [196]**우리 기업 연합 창립에 대한 소식이 지역 사회 내 관심을 불러 일으키고 있기 때문에, 우리를 홍보하기 위한 문서 자료를 만들 시기입니다.**

회의 때 회원 유치 계획을 세우는 시간을 마련했으면 합니다. 안건 초안을 첨부합니다. [197]**사업주들과 이야기를 나누는 업무를 할당하는 데 오랜 시간이 걸리지는 않겠지만, 회의 전에 이를 온라인으로 작업하면 회의 시간을 아낄 수 있을 것입니다.**

다음 몇 주 동안 언제 시간이 되는지 저에게 이메일을 보내 주세요. [199]**사샤 짐머 씨가 7월 초까지 자리를 비우실 것으로 알고 있습니다만, 그래도 모두에게 맞는 회의 날짜와 시간을 정할 수 있을 거라고 생각합니다.**

로빈 파울러

어휘 generate 발생시키다, 만들어 내다 promote 홍보하다 formulate a plan 계획을 세우다 solicit 구하다, 간청하다 assignment 임무, 업무 availability 가능 여부

조직 회의 – 안건 제안서

오전 10시	소개
오전 10시 15분	항목 1 – 강령 정의 및 3건의 연간 계획을 확인하는 논의
오전 11시	항목 2 – 브랜든 클라크* 씨의 미디어 교육 워크숍
오후 12시	항목 3 – 연합 정부 통신부 창립 업무 배정: 보도 자료, 지역 사업주에게 서신, 안내책자, 회원제 중심 웹사이트
오후 12시 30분	[197]**항목 4 – 사업주들과 이야기를 나눌 얼라이언스 직원 배정**
오후 12시 45분	휴회

* [198]**브랜든 클라크 씨는 울라니 뉴스 방송국 뉴스 앵커로, 대중 매체와의 교류에 관한 워크숍을 진행하겠다고 제안해 왔습니다.** 그는 연설 내용 준비 및 논점 유지의 중요성을 강조할 것입니다.

어휘 mission statement 강령 initiative 계획 assign 배정하다, 배분하다 press release 보도 자료 adjourn 휴회하다, 휴정하다 interact with ~와 교류하다, 상호작용하다 emphasize 강조하다

수신: 린톤 기업 연합 직원
발신: 로빈 파울러
날짜: 6월 22일
제목: 조직 회의 완료
첨부: 최종 안건

모두 의견 주셔서 감사합니다. 최종 안건을 첨부합니다. [199]**워크숍은 6월 28일 린톤 커뮤니티 도서관에서 진행하는 것으로 확정했습니다.** 도서관은 오전 10시에 개관하며 직원들이 참여해 회의실 준비를 도울 예정입니다.

함께 모일 시간이 한정되어 있으므로 안건 유지의 중요성을 강조하고

싶습니다. 다른 주제를 더 논의하고 싶은 회의 참석자는 회의 이후 점심 시간을 이용하시면 됩니다. [200]**도서관에서 남쪽으로 한 블록 떨어진 데본스 샌드위치 가게에 갈 계획입니다.** 모두 오시기 바랍니다.

로빈 파울러

어휘 confirm 확정하다 on hand 참석하는 stick to ~을 고수하다, 지키다 further 추가로, 더욱 깊이

196 추론 / 암시

번역 첫 번째 이메일에 따르면, 린톤 기업 연합에 대해 사실인 것은?

(A) 시 정책에 반대한다.
(B) 새로 생긴 조직이다.
(C) 회비를 부과한다.
(D) 시 공무원이 이끈다.

해설 첫 번째 이메일의 첫 번째 단락에서 기업 연합 창립에 대한 소식이 지역 사회 내 관심을 불러 일으키고 있다(Since news about the creation of our Business Alliances is generating interest)고 했으므로, 린톤 기업 연합이 새로 생긴 조직임을 추론할 수 있다. 따라서 (B)가 정답이다.

어휘 oppose 반대하다 charge 부과하다, 청구하다

▸▸ Paraphrasing 지문의 the creation of our Business Alliances → 정답의 a new organization

197 연계

번역 파울러 씨는 안건 제안서에서 어떤 항목을 삭제할 수 있다고 제안하는가?

(A) 항목 1
(B) 항목 2
(C) 항목 3
(D) 항목 4

해설 파울러 씨는 첫 번째 이메일의 두 번째 단락에서 지역 사업주들과 이야기를 나누는 업무를 할당하는데 오랜 시간이 걸리지는 않겠지만, 회의 전에 온라인으로 작업하면 회의 시간을 아낄 수 있다(It ~ to coordinate our assignments for speaking to local business owners, but we could probably save meeting time by doing this online before the meeting)고 했다. 안건 제안서를 보면, 파울러 씨가 온라인으로 하자고 제안한 작업이 4번째 항목(Item 4-Assign Alliance members to speak with business owners)임을 확인할 수 있으므로, (D)가 정답이다.

198 사실 관계 확인

번역 안건 제안서에서 클라크 씨에 대해 명시한 것은?

(A) 회원 신청을 할 것이다.
(B) 객원 연사이다.
(C) 은퇴한 기자이다.
(D) 논의 중에 메모를 할 것이다.

해설 안건 제안서 하단을 보면, 울라니 뉴스 방송국 뉴스 앵커인 클라크 씨가 대중 매체와의 교류에 관한 워크숍을 진행하겠다고 제안했다(Brandon Clark, a news anchor ~, has offered to lead a workshop about interacting with the media)고 했으므로, 클라크 씨가 객원 연사임을 확인할 수 있다. 따라서 (B)가 정답이다.

어휘 apply for ~를 신청하다

199 연계

번역 곧 있을 회의에 대해 어떤 결론을 내릴 수 있는가?

(A) 일반에 공개될 것이다.
(B) 매체의 큰 관심을 받을 것이다.
(C) 적어도 한 명의 조직원은 불참할 것이다.
(D) 참석자들에게 몇몇 장비를 가져오라고 요구할 것이다.

해설 파울러 씨는 첫 번째 이메일의 마지막 단락에서 짐머 씨가 7월 초까지 자리를 비우지만 모두에게 맞는 회의 날짜와 시간을 정할 수 있을 것(Sasha Zimmer is out of town until early July, but ~ we can find a meeting date and time that will work for everyone)이라고 했다. 하지만 두 번째 이메일의 첫 번째 단락을 보면, 워크숍을 6월 28일에 진행하는 것으로 확정했다(We have confirmed the workshop for June 28)고 했으므로, 짐머 씨가 그날 불참할 것임을 알 수 있다. 따라서 (C)가 정답이다.

어휘 receive attention 관심을 받다, 주목받다

200 세부 사항

번역 두 번째 이메일에서 파울러 씨는 점심 식사에 대해 어떤 정보를 제공하는가?

(A) 예약 시간
(B) 참석자 수
(C) 비용
(D) 장소

해설 두 번째 이메일의 마지막 단락에서 점심 때 도서관에서 남쪽으로 한 블록 떨어진 데본스 샌드위치 가게(Devon's Sandwich Shop, which is just one block south of the library)에 갈 계획이라고 했으므로, (D)가 정답이다.

▸▸ Paraphrasing 지문의 Devon's Sandwich Shop, which is just one block south of the library → 정답의 The location

TEST 5

기출 TEST 6

101 (B)	102 (C)	103 (A)	104 (C)	105 (C)
106 (B)	107 (B)	108 (D)	109 (A)	110 (A)
111 (D)	112 (D)	113 (C)	114 (A)	115 (B)
116 (D)	117 (D)	118 (A)	119 (D)	120 (D)
121 (C)	122 (A)	123 (B)	124 (B)	125 (A)
126 (A)	127 (D)	128 (C)	129 (B)	130 (A)
131 (B)	132 (C)	133 (A)	134 (C)	135 (B)
136 (D)	137 (D)	138 (C)	139 (A)	140 (B)
141 (D)	142 (D)	143 (A)	144 (C)	145 (D)
146 (B)	147 (C)	148 (D)	149 (A)	150 (D)
151 (C)	152 (B)	153 (A)	154 (D)	155 (D)
156 (C)	157 (C)	158 (B)	159 (C)	160 (D)
161 (A)	162 (C)	163 (D)	164 (C)	165 (A)
166 (C)	167 (C)	168 (B)	169 (C)	170 (A)
171 (D)	172 (B)	173 (A)	174 (C)	175 (C)
176 (B)	177 (C)	178 (A)	179 (D)	180 (D)
181 (C)	182 (B)	183 (D)	184 (C)	185 (B)
186 (C)	187 (A)	188 (D)	189 (B)	190 (D)
191 (A)	192 (D)	193 (C)	194 (B)	195 (B)
196 (A)	197 (D)	198 (B)	199 (C)	200 (D)

PART 5

101 인칭대명사의 격 _ 소유격

해설 빈칸은 전치사 to의 목적어 역할을 하는 명사 assistant를 한정 수식하는 자리이므로, 소유격 인칭대명사인 (B) her가 정답이다.

번역 홍보부장이 부재중일 때는, 이메일과 전화가 모두 그녀의 비서에게 전달될 것이다.

어휘 director of communications 홍보부장 forward 전달하다

102 부사 어휘

해설 빈칸은 to부정사구(for him to attend the reception)와 함께 부사 late를 적절히 수식하는 부사를 선택하는 문제이다. 문맥상 '너무 늦어서 환영회에 참석하지 못했다'는 내용이 되어야 자연스러우므로, to부정사와 함께 「too+형용사/부사(+for+목적격)+to부정사」의 구조로 쓰여, '너무 ~해서 (누가) …하지 못하다'라는 의미를 나타내는 (C) too가 정답이다.

번역 스루르 씨는 비행기가 너무 늦게 도착해서 환영회에 참석하지 못했다.

어휘 reception 환영[축하] 연회

103 명사 자리 _ 전치사의 목적어

해설 빈칸은 전치사 for의 목적어 역할을 하는 명사 자리로, 전치사구 of the flagship store의 수식을 받는다. 따라서 보기에서 명사인 (A) opening(개시, 개장)과 (B) openness(솔직함, 열려 있음) 중 하나를 선택해야 한다. 문맥상 '본점의 개장을 위한'이라는 내용이 되어야 자연스러우므로, (A) opening이 정답이다. (C) openly는 '솔직하게, 공공연히'라는 의미의 부사, (D) opens는 동사로 품사상 빈칸에 들어갈 수 없다.

번역 와그너 씨가 본점 개장 행사 일정을 세울 예정이다.

어휘 arrange 준비하다, 일정을 세우다 flagship store 본점, 대표 매장

104 접속사 자리

해설 빈칸 뒤 완전한 절(the final award had been presented)을 이끄는 접속사 자리이다. 빈칸을 포함한 절과 콤마 뒤에 나오는 절(Ms. Ryu acknowledged ~ sponsors)을 연결해 줄 접속사가 필요하므로, 부사절 접속사 (C) After가 정답이다. (A) During은 전치사, (B) Then은 부사, (D) Next는 명사/형용사/부사이므로 품사상 빈칸에 들어갈 수 없다.

번역 마지막 시상이 있은 후에, 류 씨는 행사를 후원해 준 업체들에 감사를 표했다.

어휘 present 증정하다, 주다 acknowledge 감사를 표하다 sponsor 후원자[업체]

105 형용사 자리 _ 명사 수식

해설 빈칸이 부정관사 a와 명사 way 사이에 있으므로, 빈칸에는 way를 수식하는 형용사나 way와 복합명사를 이루는 명사가 들어갈 수 있다. 따라서 보기에서 명사인 (B) success(성공)와 형용사인 (C) successful(성공적인, 효과적인) 중 하나를 선택해야 한다. '효과적인 방안'이라는 내용이 되어야 문맥상 자연스러우므로, 제시된 방안(way)을 묘사하는 형용사 (C) successful이 정답이다. (A) succeed(성공하다)는 동사, (D) successfully(성공적으로)는 부사이므로 품사상 빈칸에 들어갈 수 없다.

번역 천토 자문 회사는 연간 예산의 수지 균형을 맞추는 효과적인 방안을 제시했다.

어휘 consultancy 자문 (회사) balance the budget (예산의) 수지 균형을 맞추다

106 전치사 어휘

해설 빈칸은 명사구 the pedal을 목적어로 취하는 전치사 자리로, Press와 the pedal을 적절히 연결하는 전치사가 들어가야 한다. 문맥상 '페달 위를 밟다'라는 내용이 되어야 자연스러우므로, '~ 위에'라는 의미의 (B) on이 정답이다.

번역 왼발로 페달을 살짝 밟아서 주차 브레이크를 풀어 주세요.

어휘 release 풀어 주다 parking brake 주차 브레이크

107 to부정사

해설 빈칸 앞에 이미 동사구 are invited가 있으므로, 또 동사가 들어갈 수는 없다. 따라서 (C) visits는 제외한다. 나머지 준동사(동명사, to부정사, 분사) 중에 답이 있는데, 빈칸을 포함한 동사구는 능동의

「invite+목적어(Hikers)+to부정사: ~가 …하도록 요청하다」가 수동으로 변형된 형태이므로, to부정사 (B) to visit가 정답이다.

번역 하이킹을 하시는 분들은 안내 센터를 방문하셔서 파 밸리 공원의 오솔길 지도를 받아가시기 바랍니다.

어휘 invite 요청하다, 초청하다 trail 오솔길, 산길

108 형용사 어휘

해설 빈칸은 「help+목적어(home buyers)+목적격 보어(choose a property)」의 구조에서 home buyers를 수식하는 형용사 자리로, 부동산 선택에 있어 도움을 받는 대상인 home buyers와 가장 잘 어울리는 형용사가 빈칸에 들어가야 한다. 문맥상 '주택 매입 경험이 없는 사람들이 부동산을 선택하는 것을 도와준다'라는 내용이 되어야 자연스러우므로, '경험이 없는, 미숙한'이라는 의미의 (D) inexperienced가 정답이다. (A) unmistakable은 '명백한, 틀림없는', (B) incomplete는 '불완전한, 불충분한', (C) unused는 '사용되지 않은'이라는 뜻으로 문맥상 빈칸에 적절하지 않다.

번역 댄톤 부동산 중개사는 주택 매입 경험이 없는 사람들이 부동산을 선택하는 것을 도와주기 위해 온라인 교육프로그램을 제공한다.

어휘 estate brokerage 부동산 중개업 property 부동산, 건물

109 명사절 접속사

해설 빈칸은 to부정사구(to integrate ~ styles)와 함께 동사 knows의 목적어 역할을 하는 자리이므로, 명사절 접속사 (A) how가 정답이다. 참고로 명사절 접속사 how 뒤에는 완전한 절 또는 to부정사가 올 수 있다. (B) that도 명사절 접속사로 쓰일 수 있지만 뒤에 완전한 절만 올 수 있고, (C) since는 부사절 접속사/전치사, (D) about은 전치사로 품사상 빈칸에 들어갈 수 없다.

번역 아이올라나 무용단은 다양한 스타일의 춤을 조화롭게 엮어 내는 데 능숙하기 때문에 각광을 받고 있다.

어휘 troupe 공연단, 극단 stand out 두드러지다 integrate 통합하다, 전체로 합치다

110 명사 어휘

해설 빈칸은 수동태 현재 동사 be restricted의 주어 역할을 하는 명사 자리로, 빈칸 뒤 전치사구 of mobile phones의 수식을 받는다. 문맥상 '휴대폰 사용은 담화실 내에서만 가능하다'라는 내용이 되어야 자연스러우므로, '사용'이라는 의미의 (A) use가 정답이다. 참고로 '요구하다, 요청하다'라는 의미의 동사 require는 「require+that+주어(+should)+동사원형」의 구조로 쓰일 수 있으므로, that이 이끄는 명사절의 동사원형 be 앞에 should가 생략된 형태이다.

번역 라파예트 힐 공립 도서관은 담화실 내에서만 휴대폰 사용이 가능하게끔 규정하고 있다.

어휘 be restricted to ~로 국한되다

111 부사 자리_동사 수식

해설 빈칸은 현재완료진행 시제를 이루는 동사 have와 been using 사이에서 동사를 수식하는 부사 자리이므로, (D) increasingly가 정답이다. (A) increases는 명사/동사, (B) increasing은 동명사/현재분사, (C) increased는 동사/과거분사로 모두 품사상 빈칸에 들어갈 수 없다.

번역 대형 항공사들은 대기 시간을 줄이고자 무인 발권 시스템을 점점 더 많이 사용해 오고 있다.

어휘 increasingly 점점 더, 갈수록 더 self-serve ticketing system 무인 발권[셀프 체크인] 시스템 reduce 줄이다

112 전치사 어휘

해설 빈칸은 명사구 an undisclosed amount를 목적어로 취하는 전치사 자리로, 빈칸을 포함한 전치사구는 동사구 was sold를 수식한다. 따라서 빈칸에는 was sold와 an undisclosed amount를 적절히 연결하는 전치사가 들어가야 한다. 문맥상 '액수 미상의 금액으로 판매되었다'라는 내용이 되어야 자연스러우므로, '~의 금액으로, ~와 교환으로'라는 의미로 쓰일 수 있는 전치사 (D) for가 정답이다.

번역 파키스탄 가수 아예사 사드가 쓴 노래집이 어제 경매에서 액수 미상의 금액으로 판매되었다.

어휘 auction 경매 undisclosed 밝혀지지 않은, 비밀에 부쳐진 amount 액수, 양

113 대명사

해설 빈칸은 There is 뒤에 이어지는 주어 자리이며, 비교급 형용사구(more important ~ than brushing your teeth twice a day)의 수식을 받는다. 문맥상 '하루에 두 번 양치질을 하는 것보다 더 중요한 것은 없다(하루에 두 번 양치질하는 것이 가장 중요하다)'라는 내용이 되어야 가장 자연스러우므로, (C) nothing이 정답이다. (B) neither는 제시된 둘 중 어떤 것도 선택하지 않는 경우에 쓰일 수 있으므로, 문맥상 빈칸에 적절하지 않다. (A) other는 관사 없이 단독으로 쓰일 수 없고, (D) whatever는 명사절/부사절 접속사로 뒤에 절이 나와야 한다.

번역 치아 건강을 지키는 데 있어서 하루에 두 번 양치질을 하는 것보다 더 중요한 것은 없다.

어휘 maintain 유지하다, 지키다

114 동사 어휘

해설 빈칸 뒤 목적어 Dairysmooth's red-bean-flavored ice cream 및 목적격 보어 very appetizing과 가장 잘 어울리는 동사를 선택하는 문제이다. 문맥상 '데어리스무스의 팥 맛 아이스크림이 맛있다고 생각하다'라는 내용이 되어야 자연스러우며, 목적어와 목적격 보어를 취할 수 있는 동사가 빈칸에 들어가야 하므로, (A) find가 정답이다. 참고로 「동사+목적어+목적격 보어(형용사)」의 구조로 주로 쓰이는 동사는 find 외에 consider, keep, leave, make, think 등이 있다.

번역 시식회 결과에 따르면, 대다수가 데어리스무스의 팥 맛 아이스크림이 맛있다는 평을 했다고 한다.

어휘 suggest 나타내다, 시사하다 appetizing 구미를 돋우는, 맛있어 보이는

115 명사절 접속사

해설 빈칸은 완전한 절(a candidate is offered a job)을 이끄는 접속사 자리이다. Regardless of의 목적어 역할을 하는 명사절 접속사가 들어가야 하며, 문맥상 '지원자가 취업 제의를 받든지 못 받든지 상관 없이'라는 내용이 되어야 자연스러우므로, (B) whether(~인지 아닌지)가 정답이다. 참고로, whether는 명사절 접속사뿐만 아니라 부사절 접속사로도 쓰일 수 있다. (C) although(비록 ~이지만)는 부사절 접속사이므로 빈칸에 들어가서 명사절을 이끌 수 없다. (A) even(심지어; 균등한)는 부사/형용사, (D) including(~을 포함하여)은 전치사로 품사상 빈칸에 들어갈 수 없다.

번역 지원자의 합격 여부와 상관없이, 모든 지원서들은 6개월간 파일에 보관된다.

어휘 regardless of ~에 상관없이 application 지원(서)

116 전치사 자리 _ 어휘

해설 빈칸 뒤 명사구 the Nye Research Center를 목적어로 취하는 전치사 자리로, 빈칸을 포함한 전치사구는 콤마 뒤에 나오는 절을 수식한다. 따라서 보기에서 구전치사인 (B) In case of(~의 경우에)와 (D) According to(~에 따르면, ~에 따라) 중 하나를 선택해야 한다. 문맥상 '나이 리서치 센터에 따르면'이라는 내용이 되어야 자연스러우므로, (D) According to가 정답이다. (A) Not only는 주로 but also와 상관접속사를 이루어 쓰이고, (C) As though(마치 ~인 것처럼)는 부사절 접속사이므로 뒤에 완전한 절이 이어져야 한다.

번역 나이 리서치 센터에 따르면, 30분 정도 과업을 서서 하면 생산성이 높아진다고 한다.

어휘 perform (일·의무 등을) 수행하다 assigned 할당된, 주어진 productivity 생산성

117 명사 자리 _ 전치사의 목적어

해설 빈칸은 전치사 of의 목적어 역할을 하는 명사 자리이므로, 보기에서 전치사의 목적어 역할을 할 수 있는 동명사 (B) restricting과 명사 (D) restrictions 중 하나를 선택해야 한다. 빈칸이 뒤에 나오는 전치사구 on bridge travel for oversized vehicles의 수식을 받고 있으므로, 명사 (D) restrictions가 정답이다. 타동사 restrict의 동명사인 (B) restricting은 전치사 on 없이 바로 규제 대상을 목적어로 취해야 하므로 답이 될 수 없고, (A) restricts는 동사, (C) restrictive는 형용사로 품사상 빈칸에 들어갈 수 없다.

번역 이 소책자는 운전자에게 초대형 차량의 교량 통행 관련 규제를 안내하기 위한 것이다.

어휘 booklet 소책자 be intended to ~하기 위함이다 oversized 초대형의 restrict 제한하다 restriction 규제, 제한 restrictive 제한적인

118 형용사 어휘

해설 빈칸은 명사 food를 수식하는 형용사 자리로, 빈칸을 포함한 명사구는 동사 enjoy의 목적어 역할을 한다. 따라서 빈칸에는 enjoy 및 food와 잘 어울리는 형용사가 빈칸에 들어가야 한다. 문맥상 '빼어난 별미를 즐길 수 있다'라는 내용이 되어야 자연스러우므로, '뛰어난'이라는 의미의 (A) exceptional이 정답이다. (B) surpassing도 '뛰어난, 출중한'이라는 의미이지만, food와 같이 명확한 실체가 있는 사물 명사가 아닌, quality(품질), ability(능력), skill(솜씨, 기술), beauty (아름다움), performance(연기, 성과) 등과 같이 추상적인 대상을 주로 수식한다. (C) effective는 '효과적인', (D) dominant는 '지배적인, 우세한'이라는 뜻으로 문맥상 빈칸에 적절하지 않다.

번역 이제 손님들은 최근 새로 단장한 노바니 그릴에서 매일 빼어난 별미를 즐기실 수 있습니다.

어휘 renovate 개조[보수]하다, 새롭게 하다

119 부사 자리 _ 동사 수식 _ 비교급

해설 빈칸은 동사 campaigned를 수식하는 부사 자리이므로, 보기에서 부사의 원급인 (C) energetically(열정적으로)와 비교급인 (D) more energetically 중 하나를 선택해야 한다. 문장 끝에 비교급과 어울려 쓰이는 than이 있으므로 비교급인 (D) more energetically가 정답이다. 형용사의 원급인 (A) energetic과 최상급인 (B) most energetic은 품사상 빈칸에 들어갈 수 없다.

번역 안셀트사에서 멜로디 안보다 더 열정적으로 인턴사원 제도를 확대하자고 주창한 사람은 아무도 없었다.

어휘 campaign 운동[캠페인]을 벌이다 expansion 확대, 확장

120 동사 어휘

해설 빈칸은 「help+목적어(restaurant owners)+(to)부정사: ~가 …하도록 돕다」의 구조에서 restaurant owners의 행위를 설명하는 (to)부정사 자리로, 명사구 their ability to effectively recruit, train and retain staff를 목적어로 취한다. 문맥상 '요식업자들이 효과적으로 직원을 채용하고 훈련시켜 근속하게 만드는 스스로의 역량을 평가하는 데 도움을 준다'라는 내용이 되어야 자연스러우므로, '평가하다'라는 의미의 타동사 (D) evaluate가 정답이다. (C) progress는 '진척시키다', (A) cover는 '덮다, 다루다', (B) prepare는 '준비하다'라는 뜻으로 문맥상 빈칸에 적절하지 않다.

번역 월요일의 워크숍은 직원을 새로 채용하고 훈련시켜 근속하게 만드는 일을 효과적으로 해내고 있는지, 요식업자들이 스스로의 역량을 평가하는 데 도움을 줄 것이다.

어휘 recruit (신입 직원을) 모집하다 retain 유지하다

121 형용사 자리 _ 명사 수식

해설 빈칸이 동사구 has generated의 목적어 역할을 하는 명사 interest 앞에 있으므로, 빈칸에는 interest를 수식하는 형용사나 interest와 복합명사를 이루는 명사가 들어갈 수 있다. 따라서 보기에서 명사인 (A) substance(물질, 본질)와 (B) substances, 형용사인 (C) substantial(상당한, 많은) 중 하나를 선택해야 한다. 문맥상 '상당한 관심을 불러 일으켰다'라는 내용이 되어야 자연스러우므로, (C) substantial이 정답이다. (D) substantially(상당히)는 부사로 품사상 빈칸에 들어갈 수 없다.

번역 디지털 광고로 인하여 의류 상품들에 많은 관심이 쏠리게 되었다.

어휘 generate 일으키다[초래하다]

122 부사 어휘

해설 빈칸 앞에 있는 동명사구 addressing customer concerns를 적절히 수식하는 부사를 선택하는 문제이다. 고객의 고민을 해결하려는 방식과 관련된 부사가 빈칸에 들어가야 자연스러우므로, '끊임없이, 일관성 있게'라는 의미의 (A) consistently가 정답이다. (B) largely는 '주로, 대체로', (C) hugely는 '엄청나게, 아주', (D) identically는 '똑같이, 동일하게'라는 뜻으로 문맥상 빈칸에 적절하지 않다.

번역 세미나 진행자는 끊임없이 고객의 고민을 해결하려 노력하는 일이야말로 재정적 성공에 있어 중요한 요소 중 하나라고 단언했다.

어휘 state (분명하게) 말하다 address (문제 등을) 다루다, 해결하(려 노력하)다 concern 고민(거리), 관심사 crucial 결정적인, 중대한 financial 재정적인, 재무의

123 형용사 자리 _ 주격 보어

해설 빈칸은 주어 it(the desk)을 보충 설명하는 주격 보어 자리로 부사 still의 수식을 받으므로 형용사가 들어가야 한다. 또한 '책상은 아직 쓸 만하다'라는 내용이 되어야 자연스러우므로, (B) functional (작동하는, 쓸 만한)이 정답이다. (D) functioned가 들어가서 수동태 문장이 될 수도 있다고 생각할 수 있으나, function은 '작동하다, 기능하다'라는 의미의 자동사이기 때문에 수동태로 쓰일 수 없다. (A) function은 명사/동사, (C) functionally는 부사이므로 품사상 빈칸에 들어갈 수 없다.

번역 조립 과정에서 약간 손상되긴 했지만, 그 책상은 아직 쓸 만하다.

어휘 slightly 약간, 가볍게 assembly 조립

124 전치사 어휘

해설 빈칸 뒤 명사구 its discounts for new customers를 목적어로 취하는 전치사 자리로, 빈칸을 포함한 전치사구는 콤마 뒤에 나오는 절을 수식한다. 따라서 빈칸에는 '신규 고객을 위한 할인'과 '요금제가 별로라고 여긴다'는 문장을 적절히 연결하는 전치사가 들어가야 한다. 문맥상 '신규 고객을 위한 할인에도 불구하고, 요금제가 별로라고 여긴다'라는 대조적인 내용이 되어야 자연스러우므로, (B) Despite(~에도 불구하고)가 정답이다. (A) Far from(결코 ~가 아닌), (C) Among(~ 중에), (D) Instead of(~ 대신에)는 모두 문맥상 적절하지 않다.

번역 신규 고객에 대한 할인 정책에도 불구하고, 테라트란 폰의 요금제가 별로라고 생각하는 사람들이 많다.

어휘 consider ~로 여기다[생각하다] inferior 질이 낮은, 열등한

125 동사 어형 _ 수 일치

해설 빈칸은 부사절 접속사 Now that이 이끄는 부사절의 동사 자리이므로, 보기에서 동사 자리에 들어갈 수 있는 (A) has transferred와 (C) transfer 중 하나를 선택해야 한다. 빈칸 앞 주어 Ms. Nakamura가 3인칭 단수이므로, 3인칭 단수 동사인 (A) has transferred가 정답이다. 동명사/현재분사 (B) transferring과 to 부정사 (D) to transfer는 동사 자리에 들어갈 수 없다.

번역 나카무라 씨가 런던 본사로 전근을 갔기 때문에, 새 지부장이 도쿄 지사를 관리하고 있다.

어휘 now that ~이므로, ~이기 때문에 transfer 이동하다, 전근하다 headquarters 본사 run 운영[관리]하다

126 접속사 자리

해설 빈칸 뒤 완전한 절(the kitchen cabinets arrived late)을 이끄는 접속사 자리이다. 빈칸을 포함한 절이 콤마 뒤에 나오는 주절(the contract installed ~ schedule)을 수식하므로, 빈칸에는 부사절 접속사가 들어가야 한다. 따라서 '~이긴 하지만'이라는 의미의 부사절 접속사 (A) Even though가 정답이다. (B) Instead of(~ 대신에), (C) In addition to(~에 더하여), (D) On top of(~ 위에)는 모두 전치사이므로 빈칸에 들어갈 수 없다.

번역 주방 찬장들이 늦게 배달되었지만, 도급 업자는 일정에 뒤처지지 않고 설치를 마쳤다.

어휘 contractor 도급 업자[업체], 하청 업자[업체] install 설치하다 behind schedule 예정[계획]보다 늦게

127 부사절 접속사

해설 빈칸은 앞뒤 완전한 절을 이어주는 접속사 자리이다. '오늘 중으로 예산 분석 보고서를 받게 된다면 내일 제안서가 준비될 것이다'라는 내용이 되어야 자연스러우므로, 부사절 접속사 (D) as long as(~하기만 하면, ~하는 한)가 정답이다. 빈칸 뒤에 that이 생략되었다고 가정할 경우 현재분사인 (A) expecting(기대하며)도 빈칸에 들어갈 수 있으나, 의미상 어색하므로 정답이 될 수 없다. (B) if not(~하지 않으면)은 완전한 두 절을 이어줄 수 없고, (C) unlike(~와 달리, 다른)는 전치사/형용사로 품사상 빈칸에 들어갈 수 없다.

번역 오늘 중으로 예산 분석 보고서를 받게 된다면, 내일 씨스케이프 프로젝트 제안서가 준비될 것이다.

어휘 proposal 제안(서) budget analysis 예산 분석 (보고서)

128 부사 어휘

해설 빈칸 앞 최상급 표현 most와 함께 priced(가격이 매겨진)를 가장 잘 수식하는 부사를 선택하는 문제이다. 문맥상 '가장 적정한 가격의'라는 내용이 되어야 자연스러우므로, '합리적으로, 타당하게'라는 의미의 (C) reasonably가 정답이다. (A) closely(면밀히), (B) sparsely(드물게), (D) absolutely(절대적으로)는 의미상 빈칸에 적절하지 않다.

번역 오티메이트 3 홈 시어터 시스템은 형 일렉트로닉스에서 가장 적정한 가격의 구성 사양을 갖춘 제품이다.

어휘 home theater system 가정용 영사 시스템 configuration (장비의) 조합[구성]

129 동사 어형 _ 시제

해설 빈칸은 주어 The Oakwood Restaurant 뒤에 나오는 동사 자리로, 과거 10년 전부터 현재까지의 기간을 나타내는 전치사구 for the past decade의 수식을 받는다. 따라서 현재완료 시제 동사 (B) has been offering이 정답이다.

TEST 6

번역 오크우드 레스토랑은 지난 십 년간 토요일마다 특별 저녁 메뉴를 제공해 오고 있습니다.

어휘 offer 제공하다, 내놓다 decade 10년

130 명사 어휘

해설 빈칸 앞 명사 speaking과 복합명사를 이루어 동사 has의 목적어 역할을 하는 명사 자리로, 빈칸을 포함한 동사구는 특정 시간을 나타내는 전치사구 on Tuesday, November 15의 수식을 받는다. 문맥상 '11월 15일 화요일에 강연 약속이 있다'라는 내용이 되어야 자연스러우므로, '약속, 업무'라는 의미의 (A) engagement가 정답이다. (B) term은 '기간, 용어', (C) subject는 '주제, 과목', (D) employment는 '고용, 근무'라는 뜻으로 문맥상 빈칸에 적절하지 않다.

번역 드 토넌커 씨는 11월 15일 화요일에 강연 약속이 잡혀 있습니다.

PART 6

131-134 기사

도도마 (5월 21일) – 도도마 가스·전기(DGE)와 아루샤 전력(아루포)은 양사가 [131]**합병할 예정이라고** 오늘 발표했다. 합병 효력 발생일은 7월 1일이다. 곧 [132]**창립될** 이 기업은 탄자니아 에너지 솔루션즈라는 새로운 이름으로 운영될 예정이다. 현재 DGE는 약 25만, 아루포는 약 9만 곳에 달하는 가구 및 기업에 서비스를 제공하고 있다. [133]**계약상의 재무 조건은 아직 공개되지 않았다.** DGE의 대표이사 조나단 가샤자와 아루포의 대표이사 코레타 콤바는 공동 성명을 통해 서비스에는 어떤 변화도 없을 것이라고 고객들에게 약속했다. [134]**그들은** 또한 직원 해고도 없을 것이라고 밝혔다.

어휘 announce 발표하다 effective date 유효일, 시작 일자 merger 합병 soon-to-be 곧 ~할 operate 영업하다, 운영되다 serve (상품·서비스를) 제공하다 joint statement 공동 성명 assure 확약하다 layoff 해고

131 동사 어형_태_시제

해설 빈칸은 주어 they 뒤에 나오는 동사 자리이다. 주어 they가 앞에서 언급된 Dodoma Gas and Electric (DGE) and Arusha Power (Arupo)를 대신하므로, they는 합병(merge)의 주체이다. 따라서 수동태인 (D) are merged는 제외하고, 능동태 표현인 (A) have been merging, (B) will be merging, (C) have merged 중 하나를 선택해야 한다. 이어지는 문장에서 합병의 효력이 기사를 쓴 날짜인 5월 21일보다 늦은 7월 1일에 발생할 예정(The effective date ~ 1 July)이라고 했으므로, 미래진행 시제 동사 (B) will be merging이 정답이다.

어휘 merge 합병하다

132 동사 어휘

해설 빈칸 앞 The soon-to-be와 결합하여 명사 company를 적절히 수식하는 과거분사를 선택하는 문제이다. 앞 문장에서 두 회사의 합병 발효일이 7월 1일(The effective date ~ 1 July)이라고 했고, 뒤에서 새로운 이름으로(under the new name) 운영될 예정이라고 했으므로, 문맥상 합병으로 인해 '곧 창립될 회사'라는 내용이 되어야 자연스럽다. 따라서 '만들다, 창조하다'라는 의미인 create의 과거분사형 (C) created가 정답이다. (A) renovated(개조된, 수리된) (B) informed(정보가 제공된), (D) acquired(습득된, 취득된)는 모두 문맥상 빈칸에 적절하지 않다.

133 문맥에 맞는 문장 고르기

번역 (A) 계약상의 재무 조건은 아직 공개되지 않았다.
(B) 에너지 부문은 탄자니아의 발전에 필수적이다.
(C) 양사는 해외 금융 시장을 매우 잘 파악하고 있다.
(D) 양사는 각자의 업계에서 평판이 우수하다.

해설 빈칸 앞 문장에서 곧 합병할 두 회사의 서비스 범위(DGE serves about 250,000 households and businesses, while Arupo serves about 90,000)를 언급했고, 빈칸 뒤 문장에서 공동 성명을 통해 어떤 서비스 변화도 없을 것임을 고객들에게 확약했다(In a joint statement, ~ assured customers they will not see any service changes)고 했으므로, 빈칸에도 합병 관련 내용이 들어가는 것이 문맥상 자연스럽다. 따라서 계약상의 재무 조건(The financial terms of the agreement)을 언급한 (A)가 정답이다.

어휘 terms 조건 agreement 계약, 합의 yet to be 아직 ~ 아닌 disclose 공개하다, 밝히다 vital 굉장히 중요한 exceptional 우수한 have a grasp of ~를 잘 이해하고 있다 reputation 평판, 명성 respective 각자의

134 대명사 어휘

해설 빈칸은 동사 said의 주어 자리이다. '또한'이라는 의미의 부사 also가 동사 said를 수식하므로, 앞 문장의 주어 CEOs Johnathan Gashaza of DGE and Coretha Komba of Arupo가 동사 assured의 주어인 동시에 said의 주어가 되어야 문맥상 자연스럽다. 따라서 복수명사구를 대신하는 (C) They가 정답이다.

135-138 편지

8월 29일

앨빈 망구바트
인사부장
파스턴 프로덕츠 유한회사
캐스터 대로 549번지
위니펙, 매니토바 주 R3E 2S2

망구바트 씨께,

저는 귀사의 웹사이트에 공지된 기계 기술자 자리에 지원하고자 이 편지를 씁니다. 제가 직원이 되면 파스턴 프로덕츠의 설계 [135]**부서**에 커다란 기여를 할 수 있다고 생각합니다.

[136]**저는 경험이 풍부하므로 귀사에 적임자라고 할 수 있습니다.** 현재 저는 욘트 시스템즈에서 기술자로 근무하고 있으며, 지난 6년간 기계 및 엔진 설계를 담당해 왔습니다. 그 [137]**이전에는**, 젤렌카 인더스트리즈에서 근무했고, 효율적인 고철 재활용법 개발 프로젝트에 참여했습니다.

제 근무 경력과 학력에 대해 상세히 [138]**기술한** 이력서를 동봉합니다. 제 기술과 경험이 파스턴 프로덕츠에 어떻게 도움이 될 수 있을지, 인사 부장님을 만나 뵙고 논의할 수 있게 되기를 바랍니다.

게일 백

이력서 동봉

어휘 apply for ~에 지원하다 design 디자인, 설계 efficient 효율적인 scrap steel 고철 enclose 동봉하다 educational background 학력 look forward to -ing ~하기를 고대하다

135 명사 어휘

해설 빈칸은 명사 design과 복합명사를 이루는 명사 자리로, 빈칸을 포함한 복합명사는 to offer의 목적어 역할을 하고, 해당 to부정사구는 대명사 much를 수식한다. 문맥상 '직원으로서 파스턴 프로덕츠의 설계 부서에 기여할 많은 것이 있다'라는 내용이 되어야 자연스러우므로, '부서'라는 의미의 (B) department가 정답이다. (A) phase는 '단계, 양상', (C) consultant는 '고문, 컨설턴트', (D) expertise는 '전문 지식'이라는 뜻으로 모두 문맥상 빈칸에 적절하지 않다.

136 문맥에 맞는 문장 고르기

번역 (A) 귀사의 웹사이트에는 좋은 기회가 될 인턴십 제도도 나열되어 있습니다.
(B) 직무 기술서에 지원자는 상급 학위가 있어야 한다고 쓰여 있었습니다.
(C) 귀사의 요청에 대해 제 관리자가 지난 주에 답신을 드렸습니다.
(D) 저는 경험이 풍부하므로 귀사에 적임자라고 할 수 있습니다.

해설 빈칸 뒤에서 직책과 관련된 자신의 경력(I am currently an engineer at Yount Systems ~ I was employed by Zelenka Industries)을 구체적으로 열거하고 있으므로, 빈칸에는 이를 포괄하는 내용이 들어가야 자연스럽다. 따라서 풍부한 경험을 언급하며 자신이 적임자임을 어필한 (D)가 정답이다.

어휘 job description 직무 기술(서) advanced degree 상급 학위(석사·박사) extensive 폭넓은 ideal 이상적인 fit 딱 맞는 것[사람]

137 전치사 어휘

해설 빈칸 뒤 지시대명사 that을 목적어로 취하는 전치사 자리로, 전치사의 목적어인 that은 현재의 직장(I am currently an engineer)을 설명하는 앞 문장 전체를 대신한다. 또한 빈칸을 포함한 전치사구가 과거 시제 동사를 포함한 문장(I was employed ~ recycling scrap steel)을 수식하므로, 시간을 현재에서 과거로 적절히 연결하는 전치사가 빈칸에 들어가야 한다. 따라서 '~ 전에'라는 의미의 (D) Prior to가 정답이다. (A) Regarding(~에 관해), (B) Following(~ 이후에), (C) Contrary to(~에 반해, ~에 상반되는)는 문맥상 빈칸에 적절하지 않다.

138 동사 어형 _ 수 일치 _ 시제

해설 빈칸은 주격 관계대명사 which가 이끄는 관계사절의 동사 자리이다. 빈칸의 주어 역할을 하는 주격 관계대명사 which는 선행사 my résumé를 대신하므로, 보기에서 단수명사와 수가 일치하는 (B) gave, (C) gives, (D) is giving 중 하나를 선택해야 한다. 이력서는 사실을 기술한 것이므로, 빈칸에 단순 현재 시제 동사가 들어가야 자연스럽다. 따라서 (C) gives가 정답이다.

139-142 이메일

수신: 라시파 수르야니 〈lsuryani@cmail.com〉
발신: 자바리 에버스 〈eversj@pems.com〉
발신일: 5월 18일
제목: 문자 메시지

수르야니 씨께,

저희는 환자분들께 최대한 효과적이면서도 신뢰할 수 있는 [139]**서비스를 제공**하기 위해, 이제 예약 알림 및 기타 관련 정보를 문자 메시지로 수신할 수 있는 선택권을 드립니다. 현재 귀하는 저희 자료를 이메일로 수신하게끔 등록되어 있습니다. [140]**현재 서비스 그대로가 좋으시면, 아무런 조치를 취하실 필요가 없습니다.** 만일 연락 방식에 문자 메시지 서비스를 추가하고 싶으시거나, 이메일 수신에서 문자 메시지 수신으로 [141]**선호** 방식을 변경하고 싶으시다면, 가급적 빨리 알려 주시기 바랍니다. [142]**저희의** 목표는 귀하의 건강, 그리고 저희가 제공하는 제품 및 서비스에 대해 적절하고 유용한 정보를 시기적절하게 알려 드리는 것입니다.

자바리 에버스
고객 서비스 담당
전문 눈 건강 관리 서비스

어휘 effectively 효과적으로 reliably 신뢰할 수 있게 appointment 예약 reminder 상기시켜 주는 것, 알림 relevant 관련 있는 materials 자료 mode 방식 at your earliest convenience 가급적 빨리 in a timely fashion 시기적절하게 representative 직원, 대표

139 동사 어휘

해설 빈칸은 명사구 our patients를 목적어로 취하는 타동사 자리로, 부사구 as effectively and reliably as possible의 수식을 받는다. 문맥상 '환자분들께 최대한 효과적이면서도 신뢰할 수 있는 서비스를 제공하기 위해'라는 내용이 되어야 자연스러우므로, '서비스를 제공하다, 섬기다'라는 의미의 (A) serve가 정답이다. 타동사로 쓰일 경우 (B) care는 '~를 신경 쓰다, (to부정사)하고 싶어하다', (C) work는 '일하게 하다, 작동시키다' 등의 의미를 나타내므로 문맥상 빈칸에 적절하지 않다. (D) provide는 '제공하다'라는 뜻으로 의미상 자연스러워 보이지만, 「provide A(제공 받는 대상) with B(제공하는 것)」 혹은 「provide B for/to A」 구조로 쓰이므로 빈칸에는 들어갈 수 없다.

TEST 6

140 문맥에 맞는 문장 고르기

번역 (A) 최근에 저희 사무실을 방문하신 적이 없으시군요.
(B) 현재 서비스 그대로가 좋으시면, 아무런 조치를 취하실 필요가 없습니다.
(C) 구매하실 수 있는 좋은 상품이 준비되어 있습니다.
(D) 이메일 메시지가 모든 환자분들께 제공되지는 않습니다.

해설 이 지문은 문자 메시지 서비스를 실시한다는 내용인데, 빈칸 앞 문장에서 편지 수신인이 현재 이메일로 정보를 받고 있다고 했고, 빈칸 뒤에서는 문자 메시지 서비스를 추가하거나 이메일 대신 문자로 정보를 받고 싶다면 연락하라(If you would like to add text messaging ~ to change ~ to text messaging, please let us know)고 했으므로, 빈칸에도 정보 제공 서비스 관련 내용이 들어가야 한다. (B)와 (D) 중에 (B) 문장이 문맥상 더 자연스러우므로 (B)가 정답이다.

어휘 require 필요로 하다 current 현재의, 지금의 available 이용 가능한

141 명사 자리 _ 동사의 목적어

해설 빈칸은 소유격 your의 한정 수식을 받는 명사 자리이다. 또한 your -------는 to change의 목적어 역할을 한다. 따라서 '선호, 애호'라는 의미의 명사 (D) preference가 정답이다. (A) prefer(선호하다)는 동사, (B) preferential(우선권이 있는)은 형용사, (C) preferred는 동사/과거분사로 모두 품사상 빈칸에 들어갈 수 없다.

142 대명사 어휘

해설 문장의 주어 goal을 수식하는 소유격 인칭대명사를 선택하는 문제로, 주어 goal은 be동사 is 뒤에 있는 to부정사구(to give you relevant and useful information ~ we offer in a timely fashion)와 동격 관계를 이룬다. 문맥상 발신인 에버스 씨가 속한 회사가 관련 정보를 제때 제공하는 것이 '회사의 목표(goal)'라는 내용이 되어야 자연스러우므로, (D) Our가 정답이다.

143-146 기사

토프틀룬드 (6월 10일) - 지역 내 주차 구역 곳곳에 줄지어 서 있는 전기 자동차들은 토프틀룬드 시민들이 휘발유 자동차를 단념하기 시작했다는 사실을 보여 주는 듯하다. 실제로, 토프틀룬드 시내 거리에 보이는 차량 중 20퍼센트가 전기차이지만, 이러한 수치는 143**빠른** 속도로 변화하고 있다.

어느 정도는 전기차 운전자들에게 주어지는 토프틀룬드 시의 많은 세금 144**혜택** 때문이다. 토프틀룬드 그린 비즈니스의 앤 라스무센 회장에 따르면, 더 매력적인 디자인과 더 오래가는 배터리 145**역시** 영향을 끼쳤다고 한다. 라스무센 회장은 향후 토프틀룬드의 전기차 수가 두 배 이상 늘어날 것으로 예견한다. 146**사실, 그녀는 20년 후에는 이곳에서 전기차만 판매될 것이라고 생각한다.**

어휘 row after row 줄지어 indicate 나타내다 give up on ~을 단념하다 to some extent 어느 정도로 due to ~ 때문에 generous 관대한, 많은 longer-lasting 더 오래 지속되는 make a difference 영향을 끼치다 double 두 배가 되다

143 형용사 어휘

해설 명사 pace를 적절히 수식하는 형용사를 선택하는 문제이다. 빈칸을 포함한 전치사구가 동사구 is changing을 수식하여 수치가 특정 속도로 변하고 있다는 의미가 되어야 자연스러우므로, '빠른'이라는 의미의 (A) rapid가 정답이다. (B) brief는 '짧은, 간결한', (C) narrow는 '좁은, 아슬아슬한', (D) valuable은 '귀중한, 소중한'이라는 뜻으로 문맥상 빈칸에 적절하지 않다.

144 명사 자리 _ 복합명사

해설 빈칸은 tax와 복합명사를 이루어 소유격 the city's(시의) 및 형용사 generous(많은)의 수식을 받는 동시에, 뒤에 오는 과거분사구 offered to electric car drivers(전기차 운전자에게 주어지는)의 수식도 받고 있다. 따라서 빈칸에는 명사가 들어가야 하므로, (C) benefits(혜택)가 정답이다. (A) beneficial(이로운, 유익한)은 형용사, (B) benefitting은 동명사/현재분사, (D) to benefit은 to부정사로 구조상 빈칸에 들어갈 수 없다.

145 부사 어휘

해설 현재완료 시제 동사 have made a difference를 적절히 수식하는 부사를 선택하는 문제이다. 앞에서 먼저 전기 자동차 수가 증가하는 이유로 '시의 많은 세금 혜택(the city's generous tax benefits)'을 언급했고, 동사 have made a difference의 주어 more attractive designs and longer-lasting batteries도 전기 자동차 수의 변화에 영향을 주는 요인 중 하나이므로, '또한, 역시'라는 의미의 (D) also가 정답이다. (C) very는 형용사 또는 부사를 수식하는 부사이므로, 빈칸에는 들어갈 수 없다.

146 문맥에 맞는 문장 고르기

번역 (A) 더욱이, 그녀는 고속도로에 충전소가 있어 편리하다는 점이 마음에 든다.
(B) 사실, 그녀는 20년 후에는 이곳에서 전기차만 판매될 것이라고 생각한다.
(C) 따라서, 그녀는 전기차 가격이 너무 높다고 생각한다.
(D) 그녀는 토프틀룬드의 인구가 꾸준히 감소하고 있다는 점에 주목한다.

해설 빈칸 앞 문장에서 향후 전기 자동차 수에 관한 라스무센 씨의 예측(Ms. Rasmussen predicts the number of electric cars ~ double in the coming years)을 언급했으므로, 빈칸에도 그녀의 예측과 관련된 내용이 이어지는 것이 문맥상 자연스럽다. 따라서 20년 후에 대한 라스무센 씨(she)의 생각을 서술한 (B)가 정답이다.

어휘 moreover 게다가, 더욱이 convenience 편의, 편리한 것 recharging station (전기차) 충전소 note 주목하다, 특별히 언급하다 steadily 꾸준히

PART 7

147-148 초대장

자틴 사치데바 박사 추모 강연회에
여러분을 정중히 초대합니다.

강연자:

시마 라즈단 박사
국립연구센터장, 〈진료 태도 개선: 의료 서비스 필수 기술〉의 저자

주제: 환자 관리
일자: 5월 15일 오전 9시 30분-10시 30분
장소: 나드카르니 강당

[147]**본 강연회는 매일 환자를 대하는 잘란다르 병원 의료진에 한해서만 참석 가능합니다.** 좌석이 한정되어 있습니다. [148]**자리를 예약하시려면 아르나브 고팔 씨에게 이메일을 보내세요.**

어휘 cordially 진심으로, 정중히 memorial 추모의 bedside manner (의사 등이) 환자를 대하는 태도 venue 장소, 개최 예정지 personnel 인원, 직원(들) interact 교류하다, 소통하다 spot 위치, 자리

147 추론 / 암시

번역 초대장의 대상자는 누구인가?
(A) 건강 보험 제공 업체
(B) 병원 선물 가게 직원
(C) 의사와 간호사
(D) 관리 및 운영 관계자

해설 마지막 단락에서 강연회는 병원 소속 의료진에 한해서만 참석 가능하다(This lecture is open only to Jalandhar Hospital medical personnel)고 했으므로, 의사와 간호사가 초대 대상임을 추론할 수 있다. 따라서 (C)가 정답이다.

▸▸ Paraphrasing 지문의 medical personnel
→ 정답의 Doctors and nurses

148 세부 사항

번역 참석 희망자에게 권하는 행동은?
(A) 강연 메모 검토하기
(B) 라즈단 박사 저서 읽어 보기
(C) 강당에 일찍 도착하기
(D) 고팔 씨에게 연락하기

해설 마지막 단락에서 자리를 예약하려면 고팔 씨에게 이메일로 신청할 것(E-mail Mr. Arnav Gopal to hold your spot)을 권하고 있으므로, (D)가 정답이다.

▸▸ Paraphrasing 지문의 E-mail Mr. Arnav Gopal
→ 정답의 Contact Mr. Gopal

149-150 안내문

[149]**로젠 밸리 은행에 오신 것을 환영합니다! 온라인으로 귀하의 직불카드를 사용 등록하시려면, 아래 절차를 따라 주십시오:**

1. www.rosenvalleybank.com을 방문하셔서 "직불카드" 탭을 클릭하십시오.
2. 귀하의 직불카드 번호 16자리를 모두 입력하십시오.
3. 귀하의 임시 비밀번호를 입력하십시오. 보안상의 이유로, 카드 사용 등록에 필요한 4자리 숫자의 임시 비밀번호가 별도로 발송되었을 것입니다. 해당 우편을 수신하지 못했다면, 가까운 지점에 연락하시기 바랍니다.
4. [150]**본인 고유의 직불카드 비밀번호 4자리를 만들라는 요청을 받으실 겁니다.** 물건을 구입하거나 현금을 인출하기 위해 카드를 사용할 때마다 이 비밀번호를 입력하셔야 합니다.
5. 화면 하단의 "사용 등록" 아이콘을 클릭하십시오. 이제 로젠 밸리 직불카드를 사용하실 수 있을 것입니다.

로젠 밸리 은행

어휘 activate 활성화하다, 작동시키다 digit (숫자의) 자리 temporary 임시의 PIN number (= Personal Identification Number) 개인 비밀번호 separate 별개의 prompt (컴퓨터 상에서) ~하라고 요청하다 unique 고유한 access cash 현금을 인출하다

149 추론 / 암시

번역 안내문의 대상자는 누구인가?
(A) 신규 고객
(B) 은행 대출 신청자
(C) 교육 대상 직원
(D) 고객 서비스 담당자

해설 안내문의 초반부에서 '로젠 밸리 은행에 오신 것을 환영합니다!(Welcome to Rosen Valley Bank!)'라고 한 후 직불카드 사용 등록을 위한 절차(To activate your debit card online, follow these steps)를 설명하고 있으므로, 신규 고객을 위한 안내문임을 추론할 수 있다. 따라서 (A)가 정답이다.

150 세부 사항

번역 독자는 무엇을 하라고 요청받는가?
(A) 서명 후 서류 제출
(B) 온라인 사용자 이름 등록
(C) 연락처 확인
(D) 보안 코드 갱신

해설 네 번째 절차에서 본인 고유의 직불카드 비밀번호 4자리를 만들라는 요청을 받을 것(You will be prompted to create your own unique 4-digit debit card PIN)이라고 했으므로, (D)가 정답이다.

어휘 verify (정확한지를) 확인하다 secure code 보안 코드, 암호

▸▸ Paraphrasing 지문의 create your own unique 4-digit debit card PIN
→ 정답의 Update a secure code

TEST 6

151-152 문자 메시지

(오후 5시 34분) 대니얼 헤이니
압둘, 아직도 사무실에 있어요?

(오후 5시 35분) 압둘 아흐메드
네. 이제 곧 퇴근하려고요. 왜요?

(오후 5시 36분) 대니얼 헤이니
[151]**원격 컴퓨터 시스템의 제 새 비밀번호가 기억이 안 나요.**
회사에서 왜 이렇게 자주 바꾸라고 하는 건가요!

(오후 5시 37분) 압둘 아흐메드
어딘가 적어 놨나요?

(오후 5시 38분) 대니얼 헤이니
네. 제 책상 위의 종이 쪽지에요.

(오후 5시 40분) 압둘 아흐메드
책상 위에 종이가 너무 많은데요.

(오후 5시 41분) 대니얼 헤이니
[152]**미안해요! 조그만 노란색 쪽지예요. 왼쪽 아래 구석을 전부 봐 줘요.**

(오후 5시 43분) 압둘 아흐메드
알았어요. 찾은 것 같아요. RV5cc라고 적혀 있는데요. 이게 찾던 거예요?

(오후 5시 44분) 대니얼 헤이니
네. 정말 고마워요, 압둘. 덕분에 살았어요!

어휘 write down 적다, 기록하다 all the way 완전히, 전부
lifesaver 궁지를 벗어나게 해 주는 것

151 세부 사항

번역 헤이니 씨의 문제는 무엇인가?

(A) 사무실 문이 잠겨 들어가지 못한다.
(B) 보고서를 찾는 데 도움을 필요로 한다.
(C) 중요한 정보를 잊어버렸다.
(D) 회사 컴퓨터 전원을 끄지 않았다.

해설 헤이니 씨가 오후 5시 36분 메시지에서 원격 컴퓨터 시스템에 접근하는 자신의 새 비밀번호가 기억이 안 난다(I can't remember my new password to the remote computer system)고 했으므로, (C)가 정답이다.

▸▸ **Paraphrasing** 지문의 **can't remember my new password to the remote computer system**
→ 정답의 **has forgotten important information**

152 의도 파악

번역 오후 5시 40분에 아흐메드 씨가 "책상 위에 종이가 너무 많은데요"라고 쓸 때, 그 의도는 무엇인가?

(A) 자신은 헤이니 씨의 책상에서 일을 할 수가 없다.
(B) 좀 더 자세한 설명이 필요하다.
(C) 헤이니 씨는 정리를 좀 더 잘 해야 한다.
(D) 헤이니 씨가 일을 끝마치지 않았다.

해설 아흐메드 씨의 '당신의 책상 위에 종이가 너무 많다(There's a lot of paper on your desk)'라는 메시지에 대해 헤이니 씨가 오후 5시 41분 메시지에서 사과(Sorry!)를 한 후 자신이 찾는 쪽지에 대한 세부적인 정보(It's a little yellow piece ~ at the bottom-left corner)를 제공했으므로, 아흐메드 씨에게 좀 더 자세한 정보가 필요했다는 것을 추론할 수 있다. 따라서 (B)가 정답이다.

153-154 이메일

발신: 트레이시 펠젠탈
수신: 존 데이비스
날짜: 12월 8일
제목: 정보
첨부: 문서

데이비스 씨께:

[153]**귀하의 슬로바키아 브라티슬라바 여행 세부 사항을 첨부해 드렸으니 확인 바랍니다.** 첨부 서류에는 귀하의 여행 일정표와 호텔 예약 확인서, 그리고 국제 항공 승무원 연맹(WFFA) 컨퍼런스 참가 확인서가 포함되어 있습니다. 발생할 비용 청구에 관한 설명도 들어 있습니다. [154]**첨부 문서를 인쇄하여 서명하신 다음 가급적 빨리 다시 보내 주시기 바랍니다.** 보내 주시는 서류는 해당 정보를 수령하셨다는 증빙이 될 것입니다. 기록 보관을 위해 사본을 출력해 두셔도 됩니다.

궁금한 사항이 있으시면, 제게 말씀해 주십시오.

트레이시 펠젠탈
인력 개발 코디네이터
에일론 항공

어휘 itinerary 여행 일정표 confirmation 확인(서), 확정
flight attendant 항공 승무원 reimbursement 상환, 변제
expense 비용, 경비 incur 비용을 발생시키다
acknowledgment 접수[수령] 증빙(서) as well 또한

153 주제 / 목적

번역 이메일의 목적 중 하나는?

(A) 출장 준비가 완료되었음을 알리기 위해
(B) 출장 정책의 시행을 발표하기 위해
(C) 국제 항공 승무원 연맹 관련 정보를 제공하기 위해
(D) 컨퍼런스 발표 승인을 요청하기 위해

해설 첫 번째 문장에서 여행 준비와 관련된 자세한 사항을 첨부했으니 확인하라(Attached please find the details for your trip)고 요청했으므로, 이메일의 목적 중 하나가 여행 관련 준비가 완료되었다는 것을 알리기 위함임을 알 수 있다. 따라서 (A)가 정답이다.

어휘 acknowledge (편지 등을 받았음을) 알리다 arrangement 준비, 주선 implementation (정책 등의) 시행

▸▸ **Paraphrasing** 지문의 **the details for your trip**
→ 정답의 **travel arrangements**

154 세부 사항

번역 데이비스 씨가 지시받은 사항은?

(A) 자신의 기록이 최신 내용인지 확인해 주기
(B) 컨퍼런스 세부 사항 제출하기
(C) 호텔 객실 예약하기
(D) 서류에 서명하기

해설 첫 번째 단락의 후반부에서 수신인(You)인 데이비스 씨에게 첨부 문서를 인쇄하여 서명한 후 다시 보내 줄 것(Please print and sign a copy of the attached letter and return it)을 요청했으므로, (D)가 정답이다.

어휘 instruct 지시하다 current 가장 최근의, 현재 통용되는 book (호텔 등에) 예약하다

▸▸ Paraphrasing 지문의 **sign a copy of the attached letter**
→ 정답의 **Sign a document**

155-157 양식

작업 계약서 모리츠-코넬리 조경 이메일: info@moritzconnelly.com 웹사이트: www.moritzconnelly.com 전화: 215-555-0128	
고객 성명:	애나 아렐라노
고객 전화번호:	215-555-0193
작업 장소:	마켓 가 4번지, 필라델피아, 펜실베이니아 주
156**작업 유형:**	**주택 정원**
157**작업일:**	**5월 9일**
도착 시간:	오전 9시
157**작업 완료 예상 시간:**	**정오**
작업 내용	작업 비용
155**매월 잔디 관리 (5월)**	39.95달러
토양 개선 작업	150달러
화초 운반 및 식재	395달러
총 작업비:	584.95달러
선금 (5월 1일 지불 완료)	200달러
157**작업 완료 시 지불해야 하는 잔금**	**384.95달러**

어휘 landscaper 조경사 fertilization 토양을 기름지게 함, 비옥화 deposit 착수금, 보증금 balance due 지불해야 할 금액, 미지급액

155 사실 관계 확인

번역 작업에 대해 명시된 것은?

(A) 오후에 작업이 시작될 것이다.
(B) 작업비는 이미 완불되었다.
(C) 초목 제거 작업이 필요하다.
(D) 정기적으로 제공되는 서비스가 포함되어 있다.

해설 작업 내용(Service)에서 매월 잔디 관리를 한다는 것(Monthly lawn maintenance)을 확인할 수 있으므로, (D)가 정답이다.

▸▸ Paraphrasing 지문의 **Monthly lawn maintenance**
→ 정답의 **a service offered regularly**

156 세부 사항

번역 작업은 어디에서 이루어질 것인가?

(A) 공원
(B) 화원
(C) 아렐라노 씨 자택
(D) 모리츠-코넬리 조경 업체 사무실

해설 작업 유형(Type of project)에 주택 정원(Home garden)이라고 나와 있으므로, 작업이 이루어지는 장소가 아렐라노 씨의 자택임을 알 수 있다. 따라서 (C)가 정답이다.

▸▸ Paraphrasing 지문의 **Home** → 정답의 **residence**

157 세부 사항

번역 모리츠-코넬리 조경이 5월 9일에 받을 금액은?

(A) 39.95달러
(B) 200달러
(C) 384.95달러
(D) 584.95달러

해설 질문에서 언급한 5월 9일은 작업일(Project date: May 9)로, 당일 작업이 완료될 예정(Anticipated time of completion: 12:00 Noon)이다. 작업 계약서의 마지막 부분에서 작업 완료시 지불해야 하는 잔금(Balance due upon completion)이 384.95달러라고 명시하고 있으므로, (C)가 정답이다.

158-160 보도 자료

즉시 배포용
연락처: 엘로이즈 배셋, bassett@edmond.com.jm

몬테고베이 (7월 23일) – 158**에드몬드 유한회사는 당사의 최신 프로젝트인 사우스 몬테고베이 코트의 완공을 알리게 되어 기쁩니다. 이 단지는 착공 당시 대부분의 세대가 선 분양되어 현재는 타운하우스 200세대만 공급 가능합니다.**

타운하우스 각 세대는 설비가 잘 갖춰진 주방과 널찍한 가족실, 아늑한 침실 두세 개, 그리고 욕조가 딸린 화장실도 두 개씩 갖춰져 있습니다. 가족실은 테라스와 연결되어 있어서 평온한 주거 환경을 누리실 수 있습니다. 159**또한 세대마다 중앙 냉방, 에너지 효율이 높은 오븐, 식기세척기, 세탁기 및 건조기 등 현대식 편의 시설도 갖추고 있습니다.**

사우스 몬테고베이 코트 단지는 유명 해변들은 물론, 상가와 음식점들도 인접해 있어 입지 조건도 이상적입니다. 게다가, 주민들이 이용할 수 있는 야외 수영장과 놀이터도 단지 내에 마련되어 있습니다.

160**사우스 몬테고 코트에 오셔서 분양 가능한 세대들을 둘러보시기 바랍니다.**

TEST 6

방문 가능 시간은 화요일부터 토요일까지, 오전 10시에서 오후 7시 사이입니다. 개인적으로 둘러보길 원하실 경우에는, 876-555-0176으로 전화 주세요.

어휘 release 발표, 공개 complex 주택 단지 unit (공동 주택 내의) 한 세대 presold 사전에 판매된 well-equipped 설비를 잘 갖춘 spacious 널찍한 patio (옥외) 테라스 amenities (생활) 편의 시설 situate (어떤 위치에) 짓다, 두다 property (주택 단지의) 부지 drop in (잠깐) 들르다

158 추론 / 암시

번역 에드몬드 유한회사는 어떤 곳이겠는가?

(A) 인테리어 설계 업체
(B) 주택 개발 업체
(C) 주택 담보 대출 업체
(D) 주택 검사 업체

해설 첫 번째 단락에서 에드몬드 유한회사가 완공(completion)한 사우스 몬테고베이 코트의 타운하우스 분양 상황(The complex has only 200 townhouses still available; most of the units were presold when construction first began)을 언급하고 있으므로, 에드몬드 유한회사가 주택 개발 업체임을 추론할 수 있다. 따라서 (B)가 정답이다.

159 사실 관계 확인

번역 타운하우스에 대해 알 수 있는 내용은?

(A) 전부 다 매매되었다.
(B) 개별 정원이 딸려 있다.
(C) 가전 제품도 일부 갖추고 있다.
(D) 세대마다 두 대의 주차 공간이 있다.

해설 두 번째 단락에서 타운하우스의 세대마다 중앙 냉방, 에너지 효율이 높은 오븐, 식기세척기, 세탁기 및 건조기 등 현대식 편의 시설을 갖추고 있다(Every unit also includes modern amenities, such as central air conditioning ~ and clothes washer/dryer)고 했으므로, (C)가 정답이다.

▸▸ Paraphrasing 지문의 **amenities, such as central air conditioning and an energy-efficient oven, dishwasher, and clothes washer/dryer** → 정답의 **some appliances**

160 문장 삽입

번역 [1], [2], [3], [4]로 표시된 곳 중에서 다음 문장이 들어가기에 가장 적합한 곳은?

"방문 가능 시간은 화요일부터 토요일까지, 오전 10시에서 오후 7시 사이입니다."

(A) [1]
(B) [2]
(C) [3]
(D) [4]

해설 주어진 문장에서 방문 가능 시간이 화요일부터 토요일까지, 오전 10시에서 오후 7시 사이(They are open for viewing Tuesday through Saturday from 10:00 A.M. to 7:00 P.M.)라고 했으므로, 앞에서 먼저 They가 가리키는 대상(방문 가능한 곳)이 언급되어야 한다. [4] 앞에서 사우스 몬테고 코트에 와서 분양 가능한 세대들을 둘러보길 바란다(You are welcome to drop in at South Montego Court and visit any of the available units)고 했으므로, (D)가 정답이다. 참고로 주어진 문장의 They는 any of the available units를 가리킨다.

161-163 구인 공고

현장 학습 코디네이터 구함

서머셋 폴스 공원 관리실에서 환경 교육 학교의 현장 학습 프로그램을 지도할 야외 활동 애호가를 찾습니다. 담당 업무에는 현장 학습 수업 연구 및 준비, 각 프로그램 실시 후 평가, 모든 현장 학습 단체 조직 및 일정 관리 보조 등이 포함됩니다.

자격 요건에는 생물학, 환경 과학, 혹은 관련 분야의 학위도 포함됩니다. [161]**또한 이전에 팀을 관리한 경험도 있어야 하며, 우리 시의 공원, 자연보호 단체들 및 환경 자원을 잘 아시는 분이어야 합니다.** 마케팅과 지역 봉사활동에 기여하는 능력은 필수 요건은 아니지만 [162]**가점 요인**입니다.

지원을 희망하시는 분은 자기소개서와 이력서, 추천서를 3월 25일까지 이메일, jobs@somersetfallsparks.com으로 보내 주시기 바랍니다.

[163]**공석 및 채용 절차와 관련된 FAQ(자주 묻는 질문)을 보시려면 www.somersetfallsparks.com/jobs/FAQs를 방문하시기 바랍니다.**

어휘 field trip 현장 학습 outdoor enthusiast 야외 활동을 좋아하는 사람 job description 직무 기술 facilitate (일 등을) 원활히 진행시키다 qualification 자격 (요건) biology 생물학 environmental science 환경 과학 be familiar with ~에 익숙하다 outreach 봉사활동 cover letter 자기소개서

161 세부 사항

번역 지원 자격 필수 요건은 무엇인가?

(A) 지역 내 공원에 대한 지식
(B) 교직 경력
(C) 광고 부문 경력
(D) 운전 면허

해설 두 번째 단락에서 지원자는 시의 공원, 자연보호 단체들 및 환경 자원을 잘 알아야 한다(Qualified applicants ~ should be familiar with the parks, nature organizations, and environmental resources in the city)고 했으므로, (A)가 정답이다.

▸▸ Paraphrasing 지문의 **familiar with the parks ~ in the city** → 정답의 **Knowledge of the area's parks**

162 동의어 찾기

번역 두 번째 문단 5행의 "plus"와 의미가 가장 가까운 단어는?

(A) 보상
(B) 추가
(C) 이점
(D) 정보

해설 "plus"를 포함한 문장은 '마케팅과 지역 봉사활동에 기여하는 능력은 필수 요건은 아니지만, 가점 요인이다(The ability to assist in marketing and outreach is a plus, though not required)'라는 의미로, 여기서 plus는 '가점 요인, 이점'이라는 뜻으로 쓰였다. 따라서 '이점, 이득'이라는 의미의 (C) benefit이 정답이다.

163 세부 사항

번역 해당 직무에 대한 정보를 더 얻으려면 어떻게 해야 하는가?

(A) 일정을 확인한다.
(B) 현장 학습 담당자에게 연락한다.
(C) 이메일을 보낸다.
(D) 웹사이트를 방문한다.

해설 마지막 단락에서 지원 가능한 자리 및 채용 절차와 관련된 자주 묻는 질문은 웹사이트를 참조할 것(Visit www.somersetfallsparks.com/jobs/FAQs for a list of frequently asked questions about available positions and our hiring process)을 권하고 있으므로, (D)가 정답이다.

▸▸ Paraphrasing 지문의 a list of frequently asked questions about available positions and our hiring process
→ 질문의 more information about the job
지문의 www.somersetfallsparks.com/jobs/FAQs → 정답의 a Web site

164-167 온라인 채팅

한나 워드 [오후 2시 1분] 코랄 시청 관계자들과의 회의에 대해 논의하기 전에, 기쁜 소식을 전할 게 있어요. 164**우리가 최근에 설계했던 채틸리온 주택이 <레지덴셜 라이프>지의 다음달 호에 특집으로 실리게 되었어요.**

마흐디 나세르 [오후 2시 2분] 와, 정말 좋은 소식이군요! 저도 그 일이 정말 재미있었어요.

엘레인 라우 [오후 2시 2분] 멋져요! 165**우리 회사 이름이 더 많이 알려지겠네요.**

마흐디 나세르 [오후 2시 3분] 제 생각도 그렇습니다. 165**그 잡지는 많은 나라에 독자층을 확보하고 있으니까요.**

한나 워드 [오후 2시 4분] 비스타라마사 직원들이 대단한 역할을 했다는 사실을 간과하면 안 되겠죠.

엘레인 라우 [오후 2시 5분] 그 회사가 우리 일에 정말 중요한 역할을 했어요.

한나 워드 [오후 2시 7분] 특히 주택이 주변을 장식하는 푸른 나무들과 어우러지게 만드는 게 우리 의도였으니까요. 166**다양한 식물, 나무, 꽃을 활용해서, 비스타라마 팀은 정말이지 멋진 풍경을 만들어 냈어요.**

마흐디 나세르 [오후 2시 8분] 맞아요, 집 주변이 너무나 근사해 보여요.

한나 워드 [오후 2시 8분] 좋아요, 다음으로 넘어가죠. 엘레인, 코랄 시 법원 신청사 요구 사항들과 관련해서 무슨 새로운 정보가 있나요?

엘레인 라우 [오후 2시 9분] 예, 있어요. 167**오늘 아침 시청 공무원 제리카 오길비와 그 문제에 대해 이야기를 나눴어요. 지금 바로 함께 검토하시죠.**

어휘 feature 특집으로 다루다 issue (출판물의) 호 assignment 일, 임무 exposure 노출, 알려짐 readership 독자 수 vital 필수적인, 매우 중대한 blend in 조화를 이루다 greenery 푸른 나무들, 녹음 adorn 꾸미다, 장식하다 crew (함께 일을 하는) 팀 stunning 굉장히 멋진 fabulous 기막히게 멋진 requirements 필요 사항[요건] courthouse 법원 청사

164 세부 사항

번역 워드 씨는 동료들과 어떤 정보를 공유했는가?

(A) 보고서 결과에 대한 세부 사항
(B) 최근 마무리한 연구 결과
(C) 회사의 소중한 기회
(D) 앞으로 수행할 프로젝트에 관한 새로운 소식

해설 워드 씨가 오후 2시 1분 메시지에서 회사의 최근 프로젝트가 잡지에 특집으로 다뤄질 예정(one of our most recent designs ~ will be featured in next month's issue of Residential Life)이라고 했는데, 이는 회사를 알릴 좋은 기회가 될 수 있으므로, (C)가 정답이다.

어휘 findings 연구 결과 forthcoming 다가오는, 앞으로 있을

165 의도 파악

번역 오후 2시 3분에 나세르 씨가 "제 생각도 그렇습니다"라고 쓸 때, 그 의도는 무엇인가?

(A) 회사의 지명도가 더 높아질 것이다.
(B) 회사의 작품을 세계 여러 곳에서 볼 수 있게 될 것이다.
(C) 회사의 최신 프로젝트에 참여해서 기뻤다.
(D) 회사 내 발전 사항을 이야기하는 것이 중요하다.

해설 라우 씨가 오후 2시 2분 메시지에서 잡지에 실리게 되면 회사 이름이 더 많이 알려지겠다(This will mean increased exposure for the firm)는 의견을 밝혔고, 이에 대해 나세르 씨가 '제 생각도 그렇습니다(My thoughts exactly)'라며 라우 씨의 의견에 동의를 표한 후, 그 잡지가 세계 여러 나라에 독자층을 확보하고 있기 때문(The magazine has a readership that spans many countries)이라는 근거를 제시했으므로, (A)가 정답이다.

어휘 visibility 가시성 gratifying 기쁜, 만족한

TEST 6

166 추론 / 암시

번역 비스타라마는 어떤 일을 하는 회사인가?

(A) 건축 설계
(B) 법률 서비스
(C) 조경
(D) 출판

해설 워드 씨가 오후 2시 7분 메시지에서 비스타라마 팀이 다양한 식물, 나무, 꽃을 활용해서 멋진 풍경을 만들어 냈다(Using a variety of plants, trees, and flowers, the crew from Vistarama created a scenery that is absolutely stunning)고 했으므로, 비스타라마가 조경 회사임을 추론할 수 있다. 따라서 (C)가 정답이다.

167 추론 / 암시

번역 라우 씨는 다음에 무엇을 할 것 같은가?

(A) 오길비 씨에게 법원 청사 관련 정보를 제공해 달라고 요청한다.
(B) 채틸리온 주택 주변 경관에 대한 세부 사항을 제공한다.
(C) 코랄 시청 공무원의 요구 사항에 대해 논의한다.
(D) 코랄 시청의 다른 공무원들에게 연락한다.

해설 라우 씨가 오후 2시 9분 메시지에서 시청 공무원과 요구 사항 관련해서 이야기를 나눴다(This morning I discussed them(requirements) with ~ a city official)고 한 후, 워드 씨에게 바로 함께 검토할 것(I'll go over them(requirements) with you right away)을 제안했으므로, (C)가 정답이다.

Paraphrasing 지문의 **go over them(requirements)**
→ 정답의 **Discuss the requests**

168-171 이메일

수신: team@comlor.com
발신: theo_shanner@comlor.com
날짜: 7월 9일 토요일
제목: 바닥 공사 상황
첨부: 문서 1

직원 여러분께,

[169]**월요일에 사무실을 다시 폐쇄하게 되었음을 양지하시기 바랍니다.** [168]**도급 업체가 바닥 설치 공사를 완료하는 데 당초 예상했던 것보다 시간이 더 필요하기 때문입니다.** 공사 진척 상황은 자세한 내용이 들어오는 대로 알려 드리겠습니다. [169]**그러나, 집에서 계속 프로젝트 관련 사항을 파악하고 고객사 지원 업무를 수행해 주시기 바랍니다.**

확실한 것은, 월요일로 예정되었던 회의를 그 주 중후반으로 연기해야 한다는 겁니다. [170]**그때 이전 분기의 수익과 수입을 검토해 보기로 하겠습니다. 여러분들이 미리 확인할 수 있도록 관련 자료를 첨부합니다.** 그리고 추가적으로, [171]**친환경 설계 및 시공의 최근 몇몇 동향에 대해서도 살펴보도록 하겠습니다.**

마지막으로, 이번 사무실 보수 공사로 업무에 지장이 생긴 것에 대해 사과드립니다. 모쪼록 이번 기회를 이용해서 업무 효율성을 높이는 새로운 방법을 찾아 내고, 일과 삶의 균형을 도모하시기 바랍니다.

테오 섀너
컴로 유한회사

어휘 contractor 도급 업자[업체] initially 처음에 anticipate 예상하다 installation 설치 follow up on 후속 조치를 하다, 더 알아보다 customer account 고객사 obviously 분명히, 명백히 earnings 수익 revenue 수입 relevant 관련 있는 sustainable 지속 가능한, 친환경의 disruption 혼란, 지장 seize 잡다

168 사실 관계 확인

번역 바닥 설치 공사에 대해 언급된 것은?

(A) 더 큰 보수 공사의 일부분이다.
(B) 예상보다 더 오래 걸리고 있다.
(C) 공사가 완료되면 검사가 이루어질 것이다.
(D) 일시적으로 중단된 상태이다.

해설 첫 번째 단락에서 도급 업체가 바닥 설치 공사를 완료하는 데 당초 예상했던 것보다 시간이 더 필요하다(the contractor needs more time than initially anticipated to complete the floor installation)고 했으므로, (B)가 정답이다.

Paraphrasing 지문의 **floor installation**
→ 질문의 **flooring installation project**
지문의 **needs more time than initially anticipated**
→ 정답의 **is taking longer than anticipated**

169 세부 사항

번역 직원들이 월요일에 할 것으로 예상되는 일은?

(A) 다른 시간대에 일을 시작한다.
(B) 고객에게 세부 사항을 요청한다
(C) 멀리 떨어진 장소에서 일을 한다.
(D) 회의 안건을 제출한다.

해설 첫 번째 단락에서 월요일에 사무실을 폐쇄할 예정이므로(the office will be closed again on Monday) 집에서 프로젝트 관련 사항을 파악하고 고객사 지원 업무를 수행해 줄 것(While at home, though, continue to follow up on project leads and to support your customer accounts)을 요청했다. 따라서 (C)가 정답이다.

170 세부 사항

번역 섀너 씨가 이메일에 첨부한 서류는?

(A) 재무 제표
(B) 교육용 문서
(C) 판매처 목록
(D) 프로젝트 세부 일정

해설 두 번째 단락에서 회의에서 이전 분기의 수익과 수입을 검토할 예정(On that occasion we will go over our earnings and revenue of the previous quarter)이고 미리 확인할 수 있도록 관련 자료를 첨부한다(I have attached the relevant information ~ ahead of time)고 했으므로, (A)가 정답이다.

▸▸ Paraphrasing 지문의 have attached → 질문의 include
지문의 our earnings and revenue of the previous quarter → 정답의 financial

171 추론 / 암시

번역 컴로 유한회사는 어떤 종류의 업체이겠는가?

(A) 사무용 가구 업체
(B) 산업 부품 제조 업체
(C) 금융 자문 회사
(D) 건축 회사

해설 두 번째 단락에서 친환경 설계 및 시공의 최근 몇몇 동향에 대해서 회의에서 살펴볼 예정(we will be looking at some recent trends in sustainable building design and construction)이라고 했으므로, 컴로 유한회사가 건축 관련 회사임을 추론할 수 있다. 따라서 (D)가 정답이다.

▸▸ Paraphrasing 지문의 building design and construction → 정답의 architecture

172-175 기사

탄력근무제 도입을 고려하십니까?

로미 존슨

"탄력근무제"라는 제도를 통해, 통상적인 정규 근무와는 다른 형태로 근무하기를 바라는 직장인들이 많습니다. 탄력근무제는 기존과는 다른 시간대에 근무를 하거나, 어떤 날은 근무 시간을 늘리는 대신 어떤 날은 근무 시간을 줄이는 식의 형태가 될 수도 있습니다. 일반적으로 보기에는 직원에게 혜택이 가는 제도 같지만, 탄력근무제는 [173(D)]**피고용인의 만족도를 높여 주고,** [173(B)]**새로운 인재 채용에도 도움이 되며,** [173(C)]**직원 수를 늘리거나 초과 근무 수당을 발생시키지 않고서도 근무 시간대를 늘릴 수 있다는 측면에서** 고용주에게도 이득이 되는 제도입니다.

[172]**이러한 방식에 관심이 있는 고용주라면, 우선 먼저 몇 가지 요소들을 고려해야 합니다.** 이 제도를 이용하고자 하는 직원들이 얼마나 되는지, 그리고 직원들의 근무 시간을 어떻게 파악할 것인지, 또 탄력근무제가 일상 업무에 지장을 주는 것은 아닌지의 여부 등입니다.

그 다음에는, [175]**회사가 필요로 하고 선호하는 바에 따라 특별한 세부 사항들이 포함된 정책을 마련해야 할 것입니다.** 예를 들면, 고용주가 특정 직책의 직원들만 참여하게 만들 수도 있습니다. [174]**고용주들은 가끔씩 이 내용을 재검토하고, 필요하다면 수정을 해야 할 것입니다.** 그리고 물론, 제도 시행에 앞서, 제안된 정책이 임금 및 근무 시간 관련 법에 저촉되는 부분이 없는지 확실히 해 두려면, 자사의 법무팀에 자문을 구할 필요도 있을 것입니다.

어휘 flextime 탄력근무제 nonstandard 비표준의 nontraditional 비전통적인 view ~로 여기다, 보다 recruitment 채용 talent 인재 coverage 범위 incur 발생시키다 arrangement 방식 take advantage of ~을 이용하다 track 파악하다 interfere with ~을 방해하다 specific to 특유한, 독특한 revisit 다시 논의하다 implementation 이행, 시행 legal team 법무팀 comply with 지키다, 준거하다

172 추론

번역 기사는 주로 누구를 위해 쓰인 것인가?

(A) 법무팀
(B) 회사 경영자들
(C) 급여 담당자들
(D) 신문 기자들

해설 두 번째 단락 첫 번째 문장에서 탄력근무제 운영 방식에 관심이 있는 고용주라면, 우선 먼저 몇 가지 요소들을 고려해야 한다(Employers who are interested in such arrangements should first consider several factors)고 했으므로, 회사 경영자들을 위한 기사임을 추론할 수 있다. 따라서 (B)가 정답이다.

▸▸ Paraphrasing 지문의 Employers
→ 정답의 Leaders of companies

173 사실 관계 확인

번역 탄력근무제의 이점으로 언급되지 않은 것은?

(A) 시행에 착수하기 쉽다.
(B) 회사가 구직자들에게 관심을 끌게 한다.
(C) 회사 운영 시간을 늘릴 수 있게 해 준다.
(D) 직원들의 만족도를 높여 준다.

해설 첫 번째 단락의 '새로운 인재 채용에도 도움이 된다(helping in recruitment of new talent)'에서 (B)를, '직원 수를 늘리거나 초과 근무 수당을 발생시키지 않고서도 근무 시간대를 늘릴 수 있다(permitting longer hours of coverage at the business without increasing the number of employees or incurring overtime costs)'에서 (C)를, '피고용인의 만족도를 높여 준다(increasing employee satisfaction)'에서 (D)를 확인할 수 있다. 하지만 시행에 착수하기가 쉬운지는 언급되지 않았으므로, (A)가 정답이다.

▸▸ Paraphrasing 지문의 helping in recruitment of new talent
→ 보기 (B)의 makes a company appealing to job applicants
지문의 permitting longer hours of coverage at the business → 보기 (C)의 enable a company to extend its operating hours
지문의 increasing employee satisfaction
→ 보기 (D)의 increases workers' happiness

174 세부 사항

번역 기사에 따르면, 정기적으로 어떤 일을 해야 하는가?

(A) 결제 간소화
(B) 업무 내용 조정
(C) 정책 검토
(D) 근무 시간 축소

해설 마지막 단락에서 고용주들은 가끔씩 정책 내용을 재검토하고, 필요하다면 수정해야 할 것(Employers should revisit this information from time to time and make changes as necessary)이라고 했으므로, (C)가 정답이다.

어휘 periodically 정기적으로 simplification 단순화, 간소화 adjustment 수정, 조정

▸▸ Paraphrasing 지문의 from time to time
→ 질문의 periodically
지문의 revisit this information
→ 정답의 A review of policies

175 문장 삽입

번역 [1], [2], [3], [4]로 표시된 곳 중에서 다음 문장이 들어가기에 가장 적합한 곳은?

"예를 들면, 고용주가 특정 직책의 직원들만 참여하게 만들 수도 있습니다."

(A) [1]
(B) [2]
(C) [3]
(D) [4]

해설 주어진 문장이 '예를 들어(For example)'라는 표현을 사용하여 앞에 언급된 내용을 부연 설명하고 있으므로, 앞에서 먼저 예시를 포함할 수 있는 전체적인 내용이 언급되어야 한다. [3] 앞 문장에서 회사가 필요로 하고 선호하는 바에 따라 특별한 세부 사항들이 포함된 정책을 마련해야 할 것(Then a policy must be created that includes details specific to the company's needs and preferences)이라고 했으며, 주어진 문장이 정책(policies)의 세부 사항(details)에 해당하는 하나의 예시(example)라고 볼 수 있다. 따라서 (C)가 정답이다.

어휘 job title 직위, 직책

176-180 웹페이지 + 이메일

몰렌 박물관 관람객 안내문

환영합니다! [176]**리치포드 쇼핑 지역의 하이 스트리트 역 가까이에 위치한 몰렌 박물관은, 관람객들의 참여를 유도하는 체험 전시들을 통해 과학의 세계를 탐험할 수 있는 기회를 제공합니다.** 더욱 자세한 내용을 알고 싶어 하는 분들을 위해 견학 프로그램을 마련해 드릴 수도 있습니다. 주차는 인근의 시립 주차장에 하시면 됩니다. 또한, 독특하고 흥미로운 상품들을 다양하게 갖추고 있는 박물관 기념품 매장도 잊지 말고 꼭 들려보시기 바랍니다.

입장권:

종류	입장료	제공
기본 관람	15파운드	상설 전시관 입장
기본 추가 관람	20파운드	기본 관람 및 밴잰트 천체투영관 쇼 입장
특별 할인 관람	25파운드	기본 추가 관람 및 지질학 연구소 입장
[179]**전체 관람**	30파운드	[179]**특별 할인 관람 및 특별 전시관 입장**

특별 전시:

- 스포츠: 우리가 움직이는 방식 (1월 1일–3월 31일)
- 나비: 움직이는 색채 (4월 1일–6월 30일)
- 수학의 묘미: 숫자는 어떻게 우리 세계를 구성하는가 (7월 1일–9월 30일)
- [180]**흙, 불, 물, 바람: 미래 동력원 (10월 1일–12월 31일)**

어휘 engaging 끌어당기는, 눈길을 끄는 hands-on 직접 해 보는 arrange 마련하다, 준비하다 permanent exhibits 상설 전시(관) planetarium 천체 투영관 geology 지질학

수신: tlin@morlenmuseum.org
발신: acordell@talvix.com
날짜: 10월 2일
제목: 곧 있을 단체 견학

린 씨께,

탤빅스 에너지 프로페셔널즈 파트너십(TEPP)을 대표하여 메일을 드립니다. [178]**TEPP는 에너지 산업 부문 취업을 희망하는 젊은이들을 탤빅스 소속 기술자 및 관리자들과 연결해 주는 프로그램입니다.** 저희는 분기마다 프로그램 참가자들에게 교육 견학을 주선하고 있습니다.

[178/180]**10월 12일, 6명의 멘토와 12명의 멘티로 구성된 저희 단체가 몰렌 박물관을 방문할 예정입니다.** 지질학 연구소에 방문하여 화석 연료의 기원을 살펴보려고 합니다. 저희는 심도 있는 박물관 견학이 멘티들에게 상당히 유익할 것으로 보고 있습니다. [177/179/180]**혹시 연구소 견학을 주선해 주실 수 있으신지요? 만약 가능하다면, 입장료에 추가되는 비용은 어떻게 되는지요? 저희는 또한 특별 전시도 관람할 수 있기를 바랍니다.**

귀하의 도움에 대해 미리 감사를 드리는 바입니다.

앨튼 코델

TEPP 관리자

어휘 excursion 짧은 여행, 당일 여행 on behalf of ~를 대표하여 sector 부문 executive 관리자, 경영진 fossil fuel 화석 연료 in-depth 면밀한, 심도 있는 beneficial 유익한, 이로운

176 추론 / 암시

번역 몰렌 박물관에 대해 암시된 것은?

(A) 부속 주차장이 있다.
(B) 접근이 편리한 위치에 있다.
(C) 입장료가 최근에 인상됐다.
(D) 기념품 매장은 현재 영업을 하지 않는다.

해설 웹페이지의 첫 번째 단락에서 몰렌 박물관이 리치포드 쇼핑 지역의 하이 스트리트 역 가까이에 위치해 있다(Located just minutes from High Street Station in Richford's shopping district, the Morlen Museum offers ~ hands-on exhibits)고 했으므로, 박물관 접근이 편리하다는 것을 추론할 수 있다. 따라서 (B)가 정답이다.

▸▸ Paraphrasing 지문의 Located just minutes from High Street Station in Richford's shopping district → 정답의 conveniently located

177 주제 / 목적

번역 코델 씨가 이메일을 보낸 이유는?

(A) 구인 공고에 관해 문의하려고
(B) 자원봉사의 기회를 주려고
(C) 박물관 견학 관련 정보를 요청하려고
(D) 특별 전시 주제를 제안하려고

해설 이메일의 두 번째 단락에서 연구소 견학을 제공할 수 있는지(Would you be able to provide us with a tour of the lab?), 그에 따른 추가되는 입장료는 얼마인지(If so, what would be the cost in addition to the ticket price?)를 문의하고 있으므로, 박물관 견학 관련 정보를 요청하기 위한 이메일임을 알 수 있다. 따라서 (C)가 정답이다.

178 세부 사항

번역 이메일에 따르면, TEPP는 무엇인가?

(A) 멘토링 프로그램
(B) 인재 파견 업체
(C) 여행사
(D) 지질학 동아리

해설 이메일의 첫 번째 단락에서 TEPP가 에너지 산업 부문 취업을 희망하는 젊은이들을 탤빅스 소속 기술자 및 관리자들과 연결해 주는 프로그램(TEPP pairs young adults considering careers in the energy sector with engineers and executives from Talvix)이라고 설명한 후, 두 번째 단락에서 멘토와 멘티로 구성된 단체가 박물관 견학을 할 예정(we are planning for a group of six mentors and twelve mentees to visit the Morlen Museum)이라고 했으므로, TEPP가 멘토링 프로그램임을 알 수 있다. 따라서 (A)가 정답이다.

어휘 staffing company 인재 파견 회사(기업이 필요로 하는 인재를 파견하고 그 기업에서 돈을 받아 수수료를 제하고 직원에게 급여를 지급하는 형태의 회사)

179 연계

번역 TEPP 회원은 어떤 종류의 표가 필요하겠는가?

(A) 기본 관람권
(B) 기본 추가 관람권
(C) 특별 할인 관람권
(D) 전체 관람권

해설 이메일의 두 번째 단락에서 TEPP 그룹의 멤버들이 연구소 견학(Would you be able to provide us with a tour of the lab?) 및 특별 전시 관람(We also want to spend time at the special exhibit)을 희망한다고 했고, 웹페이지의 입장료(Admission)를 보면 특별 할인 관람 및 특별 전시관 입장(Super Saver access AND access to special exhibits)은 전체 관람권(Full Access)으로 이용 가능하므로, (D)가 정답이다.

180 연계

번역 TEPP 단체는 어떤 전시를 관람할 것인가?

(A) 스포츠
(B) 나비
(C) 수학의 묘미
(D) 흙, 불, 물, 바람

해설 이메일의 두 번째 단락에서 10월 12일로 예정된 박물관 견학에서 특별 전시 관람을 희망한다(We also want to spend time at the special exhibit)고 했는데, 웹페이지의 특별 전시(Special Exhibits) 목록을 보면 10월 12일에는 10월 1일부터 12월 31일까지(1 October–31 December) 예정된 '흙, 불, 물, 바람: 미래 동력원(Earth, Fire, Water, Wind: Future Power Sources)'이라는 특별 전시를 관람할 수 있으므로, (D)가 정답이다.

181-185 공지 + 이메일

HJP 운송 솔루션즈 유한회사

파월 인턴십 프로그램

181**런던에 본사를 두고 있는 HJP 운송 솔루션즈 유한회사가 파월 인턴십 프로그램(PIP)의 인턴직 10명을 선정하고자 대학생 지원자들을 모집합니다.** 인턴사원은 버밍엄, 맨체스터, 브리스톨에 있는 HJP의 세 개 지사 중 한 곳에 배치될 예정입니다. 지원을 희망하시는 분은 자기소개서와 이력서를 3월 31일까지 이메일 pip@hjp.co.uk로 보내 주시기 바랍니다. 181**합격자는 파월 인턴십 프로그램의 최초 수혜자가 되는 영광을 얻게 될 것입니다.**

배경:

PIP는 트리스탄 파월이 HJP 운송 솔루션즈 유한회사의 설립자인 헨리 J. 파월의 창의적 정신을 기리기 위해 창시한 것입니다. 184**이 프로그램은 젊은 공대생들이 헨리 J. 파월의 뒤를 이어, 배송 및 운송 관련 문제점들을 해결할 혁신적인 방안을 제시하고 개발하도록 고무하는 데 목적을 두고 있습니다.** 공학 박사 학위를 취득한 뒤, 헨리 J. 파월 씨는 HJP 운송 솔루션즈 유한회사를 설립하였습니다. 긴 시간에 걸쳐, 그는 회사를 국제적으로 명성을 떨치는 성공 기업으로 키워 냈습니다. 182**40년간 대표직을 맡았다가 지난해 퇴임하였고, 아들인 트리스탄이 그의 뒤를 이었습니다.**

어휘 headquarter 본부를 두다 recipient 수령인 initiative 계획, 창시(한 것) ingenuity 독창성, 창의력 seek to ~하도록 추구하다 inspire 격려하다, (감정 등을) 고취시키다 follow in somebody's footsteps ~의 뒤를 잇다 innovative 획기적인, 혁신적인 found 설립하다, 세우다 over time 세월이 흘러 renowned 유명한, 명성이 높은 succeed 뒤를 잇다, 승계하다

수신: 조셉 첸 〈jchen@sunnydale.ac.uk〉
발신: 파드마 비타나 〈pvithana@hjp.co.uk〉
날짜: 4월 25일
제목: 정보

첸 씨께,

인턴십 관련 서류를 빠르게 보내 주셔서 감사합니다. [184]**일주일 내로 귀하의 인턴십 서류들을 수령하실 것입니다.**

[183]**주거에 대한 귀하의 문의에 관해 말씀드리면, 런던에서 근무지까지 기차로 2시간 거리를 매일 통근하기는 무척 힘들 것이라는 귀하의 우려에 공감하는 바입니다.** 유감스럽지만, HJP는 인턴사원에게 숙소를 제공하지 않습니다. [183/185]**저희 회사 브리스톨 지사의 멘토십 프로그램 담당자이신 대니얼 앤더스 씨에게 연락해 보시기를 권해 드립니다. 앤더스 씨는 그곳에 수년간 거주하셨으니, 아마 주거 선택에 관해 조언을 해 주실 수 있을 것입니다.** 행운을 빌며, 저희 HJP에서 즐겁게 근무하시기를 바랍니다.

파드마 비타나
인재 채용 부장, HJP 운송 솔루션즈 유한회사

어휘 promptly 지체 없이 packet 소포, 서류 꾸러미 as for ~에 대해 말하자면 arduous 몹시 힘든, 고된 commute 통근 (거리) regrettably 유감스럽게도 be in charge of ~를 담당하다 presumably 아마, 짐작컨대

181 주제 / 목적

번역 공지의 목적은?

(A) 회사의 자원활동 목록을 작성하기 위해
(B) 회사 연혁을 설명하기 위해
(C) 회사의 새로운 프로그램을 홍보하기 위해
(D) 회장의 퇴임을 알리기 위해

해설 공지의 첫 번째 단락에서 HJP 운송 솔루션즈 유한회사가 파월 인턴십 프로그램(PIP)의 인턴직 10명을 선정하고자 대학생 지원자들을 모집한다(HJP Transport Solutions, Ltd. ~ seeks university students to fill ten intern positions in its Powell Internship Programme)고 한 후, 합격자는 파월 인턴십 프로그램의 최초 수혜자가 되는 영광을 얻게 될 것(Successful candidates ~ being the first recipients of the Powell Internship)이라고 했으므로, 회사의 신설 인턴십 프로그램을 알리기 위한 공지임을 알 수 있다. 따라서 (C)가 정답이다.

182 세부 사항

번역 트리스탄 파월은 누구인가?

(A) 회사 설립자
(B) 회사 대표
(C) 대학 강사
(D) 인턴십 지원자

해설 공지의 마지막 단락에서 헨리 파월 씨가 대표직에서 물러난 후, 아들인 트리스탄 파월 씨가 뒤를 이었다(Having served four decades as company president, he retired ~ was succeeded by his son, Tristan)고 했으므로, (B)가 정답이다.

▸▸ **Paraphrasing** 지문의 **company president**
→ 정답의 **head of a company**

183 주제 / 목적

번역 비타나 씨가 이메일을 보낸 이유에 해당하는 것은?

(A) 첸 씨를 축하하려고
(B) 문제점에 대해 문의하려고
(C) 첸 씨에게 서류를 보내려고
(D) 질문에 답하기 위해서

해설 이메일의 두 번째 단락에서 주거에 대한 첸 씨의 문의에 대해 응답(As for your inquiry about housing, I appreciate your concern ~ for an arduous daily commute)하고 있으므로, (D)가 정답이다.

▸▸ **Paraphrasing** 지문의 **inquiry** → 정답의 **question**

184 연계

번역 첸 씨에 대해서 옳은 설명은?

(A) 과거에 앤더스 씨와 함께 일한 적이 있다.
(B) 프로젝트와 관련해서 도움을 요청했다.
(C) 공학을 전공하는 학생이다.
(D) 다른 사무실로 옮길 예정이다.

해설 이메일의 첫 번째 단락에서 수신인(You)인 첸 씨가 인턴십 서류들을 수령할 것(You will receive your intern packet)이라고 했으므로, 첸 씨가 인턴십 참가를 신청했음을 알 수 있다. 공지의 마지막 단락에서 인턴십 프로그램은 젊은 공대생들이 배송 및 운송 관련 문제점들을 해결할 혁신적인 방안을 제시하고 개발하도록 고무하는 데 목적이 있다(The programme seeks to inspire young engineering students ~ propose and develop innovative solutions to shipping and transport problems)고 했으므로, 인턴십에 참가할 예정인 첸 씨가 공학 전공 학생임을 추론할 수 있다. 따라서 (C)가 정답이다.

185 세부 사항

번역 첸 씨가 근무하게 될 곳은?

(A) 버밍엄
(B) 브리스톨
(C) 런던
(D) 맨체스터

해설 이메일의 두 번째 단락에서 주거에 대해 문의한 첸 씨에게 브리스톨 지사의 멘토십 프로그램 담당자인 대니얼 앤더스 씨가 그곳에 오래 살았으니 그에게 연락해 보라(I suggest that you contact Mr. Daniel Anders who is in charge of the mentorship program in our Bristol office)고 조언했으므로, (B)가 정답이다.

186-190 웹페이지 + 이메일 + 도표

http://www.euroful.it/glasscontainers

유로풀 글래스

유로풀은 이탈리아와 그 외 지역에 고품질 유리 용기를 제공한 지 125년을 맞았습니다!

유리로 만든 병과 단지는 오랜 세월 동안 아름다우면서도 실용적인 용기의 기준이 되어 왔습니다. 이 유용한 재료의 훌륭한 속성을 모두 고려해 보세요.

1. 중성 유리 용기는 보관하는 물건에 영향을 미치지 않습니다. 유리는 무미무취의 재료이므로 식품, 미용 및 위생용품 보관에 이상적입니다.

2. 불투수성 유리는 공기나 물이 침투할 수 없습니다. 유리 용기에 보관되는 내용물은 잘 보호되며 더 오래 신선함을 유지합니다.

3. 환경친화성 유리는 자연에 무해한 천연 재료인 모래, 석회, 소다회로 만들어집니다. 유리는 재사용과 재활용이 가능합니다.

4. 편리성 유리는 세척이 쉽고, 식기세척기 사용도 가능합니다.

188*5. 스타일* **유리의 디자인 가능성은 무궁무진합니다.** 186/188**저희 카탈로그에서 선택하시거나, 저희 유로풀 디자이너가 여러분의 제품 용기를 주문 제작하실 수 있도록 도와 드릴 수 있습니다.**

어휘 celebrate 기념하다 quality 양질의 and beyond 그리고 그 외의 desirable 가치 있는 attribute 속성, 특질 neutrality 중(립)성 interact with ~와 상호작용을 하다 flavor 맛, 향미 odor 냄새, 향 personal care product 개인 미용 및 위생용품 impermeability 불투수성 environmentally responsible 환경을 책임지는 limestone 석회(산화칼슘) soda ash 소다회(탄산소다) ingredient 재료, 성분 customize 주문 제작하다 vessel 그릇, 용기

수신: 토마스 루짜토 〈tluzzatto@euroful.it〉
발신: 비르기트 빌라드센 〈bvilladsen@bivilla.co.dk〉
날짜: 2월 16일
제목: 새 유리병

루짜토 씨께:

188**전화를 주셔서 저희와 함께 유리병 디자인을 같이 검토해 주신 데 대해 감사드립니다.** 이 유리 용기는 꽤 독특해서 비빌라 화장품을 타 경쟁사들의 제품보다 더욱 돋보이게 할 것이 분명합니다.

저희 팀과 상의를 해 보았는데, 한 가지 더 질문이 있습니다. 저희는 유럽 전역, 그리고 때로는 아시아에도 제품을 배송합니다. 187**포장 방법과 병을 담는 케이스 안에 넣을 충전재를 추천해 주실 수 있을까요?** 190**저희 제품을 견고하게 보호하면서, 가능하면 환경 피해를 최소화할 수 있는 충전재를 찾고 있습니다.**

비르기트 빌라드센
비빌라 코스메틱스

어휘 cosmetic 화장품 stand out 두드러지다 regarding ~에 관하여 filling material 충전재 substantial 견고한, 튼튼한 if any 만약에 있다 하더라도 surroundings 환경

유리 용기 제품 운송 요령

파손되기 쉬운 물건을 안전하게 운반하는 가장 좋은 방법은 이중 포장이다. 189**이중 포장이란 제품이 든 상자를 더 큰 상자 안에 넣어 포장하는 것을 말한다.** 박스 사이 공간에는 충격을 흡수하는 충전재를 채워 넣어, 운송 중의 흔들림이나 움직임으로 인해 작은 박스에 가해지는 충격을 완화시킨다. 구체적인 필요에 따라, 다음 중 한 가지를 충전재로 쓸 수 있다.

충전재	보호 강도	친환경성
재활용된 긴 종이 조각들	하	+ +
비닐 공기 쿠션	상	−
땅콩 모양의 포장용 스티로폼	중	− −
190**팽창 바이오폼**	**상**	**+ +**

어휘 delicate 연약한, 부서지기 쉬운 absorbent (충격을) 흡수하는 cushion 충격을 완화하다 vibration 흔들림, 진동 transit 수송, 운반 depending on ~에 따라 filler 충전재

186 사실 관계 확인

번역 유로풀에 대해 명시된 것은?
(A) 신생 업체이다.
(B) 판지로 만든 상자를 판매한다.
(C) 제품을 주문 제작할 수 있다.
(D) 상품은 주로 아시아 지역에서 팔린다.

해설 웹페이지의 5번 속성인 스타일(Style)을 보면 제품 카탈로그에서 제품 용기를 선택하거나 디자이너가 제품 용기 주문 제작을 도와줄 수 있다(Choose from our catalog or work with our Euroful designers who can assist you in customizing a vessel for your product)고 했으므로, (C)가 정답이다.

▸▸ **Paraphrasing** 지문의 **customizing a vessel for your product**
→ 정답의 **make customized products**

187 주제 / 목적

번역 빌라드센 씨가 루짜토 씨에게 이메일을 보낸 이유는?
(A) 조언을 구하려고
(B) 변경을 제안하려고
(C) 절차를 설명하려고
(D) 공급 업체를 추천하려고

TEST 6

해설 이메일의 두 번째 단락에서 포장 방법과 병을 담는 케이스 안을 채우는 충전재를 추천해 줄 것(Do you have recommendations regarding packing methods and filling materials for cases in which the jars are packaged?)을 요청했으므로, 조언을 구하기 위한 이메일임을 알 수 있다. 따라서 (A)가 정답이다.

▸▸ Paraphrasing 지문의 recommendations → 정답의 advice

188 연계

번역 빌라드센 씨와 루짜토 씨가 논의한 유로풀 유리 용기의 속성은?

(A) 속성 2
(B) 속성 3
(C) 속성 4
(D) 속성 5

해설 이메일의 첫 번째 단락에서 전화로 유리 용기 디자인에 대해 루짜토 씨와 함께 검토했다(Thank you for your call during which you went over the details of the design of the jars with us)고 했는데, 웹페이지의 5번 속성인 스타일(Style)에서 디자이너가 제품 용기를 주문 제작할 수 있도록 도울 수 있다(work with our Euroful designers who can assist you in customizing a vessel for your product)고 했으므로, 빌라드센 씨와 루짜토 씨가 유리 용기의 5번 속성에 대해 함께 논의했음을 알 수 있다. 따라서 (D)가 정답이다.

▸▸ Paraphrasing 지문의 went over → 질문의 discuss
지문의 jars → 질문의 glass containers

189 세부 사항

번역 도표에 따르면, 이중 포장에 필요한 물건은?

(A) 여분의 제품 견본
(B) 크기가 다른 상자들
(C) 낱개 포장 유리병들
(D) 배송 시 특별 지시 사항

해설 도표의 두 번째 문장에서 이중 포장이란 제품이 든 상자를 더 큰 상자 안에 넣어 포장하는 것(Overpacking simply means packing the box containing the product inside another larger box)이라고 했으므로, 이중 포장을 위해 크기가 다른 상자 두 개가 필요하다는 것을 알 수 있다. 따라서 (B)가 정답이다.

190 연계

번역 비빌라 코스메틱스의 필요에 가장 부합하는 충전재는?

(A) 재활용 긴 종이 조각들
(B) 비닐 공기 쿠션
(C) 땅콩 모양의 포장용 스티로폼
(D) 팽창 바이오폼

해설 이메일의 마지막 단락에서 비빌라 코스메틱스의 제품들을 튼튼하게 보호하면서도 환경에는 해가 없는, 혹시 있다 하더라도 최소한에 그치는 충전재를 찾고 있다(We are looking for a filling material that offers substantial protection for our product, but does minimal damage, if any, to the surroundings)고 했는데, 도표를 보면 비빌라 코스메틱스의 요구 조건에 가장 부합하는 충전재는 보호 강도(Protection)가 높고(high) 친환경성(Earth friendly)이 우수한(+ +) 팽창 바이오폼(Expanding bio foam)이므로, (D)가 정답이다.

191-195 기사 + 일정표 + 이메일

노후된 가스관 개선에 나선 시 당국

(9월 1일) -10월 한 달 동안, 나이로비 에너지 서비스 주식회사(NESI)는 도시의 에너지 기반 시설 유지 보수 책임 사업의 일환으로 2킬로미터 구간의 지하 매립 주철 가스관을 플라스틱 코팅 강철관으로 교체할 계획이다.

"[191]**새 가스관이 압력을 상승시켜 현대식 고효율 보일러나 온수기, 건조기, 그리고 기타 가스 기기들의 사용이 보다 용이해질 것입니다.**" 가스 업체의 부회장 에스더 체프투모 씨의 설명이다. "새로운 시스템으로 향후 수년간 안전하고 신뢰성 높은 가스 공급이 보장될 것입니다."

[193]**나이로비의 일부 도로는 관이 교체되는 동안 오전 9시부터 오후 4시까지 교통이 통제될 예정이다.** 가스 업체는 시 공무원들과 협력하여 시민들의 불편을 최소화할 수 있는 공사 일정을 추진 중이다. [192]**공사 일정은 가스 업체 웹사이트뿐 아니라 모든 지역 신문에도 매일 업데이트될 예정이다.** 공사 일정으로 인해 중대한 문제가 있는 고객은 가스 업체에 연락하면 된다.

어휘 aging 노후한 replace with ~로 교체하다 cast-iron 주철 commitment 책무, 책임 infrastructure 사회 기반 시설 high-efficiency 고효율성 furnace 용광로, 보일러 ensure 보장하다 for years to come 앞으로 몇 년간 significant 커다란, 중대한 due to ~ 때문에 concerns 걱정[염려], 관심사

가스 배관 교체 공사 일정표

[193]**10월 16일 월요일:**	**월라스턴 가**
[194]**10월 17일 화요일:**	**모링가 로**
10월 18일 수요일:	블랙우드 가
10월 19일 목요일:	새틴우드 가
10월 20일 금요일:	작업 일정 없음 (국경일)

거주하시는 도로의 공사가 완료되면, NESI 기술자가 여러분의 가정을 방문하여 가스 공급선을 연결해 드립니다.

어휘 national holiday 국경일, 법정 공휴일 technician 기술자

수신: 피터 아보뇨 〈pabonyo@mailergrip.com〉
발신: [195]주디스 카마우 〈jkamau@nesi.co.ke〉
날짜: 10월 12일
제목: 고객 번호 A0194

아보뇨 씨께,

[194]**거주하시는 도로의 가스관 교체 공사가 10월 17일 화요일로 예정되어 있습니다.** 기술자들이 가스선을 연결하기 위해 오후 3시에서 8시 사이에 방문할 예정입니다. 555-0181로 전화 주셔서 작업 완료 시간을 정하시기 바랍니다. 재연결 작업이 완료될 때까지 귀하의 가정에 약 한 시간 가량 가스 공급이 중단될 것입니다.

감사합니다.

주디스 카마우

어휘 available 시간이 있는 interrupt (잠깐) 중단시키다

191 사실 관계 확인

번역 기사에 따르면, 새 가스관에 대해 사실인 것은?

(A) 현대식 기기의 작동에 도움이 될 것이다.
(B) 주철관보다 더 빨리 설치될 것이다.
(C) 몇 년 후 교체될 것이다.
(D) 야간에 설치될 것이다.

해설 기사의 두 번째 단락에서 새로운 파이프로 압력이 증가되면서 현대식 가스 기기들의 사용이 보다 용이해질 것(The increase in pressure provided by the new pipes will better support today's ~ gas appliances)이라고 했으므로, (A)가 정답이다.

▸▸ **Paraphrasing** 지문의 **today's** → 정답의 **modern**

192 사실 관계 확인

번역 기사에서 공사 일정에 대해 명시된 것은?

(A) 시 공무원들이 승인하지 않을 것이다.
(B) 체프투모 씨가 게시하였다.
(C) 몇 군데 오류가 있다.
(D) 최종 확정된 것은 아니다.

해설 기사의 마지막 단락에서 공사 일정은 가스 업체 웹사이트뿐 아니라 모든 지역 신문에도 매일 업데이트될 예정(The schedule will be updated daily on the company's Web site as well as in all local newspapers)이라고 했으므로, 최종 확정된 일정표가 아님을 알 수 있다. 따라서 (D)가 정답이다.

193 연계

번역 10월 16일에 무슨 일이 있을 것인가?

(A) NESI 기술자들의 회의가 열린다.
(B) 국경일을 기념할 것이다.
(C) 시내 도로 한곳의 교통이 차단될 것이다.
(D) NESI 가스 사용자가 제기한 불만이 해결될 것이다.

해설 일정표를 보면 질문에 언급된 10월 16일에는 월라스턴 가(Wollaston St.)에 가스 배관 교체 작업이 있을 예정인데, 기사의 마지막 단락에서 나이로비의 도로 일부가 파이프 교체 작업을 하는 동안 차량 통행이 차단될 것(Some streets in Nairobi will be closed to traffic ~ while pipes are replaced)이라고 했으므로, 10월 16일에 월라스턴 가의 차량 통행이 차단될 것임을 추론할 수 있다. 따라서 (C)가 정답이다.

194 연계

번역 아보뇨 씨에 대해 암시된 것은?

(A) 어떤 정보를 요청했다.
(B) 모링가 로에 살고 있다.
(C) 최근에 카마우 씨와 통화를 했다.
(D) 저녁 때 집에 없다.

해설 이메일의 첫 번째 문장에서 수신인(You)인 아보뇨 씨가 거주하는 지역의 가스관 교체 공사가 10월 17일로 예정되어 있음(Your street is scheduled for gas pipe replacement on Tuesday, October 17)을 알리고 있는데, 일정표를 보면 10월 17일에는 모링가 로(Moringa Rd)에 가스배관 교체 작업이 진행될 예정이므로, 아보뇨 씨가 모링가 로에 거주한다는 것을 추론할 수 있다. 따라서 (B)가 정답이다.

195 세부 사항

번역 카마우 씨는 누구인가?

(A) 시 공무원
(B) NESI 직원
(C) 가스 기기 기술자
(D) 공장 임원

해설 카마우 씨(Judith Kamau)의 이름은 세 번째 지문인 이메일에서 찾을 수 있다. 두 번째 칸의 발신인과 맨 마지막에 그 이름이 등장하는 것으로 보아 이메일을 쓴 사람이라는 것을 알 수 있는데, 카마우 씨의 이메일 주소 jkamau@nesi.co.ke에서 NESI 직원임을 알 수 있다. 따라서 정답은 (B)이다.

196-200 안내책자 + 이메일 + 이메일

엘비나스

바하마 수도 나소 바로 외곽에 위치하고 있는 [196]**엘비나스는 여러분의 축하 연회, 공식 만찬, 또는 비즈니스 모임을 개최하기에 적합한 장소입니다.** 도시의 번잡함을 피해서, 이곳은 다양하고 멋진 조형물들이 있는 푸르른 녹음의 정원에 둘러싸여 있습니다.

[198]**알라메다 룸은 100명에서 250명 사이의 인원을 충분히 수용할 수 있으며, 저희의 가장 큰 연회실인 부겐빌레아 룸은 300명까지 수용하기에 적합합니다.** 비즈니스 모임 용도로는, 타마린드 룸이 50명까지 수용 가능하며, 그보다 조금 더 큰 워터폴 룸은 80명까지 수용 가능합니다. 비즈니스 미팅 공간인 두 곳은, 생산적이고 효율적인 회의 진행을 위해 최신 기술 장비를 갖추고 있습니다.

TEST 6

저희의 격조 높은 식당인 캔들우드 트리는 손님들의 각종 식이 제한과 기호들을 고려하여 풍성한 메뉴를 제공하고 있습니다. 7월 10일에 이용하시려는 분들은 미리 계획해 주십시오. 그날은 독립 기념일 특별 만찬 메뉴가 준비됩니다!

행사 예약을 하시려면 elvinnas.bs를 방문해 주십시오. 특정일 최초 예약 시 15퍼센트 할인을 해 드립니다. 더 자세한 정보를 원하시면 242-555-0135로 전화 주시기 바랍니다.

어휘 venue 장소 banquet 연회 hustle and bustle 혼잡, 소란스러움 lush 무성한, 우거진 accommodate 수용하다 be outfitted with ~이 갖춰져 있다 elegant 품격 있는, 격조 높은 ample 충분한, 풍부한 take into account ~을 고려에 넣다 dietary restriction 식이 제한 preference 기호(물)

수신: 타니카 니콜스
발신: 브라이언 다빌
날짜: 2월 18일
제목: 기념일 행사 계획

안녕하세요, 타니카,

엘비나스를 방문해 당신이 창립 기념일 기념식에 적합하다고 제안한 공간을 살펴봤습니다. [198]**식사 메뉴는 현재 250명이 넘는 저희 예상 손님들의 다양한 기호를 맞출 수 있을 것으로 보였습니다.** [200]**현재 그 연회실은 7월 15일 토요일과 8월 5일 토요일, 그 두 날짜에 예약이 가능하고, 8월 23일 수요일에도 예약이 가능합니다. 특히 마지막 8월 23일은 할인도 많이 받을 수 있다는 점을 유의하시기 바랍니다.**

[197]**이 연회실 예약을 승인하시는지 알려 주시기 바랍니다.** [199]**다른 단체가 그 날짜에 예약하기 전에, 서둘러 결정해야 할 필요가 있습니다.** 5월의 시상식 일정 변경에 대해서도 곧 연락 드리겠습니다.

브라이언

어휘 suit 어울리다, 맞다 qualify for ~의 자격을 얻다 party 단체, 일행 be in touch 연락하다

수신: 브라이언 다빌
발신: 타니카 니콜스
날짜: 2월 18일
제목: 기념일 행사 계획

안녕하세요, 브라이언,

엘비나스 관련 정보 감사합니다. [200]**할인이 되는 날짜를 이용하기로 하죠.** 예산 내에서 진행하는 데 도움이 될 수도 있으니까요. 연락해서 예약을 잡아 주시기 바랍니다.

타니카 니콜스, 수석 부사장
나소 이동통신

어휘 take advantage of ~을 (기회로) 활용하다 stay within budget 예산 범위 내에서 하다

196 사실 관계 확인

번역 안내책자에서 엘비나스에 대해 언급한 내용은?
(A) 다양한 유형의 단체 행사를 주최할 수 있다.
(B) 나소 도심의 편리한 위치에 있다.
(C) 그곳의 레스토랑에 주방장을 새로 고용했다.
(D) 비즈니스 센터를 개보수할 계획이다.

해설 안내책자의 첫 번째 단락에서 엘비나스가 축하 연회, 공식 만찬, 비즈니스 모임 개최지로 최적의 장소(Elvinna's is the ideal venue for your reception, banquet, or business meeting)라고 홍보하고 있으므로, (A)가 정답이다.

▸▸ Paraphrasing 지문의 **the ideal venue for your reception, banquet, or business meeting**
→ 정답의 **host groups of various types**

197 사실 관계 확인

번역 다빌 씨가 회사 기념식 계획에 대해 명시한 것은?
(A) 행사에는 단순한 메뉴가 나와야 한다.
(B) 일정을 조정할 필요가 있을 것이다.
(C) 시상식도 같이 열릴 예정이다.
(D) 혼자서는 결정할 수 없는 사안이다.

해설 첫 번째 이메일의 두 번째 단락에서 발신인(I)인 다빌 씨가 수신인(You)인 니콜스 씨에게 연회실 예약을 승인할지 알려 달라(Let me know if I have your approval to book this room)고 했으므로, 다빌 씨 혼자 결정할 수 없는 사안임을 알 수 있다. 따라서 (D)가 정답이다.

198 연계

번역 회사 창립 기념일 행사는 어디서 개최되겠는가?
(A) 알라메다 룸
(B) 부겐빌레아 룸
(C) 타마린드 룸
(D) 워터폴 룸

해설 첫 번째 이메일의 첫 번째 단락에서 식사 메뉴도 현재 250명이 넘을 것으로 예상되는 손님들의 다양한 기호를 맞출 수 있을 것(Their catering menu would suit ~ our expected guests, now numbering over 250)이라며 장소 선정에 영향을 미치는 참가 인원을 언급했다. 소책자의 두 번째 단락에서 알라메다 룸은 100명에서 250명 사이의 인원을 충분히 수용할 수 있고, 가장 큰 연회실인 부겐빌레아 룸은 300명까지 수용하기에 적합하다(The Alameda Room seats between 100 and 250 people comfortably, and our largest space, the Bougainvillea Room, is perfect for up to 300 guests)고 했으므로, 250명 이상의 참가가 예상되는 회사의 행사는 부겐빌레아 룸에서 진행될 것으로 추론할 수 있다. 따라서 (B)가 정답이다.

199 세부 사항

번역 다빌 씨가 걱정하는 이유는?

(A) 초청장에 응답한 사람이 충분치 않다.
(B) 다른 장소가 비용이 적게 들 수 있다고 생각한다.
(C) 마음에 드는 장소를 다른 단체가 예약할지도 모른다.
(D) 오락거리를 확보하지 못한 상황이다.

해설 첫 번째 이메일의 두 번째 단락에서 다른 단체가 그 날짜에 예약하기 전에 서둘러 결정할 필요가 있다(We need to make a decision quickly before other parties reserve those dates)고 했으므로, (C)가 정답이다.

▸▸ **Paraphrasing** 지문의 **other parties reserve those dates**
→ 정답의 **A venue ~ might be reserved by another group**

200 연계

번역 나소 이동통신의 기념식은 언제 개최될 것인가?

(A) 7월 10일
(B) 7월 15일
(C) 8월 5일
(D) 8월 23일

해설 첫 번째 이메일의 첫 번째 단락에서 연회실이 토요일인 7월 15일과 8월 5일, 수요일인 8월 23일 예약이 가능하다(Currently the room is available on two Saturdays, 15 July and 5 August; it is also available on Wednesday, 23 August)고 한 후, 마지막 날인 8월 23일에는 상당한 할인을 받을 수 있다(this last date would qualify for a nice discount)는 점을 강조했다. 두 번째 이메일에서 할인을 제공하는 날짜에 연회실을 이용할 것(Let's take advantage of that discount date they are offering)을 제안했으므로, (D)가 정답이다.

기출 TEST 7

101 (D)	102 (B)	103 (B)	104 (B)	105 (C)
106 (A)	107 (B)	108 (D)	109 (D)	110 (C)
111 (C)	112 (A)	113 (C)	114 (B)	115 (D)
116 (A)	117 (C)	118 (C)	119 (D)	120 (A)
121 (C)	122 (B)	123 (A)	124 (A)	125 (D)
126 (A)	127 (C)	128 (B)	129 (C)	130 (A)
131 (D)	132 (B)	133 (A)	134 (C)	135 (A)
136 (C)	137 (D)	138 (D)	139 (A)	140 (D)
141 (A)	142 (B)	143 (B)	144 (A)	145 (D)
146 (C)	147 (D)	148 (A)	149 (D)	150 (C)
151 (C)	152 (A)	153 (C)	154 (B)	155 (C)
156 (D)	157 (B)	158 (C)	159 (A)	160 (D)
161 (A)	162 (D)	163 (C)	164 (A)	165 (B)
166 (C)	167 (B)	168 (C)	169 (D)	170 (C)
171 (B)	172 (B)	173 (A)	174 (C)	175 (D)
176 (B)	177 (B)	178 (A)	179 (D)	180 (A)
181 (B)	182 (C)	183 (C)	184 (D)	185 (B)
186 (A)	187 (D)	188 (D)	189 (C)	190 (C)
191 (B)	192 (A)	193 (C)	194 (D)	195 (D)
196 (A)	197 (A)	198 (D)	199 (D)	200 (B)

PART 5

101 동사 어형 _ 시제

해설 빈칸은 주어 Mr. Guo의 동사 자리로, 과거 시간을 나타내는 부사 yesterday의 수식을 받는다. 따라서 과거 시제 동사 (D) consulted가 정답이다. (A) consults는 현재 시제, (B) is consulting은 현재 진행 시제로 yesterday와 시제가 일치하지 않고, (C) to consult는 to부정사로 동사 자리에 들어갈 수 없다.

번역 궈 씨는 어제 전기 기술자와 배선 교체 공사에 관해 상의했다.

어휘 electrician 전기 기술자 consult 상의하다 rewire 배선을 바꾸다

102 인칭대명사의 격 _ 소유격

해설 빈칸은 동사 will complete의 목적어 역할을 하는 명사 internship을 한정 수식하는 자리이므로, 소유격 인칭대명사 (B) her가 정답이다.

번역 랑 르 씨는 다음 주에 조지 케이크 숍에서 수습 훈련을 마칠 것이다.

어휘 complete 마치다

103 동사 어휘

해설 빈칸은 to부정사구의 동사원형 자리로, 명사구 novels written by local authors를 목적어로 취한다. 또한 빈칸을 포함한 to부정사구가 동사 meets를 수식하므로, 독서 클럽이 만나는 목적을 나타내는 동사가 빈칸에 들어가야 자연스럽다. 따라서 '토론하다, 논의하다'라는 의미의 (B) discuss가 정답이다. (A) create는 '만들다, 창조하다', (C) perform은 '수행하다, 공연하다', (D) dictate는 '명령하다, 받아 쓰게 하다'라는 뜻으로 문맥상 빈칸에 적절하지 않다.

번역 평생 독서 클럽은 매주 목요일에 모여 지역 작가들이 쓴 소설에 관해 토론한다.

어휘 novel 소설 local 지역의 author 작가

104 부사 자리 _ 동사 수식

해설 빈칸은 주어 Skymills Insurance와 동사 grew 사이에서 grew를 수식하는 부사 자리이므로, 부사 (B) quickly(빨리)가 정답이다. (A) quick(빠른)은 형용사의 원급, (C) quicker는 비교급, (D) quickest는 최상급으로 모두 형용사이므로 품사상 빈칸에 들어갈 수 없다. 참고로, quick도 부사로 쓰일 수 있으나, 동사 바로 앞에 올 수는 없다.

번역 스카이밀스 보험은 소기업에서 직원 350명을 둔 중견 기업으로 빠르게 성장했다.

어휘 insurance 보험 midsize 중형의

105 명사 자리 _ 전치사의 목적어

해설 빈칸은 정관사 the 뒤에 오는 명사 자리로, 전치사구 of Clyde Bank's downtown branch의 수식을 받고, 전치사 to의 목적어 역할을 한다. 따라서 '개업식, 개장'이라는 의미의 명사 (C) opening이 정답이다. (A) open은 명사로 쓰일 경우 '야외, 드러남'을 뜻하므로 빈칸에 적절하지 않고, (B) opened는 동사, (D) openly(공공연히)는 부사로 품사상 빈칸에 들어갈 수 없다.

번역 지역 상점 주인들은 클라이드 은행 시내 지점 개업식에 초대받았다.

어휘 branch 지점

106 동사 어휘

해설 빈칸은 주어 All e-mail messages의 동사 should be 뒤에 오는 과거분사 자리로, 전치사구 in a separate folder의 수식을 받는다. '모든 이메일 메시지는 별도의 폴더에 저장되어야 한다'는 내용이 되어야 자연스러우므로, '저장하다, 보관하다'라는 의미의 동사 store의 과거분사 (A) stored가 정답이다.

번역 법적 문제에 관한 이메일 메시지는 모두 별도의 폴더에 저장되어야 한다.

어휘 regarding ~에 관한 legal 법적인 separate 별도의 escape 탈출하다, 모면하다 serve 봉사하다, 시중들다 determine 결정하다

107 명사 자리 _ 동명사의 목적어 _ 어휘

해설 빈칸은 동명사 Hiring의 목적어 역할을 하는 명사 자리로, 전치사구 for Ms. Tsai의 수식을 받는다. 따라서 명사인 (B) assistant와 (D) assistance 중 하나를 선택해야 한다. 문맥상 빈칸에는 차이 씨를 위해 채용해야 할 대상을 나타내는 사람 명사가 들어가야 하므로, '조수, 조력자'라는 의미의 (B) assistant가 정답이

다. (D) assistance는 '도움, 지원'이라는 뜻의 불가산 명사이고, (A) assist는 동사, (C) assisted는 동사/과거분사이므로 빈칸에 들어갈 수 없다.

번역 차이 씨의 업무량이 늘었기 때문에, 차이 씨의 조수를 채용하는 것이 최우선 과제가 되어야 한다.

어휘 top priority 최우선 과제 workload 업무량 increase 늘다

108 형용사 자리 _ 명사 수식 _ 어휘

해설 빈칸은 문장의 주어인 Ladoff Building을 수식하는 형용사 자리이므로, 형용사와 같은 역할을 할 수 있는 과거분사 (B) originated와 형용사 (D) original 중 하나를 선택해야 한다. 동사구 was constructed in 1923의 1923년은 건물이 최초로 건설된 연도이므로, '원래의, 본래의'라는 의미의 형용사 (D) original이 정답이다. '유래된, 발생된'이라는 의미의 과거분사 (B) originated는 문맥상 어색하고, (A) origin(유래, 기원)은 명사, (C) originally(원래)는 부사로 품사상 빈칸에 들어갈 수 없다.

번역 원래의 라도프 건물은 1923년에 건축되었고 2층 높이였다.

어휘 construct 건축하다 story 층

109 형용사 어휘

해설 빈칸은 전치사 about의 목적어 역할을 하는 명사구 credit card statement를 최상급으로 수식하는 형용사 자리로, 빈칸을 포함한 전치사구는 명사 questions를 수식한다. 따라서 빈칸에는 질문(questions)의 대상인 신용카드 명세서(credit card statement)를 적절히 묘사하는 형용사가 들어가야 하므로, most와 함께 '가장 최근의'라는 의미를 나타내는 (D) recent가 정답이다. (A) central은 '중앙의', (B) consecutive는 '연속적인', (C) actual은 '실제의'라는 뜻으로 문맥상 빈칸에 적절하지 않다.

번역 가장 최근의 신용카드 명세서에 대해 문의 사항이 있으시면 하산 씨에게 전화하십시오.

어휘 recent 최근의 statement 명세서 consecutive 연이은

110 비교급 + than

해설 빈칸 앞에 비교급인 higher가 있고, 해당 문장이 The Rinzlite dishwasher와 all other dishwashers in its class를 비교하고 있으므로, (C) than이 정답이다.

번역 린즐라이트 식기세척기는 동급의 식기세척기 중 가장 높은 순위에 올랐다.

어휘 dishwasher 식기세척기 class 종류, 급

111 동사 어형 _ 태 _ 시제

해설 알맞은 동사 형태를 선택하는 문제이다. 주어 the Grantley store는 휴대폰(mobile phones)을 판매하는 주체이므로, 일단 수동형인 (B) was sold는 제외한다. 문장 맨 앞에 '지금까지'라는 의미의 부사 표현 So far가 있으므로, 현재완료 시제 동사 (C) has sold가 정답이다.

번역 지금까지 그랜틀리 매장은 지난해보다 휴대폰을 20퍼센트 더 많이 판매했다.

112 부사 자리 _ 동사 수식

해설 빈칸은 be동사 is와 과거분사 restored 사이에서 restored를 수식하는 부사 자리이다. 따라서 '완전히'라는 의미의 부사 (A) fully가 정답이다. (B) fullness(충만함)는 명사, (C) fullest와 (D) full은 형용사로 품사상 빈칸에 들어갈 수 없다.

번역 정전이 발생할 경우 전원이 완전히 복구될 때까지 컴퓨터 플러그를 뽑으세요.

어휘 in the event of ~이 발생할 경우 power failure 정전 restore 복구하다

113 부사 어휘

해설 빈칸은 동사 visits를 수식하는 부사 자리로, 부사절(Although Mr. Akiyama retired last year) 및 each week와도 어울리는 부사가 들어가야 한다. 아키야마 씨가 지난해 은퇴했음에도 매주 사무실에 방문하고 있다는 내용이므로, '여전히'라는 의미의 (C) still이 정답이다. (B) yet은 주로 부정문에서 '아직'이라는 뜻으로 쓰이며 동사를 앞에서 꾸며 줄 수 없으므로 빈칸에 적절하지 않다.

번역 아키야마 씨는 지난해에 은퇴했지만, 여전히 매주 사무실을 방문한다.

어휘 retire 은퇴하다

114 형용사 자리 _ 분사

해설 빈칸은 부정관사 a와 명사 argument 사이에서 argument를 수식하는 형용사 자리이다. 따라서 형용사와 같은 역할을 하는 현재분사 (B) convincing(설득력 있는)과 과거분사 (C) convinced(확신하는, 납득하는) 중 하나를 선택해야 한다. 주장(argument)은 확신을 주는 주체이므로, 능동의 의미를 내포한 현재분사 (B) convincing(설득력 있는)이 정답이다. (A) convince(설득하다)는 동사, (D) convincingly(납득이 가도록)는 부사로 품사상 빈칸에 들어갈 수 없다.

번역 패널 토론에서 양 씨는 환경에 대해 책임감을 갖는 사업 관행에 관해 설득력 있는 주장을 펼쳤다.

어휘 argument 주장 environmentally 환경적으로 responsible 책임감을 갖는 practice 관행

115 명사 어휘

해설 빈칸은 동사 will hold의 목적어 역할을 하는 명사 자리로, 전치사구 for new string musicians의 수식을 받는다. 따라서 빈칸에는 새로운 현악기 연주자들을 위해 개최(hold)해야 하는 행사와 관련된 명사가 들어가야 하므로, '오디션'이라는 의미의 (D) auditions가 정답이다. (A) attention은 '주의, 관심', (B) investigations는 '조사', (C) motivation은 '동기 부여'라는 뜻으로 문맥상 빈칸에 적절하지 않다.

번역 호코도 오케스트라는 다음 주 화요일에 새로운 현악기 연주자를 뽑기 위한 오디션을 개최할 예정이다.

어휘 string 현악기

TEST 7

116 재귀대명사 _ 강조 용법

해설 빈칸이 주어 the team members와 be동사 were 사이에 있는데, Although가 이끄는 부사절은 빈칸이 없이도 문법적으로 완벽하다. 따라서 생략 가능한 대명사가 들어가야 한다는 것을 알 수 있으므로, '자신들이 직접'이라는 의미로 주어 the team members를 강조하는 재귀대명사 (A) themselves가 정답이다.

번역 경기가 끝난 뒤, 정작 팀원들은 여유가 없었지만 코치는 기꺼이 인터뷰에 응했다.

어휘 available (사람이) 만날 여유가 있는

117 부사 어휘

해설 빈칸은 부정어 not과 과거분사 reviewed 사이에서 reviewed를 수식하는 부사 자리이다. 전치사구 until November 5 또한 reviewed를 수식하므로, 11월 5일이 되어서야 검토가 끝났다는 말을 가장 자연스럽게 수식하는 부사가 빈칸에 들어가야 한다. 따라서 '완전히, 전적으로'라는 의미의 (C) completely가 정답이다. (A) relatively는 '비교적, 상대적으로', (B) occasionally는 '가끔, 때때로', (D) enormously는 '대단히, 막대하게'라는 뜻으로 문맥상 빈칸에 적절하지 않다.

번역 쉼머 씨의 지원서는 11월 5일이 되어서야 완전히 검토가 끝났다.

어휘 application 지원(서)

118 형용사 자리 _ 명사 수식

해설 빈칸이 to부정사구 「to give+간접목적어(their staff)+직접목적어(feedback)」의 직접목적어 feedback 앞에 있으므로, feedback을 수식하는 형용사나 feedback과 복합명사를 이루는 명사가 들어갈 수 있다. 문맥상 feedback의 특징을 묘사하는 형용사가 들어가야 자연스러우므로, (C) constructive(건설적인)가 정답이다. (A) construction은 '건설, 구조[물]'이라는 뜻으로 feedback과 복합명사를 이룰 수 없고, (D) constructing은 '건설하고 있는'이라는 뜻으로 문맥상 어색하다. (B) constructively(건설적으로)는 부사로 품사상 빈칸에 들어갈 수 없다.

번역 부장들은 연례 성과 검토 회의에서 직원들에게 건설적인 피드백을 하도록 권장 받는다.

어휘 be encouraged to ~하도록 권장 받다 annual 연례의 performance 성과

119 명사 어휘

해설 빈칸은 flexible scheduling and telecommuting과 함께 동사 offers의 직접목적어 역할을 하는 명사 자리이다. 따라서 빈칸에는 직원들에게 제공되는 탄력 근무 및 재택 근무 혜택에 상응하는 명사가 들어가야 하므로, '선택권'이라는 의미의 (D) options가 정답이다. (A) statements는 '진술(서)', (B) exchanges는 '교환, 환전', (C) precautions는 '예방책'이라는 뜻으로 문맥상 빈칸에 적절하지 않다.

번역 데커마크 엔터프라이즈는 직원들에게 탄력 근무와 재택 근무 선택권을 제공한다.

어휘 flexible scheduling 탄력 근무제(자유 근무 시간제) telecommuting 재택 근무

120 부사 어휘

해설 빈칸 뒤 부사절을 수식하는 부사 자리이다. 세부 사항이 확정되기 전(before the details are finalized)에 공사 비용을 추정할 수 있다(can estimate the cost for the ~ project)는 내용이므로, 이를 강조하는 부사가 들어가야 자연스럽다. 따라서 접속사 before와 함께 쓰여 '~하기 전이라도'라는 의미를 완성하는 (A) even(~조차, ~도)이 정답이다. (B) some은 '약간', (C) such는 '매우, 그런', (D) else는 '그 밖에, 달리'라는 뜻으로 문맥상 빈칸에 적절하지 않다.

번역 서머 씨는 세부 사항이 확정되기 전이라도 포스터빌의 개간 공사에 드는 비용을 추정할 수 있다.

어휘 estimate 추정하다 land-clearing 개간 finalize 확정하다

121 부사 자리 _ 형용사 수식

해설 빈칸은 be동사 was와 형용사 smooth 사이에서 smooth를 수식하는 부사 자리이므로, '인상 깊게, 대단히'라는 의미의 부사 (C) impressively가 정답이다. (A) impressive(인상적인)는 형용사, (B) impression(인상)은 명사, (D) impress(감명을 주다)는 동사로 품사상 빈칸에 들어갈 수 없다.

번역 회사가 종이 급여에서 전자 급여로 전환하는 과정은 대단히 순조로웠다.

어휘 transition 전환 smooth 순조로운

122 동사 어휘

해설 빈칸은 to부정사의 동사원형 자리로, 명사구 an identification badge를 목적어로 취한다. 또한 빈칸을 포함한 to부정사구가 동사구 should contact를 수식하므로, 빈칸에는 신분증과 관련해 연락을 취해야 하는 목적 또는 이유를 나타내는 동사가 들어가야 한다. 따라서 '손에 넣다, 획득하다'라는 의미의 (B) obtain이 정답이다. (A) combine은 '결합하다', (C) gather는 '모이다, 모으다' (D) approach는 '다가가다'라는 뜻으로 문맥상 빈칸에 적절하지 않다.

번역 임시직 직원은 모두 피에로 씨에게 연락해 신분증을 받아야 한다.

어휘 temporary 임시의 contact 연락하다 identification 신분

123 부사절 접속사

해설 두 개의 완전한 절을 자연스럽게 이어 주는 접속사를 선택하는 문제이다. 빈칸 앞 주절에서는 미래 시제를 사용하여 보험금을 지불할 것(will pay)이라고 하고, 뒤에 오는 종속절에서는 현재 시제를 사용하여 피해 신고서를 접수하는(receive) 조건을 제시하고 있다. 따라서 '일단 ~하면, ~하자마자'라는 시간/조건의 부사절 접속사 (A) once가 정답이다.

번역 공식 피해 신고를 접수하면 고객님의 청구된 보험금을 지불할 것입니다.

어휘 insurance claim 보험금 청구 receive 접수하다 report 신고

124 명사 자리 _ 전치사의 목적어

해설 빈칸은 정관사 the 뒤에 오는 명사 자리로, 전치사 of의 목적어 역할을 한다. 따라서 '정치인'이라는 의미의 명사 (A) politicians가 정답이다. (B) politicize(~을 정치화하다)는 동사, (C) political(정치적인)은 형용사, (D) politically(정치적으로)는 부사로 품사상 빈칸에 들어갈 수 없다.

번역 토론에 참가한 정치인들 중 어느 누구도 강변 개발 논란에 대해 선뜻 입장을 표명하려 하지 않았다.

어휘 debate 토론 be willing to 기꺼이 ~하다 take a stand 입장을 표명하다 riverfront 강변 controversy 논란

125 전치사 어휘

해설 빈칸은 명사구 the additional funding을 목적어로 취하는 전치사 자리로, 빈칸을 포함한 전치사구가 콤마 뒤 절을 수식한다. 따라서 명사구와 해당 절을 가장 자연스럽게 연결하는 전치사가 들어가야 한다. 추가 자금 지원은 연구팀의 규모(the size of its research team)를 키울 수단이 될 수 있으므로, '(도구·수단)을 사용해, ~을 가지고'라는 의미의 (D) with가 정답이다.

번역 센트럴시티 의대는 추가 자금 지원을 통해 연구팀의 규모를 두 배로 키울 수 있으리라 기대한다.

어휘 additional 추가의 funding 자금 지원 research 연구

126 형용사 어휘

해설 빈칸은 주어 a reception area of 60 square meters의 주격 보어 역할을 하는 형용사 자리로, 전치사구 in the new building의 수식을 받는다. 따라서 빈칸에는 60제곱미터 크기의 안내실이 새 건물에서 차지하는 정도를 묘사하는 형용사가 들어가야 자연스러우므로, '충분한, (~하기에) 족한'이라는 의미의 (A) sufficient가 정답이다. (B) flexible은 '융통성 있는, 탄력적인', (C) capable은 '~할 수 있는', (D) calculating은 '계산적인'이라는 뜻으로 문맥상 빈칸에 적절하지 않다.

번역 고객들은 새 건물에는 안내실이 60제곱미터면 충분할 것이라고 말했다.

어휘 reception area 안내실 calculate 계산하다

127 명사절 접속사

해설 빈칸 뒤에 완전한 절(Mr. Cole called the main office yesterday)이 왔으며, 빈칸 이하의 절이 to부정사 to know의 목적어 역할을 하고 있다. 따라서 빈칸에는 완전한 절을 이끌 수 있는 명사절 접속사가 들어가야 하므로, (C) why가 정답이다. (A) whatever와 (D) who도 명사절 접속사로 쓰일 수 있지만 뒤에 불완전한 절이 와야 하고, (B) while이 이끄는 부사절은 목적어 역할을 할 수 없으므로 빈칸에 들어갈 수 없다.

번역 라우 씨는 콜 씨가 어제 본사에 전화한 이유를 알고 싶어 한다.

어휘 main office 본사

128 to부정사 관용 표현

해설 빈칸은 동사원형 구문(meet its commitment to clients)과 결합하여 동사 hired를 수식하고 있다. 더 많은 변호사 보조원을 채용하는 것은 의뢰인과 약속한 바를 이행하기 위함이므로, '~하기 위해'라는 의미의 to부정사 관용 표현 (B) in order to가 정답이다. (A) consequently는 '그 결과, 따라서', (C) in any case는 '어쨌든', (D) additionally는 '게다가'라는 뜻의 부사로 구조상 빈칸에 들어갈 수 없다.

번역 코플러 법률 사무소는 의뢰인과 약속한 바를 이행하기 위해 더 많은 변호사 보조원을 채용했다.

어휘 paralegal 변호사 보조원 meet one's commitment 약속한 일을 하다, 의무를 다하다

129 명사 어휘

해설 빈칸은 전치사 for의 목적어 역할을 하는 명사 자리로, 형용사 extra의 수식을 받는다. 또한 빈칸을 포함한 전치사구는 동사구 has plastic-coated pages를 수식하는 역할을 한다. 따라서 빈칸에는 비닐로 코팅된 페이지가 있는 이유 또는 목적과 관련된 명사가 들어가야 하므로, '내구성'이라는 의미의 (C) durability가 정답이다. (A) familiarity는 '익숙함', (B) persistence는 '끈기, 지속', (D) replacement는 '교체, 대체'라는 뜻으로 문맥상 빈칸에 적절하지 않다.

번역 〈빌트마이어 로드 아틀라스〉 최신판은 내구성 강화를 위해 비닐로 코팅된 페이지들이 있다.

130 전치사 어휘

해설 빈칸은 동명사구 applying for positions를 목적어로 취하는 전치사 자리로, 빈칸을 포함한 전치사구는 앞에 있는 동사구 prepare a list of professional references를 수식한다. 따라서 빈칸에는 동사구와 동명사구를 적절히 연결하는 전치사가 들어가야 한다. 추천인 명단을 준비하는 것은 지원하기 전에 충족되어야 할 요건이므로, '~ 전에'라는 의미의 (A) prior to가 정답이다. (B) outside of는 '~ 밖에', (C) in front of는 '~의 앞쪽에', (D) according to는 '~에 따라'의 뜻으로 문맥상 빈칸에 적절하지 않다.

번역 구직자들은 직책에 지원하기 전에 직업 관련 추천인 명단을 준비해야 한다.

어휘 job seeker 구직자 reference 추천(인) apply for ~에 지원하다

TEST 7

PART 6

131-134 기사

도쿄(6월 2일) – 토다 엔터테인먼트는 오늘 아침 자사의 최신 비디오 게임을 이번 주 중으로 공개할 거라고 발표했다. 게임 시연회[131]**뿐 아니라** 개발자들의 발표회가 일본 표준시로 금요일 오후 4시 회사 웹사이트를 통해 방송될 예정이다. 지금까지 게임에 대한 자세한 내용은 공개되지 않았다. 많은 소비자들은 이미 이 게임이 회사의 인기 있는 〈토다시 어드벤처〉 시리즈의 속편일 것이라고 [132]**추측하고** 있다. 2년 전에 발매된 이 시리즈의 첫 번째 게임이 일본에서 40만 장 이상 팔리면서 회사로서는 [133]**놀라운** 성공을 거둔 바 있다. [134]**전 세계 판매량은 그 두 배였다.**

어휘 reveal 공개하다 preview 시연회, 시사회 developer 개발자 consumer 소비자 broadcast 방송하다, 광고하다 sequel 속편

131 상관접속사

해설 빈칸에는 문장의 주어 역할을 하는 두 명사구 A preview of the game과 a presentation from the developers를 연결할 수 있는 등위 또는 상관접속사가 들어가야 한다. 문맥상 게임 시연회와 개발자들의 발표회 모두 방송될 대상으로 보는 것이 자연스러우므로, '~뿐만 아니라'라는 의미의 상관접속사 (D) as well as가 정답이다. (B) even though(비록 ~이지만)는 부사절 접속사, (C) how는 부사/명사절 접속사로 두 명사구를 이어줄 수 없다.

132 동사 어휘

해설 빈칸은 be동사 are와 함께 현재진행 시제 동사를 이루는 현재분사 자리로, that이 이끄는 명사절(that it will be a sequel ~ series)을 목적어로 취한다. 앞 문장에서 지금까지 게임에 대한 자세한 내용은 공개되지 않았다(Until now, no details have been revealed about the game)고 했는데, 속편일 것이라는 소비자의 의견을 that절에서 제시했으므로, 빈칸에는 이러한 상황을 적절히 묘사하는 동사가 들어가야 한다. 따라서 '추측하고 있는'이라는 의미의 (B) speculating이 정답이다. (A) confirming은 '확인하고 있는', (C) requesting은 '요청하고 있는', (D) analyzing은 '분석하고 있는'이라는 뜻으로 문맥상 빈칸에 적절하지 않다.

133 형용사 자리_명사 수식

해설 빈칸이 부정관사 a와 명사 success 사이에 있으므로, 빈칸에는 success를 수식하는 형용사나 success와 복합명사를 이루는 명사가 들어갈 수 있다. 따라서 부사 (B) remarkably(놀랍게도)는 일단 제외한다. 문맥상 빈칸에는 성공(success)의 정도를 묘사하는 형용사가 들어가는 것이 자연스러우므로, '놀랄 만한'이라는 의미의 형용사 (A) remarkable이 정답이다.

어휘 remark 의견, 언급; 언급하다

134 문맥에 맞는 문장 고르기

번역 (A) 회사는 이 목표를 달성할 수 없었다.
(B) 토다 엔터테인먼트는 다음 주 신임 CEO를 발표할 예정이다.
(C) 전 세계 판매량은 그 두 배였다.
(D) 소비자들은 이제 처음으로 그것을 구매할 수 있다.

해설 빈칸 앞 문장에서 2년 전에 발매된 이 시리즈의 첫 번째 게임이 일본에서 40만 장 이상 팔리면서 회사가 성공을 거두었다(The first game in that series, ~ success for the company, selling over 400,000 copies in Japan)고 했으므로, 빈칸에도 게임의 판매량 또는 회사의 성과와 관련된 내용이 이어져야 문맥상 자연스럽다. 따라서 전 세계 판매량(Its worldwide sales)을 언급한 (C)가 정답이다.

어휘 purchase 구매하다

135-138 편지

7월 11일

웡 씨께:

오늘 리드버그 부동산의 채권부 공석에 관해 이야기하게 되어 즐거웠습니다. [135]**그 일은 제 역량과 관심사에 딱 맞는 것 같습니다.** 이전의 경력 덕분에 저는 이 [136]**자리**에 특별히 잘 준비할 수 있었습니다. 제 지난 직업 두 가지에서는 훌륭한 글쓰기 능력, 적극성, 그리고 정확성이 [137]**모두 요구되었습니다.** 또한 저는 특히 바삐 돌아가는 환경에서 동료들과 효과적으로 협조할 수 있습니다

시간을 내 저를 [138]**면접해** 주셔서 감사합니다. 최종 채용 결정을 내리시면 꼭 소식 전해 주시기 바랍니다.

존 트러프만

어휘 accounts receivable 채권, 미수 대금 realty 부동산 prior 이전의 experience 경력 assertiveness 적극성 accuracy 정확성 require 요구하다 effectively 효과적으로 coworker 동료 fast-paced 바삐 돌아가는 environment 환경 decision 결정

135 문맥에 맞는 문장 고르기

번역 (A) 그 일은 제 역량과 관심사에 딱 맞는 것 같습니다.
(B) 그 회사는 전국적으로 명성이 자자합니다.
(C) 저는 다수의 다른 직책에도 지원했음을 알려 드립니다.
(D) 추가 대안 일정에 관해 논의하도록 제게 연락 주십시오.

해설 빈칸 앞 문장에서 리드버그 부동산의 채권부 공석에 관해 이야기하게 되어 즐거웠다(It was good to speak ~ in the accounts receivable department at Riedeberg Realty)고 했고, 뒤 문장에서 이전의 경력으로 특별히 준비가 잘 되어 있다(My prior experience has prepared me particularly well)고 했다. 따라서 빈칸에는 해당 직책에 대한 지원자의 적합성을 언급하는 내용이 들어가야 문맥상 자연스러우므로, (A)가 정답이다.

어휘 outstanding 두드러진 reputation 명성

136 명사 어휘

해설 빈칸은 전치사 for의 목적어 역할을 하는 명사 자리로, 지시형용사 this의 한정 수식을 받는다. 또한 빈칸을 포함한 전치사구는 동사구 has prepared me particularly well을 수식한다. 문맥상 준비 대상인 this -------이 앞에서 언급한 채권부 공석(the opening in the accounts receivable department)을 가리키는 것이 자연스러우므로, 빈칸에는 '공석'과 유사한 의미의 명사가 들어가야 한다. 따라서 '직책, (일)자리'라는 의미의 (C) position이 정답이다. (A) event는 '행사, 사건', (B) incident는 '사건', (D) exception은 '예외'라는 뜻으로 문맥상 빈칸에 적절하지 않다.

137 동사 자리 _ 태

해설 빈칸은 주어 Strong writing skills, assertiveness, and accuracy의 동사 자리로, 전치사구 in my last two jobs의 수식을 받는다. 따라서 본동사 역할을 할 수 있는 (B) had all required와 (D) were all required 중 하나를 선택해야 한다. 주어 Strong writing skills, assertiveness, and accuracy는 모두 요구되는 대상이므로, 수동태 과거 동사 (D) were all required가 정답이다.

138 동사 어휘

해설 빈칸은 to부정사의 동사원형 자리로, me를 목적어로 취한다. 또한 빈칸을 포함한 to부정사구는 동사 took (the time)을 수식하여 웡 씨가 시간을 낸 목적 또는 이유를 나타낸다. 이 편지는 면접을 보고 와서 감사 인사를 하는 내용이며, 뒤 문장에서 최종 채용 결정을 내리면 알려 줄 것(hearing from you when you make your final hiring decision)을 요청했으므로, 빈칸에는 '면접하다'라는 의미의 (D) interview가 들어가야 자연스럽다. (A) train은 '훈련하다', (B) recommend는 '추천하다', (C) entertain은 '즐겁게 하다'라는 뜻으로 문맥상 빈칸에 적절하지 않다.

139-142 웹페이지

보호와 보존

가너 미술관(GMA)은 전시관의 조명을 주의 깊게 [139]**관찰해** 소장품을 안전하게 보존합니다. 수천 년 된 유물이 다수 포함된 특정 공예품은 특히 빛에 민감합니다. [140]**이런 이유로** 미술관은 창문이 있는 구역에는 어떤 작품도 전시하지 않습니다. 그리고 [141]**밝아서** 잠재적으로 해로울 수 있는 특정 종류의 전구가 있는 구역에도 예술 작품을 보관하지 않습니다. [142]**또한 플래시를 터뜨리는 사진 촬영은 허용되지 않습니다.** 이러한 조치를 취함으로써 가너 미술관은 앞으로 여러 세대에 걸쳐 소장품을 즐길 수 있을 것으로 기대합니다.

어휘 ensure 확실하게 ~하다, 안전하게 하다 preservation 보존 collection 소장품 lighting 조명 artifact 공예품 sensitive 민감한 potentially 잠재적으로 harmful 해로운 bulb 전구 measure 조치

139 동사 어휘

해설 빈칸은 전치사 by의 목적어 역할을 하는 동명사 자리로, 명사구 the lighting of its galleries를 목적어로 취하고 부사 carefully의 수식을 받는다. 또한 빈칸을 포함한 전치사구가 동사구 ensures the preservation of its collection을 수식하므로, 빈칸에는 소장품 보존을 위해 갤러리 조명에 취해야 할 조치와 관련된 동사가 들어가야 한다. 따라서 '관찰하기, 상태를 확인하기'라는 의미의 (A) monitoring이 정답이다. (B) acquiring은 '획득하기, 습득하기', (C) performing은 '수행하기, 공연하기', (D) guarding은 '보호하기'라는 뜻으로 문맥상 빈칸에 적절하지 않다.

140 접속부사

해설 빈칸 앞뒤 문장을 의미상 자연스럽게 연결하는 접속부사를 선택하는 문제이다. 빈칸 앞 문장에서 특정 공예품은 특히 빛에 민감하다(Certain artifacts ~ are particularly sensitive to light)고 했는데, 뒤 문장에서 미술관은 창문이 있는 구역에는 어떤 작품도 전시하지 않는다(the museum does not showcase any of its pieces in areas with windows)며 빛에 대한 민감성 때문에 미술관이 취하는 조치를 언급하고 있다. 따라서 빈칸에는 인과 관계의 내용을 이어주는 접속부사가 들어가야 문맥상 자연스러우므로, '이런 이유로'라는 의미의 (D) For this reason이 정답이다. (A) After all은 '결국, 어쨌든', (B) For instance는 '예를 들어', (C) On the contrary는 '그와는 반대로'라는 뜻으로 문맥상 빈칸에 적절하지 않다.

141 형용사 자리 _ 명사 수식

해설 빈칸 뒤에 콤마가 있어서 혼동이 될 수 있으나, 빈칸은 전치사 of의 목적어 역할을 하는 명사 bulbs(전구)를 수식하는 형용사 자리이다. 따라서, '밝은'이라는 의미의 형용사 (A) bright가 정답이다. 콤마로 연결된 두 개의 형용사(bright, harmful)가 bulbs를 수식하는 구조이다. (D) brightness(밝음)는 명사로 전치사 of의 목적어 역할을 할 수 있지만, bulbs와 연결해 주는 등위접속사가 없고 bulbs와 동격 관계도 이룰 수 없으므로 오답이다. (B) brightly(밝게)는 부사, (C) brighten(밝히다)은 동사로 품사상 빈칸에 들어갈 수 없다.

142 문맥에 맞는 문장 고르기

번역 (A) 따라서 박물관은 오래된 작품 중 일부를 대여할 예정입니다.
(B) 또한 플래시를 터뜨리는 사진 촬영은 허용되지 않습니다.
(C) 소수의 직원만이 이런 전문 기술을 보유하고 있습니다.
(D) 아쉽게도 대상의 연대는 판단하기 어려울 수 있습니다.

해설 빈칸 앞에서 창문이 있는 구역에는 어떤 작품도 전시하지 않고(the museum does not showcase ~ in areas with windows), 밝고 잠재적으로 해로울 수 있는 특정 종류의 전구가 있는 구역에도 예술 작품을 보관하지 않는다(Nor does it keep artwork ~, potentially harmful bulbs)며 미술관이 취하는 조치들을 언급했고, 뒤 문장이 '이러한 조치를 취함으로써(By taking such measures)'라는 전치사구로 시작하므로, 빈칸에도 미술관이 취하는 조치와 관련된 내용이 들어가야 문맥상 자연스럽다. 따라서 (B)가 정답이다.

어휘 loan 대여 permit 허용하다 possess 보유하다 determine 판단하다

TEST 7

143-146 이메일

수신: 부장 전원
발신: 버트 피사로
날짜: 10월 10일
제목: 직원 회식

부장들께,

12월이 빠르게 다가오고 있어 인사팀은 올해 직원 회식을 위한 세부 사항을 정리하고 있습니다. 알다시피, 이 [143]**연례** 행사는 전 직원의 노고에 감사하고 지난 12개월을 되짚어 볼 수 있는 기회입니다. 덧붙여 편안하고 사교적인 환경에서 동료들과 시간을 [144]**보낼** 기회를 모두에게 제공할 겁니다.

지난해 리버데일 연회장은 거리 때문에 여러 직원이 행사에 참석하기 어려웠다고 알고 있습니다. 모든 사람이 이번 행사에 더 쉽게 참여할 수 있도록, 사무실 건물과 더 가까운 [145]**장소**를 찾고 있습니다. [146]**제안이 있으시면 회신해 주세요.**

곧 자세한 내용을 보낼 계획입니다.

버트 피사로
인사부장

어휘 approach 다가오다 opportunity 기회 reflect on ~을 되짚어 보다 in addition 덧붙여 colleague 동료 distance 거리 participate in ~에 참석하다 celebration 행사 venue 장소

143 형용사 어휘

해설 빈칸은 지시형용사 this와 명사 event 사이에서 event를 수식하는 형용사 자리이다. 문맥상 this ------- event가 앞 문장에서 언급된 올해 직원 회식(this year's staff banquet)을 대신하는 것이 자연스러우므로, '연례의'라는 의미의 (B) annual이 정답이다. (A) initial은 '처음의', (C) favoring은 '형편에 맞는', (D) hiring은 '고용하고 있는'이라는 뜻으로 문맥상 빈칸에 적절하지 않다.

144 to부정사 _ 명사 수식

해설 빈칸에는 명사 time을 목적어로 취하면서 명사 opportunity를 수식할 수 있는 준동사가 들어가야 한다. 따라서 opportunity(기회)를 수식하여 '~할 기회'라는 미래 또는 잠재적 상황을 나타내는 to부정사 (A) to spend가 정답이다. (B) having spent와 (C) spending을 분사로 볼 경우, 명사를 수식할 수 있지만 주로 현재 진행 중인 상황을 나타내므로 opportunity와 어울리지 않고, (D) will spend는 본동사 역할을 하므로 빈칸에 들어갈 수 없다.

145 명사 어휘

해설 빈칸은 for의 목적어 역할을 하는 명사 자리로, 관계사절(that is closer to our office building)의 수식을 받는다. 따라서 빈칸에는 사무실 건물 가까이에 있는 곳을 나타내는 명사가 들어가야 하므로, '장소, 현장'이라는 의미의 (D) venue가 정답이다. (A) result는 '결과', (B) transport는 '수송, 이동', (C) capacity는 '수용력, 능력'이라는 뜻으로 문맥상 빈칸에 적절하지 않다.

146 문맥에 맞는 문장 고르기

번역 (A) 운전용 길 안내가 첨부되어 있습니다.
(B) 혼란을 드려 죄송합니다.
(C) 제안이 있으시면 회신해 주세요.
(D) 잊지 마시고 참석 여부를 확정해 주세요.

해설 빈칸 앞 문장에서 모든 사람이 행사에 더 쉽게 참여할 수 있도록, 사무실 건물과 더 가까운 장소를 찾고 있다(To make it easier for everyone to participate ~ is closer to our office building)고 했으므로, 빈칸에도 행사 장소와 관련된 내용이 이어져야 문맥상 자연스럽다. 따라서 장소 추천(suggestions)을 요청한 (C)가 정답이다.

어휘 confusion 혼란 attendance 참석

PART 7

147-148 공지

반품 약정

[147]**싱스 걸로어에서 구매한 제품이 기대에 부응하지 못하면 매장에 반품하시고 교환 또는 환불을 받으세요.** [148]**환불은 정상가 구매일 경우에만 가능합니다.** 자세한 내용은 Thingsgalore.com/help를 참조하세요.

어휘 pledge 약정 purchase 구매하다 expectation 기대 full-price 정상가

147 추론 / 암시

번역 공지는 어디에서 보이겠는가?
(A) 쿠폰
(B) 웹사이트
(C) 제품 라벨
(D) 판매 영수증

해설 첫 번째 문장에서, 구매한 제품에 대한 교환 또는 환불(If the products you purchased ~, please return to our store for an exchange or a refund)과 관련해 언급했으므로, 판매 영수증에서 볼 수 있는 공지로 추론할 수 있다. 따라서 (D)가 정답이다.

148 추론 / 암시

번역 싱스 걸로어에 관해 암시된 것은?
(A) 모든 품목을 환불해 주지는 않는다.
(B) 할인 제품을 판매하지 않는다.
(C) 불량품을 회수했다.
(D) 연례 할인 판매를 실시하고 있다.

해설 두 번째 문장에서 환불은 정상가 구매일 경우에만 가능하다(Refunds may be issued on full-price purchases only)고 했으므로, 정상가(full-price)가 아닌 제품은 환불이 되지 않을 수 있다고 추론할 수 있다. 따라서 (A)가 정답이다.

어휘 recall (불량품을) 회수하다 defective 결함 있는

149-150 문자 메시지

에드 싱 (오전 9시 46분)
안녕하세요 마리사, 데이비드 옌이 사무실에 들렀나요?

마리사 비텔리 (오전 9시 48분)
제가 알기로는 아니에요. 저는 방금 여기 왔어요.

에드 싱 (오전 9시 49분)
그렇군요. [149/150]**그는 프로그램 오류를 제거하느라 애를 먹고 있어요. 그래서 제가 당신한테 한번 봐 달라고 부탁하라고 했죠.** [150]**언짢게 생각하시지 않았으면 하네요.**

마리사 비텔리 (오전 9시 50분)
전혀요. 그는 잔도스 프로젝트를 맡고 있죠?

에드 싱 (오전 9시 51분)
예, [149]**주문 추적 시스템을 구축하고 있는데 몇 주 뒤에 넘겨야 한대요.**

마리사 비텔리 (오전 9시 52분)
아, 엄청난 프로그램이죠. 그가 코딩 문제에 시달리는 이유를 알겠네요.

어휘 stop by (~에) 들르다 debug (컴퓨터 프로그램의) 오류를 제거하다 deliver 넘겨주다

149 추론 / 암시

번역 글쓴이들은 어디에서 일하겠는가?

(A) 집 수리 업체
(B) 식품 배송 업체
(C) 건설사
(D) 소프트웨어 개발 회사

해설 싱 씨가 오전 9시 49분 메시지에서 옌 씨가 프로그램 오류를 제거하느라 애를 먹고 있다(He's having a hard time debugging a program)고 했고, 오전 9시 51분 메시지에서도 주문 추적 시스템을 구축하고 있다(they're building an order-tracking system)고 했으므로, 글쓴이들이 소프트웨어 개발 회사에서 일한다고 추론할 수 있다. 따라서 (D)가 정답이다.

어휘 repair 수리

▸▸ Paraphrasing 지문의 a program/an order-tracking system → 정답의 software

150 의도 파악

번역 오전 9시 50분에 비텔리 씨가 "전혀요"라고 말한 의도는 무엇인가?

(A) 데이비드 옌을 모른다.
(B) 아직 사무실에 도착하지 않았다.
(C) 기꺼이 동료를 도울 것이다.
(D) 잔도스 프로젝트 팀의 일원이다.

해설 싱 씨가 오전 9시 49분 메시지에서 옌 씨가 프로그램 오류를 제거하느라 애를 먹고 있어서 비텔리 씨에게 한번 봐 달라고 부탁할 것을 권했다(He's having a hard time ~ I told him to ask you to look at it)고 한 후, 비텔리 씨에게 언짢게 생각하지 않았으면 한다(I hope you don't mind)고 했다. 이에 대해 비텔리 씨가 전혀 그렇지 않다고 응답한 것이므로, 그녀가 기꺼이 옌 씨를 도울 것임을 알 수 있다. 따라서 (C)가 정답이다.

어휘 coworker 동료

151-152 이메일

발신: 아웃박스 〈customer_service@outbox.com〉
수신: 와리스 듀얼 〈warisduale@mailinsights.com〉
날짜: 9월 1일
제목: 매장 소식

좋은 소식입니다, 듀얼 씨. [152]**그라인드스톤 리버 밸리 지역 1위 사무용품 매장인 아웃박스가 레이크뷰 애비뉴 매장을 확장해 사무용 가구 코너까지 포함하게 되었습니다.** [151]**이를 기념하기 위해, 보상 제도 클럽 회원들은 모든 사무용 가구를 20퍼센트 할인받게 됩니다. 게다가, 이 할인 행사 기간에는 보상 포인트를 두 배로 받을 것입니다.** 주문은 모든 매장뿐 아니라 당사 웹사이트 www.outbox.com에서도 받습니다. 이 기회를 활용해 업체 사무소를 새롭게 하시고, 그 과정에서 비용을 절감하고 보상 포인트를 적립하세요. 서두르세요, 할인은 9월 30일에 끝납니다.

어휘 expand 확장하다 department 코너, 매장 mark 기념하다 occasion 기회, 행사 reward 보상 additionally 게다가 earn 받다 accept 받다 opportunity 기회 process 과정, 절차 accumulate 적립하다 offer (특히 단기간의) 할인

151 주제 / 목적

번역 이메일을 보낸 이유는?

(A) 온라인 주문 절차 소개
(B) 새 매장 위치 알림
(C) 특별 할인 언급
(D) 신규 프로그램 설명

해설 중반부에서 매장 확장 기념(To mark this occasion)으로 보상 제도 클럽 회원들은 모든 사무용 가구를 20퍼센트 할인받게 된다(members of our rewards club will receive a 20% discount on all office furniture)고 했고, 마지막 부분에서도 이 행사가 9월 30일에 끝나니 서두르라는 말을 덧붙이고 있으므로, 특별 할인 행사를 언급하기 위한 이메일임을 알 수 있다. 따라서 (C)가 정답이다.

▸▸ Paraphrasing 지문의 receive a 20% discount on all office furniture → 정답의 a special offer

152 사실 관계 확인

번역 레이크뷰 애비뉴 매장에 관해 명시된 것은?

(A) 최근 확장되었다.
(B) 웹사이트를 개선했다.
(C) 보상 제도 클럽 회원들을 위한 할인 행사를 자주 연다.
(D) 지역 최초의 아웃박스 매장이었다.

해설 초반부에서 아웃박스가 레이크뷰 애비뉴 매장을 확장해 사무용 가구 코너까지 포함하게 되었다(Outbox, ~ has expanded its store on Lakeview Avenue to include an office furniture department)고 했으므로, (A)가 정답이다.

어휘 recently 최근 enlarge 확장하다

TEST 7

▸▸ Paraphrasing 지문의 has expanded
→ 정답의 was recently enlarged

153-155 회람

회람
수신: 전 직원
발신: 도날도 마타, 시설 관리자
날짜: 7월 22일
제목: 드릴 공정

지난주 직원 회의에서 제가 보고한 바와 같이, [153]**이제 본사 건물 증축을 위한 설계가 최종 단계에 있습니다.** [153]**이 과정의 일환으로 도급 업자들이 구조 분석을 위해 내일 건물 북쪽, 동쪽, 그리고 서쪽에 구멍을 뚫을 예정입니다.** 드릴 작업에는 몇 시간이 소요될 것으로 예상되며, 매우 시끄럽겠습니다. [155]**이런 유형의 소음이 고객과 대화하거나 회의를 진행하려는 직원들이 집중하지 못하게 할 수도 있다는 점은 알고 있습니다.** 하지만 소음 수준과 관련하여 할 수 있는 일이 거의 없습니다. 고객 서비스 사무소와 가장 가까운 동쪽에서 드릴 작업을 시작해 가장 바쁜 서비스 시간 전에 작업을 마치도록 해 달라고 도급 업자들에게 요청했습니다. [154]**건물 사면의 창문을 닫아 소음을 최소화하고 드릴 장비에서 나오는 배기 가스가 건물 안으로 들어오지 않도록 하십시오.**

제가 하루 종일 여기서 이 과정을 감독하고 질문에 대답해 드리겠습니다. 불편을 끼쳐 진심으로 사과드립니다.

어휘 supervisor 관리자 addition 추가 contractor 도급 업자 structural 구조의 analysis 분석 be expected to ~하리라 예상되다 distracting 집중에 방해가 되는 prevent 막다 exhaust fume 배기가스 rig 장비 supervise 감독하다 inconvenience 불편

153 세부 사항

번역 구멍을 뚫는 이유는?
(A) 우물을 팔 최적의 장소를 찾으려고
(B) 개선된 배수 시스템을 설치하려고
(C) 건물 공사 설계를 용이하게 하려고
(D) 조경을 위해 토양 특질을 분석하려고

해설 첫 번째 단락에서 본사 건물 증축을 위한 설계가 최종 단계에 있다(we are now in the final planning stages for the new addition to our headquarters building)고 한 후, 그 과정의 일환으로 도급 업자들이 구조 분석을 위해 건물 북쪽, 동쪽, 그리고 서쪽에 구멍을 뚫을 예정(As part of the process, contractors will be drilling holes ~ to do structural analysis)이라고 했으므로, 설계를 용이하게 하기 위해 구멍을 뚫는다는 것을 알 수 있다. 따라서 (C)가 정답이다.

어휘 identify 찾다 install 설치하다 drainage 배수 facilitate 용이하게 하다 analyze 분석하다 soil 토양 landscaping 조경

▸▸ Paraphrasing 지문의 the new addition to our headquarters building
→ 정답의 a building project

154 세부 사항

번역 마타 씨가 직원들에게 내일 하라고 요청하는 일은?
(A) 재택 근무하기
(B) 모든 창문 닫기
(C) 새 사무실 공간 둘러보기
(D) 고객 면담 일정 조정하기

해설 첫 번째 단락의 마지막 문장에서 건물 사면의 창문을 닫아 소음을 최소화하고 드릴 장비에서 나오는 배기 가스가 건물 안으로 들어오지 않도록 할 것(Please keep windows on all sides of the building shut ~ prevent any exhaust fumes)을 요청했으므로, (B)가 정답이다.

▸▸ Paraphrasing 지문의 keep windows on all sides of the building shut → 정답의 Close all windows

155 문장 삽입

번역 [1], [2], [3], [4]로 표시된 곳 중에서 다음 문장이 들어가기에 가장 적합한 곳은?
"하지만 소음 수준과 관련하여 할 수 있는 일이 거의 없습니다."
(A) [1]
(B) [2]
(C) [3]
(D) [4]

해설 주어진 문장이 앞뒤 대조적인 내용을 연결하는 접속부사 However(하지만)로 시작하고, However 뒤에서 소음 수준과 관련하여 할 수 있는 일이 거의 없다(there is little that can be done regarding noise levels)고 했으므로, 앞에서 먼저 소음으로 인한 문제점이 언급되어야 한다. [3] 앞에서 소음이 고객과 대화하거나 회의를 진행하려는 직원들이 집중하지 못하게 할 수도 있다(this type of noise can be very distracting ~ to speak with customers or conduct meetings)이 소음으로 인한 문제점을 밝혔으므로, (C)가 정답이다.

156-158 보도 자료

즉시 보도용
연락처: 필라 리오스, 언론 통신, prios@belledevelopment.org

로스앤젤레스(4월 18일) – [156]**캘리포니아에 본사를 둔 벨 개발은 런던에 본사를 둔 홀든 에셋과 공동 작업하기로 합의했다.** 두 회사는 힘을 합쳐 공항, 기차역, 호텔, 소매 업체를 위한 업무용 건물의 비어 있는 [157]**공간**을 개조하고 변모시킬 것이다. 벨 대변인 이리나 카슨에 따르면, "공사로 고객들의 경험과 부동산 소유주들의 매출원 모두 개선될 것입니다." [156/158]**월요일 기자 회견 도중 카슨 씨는 두 회사가 과거 이탈리아 나폴리 공항 개조 작업을 함께했을 때 아주 성공적이었기 때문에 "장기적인 관계를 맺기로 결정했다"고 말했다.** 이번 벤처 사업은 다음 달 바르셀로나 기차역 매장과 식당의 외관을 고치는 일부터 시작된다.

어휘 agreement 합의 collaborate 공동 작업하다 transform 변모시키다 revenue stream 매출원 property 부동산 press conference 기자 회견 previously 과거 long-term 장기적인 redesign 외관을 고치다

156 주제 / 목적

번역 보도 자료가 발표하는 것은?

(A) 신상품 라인 출시
(B) 회사 본사 이전
(C) 부동산 회사의 수익 증대
(D) 장기 사업 제휴 시작

해설 초반부에서 캘리포니아에 본사를 둔 벨 개발이 런던에 본사를 둔 홀든 에셋과 공동 작업하기로 합의했다(California-based Belle Development has entered into an agreement to collaborate with the firm Holden Assets)고 했는데, 후반부에서도 두 회사가 장기적인 관계를 맺기로 결정했다(they "decided to make it a long-term relationship")고 한 번 더 언급했으므로, 장기 사업 제휴를 알리는 보도 자료임을 알 수 있다. 따라서 (D)가 정답이다.

어휘 relocation 이전 earnings 수익 real estate 부동산

▸▸ Paraphrasing 지문의 a long-term relationship
→ 정답의 a lengthy business partnership

157 동의어 찾기

번역 첫 번째 단락 4행 "spaces"와 의미가 가장 가까운 단어는?

(A) 구멍
(B) 구역
(C) 좌석
(D) 공원

해설 "spaces"가 포함된 부분은 '비어 있는 공간을 개조하고 변모시키기 위해(to remodel and transform open spaces)'라는 의미로 해석되는데, 여기서 spaces는 '공간, 장소'라는 의미로 쓰였다. 따라서 '구역, 지역'이라는 의미의 (B) areas가 정답이다.

158 사실 관계 확인

번역 보도 자료에서 프로젝트가 완공된 지역으로 명시한 곳은?

(A) 로스앤젤레스
(B) 런던
(C) 나폴리
(D) 바르셀로나

해설 후반부의 기자 회견 도중 카슨 씨가 한 말을 인용한 부분(During the press conference on Monday, Carson said)에서 두 회사가 과거 이탈리아 나폴리 공항 개조 작업을 함께했을 때 아주 성공적이었다(the two companies had been so successful when they worked together previously remodeling an airport in Naples, Italy)고 했으므로, (C)가 정답이다.

▸▸ Paraphrasing 지문의 remodeling an airport
→ 질문의 a project

159-161 공지

방문객 여러분께:

[159]**헤일린 공원은 바위투성이 야생 지대입니다. 오솔길은 풀이 무성하고 비포장이며, 나무뿌리와 바위, 그루터기가 튀어나와 있는 곳이 많습니다.** 길이 지날 수 없는 상태가 되면 허가받은 공원 경비원들이 떨어진 암석 조각을 치우지만, 그렇지 않은 경우에는 야생 동식물의 건강한 서식지를 유지하기 위해 토양은 자연 상태 그대로 유지됩니다. [160]**저희의 노력에 힘을 보태 주시려면 사진과 추억 외에는 아무것도 집에 갖고 가지 마세요. 꽃은 야생에서 자라도록 그대로 두시고 나뭇가지와 돌은 있던 곳에 두세요.**

[161]**저희 공원에서 자라는 다양한 나무, 관목, 꽃에 대해 배우고 싶으시면 공원 관리원이 안내하는 무료 하이킹에 합류하세요.** 매주 토요일 오후 2시부터 3시 30분까지 열립니다. [161]**공원 입구 근처에 있는 등록대에서 신청서에 이름만 추가하시면 됩니다.**

감사드리며 즐거운 하이킹 되십시오!

헤일린 공원 관리소

어휘 rugged 바위투성이의, 울퉁불퉁한 wilderness 황야, 자연 보호 구역 trail 오솔길 grassy 풀이 무성한 unpaved 비포장인 protruding 튀어나온 stump 그루터기 licensed 면허를 소지한, 허가받은 ranger 공원 관리원 debris 암석 조각, 잔해 impassable 지나갈 수 없는 habitat 서식지 wildlife 야생 동식물 aside from ~을 제외하고 shrub 관목

159 추론 / 암시

번역 헤일린 공원에 관해 암시된 것은?

(A) 미개발 지역이다.
(B) 최근 폭풍에 영향을 받았다.
(C) 입장료가 인상되고 있다.
(D) 많은 연구 프로젝트가 이루어지는 장소다.

해설 첫 번째 단락에서 헤일린 공원은 바위투성이 야생 지대(Heylin Park is a rugged wilderness site)라고 한 후 오솔길은 풀이 무성하고 비포장이며, 나무뿌리와 바위, 그루터기가 튀어나와 있는 곳이 많다(Our trails are grassy and unpaved, and ~ tree roots, rocks, and stumps)는 부연 설명을 했으므로, 헤일린 공원이 미개발된 지역임을 추론할 수 있다. 따라서 (A)가 정답이다.

어휘 undeveloped 미개발의

▸▸ Paraphrasing 지문의 a rugged wilderness site
→ 정답의 an undeveloped area

160 세부 사항

번역 헤일린 공원에서 금지된 것은?

(A) 하룻밤 야영
(B) 안내인 없는 하이킹
(C) 허가 없는 방문
(D) 자연물 수거하기

TEST 7

해설 첫 번째 단락에서 아무것도 집에 갖고 가지 말 것(we ask that you please take nothing home with you)을 요청한 후, 꽃은 야생에서 자라도록 그대로 두고 나뭇가지와 돌은 있던 곳에 두도록(Please allow the flowers to grow wild and leave sticks and stones where they are) 구체적인 예시를 들어 한 번 더 강소했으므로, (D)가 정답이다.

▸▸ Paraphrasing 지문의 **flowers/sticks and stones**
→ 정답의 **natural objects**

161 세부 사항

번역 등록대에서 방문객들이 할 수 있는 일은?

(A) 투어 신청하기
(B) 소식지 구독하기
(C) 식물 사진 보기
(D) 오솔길 만드는 일 돕는 자원봉사 신청하기

해설 두 번째 단락에서 공원 관리원이 안내하는 무료 하이킹에 합류할 것(you can join a free ranger-guided hike)을 권유한 후, 공원 입구 근처에 있는 등록대에서 신청서에 이름만 추가하면 된다(Just add you name to the sign-up sheet at the check-in kiosk)고 했으므로, (A)가 정답이다.

어휘 subscribe to ~을 구독하다

▸▸ Paraphrasing 지문의 **a free ranger-guided hike**
→ 정답의 **a tour**
지문의 **add your name to the sign-up sheet**
→ 정답의 **Register**

162-163 기사

브라이슨 사업 개발 네트워크, 학습 프로그램 확장

(3월 14일) – [162]**캘거리에 본사를 둔 브라이슨 사업 개발 네트워크는 10년 이상 현장 강좌를 제공한 데 이어 지난여름 최근 창업한 사람들을 위한 다양한 워크숍을 제공하기 시작했다. 신생 업체 소유주 수백 명이 웹사이트 개발, 마케팅, 광고 같은 주제에 중점을 둔 온라인 세션에 등록했다. 이번 여름 회사는 새로운 학습 기회를 도입할 예정이다.**

"각 분야 전문가들이 진행하는 다양한 심층 강좌가 개설된다는 것을 발표하게 되어 설렙니다." 로사 곤잘레스 이사가 말했다. "모두가 강좌에 대해 더 많이 알 수 있도록 각 강좌에서 다룰 주요 논점들을 강조하는 짧은 동영상을 만들었습니다. [163]**웹사이트에서 저희가 제공하는 강좌들 중 고객님의 필요에 가장 잘 맞는 강좌를 결정하는 데 도움이 되시도록 무료 소개 영상을 보시기를 권합니다.**"

www.brysonbdn.ca에서 등록을 하거나 더 자세한 내용을 볼 수 있다.

어휘 recently 최근 sign up for ~에 등록하다 opportunity 기회 launch 개시 enable 가능하게 하다 a wide variety of 다양한 in-depth 심도 있는 expert 전문가 introductory 소개의 free of charge 무료로

162 주제 / 목적

번역 기사의 목적은?

(A) 기업 합병 발표
(B) 마케팅 비법 제공
(C) 신임 이사 소개
(D) 온라인 강좌 홍보

해설 첫 번째 단락에서 브라이슨 사업 개발 네트워크가 지난여름 최근 창업한 사람들을 위한 다양한 워크숍을 제공하기 시작해서(began offering a different set of workshops for people who have recently started a business) 신생 업체 소유주 수백 명이 웹사이트 개발, 마케팅, 광고 같은 주제에 중점을 둔 온라인 세션에 등록했다(Hundreds of new business owners signed up for the online courses)고 한 후, 새로운 학습 기회 관련 정보를 제공했으므로, 온라인 강좌 홍보를 위한 기사임을 알 수 있다. 따라서 (D)가 정답이다.

어휘 publicize 홍보하다

163 세부 사항

번역 곤잘레스 씨가 사람들에게 권장하는 것은?

(A) 결제하기
(B) 양식 작성하기
(C) 동영상 보기
(D) 전문가에게 연락하기

해설 두 번째 단락에서 웹사이트에서 제공하는 강좌들 중 고객의 필요에 가장 잘 맞는 강좌를 결정하는 데 도움이 되도록 무료 소개 영상을 보기를 권한다(Customers are invited to view this introductory presentation free of charge on our Web site)는 곤잘레스 씨의 말을 인용했으므로, (C)가 정답이다.

▸▸ Paraphrasing 지문의 **view this introductory presentation**
→ 정답의 **Watch a video**

164-167 온라인 채팅

실시간 채팅

아리아나 존스 (오후 1시 18분):
안녕하세요, 리날토, 재니스. [164/165]**제가 두 사람에게 시작하라고 요청한 블로그들은 어떻게 되어 가고 있어요?**

재니스 칸토 (오후 1시 20분):
[164/165]**우리 투자 자문가팀의 팀원들 약력을 소개할까 생각하고 있어요.**

아리아나 존스 (오후 1시 22분):
좀 더 자세히 이야기해 주실래요?

재니스 칸토 (오후 1시 24분):
[166]**매달 다른 팀원과 인터뷰를 해서 특집으로 다루고 싶어요.** 약간 사적인 정보나 경력에 관한 정보를 얻을 수도 있고, 투자 전략에 대한 팀원의 견해를 물을 수도 있고, 뭐 그런 거죠.

아리아나 존스 (오후 1시 25분):
좋아요. 고객들이 정말 좋아하겠어요. 리날토는요?

리날토 페레이라 (오후 1시 27분):
[164/167]**주식 시장에서 새로 부상하는 추세에 대해 보도할까 생각하고 있어요.** 이 주제에 관한 자료도 벌써 많이 모았어요.

재니스 칸토 (오후 1시 27분):
죄송해요, 약 5분 뒤에 회의하러 가야 해요.

아리아나 존스 (오후 1시 28분):
흥미롭네요. [167]**조사하는 데 도움이 필요한가요?**

리날토 페레이라 (오후 1시 29분):
감사하지만 제가 알아서 할 수 있을 것 같아요.

아리아나 존스 (오후 1시 30분):
좋아요, [165]**두 사람 모두 월요일까지 이 아이디어가 진척된 상황을 제게 다시 이야기해 주세요.**

어휘 profile 약력을 소개하다 feature 특집으로 다루다 inquire 묻다 emerging 부상하는 stock market 주식시장 cover 해결하다

164 추론 / 암시

번역 참가자들은 어떤 업계에서 일하겠는가?

(A) 금융
(B) 의료
(C) 기술
(D) 부동산

해설 존스 씨가 오후 1시 18분 메시지에서, 블로그의 진행 상황(How are things coming along with those blogs ~?)을 문의했는데, 이에 대해 칸토 씨는 오후 1시 20분 메시지에서 투자 자문가팀 팀원들 약력 소개(profiling the members of our team of investment advisors)를, 페레이라 씨는 오후 1시 27분 메시지에서 주식 시장에서 새로 부상하는 추세에 대한 보도(reporting on emerging stock market trends)를 생각하고 있다고 응답했다. 이에 따라 참가자들이 금융 업계에서 일하고 있음을 추론할 수 있으므로, (A)가 정답이다.

165 추론 / 암시

번역 존스 씨에 관해 암시된 것은?

(A) 페레이라 씨의 연구를 도울 것이다.
(B) 칸토 씨의 업무를 감독한다.
(C) 월요일 사무실에 없을 것이다.
(D) 구직자에 관한 정보가 필요하다.

해설 존스 씨가 오후 1시 18분 메시지에서, 자신이 두 사람에게 시작하라고 요청한 블로그의 진행 상황(How are things coming along with those blogs I asked you to start?)을 물어봤는데, 칸토 씨가 오후 1시 20분 메시지에서 투자 자문가팀 팀원들 약력 소개를 생각하고 있다(I am thinking of profiling the members of our team of investment advisors)고 응답했다. 이후 존스 씨가 마지막 메시지에서 진척 상황(your progress)을 다시 이야기해 달라고 두 사람에게 요청했으므로, 그녀가 칸토 씨의 업무를 감독한다고 추론할 수 있다. 따라서 (B)가 정답이다.

어휘 supervise 감독하다 job applicant 구직자

166 사실 관계 확인

번역 칸토 씨의 블로그에 관해 명시된 것은?

(A) 오늘 안으로 준비될 것이다.
(B) 몇몇 팀원이 작성할 것이다.
(C) 한 달에 한 번 발표할 것이다.
(D) 사내 이용을 위해 기획될 것이다.

해설 칸토 씨가 오후 1시 24분 메시지에서 매달 다른 팀원과 인터뷰를 해서 특집으로 다루고 싶다(I want to feature an interview ~ every month)고 했으므로, (C)가 정답이다.

어휘 publish (신문·잡지 등에) 발표하다

▸▸ Paraphrasing 지문의 every month → 정답의 once a month

167 의도 파악

번역 오후 1시 28분에 존스 씨가 "흥미롭네요"라고 적은 의도는 무엇인가?

(A) 칸토 씨의 회의에 대해 더 알고 싶다.
(B) 페레이라 씨 블로그의 주제가 마음에 든다.
(C) 최근 주식 시장 추세에 만족한다.
(D) 긍정적인 고객 피드백을 받고 싶다.

해설 페레이라 씨가 오후 1시 27분 메시지에서 주식 시장에서 새로 부상하는 추세에 대해 보도할까 생각하고 있다(I'm thinking of reporting on emerging stock market trends)며 블로그 주제에 대해 언급했는데, 이에 대해 존스 씨가 '흥미롭네요(Sounds interesting)'라고 응답을 한 후, 조사에 도움이 필요한지(Do you need assistance with the research?) 문의하며 도움을 주겠다는 의향까지 내비쳤으므로, (B)가 정답이다.

어휘 positive 긍정적인

168-171 회의록

코르비신사

재무팀 분기 회의록
[169]**10월 18일 목요일**

참석: 로렌조 아베이타 (의장), 돌로레스 텡코, 페를라 부에나플로르, 오마르 마유가, 코라 오데빌라스

[169]불참: **후안 카를로스 세라피오 (국제 기술 회의 참석 중)**
오전 10시 30분 로렌조 아베이타가 개회를 선언했다.
6월 20일 회의록은 만장일치로 승인되었다.

재무 요약 (오마르 마유가 발표)
- 지난 분기 수익이 10퍼센트 상승했다.
- 영업 사원과 고객 서비스 직원 추가 채용을 위한 예산이 승인되었다.
- [170]**제안된 인턴십 프로그램 논의는 조사가 더 시행될 때까지 연기되었다. 페를라 부에나플로르가 이 제안을 검토해 다음 회의 때 보고서를 제출할 예정이다.**
- "우리 모두는 이야기를 한다" 마케팅 캠페인이 진행 중이다. [168]**이 프로젝트는 당사 제품 설치 후 사무실 운영이 개선된 소기업 업주들의 추천 글이 특징이다.**

TEST 7

알림

168/171**돌로레스 텡코는 신제품 프린터와 복사기 출시가 11월 10일 예정이라고 확인해 주었다.** TV, 라디오, 온라인, 인쇄 매체에 광고가 있을 예정이다. 만달루용과 타기그 매장이 전일 행사를 계획하고 있다. 기타 매장 할인 행사 정보는 곧 공개 예정이다.

오전 11시 30분 로렌조 아베이타가 산회를 선언했다.

어휘 minutes 회의록, 의사록 call to order 개회를 선언하다 revenue 수익 budget 예산 approve 승인하다 personnel 직원 associate 직원 postpone 연기하다 proposal 제안(서) testimonial 추천 글 installation 설치 commercial 광고 adjourn 산회를 선언하다

168 사실 관계 확인

번역 코르비신사에 관해 명시된 것은?

(A) 재무팀은 매달 회의를 갖는다.
(B) 영업 사원 연봉이 인상되었다.
(C) 사무 장비를 제조하고 판매한다.
(D) 최근 타기그에 매장을 열었다.

해설 재무 요약(Financial Summary) 마지막 항목에서, 진행 중인 마케팅 캠페인은 코르비신사 제품 설치 후 사무실 운영이 개선된 소기업 업주들의 추천 글이 특징(The project features testimonials ~ after installation of our products)이라고 했고, 알림(Announcements)에서 신제품 프린터와 복사기 출시가 11월 10일 예정(the launch of our new line ~ is set for 10 November)이라고 했다. 이에 따라 코르비신사가 사무실 장비를 제조 판매하는 회사임을 알 수 있으므로, (C)가 정답이다. 초반부에서 '재무팀 분기 회의록'이라고 했으므로, (A)는 오답이다.

어휘 manufacture 제조하다

▸▸ Paraphrasing 지문의 **printers and copiers**
→ 정답의 **office technology**

169 추론 / 암시

번역 세라피오 씨에 관해 암시된 것은?

(A) 회의록을 작성했다.
(B) 이전 팀 회의 일정을 잡았다.
(C) 최근 회의에서 발표했다.
(D) 10월 18일에는 출장 중이다.

해설 불참(Absent) 명단을 보면 질문에 언급된 세라피오 씨가 국제 기술 회의 참석 중(attending International Technology Conference)이어서 회의에 불참했음을 확인할 수 있다. 이에 따라 회의가 진행된 10월 18일에 세라피오 씨가 출장 중이라고 추론할 수 있으므로, (D)가 정답이다.

어휘 previous 이전의

170 세부 사항

번역 어떤 주제에 관해 추가로 정보를 수집할 사람은?

(A) 아베이타 씨
(B) 텡코 씨
(C) 부에나플로르 씨
(D) 마유가 씨

해설 재무 요약(Financial Summary) 세 번째 항목에서 제안된 인턴십 프로그램 논의는 조사가 더 시행될 때까지 연기되었다(Discussion of the proposed internship program ~ until more research has been done)고 한 후, 페를라 부에나플로르가 이 제안을 검토해 다음 회의 때 보고서를 제출할 예정(Perla Buenaflor will look into this proposal)이라고 했으므로, (C)가 정답이다.

▸▸ Paraphrasing 지문의 **more research has been done**
→ 질문의 **gather more information**

171 세부 사항

번역 11월에 있을 일은?

(A) 재무팀이 출장을 갈 것이다.
(B) 신제품이 출시될 것이다.
(C) 장비가 수리될 것이다.
(D) 사용자 안내서가 업데이트될 것이다.

해설 알림(Announcements)에서 신제품 프린터와 복사기 출시가 11월 10일 예정(the launch of our new line of printers and copiers is set for 10 November)이라고 했으므로, (B)가 정답이다.

▸▸ Paraphrasing 지문의 **the launch of our new line of printers and copiers is set**
→ 정답의 **New products will be released**

172-175 편지

하딩 환경 단체

9월 6일

젤라니 캠벨
노든 상수도 위원회
329 루트 15
노든 시, 애리조나 주 86310

캠벨 씨께,

제가 이사회의 회원으로 재직하는 것을 고려해 주신 노든 상수도 위원회에 감사드립니다. 함께 논의한 바와 같이, 현재 저는 추가로 어떤 책무도 맡을 수 없습니다. 172**하지만 이 기회를 빌어 로렌 비렐 씨가 이사로 재직하는 것을 지지하고 싶습니다.**

173**하딩 환경 단체의 개발 담당 이사인 비렐 씨는 이곳에서 수질 분석가로 경력을 시작했습니다.** 전문 지식과 역량이 두각을 드러내면서 그녀는 빠르게 여러 관리직 역할로 승진했습니다. 173**예를 들어, 비렐 씨가 주도한 최근 연구로 노든 시의 양수 시스템에 결함이 있다는 것이 드러났습니다.** 그녀는 필요한 개선책에 대한 지침을 적시에, 또한 비용 효율

적으로 제공했습니다. [174]**유지 보수가 훨씬 적게 드는 개선 시스템으로 지난 5년 동안 노든 시는 수천 달러를 절약했습니다.**

[175]**게다가, 비렐 씨는 그레이트 밸리 분수계, 노든 환경 보호부 등 기타 정부 기관들과 공고한 관계를 구축했습니다.** 이러한 연결 고리는 귀 단체에도 도움이 될 것입니다. 비렐 씨는 귀 단체에 매우 귀중한 기여자가 될 겁니다.

문의 사항이 있으시면 직통 전화 928-555-0176으로 저에게 연락 주십시오.

사니야 마서
회장, 하딩 환경 단체

어휘 board of directors 이사회 currently 현재 assume 맡다 additional 추가의 responsibility 책무 analyst 분석가 promote 승진시키다 supervisory 관리의 expert 전문적인 apparent 뚜렷한 deficiency 결함 water pumping system 양수 시스템 necessary 필요한 timely 적시의 cost-effective 비용 효율적인 maintenance 유지 보수 watershed 분수계 protection 보호 organization 단체 benefit 이득을 보다 invaluable 귀중한 contributor 기여자

172 주제 / 목적

번역 마서 씨가 편지를 보낸 이유는?

(A) 자신의 직무상 책임을 기술하기 위해
(B) 동료를 어떤 직책에 추천하기 위해
(C) 이사회 신임 회원을 환영하기 위해
(D) 동료의 승진을 축하하기 위해

해설 첫 번째 단락에서 이 기회를 빌어 로렌 비렐 씨가 이사로 재직하는 것을 지지하고 싶다(I would like to ~ to voice my support for Ms. Lauren Birrell to serve as a board member)고 했으므로, 비렐 씨를 추천하기 위해 쓴 편지임을 알 수 있다. 따라서 (B)가 정답이다.

어휘 describe 기술하다 promotion 승진

▸▸ Paraphrasing 지문의 **to voice my support for Ms. Lauren Birrell to serve as a board member**
→ 정답의 **To recommend a colleague for a position**

173 사실 관계 확인

번역 하딩 환경 단체에 관해 언급된 것은?

(A) 조사 연구를 수행한다.
(B) 법률 서비스를 제공한다.
(C) 양수 펌프를 제조한다.
(D) 정부 기관이다.

해설 두 번째 단락에서 하딩 환경 단체의 개발 담당 이사인 비렐 씨가 그곳에서 수질 분석가로 경력을 시작했다(Ms. Birrell, the Director of Development at Harding Environmental Group, began her career here as a water analyst)고 한 후, 비렐 씨가 주도한 최근의 조사 연구(a recent research study led by Ms. Birrell)를 예로(For example) 들었다. 이에 따라 비렐 씨가 속한 하딩 환경 단체가 조사 연구를 수행한다는 것을 알 수 있으므로, (A)가 정답이다.

174 추론 / 암시

번역 노든 시의 상수도에 관해 암시된 것은?

(A) 앞으로 5년 후에 개선이 되어야 한다.
(B) 비렐 씨가 정기적으로 점검한다.
(C) 유지 보수 비용이 줄었다.
(D) 그곳의 펌프를 수리해야 한다.

해설 두 번째 단락에서 유지 보수가 훨씬 적게 드는 개선 시스템으로 지난 5년 동안 노든 시는 수천 달러를 절약했다(The upgraded system, ~ has saved Norden City thousands of dollars over the past five years)고 했으므로, (C)가 정답이다.

어휘 inspect 점검하다 decrease 줄다

▸▸ Paraphrasing 지문의 **has saved ~ thousands of dollars**
→ 정답의 **costs have decreased**

175 문장 삽입

번역 [1], [2], [3], [4]로 표시된 곳 중에서 다음 문장이 들어가기에 가장 적합한 곳은?

"이러한 연결 고리는 귀 단체에도 도움이 될 것입니다."

(A) [1]
(B) [2]
(C) [3]
(D) [4]

해설 주어진 문장에서 이러한 연결 고리가 단체에 이로울 것(Your organization would benefit from these connections)이라고 했으므로, 앞에서 먼저 these connections의 구체적인 예시가 언급되어야 한다. [4] 앞에서 비렐 씨가 그레이트 밸리 분수계, 노든 환경 보호부 등 기타 정부 기관들과 공고한 관계를 구축했다(Ms. Birrell has built strong relationships with ~ and other government agencies)며 these connections의 구체적인 예시를 나열했으므로, (D)가 정답이다.

176-180 이메일 + 웹페이지

수신: 효정 조
발신: 줄리안 캐츠
날짜: 6월 14일
제목: 정보

조 씨께:

[176]**지난주에 자리를 비우셨으니, 아직 웹사이트 관련해서 자세한 상황을 모두 파악하지는 못하셨을 겁니다.** 심한 뇌우가 이 지역을 강타했을 때 우리 웹디자이너인 섀넌 게링은 사이트를 한창 수정하는 중이었습니다. 우리 서버는 벼락을 맞아서 조금 피해를 입었고, 서버를 복구하는 동안 미술관 웹사이트는 이틀 동안 정지되었습니다.

[178/180]**오늘 회원들에게 이메일을 보내 우리 회계 연도의 마지막 날인 6월 30일까지 모금 목표를** [177]**달성할 수 있도록 도와 달라고 부탁하실 계획이라고 알고 있습니다.** 우리 사이트는 이제 다시 온라인 상태이며, 이 기금 모금 행사에 사용될 수 있는 새로운 게시판이 포함되었습니다. 추가 정보가 필요하면 연락하십시오.

TEST 7

줄리안 캐츠
IT 담당자
나이트 미술관

어휘 situation 상황 revise 수정하다 severe 심한
lightning 벼락 sustain (손실 등을) 입다 repair 수리하다
fund-raising 기금 모금 fiscal year 회계 연도

http://www.knightmuseumofart.ca/comments

[180]**6월 14일**

저는 나이트 미술관의 열렬한 팬이에요! 미술관의 훌륭한 프로그램들 일부를 이용해 오고 있어요. 최근 지역 미술가 르로이 데이비스와 함께하는 수채화 강좌는 대단했어요. 이 수채화 경험으로 현재 미술관에서 전시하고 있는 일본 수채화 전시회를 제대로 감상할 수 있을 거예요. [179]**다음 주 전시회 투어를 고대하고 있어요.**

[178/180]**이미 미술관 회원으로 기부하고 있지만 미술관장님이 보내신 기금 모금 이메일을 받고 오늘 조금 전에 온라인으로 추가로 기부했어요.** 지난주에는 문제가 있었지만 이번에는 쉽게 웹사이트에 접속했어요. 다른 사람들도 마감인 6월 30일 이전에 기부해서 미술관을 도왔으면 합니다. 나이트 미술관의 프로그램은 그만한 값어치가 있어요.

–브렌다 산스

어휘 take advantage of ~을 이용하다 appreciate 감상하다
exhibition 전시(회) contribute 기부하다 donation 기부

176 주제 / 목적

번역 캐츠 씨가 조 씨에게 연락한 이유는?

(A) 신입 사원 소개
(B) 새로운 소식 제공
(C) 행사 세부 내용 요청
(D) 지원 요청

해설 이메일의 첫 번째 단락에서 지난주에 자리를 비워 아직 웹사이트 관련한 자세한 상황을 모두 파악하지는 못했을 것(Since you were away last week, you might not yet know all the details of the situation with the Web site)이라고 한 후, 단락 전반에 걸쳐 웹사이트의 상황을 설명했으므로, 새로운 소식 제공을 위한 이메일임을 알 수 있다. 따라서 (B)가 정답이다.

177 동의어 찾기

번역 이메일에서 두 번째 단락 1행의 "meet"와 의미가 가장 가까운 단어는?

(A) 연결하다
(B) 충족하다
(C) 맞닥뜨리다
(D) 모으다

해설 "meet"가 포함된 부분은 '모금 목표를 달성할 수 있도록 도와 달라고 부탁하다(asking them to help us meet a fund-raising goal)'라는 의미로 해석되는데, 여기서 meet는 '충족시키다, 달성하다'라는 뜻으로 쓰였다. 따라서 '충족시키다, 성취하다'라는 의미의 (B) fulfill이 정답이다.

178 연계

번역 조 씨는 누구인가?

(A) 미술관장
(B) IT 담당자
(C) 웹 디자이너
(D) 지역 미술가

해설 질문에 언급된 조 씨는 이메일의 수신인(you)으로, 두 번째 단락에서 회원들에게 이메일을 보내 미술관의 회계 연도 마지막 날인 6월 30일까지 모금 목표를 달성할 수 있도록 도와 달라고 부탁할 계획(you are planning to send an e-mail to members today, asking them ~ fiscal year)이라고 했는데, 웹페이지의 두 번째 단락을 보면, 산스 씨가 미술관장이 보낸 기금 모금 이메일을 받고 온라인으로 추가로 기부했다(I just made an additional donation ~ after I received a fund-raising e-mail from the museum's director)고 했으므로, 조 씨가 미술관장임을 알 수 있다. 따라서 (A)가 정답이다.

179 세부 사항

번역 산스 씨가 하려고 하는 일은?

(A) 웹사이트 지원하기
(B) 회원 투어 인도하기
(C) 미술 강좌 등록하기
(D) 전시회 참석하기

해설 웹페이지의 첫 번째 단락에서 산스 씨가 다음 주 전시회 투어를 고대하고 있다(I'm looking forward to taking a tour of the exhibition next week)고 했으므로, (D)가 정답이다.

어휘 enroll 등록하다

▸▸ Paraphrasing 지문의 **looking forward to**
→ 질문의 **is ~ eager to do**

지문의 **taking a tour of the exhibition**
→ 정답의 **Attend an exhibition**

180 연계

번역 산스 씨가 게시글에서 암시하는 것은?

(A) 회계 연도가 끝나기 전에 기부했다.
(B) 일본을 방문한 적이 있다.
(C) 최근 미술관의 온라인 미술 소장품에 접속했다.
(D) 르로이 데이비스의 그림을 구입했다.

해설 웹페이지에서 산스 씨가 미술관장이 보낸 기금 모금 이메일을 받고 오늘 조금 전에 온라인으로 추가로 기부했다(I just made an additional donation ~ today after I received a fund-raising e-mail)고 했는데, 웹페이지의 날짜에서 오늘이 6월 14일임을 확인할 수 있다. 이메일의 두 번째 단락에서 회원들에게 이메일을 보내 회계 연도 마지막 날인 6월 30일까지 모금 목표를 달성할 수 있도록 도와 달라고 부탁할 계획(you are planning to send an e-mail to members ~ by 30 June, the end of our fiscal year)이라고

했으므로, 산스 씨가 회계 연도가 끝나기 전에 추가로 기부했음을 추론할 수 있다. 따라서 (A)가 정답이다.

어휘 access 접속하다 purchase 구입하다

181-185 이메일 + 청구서

이메일 메시지

[181]**수신: ababin@babinassociates.co.nz**
발신: f_zhong@zhong.co.nz
날짜: 3월 5일
제목: 주문 번호 45368

바빈 씨께,

최근 제 주문과 관련해 몇 가지 문제를 알려 드리고자 씁니다. [181/182]**귀사에서 여러 해 동안 물건을 구매해 왔는데 이전 주문은 한 번도 오류가 없었습니다.** 그래서 최근의 주문품이 도착했을 때 깜짝 놀랐습니다. [181]**우선 청구서에 올린 수량은 2묶음이 아닌데 배송품에 티셔츠가 2묶음 밖에 없었어요. 긴소매 셔츠에 대한 메모는 보았지만 티셔츠에 대한 메모는 없었어요.**

[185]**게다가 61번 품목 가격이 카탈로그와 웹사이트에 묶음당 50달러로 나와 있는데 제게 청구된 비용은 달랐어요.** [183]**이 문제를 살펴보시고 전화 주시겠어요?** 제 번호는 +64 04 455 5212입니다.

미리 감사드립니다.

파이 중

어휘 previous 이전의 shipment 배송(품) contain 들어 있다 charge 청구하다

발신:
바빈 앤 어소시에이츠
칼레도니아 가 25번지,
스트래스모
웰링턴 6022

수신:
파이 중
중 레스토랑 앤 케이터링
로미오 가 76번지, 손던
웰링턴 6011

청구서 수령 시 대금 지불				
주문 번호 45368				
품번	설명	주문 수량	묶음 당 가격	총액
32A	티셔츠, 로고 있는 흰색, 다양한 사이즈	3묶음	125달러	375달러
32B* *아래 메모 참고*	긴소매 셔츠, 로고 있는 흰색, 다양한 사이즈	3묶음	175달러	525달러
[185]**61**	[185]**검정색 앞치마**, 한 정판, 무릎 길이	5묶음	[185]**60달러**	300달러
118	검정 바지, 다양한 사이즈	2묶음	200달러	400달러
		총액	상품용역세 포함	1,600달러

* [184]**긴소매 셔츠는 재고가 한 묶음밖에 없습니다. 이번 배송에는 한 묶음이 포함되었고 영업일 기준 7일에서 10일 이내에 나머지를 보내겠습니다.** 이 품목들에는 별도의 배송비가 없습니다.

어휘 assorted 다양한 trousers 바지 in stock 재고가 있는

181 추론 / 암시

번역 바빈 앤 어소시에이츠는 어떤 업체이겠는가?
(A) 세탁 서비스
(B) 의류 회사
(C) 출장 요리 업체
(D) 운송 서비스

해설 바빈 앤 어소시에이츠 소속인 바빈 씨에게 보낸 이메일의 첫 번째 단락에서, 중 씨는 자신이 바빈 씨의 회사에서 여러 해 동안 물건을 구매해왔는데(I have been buying items from your company for years) 최근 주문품에 오류가 많아서 놀랐다고 하며, 티셔츠 수량이 잘못된 점(the shipment contained only two packs of T-shirts) 등을 구체적으로 명시했다. 이를 통해 바빈 앤 어소시에이츠가 의류 회사임을 추론할 수 있으므로, (B)가 정답이다.

182 사실 관계 확인

번역 중 씨에 관해 명시된 것은?
(A) 여러 주소를 사용한다.
(B) 익일 배송을 선호한다.
(C) 이전에 바빈 앤 어소시에이츠에서 주문한 적이 있다.
(D) 사업을 확장하고 있다.

해설 이메일의 첫 번째 단락에서 중 씨가 바빈 앤 어소시에이츠에서 여러 해 동안 물건을 구매해 왔는데 이전 주문은 한 번도 오류가 없었다(I have been buying items from your company for years, and my previous orders have never had an error)고 했으므로, (C)가 정답이다.

어휘 expand 확장하다

▸▸ **Paraphrasing** 지문의 **have been buying items from your company for years**
→ 정답의 **has ordered from Babin and Associates before**

183 세부 사항

번역 중 씨가 요청한 것은?
(A) 수정된 카탈로그
(B) 새 로고 디자인
(C) 회신 전화
(D) 다른 장소로 배송

해설 이메일의 두 번째 단락에서 문제를 살펴본 후 자신에게 전화를 줄 것(Can you please look into this matter and give me a call?)을 요청했으므로, (C)가 정답이다.

> ▸▸ **Paraphrasing** 지문의 **give me a call**
> → 정답의 **A return phone call**

184 사실 관계 확인

번역 청구서에 의하면, 긴소매 셔츠에 관해 사실인 것은?

(A) 할인 가에 청구되고 있다.
(B) 다양한 색상으로 나온다.
(C) 일부가 창고에서 손상되었다.
(D) 일부는 나중에 배송될 예정이다.

해설 청구서 하단의 비고(*) 부분에서 긴소매 셔츠는 재고가 한 묶음밖에 없다(We had only one pack of long-sleeved shirts in stock)고 한 후, 이번 배송에는 한 묶음이 포함되었고 영업일 기준 7일에서 10일 이내에 나머지를 보내겠다(We included it ~ will send the others in 7-10 business days)고 했으므로, (D)가 정답이다.

> ▸▸ **Paraphrasing** 지문의 **will send the others in 7-10 business days** → 정답의 **Some of them will be shipped at a later date**

185 연계

번역 중 씨가 발견한 한 가지 문제는?

(A) 바지가 너무 많이 배송되었다.
(B) 앞치마에 잘못된 금액이 청구되었다.
(C) 티셔츠가 잘 맞지 않는다.
(D) 셔츠 로고가 틀렸다.

해설 이메일의 두 번째 단락에서 61번 품목 가격이 카탈로그와 웹사이트에 묶음당 50달러로 나와 있는데 청구된 비용은 달랐다(the price for item number 61 ~, but that was not what I was charged)는 문제점을 언급했는데, 청구서를 보면 61번 품목(Item Number)이 검정색 앞치마(Black aprons)임을 알 수 있고 묶음당 가격이 60달러로 기재되어 있으므로, (B)가 정답이다.

186-190 이메일 + 표 + 시간표

이메일 메시지

수신: 안드레아 윌리엄스 <a.williams@cardiocentre.co.uk>
발신: 사무엘 펜폴드 <s.penfold@cardiocentre.co.uk>
날짜: 8월 2일
제목: 회신: 심장학 학회

윌리엄스 박사님께,

맞습니다, 저는 심장학 학회에 갈 예정이며 회의를 고대하고 있습니다. [186/188]**아쉽게도 저는 8월 5일 오후 3시까지 환자들을 진료해야 해서 당신과 함께 거기로 이동할 수 없습니다.** 첫날 세션은 빠져야 하겠지만 그날 저녁과 이후 이틀 동안은 현장에 있을 겁니다.

언제 저녁 식사 같이할 수 있을까요? [186]**에브림 투르굿이 당신과 함께 하고 있는 영상 진단 기술 관련 연구에 대해 이야기했는데, 이에 관해 당신과 논의할 기회가 있으면 좋겠습니다.** 언제 시간이 되시는지 알려 주세요.

사무엘 펜폴드, 의학박사

어휘 cardiology 심장학 patient 환자 diagnostic 진단의

NTS 기차 **예약** 4JK5 4RN5 4XW8

등급	성인	승객
[187]**일반**	1	안드레아 윌리엄스
출발	**열차 번호**	**왕복 여행**
랭커스터	[189]**EX111**	[187]**포함 안 됨**
도착	**금액**	
맨체스터	[189]**18파운드**	
날짜	**좌석 번호**	**요금**
8월 5일	[187]**배정 안 됨**	[189]**예매**

8월 1일 인쇄

어휘 reservation 예약 passenger 승객 assign 배정하다 advance purchase 예매

기차 시간표 – NTS 기차
[190]**랭커스터발 맨체스터행**

열차 번호	출발 시간	운행 시간	도착 시간	금액
[189]**EX111**	오전 7:00	55분	오전 7:55	[189]**20파운드**
RN902	오전 8:30	1시간 1분	오전 9:31	20파운드
EX224	오전 10:15	1시간 15분	오전 11:30	18파운드
RN516	오후 12:30	1시간 25분	오후 1:55	18파운드
EX670	오후 2:00	1시간 35분	오후 3:35	18파운드
[188]**RN823**	[188]**오후 4:45**	1시간 05분	오후 5:50	20파운드

[189]**여행 24시간 이전에 https://www.ntsrail.co.uk에서 온라인으로 표를 구매하시면 위에 게시된 요금에서 10퍼센트 할인받을 수 있습니다.** 정상가 표는 모든 NTS 기차 판매대에서 구하실 수 있습니다.

어휘 duration 지속[운행] 시간 entitle 자격을 주다 fare 요금

186 추론 / 암시

번역 에브림 투르굿은 누구이겠는가?

(A) 의사
(B) 사무장
(C) 회의 주최자
(D) 고객 서비스 담당 직원

해설 이메일의 두 번째 단락에서 에브림 투르굿이 윌리엄스 씨와 함께 하고 있는 영상 진단 기술 관련 연구에 대해 펜폴드 씨에게 이야기했다(Evrim Turgut was telling me about your research together into diagnostic imaging technologies)고 했는데, 첫 번째 단락을 보면 펜폴드 씨가 의사임(I am seeing patients)을 알 수 있다. 따라서 그와 심장학 학회(cardiology conference)에 참석

할 예정인 윌리엄스 박사와 함께 연구를 진행하는 에브림 투르굿 씨 역시 의사임을 추론할 수 있으므로, (A)가 정답이다.

어휘 organizer 주최자 representative 직원

187 사실 관계 확인

번역 윌리엄스 박사의 여행에 관해 표에 명시된 것은?

(A) 일등석으로 여행할 것이다.
(B) 여행 도중 기차를 갈아탈 것이다.
(C) 돌아오는 여행도 같은 표를 사용할 것이다.
(D) 앉을 자리를 선택할 수 있을 것이다.

해설 표에서 좌석 번호(Seat Number)가 배정되지 않았다(NONE ASSIGNED)고 명시되어 있으므로, (D)가 정답이다. 등급(Class)은 일반(STANDARD)으로, 왕복 여행(Return Trip)은 포함되지 않았다(NOT INCLUDED)고 기재되어 있으므로 (A)와 (C)는 오답이며, (B)는 언급되지 않았으므로 정답이 될 수 없다.

▸▸ Paraphrasing 지문의 Seat Number → 정답의 where to sit
지문의 NONE ASSIGNED
→ 정답의 be able to choose

188 연계

번역 펜폴드 박사의 시간을 볼 때, 어떤 기차를 타겠는가?

(A) EX111
(B) EX224
(C) RN516
(D) RN823

해설 이메일의 첫 번째 단락에서 펜폴드 씨가 8월 5일 오후 3시까지 환자들을 진료해야 해서 윌리엄스 씨와 함께 이동할 수 없다(I will not be able to travel there with you because I am seeing patients until 3 P.M. on 5 August)고 했는데, 기차 시간표에 따르면 오후 3시 이후에 출발하는 열차 번호(Train Number)는 RN823 한 대뿐이므로, 펜폴드 씨가 RN823을 탈 것으로 추론할 수 있다. 따라서 (D)가 정답이다.

189 연계

번역 윌리엄스 박사에 관해 암시된 것은?

(A) 맨체스터에서 일한다.
(B) 정기적으로 기차로 여행한다.
(C) 할인가에 표를 구매했다.
(D) 랭커스터 기차역에서 예매했다.

해설 표에서 윌리엄스 씨가 예매(ADVANCE PURCHASE)한 EX111편의 금액이 18파운드라고 했지만, 열차 시간표를 보면 EX111편은 20파운드라고 명시되어 있다. 열차 시간표 하단에서 여행 24시간 이전에 온라인으로 표를 구매하면 위에 게시된 요금에서 10퍼센트 할인받을 수 있다(Purchasing tickets online ~ to a 10 percent discount off the above-listed fares)고 했으므로, 미리 예매한 윌리엄스 씨가 할인가에 표를 구매했음을 추론할 수 있다. 따라서 (C)가 정답이다.

▸▸ Paraphrasing 지문의 a 10 percent discount off the above-listed fares
→ 정답의 a reduced price

190 사실 관계 확인

번역 일정에 의하면, 기차 여행에 관해 사실인 것은?

(A) 걸리는 시간이 같다.
(B) 오전에는 더 저렴하다.
(C) 같은 목적지에서 끝난다.
(D) 직접 구매해야 한다.

해설 열차 시간표의 윗부분에 '랭커스터발 맨체스터행(Lancaster to Manchester)'이라고 나와 있으므로 모든 열차의 출발지와 목적지가 같다는 것을 확인할 수 있다. 따라서 (C)가 정답이다.

어휘 destination 목적지

191-195 기사 + 이메일 + 양식

포터스빌 예술가를 소개하는 지역 사회 프로젝트

글 로렌스 뒤 부아

포터스빌(5월 21일)－어제 포터스빌 센트럴 파크에서 열린 중소기업 박람회 개막식에서 포터스빌 상공회의소는 공공 예술로 포터스빌 업체들을 홍보하기 위한 지역 사회 계획인 '성공의 이미지'를 발표했다. [191]**이 프로젝트를 통해 지역 예술가들은 지역 사업주들과 협력해 도시 전역의 매장 앞에 독창적인 벽화를 만들 예정이다.**

신청하려는 사업주는 지역 사회 내에서 해당 업체의 역할에 대한 설명서를 제출하고 적어도 2년 동안 업체가 현재 장소에 있었다는 것을 문서로 입증해야 한다. 참여하고 싶은 예술가는 포터스빌과 어떤 인연이 있는지 설명하는 신청서를 작성해야 하며, 본인의 독창적인 예술품 견본을 제출해야 한다.

사업주와 예술가 모두 6월 15일까지 tfreel@pottersvillecoc.gov로 티모시 프릴에게 신청서를 제출해야 한다. [193]**시는 승인받은 용품에 대해 한도 150달러까지 예술가들에게 환급할 예정이다.**

어휘 Chamber of Commerce 상공회의소 initiative (특정한 목적을 위한) 계획 promote 홍보하다 by way of ~을 통해 mural 벽화 storefront 매장 앞 submit 제출하다 description 설명(서) document 문서로 입증하다 participate 참가하다 application 신청(서) reimburse 환급하다 approve 승인하다 supplies 용품 up to ~까지

수신: 티모시 프릴
발신: 하루카 고토
날짜: 6월 24일
제목: '성공의 이미지' 문의
첨부: 초안 #2

프릴 씨께,

이번 주 초 잼 카페에서 성공의 이미지 벽화 프로젝트 디자인에 대해 이야기 나누게 되어 즐거웠습니다. 잼 카페가 다시 문을 연 후로 한 번도

TEST 7

가 보지 못했었는데, 개조가 완료된 모습을 보니 정말 좋았습니다. 사실 카페 주인은 최근 제 그림 하나를 구매해 카페에 전시했습니다. 192/195**제안하신대로, 저는 잼 카페의 인테리어 색상만 포함하도록 색채 배합을 조정했습니다. 더 바꾸고 싶으시면 가능한 한 빨리 알려 주십시오.**

하루카 고토

어휘 renovation 개조 recently 최근 adjust 조정하다 color scheme 색채 배합 additional 추가의

포터스빌 상공회의소 환급 양식

194**양식을 전부 작성하고 구매 기록을 첨부하세요.** 처리에 2주가 소요됩니다.

이름: 하루카 고토
날짜: 6월 25일
행사: 성공의 이미지
내역:
'성공의 이미지' 벽화 프로젝트를 위해 포터스빌 미술용품에서 구입한 용품. 6월 24일자 영수증 사본 첨부함.

제품	단가	수량	총액
195**연녹색 스프레이 페인트**, 18온스 캔	11.99달러	2	23.98달러
195**진녹색 페인트**, 1/2갤런	18.99달러	1	18.99달러
195**짙은 황록색 페인트**, 1갤런	34.99달러	1	34.99달러
화필 세트	24.99달러	1	24.99달러
	193**총액(세금 포함) 111.14달러**		

승인: T. 프릴 **승인 날짜:** 7월 3일

어휘 purchase 구매(품) process 처리하다 receipt 영수증

191 세부 사항

번역 기사에 의하면, 예술가들은 어디에 작품을 전시할 것인가?

(A) 포터스빌 센트럴 파크
(B) 지역 사업체
(C) 상공회의소
(D) 정부 웹사이트

해설 기사의 첫 번째 단락에서 지역 예술가들이 지역 사업주들과 협력해 도시 전역의 매장 앞에 독창적인 벽화를 만들 예정(local artists will work with area business owners to create original murals on storefronts throughout the city)이라고 했으므로, (B)가 정답이다.

192 주제 / 목적

번역 이메일의 목적은?

(A) 디자인 승인 요청
(B) 채용 제안
(C) 미술 재료 주문
(D) 약속 잡기

해설 이메일의 두 번째 단락에서 프릴 씨가 제안한대로 고토 씨가 잼 카페의 인테리어 색상만 포함하도록 색채 배합을 조정했다(As you suggested, I have adjusted the color scheme)고 한 후, 더 바꾸고 싶으면 가능한 한 빨리 알려 줄 것(Please let me know ~ whether you would like me to make additional changes)을 당부했다. 따라서 승인을 요청하기 위한 이메일임을 알 수 있으므로, (A)가 정답이다.

어휘 appointment 약속

193 연계

번역 고토 씨가 구매한 용품에 관해 명시된 것은?

(A) 온라인으로 주문했다.
(B) 포터스빌에서는 판매되지 않는다.
(C) 비용이 전액 환급될 것이다.
(D) 승인이 거절되었다.

해설 기사에서 시는 승인받은 용품에 대해 한도 150달러까지 예술가들에게 환급할 예정(The city will reimburse artists for approved supplies up to a limit of $150)이라고 했는데, 양식을 보면 고토 씨가 용품에 대해 지불한 총액(Total)이 세금을 포함해(including tax) 111.14달러이므로, 고토 씨는 전액 환급을 받을 수 있게 된다. 따라서 (C)가 정답이다.

어휘 approval 승인 deny 거절하다

194 사실 관계 확인

번역 양식에 포함되어야 하는 것은?

(A) 세금 명세서
(B) 디자인 사본
(C) 프로젝트 신청서
(D) 판매 영수증

해설 양식의 상단에서 양식을 전부 작성하고 구매 기록을 첨부할 것(Complete the entire form and attach a record of the purchase)을 요청했으므로, (D)가 정답이다. 참고로, 고토 씨도 내역(Description)을 적는 부분에서 6월 24일자 영수증 사본을 첨부했다(Copy of receipt dated June 24 attached)고 밝혔다.

▸▸ Paraphrasing 지문의 attach → 질문의 needs to be included
지문의 a record of the purchase
→ 정답의 The sales receipt

195 연계

번역 잼 카페에 관해 무엇이 사실이겠는가?

(A) 지역 예술 작품을 판매한다.
(B) 고토 씨가 카페 로고를 디자인했다.
(C) 개보수를 위해 문을 닫았다.
(D) 실내가 녹색이다.

해설 이메일의 두 번째 단락에서 고토 씨가 잼 카페의 인테리어 색상만 포함하도록 색채 배합을 조정했다(I have adjusted the color scheme to include only the colors from Jam Café's interior)고 했는데, 양식을 보면 고토 씨가 구매한 제품(Product)이 연녹색 스프레이 페인트(Soft green spray paint), 진녹색 페

인트(Emerald green paint), 짙은 황록색 페인트(Forest green paint)이므로, 잼 카페의 실내가 녹색일 것으로 추론할 수 있다. 따라서 (D)가 정답이다.

196-200 웹페이지 + 이메일 + 기사

http://www.jaqgarza.com

소식	동영상	사진	약력	메시지 보내기

재크로 더 잘 알려진 재클린 가자는 텍사스 주 오스틴에서 나고 자랐다. 어린 시절 가자 씨는 춤추는 것과 운동을 좋아했다. 특히 농구를 잘했는데, 고등학교 졸업 이후 지역 오스틴 팀에서 프로 계약을 제안 받았다. 196**그러나 그녀는 대신 대학에서 경제학 학위를 받기로 선택했다. 가자 씨는 학위를 마친 뒤 여전히 자신이 농구를 할 때가 가장 행복하다는 것을 인정하고 마침내 오스틴 팀에 입단했다.**

가자 씨는 기량과 스피드뿐 아니라 친절함과 연대의식으로도 유명하다. 코트 밖에서 그녀는 '독서는 산들바람'이라는 단체를 설립했다. 이 단체는 인쇄 도서, 오디오 도서, 청소년 정기간행물, 그리고 디지털 독서 장비를 위한 자금이 부족한 도서관에 자원을 제공한다. 197**이 단체는 부모가 안경을 사 주기 힘든 아이들에게 안경도 제공한다.**

어휘 contract 계약(서) degree 학위 economics 경제학 admit 인정하다 found 설립하다 organization 단체 resource 자원 limited 부족한 periodical 정기간행물 device 장비

수신: 앙리 들롱 〈hdelon@bonvue.ca〉
발신: 아니타 와이어트 〈awyatt@bonvue.ca〉
제목: 유명인사 대변인
날짜: 3월 18일

앙리 씨께:

약속대로, 저는 미국 시장으로 진출하기 위해 우리와 함께 일할 수 있는 유명 홍보대사를 조사했습니다. 재클린 가자는 텍사스 주 오스틴 출신의 프로 농구 선수로, 배경도 흥미롭습니다. 197**그녀의 비영리 재단은 아이들의 읽고 쓰는 능력에 초점을 맞추고 있어 우리 봉뷔의 제품과 자연스러운 연결 고리를 가지고 있습니다.** 그녀의 웹사이트인 www.jaqgarza.com을 방문하면 그녀에 대해 자세히 알 수 있습니다. 만약 이 아이디어를 승인하신다면, 제가 그녀의 에이전트에게 연락해 보수를 협상하겠습니다.

198**오늘 아침에 로이 씨와도 이야기를 나눴습니다.** 198/199**그의 말에 따르면 홍보 캠페인이 일시적으로 지연되었기 때문에 마케팅부에서 6월까지는 대변인을 준비시킬 필요가 없다고 합니다.**

아니타

어휘 celebrity 유명 인사 spokesperson 대변인 endorser 홍보대사 expansion 확장 nonprofit 비영리의 foundation 재단 literacy 읽고 쓰는 능력 approve 승인하다 negotiate 협상하다 compensation 보수, 보상금 publicity 홍보 temporarily 일시적으로 line A up A를 준비시키다

미국으로 진출하는 봉뷔

오스틴(199**5월 11일)** – 프랑스 디자이너 안경 회사인 봉뷔가 미국 시장 진출을 발표했다. 199**오스틴에서 활약하는 농구 스타 재클린 "재크" 가자가 이 회사의 유명인 홍보대사로 계약을 맺었다.** 가자 씨가 협업을 알리는 비디오 영상이 월요일 공개되었고, 다음 주부터 전체 광고가 공개될 예정이다.

200**파리에서 설립되고 파리에 본사를 둔 이 안경 회사는 현재 CEO인 마틴 올리베이라가 이끌고 있다.** 봉뷔는 8년 전 오타와에 소매점을 열어 캐나다로 사업을 확장했다. 이 회사의 인기 있는 안경과 선글라스는 이제 미국 전역의 매장에서 판매될 것이다.

어휘 release 공개하다 roll out 발표하다 currently 현재

196 세부 사항

번역 웹페이지에 의하면, 가자 씨가 프로팀 입단 전에 받은 것은?

(A) 대학 학위
(B) 기증 도서
(C) 댄스 강좌
(D) 프로젝트 자금

해설 웹페이지의 첫 번째 단락에서 가자 씨는 프랑스 입단 제의를 받았지만 대학에서 경제학 학위(a university degree)를 받기로 했고, 학위를 마친 뒤에야 자신이 여전히 농구를 할 때가 가장 행복하다는 것을 인정하고 마침내 오스틴 팀에 입단했다(After completing her degree, Ms. Garza ~ finally joined the Austin team)고 했다. 따라서 (A)가 정답이다.

197 연계

번역 와이어트 씨가 가자 씨를 적합한 유명인 홍보대사로 생각한 이유는?

(A) 그녀의 자선 단체가 안경을 나누어준다.
(B) 팀워크 기술이 뛰어나다.
(C) 봉뷔 본사가 오스틴에 있다.
(D) 봉뷔가 농구복을 만든다.

해설 웹페이지의 마지막 문장에서 가자 씨가 설립한 단체가 부모가 안경을 사 주기 힘든 아이들에게 안경도 제공한다(It even provides glasses to children ~ on their own)고 하였는데, 와이어트 씨가 쓴 이메일의 첫 번째 단락을 보면 가자 씨의 비영리 재단이 아이들의 읽고 쓰는 능력에 초점을 맞추고 있어 봉뷔의 제품과 자연스러운 연결 고리를 가지고 있다(Her nonprofit foundation, ~ has a natural connection to our products at Bonvue)고 쓰여 있다. 이러한 점이 와이어트 씨가 가자 씨를 적합한 유명인 홍보대사로 생각한 이유라고 볼 수 있으므로 정답은 (A)이다.

▸▸ **Paraphrasing** 지문의 **provides glasses**
→ 정답의 **distributes eyeglasses**

TEST 7

198 추론 / 암시

번역 이메일이 로이 씨에 관해 암시하는 것은?

(A) 가자 씨의 연예 부문 대리인이다.
(B) 가자 씨의 웹페이지를 방문한 적이 있다.
(C) 전직 봉뷔 직원이다.
(D) 와이어트 씨 및 들롱 씨와 함께 일한다.

해설 이메일의 두 번째 단락에서 와이어트 씨가 로이 씨와도 이야기를 나눴다(I also spoke with Mr. Roy)고 한 후, 로이 씨가 한 말(Marketing does not need us to have the spokesperson lined up until June)을 인용하여(He says) 들롱 씨에게 전달했으므로, 로이 씨가 와이어트 씨 및 들롱 씨와 함께 일한다고 추론할 수 있다. 따라서 (D)가 정답이다.

199 연계

번역 가자 씨에 관해 명시된 것은?

(A) 봉뷔의 오랜 고객이다.
(B) 봉뷔에서 돈을 받지 않는다.
(C) 최근 영화에 출연했다.
(D) 일정보다 앞서 봉뷔 홍보 캠페인에 합류했다.

해설 이메일의 두 번째 단락에서 홍보 캠페인의 일시적 지연으로 인해 마케팅부에서 6월까지는 대변인을 준비시킬 필요가 없다(Marketing does not need us to have the spokesperson lined up until June)고 했지만, 5월 11일자 기사의 첫 번째 단락에서 오스틴에서 활약하는 농구 스타 재클린 "재크" 가자가 봉뷔의 유명인 홍보대사로 계약을 맺었다(Austin-based basketball star ~ Garza has signed up as the company's celebrity endorser)고 했으므로, 가자 씨가 일정보다 앞서 계약을 맺었다는 것을 알 수 있다. 따라서 (D)가 정답이다.

어휘 ahead of schedule 일정보다 앞서

▸▸ **Paraphrasing** 지문의 **signed up** → 정답의 **joined**

200 세부 사항

번역 기사에 포함된 봉뷔에 관한 정보는?

(A) 사업을 해 오고 있는 햇수
(B) 본사 위치
(C) 광고 캠페인 슬로건
(D) 최고 인기 상품의 가격

해설 기사의 두 번째 단락에서 '파리에서 설립되고 파리에 본사를 둔 안경 회사(Founded and headquartered in Paris, the eyewear company)'라는 정보를 제공했으므로, (B)가 정답이다.

▸▸ **Paraphrasing** 지문의 **headquartered in Paris**
→ 정답의 **The location of its head office**

기출 TEST 8

101 (D)	102 (C)	103 (B)	104 (D)	105 (A)
106 (D)	107 (D)	108 (C)	109 (B)	110 (A)
111 (C)	112 (B)	113 (C)	114 (A)	115 (B)
116 (C)	117 (B)	118 (D)	119 (B)	120 (B)
121 (D)	122 (D)	123 (B)	124 (D)	125 (C)
126 (A)	127 (D)	128 (B)	129 (C)	130 (A)
131 (C)	132 (A)	133 (B)	134 (B)	135 (D)
136 (D)	137 (A)	138 (B)	139 (C)	140 (A)
141 (D)	142 (C)	143 (C)	144 (A)	145 (B)
146 (D)	147 (A)	148 (C)	149 (A)	150 (C)
151 (B)	152 (D)	153 (A)	154 (B)	155 (C)
156 (A)	157 (D)	158 (A)	159 (D)	160 (B)
161 (D)	162 (B)	163 (B)	164 (D)	165 (B)
166 (A)	167 (A)	168 (D)	169 (D)	170 (A)
171 (C)	172 (C)	173 (D)	174 (D)	175 (C)
176 (B)	177 (C)	178 (C)	179 (A)	180 (D)
181 (C)	182 (A)	183 (B)	184 (D)	185 (C)
186 (A)	187 (A)	188 (C)	189 (D)	190 (B)
191 (A)	192 (B)	193 (A)	194 (C)	195 (C)
196 (B)	197 (A)	198 (D)	199 (D)	200 (C)

PART 5

101 동사 어형 _ to + 동사원형

해설 빈칸 앞의 to를 전치사로 볼 경우 동명사인 (B) increasing이, to부정사의 to로 볼 경우 동사원형인 (D) increase가 빈칸에 들어갈 수 있다. 또한 빈칸은 명사구 their market share를 목적어로 취하고, 빈칸을 포함한 구문이 동사구 have entered를 수식한다. '시장 점유율을 높이기 위해 전략적 제휴에 들어갔다'라는 내용이 되어야 자연스러우므로, 빈칸 앞의 to는 부사적 용법으로 쓰여 목적을 나타내는 to부정사의 to이다. 따라서 동사원형 (D) increase가 정답이다.

번역 케널렉사와 이븐손사는 시장 점유율을 높이기 위해 전략적 제휴에 들어갔다.

어휘 strategic 전략적인 increase 올리다 market share 시장 점유율

102 형용사 어휘

해설 빈칸은 명사 practices를 수식하는 형용사 자리로, 빈칸 앞 부사 environmentally의 수식을 받는다. 따라서 빈칸에는 환경과 관련된 관행(practices)을 가장 잘 묘사하는 형용사가 들어가야 하므로, environmentally와 함께 '환경친화적인'이라는 의미를 나타내는 (C) friendly(친화적인, 우호적인)가 정답이다. (A) exposed는 '노출된', (B) communal은 '공동의, 공용의', (D) considerable은 '상당한, 많은'이라는 뜻으로 문맥상 빈칸에 적절하지 않다.

번역 글렌워 유기농 농장은 환경친화적인 관행으로 다른 농장들에 비해 두드러진다.

어휘 stand out 두드러지다, 뛰어나다

103 명사 자리 _ 동사의 주어

해설 빈칸이 소유격 Our와 be동사 is 사이에 있으므로, 보기에서 is의 주어 역할을 할 수 있는 명사 (B) division과 동명사 (D) dividing 중 하나를 선택해야 한다. be동사 뒤 형용사 responsible이 주어인 빈칸을 보충 설명하므로, 문맥상 책임을 맡을 수 있는 주체가 빈칸에 들어가야 한다. 따라서 '부서'라는 의미의 명사 (B) division이 정답이다.

번역 우리 부서는 생산 중 품질 관리를 검토하는 일을 맡고 있다.

어휘 be responsible for ~을 맡다 perform 수행하다 quality-control 품질 관리 production 생산

104 전치사 어휘

해설 빈칸 뒤 명사구 further notice를 목적어로 취하는 전치사 자리로, 빈칸을 포함한 전치사구는 동사구 will be closed를 수식한다. 따라서 빈칸에는 will be closed와 further notice를 가장 잘 연결하는 전치사가 들어가야 한다. '추후 통지가 있을 때까지 휴업한다'라는 내용이 되어야 자연스러우므로, '~까지'라는 의미의 시간 전치사 (D) until이 정답이다. until further notice는 '추후 통지가 있을 때까지'라는 의미의 관용적인 표현으로 묶어서 기억하는 것이 좋다.

번역 생산 설비의 기계 고장으로 피지 보틀러스는 추후 통지가 있을 때까지 휴업합니다.

어휘 mechanical failure 기계 고장 facility 설비

105 재귀대명사 _ 재귀 용법

해설 빈칸은 전치사 among의 목적어 역할을 하는 자리이므로, 보기에서 목적어 자리에 들어갈 수 있는 재귀대명사 (A) themselves, 소유대명사 (B) theirs, 목적격 인칭대명사 (C) them 중 하나를 선택해야 한다. 주어인 Interviewees를 받아서 '면접 대상자들(interviewees)끼리, 자기들끼리'라는 말이 되어야 자연스러우므로, 주어와 목적어가 동일할 경우 쓰이는 재귀대명사 (A) themselves가 정답이다.

번역 면접 대상자들은 안내실에서 기다리는 동안 서로 이야기하지 말라는 요청을 받는다.

어휘 interviewee 면접 대상자

106 부사 어휘

해설 빈칸은 전치사구 after returning from a trip을 강조하는 부사 자리로, 빈칸을 포함한 전치사구가 to부정사구 to submit expense reports를 수식한다. 따라서 전치사 after를 강조하여 '직후'라는 의미를 나타내는 (D) soon이 정답이다. 참고로 (A) very는 형용사, 부사를 앞에서 수식하고, (B) enough(충분히)는 형용사, 부사, 동사를 뒤에서 수식한다. (C) rather는 '다소, 약간'이라는 부사로 문맥상 빈칸에 적절하지 않다.

번역 경리부에서는 출장에서 돌아온 직후 경비 보고서를 제출해야 된다는 것을 전 직원께 다시 알려 드립니다.

어휘 accounting department 경리부 submit 제출하다 expense 경비

107 부사 자리 _ 동사 수식

해설 빈칸이 주어 Olayinka Boutique와 동사 hosts 사이에 있으므로, 빈칸에는 동사 hosts를 수식하는 부사가 들어가야 한다. 따라서 '가끔, 때때로'라는 의미의 부사 (D) occasionally가 정답이다. (A) occasion과 (B) occasions는 명사, (C) occasional은 형용사로 품사상 빈칸에 들어갈 수 없다.

번역 올라인카 부티크는 이따금 단골 클럽 회원을 위한 특별한 쇼핑 행사를 주최한다.

어휘 host 주최하다 occasion 경우, 행사 occasional 가끔의

108 형용사 어휘

해설 빈칸은 주어 the energy-saving ideas의 주격 보어 역할을 하는 형용사 자리로, 빈칸을 포함한 주절은 전치사구 For homeowners seeking to reduce their electricity bills의 수식을 받는다. 따라서 빈칸에는 에너지 절약 아이디어가 전기 요금을 줄이려는 주택 소유자들에게 미치게 될 영향을 가장 잘 묘사하는 형용사가 들어가야 하므로, '도움이 되는'이라는 의미의 (C) helpful이 정답이다. (A) lengthy는 '너무 긴, 장황한', (B) immediate는 '즉각적인, 직속의', (D) perceptive는 '통찰력 있는'이라는 뜻으로 문맥상 빈칸에 적절하지 않다.

번역 전기 요금을 줄이려는 주택 소유자들에게, 이 소책자의 에너지 절약 아이디어는 도움이 될 것이다.

어휘 seek to ~하려고 하다 reduce 줄이다 electricity bill 전기 요금 brochure 소책자

109 동사 어형 _ 태

해설 빈칸은 주어 The Delmar Highway Department의 동사 자리이므로, 보기에서 능동태 동사인 (B) maintains와 수동태 동사인 (D) is maintained 중 하나를 선택해야 한다. 빈칸이 명사구 an online list를 목적어로 취하고, 주어인 The Delmar Highway Department는 온라인 목록을 관리하는 주체이므로, 능동태 동사 (B) maintains가 정답이다. 명사 (A) maintenance(유지 보수)와 동명사/현재 분사 (C) maintaining은 품사상 빈칸에 들어갈 수 없다.

번역 델마 고속도로 관리국은 현재 도로 폐쇄에 대한 온라인 목록을 관리하고 있다.

어휘 maintain 유지하다, 관리하다 current 현재의

110 전치사 자리

해설 빈칸 뒤 동명사구(reducing staff)를 목적어로 취하는 전치사 자리로, 빈칸을 포함한 전치사구가 콤마 뒤 절(management made the decision)을 수식한다. 따라서 '~ 대신에'라는 의미의 전치사 (A) Rather than이 정답이다. 참고로 rather than은 '~라기보다는'이라는 의미의 접속사로도 쓰일 수 있다. (B) Whether(~인지 아닌지)는 명사절 접속사, (C) Just as(~하는 대로, ~한 것처럼)는 부사절 접속사, (D) Namely(즉, 다시 말해)는 부사로 품사상 빈칸에 들어갈 수 없다.

번역 경영진은 직원을 감축하는 대신 관리직의 보너스를 줄이기로 결정했다.

어휘 reduce 줄이다 management 경영진 decision 결정 decrease 줄이다 administrative 관리의

111 부사 자리 _ 동사 수식

해설 빈칸은 주격 관계대명사 which가 이끄는 관계절의 동사 arch를 수식하는 부사 자리이므로, '우아하게, 기품 있게'라는 의미의 부사 (C) gracefully가 정답이다. (A) graceful(우아한)은 형용사, (B) grace(우아함, 은혜)와 (D) graces(예의; 장식하다)는 명사/동사로 품사상 빈칸에 들어갈 수 없다.

번역 매우 우아하게 아치형을 그리는 출입구는 유서 깊은 더스텐 빌딩의 개보수 작업 도중 온전히 남아 있었다.

어휘 intact 온전한 renovation 개보수

112 동사 어휘 _ 과거분사

해설 be동사 was와 결합하여 주어 Ms. Maeda를 가장 잘 설명하는 과거분사를 선택하는 문제이다. that이 이끄는 절(that her art submission was used on the cover)이 빈칸의 이유나 근거를 나타내므로, 빈칸에는 자신이 제출한 미술품이 표지에 사용되자 마에다 씨가 느낀 감정으로 어울리는 어휘가 들어가야 한다. 따라서 (B) flattered(기뻐하는, 우쭐한)가 정답이다. (A) performed(수행된), (C) welcomed(환영받는), (D) challenged(도전받는, 어려움이 있는)는 문맥상 빈칸에 적절하지 않다.

번역 마에다 씨는 자신이 제출한 미술품이 회사의 연례 보고서 표지에 사용되자 기뻐했다.

어휘 submission 제출 annual 연례의

113 명사 어휘

해설 빈칸은 정관사 The, 형용사 primary 뒤에 이어지는 명사 자리로, be동사 is의 주어 역할을 한다. 또한 빈칸이 주격 보어 역할을 하는 명사절(whether the cost of the car repair is reasonable)과 동격 관계를 이루므로, 빈칸에는 자동차 수리 비용이 합당한 지의 여부와 상응하는 명사가 들어가야 한다. 따라서 primary의 수식을 받아 '가장 중요한 문제'라는 의미를 완성하는 (C) concern이 정답이다. (A) method는 '방법, 방식', (B) relation은 '관계, 관련성', (D) source는 '원천, 근원'이라는 뜻으로 문맥상 빈칸에 적절하지 않다.

번역 가장 중요한 문제는 수반된 노동량을 고려해 보았을 때 자동차 수리 비용이 합당한가의 여부이다.

어휘 primary 가장 중요한, 주된 repair 수리 reasonable 합당한 amount 양 labor 노동 involved 수반된, 관련된

114 형용사 자리_명사 수식

해설 빈칸이 부정관사 an과 복합명사 client base 사이에 있으므로, 빈칸에는 client base를 수식하는 형용사가 들어가야 한다. 따라서 '인상적인, 감동적인'이라는 의미의 형용사 (A) impressive가 정답이다. (B) impress(깊은 인상을 주다)와 (D) impresses는 동사, (C) impressively(인상적으로)는 부사로 품사상 빈칸에 들어갈 수 없다.

번역 노보 금융은 단기간에 인상적인 고객층을 구축했다.

어휘 client base 고객층

115 동사 어휘

해설 「동사+목적어(all employees)+목적격 보어(to wear formal business attire)」의 구조로 쓰일 수 있는 타동사를 선택하는 문제이다. '전 직원에게 정장을 입도록 요구한다'라는 내용이 되어야 자연스러우므로, '요구하다, 필요로 하다'라는 의미의 (B) require가 정답이다. (A) monitor는 '감시하다, 상태를 살피다', (C) confirm은 '확인하다, 확실히 하다', (D) include는 '포함하다'라는 뜻으로 문맥상 어색하며, 구조상으로도 불가능하다.

번역 당사는 전 직원에게 사무실에서 고객 면담 시 정장을 입도록 요구한다.

어휘 formal business attire 정장

116 상관접속사

해설 빈칸에는 nor와 함께 상관접속사를 이루어 Ms. Chang과 Mr. Kao를 연결해 주는 단어가 들어가야 하므로, (C) Neither가 정답이다. 상관접속사 Neither A nor B는 'A도 B도 아닌'이라는 의미로 쓰인다. 참고로 (A) Both는 both A and B 형태로 쓰여 'A, B 둘다'라는 의미를 나타낸다.

번역 창 씨와 카오 씨 둘다 프로젝트 제안서를 요약한 이메일을 받지 못했다.

어휘 receive 받다 proposal 제안(서)

117 부사 어휘

해설 to부정사의 동사원형 work를 가장 잘 수식하는 부사를 선택하는 문제이다. 접속사 rather than(~하기보다는)이 work -------와 travel to the office를 연결하므로, 이 둘이 서로 반대되는 의미를 나타내야 한다. 따라서 빈칸에는 사무실에 오지 않고 근무하는 방식을 묘사한 부사가 들어가야 자연스러우므로, '원격으로, 멀리서'라는 의미의 (B) remotely가 정답이다. (A) carefully는 '주의 깊게', (C) eventually는 '결국, 마침내', (D) closely는 '면밀히'라는 뜻으로 문맥상 빈칸에 적절하지 않다.

번역 악천후일 경우, 직원들은 사무실로 오지 말고 원격으로 일하도록 권장됩니다.

어휘 inclement 궂은 be encouraged to ~하도록 권장받다

118 동사 어휘

해설 빈칸은 주어 Long-term maintenance fees의 동사 자리로, 전치사구 according to the type of industrial printing machine purchased의 수식을 받는다. 따라서 빈칸에는 주어 및 전치사구와 가장 잘 어울리는 자동사가 들어가야 한다. 구매한 공업용 인쇄기의 종류에 따라 장기 유지 보수비가 좌우된다고 볼 수 있으므로, '다르다, 다양하다'라는 의미의 (D) vary가 정답이다. (A) copy(복사하다), (B) repair(수리하다), (C) support(지지하다, 지원하다)는 문맥상 어색하며, 구조상으로도 불가능하다.

번역 장기 유지 보수비는 구매한 공업용 인쇄기의 종류에 따라 다르다.

어휘 long-term 장기적인 maintenance 유지 보수 according to ~에 따라 purchase 구매하다

119 형용사 자리_목적격 보어

해설 빈칸은 「made+가목적어(it)+목적격 보어+진목적어(that ~ approval)」의 구조에서 목적어를 보충 설명하는 형용사 자리로, 부사 absolutely의 수식을 받는다. 따라서 '분명한, 확실한'이라는 의미의 형용사인 (B) clear가 정답이다.

번역 권 씨는 채용 결정에는 자신의 승인이 필요하다는 점을 전적으로 분명히 했다.

어휘 absolutely 전적으로, 정말로 decision 결정 approval 승인

120 동사 어형_태

해설 동사구 is being 뒤에 올 수 있는 알맞은 형태를 선택하는 문제로, 전치사구 by Chung-He Park의 수식을 받는다. 주어 Sookie Choi's latest children's book은 삽화가 넣어지는 대상이므로, 수동의 의미를 내포한 과거분사 (B) illustrated가 정답이다. 능동의 의미를 내포한 현재분사 (A) illustrating과 동사 (D) illustrates는 is being 뒤에 들어갈 수 없고, (C) illustration은 명사로 주어 Sookie Choi's latest children's book과 동격 관계를 이루지 않으므로 빈칸에 적절하지 않다.

번역 숙희 최의 최신 아동 도서에는 청희 박이 삽화를 넣고 있다.

어휘 latest 최신의 illustrate 삽화를 넣다

121 명사 어휘

해설 빈칸은 동사구 is hosting의 목적어 역할을 하는 명사 자리이므로, 빈칸에는 주최될 수 있는 행사 관련 명사가 들어가야 한다. 따라서 '환영회'라는 의미의 (D) reception이 정답이다. (A) scene은 '장면, 현장', (B) society는 '사회, 단체', (C) formality는 '절차, 격식'이라는 뜻으로 문맥상 빈칸에 적절하지 않다.

번역 스톤포트 갤러리는 조각가 패브리스 페핀의 작품을 소개하는 리셉션을 다음 주에 주최한다.

어휘 showcase 소개하다 sculptor 조각가

122 동사 어휘

해설 빈칸은 to부정사의 관용 표현 in order to 뒤에 이어지는 동사원형 자리이다. 빈칸을 포함한 to부정사구가 동사구 will run 5 kilometers every other day를 수식하므로, 빈칸에는 하프 마라톤을 위해 매일 5킬로미터를 달리는 이유 또는 목적을 나타내는 동사가 들어가야 한다. 따라서, '훈련하다, 연마하다'라는 의미의 (D) train이 정답이다. (A) translate(번역하다), (B) listen(듣다), (C) wait(기다리다)는 문맥상 빈칸에 적절하지 않다.

번역 소토 씨는 리즈버그사 챌린지 하프 마라톤 경기를 대비해 훈련을 목적으로 이틀에 한 번 5킬로미터를 달릴 예정이다.

어휘 every other day 하루 걸러

123 부사 자리 _ 동사 수식

해설 빈칸은 to부정사의 동사원형 behave를 수식하는 부사 자리이므로, '책임감 있게'라는 의미의 부사 (B) responsibly가 정답이다. (A) responsible(책임이 있는)은 형용사, (C) responsibility(책임)와 (D) responsibleness(책임을 짐)는 명사로, 품사상 빈칸에 들어갈 수 없다.

번역 모든 직원은 회사 업무차 여행 시 책임감 있게 처신해야 한다.

어휘 be expected to ~할 것으로 기대되다, ~해야 한다 behave 처신하다 on business 업무차

124 부사절 접속사 _ 어휘

해설 빈칸은 완전한 절(he is now retired)을 이끄는 접속사 자리로, 빈칸을 포함한 절이 콤마 뒤 주절(Mr. Matilla is able to pursue his hobby ~)을 수식한다. 따라서 보기에서 부사절 접속사인 (C) When과 (D) Because 중 하나를 선택해야 한다. 은퇴했기 때문에 취미 활동에 심취할 수 있다는 내용이 되어야 자연스러우므로, 이유를 나타내는 부사절 접속사 (D) Because가 정답이다. (A) During(~하는 동안)은 전치사, (B) Therefore(그러므로)는 접속부사로 완전한 절을 이끌 수 없으므로 빈칸에 들어갈 수 없다.

번역 마티야 씨는 이제 은퇴했기 때문에 취미인 목공에 심취할 수 있다.

어휘 retire 은퇴하다 pursue (취미 등에) 심취하다, 추구하다 woodworking 목공

125 명사 자리 _ 어휘

해설 빈칸은 동사구 will receive의 주어 역할을 하는 명사 자리로, 전치사구 for press coverage의 수식을 받는다. 따라서 보기에서 명사인 (B) Application(신청, 지원)과 (C) Applicants(지원자들, 신청자들), 명사와 같은 역할을 할 수 있는 동명사 (D) Applying 중 하나를 선택해야 한다. 공식 답변을 받을 주체는 사람이므로, (C) Applicants가 정답이다. (A) Applies는 동사로 품사상 빈칸에 들어갈 수 없다.

번역 음악 축제 언론 보도 신청자들은 6월 30일까지 공식 답변을 받을 것이다.

어휘 press coverage 언론 보도 response 답변

126 전치사 자리 _ 어휘

해설 빈칸 뒤 동명사 구문(switching over to the new software system ~)을 목적어로 취하는 전치사 자리이므로, 보기에서 전치사인 (A) before와 (B) of 중 하나를 선택해야 한다. 내용상 자료 백업은 신규 소프트웨어 시스템으로 전환하기 전에 선행되어야 하므로, '~ 전에'라는 의미의 (A) before가 정답이다.

번역 모든 직원은 8월 5일 신규 소프트웨어 시스템으로 전환하기 전에 중요한 데이터를 백업해야 한다.

어휘 crucial 중요한

127 명사 어휘

해설 빈칸은 전치사 of의 목적어 역할을 하는 명사 자리로, 전치사구 of the contents의 수식을 받는다. 상관접속사 as well as가 the production date와 the place of ------- of the contents를 연결하고 있으므로, 빈칸을 포함한 명사구는 생산일과 더불어 라벨에 표기되어야 할 대상을 나타내야 한다. 따라서 the place of와 함께 '원산지'라는 표현을 완성하는 (D) origin(기원, 원천)이 정답이다. (A) importance(중요성), (B) safety(안전), (C) foundation(토대, 기초)은 문맥상 빈칸에 적절하지 않다.

번역 각 상자의 라벨에는 생산일뿐만 아니라 내용물의 원산지도 표시해야 한다.

어휘 indicate 표시하다 place of origin 원산지 contents 내용물

128 인칭대명사의 격 _ 주격

해설 빈칸은 접속사 that이 이끄는 명사절에서 동사구 would deliver의 주어 역할을 하므로, 보기에서 주격 인칭대명사인 (B) she와 소유대명사 (C) hers 중 하나를 선택해야 한다. 계약을 이행하는 주체는 문장의 주어인 Ms. Jha이므로, Ms. Jha를 대신하는 주격 인칭대명사 (B) she가 정답이다. 소유격/목적격인 (A) her와 재귀대명사 (D) herself는 주어 자리에 들어갈 수 없다.

번역 자 씨는 고객에게 자신이 그날 오후에 계약서를 전달하겠다고 장담했다.

어휘 assure 장담하다 deliver 전달하다 contract 계약(서)

129 형용사 자리 _ 주격 보어

해설 빈칸은 동사 appeared 뒤에서 주어 management를 보충 설명하는 주격 보어 자리로, 전치사구 to the idea of increasing the staff's wages의 수식을 받는다. 동사 appear는 형용사 보어를 취해 '~처럼 보이다'라는 의미로 쓰이므로, 형용사 (C) agreeable이 정답이다. 여기서 agreeable은 전치사 to와 함께 쓰여 '~에 동의하는'이라는 뜻을 나타낸다.

번역 협상 도중, 경영진은 직원 임금 인상에 선뜻 동의하는 듯했다.

어휘 negotiation 협상 management 경영진 increase 인상하다 wage 임금

130 전치사 어휘

해설 빈칸 뒤 명사구 several departments를 목적어로 취하는 전치사 자리로, 빈칸을 포함한 전치사구는 명사 Employees를 수식한다. 따라서 빈칸에는 Employees와 several departments를 가장 잘 연결하는 전치사가 들어가야 한다. 여러 부서에 속한 직원들 전부가 비용을 최소화하라는 권유를 받았다는 내용이 되어야 자연스러우므로, '~에 걸쳐'라는 의미의 (A) across가 정답이다. (B) into(~ 안으로), (C) between(~ 사이에), (D) despite(~에도 불구하고)는 문맥상 빈칸에 적절하지 않다.

번역 여러 부서에 걸친 직원들이 비용을 최소화하라는 권유를 받았다.

어휘 be encouraged to ~하도록 권장받다 minimize 최소화하다

PART 6

131-134 광고

이탈리아는 박물관, 정원, 아름다운 풍경, 그리고 훌륭한 음식 등 제공할 것이 아주 풍성합니다. 단 한 번의 저렴한 가격에, 올-이탈리아 패스로 전국에 걸쳐 100여 곳이 넘는 인기 명소를 이용할 수 있습니다. 패스는 많이 [131]**쓸수록** 더욱 값어치를 합니다.

[132]**이 특가 상품은 국외 방문객만 이용할 수 있습니다.** 패스는 고국을 떠나기 전에 온라인으로 구입해야 하며, 첫 번째 명소를 방문할 때 활성화됩니다. 패스는 21일 동안 [133]**유효합니다.**

패스를 구입하면 장식용 여행 핀과 컬러판 기념품 안내책자[134]**도** 포함됩니다.

어휘 scenery 풍경 access 접근 attraction 명소 purchase 구매하다 activate 활성화하다 decorative 장식용의 souvenir 기념품

131 동사 어형 _ 시제

해설 빈칸은 「the 비교급+주어+동사, the 비교급+주어+동사」의 구조로 쓰여 '~하면 할수록 점점 더 …하다'라는 의미를 나타내는 문장에서 주어 you 뒤에 오는 동사 자리이다. 보기에서 현재 동사 (C) use와 과거 동사 (D) used 중 하나를 선택해야 하는데, 두 번째 절의 동사가 미래 시제(will get)이므로, 빈칸에는 현재 동사가 들어가야 자연스럽다. 따라서 (C) use가 정답이다.

132 문맥에 맞는 문장 고르기

번역 (A) 이 특가 상품은 국외 방문객만 이용할 수 있습니다.
(B) 관광객들은 한 주에 모든 장소를 볼 수는 없습니다.
(C) 여름이면 명소들이 아주 붐빕니다.
(D) 몇몇 회사가 관광 가이드를 제공합니다.

해설 빈칸 앞 단락에서 명소 방문시 사용 가능한 올-이탈리아 패스(All-Italy Pass)를 소개했고, 빈칸 뒤 문장에서 패스는 고국을 떠나기 전에 온라인으로 구입해야 하며, 첫 번째 명소를 방문할 때 활성화된다(Passes must be purchased online ~ when you visit your first attraction)고 했으므로, 빈칸에도 패스와 관련된 내용이 들어가야 문맥상 자연스럽다. 따라서 패스의 이용 대상(international visitors)을 언급한 (A)가 정답이다.

어휘 offer 특가(상품), 할인 available 이용할 수 있는 crowded 붐비는

133 형용사 어휘

해설 빈칸은 주어 They(Passes)의 주격 보어 역할을 하는 형용사 자리로, 기간을 나타내는 전치사구 for 21 days의 수식을 받는다. 패스가 활성화된 후 21일간 사용 가능할 거라는 내용의 문장이 되어야 하므로, '유효한, 타당한'이라는 의미의 (B) valid가 정답이다. (A) open은 '열려 있는, 개방된', (C) constant는 '한결같은, 끊임없는', (D) ordinary는 '보통의, 평범한'이라는 뜻으로 문맥상 빈칸에 적절하지 않다.

134 부사 어휘

해설 빈칸에 적합한 부사를 선택하는 문제이다. 빈칸 앞 문장에서는 패스의 유효 기간(They will remain valid for 21 days)을, 빈칸을 포함한 문장에서는 패스의 혜택(Purchase of the pass ~ full-color souvenir guidebook)을 언급했으므로, 빈칸에는 추가 정보를 말할 때 쓰는 부사가 들어가야 글의 흐름이 자연스러워진다. 따라서 (B) also(또한)가 정답이다. (A) besides도 '게다가, 또한'이라는 의미이지만, 주로 문두에서 이유나 주장을 추가적으로 설명할 때 쓰인다. (C) after(~ 뒤에), (D) beyond(그 너머에)는 문맥상 빈칸에 적합하지 않다.

135-138 이메일

수신: 웨이이 샨 <wshan@strategiccomm.org>
발신: 아빈 플로레스 <aflores@floresmanufacturing.com>
날짜: 4월 5일
제목: 3월 28일 워크숍

샨 씨께,

앨라나 휴즈가 3월 28일 당사 본사에서 수행한 워크숍에 대해 [135]**감사**드리기 위해 메일을 씁니다. 일부 직원들은 업무 환경에서 즉석으로 하는 연수의 유용성에 관해 우려를 [136]**표하기도 했습니다.** 그런데 바로 이 직원들이 하루 종일 꼬박 참여했고 후속 교육 가능성까지 문의했습니다. 우리는 워크숍의 유효성을 더 잘 측정하기 위해 [137]**이후** 참가자들에게 회사의 평가 양식을 작성하도록 요청했습니다. 결과는 대체로 긍정적이었고, 90퍼센트의 참가자가 이제 의사 소통 능력이 더 강화되었다고 말했습니다. [138]**몇몇 참가자들은 연습을 더 했어도 좋았겠다고 말했습니다.** 워크숍에 대해 좀 더 자세히 논의하고 싶으시면 제게 알려 주십시오.

아빈 플로레스

어휘 deliver (연설·강연 등을) 하다 headquarters 본사 improvisation 즉석에서 하기[한 것] participate 참가하다 possibility 가능성 evaluation 평가 gauge 측정하다 effectiveness 유효성 mainly 대체로 positive 긍정적인

135 명사 자리 _ 동사의 목적어

해설 빈칸은 소유격 our 뒤에 이어지는 명사 자리로, to부정사의 동사원형 share의 목적어 역할을 한다. 따라서 '감사'라는 의미의 명사 (D) appreciation이 정답이다. (A) appreciate(감사하다)는 동사, (B) appreciative(감사하는)는 형용사, (C) appreciated는 동사/과거분사로 품사상 빈칸에 들어갈 수 없다.

136 동사 어형 _ 시제 _ 태

해설 빈칸은 주어 Some employees의 동사 자리로, 빈칸 뒤 명사구 a concern을 목적어로 취한다. 빈칸 뒤 문장에서 이 직원들이 하루 종일 꼬박 참여했다(These same employees participated fully throughout the day)고 했으므로, 우려 표명은 워크숍에 참여하기 전에 일어난 행위임을 알 수 있다. 따라서 과거(participated)보다 앞

TEST 8

서 일어난 일을 나타내는 과거완료 동사 (D) had expressed가 정답이다. 주어 Some employees는 우려를 표하는 주체이므로, 수동태 표현 (C) were to be expressed는 빈칸에 들어갈 수 없다.

137 부사 어휘

해설 빈칸 앞 절은 '참가자들에게 회사의 평가 양식을 작성하도록 요청했다'는 내용이며, 빈칸 뒤 to부정사구는 '워크숍의 유효성을 더 잘 측정하기 위해서'라는 내용이다. 워크숍의 유효성 측정을 위한 평가서 작성은 워크숍이 끝난 후 이뤄져야 하므로, '이후에, 그 뒤에'라는 의미의 (A) afterward가 정답이다. (B) often(종종), (C) since(그 이후로 줄곧), (D) instead(대신에)는 문맥상 빈칸에 적절하지 않다.

138 문맥에 맞는 문장 고르기

번역 (A) 워크숍은 이번 주 중후반으로 일정이 조정될 예정입니다.
(B) 몇몇 참가자들은 연습을 더 했어도 좋았겠다고 말했습니다.
(C) 이따금 추가로 팀워크 구축 워크숍이 제공됩니다.
(D) 귀하에게 납부를 요청하는 청구서를 드리겠습니다.

해설 빈칸 앞 문장에서 워크숍의 평가 결과(Results were mainly positive ~ their communication skills are now stronger)를 언급했고, 빈칸 뒤 문장에서 워크숍에 대해 좀 더 자세히 논의하고 싶으면 자신에게 알려 줄 것(Please let me know ~ to discuss the workshops in more detail)을 요청했으므로, 빈칸에도 워크숍의 평가 결과와 관련된 내용이 들어가야 문맥상 자연스럽다. 따라서 (B)가 정답이다.

어휘 team building 팀워크 구축 occasionally 이따금 invoice 청구서

139-142 이메일

수신: 리 청 〈lcheung@broadwayos.com〉
발신: 트래비스 주노 〈tjuno@hiraokaarchitecture.com〉
날짜: 11월 18일
제목: 월별 주문

청 씨께:

저희 히라오카 건축의 139**고정** 주문을 조정할 필요가 있습니다. 발표 시 건식으로 지우는 화이트보드를 사용하는 발표자가 줄어들고 있으며, 그 결과 건식으로 지우는 BR1608 마커를 더 적게 사용하고 있습니다. 140**따라서** 다음 달부터 주문 개수를 줄여 12개만 주문하려고 합니다. GN2280 다목적 마커 수를 14개로 늘려 주세요.

BR1608 마커는 단계적으로 줄이다가 결국에는 중단하려고 합니다. 그러나 그 전에 충분히 시간을 두어, 아마도 내년 말쯤에 귀사에 통보 141**하겠습니다**.

수정된 월 청구서와 함께 명세서를 보내 주시겠습니까? 142**당사 경리부에서 필요할 겁니다.**

트래비스 주노
히라오카 건축

어휘 adjustment 조정 presenter 발표자 dry-erase 건식으로 지우는 reduce 줄이다 all-purpose 다목적의 eventually 결국에는 phase out 단계적으로 중단하다 entirely 완전히, 전부 give ~ plenty of notice ~에게 충분한 시간을 두고 통보하나 statement 명세서 revised 수정된

139 형용사 어휘

해설 빈칸은 전치사 to의 목적어 역할을 하는 명사 order(주문)를 수식하는 형용사 자리이다. '주문을 조정할 필요가 있다'는 내용인데, 달마다 주문하는(monthly order) 문구류 개수를 줄이고 늘린다는 것으로 보아, 빈칸을 포함한 명사구가 '고정 주문'이라는 표현이 되어야 문맥상 자연스럽다. 따라서, '고정적인, 상설의'라는 의미를 갖고 있는 (C) standing이 정답이다. (A) still(정지한, 고요한), (B) overdue(기한이 지난), (D) redundant(불필요한)는 문맥상 빈칸에 적절하지 않다. 참고로 (A) still은 '여전히, 그럼에도'라는 뜻의 부사로도 쓰인다.

140 접속부사

해설 빈칸 앞뒤 문장을 의미상 자연스럽게 연결하는 접속부사를 선택하는 문제이다. 빈칸 앞 문장에서 주문 조정의 이유(Fewer of our presenters are using fewer BR1608 dry-erase markers)를, 빈칸 뒤에서 조정된 주문의 결과(I would like to reduce the number in our order)를 언급했으므로, (A) Therefore(그러므로)가 정답이다. (B) Typically는 '보통, 일반적으로', (C) Similarly는 '유사하게, 마찬가지로', (D) Nevertheless는 '그럼에도 불구하고'라는 뜻으로 문맥상 빈칸에 적절하지 않다.

141 동사 어형_시제_태

해설 빈칸은 주어 I 뒤에 이어지는 동사 자리로, 빈칸 뒤 you를 간접목적어로, plenty of notice를 직접목적어로 취한다. 뒤에 미래를 나타내는 시간 전치사구(before then, probably by late next year)가 나왔으므로, (D) will give가 정답이다.

142 문맥에 맞는 문장 고르기

번역 (A) 우리는 아직 재고를 다 쓰지 않았습니다.
(B) 이메일 수신함에서 찾으실 수 있습니다.
(C) 당사 경리부에서 필요할 겁니다.
(D) 직원들이 그 제품에 만족합니다.

해설 빈칸 앞 문장에서 수정된 월 청구서와 함께 명세서를 보내 줄 것(Can you send a statement with the revised monthly bill?)을 요청했으므로, 빈칸에도 명세서와 관련된 내용이 들어가야 문맥상 자연스럽다. 따라서 수정된 명세서를 요청한 이유를 언급한 (C)가 정답이다. 참고로 (C)의 대명사 it은 a statement with the revised monthly bill을 가리킨다.

어휘 use up 다 쓰다 inventory 재고

143-146 편지

3월 13일

데니스 카레라
레호스 배관 및 난방
샌 안토니오, 텍사스 주

카레라 씨께:

축하합니다! 저희 마요르카 건설이 카운티 법원 청사를 개선하기 위해 레호스 배관 및 난방의 입찰을 [143]**수락했습니다**. 귀사 직원들은 5월 5일 [144]**현장**에 출입할 수 있습니다. 지역 건축 법규에 명시된 바와 같이, 레호스 배관 및 난방은 필요한 허가를 확보할 책임이 있습니다. 동봉한 기획안에 공사 범위가 간략히 나와 있습니다. [145]**덧붙여**, 이 문서에는 당사가 제휴하고 있는 다른 도급 업체들이 포함되어 있어, 귀사의 작업이 전체 공사에 어떻게 들어맞는지 볼 수 있습니다.

귀사가 제안서와 함께 제출한 청사진과 시방서에서 크게 조정할 부분은 없습니다. 추가 정보가 필요하시면 제 사무실로 연락하십시오. [146]**신속하게 제공해 드리겠습니다.**

페트라 로하스, 관리자
마요르카 건설사

동봉

어휘 accept bid 입찰을 수락하다 plumbing 배관 (작업) enhancement 개선 specify 명시하다 code 법규 secure 확보하다 required 필요한 permit 허가 scope 범위 contractor 도급 업체 reveal 보이다, 나타내다 significant 상당한 adjustment 조정 specification 시방서, 사양서 submit 제출하다 additional 추가의

143 동사 어형 _ 시제

해설 빈칸은 주어 Mallorca Construction의 동사 자리로, 명사구 the bid of Lejos Plumbing and Heating을 목적어로 취한다. 뒤에 나오는 문장에서 레호스 배관 및 난방의 직원들이 현장에 출입할 수 있다(Your workers will have access to ~ on May 5)고 했는데, 이것은 입찰이 수락된 상태여야 가능한 일이므로, 현재완료 동사 (C) has accepted가 정답이다.

144 명사 어휘

해설 빈칸은 전치사 to의 목적어 역할을 하는 명사 자리로, '~로의 접근 또는 출입이 가능하다'는 의미가 되어야 한다. 앞 문장에서 마요르카 건설이 카운티 법원 청사를 개선하기 위해 레호스 배관 및 난방의 입찰을 수락했다(Mallorca Construction ~ to provide enhancements to the County Courthouse)고 했으므로, 빈칸에는 접근 권한이 주어진 카운티 법원 청사를 대신할 장소 관련 명사가 들어가는 것이 가장 자연스럽다. 따라서 (A) site(현장, 부지)가 정답이다. (B) data는 '자료', (C) results는 '결과', (D) product는 '제품'이라는 의미로 빈칸에 적절하지 않다.

145 접속부사

해설 빈칸 앞뒤 문장을 의미상 자연스럽게 연결하는 접속부사를 선택하는 문제이다. 빈칸 앞 문장에서 동봉한 기획안에 공사 범위가 간략히 나와 있다(The enclosed plan outlines the scope of the project)고 했고, 빈칸 뒤에서 동봉한 문서에 대해 추가적으로 설명(the document lists ~ into the overall project) 했으므로, 추가 정보를 말할 때 쓰는 접속부사 (B) In addition(덧붙여, 게다가)이 정답이다. (A) However(하지만), (C) As a result(결과적으로), (D) On the other hand(다른 한편으로)는 문맥상 빈칸에 적절하지 않다.

146 문맥에 맞는 문장 고르기

번역 (A) 아쉽게도, 귀사의 입찰은 마감일 이후에 도착했습니다.
(B) 곧 최종 결정을 알려 드리겠습니다.
(C) 귀사의 최근 확장에 다시 한번 행운이 깃들길 기원합니다.
(D) 신속하게 제공해 드리겠습니다.

해설 빈칸 앞 문장에서 추가 정보가 필요하면 로하스 씨의 사무실로 연락할 것(Please contact my office ~ additional information)을 요청했으므로, 빈칸에는 정보 요청을 받았을 경우 로하스 씨가 취할 후속 조치와 관련된 내용이 이어지는 것이 문맥상 자연스럽다. 따라서 (D)가 정답이다.

어휘 recent 최근의 expansion 확장 promptly 신속하게

PART 7

147-148 공지

리버 스트리트 호텔을 선택해 주셔서 감사합니다!

[147]**고객님들께 최상의 경험을 드리고자 하는 노력의 일환으로 무료 셔틀버스 서비스를 시 도심지까지 포함하도록 확대하였습니다.** [148]**셔틀은 모든 유적지, 야외 시장, 극장가 등 도심의 가장 인기 있는 관광 명소를 순환하면서 몇 군데 정차합니다. 이 목적지들은 모두 호텔에서 걸어갈 수 있는 거리지만 셔틀을 타면 더 빨리 갈 수 있습니다.** 노선은 처음 오는 방문객과 자주 오는 방문객에게 안성맞춤입니다. 또한 특별한 행사나 축제가 있을 때는 셔틀 정차지가 추가될 예정입니다.

셔틀 일정은 호텔 로비에 게시되어 있습니다. 공항 서비스와 마찬가지로, 보상제도 클럽 회원은 미리 셔틀을 예약할 수 있습니다.

어휘 extend 확대하다 complimentary 무료의 loop 고리 모양으로 이동[순환]하다 attraction 명소 destination 목적지 reward 보상

147 세부 사항

번역 제공되고 있는 것은?
(A) 무료 교통 서비스
(B) 축제 할인 입장권
(C) 보상 제도 회원권
(D) 극장가 가이드 투어

TEST 8

해설 첫 번째 단락에서 고객들에게 최상의 경험을 제공하고자 하는 노력의 일환으로 무료 셔틀 버스 서비스를 시 도심지까지 포함하도록 확대했다(In an effort to bring our guests the very best experience, we've extended our complimentary shuttle bus service)고 했으므로, (A)가 정답이다.

어휘 transportation 교통

▸▸ Paraphrasing 지문의 our complimentary shuttle bus service
→ 정답의 A free transportation service

148 추론 / 암시

번역 리버 스트리트 호텔에 관해 암시된 것은?

(A) 유서 깊은 건물이다.
(B) 등급이 높은 호텔이다.
(C) 도심지에서 가깝다.
(D) 출장 여행객들에게 인기 있다.

해설 첫 번째 단락에서 셔틀은 도심의 가장 인기 있는 관광 명소를 순환하면서 몇 군데 정차한다(The shuttle loops around the downtown's most popular tourist attractions with several stops)고 한 후, 목적지들이 모두 호텔에서 걸어갈 수 있는 거리(While these destinations are all within walking distance from the hotel)라고 했으므로, 리버 스트리트 호텔이 도심에서 가까이 있다고 추론할 수 있다. 따라서 (C)가 정답이다.

어휘 rated 등급의

▸▸ Paraphrasing 지문의 within walking distance → 정답의 near

149-150 문자 메시지

조앤 트리버스 [오전 10시 34분] 유지, 기차가 한 시간 연착이라서 [149]**발표회에 늦을 것 같아요. 제가 2시 전에 거기 도착하지 않으면 준비하고 시작해 주실래요?**

유지 오카다 [오전 10시 35분] 그럴게요. 언제 도착할 것 같으세요?

조앤 트리버스 [오전 10시 37분] 1시 20분은 되어야 오크빌 역에 도착해요. [150]**거기서 제일 먼저 오는 버스를 타고 사무실까지 갈게요.**

유지 오카다 [오전 10시 39분] 그럴 필요 없어요. [150]**제가 데리러 갈게요.** 2시 전에는 사무실에 도착할 겁니다.

조앤 트리버스 [오전 10시 41분] 좋아요, 고마워요! 그런데 발표회에 쓸 컴퓨터는 설치해 놓으세요.

어휘 delay 지연시키다 make it to ~에 도착하다

149 세부 사항

번역 트리버스 씨가 걱정하는 것은?

(A) 특정 시간까지 사무실에 도착하는 것
(B) 동료의 발표회를 놓치는 것
(C) 연결 기차 타는 것
(D) 버스 터미널 찾는 것

해설 트리버스 씨가 오전 10시 34분 메시지에서 발표회에 늦을 것 같다(I might be late for my presentation)며 자신이 2시 전에 도착하지 않으면 대신 준비하고 시작해 줄 것(Would you be able to set up and start for me if I am not there before 2:00?)을 요청했으므로, (A)가 정답이다.

어휘 colleague 동료

▸▸ Paraphrasing 지문의 before 2:00
→ 정답의 by a certain time

150 의도 파악

번역 오전 10시 39분에 오카다 씨가 "그럴 필요 없어요"라고 적은 의도는 무엇인가?

(A) 그들은 오크빌에 갈 필요가 없을 것이다.
(B) 그들은 컴퓨터가 필요 없을 것이다.
(C) 트리버스 씨는 버스를 탈 필요가 없다.
(D) 트리버스 씨는 사무실에 갈 필요가 없다.

해설 트리버스 씨가 오전 10시 37분 메시지에서 오크빌 역에서 제일 먼저 오는 버스를 타고 사무실까지 가겠다(I'll try to get the first bus from there to the office)고 했는데, 이에 대해 오카다 씨가 '그럴 필요 없어요(No need)'라고 응답한 후, 자신이 데리러 가겠다(I'll pick you up)고 했으므로, (C)가 정답이다.

▸▸ Paraphrasing 지문의 get the first bus → 정답의 take a bus

151-153 기사

셸든 업계 소식

셸든(8월 4일) – [151]**다우닝 웨이는 셸든 시에서 새로운 일자리를 많이 창출할 것이라고 화요일에 발표했다. 식당 대변인인 다니엘 바세는 식당이 9월 26일 다우닝 대로 1091번지에 문을 열 계획이라고 말했다.** [152]**경영진은 문을 열기 전에 50개의 공석을 채울 계획이다.** 직책은 서빙 담당에서 제과제빵사, 매니저까지 다양하다. [152]**공석 수 때문에 다우닝 웨이는 8월 16일 하루 동안 취업 박람회를 개최할 예정이다.** 행사에서 공개 면접을 실시한다.

[153]**다우닝 웨이의 최신 지점은 식당 부지 내 정원에서 채소와 허브를 자체 수확하는 유일한 식당이 될 것이다.** 이 식당은 현지 요리도 전문으로 한다. "지역 일자리 기반을 키우는 데 기여할 수 있어 기쁩니다." 다우닝 웨이 창업자이자 CEO인 마리 폰테인은 말했다. "음식에 대한 열정과 1급 응대 실력을 갖춘 팀원을 채용하고자 합니다. 저희는 직원에게 업계 평균 이상의 급여와 탁월한 복지 혜택을 제공합니다." 관심 있는 지원자 중 취업 박람회에 참석할 수 없는 사람은 downingway-sheldon.com에서 온라인으로 지원할 수 있다.

어휘 spokesperson 대변인 be slated to ~할 계획이다 management 경영진 range from A to B A에서 B까지 다양하다 career fair 취업 박람회 harvest 수확하다 premises 부지, 구내 regional 지역의 cuisine 요리 contribute to ~에 기여하다 hospitality 접대 competitive 경쟁력 있는, 뒤지지 않는 benefits 복지 혜택 candidate 지원자

151 주제 / 목적

번역 무엇에 관한 기사인가?

(A) 식당 이전
(B) 새 식당 취업 기회
(C) 지역 원예 경향
(D) 새로운 직무 기술 개발 교육

해설 첫 번째 단락에서 다우닝 웨이는 셸든 시에서 새로운 일자리를 많이 창출할 것이라고 발표했다(Downing Way announced ~ creating many new jobs in the city of Sheldon)고 한 후, 식당이 9월 26일 다우닝 대로 1091번지에 문을 열 계획(the restaurant is slated to open on September 26)이라고 했으므로, 새로운 식당의 취업 기회에 관한 기사임을 알 수 있다. 따라서 (B)가 정답이다.

어휘 relocation 이전

▸▸ Paraphrasing 지문의 creating many new jobs → 정답의 Job opportunities

152 사실 관계 확인

번역 8월 16일 행사에 관해 명시된 것은?

(A) 지역 식당 주인들을 위한 행사이다.
(B) 구직자들은 면접을 보려면 이 행사에 참석해야 한다.
(C) 참석자들은 식당 대표 요리를 시식할 것이다.
(D) 공석이 50개 있을 것이다.

해설 첫 번째 단락에서 경영진은 문을 열기 전에 50개의 공석을 채울 계획(Management is looking to fill 50 positions before the doors open)이라고 했고, 질문에서 언급된 8월 16일에 공석 수 때문에 취업 박람회를 개최할 예정(Because of the number of positions, Downing Way will host a one-day career fair on August 16)이라고 했으므로, (D)가 정답이다. 참고로, 마지막 단락에서 박람회에 참석할 수 없는 사람은 온라인으로 지원해도 된다(Interested candidates who are unable to attend the career fair may instead apply online)고 했으므로, (B)는 정답이 될 수 없다.

어휘 sample 시식[시음]하다 representative 대표적인

153 세부 사항

번역 다우닝 웨이가 독특한 점은?

(A) 자체 농산물을 재배한다.
(B) 최상의 급여를 제공한다.
(C) 대대로 같은 집안 소속이었다.
(D) 웹사이트가 다수의 산업상을 수상했다.

해설 두 번째 단락에서 다우닝 웨이의 최신 지점은 식당 부지내 정원에서 채소와 허브를 자체 수확하는 유일한 식당이 될 것(Downing Way's newest location will be the only restaurant ~ that harvests its own vegetables and herbs in a garden on the premises)이라고 했으므로, (A)가 정답이다.

어휘 produce 농산물

▸▸ Paraphrasing 지문의 the only restaurant → 질문의 unique
지문의 harvests its own vegetables and herbs → 정답의 grows its own produce

154-157 회람

회람

수신: 고객 서비스 담당 직원
제목: 다음 주 금요일 회의
날짜: 11월 19일

[155]**지난주에 고객 서비스에 대한 의견을 수집하기 위한 조사를 실시했습니다. 데이터가 들어왔는데 양호해 보입니다.** 대다수는 우리 직원과의 의사 소통에 만족감을 표시했습니다. [154]**포장 서비스, 배송비, 그리고 배송 진행 상황에 대한 고객의 질문에 전문적이고 신속하게 답변이 이루어졌습니다.**

[156]**우리가 해결해야 할 한 가지 부분은 추천 수가 적다는 점입니다. 우리가 접촉한 고객 중 서비스에 대해 다른 사람들에게 말한다고 한 사람은 거의 없었습니다.** [154]**답변에 근거해 보면, 대다수는 다시 찾는 고객으로, 배송 서비스가 필요할 때 언제나 우리를 이용하는 고객이거나 광고를 보고 우리를 선택하는 고객입니다.** 분명 우리는 추천을 제대로 요청하지 못하고 있습니다.

따라서 다음 주 금요일 회의는 이 주제를 중심으로 하겠습니다. 제가 이러한 단점을 시정하기 위한 자료와 실제 활동들을 기획하겠습니다. [157]**하지만 여러분이 추천율을 개선하기 위한 창의적인 방법을 생각해 오신다면 감사하겠습니다. 제안을 보내 주시면 꼭 토론에 포함시키겠습니다.** 모든 분들의 소식 기다리겠습니다.

제니스 웰스, 고객 서비스 수석 코디네이터

어휘 satisfaction 만족 representative 직원 status 상태 parcel 소포 promptly 신속하게 address 해결하다 referral 추천 repeat customer 다시 찾는 고객 rely on ~에 의존하다, ~을 필요로 하다 properly 제대로 shortcoming 단점

154 추론 / 암시

번역 웰스 씨는 어디에서 일하겠는가?

(A) 시장 조사 회사
(B) 배송 회사
(C) 보험 대리점
(D) 광고 회사

해설 첫 번째 단락에서 회사의 고객 서비스 관련 조사 결과에 따르면 포장 서비스, 배송비, 배송 진행 상황에 대한 고객의 질문에 전문적이고 신속하게 답변이 이루어졌다(Their questions about packaging services, shipping charges, and the status of their parcels were answered)고 했고, 두 번째 단락에서 대다수 고객이 배송 서비스가 필요할 때 언제나 웰스 씨의 회사를 이용한다(most people are repeat customers who always rely on us for their shipping needs)고 했으므로, 그녀가 배송 관련 회사에서 일한다고 추론할 수 있다. 따라서 (B)가 정답이다.

TEST 8

155 세부 사항

번역 웰스 씨가 검토한 정보는?

(A) 자재 가격
(B) 배송일
(C) 조사 결과
(D) 매출액

해설 첫 번째 단락에서 고객 서비스에 대한 의견을 수집하기 위해 조사를 실시했다(Last week we conducted a study to gather opinions about our customer service)고 한 후, 데이터가 들어왔는데 양호해 보인다(The data are in and they look good)며 결과를 언급했으므로, (C)가 정답이다.

▸▸ **Paraphrasing** 지문의 **a study to gather opinions** → 정답의 **Survey**
지문의 **The data** → 정답의 **results**

156 세부 사항

번역 웰스 씨가 언급한 문제는?

(A) 다른 사람에게 회사를 추천하는 고객이 거의 없다.
(B) 일부 주문이 신속하게 처리되지 않았다.
(C) 광고비가 올랐다.
(D) 고객 서비스부에 직원이 모자란다.

해설 두 번째 단락에서 해결해야 할 한 가지 부분으로 적은 추천 수(One area that we need to address is the low number of referrals)를 언급한 후, 서비스에 대해 다른 사람들에게 말한다고 한 사람이 거의 없었다(Few customers ~ reported telling others about our services)며 문제점에 대한 부연 설명을 덧붙였으므로, (A)가 정답이다.

어휘 process 처리하다 understaffed 직원이 모자라는

▸▸ **Paraphrasing** 지문의 **One area that we need to address** → 질문의 **problem**
지문의 **referrals/telling others about our services** → 정답의 **recommend the company to others**

157 세부 사항

번역 직원들이 요청받은 일은?

(A) 온라인 양식 작성
(B) 고객 서비스 담당 직원 추가 채용
(C) 대안이 되는 회의 날짜 제안하기
(D) 토론할 아이디어 제출하기

해설 마지막 단락에서 수신인(you)인 직원들에게 추천율을 개선하기 위한 창의적인 방법을 생각해서(you could come up with some creative ways to improve our referral rate) 보내 줄 것(Send me your suggestions ~ in our discussion)을 요청했으므로, (D)가 정답이다.

어휘 alternate 대안이 되는

▸▸ **Paraphrasing** 지문의 **some creative ways to/suggestions** → 정답의 **ideas**
지문의 **Send me** → 정답의 **Submit**

158-159 이메일

이메일

수신: 바바라 트렐로어 〈btreloar@questor.ca〉
발신: 에이미 던스턴 〈adunstan@bluetern.co.nz〉
제목: 표지
날짜: 4월 20일

바바라에게:

[159]**이번 주 안에 블루 턴 마케팅 팀으로부터 이메일을 받으실 겁니다.** [158/159]**이메일에는 마케팅 과정이 설명되어 있으며, 저자용 온라인 설문지 링크도 있습니다.** [158]**비록 디자인 팀이 귀하의 책 표지를 최종 결정하겠지만, 분명 어떤 의견이 있으실 겁니다.** 표지에서 꼭 보고 싶거나 혹은 보지 않았으면 하는 것이 있으신가요? 제게 알려 주시기 바랍니다.

에이미 던스턴
수석 개발 편집자

어휘 describe 설명하다 questionnaire 설문지 have the final say 최종 결정권을 갖다 input 의견, 생각

158 추론 / 암시

번역 트렐로어 씨는 누구이겠는가?

(A) 저자
(B) 홍보 담당자
(C) 광고 책임자
(D) 마케팅팀 팀원

해설 두 번째 문장에서 수신인(you)인 트렐로어 씨가 받을 이메일에 저자용 온라인 설문지 링크가 있다(The e-mail ~ gives you a link to an online questionnaire for authors)고 했고, 세 번째 문장에서 트렐로어 씨의 책 표지 디자인(Although the design team will have the final say on your book's cover)에 대해 언급했으므로, 트렐로어 씨가 책의 저자임을 추론할 수 있다. 따라서 (A)가 정답이다.

159 세부 사항

번역 이메일에 의하면, 곧 도착하는 것은?

(A) 책
(B) 표지 사진
(C) 몇 가지 편집 제안
(D) 마케팅 정보

해설 이메일의 초반부에서 이번 주 안에 블루 턴 마케팅 팀으로부터 받을 예정(You will be receiving an e-mail from the Blue Tern marketing team before the end of the week)인 이메일에 마케팅 과정이 설명되어 있다(The e-mail describes the marketing process)고 했으므로, (D)가 정답이다.

▸▸ Paraphrasing 지문의 will be receiving ~ before the end of the week → 질문의 should soon arrive
지문의 the marketing process
→ 정답의 Some marketing information

160-162 편지

줄리아 간다리아스 씨
바틀렛 가 1896번지
사우스필드, 미시간 주 48075
11월 10일

간다리아스 씨께,

리우 웹 웍스와 계약을 갱신해 주셔서 감사합니다. 저희 웹사이트 호스팅 서비스에 대한 분기별 청구서를 동봉했습니다. [160/162]**정기 유지비에 20달러의 금액이 추가된 것을 보실 겁니다.** 이번 인상과 관련해 5월에 메일을 드렸습니다. [160]**다시 알려 드리자면, 리우 웹 웍스는 고객님의 웹사이트가 최신 장비와 호환되도록 6월에 중요한 업그레이드를 수행했습니다.** 이제 귀사의 고객들은 컴퓨터를 사용하든, 태블릿이나 스마트폰을 사용하든 상관없이 동일한 콘텐츠를 보며 이와 상호 작용하게 됩니다.

이렇게 개선된 점이 귀사의 웹사이트와 사업에 어떤 영향을 미치는지 알려 주시기 바랍니다. [161]**당사 계정으로 로그인하고 페이지 상단에 나타나는 링크를 클릭해 온라인 설문 조사를 작성하세요.** 고객님의 제안에 대한 감사의 표시로, 향후 청구서에 대해 10퍼센트의 할인을 받으시게 됩니다.

계속 거래해 주셔서 감사합니다!

숀 리우
리우 웹 웍스

어휘 renew 갱신하다 quarterly 분기별 invoice 청구서 Web site hosting service 웹 서버를 임대/관리해 주는 서비스 maintenance cost 유지비 perform 수행하다 compatible with ~와 호환되는 interact with ~와 상호 작용하다 regardless of ~와 상관없이 enhancement 개선 (사항) affect 영향을 미치다 as a token of appreciation 감사의 표시로

160 세부 사항

번역 요금이 변경된 이유는?
(A) 리우 웹 웍스가 할인을 없앴다.
(B) 리우 웹 웍스가 서비스를 개선했다.
(C) 간다리아스 씨가 웹사이트에 온라인 매장을 추가했다.
(D) 간다리아스 씨가 추가 장비를 요청했다.

해설 첫 번째 단락에서 정기 유지비에 20달러의 금액이 추가되었다(the amount of $20.00 was added to the regular maintenance cost)고 한 후, 리우 웹 웍스가 간다리아스 씨의 웹사이트가 최신 장비와 호환되도록 6월에 중요한 업그레이드를 수행했다(Liu Web Works performed a major upgrade in June to ensure that your Web site is compatible with the latest devices)며 요금 변경의 이유를 언급했으므로, (B)가 정답이다.

▸▸ Paraphrasing 지문의 the amount of $20.00 was added to the regular maintenance cost
→ 질문의 the fee change
지문의 performed a major upgrade
→ 정답의 improved its services

161 세부 사항

번역 리우 씨가 간다리아스 씨에게 해 달라고 요청한 일은?
(A) 고객에게 알림 보내기
(B) 연간 계약 갱신하기
(C) 계정 정보 업데이트하기
(D) 의견 양식 작성하기

해설 두 번째 단락에서 수신인(you)인 간다리아스 씨에게 리우 웹 웍스 계정으로 로그인하고 페이지 상단에 나타나는 링크를 클릭해 온라인 설문 조사를 작성할 것(Complete our online survey by logging in to your account with us and clicking the link)을 요청했으므로, (D)가 정답이다.

▸▸ Paraphrasing 지문의 our online survey
→ 정답의 a feedback form

162 문장 삽입

번역 [1], [2], [3], [4]로 표시된 곳 중에서 다음 문장이 들어가기에 가장 적합한 곳은?
"이번 인상과 관련해 5월에 메일을 드렸습니다."
(A) [1]
(B) [2]
(C) [3]
(D) [4]

해설 주어진 문장에서 이번 인상과 관련해 5월에 메일을 보냈다(We e-mailed ~ about this increase)고 했으므로, 앞에서 먼저 this increase가 가리키는 대상이 언급되어야 한다. [2] 앞에서 정기 유지비에 20달러의 금액이 추가되었다(the amount of $20.00 was added to the regular maintenance cost)며 구체적인 인상 금액을 밝혔으므로, (B)가 정답이다.

163-166 온라인 채팅

호르헤 아빌라 오전 10시 18분
[163]**건물 일부에서 에어컨이 작동하지 않는다는 것을 알고 계실 겁니다.**

사이먼 미아노 오전 10시 19분
알고 있었어요. 여기 온도와 습도가 급속히 오르고 있네요.

호르헤 아빌라 오전 10시 20분
냉각기가 고장인데 수리가 빠르지도, 싸지도 않아요. 지난번 고장 났을 때는 교체품을 구하는 데 1주일이 걸렸어요. 이번 주는 그렇게 덥지 않아서 다행이에요. 기사가 오고 있지만 우선 자유롭게 선풍기를 켜세요.

사이먼 미아노 오전 10시 24분
컴퓨터 서버가 과열될까 걱정이에요. [164]**IT 사무실에 설치할 이동식 장치가 있나요?**

에이프릴 데너 오전 10시 25분
서버는 잘못되면 정말 안 돼요.

호르헤 아빌라 오전 10시 26분
이 건물에는 없어요. [165]**데너 씨가 허락하면 밴을 이용해서 민도네스에 있는 창고에서 가져오면 돼요.** 거기 서너 개 있을 거예요. [165]**하지만 빨라야 오늘 저녁에나 돌아올 수 있어요.**

에이프릴 데너 오전 10시 28분
[165]**호르헤, 당장 IT 사무실용 이동식 에어컨을 긴급 구매하는 것을 허가합니다.** [166]**필요한 에어컨 개수를 정하고 비용을 계산해서 구매 준비가 되는 대로 제게 보고하세요.**

호르헤 아빌라 오전 10시 28분
[166]**지금 바로 착수할게요.**

에이프릴 데너 오전 10시 29분
지역 가전 할인 매장에서 오후까지 배송해 주지 않으면 사람을 보내서 배송 밴으로 가져오도록 하세요.

어휘 function 기능하다 temperature 온도 humidity 습도 condenser 냉각기 down 고장 난 fix 수리 replacement 교체품 technician 기사 portable 이동식의 can't afford to ~할 여력이 없다 authorize 인가하다 emergency 긴급 determine 알아내다 appliance 가전 제품 outlet 할인 매장

163 세부 사항

번역 무엇이 문제인가?

(A) 배송 밴을 수리해야 한다.
(B) 냉방 시스템이 고장이다.
(C) 콘덴서가 교체하기에 너무 비싸다.
(D) 구매 승인이 거부되었다.

해설 아빌라 씨가 오전 10시 18분 메시지에서 건물 일부에서 에어컨이 작동하지 않는다(the air-conditioning is not functioning in parts of the building)는 문제점을 언급했으므로, (B)가 정답이다.

어휘 authorization 허가, 인가 deny 거절하다

▸▸ **Paraphrasing** 지문의 **the air-conditioning is not functioning**
→ 정답의 **The cooling system is not working**

164 의도 파악

번역 오전 10시 26분에 아빌라 씨가 "이 건물에는 없어요"라고 적은 의도는 무엇인가?

(A) 기사를 구할 수 없다.
(B) 그는 IT에 사무실이 없다.
(C) 그가 있는 곳은 컴퓨터 서버가 괜찮다.
(D) 근처에 이동식 에어컨이 없다.

해설 미아노 씨가 오전 10시 24분 메시지에서 IT 사무실에 설치할 이동식 장치가 있는지(Do we have any portable units we could set up in the Information Technology office?)를 문의했는데, 이에 대해 아빌라 씨가 '이 건물에는 없어요(Not in this building)'라는 응답을 했으므로, (D)가 정답이다.

165 추론 / 암시

번역 데너 씨가 민도네스에 있는 기기를 쓰지 않기로 결정한 이유는 무엇이겠는가?

(A) 기기가 충분하지 않다.
(B) 도착하려면 시간이 너무 오래 걸린다.
(C) 효율적으로 작동하지 않는다.
(D) 기기를 놓을 공간이 충분하지 않다.

해설 아빌라 씨가 오전 10시 26분 메시지에서 데너 씨가 허락하면 민도네스에 있는 창고에서 기기를 가져 오겠다(With Ms. Denner's OK, ~ to pick up the ones in the warehouse in Mindones)고 한 후, 빨라야 오늘 저녁에나 돌아올 수 있다(But the earliest I could get back is tonight)는 도착 시간 문제를 언급했는데, 이에 대해 데너 씨가 오전 10시 28분 메시지에서 아빌라 씨에게 IT 사무실용 이동식 에어컨을 긴급 구매하도록 허가한다(I'm authorizing you to make an emergency purchase ~ right away)고 했다. 따라서 데너 씨가 시간이 너무 오래 걸리는 문제를 우려했다고 추론할 수 있으므로, (B)가 정답이다.

166 추론 / 암시

번역 다음에 무슨 일이 있겠는가?

(A) 아빌라 씨가 구매 준비를 할 것이다.
(B) IT 사무실에 선풍기가 배송될 것이다.
(C) 미아노 씨가 차를 몰고 창고로 갈 것이다.
(D) 기사가 서버를 교체할 것이다.

해설 데너 씨가 오전 10시 28분 메시지에서 아빌라 씨에게 필요한 에어컨 개수를 정하고 비용을 계산해서 구매 준비가 되는 대로 보고할 것(Please decide ~ and report back to me as soon as you have set up the purchase)을 요청했는데, 이에 대해 아빌라 씨가 지금 바로 착수하겠다(I'll get started on that now)고 응답했으므로, 아빌라 씨가 구매 준비를 할 것임을 추론할 수 있다. 따라서 (A)가 정답이다.

▸▸ **Paraphrasing** 지문의 **have set up the purchase**
→ 정답의 **arrange a purchase**

167-168 이메일

이메일 메시지

수신: hhollander@helensplace.com
발신: customerservice@eaterysource.com
날짜: 1월 16일
제목: 주문 확인

홀랜더 씨께:

저희 물건을 구매해 주셔서 감사합니다! [167]**eaterysource.com에서 고객님의 주문을 접수했음을 확인하는 이메일입니다. 본사는 전 세계 식당을 상대로 하는 국제적인 장비 납품 업체라는 점에 자부심을 가지고 있습니다.**

고객님의 주문은 현재 처리 중입니다. 주문은 대개 영업일 기준으로 이틀 이내에 처리되어 창고로 전달됩니다. 그러면 직원이 주문품 배송을

준비하게 됩니다. [168]**주문품이 배송되면 현재의 추적 정보를 알리는 이메일을 다시 받으실 겁니다.**

거래해 주셔서 감사합니다.

이터리 소스 팀
주문 번호: #19998056
주문일: 1월 16일

어휘 supplier 납품 업체 equipment 장비 process 처리하다 current 현재의

167 추론 / 암시

번역 홀랜더 씨는 어떤 업종에서 일하겠는가?

(A) 식당
(B) 슈퍼마켓
(C) 음식 납품 업체
(D) 배송 회사

해설 첫 번째 단락에서 수신인(you)인 홀랜더 씨의 주문을 접수했음을 확인하는 이메일(This e-mail confirms that we have received your order)이라고 한 후, 이메일을 보낸 회사가 전 세계 식당을 상대로 하는 국제적인 장비 납품 업체(We are ~ an international supplier of equipment to restaurants worldwide)라고 설명했으므로, 주문을 한 홀랜더 씨가 식당에서 일한다고 추론할 수 있다. 따라서 (A)가 정답이다.

168 세부 사항

번역 이메일에 의하면, 홀랜더 씨는 이터리 소스에서 언제 또 이메일을 받을 것인가?

(A) 결제할 때
(B) 다른 주문을 할 때
(C) 신제품이 구매 가능해질 때
(D) 주문품이 창고에서 나갔을 때

해설 두 번째 단락에서 주문품이 배송되면 현재의 추적 정보를 알리는 이메일을 다시 받게 될 것(You will receive another e-mail once your order has shipped)이라고 했으므로, (D)가 정답이다.

▸▸ **Paraphrasing** 지문의 once your order has shipped
→ 정답의 When her order has left the warehouse

169-171 이메일

발신: 트로니카사 고객 서비스
수신: 노시스 소프트웨어 사용자
날짜: 9월 14일
제목: 버전 3.1

노시스 소프트웨어 사용자 여러분께,

[169]**이달 말, 트로니카사에서 상업용 삽화 제작에 사용되는 온라인 소프트웨어인 노시스 3.1 버전을 출시할 예정입니다.** [170]**그리니치 표준시로 9월 29일 오후 11시부터 당사 기사들이 새로운 버전을** [171]**개시하는 동안 노시스는 이용할 수 없습니다.** 여러분은 아무 조치도 취할 필요가 없습니다. 저희가 온라인 데이터베이스에 저장된 고객 파일을 포함한 모든 포트폴리오를 백업할 예정입니다. 따라서, 그 과정에서 고객 파일은 완벽하게 보호될 겁니다. 모든 이용자는 9월 30일 오전, 절차가 완료되면 통지를 받을 것입니다. 고객님은 통지를 받은 후 노시스를 다시 사용할 수 있습니다.

[169]**새로운 기능에는 간소화된 작업 흐름, 혁신적인 디자인 테마, 새로운 배경과 글꼴, 그리고 조판 지정 표시 및 수정을 위한 쌍방향 추적 도구 등 재설계된 인터페이스가 포함됩니다.** 여러분이 이 새 기능들을 즐겨 사용하실 것으로 확신합니다.

트로니카사 고객 서비스

어휘 subscriber 사용자 release 출시하다 commercial 상업용의 unavailable 이용할 수 없는 roll out 시작하다 contain 포함하다 completion 완료 resume 재개하다 feature 기능 streamlined 간소화된 workflow 작업 흐름 interactive 쌍방향의 markup 조판 지정 표시

169 주제 / 목적

번역 이메일의 목적은?

(A) 할인 광고
(B) 새 사용자 유치
(C) 프로그램 이용법 설명
(D) 고객에게 변경 사항 알림

해설 첫 번째 단락에서 트로니카사에서 온라인 소프트웨어인 노시스 3.1 버전을 출시할 예정(Tronica LLC will release version 3.1 of Nossis)이라고 했고, 마지막 단락에서 새로운 기능에는 간소화된 작업 흐름, 혁신적인 디자인 테마, 새로운 배경과 글꼴, 그리고 조판 지정과 수정을 위한 쌍방향 추적 도구 등 재설계된 인터페이스가 포함된다(New features include a redesigned interface for streamlined workflow, ~ and interactive tracking tools for markups and revisions)고 했다. 따라서 새로운 버전이 출시됨에 따라 생긴 변경 사항을 고객에게 알리기 위한 이메일이라고 볼 수 있으므로, (D)가 정답이다.

어휘 attract 유치하다

170 사실 관계 확인

번역 9월 29일에 있을 일로 이메일에 명시된 것은?

(A) 컴퓨터 응용프로그램에 접속할 수 없게 될 것이다.
(B) 트로니아사에서 새 기사들을 채용할 것이다.
(C) 노시스 사용자들에게 이메일을 보낼 것이다.
(D) 새 소프트웨어를 구매할 수 있을 것이다.

해설 첫 번째 단락에서 질문에 언급된 9월 29일 오후 11시부터 당사의 기사들이 새로운 버전을 개시하는 동안 노시스를 이용할 수 없다(Beginning at 11 p.m. GMT on 29 September, Nossis will be unavailable)고 했으므로, (A)가 정답이다.

어휘 inaccessible 접속할 수 없는

TEST 8

▸▸ **Paraphrasing** 지문의 **Nossis will be unavailable**
→ 정답의 **A computer application will become inaccessible**

171 동의어 찾기

번역 첫 번째 단락 3행의 "roll out"과 의미가 가장 가까운 단어는?

(A) 납작하게 만들다
(B) 제거하다
(C) 도입하다
(D) 펼치다

해설 "roll out"이 포함된 부분은 '당사의 기사들이 새로운 버전을 개시하는 동안(while our technicians roll out the new version)'이라는 의미로 해석되는데, 여기서 roll out은 '사용 가능하게 하다, 개시하다'라는 뜻으로 쓰였다. 따라서 '내놓다, 도입하다, 소개하다'라는 의미의 (C) introduce가 정답이다.

172-175 기사

재정적인 성공에 그렇다고 답하다

에든버러(4월 3일) – 욜란다 아바스칼은 30년 전 맨체스터에 있는 대학에 처음 입학했을 때 패션 디자인을 공부할 생각이었다. 하지만 어느 여름 작은 의류 부티크에서 일하는 동안 그녀는 자신이 소매업을 좋아한다는 것을 알게 되었다. 172/173**그녀는 새로운 꿈을 쫓기 위해 패션 디자인 대신 경영학 학위를 취득했고 고향인 에든버러에 세이 예스 투 욜란다라는 작은 가게를 열었다.**

172**오늘날까지 빠르게, 아바스칼 씨의 작은 가게는 매년 수백만 파운드를 버는 성공적인 기업으로 성장했다.** 이렇게 성공한 데에는 아바스칼 씨가 4년 전 온라인상의 병행 가상 매장인 YesYolanda.com을 개발하기 위해 고용한 비한 쿨카르니의 마법이 한몫했다. 173**온라인 상호명과 동일하게 대표 매장의 이름을 예스 욜란다로 바꾼 것은 쿨카르니 씨의 생각이었다.**

175**아바스칼 씨는 직접적인 상호 교류를 강력히 지지하며, 고객들과 소통하기를 좋아한다.** 그녀는 그들이 실제 매장에서 쇼핑할 때 필요한 것을 가장 잘 충족시킬 수 있다고 여전히 믿는다. 175**하지만 그녀는 온라인 매장의 존재가 중요하다는 사실을 인식하고 있다.** 예스 욜란다는 올해 온라인 판매 수익만 1억 4천만 파운드가 넘을 것으로 예상하고 있다. 이 매출의 약 3분의 2는 주로 스코틀랜드 외부인 미국, 싱가포르 그리고 호주에서 창출될 것이다.

그에 따라 예스 욜란다의 인력은 확대되었다. 웹사이트를 업데이트하고 운영할 기술력을 갖춘 사람들을 고용하는 것 외에도, 회사는 얼마 전 사내 사진 스튜디오를 추가했다.

"이 스튜디오는 온라인 전시용 제품을 174**적시에** 사진으로 찍을 수 있도록 합니다." 아바스칼이 말했다. "매주 신제품이 추가되므로 반드시 필요합니다."

아바스칼 씨는 미래가 어떻게 될지 모른다고 말하지만, 예스 욜란다는 상승일로를 달릴 것으로 보인다.

어휘 retail 소매업 earn 취득하다 expand 확장하다[되다] enterprise 기업 due to ~ 덕분에 parallel 병행의 virtual 가상의 identity 이름, 정체(성) proponent 지지자 personal 직접적인, 몸소 하는 engage with ~와 소통하다 presence 존재(감) earnings 수익 accordingly 그에 따라 in-house 내부의 in a timely fashion 적시에 necessity 반드시 필요한 것

172 주제 / 목적

번역 기사의 목적은?

(A) 몇몇 지역 회사 연혁 소개하기
(B) 스코틀랜드 패션 동향 논의하기
(C) 업체 성장 과정 설명하기
(D) 새로운 사진 서비스 광고하기

해설 첫 번째 단락에서 아바스칼 씨가 고향인 에든버러에 작은 가게를 열었다(she ~ opened a small store in her hometown of Edinburgh)고 한 후, 두 번째 단락에서 아바스칼 씨의 작은 가게가 매년 수백만 파운드를 버는 성공적인 기업으로 성장했다(Fast-forward to today, ~ a successful enterprise that earns millions of pounds each year)며 사업체를 소개했다. 또한 기사 전반에서 아바스칼 씨의 사업체가 성장해 온 과정을 설명하고 있으므로, (C)가 정답이다.

어휘 illustrate 설명하다

173 사실 관계 확인

번역 예스 욜란다에 관해 명시된 것은?

(A) 여러 해 동안 판매량이 꾸준했다.
(B) 맨체스터에 첫 번째 매장을 열었다.
(C) 최근 웹 디자이너가 상을 받았다.
(D) 한때는 다른 이름으로 알려졌다.

해설 첫 번째 단락에서 아바스칼 씨가 고향인 에든버러에 세이 예스 투 욜란다라는 작은 가게를 열었다(she ~ opened a small store in her hometown of Edinburgh called Say Yes To Yolanda)고 했는데, 이후 두 번째 단락에서 온라인 상호명과 동일하게 대표 매장의 이름을 예스 욜란다로 바꿨다(It was ~ to rename the flagship store Yes Yolanda to match its digital identity)고 했으므로, (D)가 정답이다.

174 동의어 찾기

번역 다섯 번째 단락 2행의 "fashion"과 의미가 가장 가까운 단어는?

(A) 형태
(B) 스타일
(C) 행사
(D) 방식

해설 "fashion"이 포함된 부분은 '온라인 전시용 제품을 적시에 사진으로 찍을 수 있다(items are photographed in a timely fashion for online display)'라는 의미로 해석되는데, 여기서 fashion은 '방식, ~하는 식'이라는 뜻으로 쓰였다. 따라서 '방식, 태도'라는 의미의 (D) manner가 정답이다. 참고로 in a timely manner[fashion]는 '시기적절하게, 적시에'라는 관용적 표현으로 묶어서 기억하도록 한다.

175 문장 삽입

번역 [1], [2], [3], [4]로 표시된 곳 중에서 다음 문장이 들어가기에 가장 적합한 곳은?

"그녀는 그들이 실제 매장에서 쇼핑할 때 필요한 것을 가장 잘 충족시킬 수 있다고 여전히 믿는다."

(A) [1]
(B) [2]
(C) [3]
(D) [4]

해설 주어진 문장은 아바스칼 씨가 생각하는 실제 매장에서 쇼핑할 때의 이점이다. 따라서 이 문장이 들어갈 앞뒤 문맥에도 이와 비슷한 생각이 언급되어야 한다. [3] 앞에서 아바스칼 씨는 직접적인 상호 교류를 강력히 지지하며, 고객들과 소통하기를 좋아한다(Ms. Abascal is a strong proponent ~ with her customers)고 하면서 실제 매장을 좋아하는 이유를 언급했으므로 (C)가 정답이다. 참고로 [3] 뒤에서는 주어진 문장과 대조적으로(However) 아바스칼 씨가 온라인 매장의 존재가 중요하다는 사실을 인식하고 있음(she realizes that an online presence is important)을 밝히고 있으므로, (C)가 답이 되는 추가적인 근거가 된다.

176-180 온라인 양식 + 이메일

http://www.quipwerxsoftware.com/support_request

퀍워스 지원 요청서

본 양식을 작성하고 제출해 지원 티켓 번호를 생성하세요. 24시간 이내에 이메일로 회신 드립니다.

이름: 아그네스 코왈스키
회사: [180]**알렉시사**
이메일 주소: akowalski@alexsycorp.net
제목: 웹기반 회의 문제

겪고 계신 문제를 설명하세요.

[177]**6월에 귀사의 웹기반 회의 소프트웨어를 사용하기 시작했고 대체로 만족합니다.** 그런데 어제 중요한 교육 세션 도중 여러 차례 서비스가 중단되었습니다. 회의가 한창일 때 갑자기 화면이 까맣게 되고 "점검을 위해 퀍워스가 작동을 멈춥니다"라는 안내문이 나타났습니다. 몇몇 직원이 해외에서 전화를 걸고 있었고 이 안내문이 여러 차례 나타난 뒤로 우리는 일정을 다시 잡기로 했습니다. [176]**점검 일정을 미리 저희에게 알려 줄 방법이 있을까요?** [177]**없다면 아마도 회원권을 해지하게 될 것 같습니다.** [178]**제가 필요할 때 언제든지 귀사 제품을 쓸 수 있다는 확신이 있어야 합니다.**

제출

어휘 response 회신 interruption 중단 in advance 미리 terminate 해지하다

수신: 아그네스 코왈스키 〈akowalski@alexsycorp.net〉
발신: 퀍워스 지원 〈support@quipwerxsoftware.com〉
날짜: 7월 29일
제목: 티켓 000125659 – 웹기반 회의 문제

코왈스키 씨께,

고객님의 우려 사항에 대해 연락 주셔서 감사합니다. 고객님이 지난 수요일에 겪은 문제는 데이터베이스 통신 문제로 서버가 다운되어 발생했습니다. 저희가 이 문제를 예측할 수 없어서 고객님께 미리 알려 드리지 못했습니다. 이런 일이 발생하는 경우는 매우 드물다는 점 확실히 말씀드립니다.

[179]**고객님의 지적을 고려하여, 알림 메시지를 "점검을 위해 작동 멈춤"에서 "기술적 문제가 발생함"으로 바꾸기로 결정했습니다.** 이렇게 하면 고객님들이 정기 점검이 아니라 예상치 못한 상황 때문에 문제가 발생했다는 점을 아실 것입니다. 사실, 저희 소프트웨어는 점검을 위해 작동을 멈추는 일이 거의 없습니다. 업그레이드 작업을 할 때 혹시 그런 일이 있다 하더라도, 소프트웨어를 사용할 수 없는 건 단 몇 분간입니다.

이번 일로 고객님께 불편을 끼쳐 드려 유감으로 생각하며 의견에 진심으로 감사드립니다. [180]**거래에 감사하는 마음으로, 귀사의 계정에 대해 이번 달 서비스 요금을 면제해 드리겠습니다.**

신디 트라우트만, 퀍워스 지원

어휘 crash (컴퓨터 등이) 갑자기 멈추다 anticipate 예측하다 assure 확언하다 occurrence 발생 rare 드문 in light of ~을 고려하여, ~에 비추어 reword 바꾸어 말하다 unforeseen 예상치 못한 circumstance 상황 routine 정기적인 if at all 혹시 ~하더라도 inconvenience 불편 waive 면제하다

176 세부 사항

번역 코왈스키 씨가 온라인 양식에서 요청한 것은?

(A) 회원권 취소
(B) 정비 일정
(C) 고객 지원부의 전화
(D) 새 교육 세션 시간

해설 온라인 양식의 문제 설명란(Please describe the problem you are experiencing) 하단에서 점검 일정을 미리 알려 줄 방법이 있는지(Is there a way for you to inform us of your maintenance schedule in advance?) 문의했으므로, (B)가 정답이다.

▸▸ Paraphrasing 지문의 your maintenance schedule
→ 정답의 A maintenance calendar

177 추론 / 암시

번역 코왈스키 씨에 관해 암시된 것은?

(A) 한때 퀍워스에서 일했다.
(B) 6월에 알렉시사에 입사했다.
(C) 웹기반 회의 소프트웨어를 정기적으로 사용한다.
(D) 매주 수요일마다 교육 세션을 수행한다.

TEST 8

해설 온라인 양식 문제 설명란(Please describe the problem you are experiencing)의 첫 번째 문장에서 6월에 컴워스의 웹기반 회의 소프트웨어를 사용하기 시작했다(We started using your Web-conferencing software in June)고 한 후, 후반부에서 정비 일정을 미리 알려 줄 수 없다면 아마도 회원권을 해지하게 될 것 같다(If not, I will probably terminate my membership)고 했으므로, 회원권을 보유한 코왈스키 씨가 웹기반 회의 소프트웨어를 정기적으로 사용한다는 것을 추론할 수 있다. 따라서 (C)가 정답이다.

178 세부 사항

번역 코왈스키 씨가 컴워스 회의 소프트웨어에 갖는 불만은?

(A) 자신의 현재 목적에 부합하지 않는다.
(B) 자신의 컴퓨터와 호환되지 않는다.
(C) 신뢰할 수 없다.
(D) 자신의 해외 고객이 쓸 수 없다.

해설 온라인 양식 문제 설명란(Please describe the problem you are experiencing)의 마지막 문장에서 코왈스키 씨가 필요할 때 언제든지 컴워스사의 제품을 쓸 수 있다는 확신이 있어야 한다(I must be confident that I can use your product anytime I need it)고 했으므로, 사용상의 신뢰 문제를 우회적으로 언급했다는 것을 알 수 있다. 따라서 (C)가 정답이다.

어휘 incompatible 호환되지 않는 unreliable 신뢰할 수 없는

179 세부 사항

번역 트라우트만 씨는 컴워스가 무엇을 바꿀 것이라고 말하는가?

(A) 오작동 메시지
(B) 고객 계약
(C) 웹기반 회의 소프트웨어
(D) 정비 일정

해설 이메일의 두 번째 단락에서 알림 메시지를 "점검을 위해 작동 멈춤"에서 "기술적 문제가 발생함"으로 바꾸기로 결정했다(we have decided to reword our alert message from "down for maintenance" to "experiencing technical difficulties")고 했으므로, (A)가 정답이다.

어휘 malfunction 오작동

▸▸ Paraphrasing 지문의 reword → 질문의 change
지문의 our alert message
→ 정답의 Its malfunction message

180 연계

번역 알렉시사에 관해 명시된 것은?

(A) 시스템을 정기적으로 점검한다.
(B) 매주 신입 사원을 채용한다.
(C) 최근 소프트웨어를 업그레이드했다.
(D) 컴워스에 월별 요금을 납부한다.

해설 온라인 양식의 회사명(Company)을 보면 질문에서 언급된 알렉시사가 코왈스키 씨가 근무하는 회사임을 확인할 수 있는데, 이메일의 마지막 단락에서 거래에 감사하는 마음으로, 코왈스키 씨 회사의 계정에 대해 이번 달 서비스 요금을 면제해 준다(In appreciation of your business, we will be waiving the service fee on your company account for this month)고 했으므로, 알렉시사가 월별 요금을 납부한다는 것을 알 수 있다. 따라서 (D)가 정답이다.

181-185 이메일 + 설명서

발신: 희란 김, 휠링 여행사
수신: 미히르 수크바라
제목: 스포츠 무역 박람회 출장 계획
보냄: 7월 3일
첨부: 시드니-퍼스 여행 일정

수크바라 씨께,

[185]**고객님의 요청에 따라, 퍼스로 가는 왕복표를 예약했습니다.** [181]**시드니에서 출발하는 날은 7월 20일이며, 퍼스에서 돌아오는 날은 7월 24일로, 7월 21~23일 무역 박람회에 완벽하게 맞출 수 있을 겁니다.** 여행 일정을 첨부합니다.

[181/182]**견본을 가지고 갈 수 있느냐는 질문에 답해 드리자면, 스키와 스노보드는 수하물로 부칠 수 있습니다. 캔버라 항공사에 연락해 보니 대형 짐 하나당 75호주 달러의 수수료가 있다고 합니다.** 이 수수료를 미리 지불하면 수속할 때 대형 품목을 위탁 수하물 전용 수속대에서 보낼 수 있습니다. 품목이 항공사의 최대 허용 중량 및 크기 요건을 초과하지 않도록 하십시오. [183]**몇 개의 품목을 부치고 싶은지 알려 주시면 제가 대신 선불로 지불하겠습니다.**

희란 김
휠링 여행사

어휘 itinerary 여행 일정 accommodate 맞추다 in reply to ~에 대한 답으로 luggage 수하물 kiosk 수속기[수속대] exceed 초과하다 allowable 허용되는 weight 무게 requirement 요건 prepayment 선불

캔버라 항공사

빠른 수하물 위탁 서비스 – 설명서

공항에 도착하시면 간단히 다음 단계를 따르십시오:

1. 터미널에 들어가면 무인 탑승 수속기에서 탑승권을 출력하십시오.
2. [184]**안내를 따라 위탁 수하물 전용 수속대로 가서 품목을 저울에 놓으십시오. 사진이 있는 신분증과 탑승권을 저희 직원에게 제시하면 직원이 가방을 몇 개 부치는지 묻습니다.**
3. 저희 직원이 가방에 수하물표를 붙이고 서류를 돌려 드리면 바로 보안 검색대로 가십시오.

주의: [185]**빠른 수하물 위탁 서비스는 현재 시드니, 멜버른, 브리즈번에서만 이용하실 수 있습니다.**

어휘 scale 저울 agent 직원 proceed 진행하다

181 추론 / 암시

번역 이메일에 의하면, 수크바라 씨가 퍼스로 가는 이유는 무엇이겠는가?

(A) 스포츠 경기 참가
(B) 회사 합병 협상
(C) 자사 제품 홍보
(D) 시 인근 고객 방문

해설 이메일의 첫 번째 단락에서 시드니에서 출발하는 날은 7월 20일이며, 퍼스에서 돌아오는 날은 7월 24일로, 7월 21~23일 무역 박람회에 완벽하게 맞출 수 있을 것(Departure from Sydney is ~ accommodate your 21-23 July Trade Show)이라고 했고, 두 번째 단락에서 견본 지참이 가능한지에 대한 수크바라 씨의 질문(In reply to your question whether your samples)을 언급했으므로, 수크바라 씨가 무역 박람회에서 자사 제품을 홍보할 것으로 추론할 수 있다. 따라서 (C)가 정답이다.

어휘 compete 경쟁하다, 겨루다 negotiate 협상하다 merger 합병

182 사실 관계 확인

번역 수크바라 씨의 대형 수하물에 관해 사실인 것은?

(A) 스포츠 장비로 구성된다.
(B) 제한 중량을 초과한다.
(C) 김 씨가 짐을 꾸릴 것이다.
(D) 무역 박람회에서 구매했다.

해설 두 번째 단락에서 견본을 가지고 갈 수 있느냐는 질문에 대한 답으로, 스키와 스노보드는 수하물로 부칠 수 있다(In reply to your question ~ the skis and snowboards can be checked as luggage)고 한 후, 대형 짐 하나당 75호주 달러의 수수료가 있다(there is a $75 AUD fee for each piece of oversized luggage)는 부연 설명을 했으므로, (A)가 정답이다.

▸▸ Paraphrasing 지문의 the skis and snowboards → 정답의 sports equipment

183 세부 사항

번역 김 씨가 수크바라 씨를 위해 하겠다고 제안한 일은?

(A) 호텔 예약
(B) 요금 처리
(C) 배송 일정 잡기
(D) 셔틀 교통 마련

해설 이메일의 두 번째 단락에서 수크바라 씨가 몇 개의 품목을 부치고 싶은지 알려 주면 김 씨가 선불로 지불하겠다(Please let me know how many items ~ make the prepayment for you)고 제안을 했으므로, (B)가 정답이다.

▸▸ Paraphrasing 지문의 make the payment → 정답의 Handle a fee

184 사실 관계 확인

번역 탑승권에 관해 명시된 것은?

(A) 김 씨의 이메일에 첨부되었다.
(B) 집에서 출력해야 한다.
(C) 항공사 직원을 통해서만 입수할 수 있다.
(D) 위탁 수하물 수속대에서 제시해야 한다.

해설 설명서의 2번 단계에서 안내에 따라 위탁 수하물 전용 수속대로 가서(Follow directions to the express drop-off kiosk) 품목을 저울에 놓은 후, 사진이 있는 신분증과 탑승권을 직원에게 제시할 것(Show your photo ID and boarding pass to one of our agents)을 요청했으므로, (D)가 정답이다. 1번 단계에서 터미널에 들어가면 무인 탑승 수속기에서 탑승권을 출력하라고 안내했으므로, (A), (B), (C)는 모두 적절하지 않다.

어휘 obtain 입수하다 present 제시하다

▸▸ Paraphrasing 지문의 Show your photo ID and boarding pass → 정답의 It must be presented

185 연계

번역 수크바라 씨의 귀국 항공편에 관해 암시된 것은?

(A) 수크바라 씨는 밤 사이에 시드니로 돌아갈 것이다.
(B) 수크바라 씨는 자신의 귀국행 티켓을 구매할 것이다.
(C) 수크바라 씨는 빠른 위탁 서비스를 이용할 수 없을 것이다.
(D) 수크바라 씨는 여행 일정을 변경할 수 없을 것이다.

해설 이메일의 첫 번째 단락에서 수크바라 씨의 요청에 따라, 퍼스로 가는 왕복표를 예약했다(Per your request, I have reserved your round-trip ticket to Perth)고 했으므로, 수크바라 씨의 귀국 항공편이 퍼스에서 출발한다는 것을 알 수 있다. 설명서의 주의 사항(NOTE)에서 빠른 수하물 위탁 서비스는 현재 시드니, 멜버른, 브리즈번에서만 이용할 수 있다(Express drop-off service is currently available only in Sydney, Melbourne, and Brisbane)고 했으므로, 귀국 항공편의 출발지인 퍼스에서는 빠른 수하물 위탁 서비스를 이용할 수 없을 것으로 추론할 수 있다. 따라서 (C)가 정답이다.

어휘 modify 변경하다

186-190 웹페이지 + 이메일 + 기사

http://www.newstarthome.org/donations

뉴 스타트 홈 매장에서 새 가구나 중고 가구, 가전 제품, 가정용품, 건축 자재를 기증받습니다. 물품은 상태가 양호해야 합니다. 수리가 필요한 물품 또는 얼룩이 있거나 찢어진 물품은 받지 않습니다. [186]**물품 판매 수익은 교육 프로그램, 주택 개조, 근린 공원 미화 같은 지역 사회 프로젝트에 자금을 지원하는 데 쓰입니다.**

기증 방법:

1. [187]**저희 메인 화면에서 검색창에 주소를 입력해 가장 가까운 뉴 스타트 홈 지점을 찾으세요.**

TEST 8

2. 필요 없는 물건을 직접 갖다주거나 가장 가까운 지점에 연락해 커다란 물품이나 대량 기부 물품을 집 또는 업체에서 수거하도록 일정을 잡으세요.

3. 각 지점의 영업 시간은 웹사이트에서 확인하세요.

어휘 donation 기부, 기증 stain 얼룩지게 하다 rip 찢다 proceeds 수익 neighborhood park 근린공원 beautification 미화

발신: bmorris@morriscountryinn.com
수신: aperez@newstarthome.org
날짜: 3월 27일
내용: 기증

페레즈 씨께,

[188]**저는 캔턴에 있는 모리스 컨트리 호텔의 주인입니다. 이곳은 제가 다음 달에 은퇴하면 영구적으로 문을 닫을 예정입니다.** 제게 침대, 책상, 안락의자 등 상태가 아주 좋은 가구들이 많습니다. 친구가 이 물품을 귀하의 단체에 기부하면 어떻겠냐고 제안했습니다. [187/189]**하트포드에 있는 뉴 스타트 홈 지점이 제 호텔과 가장 가까운 것 같은데, 귀하가 거기 지점 매니저시더군요.** 저희는 거의 35마일 떨어진 곳에 위치해 있습니다. [189]**이 물품들을 제 시설에서 수거하도록 일정을 잡을 수 있을까요?**

브렌다 모리스

모리스 컨트리 호텔

어휘 inn 여관, 호텔 permanently 영구적으로 organization 조직, 단체 establishment 시설

모리스 컨트리 호텔 문을 닫다

캔턴(4월 27일) – [189]**브렌다 모리스는 모리스 컨트리 호텔 가구를 가득 실은 뉴 스타트 홈 트럭이 멀어지는 모습을 지켜보았다.** 그녀는 40년 동안 지역의 대표적인 건물인 이 호텔의 주인이자 운영자였다. "[190]**해변과 따뜻한 날씨가 있는 씨뷰 포인트로 가게 되어 행복해요.**" 모리스 씨가 말했다. "그리고 이제 자원봉사를 하고 그저 쉬면서 시간을 보낼 계획입니다. 그러나 호텔은 제 인생에서 큰 부분을 차지해 왔기 때문에 이 지역을 떠나는 게 힘들 거예요."

모리스 컨트리 호텔이 있는 부지는 브렌트 밸리 개발 그룹에 매각되었는데, 이 그룹은 내년에 이 건물을 아파트로 바꿀 계획이다.

어휘 volunteer 자원봉사하다 property 부동산, 부지 convert 바꾸다

186 세부 사항

번역 웹페이지에 의하면, 뉴 스타트 홈은 받은 물품을 어떻게 하는가?

(A) 판매한다.
(B) 학교에 기부한다.
(C) 재활용하도록 보낸다.
(D) 수리한다.

해설 웹페이지의 첫 번째 단락에서 물품 판매 수익이 지역 사회 프로젝트에 자금을 지원하는 데 쓰인다(Proceeds from the sale of our goods are used to fund community projects)고 했으므로, 기증 받은 물품을 판매한다는 것을 알 수 있다. 따라서 (A)가 정답이다.

▸▸ Paraphrasing 지문의 **the sale of our goods**
→ 정답의 **sells them(items)**

187 연계

번역 모리스 씨가 뉴 스타트 홈 매니저 이름을 알게 된 경위는 무엇이겠는가?

(A) 온라인 검색
(B) 다른 단체에 이메일 보내기
(C) 지역 신문 기사 읽기
(D) 지역 프로젝트 참여

해설 이메일에서 하트포드에 있는 뉴 스타트 홈 지점이 모리스 씨의 호텔과 가장 가까운 것 같다(The New Start Home branch in Hartford seems to be the closest to my inn)고 한 후, 수신인(you)인 페레즈 씨가 하트포드 지점의 매니저(you are the store manager there)라고 했는데, 웹페이지의 기증 방법(How to donate)을 보면 메인 화면에서 검색창에 주소를 입력해 가장 가까운 뉴 스타트 홈 지점을 찾을 것(Using our home screen, ~ into the search box)을 지시했으므로, 온라인 검색을 통해 지점 위치와 매니저의 이름을 알았을 것으로 추론할 수 있다. 따라서 (A)가 정답이다.

▸▸ Paraphrasing 지문의 **find ~ by entering your address into the search box**
→ 정답의 **By searching online**

188 사실 관계 확인

번역 이메일에서 모리스 씨에 관해 명시된 것은?

(A) 친구와 함께 뉴 스타트 홈을 방문했다.
(B) 새 직장을 찾고 있다.
(C) 사업을 접기로 결심했다.
(D) 업체로 가는 길 안내가 필요하다.

해설 이메일의 초반부에서 모리스 씨가 자신을 캔턴에 있는 모리스 컨트리 호텔의 주인(I am the owner of the Morris Country Inn in Canton)이라고 소개한 후, 다음 달에 은퇴하면 영구적으로 호텔 문을 닫을 예정(It will be closing permanently when I retire next month)이라고 했으므로, (C)가 정답이다.

▸▸ Paraphrasing 지문의 **It(Morris Country Inn) will be closing permanently** → 정답의 **close a business**

189 연계

번역 뉴 스타트 홈 하트포드 지점에 관해 암시된 것은?

(A) 호텔에 가구를 비치한다.
(B) 학생들이 직원이다.
(C) 현재 재고가 매진되었다.
(D) 인근 지역에서 기증 물품을 수거한다.

해설 이메일의 중반부에서 모리스 씨는 자신의 호텔과 가장 가까운 뉴 스타트 홈 하트포드 지점(The New Start Home branch in Hartford seems to be the closest)의 매니저인 페레즈 씨에게 자신의 시설에서 물품들을 수거하도록 일정을 잡을 수 있는지(Can I arrange a pickup of these goods at my establishment?) 문의했는데, 기사의 첫 번째 단락에서 모리스 씨가 모리스 컨트리 호텔 가구를 가득 실은 뉴 스타트 홈 트럭이 멀어지는 모습을 지켜보았다(Brenda Morris watched ~ from the Morris Country Inn)고 했으므로, 뉴 스타트 홈 하트포드 지점이 인근 지역의 기부 물품을 수거한다고 추론할 수 있다. 따라서 (D)가 정답이다.

190 세부 사항

번역 기사에 의하면 모리스 씨는 다음에 어디에 거주할 계획인가?

(A) 하트포드
(B) 씨뷰 포인트
(C) 캔턴
(D) 브렌트 밸리

해설 기사의 첫 번째 단락에서 '해변과 따뜻한 날씨가 있는 씨뷰 포인트로 가게 되어 행복하다(I am happy to be heading to Seaview Point, with its beaches and warm weather)'라는 모리스 씨의 말을 인용했으므로, (B)가 정답이다.

191-195 이메일 + 주문서 + 이메일

수신: 이모젠 챔버스 〈ichambers@championos.com〉
발신: 레지날드 리 〈rlee@cooperandcolsonlaw.org〉
내용: 사무용품 주문
날짜: 3월 20일

챔버스 씨께,

저희는 챔피언 사무용품점에 고정 주문을 하고 있으며, 매달 1일에 당사로 자동 배송됩니다. [191]**다가오는 달에 대한 통상 주문을 첨부된 양식에 간략하게 정리한 대로 수정하고 싶어 메일을 씁니다.** [194]**과거에 주문했던 잉크 토너를 명시한 것처럼 다른 브랜드로 교체했으면 한다는 점을 유념해 주십시오.** [192]**덧붙여 저희는 최근 변호사들을 새로 채용했고 그들을 위한 사무 공간을 추가로 준비하고 있기 때문에 이번 달에만 WB918 품목을 주문에 추가하고 싶습니다.** 귀사가 파일로 가지고 있는 당사의 신용카드 계정을 사용하세요.

[193]**저희는 귀사의 제품, 특히 당사 로고가 있는 재활용 문구류 제품에 계속 만족하고 있습니다.**

감사합니다.

레지날드 리, 사무실 관리자
쿠퍼 앤 콜슨 법률사무소

어휘 standing order (취소나 변경 때까지 유지되는) 고정 주문 delivery 배송 modify 수정하다 replace 교체하다 attorney 변호사 merchandise 제품 recycled 재활용된 stationery 문구류

주문처: 쿠퍼 앤 콜슨 법률사무소 배송일: 4월 1일
연락: 레지날드 리

품목 설명	품번	수량	단가	항목별 총액
회사명과 주소가 인쇄된 편지지	LH228	10연	54.00	540.00
화이트보드 펜	WP263	4자루씩 10묶음	4.99	49.90
[194]**사이트로닉스 잉크 토너 카트리지**	[194]**CP576**	8	42.00	336.00
[195]**와이트글로우 마그네틱 화이트보드**(50"X35")	WB918	4	[195]**79.99**	319.96
챔피언 사무용품			세금:	74.75
			총액:	1320.61 달러

어휘 description 설명 letterhead 주소, 이름 등이 인쇄된 편지지

이메일 메시지

수신: 레지날드 리 〈rlee@cooperandcolsonlaw.org〉
발신: 이모젠 챔버스 〈ichambers@championos.com〉
내용: 사무용품 주문
날짜: 3월 21일

리 씨께,

주문서에 정리된 대로 요청에 기꺼이 맞춰 드리겠습니다. 그런데 아쉽게도 현재 와이트글로우 브랜드 화이트보드는 재고가 없습니다. [195]**다른 고객들의 호평을 받고 있는 다른 상표의 마그네틱 화이트보드인 스텔라 화이트보드를 추천합니다.** 이 화이트보드는 시장에서 최고라고 평가받고 있습니다. [195]**일반적으로 각각 85달러지만, 한번 써 보고 싶으시면 와이트글로우 브랜드와 같은 가격에 4개를 기꺼이 제공하겠습니다.** 말씀만 해 주세요. 감사합니다.

이모젠 챔버스

어휘 accommodate 맞추다 unfortunately 아쉽게도 recommend 추천하다 typically 일반적으로, 대체로

191 주제 / 목적

번역 첫 번째 이메일의 목적은?

(A) 정기 주문 수정하기
(B) 배송 오류 알리기
(C) 제품에 대한 불만 제기하기
(D) 배송일 확인하기

해설 첫 번째 이메일의 첫 번째 단락에서 다가오는 달에 대한 통상 주문을 첨부된 양식에 간략하게 정리한 대로 수정하고 싶어 메일을 쓴다(I am writing because we would like to modify)며 이메일을 쓴 목적을 구체적으로 밝혔으므로, (A)가 정답이다.

TEST 8

> ▸▸ Paraphrasing 지문의 modify our usual order
> → 정답의 amend a regular order

192 사실 관계 확인

번역 첫 번째 이메일에서 쿠퍼 앤 콜슨 법률사무소에 관해 명시된 것은?

(A) 얼마 전 새 복사기를 설치했다.
(B) 현재 확장되고 있다.
(C) 이전이 진행되고 있다.
(D) 얼마 전 새 사무실 관리자를 채용했다.

해설 첫 번째 이메일의 첫 번째 단락에서 쿠퍼 앤 콜슨 법률사무소가 최근 변호사들을 새로 채용했고 신입 변호사들을 위한 사무 공간을 추가로 준비하고 있다(we would like to add ~ preparing additional office spaces for them)고 했으므로, (B)가 정답이다.

어휘 relocate 이전하다

> ▸▸ Paraphrasing 지문의 preparing additional office spaces
> → 정답의 expanding

193 세부 사항

번역 리 씨가 특히 마음에 들어하는 제품은?

(A) 회사명과 주소 등이 있는 종이
(B) 화이트보드 펜
(C) 와이트글로우 마그네틱 화이트보드
(D) 사이트로닉스 잉크 토너 카트리지

해설 첫 번째 이메일의 두 번째 단락에서 챔피언 사무용품의 제품, 특히 쿠퍼 앤 콜슨 로고가 있는 재활용 문구류 제품에 계속 만족하고 있다(We continue to be pleased with ~ products with our firm's logo)고 했으므로, (A)가 정답이다. 참고로 letterhead는 편지지의 윗부분에 인쇄된 문구를 뜻하기도 하며, 개인 및 회사나 단체의 이름, 주소, 전화번호 등을 포함한다.

> ▸▸ Paraphrasing 지문의 especially → 질문의 particularly
> 지문의 the recycled stationery products with our firm's logo → 정답의 Paper with company letterhead

194 연계

번역 정기 주문 제품의 대체품을 식별하는 품목 번호는?

(A) LH228
(B) WP263
(C) CP576
(D) WB918

해설 첫 번째 이메일의 첫 번째 단락에서 과거에 주문했던 잉크 토너를 명시한 것처럼 다른 브랜드로 교체하도록(we would like the ink toner that we have ordered in the past to be replaced by a different brand as indicated) 요청했는데, 주문서를 보면 새로 주문한 잉크 토너는 사이트로닉스 잉크 토너 카트리지(Cytronics ink toner cartridge)로 품목 번호(Item Number)가 CP576임을 확인할 수 있다. 따라서 (C)가 정답이다.

> ▸▸ Paraphrasing 지문의 the ink toner that we have ordered in the past
> → 질문의 a regularly ordered product

195 연계

번역 법률사무소가 스텔라 브랜드 화이트보드 하나에 지불할 돈은?

(A) 49.90달러
(B) 54달러
(C) 79.99달러
(D) 85달러

해설 두 번째 이메일에서 다른 고객들의 호평을 받고 있는 다른 상표의 마그네틱 화이트보드인 스텔라 화이트보드를 추천한다(I can recommend another brand ~ called Stellar Whiteboards)고 한 후, 일반적으로 각각 85달러지만 와이트글로우 브랜드와 같은 가격에 제공하겠다(They are typically $85 each, but ~ at the same cost of the Witeglow brand)고 했다. 주문서를 보면 와이트글로우 마그네틱 화이트보드(Witeglow Magnetic Whiteboard)의 단가(Price Per Unit)가 79.99달러임을 확인할 수 있으므로, (C)가 정답이다.

196-200 일정표 + 이메일 + 이메일

브렌튼 솔루션즈
3동 회의실 일정
3월 매주 월요일

본 일정표는 3월 한 달간 월요일마다 회의실에 정기 예약된 회의들을 보여줍니다. 경영진이 촉박하게 사전 통보하면서 회의실을 요청할 수 있다는 점 유념하시기 바랍니다. [196]**이런 일이 있을 경우 재닛 마튼에게 jmarten@brentonsolutions.com으로 구내 다른 건물에 있는 회의실에 관해 문의하시기 바랍니다.**

시간대	3A실 (수용 인원: 35명)	3B실 (수용 인원: 50명)
오전 1 오전 9시-10시	이용 가능	[199]**영업팀** (필요 시 프로젝트 그룹별로 나누어 3A실 사용)
오전 2 오전 10시 30분-11시 45분	[199]**인사부**	여름 행사 기획
오후 1 오후 2시-2시 45분	고객 서비스부	기술 및 엔지니어링
오후 2 [198]**오후 3시-4시**	이용 가능	[199]**마케팅 그룹**

어휘 regularly 정기적으로 advance notice 사전 통보 capacity 수용 인원

수신: 팀장들
발신: 재닛 마튼
제목: 회의실 일정
날짜: 2월 27일

팀장 전원에게:

브렌튼 솔루션즈의 저희 부서가 기업 경영팀을 모실 예정이므로, 3월 12일 월요일 3동 회의실 두 곳 모두 하루 종일 이용할 수 없다는 점 알려 드립니다. [198]**이 회의들은 정확히 오전 9시 30분에 시작해 오후 회의가 보통 끝나는 시간에서 1시간 초과해 연장될 것으로 예상됩니다.** [197]**이날 회의 공간이 필요한 팀장은 늦어도 금요일까지 이 이메일로 직접 회신하여 요청서를 제게 보내셔야 합니다.** 공간은 선착순으로 예약됩니다. 감사합니다!

재닛 마튼, 기업 비서실

어휘 be expected to ~할 것으로 예상되다 promptly 정확히 제시간에 extend 연장되다[하다] no later than 늦어도 first-come, first-served basis 선착순으로

수신: 전 직원
발신: 재닛 마튼
제목: 월요일 일정 변경
날짜: 3월 5일

[199]**3월 12일 경영진 회의 때문에 회의실 일정이 아래와 같이 변경되었다는 점 유의하십시오.** 임시 회의실 배정은:

- [199]**오전 1 회의들은 5A실, 5B실에서 열립니다. 필요에 따라 공간을 나누세요.**
- [199]**마케팅 그룹은 오후 1 시간대에 4B실에서 모입니다.**

이 회의실 두 곳 모두 수용 인원이 제한되어 있다는 점을 유념하셔서 그에 따라 계획을 세우세요. [199]**위에 언급되지 않은 회의들은 취소되었습니다.** 회의나 취소와 관련된 질문은 팀장에게 문의해야 합니다. [200]**참석할 수 없는 직원들을 위해 회의록을 온라인에 통상 올리는 곳에 게시하겠습니다.**

어휘 temporary 임시의 assignment 배정 accordingly 그에 따라 address 언급하다 electronically 전자기기로, 인터넷으로, 컴퓨터로

196 사실 관계 확인

번역 일정표에 의하면, 브렌튼 솔루션즈에 관해 사실인 것은?

(A) 최대 회의실 수용 인원은 35명이다.
(B) 건물이 여러 동 있다.
(C) 연간으로 회의실 일정을 발표한다.
(D) 직원들이 한 달에 한 번 모인다.

해설 일정표의 상단에서 경영진이 촉박하게 사전 통보하면서 회의실을 요청하는 경우 재닛 마튼에게 구내 다른 건물에 있는 회의실에 관해 문의할 것(If this occurs, you may contact Janet Marten ~ to inquire about rooms in other buildings on campus)을 권고했는데, 이를 통해 브렌튼 솔루션즈에 여러 동의 건물이 있다는 것을 알 수 있다. 따라서 (B)가 정답이다.

197 세부 사항

번역 팀장들이 첫 번째 이메일에 회신해야 하는 이유는?

(A) 회의실 예약을 위해
(B) 기업 경영진과 면담하기 위해
(C) 회의록을 구하기 위해
(D) 추가 직원을 요청하기 위해

해설 첫 번째 이메일의 후반부에서 3월 12일에 회의 공간이 필요한 팀장은 늦어도 금요일까지 해당 이메일로 직접 회신하여 요청서를 보낼 것(Any team leads in need of conference space on this date should send)을 권고했으므로, (A)가 정답이다.

어휘 minutes 회의록

▸▸ Paraphrasing 지문의 conference space → 정답의 a room

198 연계

번역 기업 경영진 방문은 언제 끝나겠는가?

(A) 오전 11시 45분
(B) 오후 2시 45분
(C) 오후 4시
(D) 오후 5시

해설 첫 번째 이메일에서 기업 경영진과 진행하는 회의들이 오전 9시 30분에 시작해 오후 회의가 보통 끝나는 시간에서 1시간 초과해 연장되리라 예상된다(These meetings are expected ~ to extend one full hour past the time that afternoon meetings usually end)고 했는데, 일정표에서 시간대(Time Slot)가 정리된 부분을 보면 마지막 일정(Afternoon 2)이 오후 4시(3:00-4:00 P.M.)에 끝난다고 나와 있으므로, 기업 경영진의 방문은 1시간이 초과된 오후 5시에 끝날 것으로 추론할 수 있다. 따라서 (D)가 정답이다.

199 연계

번역 어떤 팀이 3월 12일에 회의가 없을 것인가?

(A) 영업팀
(B) 마케팅 그룹
(C) 경영진
(D) 인사부

해설 두 번째 이메일에서 3월 12일 경영진 회의로 인한 회의실 일정이 변경되었으니 유의하라고(Please make note of the following changes ~ on March 12) 한 후, 오전 1 회의와 마케팅 그룹의 회의 장소를 다시 배정하고 있다. 그리고 마지막 단락에서 '위에 언급되지 않은 회의들은 취소되었다(Meetings not addressed above are canceled)'라고 했다. 일정표를 보면, 오전 1 회의는 영업 팀(Sales Team) 회의라고 되어 있으므로, 3월 12일에는 경영진, 영업

TEST 8

팀, 마케팅 그룹이 회의를 진행할 예정이고, 인사부 회의는 취소되었음을 알 수 있다. 따라서 (D)가 정답이다.

200 사실 관계 확인

번역 회의를 놓친 직원들에 관해 명시된 것은?

(A) 재닛 마튼에게 연락해야 한다.
(B) 팀장과 면담해야 한다.
(C) 온라인으로 회의 정보를 볼 수 있다.
(D) 3B에서 두 번째 세션에 참석할 수 있다.

해설 두 번째 이메일의 마지막 단락에서 참석할 수 없는 직원들을 위해 회의록을 온라인에 통상 올리는 곳에 게시하겠다(Meeting notes will be posted electronically in the usual location for those who are unable to attend)고 했으므로, (C)가 정답이다.

▸▸ Paraphrasing 지문의 **those who are unable to attend** → 질문의 **employees who miss a meeting**

지문의 **Meeting notes will be posted electronically** → 정답의 **access meeting information online**

기출 TEST 9

101 (A)	102 (C)	103 (D)	104 (B)	105 (A)
106 (B)	107 (C)	108 (D)	109 (A)	110 (B)
111 (C)	112 (B)	113 (B)	114 (A)	115 (A)
116 (D)	117 (C)	118 (B)	119 (B)	120 (D)
121 (A)	122 (B)	123 (C)	124 (B)	125 (A)
126 (B)	127 (D)	128 (A)	129 (D)	130 (C)
131 (C)	132 (A)	133 (C)	134 (A)	135 (C)
136 (D)	137 (A)	138 (B)	139 (A)	140 (C)
141 (B)	142 (D)	143 (C)	144 (B)	145 (D)
146 (A)	147 (A)	148 (B)	149 (B)	150 (C)
151 (D)	152 (B)	153 (C)	154 (D)	155 (B)
156 (C)	157 (C)	158 (B)	159 (D)	160 (C)
161 (A)	162 (C)	163 (A)	164 (B)	165 (D)
166 (C)	167 (D)	168 (C)	169 (D)	170 (A)
171 (B)	172 (A)	173 (B)	174 (D)	175 (D)
176 (A)	177 (C)	178 (A)	179 (D)	180 (C)
181 (B)	182 (A)	183 (C)	184 (C)	185 (D)
186 (D)	187 (D)	188 (B)	189 (C)	190 (B)
191 (A)	192 (B)	193 (D)	194 (D)	195 (C)
196 (B)	197 (D)	198 (C)	199 (A)	200 (C)

PART 5

101 인칭대명사의 격 _ 주격

해설 빈칸은 목적격 관계대명사 that 또는 which가 생략된 관계사절에서 동사 considers의 주어 자리이므로, (A) it이 정답이다. 참고로, considers와 to be 사이에 들어갔던 목적어가 companies인데 관계대명사가 되어 it 앞으로 보내진 후 생략된 문장 구조이다.

번역 심의위원회는 가장 자선을 많이 베푼다고 여기는 기업 목록을 발표했다.

어휘 board 위원회 consider A to be B A를 B라고 여기다 charitable 자선을 베푸는

102 동사 어휘

해설 빈칸의 목적어 역할을 하는 yesterday's budget meeting과 가장 잘 어울리는 타동사를 선택하는 문제이다. '예산 회의에 참석하다'라는 내용이 되어야 가장 자연스러우므로 정답은 (C) attend(참석하다)이다. (A) recognize는 '인정하다, 알아보다', (B) achieve는 '성취하다, 달성하다'라는 뜻으로 문맥상 빈칸에 적절하지 않고, (D) inform은 '알리다, 통지하다'라는 뜻으로 정보를 제공받는 대상이 목적어 자리에 들어가야 한다.

번역 어제 예산 회의에 참석하지 못한 사람은 누구든지 권 씨에게 연락해 기록물을 받을 수 있다.

어휘 be unable to ~할 수 없다 budget 예산 contact 연락하다

103 명사 자리 _ 복합명사 _ 어휘

해설 빈칸은 명사 dance와 복합명사를 이루어 동사 was made의 주어 역할을 하는 명사 자리이므로, '발표'라는 의미의 (D) presentation이 정답이다. (B) presents를 동사 '보여 주다'가 아닌 명사 '선물'로 본다고 해도, 의미상 어색하고 동사 was와 수가 일치하지 않으므로 오답이다. (A) presented는 동사/과거분사, (C) presenting은 동명사/현재분사로 문장 구조상 빈칸에 들어갈 수 없다.

번역 저녁의 무용 발표회는 태글릿츠 엠포리움의 지원으로 가능했다.

104 형용사 어휘

해설 한정사 All과 명사 candidates 사이에서 명사 candidates를 수식하는 형용사 자리로, 빈칸을 포함한 명사구는 동사 should submit의 주어 역할을 한다. 따라서 빈칸에는 서류 제출 대상 지원자(candidates)를 적절히 묘사하는 형용사가 들어가야 하므로, '자격이 되는, 적격의'라는 의미의 (B) qualified가 정답이다. (A) increasing은 '증가하는', (C) beneficial은 '유익한', (D) modified는 '수정된'이라는 의미로 문맥상 빈칸에 적절하지 않다.

번역 마케팅 직책에 자격 요건이 되는 지원자는 모두 자기소개서와 이력서를 제출해야 한다.

어휘 submit 제출하다 cover letter 자기소개서 résumé 이력서

105 동사 자리 _ 태

해설 빈칸은 Because가 이끄는 부사절에서 주어 experts 뒤에 이어지는 동사 자리이므로, 보기에서 능동태 동사 (A) predict와 수동태 동사 (C) are predicted 중 하나를 선택해야 한다. '전문가(experts)'는 미래에 대해 예측하는 주체이므로, 능동태 동사 (A) predict가 정답이다. (B) prediction(예상)은 명사, (D) predictably(예상대로)는 부사로 품사상 빈칸에 들어갈 수 없다.

번역 전문가들이 알레르기가 기승을 부릴 시기가 닥칠 것으로 전망하고 있기 때문에, 차울런 제약은 예방 의약품의 재고를 늘렸다.

어휘 pharmacy 제약(업), 약국 increase 늘리다 stock 재고 preventative 예방의 medicine 약

106 전치사 어휘

해설 빈칸은 명사구 its leadership을 목적어로 취하는 전치사 자리로, 빈칸을 포함한 전치사구가 동사 applauded를 수식한다. 따라서 빈칸에는 applauded와 its leadership을 가장 잘 연결하는 전치사가 들어가야 한다. '통솔력, 주도적 역할(leadership)'은 칭찬을 받는 이유이므로, '~로, ~때문에'라는 의미로 쓰일 수 있는 (B) for가 정답이다.

번역 시장은 월턴 병원이 시의 공중 보건 프로그램을 홍보하는 데 주도적인 역할을 했다며 치하했다.

어휘 mayor 시장 applaud 칭찬하다, 갈채를 보내다 promote 홍보하다 public health 공중 보건

TEST 9

107 명사 자리 _ 주격 보어

해설 빈칸은 부정관사 a와 형용사 leading 뒤에 이어지는 명사 자리로, 주어 Liao Uniform Services를 보충 설명하는 주격 보어 역할을 한다. 따라서 주어와 동격 관계를 이루는 명사가 빈칸에 들어가야 하므로, '공급 업체'라는 의미의 단수명사 (C) supplier가 정답이다. (A) supplies는 동사/복수명사, (B) supplying은 동명사/현재분사, (D) supplied는 동사/과거분사이므로 문장 구조상 빈칸에 들어갈 수 없다.

번역 리아오 유니폼 서비스는 의료 의류 업계에서 30년 이상 선도적인 공급 업체였다.

어휘 leading 선도적인, 주도적인 apparel 의류 supply 공급하다; 공급(량) supplies 비품

108 명사 어휘

해설 빈칸은 to include의 목적어 역할을 하는 명사 자리로, 전치사구 of a fountain in the garden의 수식을 받는다. 또한 빈칸을 포함한 to부정사구가 동사구 adjust the budget을 수식하므로, to부정사구는 예산을 조정하는 목적을 나타내야 한다. 따라서 '설치'라는 의미의 (D) installation이 정답이다. (A) schedule은 '일정', (B) determination은 '결정, 결심', (C) result는 '결과'라는 뜻으로 문맥상 빈칸에 적절하지 않다.

번역 정원 분수 설치 건이 포함되도록 예산을 조정하십시오.

어휘 adjust 조정하다 budget 예산 include 포함하다 fountain 분수

109 형용사 자리 _ 명사 수식

해설 빈칸이 한정사 all과 명사 streets 사이에 있으므로, 빈칸에는 명사 streets를 수식하는 형용사 또는 명사 streets와 복합명사를 이루는 명사가 들어갈 수 있다. 따라서 보기에서 형용사 (A) residential(주택의, 주거의), 현재분사 (B) residing(거주하는), 명사 (C) residences(거주) 중 하나를 선택해야 한다. 문맥상 '주택가의 모든 도로'라는 내용이 되어야 자연스러우므로, 형용사 (A) residential이 정답이다. (D) residentially(거주 지역에 관해)는 부사로 품사상 빈칸에 들어갈 수 없다.

번역 벤튼 주택가 모든 도로의 제한 속도는 시속 40킬로미터로 변경되었다.

어휘 limit 제한 per ~당

110 부사절 접속사

해설 빈칸은 완전한 절(visitors generally prefer to set their own pace)을 이끄는 접속사 자리로, 빈칸을 포함한 절이 콤마 뒤 주절을 수식한다. 방문객들이 스스로 관람 속도를 조절하는 것을 선호하여 수족관에서 오디오 투어를 제공하게 된 것이므로, '~ 때문에'라는 의미의 부사절 접속사 (B) Since가 정답이다. '~라는 것 이외는'이라는 뜻의 (A) Except (that)은 문맥상/위치상 빈칸에 적절하지 않고, (C) How는 명사절 접속사, (D) That은 명사절/형용사절 접속사로 쓰이므로 빈칸에 들어갈 수 없다.

번역 대체로 방문객들이 본인들 나름대로 속도 조절하기를 선호하므로, 수족관은 이제 사용자 친화적인 오디오 투어를 제공한다.

어휘 aquarium 수족관 user-friendly 사용자 친화적인

111 동사 어형 _ 태

해설 빈칸은 주어 The salmon dish at Salia's Café의 동사 자리이므로, 보기에서 능동태 동사형인 (B) will serve와 (D) was serving, 수동태 동사형인 (C) is served 중 하나를 선택해야 한다. 연어 요리(The salmon dish)는 제공되는 대상이므로, 수동태 동사형인 (C) is served가 정답이다. (A) to serve는 동사 자리에 들어갈 수 없다.

번역 살리아즈 카페의 연어 요리에는 황설탕, 겨자, 후추 글레이즈가 곁들여 나온다.

어휘 salmon 연어 mustard 겨자 pepper 후추 glaze (음식에 윤을 내는) 글레이즈

112 부사 어휘

해설 수동태 동사 is recommended를 적절히 수식하는 부사를 선택하는 문제로, 문맥상 추천 또는 권장하는 정도를 나타내는 부사가 빈칸에 들어가야 자연스럽다. 따라서 '매우, 대단히'라는 의미의 (B) highly가 정답이다. (A) closely는 '면밀하게', (C) nearly는 '거의', (D) roughly는 '대략'이라는 뜻으로 빈칸에 적합하지 않다.

번역 칠먼 트레일의 울퉁불퉁한 지형 때문에 적절한 등산용 신발을 적극 권장합니다.

어휘 due to ~ 때문에 uneven 울퉁불퉁한 terrain 지형 trail 오솔길, 등산로 proper 적절한 recommend 권장하다

113 전치사 자리

해설 빈칸 뒤 the hours of 4 P.M. and 6 P.M.을 목적어로 취하는 전치사 자리로, 보기에서 등위접속사 and와 어울려 쓰이는 전치사를 선택해야 한다. 따라서 and와 함께 '~와 … 사이에'라는 의미를 나타내는 (B) between이 정답이다. (A) always와 (D) only는 부사로 품사상 빈칸에 들어갈 수 없다.

번역 방문객들은 오후 4시에서 6시 사이에 새로운 인쇄 공장 시설을 둘러볼 수 있다.

어휘 plant 공장 facility 시설

114 형용사 어휘

해설 빈칸은 주어 Playablanca Financial을 보충 설명하는 주격 보어 자리로, to부정사구 to make new acquisitions의 수식을 받는다. 또한 Given the current economic climate가 빈칸을 포함한 문장을 수식하므로, 빈칸에는 현재의 경제 상황을 감안하여 신규 인수를 결정해야 하는 회사의 태도를 묘사하는 형용사가 들어가야 자연스럽다. 따라서 '주저하는, 망설이는'이라는 의미의 (A) hesitant가 정답이다. (B) delinquent는 '태만한, 체납의', (C) worthy는 '가치 있는, ~에 어울리는', (D) empty는 '비어 있는'이라는 뜻으로 모두 문맥상 빈칸에 적절하지 않다.

번역 플레이아블랑카 파이낸셜은 지금의 경제 상황을 감안하여, 신규 인수에 주저하고 있다.

어휘 given ~을 감안할 때 current 지금의 economic 경제의 climate 상황, 분위기 acquisition 인수

115 부사 자리 _ 동사 수식

해설 빈칸은 완전한 절(Mr. Fitzpatrick memorized his lines) 뒤에서 동사 memorized를 수식하는 부사 자리이므로, (A) perfectly가 정답이다. (B) perfected는 동사/과거분사, (C) perfect는 형용사, (D) perfecting은 동명사/현재분사로 품사상 빈칸에 들어갈 수 없다.

번역 피츠패트릭 씨는 영화 촬영이 시작되기 몇 주 전에 자신의 대사를 완벽하게 외웠다.

어휘 memorize 외우다 filming 촬영 perfectly 완벽하게 perfect 완벽한; 완벽하게 하다

116 전치사 어휘

해설 빈칸 뒤 명사구 the deadline을 목적어로 취하는 전치사 자리로, 빈칸을 포함한 전치사구는 동사 will be submitted를 수식한다. 따라서 will be submitted와 the deadline을 가장 적절히 연결하는 전치사가 빈칸에 들어가야 한다. 신청서 제출은 마감일 또는 마감일 전후에 가능하므로, '~ 전에'라는 의미의 시간 전치사 (D) before가 정답이다. (A) along(~을 따라)은 방향을 나타내고, (B) over와 (C) during은 '~ 동안'이라는 뜻으로 기간을 나타내는 명사를 목적어로 취하므로 문맥상 빈칸에 적절하지 않다.

번역 아마리 씨는 보조금 신청서를 검토했고, 신청서는 마감일 전에 제출될 것이다.

어휘 scan 검토하다 grant 보조금 application 신청(서) submit 제출하다

117 부사 어휘

해설 빈칸은 주어 Good design and quality material의 주격 보어인 형용사 important를 수식하는 부사 자리이다. 우수한 디자인과 좋은 소재의 중요도를 적절히 묘사하는 부사가 빈칸에 들어가야 하므로, '똑같이, 동등하게'라는 의미의 (C) equally가 정답이다. '충분히'라는 의미의 부사 (B) enough는 형용사/부사/동사를 뒤에서 수식하고, (A) gradually(점차)와 (D) well(잘)은 문맥상 빈칸에 적절하지 않다.

번역 크래스너 연구소의 제품 개발 팀에게는 우수한 디자인과 양질의 소재가 똑같이 중요하다.

어휘 quality 좋은, 양질의 important 중요한 laboratory 연구소 development 개발

118 명사 어휘

해설 빈칸은 동사 make의 목적어 역할을 하는 명사 자리로, 전치사구 of pet treats의 수식을 받는다. 최상의 재료만으로 반려동물의 간식(treats)을 제품화한다는 내용의 문장이므로, '상품의 종류, 제품'이라는 의미의 (B) line이 정답이다. (A) usage는 '사용', (C) result는 '결과', (D) addition은 '추가, 첨가'라는 뜻으로 모두 문맥상 빈칸에 적절하지 않다.

번역 저희는 최상의 재료만으로 반려동물 간식을 만듭니다.

어휘 treat 간식 ingredient 재료

119 형용사 자리 _ 명사 수식

해설 빈칸이 부정관사 an과 명사 price 사이에 있으므로, 빈칸에는 명사 price를 수식하는 형용사 또는 명사 price와 복합명사를 이루는 명사가 들어갈 수 있다. 따라서 보기에서 형용사인 (B) affordable(가격이 알맞은, 저렴한)과 명사인 (D) affordability(감당할 수 있는 비용) 중 하나를 선택해야 한다. 문맥상 치료 비용(price)을 적절히 묘사하는 형용사가 빈칸에 들어가야 하므로, (B) affordable이 정답이다. (A) affords(제공하다)는 동사, (C) affordably(감당할 수 있게)는 부사로 품사상 빈칸에 들어갈 수 없다.

번역 우 박사는 저렴한 금액에 탁월한 치과 치료를 환자에게 제공한다.

어휘 patient 환자 exceptional 탁월한 afford 여유가 되다, 제공하다

120 부사절 접속사

해설 빈칸은 완전한 절(two additional designers are hired)을 이끄는 접속사 자리이므로, 보기에서 (A) Whether(~이든 아니든)와 (D) If(~한다면) 중 하나를 선택해야 한다. 빈칸을 포함한 절이 콤마 뒤에 나오는 주절(current staffers will not need to work ~ on time)의 조건을 나타내므로, (D) If가 정답이다. 참고로, (A) Whether는 부사절을 이끌 경우 or not과 함께 쓰여야 한다. (B) Already(이미)와 (C) Instead(대신에)는 부사로 품사상 빈칸에 들어갈 수 없다.

번역 만약 디자이너 두 명을 추가로 고용한다면, 현재 직원들은 프로젝트를 제시간에 끝내기 위해 초과 근무를 할 필요가 없을 것이다.

어휘 additional 추가의 hire 고용하다 current 현재의 staffer 직원 work overtime 초과 근무를 하다 complete 완료하다 on time 제시간에

121 부사 자리 _ 동사 수식

해설 빈칸은 수동태를 이루는 will be와 reviewed 사이에서 reviewed를 수식하는 부사 자리이므로, (A) extensively(두루, 광범위하게)가 정답이다. (B) extensive(광범위한)는 형용사, (C) extension(연장, 확대)은 명사, (D) extending(연장하기; 연장하는)은 동명사/현재분사로 모두 품사상 빈칸에 들어갈 수 없다.

번역 모든 안전 정책은 발표 전 인사부에서 두루 검토할 예정이다.

어휘 policy 정책 Human Resources Department 인사부 publication 발표

122 동사 어휘

해설 빈칸은 while(~하는 반면에, ~하는 동안)이 이끄는 부사절에서 주어 others의 동사 역할을 하며, only in the summer and fall의 수식을 받는다. 콤마 앞 주절에서 동사 run을 수식하는 year-round(일 년 내내)와 빈칸을 수식하는 only in the summer and fall(여름과 가을에만)이 대조적인 의미를 나타내므로, 빈칸에는 run과 상응하는 동사가 들어가야 자연스럽다. 따라서 '운영되다, 영업하다'라는 뜻의 (B) operate가 정답이다. (A) grow는 '재배하다,

TEST 9

자라다', (C) raise는 '들어올리다, 인상하다', (D) promise는 '약속하다'라는 의미로 문맥상 빈칸에 적절하지 않다.

번역 더블린의 일부 노상 농산물 직판장은 일 년 내내 운영되는 반면, 다른 직판장들은 여름과 가을에만 운영된다.

어휘 roadside 길가, 노상 farmers market 농산물 직판장

123 한정사

해설 ------- ones you borrowed가 동사 return의 목적어 역할을 하고 있으며, 여기서 ones는 you borrowed의 수식을 받고 있다. 따라서 빈칸에는 부정대명사 ones를 수식할 수 있는 한정사가 들어가야 하는데, '직물 견본 중 어느 것을 빌렸든 반납해달라'라는 내용이 되어야 자연스러우므로, '어느 ~이든'이라는 의미의 (C) whichever가 정답이다. (A) what과 (D) whose도 한정사로 쓰일 수 있지만 문맥상 빈칸에 적절하지 않으며, (B) whomever는 문장 구조상 빈칸에 들어갈 수 없다.

번역 직물 견본이 부족하니, 어느 것을 빌렸든 즉시 반납해 주세요.

어휘 fabric 직물 promptly 즉시

124 부사절 접속사 _ 어휘

해설 빈칸 뒤 완전한 절(it does not rain tomorrow)을 이끄는 접속사 자리로, 빈칸을 포함한 절은 콤마 뒤 주절을 수식한다. 따라서 보기에서 부사절 접속사인 (A) Though(비록 ~일지라도)와 (B) Even if (만약 ~일지라도) 중 하나를 선택해야 한다. 빈칸이 이끄는 절이 내일의 날씨를 가정한 조건을 나타내고 있으므로, (B) Even if가 정답이다. (C) Almost(거의)와 (D) Besides that(그 밖에)은 부사이므로 절을 이끌 수 없다.

번역 내일 비가 오지 않더라도 예정된 야외 행사를 위해 텐트가 설치될 예정입니다.

어휘 set up 설치하다 scheduled 예정된

125 숫자 / 양 수식 표현

해설 전치사 for의 목적어 역할을 하는 two hours를 적절히 수식하는 표현을 선택하는 문제이다. 문맥상 two hours를 강조하여 '2시간만'이라는 의미를 완성하는 표현이 빈칸에 들어가야 자연스러우므로, (A) no more than(단지 ~뿐)이 정답이다. (B) hardly any는 '거의 없는', (C) as far as는 '~에까지', (D) that many는 '그렇게 많이'라는 뜻으로 빈칸에 적절하지 않다. 참고로, (C) as far as는 '~하는 한'이라는 의미의 접속사로도 쓰일 수 있다.

번역 네트워크는 단지 2시간만 이용할 수 없을 것으로 예상된다.

어휘 be expected to ~할 것으로 예상되다 unavailable 이용할 수 없는

126 형용사 어휘

해설 빈칸은 동명사 accepting의 목적어 역할을 하는 명사 opinions를 수식하는 형용사 자리로, 빈칸을 포함한 동명사구는 부사 blindly의 수식을 받는다. 따라서 빈칸에는 맹목적으로 수용하지 말아야 할 의견을 적절히 묘사하는 형용사가 들어가야 하므로, '편향된, 선입견이 있는'이라는 의미의 (B) biased가 정답이다. (A) total은 '총, 전체의', (C) profitable은 '수익성이 있는', (D) competitive는 '경쟁적인'이라는 뜻으로 문맥상 빈칸에 적절하지 않다.

번역 소비자 보호 운동가들은 제품에 대한 편견을 맹목적으로 수용하지 말라고 조언한다.

어휘 consumer advocate 소비자 보호 운동가 blindly 맹목적으로 biased opinion 편견

127 명사 어휘

해설 전치사구 of tasks의 수식을 받으며 문장의 주어 역할을 하는 명사를 선택하는 문제이다. 관리자의 일이 수월해지고 팀원들이 새로운 기술을 배울 수 있도록 하는 방법은 관리자의 업무를 팀원에게 '위임'하는 것이므로, '위임'이라는 의미의 (D) Delegation이 정답이다. (A) Promotion은 '승진, 홍보', (B) Commission은 '위원회, 수수료', (C) Provision은 '공급, 제공'이라는 의미로 문맥상 빈칸에 적절하지 않다.

번역 업무 위임을 통해 관리자의 일은 수월해지고 팀원들은 새로운 기술을 배울 수 있다.

어휘 supervisor 관리자

128 부사 어휘

해설 빈칸 앞 과거분사 reported를 가장 적절히 수식하는 부사를 선택하는 문제이다. 빈칸의 수식을 받는 reported는 similar to의 목적어 역할을 하는 지시대명사 those(=findings)를 수식한다. 따라서 빈칸에는 립킨 제약 회사의 결과물과 유사한 결과물이 보고된 곳을 나타내는 부사가 들어가야 자연스러우므로, '다른 곳에서'라는 의미의 (A) elsewhere가 정답이다. (B) beyond는 '건너편에', (C) furthermore는 '게다가, 더욱이', (D) wherever는 '어디든지'라는 뜻으로 문맥상 빈칸에 적절하지 않다.

번역 립킨 제약 회사의 과학자들은 다른 곳에서 보고된 것과 비슷한 결과를 서술했다.

어휘 pharmaceutical 제약 회사 describe 서술하다 findings (연구) 결과 similar to ~와 비슷한

129 동사 어형 _ 태

해설 빈칸은 주어 All four walls of the greenhouse 뒤에 이어지는 동사 자리이므로, 보기에서 능동태 동사인 (A) construct와 (C) have constructed, 수동태 동사인 (D) will be constructed 중 하나를 선택해야 한다. 주어 All four walls는 시공되는 대상이므로, (D) will be constructed가 정답이다. (B) constructing은 동명사/현재분사로 동사 자리에 들어갈 수 없다.

번역 온실의 네 벽은 모두 완전 강화 유리로 시공될 예정이다.

어휘 greenhouse 온실 construct 시공하다 tempered glass 강화 유리

130 동사 어휘

해설 주어 The increase in tourism in Mariondale은 '결과'를, 전치

사 to의 목적어 the various attractions는 관광객이 증가한 '원인'을 나타내므로, 원인과 결과를 가장 잘 연결하는 동사의 과거분사 형태가 빈칸에 들어가야 한다. 따라서 전치사 to와 결합하여 '~는 … 덕분이다[때문이다]'라는 의미를 완성하는 attribute의 과거분사 (C) attributed가 정답이다.

번역 마리온데일의 관광객 증가는 최근 몇 년간 시가 추가한 다양한 관광지 덕분이라고 할 수 있다.

어휘 tourism 관광(객) attraction 관광지, 명소 deduct 공제하다, 감하다 confirm 확정하다 amplify 증폭시키다

PART 6

131-134 이메일

수신: 에리포드 호텔 직원
발신: 세스 박
제목: 자원 절약하기
날짜: 3월 15일

객실 관리 전 직원에게:

호텔 경영진은 매일 이루어지는 수건 세탁과 [131]**관련하여** 새로운 정책을 시행하기로 결정했습니다. 앞으로 고객이 바닥에 둔 수건은 매일 수거해 세탁하지만, 고리나 선반에 걸린 사용한 수건은 고객이 재사용하도록 객실에 남겨 둘 것입니다. 이 정책으로 하루치 세탁물을 [132]**최소화할 것입니다.** [133]**결과적으로,** 전기와 전력 사용이 감소할 것입니다. 고객들에게 이 정책을 알리도록 각 객실마다 안내문을 붙일 예정입니다. [134]**이러한 노력에 협조해 주시면 진심으로 감사하겠습니다.** 경영진은 절약에 심혈을 기울이고 있습니다.

감사합니다.

세스 박
접객 매니저, 에리포드 호텔

어휘 conserve 아끼다, 보존하다 resource 자원 housekeeping (호텔) 객실 관리 decide 결정하다 implement 시행하다 policy 정책 launder 세탁하다 collect 수거하다 rack 선반 reuse 재사용하다 minimize 최소화하다 load 분량 electricity 전기 reduce 줄이다 be committed to ~에 심혈을 기울이다 conservation 절약, 보존 hospitality 접대

131 전치사 자리

해설 빈칸 뒤 명사구 the daily laundering을 목적어로 취하는 전치사 자리로, 빈칸을 포함한 전치사구는 명사구 a new policy를 수식한다. 따라서 '~에 관하여'라는 의미의 전치사 (C) regarding이 정답이다. 참고로 (A) regards는 「as regards+명사구」의 형태로 '~에 관하여'라는 의미의 전치사로 쓰이며, (B) regardless는 「regardless of+명사구」의 형태로 '~에 상관없이'라는 의미로 쓰인다.

132 동사 어휘

해설 빈칸의 주어인 This policy는 앞 문장에서 언급한 수건의 세탁 및 재사용에 관한 정책(all towels left on the floor ~, but any used towels ~ to reuse)을 대신하고, 빈칸의 목적어인 our daily laundry load는 그러한 정책에 영향을 받는 대상을 나타낸다. 따라서 빈칸에는 해당 정책 시행으로 인한 세탁물 양의 변화를 묘사하는 동사가 들어가야 하므로, '최소화하다, 축소하다'라는 의미의 (A) minimize가 정답이다. (B) double은 '두배로 만들다', (C) require는 '요구하다, 필요로 하다', (D) eliminate는 '제거하다, 탈락시키다'라는 뜻으로 문맥상 빈칸에 적절하지 않다.

133 접속부사

해설 빈칸 앞뒤 문장을 의미상 자연스럽게 연결하는 접속부사를 선택하는 문제이다. 빈칸 앞 문장에서 해당 정책으로 하루치 세탁물을 최소화할 것(This policy will minimize our daily laundry load)이라고 했고, 빈칸 뒤 문장에서 그에 따른 결과로 전기와 전력 사용이 감소할 것(our electricity and power use will be reduced)이라고 했으므로, 빈칸에는 원인과 결과를 연결하는 접속부사가 들어가야 글의 흐름이 자연스러워진다. 따라서 '결과적으로'라는 의미의 (C) As a result가 정답이다. (A) Despite this는 '이러한 상황에도 불구하고', (B) However는 '하지만', (D) Evidently는 '분명히'라는 뜻으로 문맥상 빈칸에 적절하지 않다.

134 문맥에 맞는 문장 고르기

번역 (A) 이러한 노력에 협조해 주시면 진심으로 감사하겠습니다.
(B) 유지 보수가 필요한 곳이 확인되면 저희에게 알려 주십시오.
(C) 이 시간에는 샤워를 10분 이내로 제한하도록 하십시오.
(D) 직원 회의에서 아이디어를 모두 공유해 달라는 요청을 받으실 겁니다.

해설 빈칸 앞 문장에서 손님들에게 정책을 알리도록 객실마다 안내문을 붙일 예정(Notices will be posted in each room informing our guests of this policy)이라고 했으므로, 빈칸에는 정책 시행과 관련하여 이메일 수신자(you/your)인 직원들의 협조를 구하는 내용이 이어지는 것이 문맥상 자연스럽다. 따라서 (A)가 정답이다.

어휘 cooperation 협조 identify 확인하다, 식별하다 maintenance 유지 보수 limit 제한하다

135-138 공지

여행자 여러분께 알립니다:

운송 중 짐이 파손되었나요? 그렇다면 도착 후 가능한 한 빨리 클라우드 익스프레스 항공 수하물 취급소로 [135]**가져오십시오.** 국내 여행자는 목적지 도착 후 24시간 이내에 피해를 신고하고 해외 여행자는 사건 발생 후 5일 이내에 보고서를 제출해야 합니다. [136]**지시에 따라 수하물 파손 서식을 작성하십시오.** 취급소 직원이 모든 [137]**청구서**를 검토, 평가합니다. 클라우드 익스프레스 항공은 기존의 상태, 짐을 너무 많이 넣어 지퍼나 버클이 파손된 경우, 또는 [138]**일상적인** 마모에 대해서는 책임지지 않는다는 점 유의하십시오.

TEST 9

어휘 luggage 짐 transit 운송 baggage office 수하물 취급소 domestic 국내의 destination 목적지 submit 제출하다 incident 사건 personnel 직원 evaluate 평가하다 be responsible for ~에 대해 책임지다 preexisting 기존의 related to ~와 관련된 overpack 너무 많이 넣다 wear 마모

135 동사 어형 _ 명령문

해설 빈칸 앞에 주어가 없고 뒤에 목적어 it이 있는 것으로 보아, 빈칸을 포함한 문장이 주어 you가 생략된 명령문임을 알 수 있다. 따라서 동사 원형 (C) bring이 정답이다.

136 문맥에 맞는 문장 고르기

번역 (A) 클라우드 익스프레스는 최근 국제 노선을 확장했습니다.
(B) 클라우드 익스프레스는 가장 유능한 직원만 고용합니다.
(C) 수하물 취급소는 이번 주에 임시 휴무입니다.
(D) 지시에 따라 수하물 파손 서식을 작성하십시오.

해설 빈칸 앞 문장에서 국내외 여행자는 기한 내 수하물 파손에 대해 신고하거나 보고서를 제출(Domestic travelers are asked to report damage within 24 hours ~ within five days of an incident)하라고 요청했고, 빈칸 뒤 문장에서 직원들이 검토하고 평가할 것(Office personnel will review and evaluate)이라고 했으므로, 빈칸에도 수하물 파손 보고와 관련된 내용이 언급되어야 문맥상 자연스럽다. 따라서 (D)가 정답이다.

어휘 recently 최근 expand 확장하다 qualified 유능한 temporarily 임시로 as instructed 지시된 대로

137 명사 어휘

해설 빈칸은 동사 will review and evaluate의 목적어 역할을 하는 명사 자리이다. 앞에서 여행객의 수하물 파손 관련 보고서 제출(Domestic travelers are asked to report damage ~ of an incident)에 대해 언급했고, 검토하고 평가하는 대상 또한 여행객이 제출한 파손 관련 보고서이므로, 빈칸에는 파손 관련 보고서와 관련된 명사가 들어가야 한다. 따라서 '청구(서), 지불 요구'라는 의미의 (A) claims가 정답이다. (B) agendas는 '의제, 안건', (C) passports는 '여권', (D) rates는 '요금'이라는 뜻으로 문맥상 빈칸에 적절하지 않다.

138 형용사 자리 _ 명사 수식

해설 빈칸은 '마모'라는 의미의 명사 wear를 수식하는 형용사 자리이므로, 형용사 (B) normal(일상의, 정상적인)이 정답이다. (A) normality(정상 상태)는 명사, (C) normally(보통)는 부사, (D) normalize(정상화하다)는 동사로 품사상 빈칸에 들어갈 수 없다.

139-142 회람

수신: 브룸 도서관 직원
발신: 에인슬리 메이슨
제목: 커뮤니티 룸
날짜: 3월 20일

이번 달 말까지 새 커뮤니티 룸 건설이 완공된다는 것을 알려 드리게 되어 기쁩니다. 네 개의 방은 메인 로비에서 [139]**들어갈 수 있습니다**.

새로운 방들은 10명에서 25명까지 사용할 수 있으며 회의와 단체 학습을 위한 용도입니다. [140]**모든 방은 미리 예약해야 합니다.** 선드퀴스트 씨가 3월 말까지 임시로 이 공간의 예약 업무를 맡게 됩니다. [141]**그때는**, 그녀가 도서관 정보 전문가인 자신의 역할로 돌아오게 됩니다. 정규직 대민 연락 담당자를 구하는 광고를 곧 게재할 예정입니다. 이 사람은 새로운 방의 예약 [142]**관리** 업무를 담당하게 됩니다.

어휘 construction 공사, 건설 community 지역 사회, 공동체 range (범위가) A에서 B사이이다, ~에서 …에 이르다 occupancy 점유 intended for ~을 위한 temporarily 임시로 be responsible for ~을 담당하다 advertisement 광고 permanent 정규의 Community Liaison 지역 사회 연락 담당자 individual 개인, 사람 be in charge of ~을 담당하다

139 형용사 어휘

해설 빈칸은 주어 The four rooms를 보충 설명하는 주격 보어 자리로, 전치사구 from the main lobby의 수식을 받는다. 따라서 빈칸에는 방과 메인 로비의 관계를 적절히 묘사하는 형용사가 들어가야 하므로, '접근할 수 있는'이라는 의미의 (A) accessible이 정답이다. (B) assorted는 '선별된', (C) appropriate는 '적절한', (D) acceptable은 '받아들일 수 있는'이라는 뜻으로 문맥상 빈칸에 적절하지 않다.

140 문맥에 맞는 문장 고르기

번역 (A) 면접은 5월 초에 시행 예정입니다.
(B) 린 선드퀴스트는 많은 회의를 주재했습니다.
(C) 모든 방은 미리 예약해야 합니다.
(D) 직원 주차 공간은 명확하게 표시해 두겠습니다.

해설 빈칸 앞 문장에서 새로 만든 방의 규모와 용도(The new rooms range in occupancy ~ for meetings and study groups)를 밝혔고, 빈칸 뒤 문장에서 임시 예약 담당자(Ms. Sundquist will be temporarily responsible for reserving)를 언급했으므로, 빈칸에는 새로 만든 방의 예약과 관련된 내용이 들어가야 문맥상 자연스럽다. 따라서 (C)가 정답이다.

어휘 conduct 시행하다 reserve 예약하다 in advance 미리 mark 표시하다

141 접속부사

해설 빈칸 앞뒤 문장을 내용상 자연스럽게 연결하는 접속부사를 선택하는 문제이다. 빈칸 앞 문장에서 선드퀴스트 씨가 3월 말까지 임시로 예약 업무를 맡게 된다(Ms. Sundquist will be temporarily ~ reserving the spaces until the end of March)고 했고, 그후 도서관 정보 전문가인 자신의 역할로 돌아갈 예정(she will return to her role as Library Information Specialist)이라고 했으므로, 빈칸에는 3월 말을 대신하는 접속부사가 들어가야 글의 흐름이 자연스러워진다. 따라서 '그때'라는 의미의 (B) At that time이 정답이다. (A) Nonetheless는 '그럼에도 불구하고', (C) Likewise는 '마찬가지로', (D) In a word는 '한마디로'라는 뜻으로 문맥상 빈칸에 적절하지 않다.

142 동사 어형 _ 동명사

해설 빈칸은 뒤에 나오는 bookings for the new rooms를 목적어로 취하는 자리이다. 보기에 동사 oversee(관리하다, 감독하다)의 여러 가지 형태가 나오는데, 문맥상 '이 사람이 새 방의 예약 관리 업무를 담당할 것'이라는 의미가 되어야 하고, 빈칸 앞에 in charge of가 있으므로 전치사의 목적어 역할을 할 수 있는 동명사가 들어가야 한다. 따라서 (D) overseeing이 정답이다.

143-146 이메일

수신: tkhan@smolermanufacturing.co.uk
발신: lpreston@emmetestate.co.uk
날짜: 3월 9일
제목: 코랄 가 1161번지

칸 씨께,

코랄 가 1161번지에 있는 200제곱미터 창고 공간에 관해 문의해 주셔서 감사합니다. 제 부동산 데이터베이스를 확인했더니 이 건물은 판매가 중지된 [143]**것으로 보입니다.**

어떤 물건을 찾으시는지 구체적으로 알려 주시면 제가 다른 것을 찾도록 [144]**도와 드릴 수 있습니다.** 고객님의 가격대, 필요한 규모, 도시에서 선호하는 지역 및 기타 중요한 요건을 적어 이 이메일로 회신 주십시오. [145]**그러면 이런 기준에 맞는 상가 건물을 찾아 보겠습니다.**

원하시면 [146]**알림**을 신청하실 수 있습니다. 그렇게 하면 새로운 부동산 매물이 이용 가능해 질 때마다 즉시 이메일 또는 문자 메시지로 알림을 받으시게 됩니다.

로이드 프레스턴

에미트 부동산 중개소

어휘 warehouse 창고 real estate 부동산 property 부동산, 건물 take off the market 판매를 중지하다, 시장에서 회수하다 specifically 구체적으로 respond to ~에 회신하다 prefer 선호하다 requirement 요건 alert 알림 receive 받다 instant 즉각적인 notification 통보 available 이용할 수 있는

143 부사 어휘

해설 등위접속사 and가 이어 주는 앞뒤 절을 의미상 가장 잘 연결하는 부사를 선택하는 문제이다. 부동산 데이터베이스를 확인(I checked my real estate database)했는데, 해당 건물이 판매가 중지된 것(this property has been taken off the market)으로 보인다는 내용이 되어야 문맥상 자연스럽다. 따라서 '보기에, 외관상으로'라는 의미의 (C) apparently가 정답이다. (A) briefly는 '간략하게', (B) considerably는 '상당히', (D) primarily는 '주로'라는 뜻으로 문맥상 빈칸에 적절하지 않다.

144 동사 어형 _ 조동사 + 동사원형

해설 빈칸은 주어 I 뒤에 이어지는 동사 자리이다. 문맥상 부동산 중개인인 발신인(I)이 다른 부동산을 찾는 것(finding something else)을 도울 능력이 있음을 보여 주는 동사 형태가 빈칸에 들어가야 하므로, (B) can assist가 정답이다.

145 문맥에 맞는 문장 고르기

번역 (A) 예를 들어, 무엇이든 개선하기 전에는 승인이 필요합니다.
(B) 제가 목요일에 이 부동산을 잠재 구매자들에게 보여 주겠습니다.
(C) 그것은 부동산 업계에서 흥미로운 추세입니다.
(D) 그러면 이런 기준에 맞는 상가 건물을 찾아 보겠습니다.

해설 빈칸 앞에서 다른 부동산을 찾아주겠다며 가격대 등 기타 중요한 요건을 적어 이메일로 회신할 것(Just respond to this e-mail ~ any other important requirements)을 요청했으므로, 빈칸에도 부동산을 찾는 행위와 관련된 내용이 들어가야 문맥상 자연스럽다. 따라서 (D)가 정답이다.

어휘 approval 승인 potential 잠재적인 commercial 상업의 criteria 기준

146 명사 어휘

해설 빈칸은 '~을 신청하다'라는 의미의 sign up for의 목적어 역할을 하는 명사 자리이다. 빈칸 뒤 문장에서 '그렇게 하면 이메일 또는 문자 메시지로 알림을 받게 된다(This way you will receive instant e-mail or text-message notifications)'라고 했으므로, 빈칸에 notifications와 유사한 명사가 들어가야 문맥상 자연스럽다. 따라서 '알림, 경보'라는 의미의 (A) alerts가 정답이다. (B) payments는 '지불', (C) activities는 '활동', (D) inspections는 '점검, 조사'라는 뜻으로 문맥상 빈칸에 적절하지 않다.

PART 7

147-148 이메일

수신: j.parnthong@trottermail.co.uk
발신: l.florinsmith@gaseau.co.uk
날짜: 1월 22일
제목: 구매 물품
첨부: 조리법

판송 씨께,

최근 가소 대나무 조리 기구 4개를 구입해 주셔서 감사합니다. [147]**아시다시피 모든 가소 제품은 100퍼센트 천연 대나무로 제조되며 평생 쓸 수 있습니다.** 가소 제품은 가볍고 튼튼하며 눌어붙지 않는 조리 기구뿐만 아니라 금속 냄비와 팬에 써도 안전합니다. 새 조리 기구는 잊지 마시고 순한 비누와 물로 손으로 씻으십시오.

거래에 대한 감사의 표시로, 새로운 제품을 사용해 만들 수 있는 몇 가지 간단한 조리법을 첨부했습니다.

[148]**만약 아직 하지 않으셨다면, 웹사이트에 당사와 함께한 경험에 대해 후기를 남겨 주십시오.** 이 링크를 사용하시면 됩니다: www.gaseau.co.uk/reviews.

TEST 9

리안 플로린-스미스
고객 서비스 담당

어휘 recent 최근의 purchase 구매(품) bamboo 대나무 utensil 기구 durable 튼튼한 nonstick 눌어붙지 않는 concerning ~에 관하여 representative 직원

147 사실 관계 확인

번역 기구에 관해 명시된 것은?

(A) 천연 재료로 제조되었다.
(B) 금속 표면에는 사용할 수 없다.
(C) 특별한 세척제로 씻어야 한다.
(D) 가장 많이 판매되는 제품이다.

해설 첫 번째 단락에서 모든 제품은 100퍼센트 천연 대나무로 제조된다(all Gaseau products are made of 100 percent natural bamboo)고 했으므로, (A)가 정답이다.

어휘 surface 표면

▸▸ Paraphrasing 지문의 100 percent natural bamboo
→ 정답의 natural materials

148 세부 사항

번역 판송 씨가 요청받은 일은?

(A) 구매 영수증 확인
(B) 온라인에 의견 남기기
(C) 조리법 검토하기
(D) 대회에 참가하기

해설 마지막 단락에서 수신인(you)인 판송 씨에게 웹사이트에 당사와 함께 한 경험에 대해 후기를 남겨 줄 것(please leave a review on our Web site concerning your experience with us)을 요청했으므로, (B)가 정답이다.

어휘 receipt 영수증

▸▸ Paraphrasing 지문의 leave a review on our Web site
→ 정답의 Give some feedback online

149-150 제품 설명서

제브크 홍차

터키는 세계 최고급 홍차 제품 가운데 몇 가지를 자랑합니다. 제브크('즐거움'을 뜻하는 터키어)도 예외는 아니며 50년 간 상업적으로 성공을 거둔 점이 이를 증명하고 있습니다. 손님들을 진정 터키식으로 접대하고 싶으시다면 길쭉하고 투명한 유리잔에 홍차를 내십시오. 그래야 제브크 홍차가 우러나는 동안 색깔이 변하는 모습을 손님들이 감탄하며 바라볼 수 있습니다. [149]**비스킷이나 사탕을 곁들이세요.**

사용법: 봉지에 제브크 차를 채우고 유리잔에 넣는다.
끓인 물을 부어 우려낸다. 취향에 따라 단맛을 첨가한다.

터키 제품
순 중량 250그램.

[150]**ABD 수출 독점 계약 상품**
최상의 맛을 즐기시려면 포장일로부터 6개월 이내에 사용하세요.

어휘 boast 자랑하다 exception 예외 commercial 상업의 prove 증명하다 hospitable 환대하는 admire 감탄하며 보다 brew 우러나다 accompany 덧붙이다 steep (담기) 우려내다 taste 취향 weight 무게 exclusively 독점으로

149 세부 사항

번역 제브크 홍차 소비자에게 주는 조언은?

(A) 오랜 시간 신선함을 유지하는 방법
(B) 차에 곁들일 음식
(C) 추가해야 하는 설탕의 양
(D) 유리잔에 봉지를 담가 두는 시간

해설 첫 번째 단락에서 비스킷이나 사탕을 곁들일 것(Accompany with biscuits or sweets)을 권하고 있으므로, (B)가 정답이다.

▸▸ Paraphrasing 지문의 Accompany with biscuits or sweets
→ 정답의 The food items to serve with it

150 사실 관계 확인

번역 제품 설명에 의하면, 제브크 홍차에 관해 사실인 것은?

(A) 비교적 신제품이다.
(B) 과일 맛이 난다.
(C) 터키 외부에서 판매된다.
(D) 봉지 250개들이 상자로 나온다.

해설 마지막 단락에서 'ABD 수출 독점 계약 상품(Packaged exclusively for ABD Exports)'이라고 했으므로, 터키 외부에서 판매된다는 것을 알 수 있다. 따라서 (C)가 정답이다.

어휘 relatively 비교적 flavor 맛 contain 포함하다 pouch 작은 주머니

151-152 문자 메시지

비샤 푸델 [오전 9시 27분]
자이푸르행 기차를 놓쳤어요. 다른 역에서 출발하는 것 같아요. [151]**비즈니스 포럼 기조 연설 시간에 맞춰 갈 수 있는 기차가 없어요. 좋은 생각 있나요?**

슈라다 케르 [오전 9시 32분]
문제 없어요. [151/152]**제가 차를 보낼게요.**

비샤 푸델 [오전 9시 33분]
정말 다행이에요! 고마워요. [152]**만찬이 오후 7시에 시작하니까 2시간 안에 뉴델리에서 출발하면 제시간에 도착할 거예요.**

슈라다 케르 [오전 9시 34분]
기사가 어디로 모시러 가면 될까요?

비샤 푸델 [오전 9시 35분]
사프다르정 역 1번 출입구예요. 차가 언제 오는지 확인해 주세요.

어휘 apparently 보기에 keynote address 기조 연설 relief 다행, 안도 entrance 출입구

151 의도 파악

번역 오전 9시 32분에 케르 씨가 "문제 없어요"라고 적은 의도는 무엇인가?

(A) 푸델 씨가 고마워하는 것을 알고 있다.
(B) 푸델 씨가 정확한 역에 가는 것을 도울 것이다.
(C) 푸델 씨의 기조 연설 시간을 바꿀 것이다.
(D) 어떻게 하면 푸델 씨를 도울 수 있는지 안다.

해설 푸델 씨가 오전 9시 27분 메시지에서 비즈니스 포럼 기조 연설 시간에 맞춰 갈 수 있는 기차가 없으니 무슨 방법이 있는지(No other trains can get me to the business forum in time ~ Any ideas?) 문의했고, 이에 대해 케르 씨가 '문제 없어요(No problem)' 라고 응답한 후 차를 보내겠다(I'll send a car for you)는 해결책을 제시했으므로, (D)가 정답이다.

어휘 appreciate 충분히 인식하다

152 추론 / 암시

번역 푸델 씨에 관해 암시된 것은?

(A) 만찬 약속을 지키지 못할 것이다.
(B) 차를 타면 비즈니스 포럼에 갈 수 있는 거리에 있다.
(C) 다른 식당으로 갈 예정이다.
(D) 오후 7시에 동료를 데리러 가야 한다.

해설 케르 씨가 오전 9시 32분 메시지에서 차를 보내겠다(I'll send a car for you)는 해결책을 제시했고, 이에 대해 푸델 씨가 오전 9시 33분 메시지에서 2시간 안에 뉴델리에서 출발하면 제시간에 도착할 것(so if I leave New Delhi within two hours, I should arrive on time)이라고 했으므로, 푸델 씨가 차를 타면 비즈니스 포럼에 갈 수 있는 거리에 있음을 추론할 수 있다. 따라서 (B)가 정답이다.

어휘 engagement 약속

153-154 설명서

새 아페레타 모뎀 연결법

이 삽지를 설치 정보 및 경과를 확인하는 양식으로 사용하십시오.

1. 먼저, **검은색** AC 어댑터를 벽면 콘센트에 꽂은 다음 "전원"이라고 표시된 모뎀의 첫 번째 포트에 연결하십시오.
2. 다음으로, **파란색** 케이블의 한쪽 끝을 모뎀 근처 벽에 장착된 전화 단자에 연결하십시오. 다른 쪽 끝을 "서비스"라고 표시된 모뎀의 두 번째 포트에 연결하십시오.
3. [153]**마지막으로, 컴퓨터 USB 포트에 빨간색 케이블을 연결하십시오. 그런 다음 다른 쪽 끝을 "컴퓨터"라고 표시된 모뎀의 세 번째 포트에 연결하십시오.**
4. 인터넷 브라우저를 여십시오. 아페레타 홈페이지가 자동으로 로딩됩니다. "동의합니다" 버튼을 누르면 등록 절차를 안내 받을 수 있습니다. 완료하시면, 서비스 비밀번호와 함께 웹 링크를 이메일로 받게 됩니다. 여기 암호를 기록해 두십시오: R+17ya-52p
5. [154]**서비스 비밀번호를 재설정하려면 로그인 페이지 하단에 있는 "재설정" 단추를 클릭한 다음, 선택한 비밀번호를 입력하십시오. 여기 새 비밀번호를 기록해 두십시오: ____________**

어휘 insert 삽지, 부속품 keep track of ~을 확인하다 installation 설치 outlet 콘센트 connect 연결하다 browser 브라우저 load 로딩되다 automatically 자동으로 sign-up 신청, 가입 reset 재설정하다

153 세부 사항

번역 빨간색 케이블은 무엇을 연결하기 위한 것인가?

(A) 모뎀과 전원 콘센트
(B) 모뎀과 전화 단자
(C) 컴퓨터와 모뎀
(D) 컴퓨터와 전원 콘센트

해설 3번 항목에서 빨간색 케이블을 컴퓨터 USB 포트와 모뎀의 세 번째 포트에 연결할 것(plug the **red** cable into a USB port in your computer ~ other end into the third port on your modem)을 지시했으므로, (C)가 정답이다.

154 추론 / 암시

번역 설명서 사용자가 아직 수행하지 않은 일은 무엇이겠는가?

(A) "동의" 버튼 누르기
(B) 이메일 메시지 받기
(C) 케이블 전부 연결하기
(D) 서비스 비밀번호 재설정하기

해설 5번 항목에서 서비스 비밀번호를 재설정한 후 선택한 비밀번호를 입력하고 기록할 것(To reset your service password, ~ Note your new password here)을 요청했지만, 빈칸이 비어 있으므로, 아직 서비스 비밀번호를 재설정하지 않았음을 추론할 수 있다. 따라서 (D)가 정답이다.

155-157 초대장

창의성과 영감의 밤
센터 크리에이티브
9월 22일 목요일
오후 6시 30분 ~ 오후 9시

센터 크리에이티브
댄버스 로 42번지, 카디프, 웨일스

센터 크리에이티브가 이제 10년이 되었습니다! 영국 전역에서 예술을 지원해 온 10년을 기념하기 위해, 〈창의성과 영감의 밤〉을 주최합니다. [155]**지난 수년간 저희 모금 운동을 지원하신 모든 분들을 초대하니 저희와 함께 예술과 음식을 즐기시고 인맥을 쌓아보십시오.** 지금 저희 갤러리에 전시되고 있는 밍 영의 조각품을 감상하시면서 지역 예술가, 동료 미술 애호가와 어울리십시오. 또한 [156]**얼마 전** 아래층에 문을 연 선다이얼 카페 요리사 디에고 에스피나가 준비한 전채와 다양한 고급 빵과자도 맛보십시오. 큐레이터 올리비아 리처즈가 이 센터의 역사에 대해 강연할 예정입니다. 저녁 동안 판매된 다과 수익금은 지역 학교 '그림 그

TEST 9

리는 아이들' 프로그램의 지원금으로 사용될 예정입니다.

이안 그리핀(igriffin@centrecreative.co.uk)에게 연락하여 참석 등록을 하십시오. [157]**인원이 다 차면, 등록이 마감된다는 것에 유의하십시오.**

어휘 celebrate 기념[축하]하다 decade 10년 host (행사를) 주최하다 inspiration 영감 mingle with ~와 어울리다 enthusiast 애호가 sculpture 조각품 currently 현재 feature 출연하다, 특징을 이루다 appetizer 전채 요리 a variety of 다양한 gourmet 고급의, 미식가를 위한 pastry 빵과자 proceeds 수익금 refreshment 다과 purchase 구매하다 initiative (특정한 목적을 달성하기 위한) 계획, 프로그램 local 지역의

155 추론 / 암시

번역 누구를 위해 마련한 초대장이겠는가?

(A) 미술 강사
(B) 지금까지의 기부자
(C) 식당 고객
(D) 학교 관계자

해설 세 번째 문장에서 지난 수년간 모금 운동을 지원한 모든 이들을 초대한다(We invite all who have supported our fund-raising campaigns)고 했으므로, (B)가 정답이다.

어휘 previous 이전의, 과거의 patron 손님 administrator 관계자, 관리자

▸▸ Paraphrasing 지문의 all who have supported our fund-raising campaigns
→ 정답의 Previous donors

156 동의어 찾기

번역 첫 번째 단락 8행의 "just"와 의미가 가장 가까운 단어는?

(A) 꽤
(B) 정확하게
(C) 최근에
(D) 현재

해설 "just"를 포함한 부분은 '얼마 전 아래층에 문을 연 선다이얼 카페(the Sundial Café, which just opened on the lower level)'라는 의미로, 여기서 just는 '얼마 전, 방금'이라는 뜻으로 쓰였다. 따라서 '최근에'라는 의미의 (C) recently가 정답이다.

157 사실 관계 확인

번역 행사에 관해 명시된 것은?

(A) 판매용 그림을 선보일 것이다.
(B) 참석하려면 요금을 내야 한다.
(C) 참석자가 특정 인원수로 제한될 것이다.
(D) 요리 시연이 포함될 것이다.

해설 마지막 문장에서 인원이 다 차면 등록이 마감되므로 유의하라(Note that once capacity is reached, registration will close)고 했으므로, 참석자가 특정 인원수로 제한된다는 것을 알 수 있다. 따라서 (C)가 정답이다.

어휘 attendee 참석자 demonstration 시연, (시범) 설명

▸▸ Paraphrasing 지문의 capacity
→ 정답의 a specific number of attendees

158-161 기사

살바도르의 신규 철도 노선

글 레오넬 메넨데스

(11월 14일)–바이아 주 정부는 살바도르와 파리페 간 철도 사업을 누가 맡을지 마침내 결론에 도달했다. 지난해 정부는 경전철 시스템의 건설과 운영, 유지에 관한 제안서를 요청했다. [158/161]**예상외로 긴 선정 과정을 거친 후, 도시 개발 사무국은 마침내 제안서가 선정되었다고 지난주에 발표했다.**

[158]**SOA 인터내셔널과 ROOV 프로젝트 매니지먼트 합작회사가 계약 수주자로 선정되었다.** [159]**사무국은 브라질 기업이 계약에 포함되어야 한다고 주장했었다. SOA 인터내셔널은 브라질, 스페인, 중동 전역에 걸쳐 오랫동안 철도 사업에 관여해 왔다. 스위스 기업인 ROOV 프로젝트 매니지먼트는 최근 국제 프로젝트 매니지먼트 기관에 의해 올해의 프로젝트 매니지먼트 회사로 선정되었다.**

노선은 두 단계로 건설된다. 1단계는 살바도르에서 플라타포르마까지 운행하는 기존 철도 노선을 활용하되, SOA가 건설할 경전철 차량을 수용하기 위해 선로를 교체할 예정이다. [160]**2단계는 플라타포르마에서 파리페로 가는 신규 선로의 건설로 이어진다.** 업체 선정이 오래 지연되면서 사무국은 이 사업이 30개월 내에 완료되면 인센티브를 제공하겠다고 했다. 그러나 ROOV 대변인 데이비드 리오스는 예측할 수 없는 날씨, 노동력, 물자 때문에 이 사업을 완료하는 데 최소한 36개월은 필요할 것이라고 말했다.

어휘 take charge of ~을 맡다 solicit 요청하다 proposal 제안(서) maintain 유지하다 unexpectedly 예상외로 secretariat 사무국 joint venture 합작회사 contract 계약(서) insist 주장하다 recently 최근 institute 기관 phase 단계 existing 기존의 replace 교체하다 accommodate 수용하다 settle on ~을 정하다 vendor 업체 reasonable 적당한 unpredictable 예측할 수 없는 labor 노동(력) supplies 물품

158 주제 / 목적

번역 기사를 작성한 이유는?

(A) 건설 사업 응찰 요청
(B) 계약 수주 알림
(C) 합병 가능성 설명
(D) 정책 결정 비판

해설 첫 번째 단락에서 도시 개발 사무국이 마침내 제안서가 선정되었다는 발표를 했다(After an unexpectedly long selection process, ~ a proposal had finally been selected)고 한 후, 이어서 선정된 업체와 해당 사업에 관해 설명했으므로, 계약 수주를 알리기 위한 기사임을 알 수 있다. 따라서 (B)가 정답이다.

어휘 bid 입찰, 입찰 기회 merger 합병 criticize 비판하다

159 추론 / 암시

번역 SOA 인터내셔널에 관해 암시된 것은?

(A) 이전에 ROOV와 협업했다.
(B) 기존 철도 노선을 건설했다.
(C) 산업상을 다수 받았다.
(D) 브라질에 본사를 둔 기업이다.

해설 두 번째 단락에서 사무국이 계약에 브라질 기업이 포함되어야 한다고 주장했다(The Secretariat had insisted that a Brazilian firm be included in the contract)고 했는데, 뒤이어 SOA 인터내셔널은 브라질, 스페인, 중동 전역에 걸쳐 오랫동안 철도 사업에 관여해 왔다(SOA International has long been involved in rail projects throughout Brazil)고 했고, ROOV 프로젝트 매니지먼트는 스위스 기업(Swiss Company)이라고 했다. 따라서 SOA 인터내셔널이 브라질 회사임을 추론할 수 있으므로, (D)가 정답이다.

어휘 collaborate 협업하다

160 사실 관계 확인

번역 기사가 사업에 관해 명시한 것은?

(A) 브라질에서 처음 있는 사업이다.
(B) 자금 부족으로 지연되었다.
(C) 2단계에는 신규 철도 노선 건설이 포함된다.
(D) 아마 30개월 후에는 완공될 것이다.

해설 마지막 단락에서 2단계는 플라타포르마에서 파리페로 가는 신규 선로의 건설로 이어진다(The second phase will continue with the construction of a new track to Paripe)고 했으므로, (C)가 정답이다.

▸▸ Paraphrasing 지문의 **the construction of a new track**
→ 정답의 **building a new rail line**

161 문장 삽입

번역 [1], [2], [3], [4]로 표시된 곳 중에서 다음 문장이 들어가기에 가장 적합한 곳은?

"지난해 정부는 경전철 시스템의 건설과 운영, 유지에 관한 제안서를 요청했다."

(A) [1]
(B) [2]
(C) [3]
(D) [4]

해설 주어진 문장에서 지난해 정부가 제안서를 요청했다(Last year the government solicited proposals)고 했으므로, 뒤에는 제안서 선정과 관련된 내용이 이어져야 자연스럽다. [1] 뒤의 문장에서 예상외로 긴 선정 과정을 거친 후, 지난주 마침내 제안서가 선정되었다(After an unexpectedly long selection process, ~ a proposal had finally been selected)며 제안서 선정 과정을 언급했으므로, (A)가 정답이다.

162-164 게시글

http://www.dealdirect.co.ke/buyerforum

스레드〉주문품 못 받음
게시 5월 15일 오전 11시 49분, 프레드릭 왐부

저는 2주 전 dealdirect.co.ke를 통해 책 배송품을 주문했습니다. 4월 20일로 예정된 배송품을 받지 못했어요. 162(B)**배송 업체에 전화했는데** 직원이 말하길 누군가 소포를 수령한 기록이 있지만 서명을 알아볼 수 없다고 하네요. 회사가 기록해 둔 제 주소가 정확한지 확인하기 위해 162(A)**딜 다이렉트에 전화를 했는데** 주소는 정확했어요. 163**다음으로 어떤 조치를 취해야 할지 고민하고 있습니다. 여러분이 주시는 아이디어에 귀를 기울이겠습니다.** 162(D)**지금까지 아파트 건물에 공고를 붙였지만** 연락 온 사람은 없었어요. 그냥 잊어버리고 다른 회사에 책을 다시 주문해야 할지 아니면 더 시간을 들여 이 문제를 164**해결하려고** 해야 할지 모르겠네요.

어휘 thread 스레드(하나의 주제에 대해 올린 여러 가지 의견) receive 받다 shipment 배송(품) representative 직원 accept 받다 signature 서명 legible 알아볼 수 있는, 또렷한 figure out 생각해 내다 respond 응답하다 resolve 해결하다

162 사실 관계 확인

번역 왐부 씨가 한 일이 아닌 것은?

(A) 딜 다이렉트에 전화했다.
(B) 배송 업체에 확인했다.
(C) 제품을 다시 주문했다.
(D) 공고를 붙였다.

해설 '딜 다이렉트에 전화했다(I called Deal Direct)'에서 (A)를, '배송 업체에 전화했다(I called the shipping company)'에서 (B)를, '지금까지 아파트 건물에 공고를 붙였다(So far, I've put up notices in my apartment building)'에서 (D)를 확인할 수 있다. 하지만 제품을 다시 주문해야 할지 문제 해결을 위해 더 노력해야 할지는 모르겠다(I wonder if I should ~ or spend more time trying to resolve the matter)고 했으므로, (C)가 정답이다.

▸▸ Paraphrasing 지문의 **called** → 보기 (B)의 **Checked with**
지문의 **put up** → 보기 (D)의 **Posted**

163 주제 / 목적

번역 게시글의 목적은?

(A) 조언 구하기
(B) 환불 요청하기
(C) 해결책 제시하기
(D) 대답하기

해설 다음으로 어떤 조치를 취해야 할지 고민하고 있고(I'm trying to figure out what my next step should be), 포럼(forum) 이용자들의 아이디어에 귀를 기울이겠다(I'm open to your ideas)고 했으므로, 조언을 구하는 게시글임을 알 수 있다. 따라서 (A)가 정답이다.

164 동의어 찾기

번역 첫 번째 단락 15행의 "resolve"와 의미가 가장 가까운 단어는?

(A) 발견하다
(B) 해결하다
(C) 결정하다
(D) 고려하다

해설 "resolve"를 포함한 부분은 '더 시간을 들여 이 문제를 해결한다(spend more time trying to resolve the matter)'는 의미로, 여기서 resolve는 '해결하다'라는 뜻으로 쓰였다. 따라서 '해결하다, 정착하다'라는 의미의 (B) settle이 정답이다.

165-167 기사

새 모습 갖춘 애시비 로고

(7월 30일) – 애시비 시의 새로운 로고가 화요일 찰스 카바노프 시장에 의해 공개되었다. 이 로고와 로고에 딸린 슬로건인 "애시비 커넥츠"는 즉시 공식 사용될 예정이다.

[165]**새 디자인은 붉은 배너와 도시 설립 연도를 포함해 애시비 원래 로고의 요소들을 사용한다. 그러나 그림자로 된 도시 스카이라인의 이미지는 새로운 디자인에 더욱 현대적인 느낌을 부여한다.** 슬로건은 애시비가 지역 사회 연계에 주력한다는 점을 알리고 있다.

카바노프 시장은 새로운 로고가 인기 있다고 주장하지만, 모두가 만족하는 것은 아니다. 시에서 평생 거주해 온 노엘 데이비슨은 "웬 야단법석인가요?"라고 물었다. "[167]**옛날 로고는 아주 쉽게 알아볼 수 있었어요. 왜 교체하느라 사서 고생인지 모르겠어요.**" 그럼에도 불구하고 대다수 주민은 바꿀 때가 되었다며 찬성했다.

[166(A)/(B)]**지역 지도와 공식 서신을 위한 편지지 머리글에는 이미 새 로고가 인쇄되어 있다.** [166(D)]**주민들은 또한 연례 헌옷 나누기 운동, 여름 음악 축제 같은 지역 행사를 위한 홍보 캠페인에서 새 로고를 곧 보게 된다.** 로고와 슬로건은 등록 상표이며 허가 없이 사용할 수 없다. 자세한 내용은 www.ashbyconnects.co.uk 참조.

어휘 unveil 공개하다 accompany 따라오다, 딸리다 immediately 즉시 element 요소 founding 설립, 창립 contemporary 현대적인 communicate 알리다, 전달하다 insist 주장하다 fuss 야단법석 recognizable 쉽게 알아볼 수 있는 replace 교체하다 correspondence 서신 promotional 홍보의 annual 연례의 permission 허가

165 세부 사항

번역 새 디자인의 특징은?

(A) 시장 이름
(B) 현재 날짜
(C) 추가 색상
(D) 업데이트된 그림

해설 두 번째 단락에서 새 디자인은 애시비 시의 원래 로고에 있던 요소들을 그대로 사용하지만(The new design uses elements from Ashby's original logo), 그림자로 된 도시 스카이라인의 이미지는 새로운 디자인에 더욱 현대적인 느낌을 부여한다(But an image of ~ gives the new design a more contemporary feel)고 했으므로, (D)가 정답이다.

166 사실 관계 확인

번역 새 로고가 등장하는 곳으로 언급되지 않은 것은?

(A) 지역 지도
(B) 시 문구류
(C) 의류
(D) 행사 포스터

해설 마지막 단락의 '지역 지도와 공식 서신을 위한 편지지 머리글에는 이미 새 로고가 인쇄되어 있다(Local maps and the letterhead for official correspondence ~ printed with the new logo)'에서 (A)와 (B)를, '주민들은 또한 지역 행사를 위한 홍보 캠페인에서 새 로고를 곧 보게 된다(Residents will also soon see it in promotional campaigns for events in the area)'에서 (D)를 확인할 수 있다. '연례 헌옷 나누기 운동과 같은 지역 행사를 위한 홍보 자료(promotional campaigns for events in the area, such as the annual used-clothing drive)'에서 헌옷(used-clothing)이 언급되긴 했지만 의류 자체에 로고가 새겨진다는 내용은 언급되지 않았으므로, (C)가 정답이다.

어휘 stationery 문구류

▸▸ **Paraphrasing**

지문의 **local maps** → 보기 (A)의 **maps of the area**

지문의 **the letterhead for official correspondence** → 보기 (B)의 **city stationery**

지문의 **promotional campaigns for events** → 보기 (D)의 **event posters**

167 문장 삽입

번역 [1], [2], [3], [4]로 표시된 곳 중에서 다음 문장이 들어가기에 가장 적합한 곳은?

"그럼에도 불구하고 대다수 주민은 바꿀 때가 되었다며 찬성했다."

(A) [1]
(B) [2]
(C) [3]
(D) [4]

해설 주어진 문장이 앞뒤 대조적인 내용을 의미상 연결하는 접속부사 Nevertheless로 시작하므로, 앞에서 먼저 로고 변경에 대해 찬성(most residents expressed approval)하는 것과 대조적인 내용이 언급되어야 한다. [4] 앞에서 로고 변경에 반대하는 노엘 데이비슨의 의견(The old logo was very recognizable. ~ the trouble of replacing it)이 인용되었으므로, (D)가 정답이다.

어휘 nevertheless 그럼에도 불구하고 approval 찬성, 승인

168-171 이메일

수신: s.gillis@stephengillis.net
발신: pete@bartharchitecture.com
날짜: 10월 2일 목요일
제목: 회신: 계약

길리스 씨께:

[168]**서명한 계약서를 보내 주셔서 감사합니다.** 지난주에 만나 뵙고 고객님이 하고자 하는 목공 사업의 전망에 대해 듣게 되어 기뻤습니다.

[168]**고객님이 원하는 목공소의 특징을 토대로, 앞으로 믿고 진행해도 좋을만한 몇 가지 안을 생각해 냈습니다.** [169]**대화를 통해, 고객님이 비용에 대해 우려하고 있다는 점도 이해하게 되었습니다.** 저는 설계 계획서를 작성할 때 이 점을 반드시 염두에 두고, 구조적으로 견고하면서도 경제적인 자재를 사용할 것입니다. [170]**앞으로 2주 안에 스케치 초안이 나옵니다. 일단 스케치 초안을 살펴보신 후에, 다시 만날 시간을 정하면 그 때 수정도 하고 마무리지을 수 있습니다.**

대형 기계들이 들어갈 자리는 이미 알고 있습니다. [171]**하지만 고압 전기 콘센트를 어디에 설치해야 할지 생각해야 하므로, 어떤 사안이든 마음이 바뀌면 알려 주십시오. 안전을 위해 테이블 톱 같은 모든 대형 장비가 반드시 전용 회로를 갖추도록 해야 합니다.**

고객님과 협력하여 생각하고 계신 것을 실현할 수 있기를 고대하고 있습니다.

피트 바스

어휘 contract 계약(서) woodworking 목공 feature 특징 solid 믿을만한, 훌륭한 cost 비용 concern 우려 be conscious of ~을 의식하다 sound 견고한 economical 경제적인, 알뜰한 preliminary 예비의, 임시의 adjustment 수정, 조정 electrical outlet 전기 콘센트 install 설치하다 equipment 장비 saw 톱 dedicated circuit 전용 회로

168 주제 / 목적

번역 이메일의 목적은?

(A) 청구 절차 명확히 밝히기
(B) 도급 업자의 다양한 역할 설명하기
(C) 프로젝트의 다음 단계 논의하기
(D) 새로운 설계 아이디어 요청하기

해설 첫 번째 단락에서 서명한 계약서에 대해 감사(Thank you for sending me your signed contract)를 전한 후, 두 번째 단락에서 길리스 씨가 원하는 목공소의 특징을 토대로, 앞으로 믿고 진행해도 좋을만한 몇 가지 안을 생각해 냈다(Based on the features you want ~ I have some solid ideas with which to move forward)고 했으므로, 프로젝트의 다음 단계를 논의하기 위한 이메일임을 알 수 있다. 따라서 (C)가 정답이다.

어휘 clarify 분명하게 밝히다 contractor 도급 업자

169 사실 관계 확인

번역 길리스 씨에 관해 명시된 것은?

(A) 작업장을 이전할 계획이다.
(B) 확실히 자리잡은 사업체를 소유하고 있다.
(C) 허가를 갱신해야 한다.
(D) 예산이 한정되어 있다.

해설 두 번째 단락에서 길리스 씨가 비용에 대해 우려하는 점을 이해한다(I also understand that you have some cost concerns)고 했으므로, 길리스 씨의 예산이 한정되어 있음을 알 수 있다. 따라서 (D)가 정답이다.

어휘 relocate 이전하다 well-established 확실히 자리잡은 renew 갱신하다 limited 제한된 budget 예산

▸▸ Paraphrasing 지문의 **have some cost concerns** → 정답의 **has a limited budget**

170 세부 사항

번역 이메일에 의하면, 길리스 씨는 다음 면담을 어떻게 준비해야 하는가?

(A) 도면 검토
(B) 서면 안건 작성
(C) 수정된 계약서에 서명
(D) 몇몇 건축 부지 후보지 방문

해설 두 번째 단락에서 2주 안에 스케치 초안이 나올 예정(You can expect some preliminary sketches within the next two weeks)이므로, 초안을 살펴본 후 다시 만날 시간을 정해 수정을 하고 마무리지을 것(Once you have looked them(preliminary sketches) over, let's set a time ~ finalized)을 제안했으므로, (A)가 정답이다.

▸▸ Paraphrasing 지문의 **looked them(preliminary sketches) over** → 정답의 **reviewing some drawings**

171 세부 사항

번역 바스 씨가 대형 기계에 관해 알고 싶어 하는 이유는?

(A) 방의 정확한 치수를 결정하려고
(B) 안전 규정을 모두 지키려고
(C) 모집해야 하는 작업팀의 규모를 결정하려고
(D) 계획이 다른 프로젝트에 지장을 주지 않도록 하려고

해설 세 번째 단락에서 대형 기계와 관련해 어떤 사안이든 마음이 바뀌면 알려 달라(please let me know if you change your mind about anything)고 한 후, 안전을 위해 테이블 톱 같은 모든 대형 장비가 반드시 전용 회로를 갖추도록 해야 한다(For the purpose of safety, I am required to ensure that all large pieces of equipment ~ have their own dedicated circuits)고 했으므로, (B)가 정답이다.

어휘 determine 결정하다 measurement 치수 assemble 모으다 interfere with ~에 지장을 주다

TEST 9

172-175 온라인 채팅

루크 오를랑 [오전 8시 30분]
모두들 안녕하세요. [172]**카터 스트리트 몰 개장식에 관한 새 소식이 듣고 싶네요.**

파멜라 쿡 [오전 8시 31분]
개장식은 잘 진행되었어요. 상점과 식당에는 보행자 왕래도 많았고 고객들도 만족한 것 같았어요. [173]**아직 고객 만족도 조사를 취합하고 있어요.** 레드 문 식당이 인기가 많았어요.

루크 오를랑 [오전 8시 32분]
자료를 입수하면 바로 보내 주세요. 그 밖에 제가 알아야 할 건 없나요?

알레나 산티아고 [오전 8시 33분]
[174]**저, 개장식 동안 주차 구역에 문제가 좀 있었어요. 조명이 제대로 작동되지 않았거든요.** 어두워졌을 때 제대로 작동하지 않았어요.

루크 오를랑 [오전 8시 34분]
네?

알레나 산티아고 [오전 8시 34분]
알고 보니 타이머가 정확하게 설정되지 않았어요.

루크 오를랑 [오전 8시 35분]
쉽게 해결됐다니 다행이네요. 전반적인 관리는 어땠나요?

마커스 아폴라얀 [오전 8시 35분]
경영진이 관리부와 긴밀하게 협조했으면 합니다. 일상적인 시설 관리를 위해 현장에 직원을 두고 있고 조경과 에스컬레이터 유지 관리를 맡을 외부 도급 업체를 두고 있어요.

루크 오를랑 [오전 8시 36분]
[172]**모든 일이 순조롭게 돌아가는 것 같군요. 주마다 이런 온라인 회의를 계속합시다.** [175]**2월에 제가 거기로 가서 직접 모든 사안을 봤으면 합니다.** 고마워요.

어휘 pedestrian 보행자의 compile 수집하다 function 작동하다 resolve 해결하다 maintenance 관리, 유지 보수 on-site 현장에 routine 일상적인 housekeeping 시설 관리 contractor 도급 업체 landscaping 조경 travel 이동하다 firsthand 직접

172 추론 / 암시

번역 오를랑 씨는 누구이겠는가?

(A) 기업 대표
(B) 식당 요리사
(C) 건축가
(D) 관리부 직원

해설 오를랑 씨는 오전 8시 30분 메시지에서 몰의 개장식에 관한 새 소식이 듣고 싶다(I would like an update on the grand opening at the Carter Street Mall)고 한 후 다른 사람들로부터 보고를 받았다. 이후 마지막 메시지에서 모든 일이 순조롭게 돌아가는 것 같다(Everything seems to be running smoothly)며 주마다 회의를 계속하자(Let's continue these online meetings weekly)고 말했으므로, 그가 회사의 대표임을 추론할 수 있다. 따라서 (A)가 정답이다.

173 의도 파악

번역 오전 8시 32분에 오를랑 씨가 "자료를 입수하면 바로 보내 주세요"라고 적은 의도는 무엇인가?

(A) 지난주 거둔 매출액을 알고 싶다.
(B) 몰 방문객의 반응에 관심이 있다.
(C) 운영 예산 증가를 걱정한다.
(D) 최근 고용된 직원의 최신 목록이 필요하다.

해설 쿡 씨가 오전 8시 31분 메시지에서 아직 고객 만족도 조사를 취합하고 있다(We are still compiling the customer-satisfaction surveys)고 했고, 이에 대해 오를랑 씨가 '자료를 입수하면 바로 보내 주세요(Please send me that data once you have it)'라고 요청했으므로, 그가 고객의 반응에 관심이 있음을 알 수 있다. 따라서 (B)가 정답이다.

어휘 revenue 매출, 수익

▸▸ Paraphrasing 지문의 **the customer-satisfaction surveys**
→ 정답의 **visitors' reactions to the mall**

174 사실 관계 확인

번역 논의에서 언급된 문제는?

(A) 설문지가 늦게 발송되었다.
(B) 식당 한 곳이 너무 붐볐다.
(C) 경영진이 아직 조경사를 충분히 고용하지 않았다.
(D) 주차 구역에 조명이 잘 들어오지 않았다.

해설 산티아고 씨가 오전 8시 33분 메시지에서 개장식 동안 주차 구역에 조명이 제대로 작동되지 않았다(there were some issues with the parking area ~ The lighting did not work right)는 문제점을 언급했으므로, (D)가 정답이다.

▸▸ Paraphrasing 지문의 **The lighting did not work right**
→ 정답의 **was not well lit**

175 추론 / 암시

번역 카터 스트리트 몰에 관해 암시된 것은?

(A) 산티아고 씨가 인사부를 감독한다.
(B) 보수 중이다.
(C) 판매 공간 몇 군데가 비었다.
(D) 오를랑 씨는 아직 그곳을 방문하지 않았다.

해설 오를랑 씨가 오전 8시 36분 마지막 메시지에서 2월에 카터 스트리트 몰에 가서 직접 모든 사안을 봤으면 한다(I hope to travel there(the Carter Street Mall) ~ to see everything firsthand)고 했으므로, 그가 아직 카터 스트리트 몰에 방문한 적이 없음을 추론할 수 있다. 따라서 (D)가 정답이다.

어휘 oversee 감독하다 renovate 보수하다 retail 판매, 소매

176-180 구인 공고 + 이메일

보스 통신 - 현재 공석

[180]**보스 통신(VCI)은 요하네스버그에 본사를 두고 있으며 출판부는 케이프타운, 디지털 미디어부는 프리토리아에 있습니다.** [176]**당사는 아프리카의 건강 및 건강 관리에 초점을 맞춘 과학 출판물을 제작하며 창사 이후 3년 동안 빠르게 사세를 확장해 오고 있습니다.** 현재 부족한 인력을 채우기 위해 당사는 다음 직책에서 의료 통신 산업에 대한 이해가 [177]**탄탄한** 지원자를 찾고 있습니다:

의료 전문 선임 작가
독창적인 발행물 개발하기. 자격 요건은 임상 의학 석사 학위, 의료 전문 작가 경험 최소 5년 이상, 탁월한 소통 기술, [178]**독자적으로 일할 수 있는 역량 및 협력하여 일할 수 있는 역량을 모두 갖출 것**. 합격한 지원자는 출판부에 배치됨.

부편집자
[178]**출판부 편집진 일원으로 근무**. 자격 요건은 신문학과 또는 관련학과 학사 학위, 탁월한 교열 능력 및 편집 소프트웨어 사용 경험.

의료 전문 작가/품질 관리 검토 담당자
[178]**출판팀과 긴밀히 협조해 모든 출판부 발행물의 정확성을 확보해야 함**. 출판부 배치.

[179]**지원자는 자기소개서, 이력서, 작문 샘플을 lmadisha@vci.co.za로 리언 마디샤 씨에게 보내십시오.** 면접은 5월 7일부터 12일까지 본사에서 진행되며 면접 시 추천서 3부를 제출해야 합니다. 면접 대상으로 선정된 지원자들만 연락을 받게 됩니다.

어휘 publication 출판(물) expand (사세를) 확장하다 applicant 지원자 solid (지식 등이) 견실한, 탄탄한 requirement 요건 master's degree 석사 학위 independently 독자적으로 collaboratively 협력하여 candidate 지원자, 후보자 bachelor's degree 학사 학위 journalism 신문 방송학과 related 관련된 copyedit 원고를 정리[교열]하다 ensure 보장하다, 확보하다 accuracy 정확(성) submit 제출하다 recommendation 추천 present 제출하다

수신: 리언 마디샤 〈lmadisha@vci.co.za〉
발신: 아미나 바이스 〈buysam@mailworks.net.za〉
날짜: 5월 1일
제목: 보조 편집자 직
첨부: 바이스_지원_자료

마디샤 씨께,

[179]**보조 편집자 직에 관심이 있어 메일 드립니다.**

저는 리처즈베이대학에서 정보 통신학 학사 학위를 받았습니다. 더반에 있는 룩소르 출판사에서 6년째 보조 편집자로 일하고 있습니다. 제 직위를 통해 저는 고객과 장기적인 협력 관계를 발전시켜 올 수 있었습니다.

출판 업계에서 쌓은 경험과 세세한 부분에 기울이는 세심함을 갖추었기에 제가 완벽한 적임자라고 생각합니다. [179]**관련 지원 서류를 첨부합니다.** [180]**마침 예정된 면접 기간에 귀사 본사 근처에서 열리는 회의에 참석할 예정이어서, 만약 대상자로 선정된다면 문제 없이 면접에 참석할 수 있습니다.**

아미나 바이스

어휘 long-term 장기의 collaborative 협력적인 attentiveness 조심성, 세심함 fit 딱 맞음, 적합함 relevant 관련된, 적절한 incidentally 마침, 우연히

176 사실 관계 확인

번역 VCI에 관해 명시된 것은?
(A) 3년째 운영되고 있다.
(B) 현재 여러 도시에 일자리가 비어 있다.
(C) 출판물은 재정 문제가 중심이다.
(D) 직원들은 출판물 개선에 주력한다.

해설 구인 광고의 첫 번째 단락에서 VCI가 아프리카의 건강 및 건강 관리에 초점을 맞춘 과학 출판물을 제작하며 창사 이후 3년 동안 빠르게 사세를 확장해 오고 있다(We(VCI) ~ have been expanding rapidly in the three years following our launch)고 했으므로, (A)가 정답이다.

▸▸ Paraphrasing 지문의 in the three years following our launch → 정답의 in operation for three years

177 동의어 찾기

번역 광고에서 첫 번째 단락 4행의 "solid"와 의미가 가장 가까운 단어는?
(A) 단단한
(B) 변함없는
(C) 빈틈없는
(D) 밀집한

해설 "solid"를 포함한 부분은 탄탄한 이해력을 가진 지원자(applicants with a solid understanding)라는 의미로 해석되는데, 여기서 solid는 '탄탄한, 견실한'이라는 뜻으로 쓰였다. 따라서 '빈틈없는, 철저한'이라는 의미의 (C) thorough가 정답이다.

178 세부 사항

번역 모든 일자리에 요구되는 자격 요건은?
(A) 팀의 일원으로 일할 수 있는 역량
(B) 과학 분야의 석사 학위
(C) 유능한 소프트웨어 기술
(D) 의료 분야 경력

해설 구인 공고에서 의료 전문 선임 작가(Senior Medical Writer)는 '독자적으로 일할 수 있는 역량과 협력하여 일할 수 있는 역량을 모두 갖출 것(the ability to work both independently and collaboratively)'을, 보조 편집자(Assistant Editor)는 '출판부 편집진 일원으로 근무(Works as a member of the Editorial Panel in our print division)'를, 의료 전문 작가/품질 관리 검토 담당자(Medical Writer/Quality Control Reviewer)는 '출판팀과 긴밀히 협조해 모든 출판부 발행물의 정확성을 확보해야 함(Works closely with other members of the print division team ~ publications)'을 자격 요건으로 제시하고 있다. 따라서 팀의 일원으로 일할 수 있는 역량을 공통적으로 요구한다는 것을 알 수 있으므로, (A)가 정답이다.

TEST 9

179 연계

번역 바이스 씨는 어떤 지원 서류를 제출하지 않았겠는가?

(A) 작문 능력을 보여 주는 실례
(B) 해당 일에 대한 관심의 표현
(C) 자격과 경력에 대한 설명
(D) 능력과 지식에 관한 고용주의 평가

해설 이메일에서 바이스 씨는 보조 편집자 직책(assistant editor position)에 관심을 표하며 관련 지원 서류(relevant application materials)를 첨부한다고 했다. 구인 공고의 하단을 보면 지원자는 자기소개서, 이력서, 작문 샘플을 제출해야 한다(Applicants should submit a cover letter, a résumé, and a writing sample)고 했으므로, 바이스 씨가 (A), (B), (C)에 해당하는 서류를 제출했을 것으로 추론할 수 있다. 따라서 (D)가 정답이다.

어휘 illustration 실례, 예증 capability 능력 description 설명 qualification 자격(증)

▸▸ Paraphrasing 지문의 **a cover letter** → 보기 (B)의 **An expression of her interest for the job**
지문의 **a résumé** → 보기 (C)의 **A description of her qualifications and experience**
지문의 **a writing sample** → 보기 (A)의 **An illustration of her writing capabilities**

180 연계

번역 바이스 씨는 어디에서 열리는 회의에 참석할 것인가?

(A) 케이프타운
(B) 더반
(C) 요하네스버그
(D) 프리토리아

해설 이메일의 마지막 단락에서 예정된 면접 기간에 VCI 본사 근처에서 열리는 회의에 참석할 예정(I will be attending a conference near your headquarters ~ interview period)이라고 했고, 구인 공고의 첫 번째 단락을 보면 보스 통신(VCI)이 요하네스버그에 본사를 두고 있다는 것(Vos Communications, Inc. (VCI), is headquartered in Johannesburg)을 알 수 있으므로, (C)가 정답이다.

181-185 온라인 기사 + 독자 의견

http://www.thecentervilletimes.com

〈센터빌 타임스〉, 6월 1일, "[181]**수상 음악**"

황홀한 바이올린 선율이 센터빌 도심에 퍼진다. 첼로 소리도 합류한다. 궁금한 관광객들이 음악 소리가 나오는 곳을 찾아 주위를 둘러본다. [181]**관광객들은 오케스트라 단원들이 센터빌 항구에 정박된 배 위에 잘 보이게 앉아 있는 모습을 차츰 알아차린다.**

[183]**"수상 음악"은 30년 전 브리지타 칼슨이 낡은 화물선을 개조해 갑판 위에서 처음 음악 공연을 한 것이 시초였다.** 오늘날 실내악단 "수상 음악"은 같은 항구 위치에서 원래의 배 위에서 주말 공연을 펼치고 있다.

현재 음악가들을 이끌고 있는 거장 아서 실버맨은 극찬받는 바이올린 연주자로 매주 공연에서 연주한다. "저희가 일정을 늘려서 기록적인 횟수의 콘서트를 제공하게 되었습니다. 해마다 50회가 넘죠." 거장 실버맨이 설명한다. "특정 프로그램들은 이제 젊은 청취자 같은 특정 청중에 맞추고 있습니다."

"수상 음악"은 대다수 금요일, 토요일 저녁 6시에 공연한다. 티켓은 온라인 www.musiconthewater.org에서 구매할 수 있다. 가족 콘서트는 일요일 오후 2시에 열릴 예정이다. [182]**가족 콘서트에는 티켓이 필요 없지만 자리를 확보하려면 일찍 도착할 것을 권한다.**

어휘 waft (공중에서) 퍼지다 figure out 알아 내다 in plain sight 잘 보이게 cargo boat 화물선 acclaimed 찬사를 받는 expand 늘리다 tailored 맞춤의 be encouraged to ~하도록 권유받다

http://www.thecentervilletimes.com/musiconthe water/comments

[185]**저는 아이 때부터 "수상 음악"을 즐기고 있습니다.** [183/185]**사실 창시자의 첫 번째 공연, 항구를 마주보고 있는 우리 가족의 3층 아파트까지 울려 퍼지던 그녀의 플루트 선율을 결코 잊지 못할 겁니다.** 조금 더 자라자 저는 직접 선상 공연 티켓을 사려고 동전을 모았습니다. "수상 음악"은 항구 지역에 경이로운 영향을 미쳐 오고 있습니다. [184/185]**〈센터빌 타임스〉가 제가 아직도 자랑스레 고향이라고 부르는 이 지역의 역사에 관한 기사를 낼 의향은 없는지 궁금합니다.**

감사합니다.

로베르토 파딜라

어휘 float 떠오르다 purchase 구매하다 impact 영향 publish 출간하다 neighborhood 지역

181 추론 / 암시

번역 "수상 음악" 공연에 관해 암시된 것은?

(A) 최근 좌석수를 늘렸다.
(B) 의외의 장소에서 열린다.
(C) 여름에만 개최된다.
(D) 빨리 매진된다.

해설 온라인 기사의 첫 번째 단락에서 관광객들이 주위를 둘러보다 오케스트라 단원들이 센터빌 항구에 정박된 배 위에 잘 보이게 앉아 있는 모습을 차츰 알아차린다(They(tourists) gradually realize that members of an orchestra ~ seated on a boat docked in the Centerville harbor)고 했으므로, 의외의 장소에서 공연이 열린다는 것을 추론할 수 있다. 따라서 (B)가 정답이다.

어휘 seating capacity 좌석수 unexpected 의외의

182 추론 / 암시

번역 가족 콘서트에 관해 기사에서 암시한 것은?

(A) 자리가 보장되지 않는다.
(B) 음반을 구매할 수 있다.
(C) 청중은 좋아하는 작품을 요청할 수 있다.
(D) 콘서트 음악가의 인터뷰가 온라인에 실린다.

해설 온라인 기사의 마지막 단락에서 가족 콘서트에는 티켓이 필요 없지만 자리를 확보하려면 일찍 도착할 것(No tickets are needed for family concerts, but patrons are encouraged to arrive early to ensure seats are available)을 권고했으므로, 자리가 보장되지 않는다는 것을 추론할 수 있다. 따라서 (A)가 정답이다.

어휘 guarantee 보장하다 piece (음악) 한 곡

183 연계

번역 칼슨 씨에 관해 암시된 것은?

(A) 거장 실버맨과 함께 음악을 공부했다.
(B) 항구 여행을 기획했다.
(C) 플루트를 연주했다.
(D) 배 수리점을 소유했다.

해설 온라인 기사의 두 번째 단락에서 "수상 음악"은 30년 전 브리지타 칼슨이 낡은 화물선을 개조해 갑판 위에서 처음 음악 공연을 한 것이 시초였다("Music on the Water" began ~ performed the first musical performance from the boat's deck)고 했는데, 독자 의견을 보면 '창시자의 첫 번째 공연, 항구를 마주보고 있는 우리 가족의 3층 아파트까지 울려 퍼지던 그녀의 플루트 선율을 결코 잊지 못할 겁니다(I will never forget listening to the founder's very first performance, ~ the harbor)'라고 쓰여 있으므로, "수상 음악"의 창시자인 칼슨 씨가 플루트를 연주했음을 추론할 수 있다. 따라서 (C)가 정답이다.

184 세부 사항

번역 파딜라 씨가 요청한 것은?

(A) 추가 주간 공연
(B) 콘서트 음질 개선
(C) 특정 주제에 대한 기사
(D) 지역 주민 티켓 가격 할인

해설 독자 의견의 마지막 부분에서 〈센터빌 타임스〉가 지역의 역사에 관한 기사를 낼 의향은 없는지 궁금하다(I wonder if *The Centerville Times* would consider publishing a piece of history of this neighborhood)고 했으므로, (C)가 정답이다.

어휘 reduced 할인된

185 추론 / 암시

번역 독자 의견이 파딜라 씨에 관해 암시하는 것은?

(A) 최근 콘서트 티켓을 샀다.
(B) 〈센터빌 타임스〉 기자다.
(C) 영감을 받아 자신도 음악가가 되었다.
(D) 어릴 때부터 센터빌에 살고 있다.

해설 독자 의견의 첫 번째 문장에서 파딜라 씨는 자신이 아이 때부터 "수상 음악"을 즐겨 왔다(I have enjoyed "Music on the Water" ever since I was a child)고 했고, 마지막 부분에서 자신이 자랑스레 고향이라고 부르는 센터빌 지역의 역사에 관한 기사를 〈센터빌 타임즈〉에서 낼 의향이 있는지(I wonder if *The Centerville Times* ~ history of this neighborhood, which I am still proud to call home) 문의했으므로, 그가 어릴 때부터 센터빌에서 살고 있음을 추론할 수 있다. 따라서 (D)가 정답이다.

▸▸ Paraphrasing 지문의 ever since I was a child
→ 정답의 since his childhood

186-190 광고 + 양식 + 이메일

카슨 사무용품
할인 판매!
[186]5월 25-26일, 이번 주만 연중 최대 할인 판매!

50% 할인 고급 프린터	15.99달러 종이 10연	25% 할인 소나마 텔레비전 전 품목	150달러 할인 릭쿠에르 사무용 책상 전 품목	10달러 할인 허브롯 잉크 카트리지 전 품목

매장이나 온라인에서 구입하세요. 단, 재고 소진 시까지!

어휘 ream 연(전지 500장) supplies 용품, 비축품

카슨 사무용품
반품 승인 요청서

주문 번호: 300034122
계정 번호: 업체5271
이름: **[186]제인 모리**
이메일: j.mori@welsomf.com
제목: 최근 구매
반품 사유:

저는 웰소 제조의 구매부장으로 카슨 사무용품에 업체 계정이 있습니다. 지난주 저는 다음 품목을 구매했습니다: **[189]릭쿠에르 사무용 책상 3개, 허브롯 잉크 카트리지 15개, 메모지 30개, 봉투 5상자. [186]오늘 곧 있을 주말 할인 광고를 봤는데 제가 구매한 일부 품목이 대폭 할인되네요. [187]적용되는 품목에 대해 환불을 받은 다음 더 저렴한 주말 할인가로 재구매할 수 있을까요?**

어휘 account 계정 purchase 구매하다; 구매(품) upcoming 다가오는 heavily 크게, 심하게 applicable 적용 가능한

수신: 제인 모리 〈j.mori@welsomf.com〉
발신: 셰리던 호멜 〈homel@cos.com〉
날짜: 5월 22일
제목: 회신: 교환
첨부: 쿠폰, 반품 및 교환

모리 씨께:

메시지 보내 주시고 카슨 사무용품과 지속적으로 거래해 주셔서 감사합니다. 아쉽게도, 공식 할인 날짜에 구매한 품목만 할인가가 적용됩니다.

[188/189]하지만 당사에 업체 계정이 있으시므로 대량 품목(동일 품목 15개 이상 구매)은 자동으로 20퍼센트 할인되며 당사 온라인 거래 사이트를 통해 구입 시 차감됩니다. 제가 고객님 주문을 보니 일부 품목이 해당이 되는군요.

또한 다음 구매 시 10퍼센트 할인되는 쿠폰을 제공해 드릴 수 있습니다. 쿠폰을 첨부합니다. 여기에는 온라인에서 사용할 수 있는 접속 코드가 명시되어 있습니다. [190]**반품 및 교환 절차도 첨부하니 앞으로 참고해 주십시오.**

문의 사항이나 우려되는 점 있으시면 주저 없이 연락 주십시오.

셰리던 호멜
지점장
카슨 사무용품

어휘 continued 지속적인 unfortunately 아쉽게도 be eligible for ~에 자격이 되다 bulk 대량 deduct 차감하다 specify 명시하다 procedure 절차 reference 참고 hesitate 주저하다

186 연계

번역 모리 씨에 관해 사실인 것은?

(A) 업체를 소유하고 있다.
(B) 처음 오는 고객이다.
(C) 프린터를 할인받았다.
(D) 5월 25일 이전에 물품을 구매했다.

해설 양식의 반품 사유(Reason for Return)란에서 모리 씨가 곧 있을 주말 할인 광고를 보고 자신이 구매한 일부 품목이 대폭 할인된다는 것을 알게 되었다(I noticed in an advertisement ~ I purchased are going to be heavily discounted)고 했고, 광고에서 카슨 사무용품이 5월 25일과 26일에 연중 최대 할인 행사(This weekend only, ~ our biggest sale of the year)를 진행한다고 했으므로, 할인을 받지 못한 모리 씨는 25일 이전에 제품을 구매했다는 것을 알 수 있다. 따라서 (D)가 정답이다.

187 세부 사항

번역 모리 씨가 일부 품목의 반품에 대해 문의한 이유는?

(A) 엉뚱한 주문품을 받았다.
(B) 도착 시 물품이 파손되어 있었다.
(C) 주문한 책상이 너무 작다.
(D) 주말 할인 기간에 물품을 구매하고 싶다.

해설 양식의 반품 사유(Reason for Return)란에서 할인이 적용되는 품목에 대해 환불받고 더 저렴한 주말 할인가로 재구매할 수 있을지(Would it be possible for me to get a refund ~ at the lower weekend sale price?)를 문의했으므로, (D)가 정답이다.

▸▸ Paraphrasing 지문의 **rebuy them at the lower weekend sale price** → 정답의 **purchase items during the weekend sale**

188 세부 사항

번역 이메일에 의하면, 모리 씨가 대량 구매에 할인을 받은 이유는?

(A) 쿠폰을 상품으로 바꾸었다.
(B) 업체 계정을 사용했다.
(C) 온라인으로 특별 코드를 입력했다.
(D) 회원 전용 할인 기간에 구매했다.

해설 이메일의 두 번째 단락에서 카슨 사무용품에 모리 씨의 업체 계정이 있으므로 대량 품목은 자동으로 20퍼센트 할인된다(Because you have a business account with us, ~ discount on bulk items)고 했으므로, (B)가 정답이다.

어휘 redeem (쿠폰 등을) 상품으로 바꾸다 exclusive 전용의, 독점의

▸▸ Paraphrasing 지문의 **a 20 percent discount on bulk items** → 질문의 **a discount on her bulk purchases**
지문의 **have a business account** → 정답의 **used a business account**

189 연계

번역 모리 씨가 구매한 품목 중 대량 할인 대상이 되는 것은?

(A) 사무용 책상과 메모지
(B) 잉크 카트리지와 봉투 상자
(C) 잉크 카트리지와 메모지
(D) 봉투 상자와 사무용 책상

해설 이메일의 두 번째 단락에서 대량 품목(동일 품목 15개 이상 구매)은 자동으로 20퍼센트 할인된다(you automatically receive a 20 percent discount on bulk items (purchases of fifteen or more of the same item))고 했으므로, 양식의 반품 사유(Reason for Return)란에 적힌 모리 씨의 구매 품목 중 '허브롯 잉크 카트리지 15개(15 Herbrot ink cartridges)'와 '메모지 30개(30 notepads)'가 대량 할인되었다는 것을 알 수 있다. 따라서 (C)가 정답이다.

▸▸ Paraphrasing 지문의 **automatically receive a 20 percent discount on bulk items** → 질문의 **qualified for the bulk discount**

190 세부 사항

번역 이메일에 포함된 것은?

(A) 최신 반품 양식
(B) 매장 정책에 관한 문서
(C) 신규 계정 신청서
(D) 모리 씨의 구매 영수증

해설 이메일의 세 번째 단락에서 앞으로 참고하라며 카슨 사무용품의 반품 및 교환 절차를 첨부한다(I will also attach our return and exchange procedures for your future reference)고 했으므로, (B)가 정답이다.

어휘 application 신청(서) receipt 영수증

▸▸ Paraphrasing 지문의 **attach** → 질문의 **was included**
지문의 **our return and exchange procedures** → 정답의 **A document about store policy**

191-195 온라인 게시판 + 이메일 + 웹페이지

https://www.forum.askaway.com.au

포럼	로그인	가입하기

믹스 92 라디오 광고

메릴린 응우옌, 8월 13일
믹스 92 라디오에 광고해 보신 분?

제임스 드포트, 8월 15일
저는 지난 3월부터 믹스 92 라디오에 광고를 하고 있습니다. 현명한 선택이었음이 입증되었습니다. 최근 몇 달 동안 제 업소인 드포트 자동차를 방문하는 고객 수가 현저하게 늘었거든요. 많은 사람들이 라디오 광고를 듣고 왔다고 말합니다.

방송국과 계약했을 때 예상하지 못한 비용 때문에 문제가 있었습니다. 191/192**하지만 광고부 예이거 씨가 관리자에게 제 일을 얘기했고 문제는 신속하게 해결되었습니다.** 예이거 씨는 제가 결과에 만족하는지 일주일 뒤에 재차 확인까지 했습니다.

어휘 significant 현저한 increase 증가 contract 계약(서) unexpected 예상하지 못한 supervisor 관리자 outcome 결과(물)

이메일

수신: 전 직원
발신: 캐서린 예이거
날짜: 9월 29일
제목: 마지막 방송

전 직원께,

192**믹스 92 라디오에서의 제 인턴 기간이 끝나 가네요.** 여기서 일한 것이 제게 멋진 경험이 되었다는 점 알아 주셨으면 합니다. 193**지난 12개월 동안 받은 훈련과 조언에 감사드립니다.** 193/194**특히 제 상사이자 멘토인 앨리슨 앨비에게 감사드려요.** 앨비 씨에게 라디오 광고의 기본 원칙을 배웠을 뿐만 아니라 고객의 요구에 부응하는 방법을 알게 되었습니다. 앨비 씨가 올해 오스트랄리스 트로피 후보에 오른 것은 고객과 직원들에 대한 그녀의 헌신을 여실히 보여 줍니다.

또한 제가 여기에서 일하고 노는 모습을 찍은 녹화 영상을 주셔서 감사해요. 핫 스팟 카페에서 여러분과 같이 점심 먹던 일이 그리울 거예요.

캐서린 예이거

어휘 grateful 감사하는 fundamental 기본 원칙 nomination 후보에 오름, 지명 speak volumes 여실히 보여 주다 dedication 헌신

https://www.cba.com.au/aawinners/advertising_and_social_media

오스트랄리스 중소기업 트로피 수상자
광고 및 소셜 미디어 부문

195**대상:** **라비 베단탐, 소셜 미디어 기술, 믹스 92 라디오**

금상: 쯔쉬안 리, 마케팅, 스트레일러스 의류점

은상: 호르헤 벨트란, 벨트란 광고사

194/195**동상: 앨리슨 앨비, 광고, 믹스 92 라디오**

50명이 넘는 후보자 중에 수상자가 선정되었습니다. 오스트랄리스 트로피 대상 수상자는 〈캔버라 비즈니스 투데이〉 12월 호에 인물 단평이 실립니다. 10월 12일 포스 스트리트 호텔 연회장에서 열리는 축하 행사에서 캔버라 기업 연합이 상을 수여합니다.

어휘 publicity 광고, 홍보 recipient 수상자 profile 인물 단평을 싣다

191 사실 관계 확인

번역 드포트 씨가 믹스 92 라디오에 관해 명시한 것은?
(A) 그의 문제를 적절하게 해결했다.
(B) 급속히 성장 중인 회사다.
(C) 지역 업체만 광고한다.
(D) 신규 고객에게 추가 요금을 부과한다.

해설 온라인 메시지의 마지막 단락에서 드포트 씨는 광고부 예이거 씨가 관리자에게 자신의 일을 얘기한 후 문제가 신속하게 해결되었다(Ms. Jager from the advertising department brought my concerns to her supervisor, and the matter was quickly resolved)고 명시했으므로, (A)가 정답이다.

어휘 adequately 적절하게

▸▸ Paraphrasing 지문의 the matter was quickly resolved
→ 정답의 resolved his problem adequately

192 연계

번역 드포트 씨에 관해 암시된 것은?
(A) 여러 해 동안 믹스 92 라디오의 고객이었다.
(B) 믹스 92 라디오 인턴 직원의 도움을 받았다.
(C) 최근 자동차 판매가 감소했다.
(D) 그 지역에서 가장 큰 자동차 업체를 운영하고 있다.

해설 온라인 메시지의 마지막 단락에서 드포트 씨는 광고부 예이거 씨가 관리자에게 자신의 일을 얘기한 후 문제가 신속하게 해결되었다(Ms. Jager from the advertising department ~ and the matter was quickly resolved)고 했는데, 이메일의 첫 번째 단락에서 예이거 씨가 믹스 92 라디오에서 자신의 인턴 기간이 끝나 간다(As my internship at Mix 92 Radio draws to a close)고 했으므로, 드포트 씨가 믹스 92 라디오 인턴 직원의 도움을 받았음을 추론할 수 있다. 따라서 (B)가 정답이다.

어휘 decline 감소

TEST 9

193 주제 / 목적

번역 예이거 씨가 이메일을 보낸 이유는?

(A) 동료들에게 도움을 요청하려고
(B) 오찬을 준비하려고
(C) 비디오 녹화 시간을 마련하려고
(D) 직원들에게 감사하려고

해설 이메일의 첫 번째 단락에서 믹스 92 라디오에서 지난 12개월 동안 받은 훈련과 조언에 감사드린다(I am grateful for the training and advice ~ over the past twelve months)고 한 후, 특히 자신의 상사이자 멘토인 앨리슨 앨비에게 감사(I especially want to thank my boss and mentor, Alison Alvey)를 전했으므로, (D)가 정답이다.

▸▸ **Paraphrasing** 지문의 **am grateful** → 정답의 **thank**

194 연계

번역 예이거 씨의 상사에게 수여될 상은?

(A) 대상
(B) 금상
(C) 은상
(D) 동상

해설 이메일의 첫 번째 단락에서 예이거 씨가 상사이자 멘토인 앨리슨 앨비에게 감사드린다(I especially want to thank my boss and mentor, Alison Alvey)고 했는데, 웹페이지를 보면 예이거 씨의 상사인 앨비 씨에게 수여될 상이 동상(Bronze)임을 확인할 수 있으므로, (D)가 정답이다.

▸▸ **Paraphrasing** 지문의 **my boss and mentor**
→ 질문의 **Ms. Jager's supervisor**

195 추론 / 암시

번역 웹페이지가 암시하는 것은?

(A) 축하 행사는 일반에게 공개된다.
(B) 올해는 상 추천자가 적었다.
(C) 베단탐 씨와 앨비 씨는 동료다.
(D) 수상자는 〈캔버라 비즈니스 투데이〉 무료 구독권을 받는다.

해설 웹페이지의 수상자 중 대상(Platinum) 수상자인 베단탐 씨와 동상(Bronze) 수상자인 앨비 씨의 회사가 믹스 92 라디오(Mix 92 Radio)이므로, 두 사람이 회사 동료임을 추론할 수 있다. 따라서 (C)가 정답이다.

196-200 기사 + 초대장 + 이메일

올리나위는 맛의 융합

동커스터(3월 21일) – [196]**아미나 이케가미 셰프는 여러 해 동안 열심히 일한 끝에 동커스터 시내에 자신의 식당을 개업한다.**

[200]**이케가미 씨는 체스터필드 요리 학교에서 교육받았고**, 시스라 비스트로에서 3년 동안 대리급 주방장으로 일했다. 그녀는 지난 12년간 델무렐의 직원이었는데, 그곳에서 지난 4년간 총괄 요리사 직함을 갖고 있었다.

이케가미 씨는 영국 혁신 셰프상을 포함해 여러 상을 수상했다. 그녀는 델무렐을 떠나는 것이 서운하지만, 자신의 식당을 소유하고자 했던 오랜 꿈을 이루게 되어 매우 기뻐하고 있다.

이케가미 씨의 새 레스토랑인 올리나위는 그녀가 어린 시절 경험한 다양한 맛에 영향을 받은 메뉴가 특징이다. [197]**그녀는 영국에서 프랑스, 세네갈, 그리고 일본계 다문화 가정에서 자랐다. 아주 다양한 음식 전통을 접한 것이 요리사가 되도록 영감을 주었다.**

"어머니, 아버지가 훌륭한 요리사예요." 이케가미 씨가 말한다. "저는 한 집에 이 모든 요리가 있는 게 좋았고, 항상 제 요리에 문화의 융합이 이루어지도록 노력하고 있습니다."

[198]**올리나위는 4월 25일 공식 개업하며 화요일부터 일요일까지 점심과 저녁 식사를 제공할 예정이다.**

어휘 culinary 요리의 executive chef 총괄 요리사 fulfill 이루다 influence 영향을 미치다 heritage 혈통[계], 유산 be exposed to ~에 노출되다 inspire 영감을 주다 cuisine 요리 strive to ~하려고 노력하다

함께하세요!
요리사 아미나 이케가미가 여는
새로운 식당
〈올리나위〉에서
맛있는 퓨전 요리를 즐기세요

[198]**4월 2일 토요일**
오후 7시 ~ 오후 11시

모든 음식과 음료 포함입니다.
초대자 전용 행사입니다.
본 초대장을 가져 오십시오.

어휘 invitation-only (초대받은 사람만 들어갈 수 있는) 초대자 전용

수신: 아미나 이케가미 〈amina.ikegami@scomail.co.uk〉
발신: 줄리앙 오프리 〈jaupry@enukmail.co.uk〉
제목: 올리나위
날짜: 3월 26일

아미나에게,

[199]**방금 올리나위 소식 들었고, 축하 행사 초대장을 받았어요.** 정말 멋진 소식이에요! [200]**학교 다닐 때 당신이 레스토랑을 열겠다고 자주 말했던 것이 기억나는데,** 마침내 실현된다니 정말 기뻐요!

[199]**아쉽지만 이번 행사에 참석할 수가 없네요.** 그 주말에 제과제빵 수업을 하러 프랑스에 가거든요. 하지만 돌아오면 저녁 먹으러 꼭 들릴게요.

행운을 빌어요.

줄리앙

어휘 celebratory 축하하는 unfortunately 아쉽게도
definitely 꼭, 확실히

196 주제 / 목적

번역 기사의 목적은?

(A) 새로운 요리 스타일 설명하기
(B) 새로운 식당 개업 알리기
(C) 요리학교 수업 광고하기
(D) 동커스터에 있는 다양한 식당 간략하게 소개하기

해설 기사의 첫 번째 단락에서 요리사 이케가미 씨가 동커스터 시내에 자신의 식당을 개업한다(After many years of hard work, chef Amina Ikegami is opening her own restaurant in downtown Doncaster)는 소식을 전했으므로, 식당 개업을 알리기 위한 기사임을 알 수 있다. 따라서 (B)가 정답이다.

어휘 profile 소개하다 establishment 식당, 점포

197 세부 사항

번역 이케가미 씨가 요리사 직업을 갖게 된 동기는?

(A) 어린 시절의 일본 여행
(B) 델무렐의 동료 요리사
(C) 과거 학교 교수
(D) 다양한 가족 배경

해설 기사의 네 번째 단락에서 이케가미 씨가 영국에서 프랑스, 세네갈, 그리고 일본계 다문화 가정에서 자랐고(She was raised in England in a family with French, Senegalese, and Japanese heritage), 이를 통해 아주 다양한 음식 전통을 접한 것이 요리사가 되도록 영감을 주었다(Being exposed to so many different food traditions is what inspired her to become a chef)고 했으므로, (D)가 정답이다.

어휘 diverse 다양한

▸▸ **Paraphrasing** 지문의 to become a chef
→ 질문의 to enter the cooking profession
지문의 a family with French, Senegalese, and Japanese heritage
→ 정답의 Her diverse family background

198 연계

번역 4월 2일 행사에 관해 사실인 것은?

(A) 예약이 필요하다.
(B) 일반에게 공개된다.
(C) 올리나위가 공식 개업하기 전에 열린다.
(D) 시스라 비스트로가 후원한다.

해설 초대장을 보면 질문에 언급된 4월 2일(April 2)이 올리나위에서 초대 행사가 진행되는 날(Saturday, 2 April)임을 확인할 수 있고, 기사의 마지막 단락에서 올리나위는 4월 25일 공식 개업한다(Olinawe opens officially on 25 April)고 했으므로, (C)가 정답이다.

199 주제 / 목적

번역 오프리 씨가 이메일을 보낸 이유는?

(A) 초대를 거절하려고
(B) 저녁 식사를 예약하려고
(C) 프랑스에 온 이케가미 씨를 환영하려고
(D) 이케가미 씨에게 수업을 해 달라고 요청하려고

해설 이메일의 첫 번째 단락에서 축하 행사 초대장을 받았다(I received your invitation to the celebratory event)고 한 후, 두 번째 단락에서 아쉽지만 이번 행사에 참석할 수 없다(Unfortunately, I will not be able to attend this event)고 했으므로, 초대를 거절하기 위한 이메일임을 알 수 있다. 따라서 (A)가 정답이다.

어휘 decline 거절하다

▸▸ **Paraphrasing** 지문의 not be able to attend this event
→ 정답의 decline an invitation

200 연계

번역 오프리 씨에 관해 명시된 것은?

(A) 올리나위에서 식사를 한 적이 있다.
(B) 한때 이케가미 씨 밑에서 일했다.
(C) 체스터필드 요리 학교에 다녔다.
(D) 델무렐 총괄 요리사이다.

해설 이메일의 첫 번째 단락에서 학교에 다닐 때 이케가미 씨가 레스토랑을 열겠다고 자주 말했던 것을 기억한다(At school, I remember that you often talked about opening your own restaurant)고 했으므로, 오프리 씨와 이케가미 씨가 같은 학교를 다녔다는 것을 알 수 있다. 기사의 두 번째 단락에서 이케가미 씨가 체스터필드 요리 학교에서 교육을 받았다(Ms. Ikegami trained at Chesterfield Culinary Academy)고 했으므로, (C)가 정답이다.

▸▸ **Paraphrasing** 지문의 trained at → 정답의 attended

TEST 9

기출 TEST 10

101 (A)	102 (B)	103 (D)	104 (D)	105 (C)
106 (B)	107 (A)	108 (A)	109 (C)	110 (C)
111 (D)	112 (D)	113 (C)	114 (B)	115 (A)
116 (C)	117 (A)	118 (D)	119 (B)	120 (B)
121 (A)	122 (D)	123 (B)	124 (D)	125 (D)
126 (D)	127 (B)	128 (A)	129 (C)	130 (C)
131 (D)	132 (D)	133 (C)	134 (A)	135 (B)
136 (D)	137 (C)	138 (A)	139 (D)	140 (D)
141 (A)	142 (C)	143 (A)	144 (C)	145 (A)
146 (D)	147 (C)	148 (D)	149 (C)	150 (A)
151 (B)	152 (C)	153 (D)	154 (B)	155 (C)
156 (A)	157 (C)	158 (D)	159 (B)	160 (B)
161 (C)	162 (B)	163 (C)	164 (D)	165 (A)
166 (B)	167 (B)	168 (B)	169 (A)	170 (D)
171 (D)	172 (C)	173 (C)	174 (D)	175 (A)
176 (A)	177 (A)	178 (C)	179 (D)	180 (A)
181 (C)	182 (C)	183 (B)	184 (D)	185 (D)
186 (B)	187 (D)	188 (C)	189 (D)	190 (A)
191 (B)	192 (A)	193 (C)	194 (A)	195 (C)
196 (C)	197 (C)	198 (B)	199 (D)	200 (A)

PART 5

101 명사 자리 _ 동사의 목적어

해설 빈칸은 동사 has의 목적어 역할을 하는 명사 자리로, 빈칸 앞 수량 형용사 several과 수가 일치하는 복수 명사가 들어가야 한다. 따라서 '지점, 장소'라는 의미의 복수 명사 (A) locations가 정답이다. (B) locate(위치하다, 위치를 찾다)는 동사, (C) located는 동사/과거분사로 품사상 빈칸에 들어갈 수 없고, (D) location은 단수 명사로 several과 수가 일치하지 않는다.

번역 선워스 스니커즈는 더 넓은 대도시 지역에 몇 군데 지점을 보유하고 있다.

102 동사 어휘

해설 빈칸은 명사구 their invoices를 목적어로 취하면서 전치사 of의 목적어 역할을 하는 동명사 자리로, online and by mail의 수식을 받는다. 따라서 빈칸에는 청구서(대금)과 관련하여 온라인과 우편으로 할 수 있는 행위를 나타내는 동사가 들어가야 하므로, '지불하기'라는 의미의 (B) paying이 정답이다.

번역 침버 공인 회계 법인은 온라인과 우편으로 청구서 대금을 지불할 수 있도록 고객에게 편의를 제공한다.

어휘 convenience 편의 invoice 청구서, 송장

103 부사 자리 _ 동사 수식

해설 빈칸이 동사 has been working 뒤에 있으므로, 부사 (D) reliably 또는 부사 역할을 할 수 있는 to부정사 (B) to rely 중 하나를 선택해야 한다. 문맥상 작동하는 상태를 적절히 묘사하는 부사가 들어가야 자연스러우므로, '확실하게, 안정적으로'라는 의미의 부사 (D) reliably가 정답이다. (B) to rely는 '의존하기 위해'라는 목적의 의미를 나타내는 to부정사로 전치사 on과 함께 쓰여야 하며, 문맥상 빈칸에 적절하지 않다. (A) reliable은 형용사의 원급, (C) more reliable은 형용사의 비교급으로 품사상 빈칸에 들어갈 수 없다.

번역 파텔 산업의 새 소프트웨어는 지난해 설치된 이후 안정적으로 작동하고 있다.

어휘 install 설치하다

104 전치사 어휘

해설 동사 are outlined와 명사구 the training handbook을 적절히 연결하는 전치사를 선택하는 문제이다. 교육 편람은 주어 Best practices가 설명되어 있는 곳으로 볼 수 있으므로, '전반에, 도처에'라는 의미의 장소 전치사 (D) throughout이 정답이다. 참고로 throughout은 기간 명사와 함께 '동안, 내내'라는 의미로도 쓰인다. (A) along은 '~을 따라', (B) toward는 '~을 향하여', (C) over는 '~ 위에, ~을 건너'라는 의미로 문맥상 빈칸에 적절하지 않다.

번역 고객 서비스 모범 사례는 교육 편람 전반에 요약되어 있다.

어휘 practice 사례, 관례 outline 약술하다, 요약하다

105 부사 자리 _ 동사 수식

해설 빈칸은 「help+목적어(us)+목적격 보어(migrate our client records)」의 구조에서 동사원형 migrate를 수식하는 부사 자리이므로, '쉽게, 간단히'라는 의미의 부사 (C) simply가 정답이다. (A) simple은 형용사의 원급, (B) simpler는 형용사의 비교급, (D) simplicity는 명사로 품사상 빈칸에 들어갈 수 없다. 참고로 help의 목적격 보어인 migrate 앞에는 to부정사의 to를 쓸 수도 있다.

번역 스크래치 소프트웨어는 우리가 고객 기록을 쉽게 옮기는 데 도움이 될 것이다.

어휘 migrate 옮기다 simplicity 단순함

106 인칭대명사의 격 _ 소유격

해설 빈칸은 that이 이끄는 명사절의 주어 sense of humor를 한정 수식하는 자리이므로, 소유격 인칭대명사 (B) her가 정답이다.

번역 그 코미디언은 자신의 유머 감각을 조부모에게 물려받았다고 말했다.

어휘 sense of humor 유머 감각 inherit 물려받다

107 전치사 어휘

해설 전치사 to와 함께 단체 사이클 여행의 출발지(Paris)와 종착지(Berlin)를 자연스럽게 연결하는 전치사를 선택하는 문제이다. 따라서 '~에서(부터)'라는 의미의 (A) from이 정답이다.

번역 이번 8월부터 게벨튼 바이크 투어즈는 파리에서 베를린까지 단체 사이클 여행을 이끌 것이다.

어휘 starting ~부터

108 동사 어휘

해설 빈칸은 to부정사구의 동사원형 자리로, 명사구 an agreement with Mason Cooper, Inc.를 목적어로 취한다. 따라서 빈칸에는 합의와 관련하여 이루고자 하는 성과를 나타내는 동사가 들어가야 하므로, '이르다, 도달하다'라는 의미의 (A) reach가 정답이다. 참고로, reach an agreement는 '합의에 이르다'라는 의미의 표현으로 묶어서 기억해두면 좋다. (B) talk는 '말하다, 대화하다'라는 의미의 자동사로 전치사 없이 바로 목적어를 취할 수 없고, (C) reason은 '추론하다, 판단을 내리다', (D) put은 '놓다, 처하게 하다'라는 뜻으로 문맥상 빈칸에 적절하지 않다.

번역 우리는 다음 주 중에 메이슨 쿠퍼사와 합의에 이르기를 바란다.

109 전치사 자리 _ 어휘

해설 빈칸이 명사구 their shift를 목적어로 취하는 전치사 자리이므로, (B) to, (C) of, (D) as 중 하나를 선택해야 한다. 또한 빈칸을 포함한 전치사구가 앞에 있는 명사구 the end를 수식하므로, 빈칸에는 the end와 their shift를 가장 잘 연결하는 전치사가 들어가야 한다. '교대 근무를 마칠 때(교대 근무의 끝에)'라는 내용이 되어야 자연스러우므로, '~의'라는 의미의 (C) of가 정답이다. 참고로, at the end[beginning] of는 '~의 말[초]에'라는 의미의 전치사구로 묶어서 기억해야 한다. (A) if는 접속사로 빈칸에 들어갈 수 없다.

번역 공장 작업장 관리자들은 교대 근무를 마칠 때 검사 보고서를 제출해야 한다.

어휘 factory 공장 floor 작업장 submit 제출하다 inspection 검사 shift 교대 근무

110 부사 어휘

해설 Seedum International의 상황을 가장 잘 묘사하는 부사를 선택하는 문제이다. 웹사이트를 통해서만 상품을 판매할 예정(will now sell ~ through its Web site)이라는 것은 더 이상 오프라인 소매점을 운영하지 않을 것임을 나타내므로, '이전에, 예전에'라는 의미의 (C) Formerly가 정답이다. (A) Sometimes는 '때때로, 가끔', (B) Later는 '나중에, 후에', (D) Frequently는 '자주, 흔히'라는 뜻으로 문맥상 빈칸에 적절하지 않다.

번역 이전에 소매점이었던 시덤 인터내셔널은 이제 웹사이트를 통해서만 상품을 판매할 예정이다.

어휘 retail store 소매점 merchandise 상품

111 상관접속사

해설 빈칸에는 neither와 함께 상관접속사를 이루어 Ms. Chen과 Mr. Gillespie를 연결하는 접속사가 들어가야 하므로, (D) nor가 정답이다. 참고로, or는 either A or B, and는 both A and B라는 상관접속사에 쓰인다.

번역 놀랍게도, 첸 씨와 길레스피 씨 모두 이사회가 취소되었다는 통보를 받지 못했다.

어휘 remarkably 놀랍게도 neither A nor B A도 아니고 B도 아니다 notify 통보하다 board meeting 이사회 cancel 취소하다

112 형용사 자리 _ 비교급

해설 빈칸이 주어 The new microwave soup containers를 보충 설명하는 보어 자리이므로, 형용사의 원급 (A) rigid와 형용사의 비교급 (D) more rigid 중 하나를 선택해야 한다. 빈칸 뒤에 비교급과 어울려 쓰이는 than이 있으므로, (D) more rigid가 정답이다. (B) most rigidly는 부사의 최상급, (C) rigidly는 부사의 원급으로 품사상 빈칸에 들어갈 수 없다.

번역 새로 나온 전자레인지 수프 용기는 이전 것보다 더 단단하다.

어휘 previous 이전의 rigid 단단한 rigidly 단단하게, 견고하게

113 형용사 어휘

해설 빈칸은 주어 The Banly Tourism Society를 보충 설명하는 형용사 자리로, to부정사구 to present the first issue of its publication의 수식을 받는다. 따라서 빈칸에는 창간호 출판이라는 성과에 대한 관광 협회의 심정을 적절히 묘사하는 형용사가 들어가야 하므로, '자랑스러워하는, 자부심이 강한'이라는 의미의 (C) proud가 정답이다. (A) regular는 '정기적인, 규칙적인', (B) general은 '일반적인, 전반적인', (D) favorite는 '가장 좋아하는'이라는 뜻으로 문맥상 빈칸에 적절하지 않다.

번역 밴리 관광 협회는 〈계간 밴리〉라는 출판물의 창간호를 자랑스럽게 소개합니다.

어휘 society 협회 present (정식으로) 소개하다 issue (잡지 등의) 호 publication 출판물 quarterly 계간지

114 명사 자리 _ 동사의 목적어 _ 어휘

해설 빈칸은 부정관사 a와 형용사 thorough 뒤에 오는 명사 자리로, 동사 is conducting의 목적어 역할을 한다. 따라서 명사인 (B) evaluation과 (C) evaluator 중 하나를 선택해야 한다. 동사 conduct(실시하다, 수행하다)는 실시하는 행위를 목적어로 취하므로, '평가'라는 의미의 (B) evaluation이 정답이다. (C) evaluator는 '평가자'라는 뜻으로 문맥상 적절하지 않고, (A) evaluate는 동사, (D) evaluative는 형용사로 품사상 빈칸에 들어갈 수 없다.

번역 코닉서 프린터즈는 현재의 장비 개선 요청에 대해 철저한 평가를 실시하고 있다.

어휘 thorough 철저한 current 현재의 equipment 장비

115 전치사 어휘

해설 빈칸은 명사구 the addition of 300 spaces를 목적어로 취하는 전치사 자리로, 빈칸을 포함한 전치사구는 콤마 뒤 절을 수식한다. 따라서 빈칸에는 명사구와 절을 가장 자연스럽게 연결하는 전치사가 들어가야 한다. 300개의 공간을 추가했음에도 여객선 터미널 주차장이 여전히 만차 상태(the ferry terminal's parking area is still full)라는 내용이므로, '~에도 불구하고'라는 의미의 (A) Despite가 정답이다. (B) Across는 '~을 가로질러, ~ 전체에 걸쳐', (C) Besides는 '~에 더하여, ~ 외에', (D) Inside는 '~ 안에'라는 뜻으로 문맥상 빈칸에 적절하지 않다.

TEST 10

번역 300대의 (주차) 공간이 추가되었지만 아직도 매일 오전 9시가 되면 여객선 터미널 주차장은 만차 상태다.

어휘 addition 추가 ferry 여객선

116 부사 자리 _ 동사 수식

해설 빈칸은 to부정사의 동사원형 redesign을 수식하는 부사 자리이므로, '합작으로, 공동으로'라는 의미의 부사 (C) collaboratively가 정답이다. (A) collaboration은 명사, (B) collaborative는 형용사, (D) collaborate는 동사로 모두 품사상 빈칸에 들어갈 수 없다.

번역 저스트록스사는 더 나은 제품을 확보하기 위해 영국에 있는 협력사들과 합작하여 모델 543Q를 재설계할 계획이다.

어휘 ensure 확보하다

117 명사 어휘

해설 빈칸은 동사 contains의 목적어 역할을 하는 명사 자리로, 전치사구 of surprising colors의 수식을 받는다. 문맥상 유성펜 상자에 다양한 색이 모여 있다는 내용이 되어야 자연스러우므로, '모음, 각종 구색을 갖춘 것'이라는 의미의 (A) assortment가 정답이다. (B) excitement는 '흥분, 신남', (C) account는 '계좌, 계정', (D) industry는 '산업'이라는 뜻으로 빈칸에 적절하지 않다.

번역 레인 퍼머넌트 마커즈의 각 상자에는 예상치 못한 색깔들이 다양하게 들어 있다.

어휘 permanent marker 유성펜 contain 담고 있다

118 형용사 어휘

해설 빈칸은 형용사 courteous와 함께 전치사 by의 목적어 역할을 하는 명사 reply를 수식한다. 또한 빈칸을 포함한 전치사구가 과거분사 pleased를 수식하므로, 빈칸에는 courteous와 더불어 기쁜 감정을 유발하는 답변의 특성을 묘사하는 형용사가 들어가야 한다. 따라서 '신속한, 즉각적인'이라는 의미의 (D) prompt가 정답이다. (A) safe는 '안전한', (B) close는 '가까운, 정밀한', (C) clean은 '깨끗한, 흠 없는'이라는 뜻으로 문맥상 빈칸에 적절하지 않다.

번역 우리는 여행 일정 변경에 대해 아스텔라 항공사로부터 신속하고 정중한 답변을 받고 기뻤다.

어휘 courteous 정중한 reply 답변 receive 받다 concerning ~에 대해 itinerary 여행 일정

119 명사 자리 _ 전치사의 목적어

해설 빈칸은 '기여하다'라는 의미의 동사 contribute와 어울려 쓰이는 전치사 to의 목적어 역할을 하는 명사 자리이다. 따라서 '성장, 증가'라는 의미의 명사 (B) growth가 정답이다. (A) grow를 동사원형으로 볼 경우 to부정사의 to 뒤에는 올 수 있지만 전치사 to 뒤에는 들어갈 수 없으므로 빈칸에 적절하지 않고, (C) grew는 과거동사, (D) grown은 과거분사로 품사상 빈칸에 들어갈 수 없다.

번역 고용률 상승은 주택 건설 업계의 성장에 기여하는 한 가지 요인이다.

어휘 employment rate 고용률 factor 요인 contribute to ~에 기여하다 housing construction 주택 건설 trade (특정) 업계

120 동사 어형 _ 태

해설 빈칸이 was not과 전치사구 사이에 있으므로, 과거분사 (B) specified와 현재분사 (C) specifying, 명사 (D) specification 중 하나를 선택해야 한다. 주어인 The color of the new chairs는 송장에(on the invoice) 명시되어야 하는 대상이므로, 수동의 의미를 내포하는 과거분사 (B) specified가 정답이다. (A) specify는 동사원형으로 be동사 was와 함께 쓰일 수 없어 빈칸에 들어갈 수 없다.

번역 새 의자들의 색상은 송장에 명시되어 있지 않았다.

어휘 invoice 송장 specify 명시하다 specification 상술

121 형용사 어휘

해설 빈칸은 주어인 Two hours와 동격 관계를 이루는 명사구 amount of time needed를 수식하는 형용사 자리이다. 임무를 완료하는 데 최소한 2시간이 필요하다는 내용이 되어야 자연스러우므로, '최소한의'라는 의미의 (A) minimum이 정답이다. (B) temporary는 '일시적인, 임시의', (C) bottom은 '밑바닥의, 근본적인', (D) durable은 '내구성이 있는, 오래 가는'이라는 뜻으로 문맥상 빈칸에 적절하지 않다.

번역 2시간이 그 임무를 완료하는 데 필요한 최소한의 시간이다.

어휘 complete 완료하다 assignment 임무, 과업

122 동사 어형 _ 목적격 보어

해설 빈칸은 명사구 its profit margins를 목적어로 취하면서 「has helped+목적어(Fossler Electronics)+목적격 보어」 구조에서 목적격 보어 역할을 하는 자리이다. '도움이 되다'라는 의미의 help는 to부정사 또는 동사원형을 목적격 보어로 취하는 동사이므로, 동사원형 (D) stabilize가 정답이다. (A) stabilized는 과거 동사/과거분사, (B) stability(안정)는 명사, (C) stabilizing은 현재분사/동명사로 help의 목적격 보어 자리에 들어갈 수 없다.

번역 성공적인 디지털 마케팅 캠페인은 포슬러 전자의 수익률을 안정시키는 데 도움이 되었다.

어휘 stabilize 안정시키다 profit margin 수익률

123 형용사 자리 _ 명사 수식

해설 빈칸이 a minimum of three years'와 명사 experience 사이에 있으므로, 빈칸에는 experience를 수식하는 형용사나 experience와 복합명사를 이루는 명사가 들어갈 수 있다. 따라서 명사인 (A) supervisors와 형용사인 (B) supervisory 중 하나를 선택해야 한다. 문맥상 지원자(Applicants)가 갖추어야 할 경력(experience)에 대해 설명하는 형용사가 들어가야 자연스러우므로, '관리의, 감독의'라는 의미의 형용사인 (B) supervisory가 정답이다. (A) supervisors는 '관리자들, 감독자들'이라는 뜻의 명사로 experience와 복합명사를 이룰 수 없고, (C) supervise와 (D) supervises는 동사로 품사상 빈칸에 들어갈 수 없다.

번역 데이터 관리자 직에 지원하는 사람은 최소 3년의 관리 경력이 있어야

한다.

어휘 be expected to ~해야 한다

124 동사 어형 _ 태 _ 수 일치

해설 빈칸은 주어 The mayor's speech의 동사 자리이므로, (A) record와 (D) was recorded 중 하나를 선택해야 한다. 주어 The mayor's speech가 단수 명사이고, 녹화되는 대상이므로, 수동태 과거 시제 동사 (D) was recorded가 정답이다. (A) record는 The mayor's speech와 수가 일치하지 않고, (B) recording과 (C) being recorded는 동명사/현재분사로 동사 자리에 들어갈 수 없다.

번역 월요일 업무 조찬에서 시장의 연설은 녹화되었고, 이번 주 후반에 방송될 예정이다.

어휘 mayor 시장 record 기록하다, 녹음[녹화]하다 broadcast 방송하다

125 부사 어휘

해설 빈칸은 until이 이끄는 부사절(until the desired results were achieved)과 함께 동사 tested를 수식하는 부사 자리이다. 문맥상 원하는 결과를 얻을 때까지 다양한 방식을 계속 시도했다는 내용이 되어야 자연스러우므로, '되풀이하여, 거듭'이라는 의미의 (D) repeatedly가 정답이다. (A) soon은 '곧, 빨리', (B) suddenly는 '갑자기', (C) well은 '잘, 제대로'라는 의미로 빈칸에 적절하지 않다.

번역 연구원들은 원하는 결과를 얻을 때까지 여러 방식을 거듭 시험했다.

어휘 researcher 연구원 formula 방식, 공식 achieve 얻다

126 동사 어휘

해설 빈칸은 equipment purchases를 목적어로 취하면서 동사 can help의 목적격 보어 역할을 하는 동사원형 자리이다. 따라서 빈칸에는 장비 구입과 관련하여 대출 전문가들(Loan specialists)이 어떻게 도와줄 수 있는지를 표현하는 동사가 들어가야 하므로, '자금을 조달하다'라는 의미의 (D) finance가 정답이다. (A) commit는 '저지르다, 약속하다', (B) associate는 '관련시키다, 연상하다', (C) reserve는 '예약하다, 보유하다'라는 뜻으로 문맥상 빈칸에 적절하지 않다.

번역 뉴턴 은행의 대출 전문가들은 귀사가 장비 구입 자금을 조달하도록 도울 수 있습니다.

어휘 specialist 전문가 equipment 장비 purchase 구입

127 전치사 자리

해설 빈칸은 명사구 our partnership을 목적어로 취하는 전치사 자리로, 빈칸을 포함한 전치사구는 콤마 뒤 절을 수식한다. 따라서 '~ 때문에'라는 의미의 전치사 (B) Because of가 정답이다. (A) After all(결국)과 (C) For the reason(그 이유로)은 부사, (D) As long as(~하는 한)는 접속사로 품사상 빈칸에 들어갈 수 없다.

번역 우리는 쇽스 짐과 제휴했기 때문에 직원들에게 헬스장 무료 회원권을 제공할 수 있다.

어휘 be able to ~할 수 있다 provide 제공하다 employee 직원

128 대명사 자리 _ 동사의 주어

해설 빈칸이 명사절 접속사 whether와 동사 could work 사이에 있으므로, 빈칸에는 명사절의 주어 역할을 하는 대명사가 들어갈 수 있다. 따라서 대명사인 (A) anyone과 대명사/부사인 (B) anywhere 중 하나를 선택해야 한다. 시간 외 근무를 할 수 있는 주체는 사람이므로, '누구나'라는 의미로 사람을 나타내는 대명사 (A) anyone이 정답이다. (B) anywhere를 '어디, 어디든'이라는 뜻의 명사로 보더라도 동사 could work의 주체가 될 수 없으므로 빈칸에 적절하지 않고, (C) anyway와 (D) anyhow는 부사로 품사상 빈칸에 들어갈 수 없다.

번역 트란 씨는 금요일에 시간 외 근무를 할 수 있는 사람이 있는지 부서에 문의했다.

어휘 department 부서 work overtime 시간 외 근무를 하다

129 명사 어휘

해설 빈칸은 동사 will research의 목적어 역할을 하는 명사 자리로, 형용사 potential과 전치사구 of expanding its overseas market to East Africa의 수식을 받는다. 따라서 빈칸에는 해외 시장을 넓힐 경우 사전에 조사해야 할 사항을 나타내는 명사가 들어가야 하므로, '수익성'이라는 의미의 (C) profitability가 정답이다. (A) deadline은 '기한, 마감 시간', (B) availability는 '이용 가능성, 유용성', (D) emphasis는 '강조, 중점'이라는 뜻으로 문맥상 빈칸에 적절하지 않다.

번역 캐니언랜드사는 동아프리카로 해외 시장을 넓힐 경우의 잠재적 수익성을 조사할 예정이다.

어휘 research 조사하다 potential 잠재적인 expand 넓히다

130 관계대명사의 격 _ 주격

해설 빈칸 뒤 주어가 없는 불완전한 절(will be available next week)을 이끄는 접속사 자리로, 빈칸을 포함한 절은 명사구 Chef Lind's cookbook을 보충 설명한다. 따라서 빈칸에는 사물 명사를 보충 설명하는 관계사절을 이끄는 주격 관계대명사가 들어가야 하므로, (C) which가 정답이다. (A) who도 주격 관계대명사로 쓰일 수 있지만 사람 명사를 대신하고, (D) whose는 소유격 관계대명사로 뒤에 명사가 와야 하므로 빈칸에 들어갈 수 없다. (B) what은 명사절 접속사 또는 선행사를 포함한 관계대명사로, 명사 cookbook을 보충 설명할 수 없다.

번역 다음 주에 나올 요리사 린드의 요리책에는 디저트 요리법만 들어 있다.

어휘 contain 들어 있다 recipe 요리법

PART 6

131-134 공지

프로 유니스는 현재 생산, 인사, 회계 부서 내 직책에 채용을 진행하고 있습니다. 지역에서 가장 큰 회사 중 하나인 프로 유니스는 70년 넘게 노동자들에게 유니폼을 [131]**공급해 왔습니다**. 창립 이래 프로 유니스는 고용 유지 및 인력 [132]**개발**에 주력해 왔습니다. 당사는 업계 평균 이상의 임금, 직무 교육, 정기적인 승진 기회를 제공합니다. [133]**공석**에 대해 자세히 알아보시려면 prounis.com/careers를 방문하세요. 관심 있는 구직자들은 안내에 따라 온라인 지원서를 작성하고 이력서를 업로드하시면 됩니다. [134]**또한 그들은 채용 자격을 갖추려면 신원 조회를 통과해야 합니다.**

어휘 hire 채용하다 human resources 인사 accounting 회계 region 지역 employer 회사, 고용주 outfit A with B A에게 B를 공급하다 workforce 인력 founding 창립 be committed to ~에 주력하다 employee retention 고용 유지 competitive 경쟁력 있는 wage 임금 opportunity 기회 promotion 승진 job-seeker 구직자 direct 안내하다 fill out 작성하다 application 지원(서)

131 동사 어형 _ 시제

해설 빈칸은 주어 Pro Unis의 동사 자리로, 기간을 나타내는 전치사구 for over 70 years의 수식을 받는다. 따라서 과거에 발생하여 현재까지 이어지는 일을 나타내는 현재완료진행 시제 (D) has been outfitting이 정답이다.

132 명사 자리 _ 전치사의 목적어

해설 빈칸은 등위접속사 and가 연결하는 복합명사 employee retention과 함께 전치사 to의 목적어 역할을 하는 명사 자리이므로, 명사인 (B) an advance와 (D) advancement 중 하나를 선택해야 한다. 문맥상 고용 유지와 더불어 직원을 위해 회사가 주력해 왔던(has been committed to) 분야를 나타내는 명사가 들어가야 하므로, '발달, 개발'이라는 의미의 (D) advancement가 정답이다. (B) an advance는 가산 명사로 '전진, 선불'이라는 뜻이므로 빈칸에 적절하지 않고, (A) advanced는 동사/과거분사로 품사상 빈칸에 들어갈 수 없다. (C) they advance는 '그들은 전진한다'라는 뜻으로 등위접속사 and가 연결하는 앞 절과 문맥상 어울리지 않는다.

133 명사 어휘

해설 빈칸은 전치사 about의 목적어 역할을 하는 명사 자리로, 빈칸을 포함한 전치사구가 to부정사의 동사원형 learn을 수식한다. 첫 번째 문장에서 프로 유니스가 채용을 진행하고 있다(Pro Unis is now hiring for positions)고 했고, 빈칸에 대해 알아보려면 자사의 웹사이트를 방문할 것(visit prounis.com/careers)을 조언했으므로, 빈칸에는 채용과 관련된 명사가 들어가야 한다. 따라서 '공석, 빈자리'라는 의미의 (C) openings가 정답이다. (A) issues는 '쟁점, 발행', (B) events는 '행사, 사건', (D) investments는 '투자'로 문맥상 빈칸에 적절하지 않다.

134 문맥에 맞는 문장 고르기

번역 (A) 또한 그들은 채용 자격을 갖추려면 신원 조회를 통과해야 합니다.
(B) 귀사의 작업복 디자인을 프로 유니스에 맡기세요.
(C) 이제 소셜 미디어에서 당사를 지켜보실 수 있습니다.
(D) 당사는 최근 인사부장을 새로 채용했습니다.

해설 빈칸 앞 문장에서 관심 있는 구직자들은 온라인 지원서를 작성하고 이력서를 업로드하면 된다(Interested job-seekers ~ to fill out an online application and upload a résumé)고 했으므로, 빈칸에도 구직자들과 관련된 내용이 들어가야 문맥상 자연스럽다. 따라서 (A)가 정답이다. 참고로, (A)의 인칭대명사 They는 앞 문장의 Interested job-seekers를 대신하고 있다.

어휘 background check 신원 조회 be eligible for ~에 자격이 있다 employment 채용

135-138 정보문

WS 치과는 치과 영업이 [135]**확장되고 있다**는 소식을 알리게 되어 기쁩니다. 두 번째 진료실이 이제 램튼에 있는 유니언 가 242번지에 문을 열어 도시 북쪽에 사는 환자들에게 더 큰 [136]**편의**를 제공합니다. 원래 병원은 핀 가 12번지에서 계속 운영합니다. 월벡 박사와 스타이너 박사는 두 곳 모두에서 [137]**탁월한** 진료 서비스를 제공하는 데 전념합니다.

WS 치과는 양쪽 진료실에서 폭넓은 치과 진료 서비스를 제공합니다. 두 곳 모두 월요일에서 금요일 오전 8시부터 오후 5시까지 영업합니다. [138]**핀 가의 진료실은 토요일 오전에도 문을 엽니다**. 저녁 시간 연장은 다음 시즌에 고려하겠습니다.

어휘 practice (병원·변호사 등의) 영업 convenience 편의 patient 환자 continue to 계속 ~하다 operate 운영하다 provide 제공하다 a full range of 폭넓은 extended 연장된

135 동사 어휘

해설 빈칸은 that이 이끄는 명사절에서 be동사 is와 함께 주어 our practice의 동사 역할을 하는 현재분사 자리로, 빈칸을 포함한 명사절은 to announce의 목적어 역할을 한다. 따라서 빈칸에는 to부정사구가 수식하는 과거분사 pleased(기쁜)의 원인을 나타내는 동사가 들어가야 한다. 뒤에 오는 문장에서 두 번째 진료실이 이제 문을 연다(Our second office is now open)고 했는데, 이 확장 소식이 pleased의 직접적인 원인으로 볼 수 있으므로, '확장되고 있는'이라는 의미의 (B) expanding이 정답이다. (A) training은 '훈련하고 있는', (C) calling은 '소집하고 있는', (D) moving은 '움직이고 있는'이라는 뜻으로 문맥상 빈칸에 적절하지 않다.

136 명사 어휘

해설 빈칸은 현재분사 offering의 목적어 역할을 하는 명사 자리로, 비교급 형용사 greater와 전치사구 for patients living on the north side of the city의 수식을 받는다. 문맥상 빈칸을 포함한 분사구문은 두 번째 진료실 개업(Our second office is now open)이 환자들에게 제공하는 혜택과 관련된 내용이 되어야 자연스럽다. 따라서 빈칸에는 그 혜택을 나타내는 명사가 들어가야 하므로, '편리, 편의'라는 의

미의 (D) convenience가 정답이다. (A) collection은 '수집, 모금', (B) production은 '생산, 제작', (C) performance는 '수행, 성과'라는 뜻으로 문맥상 빈칸에 적절하지 않다.

137 형용사 자리 _ 명사 수식

해설 빈칸이 동명사 providing의 목적어 역할을 하는 명사 care 앞에 있으므로, 빈칸에는 care를 수식하는 형용사나 care와 복합명사를 이루는 명사가 들어갈 수 있다. 문맥상 진료 서비스(care)의 수준을 묘사하는 형용사가 들어가야 자연스러우므로, '탁월한, 이례적인'이라는 의미의 형용사 (C) exceptional이 정답이다. (A) exception과 (B) exceptions는 '예외, 이의 신청'이라는 의미의 명사로 care와 복합명사를 이룰 수 없고, (D) exceptionally는 부사로 품사상 빈칸에 들어갈 수 없다.

138 문맥에 맞는 문장 고르기

번역 (A) 핀 가의 진료실은 토요일 오전에도 문을 엽니다.
(B) 이 지역에는 다채로운 역사와 활기찬 도심이 있습니다.
(C) 시설은 편안하고 깨끗하며 밝습니다.
(D) 일단 그곳에 가면 우회전해서 마운틴 뷰 로드로 가세요.

해설 빈칸 앞 문장에서 진료실 두 곳의 현재 영업 시간(They are both open from 8 A.M. to 5 P.M., Monday through Friday)을, 빈칸 뒤 문장에서 저녁 시간 연장 계획(Extended evening hours will be considered in the coming season)을 언급하고 있으므로, 빈칸에도 진료 시간과 관련된 내용이 들어가야 문맥상 자연스럽다. 따라서 (A)가 정답이다.

어휘 vibrant 활기찬 facility 시설 comfortable 편안한

139-142 이메일

수신: jroux@xmail.com
발신: josephbelle@perilleuxrealestate.com
날짜: 3월 2일
제목: 취업 문의

루 씨께:

귀하의 이력서가 동료를 통해 제게 [139]**전달되었습니다.** [140]**아쉽게도, 접수원 직에 빈자리가 없습니다.** 페릴뢰 부동산에 대한 귀하의 관심에 감사드리며, 앞으로 전일제 공석이 생길 경우에 대비해 귀하의 [141]**서류**를 보관해 두겠습니다.

[142]**그동안**, 특별 프로젝트를 위해 시간제로 근무하실 의향이 있으신가요? 저희 최고 경영자께서 야심 찬 광고 캠페인에 행정 지원을 필요로 하십니다. 이 프로젝트는 7월 말까지 계속됩니다.

이 기회에 관심이 있으신지 알려 주십시오.

조셉 벨, 부서장
인사부

어휘 colleague 동료 appreciate 감사하다 real estate 부동산 keep on file 보관하다 in case ~할 경우에 대비해 administrative 행정의 support 지원 advertising 광고 last 계속되다 opportunity 기회

139 동사 어형 _ 태

해설 빈칸은 주어 Your résumé의 동사 자리로 전치사구 to me의 수식을 받는다. 따라서 본동사 역할을 할 수 있는 (B) will pass on, (C) is passing on, (D) was passed on 중 하나를 선택해야 한다. 주어인 Your résumé는 전달되는 대상이므로, 수동태인 (D) was passed on이 정답이다. (A) to pass on은 to부정사로 동사 자리에 들어갈 수 없다.

140 문맥에 맞는 문장 고르기

번역 (A) 인맥 쌓기 행사에서 뵙게 되어 즐거웠습니다.
(B) 당사는 이제 6년 되었습니다.
(C) 귀하를 팀의 일원으로 맞게 되어 기쁩니다.
(D) 아쉽게도, 접수원 직에 빈자리가 없습니다.

해설 빈칸 앞 문장에서 루 씨의 이력서가 전달되었다(Your résumé was passed on to me)고 했지만, 빈칸 뒤 문장에서 앞으로 전일제 공석이 생길 경우에 대비해 서류를 보관해 두겠다(will keep ~ on file in case a full-time position opens up)고 했다. 따라서 빈칸에는 루 씨가 바로 채용되지 못한 상황을 보여 주는 내용이 들어가야 문맥상 자연스러우므로, (D)가 정답이다.

어휘 firm 회사 unfortunately 아쉽게도 receptionist 접수원

141 명사 어휘

해설 빈칸은 동사 will keep의 목적어 역할을 하는 명사 자리이다. 동사 keep은 전치사구 on file과 함께 '보관하다'라는 의미를 나타내므로, 빈칸에는 보관의 대상이 들어가야 한다. 첫 번째 문장에서 루 씨의 이력서가 전달되었다(Your résumé was passed on to me)고 했고, in case가 이끄는 부사절에서 앞으로 전일제 공석이 생길 경우에 대비하겠다(in case a full-time position opens up)고 했으므로, 보관 대상이 루 씨의 이력서임을 알 수 있다. 따라서 빈칸에는 이력서를 대신할 수 있는 명사가 들어가야 하므로, '문서, 서류'라는 의미의 (A) documents가 정답이다. (B) analysis는 '분석', (C) descriptions는 '설명서, 묘사', (D) reports는 '보고서, 보도'라는 뜻으로 문맥상 빈칸에 적절하지 않다.

어휘 analysis 분석 description 설명

142 접속부사 _ 어휘

해설 빈칸이 완전한 문장 앞에 있으므로, 문장 전체를 수식하는 부사가 들어가야 한다. 빈칸 앞 문장에서 앞으로 전일제 공석이 생길 경우에 대비해 루 씨의 서류를 보관해 두겠다고 했지만, 빈칸 뒤에서 특별 프로젝트를 위해 시간제로 근무할 의향이 있는지 물었으므로, 문맥상 빈칸에는 공석이 생기기 전까지의 기간을 나타내는 접속부사가 들어가야 자연스러워진다. 따라서 '그 동안, 그 사이에'라는 의미의 (C) In

TEST 10

the meantime이 정답이다. (A) First of all은 '우선, 가장 먼저', (B) As mentioned는 '언급한 대로'라는 뜻으로 문맥상 빈칸에 적절하지 않고, (D) In order that은 '~하기 위해'라는 부사절 접속사로 품사상 빈칸에 들어갈 수 없다.

143-146 기사

허스트 항공, 고객 서비스 제공 개선한다

로스앤젤레스(9월 22일)—허스트 항공은 승객이 신분증을 스캔하고, 탑승권을 출력하고, 항공기에 실을 짐에 수하물 표를 달 수 있는 무인 탑승 수속기 설치를 시작했다. 이 새로운 [143]**기기들**은 캘리포니아에 있는 공항 두 곳에 이미 설치되어 있다. [144]**이것들은** 허스트 항공이 운항하는 모든 공항에서 곧 이용할 수 있을 것이다. 허스트 항공 CEO 록사나 가지에 따르면 회사는 올 여름까지 모든 서비스 지역에 무인 탑승 수속기를 [145]**갖추는 것이** 목표라고 한다.

이 무인 탑승 수속기의 목적은 수속 절차를 더 빨리 진행하기 위함이다. 가지 씨는 "직원이 한정되어 있고, 종종 줄이 꽤 길어지기도 합니다. [146]**가장 분주한 운영 시간에는 특히 그렇죠.** 새로운 이 무인 탑승 수속기로 줄 서서 보내는 시간이 상당히 줄어들 것으로 예상합니다."라고 말했다.

어휘 install 설치하다 self-check-in kiosk 무인 탑승 수속기 passenger 승객 identification 신분증 boarding pass 탑승권 luggage 수하물 load 싣다 aim 목표하다 be equipped with ~을 갖추다 intent 목적 process 절차 limited 한정된 be expected to ~할 예정이다 significantly 상당히 reduce 줄이다

143 명사 어휘

해설 빈칸은 지시형용사 These와 형용사 new의 수식을 받는 명사 자리로, 동사구 are already in place의 주어 역할을 한다. 첫 번째 문장에서 허스트 항공사는 무인 탑승 수속기 설치를 시작했다(Hurst Airlines has started installing self-check-in kiosks)고 했으므로, These new -------이 가리키는 대상이 무인 탑승 수속기(self-check-in kiosks)임을 알 수 있다. 따라서 빈칸에는 수속기를 대신할 수 있는 명사가 들어가야 하므로, '장치, 기기'라는 의미의 (A) devices가 정답이다. (B) positions는 '지위, 위치', (C) materials는 '재료, 자료', (D) regulations는 '규정, 규제'라는 뜻으로 문맥상 빈칸에 적절하지 않다.

144 인칭대명사

해설 빈칸은 동사구 will soon be available at all airports의 주어 역할을 하는 대명사 자리이다. 첫 번째 문장에서 허스트 항공사가 무인 탑승 수속기 설치를 시작했다(Hurst Airlines has started installing self-check-in kiosks)고 했으므로, 모든 공항에서 곧 이용할 수 있게 되는 것은 무인 탑승 수속기(self-check-in kiosks)임을 알 수 있다. 따라서 self-check-in kiosks를 대신하는 복수 인칭대명사 (C) They가 정답이다. (D) Either는 '(둘 중) 어느 하나'라는 뜻으로 문맥상 빈칸에 적절하지 않다.

145 to부정사

해설 빈칸 앞 능동태 동사 aims(목표하다)는 to부정사를 목적어로 취하거나, 「aim for+목표로 하는 대상」의 구조로 쓰인다. 앞뒤 내용을 살펴보면, 허스트 항공이 서비스 지역(service areas) 자체를 목표로 삼는 것이 아니라, 올 여름까지 자사의 모든 서비스 지역에 무인 탑승 수속기를 갖추고자(equipped with kiosks) 한다는 것을 알 수 있다. 따라서 빈칸에는 to부정사가 들어가야 하므로, (A) to be가 정답이다. 여기서 all its service areas는 to부정사의 의미상 주어 역할을 한다. (B) that are은 문맥상 빈칸에 적절하지 않으며, (C) they were와 (D) having been은 구조상 빈칸에 들어갈 수 없다.

146 문맥에 맞는 문장 고르기

번역 (A) 아쉽게도, 저희는 노선을 변경하고 있습니다.
(B) 승객은 비행 2시간 전에 도착해야 합니다.
(C) 곧 직원을 더 채용할 것으로 예상합니다.
(D) 가장 분주한 운영 시간에는 특히 그렇죠.

해설 빈칸 앞 문장에서 무인 탑승 수속기 설치 이전의 문제점(We have limited staff, and lines can often be quite long)을, 빈칸 뒤 문장에서 무인 탑승 수속기 설치로 예상되는 이점(These new kiosks are expected to significantly reduce the amount of time spent in line)을 설명하고 있다. 따라서 빈칸에도 무인 탑승 수속기 설치 이전에 발생했던 문제점과 관련된 내용이 들어가야 문맥상 자연스러우므로, (D)가 정답이다. 참고로, (D)의 지시대명사 This는 앞 문장의 lines can often be quite long을 가리킨다.

어휘 route 경로, 노선 peak 한창인 operating time 운영 시간

PART 7

147-148 구인 공고

고용 센터

홈	일자리 찾기	지원하기

관리 보조, 부동산 개발부

퍼 부동산 주식회사에서 부동산 개발부 관련 고객 서비스, 자료 입력, 일반 행정 지원을 제공할 정규직 관리 보조가 필요합니다. [147]**해당 인력은 일반인의 정보 요청에 응대하고 허가증에 관한 조사 및 진행 상황을 점검하며 부서 기록 유지 작업을 돕게 됩니다.** 이 직책에는 최소 학사 학위와 2년의 관련 사무 경력이 요구됩니다. [148]**능숙한 컴퓨터 사용 능력과 뛰어난 쓰기 및 말하기 의사 소통 능력은 필수입니다.**

지원서는 3월 30일까지 접수합니다.

어휘 property 부동산 realty 부동산 entry 입력 administrative 행정의 associated with ~와 관련된 respond 응대하다 permit 허가증 bachelor's degree 학사 학위 related 관련된 computer literacy 컴퓨터 사용 능력 communication 소통 application 지원(서) accept 받다

147 사실 관계 확인

번역 구인 공고에 포함된 것은?

(A) 퍼 부동산 주식회사의 위치
(B) 직책을 시작하는 날짜
(C) 책무에 대한 설명
(D) 고용 보조금에 관한 정보

해설 두 번째 문장에서 해당 직책의 다양한 책무(The individual will respond to requests for information from the public, research and track permits, and assist with maintaining department records)를 나열하고 있으므로, (C)가 정답이다.

어휘 description 설명 benefit 수당, 보조금

148 세부 사항

번역 직책에 필요한 자격은?

(A) 회계학 학위
(B) 전문 자격증
(C) 관리자 경력
(D) 능숙한 컴퓨터 실력

해설 후반부에서 능숙한 컴퓨터 사용 능력과 뛰어난 쓰기 및 말하기 의사 소통 능력이 필수(Strong computer literacy ~ are a must)라고 했으므로, (D)가 정답이다. 최소 학사 학위와 2년의 관련 사무 경력이 요구된다(The position requires a minimum of a bachelor's degree and two years of related office experience)고 했으므로, (A)와 (C)는 오답이고, (B)는 언급되지 않았다.

어휘 certification 자격증

▸▸ Paraphrasing 지문의 **Strong computer literacy**
→ 정답의 **Good computer skills**

149-150 문자 메시지

메리 피구에레도 (오전 10시 3분)
안녕하세요, 벤. [149/150]**그쪽 팀에서 창고 울타리 수리를 시작했나요?**

벤자민 헌터 (오전 10시 5분)
안녕하세요, 메리. 곧 시작할 거예요. 통로에 고인 물이 있어서 먼저 그것부터 치워야 해요.

메리 피구에레도 (오전 10시 6분)
비바람이 칠 때 지붕이 파손되서 그런 걸까요?

벤자민 헌터 (오전 10시 8분)
실은 우리가 원인을 찾았어요. 비품 창고에 있는 배수관이 막혔어요. 그걸 치우는 대로 바로 울타리를 손볼 거예요. 지붕은 괜찮은 것 같아요.

메리 피구에레도 (오전 10시 11분)
그래요, 좋아요, 벤. 고마워요!

어휘 repair 수리하다 warehouse 창고 standing water 고인 물 sustain (피해를) 입다 locate 찾다 drainpipe 배수관 supply closet 비품 창고

149 추론 / 암시

번역 헌터 씨의 직업은 무엇이겠는가?

(A) 접수원
(B) 실내 장식가
(C) 수리공
(D) 경비원

해설 피구에레도 씨가 오전 10시 3분 메시지에서 헌터 씨의 팀에서 창고 울타리 수리를 시작했는지(Has your team started repairing the fences at the warehouse?) 문의했다. 이에 따라 헌터 씨가 수리팀의 일원임을 추론할 수 있으므로, (C)가 정답이다.

어휘 maintenance 수리, 정비

150 의도 파악

번역 오전 10시 5분에 헌터 씨가 "곧 시작할 거예요"라고 적은 이유는 무엇인가?

(A) 그의 팀이 곧 작업을 시작할 것이다.
(B) 그의 팀이 프로젝트를 계속할 것이다.
(C) 그의 팀이 금방 장소에 도착할 것이다.
(D) 그의 팀이 물을 치울 것이다.

해설 피구에레도 씨가 오전 10시 3분 메시지에서 헌터 씨의 팀이 창고 울타리 수리를 시작했는지(Has your team started repairing the fences at the warehouse?) 문의했고, 이에 대해 헌터 씨가 '곧 시작할 거예요(We'll get to it soon)'라고 응답했으므로, 헌터 씨가 해당 작업을 곧 시작할 것임을 추론할 수 있다. 따라서 (A)가 정답이다. 참고로 인칭대명사 it은 repairing the fences at the warehouse를 대신하고 있다.

▸▸ Paraphrasing 지문의 **get to it soon**
→ 정답의 **begin a task shortly**

151-152 공지

75번 노선 승객 여러분께 알립니다

[151]**모든 메트로웨스턴 승객 여러분은 75번 버스 노선이 아래와 같이 임시 변경되었음을 숙지하시기 바랍니다.** 공사 때문에 다음 기간 동안 테일러 가와 포브스 대로 사이 8번 가에서 운행이 중단됩니다. 불편을 끼쳐 드려 죄송합니다.

월요일, 4월 5일, 오전 10:00-오후 4:00
수요일, 4월 7일, 오전 11:00-오후 4:30
[152]**금요일, 4월 9일, 오후 6:30-오후 10:00**
토요일, 4월 10일, 오전 9:00-오후 5:00

평소처럼 메트로웨스턴 버스 운행은 모두 오후 11시 30분에 끝납니다. 모든 버스가 매일 오전 5시 45분에 운행을 재개합니다.

어휘 passenger 승객 aware 알고 있는 temporary 임시의 due to ~ 때문에 suspend 중단하다 inconvenience 불편

TEST 10

151 주제 / 목적

번역 공지의 목적은?

(A) 새 고속버스 노선 소개
(B) 버스 운행 임시 변경 발표
(C) 공사 프로젝트 완료 보고
(D) 승객에게 가장 혼잡한 시간대에 이동 피하도록 요청

해설 초반부에서 메트로웨스턴 승객들에게 75번 버스 노선이 임시 변경되었음을 숙지하도록(All Metrowestern passengers should be aware of the following temporary changes for bus line 75) 권고했으므로, 버스 운행 임시 변경을 알리기 위한 공지임을 알 수 있다. 따라서 (B)가 정답이다.

어휘 completion 완료 avoid 피하다

152 세부 사항

번역 공지에 의하면, 버스 노선을 이용할 수 있는 시간은?

(A) 4월 5일 오전 11시 30분
(B) 4월 7일 오전 5시 30분
(C) 4월 9일 오후 3시
(D) 4월 10일 오후 4시

해설 운행 중단 일정표의 '금요일, 4월 9일, 오후 6:30-오후 10:00'에서 4월 9일 오후 3시에는 버스 이용이 가능하다는 것을 확인할 수 있으므로, (C)가 정답이다. (A)는 '월요일, 4월 5일, 오전 10:00-오후 4:00'에서, (D)는 '토요일, 4월 10일, 오전 9:00-오후 5:00'에서 버스 이용이 불가능하다는 것을 확인할 수 있고, 모든 버스가 매일 오전 5시 45분에 운행을 재개한다(All buses begin running again at 5:45 A.M. daily)고 했으므로, (B)는 임시 운행 중단과 상관없이 버스 노선을 이용할 수 없는 시간임을 알 수 있다.

153-154 이메일

수신: 피터 버스타인
발신: 칼 닐손
제목: 회의 일정 조정
날짜: 10월 22일

안녕하세요 피터,

다음 주 회의는 일정을 다시 잡아야 합니다. [154]**새로 온 사무 보조원 마르티나가 고객들의 사무실이 세계 도처에 있어 표준 시간대가 다양하다는 점을 고려하지 않았네요. 몇몇은 회의에 참석하려면 폐점 시간 후에도 남아 있어야 할 겁니다.** 제가 이미 원래 회의를 취소하고 불편을 끼친 데 대해 사과문을 보냈습니다.

[153]**시간을 내서 마르티나와 함께 이 건을 검토해 주시겠어요? 이 일은 그녀가 주기적으로 하게 될 일이에요.** 제가 그녀에게 약속을 잡으라고 하기 전에 당신보고 그녀와 같이 일하라고 할 걸 그랬어요.

고마워요.

칼 닐손, 사무장
크레아틱스 오브 스웨덴 AB사

어휘 take into consideration 고려하다 time zone 표준시간대 cancel 취소하다 apology 사과 perform 수행하다 regularly 주기적으로 appointment 약속

153 주제 / 목적

번역 닐손 씨가 이메일을 보낸 이유는?

(A) 면접 준비
(B) 신규 고객 추천
(C) 새 일정 체계 발표
(D) 직원 교육 요청

해설 두 번째 단락에서 시간을 내서 마르티나와 함께 검토할 것(Could you please find time to review this with Martina?)을 요청한 후, 함께 검토할 것이 마르티나가 주기적으로 하게 될 일(This is a task she will be performing regularly)이라는 부연 설명을 했다. 이에 따라 마르티나의 업무 교육을 요청하기 위한 이메일임을 알 수 있으므로, (D)가 정답이다.

154 세부 사항

번역 원래 회의 시간은 어떤 문제가 있었는가?

(A) 사무실이 쉬는 날에 일정을 잡았다.
(B) 해외 고객들에게 편리하지 않았다.
(C) 닐손 씨가 그날 시간이 없었다.
(D) 버스타인 씨가 그 방을 쓰고 있었다.

해설 첫 번째 단락에서 마르티나가 회의 일정을 잡을 때 고객들의 사무실이 세계 도처에 있어 표준시간대가 다양하다는 점을 고려하지 않았다(The new office assistant ~ did not take into consideration that the clients' offices are located throughout the world and in a variety of time zones)고 한 후, 몇몇은 회의에 참석하려면 폐점 시간 후에도 남아 있어야 한다(Several would have had to stay after closing time in order to attend the meeting)는 부연 설명을 했으므로, (B)가 정답이다.

▸▸ **Paraphrasing** 지문의 **the clients' offices are located throughout the world and in a variety of time zones** → 정답의 **international clients**

155-157 이메일

수신: 브래들리 왓킨스
발신: 아이코 야마시타
제목: 새 소프트웨어
날짜: 4월 4일

[155]**브래들리, 점검 목록을 만들어 우리 프로젝트들을 정리하는 데 아주 유용할 것 같은 새 소프트웨어 프로그램을 발견했어요. 클로즈 프로젝트라고 하는데, 사용하기가 꽤 쉬워 보여요.** [157]**사용자가 로그인하면 그들이 작업하고 있는 각 프로젝트를 위해 완료해야 할 항목 목록을 볼 수 있어요.** 그런 다음 각 과제가 완료되면 '완료'에 체크합니다. 이렇게 하면 각 프로젝트의 진행 상황을 더 잘 추적하는 데 도움이 되죠. 심지어 사용자가 사진을 찍어 부서진 파이프와 같은 실제 문제를 보여 줄 수 있는 모바일 애플리케이션도 있어요. 저는 시험용 프로그램을 다운로드했어요.

[156]오늘 오후에 제 사무실에 와서 같이 검토해 보실래요? 알려 주세요.

아이코

어휘 organize 정리하다 fairly 꽤 keep track of ~을 추적하다 progress 진행 actual 실제의 go through 검토하다

155 주제 / 목적

번역 야마시타 씨가 왓킨스 씨에게 이메일을 보낸 이유는?

(A) 약속 일정을 다시 잡으려고
(B) 그가 견본을 수령했는지 확인하려고
(C) 신제품에 대해 알려 주려고
(D) 그가 프로젝트를 끝냈는지 알아보려고

해설 초반부에서 점검 목록을 만들어 프로젝트들을 정리하는 데 아주 유용할 것 같은 새 소프트웨어 프로그램을 발견했다(I've come across a new software program ~ very useful for creating checklists to organize our projects)고 한 후, 사용하기가 꽤 쉬워 보인다(it seems fairly easy to work with)는 의견을 덧붙였다. 이에 따라 새 소프트웨어 프로그램에 대해 알려 주기 위한 이메일임을 알 수 있으므로, (C)가 정답이다.

▸▸ Paraphrasing 지문의 a new software program
→ 정답의 a new product

156 세부 사항

번역 야마시타 씨가 왓킨스 씨에게 요청한 일은?

(A) 그녀에게 연락하기
(B) 하청 업체에 전화하기
(C) 사진 몇 장 보내기
(D) 프로젝트 기록하기

해설 마지막 두 문장에서 야마시타 씨가 자신의 사무실에 와서 같이 검토해 볼 것(Would you be interested in coming to my office ~ to go through it)을 제안한 후, 확인 응답(Let me know)을 요청했으므로, (A)가 정답이다.

어휘 subcontractor 하청 업체

▸▸ Paraphrasing 지문의 Let me know → 정답의 Contact her

157 문장 삽입

번역 [1], [2], [3], [4]로 표시된 곳 중에서 다음 문장이 들어가기에 가장 적합한 곳은?

"그런 다음 각 과제가 완료되면 '완료'에 체크합니다."

(A) [1]
(B) [2]
(C) [3]
(D) [4]

해설 주어진 문장이 '그런 다음(Then)'이라는 의미의 접속부사로 시작하고, Then 뒤에서 각 과제가 완료되면 '완료'에 체크한다(they check 'Completed' when each task is finished)고 했으므로, 앞에서 완료 이전 단계가 언급되어야 한다. [3] 앞 문장에서 사용자가 로그인하면 각 프로젝트를 위해 완료해야 할 항목 목록을 볼 수 있다(Users log in to view a list of items that need to be completed for each project)고 했으므로, (C)가 정답이다.

158-160 공고

여름 맞이 무료 주스를 받아가세요!

여기 프레시 버스트에서 다가오는 여름을 축하하고자 합니다! [158]**저희가 새로운 주스 맛을 생각해 내신 고객님께 보답하겠습니다.** 행운의 우승자는 7월 1일부터 9월 30일까지 매달 250ml짜리 주스 신상품 24병이 든 상자를 받게 됩니다! [158]**또한 신상품 주스와 함께 고객님 사진을 찍어 광고 캠페인에 사용할 예정입니다.**

[160(C)]**프레시 버스트 소셜 미디어 페이지에 새로운 맛에 대한 아이디어를 설명하는 글을 남기고 친구들과 게시물을 공유하기만 하면 됩니다.** [160(D)]**게시물에 새 주스를 위해 지어낸 독창적인 이름을 넣는 것도 잊지 마세요!**

[159]**이 대회는 1월 6일부터 2월 14일까지 진행됩니다.** 우승자는 4월 25일까지 통보받게 됩니다. [160(A)]**이 대회는 18세 이상만 참가할 수 있다는 점에 유의하세요.** 또한 다른 회사에 저작권이 있는 로고, 제품 이름, 또는 기타 자료가 포함된 응모작은 접수가 불가하다는 점도 유의하세요.

어휘 celebrate 축하하다 approach 다가오다 reward 보답하다 come up with ~을 생각해 내다 receive 받다 advertising 광고 describe 설명하다 notify 통보하다 competition 대회 entry 응모작 copyright 저작권으로 보호하다

158 추론 / 암시

번역 프레시 버스트는 어떤 단체이겠는가?

(A) 지역 신문사
(B) 사진 스튜디오
(C) 소셜 미디어 플랫폼
(D) 음료 제조 업체

해설 첫 번째 단락에서 프레시 버스트가 새로운 주스 맛을 생각해 낸 고객에게 보답하겠다(We'll reward the customer who comes up with a juice flavour)고 한 후, 신상품 주스와 함께 고객의 사진을 찍어 광고 캠페인에도 사용할 예정(We'll also take photographs of you with your new juice to use in our advertising campaigns)이라고 했다. 이에 따라 프레시 버스트가 음료 제조 업체임을 추론할 수 있으므로, (D)가 정답이다.

어휘 beverage 음료 manufacturer 제조 업체

159 세부 사항

번역 대회 참가 마감일은?

(A) 1월 6일
(B) 2월 14일
(C) 4월 25일
(D) 9월 30일

해설 마지막 단락에서 대회가 1월 6일부터 2월 14일까지 진행된다(The contest runs ~ until 14 February)고 했으므로, (B)가 정답이다.

160 사실 관계 확인

번역 대회 참가 요건이 아닌 것은?

(A) 최소 18세 이상
(B) 응모작에 로고 포함하기
(C) 소셜 미디어에서 게시물 공유하기
(D) 신제품 이름 짓기

해설 마지막 단락의 '이 대회는 18세 이상만 참가할 수 있다(the competition is only open to people aged 18 and over)'에서 (A)를, 두 번째 단락의 '프레시 버스트 소셜 미디어 페이지에 새로운 맛에 대한 아이디어를 설명하는 글을 남기고 친구들과 게시물을 공유할 것(leave a comment describing your idea for a new flavour on our Fresh Burst social media page, then share your post with your friends)'에서 (C)를, '게시물에 새 주스를 위해 지어낸 독창적인 이름을 넣을 것(include the creative name you've invented for your new juice)'에서 (D)를 확인할 수 있다. 마지막 단락에서 다른 회사에 저작권이 있는 로고가 포함된 응모작은 접수 불가하다(we cannot accept entries that include logos, ~ that are copyrighted by other companies)는 금지 요건은 언급했지만, 응모작에 로고를 넣으라는 참가 요건은 명시하지 않았으므로, (B)가 정답이다.

▸▸ Paraphrasing 지문의 **aged 18 and over**
→ 보기 (A)의 **at least 18 years old**
지문의 **the creative name you've invented for your new juice** → 보기 (D)의 **Creating a name for the new product**

161-163 차트

머지스틱 산업(MI) 공장 가동 작업 흐름

1. 트럭이 재료를 MI 공장으로 배송한다. [161]**재활용 불가능한 물품은 제거한다; 재활용 가능한 물품은 컨베이어 벨트 위에 올린다.** 버린 물품은 트럭으로 옮겨 매립지에 폐기한다.
2. 회전 원반이 판지를 들어올린다. 더 작은 물품은 거름망을 통과한다. [162]**상자는 깨끗이 닦아서 납작하게 만든다.**
3. 종이는 낮은 장애물 아래로 통과해 대기 구역으로 이동하고 다른 물품들은 계속 진행한다. 종이 물품은 파쇄한다.
[163]**4. 자석으로 컨베이어 벨트에서 금속 물품을 제거한다.** 금속 물품은 유형별로 자동 분류해 찌그러뜨린다.
5. 유리 물품은 수작업으로 벨트에서 제거한다. 유리 물품은 분쇄한다.
6. 광학 스캐너로 인쇄된 코드를 스캔해 플라스틱을 유형별로 나눈다. 처리한 물품은 모두 원자재로 제조 업체에 보낸다.

어휘 deliver 배송하다 nonrecyclable 재활용 불가능한 discard 버리다 transfer 옮기다 landfill 쓰레기 매립지 disposal 폐기 flatten 납작하게 만들다 barrier 장애물 shred 조각으로 찢다 magnet 자석 crush 찌그러뜨리다 manually 수작업으로 shatter 산산이 부수다 raw material 원자재

161 추론 / 암시

번역 머지스틱 산업은 어떤 업체이겠는가?

(A) 제조 업체
(B) 포장 인쇄 업체
(C) 재활용 공장
(D) 배송 업체

해설 공장 가동 작업 1단계에서 재활용 불가능한 물품은 제거하고(Nonrecyclable items are removed), 재활용 가능한 물품은 컨베이어 벨트 위에 올린다(recyclables are put on a conveyor belt)고 했다. 이에 따라 머지스틱 산업이 재활용 공장이라고 추론할 수 있으므로, (C)가 정답이다.

162 세부 사항

번역 차트에 의하면, 과정에서 판지 상자는 어떻게 되는가?

(A) 거름망 뒤에 놓인다.
(B) 깨끗이 닦아진다.
(C) 제품으로 채운다.
(D) 찌그러뜨린다.

해설 공장 가동 작업의 2단계에서 상자를 깨끗이 닦아서 납작하게 만든다(Boxes are cleaned and flattened)고 했으므로, (B)가 정답이다.

▸▸ Paraphrasing 지문의 **Boxes** → 질문의 **cardboard boxes**

163 추론 / 암시

번역 4단계에서 컨베이어 벨트에서 제거되는 물품은 무엇이겠는가?

(A) 우유갑
(B) 유리병
(C) 철제 깡통
(D) 플라스틱 병

해설 질문에서 언급된 4단계에서 자석으로 컨베이어 벨트에서 금속 물품을 제거한다(A magnet removes metal objects from the conveyor belt)고 했으므로, 보기 중 금속 물질인 철제 깡통(Steel cans)이 제거될 것으로 추론할 수 있다. 따라서 (C)가 정답이다.

어휘 carton 종이갑, 상자 steel 강철

▸▸ Paraphrasing 지문의 **objects** → 질문의 **items**
지문의 **metal** → 정답의 **Steel**

164-167 기사

태리빌에 새롭고 주목할 만한 것

우리 소도시의 많은 이들은 식당 배달 서비스를 절대 받지 못할 것이라고 생각했다. 하지만 진취적인 두 젊은이 덕분에, 이제 TVL 딜리버즈가 생겼다! [164]**알리샤 카자리안과 테레사 조는 지역 대학에서 마지막 해를 보내다가 지난 5월에 계획을 생각해 냈다.** "어느 날 밤 시험공부를 하는데 밖에 나가 먹는 건 안하고 싶었어요. 태리빌에서 이용할 수 있는 음식 배달이 제한되어 있어서 낙담했죠. [167]**식사를 쉽게 찾고, 주문하고, 결제하는 방법을 원했어요.** 또한 다양한 음식과 가격대에서 선택할

수 있었으면 했어요. 하지만 여기에는 그런 서비스가 없었죠." 조 씨가 말했다.

[164]**태리빌의 음식 배달 공백을 메우기 위한 노력으로, TVL 딜리버즈는 식사하는 사람과 식당의 요구를 모두 충족하는 온라인 플랫폼을 통해 식사하는 사람과 식당을 연결한다.** 식당은 더 폭넓은 고객층을 만날 수 있고, [165(B)/(C)/(D)]**고객은 놀라울 정도로 다양한 판매자들 중에서 선택해, 집이나 사무실에서 편하게 음식을 골라 주문하고 수많은 온라인 결제 방식 중 하나를 통해 지불할 수 있다.** TVL 딜리버즈와 제휴하는 식당은 태리빌 인근 대부분 지역에 분포되어 있으며, 어떤 예산에도 맞는 음식을 제공한다. "출발은 좋다고 생각하지만, 우리는 벌써 개선점을 염두에 두고 있습니다." 카자리안이 말했다. "일부 음식 배달 서비스는 최소 30분 안에 주문이 배달된다고 약속하죠. 우리도 결국에는 특정 시간 안에 배달하기를 바라지만, 공식적으로 그런 약속을 하기 전에 서비스의 모든 측면이 제대로 작동하는지 확인할 필요가 있어요."

태리빌 기업 협회 대표인 배리 포터는 새 업체에 열광했다. "물론 이곳 태리빌에 새로운 업체가 문을 열면 언제나 신나죠. 그러나 이건 지역 주민들이 오랫동안 소망해 온 업체예요. [166]**더구나 최근 시 남쪽에 크리슬리 복합 상업 지구가 생겼으므로, TVL 딜리버즈가 성공하리라 확신해요.**"

어휘 enterprising 진취적인 come up with ~을 생각해 내다 avoid 피하다, ~하지 않다 frustrated 낙담한 delivery 배달 clientele 고객(층) impressively 놀랄 만한 diverse 다양한 vendor 판매자 a number of 많은 suit 맞다 budget 예산 improvement 개선(점) eventually 결국에는 specified 특정한 properly 적절하게 enthusiasm 열정 recent 최근의 office park 복합 상업 지구

164 주제 / 목적

번역 기사의 목적은?

(A) 막 개업한 식당 평가
(B) 유명한 태리빌 주민 인터뷰
(C) 시의 새 건물 건축 보도
(D) 최근 창업한 업체 설명

해설 첫 번째 단락에서 카자리안 씨와 조 씨가 최근에 TVL 딜리버즈를 창업하게 된 경위(Alicia Kazarian and Theresa Cho ~ came up with their plan last May)를, 두 번째 단락에서 TVL 딜리버즈의 운영(TVL Delivers connects diners and restaurants on an online platform that serves each of their needs)과 관련해 설명했다. 이에 따라 최근 창업한 TVL 딜리버즈를 소개하는 기사임을 알 수 있으므로, (D)가 정답이다

어휘 describe 설명하다

165 사실 관계 확인

번역 기사에 의하면, TVL 딜리버즈가 제공하지 않는 것은?

(A) 배송 시간 보장
(B) 온라인 메뉴
(C) 편리한 결제 옵션
(D) 다양한 참여 판매자

해설 두 번째 단락의 '고객은 놀라울 정도로 다양한 판매자들 중에서 선택해, 집이나 사무실에서 편하게 음식을 골라 주문하고, 수많은 온라인 결제 방식 중 하나를 통해 지불할 수 있다(customers can choose from an impressively diverse list of vendors, select and order their food, and pay through one of a number of online payment methods, all from the convenience of their home or office)'에서 (B), (C), (D)가 제공된다는 것을 확인할 수 있다. 하지만 두 번째 단락의 후반부에서 TVL 딜리버즈도 특정 시간 안에 배달하기를 바라고 있다(We hope eventually to deliver within a specified time)고 했으므로, 배송 시간 보장은 아직 제공되지 않는 서비스임을 알 수 있다. 따라서 (A)가 정답이다.

어휘 participate 참가하다

▸▸ Paraphrasing
지문의 online payment methods
→ 보기 (C)의 Convenient payment options
지문의 an impressively diverse list of vendors
→ 보기 (D)의 A variety of participating vendors

166 추론 / 암시

번역 크리슬리 복합 상업 지구의 업체들에 대해 포터 씨가 암시하는 것은?

(A) 곧 다른 장소로 옮길 것이다.
(B) TVL 딜리버즈에서 주문할 것이다.
(C) 업체 일부는 식당일 것이다.
(D) 업체 일부는 지역 대학생을 고용할 것이다.

해설 마지막 단락에서 최근 크리슬리 복합 상업 지구가 생겼으므로, TVL 딜리버즈가 성공하리라 확신한다(with the recent opening of Crisley Office Park ~ TVL Delivers will be a success)고 했다. 이에 따라 크리슬리 복합 상업 지구의 업체들이 TVL 딜리버즈에서 주문할 것으로 추론할 수 있으므로, (B)가 정답이다.

167 문장 삽입

번역 [1], [2], [3], [4]로 표시된 곳 중에서 다음 문장이 들어가기에 가장 적합한 곳은?

"또한 다양한 음식과 가격대에서 선택할 수 있었으면 했어요."

(A) [1]
(B) [2]
(C) [3]
(D) [4]

해설 주어진 문장에 '또한(also)'이라는 뜻의 접속부사가 있고, 다양한 음식과 가격대에서 선택할 수 있었으면 했다(We also wanted to be able to choose from a range of cuisines and price points)는 희망 사항이 담겼으므로, 앞에서도 이와 비슷한 희망 사항이 언급되어야 한다. [2] 앞 문장에서 식사를 쉽게 찾고, 주문하고, 결제하는 방법을 원했다(We wanted an easy way to find, order, and pay for our meals)고 했으므로, (B)가 정답이다.

어휘 a range of 다양한 cuisine 요리

TEST 10

168-171 편지

11월 3일

라이스 토마센
인사부장
슬레포이 마케팅사
7층, 엑스톤 가 500번지
시드니, 뉴사우스웨일즈 주 2000

토마센 씨께,

슬레포이 마케팅 전속 사진작가 자리에 면접 기회를 주신 것에 다시 한 번 감사드리고 싶습니다. 비록 제가 뽑히지 않아서 낙담하긴 했지만, 귀하와 직원들을 만나서 즐거웠습니다. [169]**귀하가 다른 후보자와 함께하기로 결정했다고 해서, 많은 상을 받았고 마땅히 그럴 자격이 있는 귀사가 최고의 마케팅 회사라는 제 믿음이 작아지지는 않습니다.**

[168]**그런데 만남 도중 산을 주제로 한 캠페인이 곧 있을 예정이며 귀사가 종종 프리랜서 사진 작가를 고용한다는 사실을 우연히 언급하셨죠.** 저는 앞으로 3개월 동안 아시아를 여행할 예정이며, 이 캠페인에 적합할 수도 있는 풍경 사진을 찍을 계획입니다. [168/170]**만약 관심이 있으시면, 일부 사진을 기꺼이 보내 드리겠습니다.**

만나 주셔서 다시 한번 감사합니다. [171]**올해 브리즈번에서 열리는 그래픽 아트 회의에서 귀하와 다시 이야기할 기회가 있었으면 합니다.**

예은 황

어휘 opportunity 기회 disappointed 실망한 decision 결정 candidate 지원자 diminish 줄이다 rightfully 마땅히 deserve 자격이 있다 incidentally 그런데 appropriate 적합한

168 주제 / 목적

번역 황 씨가 편지를 보낸 이유는?

(A) 일자리 제안 거절
(B) 도움 제공
(C) 일자리 문의
(D) 직책에 후보자 추천

해설 두 번째 단락에서 수신인(you)인 토마센 씨가 산을 주제로 한 캠페인이 곧 있을 예정이며 회사에서 프리랜서 사진작가를 고용한다는 사실을 언급했던 점(you happened to mention your upcoming mountain-themed campaign ~ your company often hires freelance photographers)을 상기시킨 후, 캠페인과 관련된 일부 사진을 기꺼이 보내 주겠다(I would be happy to send you some of those pictures)고 제안했다. 이에 따라 도움을 제안하기 위한 편지임을 알 수 있으므로, (B)가 정답이다.

어휘 decline 거절하다 inquire 묻다

▸▸ Paraphrasing 지문의 **send you some of those pictures**
→ 정답의 **offer her services**

169 세부 사항

번역 슬레포이 마케팅에 대한 황 씨의 의견은?

(A) 많은 상을 받을 만하다.
(B) 수요가 많은 서비스를 제공한다.
(C) 채용 관행이 훌륭하다.
(D) 직원 간 협업을 중시한다.

해설 첫 번째 단락에서 슬레포이 마케팅이 많은 상을 받았고, 마땅히 그럴 자격이 있는 최고의 마케팅 회사(your company is a first-rate marketing firm, which rightfully deserves the many awards it has won)라며 자신의 믿음을 밝혔으므로, (A)가 정답이다.

어휘 demand 수요 practice 관행 value 중시하다 collaboration 협업

▸▸ Paraphrasing 지문의 **rightfully deserves the many awards**
→ 정답의 **is worthy of its many awards**

170 세부 사항

번역 황 씨가 토마센 씨에게 보내고 싶어 하는 것은?

(A) 추천인 목록
(B) 몇 가지 마케팅 아이디어
(C) 회의 프로그램
(D) 일부 사진

해설 두 번째 단락에서 곧 있을 캠페인에 적합할 수도 있는 일부 사진을 기꺼이 보내 주겠다(I would be happy to send you some of those pictures)고 했으므로, (D)가 정답이다.

어휘 reference 추천인, 추천서

▸▸ Paraphrasing 지문의 **would be happy to send you**
→ 질문의 **want to send Mr. Tomasen**
지문의 **some of those pictures**
→ 정답의 **Some photographs**

171 세부 사항

번역 황 씨는 언제 토마센 씨를 다시 보기를 바라는가?

(A) 두 번째 면접
(B) 마케팅 회의
(C) 사진 강좌
(D) 전문 학술 회의

해설 마지막 단락에서 브리즈번에서 열리는 그래픽 아트 회의에서 토마센 씨와 다시 이야기할 기회가 있기를 기대한다(I hope to have another opportunity to speak with you at this year's Graphic Arts Conference in Brisbane)고 했으므로, (D)가 정답이다.

▸▸ Paraphrasing 지문의 **to have another opportunity to speak with you**
→ 질문의 **to see Mr. Tomasen again**
지문의 **Graphic Arts Conference**
→ 정답의 **a professional conference**

172-175 온라인 채팅

채팅

노라 오번 (오전 9시 36분) 클리멕 씨, 다음 주 마드리드 소매업자와의 발표 회의에 가려고 우리 항공권을 방금 구매했어요.

안나 클리멕 (오전 9시 37분) 잘하셨어요. 목요일에 가는 항공편으로 예약하신 건가요?

노라 오번 (오전 9시 37분) 예, 오후 4시예요. [173]**밤에 거기 도착하니까 금요일 회의 전에 쉴 시간이 충분해요. 계획대로 토요일에 더블린으로 돌아오고요.**

안나 클리멕 (오전 9시 38분) 완벽하네요. 여행 보험도 처리해 주시겠어요?

노라 오번 (오전 9시 38분) 건강과 제품 견본 모두 보장되도록 말씀인가요?

안나 클리멕 (오전 9시 39분) [172/174]**예, 천, 디자인, 그리고 제품군에서 몇 가지 골라서 가져갑니다.** 지난번과 같은 보험 회사로 해 주실래요?

노라 오번 (오전 9시 40분) 데일리 씨, 클리멕 씨와 저를 위해 보험 패키지를 준비해 주시겠어요? 해외 여행이고 건강과 우리가 가져갈 제품 견본을 보장하는 것으로요.

퍼걸 데일리 (오전 9시 40분) 그럴게요. 항공편과 수하물에 대해 상세히 알려 주실래요?

노라 오번 (오전 9시 41분) 다음 주 목요일에서 토요일까지에요. 에어 코너웨이로 더블린에서 마드리드에 갔다가 돌아와요. [174]**가벼운 짐인데 대부분 옷과 패션 액세서리고요.**

퍼걸 데일리 (오전 9시 59분) 알겠어요, 방금 전자 보험 증서를 전달했어요.

노라 오번 (오전 10시 1분) 고마워요! 방금 전자 서명을 했어요. [175]**이제 송금할게요.**

퍼걸 데일리 (오전 10시 2분) 천천히 하세요. [175]**보험회사에서 이틀 말미를 주니까 수요일까지 하면 돼요.**

보내기

어휘 purchase 구매하다 retailer 소매업자 manage to 가까스로 ~하다 insurance 보험 cover 보장하다, 보험에 가입하다 merchandise 제품 fabric 천 baggage 짐 forward 전달하다 policy 보험 증서 signature 서명 wire (전자 시스템을 이용해) 송금하다

172 추론 / 암시

번역 오번 씨와 클리멕 씨는 어떤 업계에서 일하겠는가?

(A) 보험
(B) 광고
(C) 의류
(D) 건강 관리

해설 클리멕 씨가 오전 9시 39분 메시지에서 오번 씨와 함께 참석하는 발표 회의(presentation meeting)에 천, 디자인, 그리고 제품군에서 몇 가지 골라서 가져갈 예정(we're taking fabrics, designs, and a few selections from our line)이라고 했다. 이에 따라 오번 씨와 클리멕 씨가 의류 업계에서 일한다고 추론할 수 있으므로, (C)가 정답이다.

173 추론 / 암시

번역 발표는 언제 하겠는가?

(A) 수요일
(B) 목요일
(C) 금요일
(D) 토요일

해설 오번 씨가 오전 9시 37분 메시지에서 금요일 회의 전에 쉴 시간이 충분하다(We'll arrive there ~ with enough time to rest before the Friday meeting)고 한 후, 계획대로 토요일에 더블린으로 돌아온다(Back to Dublin on Saturday, as planned)고 했으므로, 금요일에 발표를 할 것으로 추론할 수 있다. 따라서 (C)가 정답이다.

174 세부 사항

번역 오번 씨와 클리멕 씨가 비행기에 실을 계획인 것은?

(A) 고객들의 주문품
(B) 교육 자료
(C) 무거운 짐
(D) 제품 견본

해설 클리멕 씨가 오전 9시 39분 메시지에서 오번 씨와 함께 가는 발표 회의에 제품 견본(merchandise examples)으로 천, 디자인, 그리고 회사의 제품군 중 몇 가지를 가져갈 예정(we're taking fabrics, designs, and a few selections from our line)이라고 했다. 이후 데일리 씨가 항공편과 수하물 관련 정보(your flight and baggage details)를 묻자, 9시 41분 메시지에서 대부분 옷과 패션 액세서리인 가벼운 짐(Lightweight baggage, mainly apparel and fashion accessories)이라고 설명했으므로, 오번 씨와 클리멕 씨가 비행기에 실을 짐이 회사 제품 견본임을 알 수 있다. 따라서 (D)가 정답이다.

▸▸ Paraphrasing 지문의 merchandise examples
→ 정답의 Product samples

175 의도 파악

번역 오전 10시 2분에 데일리 씨가 "천천히 하세요"라고 적은 의도는 무엇인가?

(A) 당장 결제하지 않아도 된다.
(B) 서명은 다음 주에나 필요하다.
(C) 서류가 내일 발송될 것이다.
(D) 항공편이 지연되었다.

해설 오번 씨가 오전 10시 1분 메시지에서 지금 송금하겠다(I'll wire the money now)고 했는데, 이에 대해 데일리 씨가 '천천히 하세요(Take your time)'라고 응답한 후 보험 회사에서 이틀 말미를 준다(The insurance company allows two days)며 천천히 하라고 응답한 이유를 덧붙였다. 따라서 (A)가 정답이다.

어휘 payment 지불, 결제 immediately 즉시

TEST 10

176-180 기사 + 기사

새 공연장 거의 완공

나이젤 스미스

리버풀(8월 15일)—시에서 지난 20년 만에 처음으로 새 공연장이 될 건물 공사가 완공을 앞두고 있다. 이전의 플레처 신발 공장 부지에 건설되고 있는 크리켓 공연장에는 고객 400명을 수용할 수 있는 강당이 생긴다. [176]**공연장은 런던에 2곳, 요크에 1곳, 이렇게 3개의 다른 공연장을 소유한 와츠-스파이서 그룹이 운영하게 된다.**

와츠-스파이서 회장 콜린 와츠는 이곳이 10월에 개장할 것으로 예상된다고 말했다. "얼마 전 공사에서 가장 긴 [177]**단계**를 마무리했는데, 호주에서 좌석 주문이 밀려 예상보다 늦어졌죠. [178]**오는 10월 30일 뮤지컬 〈백업〉으로 문을 열 것으로 기대합니다.**" 크리켓 공연장은 전통 연극부터 모든 종류의 예술가들이 참여하는 특별 공연에 이르기까지 다양한 작품들을 주최할 예정이다.

어휘 completion 완료 site 부지 auditorium 강당 seat 수용하다 patron 고객, 후원자 venue (행사 등이 열리는) 장소 be expected to ~할 예정이다 chairperson 회장, 의장 due to ~ 때문에 back-order (재고가 없어) 주문이 밀리다 special engagements 특별 행사[공연]

정말 근사한 크리켓 공연장의 〈백업〉

클라라 케네디

리버풀([178]**12월 2일**)—[178]**크리켓 공연장의 첫 작품인 〈백업〉이 어젯밤 객석을 가득 메운 관객 앞에서 선을 보였다.** 공연장을 자주 찾는 사람들은 실화를 바탕으로 한 이 새 뮤지컬에 분명 즐거워했다. [179]**〈백업〉은 유명한 뮤지컬 공연자들의 젊은 코러스 가수였던 배벳 존스가 단독 공연자가 되기까지 23년간의 고군분투를 따라간다.** [180]**리버풀 출신 타미 맥클루어가 존스 역을 맡아 넓은 음역대의 보컬로 관객을 열광시켰다.** 그녀의 대담무쌍한 매니저 역을 맡은 폴 로빈슨 역시 열연했다. 의상 디자이너 소피 라이트의 의상 및 소품은 매우 아름다웠다.

〈백업〉이 지닌 뛰어난 작품성과 크리켓 공연장의 적당한 표 값이 이 새 공연장의 장기적이고 성공적인 미래를 가리키고 있다. 〈백업〉은 크리켓 공연장에서 2월 5일까지 연속 상연된다.

어휘 full house (공연장 등) 객석이 다 참 theatregoer 공연장을 자주 찾는 사람 act 공연자 struggle 고군분투 audience 관객 wide-ranging 폭넓은 fearless 대담무쌍한 exquisite 매우 아름다운 reasonable 적당한, 합리적인 run (극·영화 등이) 연속 상연되다

176 사실 관계 확인

번역 와츠-스파이서 그룹에 관해 명시된 것은?

(A) 공연장을 여러 개 운영한다.
(B) 플레처 신발 공장을 소유했다.
(C) 호주 회사다.
(D) 시에서 가장 오래된 공연장을 운영한다.

해설 첫 번째 기사의 첫 번째 단락에서 공연장은 3개의 다른 공연장을 소유한 와츠-스파이서 그룹이 운영하게 된다(The theatre will be operated by the Watts-Spicer Group, which owns three other theatres)고 했으므로, (A)가 정답이다.

▸▸ **Paraphrasing** 지문의 **owns three other theatres**
→ 정답의 **runs multiple theaters**

177 동의어 찾기

번역 첫 번째 기사에서 두 번째 단락 4행의 "stage"와 의미가 가장 가까운 단어는?

(A) 단계
(B) 플랫폼
(C) 장면
(D) 발표

해설 "stage"가 포함된 부분은 '공사에서 가장 긴 단계를 마무리했다(We have just completed the longest stage of the project)'라는 의미로 해석되는데, 여기서 stage는 '단계'라는 뜻으로 쓰였다. 따라서 '단계, 국면'이라는 의미의 (A) phase가 정답이다.

178 연계

번역 크리켓 공연장에 관해 암시된 것은?

(A) 가격이 아주 비싸다.
(B) 공연물은 주로 뮤지컬 코미디일 것이다.
(C) 개장 예정일이 지연되었다.
(D) 다음 작품은 1월에 시작한다.

해설 첫 번째 기사의 두 번째 단락에서 10월 30일 뮤지컬 〈백업〉으로 문을 열 것으로 기대한다(We are expecting to open with the musical *Backup* on 30 October)고 했고, 두 번째 기사의 첫 번째 단락에서 크리켓 공연장의 첫 작품인 〈백업〉이 어젯밤 객석을 가득 메운 관객 앞에서 선을 보였다(The Cricket Theatre's first production, *Backup*, opened last night to a full house)고 했는데, 기사가 쓰여진 날(2 December)의 전날은 12월 1일이다. 이에 따라 크리켓 공연장의 개장 예정일이 지연되었음을 추론할 수 있으므로, (C)가 정답이다.

어휘 mainly 주로

179 사실 관계 확인

번역 두 번째 기사에 의하면, 〈백업〉에 관해 명시된 것은?

(A) 표 판매가 저조했다.
(B) 관객을 실망시켰다.
(C) 이야기는 허구다.
(D) 수십 년에 걸쳐 일어난 이야기다.

해설 두 번째 기사의 첫 번째 단락에서 〈백업〉은 유명한 뮤지컬 공연자들의 젊은 코러스 가수가 단독 공연자가 되기까지 23년간의 고군분투를 따라간다(*Backup* follows ~ a young backup singer for famous musical acts, through her 23-year struggle to become a successful solo act)고 했으므로, (D)가 정답이다. 객석을 가득 메운 관객 앞에서 선을 보였다(opened last night to a full house)고 했으므로 (A)는 적절하지 않고, 공연장을 자주 찾는 사람들이 실화를 바탕으로 한 이 뮤지컬에 즐거워했다(Theatregoers were clearly delighted by this new musical, which is based on a true story)고 했으므로, (B)와 (C) 또한 오답이다.

어휘 disappoint 실망시키다 fictional 허구의 decade 10년

▸▸ Paraphrasing 지문의 through her 23-year struggle
→ 정답의 over several decades

180 세부 사항

번역 맥클루어 씨는 누구인가?

(A) 공연자
(B) 매니저
(C) 의상 디자이너
(D) 무대 디자이너

해설 두 번째 기사의 첫 번째 단락에서 맥클루어 씨가 존스 역을 맡아 넓은 음역대의 보컬로 관객을 열광시켰다(Tami McClure, as Ms. Jones, thrilled the audience with her wide-ranging vocals)고 했으므로, (A)가 정답이다.

181-185 기사 + 온라인 후기

켄트(2월 26일)—스텔라 초콜릿은 다양한 수제 진미를 제공하는 지역 업체다. 켄트에 두 곳의 가게가 있는 이 업체는 지역에서 유명하다. **181그러나 최근, 지난달 초콜릿 위원회에서 최고상을 받으면서 스텔라 초콜릿은 전국적으로 인정받게 되었다.**

182브라이언 마커스와 함께 이 가게를 공동 소유하는 스테파니 데이비슨은 스텔라 초콜릿의 원료와 품질을 강조한다. "브라이언과 저는 사업을 시작하기 전에 몇 달 동안 고품질 카카오 콩 생산으로 유명한 세계 각지를 여행했어요. 우리는 나무를 살펴보고 전통적인 수확 및 로스팅 과정에 대해 배웠어요." 그녀는 말했다. 사실, 공동 소유주들이 자사의 제품을 위해 183**가장 좋은** 재료를 확보한 후에야 생산이 시작되었다. 그들은 이제 고추, 바질, 심지어 고추냉이 같은 다양한 재료를 통합해 독특한 초콜릿 제품군을 만들고 있다.

184스텔라 제품군에 대한 수요는 계속 증가하고 있어 회사는 올해 말에 배스에 세 번째 가게를 열 것으로 기대하고 있다. 데이비슨 씨는 소매 용도로 바뀔 오래된 제분소에서 추가 공간을 찾았다고 말했다. 그녀는 "새 가게는 우리 가게 중 최대 규모가 될 것이고 국내는 물론 해외로도 배송이 가능하도록 우편 주문 사업을 실시할 계획"이라고 말했다.

어휘 a wide selection of 다양한 handcrafted 수제의 delicacy 진미 recently 최근 gain 얻다 recognition 인정 earn 얻다 emphasis 강조하다 inspect 살펴보다 harvest 수확하다 secure 확보하다 ingredient 재료 incorporate 통합하다 additional 추가의 mill 제분소 convert 바꾸다 retail 소매의 domestically 국내에서

www.stellarchocolates.co.uk/reviews

홈	제품군	고객 후기	연락처

184오늘 이전에 제분소였던 곳에 몇 주 전 문을 연 스텔라 초콜릿의 새 매장에 갔어요. 그저 그런 과자점이겠거니 하고요. 세상에! **185초콜릿이 수제로 만들어지는 모습을 지켜보는 동안 무료 시식품을 맛보게 되어 즐거웠어요.** 심지어 주인 중 한 분과 이야기를 나눌 기회도 있었는데 업체의 기원에 대해 얘기해 주셨어요. **182그녀는 공동 소유주를 10년 전 대학 강의에서 만났고 과제로 사업 아이디어를 생각해 냈다고 하네요.** 교수님과 학우들에게 아주 긍정적인 의견을 들어서 아이디어를 직업 프로젝트로 전환하겠다고 결심했고요. **184가게가 저희 집에서 모퉁이만 돌면 바로 있으니까 앞으로도 자주 갈 것 같아요.**

신시아 라구사

어휘 ordinary 그저 그런, 평범한 origin 기원 assignment 과제 positive 긍정적인 decide to ~하기로 결심하다

181 사실 관계 확인

번역 기사에서 스텔라 초콜릿에 관해 언급된 것은?

(A) 초콜릿뿐만 아니라 다양한 품목을 판매한다.
(B) 거래 대부분을 우편 주문으로 한다.
(C) 탁월한 초콜릿 제조 솜씨로 인정받았다.
(D) 최근 제조 과정을 자동화했다.

해설 기사의 첫 번째 단락에서 최근 스텔라 초콜릿이 초콜릿 위원회에서 최고상을 받아 전국적으로 인정받게 되었다(Recently ~ Stellar Chocolates gained national recognition by earning top awards from the Chocolate Council)고 했으므로, (C)가 정답이다.

어휘 automate 자동화하다 manufacturing 제조

▸▸ Paraphrasing 지문의 gained national recognition by earning top awards → 정답의 has been recognized for excellence

182 연계

번역 마커스 씨에 관해 사실인 것은?

(A) 기사에 실릴 인터뷰를 했다.
(B) 단골이다.
(C) 데이비슨 씨와 대학에서 만났다.
(D) 제분소 개조를 감독했다.

해설 기사의 두 번째 단락에서 데이비슨 씨가 마커스 씨와 함께 가게를 공동 소유하고 있다(Stephanie Davidson, who co-owns the shops with Brian Markus)고 했는데, 온라인 후기의 중반부를 보면 데이비슨 씨가 공동 소유주를 10년 전 대학 강의에서 만났다(She met her co-owner ten years ago in a class at university)고 나와 있다. 이에 따라 마커스 씨가 데이비슨 씨와 대학에서 만난 사실을 확인할 수 있으므로, (C)가 정답이다.

어휘 oversee 감독하다 conversion 개조

TEST 10

183 동의어 찾기

번역 기사에서 두 번째 단락 11행의 "finest"와 의미가 가장 가까운 단어는?

(A) 가장 건강한
(B) 가장 좋은
(C) 가장 얇은
(D) 가장 일반적인

해설 "finest"가 포함된 부분은 '공동 소유주들이 자사의 제품을 위해 가장 좋은 재료를 확보한 후에야(after the co-owners had secured the finest ingredients for their products)'라는 의미로 해석되는데, 여기서 finest는 '가장 좋은'이라는 뜻으로 쓰였다. 따라서 '가장 좋은, 최상의'라는 의미의 (B) best가 정답이다.

184 연계

번역 라구사 씨에 관해 암시된 것은?

(A) 초콜릿을 거의 먹지 않는다.
(B) 한때 켄트에 있는 제분소에서 일했다.
(C) 데이비슨 씨의 동료다.
(D) 배스에 산다.

해설 온라인 후기의 첫 번째 문장에서 라구사 씨가 이전에 제분소였던 곳에 문을 연 스텔라 초콜릿의 새 매장에 갔다(I visited the new Stellar Chocolates shop that opened ~ in the former mill)고 한 후, 마지막 문장에서 가게가 자신의 집에서 모퉁이만 돌면 바로 있다(as the shop is just around the corner from my home)며 위치에 대해 언급했다. 기사의 마지막 단락에서 회사가 올해 말에 배스에 세 번째 가게를 열 것으로 기대하고 있다(the firm expects to open a third shop in Bath later this year)고 한 후, 소매 용도로 바뀔 오래된 제분소에서 추가 공간을 찾았다(they have found additional space in an old mill to be converted for retail use)고 했다. 이에 따라 라구사 씨가 배스에 산다고 추론할 수 있으므로, (D)가 정답이다.

어휘 seldom 거의 ~않다 colleague 동료

185 사실 관계 확인

번역 가장 최근에 생긴 스텔라 초콜릿 가게에 관해 명시된 것은?

(A) 개장이 늦어졌다.
(B) 영업 시간이 연장되었다.
(C) 이전 우체국 자리에 위치한다.
(D) 무료 견본품을 제공한다.

해설 온라인 후기의 초반부에서 라구사 씨가 스텔라 초콜릿 새 매장에 갔다(I visited the new Stellar Chocolates shop)고 한 후, 무료 시식품을 맛보게 되어 즐거웠다(I was delighted to taste some free samples)고 했으므로, 스텔라 초콜릿 가게에서 무료 견본품을 제공한다는 것을 알 수 있다. 따라서 (D)가 정답이다.

어휘 extend 연장하다

▸▸ Paraphrasing 지문의 free samples
→ 정답의 complimentary samples

186-190 이메일 + 웹페이지 + 양식

수신: 알렉스 굴린 〈alex.gulin@senmail.ca〉
발신: 코헥 어패럴 〈orders@kohekapparel.com〉
날짜: 8월 27일
제목: 코헥 어패럴 주문 확인

알렉스 씨에게:

온라인으로 코헥 어패럴에서 주문해 주셔서 감사합니다! 주문품은 영업일 기준으로 5-10일 안에 도착합니다. 아래는 상세 내용입니다:

주문 번호: 96781
[190]**배송지: 엑서터 가 22번지, 토론토, M4B 1B3 캐나다**
주문 요약:

명세	품번	색상	[187]**사이즈**	가격
조깅복	P394	진회색	[187]**라지**	78달러
면 셔츠	S963	밝은 흰색	[187]**라지**	36달러
울 스웨터	SW852	하늘색	[187]**라지**	45달러
[189]**플리스 재킷**	[189]**J109**	황록색	[187]**라지**	65달러
			총 224달러	

거듭 거래해 주셔서 감사합니다! [186]**다음 주문 시 10퍼센트 할인 쿠폰을 받으시려면 웹사이트를 방문하셔서 판촉 코드 RC008을 입력하세요.**

어휘 description (상품) 명세 promotional 판촉의

http://www.kohekapparel.com/returns

코헥 어패럴 – 반품 규정

코헥 어패럴은 적당한 가격에 고품질의, 몸에 잘 맞는 제품을 만들고자 노력하고 있습니다. 저희는 여러분께서 주문품에 전적으로 만족하시길 바라며, 반품 절차를 가능한 한 쉽게 만들고자 합니다.

물품을 반품하시려면 이메일 customersupport@kohekapparel.com으로 배송 라벨을 요청하세요. [188]**출력할 수 있는 배송 라벨이 이메일로 발송될 겁니다. 배송 라벨을 받으시면 작성 완료한 반품 요청서(송장 뒷면에 있음)와 함께 물품을 원래 담겨 있던 상자에 넣고 배송 라벨을 상자에 붙이세요.** 원래 상자가 없다면 다른 상자에 제품을 넣으세요. 저희가 소포를 받는 대로 구매품에 대해 전액 환불해 드리겠습니다.

미국 내 반송은 전적으로 무료입니다. [190]**캐나다에서 반품하실 경우 환불 금액에서 6달러의 배송비가 차감됩니다.** 그 외 모든 국가에서 보낼 경우 배송비는 12달러입니다.

어휘 policy 규정 strive 노력하다 reasonable 적당한, 합리적인 deduct 차감하다

http://www.kohekapparel.com/returns

코헥 어패럴—반품 요청

이름: 알렉스 굴린
고객 ID: A.Gul370
주문 번호: 96781
189**반품 품번: J109**

반품 사유: 너무 컸다.
다른 사이즈로 주문하시겠습니까? 아니요. **사이즈 ___**

의견:
여러 해 동안 코헥 어패럴에서 같은 사이즈를 주문해 왔습니다. 이번에는 사이즈가 맞지 않아 놀랐습니다. 하지만 다른 제품들은 만족합니다.

어휘 request 요청 for years 수년 동안 off 잘못된, 틀린

186 추론 / 암시

번역 코헥 어패럴에 관해 암시된 것은?
(A) 물품 목록에 새 품목을 몇 가지 추가했다.
(B) 재구매 고객에게 할인을 제공한다.
(C) 여름 의류 전문이다.
(D) 물품 해외 배송은 하지 않는다.

해설 이메일의 마지막 단락에서 다음 주문 시 10퍼센트 할인 쿠폰을 받으려면 웹사이트를 방문해서 판촉 코드를 입력할 것(To receive a coupon for 10 percent off your next order, visit our website and enter the promotional code)을 조언했다. 이에 따라 재구매 고객에게 할인을 제공한다고 추론할 수 있으므로, (B)가 정답이다.

어휘 inventory 물품 목록 specialize in ~을 전문으로 하다

▸▸ Paraphrasing 지문의 **a coupon for 10 percent off your next order**
→ 정답의 **discounts to returning customers**

187 세부 사항

번역 굴린 씨가 주문한 모든 품목의 공통점은?
(A) 같은 소재로 제조되었다.
(B) 같은 가격이다.
(C) 캐나다에서 제조되었다.
(D) 같은 사이즈다.

해설 이메일의 주문 요약(Order Summary) 표에서 사이즈(Size)가 모두 라지(Large)임을 확인할 수 있으므로, (D)가 정답이다.

188 세부 사항

번역 반품할 때 고객이 해야 하는 일은?
(A) 특정 크기의 상자 사용
(B) 온라인으로 양식 제출
(C) 배송 라벨 출력
(D) 특정 배송 업체 이용

해설 웹페이지의 두 번째 단락에서 출력할 수 있는 배송 라벨이 이메일로 발송될 것(A printable shipping label will be emailed to you)이라고 한 후, 배송 라벨을 받으면 물품을 원래 담겨 있던 상자에 넣고 배송 라벨을 상자에 붙일 것(Once you receive it, place the item in the same box ~ tape the shipping label to the box)을 요청했다. 이에 따라 반품할 때 고객이 배송 라벨을 출력해야 한다는 것을 알 수 있으므로, (C)가 정답이다.

▸▸ Paraphrasing 지문의 **printable** → 정답의 **Print out**

189 연계

번역 굴린 씨가 반품하는 품목은?
(A) 조깅복
(B) 셔츠
(C) 스웨터
(D) 재킷

해설 반품 요청(Return Request) 양식에서 반품 품번(Returning Item Number)이 J109라고 했는데, 이메일의 주문 요약(Order Summary) 표를 보면 J109가 플리스 재킷(Fleece jacket)임을 확인할 수 있으므로, (D)가 정답이다.

190 연계

번역 굴린 씨에 관해 명시된 것은?
(A) 반품 배송비가 부과될 것이다.
(B) 반품 규정에 불만이 있다.
(C) 대체 물품을 주문할 것이다.
(D) 다시는 코헥 어패럴에서 옷을 구매하지 않을 것이다.

해설 이메일에서 굴린 씨의 배송지(Deliver To)가 캐나다(CANADA)임을 확인할 수 있는데, 웹페이지의 마지막 단락에서 캐나다에서 반품할 경우 환불 금액에서 6달러의 배송비가 차감된다(For returns from Canada, a $6 shipping charge will be deducted from your refund)고 했으므로, (A)가 정답이다.

어휘 dissatisfied 불만인 replacement 대체(품)

▸▸ Paraphrasing 지문의 **a $6 shipping charge**
→ 정답의 **be charged a return shipping fee**

191-195 일정표 + 소식지 기사 + 양식

쿠라키 자동차 캐나다 영업소 연례 회의
6월 8일 금요일 일정

오전 7시 30분	아침 식사	동 연회장
오전 9시	기조 연설 191**CEO 카츠히코 나카무로**	191**남 연회장**
오전 10시 30분	쿠라키 사업 전망 191**부회장 지로 히가**	191**남 연회장**
정오	점심 식사	동 연회장
193**오후 1시 30분**	193**신제품 공개** 191**수석 디자이너 유나 야마시타**	191**남 연회장**
오후 4시	영업소 주도 세미나: 194**선구적인 영업소** 194**디지털 캠페인**	 마라 룸 플로라 룸
오후 6시	저녁 식사	동 연회장

TEST 10

어휘 dealer 영업소 annual 연례의 keynote address 기조 연설 outlook 전망 dealership 판매업, 대리점

캐나다 영업소 회의

조시 홉킨스, 〈쿠라키 나우〉 전속 기자

쿠라키 자동차 임원들이 천여 명에 가까운 캐나다 쿠라키 직원들의 연례 회의를 위해 토론토로 돌아왔다. [192]**이틀간 열리는 이 행사는 금요일 아침, 토론토에 있는 회사 신규 생산 공장의 진행 상황을 강조하는 CEO 카츠히코 나카무로의 기조 연설로 시작되었다. 이어 지로 히가 부회장이 생산량 증가와 성장 전망에 대해 상세히 설명했다.** 참석자들은 이틀간의 세미나에 참석할 기회를 가졌다. [192/193]**그러나 이 행사의 하이라이트는 날렵한 다이노 세단과 쿠라키의 신형 하이브리드인 푸라, 이 두 신모델을 공개한 것이었다.** 이 모델들은 8월에 대리점에 들어올 예정이다.

어휘 executive 임원, 간부 nearly 거의 representative 직원 kick off 시작하다 progress 진행 manufacturing plant 제조 공장 expected 예상되는 growth 성장 attendee 참석자 opportunity 기회 unveil 공개하다 sleek 날렵한 roll into 들어오다

쿠라키 자동차 캐나다 영업소 연례 회의 – 설문 조사서

올해 영업소 회의에 참석해 주셔서 감사합니다. 의견에 감사드립니다. 다음 평가 척도를 이용해 참석하셨던 각 세미나를 평가해 주세요.

평가 척도: 4 = 탁월함; 3 = 매우 좋음; 2 = 만족; 1 = 나쁨

세미나	평가
[194]**선구적인 영업소**	[194]**4**
디지털 캠페인	해당 없음
영업 사원을 유치하는 검증된 방법	4
인터넷 영업 성공	해당 없음
미래의 사업 모델	해당 없음
경쟁에서 두각 나타내기	4

의견:

이틀간의 세미나 모두 언제나처럼 유익했습니다. [195]**일부 세미나가 동시에 일정이 잡히지 않고, 토요일 점심 전에 세미나가 더 많았더라면 좋았을 것 같아요. 동료 몇 사람이 오후 세미나까지 있을 수 없었거든요.**

이름: 하워드 겔맨

어휘 rating 평가 n/a 해당 없음(not applicable) proven 검증된 stand out 두각을 나타내다 competition 경쟁 informative 유익한

191 세부 사항

번역 쿠라키의 고위 임원이 발표한 장소는?

(A) 동 연회장
(B) 남 연회장
(C) 마라 룸
(D) 플로라 룸

해설 일정표를 보면 고위 임원(senior executives)인 CEO 카츠히코 나카무로(CEO Katsuhiko Nakamuro), 부회장 지로 히가(Vice President Jiro Higa), 수석 디자이너 유나 야마시타(Chief Designer Yuna Yamashita)가 '남 연회장(South Ballroom)에서 발표하는 것을 알 수 있으므로, (B)가 정답이다.

192 주제 / 목적

번역 기사의 한 가지 목적은?

(A) 연례 회의에서 열린 행사들 요약하기
(B) 신차 모델 기능 평가하기
(C) 제공되는 세미나에 관해 자세한 내용 제공하기
(D) 나카무로 씨의 승진 발표하기

해설 기사의 전반에서 신규 생산 공장의 진행 상황을 강조하는 CEO 카츠히코 나카무로의 기조 연설(CEO Katsuhiko Nakamuro, who gave a keynote address highlighting progress on the company's new manufacturing plant), 지로 히가 부사장의 생산량 증가와 성장 전망에 대한 설명(Vice President Jiro Higa detailing increased production levels and expected growth), 신형 모델의 공개(the unveiling of two new models) 등 연례 회의에서 진행된 행사들을 나열하고 있다. 이에 따라 연례 회의에서 열린 행사들을 요약하는 기사로 볼 수 있으므로, (A)가 정답이다.

어휘 summarize 요약하다 take place 일어나다, 열리다 feature 기능, 특징 announce 발표하다

193 연계

번역 다이노와 푸라는 언제 회의 참석자들에게 소개되었겠는가?

(A) 오전 7시 30분
(B) 오전 9시
(C) 오후 1시 30분
(D) 오후 6시

해설 소식지 기사의 후반부에서 행사의 하이라이트는 날렵한 다이노 세단과 쿠라키의 신형 하이브리드인 푸라를 신모델로 공개한 것이었다(the highlight of the event was the unveiling of two new models, the sleek Daino sedan and Kuraki's new hybrid, the Pura)고 했다. 일정표를 보면, 신제품 공개(New Product Debuts)는 오후 1시 30분(1:30 P.M.)에 진행되었으므로, 다이노와 푸라가 그때 소개되었다고 볼 수 있다. 따라서 (C)가 정답이다.

▸▸ Paraphrasing 지문의 **Debuts/the unveiling**
→ 질문의 **introduced**

194 연계

번역 겔맨 씨에 관해 명시된 것은?

(A) 금요일에 세미나에 참석했다.
(B) 토요일 점심 전에 떠났다.
(C) 쿠라키 디지털 광고부에서 일했다.
(D) 다음 해 회의에서 세미나를 진행할 계획이다.

해설 겔맨 씨가 설문 조사서(Survey Form)에서 평가한 세미나 중 하나가 '선구적인 영업소(The Modern Dealership)'인데, 금요일 일정표를 보면 이 세미나가 오후 4시(4:00 P.M.)에 진행되었다고 나와 있다. 따라서 겔맨 씨가 금요일 세미나에 참석했음을 알 수 있으므로, (A)가 정답이다.

195 세부 사항

번역 세미나에 대한 겔맨 씨의 불만은?

(A) 시간이 너무 길었다.
(B) 주제가 따분했다.
(C) 모든 세미나에 다 참석할 수 없었다.
(D) 발표자가 마음에 들지 않았다.

해설 겔멘 씨는 설문 조사서의 의견(Comments)란에서 일부 세미나가 동시에 일정이 잡히지 않았으면 좋겠다(I wish that some were not scheduled at the same time)는 의견을 밝혔으므로, 모든 세미나에 참석할 수 없었던 점이 겔맨 씨의 불만이라고 볼 수 있다. 따라서 (C)가 정답이다.

196-200 초대장 + 안내책자 + 이메일

창의적 기술 회의

제10회 연례 창의적 기술 회의에 함께해 주세요. 각자 분야에서 최고의 혁신가들과 함께 최신 기술을 살펴보세요. 하루 종일 발표회, 워크숍, 토론, 전시회를 즐기세요. [199]**마무리는 그루텐허 테크 창립자인 아야나 곤잘레스의 기조 연설입니다.**

[196]**5월 12일 오전 9시 - 오후 6시**
본달 대학교
마커스 가 22번지
아이온, 캘리포니아

온라인 www.creativetechcon.com/tickets에서
표를 구매하세요.

후원자가 되고 싶으신가요? 첨부한 후원자 혜택 소책자를 참고하세요.

어휘 explore 살펴보다 innovator 혁신가 exhibition 전시(회) culminate 끝나다 purchase 구매하다 benefit 혜택

창의적 기술 회의
후원자 혜택

저희는 후원자들의 지원 없이는 창의적 기술 회의를 운영할 수 없었습니다. [197]**후원은 기업가, 혁신가를 지원하는 것 외에도 다양한 기술 분야에 종사하는 500명이 넘는 회의 참석자들에게 업체의 이름을 알릴 수 있는 아주 좋은 방법입니다.** 후원 단계는 아래를 참고하세요.

[200]**혁신가—5천 달러**
- 기조 연설 중 귀사 로고가 있는 대형 배너 전시
- 전시 업체 부스 4시간 무료
- 회의 웹사이트와 회의 프로그램에 귀사 로고 표시
- [200]**회의 참석 전 직원 반값 할인권**

크리에이터—3천 달러
- 마지막 환영 연회 중 귀사 로고가 있는 대형 배너 전시
- 전시 업체 부스 4시간 무료
- 회의 웹사이트와 회의 프로그램에 귀사 로고 표시

기업가—2천 달러
- 회의 웹사이트와 회의 프로그램에 귀사 로고 표시
- 전시 업체 부스 4시간 무료

후원자—천 달러
- 회의 웹사이트와 회의 프로그램에 귀사 로고 표시

자세한 정보는 sponsors@creativetechconference.com으로 연락하세요.

어휘 in addition to ~ 외에도 entrepreneur 기업가 innovator 혁신가 feature 등장하다

수신: 올레이블 애널리틱스 전 직원
발신: 에드설 스카이어즈
제목: 창의적 기술 회의
날짜: 5월 2일

직원들께,

[198]**여러분이 5월 12일 창의적 기술 회의에 참석하셨으면 합니다.** 회의는 인근에 있는 본달 대학교에서 열립니다. 지난 2년 동안 제가 참석해 봤는데, 인맥을 쌓고 우리 분야의 최신 동향에 대한 정보를 알 수 있는 아주 좋은 방법입니다. [200]**그리고 우리가 이 행사를 후원하므로, 우리 직원은 입장권을 할인 받습니다.** [199]**게다가, 몇 분은 아시겠지만, 기조 연설자가 과거 여기 직원이었습니다!** 문의 사항 있으시면 연락 바랍니다.

에드설 스카이어즈
제품개발부장
올레이블 애널리틱스

어휘 receive 받다 former 과거의

TEST 10

196 사실 관계 확인

번역 창의적 기술 회의에 관해 초대장에서 언급한 것은?

(A) 대학 교수들이 준비한다.
(B) 대학생들은 무료 표를 요청할 수 있다.
(C) 하루 동안 열리는 회의다.
(D) 이번이 회의가 열리는 첫 해다.

해설 초대장에서 창의적 기술 회의가 5월 12일 오전 9시부터 오후 6시까지(May 12, 9 A.M.–6 P.M.) 하루 동안 진행된다는 것을 확인할 수 있으므로, (C)가 정답이다.

어휘 organize (행사 등을) 준비하다 take place 열리다, 개최되다

▸▸ Paraphrasing 지문의 **May 12, 9 A.M.–6 P.M.**
→ 정답의 **one-day**

197 세부 사항

번역 소책자에 의하면 회의 후원의 혜택은?

(A) 후원자는 회의에서 발표할 수 있다.
(B) 후원자는 특별 환영 연회에 초대받는다.
(C) 후원자는 잠재 고객들에게 자신들의 업체를 광고할 수 있다.
(D) 후원자는 무료 견본품을 받는다.

해설 소책자의 첫 번째 단락에서 후원은 다양한 기술 분야에 종사하는 500명이 넘는 회의 참석자들에게 업체의 이름을 알릴 수 있는 아주 좋은 방법(sponsorship is a great way to get the name of your business out to our 500+ attendees in various tech fields)이라고 했으므로, (C)가 정답이다.

어휘 advertise 광고하다, 홍보하다 potential 잠재적인

▸▸ Paraphrasing 지문의 **get the name of your business out to our 500+ attendees** → 정답의 **advertise the business to potential customers**

198 주제 / 목적

번역 스카이어즈 씨가 이메일을 쓴 이유는?

(A) 직원들에게 신입 사원 소개
(B) 직원들에게 행사 참석 독려
(C) 직원들에게 신기술 설명
(D) 대학과 연구 제휴 발표

해설 이메일의 첫 번째 문장에서 5월 12일 창의적 기술 회의에 참석하길 바란다(I hope you will attend the Creative Tech Conference on May 12)고 했으므로, 수신인(you)인 직원들에게 참석을 독려하는 이메일임을 알 수 있다. 따라서 (B)가 정답이다.

어휘 introduce 소개하다 encourage 독려하다

▸▸ Paraphrasing 지문의 **the Creative Tech Conference**
→ 정답의 **an event**

199 연계

번역 곤잘레스 씨에 관해 명시된 것은?

(A) 창의적 기술 회의 후원자다.
(B) 캘리포니아 아이온에 산다.
(C) 10년 전에 사업을 시작했다.
(D) 과거 올레이블 애널리틱스에서 일했다.

해설 초대장의 첫 번째 단락에서 질문에 언급된 곤잘레스 씨가 마무리로 기조 연설을 한다(culminating with a keynote address by Ayana Gonzalez)고 했는데, 세 번째 지문인, 올레이블 애널리틱스 전 직원에게 보내는 이메일의 후반부에서 기조 연설자가 과거 직원이었다(the keynote speaker is a former employee)고 했으므로, 곤잘레스 씨가 과거 올레이블 애널리틱스에서 일했다는 것을 알 수 있다. 따라서 (D)가 정답이다.

▸▸ Paraphrasing 지문의 **a former employee**
→ 정답의 **previously worked**

200 연계

번역 올레이블 애널리틱스의 후원 유형은?

(A) 혁신가
(B) 크리에이터
(C) 기업가
(D) 후원자

해설 이메일의 중반부에서 올레이블 애널리틱스가 행사를 후원하므로, 직원들이 표 값을 할인받는다(because we are a sponsor of the event, our employees receive a discount on tickets)고 했는데, 소책자를 보면 회의에 참석하는 전 직원을 위한 반값 할인권(Half-price tickets for all employees that attend the conference)은 혁신가(Innovator) 후원 유형만 받을 수 있는 혜택이므로, (A)가 정답이다.